W9-BUY-495

The University of Chicago Spanish–English Dictionary

Diccionario Universidad de Chicago Inglés–Español

The University of Chicago Spanish–English Dictionary

Diccionario Universidad de Chicago Inglés–Español

Originally Compiled by Carlos Castillo and Otto F. Bond
Compilación original de Carlos Castillo y Otto F. Bond

SIXTH EDITION · *SEXTA EDICIÓN*

David A. Pharies
Editor in Chief · *Director*

María Irene Moyna
Editor · *Editora*

Gary K. Baker
Assistant Editor · *Redactor*

Meagan M. Day
Editorial Assistant · *Redactora*

POCKET BOOKS
NEW YORK LONDON TORONTO SYDNEY NEW DELHI

The sale of this book without its cover is unauthorized. If you purchased this book without a cover, you should be aware that it was reported to the publisher as "unsold and destroyed." Neither the author nor the publisher has received payment for the sale of this "stripped book."

Pocket Books
A Division of Simon & Schuster, Inc.
1230 Avenue of the Americas
New York, NY 10020

Copyright © 2012 by The University of Chicago

Published by arrangement with The University of Chicago Press

All rights reserved, including the right to reproduce this book or portions thereof in any form whatsoever. For information, address The University of Chicago Press, 1427 East 60th Street, Chicago, IL 60637.

This Pocket Books paperback edition May 2013

POCKET and colophon are registered trademarks of Simon & Schuster, Inc.

For information about special discounts for bulk purchases, please contact Simon & Schuster Special Sales at 1-866-506-1949 or business@simonandschuster.com.

The Simon & Schuster Speakers Bureau can bring authors to your live event. For more information or to book an event, contact the Simon & Schuster Speakers Bureau at 1-866-248-3049 or visit our website at www.simonspeakers.com.

Manufactured in the United States of America

10 9

ISBN 978-1-4516-6910-7

Contents

Preface to the Sixth Edition vii

Preámbulo a la sexta edición ix

How to Use *The University of Chicago Spanish–English Dictionary* xi

Cómo usar el *Diccionario Universidad de Chicago Inglés–Español* xv

Spanish–English · Español–Inglés

List of Abbreviations 1

Spanish Pronunciation 2

Notes on Spanish Grammar 6

Common Spanish Suffixes 8

Spanish Regular Verbs 10

Spanish Irregular and Orthographic Changing Verbs 12

Spanish–English Dictionary, A–Z 31

Inglés–Español · English–Spanish

Lista de abreviaturas 291

Pronunciación inglesa 292

Notas sobre gramática inglesa 294

Sufijos comunes del inglés 296

Verbos irregulares de la lengua inglesa 298

Diccionario inglés–español, A–Z 305

Preface to the Sixth Edition

The *University of Chicago Spanish–English Dictionary* has been compiled for the general use of Spanish-speaking learners of American English and American English-speaking learners of Spanish. In step with the rapid pace of cultural and linguistic change at the beginning of the twenty-first century, we have thoroughly revised the *Dictionary* for its sixth edition to reflect the most current vocabulary and usage in both languages.

Since our goal is to ensure that users will always find the words and phrases they seek, the greatest change for this new edition is the addition of some six thousand words and meanings. In choosing among possible additions, we have paid particular attention to frequency of use in written and spoken contexts, since a user is more likely to seek a word that appears frequently (e.g., *libertad* 'liberty', number 540 in frequency according to the extensive list available at www.wordfrequency.info) than one that appears infrequently (e.g., *verdolaga* 'purslane', number 19,705).

Frequency of use cannot serve as the sole criterion for new material, however, for three reasons. First, some words become current so quickly that no frequency list can possibly capture them. Digital terminology offers good examples of this trend, such as the word *app*, which has risen from obscurity to universal acceptance in very little time. Second, some of the changes that a dictionary should reflect occur at a semantic or phrasal level not captured by frequencies. Current expressions such as *to go off on* 'to scold' and *to be down with* 'to be in agreement with' consist of extremely frequent words used in novel ways. Finally, a word can be essential without being frequent. Medical terms, for example, can be vitally important to anyone negotiating another nation's health system, even if they are used infrequently outside of medical contexts.

Medicine is in fact one of four cultural and technical areas of increasing global importance for which we have specially enhanced our coverage for this edition. Along with the 600 new words and meanings that have been added in this field, the sixth edition incorporates 750 new items from the field of business, 500 relating to digital technology, and over 400 relating to the terminology of several globally popular sports, including basketball, baseball, soccer, tennis, and golf.

In many cases, the additions in these four areas warranted completely new entries, as in the case of *allergen* (Sp. *alérgeno*), *auditing* (*auditoría*), *adapter* (*adaptador*), and *unplayable* (*injugable*). In many others, we added a meaning or an equivalent to an existing entry, as in the case of *pinza* (to whose entry was added Eng. [*medical*] *clamp*), *fraudulento* (adding *bogus*), *descifrar* (*to decrypt*), and *abanicar* (*to swing and miss*). On the English side, many additions take the form of compounds attached to existing entries—for example, *clubfoot* (*pie zambo*), added to the *club* entry; *business agreement* (*con-*

venio comercial), added to the *business* entry; *copy protection* (*protección contra copias*) added to *copy*; and *corner kick* (*córner*) added to *corner*.

To further increase the utility of the *Dictionary* for beginning learners of both Spanish and English, we have added "blind" or reference entries for irregular verb forms that differ markedly from their citation forms. These entries take the following form: *quepa*, *quepo*: ver *caber* (Spanish–English) and *frozen*: see *freeze* (English–Spanish).

Finally, we have invested considerable effort in expanding and perfecting the already well-developed set of semantic delimiters or disambiguators whose purpose is to help users differentiate among meanings in polysemic words. The English word *easy*, for example, has different Spanish equivalents according to whether it means 'simple' (*fácil*, *sencillo*), 'compliant' (*fácil*), 'comfortable' (*cómodo*), 'informal' (*desenvuelto*), or 'unworried' (*tranquilo*). Similarly, the Spanish word *gusto* has different equivalents for its several meanings: 'sentido', 'sabor', 'sentido estético' (*taste*), 'agrado' (*pleasure*), and 'preferencia personal' (*like*).

Preámbulo a la sexta edición

El *Diccionario Universidad de Chicago Inglés–Español* se ha compilado para el uso general de estudiantes hispanoparlantes que aprenden el inglés de los Estados Unidos y para estudiantes angloparlantes de los Estados Unidos que estudian español. Para acompasarse a los rápidos cambios culturales y lingüísticos que se vienen sucediendo desde comienzos del siglo XXI, se ha hecho una revisión profunda del *Diccionario* con el fin de reflejar el vocabulario y los usos más actualizados en ambas lenguas.

Ya que nuestro propósito es asegurar que los usuarios siempre encuentren los términos y expresiones que buscan, el cambio más sustancial de esta nueva edición es la inclusión de unos seis mil términos y significados nuevos. Para elegir entre las muchas posibles adiciones, se le prestó mucha atención a la frecuencia de uso en el medio escrito y oral, ya que es más probable que un usuario se encuentre con una palabra que aparece con frecuencia (v.g., *libertad*, que ocupa el puesto 540 en frecuencia según la exhaustiva lista de frecuencias disponible en www.wordfrequency.info) que con otra palabra que aparece con baja frecuencia (v.g., *verdolaga*, que ocupa el puesto 19.705 en la misma lista).

Sin embargo, la frecuencia de uso no puede ser el único criterio empleado para incluir material nuevo, por tres razones. En primer lugar, algunas palabras se generalizan tan rápidamente que no alcanzan a ser incluidas en listas de frecuencia. Un buen ejemplo de esta tendencia lo constituye la terminología digital; considérese la palabra inglesa *app* 'aplicación informática', que en muy poco tiempo ha pasado de ser casi desconocida a tener aceptación general. En segundo lugar, algunos de los cambios que debe reflejar un diccionario suceden al nivel de la frase, y estos cambios no se pueden registrar meramente a partir de las frecuencias de los términos. Algunas expresiones actuales tales como *to go off on* 'regañar' y *to be down with* 'estar de acuerdo con' están constituidas por palabras de alta frecuencia empleadas en combinaciones novedosas. Por último, una palabra puede ser esencial sin por ello ser muy frecuente. Por ejemplo, la terminología médica puede ser de importancia vital para alguien que está tratando de resolver un problema de salud mientras se encuentra en un país extranjero. Por lo tanto, esas palabras deben figurar en el *Diccionario* aunque sean de poca frecuencia fuera de los contextos médicos.

De hecho, la medicina es una de las cuatro áreas culturales y técnicas cuya cobertura se ha aumentado en esta edición, debido a su importancia cada vez mayor en el contexto internacional. Además de 600 nuevos términos y significados del área médica, la presente edición incorpora 750 nuevos términos del campo de los negocios, 500 relacionados con el mundo de la informática y la tecnología digital y más de 400

relacionados con varios deportes de popularidad mundial, incluyendo el baloncesto, el béisbol, el fútbol, el tenis y el golf.

En muchos casos, las incorporaciones a estos cuatro campos nos llevaron a crear entradas completamente nuevas, como es el caso de *alérgeno* (ing. *allergen*), *auditoría* (*auditing*), *adaptador* (*adapter*) e *injugable* (*unplayable*). En muchos otros casos, se agregó un significado o un equivalente nuevo a una entrada preexistente. Tal es el caso de *pinza* (a cuya entrada se le agregó el significado inglés de [*medical*] *clamp*), *fraudulento* (*bogus*), *descifrar* (*decrypt*) y *abanicar* (con el significado en béisbol de *to swing and miss*). En el lado inglés, se incorporaron muchos términos compuestos a entradas ya existentes, tales como *clubfoot* (*pie zambo*), que fue agregado a la entrada de *club*; *business agreement* (*convenio comercial*), que fue agregado a la entrada de *business*; *copy protection* (*protección contra copias*) agregado a *copy*; y *corner kick* (*córner*) agregado a *corner*.

Para hacer todavía más útil el *Diccionario* para los estudiantes principiantes tanto de español como de inglés, se han agregado entradas "ciegas" o de referencia, para las formas verbales irregulares que son muy diferentes de sus formas infinitivas. Estas entradas tienen la siguiente estructura: *quepa*, *quepo*: ver *caber* (español–inglés) y *frozen*: see *freeze* (inglés–español).

Por último, se ha hecho un esfuerzo considerable para expandir y perfeccionar todavía más los delimitadores semánticos o desambiguadores, que tienen como propósito asistir a los usuarios a distinguir entre los diversos significados de palabras polisémicas. Por ejemplo, la palabra inglesa *easy* tiene diferentes equivalentes en español según signifique 'simple' (*fácil* o *sencillo*), 'compliant' (*fácil*), 'comfortable' (*cómodo*), 'informal' (*desenvuelto*) o 'unworried' (*tranquilo*). Del mismo modo, la palabra española *gusto* tiene diferentes equivalentes ingleses para sus múltiples significados: *taste* para 'sentido', 'sabor', 'sentido estético', *pleasure* para 'agrado' y *like* para 'preferencia personal'.

How to Use *The University of Chicago Spanish–English Dictionary*

Order of Entries

Alphabetical order is observed irrespective of hyphens or spaces, such that *air conditioner* precedes *aircraft* and *middle school* precedes *middle-sized*. Homographs are placed under a single entry (*lie* 'to prevaricate', *lie* 'to recline', both pronounced [laɪ]), unless they are pronounced differently (e.g., *bow* [baʊ] 'forward end of a vessel', *bow* [bo] 'bend, curve'). Regarding Spanish, according to the current policy of the Spanish Royal Academy,[1] *ch* and *ll* are no longer recognized as separate letters, such that *ch* now follows *ce* and precedes *ci*, and *ll* follows *li* and precedes *lo* in alphabetization.

Compounds listed within entries are also alphabetized. However, the need to list compounds under their first element sometimes interferes with alphabetization, as when *slumlord*, a compound listed under *slum*, comes before the next headword, *slumber*, even though strict alphabetization would require the reverse.

Spelling

Spelling of English words reflects common American usage, variants being noted where applicable (*ax*, *axe*; *sulfur*, *sulphur*; *stymie*, *stymy*). The spelling of Spanish words, where possible, follows the conventions of the Spanish Royal Academy. For the orthography of problematic Spanish words such as recent borrowings (*escáner*, *scooter*), country names (*Malí*, *Irak*) and adjectives of nationality (*zimbabuo*), a variety of authorities were consulted, including the *Diccionario del español actual*, the *Diccionario de dudas*, the *Libro de estilo* published by the Madrid newspaper *El País*, and various Internet sources.[2] It should be noted that there is vacillation in some cases, such as *Bahrain*, which is listed as *Bahrein* in the *Libro de estilo* and as *Bahráin* or *Bahréin* in the *Diccionario de dudas*. In these cases, we either opt for the form that appears to be most generally accepted or provide multiple equivalents.

1. Real Academia Española, *Ortografía de la lengua española* (Madrid: Espasa-Calpe, 1999), 2.

2. Manuel Seco, Olimpia Andrés, and Gabino Ramos, *Diccionario del español actual* (Madrid: Aguilar, 1999); Manuel Seco, *Diccionario de dudas y dificultades de la lengua española*, 10th ed. (Madrid: Espasa-Calpe, 1998); *El País: Libro de estilo*, 9th ed. (Madrid: Ediciones El País, 1990).

Omissions

Some categories of words are systematically omitted from the vocabulary entries. Adverbial forms ending in *-ly* (English) and *-mente* (Spanish) are included only when their usage and meaning are not transparently derivable from their adjectival bases. Thus, *clearly* is omitted, as its usage is predictable from its adjectival base ('in a clear way'), while *surely* is included, since in addition to 'in a sure way', it means 'undoubtedly' or 'without fail'. Similarly, *claramente* 'clearly' is omitted, while *atentamente* is retained, since the latter, in addition to meaning 'in an attentive manner', is used as a farewell, equivalent to 'yours truly'. Also, English nouns ending in *-ing* and adjectives in *-ed*, which may appear as glosses of Spanish words, are not always accorded separate entries on the English–Spanish side, due to their derivational regularity and to considerations of space.

Structure of Entries

1. HEADWORD. Spelling variants, if any, follow the most frequent form, which appears first. In Spanish, occupational designations, titles, and kinship terms are shown in both masculine and feminine forms, as in *abogado -da*.
2. PRONUNCIATION. Pronunciation of English words is indicated through a modified version of the International Phonetic Alphabet, whose conventions are explained on pp. 292–93. No individual transcription of Spanish words is required, given the simplicity and consistency of the Spanish orthographic system. See "The Spanish Spelling System and the Sounds Represented" (p. 2) for an explanation.
3. GRAMMATICAL CATEGORY. Meanings are marked according to whether they reflect usage as a noun (N), adjective (ADJ), adverb (ADV), conjunction (CONJ), preposition (PREP), pronoun (PRON), interjection (INTERJ), transitive verb (VT), or intransitive verb (VI). The exception to this rule is that nouns on the Spanish–English side are marked only by gender, M (masculine noun) or F (feminine noun).

   Order of meanings within an entry reflects frequency of usage. Where more than one grammatical category can be rendered by the same gloss, the two are listed together, cf. Eng. *red*, which can be glossed as Sp. *rojo* in both its adjective and noun meanings.

   Traditionally, Spanish adjectives are listed in their masculine form only. However, where the adjective normally functions as a noun as well, it is shown with both masculine and feminine forms if both are possible, cf. the case of *africano -na*, which can mean *African* in the adjectival sense as well as *African* (*man*) and *African* (*woman*).

   Special mention must be made of the combination "VI/VT." Occasionally, a single verb form may function both transitively and intransitively, e.g., both *to eat* and its Spanish equivalent *comer*. Not infrequently, however, Spanish glosses of English intransitives require the addition of the pronominal particle *-se*. Thus, in cases such as *to bathe*, marked "VI/VT" and glossed *bañar(se)*, it should be under-

stood that the bare form is transitive and the *-se* form intransitive. Finally, where transitivity differs between a headword and its equivalent in the second language, particles must be added to reflect this, as in the case of the transitive English verb *to regret*, which is glossed in Spanish as *arrepentirse de*, since *arrepentirse* alone is intransitive. Where an English verb can be used both transitively and intransitively and its Spanish equivalent is only intransitive, the latter may sometimes be made transitive through the addition of a preposition, which appears in brackets. Thus, English *fight* is glossed as *pelear* [*con*] to show that its intransitive equivalent is *pelear*, whereas its transitive equivalent is *pelear con*.

Again for reasons of economy, pronominal forms of Spanish verbs are omitted in two cases: first, when the particle *-se* functions as a direct object, either reflexive or reciprocal, cf. *mirarse*, which can mean both *to look at oneself* and *to look at each other*, and second, when the addition of *-se* does not affect the English translation, cf. *bañar(se)*, glossed in both meanings as *to bathe*. In contrast, pronominal forms of verbs are included when they differ substantially in meaning from the bare forms, cf. *ir*, glossed as *to go*, vs. *irse*, which means *to leave*.

4. DELIMITERS. Whenever a word, within a grammatical category, is considered to have two or more meanings, these are differentiated by means of delimiters, that is, explanatory markers. Most commonly, synonyms are used, cf. *retort*, which in the meaning 'reply' is glossed as *réplica* and in the meaning 'vessel' as *retorta*. On occasion, however, other strategies may be adopted. Thus, transitive verbs are sometimes best differentiated according to the objects they take, cf. *to negotiate* (a contract), which is glossed *negociar*, while *to negotiate* (an obstacle) is glossed *salvar*. Similarly, adjectives may be most easily distinguished by showing the referents to which they regularly apply, cf. *refreshing*, which applied to drink is *refrescante*, to sleep is *reparador*, and to honesty is *amable*. Not infrequently, a single equivalent covers almost all meanings of a headword in a single grammatical category. In such cases, only the "exceptional" meaning, placed second, is delimited. For example, the equivalent of Eng. *net* in almost all its meanings is Sp. *red*, but when it refers specifically to a hairnet it is *redecilla*. Although delimiters typically precede the gloss they are meant to distinguish, occasionally they are placed afterward. In these cases they are meant to erase doubts about the applicability of a given gloss in a specific secondary context, cf. *site*, whose gloss *sitio* is followed by the delimiter "also Internet."

5. GLOSSES. Insofar as is possible, glosses are intended to match the headword in terms of meaning, register, and frequency. Thus, *cop* is glossed as *poli* rather than the more formal *policía*. Similarly, *orinar* is glossed as *to urinate* rather than the informal and vulgar *to pee*. Glosses separated by a comma are to be considered interchangeable, if not perfectly synonymous. Semicolons, on the other hand, indicate separate meanings.

6. REGIONAL USAGE. No systematic attempt has been made to reflect regional usage in either English or Spanish, since in the great majority of cases a word of more general currency is available as a gloss. Thus, among the many Spanish equivalents of Eng. *peasant*, Sp. *campesino* is understood everywhere, even where a local term also exists, such as Puerto Rican *jíbaro*, Cuban *guajiro*, and Chilean

guaso. However, Spanish regional usage is marked where any of the following conditions are met: (1) there is no term of international currency, or it might not be understood in a given location (cf. the various regional Spanish equivalents of Eng. *bean*) or (2) a specific regionalism is known throughout the Spanish-speaking world to be typical of a given dialect, cf. River Plate *che* 'hey!', Mexican *ándale* 'come on!', *cuate* 'pal'.

7. STYLISTIC MARKERS. Because, as mentioned earlier, equivalents are chosen in order to match headwords in all aspects of their meaning, including register and frequency, stylistic markers are only infrequently employed. For example, there is no need to mark the Spanish gloss *tonto* as familiar, since it is meant to be equivalent to the equally familiar Eng. *fool*. Only five register markers are employed: literary (*lit*), which also includes poetic and formal language; familiar (*fam*), which designates words used among family and friends; vulgar (*vulg*), for words whose use is socially censured; pejorative (*pej*), which implies a negative evaluation; and *offensive* (not abbreviated), for words meant to insult people.
8. COMPOUNDS. Ease of usage would dictate that each lexical item receive its own entry, but for reasons of economy this is not possible in a concise dictionary. This explains why compound words, which are composed of two or more preexisting words, are listed in almost all cases under the entry of their initial constituent, at the end of the corresponding grammatical category. Thus, *doghouse* is listed as *—house*, under *dog*. There are certain exceptions to this convention, however. First, compounds are listed under the headword of their second constituent when the first is extremely frequent, as are the so-called empty verbs such as Eng. *keep*, *take*, *turn*, Sp. *hacer*, *tener*, *tomar*. Thus, *to have a good time*, glossed *divertirse*, is listed under *time* rather than *have*, and *tener paciencia*, glossed *to be patient*, is under *paciencia* rather than *tener*. Second, English compounds whose first element is a preposition (*offsides*, *outcast*, *overcome*) are listed as separate headwords, chiefly because of their frequent grammatical complexity, cf. *overhead*, which can be an adverb (*it flew overhead*), an adjective (*overhead projector*), or a noun (*overhead from grant money*). Conversely, derived words, that is, words that contain one or more affixes (e.g., *antiabortion*, composed of the prefix *anti-* plus *abortion*, and *kingdom*, composed of *king* plus the suffix *-dom*), are listed as separate headwords.
9. ILLUSTRATIVE PHRASES. Appearing together with the compound words pertinent to any given grammatical category are illustrative phrases, a category defined so as to include idioms, collocations, proverbs, and, especially, sentences required to clarify usage in some way, as when the usage of *gustarle a uno* as a gloss of *to like* is illustrated by the phrase *he likes dogs*, with the translation *le gustan los perros*.

Cómo usar el *Diccionario Universidad de Chicago Inglés–Español*

Orden de las entradas

Se respeta el orden alfabético, independientemente de la presencia de guiones o espacios, de tal manera que *air conditioning* precede a *aircraft* y *middle school* precede a *middle-sized*. Los homógrafos se ubican en una sola entrada (*lie* 'mentir' y *lie* 'yacer', ambos con la pronunciación [laɪ]), a no ser que se pronuncien de forma diferente (e.g., *bow* [baʊ] 'proa' y *bow* [bo] 'curva'). En cuanto al español y siguiendo la política oficial de la Real Academia Española,[1] *ch* y *ll* ya no se reconocen como letras independientes, de tal manera que *ch* ahora sigue a *ce* y precede a *ci*, y *ll* sigue a *li* y precede a *lo* en el orden alfabético.

Asimismo, los compuestos incluidos dentro de una entrada determinada aparecen en orden alfabético a continuación de su primer elemento, lo cual a veces interfiere con el orden alfabético general. Así, por ejemplo, *rompeolas* aparece a continuación de *romper*, porque se trata de un compuesto de dicho verbo, si bien el orden alfabético requeriría lo contrario.

Ortografía

La ortografía de los vocablos ingleses refleja el uso general en inglés americano, y las variantes se incluyen en los casos pertinentes (*ax*, *axe*; *sulfur*, *sulphur*; *stymie*, *stymy*). La ortografía española sigue las convenciones de la Real Academia Española. Para la grafía española de palabras problemáticas, tales como préstamos recientes (*escáner*, *scooter*), nombres de países (*Malí*, *Irak*) y gentilicios (*zimbabuo*), se consultaron fuentes tales como el *Diccionario del español actual*, el *Diccionario de dudas*, el *Libro de estilo* de *El País* de Madrid y varios sitios en el internet.[2] Corresponde hacer notar que la grafía de algunos términos vacila entre varias posibles, cf. la versión española de *Bahrain*, que aparece como *Bahrein* en el *Libro de estilo* y como *Bahráin* o *Bahréin* en el *Diccionario de dudas*, en cuyo caso damos la forma que parece más generalmente aceptada u ofrecemos varias.

1. Real Academia Española, *Ortografía de la lengua española* (Madrid: Espasa-Calpe, 1999), 2.

2. Manuel Seco, Olimpia Andrés y Gabino Ramos, *Diccionario del español actual* (Madrid: Aguilar, 1999); Manuel Seco, *Diccionario de dudas y dificultades de la lengua española*, 10ª ed. (Madrid: Espasa-Calpe, 1998); *El País: Libro de estilo*, 9ª ed. (Madrid: Ediciones El País, 1990).

Omisiones

Algunas categorías de palabras se omiten sistemáticamente de las entradas del diccionario. Las formas adverbiales que terminan en *-mente* (español) y en *-ly* (inglés) se incluyen solamente cuando su uso y significado no pueden deducirse claramente de sus bases adjetivas. De esta forma, *claramente* se omite, ya que su significado es predecible a partir de su base adjetiva ('de manera clara'), mientras que *atentamente* se incluye, ya que además de significar 'de manera atenta', también se usa como fórmula de despedida epistolar. Del mismo modo, se omite *clearly*, porque su equivalente, 'de manera clara', se deduce de su base adjetiva, mientras que se incluye *surely* porque además de significar 'de forma segura' también quiere decir 'sin duda'. Debe notarse también que los sustantivos ingleses terminados en *-ing* y los adjetivos en *-ed*, que pueden aparecer como traducción de palabras españolas en la parte español–inglés, no figuran siempre como cabezas de artículo en la parte inglés–español debido a la total regularidad de su formación y a consideraciones de espacio.

Estructura de las entradas

1. PALABRAS CABEZA DE ARTÍCULO. Las variantes ortográficas, si las hay, siguen a la forma más frecuente, que aparece en primer término. En español, las designaciones de profesiones y oficios, los títulos y las relaciones de parentesco aparecen tanto en la forma masculina como en la femenina, como por ejemplo, *abogado -da*.
2. PRONUNCIACIÓN. La pronunciación de las palabras inglesas se indica mediante una versión modificada del Alfabético Fonético Internacional, cuyas convenciones se explican en las pgs. 292–93. No se requiere transcripción individual de las palabras españolas, gracias a la simplicidad y sistematicidad de la ortografía española. Para detalles, ver la sección titulada "The Spanish Spelling System" en la p. 2.
3. CATEGORÍA GRAMATICAL. Los significados se marcan según reflejen el uso de la palabra como sustantivo masculino (*m*), sustantivo femenino (*f*), adjetivo (*adj*), adverbio (*adv*), conjunción (*conj*), preposición (*prep*), pronombre (*pron*), interjección (*interj*), verbo transitivo (*vt*) o verbo intransitivo (*vi*). En inglés, en cambio, los sustantivos se marcan con *n*, abreviación de *noun*.

   Los significados dentro de una entrada aparecen ordenados de manera que el más frecuente figure primero. Cuando la misma traducción cubre el significado de dos categorías gramaticales, ambas aparecen juntas, cf. el inglés *red*, que puede traducirse como *rojo* tanto en su significado sustantivo como en el adjetivo.

   Siguiendo la tradición, los adjetivos españoles aparecen exclusivamente en su forma masculina. Sin embargo, cuando el adjetivo frecuentemente funciona además como sustantivo, se muestra tanto en la forma masculina como en la femenina si ambas son posibles, cf. el caso de *africano -na*, traducido al inglés como *African*, forma adecuada para todos sus usos.

   La combinación *vi/vt* merece mención especial. En ocasiones, una única forma verbal funciona tanto transitiva como intransitivamente, v.g., tanto *comer*

como su equivalente inglés *to eat*. Sin embargo, es también frecuente que las traducciones españolas de verbos intransitivos ingleses requieran el agregado de una partícula pronominal *-se*. Así, en casos tales como *to bathe*, que se marca "vi/vt" y se traduce como *bañar(se)*, debe entenderse que la forma no pronominalizada es transitiva y la forma con *-se* es intransitiva. En aquellos casos cuando la palabra cabeza de artículo y su equivalente en la otra lengua difieren en transitividad, se deben agregar partículas para reflejar esta diferencia. Tal es el caso del verbo *aprobar*, que se traduce al inglés como *to approve of* en algunos de sus significados, ya que *to approve* es intransitivo si no va acompañado de preposición. Finalmente, en los casos en los que un verbo español puede usarse tanto intransitiva como transitivamente y su equivalente inglés es exclusivamente intransitivo, este último puede a veces volverse transitivo mediante el agregado de una preposición entre corchetes. Así, el esp. *chivar* se traduce como *to snitch* [*on*] para mostrar que su forma intransitiva en inglés es *to snitch* mientras que el equivalente transitivo es *to snitch on*.

Por razones de espacio se omiten las formas pronominales de los verbos españoles en dos casos. En primer lugar, se omiten si la partícula pronominal hace las veces de complemento directo reflexivo o recíproco, cf. *mirarse* (a sí mismo o el uno al otro). En segundo lugar no se incluyen tampoco si la partícula pronominal no afecta la traducción al inglés, como en el caso de *bañar* y *bañarse*, ambos *to bathe*. Sí se incluyen aquellas formas pronominales que difieren semánticamente de sus verbos de base, cf. *ir* vs. *irse*.

4. INDICADORES SEMÁNTICOS. En aquellos casos en los que una palabra, dentro de una misma categoría gramatical, tiene dos o más acepciones, estas se distinguen por medio de indicadores semánticos, o sea, explicaciones parentéticas. Lo más frecuente es que se empleen sinónimos, cf. *arco*, que se traduce *arc* cuando se trata de una curva, como *arch* cuando se refiere a una estructura arquitectónica, y como *bow* cuando se trata de un arma, aunque en otras ocasiones se adoptan otras estrategias. Así, los verbos transitivos a veces se distinguen con mayor facilidad mediante los tipos de complementos directos que los acompañan, cf. *acordonar* (un zapato) *to lace*, (un lugar) *to rope off*, (una moneda) *to mill*, mientras que la forma más sencilla de distinguir adjetivos es mostrar los tipos de referentes a los cuales se aplican con mayor frecuencia, cf. *inseguro*, que aplicado a una personalidad se traduce por *insecure*, a un vehículo por *unsafe*, y al andar por *unsteady*. Es frecuente que un único equivalente abarque casi todas las acepciones de una palabra cabeza de artículo dentro de una categoría gramatical determinada. En esos casos, solamente el significado "excepcional", que aparece en segundo lugar, se acompaña de un indicador semántico. Por ejemplo, el equivalente de *acceso* en casi todas sus acepciones es *access*, excepto cuando se refiere a un ataque de tos o rabia, en cuyo caso se traduce como *fit*. Aunque los indicadores semánticos normalmente preceden a la traducción que les corresponde, en ocasiones se ubican después. En estos casos tienen como objetivo eliminar dudas acerca del empleo de una traducción determinada en un contexto secundario específico, cf. *acompañar*, cuya traducción *to accompany* va seguida de un indicador semántico "también en música" para confirmar al lector su aplicación a ese contexto.

5. TRADUCCIONES. En la medida de lo posible, se ha tratado de que las traducciones sean equivalentes a la palabra cabeza de artículo en cuanto a su significado, registro y frecuencia. Así, *poli* se traduce como *cop* y no como *policeman*, palabra más formal. De la misma forma, *to urinate* se traduce como *orinar* y no como *hacer pipí*, palabra más familiar. Las traducciones separadas por una coma deben considerarse equivalentes, aunque no sean exactamente sinónimas. El uso del punto y coma indica acepciones distintas.
6. USO REGIONAL. No se ha hecho ningún esfuerzo sistemático por reflejar usos regionales, ni en inglés ni en español, ya que en la gran mayoría de los casos existe una palabra de uso general. Así, entre los muchos equivalentes españoles de la palabra inglesa *peasant*, su equivalente español *campesino* se entiende en todo el mundo de habla hispana, aun cuando existan términos locales, tales como *jíbaro* en Puerto Rico, *guajiro* en Cuba y *guaso* en Chile. Sin embargo, el uso regional se indica para el español en tres casos específicos. En primer lugar se encuentran los casos en los que una palabra determinada podría resultar desconocida en una región dada, como los varios equivalentes españoles del ingl. *bean*. En segundo término, se han incluido regionalismos que se reconocen en todo el mundo de habla hispana como típicos de un dialecto determinado, cf. español rioplatense *che*, mexicano *ándale*, *cuate*.
7. INDICADORES DE ESTILO. Ya que, como se mencionó anteriormente, los equivalentes se eligen para que correspondan a las palabras cabeza de artículo en todos los aspectos de su significado, incluyendo nivel de lengua y frecuencia, los indicadores de estilo se usan poco. Por ejemplo, no hay necesidad de indicar que la palabra inglesa *fool* es familiar, ya que figura como equivalente del español *tonto*. Se han empleado cinco indicadores de estilo: literario (*lit*), que incluye lenguaje poético y formal, familiar (*fam*), que designa palabras que se usan en situaciones de intimidad, vulgar (*vulg*), que designa términos cuyo uso está censurado socialmente, peyorativo (*pey*), que designa palabras que tienen una carga connotativa negativa hacia el referente, y *ofensivo* (sin abreviar), que designa insultos.
8. COMPUESTOS. El criterio de facilidad de uso requeriría que cada palabra recibiera su propia entrada, pero por razones de economía de espacio esto no es posible en un diccionario conciso. Por lo tanto, las palabras compuestas, formadas por dos o más vocablos preexistentes, aparecen en casi todos los casos en la entrada de su primer constituyente, al final de la categoría gramatical correspondiente. De tal forma, *hombre rana* aparece como — *rana*, en la entrada de *hombre*. Hay ciertas excepciones a esta regla, sin embargo. En primer lugar, los compuestos aparecen bajo la cabeza de artículo de su segundo constituyente cuando el primero es extremadamente frecuente, tal como lo son los verbos semánticamente "vacíos" como el español *hacer*, *tener*, *tomar* y el inglés *to keep*, *to take*, *to turn*. De este modo, *tener paciencia* aparece en la entrada de *paciencia* y no en la de *tener*, y *to have a good time* figura bajo *time* y no bajo *to have*. En segundo lugar, los compuestos ingleses cuyo primer elemento es una preposición (*offsides*, *overcome*, *outcast*) aparecen como cabezas de artículo independientes, sobre todo debido a su complejidad gramatical, cf. *overhead*, que puede ser adverbio (*it flew overhead*, que equivale a *voló en lo alto*), adjetivo (*overhead projector*, es decir, *retroproyector*) y sustantivo (*overhead from*

grant money, o sea, *gastos generales de una subvención*). No obstante, las palabras derivadas, i.e., aquellas que contienen uno o más afijos (e.g., *anticuerpo*, compuesta del prefijo *anti-* y *cuerpo*, y *cabezón*, compuesta por *cabeza* y el sufijo *-ón*), figuran como cabezas de artículo independientes.

9. FRASES ILUSTRATIVAS. Junto con las palabras compuestas de una determinada categoría gramatical figuran las frases ilustrativas, una categoría que incluye expresiones idiomáticas, colocaciones típicas, refranes y, especialmente, oraciones necesarias para aclarar el uso de alguna palabra, como cuando el uso de *like* como traducción de *gustar* se ilustra con la frase *he likes dogs*, que se traduce *le gustan los perros*.

Spanish–English · Español–Inglés

List of Abbreviations / Lista de abreviaturas

adj	adjective	adjetivo
adv	adverb, adverbial	adverbio, adverbial
Am	America	América
art	article	artículo
Carib	Caribbean	Caribe
conj	conjunction	conjunción
def	definite	definido
dem	demonstrative	demostrativo
Esp	Spain, Spanish	España, español
f	feminine	femenino
fam	familiar	familiar
indef	indefinite	indefinido
interj	interjection	interjección
interr	interrogative	interrogativo
inv	invariable	invariable
lit	literary	literario
loc	locution	locución
m	masculine	masculino
Méx	Mexico	México
num	numeral	numeral
pej, pey	pejorative	peyorativo
pers	personal	personal
pl	plural	plural
pos	possessive	posesivo
prep	preposition, prepositional	preposición, preposicional
pron	pronoun	pronombre
rel	relative	relativo
RP	River Plate	Río de la Plata
sg	singular	singular
Sp	Spain, Spanish	España, español
v aux	auxiliary verb	verbo auxiliar
vi	intransitive verb	verbo intransitivo
vt	transitive verb	verbo transitivo
vulg	vulgar	vulgar

Spanish Pronunciation

Spanish orthography very closely mirrors Spanish pronunciation, much more so than is the case in English. This explains why, in bilingual dictionaries such as this, each English entry must be accompanied by a phonetic representation, while Spanish pronunciation may be presented in synoptic form.

This synopsis is meant only as an introduction, however. In spite of the clarity of the orthographical system of Spanish, the individual sounds of the language are difficult for adult native speakers of English to pronounce, and this difficulty is compounded by the syllabic structure of the language. For these reasons, readers who wish to perfect their pronunciation of Spanish are strongly advised to seek the help of a competent teacher.

To say that orthography mirrors pronunciation means that there is a close correlation between letters and sounds. Thus, most Spanish letters correspond to a single sound, or to a single family of closely related sounds, as is the case for all vowels and the consonants *f*, *l*, *m*, *n*, *p*, *t*, and *s*. In a few cases a single letter represents two very different sounds, as *c*, which is pronounced as *k* before *a*, *o*, and *u*, but *th* (as in *thin*, in parts of Spain, or as *s* in America) before *e* or *i*. Rarely, two letters represent a single sound, as in the case of *ch*.

The overarching differences between Spanish and English pronunciation are tenseness of articulation and syllabification within the breath group. Due to the tenseness of their articulation, for example, all Spanish vowels have a clear nondiphthongal character, unlike English long vowels, which tend to be bipartite (e.g., *late*, pronounced [le^{i}t]). Syllabification is a problem for English speakers because in Spanish, syllables are formed without respect to word boundaries, such that *el hado* 'fate' and *helado* 'ice cream' are both pronounced as e-la-do, and the phrase *tus otras hermanas* 'your other sisters' is syllabified as tu-so-tra-ser-ma-nas. In fast speech, vowels may combine, as in *lo ofendiste* 'you offended him', pronounced lo-fen-dis-te. Finally, when Spanish consonants occur in clusters, very often the articulation of the second influences that of the first, as when *un peso* 'one peso' is pronounced um-pe-so, and *en que* 'in which' is pronounced eŋ ke, where ŋ represents the sound of the letters *ng* in English.

The Spanish Spelling System and the Sounds Represented

I. VOWELS

i as a single vowel always represents a sound similar to the second vowel of *police*. Examples: **hilo, camino, piso.** As a part of a diphthong, it sounds like the *y* of English *yes*, *year*. Examples: **bien, baile, reina.**

e is similar to the vowel of *late* ([le^{i}t]), but without the diphthong. Examples: **mesa, hablé, tres.**

a is similar to the vowel of *pod*. Examples: **casa, mala, América.** Notably, **a** is always pronounced this way, even when not stressed. This contrasts with the English tendency to reduce unstressed vowels to schwa ([ə]), as in *America*, pronounced in English as [ə-mé-ri-kə].

o has a value similar to that of the vowel in Eng. *coat* [koʷt], but without the diphthong. Examples: **no, modo, amó.**

u has a value similar to that of English *oo*, as in *boot* [buʷt], but without the diphthong. Examples: **cura, agudo, uno.** Note that the letter **u** is not pronounced in the syllables **qui, que, gui,** and **gue** (unless spelled with dieresis, as in *bilingüe*). When **u** occurs in diphthongs such as those of **cuida, cuento, deuda,** it has the sound of *w* (as in *way*).

II. CONSONANTS

b and **v** represent the same sounds in Spanish. At the beginning of a breath group or when preceded by the *m* sound (which may be spelled *n*), they are both pronounced like English *b*. Examples: **bomba, en vez de, vine, invierno.** In other environments, especially between vowels, both letters are pronounced as a very relaxed *b*, in which the lips do not completely touch and the air is not completely stopped. This sound has no equivalent in English. Examples: **haba, uva, la vaca, la banda.**

c represents a *k* sound before **a, o, u, l,** and **r.** However, this sound is not accompanied by a puff of air as it is in Eng. *can* and *coat* (compare the *c* in *scan*, which is more similar to the Spanish sound). Examples: **casa, cosa, cuna, crudo, aclamar.** In contrast, when appearing before the vowels **e** and **i, c** is pronounced as s in Spanish America and the southwest of Spain, and as *th* (as in *thin*) in other parts of Spain (see **s** for more information).

ch is no longer considered to be a separate letter in the Spanish alphabet. However, it represents a single sound, which is similar to the English *ch* in *church* and *cheek*. Examples: **chato, chaleco, mucho.**

d is phonetically complex in Spanish. In terms of articulation, it is pronounced by the tongue touching the teeth rather than the alveolar ridge as in English. Second, it is represented by two variants. The first of these, which is similar to that of English *dame* and *did*, occurs at the beginning of breath groups or after **n** and **l.** Examples: **donde, falda, conde.** In all other situations the letter represents a sound similar to the *th* of English *then*. Examples: **hado, cuerda, cuadro, usted.** This sound tends to be very relaxed, to the point of disappearing in certain environments, such as word-final and intervocalic.

f is very similar to the English *f* sound. Examples: **faro, elefante, alfalfa.**

g is phonetically complex. Before the vowels **e** and **i,** it is pronounced as *h* in many American dialects, while in northern Spain it is realized like the *ch* in the German word *Bach*. Examples: **gente, giro.** At the beginning of breath groups and after nasals before the vowels **a, o, u,** and the consonants **l** and **r,** it is pronounced like the **g** of English *go*. Examples: **ganga, globo, grada.** In all other environments it is pronounced as a very relaxed *g*. Examples: **lago, la goma, agrado.**

h is silent. Examples: **hoja, humo, harto.**

j is realized in most American dialects as *h*, while in northern Spain it is pronounced like the *ch* in the German word *Bach*. Examples: **jamás, jugo, jota.**

k sounds like Eng. *k*, but without the accompanying puff of air. Examples: **kilo, keroseno.**

l is pronounced forward in the mouth, as the *l* in *leaf*, *leak*, never in the back, as in *bell*, *full*. Examples: **lado, ala, sol.**

ll is no longer considered to be a separate letter in the Spanish alphabet. However, it does represent a single sound, which differs widely in pronunciation throughout the Spanish-speaking world. In most areas, it is pronounced like the *y* of Eng. *yes*, though with greater tension. In extreme northern Spain and in parts of the Andes, it sounds like the *lli* in Eng. *million*. In the River Plate area it is pronounced like the *g* in *beige* or the *sh* in *ship*. Examples: **calle, llano, olla.**

m is essentially the same as in English. Examples: **madre, mano, cama.** However, in final position, as in **álbum** 'album', it is pronounced as [ŋ], the final sound of Eng. *sing*.

n is normally pronounced like Eng. *n*. Examples: **no, mano, hablan.** There are exceptions, however. For example, before **b, v, p,** and **m,** it is pronounced *m*, as in **en Barcelona, en vez de, un peso,** while before **k, g, j, ge-,** and **gi-,** it is realized as [ŋ], the final sound of Eng. *sing*, as in **anca, tengo, naranja, engendrar.**

ñ is similar to but more tense than the *ny* of Eng. *canyon*. Examples: **cañón, año, ñato.**

p is like English *p* except that it is not accompanied by a puff of air, as it is in Eng. *pill* and *papa* (compare the *p* in *spot*, which is more similar to the Spanish sound). Examples: **padre, capa, apuro.**

q combined with **u** has the sound of *k*. Examples: **queso, aquí, quien.**

r usually represents a sound similar to that of the *tt* in Eng. *kitty* and the *dd* in *ladder*. Examples: **caro, tren, comer.** In contrast, at the beginning of words and after **n, l, s,** the letter **r** is realized as a trill, as in **rosa, Enrique, alrededor, Israel.** The double letter **rr** always represents a trill, as in **carro, correr, guerrero.**

s is pronounced the same as in standard American English in most parts of Spanish America and in parts of southern Spain. In most of Spain, in contrast, it is realized with the tip of the tongue against the alveolar ridge, producing a whistling sound that is sometimes heard in southern dialects of American English. Examples: **solo, casa, es.** In the Caribbean and in coastal Spanish generally, there is a strong tendency to pronounce **s** in certain environments (usually preconsonantal) as *h*, or to eliminate it entirely. In these dialects, *esta* may be pronounced as *ehta* or *eta*.

t differs from English *t* in two respects: first, it is articulated by the tongue touching the teeth rather than the alveolar ridge, and second, it is not accompanied by a puff of air, as it is in English *too* and *titillate* (compare the *t* in *stop*, which is more similar to the Spanish sound). Examples: **tela, tino, tinta.**

x has a wide range of phonetic realizations. Between vowels, it is usually pronounced *ks* or *gs* (but never *gz*), as in **examen, próximo,** though in a few words it is pronounced as *s*, e.g., *exacto*, *auxilio*. Before a consonant, **x** is almost always pronounced *s*, as in **extranjero, experiencia.** In many Mexican and Central American words of indigenous origin, **x** represents *h*, as in **México.**

y varies regionally in its pronunciation. In most areas it is pronounced like the *y* of Eng. *yes*, though with greater tension. In the River Plate area it is pronounced like the *g* in *beige* or the *sh* in *ship*. Examples: **yo, ayer.**

z is subject to dialectal variation as well. In most parts of Spain, except the southwest, it is pronounced as the *th* in Eng. *thin*, *cloth*. In southwestern Spain and all of Spanish America, in contrast, it is pronounced *s*. Examples: **zagal, hallazgo, luz.**

Stress Assignment in Spanish and the Use of the Written Accent

Spanish words are normally stressed on the next-to-last syllable when they end in a vowel or the consonants **n** or **s**. Examples: **mesa, zapato, acontecimiento, hablan, mujeres.** Words whose pronunciation does not conform to this rule are considered exceptions, and their stressed syllable is indicated with an accent mark. Examples: **lámpara, estómago, género, acá, varón, además.**

Conversely, Spanish words are normally stressed on the final syllable when they end in a consonant other than **n** or **s**. Examples: **mujer, actualidad, pedal, voraz.** Words whose pronunciation does not conform to this rule are considered ex-

ceptions, and their stressed syllable is indicated with an accent mark. Examples: **nácar, volátil, lápiz.**

For the purposes of stress assignment, diphthongs are considered the same as simple vowels. Thus, **arduo** and **industria** are considered to have two and three syllables respectively, with regular stress on the penultimate syllable. However, some sequences of vowels are not considered diphthongs. For example, **alegría** and **continúo** are both considered to have four syllables, with the stress mark indicating the absence of a diphthong.

Until recently certain words received written accents in order to differentiate functions, even though they are pronounced identically (this is still true in certain cases, such as **de** 'of', **dé** 'give'). Thus, the orthography **esta** was assigned to the demonstrative adjective ('this', fem.), while the demonstrative pronoun ('this one', fem.) was written **ésta.** This convention is no longer observed by most writers.

Notes on Spanish Grammar

The Noun

Gender. All Spanish nouns, not just those that denote male or female beings, are assigned either masculine or feminine gender. As a general rule, male beings (**muchacho** 'boy', **toro** 'bull') and all nouns ending in **-o** (**lodo** 'mud') are assigned masculine gender (exceptions: **mano** 'hand', **foto** 'photo', both feminine). Similarly, female beings (**mujer** 'woman', **vaca** 'cow') and nouns ending in **-a** (**envidia** 'envy') tend to be assigned feminine gender (exceptions: **mapa** 'map', **drama** 'drama', **día** 'day', all masculine). In addition, nouns ending in **-ción, -tad, -dad, -tud,** and **-umbre** are always feminine: **canción** 'song', **facultad** 'college', **ciudad** 'city', **virtud** 'virtue', and **muchedumbre** 'crowd'. Otherwise, nouns ending in consonants and vowels other than **-o** and **-a** are of unpredictable gender. Some are feminine (**barbarie** 'savagery', **clase** 'class', **nariz** 'nose', **tribu** 'tribe'), while others are masculine (**antílope** 'antelope', **corte** 'cut', **mesón** 'lodge', **nácar** 'mother of pearl').

Nouns in **-o** that denote human beings (and to some extent, animals) form the feminine by replacing **-o** with **-a,** as in **tío** 'uncle' / **tía** 'aunt', **niño** 'boy' / **niña** 'girl', **oso** 'bear' / **osa** 'she-bear'. Where the masculine noun does not end in **-o,** the rules of formation are more complex. For example, nouns ending in **-ón, -or,** and **-án** require the addition of **-a,** as in the pairs **patrón / patrona** 'patron', **pastor / pastora** 'shepherd', **holgazán / holgazana** 'lazy person'. In other cases the difference is more unpredictable: **emperador** 'emperor' / **emperatriz** 'empress', **abad** 'abbot' / **abadesa** 'abbess'.

Some nouns have different genders according to their meanings: **corte** (m) 'cut', (f) 'court', **capital** (m) 'money capital', (f) 'capital city', while others have invariable endings which are used for both the masculine and the feminine: **artista** 'artist' (and all nouns ending in **-ista**), **amante** 'lover', **aristócrata** 'aristocrat', **homicida** 'murderer', **cliente** 'customer'. Finally, some words vacillate as to gender, e.g., **mar** 'sea', which is normally masculine but is feminine in certain expressions (**en alta mar** 'on the high seas') and in

poetic contexts, and **arte,** which is masculine in the singular but feminine in the plural. Some words, such as **armazón** and **esperma,** can be both masculine and feminine.

Pluralization. Nouns ending in an unaccented vowel and **-é** add **-s** to form the plural: **libro / libros, casa / casas, café / cafés.** Nouns ending in a consonant, in **-y,** or in an accented vowel other than **-é** add **-es: papel / papeles, canción / canciones, ley / leyes, rubí / rubíes.** Exceptions to this rule include the words **papá / papás** and **mamá / mamás,** as well as the small group of nouns ending in unaccented **-es** or **-is,** which do not change in the plural: **lunes** 'Monday', 'Mondays', **tesis** 'thesis', 'theses'.

Articles

Definite Article. The equivalent of English **the** is as follows: masculine singular, **el;** feminine singular, **la;** masculine plural, **los;** feminine plural, **las.** Feminine words beginning with stressed **a** or **ha** take **el** in the singular and **las** in the plural: **el alma** 'the soul' / **las almas** 'the souls', **el hacha** 'the hatchet' / **las hachas** 'the hatchets'. In spite of this, these nouns remain feminine in the singular, as shown by adjective agreement: **el alma bendita** 'the blessed soul'. When preceded by the prepositions **a** and **de,** the masculine singular article **el** forms the contractions **al** and **del.**

Indefinite Article. The equivalent of English **a, an** is as follows: masculine singular, **un;** feminine singular, **una.** In the plural, masculine **unos** and feminine **unas** are equivalent to English **some.** Feminine words beginning with stressed **a** or **ha** take **un** in the singular and **unas** in the plural: **un alma** 'a soul' / **unas almas** 'some souls', **un hacha** 'a hatchet' / **unas hachas** 'some hatchets'.

Adjectives

Agreement. The adjective in Spanish agrees in gender and number with the noun it modifies: **el lápiz rojo** 'the red pencil', **la casa blanca** 'the white house', **los libros interesantes** 'the interesting books', **las flores hermosas** 'the beautiful flowers'.

Formation of the Plural. Adjectives follow the same rules as nouns for the formation of the plural: **pálido, pálidos** 'pale', **fácil, fáciles** 'easy', **cortés, corteses** 'courteous', **capaz, capaces** 'capable'.

Formation of the Feminine. Adjectives ending in **-o** change to **-a: blanco, blanca** 'white'. Adjectives ending in other vowels are invariable: **verde** 'green', **fuerte** 'strong', **indígena** 'indigenous, native', **pesimista** 'pessimistic', **baladí** 'trivial', as are adjectives ending in a consonant: **fácil** 'easy', **cortés** 'courteous', **mayor** 'older', 'larger'. Some cases are more complex: (a) adjectives ending in **-ón, -án, -or** (except comparatives like **mayor**) add **-a** to form the feminine: **holgazán, holgazana** 'lazy', **preguntón, preguntona** 'inquisitive', **hablador, habladora** 'talkative'; (b) ad-

jectives of nationality ending in a consonant add **-a** to form the feminine: **francés, francesa** 'French', **español, española** 'Spanish', **alemán, alemana** 'German'.

Adverbs

Most adverbs are formed by adding **-mente** to the feminine form of the adjective: **clara** 'clear' / **claramente** 'clearly', **fácil** 'easy' / **fácilmente** 'easily'.

Comparison of Inequality in Adjectives and Adverbs

The comparative of inequality is formed by placing **más** or **menos** before the positive form of the adjective or adverb: **más rico que** 'richer than', **menos rico que** 'less rich than', **más tarde** 'later', **menos tarde** 'less late'. The superlative is formed by placing the definite article **el** before the comparative: **el más rico** 'the richest', **el menos rico** 'the least rich'.

The following adjectives and adverbs have irregular forms of comparison:

Positive	*Comparative*	*Superlative*
bueno	mejor	el (la) mejor
malo	peor	el (la) peor
grande	mayor	el (la) mayor
pequeño	menor	el (la) menor

Common Spanish Suffixes

-aco is a pejorative suffix: **pajarraco** 'ugly bird' (from **pájaro** 'bird'), **libraco** 'large, bulky book' (**libro** 'book')

-ada
a. attaches to verbal stems to indicate an action: **mirada** 'look' (**mirar** 'to look'), **empujada** 'push' (**empujar** 'to push')
b. attaches to noun stems to indicate a blow: **cachetada** 'blow on the cheek' (**cachete** 'cheek'), **puñalada** 'stab with a dagger' (**puñal** 'dagger')
c. attaches to nominal stems to indicate an action characteristic of a person or group: **bobada** 'foolish act' (**bobo** 'fool'), **niñada** 'childish act' (**niño** 'child')

-al, -ar attach to nouns indicating trees to form nouns that denote a grove: **naranjal** 'orange grove' (from **naranjo** 'orange tree'), **pinar** 'pine grove' (**pino** 'pine tree')

-azo attaches to noun stems, forming nouns that indicate
a. augmentation: **hombrazo** 'big man' (**hombre** 'man'), **marranazo** 'large hog' (**marrano** 'hog')

b. a blow or explosion: **porrazo** 'blow with a club' (**porra** 'club'), **cañonazo** 'cannon shot' (**cañón** 'cannon')

-cito is a diminutive suffix: **cochecito** 'a little car' (**coche** 'car'), **mujercita** 'little woman' (**mujer** 'woman')

-dor forms agent nouns from verbs: **hablador** 'talker' (**hablar** 'to talk'), **regulador** 'regulator' (**regular** 'to regulate'), which are sometimes used as adjectives: **hablador** 'talkative', **regulador** 'regulating'

-ejo is a pejorative suffix: **librejo** 'worthless book' (**libro** 'book'), **lugarejo** 'Podunk' (**lugar** 'place')

-ería attaches to noun stems to denote

a. a place where something is made or sold: **zapatería** 'shoestore' (**zapato** 'shoe'), **pastelería** 'pastry shop' (**pastel** 'pastry')

b. a profession, business, or occupation: **carpintería** 'carpentry' (**carpintero** 'carpenter'), **ingeniería** 'engineering' (**ingeniero** 'engineer')

c. a group: **chiquillería** 'bunch of children' (**chiquillo** 'little kid')

-ero *a.* attaches to nouns to indicate a person who makes, sells, or is in charge of something: **librero** 'bookseller' (**libro** 'book'), **zapatero** 'shoemaker' (**zapato** 'shoe'), **carcelero** 'jailer' (**cárcel** 'jail')

b. attaches to nominal stems to form adjectives: **guerrero** 'warlike' (**guerra** 'war'), **conejero** 'for hunting rabbits' (**conejo** 'rabbit')

-ez, -eza are used to make abstract nouns from adjectival bases: **vejez** 'old age' (**viejo** 'old'), **niñez** 'childhood' (**niño** 'child'), **grandeza** 'greatness' (**grande** 'large, great'), **rareza** 'rarity' (**raro** 'rare')

-ía forms abstract nouns from adjectival bases: **valentía** 'courage' (**valiente** 'brave'), **cobardía** 'cowardice' (**cobarde** 'coward')

-ico is a diminutive suffix: **ratico** 'little while' (**rato** 'while'), **momentico** 'brief moment' (**momento** 'moment')

-(i)ento attaches to adjectives to indicate attenuation, as in **amarillento** 'yellowish' (**amarillo** 'yellow'), or an undesirable quality, as in **hambriento** 'hungry' (**hambre** 'hunger')

-illo is sometimes a diminutive suffix: **politiquillo** 'insignificant politician' (**político** 'politician'), **chiquillo** 'little kid' (**chico** 'child')

-ísimo attaches to adjectives to indicate an extreme degree of a quality: **hermosísimo** 'very beautiful' (**hermoso** 'beautiful')

-ito is a diminutive suffix: **librito** 'small book' (**libro** 'book'), **casita** 'little house' (**casa** 'house')

-izo forms adjectives from nominal stems, indicating a tendency or attenuation: **rojizo** 'reddish' (**rojo** 'red'), **olvidadizo** 'forgetful' (**olvidar** 'to forget')

-mente is the adverbial ending attached to the feminine form of the adjective: **generosamente** 'generously' (**generoso** 'generous'), **claramente** 'clearly' (**claro** 'clear')

-ón *a.* is an augmentative adjectival suffix: **barrigón** 'potbellied' (**barriga** 'belly'), **cabezón** 'large-headed' (**cabeza** 'head')
b. attaches to verb stems to denote sudden actions: **tirón** 'pull, jerk' (**tirar** 'to pull'), **apretón** 'push' (**apretar** 'to push')

-oso forms adjectives from nouns, indicating abundance or character: **rocoso** 'rocky' (**roca** 'rock'), **tormentoso** 'stormy' (**tormenta** 'storm')

-ote, -ota is an augmentative and pejorative suffix attached to nouns: **discursote** 'long, boring speech' (**discurso** 'speech'), **narizota** 'big ugly nose' (**nariz** 'nose')

-udo forms adjectives from nouns, indicating an excess: **peludo** 'hairy' (**pelo** 'hair'), **panzudo** 'big-bellied' (**panza** 'belly')

-ura forms abstract nouns from adjectives: **negrura** 'blackness' (**negro** 'black'), **altura** 'height' (**alto** 'high')

-uzco forms adjectives from other adjectives, indicating attenuation: **blancuzco** 'whitish' (**blanco** 'white'), **negruzco** 'blackish' (**negro** 'black')

Spanish Regular Verbs

First Conjugation

infinitive	**hablar**
pres. indic.	hablo, hablas, habla, hablamos, habláis, hablan
pres. subj.	hable, hables, hable, hablemos, habléis, hablen
pret. indic.	hablé, hablaste, habló, hablamos, hablasteis, hablaron
imp. indic.	hablaba, hablabas, hablaba, hablábamos, hablabais, hablaban

imp. subj.	hablara, hablaras, hablara, habláramos, hablarais, hablaran, *or* hablase, hablases, hablase, hablásemos, hablaseis, hablasen
fut. indic.	hablaré, hablarás, hablará, hablaremos, hablaréis, hablarán
cond.	hablaría, hablarías, hablaría, hablaríamos, hablaríais, hablarían
imper.	habla (tú), hable (usted), hablemos (nosotros), hablad (vosotros), hablen (ustedes)
pres. part.	hablando
past part.	hablado

Second Conjugation

infinitive	**comer**
pres. indic.	como, comes, come, comemos, coméis, comen
pres. subj.	coma, comas, coma, comamos, comáis, coman
pret. indic.	comí, comiste, comió, comimos, comisteis, comieron
imp. indic.	comía, comías, comía, comíamos, comíais, comían
imp. subj.	comiera, comieras, comiera, comiéramos, comierais, comieran, *or* comiese, comieses, comiese, comiésemos, comieseis, comiesen
fut. indic.	comeré, comerás, comerá, comeremos, comeréis, comerán
cond.	comería, comerías, comería, comeríamos, comeríais, comerían
imper.	come (tú), coma (usted), comamos (nosotros), comed (vosotros), coman (ustedes)
pres. part.	comiendo
past part.	comido

Third Conjugation

infinitive	**vivir**
pres. indic.	vivo, vives, vive, vivimos, vivís, viven
pres. subj.	viva, vivas, viva, vivamos, viváis, vivan
pret. indic.	viví, viviste, vivió, vivimos, vivisteis, vivieron
imp. indic.	vivía, vivías, vivía, vivíamos, vivíais, vivían
imp. subj.	viviera, vivieras, viviera, viviéramos, vivierais, vivieran, *or* viviese, vivieses, viviese, viviésemos, vivieseis, viviesen
fut. indic.	viviré, vivirás, vivirá, viviremos, viviréis, vivirán
cond.	viviría, vivirías, viviría, viviríamos, viviríais, vivirían
imper.	vive (tú), viva (usted), vivamos (nosotros), vivid (vosotros), vivan (ustedes)
pres. part.	viviendo
past part.	vivido

Spanish Irregular and Orthographic Changing Verbs

The superscript number or numbers listed as part of a verb entry indicate that the verb is to be conjugated like the model verb in this section that has the corresponding number. Only the tenses that have irregular forms or spelling changes are given, and these irregular forms and spelling changes are shown in boldface type.

1. **pensar**
   pres. indic. **pienso, piensas, piensa,** pensamos, pensáis, **piensan**
   pres. subj. **piense, pienses, piense,** pensemos, penséis, **piensen**
   imper. **piensa** (tú), **piense** (usted), pensemos (nosotros), pensad (vosotros), **piensen** (ustedes)

2. **perder**
   pres. indic. **pierdo, pierdes, pierde,** perdemos, perdéis, **pierden**
   pres. subj. **pierda, pierdas, pierda,** perdamos, perdáis, **pierdan**
   imper. **pierde** (tú), **pierda** (usted), perdamos (nosotros), perded (vosotros), **pierdan** (ustedes)

3. **discernir**
   pres. indic. **discierno, disciernes, discierne,** discernimos, discernís, **disciernen**
   pres. subj. **discierna, disciernas, discierna,** discernamos, discernáis, **disciernan**
   imper. **discierne** (tú), **discierna** (usted), discernamos (nosotros), discernid (vosotros), **disciernan** (ustedes)

4. **adquirir**
   pres. indic. **adquiero, adquieres, adquiere,** adquirimos, adquirís, **adquieren**
   pres. subj. **adquiera, adquieras, adquiera,** adquiramos, adquiráis, **adquieran**
   imper. **adquiere** (tú), **adquiera** (usted), adquiramos (nosotros), adquirid (vosotros), **adquieran** (ustedes)

5. **contar**
   pres. indic. **cuento, cuentas, cuenta,** contamos, contáis, **cuentan**
   pres. subj. **cuente, cuentes, cuente,** contemos, contéis, **cuenten**
   imper. **cuenta** (tú), **cuente** (usted), contemos (nosotros), contad (vosotros), **cuenten** (ustedes)

6. **volver**
   pres. indic. **vuelvo, vuelves, vuelve,** volvemos, volvéis, **vuelven**
   pres. subj. **vuelva, vuelvas, vuelva,** volvamos, volváis, **vuelvan**

imper. **vuelve** (tú), **vuelva** (usted), volvamos (nosotros) volved (vosotros), **vuelvan** (ustedes)
past part. **vuelto**

7. **dormir**
pres. indic. **duermo, duermes, duerme,** dormimos, dormís, **duermen**
pres. subj. **duerma, duermas, duerma, durmamos, durmáis, duerman**
pret. indic. dormí, dormiste, **durmió,** dormimos, dormisteis, **durmieron**
imp. subj. **durmiera, durmieras, durmiera, durmiéramos, durmierais, durmieran,** or **durmiese, durmieses, durmiese, durmiésemos, durmieseis, durmiesen**
imper. **duerme** (tú), **duerma** (usted), **durmamos** (nosotros), dormid (vosotros), **duerman** (ustedes)
pres. part. **durmiendo**

8. **sentir**
pres. indic. **siento, sientes, siente,** sentimos, sentís, **sienten**
pres. subj. **sienta, sientas, sienta, sintamos, sintáis, sientan**
pret. indic. sentí, sentiste, **sintió,** sentimos, sentisteis, **sintieron**
imp. subj. **sintiera, sintieras, sintiera, sintiéramos, sintierais, sintieran,** or **sintiese, sintieses, sintiese, sintiésemos, sintieseis, sintiesen**
imper. **siente** (tú), **sienta** (usted), **sintamos** (nosotros), sentid (vosotros), **sientan** (ustedes)
pres. part. **sintiendo**

9. **pedir**
pres. indic. **pido, pides, pide,** pedimos, pedís, **piden**
pres. subj. **pida, pidas, pida, pidamos, pidáis, pidan**
pret. indic. pedí, pediste, **pidió,** pedimos, pedisteis, **pidieron**
imp. subj. **pidiera, pidieras, pidiera, pidiéramos, pidierais, pidieran,** or **pidiese, pidieses, pidiese, pidiésemos, pidieseis, pidiesen**
imper. **pide** (tú), **pida** (usted), **pidamos** (nosotros), pedid (vosotros), **pidan** (ustedes)
pres. part. **pidiendo**

10. **reír**
pres. indic. **río, ríes, ríe,** reímos, reís, **ríen**
pres. subj. **ría, rías, ría, riamos, riáis, rían**
pret. indic. reí, reíste, **rió,** reímos, reísteis, **rieron**

imp. subj. **riera, rieras, riera, riéramos, rierais, rieran,** or **riese, rieses, riese, riésemos, rieseis, riesen**
imper. **ríe** (tú), **ría** (usted), **riamos** (nosotros), reíd (vosotros), **rían** (ustedes)
pres. part. **riendo**
past part. **reído**

11. **reñir**
pres. indic. **riño, riñes, riñe,** reñimos, reñís, **riñen**
pres. subj. **riña, riñas, riña, riñamos, riñáis, riñan**
pret. indic. reñí, reñiste, **riñó,** reñimos, reñisteis, **riñeron**
imp. subj. **riñera, riñeras, riñera, riñéramos, riñerais, riñeran,** or **riñese, riñeses, riñese, riñésemos, riñeseis, riñesen**
imper. **riñe** (tú), **riña** (usted), **riñamos** (nosotros), reñid (vosotros), **riñan** (ustedes)
pres. part. **riñendo**

12. **seguir**
pres. indic. **sigo, sigues, sigue,** seguimos, seguís, **siguen**
pres. subj. **siga, sigas, siga, sigamos, sigáis, sigan**
pret. indic. seguí, seguiste, **siguió,** seguimos, seguisteis, **siguieron**
imp. subj. **siguiera, siguieras, siguiera, siguiéramos, siguierais, siguieran,** or **siguiese, siguieses, siguiese, siguiésemos, siguieses, siguiesen**
imper. **sigue** (tú), **siga** (usted), **sigamos** (nosotros), seguid (vosotros), **sigan** (ustedes)
pres. part. **siguiendo**

13. **erguir**
pres. indic. **yergo, yergues, yergue,** erguimos, erguís, **yerguen** or **irgo, irgues, irgue,** erguimos, erguís, **irguen**
pres. subj. **yerga, yergas, yerga, irgamos, irgáis, yergan** or **irga, irgas, irga, irgamos, irgáis, irgan**
pret. indic. erguí, erguiste, **irguió,** erguimos, erguisteis, **irguieron**
imp. subj. **irguiera, irguieras, irguiera, irguiéramos, irguierais, irguieran,** or **irguiese, irguieses, irguiese, irguiésemos, irguieseis, irguiesen**
imper. **yergue** or **irgue** (tú), **yerga** or **irga** (usted), **irgamos** (nosotros), erguid (vosotros), **yergan** or **irgan** (ustedes)
pres. part. **irguiendo**

14. **elegir**
pres. indic. **elijo, eliges, elige,** elegimos, elegís, **eligen**
pres. subj. **elija, elijas, elija, elijamos, elijáis, elijan**

pret. indic. elegí, elegiste, **eligió,** elegimos, elegisteis, **eligieron**
imp. subj. **eligiera, eligieras, eligiera, eligiéramos, eligierais, eligieran,** or **eligiese, eligieses, eligiese, eligiésemos, eligieseis, eligiesen**
imper. **elige** (tú), **elija** (usted), **elijamos** (nosotros), elegid (vosotros), **elijan** (ustedes)
pres. part. **eligiendo**

15. **tañer**
pret. indic. tañí, tañiste, **tañó,** tañimos, tañisteis, **tañeron**
imp. subj. **tañera, tañeras, tañera, tañéramos, tañerais, tañeran,** or **tañese, tañeses, tañese, tañésemos, tañeseis, tañesen**
pres. part. **tañendo**

16. **bullir**
pret. indic. bullí, bulliste, **bulló,** bullimos, bullisteis, **bulleron**
imp. subj. **bullera, bulleras, bullera, bulléramos, bullerais, bulleran,** or **bullese, bulleses, bullese, bullésemos, bulleseis, bullesen**
pres. part. **bullendo**

17. **gruñir**
pret. indic. gruñí, gruñiste, **gruñó,** gruñisteis, **gruñeron**
imp. subj. **gruñera, gruñeras, gruñera, gruñéramos, gruñerais, gruñeran,** or **gruñese, gruñeses, gruñese, gruñésemos, gruñeseis, gruñesen**
pres. part. **gruñendo**

18. **creer**
pret. indic. creí, creíste, **creyó,** creímos, creísteis, **creyeron**
imp. subj. **creyera, creyeras, creyera, creyéramos, creyerais, creyeran,** or **creyese, creyeses, creyese, creyésemos, creyeseis, creyesen**
pres. part. **creyendo**
past part. **creído**

19. **huir**
pres. indic. **huyo, huyes, huye,** huimos, huís, **huyen**
pres. subj. **huya, huyas, huya, huyamos, huyáis, huyan**
pret. indic. hui, huiste, **huyó,** huimos, huisteis, **huyeron**
imp. subj. **huyera, huyeras, huyera, huyéramos, huyerais, huyeran,** or **huyese, huyeses, huyese, huyésemos, huyeseis, huyesen**

	imper.	**huye** (tú), **huya** (usted), **huyamos** (nosotros), huid (vosotros), **huyan** (ustedes)
	pres. part.	**huyendo**
20.	**argüir**	
	pres. indic.	**arguyo, arguyes, arguye,** argüimos, argüís, **arguyen**
	pres. subj.	**arguya,arguyas, arguya, arguyamos, arguyáis, arguyan**
	pret. indic.	argüí, argüiste, **arguyó,** argüimos, argüisteis, **arguyeron**
	imp. subj.	**arguyera, arguyeras, arguyera, arguyéramos, arguyerais, arguyeran,** or **arguyese, arguyeses, arguyese, arguyésemos, arguyeseis, arguyesen**
	imper.	**arguye** (tú), **arguya** (usted), **arguyamos** (nosotros), argüid (vosotros), **arguyan** (ustedes)
	pres. part.	**arguyendo**
21.	**errar**	
	pres. indic.	**yerro, yerras, yerra,** erramos, erráis, **yerran**
	pres. subj.	**yerre, yerres, yerre,** erremos, erréis, **yerren**
	imper.	**yerra** (tú), **yerre** (usted), erremos (nosotros), errad (vosotros), **yerren** (ustedes)
22.	**oler**	
	pres. indic.	**huelo, hueles, huele,** olemos, oléis, **huelen**
	pres. subj.	**huela, huelas, huela,** olamos, oláis, **huelan**
	imper.	**huele** (tú), **huela** (usted), oled (vosotros), **huelan** (ustedes)
23.	**avergonzar**	
	pres. indic.	**avergüenzo, avergüenzas, avergüenza,** avergonzamos, avergonzáis, **avergüenzan**
	pres. subj.	**avergüence, avergüences, avergüence, avergoncemos, avergoncéis, avergüencen**
	pret. indic.	**avergoncé,** avergonzaste, avergonzó, avergonzamos, avergonzasteis, avergonzaron
	imper.	**avergüenza** (tú), **avergüence** (usted), **avergoncemos** (nosotros), avergonzad (vosotros), **avergüencen** (ustedes)
24.	**degollar**	
	pres. indic.	**degüello, degüellas, degüella,** degollamos, degolláis, **degüellan**
	pres. subj.	**degüelle, degüelles, degüelle,** degollemos, degolléis, **degüellen**
	imper.	**degüella** (tú), **degüelle** (usted), degollemos (nosotros), degollad (vosotros), **degüellen** (ustedes)

25. **averiguar**

pres. subj. **averigüe, averigües, averigüe, averigüemos, averigüéis, averigüen**

pres. indic. **averigüé,** averiguaste, averiguó, averiguamos, averiguasteis, averiguaron

imper. averigua (tú), **averigüe** (usted), **averigüemos** (nosotros), averiguad (vosotros), **averigüen** (ustedes)

26. **continuar**

pres. indic. **continúo, continúas, continúa,** continuamos, continuáis, **continúan**

pres. subj. **continúe, continúes, continúe,** continuemos, continuéis, **continúen**

imper. **continúa** (tú), **continúe** (usted), continuemos (nosotros), continuad (vosotros), **continúen** (ustedes)

27. **reunir**

pres. indic. **reúno, reúnes, reúne,** reunimos, reunís, **reúnen**

pres. subj. **reúna, reúnas, reúna,** reunamos, reunáis, **reúnan**

imper. **reúne** (tú), **reúna** (usted), reunamos (nosotros), reunid (vosotros), **reúnan** (ustedes)

28. **enviar**

pres. indic. **envío, envías, envía,** enviamos, enviáis, **envían**

pres. subj. **envíe, envíes, envíe,** enviemos, enviéis, **envíen**

imper. **envía** (tú), **envíe** (usted), enviemos (nosotros), enviad (vosotros), **envíen** (ustedes)

29. **prohibir**

pres. indic. **prohíbo, prohíbes, prohíbe,** prohibimos, prohibís, **prohíben**

pres. subj. **prohíba, prohíbas, prohíba,** prohibamos, prohibáis, **prohíban**

imper. **prohíbe** (tú), **prohíba** (usted), prohibamos (nosotros), prohibid (vosotros), **prohíban** (ustedes)

30. **buscar**

pres. subj. **busque, busques, busque, busquemos, busquéis, busquen**

pret. indic. **busqué,** buscaste, buscó, buscamos, buscasteis, buscaron

imper. busca (tú), **busque** (usted), **busquemos** (nosotros), buscad (vosotros), **busquen** (ustedes)

31. **trocar**

pres. indic. **trueco, truecas, trueca,** trocamos, trocáis, **truecan**
pres. subj. **trueque, trueques, trueque, troquemos, troquéis, truequen**
pret. indic. **troqué,** trocaste, trocó, trocamos, trocasteis, trocaron
imper. **trueca** (tú), **trueque** (usted), **troquemos** (nosotros), trocad (vosotros), **truequen** (ustedes)

32. **convencer**

pres. indic. **convenzo,** convences, convence, convencemos, convencéis, convencen
pres. subj. **convenza, convenzas, convenza, convenzamos, convenzáis, convenzan**
imper. convence (tú), **convenza** (usted), **convenzamos** (nosotros), convenced (vosotros), **convenzan** (ustedes)

33. **esparcir**

pres. indic. **esparzo,** esparces, esparce, esparcimos, esparcís, esparcen
pres. subj. **esparza, esparzas, esparza, esparzamos, esparzáis, esparzan**
imper. esparce (tú), **esparza** (usted), **esparzamos** (nosotros), esparcid (vosotros), **esparzan** (ustedes)

34. **cocer**

pres. indic. **cuezo, cueces, cuece,** cocemos, cocéis, **cuecen**
pres. subj. **cueza, cuezas, cueza, cozamos, cozáis, cuezan**
imper. **cuece** (tú), **cueza** (usted), **cozamos** (nosotros), coced (vosotros), **cuezan** (ustedes)

35. **conocer**

pres. indic. **conozco,** conoces, conoce, conocemos, conocéis, conocen
pres. subj. **conozca, conozcas, conozca, conozcamos, conozcáis, conozcan**
imper. conoce (tú), **conozca** (usted), **conozcamos** (nosotros), conoced (vosotros), **conozcan** (ustedes)

36. **placer**

pres. indic. **plazco,** places, place, placemos, placéis, placen
pres. subj. **plazca, plazcas, plazca, plazcamos, plazcáis, plazcan**
imper. place (tú), **plazca** (usted), **plazcamos** (nosotros), placed (vosotros), **plazcan** (ustedes)

37. **yacer**

pres. indic. **yazco** or **yazgo** or **yago,** yaces, yace, yacemos, yacéis, yacen

pres. subj. **yazca, yazcas, yazca, yazcamos, yazcáis, yazcan,** or **yazga, yazgas, yazga, yazgamos, yazgáis, yazgan** or **yaga, yagas, yaga, yagamos, yagáis, yagan**

imper. yace or **yaz** (tú), **yazca** or **yazga** or **yaga** (usted), **yazcamos** or **yazgamos** or **yagamos** (nosotros), yaced (vosotros), **yazcan** or **yazgan** or **yagan** (ustedes)

38. **conducir**

pres. indic. **conduzco,** conduces, conduce, conducimos, conducís, conducen

pres. subj. **conduzca, conduzcas, conduzca, conduzcamos, conduzcáis, conduzcan**

pret. indic. **conduje, condujiste, condujo, condujimos, condujisteis, condujeron**

imp. subj. **condujera, condujeras, condujera, condujéramos, condujerais, condujeran,** or **condujese, condujeses, condujese, condujésemos, condujeseis, condujesen**

imper. conduce (tú), **conduzca** (usted), **conduzcamos** (nosotros), conducid (vosotros), **conduzcan** (ustedes)

39. **lucir**

pres. indic. **luzco,** luces, luce, lucimos, lucís, lucen

pres. subj. **luzca, luzcas, luzca, luzcamos, luzcáis, luzcan**

imper. luce (tú), **luzca** (usted), **luzcamos** (nosotros), lucid (vosotros), **luzcan** (ustedes)

40. **llegar**

pres. subj. **llegue, llegues, llegue, lleguemos, lleguéis, lleguen**

pret. indic. **llegué,** llegaste, llegó, llegamos, llegasteis, llegaron

imper. llega (tú), **llegue** (usted), **lleguemos** (nosotros), llegad (vosotros), **lleguen** (ustedes)

41. **negar**

pres. indic. **niego, niegas, niega,** negamos, negáis, **niegan**

pres. subj. **niegue, niegues, niegue, neguemos, neguéis, nieguen**

pret. indic. **negué,** negaste, negó, negamos, negasteis, negaron

imper. **niega** (tú), **niegue** (usted), **neguemos** (nosotros), negad (vosotros), **nieguen** (ustedes)

42. **colgar**

pres. indic. **cuelgo, cuelgas, cuelga,** colgamos, colgáis, **cuelgan**
pres. subj. **cuelgue, cuelgues, cuelgue, colguemos, colguéis, cuelguen**
pret. indic. **colgué,** colgaste, colgó, colgamos, colgasteis, colgaron
imper. **cuelga** (tú), **cuelgue** (usted), **colguemos** (nosotros), colgad (vosotros), **cuelguen** (ustedes)

43. **jugar**

pres. indic. **juego, juegas, juega,** jugamos, jugáis, **juegan**
pres. subj. **juegue, juegues, juegue, juguemos, juguéis, jueguen**
pret. indic. **jugué,** jugaste, jugó, jugamos, jugasteis, jugaron
imper. **juega** (tú), **juegue** (usted), **juguemos** (nosotros), jugad (vosotros), **jueguen** (ustedes)

44. **distinguir**

pres. indic. **distingo,** distingues, distingue, distinguimos, distinguís, distinguen
pres. subj. **distinga, distingas, distinga, distingamos, distingáis, distingan**
imper. distingue (tú), **distinga** (usted), **distingamos** (nosotros), distinguid (vosotros), **distingan** (ustedes)

45. **coger**

pres. indic. **cojo,** coges, coge, cogemos, cogéis, cogen
pres. subj. **coja, cojas, coja, cojamos, cojáis, cojan**
imper. coge (tú), **coja** (usted), **cojamos** (nosotros), coged (vosotros), **cojan** (ustedes)

46. **dirigir**

pres. indic. **dirijo,** diriges, dirige, dirigimos, dirigís, dirigen
pres. subj. **dirija, dirijas, dirija, dirijamos, dirijáis, dirijan**
imper. dirige (tú), **dirija** (usted), **dirijamos** (nosotros), dirigid (vosotros), **dirijan** (ustedes)

47. **abrazar**

pres. subj. **abrace, abraces, abrace, abracemos, abracéis, abracen**
pret. indic. **abracé,** abrazaste, abrazó, abrazamos, abrazasteis, abrazaron
imper. abraza (tú), **abrace** (usted), **abracemos** (nosotros), abrazad (vosotros), **abracen** (ustedes)

48. **empezar**

pres. indic. **empiezo, empiezas, empieza,** empezamos, empezáis, **empiezan**

pres. subj. **empiece, empieces, empiece, empecemos, empecéis, empiecen**

pret. indic. **empecé,** empezaste, empezó, empezamos, empezasteis, empezaron

imper. **empieza** (tú), **empiece** (usted), **empecemos** (nosotros), empezad (vosotros), **empiecen** (ustedes)

49. **forzar**

pres. indic. **fuerzo, fuerzas, fuerza,** forzamos, forzáis, **fuerzan**

pres. subj. **fuerce, fuerces, fuerce, forcemos, forcéis, fuercen**

pret. indic. **forcé,** forzaste, forzó, forzamos, forzasteis, forzaron

imper. **fuerza** (tú), **fuerce** (usted), **forcemos** (nosotros), forzad (vosotros), **fuercen** (ustedes)

50. **asir**

pres. indic. **asgo,** ases, ase, asimos, asís, asen

pres. subj. **asga, asgas, asga, asgamos, asgáis, asgan**

imper. ase (tú), **asga** (usted), **asgamos** (nosotros), asid (vosotros), **asgan** (ustedes)

51. **bendecir**

pres. indic. **bendigo, bendices, bendice,** bendecimos, bendecís, **bendicen**

pres. subj. **bendiga, bendigas, bendiga, bendigamos, bendigáis, bendigan**

pret. indic.. **bendije, bendijiste, bendijo, bendijimos, bendijisteis, bendijeron**

imp. subj. **bendijera, bendijeras, bendijera, bendijéramos, bendijerais, bendijeran** or **bendijese, bendijeses, bendijese, bendijésemos, bendijeseis, bendijesen**

fut. indic. bendeciré, bendecirás, bendecirá, bendeciremos, bendeciréis, bendecirán

cond. bendeciría, bendecirías, bendeciría, bendeciríamos, bendeciríais, bendecirían

imper. **bendice** (tú), **bendiga** (usted), **bendigamos** (nosotros), bendecid (vosotros), **bendigan** (ustedes)

pres. part. **bendiciendo**

past part. bendecido

52. **caer**

pres. indic. **caigo,** caes, cae, caemos, caéis, caen

pres. subj. **caiga, caigas, caiga, caigamos, caigáis, caigan**

pret. indic.	caí, caíste, **cayó,** caímos, caísteis, **cayeron**
imp. subj.	**cayera, cayeras, cayera, cayéramos, cayerais, cayeran,** or **cayese, cayeses, cayese, cayésemos, cayeseis, cayesen**
imper.	cae (tú), **caiga** (usted), **caigamos** (nosotros), caed (vosotros), **caigan** (ustedes)
pres. part.	**cayendo**
past part.	**caído**

53. **decir**[1]

pres. indic.	**digo, dices, dice,** decimos, decís, **dicen**
pres. subj.	**diga, digas, diga, digamos, digáis, digan**
pret. indic.	**dije, dijiste, dijo, dijimos, dijisteis, dijeron**
imp. subj.	**dijera, dijeras, dijera, dijéramos, dijerais, dijeran,** or **dijese, dijeses, dijese, dijésemos, dijeseis, dijesen**
fut. indic.	**diré, dirás, dirá, diremos, diréis, dirán**
cond.	**diría, dirías, diría, diríamos, diríais, dirían**
imper.	**di** (tú), **diga** (usted), **digamos** (nosotros), decid (vosotros), **digan** (ustedes)
pres. part.	**diciendo**
past part.	**dicho**

54. **hacer**

pres. indic.	**hago,** haces, hace, hacemos, hacéis, hacen
pres. subj.	**haga, hagas, haga, hagamos, hagáis, hagan**
pret. indic.	**hice, hiciste, hizo, hicimos, hicisteis, hicieron**
imp. subj.	**hiciera, hicieras, hiciera, hiciéramos, hicierais, hicieran,** or **hiciese, hicieses, hiciese, hiciésemos, hicieseis, hiciesen**
fut. indic.	**haré, harás, hará, haremos, haréis, harán**
cond.	**haría, harías, haría, haríamos, haríais, harían**
imper.	**haz** (tú), **haga** (usted), **hagamos** (nosotros), haced (vosotros), **hagan** (ustedes)
past part.	**hecho**

55. **oír**

pres. indic.	**oigo, oyes, oye,** oímos, oís, **oyen**
pres. subj.	**oiga, oigas, oiga, oigamos, oigáis, oigan**
pret. indic.	oí, oíste, **oyó,** oímos, oísteis, **oyeron**

1. The compound verbs of *decir* have the same irregularities with the exception of the following: The future and conditional forms of the compound verbs *contradecir, desdecir,* and *predecir* are used interchangeably in both their irregular and regular forms (see 51 **bendecir**). However, their past participles are always irregular (see 74 **Irregular Past Participles**).

imp. subj. **oyera, oyeras, oyera, oyéramos, oyerais, oyeran,** or **oyese, oyeses, oyese, oyésemos, oyeseis, oyesen**
imper. **oye** (tú), **oiga** (usted), **oigamos** (nosotros), oíd (vosotros), **oigan** (ustedes)
pres. part. **oyendo**
past part. **oído**

56. **poner**
pres. indic. **pongo,** pones, pone, ponemos, ponéis, ponen
pres. subj. **ponga, pongas, ponga, pongamos, pongáis, pongan**
pret. indic. **puse, pusiste, puso, pusimos, pusisteis, pusieron**
imp. subj. **pusiera, pusieras, pusiera, pusiéramos, pusierais, pusieran,** or **pusiese, pusieses, pusiese, pusiésemos, pusieseis, pusiesen**
fut. indic. **pondré, pondrás, pondrá, pondremos, pondréis, pondrán**
cond. **pondría, pondrías, pondría, pondríamos, pondríais,pondrían**
imper. **pon** (tú), **ponga** (usted), **pongamos** (nosotros), poned (vosotros), **pongan** (ustedes)
past part. **puesto**

57. **salir**
pres. indic. **salgo,** sales, sale, salimos, salís, salen
pres. subj. **salga, salgas, salga, salgamos, salgáis, salgan**
fut. indic. **saldré, saldrás, saldrá, saldremos, saldréis, saldrán**
cond. **saldría, saldrías, saldría, saldríamos, saldríais, saldrían**
imper. **sal** (tú),[2] **salga** (usted), **salgamos** (nosotros), salid (vosotros), **salgan** (ustedes)

58. **tener**
pres. indic. **tengo, tienes, tiene,** tenemos, tenéis, **tienen**
pres. subj. **tenga, tengas, tenga, tengamos, tengáis, tengan**
pret. indic. **tuve, tuviste, tuvo, tuvimos, tuvisteis, tuvieron**
imp. subj. **tuviera, tuvieras, tuviera, tuviéramos, tuvierais, tuvieran,** or **tuviese, tuvieses, tuviese, tuviésemos, tuvieseis, tuviesen**
fut. indic. **tendré, tendrás, tendrá, tendremos, tendréis, tendrán**

2. The compound *sobresalir* is regular in the familiar imperative: *sobresale.*

cond. **tendría, tendrías, tendría, tendríamos, tendríais, tendrían**

imper. **ten** (tú), **tenga** (usted), **tengamos** (nosotros), tened (vosotros), **tengan** (ustedes)

59. **traer**

pres. indic. **traigo,** traes, trae, traemos, traéis, traen

pres. subj. **traiga, traigas, traiga, traigamos, traigáis, traigan**

pret. indic. **traje, trajiste, trajo, trajimos, trajisteis, trajeron**

imp. subj. **trajera, trajeras, trajera, trajéramos, trajerais, trajeran,** or **trajese, trajeses, trajese, trajésemos, trajeseis, trajesen**

imper. trae (tú), **traiga** (usted), **traigamos** (nosotros), traed (vosotros), **traigan** (ustedes)

pres. part. **trayendo**

past part. **traído**

60. **valer**

pres. indic. **valgo,** vales, vale, valemos, valéis, valen

pres. subj. **valga, valgas, valga, valgamos, valgáis, valgan**

fut. indic. **valdré, valdrás, valdrá, valdremos, valdréis, valdrán**

cond. **valdría, valdrías, valdría, valdríamos, valdríais, valdrían**

imper. **val** *or* vale (tú), **valga** (usted), **valgamos** (nosotros), valed (vosotros), **valgan** (ustedes)

61. **venir**

pres. indic. **vengo, vienes, viene,** venimos, venís, **vienen**

pres. subj. **venga, vengas, venga, vengamos, vengáis, vengan**

pret. indic. **vine, viniste, vino, vinimos, vinisteis, vinieron**

imp. subj. **viniera, vinieras, viniera, viniéramos, vinierais, vinieran,** or **viniese, vinieses, viniese, viniésemos, vinieseis, viniesen**

fut. indic. **vendré, vendrás, vendrá, vendremos, vendréis, vendrán**

cond. **vendría, vendrías, vendría, vendríamos, vendríais, vendrían**

imper. **ven** (tú), **venga** (usted), **vengamos** (nosotros), venid (vosotros), **vengan** (ustedes)

pres. part. **viniendo**

62. **dar**

pres. indic. **doy,** das, da, damos, dais, dan

pres. subj.	**dé,** des, **dé,** demos, deis, den
pret. indic.	**di, diste, dio, dimos, disteis, dieron**
imp. subj.	**diera, dieras, diera, diéramos, dierais, dieran,** or **diese, dieses, diese, diésemos, dieseis, diesen**
imper.	da (tú), **dé** (usted), demos (nosotros), dad (vosotros), den (ustedes)

63. **estar**

pres. indic.	**estoy, estás, está,** estamos, estáis, **están**
pres. subj.	**esté, estés, esté,** estemos, estéis, **estén**
pret. indic.	**estuve, estuviste, estuvo, estuvimos, estuvisteis, estuvieron**
imp. subj.	**estuviera, estuvieras, estuviera, estuviéramos, estuvierais, estuvieran,** or **estuviese, estuvieses, estuviese, estuviésemos, estuvieseis, estuviesen**
imper.	**está** (tú), **esté** (usted), estemos (nosotros), estad (vosotros), **estén** (ustedes)

64. **ir**

pres. indic.	**voy, vas, va, vamos, vais, van**
pres. subj.	**vaya, vayas, vaya, vayamos, vayáis, vayan**
imp. indic.	**iba, ibas, iba, íbamos, ibais, iban**
pret. indic.	**fui, fuiste, fue, fuimos, fuisteis, fueron**
imp. subj.	**fuera, fueras, fuera, fuéramos, fuerais, fueran,** or **fuese, fueses, fuese, fuésemos, fueseis, fuesen**
imper.	**ve** (tú), **vaya** (usted), **vayamos** (nosotros), id (vosotros), **vayan** (ustedes)
pres. part.	**yendo**

65. **ser**

pres. indic.	**soy, eres, es, somos, sois, son**
pres. subj.	**sea, seas, sea, seamos, seáis, sean**
imp. indic.	**era, eras, era, éramos, erais, eran**
pret. indic.	**fui, fuiste, fue, fuimos, fuisteis, fueron**
imp. subj.	**fuera, fueras, fuera, fuéramos, fuerais, fueran,** or **fuese, fueses, fuese, fuésemos, fueseis, fuesen**
imper.	**sé** (tú), **sea** (usted), **seamos** (nosotros), sed (vosotros), **sean** (ustedes)

66. **andar**

pret. indic.	**anduve, anduviste, anduvo, anduvimos, anduvisteis, anduvieron**

imp. subj. **anduviera, anduvieras, anduviera, anduviéramos, anduvierais, anduvieran,** or **anduviese, anduvieses, anduviese, anduviésemos, anduvieseis, anduviesen**

67. **caber**

pres. indic. **quepo,** cabes, cabe, cabemos, cabéis, caben
pres. subj. **quepa, quepas, quepa, quepamos, quepáis, quepan**
pret. indic. **cupe, cupiste, cupo, cupimos, cupisteis, cupieron**
imp. subj. **cupiera, cupieras, cupiera, cupiéramos, cupierais, cupieran,** or **cupiese, cupieses, cupiese, cupiésemos, cupieseis, cupiesen**
fut. indic. **cabré, cabrás, cabrá, cabremos, cabréis, cabrán**
cond. **cabría, cabrías, cabría, cabríamos, cabríais, cabrían**
imper. cabe (tú), **quepa** (usted), **quepamos** (nosotros), cabed (vosotros), **quepan** (ustedes)

68. **haber**

pres. indic. **he, has, ha, hemos,** habéis, **han**
pres. subj. **haya, hayas, haya, hayamos, hayáis, hayan**
pret. indic. **hube, hubiste, hubo, hubimos, hubisteis, hubieron**
imp. subj. **hubiera, hubieras, hubiera, hubiéramos, hubierais, hubieran,** or **hubiese, hubieses, hubiese, hubiésemos, hubieseis, hubiesen**
fut. indic. **habré, habrás, habrá, habremos, habréis, habrán**
cond. **habría, habrías, habría, habríamos, habríais, habrían**

69. **poder**

pres. indic. **puedo, puedes, puede,** podemos, podéis, **pueden**
pres. subj. **pueda, puedas, pueda,** podamos, podáis, **puedan**
pret. indic. **pude, pudiste, pudo, pudimos, pudisteis, pudieron**
imp. subj. **pudiera, pudieras, pudiera, pudiéramos, pudierais, pudieran,** or **pudiese, pudieses, pudiese, pudiésemos, pudieseis, pudiesen**
fut. indic. **podré, podrás, podrá, podremos, podréis, podrán**
cond. **podría, podrías, podría, podríamos, podríais, podrían**
pres. part. **pudiendo**

70. **querer**

pres. indic.	**quiero, quieres, quiere,** queremos, queréis, **quieren**
pres. subj.	**quiera, quieras, quiera,** queramos, queráis, **quieran**
pret. indic.	**quise, quisiste, quiso, quisimos, quisisteis, quisieron**
imp. subj.	**quisiera, quisieras, quisiera, quisiéramos, quisierais, quisieran,** or **quisiese, quisieses, quisiese, quisiémos, quisieseis, quisiesen**
fut. indic.	**querré, querrás, querrá, querremos, querréis, querrán**
cond.	**querría, querrías, querría, querríamos, querríais, querrían**
imper.	**quiere** (tú), **quiera** (usted), queramos (nosotros), quered (vosotros), **quieran** (ustedes)

71. **saber**

pres. indic.	**sé,** sabes, sabe, sabemos, sabéis, saben
pres. subj.	**sepa, sepas, sepa, sepamos, sepáis, sepan**
pret. indic.	**supe, supiste, supo, supimos, supisteis, supieron**
imp. subj.	**supiera, supieras, supiera, supiéramos, supierais, supieran,** or **supiese, supieses, supiese, supiésemos, supieseis, supiesen**
fut. indic.	**sabré, sabrás, sabrá, sabremos, sabréis, sabrán**
cond.	**sabría, sabrías, sabría, sabríamos, sabríais, sabrían**
imper.	sabe (tú), **sepa** (usted), **sepamos** (nosotros), sabed (vosotros), **sepan** (ustedes)

72. **ver**[3]

pres. indic.	**veo,** ves, ve, vemos, veis, ven
pres. subj.	**vea, veas, vea, veamos, veáis, vean**
pret. indic.	**vi, viste, vio, vimos, visteis, vieron**
imp. indic.	**veía, veías, veía, veíamos, veíais, veían**
imp. subj.	**viera, vieras, viera, viéramos, vierais, vieran** or **viese, vieses, viese, viésemos, vieseis, viesen**
imper.	ve (tú), **vea** (usted), **veamos** (nosotros), ved (vosotros), **vean** (ustedes)
past part.	**visto**

3. The verb *prever* differs orthographically in the second- and third-person forms of the present indicative (*prevés, prevéis, prevé, prevén*), the first- and third-person singular forms of the preterit indicative (*preví, previó*), and the familiar imperative form (*prevé*).

73. Defective Verbs

The following verbs are used only in the forms that have an **i** in the ending: **abolir, agredir, aterirse, empedernirse, transgredir.**

The verb **atañer** is used only in the third person, most frequently in the present indicative: atañe, atañen.

The verb **concernir** is used only in the third person of the following tenses:

pres. indic.	**concierne, conciernen**
pres. subj.	**concierna, conciernan**
imp. indic.	concernía, concernían
imp. subj.	concerniera *or* concerniese, concernieran *or* concerniesen
fut. indic	concernirá, concernirán
cond.	concerniría, concernirían

The verb **roer** (also **corroer**) has three forms in the first person of the present indicative: **roo, royo, roigo,** all of which are infrequently used. In the present subjunctive the preferable form is **roa, roas, roa,** etc., although the forms **roya** and **roiga** are found.

The verb **soler** is used most frequently in the present and imperfect indicative. It is less frequently used in the present subjunctive.

pres. indic.	**suelo, sueles, suele,** solemos, soléis, **suelen**
pres. subj.	**suela, suelas, suela,** solamos, soláis, **suelan**
imp. indic.	solía, solías, solía, solíamos, solíais, solían

74. Additional Irregular Past Participles

absolver—**absuelto**
abrir—**abierto**
anteponer—**antepuesto**
circunscribir—**circunscrito**
componer—**compuesto**
contradecir—**contradicho**
cubrir—**cubierto**
decir—**dicho**
deponer—**depuesto**
descomponer—**descompuesto**
describir—**descrito**
descubrir—**descubierto**
desdecir—**desdicho**
desenvolver—**desenvuelto**
deshacer—**deshecho**
devolver—**devuelto**
disolver—**disuelto**

disponer—**dispuesto**
encubrir—**encubierto**
entreabrir—**entreabierto**
entrever—**entrevisto**
envolver—**envuelto**
escribir—**escrito**
exponer—**expuesto**
freír—**frito** (often regular, **freído**)
hacer—**hecho**
imponer—**impuesto**
imprimir—**impreso** (often regular, **imprimido**)
indisponer—**indispuesto**
inscribir—**inscrito**
interponer—**interpuesto**
morir—**muerto**
oponer—**opuesto**
poner—**puesto**
posponer—**pospuesto**
predecir—**predicho**
predisponer—**predispuesto**
prescribir—**prescrito**
presuponer—**presupuesto**
prever—**previsto**
proponer—**propuesto**
proscribir—**proscrito**
proveer—**provisto** (often regular, **proveído**)
pudrir—**podrido**
reabrir—**reabierto**
recubrir—**recubierto**
reescribir—**reescrito**
rehacer—**rehecho**
reponer—**repuesto**
resolver—**resuelto**
revolver—**revuelto**
romper—**roto**
satisfacer—**satisfecho**
sobreponer—**sobrepuesto**
suscribir—**suscrito**
superponer—**superpuesto**
suponer—**supuesto**
transcribir—**transcrito**
trasponer—**traspuesto**
ver—**visto**
volver—**vuelto**
yuxtaponer—**yuxtapuesto**

Aa

a PREP **voy — Londres** I'm going to London; **te lo doy — ti** I'm giving it to you; **se sentó — la sombra** she sat down in the shade; **tumbarse —l sol** to lie down in the sun; **una soga —l cuello** a rope around his neck; **lo miraba — la luz de una vela** she looked at him by the light of a candle; **— dos pesetas cada uno** at two pesetas each; **— las tres y media** at three-thirty; **sentarse — la mesa** to sit down at the table; **prestar dinero —l 15%** to lend money at 15%; **en grupos de — cinco** in groups of five; **cocina — gas** gas cooker; **fotos — todo color** full-color photos; **nadie le gana — testaruda** no one touches her for stubbornness; **terminaron — puñetazos** they ended up fighting; **¡— jugar!** let's play! **¿— qué vienen?** what are they coming for? **veo — mi mamá** I see my mother

AA [Alcohólicos Anónimos] F AA

abacá M manila

abad -esa M abbot; F abbess

abadejo M cod

abadía F abbey

abajo ADV (dirección) down; (posición relativa) below; **mirar para —** to look down; **el piso de —** the apartment below; **véase —** see below; **— de** under, underneath; **Stefan está — del coche** Stefan is under/underneath the car; **¡— el rey!** down with the king! **— firmante** undersigned; **echar —** to knock down; **río —** downstream; **venirse —** to go to ruin

abalanzarse[47] VI **— sobre** to lunge at, to swoop down upon

abanderado -da MF standard-bearer

abandonado ADJ abandoned; **es una persona muy abandonada** she's very unkempt

abandonar VT (a una persona, a una familia) to leave, to desert; (el hogar, un partido) to abandon; (una competencia, el poder) to give up; (una competencia, a un enamorado, el hábito de fumar) to quit; (en los naipes) to fold; (un curso) to drop out of

abandono M (descuido) neglect; (acción de abandonar, condición de abandonado) abandonment; **— de funciones** dereliction of duties

abanicar[30] VT (contra el calor) to fan; (en béisbol) to swing and miss

abanico M (accesorio) fan; (rango) array; (en béisbol) swing and a miss; **abrirse en —** to fan out

abaratar VT (bajar el precio) to lower the price of; (desprestigiar) to cheapen

abarcar[30] VT (categorías) to embrace, to encompass; (tiempo) to span

abarrotería F *Méx* grocery store

abarrotero -ra MF *Méx* grocer

abarrotes M PL *Méx* groceries; **tienda de —** *Méx* grocery store

abastecedor -ora MF supplier

abastecer[35] VT (un ejército, una ciudad) to supply; (una tienda) to stock

abastecimiento M supply

abasto M supply; **mercado de —s** farmers' market; **yo sola no doy —** I can't cope alone

abatido ADJ dejected, despondent, downcast

abatimiento M dejection, despondency

abatir VT (bajar) to lower; (derribar) to knock down; (desanimar) to depress; (matar a tiros) to shoot; **—se** to swoop down

abdicar[30] VI/VT to abdicate

abdomen M abdomen

abdominal ADJ abdominal; M sit-up

abecedario M alphabet

abedul M birch

abeja F bee; **— asesina** killer bee

abejón M bumblebee

abejorro M bumblebee

aberración F aberration

abertura F (acción) opening; (cualidad) openness

abeto M fir

abierto ADJ (no cerrado, no determinado, destapado) open; (franco) frank; **— de par en par** wide open

abierto *ver* abrir

abigarrado ADJ motley

abigeato M cattle rustling

abismal ADJ abysmal

abismo M abyss, chasm; **— generacional** generation gap

ablandar VT to soften

abnegación F self-denial

abobado ADJ silly

abocar[30] VI to turn onto; **—se a** to devote oneself to

abochornar VT (avergonzar) to embarrass; **—se** to become embarrassed

abocinar VT to flare

abofetear VT to slap

abogacía F legal profession; **estudiar —** to study law

abogado -da MF lawyer, attorney; **— tributarista** tax attorney, tax lawyer

abogar[40] VI **— por** to advocate, to plead for

abolengo M ancestry

abolición F abolition

abolir[73] VT to abolish

abollado ADJ dented

abolladura F dent

abollar VT to dent; **—se** to become dented
abolsarse VI to sag
abombar VT to make bulge
abominable ADJ abominable, loathsome
abominación F abomination
abominar VI to detest
abonado -da MF subscriber
abonar VT (suscribir) to subscribe; (pagar) to make a payment; (poner fertilizante) to fertilize; **—se** to subscribe; **— a una cuenta** credit an account
abono M (a una revista) subscription; (para una temporada deportiva) season ticket; (de autobús) pass; (para la tierra) fertilizer; (de dinero) payment
abordar VT (un avión, un buque) to board; (un problema) to tackle, to approach; (a una persona) to accost
aborigen ADJ aboriginal; MF native inhabitant; **— australiano** Australian aborigine
aborrascarse[30] VI to become stormy
aborrecer[35] VT to abhor, to loathe
aborrecible ADJ hateful, abhorrent
aborrecimiento M abhorrence
abortador -ora MF abortionist
abortar VI (naturalmente) to miscarry, to have a miscarriage; VI/VT (intencionadamente) to abort
abortero -ra MF abortionist
aborto M (espontáneo) miscarriage; (provocado) abortion; **— espontáneo** spontaneous abortion
abotargarse[40] VI to bloat
abotonar VT to button; **—se** to button up
abovedar VT (una iglesia) to vault, to cover with a vault; (una calle) to arch, to cover as a vault
abozalar VT to muzzle
abracadabra M abracadabra
abrasador ADJ burning
abrasar VT to burn; **—se** to be consumed
abrasión F abrasion; **— cutánea** dermabrasion
abrasivo ADJ abrasive
abrazadera F clamp
abrazar[47] VT (rodear con los brazos) to hug, to embrace; (rodear una cosa sujetando) to clasp; (una opinión) to espouse
abrazo M hug, embrace
abrevadero M trough
abrevar VT (dar de beber) to water; (beber) to drink
abreviación F abbreviation
abreviar VT to abbreviate, to abridge
abreviatura F abbreviation
abridor M opener
abrigado ADJ (ropa) warm; (lugar) sheltered
abrigar[40] VT (refugiados) to shelter; (emociones) to harbor; **—se** to bundle up
abrigo M (refugio) shelter; (prenda de vestir) coat, wrap; **— impositivo** tax shelter
abril M April
abrillantar VT to make shiny
abrir[74] VI/VT (una puerta) to open; VT (un candado) to unlock; (un grifo) to turn on; **— el apetito** to whet one's appetite; **— la sesión** call a meeting to order; **— paso** to make way; M SG **abrebotellas** bottle opener; M SG **abrelatas** can opener; VI (el cielo) to clear up; **—se** to open up; **—se paso** to press through; **en un — y cerrar de ojos** in the twinkle of an eye
abrochar VT to fasten; **—se** to buckle [up]
abrogación F repeal
abrogar[40] VT to repeal
abrojo M bur, sticker
abrumador ADJ overwhelming, overpowering
abrumar VT to overwhelm, to weigh down; **—se** to become foggy
abrupto ADJ abrupt
absceso M abscess
absolución F acquittal
absolutamente ADV, INTERJ absolutely
absoluto ADJ absolute; **en —** absolutely not
absolver[6,74] VT to absolve, to acquit
absorbente ADJ absorbent
absorber VT to absorb
absorción F absorption
absorto ADJ absorbed, engrossed
abstemio -mia ADJ abstemious; MF teetotaler
abstención F abstention
abstenerse[58] VI to abstain; **— de** to abstain from, to refrain from, to forego
abstinencia F abstinence
abstracción F abstraction
abstracto ADJ abstract
abstraer[59] VT to abstract
abstraído ADJ lost in thought
absurdo ADJ absurd, preposterous; M absurdity
abuchear VI/VT to boo, to jeer
abucheo M boo, jeer
abuelo -la M grandfather; F grandmother; **—s** grandparents
abulia F apathy
abultado ADJ bulgy
abultar VI to bulge
abundancia F abundance, plenty
abundante ADJ abundant, plentiful
abundar VI to abound; **— en** to abound in
aburrido ADJ (sin entretenimiento) bored; (pesado) boring, tiresome
aburrimiento M boredom
aburrir VT to bore; **—se** to become bored
abusar VT **— de** to abuse; (sexualmente) to molest
abuso M abuse; **— conyugal** spousal abuse; **— de confianza** breach of trust; **— de drogas** drug abuse; **— de sustancias** substance abuse
abyecto ADJ abject

acá ADV (en este lugar) here; (hacia este lugar) over here, *lit* hither; — **y allá** here and there
acabado ADJ finished; M finish
acabar VT to finish; VI to end; — **de comer** to have just eaten; — **por** to end up by; — **con** (la corrupción) to put an end to; (las cucarachas) to get rid of; **él y yo hemos acabado** he and I are through; **se acabaron los dulces** the candy is all gone; **se nos acabaron las ideas** we ran out of ideas; **y se acabó** and that's that
academia F (corporación, escuela militar) academy; (centro privado de enseñanza) private school
académico ADJ academic
acallar VT to silence, to quiet
acalorado ADJ heated
acaloramiento M **sufrió un** — he got too hot
acalorarse VI/VT (sofocarse) to overheat; (emocionarse) to get excited
acampada F camping trip
acampante MF camper
acampar VT to camp
acanalar VT to groove
acantilado ADJ sheer, steep; M bluff, cliff
acantonarse VT to be quartered
acaparar VT (productos) to hoard; (atención) to capture; (monopolizar) *fam* to hog; — **el mercado** to corner the market
acaramelar VT to candy
acariciar VT to caress; — **una esperanza** to harbor a hope
ácaro M mite
acarrear VT (transportar) to transport; (transportar en carro) to cart; (ocasionar) to bring about
acarreo M transport
acaso ADV perhaps; **por si** — just in case
acatamiento M compliance
acatar VT to abide by, to comply with
acatarrar VI to chill; —**se** to catch cold
acaudalado ADJ wealthy
acceder VI — **a** (un pedido) to accede to; VI (una invitación) to accept
accesibilidad F accessibility
accesible ADJ accessible, convenient
acceso M (entrada) access; (de ira) fit; — **a internet** Internet access; — **denegado** access denied; — **remoto** remote access, remote login; **de** — **prohibido** off limits
accesorio ADJ & M accessory
accidentado -da ADJ (viaje) eventful; (terreno) uneven; MF accident victim
accidental ADJ accidental
accidentarse VI to have an accident
accidente M (suceso imprevisto) accident; (del terreno) feature; (automovilístico) wreck; — **de tránsito** traffic accident; **por** — by accident
acción F (acto) action; (valor de bolsa) share of stock; — **de gracias** thanksgiving; **buenas acciones** good deeds; **acciones preferenciales** preferred stock; **acciones ordinarias** common stock
accionable ADJ actionable
accionar VT to operate
accionista MF shareholder, stockholder
acebo M holly
acechar VT (emboscar) to lie in ambush; (amenazar) to stalk
acecho M **rondar en** — to prowl; **estar al** — to lie in wait
aceitar VT to oil
aceite M oil; — **de linaza** linseed oil; — **de oliva** olive oil; — **de ricino** castor oil; — **vegetal** vegetable oil
aceitera F (recipiente) oilcan; (fábrica) oil factory
aceitoso ADJ oily
aceituna F olive
aceleración F acceleration
acelerador M accelerator
acelerar VT to accelerate, to speed up; VI to accelerate, to step on the gas; — **en vacío** to rev, to race; —**se** *Am* to get nervous
acémila F pack animal
acento M (pronunciación, signo) accent; (intensidad mayor, de voz) stress
acentuar[26] VT (aumentar) to accentuate; (poner tilde) to accent; (reforzar la voz) to stress; —**se** to accentuate
acepción F gloss, meaning
aceptable ADJ acceptable
aceptación F acceptance
aceptar VT to accept; — **entrega** to take delivery
acequia F irrigation ditch
acera F sidewalk
acerado ADJ made of steel
acerar VT to steel
acerca PREP — **de** about, concerning
acercamiento M approach
acercar[10] VT to bring near; **os acerco a la estación** I'll give you a ride to the station; —**se** to come near, to approach
acería F steel mill
acero M steel; — **inoxidable** stainless steel
acérrimo ADJ bitter
acertado ADJ right
acertar[1] VT to hit; VI to be right; — **con** to hit upon; — **a pasar** to happen to go by; **no** — to miss the mark
acertijo M riddle, conundrum
acervo M heritage
acetaminofén M acetaminophen
acetona F acetone
achacar[10] VI to blame
achacoso ADJ infirm, ailing

achaparrado ADJ (planta) stunted; (persona) squat
achaque M affliction, ailment; **—s** aches and pains
achicado ADJ weak-kneed
achicar[30] VT (de tamaño) to make small; (un vestido) to take in; (agua) to bail; **—se** (acobardarse) to feel intimidated; (empequeñecerse) to get smaller
achicoria F chicory
aciago ADJ unlucky
acicalado ADJ clean-cut
acicalarse VI to dress up
acicate M incentive
acidez F (de una solución) acidity; (del vinagre) sourness; **— de estómago** heartburn
ácido M acid; **—s grasos** fatty acids; ADJ (propio del ácido) acidic; (fruta) sour, tart
acierto M (contestación) right answer; (elección) felicitous choice
aclamación F acclamation, acclaim; **por —** by acclamation
aclamar VT to acclaim, to hail
aclaración F clarification
aclarar VT (con explicaciones) to clarify; (con agua) to rinse; (la voz) to clear; VI to dawn; **aclaró después de la tormenta** it cleared up after the storm; **—se** to lighten
aclimatar VT to acclimate
acné M acne
acobardar VT to intimidate
acogedor ADJ (persona) hospitable; (cuarto) cozy
acoger[45] VT (una sugerencia) to receive; (a un refugiado) to shelter; **—se** to take refuge; **—se a la ley** to have recourse to the law
acogida F reception
acogimiento M reception
acolchar VT to pad
acollarar VT to collar
acometer VT (atacar) to attack; (emprender) to undertake
acometida F attack
acomodado ADJ well-off
acomodador -ora MF usher
acomodar VT (arreglar) to arrange; (ajustar) to adjust; (adaptar) to adapt; **—se** (ponerse cómodo) to make oneself comfortable; (adaptarse) to adapt oneself
acomodo M position; **no tengo —** I can't find a comfortable position
acompañamiento M (acción, música) accompaniment; (grupo de personas que acompaña) retinue; (comida) side dish; (tenis) follow-through
acompañante ADJ accompanying; MF (compañero) companion; (en música) accompanist
acompañar VI/VT to accompany (también en música); (escoltar) to escort; (en una carta) to enclose; **—se de** to be accompanied by; **esperemos que el tiempo acompañe** let's hope the weather cooperates; **te acompaño en el sentimiento** my thoughts are with you
acompasado ADJ (rítmico) rhythmical; (mesurado) measured
acomplejado ADJ self-conscious
acondicionar VT to prepare
acongojado ADJ grief-stricken
acongojar VT to distress; **—se** to become distressed
aconsejable ADJ advisable
aconsejar VT to advise, to counsel
acontecer[35] VI to take place
acontecimiento M event; **todo un —** quite a happening; **a esta altura de los —s** at this point in the proceedings
acopiar VT to stockpile
acopio M (acción de guardar) storing; (cosas guardadas) stockpile
acoplamiento M coupling; **— universal de cardán** universal joint
acoplar VT to couple; **—se** (piezas complementarias, partes) to couple, to join; (altavoces) to have feedback
acople M coupling, connection
acorazado ADJ armored; M battleship, warship
acorazar[47] VT to armor
acordado VI agreed-upon
acordar[5] VT to agree; VI **— en** to arrange to; **—se [de]** to remember
acorde M chord; ADJ in agreement; **en — con** in agreement with
acordeón M accordion
acordonar VT (un zapato) to lace; (un lugar) to rope off, to seal off; (una moneda) to mill
acorralar VT (meter en un corral) to corral; (arrinconar) to corner
acortamiento M shortening
acortar VT to shorten
acosar VT (perseguir) to harry; (atacar) to beset; (atormentar) to badger; (importunar sexualmente) to harass
acoso M (de presa) hunting down, pursuit; (de una persona) harassment, hounding
acostar[5] VT to put to bed; **—se** to go to bed; **—se con** to sleep with
acostumbrado ADJ (normal) accustomed; (habitual) customary; **estar — a** to be used / accustomed to
acostumbrar VT to accustom; (soler) to be accustomed to; **—se [a]** to get accustomed [to]; **acostumbraban ir al teatro** they used to go to the theater
acotación F (anotación) marginal note; (en una obra de teatro) stage directions
acotar VT (un terreno) to mark off; (un texto) to

make marginal notes on
acre ADJ acrid, pungent, sharp; M acre
acrecentamiento M growth, increase
acrecentar[1] VT to grow; **—se** to grow
acreditar VT (una cuenta) to credit; (a un profesional) to accredit; **— a una cuenta** to credit an account; **a quien pueda — ser el dueño de** to whoever can prove to be the owner of
acreedor -ora ADJ deserving; **saldo —** positive balance; MF creditor
acribillar VI (a balazos) to riddle [with]; (a pedradas) to pelt
acrílico ADJ & M acrylic
acritud F acrimony
acrobacia F (arte) acrobatics; (pirueta) stunt
acróbata MF acrobat
acrobático ADJ acrobatic
acrofobia F acrophobia
acrónimo M acronym
acta F (de nacimiento) certificate; (de una reunión) minutes; (de un congreso) proceedings
actitud F attitude, mind-set
activar VT to activate
actividad F activity
activismo M activism
activista MF activist
activo ADJ active; **en —** working; M assets; **— líquido** liquid assets; **— convertible** convertible assets
acto M (solemne, dramático) act; (acción) action; **— seguido** immediately after; **— fallido** Freudian slip; **en el —** on the spot; **hacer — de presencia** to show up
actor M actor, performer; **— de carácter** character actor
actriz F actor, actress, performer
actuación F (acción) acting; (rendimiento, desempeño) performance
actual ADJ current, present
actualidad F present time; **—es** latest news; **de —** up-to-date
actualización F (de información) update; (de ordenador) upgrade
actualizado ADJ (al día) up-to-date; (al minuto) up-to-the-minute
actualizar[47] VT to update; (programa de ordenador) to upgrade; (pantalla de ordenador) to refresh
actualmente ADV presently, currently
actuar[26] VI (comportarse) to act; (dar una representación) to perform
actuario -ria MF (judicial) clerk; (de seguros) actuary
acuarela F watercolor
acuario M aquarium
acuartelar VT to quarter
acuático ADJ aquatic
acuchillar VT (penetrar) to stab; (cortar) to slash
acuclillado ADJ squatting
acuclillarse VI to squat
acudir VI (ir) to go; (asistir) to attend; **— a** to turn to; **— al llamado** to respond to the call; **— al socorro de** to go to the rescue of; **— en masa** to flock
acueducto M aqueduct
acuerda, acuerde *ver* acordar
acuerdo M agreement; **— comercial** trade agreement; **— contractual** contractual agreement; **— global** package deal agreement; **estar de —** to be in agreement; **ponerse de —** to come to an agreement; **de — con** in accordance with
acumulación F (de dinero) accumulation; (de tensión) buildup
acumulador M storage battery
acumular VT (desperdicios) to accumulate; (fortuna) to amass; (deudas) to accumulate, to run up; **—se** to collect; **rabia acumulada** pent-up rage
acumulativo ADJ cumulative
acuñación F coinage, minting
acuñar VT (monedas, una expresión) to coin; (meter cuñas) to wedge
acuoso ADJ watery
acupuntor -ora MF acupuncturist
acupuntura F acupuncture
acurrucarse[30] VI to nestle, to huddle
acusación F accusation, charge
acusado -da MF accused; (en un juicio) defendant
acusador -ora MF accuser
acusar VT (culpabilizar) to accuse; (detectar) to detect; (revelar) to betray; (entre niños) to tattle, to tell; **— el golpe** to feel the blow; **— recibo** to acknowledge receipt
acuse M acknowledgment
acusetas MF SG tattletale
acusica MF tattletale
acústica F acoustics
acústico ADJ acoustic
adagio M adage
adaptabilidad F resilience, adaptability
adaptación F adaptation
adaptador M adapter
adaptar VT to adapt
adecuado ADJ appropriate
adecuar VT to adapt; **—se a** to be suitable for
adefesio M sight, hideous thing
adelantado ADJ (economía, alumno) advanced; (reloj) fast; (tren) ahead of time, ahead of schedule; **por —** in advance
adelantamiento M (de una fecha) bringing forward; (de un coche) overtaking
adelantar VT (una fecha, dinero) to advance; (la mano) to move forward; (un coche) to pass; (una noticia) to have a scoop; VI (un reloj) to

gain; **— en** to make progress in; **—se** (sacar ventaja) to get ahead; (actuar antes) to go first; (innovar) to be ahead; (hablar antes de tiempo) to get ahead of oneself

adelante ADV forward; **— con los faroles** let's get started; **— de mí** in front of me; **de aquí en —** from now on; **hacia —** forward; **ir —** to go ahead; **más —** later; **sacar —** to make prosper; **seguir —** to go on; INTERJ go for it!

adelanto M (de la ciencia) advance, breakthrough; (de un coche) passing; (pago) advance; **el — de los relojes** setting the clocks forward

adelfa F oleander

adelgazar[47] VI to lose weight; VT to lose; (hacer perder peso) to make one lose weight; (hacer menos espeso) to thin; (hacer parecer delgado) to make one look thinner; **— cinco kilos** to lose five kilos; **—se** to get thinner

ademán M gesture; **hacer un — a alguien** to motion to someone

además ADV moreover, besides, in addition; **— de deberme dinero** besides / in addition to owing me money

adentrarse VI **— en** (un asunto) to go deeply into; (un lugar) to go deep into, to penetrate into; (una edad) to enter

adentro ADV inside; **ir para/hacia —** to go inside; **hablar para sus —s** to talk to oneself; **con lo de — para afuera** inside out

aderezar[47] VT (embellecer) to adorn; (condimentar) to season, to garnish

aderezo M (adorno) adornment; (de un alimento) seasoning; (de una ensalada) dressing

adeudar VT (deber) to owe; **— una cuenta** to debit an account

adeudo M (endeudamiento) indebtedness; (a una cuenta) debit

adherencia F adhesion

adherir[8] VI to adhere; **—se a** (una cosa) to stick to; (una huelga) to join; (una idea) to subscribe to

adhesión F (a una cosa) adhesion; (a una doctrina) adherence

adhesivo ADJ adhesive; M (pegamento) cement, adhesive; (calcomanía) sticker

adicción F addiction

adición F addition

adicional ADJ additional

adictivo ADJ addictive, habit-forming

adicto -ta ADJ addicted; MF addict; **— al trabajo** workaholic

adiestramiento M training

adiestrar VT to train

adinerado ADJ wealthy, well-to-do, moneyed

adiós INTERJ good-bye; **hacer — con la mano** to wave good-bye

adiposo ADJ fatty

aditivo M additive

adivinanza F riddle

adivinar VT to guess

adivino -na MF fortune-teller

adjetivo ADJ & M adjective

adjudicación F award

adjudicar[30] VT to award; **—se** to be awarded

adjuntar VT (incluir en una carta) to enclose; (añadir) to add, to attach, to append

adjunto ADJ (unido) attached; (incluido) enclosed; (asistente) adjunct; ADV herewith; M attachment

adminículo M gadget

administración F administration, management; **— pública** civil service; **— intermedia** middle management

administrador -ora MF administrator, manager; **— de cuentas** account manager; **— de un sitio web** webmaster

administrar VT (un medicamento) to administer; (una empresa) to administer, to manage; (justicia) to dispense; **—se** to budget

administrativo ADJ administrative

admirable ADJ admirable

admiración F admiration

admirador -ora MF admirer; (de una estrella de cine) fan

admirar VT to admire; **—se** to be amazed; **—se de** to wonder at

admisible ADJ admissible, allowable

admisión F (aceptación) admission; (reconocimiento) acknowledgment

admitir VT (dejar entrar, reconocer) to admit; (aceptar) to accept; (permitir) to allow

ADN [ácido desoxirribonucleico] M DNA

adobar VT (aderezar carne) to season; (curtir una piel) to tan; (encurtir) to pickle

adobe M adobe

adobo M sauce for seasoning

adoctrinar VT to indoctrinate

adolecer[35] VI **— de** to suffer from

adolescencia F adolescence

adolescente ADJ adolescent; MF adolescent, teenager

adonde ADV REL **esa es la casa — vamos** that's the house [that] we're going to, that's the house where we're going

adónde ADV INTERR & PRON where

adopción F adoption

adoptar VT to adopt

adoptivo ADJ adoptive

adoquín M cobblestone

adorable ADJ adorable

adoración F (a una persona) adoration; (a un dios) worship

adorador -ora MF worshiper

adorar VT (a una persona) to adore; (a un dios) to worship

adormecer[35] VT (dar sueño) to make drowsy;

(entumecer) to numb; **—se** (de sueño) to become drowsy; (de frío) to go numb
adormilado ADJ sleepy
adornar VT to adorn, to embellish
adorno M adornment, ornament, decoration
adquirir[4] VT (un bien) to acquire; (una característica) to take on
adquisición F (compra) acquisition; (nuevo miembro) addition; (compra de una compañía) takeover
adquisitivo ADJ purchasing
adrede ADV on purpose
adrenalina F adrenaline
aduana F (control) customs; (edificio) customshouse
aduanero-ra ADJ customs; **control —** customs control; MF customs officer
aducir[38] VT to adduce
adueñarse VI to take possession
adulación F flattery
adulador-ora ADJ flattering; MF flatterer
adular VI/VT to flatter
adulón-ona ADJ flattering; MF *fam* brown-noser
adulterar VT to adulterate
adulterio M adultery
adúltero-ra MF adulterer
adulto-ta ADJ & MF adult
adusto ADJ stern
advenedizo ADJ upstart
advenimiento M advent
adverbio M adverb
adversario-ria MF adversary, opponent
adversidad F adversity
adverso ADJ adverse
advertencia F (aviso) notice; (amonestación) warning, admonition
advertir[8] VT (avisar) to warn; (notar) to notice; (notificar) to advise, to tip off
Adviento M Advent
advierta, advierte *ver* advertir
adyacente ADJ adjacent
aéreo ADJ aerial; **correo —** airmail
aeróbico ADJ aerobic
aeróbic M aerobics
aerobio ADJ aerobic
aerodeslizador M hovercraft
aerodinámica F aerodynamics
aerodinámico ADJ aerodynamic, streamlined
aeródromo M airport
aeroespacial ADJ aerospace
aerolínea F airline
aeronáutica F aeronautics
aeronave F aircraft
aeropuerto M airport
aerosol M (suspensión) aerosol; (aparato) spray can
aerotransportado ADJ airborne
aerotransportar VT to airlift
afabilidad F affability, friendliness
afable ADJ affable, friendly
afamado ADJ famed
afán M eagerness
afanar VT *fam* to swipe; VI **—se** to work hard
afanoso ADJ hardworking
afasia F aphasia
afear VT to make ugly; **—se** to become ugly
afección F condition
afectación F affectation
afectado ADJ (dañado, lastimado) affected, stricken; (artificial) affected, unnatural
afectar VT to affect
afecto M affection, fondness; **— a** fond of
afectuoso ADJ affectionate, loving
afeitado-da ADJ clean-shaven; M shave
afeitadora F shaver
afeitar VT to shave
afelpado ADJ & M plush
afeminado ADJ effeminate
aferrado ADJ stubborn, obstinate
aferrar VT (agarrar) to grasp; (atar) to grapple; **—se** to cling
affaire M affair
Afganistán M Afghanistan
afgano-na ADJ & MF Afghan, Afghani
afianzado ADJ (garantizado) bonded; (apuntalado, amarrado) secured, firmed up
afianzar[47] VT (una pared) to secure; (un préstamo) to secure, to guarantee; (una amistad) to build up
afiche M poster
afición F (inclinación) inclination; (afecto) fondness; (hinchada) fans
aficionado-da ADJ **— a** fond of; MF (no profesional) amateur; (hincha) fan
aficionarse VI **— a** to become fond of
afilado ADJ sharp; M sharpening
afilador-ora MF grinder, sharpener
afilar VT to sharpen, to grind
afiliación F affiliation; **sin — política** nonpartisan
afiliarse VI **— con** to affiliate oneself with
afín ADJ kindred, related
afinación F tune-up
afinado ADJ in tune
afinador-ora MF tuner
afinar VT (una destreza) to perfect; (un plan) to fine-tune; (un piano) to tune; **—se** to become thinner
afinidad F (afecto) affinity; (parentesco) kinship
afirmación F (aseveración) assertion; (aseveración positiva) affirmation
afirmar VT (decir) to assert, to declare; (aseverar) to affirm; (sujetar) to secure; **—se** to steady oneself
afirmativa F affirmative answer
afirmativo ADJ affirmative
aflicción F affliction, woe

afligir[46] VT (dar dolor) to afflict; (entristecer) to distress
aflojar VT (una soga) to slacken, to loosen; (la vigilancia) to relax; **— el dinero** to hand over the money; VI to ease up, to slack off; **—se** to work loose, to loosen up
afluencia F influx
afluente M tributary
afluir[19] VI (río) to flow [into]; (turistas) to flock
afortunadamente ADV fortunately, luckily
afortunado ADJ fortunate, lucky
afrecho M bran
afrenta F affront
afrentar VT to offend
África F Africa
africano -na ADJ & MF African
afroamericano -na ADJ & MF African American
afrontar VT to face
afuera ADV (de un edificio) outdoors; (de un recipiente) outside; F PL **las —s** outskirts
agachar VT to lower; **—se** to crouch, to stoop
agalla F (de pez) gill; (de roble) gallnut; **tener —s** to have guts/spunk
agarrado ADJ tight-fisted
agarrar VT (sujetar) to seize, to grasp, to grab; (capturar) to catch; (adherirse) to grip; **— por sorpresa** to catch by surprise; **—le la onda a algo** to get the swing of something; **—se una neumonía** to catch a case of pneumonia; **—se** to hold on; **—se de** to latch onto; **agarré por la calle ocho** I took Eighth Street; **agarró y se fue** he up and went
agarre M (también golf) grip
agarrón M grab
agarrotarse VI (el cuerpo) to stiffen up; (un motor) to seize [up]
agasajar VT to entertain
agasajo M (acogida) welcome; (regalo) gift
agazaparse VI to crouch
agencia F agency, bureau; **— de empleo** employment agency; **— de publicidad** advertising agency; **— de viajes** travel agency; **— gubernamental** government agency
agenciar VT to wrangle
agenda F (cuaderno) daily planner; (orden del día) agenda
agente MF (representante) agent; (espía) operative; **— de policía** police officer; **— de compras** purchasing agent
ágil ADJ agile, nimble
agilidad F agility
agilizar VT to expedite
agitación F (acción de agitar, nerviosismo) agitation; (protesta) turmoil, unrest
agitado ADJ (estado) agitated; (vida) eventful, hectic; (mar) choppy; (sueño) uneasy
agitador -ora M (aparato) agitator; MF (rebelde) agitator, troublemaker
agitar VT (sacudir) to agitate, to shake up; (incitar a la protesta) to agitate; **—se** (ponerse nervioso) to get worked up; (moverse) to thrash around
aglomeración F crowd
aglomerado M particle board
aglomerarse VI to crowd together
agnóstico -ca ADJ & MF agnostic
agobiado ADJ (por los enemigos) embattled; (por el trabajo) overwhelmed
agobiante ADJ overwhelming
agobiar VT (con una carga excesiva) to weigh down; (con trabajo) to overwhelm; (con impuestos) to burden
agolparse VI to crowd together
agonía F throes of death; **ser un —s** to be a whiner
agonizante ADJ dying
agonizar[47] VI to be in the throes of death
agorafobia F agoraphobia
agorero -ra ADJ ominous; MF soothsayer
agosto M August; **hacer su —** to make hay while the sun shines
agotado ADJ (persona) worn-out, tired out; (libro) out-of-print; (mercancía) out-of-stock
agotador ADJ exhausting
agotamiento M (de una persona) exhaustion; (de un recurso) depletion
agotar VT (recurso) to exhaust, to use up, to deplete; (energía) to sap; (a una persona) to wear down; **—se** (acabarse) to be all gone; (venderse) to sell out; (secarse) to dry up; (libro) to go out of print
agraciado ADJ attractive
agraciar VT to grace
agradable ADJ (persona) agreeable, pleasant, congenial; (situación) pleasant, enjoyable
agradar VT to please
agradecer[35] VT (dar gracias) to thank; (sentir gratitud) to be grateful for; **se agradece** thank you
agradecido ADJ thankful, grateful
agradecimiento M thankfulness, appreciation; (en un libro) acknowledgment
agradezca, agradezco *ver* agradecer
agrado M pleasure; **de su —** to his liking
agrandamiento M enlargement
agrandar VT to enlarge
agrario ADJ agrarian
agravar VT to aggravate, to make worse; **—se** to get worse
agraviar VT to outrage
agravio M outrage
agredir[73] VT to assault
agregado -da MF (funcionario de embajada) attaché; (profesor) adjunct; M (mezcla) aggregate
agregar[40] VT to add

agresión F (violencia) aggression; (ataque) assault; **— con lesiones** assault and battery
agresividad F (actitud) aggressiveness; (propensión violenta) aggression
agresivo ADJ aggressive
agresor -ora MF aggressor, assailant
agreste ADJ (recio) rough; (silvestre) wild
agriar[28] VT to make sour; **—se** to go sour
agrícola ADJ agricultural
agricultor -ora MF agriculturist, farmer
agricultura F agriculture, farming
agridulce ADJ (sabor) sweet-and-sour; (memoria) bittersweet
agrietarse VI (cristales) to crack; (los labios) to chap
agrimensor -ora MF surveyor
agrimensura F surveying
agrio ADJ sour
agrisarse VI to gray
agropecuario ADJ agricultural
agrumarse VI to lump
agrupación F group
agrupamiento M grouping
agrupar VT (objetos, personas) to group; (documentos digitales) to queue
agua F water; **— con gas** sparkling water; **— corriente** running water; **— de colonia** cologne; **— de grifo** tap water; **— de manantial** spring water; **— dulce** fresh water; **—marina** aquamarine; **— mineral** mineral water; **— oxigenada** hydrogen peroxide; **— potable** drinking water; **— salada** salt water; **—s abajo** downstream; **—s arriba** upstream; **—s negras** sewer water; **hacer —** *fam* to take a leak; **se me hace — la boca** my mouth is watering
aguacate M avocado
aguacero M shower, cloudburst, downpour
aguada F watering hole
aguadero M watering hole
aguado ADJ (fruta) watery; (vino, sopa) watered-down
aguantar VT (miserias) to endure; (a una persona molesta) to bear, to stand; (un peso) to bear; (la respiración) to hold; VI (mantenerse) to stand; (durar) to last; (esperar) to wait; (no pudrirse) to keep; **aguántate** grin and bear it
aguante M (para el trabajo) endurance, stamina; (para el vino) tolerance
aguar[25] VT (añadir agua, despojar de fuerza) to water down; (estropear) to spoil; **— una fiesta** to ruin a party; **—se** to become diluted; MF SG **aguafiestas** killjoy, wet blanket
aguardar VI to wait; VT to wait for, to await
aguardentoso ADJ hoarse
aguardiente M brandy
aguarrás M turpentine
agudeza F (visual) sharpness, keenness; (del ingenio) quickness; (para los negocios) acumen; (dicho agudo) witticism
agudo ADJ (dolor, enfermedad, ángulo) acute; (vista, mente) sharp, keen; (mentón) pointed; (voz) high-pitched; (chiste) witty
agüero M portent, omen; **de mal —** portentous
aguijada F goad
aguijar VT to goad
aguijón M (de planta) spur; (de insecto) sting, stinger
aguijonear VT (a un buey) to goad, to prod; (insecto) to sting
águila F eagle; **es un —** he is sharp
aguilucho M eaglet
aguinaldo M Christmas bonus
aguja F (de coser, tejer, tocadiscos, pino, velocímetro) needle; (de reloj) hand; (riel móvil) railroad switch; (chapitel) steeple, spire; **— de croché** crochet hook; **— de punto** knitting needle; **— de zurcir** darning needle; **— hipodérmica** hypodermic needle; **como una — en un pajar** like a needle in a haystack
agujerear VT to pierce
agujero M (orificio) hole; (vacío legal) loophole; (déficit) shortfall; **— negro** black hole; **tapar —s** (reparar orificios) to plug holes; (pagar deudas) to pay debts
aguzar[47] VT to sharpen; **— el oído** to prick up one's ears
ahechaduras F PL chaff
ahí ADV there; **por —** over there, thereabouts; **de —** hence; **— te quiero ver** I want to see you in that situation
ahijado -da M godson; F goddaughter
ahínco M **trabajar con —** to work hard
ahogamiento M drowning
ahogar[40] VT (asfixiar en agua) to drown; (inundar con combustible) to flood; (asfixiar por falta de aire) to smother; (reprimir) to stifle; (asfixiar por presión al cuello) to throttle, to strangle, to choke; **— las penas bebiendo** to drown one's sorrows in drink; **—se** (en agua) to drown; (por falta de aire) to asphyxiate
ahogo M (por calor, falta de aire) suffocation; (por un esfuerzo) breathlessness; **vivir sin —s** to live a comfortable life
ahondar VT (hoyo) to deepen; (asunto) to dig deeper into; **—se** to become deeper
ahora ADV now; **— bien** now then; **— mismo** right now; **— sí** now we're cooking; **por —** for the present, for now; **hasta —** to date, up to now, so far
ahorcar[30] VT to hang; *fam* to string up
ahorita ADV (ahora mismo) right now; (dentro de poco) in a second
ahorrar VT (dinero) to save; (molestias) to spare

ahorrativo ADJ frugal, thrifty
ahorro M thriftiness; **—s** savings; **—s de toda la vida** life savings
ahuecar[30] VT to hollow out; **— la voz** to speak in a hollow voice
ahumado ADJ smoked; M smoking
ahumar VT to smoke
ahuyentar VT to drive away, to scare away; **—se** to get scared
airado ADJ irate
airarse VI to get angry
airbag M airbag
aire M air; (melodía) tune; (manera de ser) manner; **— acondicionado** air conditioning; **— libre** outdoors; **al — libre** outdoors; **cambiar de —s** to change surroundings; **darse —s** to posture; **en el —** up in the air; **estar en el —** to be on the air; **tener — de** to look like; **tomar —** to breathe in, to get some air
airear VT to air out
airoso ADJ graceful; **salir —** to come out smelling like a rose
aislacionismo M isolationism
aislado ADJ (persona) isolated; (lugar) secluded
aislador M insulator; ADJ insulating
aislamiento M (acción de aislarse) isolation; (cosa que aísla) insulation; (soledad) seclusion
aislante M insulator
aislar[28] VT (separar) to isolate; (envolver) to insulate; (rechazar socialmente) to ostracize
ajar VT (una planta) to wither; (las manos) to make rough; (la piel) to age
ajedrez M chess
ajeno ADJ (de otro) belonging to someone else; (extraño) alien; **— a un peligro** oblivious to a danger; **— a mi voluntad** beyond my control; **— a mi experiencia** foreign to my experience
ajetrearse VI to bustle about
ajetreo M bustle, hustle and bustle
ají M chile
ajo M garlic
ajonjolí M sesame
ajuar M (de novia) trousseau; (mobiliario) furnishings
ajustado ADJ tight, snug; **— a la ley** in accordance with the law
ajustar VT (una prenda) to adjust; (un contrato) to tweak; (una tuerca) to tighten; **— cuentas** to settle accounts; VI to fit tight; **—se a derecho** to be in accordance with the law
ajuste M (de horarios, planes) adjustment; (del cinturón) tightening; (de una máquina) fine-tuning; (de cuentas) settlement; (de una prenda) alteration; **hacer —s** to tinker with
ala F (de ave) wing; (de sombrero) brim; (en fútbol) winger; **cortarle las —s a alguien** to clip someone's wings
alabanza F praise
alabar VT to praise
alabeo M warp
alacena F pantry
alacrán M scorpion
alamar M (adorno) frog; (presilla) clasp
alambique M still
alambrada F wire fence
alambrado M (barrera) wire fence; (acción de alambrar) wiring
alambrar VT to wire
alambre M wire; **— de púas** barbed wire
alameda F poplar grove
álamo M poplar tree
alancear VT to wound with a lance, to spear
alano M mastiff
alarde M show; **hacer — de** to boast of, to show off
alardear VI **— de** to boast about
alargar[40] VT (hacer más largo) to lengthen; (un brazo, un guiso) to stretch [out]; **— la vista** to peer into the distance; **—se** to go on [longer than expected]
alargue M (fútbol) extra time
alarido M scream, howl
alarma F alarm; **— antirrobo** burglar alarm; **— contra incendios** fire alarm
alarmante ADJ alarming
alarmar VT to alarm
alba F dawn
albacea MF executor
albanés -esa ADJ & MF Albanian
Albania F Albania
albañal M sewer
albañil M mason, bricklayer
albañilería F masonry
albaricoque M apricot
albatros M albatross
alberca F (depósito) reservoir; (piscina) *Méx* swimming pool
albergar[40] VT (refugiar) to shelter; (hospedar) to lodge; (ser sede de) to house; (guardar rencor, un secreto) to harbor; **—se** (protegerse) to take shelter; (alojarse) to lodge
albergue M lodging; **dar —** (a un refugiado) to give refuge; (a un criminal) to harbor
albinismo M albinism
albino -na MF albino
albóndiga F meatball
albor M dawn
alborada F dawn
albornoz M bathrobe
alborotador -ora ADJ rowdy; MF troublemaker
alborotar VT (el pelo) to muss; (la casa) to mess up; (una turba) to rouse; (a los niños) to excite; **—se** to get excited
alboroto M hubbub, fuss
alborozado ADJ joyful
alborozar[47] VT to gladden; **—se** to rejoice

alborozo M joy
albricias F PL & INTERJ congratulations
álbum M album
alcachofa F artichoke
alcahuete -ta MF (soplón) tattletale; (mediador, encubridor) procurer
alcaide M warden
alcalde -esa MF mayor
alcaldía F (edificio) city hall; (oficio) mayoralty
álcali M alkali
alcalino ADJ alkaline
alcance M (de una persona) reach; (de los deseos) attainment; (de un misil) range; (de una ley) scope; **de corto[s] —[s]** of meager intellect; **al —** at hand, within reach; **a su —** within his reach; **al — del oído** within hearing; **dar — a** to catch up with; **de gran —** far-reaching; **de largo —** long-range
alcancía F piggybank
alcanfor M camphor
alcantarilla F (para agua sucia) sewer; (para lluvias) gully, gutter
alcantarillado M sewage system
alcanzar[47] VT (llegar, cumplir) to reach; (igualar) to catch up with; (pasar, poner en la mano) to pass; (herir a balazos) to get; **no alcanzo a verlo** I can't quite see it; **no me alcanza el dinero** I don't have enough money; **alcancé a conocer a mi abuela** I was born soon enough to meet my grandmother
alcaparra F caper
alcaucil M artichoke
alcázar M fortress
alce M (europeo, asiático) elk; (norteamericano) moose
alcoba F bedroom
alcohol M alcohol; **— etílico** ethyl alcohol; **— para fricciones** rubbing alcohol
alcohólico -ca ADJ & MF alcoholic
alcoholismo M alcoholism
alcornoque M (árbol) cork tree; (persona) blockhead
alcuza F oilcan
aldaba F (para llamar) knocker; (para cerrar) bolt
aldabón M large knocker
aldea F village, hamlet
aldeano -na MF villager; ADJ **joven aldeana** village girl
aleación F alloy
alear VT (metales) to alloy; VI (aves) to flap wings
aleatorio ADJ random
aleatorizar VT to randomize
aleccionar VT to teach a lesson
aledaños M PL vicinity
alegar[40] VT (aducir) to adduce; (pretender) to claim
alegato M (a favor de) plea; (en contra de) allegation
alegoría F allegory
alegrar VT (a una persona) to gladden; (una fiesta) to brighten up; **—se** to be glad; (por efecto del alcohol) to get tipsy
alegre ADJ (contento) joyful, cheerful, lighthearted; (ebrio) tipsy, lit
alegría F joy, merriment, cheer
alejamiento M (distanciamiento) withdrawal; (separacion de un cargo) dismissal
alejar VT (distanciar) to move away; (ahuyentar) to scare off; **—se** (físicamente) to move away; (emocionalmente) to withdraw
alelar VT to stupefy
alemán -ana ADJ & MF German; M (lengua) German
Alemania F Germany
alentador ADJ encouraging
alentar[1] VT (animar) to encourage, to cheer up; VI to breathe
alergeno/alérgeno M allergen
alergia F allergy
alérgico ADJ allergic
alergólogo -ga MF allergist
alero -ra MF (baloncesto) forward; M eaves
alerón M (de avión) aileron, flap; (de coche) spoiler
alerta ADJ & F alert
alertar VT to alert
aleta F (de pez) fin; (de ballena) fluke; (de buceador, delfín) flipper
aletargado ADJ sluggish, lethargic
aletargarse[40] VI to fall into lethargy, to become lethargic
aletazo M flap of a wing
aletear VI to flap, to flutter
aleteo M flapping, flutter
alevín M small fry
alevosía F treachery
alevoso ADJ treacherous
alfabetismo M literacy; **— digital** computer literacy
alfabetización F literacy; **— digital** computer literacy
alfabetizar[47] VI (enseñar) to teach to read and write; VT (ordenar) alphabetize
alfabeto M alphabet
alfalfa F alfalfa
alfanumérico ADJ alphanumeric
alfarería F pottery
alfarero -ra MF potter
alféizar M windowsill
alfeñique M (golosina) sugar paste; (persona) weakling
alférez MF second lieutenant; **— de fragata** ensign
alfil M bishop
alfiler M pin; **— de corbata** tie tack; **no cabe un —** it's totally full

alfiletero M pincushion
alfombra F (de pared a pared) carpet; (suelta) rug
alfombrar VT to carpet
alfombrilla F (en el suelo) mat; (para ordenador) mouse pad
alforja F saddlebag
alga F seaweed; **—s** algae
algarabía F uproar
algarrobo M locust tree
algazara F merriment
álgebra F algebra
algo PRON something; **— es —** something is better than nothing; **por — será** there must be reason; ADV somewhat, slightly
algodón M cotton; **— de azúcar** cotton candy; **se crió entre algodones** he had a protected childhood
algoritmo M algorithm
alguacil M (de policía) sheriff, marshal; (en un tribunal) bailiff
alguien PRON INDEF somebody, someone; **vino — a hablarte** someone came to talk to you; (en preguntas) anybody, anyone; **¿— lo vio?** did anyone see him?
alguno ADJ some; **—s** some, a few; **sin ruido —** without a sound; **en alguna parte** somewhere; **de alguna manera** somehow; **en algún momento** sometime; **¿lo has visto alguna vez?** have you ever seen him? **¿hay alguna forma de hacer esto?** is there any way to do this? PRON someone, something
alhaja F jewel (también persona); **—s** jewelry
alhajero M jewelry box
alharaca F fuss
alhelí M wallflower
aliado -da ADJ allied; MF ally
alianza F (con aliados, socios) alliance
aliar[28] VT to ally
alias M alias, assumed name; (uso policial) a k a
alicaído ADJ crestfallen
alicates M PL pliers
aliciente M inducement
aliento M (aire respirado) breath; (ánimo) encouragement; **cobrar —** to catch one's breath; **contener el —** to hold one's breath; **sin —** out of breath, breathless
aligerar VT to lighten; **— el paso** to quicken one's pace
alijo M cache, stash
alimentación F (comida) nourishment, food; (acción de dar de comer) feeding; **— intravenosa** intravenous feeding
alimentador M feeder; **— de hojas** paper feeder; **— de impresora** printer feeder
alimentar VT (a una persona) to feed, to nourish; (un fuego) to stoke
alimentario ADJ alimentary; **canal —** alimentary canal
alimenticio ADJ (nutritivo) nutritious, nourishing; (relativo a los alimentos) alimentary; **industria alimenticia** food industry; **pensión alimenticia** alimony
alimento M food, nourishment
alineación F (deportes) lineup; (coche) alignment; **— a la derecha** right justification; **— a la izquierda** left justification
alinear VT (objetos) to line up; (a un deportista) to put in the lineup; **—se con** to align oneself with
aliño M condiment, seasoning
alisar VT (tela) to smooth; (pelo) to straighten
alistamiento M enlistment
alistar VT to enlist
aliviar VT (aligerar) to lighten; (mitigar) to alleviate, to relieve; (tranquilizar) to relieve; **—se** (mejorarse) to get better; (hacer sus necesidades) to relieve oneself
alivio M relief (también golf); **— de la deuda** debt relief
aljaba F quiver
aljibe M cistern
allá ADV there, over there; **más —** farther, beyond; **el más —** the hereafter; **— tú** that's your problem
allanamiento M raid; **— de morada** forcible entry
allanar VT (la tierra) to level, to smooth; (una dificultad) to iron out; (una casa) to raid; **— el camino** to smooth the way
allegado -da ADJ close to; MF relative
allegar[40] VT to gather; **—se** to arrive
allí ADV (espacial) there; (temporal) then; **por —** through there
alma F soul; **con toda el —** from the bottom of one's heart; **hasta el —** to the bone; **ni un —** not a soul; **no me cabía el — en el cuerpo** I was overjoyed; **se me fue el — al piso** my heart sank
almacén M (depósito) warehouse, storehouse, depot; (negocio) department store; **grandes almacenes** department store
almacenaje M storage
almacenamiento M storage; **— de datos** data storage; **— masivo** mass storage, bulk storage
almacenar VT to store, to stock up on; **— como** to save as
almacenista MF wholesaler
almáciga F nursery
almádena F sledgehammer
almanaque M (anuario) almanac; (calendario) calendar
almeja F clam
almendra F almond
almendro M almond tree

almiar M haystack
almíbar M syrup
almidón M starch
almidonado ADJ (persona) stiff; (camisa) starched
almidonar VT to starch
almirante M admiral
almohada F pillow; **consultarlo con la —** to sleep on it
almohadilla F (para sellos) cushion; (en las patas de los perros) pad; **— eléctrica** heating pad
almohadón M cushion
almohaza F currycomb
almohazar[47] VT to groom
almorranas F PL piles, hemorrhoids
almorzar[49] VT to lunch, to eat lunch
almuerzo M lunch
alocado ADJ wild
áloe M aloe vera
alojamiento M (residencia) lodging, accommodations; (militar) quarters; **— web** web hosting
alojar VT (a un invitado) to lodge, to accommodate; (a unos huérfanos) to house; (a las tropas) to quarter; **—se** (una bala) to lodge; (una persona) to board, to room
alondra F lark
alpaca F alpaca
alpinismo M mountain climbing
alpinista MF mountain climber, mountaineer
alpino ADJ alpine
alpiste M birdseed
alquería F farmhouse
alquilar VT to rent; **se alquila** for rent
alquiler M (pago mensual) rent; (acción de alquilar) renting; **coche de —** rental car; **dar en —** to hire out
alquitrán M tar
alquitranar VT to tar
alrededor ADV around; **— de la casa** around the house; M **—es** (de un área) surroundings; (de una ciudad) outskirts
alta F discharge; **dar de —** to discharge
altamente ADV highly
altanería F haughtiness
altanero ADJ haughty
altar M altar
alteración F alteration; **alteraciones al orden público** public disturbances
alterar VT to alter; **— el ánimo** to upset; **—se** to get upset
altercado M altercation
altercar[30] VT **— con** to quarrel with
alternador M alternator
alternancia F alternation
alternar VT to alternate; **— con** to rub elbows with
alternativa F alternative
alternativo ADJ (cambiante) alternating; (optativo) alternative
alterno ADJ alternate; **alterna y continua** AC/DC
alteza F highness
altibajos M PL ups and downs
altillo M attic
altímetro M altimeter
altiplano M high plateau
altisonante ADJ high-sounding
altitud F altitude
altivez F haughtiness
altivo ADJ haughty
alto ADJ (que está arriba) high; (que tiene altura vertical) tall; **altas finanzas** high finance; **— contraste** high contrast; **de alta calidad** high-quality; **de alta fidelidad** high-fidelity; **de — nivel** high-level; **de alta potencia** high-powered; **de — riesgo** high-risk; **de alta velocidad** high-speed; **en voz alta** aloud; **en — grado** to a great extent; **en alta mar** on the high seas; M **altavoz** loudspeaker; M **altoparlante** loudspeaker; M (altura) height; (piso) upper story; **— el fuego** cease-fire; ADV loud; **hablar —** to talk loud; **cotizarse —** to be set high; INTERJ halt!
altruismo M altruism
altura F (de persona, edificio, ola, epidemia) height; (de avión) altitude; (sobre el nivel del mar, lugar alto) elevation; **a estas —s** at this stage; **a la — de la calle ocho** at Eighth Street; **a la — de las circunstancias** equal to the circumstances
alubia F bean
alucinación F hallucination
alucinar VT (causar alucinaciones) to hallucinate; (fascinar) to fascinate; (deslumbrar) to bowl over; VI (sufrir alucinaciones) to hallucinate
alucinógeno M hallucinogen
alud M avalanche
aludir VI **— a** to allude to, to refer to
alumbrado M lighting; **— público** street lighting; ADJ lit
alumbramiento M childbirth
alumbrar VT encender, to light up; (dar a luz) to give birth to
aluminio M aluminum
alumnado M student body
alumno -na MF (de enseñanza primaria) pupil; (de enseñanza secundaria) student
alusión F allusion
aluvión M (de preguntas, pedidos) barrage; (de personas) flood
alza F appreciation; **— de precios** boost in prices
alzado ADJ elevated; MF insurgent
alzamiento M (acción de alzar) raising;

(insurrección) uprising
alzaprima F crowbar
alzar[47] VT (la mano, la voz, una casa) to raise; (a un niño) to lift up; — **la vista** to look up; —**se** to rise up in rebellion; —**se con** to make off with
amabilidad F kindness; **¿tendría la — de . . . ?** would you mind . . . ?
amable ADJ kind, nice
amado -da MF beloved
amaestrador -ora MF trainer
amaestramiento M training
amaestrar VT to train
amagar[40] VI/VT threaten; **amagó que iba a llover** it looked like it was going to rain; **amagó con golpearla** he made as if he was going to hit her
amago M **hacer** — to make as if
amague M (baloncesto) fake, juke
amalgamar VT to amalgamate
amamantar VT to nurse, to breast-feed
amanecer[35] VI to dawn; — **enfermo** to wake up ill; **amanecí en Londres** I woke up in London; M dawn, sunrise, daybreak
amanerado ADJ effete
amansar VT to tame
amante MF lover; — **de** fond of
amañar VT (una elección) to rig; (un documento) to tamper with
amapola F poppy
amar VT to love
amargar[40] VT to embitter
amargo ADJ bitter
amargor M bitterness
amargura F bitterness
amarillear VI/VT to yellow, to turn yellow
amarillento ADJ yellowish
amarillo -lla ADJ yellow; MF (esquirol) scab
amarra F cable, rope; —**s** moorings; **soltar** —**s** to cast off
amarrar VT (un barco) to moor; (una cosa) to secure, to tie down
amartillar VT (pegar con martillo) to hammer; (un arma) to cock
amasar VT (masa) to knead; (una fortuna) to amass
amateur ADJ INV & MF amateur
amatista F amethyst
Amazonas M Amazon River
Amazonia M Amazon Forest
ambages M PL **hablar sin** — to not mince words, to speak plainly
ámbar M amber
ambición F ambition
ambicionar VT to have the ambition to
ambicioso ADJ (emprendedor) ambitious; (codicioso) overambitious
ambidiestro ADJ ambidextrous
ambiental ADJ (limpieza) environmental; (temperatura) ambient
ambiente ADJ ambient; M (condiciones biológicas) environment; (atmósfera) atmosphere, ambience, ambiance; (sector social) milieu
ambigüedad F ambiguity
ambiguo ADJ ambiguous
ámbito M (ambiente) scene; (alcance) scope; (esfera) sphere
ambivalente ADJ ambivalent
ambos ADJ & PRON both
ambulancia F ambulance
ambulante ADJ itinerant
ambulatorio ADJ ambulatory
ameba F amoeba
amedrentar VT to scare
amén INTERJ amen; **decir** — to approve without discussion; — **de** besides
amenaza F threat, menace
amenazador ADJ threatening
amenazante ADJ threatening
amenazar[47] VT to threaten; — **con** to threaten to
amenidad F (cualidad de ameno) pleasantness
amenizar[47] VI to make entertaining
ameno ADJ enjoyable, entertaining
América F America
americano -na ADJ & MF American; F sport coat
ametrallador -ora MF gunner; F machine gun
ametrallar VT to strafe, to machine-gun
amianto M asbestos
amigable ADJ friendly
amígdala F (faríngea) tonsil; (cerebral) amygdala
amigdalitis F tonsillitis
amigo -ga ADJ friendly; — **de** fond of; — **de lo ajeno** thieving; MF friend
amiguismo M cronyism
aminoácido M amino acid
aminorar VT to lessen
amistad F (relación) friendship; (amigo) friend; **trabar** — to strike up a friendship
amistoso ADJ friendly, amicable
amnesia F amnesia
amniocentesis F amniocentesis
amnistía F amnesty
amo -ma M (de esclavo, sirviente) master; (de animal) owner; F (de esclavo, de sirviente) mistress; (de animal) owner; **ama de leche** wet nurse; **ama de llaves** housekeeper; **ama de casa** homemaker
amodorrado ADJ drowsy
amodorrar VI to make drowsy; —**se** to become drowsy
amolar[5] VT to annoy
amoldar VT to mold
amonestación F admonition, warning
amonestar VT to admonish, to warn
amoníaco M ammonia

amontonamiento M pile
amontonar VT to pile up
amor M love; **— propio** self-esteem; **de mil —es** gladly; **hacerle el — a** to make love to; **por el — de Dios** for God's sake; **por — al arte** unremunerated
amoral ADJ amoral
amoratado ADJ (de golpes) black-and-blue; (de frío, por falta de oxígeno) blue
amordazar[47] VT (a una persona) to gag; (a un perro, a los críticos) to muzzle
amorfo ADJ amorphous
amorío M love affair
amoroso ADJ loving, amorous
amortajar VT to shroud
amortiguador M shock absorber
amortiguar[25] VT (un sonido) to muffle, to absorb; (un golpe) to cushion, to absorb; (un dolor) to deaden, to dull
amortización F (desvalorización periódica) depreciation; (recuperación de una inversión) recovery; (reembolso gradual) amortization, paying off
amortizar[47] VT (recuperar a plazos) to amortize; (depreciar) to depreciate
amoscarse[30] VI to get peeved
amostazarse[47] VI to get peeved
amotinarse VI (en un barco) to mutiny; (en una cárcel) to riot
amparar VT (proteger) to protect; (refugiar) to shelter; **—se** to protect oneself
amparo M (protección) protection; (refugio) shelter; **al — de** under the protection of
amperio M ampere
ampicilina F ampicillin
ampliación F (de una foto) enlargement; (de una casa) extension
ampliar[28] VT (una foto) to enlarge; (una calle) to extend; (una explicación) to expand; (un volumen) to amplify; **— una imagen** to zoom in
amplificador M amplifier
amplificar[30] VT (un sonido) to amplify; (una imagen) to magnify
amplio ADJ (información, tiempo) ample; (piso) spacious, roomy; (región, resonancia, sonrisa) broad; (vestido) full; **de amplias miras** open-minded
amplitud F (de comprensión) breadth; (de onda) amplitude
ampolla F (de la epidermis) blister; (vasija) vial
ampollar VT to blister
ampuloso ADJ bombastic
amputar VT to amputate
amueblar VT to furnish
amuleto M amulet, charm
anacronismo M anachronism
ánade M duck
anadear VI to waddle
anadeo M waddle
anaerobio ADJ anaerobic
anal ADJ anal
anales M PL annals
analfabetismo M illiteracy
analfabeto -ta ADJ & MF illiterate
analgésico ADJ & M analgesic
análisis M analysis; **— costo-beneficio** cost-benefit analysis; **— de mercado** market analysis; **— de orina** urinalysis
analista MF analyst
anotación F (béisbol) run; (básquetbol) point; (fútbol americano) touchdown; (glosa) note
analítico ADJ analytical, analytic
analizador M parser
analizar[47] VT (datos) to analyze; (secuencia) to parse
analogía F analogy
analógico ADJ (relativo a la analogía) analogical; (no digital) analog
análogo ADJ analogous
ananá[s] M SG pineapple
anaquel M shelf
anaranjado ADJ & M (color) orange
anarquía F anarchy
anarquista MF anarchist
anatema M anathema
anatomía F anatomy
anatómico ADJ anatomical
anca F haunch, rump
ancho ADJ wide, broad; **a sus anchas** at his ease; **me viene —** it's too wide for me; M width, breadth; **a lo —** widthwise; **tiene un metro de —** it's one meter wide
anchoa F anchovy
anchura F width, breadth
ancianidad F old age
anciano -na ADJ elderly, aged; MF old person
ancla F anchor
anclar VI/VT to anchor
andada F **volver a las —s** to backslide
andador -ora MF walker
Andalucía F Andalusia
andaluz -za ADJ & MF Andalusian; M (dialecto) Andalusian
andamiaje M (para construcción) scaffolding; (fundamento) framework
andamio M scaffold
andanada F broadside; **una — de insultos** a barrage of insults
andante ADJ walking
andanzas F PL adventures
andar[66] VI to walk; (coche, motor, reloj) to run; (el tiempo) to pass; (un aparato) to work; **— con cuidado** to be careful; **— en coche** to travel by car, to ride in a car; **— mal** to be in bad shape, to be a mess; **— mal del corazón** to have heart trouble; **—se por las ramas / con vueltas** to beat around the bush; **no**

—**se con rodeos** to make no bones about it; **en eso ando** that's what I'm up to; **¡andando!** move on! **¿dónde anda a estas horas?** where is he at this hour? **¡ándale!** *Méx* (apresúrate) come on! (de acuerdo) OK; M gait

andariego ADJ fond of walking

andas F **llevar en —** *RP* to carry on one's shoulders

andén M (de tren) platform; (para peatones) sidewalk

Andes M PL Andes

andino ADJ Andean

Andorra F Andorra

andorrano-na ADJ & MF Andorran

andrajo M rag, tatter

andrajoso ADJ ragged, tattered

andrógino ADJ androgynous

anduve, anduviera, anduviese *ver* andar

anécdota F anecdote

anegar[40] VT to flood

anejo ADJ attached; M accompanying volume

anemia F anemia; — **falciforme** sickle cell anemia; — **por deficiencia de hierro** iron deficiency anemia

anémico ADJ anemic

anestesia F (acción de anestesiar) anesthesia; (sustancia) anesthetic

anestesiar VT to anesthetize

anestésico ADJ & M anesthetic

anestesiología F anesthesiology

anestesiólogo-ga MF anesthesiologist

anestesista MF anesthesiologist

aneurisma M aneurysm

anexar VT (un territorio) to annex; (con una carta) to enclose

anexión F annexation

anexo ADJ attached; M (de un edificio) annex, extension; (a una ley) rider

anfeta F *fam* speed

anfetamina F amphetamine

anfibio ADJ & M amphibian

anfiteatro M amphitheater

anfitrión-ona M host (también informático); F hostess

ángel M angel; — **de la guarda** guardian angel

angelical ADJ angelic

angélico ADJ angelic

angina F —**s** tonsillitis; — **del pecho** angina pectoris; — **laríngea** laryngeal angina

angiocardiografía F angiocardiography

angiograma M angiogram

angioplastia F angioplasty

anglosajón-ona ADJ & MF Anglo-Saxon

Angola F Angola

angolano-na, angoleño-ña, angolés-esa ADJ & MF Angolan

angostar VT to narrow, to contract

angosto ADJ narrow

angostura F (cualidad de angosto) narrowness; (desfiladero) narrows

anguila F eel; — **eléctrica** electric eel

angular ADJ angular

ángulo M (figura geométrica, enfoque) angle; (rincón, esquina) corner; — **muerto** blind spot; — **recto** right angle

anguloso ADJ angular

angustia F (desasosiego) anguish, anxiety, distress; (congoja) heartache; (desazón existencial) angst

angustiado ADJ (desasosegado) anguished, anxious; (acongojado) distraught

angustiante ADJ nerve-wracking

angustiar VT to distress; —**se** to feel distressed

angustioso ADJ distressing

anhelante ADJ longing

anhelar VT to long for, to yearn for

anhelo M longing, yearning

anidar VI to nest

anillas F PL gymnastics rings

anillo M ring; — **de boda** wedding ring; **me queda como — al dedo** it fits me like a glove

ánima F soul of the departed

animación F (viveza) animation, liveliness; (en películas) animation

animado ADJ (vivo) animate; (bullicioso) lively

animador-ora MF (de un espectáculo) host; (de un equipo) cheerleader

animal ADJ & M animal

animar VT (dar vida) to animate, to enliven; (incitar) to encourage, to urge on; (dar aliento) to cheer up; —**se** (alegrarse) to cheer up; (atreverse) to gather courage

ánimo M (espíritu) spirit; (aliento) encouragement; (humor) mood; (intención) intention; **no estoy de — para eso** I'm not in the mood for that; INTERJ hang in there!

animosidad F animosity

animoso ADJ spirited

aniñado ADJ childlike

aniquilar VT to annihilate, to wipe out

anís M anise

aniversario M anniversary

anoche ADV last night

anochecer[35] VI to get dark; **anochecimos en París** night found us in Paris; M nightfall, dusk

anomalía F anomaly

anómalo ADJ anomalous

anonadado ADJ dumbfounded

anonadar VT (aniquilar) to annihilate; (vencer) overwhelm; (desconcertar) to dumbfound; —**se** to become dumbfounded

anónimo ADJ anonymous, nameless; M anonymous letter

anorak M anorak

anorexia F anorexia

anoréxico ADJ anorexic
anormal ADJ abnormal; MF freak
anotación F (nota) annotation, notation; (en fútbol) goal
anotar VT (apuntar) to note; (marcar un tanto) to score; **—se** to sign up
anquilosarse VT (las articulaciones) to become stiff; (una institución) to become stagnant
ansia F (deseo) eagerness; (congoja) anguish
ansiar[28] VT to covet
ansiedad F anxiety
ansioso ADJ (ávido) anxious, eager; (inquieto) fretful
antagonismo M antagonism
antagonista MF antagonist
antagonizar[47] VT to antagonize
antaño ADV in the old days
antártico ADJ antarctic
Antártida F Antarctica
ante PREP before; **— este problema** in the face of this problem; **— todo** above all; M suede
anteanoche ADV night before last
anteayer ADV day before yesterday
antebrazo M forearm
antecedente ADJ & M antecedent; **—s** (profesionales) background; (criminales) record; **—s delictivos** criminal record
antecesor -ora MF (antepasado) ancestor; (predecesor) predecessor
antedatar VT to backdate
antedicho ADJ aforesaid
antelación LOC ADV **con —** beforehand
antemano LOC ADV **de —** beforehand
antena F (de radio) antenna, aerial; (de insecto) antenna, feeler
anteojera F blinder
anteojos M PL glasses, spectacles; **— de sol** sunglasses; **— bifocales** bifocals
antepasado -da MF ancestor, forebear
antepecho M sill
anteponer[56, 74] VT (poner delante, poner antes) to place before; (dar preferencia) to give priority to
anterior ADJ (en el tiempo) previous; (en el espacio) anterior, front; **— a** prior to
anterioridad F **con —** before
anteriormente ADV (antes) previously, formerly; (en la parte delantera) in front
antes ADV (previamente) before, formerly; (más temprano) sooner; **llegó —** he arrived sooner; **— de** before; **— la muerte** I'd rather die; **— bien** rather; **— de impuestos** pretax; **— del cierre** before closing; **lo — posible** ASAP, as soon as possible
antesala F (habitación) anteroom; (preludio) prelude; (béisbol) third base
antesalista MF third baseman
antiaborto ADJ INV antiabortion, right-to-life
antiácido ADJ & M antacid
antiaéreo ADJ antiaircraft
antialérgico ADJ antiallergic
antibacteriano ADJ antibacterial
antibalas ADJ INV bulletproof
antibalístico ADJ (misil) antiballistic; (chaqueta) bulletproof
antibiótico ADJ & M antibiotic; **— de amplio espectro** broad-spectrum antibiotic
antibloqueo ADJ INV antilock
anticipación LOC ADV **con —** in advance
anticipado LOC ADV **por —** in advance
anticipar VT (una fecha) to move up; (dinero) to advance; (el porvenir) to anticipate; **—se a los acontecimientos** to jump the gun
anticipo M advance, deposit
anticoagulante M anticoagulant
anticoncepción F contraception
anticonceptivo ADJ & M contraceptive
anticongelante M antifreeze
anticonvulsivo M anticonvulsant
anticuado ADJ antiquated, out-of-date
anticuerpo M antibody
antideportivo ADJ unsportsmanlike
antidepresivo ADJ & M antidepressant
antidiarreico M antidiarrheal
antidiurético M antidiuretic
antídoto M antidote
antieconómico ADJ wasteful
antiespasmódico M antispasmodic
antiestético ADJ unsightly
antígeno M antigen
antigualla F old piece of junk
antiguano -na ADJ & MF Antiguan
Antigua y Barbuda F Antigua and Barbuda
antigüedad F (cualidad de antiguo) antiquity; (objeto) antique; (tiempo en un cargo) seniority
antiguo ADJ (era, historia) ancient; (ropa) old; (mueble) antique; **a la antigua** in the old style; **la antigua capital** the former capital; **más —** with more seniority
antihigiénico ADJ unsanitary
antihistamínico M antihistamine
antiinflamatorio ADJ & M anti-inflammatory
Antillas F PL West Indies
antílope M antelope
antimonio M antimony
antimonopolio ADJ INV antitrust
antioxidante ADJ & M antioxidant
antiparras F PL goggles
antipatía F antipathy
antipático ADJ unfriendly, unkind
antipoliomielítico ADJ antipolio
antipsicótico M antipsychotic
antireflejante ADJ anti-glare
antisemitismo M anti-Semitism
antiséptico ADJ & M antiseptic
antisocial ADJ antisocial
antítesis F antithesis

antitoxina F antitoxin
antitranspirante M antiperspirant
antitrust ADJ INV antitrust
antiviral M antiviral
antojadizo ADJ whimsical
antojarse VI **se le antojó comer salchicha** he took a notion to eat sausage; **esa tarea se me antoja difícil** that task seems hard to me
antojo M (deseo) whim, craving; (mancha de nacimiento) birthmark
antología F anthology, reader
antónimo M antonym
antorcha F torch
antracita F anthracite
ántrax M anthrax
antro M (bar) dive, joint; **— de perdición** den of iniquity
antropología F anthropology
antropólogo -ga MF anthropologist
anual ADJ annual, yearly
anualidad F annuity; **— variable** variable annuity
anuario ADJ annual; M yearbook
anudar VT to knot; **se le anudó la garganta** he got all choked up
anulación F (de un contrato) cancellation; (de un matrimonio) annulment
anular VT (un matrimonio) to annul; (un contrato, un evento) to cancel; (una sentencia) to overrule, to overturn; (un talón) to void; (un comando de computadora) to undo; **— una selección previa** to deselect; M ring finger
anunciador -ora MF announcer
anunciante MF advertiser
anunciar VT (información) to announce; (un producto) to advertise
anuncio M (de información) announcement; (de un producto) advertisement; **— clasificado** classified advertisement, want ad; **— publicitario** advertisement, ad; **poner un —** to place an ad
anzuelo M fishhook; **morder/picar el —** to take the bait
añadidura F addition; **por —** in addition
añadir VT to add
añejo ADJ aged, vintage
añicos M **hacerse —** to break into a thousand pieces
añil M indigo, bluing
año M year; (de la escuela) grade; (de vino) vintage; **— bisiesto** leap year; **— luz** light-year; **de cuarenta —s** aged forty; **del — hasta la fecha** year-to-date; **el — en curso** the current year; **el — pasado** last year; **en los —s veinte** in the 1920s; **entrado en —s** getting on in years; **¿cuántos —s tienes?** how old are you?
añojo -ja MF yearling
añoranza F longing; (del hogar) homesickness
añorar VT to long for, to be homesick for
añoso ADJ old
añublo M blight
aorta F aorta
apabullar VT (impresionar) to bowl over; (derrotar) to crush
apacentar[1] VI to graze, to pasture
apacible ADJ good-natured, laid-back
apaciguar[25] VT (pacificar) to pacify; (aplacar) to mollify, to appease; **—se** to calm down
apadrinar VT to sponsor; (en un bautismo) to act as godfather to; (en una boda) to act as best man for; (en un duelo) to second
apagado ADJ (no llamativo) flat; (no intenso) dull
apagar[40] VT (un fuego) to put out, to extinguish; (una luz) to turn off, to turn out; (motor) to turn off, to kill; (una computadora) to power down; (una vida) to kill, to snuff out; (la sed) to quench; **—se** (luz) to go out; (un color) to fade; (una voz) to trail off; (un volcán) to become extinct
apagón M blackout, outage
apalabrarse VI **— con** to make a verbal agreement with
apalancamiento M leverage
apalear VT to thrash
aparador M sideboard, buffet, cupboard
aparato M (de gimnasia artística) apparatus; (para ejercicio) machine; (de cocina) appliance; (de teléfono) telephone; (máquina, dirigencia política) machine; (boato) pomp; **— circulatorio** circulatory system; **— de televisión** television set; **— ortodóntico** braces; **— ortopédico** leg brace
aparatoso ADJ pompous
aparcamiento M (lugar para aparcar) parking lot; (acción de aparcar) parking
aparcar[30] VI/VT to park; MF SG **aparcacoches** valet
aparcero -ra MF sharecropper
aparear VT (animales) to mate; (calcetines) to match, to pair; **—se** (animales) to mate; (en un baile) to pair off
aparecer[35] VI (ponerse a la vista, publicarse) to appear; (hacer acto de presencia) to show up; **se me apareció un ángel** an angel appeared to me
aparejar VT (un cuarto, un ejército) to prepare; (problemas) to entail; (una embarcación) to rig
aparejo M (de caballo) harness; (de buque) rigging; (para pescar) tackle; **—s** equipment
aparentar VT to feign; VI to show off; **aparenta la edad que tiene** she looks her age
aparente ADJ apparent
aparezca, aparezco *ver* aparecer

aparición F (fantasma) apparition; (acción de aparecer) appearance
apariencia F (aspecto) appearance; (fingimiento) pretense, semblance; **las —s engañan** appearances are deceiving; **guardar las —s** to keep up appearances
apartado M section; **— postal** post office box; ADJ (recóndito) secluded; (distante) distant; **muy —** far apart
apartamento M apartment
apartamiento M separation
apartar VT (separar) sort out; **aparta las monedas de veinticinco centavos** set aside the quarters; (mover) to move away; **apartó la silla de la pared** he moved the chair away from the wall; (empujar) to push away/aside; **lo apartó de un empujón** she pushed him away; (aislar) to take aside; **lo aparté para hablarle** I took him aside to talk to him; (retirar) to take off; **apartó la cacerola del fuego** she took the pan off the fire; (alejar del cargo) to remove from office; **apartaron al ministro de su cargo** they removed the minister from his post; **apartó la vista** he looked away; VI **—se** to stray; **se apartaron del buen camino** they strayed from the straight and narrow; **los resultados se apartan de lo esperado** the results depart/deviate from the norm; **se apartó para que no lo atropellara el coche** he got out of the way so the car wouldn't hit him
aparte ADJ separate; ADV **bromas —** kidding aside; **dejar —** to exclude; **punto y —** new paragraph; M aside; PREP **— de** (además de) besides; (salvo) except for
apasionado ADJ (amor, hombre) passionate; (defensa, comentario) impassioned
apasionante ADJ exciting
apasionar VT **eso me apasiona** I love that; **—se por** to be passionate about
apatía F apathy
apático ADJ apathetic
apear VT to get down; **—se** to dismount
apechugar[40] VI **— con** to put up with
apedrear VT to stone
apegado ADJ attached
apegarse[40] VI to become attached
apego M attachment
apelación F appeal
apelar VI/VT to appeal
apellidarse VI to have the surname of
apellido M surname, last name
apelotonarse VI (una almohada) to ball up; (gente) to bunch together
apenado ADJ (dolorido) grieved; (avergonzado) embarrassed
apenar VT to grieve, to pain; **—se** to be grieved
apenas ADV hardly, scarcely, barely; **— llegó, se desmayó** no sooner had he arrived than he fainted; **— comienza la reunión** the meeting is just starting
apéndice M (órgano, parte de un libro) appendix; (añadido) appendage
apendicectomía F appendectomy
apendicitis F appendicitis
apercibir VT to warn; **—se de** to notice
aperitivo M appetizer
apero M farm implement
apertura F (transparencia) openness; (oportunidad) opening; **a la —** at the opening
apesadumbrado ADJ doleful
apestar VT (hacer heder) to stink up; (causar la peste) to plague; VI to stink, to reek
apestoso ADJ (hediondo) smelly; (apestado) pestilent
apetecer[35] **no me apetece ir contigo** I don't feel like going with you
apetecible ADJ appetizing
apetito M appetite
apetitoso ADJ appetizing
apiadarse VI **— de** to pity, to take pity on
ápice M apex; (de la lengua) tip; **no apartarse ni un —** not to diverge a jot
apio M celery
apisonadora F steamroller
apisonar VT to pack down
aplacamiento M appeasement
aplacar[30] VT (a una persona) to appease, to mollify; (miedo) to allay; (sed, pasión) to quench; **—se** to relent
aplanadora F steamroller
aplanamiento M flattening, leveling
aplanar VT (un terreno) to level, to flatten; (con una aplanadora) to roll
aplastado ADJ flattened
aplastamiento M crushing
aplastante ADJ (derrota) crushing; (victoria) sweeping
aplastar VT (achatar) to squash, to crush; (derrotar) to plaster, to stomp; (una revolución) to squelch, to smash, to crush; **—se** to crumple
aplaudir VI/VT to applaud
aplauso[s] M SG/PL applause
aplazamiento M postponement, deferral; (de un proceso legal) continuance
aplazar[47] VT to postpone, to put off
aplicable ADJ applicable
aplicación F (acción de aplicarse) application; (de un castigo) administration; (de computadora) application, app; **— de fondo** background application
aplicado ADJ (conocimiento, ciencia) applied; (trabajador) industrious
aplicador M applicator
aplicar[30] VT to apply; **—se** to work hard, to apply oneself

aplomado ADJ (equilibrado) poised; (vertical) plumb
aplomar VT to plumb
aplomo M poise
apnea M apnea; **— obstructiva del sueño** sleep apnea
apocado ADJ timid
apocalipsis MF (desastre) apocalypse; (Biblia) Revelation
apocamiento M timidity
apocarse[30] VI to become intimidated
apodar VT to nickname
apoderado -da MF proxy, agent
apoderarse VI **— de** to take possession of, to seize
apodo M nickname
apogeo M apogee; **en su —** (una fiesta) in full swing; (un estilo) in its heyday, at its peak
apolillado ADJ (comido por las polillas) moth-eaten; (anticuado) antiquated
apología F apology
apoplejía F apoplexy
aporrear VT to club, to cudgel
aportación F contribution
aportar VT (evidencia) to provide; (dinero) to contribute
aporte M contribution
aposento M chamber
apostador -ora MF bettor
apostar[5] VI/VT (a los caballos) to bet, to wager; (a un centinela) to station, to post; **— por** (caballo) to bet on; (cambio) to commit to
apóstol M apostle
apóstrofe MF apostrophe, invocation
apóstrofo M (ortografía) apostrophe
apostura F bearing
apoyar VT (sostener) to rest; (respaldar) to support, to back; (votar por) to second; (respaldar un argumento) to buttress; **—se en** (recostarse contra) to lean on, to prop against; (basarse en) to be based on; M SG **apoyabrazos** armrest
apoyo M support
apreciable ADJ (digno de aprecio) esteemed; (perceptible) noticeable; (registrable) appreciable
apreciablemente ADV significantly
apreciación F appreciation
apreciado ADJ (amigo) dear; (tesoro) valued, prized
apreciar VT (valorar) to appreciate; (percibir) to notice; (registrar) to measure; (considerar) to take into consideration; (sentir afecto) to cherish; **—se** (un fenómeno) to be noticeable; (moneda) to appreciate
aprecio M appreciation
aprehender VT (a un delincuente) to apprehend; (contrabando) to seize; (una idea) to grasp
aprehensión F (arresto) apprehension; (incautación) seizure
apremiante ADJ pressing
apremiar VT to pressure
apremio M pressure
aprender VI/VT to learn; **— de memoria** to memorize, to learn by heart
aprendiz -za MF (de un oficio) apprentice, trainee; (de una lengua, canto) learner
aprendizaje M (de un oficio) apprenticeship; (acto de aprender) learning
aprensión F apprehension, misgivings
aprensivo ADJ apprehensive
apresar VT (aprisionar) to imprison; (incautar) to seize
aprestar VT to prepare; **—se a** to get ready to
apresurado ADJ hasty, hurried
apresurar VT to hurry, to hasten
apretado ADJ (zapato) tight; (beso) hard; (racimo) compact; (síntesis) succinct; (jornada) busy; (situación) difficult, dangerous
apretar[1] VT (un botón) to press; (un gatillo) to squeeze; (un tornillo) to tighten; (los dientes, puños) to clench; (a un bebé) to clasp; **me apretó para que le diera dinero** he pressured me to give him money; **ese profesor nos aprieta mucho** that teacher demands a lot of us; VI (zapatos) to be tight, to pinch; (sol) to be intense; (esforzarse) to try hard, to bear down; **—se** to crowd together
apretón M squeeze; **— de manos** handshake
aprieta, apriete *ver* apretar
aprieto M jam, fix, predicament; **en —s** in need, hard-pressed, in dire straits; **estar en un —** to be in a tight spot, to be in trouble, to be in a pickle; **poner en —s** to embarrass
aprisa ADV quickly
aprisco M (para el ganado) fold
aprisionar VT to trap
aprobación F (aceptación) approval; (adopción, promulgación) passage, adoption; (calificación) passing grade; **— de crédito** credit approval
aprobar[5] VT (una medida, una opinión) to approve of; (una ley) to pass, to approve; (un examen) to pass; (un crédito) to sign off on; VI to pass
aprontar VT to ready
apropiación F appropriation; **— indebida** embezzlement
apropiadamente ADV properly, appropriately
apropiado ADJ appropriate, suitable
apropiarse VT **— de** to appropriate
aprovechable ADJ usable
aprovechado ADJ opportunistic
aprovechamiento M use
aprovechar VT (una ocasión) to take advantage of; (el espacio) to utilize; (la enseñanza) to

profit from; VI to be useful; **—se de** to take advantage of; INTERJ **¡que aproveche!** enjoy your meal!

aproximación F (acercamiento) approach; (estimado) rough estimate

aproximado ADJ approximate

aproximar VT to bring near; **—se** to approach; **— a** to approximate

aprueba, apruebe *ver* aprobar

aptitud F aptitude; **—es musicales** musical aptitude

apto ADJ apt, suitable; **— para menores** for general audiences

apuesta F bet, wager

apuesto ADJ good-looking

apuntalar VT to prop up, to shore up

apuntar VT (señalar) to point out; (dirigir sobre un blanco) to aim; (matricular) to enroll; (escribir) to write down, to note; (ayudar a un actor) to prompt; (marcar puntos) to score; VI (una flecha) to point; (canas) to sprout; **— a un blanco** to aim at a target; **me apunto para ir con vosotros** I'm game to go with you

apunte M notation; **—s** notes; **tomar —s** to take notes; **llevar el — a alguien** to pay attention to someone

apuñalar VT to stab

apurado ADJ (situación) difficult; (persona) in dire straits; (apresurado) in a hurry

apurar VT (consumir) to drink up; (apremiar) to put under pressure; **—se** *Am* to hurry

apuro M predicament, fix; (prisa) hurry; **estar en —s** to be in distress

aquejado ADJ stricken

aquejar VT to afflict, to trouble

aquel ADJ that; **aquella chica se llama María** that girl is named María; **aquellas ciudades son antiguas** those cities are old; PRON that one; **— es el mayor** that one is the oldest; **aquellos son mis hijos** those are my children; **de mis dos hijos, Juan y Pedro, este es gordo y — es flaco** of my two sons, Juan and Pedro, the latter is fat and the former is thin; **en/por — entonces** back then

aquí ADV here; **está por —** it is around here; **ven por —** come this way; **hasta —** this far; **de — a cuatro horas** four hours from now; **de — en adelante** from now on; **de — para allá** to and fro, back and forth; **— y ahora** here and now

aquietar VT to quiet; **—se** (los nervios) to calm down; (una tormenta) to subside

ara LOC ADV **en —s de** for the sake of

árabe MF (persona) Arab; M (caballo) Arabian; (lengua) Arabic; ADJ (caballo) Arabian; (costumbre, arte) Arab

Arabia Saudí, Arabia Saudita F Saudi Arabia

arácnido M arachnid

arado M plow

Aragón M Aragon

aragonés -esa ADJ Aragonese; MF (persona) Aragonese; M (dialecto) Aragonese

arancel M (impuesto) tariff; (lista de honorarios) list of fees

arancelario ADJ **acuerdo —** tariff agreement

arándano M blueberry; **— rojo** cranberry

arandela F washer

araña F (arácnido) spider; (candelabro) chandelier

arañar VT (rayar) to scratch; (herir con garras) to claw, to scratch; (raspar) to scrape, to score

arañazo M scratch

arañero M warbler

arar VI/VT to plow, to till

arbitraje M arbitration

arbitrar VT (un desacuerdo) to arbitrate; (un partido) to referee, to officiate; (un partido de béisbol) to umpire

arbitrariedad F (acción) arbitrary action; (cualidad) arbitrariness

arbitrario ADJ arbitrary

arbitrio M (libre albedrío) free will; (capricho) whim; (decisión) discretion; (deseos) wishes

árbitro -tra MF (del buen gusto) arbiter; (de conflictos) arbitrator; (de encuentros deportivos) referee

árbol M tree; (mástil) mast; **— de Navidad** Christmas tree; **— de levas** camshaft; **— genealógico** family tree

arbolado ADJ woody, wooded

arboleda F grove, clump

arbóreo ADJ arboreal

arbusto M shrub, bush

arca F ark; **— de Noé** Noah's ark; **las —s municipales** municipal coffers

arcada F arcade, archway; **tener/dar —s** to gag

arcaico ADJ archaic

arcaísmo M archaism

arcano ADJ arcane

arce M maple [tree]

arcén M shoulder of a road

archienemigo -ga MF archenemy

archipiélago M archipelago

archisabido ADJ very well-known

archivado ADJ on file

archivador M filing cabinet

archivar VT (guardar en un archivo) to file; (arrumbar) to shelve

archivo M (repositorio de documentos) archive; (fichero de ordenador) file; (acción de archivar) filing; **— comprimido** compressed file; **— cookie** cookie; **— corrupto** corrupted file; **— de datos** data file; **— de lectura/escritura** read/write file

arcilla F clay

arco M (geométrico, eléctrico) arc; (estructura

arquitectónica) arch; (arma, varilla de violín) bow; — **iris** rainbow
arder VT to burn; **la cosa está que arde** things are really getting hot; **el trigo se ardió** the wheat spoiled
ardid M scheme, artifice
ardiente ADJ (deseo) ardent; (calor, fuego, deseo) burning
ardilla F squirrel; — **de tierra** gopher; — **listada** chipmunk
ardite M **no valer un** — not to be worth a penny
ardor M (de pasión) ardor; (de fuego) heat; (por ácido) burning; — **de estómago** heartburn
arduo ADJ arduous, grueling
área F area; — **de penales** (fútbol) penalty area, box
arena F (tierra) sand; (plaza) arena; — **movediza** quicksand
arenero M sandbox
arenga F harangue
arengar[40] VT to harangue
arenisca F sandstone
arenisco ADJ sandy
arenoso ADJ sandy
arenque M herring
arete M earring
argamasa F mortar
Argelia F Algeria
argelino -na ADJ & MF Algerian
Argentina F Argentina
argentino -na ADJ Argentine, Argentinian; (como la plata) silvery; MF Argentine, Argentinian
argolla F iron ring
argón M argon
argot M slang
argucias F PL trickery
argüir[20] VT to argue
argumentar VT to argue
argumento M (razonamiento) argument; (conjunto de sucesos) plot
aridez F dryness
árido ADJ (seco) arid, dry, barren; (aburrido) dry; —**s** dry goods
ariete M (militar) battering ram; (fútbol) center forward
arisco ADJ surly
arista F (borde) edge; (de trigo) beard; **limar —s** to overcome difficulties
aristocracia F aristocracy
aristócrata MF aristocrat
aristocrático ADJ aristocratic
aritmética F arithmetic
aritmético ADJ arithmetical
arma F (instrumento bélico) arm, weapon; (división del ejército) branch; — **blanca** sharp weapon; — **de fuego** firearm; **a las —s** to arms; **de —s tomar** resolute; **tomar las —s** to take up arms
armada F armada, fleet
armado ADJ armed; **a mano armada** at gunpoint; M assembly, putting together
armador -ora MF (naviero) shipowner; (en fútbol) playmaker; (en vóleibol) setter
armadura F (cobertura de hierro) armor; (de un edificio) framework; (de gafas) frame; (de música) key signature
armamento M armament
armar VT (proveer de armas) to arm; (abastecer una embarcación) to equip; (reforzar) to reinforce; (ensamblar) to assemble, to put together; (levantar una tienda de campaña) to pitch; — **jaleo** to whoop it up; — **relajo** to make a mess; —**se de** to arm oneself with; — **una pendencia** to pick a fight, to start a quarrel
armario M (de ropa) wardrobe, closet; (de cocina) cabinet, armoire
armatoste M unwieldy object
armazón MF framework, skeleton
Armenia F Armenia
armenio -nia ADJ & MF Armenian
armería F (depósito) armory; (tienda) gun shop
armiño M ermine
armisticio M armistice
armonía F harmony
armónico ADJ & M harmonic
armonioso ADJ harmonious
armonizar[47] VI/VT to harmonize, to blend
ARN [ácido ribonucleico] M RNA
arnés M harness
aro M (de rueda) rim; (de baloncesto) hoop; **no tocó ni** — it was an airball
aroma M (olor agradable) aroma; (del vino) bouquet
aromático ADJ aromatic
arpa F harp
arpía F shrew
arpillera F burlap
arpón M harpoon
arponear VT to harpoon
arqueado ADJ arched
arquear VT to arch
arqueología F archaeology
arqueológico ADJ archaeological
arquero -ra MF (tirador de flechas) archer; (guardametas) goalkeeper
arquetipo M archetype
arquitecto -ta MF architect
arquitectónico ADJ architectural
arquitectura F architecture
arrabal M outlying slum
arraigar[40] VT to take root
arrancar[30] VT (una planta) to uproot; (el pelo) to tear out; (un diente) to pull; (un vicio) to eradicate; (una flor) to pick; (una confesión) to extract; — **de** to wrest from; VI/VT (un

vehículo) to start; **arrancó para el valle** he took off for the valley; **arrancó a sudar** he began to sweat; **sus problemas arrancan de su niñez** his problems are rooted in his childhood; **—se los cabellos** to tear one's hair [out]

arranque M (proceso de arrancar) starting; (dispositivo para arrancar) starter; (decisión, empuje) gumption; **— de ira** fit of rage

arrasar VT (destruir) to level, to raze; (derrotar) to crush; **— con** to obliterate; VI to win

arrastrado ADJ wretched

arrastrar VT (mover por el suelo) to drag; (llevarse consigo) to sweep away; (atraer) to draw; (soportar) to bear; (pronunciar lentamente) to draw out; **— los pies** (moverse con dificultades) to shuffle; (ser renuente) to stall; VI (cortinas) to hang down to the floor; **—se** (una serpiente) to slither; (una lagartija, un insecto) to crawl; (una persona) to grovel; **— y soltar** to drag and drop, to drag and release; M SG **arrastrapiés** shuffle

array M array

arrayán M myrtle

arrear VT to drive, to herd

arrebatar VT (quitar) to snatch away, to wrest away; (quemar) to burn on the outside; **—se** to have a fit

arrebatiña F mad scramble

arrebato M fit, outburst

arreciar VI to increase in intensity

arrecife M reef

arreglar VT (poner en orden, concertar, adaptar música) to arrange; (ordenar) to tidy up; (reparar) to fix, to repair; (resolver) to settle; **— cuentas** to settle accounts; **ya te arreglo** I'll fix you; **—se** (embellecerse) to fix oneself up; (llevarse bien con) to get along with; (entablar relaciones amorosas) to start dating; (reconciliarse) to make up; (conformarse) to make do; (despejarse) to clear up; **arreglárselas** to cope, to manage

arreglo M arrangement; **con — a** in accordance with; **no tiene —** it can't be helped; **llegar a un —** to settle; **—s** alterations

arrellanarse VI to lounge, to loll

arremangado ADJ turned up, rolled up

arremangar[40] VT to roll up; **—se** to roll up one's sleeves, to knuckle down

arremeter VI to attack; **— contra** to lunge at

arremetida F thrust, lunge

arremolinarse VT (viento) to whirl around; (agua) to eddy

arrendajo M bluejay

arrendamiento M rental

arrendar VI/VT to rent, to lease; **se arrienda** for lease

arrendatario -ria MF tenant

arreo M adornment; **—s** tack, harness

arrepentido ADJ repentant, rueful

arrepentimiento M (contrición) repentance; (disgusto) regret

arrepentirse[8] VI (de los pecados) to repent; (de los errores) to regret

arrestar VT to arrest

arresto M arrest

arriar[28] VT (la bandera) to lower; (un cabo) to slacken

arriate M flower bed

arriba ADV above; **¡—!** get up! **¡— las manos!** stick 'em up! **¡— Juan!** long live Juan! **de — abajo** from top to bottom; **lleno hasta —** full to the brim; **te vas para —** you are doing well; **viven —** they live upstairs

arribar VI LIT to arrive; (buque) to put into port

arribista MF social climber

arribo M LIT arrival

arriendo M leasing, rental

arriero -ra MF animal driver

arriesgado ADJ (peligroso) risky; (valiente) daring

arriesgar[40] VT to risk; **—se** to take a chance

arrimar VT (acercar) to bring near; (golpear) to strike; **—se a** (apoyarse) to lean on; (acercarse) to get near

arrinconar VT (acorralar) to corner; (poner en un rincón) to put in a corner; (abandonar) to abandon

arritmia F arrhythmia

arrobamiento M rapture

arrobarse VI to be enraptured

arrodillarse VI to kneel

arrogancia F arrogance

arrogante ADJ arrogant

arrogarse[40] VT to claim

arrojadizo ADJ for throwing

arrojar VT (lanzar) to throw, to hurl; (expulsar) to throw out; (botar) to throw away; (vomitar) to throw up, to vomit; (proyectar una luz) to shed, to throw; **— un saldo de** to show a balance of; **—se** to hurl oneself

arrojo M boldness, daring

arrollador ADJ overwhelming

arrollar VT (enrollar) to roll up; (arrastrar) to run over; (derrotar) to defeat

arropar VT (con ropa) to wrap up; (en la cama) to tuck in; **—se** to pull up the covers

arroyo M stream, creek

arroz M rice; **— integral** brown rice

arrozal M rice field

arruga F wrinkle

arrugar[40] VT to wrinkle; **— el ceño** to knit one's brow; **—se** (pasar a tener arrugas) to get wrinkles; (asustarse) to be afraid

arruinar VT (estropear) to ruin; (destruir) to destroy, to ravage; (aguar) to spoil; (dejar en la quiebra) to bankrupt, to ruin; **—se** to go to

ruin

arrullar VI (una paloma) to coo; VT (a un enamorado) to whisper sweet nothings to; (a un niño) to rock to sleep, to lull to sleep

arrullo M (de la tórtola) cooing; (del agua) babbling

arrumbar VT (arrinconar) to put aside; (marginalizar) to marginalize

arsenal M (depósito) arsenal; (astillero) navy yard

arsénico M arsenic

arte M SG art; F PL arts; M (destreza) skill, ability; (actividad manual) craft; **bellas —s** fine arts; **el — por el —** art for art's sake; **malas —s** wiles; **no tener ni — ni parte en algo** to have nothing to do with something; **por — de** by means of; **por — de magia** by magic

artefacto M (aparato) contrivance, device; (bomba) bomb

arteria F artery

arterial ADJ arterial

arteriosclerosis F arteriosclerosis

artero ADJ artful, wily

artesanía F (trabajo, obra) craft; (habilidad) craftsmanship

artesano -na MF artisan; M craftsman; F craftswoman

ártico ADJ arctic

articulación F (acción de articular) articulation; (juntura) joint

articular VT (pronunciar) to articulate, to enunciate; (unir) to join

artículo M (de revista) article; (de diccionario) article, entry; **— de fondo** editorial; **— definido** definite article; **hacer el —** to give a sales pitch

artífice MF (autor) architect; M (artesano) craftsman; F craftswoman

artificial ADJ artificial

artificio M artifice

artificioso ADJ affected, contrived

artillería F artillery

artillero -ra MF (militar) gunner; (en fútbol) striker

artimaña F trick, wile

artista MF (plástica) artist; (drama, música) performer

artístico ADJ artistic

artritis F arthritis

artroscopia F arthroscopy

artroscópico ADJ arthroscopic

artrosis F degenerative joint disease

Aruba F Aruba

arveja F pea

arzobispo M archbishop

arzón M saddletree

as M ace (también atleta)

asa F handle

asado ADJ roasted; M (carne asada) roast; (carne asada al aire libre) barbecue; (acción de asar) roasting

asador -ora M spit; MF barbecue cook

asalariado -da MF wage earner

asaltante MF mugger

asaltar VT (a una persona) to assault, to assail; (un banco) to hold up; (con preguntas) to assail; **—le a uno una idea** to be struck by an idea

asalto M (ataque) assault; (de un banco) holdup, stickup; **tomar por —** to storm

asamblea F assembly, gathering

asar VT to roast; **— a la parrilla** to grill; **— con adobo** to barbecue

asbesto M asbestos

ascendencia F ancestry

ascendente ADJ (que incrementa) ascending, rising; (que sube) upward

ascender[2] VT (a un empleado) to promote; (una montaña) to climb; VI to ascend; **— a** to amount to

ascendiente MF ancestor

ascenso M (acción de ascender) ascent; (en el trabajo) promotion

ascensor M elevator

asceta MF ascetic

ascético ADJ ascetic

ascienda, asciende *ver* ascender

asco M disgust, revulsion; **hacer —s a** to reject; **me da —** it makes me sick, it disgusts me; **ese hombre está hecho un —** that man is a mess; **su acné me da —** his acne is a turnoff

ascórbico ADJ ascorbic; **ácido —** ascorbic acid

ascua F ember; **estar en —s** to be on pins and needles; **tener a alguien en —s** to string someone along

aseado ADJ well-groomed

asear VT to clean up

asediar VT to besiege

asedio M siege

asegurable ADJ insurable

asegurador -ora MF underwriter

asegurar VT (una victoria) to assure; (una frontera, una cerradura) to secure; (con un contrato de seguros) to insure; **—se [de]** to make sure [of]; **te lo aseguro** I assure you

asemejarse VI **— a** to resemble

asentaderas F PL buttocks

asentamiento M (de una comunidad) settlement; (de un edificio) settling

asentar VT (datos) to enter; (una población) to establish; **—se** (posarse) to settle; (madurar) to settle down

asentimiento M assent, acquiescence

asentir[8] VI to assent, to acquiesce; **— con la cabeza** to nod

aseo M (acción de asearse) cleaning; (cualidad de aseado) cleanliness; (cuarto de baño) bathroom; (servicio) toilet, restroom

aséptico ADJ aseptic
asequible ADJ (disponible) available; (barato, económico) affordable
aserción F assertion
aserradero M sawmill, lumber mill
aserrado ADJ serrated; M sawing
aserrar[1] VT to saw
aserrín M sawdust
aserto M assertion
asesinar VT to murder; (a una figura pública) to assassinate
asesinato M murder, killing; (de una figura pública) assassination
asesino -na ADJ murderous; MF killer, murderer; (de una figura pública) assassin; — **en serie** serial killer
asesor -ora MF consultant, advisor/adviser
asesoramiento M (profesional, legal) consulting, advising; (académico) counseling; — **de crédito** credit counseling
asesorar VT to advise
asesor -ora MF aide
asestar VT — **un golpe** to inflict/deal a blow
aseveración F assertion
aseverar VT to assert
asexual ADJ asexual
asfalto M asphalt
asfixia F suffocation, asphyxiation, asphyxia
asfixiar VT to suffocate, to smother
así ADV so, thus, like this; — — so-so; — **como** in the same way that; — **de grande** that big; — **que** so that; **¿— que no vienes?** so you're not coming?
Asia F Asia
asiático -ca ADJ & MF Asian
asidero M hold; **eso no tiene — en la realidad** that has no basis in reality
asiduo ADJ (lector) assiduous; (cliente) steady
asiento M (lugar donde sentarse, parte de una silla, válvula) seat; (de nóminas) entry, record; **tomar** — to take a seat
asignación F (acción de asignar) assignment; (acción de dar fondos) appropriation; (lo asignado) allotment; (pago) allowance
asignar VT (una tarea) to assign; (fondos) to allot, to allocate, to earmark
asignatura F subject
asilado -da MF inmate; — **político -ca** political refugee
asilar VT (a un político) to give asylum to; (un animal) to shelter
asilo M (para los perseguidos) asylum; (para huérfanos, ancianos) home
asimétrico ADJ asymmetric, asymmetrical
asimilar VT (vitaminas, un grupo étnico) to assimilate; (información) to absorb
asimismo ADV likewise
asintomático ADJ asymptomatic
asir[50] VT to grasp, to grip; **—se a** to hold onto
asistencia F (presencia, personas presentes) attendance; (ayuda) assistance, aid; (servicio de averías) roadside assistance; (deporte) assist; — **médica** health care; — **social** (ayuda) welfare; (profesión) social work
asistente -ta ADJ assistant; MF assistant, helper; — **social** social worker
asistir VT — **a** (estar presente) to attend; (ayudar) to help, to assist
asma F asthma
asmático ADJ asthmatic
asno M ass, donkey
asociación F association; — **de propietarios** homeowners' association
asociado -da MF associate
asociar VT to associate; **—se** to join; **—se con** to fall in with
asolamiento M desolation
asolar VT to desolate, to devastate
asomar VI to show; VT to poke out, to stick out; **—se a** to look out
asombrar VT to astonish, to amaze, to astound; **—se** to be astonished
asombro M astonishment, amazement
asombroso ADJ astonishing, amazing
asomo LOC ADV **ni por** — by no means
asonancia F assonance
aspa F (de hélice) blade; (de ventilador) vane
aspartamo M aspartame
aspecto M (faceta) aspect, feature; (apariencia) looks
aspereza F roughness, harshness; **con** — sharply; **limar —s** to smooth over disagreements
áspero ADJ (terreno, mano) rough; (lucha) bitter; (tiempo, voz) harsh
aspiración F (ambición) aspiration, ambition; (respiración) breathing in; (succión) suction
aspiradora F vacuum cleaner
aspirante MF applicant, candidate
aspirar VT (inhalar) to breathe in, to inhale; (a un empleo) to apply for; — **a** to aspire to
aspirina F aspirin
asqueado ADJ disgusted
asquear VT to disgust
asquerosidad F nastiness; **¡estás hecho una —!** you're gross!
asqueroso ADJ nasty, disgusting, gross
asta F (de toro) horn; (de ciervo) antler; (de bandera) flagpole; (de lanza) shaft; **a media** — at half mast
asterisco M asterisk, star
asteroide M asteroid
astigmatismo M astigmatism
astilla F (de madera) chip, splinter; (de vidrio) sliver; **—s** kindling
astillar VT to chip, to splinter
astillero M shipyard
astringente ADJ & M astringent

astro M (del cielo) celestial body; (de cine) movie star
astrofísica F astrophysics
astrología F astrology
astronauta MF astronaut
astronáutica F astronautics
astronomía F astronomy
astronómico ADJ (relativo a las estrellas) astronomical; (muy elevado) astronomic, astronomical
astrónomo -ma MF astronomer
astucia F (listeza) cunning, guile; (treta) trick
asturiano -na ADJ & MF Asturian; (dialecto) Asturian
Asturias F SG Asturias
astuto ADJ shrewd, wily, cunning
asueto M (día libre) day off; (licencia) time off
asumir VT (una responsabilidad) to assume, to shoulder; (una mala noticia) to accept; **— un cargo** to take office
asunción F assumption; **— presidencial** presidential inauguration
asunto M (cuestión) matter; (tema de una obra) theme
asustadizo ADJ easily frightened, jumpy
asustado ADJ frightened, scared
asustar VT to frighten, to scare; **—se** to become frightened
atacante ADJ attacking; MF assailant
atacar[30] VT to attack, to assault; **—se de risa** to have a laughing fit
atado M bundle
atadura F **sin —s** with no strings attached
atajador M tackle
atajar VT (interrumpir) to cut off; VI (cortar camino) to take a shortcut
atajo M shortcut
atalaya F watchtower
atañer[15, 73] VI to concern, to pertain to
ataque M (de violencia, asma) attack; (de rabia, de tos) fit; (de epilepsia) seizure; (en fútbol americano) offensive series; **— cardíaco** heart attack; **— de nervios** nervous breakdown; **— relámpago** blitz
atar VT (sujetar) to tie, to bind; **— cabos** to put two and two together; **—se los zapatos** to tie one's shoes
atardecer[35] VI to get dark; M late afternoon, dusk, evening; **al —** at dusk
atareado ADJ busy
atarearse VI to busy oneself
atascadero M (lodazal) quagmire; (de tránsito) bottleneck
atascado ADJ stuck
atascar[30] VT (un tubo) to stop up; (una máquina) to jam; (el tráfico) to obstruct; **—se** (un vehículo) to get stuck; (una máquina) to get jammed
ataúd M coffin, casket
ataviar[28] VT to attire, to array; **—se** to dress up
atavío M attire, garb
ateísmo M atheism
atemorizar[47] VT to frighten
atención F attention; (médica) care; (acto de cortesía) courtesy; **— al cliente** customer care; **— médica a largo plazo** long-term care; **— prenatal** prenatal care; **— primaria** primary care; **a la — de** to the attention of; **llamar la —** (hacer notar) to call attention; (ser llamativo) to attract attention; (interesar) to interest; INTERJ watch out!
atender[2] VT (a un enfermo) to take care of, to look after; (una súplica) to heed; (a un cliente) to serve; (el trabajo) to attend to, to take care of; VI **— a** to pay attention to
atenerse[58] VI **— a los hechos** to bear the facts in mind, to limit oneself to the facts; **— a la ley** to abide by the law
atentado M (asesinato) assassination; (ataque fracasado) assassination attempt; (con bomba) bombing; **un — contra** an affront to
atentamente ADV (con atención) attentively; (despedida en cartas) yours truly / yours sincerely
atentar[1] VI **— contra la vida de alguien** to make an attempt on someone's life
atento ADJ (que presta atención) attentive; (amable) thoughtful
atenuar[26] VT (la violencia) to attenuate; (una luz) to dim; **—se** to abate
ateo -a MF atheist
aterciopelado ADJ velvety
aterido ADJ stiff with cold
aterirse[73] VI to become stiff with cold
aterrador ADJ terrifying
aterrar VT to terrify
aterrizaje M landing; **— forzoso** crash landing
aterrizar[47] VI/VT to land
aterrorizar[47] VT (intimidar) to terrorize; (dar miedo) to terrify
atesorar VT (memorias) to treasure; (dinero) to hoard
atestado ADJ crowded, crammed
atestar VT (certificar) to attest to; (llenar) to jam, to pack
atestiguar[25] VT to bear witness, to testify
atiborrar VT to stuff; **—se** to stuff one's face
atienda, atiende *ver* atender
atiesar VT to stiffen
atildado ADJ spruced up
atinar VT (acertar) to hit the mark; (adivinar) to guess right; **no — a decir palabra** not to manage to get a word out
atípico ADJ atypical
atisbar VT (mirar con disimulo) to peek at, to peep at; (vislumbrar) to catch a glimpse of; VI to peek

atisbo M glimpse, hint
atizar[47] VT (fuego) to poke, to stoke; (pasiones) to stir up, to stoke
atlántico ADJ Atlantic; M **Océano Atlántico** Atlantic Ocean
atlas M atlas
atleta MF athlete
atlético ADJ athletic
atletismo M track and field
atmósfera F atmosphere
atmosférico ADJ atmospheric
atolladero M quagmire
atolondrado ADJ scatterbrained; (muchacha) ditsy
atómico ADJ atomic
atomizador M atomizer
atomizar[47] VT to atomize
átomo M atom
atónito ADJ dumbfounded
atontado ADJ stupefied
atontar VT to stupefy
atorar VT to jam; **—se** to choke
atormentar VT to torment; **—se por** to agonize over
atornillar VT to bolt
atracadero M dock
atracar[30] VT (amarrar) to dock; (robar) to hold up, to mug; **—se** to gorge oneself
atracción F attraction
atraco M holdup, stickup
atracón M **darse un —** to gorge
atractivo ADJ attractive, fetching; M (capacidad de atraer) attractiveness, appeal; (cosa que atrae) attraction; **— sexual** sex appeal
atraer[59] VT to attract
atragantarse VI to choke
atraiga, atraigo, atrajo, atrajera, atrajese *ver* atraer
atrancar[30] VT to bolt, to bar
atrapada F catch
atrapar VT (en una trampa) to trap, to ensnare, to catch; (una pelota, el interés) to catch
atrás ADV **— de la casa** behind the house; **cuatro años —** four years back; **hacia —** backward; **para —** back/backwards; **quedarse —** to fall behind
atrasado ADJ (de tiempo) late; (en el pago) in arrears, behind; (país) backward; (un libro de biblioteca) overdue; **tengo sueño —** I'm behind in my sleep; **el reloj anda —** the clock is slow; **feliz cumpleaños —** belated happy birthday
atrasar VT (un plazo) to delay; (un objeto) to push back; (un reloj) to turn back; VI (un reloj) to run slow; **—se** to fall behind, to lag
atraso M (condición de atrasado) backwardness; (pago) back payment; (de trabajo) backlog; **con dos meses de —** two months in arrears
atravesar[1] VT (cruzar) to cross; (estar tendido) to span; (penetrar) to impale, to run through; **— un momento difícil** to go through a difficult moment; **se me atravesó un caballo** a horse crossed in front of me; **—se en la cama** to lie crossways in bed
atraviesa, atraviese *ver* atravesar
atrayendo *ver* atraer
atreverse VI to dare, to go for it; **¡atrévete!** go for it!
atrevido ADJ (audaz) bold, daring; (insolente) insolent
atrevimiento M (cualidad de atrevido) boldness, daring, audacity; (acción atrevida) daring act
atribución F attribution; **atribuciones** powers
atribuir[19] VT (imputar) to attribute, to ascribe; (conferir) to confer; VI **—se** to claim
atribular VT to distress; **—se** to be distressed
atributo M attribute
atribuya, atribuye, atribuyendo, atribuyera, atribuyese *ver* atribuir
atril M stand
atrincherar VT to entrench
atrio M atrium
atrocidad F atrocity
atrofia F atrophy
atrofiar VT to atrophy, to stunt
atronador ADJ thunderous, deafening
atronar[5] VI to make a racket
atropellar VT (a un peatón) to run over, to run down; (los derechos de alguien) to trample upon
atropello M (arrollamiento) running over; (ultraje) outrage; (abuso) trampling
atroz ADJ (modales, crimen) atrocious; (dolor) excruciating; (ofensa) grievous
atuendo M getup
atún M tuna
aturdido ADJ bewildered; **estar —** to be in a daze
aturdimiento M bewilderment
aturdir VT to bewilder, to daze
atusar VT to smooth, to fix
audacia F audacity, boldness
audaz ADJ audacious, bold
audible ADJ audible
audición F audition; **— radial** radio program
audiencia F (tribunal) court; (público) audience; (en un pleito, proceso legal) hearing
audífono M (para sordos) earphone; (para música) headphone
audio M audio; **—libro** audio book
audiología F audiology
audiovisual ADJ audiovisual; M audiovisual presentation
auditar VI/VT to audit
auditivo ADJ auditory
auditor-ora MF auditor
auditoría F (revisión) audit; (trabajo de auditor)

auditing
auditorio M (público) audience; (local) auditorium
auge M (del mercado) boom; (de una moda) heyday; (de una carrera) peak
augurar VT to foretell; **no — nada bueno** not to bode well
aula F (de clase) classroom; (de conferencia) lecture hall
aullar VI to howl
aullido M howl
aumentar VT to augment, to increase; **— los salarios** to raise pay; VI (precios) to rise, to escalate; (población) to grow; (violencia) to escalate
aumento M increase; (de expectativas) buildup; (de población) growth; (de precios) rise, upturn; (de peso) gain; **— por mérito** merit raise; **— salarial / de sueldo** pay raise
aun ADV even; **— así** even so; **— cuando** even though/if
aún ADV still
aunque CONJ though, although
aura F aura
áureo ADJ golden
aureola F halo
auricular M (de teléfono) receiver; **—es** headphones, earphones
aurora F dawn, aurora; **— boreal** aurora borealis, northern lights
auscultar VT to listen to with a stethoscope
ausencia F absence
ausentarse VT to absent oneself
ausente ADJ absent, missing
ausentismo M absenteeism
auspicios M PL auspices
austeridad F austerity
austero ADJ austere, stern
Australia F Australia
australiano -na ADJ & MF Australian
Austria F Austria
austríaco -ca ADJ & MF Austrian
autenticar[30] VT to authenticate
autenticidad F authenticity
auténtico ADJ authentic
autismo M autism
autista ADJ autistic
auto M (coche) auto; (orden judicial) writ; **— de choques** bumper car
autoadhesivo M decal; (para el parachoques) bumper sticker
autoayuda F self-help
autobiografía F autobiography
autobomba M RP fire engine
autobús M bus
autocine M drive-in movie theater
autocompasión F self-pity
autocontrol M self-control
autócrata MF autocrat
autóctono ADJ indigenous
autodestructivo ADJ self-destructive
autodeterminación F self-determination
autodisciplina F self-discipline
autoedición F desktop publishing
autoescuela F driving school
autoestima F self-esteem
autogobierno M self-government
autogol M own goal
autógrafo M autograph
autoimagen F self-image
automático ADJ automatic
automatización F automation
automatizar[47] VT (mecanizar) to automate; (hacer automáticamente) to do automatically
automóvil M automobile
automovilista MF motorist
automovilístico ADJ automotive
autonomía F autonomy; (de un vehículo) range
autonómico ADJ autonomic
autónomo ADJ (independiente) autonomous, independent; (que trabaja por su cuenta) self-employed; (que se presenta solo) stand-alone
autopista F freeway, turnpike; **— de la información** information superhighway
autopropulsado ADJ self-propelled
autopsia F autopsy
autor -ora MF author
autoridad F authority
autoritario ADJ (tiránico) authoritarian; (respetado) authoritative
autorización F authorization
autorizar[47] VT (permitir) to authorize; (dar propiedad intelectual) to license
autosatisfacción F self-satisfaction
autoservicio M (sistema de venta) self-service; (tienda) convenience store
autosuficiencia F self-reliance
autosuficiente ADJ (independiente) self-sufficient; (presumido) smug
autovía F freeway
auxiliar VT to help; ADJ auxiliary; MF assistant; **— de vuelo** flight attendant
auxilio M help
avalancha F avalanche
avalar VT to guarantee, to cosign
avaluar[26] VT to appraise
avalúo M appraisal
avance M (acción de avanzar, adelanto) advance, headway; (sinopsis de película) trailer
avanzada F scouting party
avanzado ADJ advanced
avanzar[47] VI (ir hacia adelante) to advance; (progresar) to make headway; **a medida que avanzaba la mañana** as the morning progressed; VT (un vehículo) to move forward; (una grabación) to fast-forward
avaricia F avarice

avariento ADJ avaricious, miserly
avaro ADJ miserly, avaricious
avasallar VT to subjugate
avatar M (vicisitud) vicissitude; (encarnación de un dios, personaje digital) avatar
ave F bird; **— de corral** poultry; **— de rapiña** bird of prey; **— canora** songbird; **— zancuda** wading bird
avecindarse VI to take up residence
avellana F hazelnut
avellano M hazel
avena F oats
avenencia F agreement
avenida F avenue
avenir[61] VI to reconcile; **—se a** to come around to; **—se bien** to get along
aventadora F fan, blower
aventajar VT (ser mejor) to be superior to; (sobrepasar) to get ahead of
aventón M **dar un —** *Méx* to give a lift
aventura F (suceso) adventure; (relación amorosa) fling, affair
aventurado ADJ (arriesgado) risky; (atrevido) daring
aventurar VT (arriesgar) to risk; (sugerir) to venture; **—se a** to dare to
aventurero -ra ADJ adventurous; MF adventurer
avergonzado ADJ (tímido) abashed; (arrepentido) ashamed, embarrassed
avergonzar[23] VT to shame, to embarrass; **—se** to be ashamed/embarrassed
avería F (de frutas) damage, bruise; (de coche) breakdown, mechanical trouble
averiado ADJ (un coche) broken-down; (un televisor) on the blink; (un ascensor) out of service; (fruta) bruised, damaged
averiarse[28] VI (fruta) to become damaged; (un coche) to break down
averiguar[25] VT to find out, to ascertain
aversión F aversion, dislike
avestruz MF ostrich
avezado ADJ seasoned
aviación F aviation
aviador -ora MF aviator
aviar[28] VT to fix
avidez F eagerness
ávido ADJ eager, avid
avinagrado ADJ sour
avinagrar VT to sour; **—se** to become sour
avío M tidying up; **—s de pescar** fishing tackle
avión M (máquina) airplane; (ave) martin; **— comercial** airliner; **— a reacción** jet airplane; **— caza** fighter airplane
avisar VT (notificar) to advise; (alertar) to alert
aviso M notice; **— publicitario** advertisement; **estar sobre —** to be forewarned; **poner sobre —** to forewarn; **sin previo —** without warning
avispa F wasp
avispado ADJ (despierto) lively; (inteligente) smart
avisparse VI to wise up
avispero M wasp's nest; **alborotar el —** to stir up a wasp's nest
avispón M hornet
avistar VT to catch sight of
avivar VT (una llama) to fan; (una fiesta) to enliven; (un fuego, un debate) to fuel
avizorar VT to spy on
axila F underarm
ay INTERJ (de dolor) ouch; (de decepción) oh, no; (de sorpresa desagradable) oh; **¡— de mí!** poor me; **¡ay, no!** oh, no!
ayer ADV yesterday
ayuda F (asistencia) help; (después de una catástrofe) relief; **— en línea** online help
ayudante -ta MF assistant, helper, aide; **— de médico** physician's assistant
ayudantía F assistantship
ayudar VT to help, to aid
ayunar VI to fast
ayunas F PL **en —** (antes de comer) without having eaten; (despistado) clueless; **estoy en —** I am fasting
ayuno M fast, fasting
ayuntamiento M (gobierno) municipal government; (edificio) city hall
azabache M jet; ADJ jet-black, raven
azada F hoe
azadón M hoe
azafato -ta MF (en aviones) flight attendant; (en ferias) host
azafrán M saffron
azahar M orange blossom
azar M chance; **al —** by chance, at random
azaroso ADJ (arriesgado) risky; (aleatorio) random
azerbaiyano -na, azerbaijano -na ADJ & MF Azerbaijani, Azerbaijanian
Azerbaiyán F Azerbaijan
azogar[40] VT to silver
azogue M (sustancia) quicksilver, mercury; (niño inquieto) restless child; **tener — en el cuerpo** to be restless
azorar VT (alarmar) to alarm; (avergonzar) to embarrass
azotaina F flogging
azotar VT (con azote) to whip, to lash, to flog; VI/VT (el viento) to whip, to buffet; (el sol) to beat down; (la lluvia) to sting
azote M (instrumento) whip; (golpe) lash; (aflicción) scourge; (golpe de viento) buffet
azotea F flat roof
azteca ADJ, MF Aztec
azúcar MF sugar; **— moreno -na** brown sugar
azucarar VT to sugar
azucarera F (fábrica) sugar mill; *Am* (recipiente)

sugar bowl
azucarero M sugar bowl
azucena F white lily
azufre M sulfur, sulphur
azul ADJ blue; **— acero** steel blue; **— celeste** sky blue; **— claro** light blue; **— marino** navy blue
azulado ADJ bluish
azular VT to color blue
azulear VI (tener color azul) to be blue; (ponerse azul) to become blue; VT (dar color azul) to color blue
azulejar VT to tile
azulejo M tile
azuzar[47] VT (a un perro) to to sic; (a una persona) to egg on

Bb

baba F drivel, drool, slobber; (de un caracol, de agua estancada) slime; **se le cae la — por el coche nuevo** he's drooling over the new car
babear VI to drivel, to drool
babero M bib
babor M portside
babosa F slug
babosear VI/VT to slobber [on]
baboso ADJ (caracol) slimy; (persona que babea) driveling; (persona tonta) idiotic; (adulador) fawning
babuino M baboon
baca F luggage rack
bacalao M cod
bache M (pozo) pothole; (momento) bad time; (de aire) air pocket
bacheado ADJ bumpy
bachiller -ra M (graduado) high school graduate; (alumno) high school student
bachillerato M baccalaureate
bacilo M bacillus
backgammon M backgammon
bacteria F bacteria
bacteriano ADJ bacterial
bacteriología F bacteriology
badajo M bell clapper
badana F sheepskin
bagaje M baggage
bagatela F trifle
bagazo M pulp
Bahamas F PL Bahamas
bahameño -ña ADJ & MF Bahamian
bahía F (geography) bay; (computer) slot
Bahrein M Bahrain
bahreiní ADJ & MF Bahraini
bailador -ora MF folk dancer; ADJ dancing
bailar VI/VT to dance; **me bailan los pantalones** my pants are falling off; **me tocó — con la más fea** I was left holding the bag; **que me quiten lo bailado** I enjoyed it anyway
bailarín -ina MF dancer
baile M (actividad) dance; (fiesta) dance, ball; **— aeróbico** aerobic dance; **— de máscaras** masked ball; **— folklórico** folk dance; **— zapateado** clog dance
bailongo M hop
bailotear VI to dance around
baivel M bevel
baja F (de temperatura, presión) drop; (de precios) decline; (de guerra) casualty; (del ejército) discharge, dismissal; (del trabajo) leave; **dar de —** to discharge; **darse de —** to call in sick
bajada F (acción de bajar, pendiente) descent; (de un caballo) dismount; **— contra-reloj** downhill ski race
bajar VI (descender) to go down; (correr) to run down; (de un árbol) to climb down; (de un caballo) to get down; (de un ómnibus) to step off, to get off; (en calidad) to worsen; (la marea) to ebb; (una creciente) to subside; VT (las escaleras) to go down; (un avión de un tiro) to shoot down; (comida con agua) to wash down; (la cabeza) to lower; (un cargamento) to let down; (el volumen) to turn down; (focos) to dim; (la voz) to lower, to soften; (los precios) to cut; **— de categoría** to demote; **— el cursor** to scroll down; **— en picado** to dive; **—se los pantalones** to pull down one's pants
bajeza F (cualidad) baseness; (acción) vile act
bajío M shoal
bajista ADJ (bolsa) bearish; MF (músico) bassist
bajo ADJ (nubes, estante, precio, voz grave) low; (persona) short; (voz débil) soft; (río) lower; (vista, persianas) lowered; (acto) base; **baja espalda** small of the back; **de baja calidad** low-end; **de baja ley** base; **de — precio** low-cost; **de — presupuesto** low-budget; **de —s ingresos** low-income; PREP under; **— contrato** under contract; **— control** under control, in hand; **— cuerda** under-the-table; **— fianza** on bail; **— fuego** under fire; **— sospecha** under a cloud; **— tierra** underground; **poner — llave** to lock up; **por lo —** under one's breath; M (en un coro, contrabajo) bass; (de pantalón) cuff; **hacer los —s** to cuff; ADV low
bala F (de pistola) bullet; (atletismo) shot; (de cañón) ball
balada F ballad
baladí ADJ trivial
balance M (cálculo) balance; (documento)

balance sheet; (número de víctimas) toll; (movimiento) sway; **hacer un —** to take stock

balancear VT to swing; VI to sway; **—se** to sway

balanceo M (de un cuerpo) swinging, swing; (de un barco) rolling, roll

balancín M seesaw

balanza F scale; **— comercial** balance of trade; **— de pagos** balance of payments

balar VI to bleat

balasto M ballast

balazo M (disparo) shot; (herida) bullet wound

balbucear VI (un adulto) to stammer; (un bebé) to babble

balbuceo M (tartamudeo) stammer; stammering; (de bebé) babble, babbling

balcón M balcony

balde M pail, bucket; **de —** gratis; **en —** in vain

baldear VT to flush

baldío ADJ (terreno) fallow; (acción) useless

baldosa F (en una casa) floor tile; (en una calle) flagstone

balido M bleat, bleating

balística F ballistics

balístico ADJ ballistic

ballena F (animal) whale; (para corsé) whalebone

ballenato M whale calf

ballet M ballet

balneario M (de veraneo) seaside resort; (con aguas medicinales) spa

balón M ball; **baloncesto** basketball; **balonmano** handball; **— de angioplastia** angioplasty balloon; **se le fue el —** (fútbol americano) he fumbled; (fútbol) he lost the ball; M **balonvolea** volleyball

balsa F (embarcación) raft, balsa; (lago) pond

bálsamo M balsam, balm

baluarte M bulwark, stronghold

bambolear VT to sway, to swing; **—se** to sway, to swing

bamboleo M swinging, swaying

bambú M bamboo

banal ADJ banal; **una respuesta —** a pat answer

banana F banana

banano M (tree) banana tree; (fruit) banana

banca F (industria) banking; (en el juego) bank; **— electrónica** e-banking; **— en línea** online banking; **— por internet** Internet banking

bancario -ria ADJ bank, banking; MF banker

bancarrota F bankruptcy

banco M (establecimiento) bank; (asiento) bench; (de peces) school; (de arena) shoal, spit; (de suplentes) bench; **— de datos** data bank; **— de niebla** fog bank; **Banco Mundial** World Bank

banda F (de músicos) band; (cinta ancha, también de computadora) band; (cinta de vestido) sash; (de delincuentes) gang, band, ring; (dibujo) stripe; (de neumático) tread; (lindero) side, edge, border; (de un barco) side; (en deporte) sideline; **— ancha** broadband; **— de frecuencia** frequency band; **— horaria** time slot; **— magnética** magnetic strip; **— sonora** soundtrack

bandada F (de aves) flock, flight; (de peces) school

bandeja F tray; **me lo sirvieron en — [de plata]** they served it to me on a silver platter

bandera F flag; **jurar la —** to pledge allegiance to the flag

banderín M pennant

banderola F pennant

bandido -da MF (delincuente) bandit, outlaw; (niño terrible) rascal

bando M (decreto) edict; (partido) camp

bandolero -ra MF bandit

Bangladesh M Bangladesh

bangladeshí, bangladesí ADJ & MF Bangladeshi

banjo M banjo

banquero -ra MF banker

banqueta F (taburete) stool; (acera) *Méx* sidewalk

banquete M banquet

banquetearse VI to feast

banquillo M bench (también en fútbol)

bañar VT (a un bebé) to bathe; (una torta) to ice, to frost; **—se** (en una bañera) to take a bath; (en el mar) to swim

bañera F bathtub

bañista MF bather

baño M (acción) bath; (cuarto) bathroom, lavatory; (de torta) icing, frosting; **darse un —** (bañarse) to take a bath; (nadar) to take a swim; **— de asiento** sitz bath; **— de esponja** sponge bath; **— [de] María** double boiler; **— de remolino** whirlpool bath; **— de sangre** bloodbath

bar M bar

barahúnda F ruckus, racket

baraja F pack/deck of cards

barajada F shuffle

barajar VI/VT (naipes) to shuffle; (alternativas) to weigh

baranda F railing, guard rail

barandal M banister

barandilla F rail, railing

barata F *Méx* sale

baratear VT to sell cheap

baratija F trinket, knickknack

barato ADJ cheap

baratura F cheapness

barba F beard; **—s** whiskers; **hacer algo en las —s de alguien** to do something right under someone's nose

barbacoa F barbecue
barbadense ADJ & MF Barbadian
barbado ADJ bearded
Barbados M Barbados
barbaridad F atrocity; **una — de** a lot of; **¡qué —!** what nonsense!
barbarie F savagery
bárbaro -ra ADJ (salvaje) barbarous, barbaric; (estupendo) cool, super; MF barbarian
barbecho M fallow land
barbería F barbershop
barbero -ra MF barber
barbilla F chin
barbitúrico M barbiturate
barbudo ADJ bearded
barca F rowboat
barcaza F barge
barco M boat; **— petrolero** oil tanker
bardo M bard
bario M barium
barítono ADJ & M baritone
barlovento M windward
barniz M (para madera) varnish; (para cerámica) glaze; (de cultura) veneer
barnizar[47] VT (madera) to varnish; (cerámica) to glaze
barómetro M barometer
barón M baron
barquero -era M boatman; F boatwoman
barquillo M rolled wafer
barquinazo M **dar —s** to lurch
barra F (de hierro, arena, chocolate, en un bar) bar; (en gimnasia) crossbar; (signo ortográfico) slash; **— de estado** status bar; **— de herramientas** toolbar; **— de jabón** bar of soap; **— de menú** menu bar; **— de tareas** task bar; **— espaciadora** space bar; **— invertida** backslash
barrabasada F mischief
barraca F (de feria) stall, stand; (casucha) hovel; (depósito) shed
barracuda F barracuda
barranca M ravine
barranco M gully, ravine
barrena F (de un taladro) bit; (de un avión) tailspin; **entrar en —** to go into a tailspin
barrenar VT to drill
barredora F sweeper
barrendero -ra MF street sweeper
barrer VI/VT (pasar èscoba) to sweep; (derrotar) to defeat decisively; M SG **barreminas** minesweeper
barrera F (protección) barrier; (valla) barrier, bar; **— arancelaria** tariff barrier; **— comercial** trade barrier; **— de coral** barrier reef; **— del sonido** sound barrier
barrica F vat
barricada F barricade
barrida F sweep
barrido M (acción de barrer) sweeping; (movimiento) sweep
barriga F (abdomen) belly; (panza) paunch; **rascarse la —** to do nothing
barrigón ADJ potbellied
barril M barrel, keg, drum
barrio M neighborhood, quarter; **— residencial** residential neighborhood; **—s bajos** slums
barritar VI to trumpet
barro M (lodo) mud; (arcilla) clay; (acné) pimple; **de —** earthen
barroco ADJ & M baroque
barroso ADJ muddy
barrote M bar
barruntar VT to suspect
barrunto M suspicion
bártulos M PL stuff
barullo M hubbub
basal ADJ basal
basalto M basalt
basar VT to base; **—se en** (depender de) to rely on; (fundamentar en) to be based on
basca F nausea
báscula F scale
base F (apoyo, área militar, en química, en béisbol) base; (punto de partida) basis; (de maquillaje) foundation; (de una campaña) plank; MF (baloncesto) point guard; **—s de concurso** contest rules; **— de datos** database; **— de lanzamiento** launching pad; **con — en** on the basis of; **en — a** on the basis of; **las —s** (de un partido) base, grass roots; (de un sindicato) rank and file; **salario —** base salary; **tener una — sólida** to be on a strong footing; **—s llenas** (béisbol) bases loaded; **— por bolas [intencional]** [intentional] base on balls
basic M (lenguaje de programación) BASIC
básico ADJ (fundamental) basic; (sin lujos) no-frills, bare-bones
básquet M basketball
básquetbol M basketball
bastante ADJ & PRON enough, sufficient; **tiene bastante dinero como para ser feliz** she has enough money to be happy; ADV (suficientemente) enough; **me lo has dicho bastante** you've told me that enough times; (mucho) quite a lot; **la herida me duele bastante** my injury is hurting a lot; (algo) quite, pretty; **la película estuvo bastante bien** the movie was quite good
bastar VI to be enough, to suffice; **¡basta!** enough!
bastardilla F italics
bastedad F coarseness
bastidor M (de teatro) wing; (para bordado) frame; (de coche) chassis; (de ventana) sash; **entre —es** (en teatro) offstage; (en privado)

behind the scenes
bastimentos M PL provisions
basto ADJ coarse, crude; M suit in the Spanish deck of cards
bastón M cane, walking stick; **— de esquí** ski pole
basura F rubbish, garbage, trash
basural M *Am* dump
basurero -ra MF (persona) garbage collector; M (lugar) dump
bata F (para llevar en casa) robe, housecoat; (de laboratorio) lab coat; (de pacientes) hospital gown; **— de baño** bathrobe
batahola F racket, din
batalla F battle; (de un carro) wheelbase; **— naval** sea battle; **ropa de —** everyday clothing; **trabar —** to engage in battle
batallar VI to battle
batallón M battalion
batata F sweet potato
bate M baseball bat; **al —** at bat
batea F tray
bateador -ora MF batter; **— ambidiestro -ra** switch hitter; **— designado -da** designated hitter; **— emergente** pinch hitter
batear VT to bat, to hit; **— un jonrón** to hit a homerun; **— un sencillo** to hit a single
batería F (de coche, artillería, béisbol) battery; (de cocina) pots and pans; (musical) drums; **— de iones de litio** lithium-ion battery
baterista MF drummer
batiburrillo M hodgepodge
batido M shake, milk shake
batidor M whisk, beater
batidora F mixer
batintín M gong
batir VT (una alfombra) to beat; (un terreno) to comb; (mantequilla) to cream, to churn; (un récord) to break; (huevos) to beat; (crema) to whip; (alas) to flap, to beat; **— palmas** to clap, to applaud; **—se en duelo** to duel; **—se en retirada** to retreat
batuta F baton; **llevar la —** to call the shots
baudio M baud
baúl M trunk
bautismo M baptism, christening; **— de fuego** baptism of fire
bautizar[47] VT to baptize, to christen
bautizo M christening, baptism
baya F berry
bayeta F cleaning cloth
bayo ADJ bay
bayoneta F bayonet
baza F card trick; **meter — en una conversación** to participate in a conversation
bazar M bazaar
bazo M spleen
bazofia F slop
bazuca F bazooka
beagle M beagle
beato ADJ (bendito) blessed; (piadoso) beatified; (santurrón) overly pious
bebé M baby, infant
bebedero M (en un corral) drinking trough; (en el campo) watering hole; (para personas) water fountain
bebedor -ora MF drinker
beber VI/VT to drink
bebercio M *fam* booze
bebida F drink, beverage
beca F scholarship, fellowship
becario -ria MF scholar, fellow
becerro M (animal) calf; (piel) calfskin
becuadro M natural sign
befa F jeer
befar VT to jeer at
beicon M *Esp* bacon
beige ADJ & M beige
béisbol M baseball
beisbolista M baseball player
beldad F beauty
belga ADJ & MF Belgian
Bélgica F Belgium
Belice M Belize
beliceño -ña ADJ & MF Belizean
bélico ADJ warlike
belicoso ADJ (guerrero) bellicose; (peleador) feisty
beligerante ADJ & MF belligerent
bellaco M rascal, scoundrel
bellaquería F mischief
belleza F beauty
bello ADJ beautiful
bellota F acorn
bemol M (música) flat; **tener —es** to be tricky
bencina F benzine
bendecir[51] VT to bless
bendición F (parte de la misa) benediction; (acción de bendecir) blessing; (beneficio) boon, blessing
bendito ADJ (agua) holy; (alma) blessed; **— sea** may he be blessed; **dormir como un —** to sleep like a log; **es un —** he is a saint
benefactor -ora MF benefactor, patron
beneficencia F charity; **— pública** welfare
beneficiar VT to benefit; **—se de** to benefit from
beneficiario -ria MF (de una herencia, perdón, acto de bondad) beneficiary; (de un cheque) payee
beneficio M benefit (también espectáculo); **—s adicionales** perks; **—s por fallecimiento** death benefits
beneficioso ADJ beneficial
benéfico ADJ beneficent
benemérito ADJ worthy of esteem
benevolencia F benevolence

benévolo ADJ benevolent
bengala F flare
bengalés-esa ADJ & MF Bangladeshi
benigno ADJ benign
Benín M Benin
beninés-esa ADJ & MF Beninese
benjamín-ina MF youngest child
beodo ADJ drunk
berbiquí M carpenter's brace
berenjena F eggplant
bermejo ADJ reddish
bermellón M vermilion
berrear VI (animal) to bellow, to bawl; (bebé) to squall
berrido M (de animal) bellowing, bawling; (de bebé) squall, squalling
berrinche M tantrum
berro M watercress
berza F cabbage
besar VT to kiss
beso M kiss
bestia F beast
bestial ADJ bestial
best-seller M best seller
besuquear VT to kiss repeatedly; **—se** to make out
betabel M *Méx* beet
betabloqueador M beta blocker
betabloqueante M beta blocker
betún M shoe polish
Biblia F Bible
bíblico ADJ biblical
bibliografía F bibliography
biblioteca F (edificio) library; (anaquel) bookcase
bibliotecario-ria MF librarian
bicarbonato M bicarbonate; **— de sosa/soda** bicarbonate of soda
bíceps M SG bicep[s]
bicho M (insecto) bug (también en informática); (animal) *fam* critter; **— raro** odd bird; **mal —** creep; **¿qué — te ha picado?** what's gotten into you? **—s** vermin
bici F bike
bicicleta F bicycle; **— de montaña** mountain bike; **— estática** stationary bike
bicúspide ADJ bicuspid
biela F connecting rod
Bielorrusia F Belarus
bien ADV well; **—aventurado** blessed; **— arreglado** well-groomed; **— conocido** well-known; **— hecho** well-made, well-done; **— poco** very little; **agarrarse —** to hold on tight; **ahora —** now then; **apretar —** to press hard; **está —** she is fine; **más —** rather; **me doy — cuenta** I'm perfectly aware; **pues —** now; **qué —** how wonderful; **si —** although; **ya está —** that's enough; M good; **—es** property, assets; **—es consumibles** consumable goods; **—es inmuebles** real estate; **—es muebles** personal property; **—es raíces** real estate; **—estar** well-being, welfare; **—hechor** benefactor; **persona de —** a good person; INTERJ OK!
bienio M biennium
bienvenida F welcome
bienvenido ADJ welcome
bifurcación F (en un camino) fork, forking; (en un programa de computadora) branch
bifurcarse[30] VI to fork, to branch off
bigamia F bigamy
bigote M (de hombre) mustache; (de animal) whisker
bikini M bikini
bilateral ADJ bilateral
bilingüe ADJ & MF bilingual
bilingüismo M bilingualism
bilis F bile
billar M (juego) billiards, pool; (mesa) pool table
billete M (de viaje, para espectáculos) ticket; (de banco) bill, banknote; (financiero) note; **— de ida solo** one-way ticket; **— de ida y vuelta** return ticket
billetera F billfold
billón M trillion
bimestral ADJ bimonthly
bimestre M two-month period
binario ADJ binary
bingo M bingo
binomial ADJ binomial
binomio M binomial
biodegradable ADJ biodegradable
biofeedback M biofeedback
biografía F biography
bioingeniería F bioengineering
biología F biology
biológico ADJ biological
biólogo-ga MF biologist
biombo M folding screen
biopsia F biopsy
bioquímica F biochemistry
biorritmo M biorhythm
biotecnología F biotechnology
bipartidista ADJ bipartisan
bipolar ADJ bipolar
birlar VT *fam* to pinch, to swipe
Birmania F Burma
birmano-na ADJ & MF Burmese, from Myanmar
birrete M mortarboard
bis M encore
bisabuelo-la M great-grandfather; F great-grandmother
bisagra F hinge
bisecar[30] VT to bisect
biselado ADJ beveled
biselar VT to bevel

bisemanal ADV biweekly
bisiesto ADJ **año** — leap year
bisnieto -ta M great-grandson; F great-granddaughter
bisonte M bison, buffalo
bistec M beefsteak
bisturí M scalpel
bisutería F costume jewelry
bit M bit
bizarría F gallantry
bizarro ADJ gallant
bizco ADJ cross-eyed
bizcocho M (pastel) sponge cake; (pastelillo) pastry
bizcochuelo M sponge cake
bizquear VI to be cross-eyed
black-jack M blackjack
blanca ADJ half note
blanco ADJ (color) white; (tez) fair; M (color) white (también clara de huevos, ojos); (de tiro) target; (de una burla) butt; — **fácil** sitting duck; **dar en el** — to hit the target; **en** — (hoja de papel, mente) blank; (sin dormir) sleepless; **en** — **y negro** in black and white
blancura F whiteness; (de tez) fairness
blancuzco ADJ whitish
blandir VT to brandish, to wield
blando ADJ (sin dureza, sin rigor) soft; (sensiblero) mushy
blandura F softness
blanqueador ADJ whitening; M bleach, whitener
blanquear VT (una pared) to whitewash; (dinero) to launder; (verduras) to blanch; —**se** to whiten
blanquecino ADJ whitish
blanqueo M whitening
blasfemar VI to blaspheme
blasfemia F blasphemy
blasón M coat of arms
blasonar VI to boast
blazer M blazer
blindado ADJ armored
blindaje M armor
blindar VT to armor
bloc M writing tablet, pad of paper
blog M blog
bloguear VI to blog
bloguero -ra MF blogger
bloque M block (también de motor, político); (edificio) building; **en** — together
bloquear VT (carretera, asalto, pase, virus digital) to block; (puerto) to blockade; (cuentas bancarias) to freeze; —**se** to choke
bloqueo M (deporte) block; (computadoras) block, blocking; (militar) blockade
blues M PL blues
bluff M bluff
blusa F blouse, top
boa F boa constrictor
boato M pomp
bobada F (tontería) foolish act; (fruslería) trifle
bobalicón -ona ADJ goofy; MF nincompoop
bobear VI to fool around, to monkey around
bobería F (cualidad) foolishness; (dicho) foolish remark; (hecho) foolish act
bobina F (de hilo) bobbin; (de alambre, de coche) coil; (de película) reel
bobinar VT to reel
bobo -ba ADJ (tonto) dumb, dimwitted, silly; (estupefacto) flabbergasted; MF dimwit, booby, fool
boca F mouth (también de río); (de un arma de fuego) muzzle; (del estómago) pit; (de una cueva) opening; —**calle** intersection; — **a** — mouth-to-mouth; — **abajo** face down; — **arriba** face up; **a** — **de jarro** at close range; **callarse la** — to shut up
bocadillo M snack; *Esp* sandwich
bocado M (de comida) bite, morsel, mouthful; (de una brida) bit
bocanada F (de líquido) mouthful; (de humo) puff; (de aire) sniff
bocazas MF SG loudmouth
boceto M sketch
bochorno M (calor) oppressive heat; (vergüenza) embarrassment
bochornoso ADJ (caluroso) sultry, oppressive, muggy; (vergonzoso) embarrassing
bocina F (de coche) horn; (megáfono) megaphone
bocinazo M honk, toot
bocio M goiter
boda F wedding; —**s de oro** golden anniversary; —**s de plata** silver anniversary
bodega F (despensa subterránea) cellar; (para vinos) wine cellar; (vinería) winery; (espacio en un barco, avión) hold; (tienda de comestibles) *Carib, Am Central* grocery store
bodeguero -ra MF (viñatero) wine producer; (almacenero) *Carib, Am Central* grocer
bofe M [de animal] lung; **echar los** —**s** to tire oneself out
bofetada F slap
boga LOC ADV **en** — in vogue, fashion
bogar[40] VI/VT to row
bogey M bogey
bohemio -mia ADJ & MF (nacionalidad) Bohemian; (estilo) bohemian
boicot M boycott
boicotear VT to boycott
boicoteo M boycott
boina F beret
bol M bowl
bola F (golf, tenis, béisbol) ball; (canica) marble; (de helado) dip; (de algodón) wad; (jugada de béisbol) ball; — **blanca** cue ball; **en** —**s** in the buff; **no dar pie con** — to be lost; **no**

dar ni — not to pay attention; — **de nudillos** knuckleball; **darle una base por —s** to walk someone; **sacar una base por —s** to walk; — **de break** break point; — **de partido** match-ball; — **de ruptura** break point

bolera F bowling alley

boleta F (de lotería) ticket; (de votación) *Méx* ballot

boletín M bulletin

boleto M ticket; — **de ida solo** one-way ticket; — **de ida y vuelta** return ticket

boliche M (juego) bowling; (bolera) bowling alley

bolígrafo M ballpoint pen; — **computadora portátil** pen computer; — **ordenador portátil** pen computer

bolita F pellet

Bolivia F Bolivia

boliviano -na ADJ & MF Bolivian

bollo M bun, roll

bolo M bowling pin; **jugar a los —s** to bowl

bolsa F (saco) bag; (cartera) purse; (órgano) sac; (marsupio) pouch; — **de valores** stock market; — **de aire** airbag; — **de estudio** scholarship; — **de miseria** pocket of poverty; **hace —s** it pooches out

bolsillo M pocket; **de** — pocket-sized

bolsista MF stockbroker

bolso M (grande) bag; (pequeño) purse

bomba F (para agua, gasolina) pump; (artefacto explosivo) bomb; (noticia, mujer) *fam* bombshell; — **atómica** atomic bomb; — **de hidrógeno** hydrogen bomb; — **de neutrones** neutron bomb; — **de tiempo** time bomb; — **fétida** stink bomb; — **incendiaria** incendiary bomb; — **inteligente** smart bomb; **lo pasamos** — we had a blast

bombacha F *RP* panties, underpants

bombardear VT to bombard

bombardeo M bombardment, bombing

bombardero -ra MF (tripulante) bombardier; M (avión) bomber

bombear VT to pump

bombero -ra MF firefighter

bombilla F lightbulb

bombo M (en música) bass drum; (en béisbol) fly ball; **dar** — to extol; **con —s y platillos** with great fanfare

bombón M (chocolate) bonbon; (mujer atractiva) *fam* dish

bombonería F candy store

bonachón ADJ (amable) good-natured; (inocente) naive

bonaerense ADJ from the city of Buenos Aires; MF person from Buenos Aires

bonanza F (buen tiempo) fair weather; (prosperidad) prosperity

bondad F goodness, kindness; **—es** virtues; **tenga la** — **de** would you please

bondadoso ADJ kind, kindly

boniato M sweet potato

bonito ADJ pretty; M tuna

bono M (título de deuda) bond; (vale) voucher

boñiga F dung

boqueada F gasp

boquear VI to gasp

boquete M opening

boquiabierto ADJ (de boca abierta) openmouthed; (asombrado) astonished

boquilla F (para cigarros) cigarette holder; (para trompeta) mouthpiece; **defender de** — to pay lip service to

bórax M borax

borbollar VI to bubble

borbollón M (burbujeo) bubbling; (alboroto) commotion; **a borbollones** bubbling over

borbotar VI to bubble, to gurgle

borboteo M bubbling, gurgling

bordado M embroidery, needlework

bordar VI/VT to embroider

borde M (de una superficie) edge, border; (de un vaso) rim, brim; (de un desastre) brink; (de una calle) *Méx* curb

bordear VT (rodear) to skirt, to go along the edge of; (adornar) to trim

bordillo M curb

bordo LOC ADV **a** — on board

bordó, bordeaux ADJ INV & M maroon

borla F (de birrete) tassel; (de algodón) powder puff

boro M boron

borra F dregs

borrachera F (estado) drunkenness; (juerga) drunken spree

borrachín -ina M drunkard

borracho -cha ADJ drunk, wasted; **no lo hago ni** — I would never do such a thing; MF drunkard, wino

borrado M erasure

borrador M (bosquejo) rough draft; (goma) eraser

borrar VT (texto escrito) to erase; (texto digital) to cut, to erase; **—se de un club** to withdraw from a club

borrasca F squall

borrego M lamb

borrico M donkey

borrón M blot, blotch, smudge; **hacer** — **y cuenta nueva** to start over at square one

borronear VT to smudge

borroso ADJ (imagen) blurry, blurred; (memoria) fuzzy

boscaje M thicket

Bosnia-Herzegovina F Bosnia and Herzegovina

bosnio -nia ADJ & MF Bosnian

bosque M forest, woods
bosquecillo M grove
bosquejar VT to sketch, to outline
bosquejo M sketch, outline
bosta F dung
bostezar[47] VI to yawn
bostezo M yawn
bota F (calzado) boot; (para vino) leather wine bag
botadura F launch
botánica F botany
botánico ADJ botanical
botar VT (una pelota) to bounce; (un buque) to launch; (basura) to throw out
botarate M fool
bote M (jarro) can; (embarcación) boat; (rebote) bounce; **— de basura** garbage can; **— de remos** rowboat; **— de salvamento** lifeboat; **de — en / a —** filled to overflowing; (tenis) **— pronto** half volley
botella F bottle
botero -ra M boatman; F boatwoman
botija F earthen jug
botijo M earthen jar
botín M (de guerra) booty, plunder; (de ladrón) loot, haul
botiquín M (en el baño) medicine cabinet; (de primeros auxilios) first-aid kit
botón M (de aparato, de camisa) button; (remache) stud; (de planta) bud; **botones** bellboy, page; **— de inicio** start button
bótox M botox
Botsuana F Botswana
botsuano -na MF Botswanan
botulismo M botulism
bouquet M bouquet
boutique F boutique
bóveda F (techo) arched roof, vault; **— celeste** the vault of heaven
bowling M bowling
box M (para coches de carrera) pit
boxeador -ora MF boxer, prizefighter
boxear VI/VT to box
boxeo M boxing
bóxer M boxer
boya F (en el mar) buoy; (corcho) float
boyante ADJ buoyant
boyar VI to buoy
bozal M muzzle
bozo M fuzz on the lip
bracear VI to move one's arms
bracero -ra MF migrant worker
bragas F PL underpants, panties
bragueta F fly
brainstorming M brainstorming
bramar VI (ciervo, cochino) to bellow; (león, viento) to roar
bramido M (de ciervo, cochino) bellow; (de león, viento) roar
brandy M brandy
brasa F ember
brasero M brazier
Brasil M Brazil
brasileño -ña ADJ & MF Brazilian
brasilero -ra ADJ & MF Brazilian
bravata F act of bravado
bravío ADJ wild
bravo ADJ (animal, río) wild; (terreno) rugged; (persona) brave; (barrio) tough; INTERJ bravo!
bravucón -ona ADJ bullying; MF bully
bravuconería F bullying
bravura F (de bestia) fierceness; (de persona) courage
braza F fathom
brazada F (cantidad) armful; (en natación) stroke
brazalete M bracelet
brazo M arm (también de silla); (de cornamenta) branch; (de balanza) beam; **— de mar** sound; **— derecho** right-hand man; **—s** day laborers; **con los —s abiertos** with open arms; **con los —s cruzados** with crossed arms; **ir del —** to go arm in arm; **luchar a — partido** to fight to the end
brea F pitch, tar
brecha F (en un muro) breach, gap; (entre generaciones) gap
brécol M broccoli
bregar[40] VI to struggle, to toil
breña F scrub
breve ADJ (cuento) brief, short; (bikini) scanty; **en —** shortly
brevedad F brevity, shortness; **a la —** as soon as possible
bribón -ona ADJ roguish; MF rascal, rogue, scoundrel
brida F bridle
brigada F brigade
brillante ADJ brilliant, bright; M diamond, gem
brillantez F brilliance
brillantina F glitter
brillar VI (oro) to shine; (ojos) to sparkle, to twinkle; (nieve) to glisten; **— por su ausencia** to be conspicuous by its absence
brillo M (de metal, piedras preciosas) shine, luster, sparkle; (de los ojos) twinkle; (de nieve) glistening; (del pelo, plumas) sheen; (de diamantes) sparkle; (de una pantalla) brightness; **dar —** to give luster; **sacar —** to polish
brilloso ADJ shiny
brincar[30] VI to hop, to skip
brinco M hop, skip
brindar VI (beber) to toast; (proporcionar) to provide; **— por alguien** to toast someone; **—se a hacer algo** to volunteer to do something
brindis M toast

brío M spirit
brioso ADJ spirited
brisa F breeze
británico ADJ British
brizna F blade of grass
broca F drill bit
brocado M brocade
brocal M (borde) rim; (boca de pozo) curb
brocha F paintbrush; **de — gorda** coarse
broche M (alhaja) brooch; (sujetador) clasp, clip; (para el pelo) barrette; **— de oro** grand finale
brocheta F skewer
brócoli, bróculi M broccoli
broma F (chiste) joke; (réplica) jest, wisecrack; **— pesada** practical joke; **—s aparte** kidding aside; **en —** in jest; **gastar una —** to play a joke; **ni en —** no way; **no estoy para —s** I'm not in the mood for kidding
bromear VI to joke, to kid
bromista MF wag, joker
bromo M bromine
bromuro M bromide
bronca F row; **armar una —** to cause a disturbance, to raise a rumpus; **echarle la — a alguien** to bawl someone out; **tener —** to be angry
bronce M bronze
bronceado ADJ (cubierto de bronce) bronzed; (tostado) tanned; (de color bronce) bronze; M suntan
broncear VT (un objeto) to bronze; **—se** to get a tan
bronco ADJ (voz) gruff; (terreno) rough; (caballo) wild
bronquial ADJ bronchial
bronquio M bronchial tube
bronquitis F bronchitis
brotar VI (planta) to sprout; (enfermedad eruptiva) to break out; (agua) to gush, to flow, to issue
brote M (de una enfermedad) outbreak; (retoño) sprout, spear
broza F brushwood
bruces LOC ADV **de —** face down
brujería F witchcraft, devilry
brujo -ja M wizard, sorcerer; F witch
brújula F compass
bruma F mist
brumoso ADJ misty
brunch M brunch
bruneano -na ADJ & MF Bruneian
Brunéi M Brunei
bruñir[17] VT to burnish
bruscamente ADV (girar, responder) sharply; (hablar) brusquely
brusco ADJ (descortés) brusque, curt; (repentino) sudden
brusquedad F (descortesía) brusqueness; (lo repentino) suddenness
brutal ADJ brutal
brutalidad F brutality
bruto -ta ADJ (ignorante) ignorant; (maleducado, burdo) uncouth; (violento) brutish; (sin descuentos) gross; **a lo —** roughly; **en —** in the rough; **recaudar en —** to gross; MF (ignorante) blockhead; (persona violenta) brute; (mal educado) lout, brute
bucal ADJ oral
bucear VI (sumergirse) to scuba dive; (indagar) to explore
buceo M scuba diving
buche M (en las aves) crop; (bocado) mouthful
bucle M (de pelo) curl, ringlet; (en informática) loop
budín M pudding
budismo M Buddhism
budista ADJ, MF Buddhist
bueno ADJ good; **buena fe** good faith; **a la buena de Dios** haphazardly; **de buenas a primeras** out of the blue; **estar —** to be sexy; **hace buen tiempo** it is fine weather; **lo —** the good thing; **por las buenas o por las malas** by hook or by crook; **ser — con los números** to be good at figures; INTERJ OK! **—s días** good day/morning; **buenas noches** good night/evening; **buenas tardes** good afternoon
buey M ox, steer
búfalo M buffalo, bison
bufanda F scarf, muffler
bufar VI to snort; **está que bufa** he is incensed
bufete M (despacho) lawyer's office; (negocio) practice
buffet M buffet
bufido M snort
bufón -ona MF buffoon, jester
bufonear VI to clown
buhardilla F (desván) attic, garret
búho M owl
buhonero -ra MF peddler
buitre M vulture, buzzard
buje M bushing
bujía F spark plug
bulbo M bulb
bulldog M bulldog
bulevar M boulevard
Bulgaria F Bulgaria
búlgaro -ra ADJ & MF Bulgarian
bulimia F bulimia
bulla F uproar, fuss, bustle
bulldozer M bulldozer
bullicio M uproar, racket, bustle
bullicioso ADJ boisterous, rowdy
bullir[16] VI (hervir) to boil; (hacer burbujas) to bubble; (ajetrearse) to bustle; (moverse) to stir
bullón M puff
bullpen M bullpen

bulto M (paquete) bundle; (tumor) lump, growth; (silueta) shape; (saliente) bulge; **a —** approximately; **escurrir el —** to slack off
bungaló M bungalow
bungee M bungee jumping
búnker M bunker
buñuelo M fritter
buque M ship; **— de carga** freighter
burbuja F bubble
burdo ADJ coarse
burgués ADJ bourgeois
burguesía F bourgeoisie, middle class
burla F ridicule, mockery; **hacer — a alguien** to mock someone
burlar VT to mock; **—se de** to scoff at, to make fun of
burlesco ADJ burlesque
burlón ADJ mocking
burocracia F bureaucracy
burócrata MF bureaucrat
burrez F stupidity
burro M (animal) donkey, ass; (persona) dunce; ADJ dense
bursátil ADJ **mercado —** stock market
bursitis F bursitis
burundés -esa ADJ & MF Burundian
Burundi M Burundi
bus M bus; **— en serie** serial bus
busca LOC ADV **en — de** in search of
buscar[30] VT (objetos perdidos) to seek, to look for, to search for; (datos, palabras) to look up; (provocar) to provoke; (la verdad) to seek after; (minerales) to prospect for; (talento) to scout for; **—se problemas** to invite trouble; **— y reemplazar** to search and replace; **tú te lo buscaste** you asked for it; **ir a —** to fetch; M SG **buscapersonas** beeper, pager
búsqueda F search; **— del tesoro** treasure hunt; **— hacia atrás** backward search; **— por palabra clave** keyword search
busto M bust
butaca F (en la casa) armchair; (en el teatro) seat
Bután M Bhutan
butanés -esa ADJ & MF Bhutanese
butano M butane
buzo M diver
buzón M mailbox; **— de sugerencias** suggestion box
bypass M bypass operation, coronary bypass
byte M byte

Cc

cabal ADJ (completo) complete; (exacto) exact; (honrado) upright; **estar uno en sus —es** to be in one's right mind
cabalgar[40] VI to ride horseback
caballa F mackerel
caballada F herd of horses
caballejo M nag
caballeresco ADJ chivalrous
caballería F (tropas) cavalry; (equino) equine; (condición de caballero) knighthood
caballeriza F stable
caballerizo M groom
caballero M (señor) gentleman; (hidalgo) knight; **— andante** knight errant; ADJ gentlemanly
caballerosidad F chivalry
caballeroso ADJ chivalrous, gentlemanly
caballete M (soporte de madera) sawhorse; (de la nariz) bridge; (de pintor) easel; (de tejado) ridge
caballo M (animal) horse; (en ajedrez) knight; (heroína) *fam* smack; **a —** on horseback; **— de carreras** racehorse; **— de batalla** hobbyhorse; **— de fuerza** horsepower; **— de Troya** Trojan horse
cabaña F (casucha) hovel; (casa de campo) cabin, cottage; (conjunto de ganado) livestock
cabaret M cabaret
cabecear VI (mover la cabeza) to nod; (dormirse) to nod off; (un barco) to bob, to pitch; VT (balón) to head
cabeceo M (de la cabeza) nodding; (de un barco) pitching
cabecera F (de cama) headboard; (de mesa) head
cabecilla MF ringleader
cabellera F head of hair
cabello M hair; **traido por los —s** far-fetched
caber[67] VI to fit; **no cabe duda** there is no doubt; **no cabe nadie más** there is no room for anybody else; **no — uno en sí** to be puffed up with pride; **no cabe en lo posible** it is absolutely impossible; **¿en qué cabeza cabe?** who would believe that?
cabestrillo M sling
cabestro M halter
cabeza F head; **— de chorlito** scatterbrain, airhead; **— de playa** beachhead; **— de puente** bridgehead; **— de turco** scapegoat, fall guy; **— de serie** seed; **— rapada** skinhead; **a la —** at the forefront; **caerse de —** to fall head first; **echarse de —** to plunge headlong; **ir a la —** to lead the way; **por —** each; **romperse la —** to rack one's brains; **la fama se le fue a la —** fame went to his head; **sentar —** to settle down; **tiene la — cuadrada** she's a square
cabezada F nod; **dar —s** to nod off
cabezal M magnetic head
cabezazo M (golpe) head butt; (jugada de fútbol) header
cabezón ADJ (de cabeza grande) big-headed;

(testarudo) pig-headed; (con mucho alcohol) strong
cabezudo ADJ (de cabeza grande) big-headed; (testarudo) pig-headed
cabida F capacity; **dar —** to include; **tener — en** to fit in
cabina F (de pasajeros) cabin; (de piloto) cockpit; (de camión) cab; (de teléfono, control) booth
cabizbajo ADJ crestfallen, downcast
cable M cable; **— coaxial** coaxial cable; **—s del ordenador / de la computadora** media
cableado M wiring
cablevisión F cable television
cabo M (parte extrema) end; (hilo) thread; (cuerda) rope; (saliente de la costa) cape; MF (rango militar) corporal; **— suelto** loose end; **al — de** at the end of; **atar —s** to put two and two together; **de — a rabo** from beginning to end; **llevar a —** to carry out
cabotaje M coastal trade
Cabo Verde M Cape Verde
caboverdiano -na ADJ & MF Cape Verdean
cabra F goat; **— montés** mountain goat; **[loco] como una —** completely crazy
cabrá, cabría *ver* caber
cabrearse VI to get mad
cabrestante M winch
cabrillas F PL whitecaps
cabrio M rafter
cabrío ADJ **macho —** he-goat
cabriola F caper
cabriolar VI to cavort
cabritilla F kid [leather]
cabrito M kid [goat]
cabrón M (macho de cabra) he-goat; (cornudo) cuckold; MF (cobarde) wimp
caca F poop; **hacer —** to poop
cacahuate M *Méx* peanut
cacahuete M *Esp* peanut
cacao M cocoa
cacarear VI to cackle, to squawk
cacareo M cackling, squawking
cacatúa F cockatoo
cacería F hunt; **— de brujas** witch hunt
cacerola F saucepan
cacha F (de navaja) handle; (nalga) thigh, butt; **hasta la —** completely
cachalote M sperm whale
cacharro M (vasija) earthen pot; (coche viejo) clunker, jalopy
cachaza F slowness
cachazudo ADJ slow
caché M (en informática) cache; (distinción) cachet; **— de memoria** memory cache
cachear VT to body-search, to frisk
cachet M artist's fee
cachetada F slap
cachete M cheek
cachiporra F blackjack
cachivaches M PL stuff, odds and ends
cacho M hunk
cachorro M (de oso, lobo, tigre, león) cub; (de perro) puppy
cacique -ca M (de indios) chief, chieftain; MF (caudillo) political boss
cacofonía F cacophony
cacto/cactus M cactus
cada ADJ each; **— uno** each one; **— vez más** more and more; **— vez menos gente** fewer and fewer people; **— vez menos harina** less and less flour; **— vez peor** worse and worse; **doscientas pesetas — una** two hundred pesetas each/apiece
cadalso M gallows
cadáver M (para enterrar) corpse; (para disecar) cadaver
cadavérico ADJ ghastly
caddie, caddy MF caddie
cadena F (serie de piezas) chain; (de televisión) network; (cordillera) mountain range; **— alimenticia** food chain; **— de montaje** assembly line; **— perpetua** life sentence; **—s** shackles; **tirar la —** to flush
cadencia F cadence
cadera F hip
cadete M cadet
cadmio M cadmium
caducar[30] VI to lapse, to expire
caducidad F expiration
caduco ADJ (deciduo) deciduous; (decrépito) decrepit
caer[52] VI to fall; (desplomarse) to fall down; (colgar) to hang; (ir a parar) to end up; **al — la noche** at nightfall; **— en desgracia** to fall into disfavor, to fall out of favor; **— en desuso** to fall into disuse; **— en cama** to fall ill; **— en cuenta** to catch on; **— en ruina** to fall into disrepair; **—le bien/mal a uno** (una persona) to make a good/bad impression; (una comida) to agree with; **—le en suerte a uno** to fall to one's lot; **— tan bajo** to fall so low; **caiga quien caiga** let fall who may; **dejar —** to drop; **está al —** he's about to show up; **—se** (persona) to fall down; (computadora, ordenador) to crash; **se cayó el sistema** the system crashed
café M (bebida) coffee; (color) brown; (establecimiento) coffee shop, café
cafeína F caffeine
cafetal M coffee plantation
cafetera F coffeepot
cafetería F snack bar, cafeteria, diner
cafetero -ra MF coffee dealer; ADJ **industria cafetera** coffee industry
cafeto M coffee bush
caída F (acción de caer) fall, tumble, spill; (de presión arterial) drop; (de un ordenador) crash; (de una cortina) hang; (de precios)

drop; — **libre** free fall; — **del sol** sunset; — **en picado** nosedive; —**s del sistema** system crashes

caído ADJ (orejas) floppy; (arco del pie) fallen; **los** —**s** the fallen

caiga, caigo *ver* caer

caimán M alligator

caja F box; — **chica** petty cash; — **de ahorros** savings bank; — **de bateo** batter's box; — **de cambios** transmission; — **de escalera** stairwell; — **de fusibles** fuse box; — **de herramientas** toolkit; — **de jubilaciones** pension fund; — **de música** music box; — **de seguridad** safe deposit box; — **de reloj** watchcase; — **fuerte** safe; — **negra** flight recorder; — **registradora** (aparato) cash register, till; (mostrador) checkout counter; — **tonta** idiot box; — **torácica** rib cage; **entrar en** — (comenzar) to get going; (establecerse) to settle down

cajero -ra MF cashier; (en un banco) teller; — **automático** ATM

cajetilla F pack [of cigarettes]

cajilla F pack [of cigarettes]

cajón M (para transportes) crate; (parte de un mueble) drawer; **eso es de** — that's a foregone conclusion

cajuela F *Méx* car trunk

cal F lime; **cerrar a** — **y canto** to close hermetically

calabacín M zucchini

calabaza F (grande y redonda) pumpkin; (pequeña y/o alargada) squash; (vaciada) gourd; **dar** —**s** to turn down

calabozo M dungeon

calado M draft

calamar M squid

calambre M cramp

calamidad F calamity

calamina F calamine

calandria F lark

calar VT (agujerear) to perforate; (empapar) to soak, to drench; — **a alguien** to see through someone; — **hondo** to resonate; —**se** to get drenched

calavera F skull; M libertine

calcar[30] VT (sobre papel) to trace; (imitar) to copy

calcetería F hosiery

calcetín M sock

calcinar VT to bake

calcio M calcium

calco M (acción de calcar) tracing; **es el** — **de su padre** he's the spitting image of his father

calcomanía F decal

calculador ADJ calculating

calculadora F calculator

calcular VT (computar) to calculate, to figure; (sopesar) to weigh; (prever) to reckon

cálculo M (cómputo) calculation; (aritmética) arithmetic; (integral, diferencial) calculus; — **biliar** gallstone; — **renal** kidney stone

caldear VT to warm up; — **los ánimos** to get everyone upset

caldera F (en una máquina de vapor) boiler; (recipiente con asas) kettle; (de calefacción) furnace

calderón M hold

caldo M broth, stock; — **de cultivo** culture medium

calefacción F heat, heating; — **central** central heating

calendario M calendar

caléndula F marigold

calentador M heater; — **de agua** water heater

calentamiento M warming; (en deportes) warm-up; — **global** global warming

calentar[1] VI/VT (poner caliente) to warm, to heat; —**se** (ponerse caliente, prepararse para un partido) to warm up, to heat up

calentura F fever

calesa F buggy

caletre M **no tener** — to have no brains

calibrador M caliper

calibrar VT to gauge, to calibrate

calibre M (de pistola, tubo) caliber; (de alambre) gauge; (calibrador) caliper

calicó M calico

calidad F quality; **baja** — low quality; **de** — of good quality; **de** — **inferior** substandard; **estoy aquí en** — **de representante** I'm here in my capacity as representative

cálido ADJ warm

caliente ADJ (agradable) warm; (excesivo) hot

calificación F (nota) grade, mark; (acción de asignar notas) grading; (comparación) rating; — **crediticia** credit rating; **le dieron la** — **de genio** they called him a genius

calificar[30] VT (juzgar la calidad) to rate, to adjudge; (asignar nota) to grade; —**se como** to be characterized as

calificativo ADJ qualifying; M label

caligrafía F (letra) penmanship; (arte) calligraphy

calina F haze

callado ADJ silent, quiet; **estarse** — to keep quiet

callar VT (no manifestar, no dejar decir) to quiet; VI (no hablar) to remain silent; (dejar de hablar) to go quiet; —**se la boca** to shut up, to pipe down

calle F (de ciudad) street; (golf) fairway; — **abajo** down the street; — **arriba** up the street; — **de sentido único** one-way street; **no pisar la** — to stay home

calleja F narrow street

callejear VI to walk the streets

callejero ADJ **perro** — stray dog; **caos** — chaos

in the streets
callejón M alley; **— sin salida** blind alley, dead end
callo M callus, corn
calloso ADJ callous
calma F calm; **— chicha** absolute calm; **mantener la —** (no enojarse) to keep one's temper; (no ponerse nervioso) to stay calm; **tomar las cosas con —** to take things easy
calmante ADJ & M sedative
calmar VT (nervios) to calm; (dolor) to sooth; (miedo) to allay, to quell; (sed) to quench; **—se** (una persona) to calm down; (una tormenta, la ira) to subside, to abate
calmo ADJ calm
calmoso ADJ easygoing
calor M (temperatura alta) heat; (temperatura templada) warmth; (actitud acogedora) warmth; **hace — hoy** it's hot today; **los —es** hot flashes; **tengo —** I'm hot
caloría F calorie
calumnia F calumny, slander
calumniar VT to slander, to malign
calumnioso ADJ slanderous
caluroso ADJ (día) hot; (recepción) warm
calva F bald spot
calvario M **mi vida es un —** *fam* my life is hell
calvicie F baldness
calvo ADJ bald, baldheaded; **ni tanto ni tan —** *fam* it ain't necessarily so; **quedarse —** to go bald
calza F long sock
calzada F pavement
calzado M footwear
calzador M shoehorn
calzar[47] VT (poner zapatos) to shoe; (hacer zapatos para) to make shoes for; **— a la familia** to buy shoes for the family; **calzo 42** I take size 10; **—se** to put on shoes
calzones M PL (de mujer) panties; (de hombre) shorts
calzonazos M SG henpecked man
calzoncillos M PL underpants, briefs; **— largos** long johns
cama F bed; **— de agua** waterbed; **— doble** double bed; **— elástica** trampoline; **— individual** twin bed; **guardar —** to be confined to bed; **meterse en la — con** to sleep with
camada F litter
camafeo M cameo
camaleón M chameleon
cámara F (espacio) chamber; (de neumático) inner tube; (fotográfica) camera; **— de comercio** chamber of commerce; **— de diputados** lower house; **— de gas** gas chamber; **— digital** digital camera; **— de oxígeno** oxygen tent; **— frigorífica** cold-storage locker; **— legislativa** legislature; **— hiperbárica** hyperbaric chamber; **en — lenta** in slow motion; MF (persona que maneja una cámara) camera operator
camarada MF comrade
camarero -ra M (restaurante) waiter, server; (coche cama) steward; F (restaurante) waitress, server; (coche cama) stewardess; (hotel) maid; MF (béisbol) second baseman
camarilla F clique
camarógrafo -fa M cameraman; F camerawoman
camarón M shrimp
camarote M cabin, stateroom
cambalache M (intercambio) fraudulent swap; (tienda) secondhand store
cambalachear VI/VT to swap fraudulently
cambiante ADJ (que cambia) changing; (propenso a cambiar) changeable; (temperamento) volatile
cambiar VI/VT to change; VT (una cosa por otra) to exchange, to swap, to trade; **— de marcha** to shift gears; **— de opinión/parecer** to change one's mind; **— de sitio** to move places
cambiario ADJ **sistema —** foreign exchange system
cambio M (acción de cambiar) change; (marcha) gear; (cotización) exchange rate; (de ferrocarril) railway switch; (béisbol) changeup; **— de velocidad** (en béisbol) change-up; **— de lado** (tenis) changeover; **— de divisas** foreign exchange; **— para peor** a turn for the worse; **— y fuera** over and out; **a — [de]** in return [for]; **en —** on the other hand
cambista MF money changer
Camboya F Cambodia
camboyano -na ADJ & MF Cambodian
camellear VT to push [drugs]
camello -lla MF (animal) camel; (vendedor de droga) pusher
camerino M dressing room
Camerún M Cameroon
camerunés -esa ADJ & MF Cameroonian
camilla F stretcher, litter
camillero -ra MF hospital orderly
caminante MF walker, wayfarer
caminar VI/VT to walk; (baloncesto) to travel
caminata F long walk; (por un lugar agreste) hike
camino M (carretera) road; (itinerario, dirección a seguir) way; **— de** on the way to; **— de mesa** table runner; **— de rosas** bed of roses; **abrirse —** to make way; **a medio —** halfway; **en — [a]** on the way [to]; **llevar por mal —** to lead astray; **mostrar el —** to lead the way; **ponerse en —** to set out; **señalar el —** to show the way

camión M (de cargas) truck; (para transporte de personas) *Méx* bus; **— de la basura** garbage truck; **— de mudanzas** moving van; **— de remolque** tow truck, wrecker; **— de reparto** delivery truck; **— volteador** dump truck
camionero -ra MF truck driver; *Méx* bus driver
camioneta F (furgoneta) van, minivan; (camioncito) pickup truck; (coche sin maletero) station wagon
camisa F shirt; **— de fuerza** straitjacket; **meterse en — de once varas** to get into a jam
camiseta F (exterior) T-shirt; (interior) undershirt
camisón M nightgown
camorrista ADJ rowdy
campamento M (de refugiados, exploradores) camp; (recreativo) campground
campana F bell; **tocar una —** to ring a bell
campanario M belfry, bell tower
campanilla F (campana pequeña) small bell; (flor) bluebell; (órgano en la boca) uvula
campanilleo M ringing
campánula F bellflower
campaña F campaign; **— publicitaria** advertising campaign; **hacer —** to campaign; **el ejército estaba de —** the army was on the front
campechano ADJ straightforward
campeón -ona MF champion
campeonato M championship; **— Mundial de Fútbol** Soccer World Cup
campero ADJ **hombre —** a man from the country
campesino -na MF peasant; ADJ **casa campesina** peasant house
campestre ADJ rural
camping M (lugar) campground; (actividad) camping
campiña F open country
campista MF camper
campo M (fuera de la ciudad) country, countryside; (para cultivos, deportes, ámbito del saber) field; (grupo en un conflicto) camp; **— abierto** range; MF **—corto** (béisbol) shortstop; **— de acción** field of action; **— de batalla** battlefield; **— de concentración** concentration camp; **— de golf** golf course; **— de juego** athletic field; **— de tiro** shooting range; **— libre** free rein; **— magnético** magnetic field; **— minado** minefield; **— petrolífero** oil field; **— visual** visual field; **a — traviesa** cross-country; **—santo** churchyard
campus M campus
camuflaje M camouflage
camuflar VT to camouflage
can M dog
cana F white hair; **echar una — al aire** to go out for a good time
Canadá M Canada
canadiense ADJ & MF Canadian
canal M (cauce artificial de agua) canal; (estrecho marítimo, banda de frecuencia) channel; (emisora) station; **— de parto** birth canal; **— radicular** root canal
canalé M ribbed fabric
canalizar[47] VT to channel
canalón M spout
canana F cartridge belt
canapé M (mueble) divan; (aperitivo) canape, starter
canario -ria M canary; ADJ of/from the Canary Islands; MF Canary Islander
canasta F basket (también en baloncesto)
canasto M hamper
cancelación F cancellation
cancelar VT (contrato, sello) to cancel; (deuda) to pay off; (evento) to call off
cáncer M cancer; **— de mama** breast cancer; **— de colon** colorectal cancer
cancerígeno ADJ carcinogen
canceroso -sa MF cancer patient; ADJ cancerous
cancha F (de baloncesto, tenis) court; (de fútbol) field; **¡abran —!** gangway! **falta —** there's no room
canciller MF (de Alemania, de universidades) chancellor; (de EEUU) secretary of state
canción F song; **— de cuna** lullaby
candado M padlock
candela F (vela) candle; (fuego) fire
candelabro M candelabrum
candelero M candlestick; **en el —** in the limelight
candente ADJ red-hot
candidato -ta MF candidate
candidatura F (hecho de ser candidato) candidacy; (conjunto de candidatos) ticket
candidez F innocence
cándido ADJ naive
candil M oil lamp
candilejas F PL footlights
candor M innocence
canela F (especia) cinnamon; (árbol) cinnamon tree
canesú M yoke of a shirt
cangrejo M crab
canguro M kangaroo; MF *Esp* baby-sitter
caníbal ADJ & MF cannibal
canica F toy marble
caniche M poodle; **— enano** toy poodle
canilla F (espinilla) shin; (pantorrilla) calf; (grifo) faucet
canino ADJ canine; **tener un hambre canina** to be ravenous; M canine [tooth]
canje M exchange
canjear VT (prisioneros, libros) to exchange; (un

cupón) to redeem
cano ADJ gray-haired
canoa F canoe
canon M (regla, modelo) canon; (canción) round
canónigo M canon
canoso ADJ gray-haired
cansado ADJ (fatigado) tired, weary; (fatigoso) wearing, tiring
cansancio M weariness
cansar VT (fatigar) to tire, to tire out; (aburrir) to bore; **—se** to get tired
cantante MF singer
cantar VI/VT (hacer música) to sing; VT (anunciar) to call out; (revelar secretos) to squeal; **— a tono** to sing on key; **—le a alguien las cuarenta** to give someone a piece of one's mind; **— victoria** to declare victory; **en menos que canta un gallo** before you can say Jack Robinson; M epic poem; **eso es otro —** that's another story
cántaro M pitcher; **llover a —s** to rain cats and dogs
cantera F quarry
cantero M *RP* flower bed
cántico M chant
cantidad F quantity, amount; (de dinero) amount, sum; **— a pagar** amount payable; **— debida** amount due; **— pagada** amount paid; **— de gente** a lot of people
cantimplora F canteen, water bottle
cantina F (lugar donde comer) mess hall, mess, canteen; (bar) tavern
cantinela F chant
cantinero -ra MF bartender
canto M (cosa cantada) song; (piedra) pebble; **— de cisne** swan song; **— llano** chant; **— rodado** rounded pebble; **de —** on edge
cantor -ora MF singer
canturrear VI to hum
canturreo M hum, humming
caña F (planta gramínea) reed; (de azúcar) cane; (cerveza) *Esp* beer; (vaso) *Esp* beer glass; **— de pescar** fishing pole; **dale —** floor it
cañada F (barranco) ravine; (arroyo) brook
cáñamo M hemp
cañaveral M reed patch
cañería F (en la calle) piping; (en la casa) plumbing
caño M (tubo) pipe; (grifo) spout; (de arma) barrel; **de doble —** double-barreled
cañón M (arma) cannon; (pieza hueca) barrel; (cañada profunda) canyon; (de pluma, bolígrafo) shaft
cañonero M gunboat
caoba F mahogany
caos M chaos
caótico ADJ chaotic
capa F (prenda) cape, cloak; (de pintura, animal) coat; (de tierra) layer; (de hielo) sheet; **— de ozono** ozone layer; **— freática** water table; **de — y espada** cloak and dagger
capacidad F capacity; **—es** aptitude, ability, capability; **— de almacenamiento de disco** disk capacity
capacitación F training; **— para empleados** in-service training
capacitar VT (entrenar) to train; (habilitar) to qualify
capar VT to castrate
caparazón M shell
capataz -za MF boss, overseer
capaz ADJ (habilidoso) capable, able; (apto) apt; (espacioso) spacious, roomy; (competente) competent
capear VT to ride out, to weather
capellán M chaplain
caperuza F pointed hood
capilar ADJ & M capillary
capilla F chapel; **estar en —** (castigado) to be in the doghouse; (en ascuas) to be on pins and needles
capital M (dinero) capital; (de préstamo) principal; **— de riesgo** venture capital; **— inicial** start-up funds; **el gran —** big business; F capital [city]; ADJ main
capitalino ADJ **atmósfera capitalina** capital city atmosphere
capitalismo M capitalism
capitalista MF capitalist; ADJ capitalistic
capitalización F capitalization
capitalizar[47] VT (aportar capital) to capitalize; (aprovechar) to capitalize on
capitán -ana MF captain
capitanear VT to captain
capitel M capital
capitolio M capitol
capitulación F (militar) capitulation, surrender; **capitulaciones matrimoniales** prenuptial agreement
capitular VI to capitulate
capítulo M chapter
capó M hood [of a car]
capo M mafia boss
capota F top [of a car]
capote M cloak; (de coche) *Méx* hood; **decir para su —** to say under one's breath
capricho M caprice, whim, notion
caprichoso ADJ (impredecible) capricious; (impulsivo) whimsical, fanciful; (malcriado) willful
cápsula F capsule
captación F (de agua) collection; (de clientes) attraction; (de inversiones, fondos) raising
captar VT (un concepto) to grasp; (atención, interés) to capture; (una emisión) to receive; (una indirecta) to get; **— la onda** to get the drift
captor -ora MF captor

captura F (acción de capturar) capture; (pesca capturada) catch; (fútbol americano) sack; **— de video/vídeo** video capture
capturar VT to capture; (pescado) to catch
capucha F (de cabeza) hood, cowl; (de lapicero) cap
capuchina F nasturtium
capuchino M cappuccino
capullo M (de insecto) cocoon; (de flor) bud
caqui M khaki
cara F (rostro) face; (de cubo) surface; (de papel, moneda) side; (morro) nerve; **— a —** face to face; **— o cruz** heads or tails; **dar la —** to face up to things; **de — al sur** facing south; **decir en la —** to tell to one's face; **de dos —s** two-sided; **la otra — de la moneda** the other side of the coin; **poner buena —** to put on a good face; **se le ve en la —** it's written all over his face; **tener — [dura]** to have a lot of nerve; **un ojo de la —** an arm and a leg; **volverle la — a** to snub
carabinero -ra MF (oficial de aduana) border patrol officer; (agente de policía) police officer; M (crustáceo) red prawn
caracol M (molusco) snail; (concha) snail shell; INTERJ **¡—es!** *fam* darn!
carácter M (temperamento, signo) character; (rasgo) characteristic; (índole) kind
característica F characteristic, feature; (en informática) feature
característico ADJ characteristic
caracterización F (descripción) characterization, description; (retrato) portrayal
caracterizar[47] VT to characterize
caramba INTERJ *fam* darn! good grief! heck!
carámbano M icicle
carambola F carom; **por —** indirectly
caramelo M (azúcar fundido) caramel; (dulce pequeño) bonbon
caramillo M reed pipe
carátula F (máscara) mask; (portada) title page
caravana F (en el desierto, convoy) caravan; (remolque) trailer
caray INTERJ *fam* shoot! darn!
carbohidrato M carbohydrate
carbón M (sustancia) coal; (pedazo) piece of coal; **— de leña** charcoal
carboncillo M charcoal drawing
carbonera F coal bin
carbono M carbon
carburador M carburetor
carburante M fuel
carca ADJ old-fashioned; MF *fam* fossil, old fogey
carcaj M quiver
carcajada F burst of laughter, guffaw
carcamal M *fam* fossil, old fogey
cárcel F jail, prison
carcelero -ra MF jailer
carcinógeno M carcinogen
carcinoma M carcinoma; **— de célula basal** basal cell carcinoma
carcomido ADJ worm-eaten
carda F card, comb
cardán M universal joint
cardar VT (lana) to card, to comb; (pelo) to rat, to tease
cardenal M (pájaro, prelado) cardinal; (moretón) bruise
cardíaco -ca ADJ cardiac; MF heart patient
cardinal ADJ cardinal
cardioangiograma M cardioangiogram
cardiograma M cardiogram
cardiología F cardiology
cardiólogo -ga MF cardiologist
cardiopulmonar ADJ cardiopulmonary
cardiovascular ADJ cardiovascular
cardo M thistle
cardumen M school of fish
carear VT to bring face to face; **—se** to meet face to face
carecer[35] VI **— de** to lack
carencia F (falta) lack; (deficiencia alimenticia) deficiency
carenciado ADJ disadvantaged
carente ADJ lacking; **— de** lacking in
carero ADJ expensive
carestía F (escasez) scarcity; (costo alto) high cost
careta F mask
carezca, carezco *ver* carecer
carga F (cosa cargada) load, freight; (de la prueba, impuesto) burden; (hipoteca) lien; (de encendedor) refill; (de explosivo, electricidad) charge; (de programas) upload; **— de municiones** round of ammunition; **— útil** payload; **volver a la —** to insist
cargado ADJ (bebida) stiff; (pausa) pregnant; (cartucho) live; **— de deudas** deep in debt; **— de espaldas** stooping
cargador M (de batería) charger; (de arma de fuego) clip, magazine
cargamento M cargo, load, shipment
cargar[40] VT (cargamentos, dados, arma, programa de ordenador) to load; (batería, a una cuenta, en baloncesto) to charge; (de obligaciones) to burden with; (a un niño) to carry; (a un estudiante) *Esp* to flunk; (molestar) to bother; **— a alguien de responsabilidades** to saddle someone with responsibilities; **— al hombro** to shoulder; **— de combustible** to fuel; **— un programa** to upload; VI to charge; **— con la culpa** to be saddled with blame; **— sobre** to charge, to attack
cargo M (función en una empresa) position; (en una factura, a una cuenta) charge; (acusación) count, charge; **— de conciencia** guilt

feelings; **—s atrasados** back charges; **— de tramitación** handling charges; **a mi —** under my charge; **hacerse — de** (responsabilizarse de) to take charge of; (ser consciente de) to understand; **investir de un —** to induct into office; **los niños están a — de la maestra** the children are under the care of the teacher; **la maestra está a[l] — de los niños** the teacher is in charge of the children

cargoso ADJ fussy

carguero ADJ freight-carrying

cariado ADJ decayed

caribeño ADJ Caribbean

caricatura F (dibujo) caricature; (con texto) cartoon

caricaturista MF cartoonist

caricaturizar[47] VT to caricature

caricia F caress

caridad F charity

caries F INV cavity, tooth decay

carillón M chimes

cariño M (amor) affection, fondness; (apodo) honey; **darle —s a alguien** to send love to someone; **ella y el perro se hacen —s** she and the dog nuzzle each other; **hacer algo con —** to do something with great care; **tenerle — a alguien** to be fond of someone

cariñoso ADJ affectionate, loving

carisma M charisma

caritativo ADJ charitable

cariz M complexion; **no me gusta el — que está tomando la situación** I don't like the look of this

carmesí ADJ INV & M crimson

carmín M (carmesí) crimson; (lápiz de labios) lipstick

carnal ADJ carnal

carnaval M carnival

carne F (para comer) meat; (de animal vivo, de persona, de tomate) flesh; **— de cañón** cannon fodder; **— de cerdo** pork; **— de cordero** mutton; **— de gallina** (comida) chicken; (reacción de la piel) goose bumps; **— de res** beef; **— de venado** venison; **— y hueso** flesh and blood; **como — y uña** *fam* thick as thieves; **en — viva** raw; **metido en —s** overweight

carnear VT to butcher

carnero M ram

carnet/carné M **— de conducir** driver's license; **— de identidad** ID

carnicería F (tienda) butcher's shop; (matanza) carnage, bloodbath

carnicero -ra MF butcher; ADJ (carnívoro) carnivorous; (cruel) cruel

carnívoro ADJ carnivorous

carnoso ADJ fleshy

caro ADJ expensive, high-priced, *fam* pricey; ADV at a high price

carona F saddle pad

carótida F carotid artery

carozo M *RP* pit, stone

carpa F (pez) carp; (tienda) tent

carpeta F (para documentos, también de ordenador) folder; (cartera) portfolio

carpintería F (oficio) carpentry; (taller) carpenter's shop

carpintero -ra MF carpenter

carraspear VI to clear one's throat

carraspera F scratchy throat

carrera F (conjunto de estudios) major; (trayectoria profesional) career; (competición) race; (en las medias) run; (recorrido corto) run, dash; (en fútbol americano, béisbol) run; (de pistón) stroke; **— a pie** footrace; **— de caballos** horse race; **— de relevos** relay race; **a la —** running; **hacer —** to succeed in a profession; **tomar —** to get a running start; **— impulsada** (en béisbol) run batted in; **— limpia** (en béisbol) earned run; **— sucia** (en béisbol) unearned run

carreta F wagon

carrete M (de película) reel; (de hilo) bobbin; (de alambre) spool

carretera F highway; **— de circunvalación** bypass; **— de peaje** toll road

carretero ADJ **sistema —** highway system

carretilla F (de una rueda) wheelbarrow; (de más de una rueda) dolly; **de —** by memory

carretón M large wagon

carril M (de ferrocarril) rail; (de calle) lane

carrillo M cheek, jowl; **a dos/cuatro —s** voraciously

carrillón M chimes

carrizo M reed

carro M (automóvil) car; (vehículo de dos ruedas, de golf) cart; (de máquina de escribir) roll; **— alegórico** parade float; **— blindado** armored car; **— de guerra** chariot; **poner el — delante de los bueyes** to put the cart before the horse; **subirse al —** to get on the bandwagon

carrocería F auto body

carroña F carrion

carroza F (de caballos) coach; (de desfile) parade float; (fúnebre) hearse

carruaje M carriage, coach

carta F (misiva) letter; (naipe) card; (de restaurante) menu; (constitución) charter; (mapa) chart; **— blanca** freehand; **— con anexos** cover letter; **— de agradecimiento** thank-you letter; **— de remisión** cover letter; **— de renuncia** resignation letter; **a la —** à la carte; **echarle las —s a alguien** to do a card-reading for someone; **tomar —s en la situación** to

take charge of a situation
cartearse VI to correspond
cartel M poster, placard; **en —** showing; **— de la droga** drug cartel
cartelera F (de periódico) entertainment section; (publicitaria) billboard; (tablón para anuncios) bulletin board
cárter M oil pan
cartera F (para dinero) wallet, billfold; (para papeles) briefcase; (escolar) satchel; (bolsa) handbag; (de valores) portfolio
carterista MF pickpocket
cartero -ra MF letter carrier; M mailman, postman
cartílago M cartilage
cartilla F (para aprender a leer) reader; (de información) booklet; **— de racionamiento** ration book; **— de examen de vista** eye chart
cartografiar[28] VT to chart
cartón M cardboard, pasteboard; **— de cigarrillos** carton of cigarettes
cartuchera F cartridge belt
cartucho M (de pistola) cartridge, shell; (de monedas) roll; (de dinamita) stick; **— de fogueo** blank cartridge; **— de tinta / tóner** toner cartridge; **quemar el último —** to exhaust one's resources
cartulina F thin cardboard
casa F (edificio) house; (hogar) home; (negocio) business firm; **— de ancianos** old folks' home; **— de citas** cheap motel for rendezvous; **— de empeños** pawnshop; **— de la moneda** mint; **— de muñecas** dollhouse; **— de pompas fúnebres** funeral home; **— de reposo** rest home; **— de rehabilitación** halfway house; **— de subastas** auction house; **— embrujada** haunted house; **— rodante** house trailer; **— solariega** manor house; **de — en —** from house to house; **en —** at home; **entró como Perico por su —** he made himself right at home; **estás en tu —** make yourself at home; **ir a —** to go home; **la — paga** on the house; **poner una —** to set up a household; **quedarse en —** to stay home; **tirar la — por la ventana** to live it up
casaca F riding jacket
casadero ADJ marriageable
casado ADJ married
casamentero -ra MF matchmaker
casamiento M wedding, marriage ceremony
casar VT to marry off; **—se** to get married, to wed; **—se con** to get married to; **no —se con nadie** to remain independent
cascabel M (campanita) jingle bell; (de víbora) rattle; **ser un —** to be lively; **ponerle el — al gato** to stick one's neck out
cascada F cascade, waterfall
cascajo M old wreck
cascar[30] VT (quebrar) to crack; (dar bofetadas) to slap around; **—se** to crack open; M SG **cascanueces** nutcracker; MF SG **cascarrabias** crab, grouch; ADJ INV grouchy
cáscara F (de huevo, fruto seco) shell; (de granos, arvejas) husk; (de fruto seco) hull; (de fruta) rind; (de naranja, manzana) peel
casco M (de ciclista, militar) helmet; (de obrero) hard hat; (de barco) hull; (de naranja) shell; (uña del pie de caballería) hoof; **— urbano** built-up area
cascote M rubble
caserío M (aldea) hamlet; (casa) *Esp* farmhouse
casero -ra ADJ (doméstico) domestic; (hecho en casa) homemade; MF (cuidador) caretaker; M (propietario) landlord; F landlady
caseta F (en un mercado) booth, stall; (de guardia) guardhouse; (de perro) doghouse
casete MF cassette
casi ADV almost, nearly; **— diez mil** almost/nearly ten thousand; **— lo hago** I almost did it; **— siempre** almost always; **— nadie** hardly anyone; **— nunca** hardly ever
casilla F (en el tablero de ajedrez) square; (en una tabla) box; (en un casillero) pigeonhole, cubbyhole; **— de perro** doghouse; **sacarle a alguien de sus —s** to drive someone up the wall
casino M (club) men's club; (lugar de apuestas) casino
caso M case; **— de fuerza mayor** act of God; **— perdido** (persona incapacitada) basket case; (persona incorregible) lost cause; **en — de** in the event of; **en — de que** in case that; **el — es que** the deal is that; **en todo —** in any case, at any rate; **en último —** as a last resort; **eso no viene al —** that is beside the point; **hacer — [de]** to pay attention [to]; **hacer — omiso de** to disregard; **no hay —** there's no point; **pongamos por —** let's suppose that; **venir al —** to come to the point
caspa F dandruff
casquillo M (de bala) case; (de lámpara) socket
cassette MF cassette
casta F caste
castaña F chestnut; **— de cajú** cashew
castañetear VI to chatter; **— con los dedos** to snap one's fingers
castañeteo M (de dientes) chattering; (de dedos) snapping
castaño M (árbol) chestnut tree; (color, madera) chestnut; ADJ chestnut-colored, brown
castañuela F castanet
castellano ADJ & MF Castilian; M (lengua) Castilian
castidad F chastity
castigar[40] VT to chastise, to punish
castigo M chastisement, punishment; **¡qué —!**

what a nuisance!
Castilla F Castile
castillo M castle; **— de arena** sandcastle; **—s en el aire** *fam* pie in the sky
casting M casting
castizo ADJ traditional
casto ADJ chaste
castor M beaver
castrar VT (a un hombre, animal) to castrate; (a una mascota) to neuter, to fix; (a mascotas hembras) to spay
casual ADJ chance, accidental
casualidad F chance, coincidence; **da la — que** it so happens that; **oír por —** to overhear; **por —** by chance
casucha F shack
cata F **— de vinos** wine-tasting
catalán -ana ADJ (del catalán) Catalan; (de Cataluña) Catalonian; MF Catalan; M (lengua) Catalan
catalejo M spyglass
catalizador M catalyst
catalogar[40] VT to catalog/catalogue
catálogo M catalog, catalogue
Cataluña F Catalonia
catar VT to taste
catarata F (cascada) cataract, waterfall; (de los ojos) cataract
catarí ADJ & MF Qatari
catarro M cold
catástrofe F catastrophe
catatonia F catatonia
catecismo M catechism
cátedra F (puesto de profesor) chair, professorship; (enseñanza) teaching; (división académica) department; **sentar —** to hold forth, to pontificate
catedral F cathedral
catedrático -ca MF [full] professor
categoría F category; **de —** important; **de — mundial** world-class; **de poca —** third-rate
caterpillar M caterpillar
catéter M catheter
cateterización F catheterization
cateterizar VT to catheterize
cátodo M cathode
catolicismo M Catholicism
católico -ca ADJ Catholic; MF Catholic
catorce NUM fourteen
catre M cot
cátsup M catsup, ketchup
cauce M channel; **— de río** riverbed
cauchero -ra MF rubber gatherer; ADJ **industria cauchera** rubber industry
caucho M rubber; **— sintético** synthetic rubber
caución F security payment
caudal M (de bienes) wealth; (de agua) volume of water
caudaloso ADJ mighty
caudillo M leader
causa F (motivo) cause; (proceso) case; **— noble** worthy cause; **— perdida** lost cause; **a — de** on account of, because of; **con conocimiento de —** wittingly; **hacer — común** to work together
causante ADJ causing; MF instigator
causar VT to cause; **— problemas** to make trouble
cáustico ADJ caustic
cautela F caution
cautelar ADJ preventive
cauteloso ADJ cautious, wary
cauterizar[47] VT to cauterize
cautivar VT (capturar) to capture; (atraer) to captivate
cautiverio M captivity
cautivo -va MF captive
cauto ADJ cautious, wary
cava F (acción de cavar) digging; (sótano) cellar; (vino) cava
cavar VT to dig
caverna F cavern, cave
cavidad F cavity
cavilar VI to muse
cayado M shepherd's crook, staff
cayendo, cayera, cayese, cayeron *ver* caer
cayo M key
caza F (acción de cazar) hunt, hunting; (conjunto de animales) wild game; **— mayor** big game; **— menor** small game; **andar a la — de** to hunt for; **dar — a** to hunt down; M (avión) fighter
cazador -ora ADJ hunting; MF hunter; F Windbreaker™
cazar[47] VI/VT (buscar presas) to hunt; (matar presas) to shoot, to bag; (atrapar presas) to trap; MF SG **cazatalentos** talent scout, headhunter; M **cazatorpedero** destroyer, torpedo boat
cazo M (cacerola) pan; (cucharón) ladle, dipper
cazoleta F pipe bowl
cazuela F (recipiente) casserole; (cazo) pan
CD M CD; **— ROM** CD-ROM
cebada F barley
cebador M pump primer
cebar VT (un animal) to fatten; (bombas) to prime; (anzuelos) to bait; **—se** to vent one's anger
cebo M (para peces) bait, lure; (para animales) feed
cebolla F onion
cebollar M onion patch
cebollino M scallion
cebra F (animal) zebra; (paso) crosswalk
cecear VI to lisp
ceceo M lisp
cecina F jerky
cedazo M sieve

ceder VT (propiedad) to cede, to assign; (un sitio) to yield, to give up; VI (el frío) to diminish; (la resistencia) to give way
cedro M cedar
cédula F document; **— de identidad** identification card
céfiro M zephyr
cegar[41] VT to blind
ceguera F blindness; **— cromática** color blindness
ceja F (sobre el ojo) eyebrow; (en una encuadernación) tab; **quemarse las —s** to cram for an exam; **cejijunto** with thick eyebrows
cejar VI to back down
celada F ambush
celador -ora MF (en una escuela) school monitor; (en un barrio) security officer
celar VT to guard
celda F cell
celebración F (fiesta) celebration; (acto solemne) performance
celebrar VT (una fiesta) to celebrate; (una reunión) to hold; (un rito) to perform
célebre ADJ famous, noted
celebridad F celebrity
celeste ADJ (relativo al firmamento) celestial; (del color del cielo) azure, light blue
celestial ADJ celestial, heavenly
célibe ADJ celibate; MF unmarried person
cellisca F sleet; **caer —** to sleet
celo M (diligencia) zeal; (excitación sexual) heat; **estar en —** to be in heat; **—s** jealousy; **tener —s** to be jealous
celofán M cellophane
celosía F window lattice
celoso ADJ (que tiene celos) jealous; (diligente) zealous
célula F cell; **— adiposa** fat cell; **— estaminal embrional** stem cell
celular ADJ cellular; M mobile phone
celulitis F cellulite
celuloide M celluloid
celulosa F cellulose
cementar VT to cement
cementerio M cemetery, graveyard
cemento M cement; **— armado** reinforced concrete
cena F supper, dinner
cenagal M quagmire, swamp
cenagoso ADJ marshy, swampy
cenar VI to eat supper, to eat dinner; **vamos a — pescado** we're having fish for dinner
cencerro M cowbell
cenicero M ashtray
ceniciento ADJ ashen
cenit M zenith
cenizas F PL ashes, cinders
censar VI/VT to take a census [of]
censo M census
censor -ora MF censor; **— de cuentas** auditor
censura F (reprobación) censure; (control) censorship
censurador ADJ censuring
censurar VT (criticar) to censure; (examinar) to censor
centavo M cent
centella F sparkle; **pasar como una —** to go by in a flash
centelleante ADJ sparkling
centellear VI to sparkle, to scintillate
centelleo M sparkle
centenar M group of a hundred; **—es** hundreds
centenario M centennial; ADJ centenarian
centeno M rye
centésimo ADJ & M hundredth
centígrado ADJ centigrade
centímetro M centimeter
céntimo M cent
centinela MF sentry, sentinel
centrado ADJ (un tablón) true; (un cuadro) centered; (una persona) focused; M truing
central ADJ central; F plant; **— de teléfonos** telephone exchange; **— eléctrica** power plant; **— lechera** milk processing plant; **— nuclear** nuclear power plant
centralita F switchboard
centralizar[47] VT to centralize; **—se** to become centralized
centrar VT to center; **—se** to focus, to be focused
céntrico ADJ central
centrífugo ADJ centrifugal
centrípeto ADJ centripetal
centro M center (también de baloncesto); (de ciudad) downtown; **— comercial** shopping center; **— de gravedad** center of gravity; **— de mesa** centerpiece; MF **—campista** (fútbol) midfield player
Centroamérica F Central America
centroamericano -na M Central American
ceñido ADJ tight
ceñir[11] VT (rodear) to gird; (abrazar) to encircle; **— la corona** to be crowned; VI (estar apretado) to be tight; **—se a** (limitarse) to limit oneself to; (arrimarse) to get close to
ceño M **fruncir el —** to frown, to scowl
cepa F (de árbol) stump; (de viña) stock; (de bacteria) strain; **de pura —** of good stock
cepillar VT (dientes, pelo) to brush; (madera) to plane, to shave
cepillo M (para pelo, dientes) brush; (para madera) carpenter's plane; **— de dientes** toothbrush
cepo M (para cazar) trap; (para inmovilizar coches) boot
cera F wax; **— de oídos** earwax; **— para muebles** polish
cerámica F (arte) ceramics; (conjunto de

artículos) pottery, earthenware
cerámico ADJ ceramic
cerbatana F blowpipe
cerca ADV near, nearby, close; **— de** near, close to; **de —** close up; F fence
cercado M (terreno cercado) enclosure; (cerca) fence
cercanía F proximity, nearness, closeness
cercano ADJ (lugar) near, nearby; (pariente) close; **— Oriente** Near East
cercar[30] VT (rodear con una cerca) to fence, to enclose; (sitiar) to besiege
cercenar VT (cortar) to chop off; (reducir) to curtail, to encroach upon
cerciorarse VI **— [de]** to make sure [of]
cerco M (sitio) siege; (cerca) fence
cerdo -da M (animal, persona sucia) hog, pig; (carne) pork; F (puerca) sow; (de cepillo) bristle
cerdoso ADJ bristly
cereal M cereal; **—es** breakfast cereal; **cultivo —** cereal crop
cerebral ADJ cerebral
cerebro M (órgano, genio) brain; (organizador de un plan) mastermind; **lavarle el — a** to brainwash
ceremonia F ceremony
ceremonial ADJ & M ceremonial
ceremonioso ADJ ceremonious
cereza F cherry
cerezo M cherry tree
cerilla F match
cerner[2] VT to sift; **—se** (un ave) to hover; (un desastre) to loom
cernícalo M kestrel
cero M (cifra) zero; (en deportes) nothing, goose egg, zip; (en tenis) love; **— absoluto** absolute zero; **partir de —** to start from scratch; **ser un — a la izquierda** to be a nobody
cerrado ADJ (no abierto) closed; (tonto) dense; (poco comunicativo) reserved; (intransigente) closed-minded; (anguloso) sharp; M enclosure
cerrador -ora MF closer
cerradura F lock; **— de combinación** combination lock
cerrajería F locksmith's shop
cerrajero -ra MF locksmith
cerrar[1] VT (la puerta, un cajón) to close, to shut; (un trato) to close, to clinch; (un terreno) to enclose; (el gas, un grifo) to turn off; (una fábrica) to shut down, to close; **— filas** to close ranks; **— el paso** to block passage; VI to close; **—se** (una flor, una tienda) to close; (un plazo) to end; **—se el cielo** to become overcast
cerrazón F (de la mente) closed-mindedness; (del cielo) stormy skies
cerro M hill
cerrojo M bolt
certamen M contest; **— de belleza** beauty contest
certero ADJ sure
certeza F certainty
certidumbre F certainty
certificación F certification
certificado ADJ certified; M certificate; **— de nacimiento** birth certificate
certificar[30] VT (la autenticidad) to certify; (una carta) to register
cervatillo M fawn
cervecera F brewery
cervecería F bar
cerveza F beer; **— de barril** draft beer
cervical ADJ cervical
cérvix M cervix
cerviz F cervix
cesar VI to cease; **— de trabajar** to stop working; **— en un cargo** to resign from a position; **— a** to dismiss
cesárea F cesarean [section]
cese M cessation; **— el fuego** ceasefire; **— de actividades** shutdown
cesión F (de propiedad) assignment; (de derechos) waiver
césped M (ante una casa) lawn; (hierba, también para tenis) grass
cesta F basket
cestería F basketry
cesto M (cesta) basket; (para ropa) hamper
cetrino ADJ olive-colored
chabacano ADJ (modales) crude; (gustos) tacky; M *Méx* apricot
chacal M jackal
chacha F servant girl
cháchara F small talk
chacota F joke; **tomarse algo a la —** to take lightly
chacra F (establecimiento agrícola) small farm; (terreno) small plot
Chad M Chad
chadiano -na ADJ & MF Chadian
chal M shawl, wrap
chala F *Am* husk; **quitar la —** to husk
chalán M horse trader
chalé M cottage
chaleco M waistcoat, vest; **— antibalas** bulletproof vest; **— de fuerza** straitjacket; **— salvavidas** life jacket
chalupa F small canoe; *Méx* tortilla with sauce
chamaco -ca M *Méx* boy; F *Méx* girl
chamarra F sheepskin jacket
chambergo M wide-brimmed hat
chambón ADJ clumsy
champán/champaña M champagne
champiñón M mushroom
champú M shampoo

chamuscadura F scorch
chamuscar[30] VT to scorch, to singe; **—se** to get scorched, to get singed
chamusquina F scorching, singeing
chance MF chance
chancearse VI **— de** to make fun of
chancho M hog
chanchullo M *fam* monkey business
chancleta F thong, flipflop; **tirar la —** to kick up one's heels
chanclo M galosh, overshoe; **—s** rubbers
chándal M sweatsuit
chantaje M blackmail
chantajear VT to blackmail
chanza F jest
chao INTERJ bye-bye
chapa F (de metal) sheet metal; (de policía) badge; (de botella) bottle top; (de madera) veneer; **— en la puerta** shingle on the door; **hacerle — y pintura a un coche** to fix the bodywork and paint of a car
chapado ADJ **— a la antigua** old-fashioned
chapalear VI to splash
chapar VT to plate
chaparral M dry rangeland, chaparral
chaparro M scrub oak; ADJ *Méx* short
chaparrón M cloudburst
chaperón -ona MF chaperon[e]; **ir de —** to chaperon[e]
chapitel M spire, steeple
chapotear VI to splash
chapoteo M splash, splashing
chapucear VT to botch, to bungle
chapucería F (trabajo, obra) botched job; (cualidad) sloppiness
chapucero ADJ shoddy, slipshod
chapurrear VT to speak a language poorly
chapuz M dive
chapuza F botched job
chapuzar[47] VI to dive
chaqueta F jacket; **— de sport** sport jacket
charada F charades
charca F pond
charco M puddle, pool; **cruzar el —** to cross the ocean
charcutería F (tienda) delicatessen; (industria) sausage-making
charla F chat, talk
charlar VI to chat, to gab
charlatán -ana ADJ talkative; MF (parlanchín) chatterbox, windbag; (curandero) charlatan, quack
charlotear VI to chatter, to jabber
charloteo M chatter, jabber
charol M (barniz) varnish; (cuero barnizado) patent leather
charolar VT to varnish
charqui M beef jerky
charro ADJ flashy, tawdry
chárter M charter flight
chascar VT (los nudillos, un hueso) to crack; (los labios) to smack; (la lengua) to click
chascarrillo M funny anecdote
chasco M (broma) prank, practical joke; (decepción) dud; **llevarse un —** to be disappointed
chasis M frame, chassis
chasquear VT (decepcionar) to disappoint; (una cerradura, la lengua) to click; (un látigo) to crack; (los labios) to smack; (los dedos) to snap; **—se** to be disappointed
chasquido M (de látigo, madera, articulaciones) crack; (de labios) smack; (de la lengua, una cerradura) click; (de los dedos) snap
chata F bedpan
chatarra F scrap iron
chatarrería F junkyard
chatear VI to chat
chato ADJ (nariz) snub-nosed; (zapatos, pecho) flat; **— como una tabla** as flat as a pancake
chaucha F green bean
chaval -la M *Esp* boy; F *Esp* girl
chaveta F cotter pin; **perder la —** *fam* to go bonkers
che INTERJ *RP* say! hey!
checo -ca ADJ & MF Czech
chef MF chef
cheque M check; **— de viajero** traveler's check; **— de caja** bank check; **— sin fondos** bad check, worthless check
chequear VT to check
checar VT to check
chequera F checkbook
chic ADJ INV & M chic
chicha F (bebida alcohólica) *Am* corn liquor; (carne) *Esp fam* meat; **de — y nabo** two-bit; **ni — ni limonada** neither fish nor fowl
chicharra F (insecto) cicada; (timbre) buzzer
chichón M bump, lump, knot
chicle M chewing gum; **— de globo** bubblegum
chico -ca ADJ small, little; M boy; F girl; **mis —s** my kids
chicote M *Am* whip
chicotear VT *Am* to whip
chicoteo M *Am* whipping
chiflado ADJ *fam* nuts, cuckoo, loony; MF (persona loca) *fam* basket case, loon
chifladura F craziness
chiflar VI (silbar) to whistle; VT (volver loco) to drive crazy; **—se** to go crazy
chiflido M whistle
chifón M chiffon
chile M chile
Chile M Chile
chileno -na ADJ & MF Chilean
chillar VI (persona) to shriek; (puerta, ratón) to squeak; (cerdo) to squeal
chillido M (de persona) shriek; (de puerta,

ratón) squeak; (de cerdo) squeal
chillón ADJ (sonido) shrill; (color) loud, gaudy, flashy
chimenea F (salida de humo) chimney; (hogar) fireplace; (de volcán, baño, mina) vent; (de fábrica) smokestack
chimpancé M chimpanzee
china F (porcelana) china; (piedra) pebble
China F China
chinche F (insecto) bedbug; (chincheta) thumbtack; MF (persona molesta) pain
chinchilla F chinchilla
chinchorro M rowboat
chino -na ADJ Chinese; M (lengua) Chinese; MF Chinese; **vi a un chino** I saw a Chinese person; **los chinos no están de acuerdo** the Chinese don't agree; **eso es —** that's Greek to me
chip M (de ordenador, en golf) chip; (de papa/patata) potato chip; **— de silicio** silicon chip
Chipre M Cyprus
chipriota ADJ & MF Cypriot[e]
chiquilín -ina M little boy; F little girl
chiquito ADJ tiny, wee
chiripa F stroke of good luck; **por/de —** by a fluke
chirivía F parsnip
chirona F jail
chirriante ADJ squeaky
chirriar[28] VI (puerta, freno) to squeak; (ave, freno) to screech
chirrido M (de puerta, freno) squeak; (de ave, freno) screech
chisgarabís M pipsqueak
chisguete M squirt
chisme M (rumor) gossip, piece of gossip; (objeto) *fam* gizmo, thingamajig
chismear VI to gossip
chismoso -sa ADJ gossipy; MF gossip
chispa F (partícula incandescente) spark; (ingenio) wit; **echar —s** to be furious; **pasar echando —s** to whiz by
chispeante ADJ (que echa chispas) sparkling; (ingenioso) witty
chispear VI (echar chispas) to spark; (lloviznar) to sprinkle
chisporrotear VI (fuego) to sputter; (cigarrillo) to fizzle; (carne) to sizzle
chisporroteo M (de fuego) sputter; (de carne) sizzle
chiste M (verbal) joke; (visual) cartoon; (ocurrencia) wisecrack; **— verde** dirty joke; **no le veo el —** I don't see the humor in it
chistera F top hat
chistoso ADJ funny, amusing, humorous
chivar VI/VT to snitch [on], to rat [on]
chivatar VI/VT to squeal [on], to snitch [on]
chivato -ta MF (delator) informer, snitch, stool pigeon; (chivito) kid
chivo M kid; **— expiatorio** scapegoat; **estar como un —** to be crazy as a loon
chocante ADJ shocking, jarring
chocar[30] VI (golpearse) to bump, to collide; (antagonizar) to clash; VT (sorprender) to shock; (destrozar) to wreck; **— los cinco** to shake hands
chocarrería F coarseness
chochear VI to be in one's dotage
chochera F senility, dotage
chochez F senility, dotage
chocho ADJ senile; **estar —** to be in one's dotage; **estar — con** to dote on
choclo M ear of corn
chocolate M (planta, dulce) chocolate; (bebida) cocoa, drinking chocolate
chocolatera F chocolate pot
chocolatina F chocolate bar
chófer, chofer MF chauffeur, driver
cholo -la MF (mestizo) person of mixed race; (indio) Europeanized Indian
chopo M poplar
choque M (de objetos móviles) collision, bump, crash; (eléctrico, emocional, cultural) shock; **— insulínico** insulin shock
chorizo M sausage
chorlito M plover
chorrear VI/VT (poco) to drip; (mucho) to gush
chorro M spurt, jet; **a —s** in buckets
chotearse VI **— de** to make fun of
choteo M mocking
chovinismo M chauvinism
choza F hut, shack, hovel
chubasco M squall, shower
chuchería F trinket, knickknack
chueco ADJ *Am* crooked
chuleta F (papel para copiar) cheat sheet; (golf) divot; **— de cerdo** pork chop; **— de ternera** veal cutlet
chulo -la M (dandi) dandy, dude; (bravucón) tough guy; MF working-class resident of Madrid; ADJ (fanfarrón) boastful; (bonito) cute
chupada F (de cigarro) puff; (de bebida) sip
chupar VI/VT (succionar) to suck; (fumar) to puff [on]; VT (absorber) to absorb; (vivir a costa de) to sponge off; **chúpate esa** put that in your pipe and smoke it; M SG **chupasangre** leech
chupete M pacifier
chupetín M *RP* lollipop, sucker
churrasco M *Am* barbecued steak
churro M fritter
chusma F rabble, riffraff
chut M hard shot
chutar VI (drogas) to shoot up; VT (un balón) to shoot; *Esp* **— la bola** to kick the ball hard
chute M narcotic fix
chuzo M watchman's pike
CIA F CIA

cianotipo M blueprint
cianuro M cyanide
cibercafé M cybercafe
ciberespacio M cyberspace
cibernética F cybernetics
ciberpunk MF cyberpunk
cicatero ADJ stingy
cicatriz F scar
cicatrizar VI (formar cicatriz) to form a scar; (curarse) to heal up
cíclico ADJ cyclical
ciclista MF bicycle rider, cyclist, biker
ciclo M cycle; **—motor** moped; **— vital** life cycle; **— de auditoría** audit cycle; **— de facturación** billing cycle; **— presupuestario** budget cycle
ciclón M cyclone
ciclotrón M cyclotron
cicuta F hemlock
ciego ADJ (no vidente) blind; (por borrachera) plastered; (por drogas) high; **quedarse —** to go blind; **a ciegas** blindly
cielo M (firmamento) sky; (paraíso) heaven; **a — abierto** under the open sky; **minería a — abierto** open pit mining; **— raso** ceiling; **¡—s!** good heavens! **estar en el séptimo —** to be in seventh heaven; **me cayó del —** it's a godsend; **poner el grito en el —** *fam* to hit the ceiling
ciempiés M centipede
cien, ciento NUM hundred; **por ciento** percent
ciénaga F swamp, mire, marsh
ciencia F (campo de investigación) science; (conocimiento) knowledge; (arte) art; **— ficción** science fiction; **—s políticas** political science; **a — cierta** with certainty; **las —s ocultas** the occult; **no tiene —** there's nothing to it
cieno M mud, mire
científico -ca ADJ scientific; MF scientist
cierra, cierre *ver* cerrar
cierre M (traba) clasp, fastener; (cremallera) zipper; (acción de cerrar) closing, closure; **— patronal** lockout; **al —** (noticias) at press time; (acciones) at the close
ciertamente ADV certainly
cierto ADJ certain; (verdadero) true; (seguro) sure; **en — sentido** in a sense; **hasta — punto** to a certain extent; **por —** by the way; INTERJ you're right!
ciervo -va M (animal) deer; (macho) stag; **— volante** stag beetle; F (hembra) doe, hind
cierzo M north wind
cifra F (numeral) digit; (número) figure; (clave) cipher, key; **— aproximada** ballpark estimate; **poner en —** to encode
cifrado M encryption; **— de datos** data encryption
cifrar VT to write in code, to encrypt; **— las esperanzas en** to place one's hopes on; **el monto se cifra en veinte millones de pesos** the figure amounts to twenty million pesos
cigarra F cicada
cigarrera F cigar case, cigarette case
cigarrillo M cigarette
cigarro M (cigarrillo) cigarette; (puro) cigar
cigoto M zygote
cigüeña F stork
cigüeñal M crankshaft
cilíndrico ADJ cylindrical
cilindro M cylinder
cima F summit
cimarrón -ona ADJ wild; MF runaway slave
címbalo M cymbal
cimbel M decoy
cimbrar VT to sway, to vibrate
cimentar VT (una casa) to lay the foundation of; (una victoria) to secure
cimiento M foundation
cinc M zinc
cincel M chisel
cincelar VT to chisel
cincha F cinch, girth
cinchar VT to cinch, to girth
cinco NUM five
cincuenta NUM fifty
cine M cinema, movies
cineasta MF filmmaker
cinematografía F cinematography, movie-making
cinematografiar[28] VI/VT to film
cinematográfico ADJ cinematographic; **industria cinematográfica** motion-picture industry
cinestesia F kinesthesia
cingalés -esa ADJ & MF Sri Lankan
cínico -ca ADJ cynical; MF cynic
cinismo M cynicism
cinta F (de adorno) ribbon; (adhesiva) tape; (cinematográfica) film; **— aislante** electrical tape; **— de vídeo** videotape; **— magnetofónica** recording tape; **— métrica** tape measure; **— rodante** treadmill; **— transportadora** conveyor belt
cinto M belt
cintura F (de persona) waist; (de cosa) middle
cinturón M belt; **— de seguridad** safety belt
ciprés M cypress
circo M circus
circonio M zirconium
circuitería F circuitry
circuito M circuit; **— cerrado** closed circuit; **— impreso** circuit board; **— integrado** integrated circuit
circulación F (de sangre, de bienes) circulation; (de vehículos) traffic; **poner en —** to circulate

circular VI to circulate; **hay que — por la derecha** you have to drive on the right; F circular letter
circulatorio ADJ circulatory; **problemas —s** cardiovascular problems; **atasco —** traffic jam
círculo M circle; **— vicioso** vicious circle
circuncidar VT to circumcise
circundante ADJ surrounding
circundar VT to surround
circunferencia F circumference
circunlocución F circumlocution
circunscribir[74] VT to circumscribe
circunspecto ADJ circumspect
circunstancia F circumstance
circunstancial ADJ circumstantial
cirio M candle
cirro M cirrus
cirrosis F cirrhosis
ciruela F plum; **— pasa** prune
ciruelo M plum tree
cirugía F surgery; **— de corazón abierto** open-heart surgery; **— plástica/estética** plastic surgery, cosmetic surgery
cirujano -na MF surgeon
cisne M swan
cisterna F cistern
cita F (romántica) date; (con el médico) appointment; (textual) quotation, quote; **— a ciegas** blind date; **darse —** to meet
citación F citation, summons
citar VT (a un testigo) to summon; (a un autor) to cite, to quote; **—se con** (el médico) to make an appointment with; (un amigo) to make a date with
citología F (ciencia) cell biology, cytology; (toma de células vaginales) pap smear
cítrico ADJ citric; M citrus
ciudad F city
ciudadanía F citizenship
ciudadano -na MF citizen
Ciudad del Vaticano F Vatican City
ciudadela F citadel
cívico ADJ civic
civil ADJ (no criminal, no religioso) civil; (no militar) civilian
civilidad F civility
civilización F civilization
civilizador ADJ civilizing
civilizar[47] VT to civilize; **—se** to become civilized
cizalla F metal shears
cizaña F **sembrar —** to sow discord
clamar VT/VI to demand; **— por** to clamor for
clamor M clamor, outcry
clamorear VI/VT to shout
clamoreo M shouting
clamoroso ADJ clamorous
clan M clan
clandestino ADJ clandestine
claqué M tap dance
clara F egg white; **— de huevo** egg white
claraboya F skylight
clarear VI (aclararse) to become clear; (amanecer) to grow light; (desenturbiarse) to thin; VT to illuminate; **—se** to grow light
claridad F (de ideas) clarity; (de la luz) brightness, lightness
clarificar[30] VT to clarify, to clear
clarín M bugle
clarinete M clarinet
clarividente MF & ADJ clairvoyant
claro ADJ clear; (franco) straightforward; (iluminado) light, bright; **azul —** light blue; **a las claras** clearly; ADV clearly; INTERJ of course! M (espacio) gap; (en un bosque) clearing; **— de luna** moonlight
clase F (tipo) kind, sort; (grupo social, sesión docente, alumnado) class; (aula) classroom; **— alta** upper class; **— media** middle class; **— obrera** working class; **— turista** economy class; **dar —** to teach a class; **toda — de** all sorts of
clasicismo M classicism
clásico ADJ (destacado, consabido) classic; (de un período histórico) classical; M classic
clasificación F (taxonómica) classification; (deportiva) qualification; **— descendiente** descending sort
clasificado M want ad
clasificar[30] VT (ordenar) to classify; (en deportes) to qualify; **—se para** to qualify for; **—se segundo** to come in second
claustro M cloister; **— de profesores** university faculty
claustrofobia F claustrophobia
claustrofóbico ADJ claustrophobic
cláusula F clause
clausura F closing
clausurar VT (una sesión) to bring to a close, to conclude; (una tienda) to close [down]
clavadista MF diver
clavado ADV exactly; M (de clavos) nailing; (en una piscina) dive; **tirarse un —** to dive
clavar VT (perforar con un clavo) to nail, to drive a nail into; (pinchar) to stick, to poke; **—le la mirada / los ojos a alguien** to stare at someone; **— los frenos** to stomp on the brakes; **me clavaron** I got a raw deal
clave F (sistema de signos) code; (tabla de correspondencias) key; (signo musical) clef; (clavicémbalo) harpsichord; (de mapa) legend; **— de fa** bass clef; **— de seguridad** password; **— de sol** treble clef; ADJ key
clavel M carnation
clavetear VT to put pegs on
clavicémbalo M harpsichord
clavícula F collarbone, clavicle

clavija F (de guitarra) peg; (de enchufe) pin
clavo M (pieza de metal) nail; (capullo) clove; (de zapato) spike; **dar en el** — to hit the nail on the head
claxon M car horn
clearing M clearing
clemencia F clemency, mercy
clemente ADJ forgiving, merciful
cleptomanía F kleptomania
cleptómano -na MF kleptomaniac
clerecía F (funciones) ministry; (clérigos) clergy
clerical ADJ clerical
clérigo M clergyman, minister
clero M clergy
clic M click; **hacer** — to click; **hacer doble** — to double-click
cliché M (placa fotográfica) photographic plate; (expresión muy usada) cliché
cliente MF, **clienta** F (de un profesional) client; (de un negocio) customer; (de un restaurante) patron; (de un hotel) guest
clientela F clientele, customer base
clientelismo M patronage
clima M climate
climático ADJ climatic; **cambio** — climate change
climatización F air conditioning
clímax M climax
clinch M clinch
clínica F clinic
clínico ADJ clinical
clip M paper clip
cloaca F sewer
clon M clone
clonación F cloning
clonaje M cloning
clonar VT to clone
cloquear VI to cluck
cloqueo M cluck, clucking
clorhidrato M hydrochloride; — **de Ritalina** Ritalin hydrochloride
cloro M chlorine
clorofila F chlorophyll
cloroformo M chloroform
cloruro M chloride
club M club (también palo de golf); — **nocturno** nightclub
coacción F compulsion, coercion; **bajo** — under duress
coagulación F (de sangre) clotting; (por productos químicos) coagulation
coagulante M coagulant
coagular VI (con productos químicos) to coagulate; (sangre) to clot
coágulo M clot
coalición F coalition
coartada F alibi
coartar VT (una libertad) to restrict; (a una persona) to inhibit; (la creatividad) to strangle
cobalto M cobalt
cobarde ADJ cowardly; MF coward
cobardía F cowardice
cobertizo M shed
cobertor M cover
cobertura F (de nieve, aérea) cover; (de seguros, noticias, televisión) coverage; — **extendida** extended coverage
cobija F (cubierta) cover; (manta) blanket
cobijar VT to shelter; — **se** to seek shelter
cobra F cobra
cobrador -ora MF (persona) collector; M (perro) retriever
cobranza F collection
cobrar VT (impuestos) to collect; (una factura) to charge; (un cheque) to cash; (el sueldo) to earn; (víctimas) to claim; — **al entregar** to collect on delivery; — **ánimo** to take heart; — **caro** to charge a lot; — **de más** to overcharge; — **de menos** to undercharge; — **valor** to gain importance; **a** — receivable; **vas a** — you're in for it
cobre M (elemento) copper; (utensilios) copper utensils
cobrizo ADJ copper-colored
cobro M collection, charge; — **excesivo** overcharge
coca F (planta, hoja) coca; (cocaína) *fam* coke
cocaína F cocaine
cóccix M coccyx
cocear VI/VT to kick
cocer[34] VI/VT (huevos) to boil; (verduras) to cook; (cerámica) to fire; — **al vapor** to steam; **a medio** — half-cooked; **romper a** — to break into a boil; **¿qué se cuece aquí?** what's up?
coche M (automóvil, vagón) car; (autobús) coach; (vehículo tirado por caballerías) carriage; — **bomba** car bomb; — **cama** sleeper; — **-comedor** dining car; — **de bebé** stroller, baby carriage; — **de bomberos** fire engine; — **de choque** bumper car; — **de golf** golf cart; — **de línea** city bus; — **deportivo** sports car; — **fúnebre** hearse; **ir en** — to go by car, to drive; **pasear en** — to go on a drive
cochera F carport
cochinada F (asquerosidad) filthy action; (maldad) dirty trick
cochinilla F woodlouse
cochino -na ADJ filthy; MF pig
cocido M stew
cociente M quotient; — **intelectual** IQ
cocina F (habitación) kitchen; (electrodoméstico) range, stove; (arte) cuisine, cookery
cocinar VI/VT to cook; (tramar) to cook up
cocinero -ra MF cook
cócker MF cocker spaniel

coco M (fruto) coconut; (cabeza) *fam* dome; (fantasma) bogeyman; **comerse el —** to get all worked up
cocodrilo M crocodile
cóctel M (bebida) cocktail, mixed drink; (fiesta) cocktail party
codazo M jab with the elbow; **dar —s** to elbow
codear VI/VT to elbow, to jab; **—se** to nudge one another; **—se con** to rub elbows with
codeína F codeine
codicia F (avaricia) greed; (deseo sexual) lust
codiciar VT (una cosa) to covet; (a una persona) to lust after
codicioso ADJ covetous, greedy
codificación F coding, encoding
codificar[30] VT (mensaje) to codify, to encrypt; (programa de computadora) to code
código M code; **— abierto** open code; **— de acceso** access code; **— de barras** bar code; **— de país** country code; **— fuente** source code; **— genético** genetic code; **— impositivo** tax code; **— postal** zip code
codo M elbow; **— a —** side by side; **— de tenista** tennis elbow; **empinar el —** to drink too much; **hablar por los —s** to talk one's head off; **hasta los —s** up to one's elbows
codorniz F quail
coeficiente M coefficient; **— de inteligencia** intelligence quotient
coerción F coercion
coetáneo ADJ contemporary
coexistencia F coexistence; **— pacífica** peaceful coexistence
cofre M coffer
coger[45] VT (a un criminal, una pelota) to catch; (con las manos) to grasp; (flores) to gather; to pick; (a un empleado) to hire; (una emisora) to receive; (cosas del suelo) to pick up; (espacio) to take up; (un pez) to land, to catch; (un camino, tren, curso) to take; **— por/de sorpresa** to catch by surprise; **— el sueño** to fall asleep; **— hacia el castillo** to turn toward the castle; **—le miedo a algo** to become scared of something; **—le el tranquillo a algo** to get into the swing of things; **—se un resfriado** to come down with a cold; **coge y le dice** he up and says
cognado ADJ & M cognate
cognitivo ADJ cognitive
cogollo M heart
cogote M neck
cohabitar VI (amigos) to live [with]; (una pareja) to cohabitate
cohecho M bribe
coheredero -ra MF joint heir
coherencia F (consecuencia) consistency; (lógica) coherence
coherente ADJ (consecuente) consistent; (lógico) coherent; (con significado) meaningful; **lo que dices no es —** you're not making any sense
cohesión F cohesion
cohesivo ADJ coherent
cohete M rocket
cohetería F rocketry
cohibición F inhibition
cohibido ADJ inhibited, self-conscious
cohibir VT to inhibit
coincidencia F coincidence
coincidir VI to coincide
coito M coitus
cojear VI to limp; **saber de qué pie cojea alguien** to know someone's weaknesses
cojera F limp
cojín M cushion
cojinete M bushing; **— de bolas** ball bearing
cojo ADJ lame, crippled
cok M coke
col F cabbage; **—es de Bruselas** Brussels sprouts
cola F (de perro, ave, avión) tail; (de vestido) train; (hilera de gente) line; (secuencia de datos o programas) queue; (pegamento) glue; **— de caballo** ponytail; **hacer —** to stand in line; **no pegar ni con —** not to go together; **traer —** to have consequences
colaboración F collaboration
colaborador -ora MF (con el gobierno) collaborator; (de periódico) contributor
colaborar VI to collaborate; (con un periódico) to contribute
colación F **sacar a —** to bring up
colacionar VT to collate
colador M (para té) strainer; (para verduras) colander
colágeno M collagen
colapso M (de puente, edificio) collapse; (de nervios) breakdown; (de mercado) crash
colar[5] VT (té) to strain; (metal líquido) to pour; VI to go through, to slip through; **esa excusa no va a —** that excuse won't wash; **—se en una fiesta** to crash a party
colateral ADJ collateral
colcha F bedspread
colchón M (para dormir) mattress; (para emergencias) cushion
colchoneta F mat
colear VI (un perro) to wag the tail; (un tema) to be pending; (un auto) to fishtail
colección F collection
coleccionar VT to collect
coleccionista MF collector
colecta F charity collection
colectividad F collective, community
colectivo M (grupo) collective; (autobús) *Am* bus
colector M (de aguas negras) sewer; (eléctrico) collector; (de coche) manifold
colega MF colleague

colegio M (escuela privada) private school; (escuela primaria) elementary school; (centro de educación secundaria) high school; (asociación profesional) association, college
colegir[14] VI to gather
cólera F rage, wrath; **montar en —** to fly into a rage; M cholera
colérico ADJ irritable, choleric
colesterol M cholesterol
coleta F pigtail
coletilla F tag
coleto M **decir para su —** to say to oneself
colgadero M hanger; ADJ hanging
colgado ADJ high and dry
colgadura F drapery; **—s** hangings
colgante ADJ hanging; M pendant
colgar[42] VT (suspender, ahorcar) to hang; (un teléfono, un abrigo) to hang up; VI (un espejo) to hang; (un andrajo) to dangle; (un asunto) to be pending; **esa falda te cuelga por atrás** that dress hangs down in the back; **—se [un ordenador]** to crash; **—se de** to get hooked on; **—se del teléfono** to tarry on the phone
colibrí M hummingbird
cólico M colic
coliflor F cauliflower
colilla F cigarette butt
colina F hill, knoll
colindante ADJ neighboring
colindar VI **— con** to border [on], to adjoin
colirio M eyedrops
coliseo M coliseum
colisión F collision
collage M collage
collar M (de perlas) necklace; (de perro) collar; **— antipulgas** flea collar
collera F horse collar
collie M collie
colmar VT (un vaso) to fill; (una demanda) to satisfy; **— de alabanzas** to lavish praise upon
colmena F beehive
colmillo M (de persona) eyetooth, cuspid; (de elefante) tusk; (de víbora) fang
colmo M **— de la locura** height of folly; **¡eso es el —!** that takes the cake; **para —** to top it all
colocación F (ubicación) placement; (puesto) position
colocar[30] VT (poner, encontrar lugar para) to place; (casar) to marry off; (invertir) to invest; **—se** (encontrar empleo) to get a job; (ubicarse) to place oneself
coloide M colloid
Colombia F Colombia
colombiano -na ADJ & MF Colombian
colon M colon
colón M (moneda) colon
colonia F (territorio, grupo de insectos) colony; (comunidad de inmigrantes) community, settlement; (vivienda) development; (perfume) cologne
colonial ADJ colonial
colonización F colonization
colonizador -ora MF colonist
colonizar[47] VT to colonize, to settle
colono -na MF (habitante de una colonia) colonist, settler; (arrendatario) tenant farmer
colonoscopia F colonoscopy
coloquial ADJ colloquial
coloquio M colloquium
color M (tono) color; (pintura) paint; (maquillaje) rouge; (de naipes) flush; **—es primarios** primary colors; **a todo —** full color; **persona de —** person of color
coloración F coloring
colorado ADJ & M red; **ponerse —** to blush
colorante ADJ & M coloring
coloreado ADJ colored; M coloring
colorear VT to color
colorete M rouge
colorido M (de un caballo) coloring; (de un comentario, paisaje) color; ADJ colorful
colosal ADJ (grande) colossal; (estupendo) wonderful
colostomía F colostomy
columbrar VT to glimpse
columna F column; **— de dirección** steering column; **— vertebral** spinal column, backbone
columnista MF columnist
columpiar VI/VT to swing
columpio M swing
colza F (planta) rape; (aceite) rapeseed oil
coma F (signo) comma; M (falta de conciencia) coma
comadre F (mujer chismosa) gossip; (partera) midwife; (parienta) godmother of one's child
comadreja F weasel
comadrona F (mujer chismosa) gossip; (partera) midwife
comandancia F command
comandante MF (rango militar) major; (militar que ejerce el mando) commander; **— en jefe** commander in chief
comandar VT to command; **— un avión** to pilot an airplane
comando M (grupo militar) commando; (orden dada al ordenador) command
comarca F district
comatoso ADJ comatose
comba F (de una pared) bulge; (de madera) warp; **saltar a la —** to jump rope
combar VI (una pared) to sag; (madera) to warp; (trayectoria de pelota) to curve
combate M combat, fight; **fuera de —** out of combat / the competition
combatiente MF combatant

combatir VI/VT to combat
combativo ADJ combative
combinación F (mezcla) combination; (billete) transfer ticket
combinar VT to combine; **—se para hacer algo** to agree to do something; **esos colores no combinan** those colors don't match
combo M combo
combustible ADJ combustible; M fuel
combustión F combustion
comedero M trough
comedia F (obra teatral) comedy; (farsa) farce; **— de situación** situation comedy, sitcom; **hacer la — de** to play the part of
comediante MF comedian
comedido ADJ moderate; *Am* obliging
comedirse[9] VI to show restraint; **— a hacer algo** *RP* to volunteer to do something
comedor M (habitación) dining room; (de empresa) cafeteria
comensal MF [fellow] diner
comentador -ora MF commentator
comentar VI/VT to comment [on], to remark [on]
comentario M (análisis) commentary; (observación) comment, remark
comentarista MF commentator
comenzar[48] VI/VT to begin, to start; **— a comer** to begin to eat; **— preguntando** to begin by asking
comer VI/VT to eat; (al mediodía) to have lunch; (en ajedrez) to take; (en el juego de damas) to jump; **dar de —** to feed; **sin —lo ni beberlo** through no fault of one's own; **—se** (corroer) to eat away; (terminar la comida) to eat up; **—se las eses** to drop one's esses; **—se las palabras** to eat one's words; **—se un semáforo en rojo** to run a red light
comercial ADJ & M commercial
comercialización F marketing, merchandising
comercializar[47] VT (volver comercial) to commercialize; (vender) to market, to merchandise
comerciante MF merchant, trader, dealer
comerciar VI to trade
comercio M commerce, trade; **— electrónico** e-business; **— exterior** foreign trade; **— minorista** retail trade; **— mayorista** wholesaler
comestible ADJ edible; M PL groceries
cometa M (cuerpo celeste) comet; F (juguete) kite
cometer VT to commit
cometido M purpose, objective
comezón F itch, itching; **tener —** to itch
cómic M comic book
comicios M PL polls
cómico -ca ADJ comic, comical; MF comedian
comida F (ocasión) meal; (alimento) food; (al mediodía) lunch; **— basura** junk food; **— macrobiótica** health food; **— rápida** fast food
comience, comienza *ver* comenzar
comienzo M beginning; **a —s de** toward the beginning of; **al —** at first, initially; **desde un/el —** from the start
comilla F quotation mark; **entre —s** in quotes
comilón -ona MF big eater; F binge
comino M cumin; **me importa un —** *fam* I don't give a hoot; **no vale un —** *fam* it's not worth a hoot
comisaría F **— de policía** police station, precinct
comisario -ria MF (comisionado) commissioner; (jefe de policía) police chief
comisión F (acción de cometer, porcentaje ganado) commission; (comité) committee
comisionar VT to commission
comistrajo M bad food
comisura F **— de los labios** corner of the mouth
comité M committee
comitiva F retinue
como ADV (del mismo modo que) as, like; **ella pinta — yo** she paints like I do; (aproximadamente) about; **pesa — diez kilos** it weighs about ten kilos; CONJ (puesto que) since; **— no tenemos dinero** since we have no money; **— no me pagues** if you don't pay me; **era — que muy viejo** he was, like, real old; **— que te voy a permitir** as if I would let you; **— quieras** as you please; **— si** as if; **¡— si me lo fuera a creer!** a likely story!
cómo ADV INTERR & PRON (de qué manera) how; (¿perdón?) excuse me? what? **¡— brillan las estrellas!** how the stars are shining! **¡— no!** of course! **¿a — me lo vende?** what does that cost?
cómoda F chest of drawers, dresser, bureau
comodidad F (cualidad) comfort; (cosa cómoda) convenience; **—es** amenities
comodín M joker, wild card
cómodo ADJ (mueble) comfortable; (horario) convenient; (persona) lazy
Comoras F PL Comoros
compactar VT to compact
compacto ADJ compact
compadecer[35] VT to pity; **—se de** to take pity on
compadre M (amigo) pal, crony; (pariente) godfather of one's child
compañero -ra MF (camarada) companion; (de un zapato) mate; **— de clase** classmate; **— de cuarto** roommate; **— de equipo** teammate
compañía F company; **— de importación y exportación** import-export company; **— fantasma** bogus company; **— recién establecida** start-up; **en — de** in the

company of
comparable ADJ comparable
comparación F comparison
comparar VI/VT to compare; **—se con** to compare [oneself] with
comparativo ADJ comparative
comparecencia F appearance
comparecer[35] VI to appear
compartimiento M compartment
compartir VT (bienes) to share; (tiempo) to divide
compás M (instrumento de geometría) compass; (ritmo) beat; (espacio entre barras) measure, bar; (división de música) time signature; **marcar el —** to beat time
compasión F compassion
compasivo ADJ compassionate, sympathetic
compatibilidad F compatibility
compatible ADJ compatible
compatriota MF compatriot
compeler VT to compel
compendiar VT to summarize
compendio M digest, condensation
compenetración F bonding
compensación F compensation
compensar VT (un daño) to compensate; (un gasto) to offset; **compensa su falta de inteligencia con mucha disciplina** he makes up for his lack of intelligence with a lot of discipline; **te voy a — por esto** I'll make it up to you
competencia F (pugna, competición, competidores) competition; (cualidad de competente) competence
competente ADJ competent
competición F athletic competition, meet
competidor -ora ADJ competing; MF (comercial) competitor; (deportivo) athlete, participant
competir[9] VI to compete, to vie
competitividad F competitiveness
competitivo ADJ competitive
compilador M compiler
compilar VT to compile
compinche M chum, crony
compita, compite, compitiendo, compitiera, compitiese *ver* competir
complacencia F satisfaction
complacer[36] VT to please, to gratify; **—se [en]** to take pleasure [in]
complaciente ADJ (que complace) obliging; (que consiente) indulgent
complejidad F complexity
complejo ADJ complex; M complex; **— de inferioridad** inferiority complex
complementar VT to complement, to supplement
complementario ADJ complementary
complemento M complement; **— alimenticio** dietary supplement; **— directo** direct object; **— indirecto** indirect object; **—s** fringe benefits
completar VT (terminar) to complete; (en fútbol americano) to complete [passes]; **—se** to be completed
completo ADJ (terminado) complete; (lleno) full; **hoy tenemos el —** today we have a full house; **por —** completely
complexión F build
complicación F complication
complicado ADJ complicated
complicar[30] VT to complicate; **—le a alguien la vida** to give someone trouble
cómplice MF accomplice
complicidad F complicity
complot M plot
compondrá, compondría *ver* componer
componenda F (arreglo provisional) quick fix; (arreglo ilegal) shady deal
componente ADJ & M component
componer[56, 74] VT (un grupo) to compose, to make up; (imprenta) to set; (un coche descompuesto) to fix; (música) to compose; **—se de** to be composed of; **componérselas** to deal with one's problems alone
componga, compongo *ver* componer
comportamiento M conduct, behavior
comportarse VI/VT to conduct oneself, to behave
composición F composition
compositor -ora MF composer
compostura F (arreglo) repair; (dignidad) composure
compra F purchase; **— apalancada** LBO; **ir de —s** to go shopping; **— hostil** hostile takeover
comprador -ora MF (comercial) buyer, purchaser; (en una tienda) shopper
comprar VT to buy, to purchase; **compró su silencio** he gave her hush money
comprender VT (entender) to understand, to comprehend; (abarcar) to cover, to include
comprensible ADJ comprehensible, understandable
comprensión F (intelectual) understanding, comprehension; (emocional) sympathy, understanding
comprensivo ADJ understanding
compresa F compress
compresión F compression; **— de archivos** file compression
comprimido ADJ compressed; M tablet
comprimir VT to compress
comprobación F verification, check
comprobante M proof; **— de compra** proof of purchase
comprobar[5] VT (verificar) to verify, to check; (probar) to prove; (darse cuenta) to realize
comprometer VT (obligar) to commit; (poner

en peligro) to jeopardize, to compromise; **—se** (prometer) to promise; (tomar partido) to commit oneself; (para casarse) to get engaged

comprometido ADJ (obligado) obligated; (arriesgado) risky; (implicado) compromised; (con planes de casarse) engaged; (entregado, dedicado) committed, engaged

compromiso M (ideología, obligación, promesa) commitment; (acuerdo) agreement; (cita) appointment, engagement; (de matrimonio) engagement; (solución negociada) compromise; **no me pongas en —** don't compromise me; **sin — de compra** without obligation to buy

comprueba, compruebe *ver* comprobar

compuerta F sluice gate, floodgate

compuesto ADJ (ojos, tiempo, interés) compound; **estar — de** to be composed of; M compound

compuesto *ver* componer

compulsión F compulsion

compulsivo ADJ compulsive

compungirse[46] VI to feel sorry

computación F computing

computadora F computer; **— personal** personal computer; **— de escritorio** desktop computer; **— de mano** palmtop, handheld computer; **— digital** digital computer; **— portátil** laptop computer; **— torre** tower model

computar VT to compute

computarizar[47] VT to computerize

cómputo M computation

comulgar[40] VI (recibir el sacramento) to take Communion; (estar de acuerdo) to agree

común ADJ common; **en —** in common; **por lo —** generally; **el — de las gentes** the majority of the people

comuna F commune

comunicable ADJ communicable

comunicación F (interacción) communication; (ponencia) presentation; **se nos cortó la —** we got disconnected

comunicado M communiqué, report

comunicar[30] VI/VT to communicate; **—se con** (entenderse) to communicate with; (ponerse en contacto con) to reach; (desembocar en) to open into

comunicativo ADJ communicative

comunidad F community; **— internauta** Internet community; **— virtual** virtual community

comunión F communion

comunismo M communism

comunista ADJ & MF communist

comunitario ADJ (en común) communal; **espíritu —** community spirit; **presupuesto —** European Union budget

con PREP with; **— lo que come, tendría que estar obesa** given what she eats, she should be obese; **— mucho** by far; **— que le digas alcanza** just telling him is enough; **— tal [de] que** provided that; **— todo** all things considered

conato M attempt

concavidad F hollow

cóncavo ADJ concave

concebible ADJ conceivable

concebir[9] VT (engendrar) to conceive; (entender) to conceive of

conceder VT (dar) to grant; (admitir) to concede, to allow

concejal MF councilor

concejo M council

concentración F (densidad, atención, cantidad) concentration; (manifestación) rally, demonstration

concentrar VT to concentrate; **—se** (prestar atención) to concentrate, to focus; (manifestar) to rally

concepción F conception

concepto M (idea) concept; (artificio) conceit

conceptual ADJ conceptual

concernir[73] VT to concern

concertación F agreement

concertar[1] VT (arreglar) to arrange; (concretar) to finalize; (planear) to concert; **—se** to agree

concesión F (admisión) concession; (otorgamiento) grant; (permiso comercial) franchise

concesionario M dealership

concha F shell

conchabarse VI to conspire

conciba, concibe, concibiendo, concibiera, concibiese *ver* concebir

conciencia F (moral) conscience; (mental) consciousness, awareness; **tomar — de** to come to grips with; **— de marca** brand awareness

concienzudo ADJ conscientious, thorough

concierto M (música) concert; (armonía) harmony; (acuerdo) agreement

conciliación F conciliation

conciliar VT (personas) to conciliate; (ideas) to reconcile; **— el sueño** to fall sleep

concilio M council

concisión F conciseness

conciso ADJ concise, brief

conciudadano -na MF fellow citizen

concluir[19] VI/VT to conclude

conclusión F conclusion

concluya, concluye, concluyendo, concluyera, concluyese *ver* concluir

concluyente ADJ conclusive

concomitante ADJ attendant

concordancia F agreement

concordar[5] VI to agree

concordia F concord
concretamente ADV specifically; **tiene un perro, — un chihuahua** he has a dog, a chihuahua, to be precise
concretar VT (cerrar) to finalize; (especificar) to be specific about; (realizar) to realize; **—se a** to focus on
concreto ADJ concrete; **en —** specifically; M *Am* concrete
concubina F concubine
concurrencia F (reunión) gathering; (asistencia) attendance
concurrido ADJ well-attended
concurrir VI (confluir) to come together; (asistir) to attend
concursante MF contestant
concurso M (para un premio) contest; (en una licitación) call for bids; (para un puesto de trabajo) competitive examination; **— de belleza** beauty pageant
concusión F graft
concusionario -ria MF grafter
condado M county
conde M count
condecoración F decoration
condecorar VT to decorate
condena F (castigo) sentence; (crítica) condemnation; **¡qué —!** what a pain!
condenación F condemnation
condenado ADJ (perdido) damned; (sentenciado) sentenced; **está — a muerte** he's on death row
condenar VT (criticar) to condemn; (sentenciar) to sentence; **eso le condenó al fracaso** that doomed him to failure; **—se** to go to hell
condensación F condensation
condensar VT to condense
condesa F countess
condescendencia F (tolerancia) acquiescence; (superioridad) condescension
condescender[2] VI (acomodarse) to acquiesce; (dignarse) to condescend
condición F condition; **— social** social station; **a — de que** on the condition that; **condiciones** (físicas) condition; (de un contrato) terms, provisos
condicional ADJ & M conditional
condicionamiento M conditioning
condicionar VT to condition
condimentar VT to season
condimento M condiment, seasoning
condiscípulo -la MF classmate
condolencias F PL condolences; **dar las —** to offer one's condolences
condolerse[6] VI to offer one's condolences
condominio M condominium
cóndor M condor
conducción F (de electricidad) conduction; (de un difunto o prisionero) transport
conducente ADJ conducive
conducir[38] VT (a un grupo) to lead; (una orquesta, electricidad) to conduct; (un coche) to drive, to steer; **—se** to behave
conducta F (moral) conduct, behavior; (biológica) behavior; **— de alto riesgo** high-risk behavior
conducto M (de agua) conduit; (anatómico) duct; **— de aire** airway; **por — de** through
conductor -ora ADJ (de electricidad) conductive; M (de electricidad) conductor; MF (de coches) driver; (en baloncesto) point guard
conductual ADJ behavioral
conduje, condujera, condujese *ver* conducir
conectar VI/VT to connect
conectividad F connectivity
conector M connector; **— en serie** serial connector
conejillo M **— de Indias** guinea pig
conejo M rabbit
conexión F connection
confabulación F collusion
confección F (fabricación de ropa) dressmaking, tailoring; (calidad) workmanship; **de —** ready-made
confeccionar VT (productos) to manufacture; (ropa) to tailor, to sew
confederación F confederation
confederado -da ADJ & MF confederate
confederar VI to form a confederacy
conferencia F (discurso) lecture; (reunión) conference; **— de prensa** press conference; **dar una —** to give a lecture
conferenciante MF lecturer, speaker
conferenciar VI to confer
conferencista MF lecturer, speaker
conferir[8] VT to confer, to bestow; (un título) to confer
confesar[1] VI/VT to confess
confesión F confession
confesionario M confessional
confesor -ora MF confessor
confiabilidad F reliability
confiable ADJ reliable
confiado ADJ (seguro de sí) confident; (crédulo) trusting
confianza F confidence, trust; **en —** in confidence; **tener —** to be confident; **tener — en** to have confidence in; **tomar —s** to be overly familiar with
confianzudo ADJ overfamiliar
confiar[28] VT (un secreto) to confide; (un valor, bien) to entrust; **— en** to rely on; **confío que Dios me proteja** I trust that God will protect me
confidencia F confidence
confidencial ADJ confidential; **altamente —** top-secret

confidente MF (amigo) confidant; M (mueble) love seat
confiesa, confiese *ver* confesar
configuración F configuration
configurar VT to configure (también computadoras); **—se** to take shape
confinamiento M confinement
confinar VT to confine
confines M PL bounds, confines
confirmación F confirmation
confirmar VT to confirm
confiscación F (de una propiedad) confiscation, seizure; (de un monto) forfeiture
confiscar[30] VT to confiscate
confitar VT to candy
confite M candy
confitería F confectionery
confitura F confection
conflictivo ADJ (persona, tema) contentious; (región) volatile
conflicto M conflict
confluencia F (de calles) junction; (de ríos) confluence
conformación F creation, establishment
conformar VT to adapt; **—se** to go along; **—se con** to settle for
conforme ADJ in agreement, content; **— a** in accordance with; CONJ **— amanece** as dawn breaks
conformidad F conformity, agreement; **estar de/en — con** to be in accordance with
conformismo M conformity
confort M comfort
confortable ADJ comfortable
confortar VT to comfort
confraternidad F fraternity, fellowship
confraternizar[47] VI to fraternize
confrontación F confrontation
confrontar VT (a un enemigo) to confront; (dos listas) to compare
confundido ADJ confused, mixed-up
confundir VT to confuse, to perplex, to baffle; **—se** (personas) to become confused; (cosas) to mingle
confusión F (mental) confusion; (de cosas) clutter, disarray
confuso ADJ (que no comprende, desordenado) confused; (difícil de comprender) confusing
congelación F freezing; **— salarial** pay freeze
congelado ADJ frozen
congelador M freezer
congelar VT to freeze
congeniar VI **— con** to get along with
congénito ADJ congenital
congestión F congestion
conglomeración F conglomeration
conglomerado M conglomeration
Congo M Congo
congoja F anguish, grief
congoleño -ña ADJ & MF Congolese
congregación F (feligreses) congregation; (orden) order
congregar[40] VI to congregate
congresista MF (legislador) member of Congress; (asistente a un congreso) conference attendee, conventioneer
congreso M (cuerpo legislativo, edificio) congress; (reunión periódica) conference, convention
congresual ADJ congressional
congruencia F congruence
conífera F conifer
conjetura F conjecture, surmise
conjeturar VT to conjecture, to surmise
conjugación F conjugation
conjugar[40] VT to conjugate
conjunción F conjunction
conjuntamente ADV jointly
conjuntivitis F conjunctivitis, pinkeye
conjunto M (grupo de cosas) set; (totalidad) total, aggregate; (de ropa) outfit; **— musical** ensemble; **en —** as a whole, all told; ADJ joint
conjuración F conspiracy
conjurado -da MF conspirator
conjurar VT (conspirar) to conspire, to plot; (evitar, cancelar) to ward off
conjuro M incantation, spell
conllevar VT to entail, to involve
conmemoración F commemoration
conmemorar VT to commemorate
conmemorativo ADJ commemorative, memorial
conmigo PRON with me
conmiseración F commiseration
conmoción F commotion; **— cerebral** brain concussion, cerebral concussion
conmovedor ADJ moving, touching
conmover[6] VT to move, to touch
conmovido ADJ moved, touched
conmutador M switch
conmutar VT to commute
connatural ADJ inborn
connotación F connotation
cono M cone
conocedor -ora ADJ who know[s], aware; **muy — de la situación** well aware of the situation; MF connoisseur, expert
conocer[35] VT to know (también en sentido carnal); (reconocer) to recognize; (tratar por primera vez) to meet; **— el paño** to know the ropes; **se conoce que** it is clear that
conocido -da ADJ well-known; MF acquaintance
conocimiento M knowledge, acquaintance; **— de embarque** bill of lading; **perder el —** to lose consciousness; **poner en —** to inform; **—s** knowledge
conozca, conozco *ver* conocer
conque CONJ so

conquista F conquest
conquistador -ora MF conqueror; ADJ conquering
conquistar VT (un terreno) to conquer; (el amor de alguien) to win
consabido ADJ habitual
consagración F consecration
consagrar VT (declarar consagrado) to consecrate; (dedicar) to devote
consciente ADJ conscious; **— del problema** aware of the problem
conscribir VT to draft
consecución F attainment, achievement
consecuencia F (hecho que resulta de otro) consequence; (cualidad de consecuente) consistency; **a — de** as a result of
consecuente ADJ (que se sigue de) consequent, logical; (fiel en sus actos) consistent
consecutivo ADJ consecutive
conseguible ADJ obtainable
conseguir[12] VT (un derecho) to attain, to get; (un objetivo) to achieve; (un puesto de trabajo) to land, to get; **— hacer algo** to manage to do something
consejero -ra MF (asesor) adviser; (miembro del consejo) board member; **consejero -ra delegado -da** *Esp* CEO
consejo M (opinión) counsel, advice; (comité) council; **— de guerra** court-martial
consenso M consensus
consentimiento M consent, acquiescence
consentir[8] VT (permitir) to consent to, to acquiesce to; (mimar) to pamper, to indulge; **— en** to permit
conserje MF (limpiador) janitor; (portero) superintendent; (recepcionista) hotel clerk
conserva F canned food; **en —** canned
conservación F conservation, preservation
conservador -ora MF (en política) conservative; (de museo) curator; ADJ (de tradiciones) conservative; (de alimentos) preservative
conservadurismo M conservatism
conservante M preservative
conservar VT (guardar) to keep; (mantener) to retain; (preservar) to preserve; (ahorrar) to conserve
conservatorio M conservatory
considerable ADJ considerable
considerablemente ADV significantly
consideración F consideration; **de —** considerable; **tomar/tener en —** to take into consideration
considerado ADJ considerate, thoughtful
considerar VT to consider
consiga *ver* conseguir
consigna F (eslogan) motto, watchword; (orden) order
consignación F consignment; **a/en —** on consignment
consignar VT to consign
consignatario -ria MF consignee
consigo PRON with oneself/himself/herself/themselves
consigo, consiguiendo, consiguiera, consiguiese *ver* conseguir
consiguiente ADJ consequent; **por —** consequently
consistencia F consistency
consistente ADJ (firme) consistent; **— de** consisting of
consistir VI **— en** to consist of
consocio -cia MF fellow member
consola F console; **— de juegos** game console
consolación F consolation
consolar[5] VT to console
consolidación F consolidation
consolidar VT to consolidate
consonante ADJ & F consonant
consorcio M consortium
consorte MF consort
conspicuo ADJ conspicuous
conspiración F conspiracy, plot
conspirador -ora MF conspirator, plotter
conspirar VI to conspire, to plot
constancia F (en el amor) constancy; (en el esfuerzo) perseverance; (en el trabajo) steadiness; (prueba) documentary proof
constante ADJ & F constant; **—s vitales** vital signs
constar VI to be stated; **aquí consta que me debes cien dólares** here it states that you owe me a hundred dollars; **— de** to consist of, to be composed of; **hacer —** to mention; **me consta que** I am aware that; **que conste** let it be known
constatar VT to verify
constelación F constellation
consternación F consternation, dismay
consternar VT to dismay
constipación F constipation
constipado ADJ *Esp* (resfriado) suffering from a cold; *Am* (seco de vientre) constipated; M *Esp* head cold
constitución F constitution
constitucional ADJ constitutional
constituir[19] VT to constitute
constitutivo ADJ (constituyente) constituent; (inherente) inherent; **— de un delito** which constitutes a crime
constituya, constituye *ver* constituir
constituyente ADJ constituent
constreñimiento M constraint
constreñir[11] VT (limitar) to constrain; (apretar) to constrict, to constrain
constricción F constriction
construcción F (actividad de construir, cosa construida) construction, building;

(gramatical) construction
constructivo ADJ constructive
constructor -ora MF builder; F construction company
construir[19] VI/VT to construct, to build
construye, construyendo, construyera, construyese *ver* construir
consuelo M consolation, comfort, solace
consuetudinario ADJ (acción) habitual; (derecho) common
cónsul MF consul
consulado M consulate
consulta F (acción de consultar) consultation; (pregunta) question; (consultorio) doctor's office
consultar VT to consult; **—lo con la almohada** to sleep on it
consultivo ADJ consultative
consultor ADJ consulting
consultoría F consulting firm
consultorio M doctor's office
consumado ADJ consummate, accomplished
consumar VT to consummate
consumidor -ora MF consumer; ADJ consuming
consumir VT to consume; **—se** (agua) to boil off; (neumático) to wear out; **—se de** to be consumed by
consumismo M consumerism
consumo M consumption
consunción F consumption
contabilidad F accounting, bookkeeping
contable MF accountant, bookkeeper
contactar VI/VT to contact; **—[se] con** to get in contact/touch with
contacto M contact; **— visual** eye contact; **en — con** in touch with
contado M **al —** in cash; ADJ **—s** few
contador -ora ADJ counting; M (de dinero) counter; (de electricidad) meter; **— Geiger** Geiger counter; MF accountant; **— público -ca** CPA
contaduría F accountant's office
contagiar VT to infect
contagio M (de enfermedad) contagion; (de ordenador) infection
contagioso ADJ contagious, catching, infectious
contaminación F (del agua, de la comida) contamination; (del medio ambiente) pollution; **— sonora** noise pollution
contaminante M contaminate
contaminar VT (agua, alimentos, cultura) to contaminate; (el medio ambiente) to pollute; **—se** (agua) to become contaminated; (medio ambiente) to become polluted
contar[5] VI/VT (medir una cantidad) to count; (decir historias) to tell; **el hotel cuenta con una piscina** the hotel has a swimming pool; **cuento con mi hermano** I count on my brother; **esto no cuenta** this doesn't count; **¿me lo vas a contar a mí?** you can say that again; **tienes que — el tiempo** you have to watch the time; M SG **cuentakilómetros** (marcador de kilómetros) odometer; (velocímetro) speedometer
contemplación F contemplation
contemplar VT (mirar, tener en cuenta) to contemplate; (consentir) to spoil; VI to contemplate
contemporáneo ADJ contemporary
contención F containment
contender[2] VI to contend
contendrá, contendría *ver* contener
contenedor M container
contenedorizar VT containerize
contener[58] VT (un líquido) to contain; (risa, lágrimas) to hold back; (entusiasmo) to restrain; (el aliento) to hold
contenga, contengo *ver* contener
contenido ADJ restrained; M content[s]
contentar VT to satisfy; **—se** to be satisfied
contento ADJ (conforme) content, contented; (feliz) happy; M contentment
conteo M count
contera F (de paraguas) tip; (de bolígrafo) cap
contestación F answer, reply
contestador M answering machine
contestar VT to answer; VI to talk back, to mouth off
contexto M context
contextura F (de un objeto) makeup; (de persona) build
contienda F (guerra) conflict; (encuentro deportivo) competition
contiene, contienes *ver* contener
contigo PRON with you
contiguo ADJ contiguous; **estar — a** to adjoin
continental ADJ continental
continente M (masa geográfica) continent; (opuesto a isla) mainland; ADJ continent
contingencia F contingency
contingente ADJ & M contingent
continuación F (de una acción) continuation; (de una película) sequel; (tenis) follow-through; **a —** after that; **a — hubo una guerra** there ensued a war
continuado ADJ continuing
continuar[26] VI/VT to continue
continuidad F continuity
continuo ADJ (ininterrumpido) continuous; (repetido) continual
contonearse VI (mujer) to swing one's hips; (hombre) to swagger
contoneo M (de mujer) swinging of the hips; (de hombre) swagger
contorno M (forma) outline, contour; (tamaño de árbol, persona) girth
contorsión F contortion

contra PREP against; M **los pro y los** — the pros and cons; **en** — against; F drawback; **llevarle la** — **a alguien** to contradict someone
contraatacar[30] VI/VT to counterattack
contraataque M (militar) counterattack; (en baloncesto) fast break
contrabajo M double bass; MF double bass player
contrabandear VI/VT to smuggle
contrabandista MF smuggler
contrabando M (actividad) smuggling; (mercancías) contraband; **hacer** — to smuggle
contracción F contraction
contrachapado M plywood
contractual ADJ contractual
contracultura F counterculture
contradecir[53, 74] VT to contradict
contradicción F contradiction
contradictorio ADJ contradictory
contraejemplo M counterexample
contraer[59] VT (enfermedad) to contract; (derechos) to limit; (deudas) to incur; — **matrimonio** to get married
contraespionaje M counterespionage
contrafuerte M (de muro) buttress; (de zapato) counter
contrahecho ADJ deformed
contralor M (control) comptroller, controller; (auditor) auditor
contralto M (voz) alto; MF (persona) alto
contramandar VT to countermand
contramedida F countermeasure
contraoferta F counteroffer
contraorden F countermand
contrapartida F compensation
contrapelo LOC ADV **a** — against the grain
contrapesar VT to counterbalance
contrapeso M counterbalance
contraproducente ADJ counterproductive
contrariar[28] VT to annoy; —**se** to get annoyed
contrariedad F (fastidio) annoyance; (dificultad) snag
contrario ADJ (opuesto) opposite; (discrepante) conflicting; **al** — on the contrary; **de lo** — otherwise; **llevar la contraria** to be contrary; **por el** — on the contrary; **soy** — **al doblaje de películas** I'm against the dubbing of films; **todo lo** — just the opposite
contrarrestar VT to counteract
contrarrevolución F counterrevolution
contraseña F password, watchword
contrastar VI/VT to contrast
contraste M contrast
contrata F contract
contratación F hiring; — **externa** outsourcing
contratar VT (a un empleado) to hire; (un servicio) to contract for; —**se** to be hired; — **y despedir** hire and fire
contratiempo M mishap
contratista MF contractor, builder
contrato M contract; — **de alquiler** rental agreement; **por** — by contract
contravenir[61] VT to contravene
contraventana F shutter
contribución F (regalo, participación) contribution; (impuesto) tax; — **alternativa mínima** alternative minimum tax
contribuir[19] VT to contribute
contribuya, contribuye, contribuyendo, contribuyera, contribuyese *ver* contribuir
contribuyente MF taxpayer
contrincante MF opponent
contrito ADJ contrite
control M (dominio, dirección) control; (contralor médico) checkup; (vigilancia) check; (puesto) checkpoint; — **de calidad** quality control; — **de daños** damage control; — **de la natalidad** birth control; — **fronterizo** border control; — **paternal** parental control; — **remoto** remote control; **bajo** — under control
controlador -ora MF comptroller; M driver; — **de impresora** printer driver
controlar VT (restringir) to control; (vigilar) to check on
controversia F controversy
controvertido ADJ controversial
contumacia F obstinacy
contumaz ADJ stubborn
contundente ADJ (argumento) forceful; (objeto) blunt; (prueba) convincing; (victoria) resounding
contusión F bruise, contusion
contuve, contuviera, contuviese *ver* contener
convalecencia F convalescence
convalecer[35] VI to convalesce
convaleciente MF convalescent
convección F convection
convencer[32] VT (por lógica) to convince; (por insistencia) to persuade
convencimiento M (creencia) conviction; (acción) convincing
convención F convention
convencional ADJ conventional
convendrá, convendría, convenga, convengo *ver* convenir
convenido ADJ agreed-upon
conveniencia F (algo cómodo) convenience; (algo aconsejable) desirability; **a su** — at your convenience
conveniente ADJ (cómodo) convenient; (aconsejable) advisable
convenio M agreement; — **colectivo** collective bargaining; — **comercial** business agreement

convenir[61] VI (ser apropiado) to be suitable; (llegar a un acuerdo) to agree
convento M convent
convergencia F convergence
converger[45] VI to converge
conversación F conversation; **trabar — con** to engage in a conversation with
conversar VI to converse
conversión F conversion; **— de dos puntos** two-point conversion
converso -sa MF convert
convertible ADJ convertible
convertidor M converter
convertir[8] VT to convert; **—se en** to become
convexo ADJ convex
convicción F conviction
convicto -ta ADJ convicted; MF convict
convidar VT to invite; *Am* to offer
convierta, convierte *ver* convertir
convincente ADJ convincing, compelling
convine, conviniendo, conviniera, conviniese *ver* convenir
convirtiendo, convirtiera, convirtiese *ver* convertir
convite M (invitación) invitation; (banquete) banquet
convivencia F (coexistencia) coexistence; (cohabitación) cohabitation, living together
convivir VI (coexistir) to coexist; (cohabitar) to cohabitate, to live together
convocación F convocation
convocar[30] VT to convoke, to call together; (una reunión, un concurso) to convene
convocatoria F (anuncio) announcement; (llamamiento) call
convoy M convoy
convoyar VT to convoy
convulsión F convulsion
conyugal ADJ conjugal, marital
cónyuge MF spouse
coñac M cognac, brandy
cooperación F cooperation
cooperar VI to cooperate
cooperativa F cooperative, co-op
cooperativista MF member of a cooperative
cooperativo ADJ cooperative
coordenada F coordinate
coordinación F coordination
coordinado ADJ coordinate
coordinador -ora MF coordinator; ADJ coordinating
coordinar VT to coordinate
copa F (vaso) goblet, wineglass; (de árbol) top; (de sombrero) crown; (palo de la baraja) card in the suit of *copas*; (trofeo, parte de un sujetador) cup; **ir de —s** to go for a drink; **— del Mundo** World Cup
copago M copayment
copete M (de pelo) tuft; (de plumas) crest; **estar hasta el —** to be fed up
copia F (réplica) copy; (de foto) print; **— de respaldo** backup copy; **— de respaldo automático** automatic backup copy; **— de seguridad** backup copy; **— en papel** hard copy; **— impresa** hard copy
copiadora F copy machine
copiar VT (reproducir) to copy; (en un examen) to cheat
copión -ona MF copycat
copioso ADJ copious, plentiful
copla F (canción) popular song; (estrofa) stanza
copo M (de nieve) snowflake; (de lana, algodón) wad; **—s de maíz** cornflakes
copropietario -ria MF joint owner
coprotagonista MF costar
cópula F copula
copulación F copulation
copular VI to copulate
copyright M copyright
coque M coke
coqueta F (mujer) coquette; (mueble) dressing table
coquetear VI to flirt, to dally
coquetería F flirtation
coqueto ADJ flirtatious
coraje M (valentía) courage; (enojo) anger
coral M (marino) coral; (musical) chorale
coralino ADJ coral
coraza F armor
corazón M (órgano) heart; (de manzana) core; (vocativo) honey; **con el — en la boca** (cansado) really tired; (nervioso) on edge; **de buen —** kindhearted; **de todo —** wholeheartedly; **romperle el — a alguien** to break someone's heart
corazonada F hunch
corbata F necktie, tie, cravat
corcel M charger, steed
corchea F eighth note; **— con puntillo** dotted eighth note
corchete M (en costura) hook and eye; (paréntesis recto) square bracket; (llave) brace
corcho M (para botella) cork; (para pescar) float
corcova F hump, hunchback
corcovear VI to buck
cordaje M strings
cordel M string
cordero M (animal) lamb; (piel, cuero) lambskin
cordial ADJ cordial
cordillera F mountain range
cordobés -esa ADJ from Cordoba; MF person from Cordoba
cordón M (cinta) cord; (al borde de la calle) *Am* curb; **— de apertura** ripcord; **— de zapatos** shoelace, shoestring; **— policial** police cordon; **— umbilical** umbilical cord
cordoncillo M ridge, rib
cordura F sanity

Corea F Korea; **— del Norte** North Korea; **— del Sur** South Korea
coreano -na ADJ & MF Korean
corear VI/VT to chant
coreografía F choreography
cornada F goring
cornear VT to gore
corneja F crow
córner M corner kick
corneta F cornet; MF bugler
cornisa F cornice, ledge
corno M horn; **— francés** French horn
cornudo ADJ horned; M cuckold
coro M (cantantes) choir, chorus; (música) chorus; (parte de la iglesia) loft; **cantar a —** to sing in unison
corolario M corollary
corona F crown
coronación F coronation
coronar VT to crown
coronario ADJ coronary
coronel M colonel
coronilla F crown of the head; **estar hasta la —** to be fed up
corpiño M (almilla) bodice; (sujetador) *Am* bra
corporación F guild
corporal ADJ corporal, bodily
corporativo ADJ corporate
corpulento ADJ stout, corpulent
corpus M corpus
corpúsculo M corpuscle
corral M (de granja) barnyard, farmyard; (para ganado) corral, pen
correa F (de cuero) leather strap; (de ventilador) belt; (de perro) leash
corrección F (acción de corregir) correction; (cualidad de correcto) correctness
correctamente ADV correctly, properly
correcto ADJ (apropiado) correct, proper; (acertado) right
corrector -ora MF editor; **— de pruebas** proofreader
corredizo ADJ sliding
corredor -ora ADJ running; MF (persona que corre, también en deportes) runner; (deportista automovilístico, ciclista) racer; (intermediario) broker, agent; M (pasillo) hallway, corridor
correduría F brokerage
corregir[14] VT (errores) to correct; (exámenes) to grade; **—se** (en lo moral) to mend one's ways; (en los errores) to correct oneself
correlación F correlation
correlacionar VT to correlate
correlato M correlate
correo M mail; (edificio) post office; **— aéreo** air mail; **— certificado** certified mail; **— de voz** voice mail; **— electrónico** e-mail; **— electrónico basura** junk e-mail, spam; **echar al —** to mail
correoso ADJ tough
correr VI (persona, agua, calle) to run; (coche) to go fast; (una puerta) to slide; (dinero, tiempo) to pass; **— con los gastos** to take on the costs; VT (una cortina) to draw; (una carrera, un riesgo) to run; **—se** (moverse) to scoot over; (desteñir) to run, to bleed; (manchar) to smear
correría F foray
correspondencia F correspondence
corresponder VI (ser adecuado, estar en consonancia) to correspond; (pertenecer) to belong; VT (amor, favores) to reciprocate; **a mí me corresponde llamarla** it's up to me to call her, it behooves me to call her
correspondiente ADJ corresponding; MF correspondent
corresponsal MF correspondent
corretaje M broker's/agent's commission
corretear VI to run around
corrida F (acción de correr) running; (competición) race; (de banco) run; **— de toros** bullfight; **de —** without stopping
corrido ADJ (experimentado) worldly; (continuo) uninterrupted; **de —** without stopping; M ballad
corriente ADJ (que corre) running; (común) usual; (franco) frank; **el — mes** the current month; **estar al —** to be up to date; F (de agua, electricidad) current; (de dinero) flow; (de pesimismo) wave; (de aire) draft; (de computadora) streaming; **— alterna** alternating current; **— continua** direct current; **— del Golfo** Gulf Stream; **al —** in the loop; **dejarse llevar por la —** to conform; **llevarle la — a alguien** to humor someone
corrija, corrijo, corrigiendo, corrigiera, corrigiese, corrigió *ver* corregir
corrillo M group of gossips
corro M circle of people
corroborar VT to corroborate
corroer[73] VT to corrode
corromper VT (a una persona) to corrupt; (un alimento) to rot; **—se** (una persona) to become corrupt; (un alimento) to rot
corrompido ADJ corrupt
corrosión F corrosion
corrupción F corruption
corrupto ADJ corrupt
corsé M corset
cortada F shortcut
cortado ADJ (abreviado, sucinto) clipped; (tímido) shy; M (café) coffee with some milk; (desnivel) slope; (tenis) backspin, slice
cortador -ora MF (persona) cutter; F (aparato) cutter; **cortadora de césped** lawn mower
cortadura M cut

cortante ADJ (comentario, instrumento) cutting; (frío, viento) biting; (tono, instrumento) sharp
cortar VT to cut (también un texto digital); (un vestido, el uso de algo) to cut out; (a un locutor, una rama, el gas) to cut off; (un árbol) to cut down; (las uñas) to clip; (el césped) to mow; **— el paso** to block; **— por lo sano** to take drastic action; M SG **cortacésped** lawn mower; M SG **cortacircuitos** circuit breaker; M SG **cortafuego** fire line; M SG **cortafuegos** firewall; M SG **cortapapeles** paper cutter; M SG **cortaplumas** penknife; M SG **cortauñas** nail clipper; VI (el frío) to bite; (la piel) to crack; **—se** (lastimarse) to cut oneself; (intimidarse) to be intimidated; (cuajarse) to curdle, to sour; **—se el pelo** to get a haircut; **— y pegar** cut and paste
corte M (de un traje, herida) cut; (acción de cortar) cutting; (de televisión) commercial break; (estilo) style; **— de pelo** haircut; **— transversal** cross section; **— y confección** dressmaking; **eso me da —** that embarrasses me; F (real, judicial) court; (séquito) retinue; **las —s** Spanish parliament; **hacer la —** to court
cortedad F shortness
cortejar VT to court, to woo
cortejo M (séquito) entourage; (acción de cortejar) courtship
cortés ADJ courteous, polite
cortesano -na MF courtier
cortesía F courtesy, politeness
córtex M cortex
corteza F (de árbol) bark; (de pan, de la Tierra) crust; (de queso, fruta) rind; **— cerebral** cerebral cortex
corticoesteroide M corticosteriod
cortijo M country house
cortina F (de ventana) curtain; (de lluvia) sheet; **— de humo** smoke screen
cortisona F cortisone
corto ADJ (breve) short; (tonto) short on brains; (encogido) bashful; **— de vista** short-sighted; **a — plazo** in the short run, in the short term; **quedarse —** to come up short; **vestirse de —** to wear a short dress; M short [film]; M **—circuito** short circuit
cosa F thing; **como quien no quiere la —** without realizing it; **como si tal —** as cool as a cucumber; **¡cómo son las —s!** what a surprise; **decir una — por otra** to tell a lie; **esperamos — de cinco minutos** we waited about five minutes; **las —s como son** let's be honest; **las —s de la vida** that's life; **no es gran —** it's no big deal; **otra —** something else
cosecha F crop, harvest; **de su —** of his invention; **vino — 1975** wine of 1975 vintage
cosechadora F combine
cosechar VT (cultivos) to harvest; (resultados) to reap
coser VI/VT to sew
cosignatario -ria MF cosigner
cosmético ADJ & M cosmetic
cósmico ADJ cosmic
cosmología F cosmology
cosmonauta MF cosmonaut
cosmopolita ADJ cosmopolitan
cosmos M cosmos
cosmovisión F worldview
coso M doodad
cosquillas F **hacer —** to tickle; **tener —** to be ticklish
cosquillear VT to tickle
cosquilleo M tickle
cosquilloso ADJ ticklish
costa F (del mar) coast, shore; **a toda —** at all costs; **—s** costs
Costa de Marfil F Ivory Coast
costado M side; **al —** alongside; **de —** edgewise; **por los cuatro —s** from all sides
costal M sack
costanero ADJ coastal
costar[5] VI/VT to cost; **— trabajo** to be difficult; **— un dineral** to cost a fortune; **— un ojo de la cara** to cost an arm and a leg
Costa Rica F Costa Rica
costarricense, costarriqueño -ña ADJ & MF Costa Rican
coste M cost; **— de [la] vida** cost of living; **al —** at cost
costear VT to defray costs; VI to sail along the coast
costero ADJ coastal
costilla F rib; **lo hizo a —s de su padre** he did it at his father's expense
costo M cost; **— adicional** added cost, extra cost; **— de [la] vida** cost of living; **al —** at cost; **— de mantenimiento** maintenance cost; **— de operación** operating cost
costoso ADJ costly
costra F (de pan) crust; (de herida) scab
costroso ADJ (pan) crusty; (heridas) scabby
costumbre F (hábito) habit; (tradición) custom; **de —** habitual; **tener la — de** to have the habit of; **está más cansado que de —** he's especially tired today
costura F (acción de coser) sewing; (línea de puntadas) stitching; (unión de dos piezas) seam; **alta —** high fashion, haute couture
costurero -ra M (caja) sewing box; (sastre) tailor; F seamstress
costurón M (puntada) large stitch; (cicatriz) large scar
cota F (nivel del agua) height above sea level; (estándar) benchmark
cotejar VT to check against

cotejo M comparison
cotidiano ADJ everyday
cotización F price quote, price quotation
cotizar[47] VT to quote
coto M — **de caza** game preserve; **poner — a** to put an end to
cotorra F (loro) parrot; (persona) chatterbox
cotorrear VI to chatter
covacha F small cave
coyote M coyote
coyuntura F (articulación) joint; (situación) juncture; **aprovechar la —** to take advantage of the situation
coz F kick; **dar coces** to kick
crack M (cocaína) crack; (deportista) ace
cráneo M cranium, skull
craso ADJ crass
cráter M crater
crayola® F crayon
creación F creation
creacionismo M creationism
creador-ora MF creator; ADJ creative
crear VI/VT to create
creatividad F creativity
creativo ADJ creative
crecer[35] VI (un niño) to grow; (masa, río) to rise; (madera, mar) to swell; (la luna) to wax
crecida F rise of a river
crecido ADJ (adulto) grown; (grande) large; (demasiado alto) overgrown
creciente ADJ (que crece) growing; (luna) crescent; M (luna) crescent; (marea) high tide; (de un río) flood
crecimiento M growth
credencial F credential
credibilidad F credibility
crédito M (solvencia, unidad de estudios) credit; (hecho de creer) credence; (fama) reputation; (préstamo) loan; **— al consumidor** consumer credit; **— rotativo** revolving credit; **dar — a** to believe; **—s** film credits; **vender a —** to sell on credit
credo M creed
crédulo ADJ credulous, gullible
creencia F belief
creer[18] VI/VT (tomar como cierto) to believe; (opinar) to think, to feel; **—se** to fall for; **¿quién se cree que es?** who does he think he is? **se cree artista** he fancies himself an artist; **¡ya lo creo!** I should say so!
creíble ADJ credible, believable
crema F cream (también cosmético); **— de espárragos** cream of asparagus; **— para [los] labios** lip balm, Chapstick®
cremallera F (de coche) rack; (de prenda) zipper; **— y piñón** rack and pinion
cremar VT to cremate
cremoso ADJ creamy
creosota F creosote
crepitación F crackle
crepitar VI to crackle
crepúsculo M twilight
crespo ADJ wiry, kinky
crespón M crepe
cresta F (de ola, montaña) crest; (de ave) tuft; (de gallo) comb
creyendo, creyera, creyese, creyó *ver* creer
creyente MF believer; ADJ believing
crezca, crezco *ver* crecer
cría F (acción de criar) breeding; (camada) litter; (animal joven) young
criada *ver* criado
criadero M **— de peces** hatchery; **— de pollos** chicken farm
criado-da MF servant; F maid
criador-ora MF breeder
crianza F (de animales) breeding; (de hijos) upbringing; (modales) manners
criar[28] VT (animales) to breed; (hijos) to bring up, to rear, to raise; **estar criando malvas** *fam* to be pushing up daisies; **—se** to grow up
criatura F (ser extraño) creature; (bebé) baby
criba F sieve
cribar VT to sift
crimen M (delito grave) serious crime, felony; (asesinato) murder; **— de guerra** war crime
criminal ADJ & MF criminal
criminalidad F serious crime
crin F mane
criogénico ADJ cryogenic
criollo ADJ (nacido en América) born in Spanish America; (tradicionalmente americano) traditionally Spanish American; M (lengua) creole
críquet M cricket
crisálida F chrysalis
crisantemo M chrysanthemum
crisis F crisis; **— de la edad madura** midlife crisis
crisma F crown of the head
crisol M crucible, melting pot
crisparse VI (un músculo) to contract; (los puños) to clench; (los nervios) to be on edge
cristal M (mineral, vidrio fino) crystal; (vidrio de ventana) *Esp* glass, pane; (lente) lens; **— labrado** cut glass
cristalería F (objetos) glassware; (establecimiento) glassware store; (fábrica) glassworks
cristalino ADJ (de cristal) crystalline; (transparente) crystal-clear; M lens of the eye
cristalizar[47] VI/VT to crystallize
cristiandad F Christendom
cristianismo M Christianity
cristiano-na ADJ & MF Christian; **hablar en —** (claramente) to speak clearly; (español) to speak Spanish
criterio M criterion

crítica F criticism; (de un libro) review
criticar[30] VT to criticize
crítico-ca ADJ critical; MF critic; (de un libro) reviewer
criticón-ona ADJ critical; MF faultfinder
Croacia F Croatia
croar VI to croak
croata ADJ & MF Croatian
crocante ADJ crisp, crunchy
croché, crochet M crochet; **hacer —** to crochet
croissant M croissant
crol M (estilo de natación) crawl, freestyle
cromado ADJ chroming
cromo M chromium, chrome
cromosoma M chromosome
crónica F (narración de eventos) chronicle; (reportaje) feature; **— policial** police report
crónico ADJ chronic
cronista MF (deportivo) reporter; (histórico) chronicler
cronología F chronology
cronológico ADJ chronological
cronometrador-ora MF timer, timekeeper
cronometraje M timing
cronometrar VT to time
cronómetro M chronometer, stopwatch
croquet M croquet
croquis M rough sketch
cross M cross-country race
cruasán M croissant
cruce M (acción, lugar) crossing; (de dos calles) crossroads, intersection; (de razas) crossbreeding; (de palabras) blend; (animal híbrido) cross; **— peatonal** crosswalk
crucero M (buque de guerra) cruiser; (viaje de placer) cruise
cruceta F crosspiece
crucial ADJ crucial
crucificar[30] VT to crucify
crucifijo M crucifix
crucigrama M crossword puzzle
crudo ADJ (comida, seda) raw; (tiempo, invierno, imágenes) harsh; (petróleo, lenguaje) crude; **agua cruda** hard water; **color —** yellowish white
cruel ADJ cruel, mean
crueldad F cruelty, meanness
cruento ADJ grisly, gruesome
crujido M (de puerta, piso) creak; (de un tallo al quebrarse) crack; (de hojas) rustle; (de un fuego) crackle
crujiente ADJ (manzana, tocino) crisp, crispy; (nueces) crunchy
crujir VI (puerta, piso) to creak; (dientes) to grate; (hojas) to rustle; (nueces) to crunch; (fuego) to crackle
cruz F (cristiana) cross; (de moneda) tails; **hacerse cruces** to dread
cruzada F crusade
cruzado M (soldado) crusader; ADJ (tenis) crosscourt; (boxeo) cross; (traje) double-breasted
cruzamiento M (de piernas, razas) crossing; (de calles) crossroads; (de razas) cross
cruzar[47] VT (la calle) to cross; (un cheque) to write across; **—le la cara a alguien** to backhand someone's face; **cruzo los dedos** I'll keep my fingers crossed; **—se con alguien** to bump into someone; **—se de brazos** to fold one's arms; **se me cruzó un ciervo** a deer crossed in front of me
cuaderno M notebook; **— de bitácora** logbook; **— de espiral** spiral notebook
cuadra F (establo) stable; (distancia) *Am* block
cuadrado ADJ square; **estar —** to be fat; M square; **es [un] —** he's a square; **dos al —** two squared; **elevar al —** to square
cuadrangular ADJ (geometría) quadrangular; M (béisbol) home run
cuadrar VT (estar en ángulo recto) to square; VI (corresponder) to fit; (ser conveniente) to be convenient; (ser iguales) to balance, to add up; **— con** to be in agreement with
cuadricular VT to divide into squares
cuadrilátero ADJ quadrilateral; M (en boxeo) ring; (polígono) quadrilateral
cuadrilla F (de ladrones) gang; (de obreros) crew; (baile) square dance
cuadro M (cuadrado) square; (pintura) picture; (de bicicleta) frame; (de jardín) bed; (en tela) checker; (de fútbol) team; **— clínico** symptoms; **— interior** (béisbol) infield; **— sinóptico** summary table; **a/de —s** checked
cuadrúpedo ADJ & M quadruped
cuajada F curd
cuajar VI (leche) to curdle; (queso, cemento) to set; (gelatina) to jell; (un grupo, una organización) to come about; **—se** to curdle; **la cosa no cuajó** that didn't pan out
cuajarón M clot
cual PRON REL which; **el/la —** (cosa) which; (persona) who; **lo —** which; **sea — sea** whichever it may be; ADV like; **— hoja al viento** like a leaf in the wind
cuál PRON INTERR which; **¿cuáles son los tuyos?** which ones are yours?
cualidad F quality, trait
cualitativo ADJ qualitative
cualquiera ADJ INDEF any; **de cualquier manera/forma** anyhow; **en cualquier lado** anywhere; PRON INDEF (cosa) any; (persona) anyone; **— que sea su nacionalidad** whatever his nationality may be; **— que elijas** whichever one you choose; **— podría hacer eso** anyone could do that
cuando ADV REL when; **— menos** at least; **— mucho** at most; **se rompió — lo usaba** it broke while she was using it; PREP **— la**

guerra during the war
cuándo ADV INTERR & PRON when
cuantía F (cantidad) quantity; (importancia) importance
cuántico ADJ quantum
cuantificar[30] VT to quantify
cuantioso ADJ considerable
cuantitativo ADJ quantitative
cuanto ADJ REL any; **lee — libro ve** she reads any book she sees; PRON REL **unos —s** a few; CONJ **hice — pude** I did as much as I could; ADV **— antes** as soon as possible; **— más trabajo, menos consigo** the more I work, the less I accomplish; **en —** as soon as possible; **en — a** regarding; **en — que** as
cuánto ADJ, ADV & PRON INTERR (dinero, agua) how much; (personas, libros) how many; **¿cada —?** how often? **¿— piensas quedarte?** how long do you plan to stay?
cuarenta NUM forty; **cantarle las — a alguien** to bawl someone out; **— iguales** (tenis) deuce
cuarentena F quarantine; **una — de libros** forty-odd books
cuarentón -ona MF person in his or her forties
cuaresma F Lent
cuarta F (marcha) fourth gear; (palmo) span of a hand
cuartear VT (una res) to quarter; (los labios) to chap; **—se** to chap
cuartel M barracks; **— general** headquarters; **no dar —** to give no quarter
cuartelada F military coup
cuartelazo M military coup
cuarteto M quartet
cuartilla F sheet of paper
cuarto ADJ one-fourth, quarter; M (habitación) room; (cantidad) quarter, one-fourth; **— de baño** bathroom; **— de estar** living room; **— de final** quarter finals; **— oscuro** darkroom; **¡ni que ocho —s!** no way! **tres —s** three-fourths
cuarzo M quartz
cuásar M quasar
cuate M *Méx* pal, buddy
cuatrero -ra MF cattle rustler
cuatrillizo -za MF quadruplet
cuatro NUM four; **— ojos** four-eyes; **más de —** a good number
cuba F (barril) cask, barrel; (tina) tub, vat
Cuba F Cuba
cubano -na ADJ & MF Cuban
cubeta F (recipiente rectangular) tray; (balde) pail; **— de hielo** ice tray
cúbico ADJ cubic
cubículo M cubicle
cubierta F (de libro) cover; (cosa para cubrir) covering; (neumático) tire; (de buque) deck
cubierto M place setting; **— de plata** silverware; **a —** sheltered
cubierto *ver* cubrir
cubismo M cubism
cúbito M ulna
cubo M (cuerpo geométrico, tercera potencia) cube; (balde) bucket; (de rueda) hub; (juguete) building block; **— de basura** trash can
cubrir[74] VT (con una manta) to cover; (con carteles) to plaster; (una vacante) to fill; (con pintura) to coat; (con crema batida) to smother; (de niebla) to shroud; **—se** (nublarse) to fog up; (ponerse el sombrero) to put on one's hat
cucaracha F cockroach
cuchara F (cubierto) spoon; (de excavadora) bucket; (para helado) scoop; **— sopera** soup spoon; **meter la —** to butt in
cucharada F (lo que cabe en una cuchara) spoonful; (medida) tablespoonful; (de helado) dip
cucharadita F teaspoonful
cucharear VT to spoon
cucharita F teaspoon
cucharón M (para helado) scoop, dipper; (para sopa) ladle
cuchichear VI/VT to whisper
cuchicheo M whisper
cuchilla F (cuchillo grande) large knife, cleaver; (de afeitar, de licuadora) blade; (de patín) runner
cuchillada F (golpe) stab, slash; (herida) stab wound, gash
cuchillería F (conjunto de cuchillos) cutlery; (tienda) cutlery store
cuchillo M knife; **pasar a —** to kill with a knife
cuclillas LOC ADV **en —** squatting; **sentarse en —** to squat
cuclillo M cuckoo
cuco ADJ cute
cucú INTERJ cuckoo
cucurucho M (de papel) paper cone; (para helado) ice-cream cone; (capirote) hood
cuelga, cuelgue *ver* colgar
cuello M (del cuerpo) neck; (de una prenda) collar; **— de botella** bottleneck; **— uterino** cervix; **— vuelto** turtleneck; **estoy hasta el — en deudas** I'm up to my neck in debts
cuenca F (de un río) basin; (del ojo) eye socket
cuenco M earthen bowl
cuenta F (cálculo) count, calculation; (factura) bill, check; (relación de ingresos y gastos) account; (bolita) bead; (depósito bancario) bank account; **— conjunta** joint account; **— corriente** checking account; **— de ahorros** savings account; **— de contrapartida** contra account; **— de crédito** charge account; **— de depósito en garantía** charge account; **— de gastos** expense account; **— de mercado monetario** escrow

account; **— en un paraíso fiscal** offshore account; **—s por/a cobrar** accounts receivable; **—s por/a pagar** accounts payable; **— regresiva/atrás** countdown; **abrir/cerrar una —** to open/close an account; **a fin de —s** when all is said and done; **ajustar —s** to settle old scores; **caí en [la] — de que** it just dawned on me that; **dar — de** to finish off; **dar —s** to give an accounting; **darse —** to realize; **en — de margen** on margin; **en resumidas —s** in short; **eso corre por mí —** that is my responsibility; **habida — de** bearing in mind; **más de la —** more than necessary; **pasar la —** to call in a favor; **tomar/tener en —** to take into account; **trabajar por — propia** to freelance; M SG **cuentagotas** eyedropper

cuenta, cuente *ver* contar

cuento M story, tale; **— chino** tall tale; **— de hadas** fairy tale; **— de nunca acabar** never-ending story; **déjese de —s** come to the point; **traer a —** to bring up; **venir a —** to be to the point

cuerda F (soga) cord, rope; (de arco) bowstring; (de guitarra) string; (de reloj) spring; **— floja** tightrope; **—s vocales** vocal cords; **bajo —** under the table; **contra las —s** on the ropes; **dar — a** to wind; **no le des —** don't get him started

cuerdo ADJ sane

cuerno M horn (también instrumento de viento); (de caracol) feeler; (de ciervo) antler; **— de la abundancia** horn of plenty; **coger el toro por los —s** to take the bull by the horns; **poner —s a** to be unfaithful to

cuero M (piel de animal) hide; (piel curtida) leather; **— cabelludo** scalp; **en —s** naked

cuerpo M body; (torso) torso; **¡— a tierra!** hit the deck! **— de bomberos** fire department; **— de policía** police force; **— de prensa** press corps; **— docente** teaching staff; **a — de rey** in great luxury; **— extraño** foreign body; **dar — a** to flesh out; **de — entero** through and through; **ganó por tres —s de ventaja** he won by three lengths; **ir de —** to have a bowel movement

cuervo M crow, raven

cuesta F slope; **— abajo** downhill; **— arriba** uphill; **a —s** piggyback

cuesta, cueste *ver* costar

cuestión F question; **en — de segundos** in a matter of seconds; **poner en —** to question; **ser — de** to be a matter of

cuestionable ADJ questionable

cuestionador ADJ questioning

cuestionar VT to question

cuestionario M questionnaire

cueva F cave

cuidado M (atención) care; (preocupación) worry; **— con el perro** beware of the dog; **— de la casa** housekeeping; **— dental** dental care; **— posparto** postnatal care; **— prenatal** prenatal care; **— terminal** end-of-life care; **al — de** under the care of; **con —** carefully; **eso me trae sin —** I don't care about that; **tener —** to be careful; **un enfermo de —** a severely ill patient; INTERJ look out!

cuidador -ora MF caregiver, caretaker

cuidadoso ADJ careful

cuidar VT to take care of, to look after; **— de** to take care of; **— la casa** to keep house; **— niños** to babysit; **—se de** to beware of

culata F (anca) haunch; (de rifle) butt; (de motor) cylinder head

culatazo M (golpe) blow with the butt of a rifle; (rebote al disparar) recoil

culebra F snake

culebrear VI to slither

culebrilla F shingles

culinario ADJ culinary

culminación F (de carrera, ceremonia) culmination, high point; (de un sueño) fulfillment

culminante ADJ climactic

culminar VI to culminate

culpa F (responsabilidad) fault, blame; (sentimiento) guilt; **echar la — a** to blame; **por — de** because of; **tener la —** to be to blame

culpabilidad F guilt

culpable ADJ guilty; MF culprit

culpar VT to blame

cultivable ADJ (planta) cultivable; (tierra) arable

cultivado ADJ (tierra) cultivated; (perlas, persona) cultured

cultivador -ora MF (persona) cultivator; F (aparato) cultivator

cultivar VT (cosecha) to grow, to raise; (la tierra) to farm; (relaciones, inteligencia) to cultivate; (microbios) to culture

cultivo M (de plantas) growing; (de la tierra) farming; (de microbios) culture; (de relaciones) cultivation; **de —** cultured

culto ADJ educated, cultured; M worship; **libertad de —** freedom of religion

cultura F culture; **— general** general knowledge

cultural ADJ cultural

culturismo M body-building

cumbre F summit

cumpleaños M SG birthday

cumplido ADJ (cortés) polite; (perfecto) perfect; M compliment; **hacer algo de —** to do something out of duty; **hacer un —** to pay a compliment

cumplimiento M (de un contrato)

performance; (de una promesa, obligación) fulfillment; (de un plazo) expiration
cumplir VT (una obligación) to fulfill, to discharge; (una promesa) to keep, to honor; (una condena) to complete, to serve; **— diez años** to turn ten; **hacer —** to enforce; VI (vencer) to expire; **— con** to meet [a goal]; **me cumple informarle que** it is my duty to inform you that
cúmulo M (grupo) host; (tipo de nube) cumulus
cuna F (que se mece) cradle; (con barandas) crib
cundir VI (extenderse) to spread; (rendir) to go a long way
cuneta F roadside ditch; **en la —** out to pasture
cuña F (pieza para hender) wedge; (bacinilla) bedpan
cuñado -da M brother-in-law; F sister-in-law
cuño M die-stamp; **de — hispano** with a Hispanic stamp
cuota F (cantidad que le corresponde a uno) quota, allotment; (cantidad que hay que pagar) dues; (mensualidad) installment; **—s del coche** car payments; **—s sindicales** union dues
cupé M coupé
cupe, cupiera, cupiese *ver* caber
cupo M (cantidad) quota; (capacidad) *Am* room
cupón M coupon
cúpula F dome
cura F cure, remedy; M priest
curable ADJ curable
curación F cure
curanderismo M faith healing
curandero -ra MF healer
curar VT (una enfermedad, carne) to cure; (una herida) to heal; **—se** to heal; **—se en salud** to take precautionary measures
curiosear VI to look around; (en asuntos ajenos) to pry
curiosidad F curiosity
curioso ADJ curious
Curita® F *Am* adhesive bandage, Band-aid®
currículo/currículum M résumé; **— vitae** CV
curro M *Esp* job
curruca F warbler
curry M curry
cursar VT (estudios) to take; (mensaje, invitación) to send
cursi ADJ (afectado) affected; (de mal gusto) tacky
cursillo M (individual) tutorial; (corto) short course
cursivo ADJ cursive; **escribir en cursiva** to write in cursive
curso M (de río, enfermedad, acontecimientos, moneda) course; (período docente) academic year; (grupo de estudiantes) class; (libro) textbook; **— legal** legal currency; **el mes en —** the current month
cursor M cursor
curtiduría F tannery
curtiembre F tannery
curtir VT (cuero) to tan; (cutis) to weather; (el carácter) to harden; **—se** (envejecerse) to get weathered; (acostumbrarse) to become accustomed to hardships
curva F curve (también béisbol); **— de campana** bell curve
curvatura F curvature
curvo ADJ curved
cúspide F summit
custodia F custody, keeping; **en —** (un monto de dinero) in escrow; (un prisionero) in custody
custodiar VT to guard
custodio -dia MF guardian
cutáneo ADJ cutaneous
cutícula F cuticle
cutis M facial skin
cuyo ADJ REL whose
cyborg M cyborg

Dd

dádiva F gift
dadivoso ADJ generous
dado ADJ given; M die; **jugar a los —s** to throw dice
dador -ora MF giver; **— de sangre** blood donor
daga F dagger
dalia F dahlia
daltónico ADJ color-blind
dama F lady; (en el juego de mesa) king; **jugar a las —s** to play checkers; **— de honor** bridesmaid
damajuana F demijohn
damasco M (fruta) apricot; (árbol) apricot tree
damisela F damsel
dandi M dandy
danés -esa ADJ Danish; MF Dane; M (lengua) Danish
danza F dance; **— del vientre** belly dance; **en —** in action
danzante MF dancer
danzar[47] VI/VT to dance
dañar VT to harm, to damage; **—se** to suffer harm
dañino ADJ harmful
daño M damage, harm; **— colateral** collateral damage; **— emergente** actual damage; **— físico** bodily harm; **—s materiales** property damage; **—s y perjuicios** damages; **hacer —** to harm
dañoso ADJ harmful
dar[62] VT (un regalo) to give; (un golpe, naipes) to

deal; (sal) to add; (una fiesta) to throw; (la hora) to strike; (un olor) to give off; (la alarma) to raise; (un paseo) to take; **— a** (un edificio) to face; (una calle) to lead to; **— a conocer** to announce; **— a entender** to intimate; **— con** to hit upon, to find; **— de alta** to discharge, to release from the hospital; **— de baja** to discharge; **— de comer** to feed; **— de sí** to perform at capacity; **esta tela da de sí** this fabric gives; **— en la pared** to hit the wall; **—le con** to scrub with; **lo misma da** it makes no difference; **¿qué más da?** what difference does it make? **dale que dale** on and on; **hoy no doy una** today I can't get anything right; **le doy cincuenta años** he must be about fifty; **me da rabia/miedo** that makes me angry/afraid; **no me da el tiempo para ir al cine** I don't have time to go to the movies; **que no le dé el sol** don't let the sun shine on it; **y dale** enough already; **—se a la bebida** to indulge in drinking; **—se por conforme** to be satisfied; **—se prisa** to hurry; **dárselas de** to boast of being; **en este lugar se dan las flores silvestres** in this location wildflowers are found

dardo M dart

dársena F dock

datar VT to date; **— de** to date from

dátil M date

dato M piece of information; **—s** data

d.C. ADV AD

de PREP **— la familia** of the family; **— Madrid** from Madrid; **habló — la guerra** he talked about the war; **el hombre — gafas** the man with glasses; **el mejor estudiante — la clase** the best student in the class; **fácil — hacer** easy to do; **más — tres** more than three; **llevar — la mano** to lead by the hand; **— regreso a España** upon returning to Spain; **— venta en farmacias** on sale in pharmacies; **ancianos — respeto** older people to be respected; **— lo más lindo** really pretty; **tonto — mí** silly me

dé *ver* dar

deambular VI to amble, to saunter; **— por** (el bosque) to wander about; (el internet) to surf

deán M dean

debacle M debacle

debajo ADV under, underneath; PREP **— de** under, below; **por — de** under

debate M debate

debatir VT to debate; **—se** to struggle

debe M debit

deber VT **deben apoyarme** they should support me; **debe de ser** it must be; **deberías sentarte** you should sit down; VT to owe; **me debes una** you owe me one; **me debo a mis alumnos** I'm devoted to my students; M duty; **—es** homework

debidamente ADV duly

debido ADJ due; **— a** due to, owing to; **a su — tiempo** in due time

débil ADJ (sin fuerza) weak; (endeble) frail, feeble; (sonido) faint

debilidad F (falta de fuerza) weakness; (cualidad de endeble) frailty; (de un sonido) faintness

debilitamiento M weakening

debilitante ADJ debilitating

debilitar VT to weaken, to debilitate

débito M debit

debutar VI to make a debut

década F decade

decadencia F (moral) decadence, decay; (cultural, económica) decline

decadente ADJ decadent

decaer[52] VI (fuerza) to weaken; (energía) to ebb; (salud) to fail; (ánimo) to flag

decaimiento M (decadencia) decline; (debilidad) weakness

decano -na ADJ senior; MF dean

decapitar VT to behead, to decapitate

decatlón M decathlon

decena F **—s de candidatos** tens of candidates

decencia F decency

decenio M decade

decente ADJ decent; **muy —** rather good

decepción F disappointment

decepcionante ADJ disappointing

decepcionar VT to disappoint

decibelio M decibel

decidido ADJ resolute, determined; **una decidida preferencia** a decided preference

decidir VI/VT to decide; **—se** to make up one's mind; **—se a** to resolve to

deciduo ADJ deciduous

décima F tenth

decimal ADJ decimal

décimo ADJ & M tenth

decir[53, 74] VT (palabras, oraciones) to say; (una mentira, un chiste, la verdad) to tell; **— tonterías** to talk nonsense; **con —te que** suffice it to say that; **este tipo no me dice nada** this guy leaves me cold; **¡que me lo digan a mí!** you're telling me that? VI to say; **diga** hello (al contestar el teléfono); **es —** that is to say; **he dicho** I have spoken; **no es prometedor que digamos** it's hardly promising; **no me digas** you don't say; **querer —** to mean; M saying

decisión F decision; **tomar una —** to make a decision

decisivo ADJ decisive

declaración F (de amor, independencia, guerra) declaration; (de un hecho) statement; (de un testigo) deposition; **— de derechos** bill of rights; **— de impuestos / de la renta** tax return; **— de impuestos sobre la renta**

income tax return; — **jurada** affidavit; — **de la misión** mission statement; — **errónea/falsa** misstatement; — **sobre la privacidad** privacy statement

declarar VT (amor, independencia, ingresos) to declare; (un hecho) to state; — **culpable** to find guilty; **os declaro marido y mujer** I pronounce you man and wife; VI (como testigo) to testify; —**se** (un amante) to declare one's love; —**se culpable** to plead guilty; —**se en huelga** to go on strike; —**se en quiebra** to declare bankruptcy

declinar VI/VT to decline

declive M (pendiente) slope, drop; (decadencia) decline

decoración F decoration; — **de interiores** interior decorating

decorado M (de casa) decoration; (de escenario) scenery

decorar VT to decorate

decorativo ADJ decorative

decoro M decorum, propriety

decorosamente ADV decorously, properly

decoroso ADJ decorous, proper

decrépito ADJ decrepit

decrepitud F decrepitude

decretar VT to decree

decreto M (disposición ejecutiva) decree; (ley) act

dedal M thimble

dedicación F dedication

dedicar[30] VT (la vida) to dedicate, to devote; (un libro) to dedicate; —**se** to dedicate oneself; (a los estudios) to apply oneself

dedicatoria F dedication

dedo M (de la mano) finger; (del pie) toe; — **anular** ring finger; — **índice** index finger; — **mayor / del corazón** middle finger; — **meñique** little finger; — **pulgar** thumb; **chuparse el** — to be a fool; **chuparse los** —**s** to lick one's fingers; **cruzar los** —**s** to keep one's fingers crossed; **elegir a** — to appoint directly; **hacer** — to hitch a ride; **no mover un** — not to lift a finger

deducción F deduction; — **impositiva** tax deduction

deducible ADJ deductible

deducir[38] VT (concluir) to deduce, to conclude; (descontar) to deduct

defecación F bowel movement

defecar[30] VI/VT to defecate

defección F defection

defecto M defect, flaw; **por** — by default

defectuoso ADJ defective, faulty

defender[2] VT (un fuerte) to defend; (una causa) to champion; (los derechos) to stand up for, to stick up for; **se defiende en francés** he can hold his own in French

defendible ADJ defensible

defensa F defense (también deportes); MF (fútbol) defender; — **individual** man-to-man defense; — **en zonas** zone defense; **aprende** — **personal** he's learning self-defense; **lo dijo en** — **propia** he said it in self-defense

defensivo ADJ defensive; **a la defensiva** on the defensive

defensor -ora MF (en la guerra) defender; (de una causa) champion

deferencia F deference

deficiencia F deficiency

deficiente ADJ deficient

déficit M deficit, shortfall; — **presupuestario** budget deficit

defienda, defiende *ver* defender

definición F definition; — **por penales** penalty shoot-out

definido ADJ definite

definir VT to define

definitivamente ADV definitely; once and for all; — **voy a comprar una impresora** I am definitely going to buy a printer; **lo arreglaremos todo** — we will take care of everything once and for all

definitivo ADJ (superior) definitive; (final) final; **en definitiva** all things considered

deflación F deflation

deflector M baffle

deforestación F deforestation

deformación F deformation

deformar VT to deform; —**se** to become deformed

deforme ADJ deformed, misshapen

deformidad F deformity

defraudar VT (cometer fraude) to defraud; (decepcionar) to disappoint

defunción F death

degenerado -da ADJ & MF degenerate

degenerar VI to degenerate

degenerativo ADJ degenerative

deglución F swallowing

degollar[24] VT to slash someone's throat

degradación F degradation

degradar VT (envilecer) to degrade, to debase; (rebajar el rango) to demote; —**se** to degrade

degüello M throat-slashing; **lucha a** — fight to the death

dehesa F pasture

deidad F deity

dejada F — **de volea** drop shot, stop-volley

dejadez F slovenliness

dejado ADJ slovenly

dejar VT (abandonar, no comer, legar) to leave; (a un enamorado) to leave, to dump; (permitir) to let; (soltar) to let go; — **de** to stop; — **caer** to drop; — **pasar** to pass up; **déjame en paz** leave me alone; **me dejó atónito** it left/rendered me speechless; **no**

dejes de venir don't fail to come; **te lo dejo en mil dólares** I'll sell it to you for one thousand dollars; **—se** to let oneself go; **—se crecer la barba** to grow a beard
deje M slight accent
dejo M (sabor) aftertaste; (acento) slight accent; (toque) hint; **tener un — de** to smack of
delantal M apron
delante ADV in front; **— de** in front of, ahead of
delantera F (de carrera) lead; (de vestido) front; **llevar la —** to be in the lead; **tomar la —** to take the lead
delantero-ra ADJ (pata) front; MF (línea, deportista) forward; M front
delatar VT to inform against, to squeal on; **— la edad** to betray one's age
delator-ora MF accuser, informer
delegación F delegation
delegado-da MF delegate
delegar[40] VT to delegate
deleitar VT to delight; **—se en algo** to revel in something; **—se la vista con** to feast one's eyes on
deleite M delight
deletrear VT to spell; **— mal** to misspell
deleznable ADJ despicable
delfín M dolphin
delgadez F thinness
delgado ADJ thin, slender, slim
deliberación F deliberation
deliberadamente ADV deliberately
deliberado ADJ deliberate
deliberar VI/VT to deliberate
delicadeza F (tacto) gentleness; (fineza) delicacy; **con —** gently; **tuvo la — de llamar** he was kind enough to call
delicado ADJ (suave, frágil, controvertido) delicate; (enfermizo) frail; (exquisito) dainty; (quisquilloso) squeamish
delicatessen F PL delicacies
delicia F delight
delicioso ADJ delicious, delectable
delimitar VT to delimit
delincuencia F crime
delincuente ADJ & MF delinquent, criminal; **— juvenil** juvenile delinquent
delineador M eyeliner
delinear VT to delineate, to outline
delirante ADJ delirious, raving
delirar VI to be delirious, to rave
delirio M delirium; **— paranoico** paranoid delusion; **—s de grandeza** delusions of grandeur
delito M crime, offense
deltoides M SG deltoids
demacrado ADJ drawn, gaunt, haggard
demagogo-ga MF demagogue
demanda F (de mercancías) demand; (de seguros) insurance claim; (pleito) lawsuit; **por —** on demand; **entablar una —** to file a lawsuit
demandado-da MF (en un pleito) defendant; (en un arbitraje) respondent
demandante MF plaintiff
demandar VT (pedir) to ask for; (poner pleito) to sue, to file a suit against
demarcar[30] VT to demarcate
demás ADJ (restante) remaining; PRON the others, the rest; **lo —** the rest; **y —** and whatnot; ADV **por lo —** moreover; **por —** useless
demasía LOC ADV **en —** excessively
demasiado ADV too; too much; **eso es — para mí** that's too much for me; **él es — alto** he's too tall; ADJ too much; too many; **— dinero** too much money; **demasiadas cosas** too many things
demencia F (locura) insanity; (senilidad) senility; (enfermedad mental) dementia
demente ADJ demented, insane, deranged
democracia F democracy
demócrata MF democrat; **Partido —** Democratic Party
democrático ADJ democratic; (del Partido —) Democrat, Democratic
democratización F democratization
demografía F demographics
demográfico ADJ demographic
demoler[6] VT to demolish, to tear down
demonio M demon; **¿qué —s haces?** what the heck are you doing? **un frío del —** bitter cold
demora F delay
demorar VT to delay; **—se** to linger
demostración F (prueba) demonstration; (de un programa digital) demo; **— de fuerza** show of force
demostrar[5] VT (mostrar) to demonstrate, to show; (comprobar) to prove, to demonstrate
demostrativo ADJ demonstrative
demudar VT to change, to alter
demuestra, demuestre *ver* demostrar
denegación F (de una petición) denial
dengue M dengue fever
denigrar VT to denigrate, to disparage
denodado ADJ untiring
denominación F (valor) denomination; (nombre) designation
denominador M denominator; **— común** common denominator
denominar VT to designate, to term
denostar[5] VT to revile
denotación F denotation
denotar VT to denote
densidad F density; **alta —** high density
denso ADJ (sólido) dense; (líquido) heavy
dentado ADJ (rueda) toothed; (montaña) ragged
dentadura F set of teeth; **— postiza** false teeth
dental ADJ dental

dentellada F (mordedura) bite; (señal de diente) tooth mark; **a —s** biting
dentífrico M toothpaste, dentifrice
dentista MF dentist
dentro ADV inside; (tenis) in; PREP **— de la casa** inside the house; **— de la ley** within the law; **— de quince días** (en el plazo de) within two weeks; (al cabo de) in two weeks; **por —** within
denuncia F (acusación) denunciation; (de mina, de seguro) claim
denunciar VT (un hecho negativo) to denounce; (una mina) to claim; (un delito) to report
deparar VT (tener preparado) to have in store; (proporcionar) to afford; **el destino me deparaba una sorpresa** fate had a surprise in store for me
departamento M (división) department; (piso) small apartment; (provincia) province
departir VI *lit* to commune
dependencia F (hecho de depender) dependence; (habituación) dependency; (filial) branch office
depender VI to depend; **— de** to depend on
dependiente -ta ADJ dependent; MF sales clerk, salesperson
depilación F hair removal
depilar VT to remove hair; (con cera) to wax
depilatorio ADJ & M depilatory
deplorable ADJ deplorable
deplorar VT to deplore
deponer[56, 74] VT (las armas) to lay down; (a un ministro) to depose, to remove; VI to defecate
deportar VT to deport
deporte M sport; **me gusta el —** I like sports/athletics
deportista ADJ athletic; MF athlete
deportivo ADJ athletic; **revista deportiva** sports magazine
deposición F (de un testigo) deposition; (de un ministro) removal; (movimiento de vientre) bowel movement
depositante MF depositor
depositar VT to deposit; **—se** to settle
depositario -ria MF repository
depósito M (en el banco) deposit; (de gasolina) tank; (de agua) reservoir; (de armas) depot, dump; (de mercancías) stock room, storehouse; **— de cadáveres** morgue; **— de garantía** security deposit; **hacer un —** to make a deposit; **en —** on consignment
depravado ADJ depraved
depreciar VI to depreciate
depredador -ora MF predator
depresión F depression
depresor M depressor; **— de lengua** tongue depressor
deprimente ADJ depressing
deprimido ADJ depressed
deprimir VT to depress
deprisa ADV quickly
depuración F (de agua) purification; (de un programa) debugging
depurador M debugger
depurar VT to purify; (un programa) to debug
derby M derby
derecha F (política) right wing; (tenis) forehand; **a la —** to the right; **de —s** right-wing
derechista ADJ right-wing; MF rightist
derecho ADJ (no izquierdo) right; (recto) straight; **ponerse —** to hold oneself erect, to stand up straight; ADV straight; **volver — a casa** to go straight home; **todo —** straight ahead; M (preceptos, disciplina) law; (prerrogativa) right; **— al trabajo** right to work; **— consuetudinario** common law; **— de admisión** fee; **—s del cliente** customer rights; **— internacional** international law; **—s** fees; **—s aduaneros** tax on imports; **—s civiles** civil rights; **—s de autor** royalties; **—s de la mujer** women's rights; **—s de los animales** animal rights; **—s mineros** mineral rights; **estar en su —** to be entitled; **poner al —** to put on right side out; **registrar los —s** to copyright
derechura F straightness
deriva F drift; **ir a la —** to be adrift
derivación F derivation
derivado M (subproducto) by-product; (palabra) derivative
derivar VT to derive
dermabrasión F dermabrasion
dermatología F dermatology
dermatólogo -ga MF dermatologist
derogación F repeal
derogar[40] VT to repeal
derramamiento M spill, spilling; **— de sangre** bloodshed
derramar VT (un líquido) to spill; (sangre, lágrimas) to shed; **—se** to spill over, to run over
derrame M spill; **— cerebral** stroke, cerebral hemorrhage
derredor LOC ADV **en —** all around
derrengar[40] VT (dañar la espalda) to sprain one's back; (cansar) to exhaust
derretir[9] VT to melt; **—se por alguien** to be crazy about someone
derribar VT (un edificio) to demolish, to tear down; (a una persona) to knock down; (un gobierno) to topple, to overthrow; (un avión) to shoot down, to down
derrocamiento M overthrow
derrocar[30] VT (un gobierno) to overthrow, to topple; (a un dictador) to depose
derrochador -ora ADJ extravagant; MF (de dinero) spendthrift; (de recursos) squanderer
derrochar VT (dinero) to squander; (salud) to

radiate
derroche M (de recursos) waste, extravagance; (de color) profusion
derrota F defeat
derrotar VT to defeat
derrotero M course
derrubio M washout
derruido ADJ dilapidated
derrumbadero M precipice
derrumbamiento M collapse
derrumbar VT to demolish; **—se** (edificio) to collapse; (túnel, caverna) to cave in
derrumbe M (de tierra) landslide; (de un edificio) collapse
desabotonar VT to unbutton, to undo
desabrido ADJ (comida) tasteless; (persona) *Am* dull; *Esp* surly
desabrigado ADJ exposed; **no salgas tan —** put on some warm clothes before you go out
desabrochado ADJ undone, unfastened
desabrochar VT (botones) to undo; (ganchos) to unhook; (hebillas, cinturones) to unbuckle; (botones) to unbutton; **—se** to come undone
desacato M disrespect; **— al tribunal** contempt of court
desacelerar VI to decelerate
desacierto M mistake
desaconsejable ADJ inadvisable
desaconsejar VT to caution against
desacoplar VT to uncouple, to disconnect
desacostumbrado ADJ unusual
desacostumbrar VT to break of a habit; **—se** to lose a habit
desacreditar VT to discredit
desactivación F deactivation
desactivar VT (explosivo, situación) to defuse; (mecanismo) to disable; (virus) to deactivate
desacuerdo M disagreement; **estar en —** to be at odds
desafiante ADJ defiant
desafiar[28] VT (retar) to challenge, to dare; (enfrentar) to defy
desafilado ADJ dull
desafilar VT to dull; **—se** to become dull
desafinado ADJ out of tune, off-key
desafinar VT to be out of tune
desafío M (reto) challenge; (desobediencia) defiance
desafortunadamente ADV unfortunately
desafortunado ADJ unfortunate, unlucky
desafuero M (de un diputado) withdrawal of immunity; (atropello) outrage
desagradable ADJ disagreeable, unpleasant
desagradar VT to displease
desagradecido ADJ ungrateful
desagrado M displeasure
desagraviar VI to make amends, to redress
desagravio M redress
desaguadero M drainpipe
desaguar[25] VI to drain
desagüe M (acción de desaguar) drainage; (de lavabo) drain, drainpipe; (en la azotea) gutter
desaguisado M mess
desahogado ADJ (cómodo) comfortable; (espacioso) spacious
desahogar[40] VT (aliviar) to relieve; **—se** to pour out one's feelings
desahogo M relief; **vivir con —** to live an easy life
desairar VT to slight, to snub, to rebuff
desaire M slight, snub, rebuff
desajustar VT to loosen; **—se** to come loose
desalentado ADJ despondent
desalentador ADJ disheartening
desalentar[1] VT to discourage, to dishearten; **—se** to get discouraged
desaliento M discouragement, dismay
desaliñado ADJ disheveled, slovenly, unkempt
desaliño M slovenliness
desalmado ADJ heartless
desalojar VT (una piedra) to dislodge; (un tribunal) to clear; (un edificio) to evacuate; (a un inquilino) to evict; (una vivienda) to vacate
desamparado ADJ helpless, forlorn
desamparar VT to forsake
desamparo M abandonment, helplessness
desamueblado ADJ unfurnished
desangrar VT to bleed; **—se** to bleed to death
desanimado ADJ (persona) discouraged; (jornada) dull
desanimar VT to discourage
desánimo M discouragement
desaparecer[35] VI (perderse) to disappear, to vanish; (morir) to pass away
desaparezca, desaparezco *ver* desaparecer
desaparición F disappearance; (muerte) demise
desapasionado ADJ dispassionate
desapego M detachment
desapercibido ADJ unnoticed
desaprobación F disapproval
desaprobar[5] VT to disapprove of
desarmado ADJ unarmed
desarmar VT (quitar las armas) to disarm; (desmontar) to take apart
desarme M disarmament
desarraigar[40] VT to uproot
desarreglar VT to disturb, to mess up
desarreglo M (trastorno, enfermedad) disorder; (desorden) mess
desarrollador-ora MF developer
desarrollar VT (aumentar) to develop; (extender algo enrollado) to unroll; (llevar a cabo) to carry out; (aclarar) to elaborate, to flesh out; **—se** to unfold
desarrollo M development; (de una ecuación) expansion; **en —** developing
desarticulado ADJ disjointed
desaseado ADJ slovenly

desaseo M slovenliness
desasir[50] VT to let go of
desasosiego M uneasiness
desastrado ADJ (desaseado) untidy; (funesto) ill-fated
desastre M disaster
desastroso ADJ disastrous
desatado ADJ (ambición) unfettered; (zapatos) untied
desatar VT (un nudo) to untie, to loosen; (una ola de violencia) to unleash; **—se** to come untied; **—se en insultos** to let out a string of insults
desatascador M plunger
desatascar[30] VT (un inodoro) to unclog; (un objeto atrapado) to dislodge
desatención F lack of attention
desatender[2] VT (no ocuparse de algo) to neglect; (ignorar) to ignore
desatendido ADJ (descuidado) neglected; (ignorado) ignored
desatento ADJ inattentive
desatinado ADJ imprudent
desatornillar VT to unscrew
desatracar[30] VI/VT to cast off, to shove off
desavenencia F discord
desayunar VT **desayuné huevos** I had eggs for breakfast; **—se** to have breakfast; **—se [con que]** to find out [that]
desayuno M breakfast
desazón F uneasiness
desbandarse VI to disband
desbaratar VT (un plan) to disrupt; (un hechizo) to break; **—se** to break down
desbocado ADJ (caballo) runaway; (collar) loose
desbordamiento M overflow
desbordante ADJ overflowing
desbordar VI (derramar) to overflow; VT (abrumar) to overwhelm; **—se** to overflow, to spill over
desbravar VT to break
descabalgar[40] VI to dismount
descabellado ADJ harebrained
descabezar[47] VT to behead; **— un sueño** to take a nap
descafeinado ADJ decaffeinated
descalabrar VT (la cabeza) to split someone's head open; (a una persona) to hurt
descalabro M disaster
descalcificación F decalcification
descalificar VT to disqualify
descalzar[47] VT to take off someone's shoes; **—se** to take off one's shoes
descalzo ADJ barefoot
descaminado ADJ **andar/ir —** to be on the wrong track
descamisado ADJ (sin camisa) shirtless; (pobre) poor
descansar VI/VT to rest; **— en paz** to rest in peace; **—se en** to rely on
descanso M (acción de descansar) rest; (de escalera) landing; (intermisión, receso) break; (en fútbol) halftime; **en —** at ease
descapotable ADJ & M convertible
descarado ADJ shameless, impudent, brazen; **a la descarada** shamelessly
descarga F (de batería, agua, armas) discharge; (de buques) unloading; (emocional) outpouring; (de electricidad) shock; (de internet) download
descargar[40] VT (una batería, agua) to discharge; (un buque, un arma de fuego) to unload; (bomba) to drop; (un programa de computadora) to download; **—se** (una batería) to drain; (ira) to vent
descargo M **en su —** in his defense
descarnado ADJ (realidad) stark; (cara) emaciated
descaro M effrontery, impudence, nerve
descarriar[28] VT to lead astray; **—se** to go astray
descarrilarse VI to derail, to jump the track
descartar VT (un naipe) to discard; (una posibilidad) to dismiss, to discard
descarte M discard; **por —** by elimination
descascararse VI (en jirones) to peel; (en fragmentos) to chip, to flake
descendencia F (linaje) descent; (descendientes) descendants
descendente ADJ descending, downward
descender[2] VI to descend; **— de** to descend from
descendiente MF descendant
descenso M descent
descentralización F decentralization
descienda, desciende *ver* descender
descifrado M deciphering
descifrar VT to decipher
descodificación F decoding, decryption
descodificar[30] VT to decode, to decrypt
descolgar[42] VT (una cortina) to take down; (un teléfono) to pick up; **—se con** to come up with; **—se de** to come down from
descollar[5] VI to excel
descolorido ADJ (persona) pale; (cosa) colorless
descomponer[56, 74] VT (disgustar) to upset; (dar diarrea) to give diarrhea; (dar náuseas) to make nauseous; (separar) to break down; (cadáveres) to decompose; (un reloj) to break; **— en factores** to factor; **—se** (productos químicos) to break down; (cadáveres) to decompose; (un reloj) to break; (sentir náuseas) to be nauseous; (tener diarrea) to have diarrhea; (disgustarse) to go to pieces
descomposición F (de cadáveres) decomposition; (de productos químicos) breaking down; (diarrea) diarrhea
descomprimir VT to decompress
descompuesto ADJ (roto) broken; (caótico)

chaotic; (con diarrea) having diarrhea
descomunal ADJ enormous
desconcertado ADJ disconcerted
desconcertante ADJ disconcerting
desconcertar[1] VT to disconcert, to puzzle, to baffle; **—se** to become disconcerted
desconchar VT to chip
desconcierto M confusion
desconectado ADJ disconnected
desconectar VT to disconnect
desconexión F (acción de desconectar) disconnecting; (incomunicación) disconnect
desconfiado ADJ mistrustful, suspicious
desconfianza F mistrust
desconfiar[28] VT to distrust, to mistrust, to be wary of
descongelación F thawing
descongestionante M decongestant
descongestionar VT to decongest
desconocer[35] VT (no reconocer) to fail to recognize; (no saber) not to know; **te desconozco** you are not acting like yourself today
desconocido -da ADJ unknown; MF stranger
desconocimiento M ignorance
desconsideración F thoughtlessness
desconsiderado ADJ thoughtless, inconsiderate
desconsolado ADJ disconsolate, dejected
desconsolador ADJ disheartening
desconsolar[5] VT to dishearten; **—se** to become disheartened
desconsuelo M dejection
descontaminación F decontamination
descontaminar VT to decontaminate
descontar[5] VT (bajar el precio) to discount; (excluir) to exclude; (quitar) to dock
descontentadizo ADJ hard to please
descontentar VT to displease
descontento ADJ & M discontent
descorazonado ADJ disheartened
descortés ADJ discourteous, impolite
descortesía F discourtesy, impoliteness
descortezar[47] VT to strip the bark from
descoser VT to rip; **—se** to come unsewn
descosido ADJ unsewn; M unsewn place; **hablar como un —** to talk one's head off
descostrar VT to remove the crust from
descoyuntado ADJ dislocated, out of joint
descoyuntar VT to dislocate; **—se** to become dislocated
descrédito M discredit
descreído -da ADJ unbelieving; MF unbeliever
descreimiento M unbelief
describir[74] VT to describe
descripción F description
descriptivo ADJ descriptive
descrito *ver* describir
descuartizar[47] VT to quarter
descubierto ADJ (destapado) uncovered; (sin sombrero) hatless; **al —** in the open; **estar al —** to be exposed; **poner al —** to expose, to lay bare; **en —** overdrawn; M overdraft
descubierto *ver* descubrir
descubridor -ora MF discoverer
descubrimiento M discovery
descubrir[74] VT (hallar) to discover; (destapar) to uncover; **—se** to take off one's hat; **— el pastel** to spill the beans
descuento M discount; **— por grupo** group discount; **con —** at a discount; **los —s** extra time, injury time
descuidado ADJ (en una tarea) careless, negligent; (en el aspecto personal) slovenly
descuidar VT to neglect; **descuida, yo me ocupo de eso** don't worry, I'll take care of that; **—se** to be negligent
descuido M (falta de cuidado) neglect; (acción descuidada) oversight; **al —** offhand; **por —** by chance
desde PREP (origen) from; (tiempo) since; **— Madrid** from Madrid; **— el martes** since Tuesday; **— luego** of course; **— el principio** from the start; **— el vamos** from the get-go; **— entonces** ever since
desdecirse[53, 74] VI (contradecirse) to contradict oneself; (retractarse) to retract
desdén M disdain, scorn
desdentado ADJ toothless
desdeñar VT to disdain, to scorn
desdeñoso ADJ disdainful, scornful
desdicha F misfortune; **por —** unfortunately
desdichado ADJ wretched
desdoblamiento M division
desdoblar VT (desplegar) to unfold; (dividir) to divide
deseabilidad F desirability
deseable ADJ desirable
desear VT to desire
desecación F drying
desecar[30] VT to dry, to desiccate; **—se** to dry up, to desiccate
desechable VT disposable, throwaway
desechar VT (ropa vieja) to discard; (una oferta) to refuse; (una posibilidad) to dismiss
desecho M waste material; **—s** refuse, waste
desembalar VT to unpack
desembarazar[47] VT to rid of; **—se** to get rid of
desembarcadero M dock
desembarcar[30] VI (de un buque) to disembark, to go ashore; (de un avión) to deplane
desembarco M landing
desembarque M landing
desembocadura F mouth
desembocar[30] VI to flow; **— en** to flow into; **la calle Ocho desemboca en la avenida A** Eighth Street feeds into Avenue A
desembolsar VT to disburse, to pay out

desembolso M disbursement, outlay
desembragar[40] VI/VT to disengage [the clutch]
desempacar[30] VT to unpack
desempañar VT to wipe clean
desempate M (tenis) tie-break; **[partido de] desempate** playoff [game]
desempeñar VT to redeem; **— un cargo** to perform the duties of a position; **— un papel** to play a part; **—se** to get out of debt
desempeño M (de un cargo o papel) performance; (de una cosa en prenda) redemption
desempleado ADJ unemployed
desempleo M unemployment
desempolvar VT to dust off
desencadenar VT (quitar las cadenas) to unchain; (provocar, causar) to trigger, to spark
desencajado ADJ (mandíbula) dislocated; (mirada) wild; **estaba — en el funeral** he was deeply disturbed at the funeral
desencajar VT (un cajón) to unstick; (la mandíbula) to dislocate
desencantar VT (desilusionar) to disillusion; (quitar un hechizo) to remove a spell from
desencanto M disillusion
desenchufar VI/VT to unplug
desenfadado ADJ uninhibited
desenfado M lack of inhibition
desenfrenadamente ADV with wild abandon
desenfrenado ADJ (sin moderación) unbridled, wanton, rampant; (muy rápido) reckless
desenganchar VT to unhook
desengañar VT to disabuse; **—se** (de un error) to become disabused; (de una ilusión) to become disillusioned
desengaño M disillusion
desengranar VT to take out of gear
desenlace M (de un libro) ending; (de un suceso) outcome
desenmarañar VT to disentangle
desenmascarar VT to unmask, to expose
desenredar VT (el cabello) to disentangle; (una historia) to disentangle
desenrollar VT to unroll
desenroscar VT to untwist
desentenderse[2] VI to pay no attention
desentendido ADJ **hacerse el —** to pretend not to notice/know
desenterrar[1] VT (un tesoro) to unearth, to dig up; (un cadáver) to disinter
desentonado ADJ out of tune
desentonar VI (cantar mal) to sing off key; (estar fuera de lugar) to be out of place
desentrañar VT to unravel
desenvoltura F self-assurance
desenvolver[6, 74] VT (desenrollar) to unroll; (quitar la envoltura) to unwrap; **—se** to behave
desenvuelto ADJ self-assured
deseo M desire, wish; (sexual) desire; **pedir un —** to make a wish
deseoso ADJ desirous
desequilibrado -da ADJ unbalanced; MF unbalanced person
desequilibrar VT to unbalance
desequilibrio M imbalance
deserción F desertion; **— escolar** school dropout rate
desertar VI/VT to desert; **— de** to defect from
desértico ADJ desert
desertor -ora MF (militar) deserter; (escolar) drop-out
desesperación F desperation
desesperadamente ADV desperately
desesperado ADJ desperate
desesperanza F despair, hopelessness
desesperanzado ADJ hopeless
desesperanzar[47] VT to discourage, to deprive of hope; **—se** to despair
desesperar VI to despair; VT to drive crazy
desestabilizar[47] VT to destabilize
desestimación F rejection
desestimar VT to reject
desfachatez F audacity
desfalcar[30] VT to embezzle
desfalco M embezzlement
desfallecer[35] VI (debilitarse) to grow weak; (desmayarse) to faint
desfallecimiento M (debilidad) weakness; (desmayo) faint
desfavorable ADJ unfavorable
desfibrilación F defibrillation
desfibrilador M defibrillator
desfibrilar VT to defibrillate
desfigurar VT (el rostro) to disfigure; (una estatua) to deface
desfiladero M narrow passage
desfilar VI (coches) to file by; (soldados, modelos) to parade
desfile M parade
desgana F (falta de apetito) lack of appetite; (falta de entusiasmo) lack of enthusiasm
desganado ADJ apathetic, without enthusiasm
desgarbado ADJ ungainly, gawky
desgarrado ADJ (prenda, músculo) torn; (grito) heartrending
desgarradura F tear
desgarrar VT (rasgar) to tear; (un escándalo) to dredge up; **—le el corazón a alguien** to break someone's heart; **—se** to tear, to pull
desgarro M muscle pull
desgarrón M tear
desgastar VT to wear away; **—se** to get worn away
desgaste M wear and tear
desglosar VT (una suma) to itemize; (un tema) to break down

desglose M (de una suma) itemization; (de un tema) breakdown
desgracia F (infortunio) misfortune; (infelicidad) unhappiness; **—s personales** casualties; **caer en —** to fall into disgrace/disfavor
desgraciadamente ADV unfortunately
desgraciado -da ADJ (desafortunado) unfortunate; (infeliz) unhappy; MF (persona desafortunada) unfortunate person
desgranar VT (granos) to thrash, to thresh; (guisantes) to shell
desgravable ADJ tax-deductible
desgreñado ADJ disheveled, unkempt
desgreñar VT to dishevel; **—se** to muss up one's hair
desguazar[47] VT to scrap
deshabitado ADJ (territorio) uninhabited; (casa) vacant
deshacer[54, 74] VT (una acción, comando a la computadora) to undo; (una cama) to strip; (un plato, un jarrón) to destroy; (un sólido en un líquido) to dissolve; (un nudo) to untie; **—la maleta** to unpack the suitcase; **—se de** to get rid of; **—se en elogios** to rave about
deshaga, deshago, deshará, desharía *ver* deshacer
desharrapado ADJ ragged
deshecho *ver* deshacer
deshelar[1] VT to thaw
desheredar VT to disinherit
deshice, deshiciera, deshiciese *ver* deshacer
deshielo M thaw
deshierbar VT to weed
deshilachar VT to unravel, to fray
deshojado ADJ leafless
deshojar VT to strip of leaves; **—se** (un árbol) to shed leaves; (un libro) to lose pages
deshonestidad F (falta de honradez) dishonesty; (falta de recato) immodesty
deshonesto ADJ (no honrado) dishonest; (no modesto) immodest
deshonra F dishonor, disgrace
deshonrar VT to dishonor, to disgrace
deshonroso ADJ dishonorable
deshora LOC ADV **a —** at an inopportune time; **comer a —** to eat between meals
deshuesar VT (un fruto) to stone; (un animal) to bone
deshumanizar[47] VT to dehumanize
deshumidificador M dehumidifier
desidia F indolence
desierto ADJ (lugar) deserted; (premio) unawarded; M (región árida) desert; (región poco fértil y no habitada) wilderness
designación F (acción de designar, nombre) designation; (nombramiento) appointment
designar VT to designate; (a un funcionario) to appoint
designio M design
desigual ADJ (pelea) one-sided; (actuación) uneven; (números) not equal; (rango) unequal; (terreno) uneven
desigualdad F inequality; (del terreno) roughness
desilusión F disillusion, disappointment
desilusionar VT to disillusion, to disappoint; **—se** to become disillusioned/disappointed
desinencia F ending
desinfección F disinfection
desinfectante ADJ & M disinfectant
desinfectar VT to disinfect
desinfestación F disinfestation
desinflado ADJ (globo, persona) deflated; (neumático) flat; M flat tire
desinflar VT to deflate
desinformación F (falta de información) disinformation; (mala información) misinformation
desinformar VT to misinform
desinhibido ADJ uninhibited
desinstalar VT to uninstall
desintegración F disintegration; **— atómica** atomic decay
desintegrarse VI to disintegrate; (material radiactivo) to decay
desinterés M (falta de interés) lack of interest; (generosidad) unselfishness
desinteresado ADJ (apático) disinterested; (generoso) unselfish, selfless
desistir VI to desist
deslavado ADJ faded
deslavar VT (quitar color) to fade; (lavar ligeramente) to wash superficially
desleal ADJ (persona) disloyal, faithless; (competencia) unfair
desleír[10] VT to mix with a liquid
deslindar VT to mark off
desliz M slipup
deslizamiento M slide, glide
deslizar[47] VT (un patín) to slip, to slide, to glide; (una tarjeta) to swipe; **—se** (un patín) to slide, to glide; (un error) to slip by
deslucido ADJ (actuación) dull; (color) dingy
deslucir[39] VT (un espectáculo) to tarnish; (color) to make dingy
deslumbramiento M dazzle
deslumbrante ADJ dazzling
deslumbrar VT to dazzle; **—se** to be dazzled
deslustrar VT to tarnish
deslustre M tarnish
desmadejado ADJ (fatigado) exhausted; (desgarbado) ungainly
desmadejar VT to exhaust
desmán M abuse
desmantelar VT to dismantle
desmañado ADJ awkward, clumsy
desmayar VI to lose courage; **—se** to faint, to

pass out
desmayo M faint, swoon; **peleó sin —** he fought unflaggingly
desmedido ADJ excessive
desmejorar VI (empeorar el aspecto) to look worse; (debilitarse) to get worse
desmembrar VT to dismember
desmentido M denial
desmentir[8] VT to deny
desmenuzar[47] VT (pan) to crumble; (zanahorias) to mince
desmerecer[35] VI **— en valor** to not do justice; **no — de** to compare favorably with
desmesurado ADJ (esfuerzo) inordinate; (orejas) too large
desmigajar VT to crumb, to crumble
desmitificar[30] VT to debunk
desmochar VT to top, to cut the top off of
desmontar VT (limpiar un monte) to clear; (desarmar) to dismantle, to take apart; (derribar de una caballería) to throw; **—se** to dismount
desmoralizar[47] VT to demoralize; **—se** to become demoralized
desmoronar VT to crumble
desmovilizar[47] VT to demobilize
desnatar VT to skim
desnaturalizado ADJ (madre) unnatural; (aceite) denatured
desnudar VT to undress; **—se** to get undressed
desnudez F nakedness
desnudo ADJ nude, naked
desnutrición F malnutrition
desnutrido ADJ underfed, undernourished
desobedecer[35] VT to disobey
desobediencia F disobedience; **— civil** civil disobedience
desobediente ADJ disobedient
desocupación F (paro) unemployment; (abandono de vivienda) vacating
desocupado ADJ (asiento, casa) unoccupied, empty; (tiempo) idle; (que no trabaja) unemployed
desocupar VT to vacate; **—se** to become free
desodorante M deodorant
desodorizar VT to deodorize
desoír[55] VT to turn a deaf ear to
desolación F desolation
desolado ADJ desolate, bleak
desolar VT to lay waste to, to desolate; **—se** to be desolated
desollar[5] VT to skin; **— vivo** to skin alive
desorbitado ADJ (precio, reacción) out of proportion; (ojos) bulging
desorden M disorder, disarray; **— público** public disturbance; **en —** in disarray
desordenado ADJ (persona, situación) messy; (persona, estilo de vida) wild; (cuarto) untidy, disorderly; (archivo) disorganized
desordenar VT to mess up
desorganización F disorganization
desorganizado ADJ disorganized
desorientar VT (marear, hacer perder) to disorient; (confundir) to confuse; **—se** to lose one's bearings, to become disoriented
desovar VT to spawn
desoxidar VT to deoxidize
despabilado ADJ (despierto) wide-awake; (listo) on the ball
despabilar VT (cortar el pabilo) to trim the wick of; (despertar) to awaken; **—se** to wake up
despachar VT (problemas) to dispatch; (una carta) to mail; (a un cliente) to take care of; (mercancías) to ship; (a una víctima) to bump off; (un pedido) to fill; **— al público** to sell to the public; **—se a su gusto** to speak one's mind
despacho M (oficina) office; (comunicación) dispatch; (envío de cartas) mailing; (envío de mercancías) shipping
despachurrar VT to squash
despacio ADV slow, slowly
desparasitar VT to worm
desparejo ADJ uneven
desparpajo M (desenvoltura) ease; (descaro) impudence
desparramar VT to scatter; **—se** to be scattered
desparramo M (lío) commotion; (de libros) clutter
despatarrarse VT (caerse) to sprawl; (abrirse de piernas) to spread one's legs
despecho M spite; **por —** out of spite
despectivo ADJ derogatory, pejorative
despedazar[47] VT to tear to pieces
despedida F farewell; **— de soltero** bachelor party
despedir[9] VT (decir adiós) to see off; (echar de un empleo) to fire, to dismiss; (emitir un dolor) to emit, to give off; **despídeme de tus padres** say good-bye to your parents for me; **—se [de]** to take leave [of], to say good-bye [to]
despegar[40] VT (dos cosas pegadas) to detach; VI (un avión) to take off; (un cohete) to blast off; **—se** to become detached
despegue M (de avión) takeoff; (de cohete) blastoff, liftoff
despeinado ADJ unkempt
despejado ADJ (el cielo) clear, cloudless; (un camino) clear; (la frente) with one's hair pulled back; (una persona) bright
despejador M (fútbol americano) punter
despejar VT (el campo, una pelota) to clear; (en fútbol americano) to punt; VI (una duda, el cielo) to clear up; **—se** to sober up
despellejar VT to skin
despensa F pantry
despeñadero M cliff

despeñar VT to push off a precipice; **—se** to fall down a precipice
despepitar VT (una granada) to seed; (una manzana) to core; **—se por una cosa** to be crazy about something
desperdiciar VT to waste; **—se** to go to waste
desperdicio M waste; **—s** scraps
desperdigar[40] VT to scatter; **—se** to be scattered
desperezarse[47] VI to stretch
desperezo M stretch
desperfecto M damage; **— mecánico** mechanical breakdown
despertador M alarm clock
despertar[1] VT (a una persona) to awaken, to wake up; (sospecha) to arouse; (interés, deseo) to kindle; **—se** to wake up
despiadado ADJ merciless, heartless, ruthless
despida, despide, despidiendo, despidiera, despidiese *ver* despedir
despido M dismissal, termination; **— temporal de un empleado** layoff
despierta, despierte *ver* despertar
despierto ADJ (no dormido) awake; (vivaracho) alert
despilfarrador ADJ wasteful
despilfarrar VT to squander
despilfarro M waste
despistado ADJ absent-minded, out of it
despistar VT (confundir) to throw off the track; (deshacerse de) to lose; **—se** to get confused
desplantador M trowel
desplante M rude remark
desplazado-da MF displaced person
desplazamiento M (de tropas) movement; (de refugiados) displacement
desplazar[47] VT to displace; **—se** to move
desplegar[41] VT (papel plegado) to unfold; (una bandera) to unfurl; (tropas) to deploy; (interés) to display
despliegue M display
desplomarse VI (edificio, precios) to collapse; (una persona) to slump; (esperanzas) to be dashed
desplome M collapse
desplumar VT (un ave) to pluck; (a un incauto) to fleece
despoblado ADJ uninhabited; **— de árboles** treeless; M open country
despojar VT to despoil; **—se** to shed leaves
despojos M PL (de batalla) spoils; (mortales) remains
desportilladura F chip
desportillar VT to chip
desposeer VT to dispossess
déspota MF despot
despótico ADJ despotic
despotismo M despotism
despotricar[30] VI to rant
despreciable ADJ (vil) contemptible, despicable, worthless; (insignificante) negligible
despreciar VT (menospreciar) to despise, to look down on; (rechazar) to snub
desprecio M (menosprecio) contempt, disdain; (rechazo) snub
desprender VT (un cierre) to unfasten; (algo prendido) to detach; (gases) to give off; **—se de algo** to part with something; **—se la ropa** to undo one's clothes; **de lo dicho se desprende que** from what has been said it follows that
desprendimiento M (de retina) detachment; (de energía) release; (de tierra) landslide; (generosidad) generosity
despreocupado ADJ carefree
desprestigiar VT to discredit; **—se** to lose one's prestige
desprestigio M loss of prestige
desprevenido ADJ unprepared; **tomar —** to take by surprise
desproporcionado ADJ disproportionate, out of proportion
despropósito M nonsense
desprovisto ADJ **— de** lacking in
después ADV after, afterward; **— de** after; **— de todo** after all; **— de horas hábiles** after hours
despuntar VI/VT to blunt; **—se** to become blunt
desquiciar VT to unhinge; **—se** to come unhinged
desquitarse VI to get even
desquite M getting even, revenge
desregular VT to deregulate
destacable ADJ notable, noteworthy
destacado ADJ outstanding
destacamento M military detachment, military detail
destacar[30] VT (tropas) to detach; (una cualidad) to highlight, to accentuate; VI to stand out; **—se** to stand out
destajo LOC ADV **a —** by the job
destapar VT (una cacerola) to take the top off; (un plan, a un niño en cama) to uncover; **—se** (en la cama) to uncover; (desnudarse) to bare all
destartalado ADJ dilapidated
destellar VI to flash
destello M flash
destemplado ADJ (persona) feverish; (sonido) out of tune
desteñido ADJ washed-out
desteñir[11] VI/VT to fade; VI to run; **—se** to fade
desternillarse VI **— de risa** to die laughing
desterrado-da ADJ exiled, banished; MF (persona) exile
desterrar[1] VT to exile, to banish
destetar VT to wean

destierro M exile, banishment
destilación F distillation
destilar VT to distill
destilería F distillery
destinar VT (determinar el destino) to destine; (dirigir) to address; (asignar) to commit
destinatario -ria MF addressee, recipient
destino M (hado) destiny, fate, lot; (uso) use; (final de viaje) destination
destitución F dismissal
destituir[19] VT to dismiss
destornillador M screwdriver
destoxificación F detoxification
destrabar VT to untie
destreza F dexterity, skill
destripar VT to gut
destronar VT to dethrone
destrozar[47] VT (estropear) to ruin; (causar grandes daños) to destroy; (derrotar) to rout
destrozo M damage
destrucción F destruction
destructible ADJ destructible
destructivo ADJ destructive
destructor -ra ADJ destructive; M (buque) destroyer; MF (persona) destroyer
destruir[19] VT (destrozar) to destroy, to obliterate; (estropear) to ruin
destruya, destruya, destruyendo, destruyera, destruyese *ver* destruir
desunir VT to divide; **—se** to come apart
desusado ADJ (no frecuente) unusual; (no usado) obsolete
desuso M disuse, obsolescence; **caer en —** to fall into disuse
desvaído ADJ faded
desvainar VT to hull, to husk
desvalido ADJ helpless
desvalijar VT (un cuarto) to ransack; (a una persona) to clean out
desvalimiento M helplessness
desván M attic
desvanecer[35] VT (un color) to fade; (un contorno) to blur; **—se** (una persona) to faint; (un color, arrugas) to fade; (un sonido) to trail off
desvanecido ADJ (una persona) fainted; (un color) faded; (un contorno) blurred
desvanecimiento M (de una persona) fainting; (de colores) fading; (de un contorno) blurring
desvariar[28] VI to rave
desvarío M raving
desvelado ADJ sleepless
desvelar VT to keep awake; **—se** to be sleepless
desvelo M (falta de sueño) sleeplessness; **—s** (esfuerzos) efforts
desvencijado ADJ dilapidated, rickety; **estoy —** I'm all beat up
desventaja F disadvantage; **estar en —** to be at a disadvantage
desventura F misfortune
desventurado ADJ unfortunate
desvergonzado ADJ shameless
desvergüenza F shamelessness
desvestir[9] VT to undress; **—se** to get undressed, to undress
desviación F (de una norma) deviation, divergence; (en ruta) detour; (de fondos) diversion; (de la columna vertebral) curvature; **— estándar** standard deviation
desviar[28] VT (la vista) to avert; (fondos, tráfico) to divert; (un golpe) to ward off; (una conversación) to steer; (un tren) to sidetrack; **—se de** (un camino) to stray from; (una norma) to deviate from
desvío M (camino secundario) side road; (desviación) detour
desvirtuar[26] VT to distort; **—se** to become distorted
desvivirse VI **— por hacer algo** to bend over backward to do something; **— por alguien** to go out of one's way for someone
detallado ADJ detailed
detallar VT to detail, to go into detail about
detalle M (pormenor) detail; (venta al por menor) retail; (lista) list; **¡qué —!** how thoughtful! **con/al/en —** in detail
detallista ADJ (cuidadoso) meticulous; (considerado) thoughtful; M (comercio) retail; MF retailer
detección F detection
detectar VT to detect
detective M detective; **— privado** private eye
detector M detector; **— de incendios** smoke detector; **— de mentiras** lie detector; **— de metales** metal detector
detención F (arresto) detention, arrest; (de un vehículo) stop; **— domiciliaria** house arrest; **— ilegal** false arrest
detendrá, detendría *ver* detener
detener[58] VT (arrestar) to detain, to arrest; (parar) to stop; **—se** to stop; **—se en** to linger on; **—se a pensar** to stop to think
detenga, detengo *ver* detener
detenidamente ADV closely
detenido ADJ thorough
detenimiento LOC ADV **con —** with care
detergente ADJ & M detergent
deteriorado ADJ in disrepair
deteriorar VT to deteriorate
deterioro M deterioration, disrepair
determinación F determination; **— del grupo sanguíneo** blood typing
determinado ADJ (cierto) certain; **es lo que suponen determinadas personas** that is what certain people suppose; (específico) definite, specific; **pidió una cantidad determinada** he asked for a specific amount
determinante ADJ determining; M determiner

determinar VT to determine
detestable ADJ detestable
detestar VT to detest
detiene, detienes *ver* detener
detonación F detonation; **hacer detonaciones** to backfire
detonar VI/VT to detonate
detrás ADV behind; **— de** (en el espacio) behind; (en el tiempo) after; **por —** behind
detritus M INV debris
detuve, detuviera, detuviese *ver* detener
deuce M deuce
deuda F debt; **— incobrable** bad debt
deudor -ora ADJ & MF debtor; **— hipotecario** mortgagor
devaluación F devaluation
devanar VT to spool; **—se los sesos** to rack one's brain
devaneo M (pasatiempo) idle pursuit; (amorío) fling
devastador ADJ devastating
devastar VT to devastate
devengar[40] VT to earn
devoción F devotion
devolución F (de un producto) return; (de poder político) devolution
devolver[6, 74] VT (dar al dueño) to return; (enviar por correo) to send back; **— al remitente** to return to sender; **— la llamada** to call back; VI (vomitar) to throw up
devorar VT to devour
devoto ADJ (pío) devout; (que muestra devoción) devoted
devuelto, devuelva, devuelve *ver* devolver
dextrosa F dextrose
di *ver* dar, decir
día M day; **— a —** day-to-day; **— tras —** day after day; **al —** up-to-date; **al otro —** on the next day; **de —** by day; **de todos los —s** everyday; **el — de mañana** in the future; **hoy —** nowadays; **no veo el —** I can't wait; **ponerse al —** to catch up; **por —** by the day; **todo el —** all day; **todos los —s** every day; **un — sí y otro no** every other day; **vivir al —** to live from hand to mouth
diabetes F SG diabetes
diablo M devil; **pobre —** poor devil; **¿por qué —s dices eso?** *fam* why the heck are you saying that?
diablura F devilry, mischief
diabólico ADJ (ritual) diabolic, devilish; (perverso) diabolical
diácono M deacon
diacrítico ADJ & M diacritic
diafragma M diaphragm
diagnosis F diagnosis
diagnosticar[30] VT to diagnose
diagnóstico ADJ diagnostic; M diagnosis
diagonal ADJ & F diagonal
diagrama M diagram; **— de flujo** flow chart; **— de pastel** pie chart
dial M dial
dialéctica F dialectic
dialéctico ADJ dialectic
dialecto M dialect
dialectología F dialectology
diálisis F dialysis
dialogar[40] VI to dialogue, to hold talks
diálogo M dialogue, conversation; **fue un — de sordos** they talked past each other
diamante M diamond; **— en bruto** diamond in the rough
diámetro M diameter
diana F bull's-eye
diapasón M tuning fork
diapositiva F slide
diario ADJ daily; M (periódico) newspaper; (de sucesos personales) journal, diary; (de navegación) log; **a —** every day; **de —** everyday; **llevar un —** to keep a diary
diarrea F diarrhea
diastólico ADJ diastolic
diatriba F diatribe
dibujante MF illustrator
dibujar VT to draw; **—se** to appear, to loom
dibujo M (arte de dibujar, cosa dibujada) drawing; (diseño) design; **— al carbón** charcoal drawing; **—s animados** animated cartoon
dicción F diction
diccionario M dictionary
dice, dicen *ver* decir
dicha F happiness
dicharachero ADJ witty
dicho ADJ aforementioned; M saying
dicho *ver* decir
dichoso ADJ happy; **todo el — día** the whole blessed day
diciembre M December
diciendo *ver* decir
dicotomía F dichotomy
dictado M (ejercicio) dictation; (orden) dictate; **escribir al —** to take dictation
dictador -ora MF dictator
dictadura F dictatorship
dictamen M (opinión) report; (judicial) ruling
dictaminar VI (dar una opinión) to report; (fallar) to rule
dictar VT to dictate; **— clase** to teach class; **— sentencia** to rule
diecinueve NUM nineteen
dieciocho NUM eighteen
dieciséis NUM sixteen
diecisiete NUM seventeen
diente M (de persona, sierra) tooth; (de víbora) fang; (de rueda dentada) cog; (de tenedor) prong; **— de león** dandelion; **— de leche** baby tooth; **—s postizos** false teeth; **entre**

—**s** under one's breath; **tener buen** — to have a good appetite
diera, diese *ver* dar
diesel M diesel
diestra F right hand
diestro -tra ADJ (habilidoso) skillful, deft; (no zurdo) right-handed; MF right-handed person; **a diestra y siniestra** on all sides
dieta F (ingesta) diet; (dinero para gastos) per diem; **estar a** — to be on a diet
dietético ADJ dietary
dietista MF dietitian
diez NUM ten
diezmar VT to decimate
diezmo M tithe; **pagar el** — to tithe
difamación F (oral) slander; (escrita) libel
difamar VT to defame, to malign; (oralmente) to slander; (por escrito) to libel
difamatorio ADJ slanderous
diferencia F difference; **a** — **de** unlike; **hacer** —**s entre** to treat differently; **partir la** — to split the difference
diferenciación F differentiation, distinction
diferencial ADJ & M (distancia, pieza de coche) differential; F (matemática) differential
diferenciar VT to differentiate; —**se de** to differ from
diferente ADJ different
diferir[8] VT (aplazar) to defer; VI (ser diferente) to differ
difícil ADJ difficult, hard
difícilmente ADV (apenas) hardly; (con dificultad) with difficulty
dificultad F difficulty
dificultar VT to make difficult
dificultoso ADJ difficult
difteria F diphtheria
difundir VT (luz) to diffuse; (noticias) to broadcast
difunto -ta ADJ & MF deceased
difusión F (de luz) diffusion; (de noticias) broadcasting
difuso ADJ diffuse
diga *ver* decir
digerible ADJ digestible
digerir[8] VT to digest
digestible ADJ digestible
digestión F digestion
digestivo ADJ digestive
digesto M digest
digital ADJ digital
digitalizar[47] VT to digitalize, to digitize
digitar VI/VT to type
dígito M digit
dignarse VI to deign
dignatario -ria MF dignitary
dignidad F dignity
digno ADJ (respetable) worthy; (orgulloso) dignified; — **de confianza** trustworthy; — **de elogio** praiseworthy
digo *ver* decir
digresión F digression
dije M charm
dije, dijera, dijese *ver* decir
dilación F delay; **sin** — without delay
dilatación F (de un metal, parte dilatada) expansion; (del ojo) dilation
dilatar VT (pupilas, capilares) to dilate; (metal, músculo) to expand; (tiempo, plazo) to defer; (prolongar) to prolong; —**se en un asunto** to dwell on a subject
dilema M dilemma
diletante MF dilettante
diligencia F (laboriosidad) diligence, industry; (vehículo) stagecoach; (tarea) errand; — **debida** due diligence
diligente ADJ diligent, industrious
dilucidar VT to elucidate
diluido ADJ dilute
diluir[19] VT (una solución) to dilute; (pintura, sopa) to thin
diluvio M deluge
dimensión F dimension
dimes M PL — **y diretes** gossip; **andar en** — **y diretes** to quibble
diminutivo ADJ & M diminutive
diminuto ADJ (tamaño) diminutive; (cantidad) minute
dimisión F resignation
dimitir VI to resign
Dinamarca F Denmark
dinámica F dynamics
dinámico ADJ dynamic
dinamismo M vigor
dinamita F dynamite
dinamitar VT to dynamite
dínamo M dynamo
dinastía F dynasty
dineral M fortune
dinero M money; — **contante y sonante** ready cash, hard cash; — **de plástico** plastic, credit card; — **sucio** dirty money
dinosaurio M dinosaur
diodo M diode; — **electroluminiscente** light-emitting diode
Dios M God; **dios** god; — **dirá** we'll see; — **los cría y ellos se juntan** birds of a feather flock together; — **mediante** God willing; **¡**— **mío!** my God! — **te lo pague** may God reward you; — **y su madre** everybody and their dog; **a la buena de** — any old way; **como** — **manda** as it should be; **¡por** —**!** oh, my! **que** — **te oiga** I hope you're right
diosa F goddess
diploma M diploma
diplomacia F diplomacy
diplomático -ca ADJ diplomatic; MF diplomat
diptongo M diphthong

diputación F council
diputado -da MF representative
dique M (presa) dike; (al lado de un río) levee; — **seco** dry dock
dirá *ver* decir
dirección F (sentido, rumbo) direction; (domicilio) address; (administración) management; (administración de una escuela) principal's office; (mecanismo, acción de conducir) steering; — **asistida** power steering; — **de correo electrónico** e-mail address
directiva F (orden) directive; (norma) guidelines; (junta de directores) board of directors
directrices F PL guidelines
directivo -va ADJ leadership; MF officer
directo ADJ (sin desviaciones, intermediarios) direct; (derecho) straight; **en** — live
director -ora MF (de una empresa) director, manager; (de una escuela) principal; (de orquesta) conductor; — **de correos** postmaster; — **general** CEO; — **técnico** coach
directorio M (índice) directory; (junta directiva) board of directors; — **[de] raíz** root directory; — **padre** parent directory
diría *ver* decir
dirigente MF leader; — **sindical** union leader
dirigible M dirigible
dirigir[46] VT (una obra teatral) to direct; (una empresa) to manage; (una orquesta) to conduct; (a un turista) to guide; (un saludo, una carta, una pregunta, una crítica) to address; —**se a** (hablar con) to address; (ir a) to go to; (tratar de) to be aimed at
discapacidad F disability
discapacitado ADJ disabled
discar[30] VI/VT *Am* to dial
discernimiento M discernment, insight
discernir[3] VT to discern
disciplina F discipline
disciplinar VT to discipline
discípulo -la MF disciple
disco M (cartílago, objeto plano y circular) disk; (fonográfico) record; — **compacto** compact disc; — **comprimido** compressed disk; — **de iniciación** boot disk; — **duro** hard disk; — **duro interno** internal hard disk; — **volador** Frisbee®; **es un** — **rayado** he's a broken record
díscolo ADJ unruly
disconforme ADJ dissatisfied
discontinuo ADJ discontinuous
discordancia F discord
discordia F discord
discoteca F (lugar donde bailar) discotheque; (colección de discos) record collection
discreción F discretion; **a** — at one's own discretion
discrepancia F discrepancy
discrepar VI to disagree; — **de** to take issue with
discreto ADJ (prudente) discreet; (separado) discrete; **un partido** — a sorry game
discriminación F discrimination; — **por edad** age discrimination; — **positiva** affirmative action; — **sexual** sexual discrimination
discriminar VI to discriminate; — **a** to discriminate against
disculpa F (excusa) excuse; (perdón) apology
disculpable ADJ excusable
disculpar VT (excusar) to excuse; (perdonar) to forgive, to pardon; —**se** to apologize
discurrir VI (transcurrir) to pass; (exponer) to discourse
discursear VI to make speeches
discurso M (enunciado) discourse; (disertación pública) speech, address; — **de apertura** keynote address
discusión F (charla) discussion; (riña) argument
discutible ADJ debatable, questionable
discutir VT (hablar sobre) to discuss; (oponerse a) to dispute; VI (reñir) to argue
disecar[30] VT (cortar) to dissect; (preparar para conservar) to stuff
diseminación F dissemination
diseminar VT to disseminate
disensión F dissension, dissent
disenso M dissent
disentería F dysentery
disentir[8] VI to dissent, to disagree
diseñador -ora MF designer
diseñar VT to design
diseño M design; — **de interiores** interior design; — **de página** page layout; — **gráfico** graphic design
disertación F lecture
disertar VI to lecture
disfraz M (para ocultarse) disguise; (de carnaval) costume
disfrazar[47] VT to disguise
disfrutar VI/VT to enjoy; — **de** to enjoy
disfrute M enjoyment
disfunción F dysfunction
disgustado ADJ (molesto) upset; (enojado) angry
disgustar VT to upset; —**se** (molestarse) to get upset; (enfadarse) to get angry
disgusto M (desagrado) unpleasantness; (discusión) quarrel; **a** — (con desgana) against one's will; (con incomodidad) uncomfortably; (en disconformidad) in conflict; **esa niña no da más que** —**s** that girl keeps us upset all the time
disidente ADJ & MF dissident
disimulado ADJ **hacerse el** — to pretend not to notice
disimular VI (fingir) to dissemble; (ocultar) to

conceal
disimulo M (fingimiento) dissimulation; (ocultamiento) concealment
disipación F dissipation
disipar VT (niebla, calor) to dissipate; (dudas) to dispel; (miedo) to allay; (dinero) to squander; **—se** to dissipate; (miedo, dudas) to allay, to lift
dislexia F dyslexia
dislocación F dislocation
dislocar[30] VT to dislocate; **—se** to get dislocated
disminución F (acción de disminuir) decrease, lessening; (desprecio) belittling; (de ventas) dip, decrease
disminuir[19] VT (menguar) to diminish, to decrease, to lessen; (despreciar) to belittle
disminuya, disminuye, disminuyendo, disminuyera, disminuyese *ver* disminuir
disolución F dissolution
disoluto ADJ dissolute, loose
disolvente M solvent; **— de pintura** paint thinner
disolver[6, 74] VT (sal) to dissolve; (reunión) to break up
disonancia F discord
dispar ADJ disparate
disparar VT (un arma de fuego) to shoot, to fire; (una cámara) to click; (la inflación) to trigger; VI (en fútbol) to shoot; **—le a alguien** to shoot at someone; **—se** (aumentar) to take off; (salir) to shoot out
disparatado ADJ absurd
disparatar VI to talk nonsense
disparate M absurdity, nonsense; **decir —s** to talk nonsense; **un — de plata** a ton of money
disparo M (acción de disparar) shooting; (tiro, herida) shot, gunshot; (tiro de fútbol) shot at goal
dispensa F dispensation
dispensación F dispensation
dispensar VT to dispense; **— de** to exempt from
dispensario M dispensary
dispersar VT to disperse
dispersión F dispersal
disperso ADJ (diseminado) dispersed, scattered; (distraído) absent-minded, distracted; (no concentrado) disperse
display M display
displicencia F flippancy
displicente ADJ (comportamiento) flippant; (actitud) cavalier
dispon, dispondrá, dispondría *ver* disponer
disponer[56, 74] VT (colocar) to arrange; (preparar) to prepare, to dispose; (mandar) to order; **— de** to have; **—se** to set about; **—se para** to get ready for
disponga, dispongo *ver* disponer
disponibilidad F availability
disponible ADJ (asiento, taxi) available; (dinero) on hand; (inventario) in stock
disposición F (voluntad) disposition; (colocación) arrangement; (de ánimo) mood; **a — de** at the disposal of
dispositivo M device; **— analógico** analog device; **— de almacenamiento** storage device; **— de salida** output device; **— intrauterino** intrauterine device
dispuesto ADJ ready; **bien —** willing; **no estar — a** to be unwilling to
dispuesto, dispuse, dispusiera, dispusiese *ver* disponer
disputa F (controversia) dispute; (riña) argument
disputar VI/VT to dispute; **—se el poder** to vie/challenge/contend for power; **—se la posición** to jockey for position
disquete M floppy disk; **— de iniciación** bootable diskette
disquetera F disk drive
distancia F distance; **a —** at arm's length; **guardar —s** to keep at a distance; **¿a qué — está?** how far away is it?
distanciarse VT to distance oneself
distante ADJ distant
distar VI **dista mucho de** it's a far cry from; **dista diez kilómetros de** it's ten kilometers from
distender[2] VT (aflojar) to relax; (dilatar) to expand
distensión F distension; **— muscular** muscle strain
distinción F distinction
distinguido ADJ distinguished
distinguir[44] VT to distinguish
distintivo ADJ distinctive, distinguishing; M distinguishing characteristic
distinto ADJ (diferente) different; (claro) distinct
distorsión F distortion
distorsionar VT to distort
distracción F distraction
distraer[59] VT (la atención) to distract; (fondos, mano de obra) to divert; **—se** (divertirse) to entertain oneself; (dispersarse) to become distracted, *fam* to space out
distraído ADJ distracted, absent-minded; **hacerse el —** to play dumb
distribución F distribution
distribuidor-ora MF (persona) distributor; M (pieza de un motor) distributor
distribuir[19] VT to distribute
distrito M district
Distrito de Columbia M District of Columbia
distrofia F dystrophy; **— muscular** muscular dystrophy
disturbio M disturbance, trouble
disuadir VT (mediante palabras) to dissuade; (mediante acciones) to deter

DIU [dispositivo intrauterino] M IUD
diurético ADJ & M diuretic
diurno ADJ (actividad) daytime; (animal) diurnal
divagación F rambling
divagar[40] VI to ramble on, to digress
diván M divan; (de psiquiatra) couch
divergencia F divergence
divergir[46] VI to diverge
diversidad F diversity
diversión F (pasatiempo) amusement, entertainment, fun; (hecho de distraer la atención) diversion
diverso ADJ diverse; **—s** various
diverticulitis F diverticulitis
divertido ADJ amusing, entertaining
divertir[8] VT to amuse, to entertain; **—se** to have a good time, to have fun
dividendo M dividend
dividir VT to divide; (un territorio) to partition
divierta, divierte *ver* divertir
divieso M boil
divinidad F divinity
divino ADJ divine; **estuvo —** it was heavenly; **lo pasé —** I had a wonderful time
divirtiendo, divirtiera, divirtiese, divirtió *ver* divertir
divisa F (señal) emblem; (moneda) currency; (moneda extranjera) foreign currency
divisar VT to make out, to catch sight of
división F division; (de un territorio) partition
divisorio ADJ dividing
divorciar VT to divorce; **—se** to get divorced
divorcio M divorce
divulgación F dissemination; **— financiera** financial disclosure
divulgar[40] VT (un secreto) to divulge; (información) to disseminate
dobladillo M hem; **hacer —s** to hem
doblado ADJ (hipócrita) hypocritical; M (de tela, papel) folding; (de tubos) bending
doblaje M dubbing
doblar VT (una sábana) to fold; (el capital) to double; (una esquina) to turn; (la voz de un actor) to dub; VI (un coche) to turn; (una campana) to knell; **—se** to bend over
doble ADJ double (también en tenis); **— agente** double agent; **— falta** double fault; **— indemnización** double indemnity; **— matanza** double play; **— pulsación** double click; **— personalidad** split personality; **— visión** double vision; **de — caño** double-barreled; **de — filo** double-edged; **de — sentido** two-way; MF (persona muy parecida, actor sustituto) double; M (repique) knell; **—s** doubles; **—s mixtos** mixed doubles; **el —** double
doblegar[40] VT to break
doblete M double
doblez M fold; F deceitfulness
doce NUM twelve
docena F dozen; **— del fraile** baker's dozen
docente ADJ teaching
dócil ADJ (persona, animal) docile, pliant; (pelo) manageable
docto ADJ learned
doctor-ora MF doctor; **— en medicina** MD
doctorado M doctorate
doctrina F doctrine
documentación F documentation (también para computadoras)
documental ADJ & M documentary
documentar VT to document
documento M document; **— de instrucciones previas** living will; **— de voluntad anticipada** living will
dogma M dogma
dogmático ADJ dogmatic
dogo M pug
dólar M dollar
dolencia F ailment
doler[6] VI to ache, to hurt; **me duele el brazo** my arm aches, my arm is sore; **—se de** (compadecerse) to feel sorry for; (arrepentirse) to regret
doliente ADJ aching; MF mourner
dolor M (físico) pain, ache; (espiritual) sorrow, pain; **— de barriga** bellyache; **— de cabeza** headache; **— de espalda** backache; **— de muela** toothache; **— de oídos** earache; **— de garganta** sore throat; **—es del crecimiento** growing pains; **— de garganta** sore throat; **—es de parto** labor pains
dolorido ADJ aching, sore
doloroso ADJ painful
doma F (de caballos) breaking; (de leones) taming
domado ADJ (caballo) broken; (león) tamed
domador-ora MF (de perros) trainer; (de leones) lion tamer
domar VT (caballos, personas) to break; (leones) to tame
domesticar[30] VT to domesticate, to tame
doméstico-ca ADJ domestic; MF servant
domiciliarse VI to take up residence; **¿dónde se domicilia usted?** where do you reside?
domicilio M (casa) dwelling; (dirección) address
dominación F domination
dominador ADJ (predominante) dominant; (tiránico) domineering, overbearing
dominante ADJ (predominante) dominant; (tiránico) domineering, overbearing
dominar VT (tener bajo su autoridad, ser más alto) to dominate; (reprimir) to control, to rein in; (tener sometido a su voluntad) to domineer
domingo M Sunday; **— de Ramos** Palm Sunday; **— de Pascua** Easter Sunday

Dominica F Dominica
dominicano-na ADJ & MF Dominican [de la República Dominicana]
dominio M (sobre una tierra, derecho de usar una cosa) dominion; (de sí mismo) control; (de una lengua) mastery, command; (hecho de dominar) domination; (ámbito, campo) domain; **— público** public domain
dominiqués-esa ADJ & MF Dominican [de Dominica]
dominó M (pieza) domino; (juego) dominoes
domo M dome
don M (gracia) gift; (título, jefe mafioso) don; **un — nadie** a nobody
dona F *Méx* doughnut, donut
donación F donation
donador-ora MF donor
donaire M grace
donante MF donor; **— universal** universal donor
donar MF to donate
doncella F *lit* maiden
donde ADV REL where; **de —** whence, from which; **ir — el herrero** to go to the blacksmith's shop; **— no** otherwise; **—quiera** wherever; **donde no comas, no te dejo salir a jugar** if you don't eat, I won't let you go out to play
dónde ADV INTERR where
donoso ADJ graceful
donut M *Esp* doughnut, donut
doña F doña
dopamina F dopamine
dopar VT to dope
dorado ADJ (cubierto de oro) gilt; (de color oro) golden; M dolphin fish
dorar VT to gild; **— la píldora** to sweeten the pill
dormido ADJ asleep
dormir[7] VI/VT to sleep; **— a** to put to bed; **— a un paciente** to anesthetize a patient; **— la mona** to sleep it off; **— la siesta** to take a nap; **se me ha dormido el brazo** my arm has fallen asleep; **—se** to fall asleep
dormitar VI to doze, to snooze
dormitorio M bedroom
dorso M back, reverse
dos NUM two; **— puntos** colon; **— veces** twice; **cada — por tres** constantly; **en un — por tres** in a jiffy; **los —** both of them
DOS M DOS
doscientos NUM two hundred
dosel M canopy
dosificar[30] VT to dose
dosis F (de medicamento) dose; (de droga) hit
dotación F (de fondos) endowment; (de personal) complement
dotar VT to endow
dote F dowry; **—s** talents
doy *ver* dar
draga F dredge
dragado M dredging
dragar[40] VT (para limpiar) to dredge; (para buscar objetos) to drag; M SG **dragaminas** minesweeper
dragón M (animal fantástico) dragon; (planta) snapdragon
drama M drama
dramático ADJ dramatic
dramatizar[47] VT to dramatize
dramaturgo-ga MF playwright, dramatist
drapear VI to drape
drástico ADJ drastic
drenaje M drainage
drenar VI/VT to drain
dribbling M dribble, dribbling
driblar VI/VT to dribble
drible M dribble
dril M drill
drive M drive
drive-in M drive-in
driver M driver
droga F drug; **— anticancerosa** anticancer drug; **—s de diseño** designer drugs; **tomar —s** to do drugs; MF **drogadicto-ta** drug addict
drogar[40] VT to drug
drogata MF junkie
drogota MF junkie
droguería F (tienda) drugstore; (industria) drug industry
droguero-ra MF druggist
dropar VI to drop
ducado M dukedom
ducha F shower
ducharse VI to shower
ducho ADJ skillful
dúctil ADJ (metal) ductile; (persona) flexible, supple
duda F doubt; **en —** in doubt; **fuera de —** beyond doubt; **no cabe —** there's no doubt; **poner en —** to cast doubt on; **sin —** without a doubt, undoubtedly; **sin lugar a —s** without doubt; **tengo una —** I have a question
dudar VT (no creer) to doubt; (vacilar) to hesitate; **— de** to have doubts about
dudoso ADJ doubtful; **de dudosa honestidad** of dubious honesty
duela F stave
duela, duele *ver* doler
duelo M (combate) duel; (luto) mourning; (pena) grief; (dolientes) mourners; **estar de —** to be in mourning
duende M (gnomo) goblin, gremlin; (gracia) charm
dueño-ña MF owner; **me sentí — de la situación** I felt like I was in control of the

situation; M landlord; F landlady
duerma, duerme *ver* dormir
dueto M duet
dulce ADJ (sabor, personalidad) sweet; (clima) pleasant; (agua) fresh; **—amargo** bittersweet; M (cosa dulce) sweet; (mermelada) preserves, conserve
dulcería F confectionery
dulcificar[30] VT to sweeten
dulzón ADJ unpleasantly sweet
dulzor M sweetness
dulzura F sweetness
duna F dune
dúo M duet; **decir a —** to say in unison
duodeno M duodenum
dúplex M duplex
duplicado ADJ & M duplicate; **por —** in duplicate
duplicar[30] VT to duplicate
duplicidad F duplicity
duque M duke
duquesa F duchess
durabilidad F durability
duración F duration; (de una película, vocal) length; **— de la vida** lifespan
duradero ADJ (ropa) durable, serviceable; (pilas) long-lasting
durante PREP during; **— el mandato de los Demócratas** under the Democrats; **— muchos años** for/over many years
durar VI/VT to last
duraznero M peach tree
durazno M (fruto) peach; (árbol) peach tree
dureza F (de metal) hardness; (del clima, de la expresión, de una tempestad) severity; (del invierno) harshness; (de un boxeador) toughness; (del cuero) stiffness
durmamos, durmiendo *ver* dormir
durmiente ADJ sleeping; M railroad tie, sleeper
durmiera, durmiese *ver* dormir
duro ADJ (metal, golpe, droga, agua) hard; (clima, tormenta) severe; (invierno, expresión, sonido) harsh; (soldado) tough; (grifo) stuck; (viento) strong; (autoridad) inflexible; (pan) stale; (cuero) stiff; **— de corazón** hard-hearted; **— de entendederas** slow on the uptake; **a duras penas** barely; M five-peseta coin; **no tengo un —** I'm flat broke
DVD M DVD

Ee

e CONJ and
ebanista MF cabinetmaker
ébano M ebony
ebrio ADJ drunk, inebriated
ebullición F boiling
eccema M eczema
echar VT (una pelota, redes) to throw, to cast; (yemas, hojas) to sprout; (a un empleado) to fire; (humo, olor) to give off; (un líquido) to pour; (a un borracho) to throw out; **— abajo** to knock down; **— a la basura** to throw away; **— al mar** to put to sea; **— al correo** to mail; **— anclas** to drop anchor; **— a pique** to sink; **— carnes** to get fat; **— de menos** to miss; **— de ver** to notice; **— mano de** to seize upon; **— la culpa** to blame; **— por la borda** to jettison; **— raíces** to take root; **— sangre** to bleed; **— suertes** to draw lots; **— una carta** to mail a letter; **— una siesta** to take a nap; **— un vistazo a** to glance at, to take a look at; **te echo una carrera** I'll race you; **—le el muerto a alguien** to pass the buck to someone; **—se** to lie down; **—se a** to start to; **—se a correr** to bolt; **—se a perder** to spoil; **—se a reír** to burst out laughing; **—se a un lado** to dodge; **—se atrás** to back down/off; **—se para atrás** to lean back
ecléctico ADJ eclectic
eclesiástico ADJ & M ecclesiastic
eclipsar VT (ocultar) to eclipse; (superar) to eclipse, to outshine, to overshadow; **—se** to fade
eclipse M eclipse; **— de sol** solar eclipse; **— de luna** lunar eclipse
eco M echo; **hacer —** to echo; **hacerse — de** to repeat
ecocardiograma M echocardiogram
ecología F (medio ambiente) environment; (ciencia) ecology
ecológico ADJ (ambiental) environmental, ecological; (bueno para la naturaleza) eco-friendly
ecologista ADJ environmental; MF environmentalist
economato M commissary
economía F (actividades de producción) economy; (ciencia) economics; (familiar) finances; **— doméstica** home economics; **—s** savings; **hacer —s** to be thrifty
económico ADJ (relativo a la economía) economic; (frugal) frugal, thrifty; (barato) economical
economista MF economist
economizar[47] VT to economize, to save
ecosistema M ecosystem
ecuación F equation
ecuador M equator
Ecuador M Ecuador
ecualizar[47] VT to equalize
ecuatoriano -na ADJ & MF Ecuadorian
ecuménico ADJ ecumenical

edad F age; **— avanzada** ripe old age; **— de merecer** marriageable age; **— de Piedra** Stone Age; **— del consentimiento sexual** age of consent; **— Media** Middle Ages; **— mental** mental age
edición F (ejemplar) edition; (acción de editar) publication; **— de sobremesa** desktop publishing
edicto M edict
edificación F building
edificar[30] VT (construir) to build; (infundir sentimientos morales) to edify, to uplift
edificio M building
editar VT to edit, to publish
editor -ora ADJ publishing; MF editor
editorial ADJ publishing; F publishing house; M editorial
editorializar[47] VI to editorialize
edredón M comforter
educación F (escolar) education; (social) breeding; **— a distancia** distance learning; **— cívica** civics; **— especial** special education; **— en línea** e-learning; **— física** physical education; **— para adultos** continuing education; **— superior** higher education
educado ADJ (cortés) well-bred; (instruido) educated
educador -ora MF educator
educar[30] VT (desarrollar conocimientos) to educate; (entrenar) to train
educativo ADJ educational
edulcorante M sweetener
EEUU [Estados Unidos] M SG/PL USA
efectivamente ADV actually; **más de los que — encuentran** more than they actually find; INTERJ exactly
efectividad F effectiveness; **tener —** to be valid, to become valid
efectivo ADJ (eficaz) effective; (real) actual; **hacer —** (un cheque) to cash; (una deuda) to pay off; (una amenaza) to make good on; M cash; **en —** in cash; **—s** troops
efecto M (resultado) effect, result; (letra comercial) bill of exchange; (rotación) English, spin; **en —** in fact; **llevar a —** to carry out; **surtir —** to work; **— invernadero** greenhouse effect; **—s especiales** special effects; **—s personales** personal effects; **perder —** to wear off; **rebotar con —** to glance off; **a estos —s** to this effect; **para los —s** to all intents and purposes; **por — de** as a consequence of
efectuar[26] VT to effect; **—se** to be carried out
eficacia F efficacy, effectiveness; **— de una ley** force of law
eficaz ADJ effective
eficiencia F efficiency
eficiente ADJ efficient
efigie F effigy; **quemar en —** to burn in effigy
efímero ADJ ephemeral, fleeting
efusivo ADJ effusive
egipcio -cia ADJ & MF Egyptian
Egipto M Egypt
égloga F pastoral
ego M ego
egocéntrico ADJ egocentric, self-centered
egoísmo M selfishness
egoísta ADJ selfish; MF selfish person
egotismo M egotism
egresado -da MF graduate
eje M (de la Tierra) axis; (de un vehículo) axle; **— del pistón** piston rod; **eso me parte por el —** that messes up my plans
ejecución F (de un condenado) execution; (de un plan, una orden) carrying out, execution; (de una tarea) performance; (de una propiedad) foreclosure
ejecutable ADJ executable
ejecutar VT (a un condenado) to execute; (un plan, una orden) to carry out; (una tarea, música) to perform; (una propiedad) to foreclose on
ejecutivo -va ADJ & MF executive; **— de empresa** corporate officer
ejemplar ADJ exemplary, model; M (libro) copy; (individuo) specimen
ejemplario M handout
ejemplificar[30] VT to exemplify
ejemplo M (cosa típica) example; (modelo) model; **a — de** on the example of; **dar —** to set an example; **por —** for example
ejercer[32] VT (una profesión) to practice; (influencia, fuerza) to exert; (poder) to wield
ejercicio M exercise; (de una profesión) practice; **hacer —** to exercise; **— contable** accounting period; **— físico** physical exercise; **—s de Kegel** Kegel exercises; **en —** active
ejercitar VT (la vista, los músculos) to exercise; (a soldados) to drill; (a alumnos) to train; **—se** to train
ejército M army; **el —** the military
ejido M common
ejote M *Méx* green bean
el ART DEF M the; **— de la derecha** the one on the right; **— que** the one that; **— que sepa** whoever knows
él PRON PERS M SG (como sujeto) he; **— dijo** he said; (como objeto) him; **para —** for him; **le di el libro a —** I gave the book to him; **estamos hablando de —** we're talking about him; **el libro de —** his book
elaboración F (de miel, comida) making; (de un método) development; (de un informe) drafting
elaborado ADJ elaborate
elaborar VT (un método) to elaborate, to

develop; (comida) to make; (un informe) to draft
elasticidad F elasticity
elástico ADJ (sustancia) elastic; (cuerpo) supple; (horario) flexible; M elastic
elección F (votación) election; (selección) choice, selection; **no tuve —** I had no choice
electo ADJ elect
elector-ora ADJ electoral; MF elector
electoral ADJ electoral
electricidad F electricity; **— estática** static electricity
electricista MF electrician
eléctrico ADJ (aparato) electric; (instalación, corriente) electrical
electrificar[30] VT to electrify
electrizado ADJ electrified
electrizante ADJ electrifying
electrizar[47] VT (suministrar electricidad) to electrify; (emocionar) to galvanize, to electrify
electrocardiograma M electrocardiogram
electrocutar VT to electrocute
electrodo M electrode
electrodoméstico M electrical appliance
electroencefalograma M electroencephalogram
electroimán M electromagnet
electrólisis F electrolysis
electromagnético ADJ electromagnetic
electrón M electron
electrónica F electronics
electrónico ADJ electronic
elefante M elephant
elegancia F elegance
elegante ADJ (armonioso) elegant; (bien vestido) stylish, classy
elegibilidad F eligibility
elegible ADJ eligible
elegir[14] VT (seleccionar) to choose, to select; (votar) to elect
elemental ADJ (sencillo) elementary; (básico) elemental
elemento M element
elenco M cast
elevación F elevation; **tirar por —** to throw high in the air
elevado ADJ (pensamiento, estilo) elevated; (fiebre, montaña) high; (precios) high; M (béisbol) fly ball
elevador M elevator
elevar VT (en una jerarquía) to elevate; (precios, voz, objeto) to raise; (el espíritu) to uplift; **— la vista** to look up; **— al cuadrado** to square; **— al cubo** to cube; **—se a** to go up to, to rise to; **el rascacielos se eleva sobre la ciudad** the skyscraper towers over the city
elfo M elf
eliminación F elimination
eliminar VT to eliminate
eliminatoria F (atletismo, natación) heat; **—s** (fútbol) playoffs
elíptico ADJ elliptical
elite/élite F elite
elitista ADJ & MF elitist
ella PRON PERS F SG (como sujeto) she; **— dijo** she said; (como objeto) her; **para —** for her; **le di el libro a —** I gave the book to her; **el libro de —** her book
ellas PRON PERS F PL (como sujeto) they; **— dijeron** they said; (como objeto) them; **para —** for them; **les di el libro a —** I gave them the book; **el libro de —** their book
ello PRON NEUTRO it; **— es que** the fact is that
ellos PRON M PL (como sujeto) they; **— dijeron** they said; (como objeto) them; **para —** for them; **les di el libro a —** I gave them the book; **el libro de —** their book
elocuencia F eloquence
elocuente ADJ eloquent; **las estadísticas son —s** the statistics speak for themselves
elogiar VT to praise
elogio M praise
elote M *Méx* corn on the cob
elucidación F elucidation
elucidar VT to elucidate
eludir VT to elude, to avoid, to dodge
emanación F emanation, flow
emanar VI/VT to emanate
emancipación F emancipation
emancipar VT to emancipate; **—se** to become free
emascular VT to emasculate
embadurnar VT to daub
embajada F embassy
embajador-ora MF ambassador
embalador-ora MF packer
embalaje M packing, packaging
embalar VT to pack; VI to accelerate
embaldosar VT to tile
embalsamar VT (a un muerto) to embalm; (un animal) to stuff
embalse M reservoir
embanderar VT to adorn with flags
embarazada ADJ pregnant
embarazar[47] VT (impedir) to hamper; (fecundar) to make pregnant; **—se** to get pregnant
embarazo M (obstáculo) impediment; (estado de embarazada) pregnancy
embarazoso ADJ embarrassing, awkward
embarcación F boat, embarkation, craft
embarcadero M wharf, pier
embarcar[30] VT (pasajeros) to embark; (mercancías) to load; **—se** to embark, to go aboard; **—se en** to embark upon
embargar[40] VT to seize; **estar embargado de emoción** to be overcome with emotion

embargo M embargo; **— judicial** seizure; **imponer un —** to embargo; **sin —** nevertheless, however
embarque M (de mercancías) loading; (de pasajeros) embarkation
embarrado ADJ smeared with mud
embarrar VT to smear with mud, to muddy
embate M lashing
embaucador M confidence man
embaucar[30] VT to dupe
embeber VT to soak up; **—se** to be absorbed
embelesar VT to enrapture
embeleso M rapture
embellecer[35] VI/VT to beautify
embestida F charge
embestir[9] VI/VT to charge
embetunar VT to polish
emblanquecer[35] VI/VT to whiten
emblema M emblem
embobar VT to amaze; **—se** to be amazed
embolia F embolism; **— cerebral** cerebral embolism
émbolo M piston, plunger
embolsar VT (dinero) to pocket; (una compra) to bag
emborrachar VT (a una persona) to intoxicate; (el carburador) to flood; **—se** to get drunk
emborronar VT (manchar) to blot; (hacer impreciso) to blur
emboscada F ambush; **tender una —** to lie in ambush
emboscar[30] VT to ambush; **—se** to lie in ambush
embotamiento M (efecto de embotar) dullness, bluntness; (acción de embotar) dulling
embotar VT to dull
embotelladora F bottling plant
embotellamiento M (de cerveza) bottling; (de tráfico) traffic jam, bottleneck
embotellar VT (cerveza) to bottle; (tráfico) to bottle up
embozar[47] VT to conceal
embragar[40] VI to engage the clutch
embrague M clutch
embriagado ADJ drunken
embriagar[40] VT to intoxicate; **—se** to become intoxicated
embriaguez F intoxication, drunkenness
embridar VT to bridle
embrión M embryo
embrionario ADJ embryonic
embriónico ADJ embryonic
embrollar VT (involucrar) to embroil; (confundir) to muddle
embrollo M muddle
embromar VT to kid
embrujar VT to bewitch
embrujo M spell
embrutecer[35] VT to stupefy
embudo M funnel
embuste M lie
embustero -ra MF liar, trickster
embutido M sausage
embutir VT to cram, to jam
emergencia F emergency
emergente ADJ emergent, emerging
emerger[45] VI (surgir) to emerge; (salir del agua) to surface
emigración F (de personas) emigration; (de animales) migration
emigrante ADJ & MF emigrant
emigrar VI (personas) to emigrate; (animales) to migrate
eminencia F eminence; **— gris** gray eminence
eminente ADJ eminent
emisario -ria MF emissary; M outlet
emisión F (de acciones, billetes) issue; (de un olor) discharge; (de programas) broadcast; (de gas) emission
emisor ADJ emitting; M transmitter
emisora F radio/television station
emitir VT (un olor, vapor) to emit; (juicios) to pronounce; (dinero, acciones) to issue; VI/VT (programas) to broadcast; **—se** to be on the air; **el programa se emite en horas de la mañana** the program airs in the morning
emoción F emotion; **¡qué —!** what a thrill!
emocional ADJ emotional
emocionante ADJ (conmovedor) touching; (apasionante) exciting
emocionar VT (apasionar) to excite; (conmover) to move, to touch; **—se** (estar ilusionado) to be excited; (estar conmovido) to be touched
emoticón M emoticon
emoticono M emoticon
emotivo ADJ emotional
empacador -ora MF packer
empacar[30] VT (regalos, mercancías) to pack; (algodón) to bale
empachar VI to cause indigestion; **—se** to suffer indigestion; **—se de** to get sick on, to stuff oneself with
empacho M (indigestión) indigestion; (cohibición) inhibition; **no tener — en** to have no qualms about
empalagar[40] VI/VT to cloy
empalagoso ADJ cloying, saccharine
empalar VT to impale
empalizada F stockade, palisade
empalmar VT to splice; **— con** to join
empalme M (de caminos) junction; (de cuerdas) splice; **— genético** gene splicing
empanada F turnover, pie
empanar VT to bread
empañado ADJ (vidrio) misty, foggy; (metal, reputación) tarnished
empañar VT (vidrio) to fog up; (metal, reputación) to tarnish
empapado ADJ soggy, sopping wet

empapamiento M soaking
empapar VT (mojar) to soak, to drench; (recoger con algo) to soak up; **—se** (mojarse) to get soaked; (enterarse) to find out all about
empapelado M wallpapering
empapelar VT to paper, to wallpaper; **— las calles** to plaster the streets
empaque M (acción de empacar) packing; (envoltorio) packaging
empaquetadura F gasket
empaquetar VT to pack, to package; **—se** to get dolled up
emparedado M sandwich
emparejar VT (una carga, un partido) to even up; VI/VT (los enamorados) to pair up; (calcetines, zapatos) to match up
emparentado ADJ akin, related
emparentar VT to relate by marriage; **—se** to become related by marriage
empastar VT to fill
empaste M filling
empatar VI to tie; **— una marca** to tie a record
empate M tie, draw
empatía F empathy
empecinado ADJ stubborn
empedernido ADJ (criminal) hardened; (mujeriego) incorrigible; (solterón) confirmed
empedernirse[73] VI to become hardened
empedrado M (acción) paving with stones; (cosa) cobblestone pavement; ADJ paved with stones
empedrar[1] VT to pave with stones
empeine M (del pie) instep; (del vientre) groin
empellón M shove; **a empellones** with shoves, shoving
empeñar VT to pawn; **— la palabra** to pledge; **—se** (endeudarse) to go into debt; (obstinarse) to insist; (esforzarse) to apply oneself; **—se en** to engage in
empeño M (prenda) pawn; (insistencia) insistence; (deseo) desire; (esfuerzo) exertion; **poner — en** to strive for
empeorar VT to make worse, to aggravate; VI to worsen; **—se** to get worse
empequeñecer[35] VT to make smaller; VI to get smaller
emperador -triz M emperor; F empress
emperifollarse VI to deck oneself out, to doll oneself up
empezar[48] VI/VT to begin, to start; **— a** to start to; **— de cero** to start from scratch; **para —** for starters; **no tengo ni para — con él** I can't touch him; **— por** to begin with; **empezamos mal** we got off to a bad start; **un paquete sin —** an unopened box; **por algo se empieza** you have to start somewhere
empinado ADJ steep
empinar VT to raise; **— el codo** to drink; **—se** (una persona) to stand on tiptoes; (un caballo) to rear; (una torre) to tower
empírico ADJ empirical
empizarrar VT to cover with slate
emplastar VT to plaster
emplasto M plaster
emplazamiento M (colocación) placement; (lugar) location
empleado -da MF employee; **— temporal** temp
emplear VT (usar) to employ, to use; (dar trabajo) to employ; **—se en** to be employed in
empleo M (ocupación) employment, work; (puesto de trabajo) job; (utilización) use
emplumado ADJ feathery
emplumar VT (adornar) to adorn with feathers; (pegar plumas en el cuerpo) to tar and feather; VI (echar plumas) to grow feathers
empobrecer[35] VI/VT to impoverish
empollar VT (huevos) to hatch, to brood; VI/VT (para un examen) to cram
empollón -ona MF *fam* egghead, overachiever
empolvar VT to cover with dust; **—se** (con cosméticos) to powder oneself; (con polvo) to get dirty
emponzoñar VT to poison
empotrado ADJ built-in
emprendedor ADJ enterprising
emprender VT (una tarea) to undertake; (un viaje) to embark on; **—la con alguien** to attack someone
empresa F (cosa que se emprende) undertaking; (compañía) company, enterprise; **libre —** free enterprise; **— privada** private enterprise; **— pública** public company; **— tiburón** raider
empresarial ADJ **—es** business administration studies; **grupo —** business group
empresario -ria MF entrepreneur
empréstito M loan
empujar VT (mover) to push; (mover con violencia) to shove; (apresurar) to hurry
empuje M (ánimo) drive; (fuerza de propulsión) thrust; (fuerza hacia arriba) lift
empujón M shove, push; **dar empujones** to jostle
empuñadura F (espada) hilt; (cuchillo) handle; (palo de golf, raqueta) grip
empuñar VT to grasp
emular VT to emulate
en PREP in; **— Asturias** in Asturias; (sobre una superficie) on, upon; **— la mesa** on the table; **sentarse — el suelo** to sit down on the floor; **me lo vendió — mil pesetas** she sold it to me for a thousand pesetas; **— la parada del autobús** at the bus stop; **— la noche** at night; **ir — tren** to go by train

enaguas F PL petticoat
enajenación M (locura) insanity; (transferencia) transfer
enajenar VT (trasladar) to transfer; (alienar) to alienate; **—se** to become alienated
enaltecer[35] VT to extol
enamorado -da ADJ in love; MF lover
enamoramiento M crush
enamorar VT to make fall in love; **—se [de]** to fall in love [with]
enanismo M dwarfism
enano -na MF (personaje imaginario, persona deforme) dwarf; (persona pequeña bien proporcionada) midget
enarbolar VT (una bandera) to raise on high; (un garrote) to brandish
enardecer[35] VT to inflame; **—se** to become inflamed
enardecimiento M inflaming
encabezado M header
encabezamiento M heading
encabezar[47] VT (una carta, una obra, un gobierno) to head; (un desfile) to lead
encabritarse VI (un caballo) to rear [up]; (una persona) to get furious
encadenar VT (poner en cadenas) to chain; (unir) to link
encajar VI/VT (colocar) to fit; VI (un gol) to allow; **el policía me encajó una multa** the policeman stuck me with a fine; **tu historia no encaja** your story doesn't hold water
encaje M (tejido) lace; (reserva bancaria) reserve; (acción de encajar) fitting together
encajonar VT (meter en una caja) to box; (apretar) to squeeze in
encallar VI to run aground, to strand; (una ballena) to beach; VT to ground
encamarse VI **— con** to go to bed with, to sleep with
encaminar VT to direct; **—se hacia** to head for
encanecer[35] VI to go gray; VT to cause to go gray
encanijado ADJ sickly
encanijarse VI to become sickly
encantado ADJ (contento) delighted; (hechizado) enchanted; **— de conocerla** pleased to meet you
encantador -ora ADJ charming, delightful; MF charmer
encantamiento M enchantment
encantar VT to enchant; **eso me encanta** I love that
encanto M (encantamiento) enchantment; (atractivo) charm; **un — de persona** a delightful person; **como por —** as if by magic
encapotado ADJ overcast
encapotarse VI to become overcast
encapricharse VI **— con/de/por** to become infatuated with
encapuchar VT (a una persona) to hood; (un bolígrafo) to put the top on
encaramar VT to raise; **—se** to climb up on; **—se al primer puesto** to rise to first place
encarar VT to face; **me encaró el fusil** he pointed the rifle at me; **—se con** to face
encarcelamiento M imprisonment
encarcelar VT to imprison, to jail, to incarcerate
encarecer[35] VI (subir de precio) to increase in price; VT (rogar) to beg
encarecidamente ADV earnestly
encargado -da ADJ on order; MF person in charge; **— de curso** lecturer
encargar[40] VT (responsabilizar) to put in charge; (pedir) to order; (mandar) to commission, to order; **— a alguien una tarea** to charge someone with a task; **—se de** to take care of
encargo M (pedido) order; (tarea) assignment, charge, errand; **construido por/de —** custom-built; **hecho por —** made to order
encariñarse VI **— de** to become fond of
encarnación F incarnation
encarnado ADJ (color) red; (uña) ingrown
encarnar VT (un ideal) to embody; (a un personaje) to play; **se me encarnó una uña** one of my nails got ingrown
encarnizado ADJ fierce
encarnizarse[47] VI **— con alguien** to attack someone viciously
encarte M insert
encasillar VT to pigeonhole
encauzamiento M channeling
encauzar[47] VT to channel
encefalitis F encephalitis; **— espongiforme bovina** mad cow disease
encendedor M cigarette lighter
encender[2] VT (un cigarro, fuego) to light; (un fósforo) to strike; (una luz, radio) to switch on, to turn on; (una computadora) to power on, to power up; (pasión) to arouse; VI **—se** (una persona, sexualmente) to become aroused; (una lámpara) to turn on
encendido ADJ (rojo) bright; (excitado) aroused; M ignition
encerado M (pizarrón) blackboard; (acción de encerar) waxing; (capa de cera) wax coating; ADJ waxed
encerar VT to wax, to polish
encerrar[1] VT (palabras entre paréntesis) to enclose; (una oveja) to pen; (a una persona) to lock up; (un contenido) to contain; (un peligro) to involve; **—se** (aislarse) to isolate oneself; (obstinarse) to become fixated
encestar VI to make a basket
enchapar VT (metal) to plate; (madera) to veneer
enchilada F enchilada
enchufar VT (un aparato eléctrico) to plug in; (a un protegido) to fix up; **— un tubo con otro** to fit one pipe into another

enchufe M (entrada eléctrica) socket, plug-in, electrical outlet; (situación ventajosa) connection
encías F PL gums
enciclopedia F encyclopedia
encienda, enciende *ver* encender
encierra, encierre *ver* encerrar
encierro M (confinamiento) confinement; (lugar) enclosure
encima ADV (arriba) on top; (además) in addition; **— de** on top of, atop; **por — de** above; **sacarse de —** to get rid of; **orinarse —** to urinate on oneself; **ya tenía el coche —** the car was already on top of me; **no lleves tanto dinero —** don't carry so much money on you; **se nos vienen — los exámenes** the exams are upon us; **mi madre siempre me está —** my mother is always on me; **lo leí por —** I scanned it
encimera F counter
encina F oak
encinta ADJ pregnant
enclaustrar VT to cloister
enclavarse VI to be located
enclave M enclave
enclenque ADJ (endeble) sickly; (desvencijado) rickety
encoger[45] VI/VT to shrink; **—se** (una prenda) to shrink; (una persona) to be intimidated; **—se de hombros** to shrug one's shoulders
encogido ADJ (tímido) shy; M (encogimiento) shrinkage, shrinking
encogimiento M (acción de encoger) shrinkage, shrinking; **— de hombros** shrug
encolar VT to glue
encolerizar[47] VT to incense; **—se** to become incensed, to lose one's temper
encomendar[1] VT to entrust; **—se** to commend oneself
encomienda F (encargo) assignment, task; (colonial) encomienda [colonial land grant]
enconar VT to inflame; VI **—se** (discusión) to become inflamed; (herida) to fester
encono M animosity
encontrado ADJ contrary, opposing
encontrar[5] VT (hallar) to find; (verse con) to meet; **— a** to run into; **—se** (estar ubicado) to be located; (hallarse) to feel; **—se con** (verse por acuerdo) to meet with; (verse, por coincidencia) to run into; (enterarse) to find out; **vas a encontrarte la casa en obras** you'll find the house under construction
encontronazo M collision
encordado M strings
encordar[5] VT to string
encorvado ADJ stoop-shouldered
encorvamiento M slouch, stoop
encorvar VT to stoop; **—se** to bend over
encostrarse VI to scab
encrespar VT (el pelo) to curl; (el mar) to make choppy; **—se** (el pelo) to get curly; (el mar) to get choppy
encrucijada F crossroads
encuadernación F (oficio) bookbinding; (producto) binding
encuadernar VT to bind
encuadrar VT to frame; **la poesía de esta época se encuadra en tres tendencias** the poetry of this period can be classified into three tendencies
encubierto ADJ covert
encubrimiento ADJ (de un delincuente) concealment; (de un escándalo) cover-up
encubrir[74] VT (un secreto) to conceal; (un escándalo) to cover up, to hush up
encuentra, encuentre *ver* encontrar
encuentro M (casual) encounter; (planeado) meeting; (partido) game; (de atletismo) meet; **salir al — de** (ir a encontrar) to go out to meet; (contradecir) to counter
encuerar VT to strip
encuesta F survey, poll
encuestado -da MF respondent
encuestar VI/VT to survey, to poll
encumbrado ADJ elevated, lofty
encumbramiento M elevation
encumbrar VT to elevate
encurtido M pickle
encurtir VT to pickle
ende LOC ADV **por —** hence
endeble ADJ (persona) feeble; (material, argumento) flimsy; (mesa) rickety
endémico ADJ endemic
endemoniado ADJ (poseído por el diablo) possessed by the devil; (niño) devilish; (pregunta) tough
enderezar[47] VT to straighten; **enderézate** stand up straight; **la niña se enderezó con los años** the girl straightened out after a few years
endeudamiento M indebtedness
endeudarse VI to get into debt
endiablado ADJ devilish
endocrino ADJ endocrine
endocrinología F endocrinology
endodermo M endoderm
endomingado ADJ dressed in one's Sunday best
endorfina F endorphin
endosante MF endorser
endosar VT to endorse
endoso M endorsement
endrogar VT to drug
endulzante M sweetener
endulzar[47] VT to sweeten; **se endulzó el tiempo** the weather became milder
endurecer[35] VT to harden, to stiffen; VI **—se** (músculos) to get hard; (pegamento) to set
endurecimiento M hardening

enebro M juniper
eneldo M dill
enema MF enema
enemigo-ga ADJ & MF enemy; **buques —s** enemy ships; **ser — de algo** to dislike something
enemistad F enmity
enemistar VT to cause enmity between; **—se con** to become an enemy of
energético ADJ **política energética** energy policy
energía F energy; **— eólica** wind power; **— hidráulica** water power; **— nuclear** nuclear energy; **— solar** solar energy; **— térmica** thermal energy
enérgicamente ADV strongly
enérgico ADJ (persona) energetic; (protesta, medida, tono) forceful
enero M January
enervar VT (debilitar) to enervate; (irritar) to irritate
enfadado ADJ angry
enfadar VT to anger; *fam* to piss off; VI **—se** to get angry
enfado M anger
enfadoso ADJ annoying
enfardar VT to bale
énfasis M emphasis
enfático ADJ emphatic
enfatizar[47] VT to emphasize
enfermar VT to sicken; VI to become sick; **—se** to become ill
enfermedad F (malestar) sickness, illness; (cardiovascular, de Parkinson) disease; (social) ill; **— contagiosa** contagious disease; **— coronaria** heart disease; **— de altura** altitude sickness; **— de Alzheimer** Alzheimer's disease; **— de las vacas locas** mad cow disease; **— del legionario** legionnaire's disease; **— de Lou Gehrig** Lou Gehrig's disease; **— de Lyme** Lyme disease; **— de Parkinson** Parkinson's disease; **— degenerativa articular** degenerative joint disease; **— mental** mental illness; **— parasitaria** parasitic disease; **— por radiación** radiation sickness
enfermería F infirmary
enfermero-ra M male nurse; F nurse
enfermizo ADJ (persona) sickly, infirm; (obsesión, aspecto) unhealthy; (imaginación) sick
enfermo-ma ADJ sick, ill; **me tiene — que vengan tarde** I'm sick of them coming late; MF patient; **— del corazón** heart patient
enfisema M emphysema
enflaquecer[35] VI to get thin
enfocar[30] VT (los ojos) to focus; (un faro) to point; (una cámara) to train; (un tema) to approach
enfoque M (método) approach; (acción de enfocar) focusing
enfrentamiento M clash, confrontation
enfrentar VT (enemigos) to confront; (una dificultad) to face, to tackle; **— a dos personas** to pit two people against each other; **—se con** to clash with
enfrente ADV opposite; **— de** in front of, opposite
enfriamiento M (del aire) cooling; (de una persona) chill; (de la economía, las relaciones) cooling off
enfriar[28] VT to cool, to chill; VI **—se** to cool off
enfundar VT to sheathe
enfurecer[35] VT to infuriate, to enrage; VI **—se** to become enraged, to rage
enfurruñado ADJ sulky
enfurruñarse VI to sulk
engalanar VT (una mesa) to decorate; (a una muchacha) to dress up; **—se** to dress up
enganchar VT (bueyes) to hitch; (una red) to snag; (un teléfono) to hook up; (a los televidentes, a un adicto) to hook; VI **—se** to get hooked
enganche M (del gas, teléfono) connection, hookup; (de drogas) addictiveness; (de vagones) coupling; (de caballos) team; (primer pago) *Méx* down payment
enganchón M snag
engañador ADJ deceitful
engañar VT (mentir) to deceive; (ser infiel) to cheat on; **— el hambre** to ward off hunger; **—se** to deceive oneself
engaño M deceit, deception
engañoso ADJ (una persona) deceitful; (un hecho) misleading
engastar VT to set
engaste M setting
engatusar VT to coax, to cajole
engendrar VT (emociones) to engender; (hijos) to father
englobar VT to encompass
engomar VT to glue
engordar VI to get fat, to put on weight; VT to make fat, to fatten; **esta semana he engordado dos kilos** I gained two kilos this week
engorroso ADJ irksome
engoznar VT to hinge
engranado ADJ meshed, interlocking; **estar —** to be in gear
engranaje M gears, gearing; **el — del partido** the party apparatus
engranar VT (meter una marcha) to put in gear, to throw into gear; (encajar) to mesh; **— la marcha atrás** to put [the car] in reverse
engrandecer[35] VT (a una persona) to aggrandize; (un palacio) to make more grandiose

engrapar VT to staple, to cramp
engrasar VT (untar) to grease; (manchar) to make greasy; (sobornar) to grease someone's palm; **—se** to get greasy
engrase M grease job
engreído ADJ conceited
engreírse[10] VI to become conceited
engrillar VT to shackle
engrosar VT (una manifestación) to swell; (un volumen) to grow; (una persona) to get fat
engrudo M paste
engullir[16] VT to gobble
enhebrar VT (un hilo) to thread; (cuentas) to string; **— idioteces** to string together a bunch of idiocies
enhorabuena F congratulation; INTERJ congratulations
enigma M (misterio) enigma, conundrum; (adivinanza) riddle; (problema) puzzle
enjabonar VT (poner jabón) to soap, to lather; (adular) to flatter
enjaezar[47] VT to harness
enjalbegar[40] VT to whitewash
enjambre M swarm
enjaular VT (un animal) to cage; (a una persona) to jail
enjuagar[40] VT to rinse; (ropa) to rinse out; (platos) to rinse off
enjuague M (limpieza) rinse, rinsing; (trama) scheme; **— bucal** mouthwash
enjugar[40] VT (la frente) to wipe; (lágrimas) to wipe away
enjuiciar VT to prosecute, to try
enjuto ADJ dry; (delgado) thin
enlace M (de trenes, web) link; (químico) bond; (boda) marriage; (persona) liaison; **— muerto** dead link
enladrillado M brick pavement
enladrillar VT to brick, to pave with bricks
enlatar VT to can
enlazar[47] VT (unir) to link (también en la web); (sujetar con lazo) to rope, to lasso; VI to connect; **—se** to connect
enlodar VT to muddy; **—se** to get muddy
enloquecedor ADJ maddening
enloquecer[35] VT to drive crazy; VI to go crazy; **—se** to go crazy
enlosado M flagstone pavement
enlosar VT to pave with flagstones
enmantecar[30] VT to butter
enmarañar VT (pelo) to entangle; (problema) to complicate
enmarcar[30] VT (un cuadro) to frame; **se enmarca dentro de** it takes place in the context of
enmascarar VT to mask
enmendar[1] VT (una ley) to amend; (un texto) to revise; **— la situación** to mend matters; **no me enmiendes la plana** don't correct me; VI **—se** to mend one's ways
enmienda F (de una ley) amendment; (de un texto) revision
enmohecer[35] VT to mold; **—se** to get moldy, to mold
enmudecer[35] VT to silence; VI to go silent
ennegrecer[35] VI/VT to blacken
ennoblecer[35] VT to ennoble
enojadizo ADJ hotheaded
enojado ADJ angry, mad
enojar VT to anger; **—se** to get angry
enojo M anger
enojoso ADJ bothersome
enorgullecer[35] VT to fill with pride; **—se de** to take pride in
enorme ADJ enormous
enormemente ADV vastly
enramada F bower
enrarecido ADJ thin, rare
enrarecimiento M rarity, thinness
enredadera F creeper
enredar VT (enmarañar) to entangle; (complicar) to complicate; (involucrar) to mix up; VI to cause trouble; **—se** to get tangled up; **—se con** to become involved with
enredijo M tangle, snarl
enredo M (enredijo) snarl; (lío) mess; (amancebamiento) affair
enredoso ADJ complicated
enrejado M (de metal) grating, grate; (de varillas) lattice
enrejar VT to install a grate on
enrevesado ADJ involved
enriquecer[35] VT to enrich; **—se** to become rich
enriquecimiento M enrichment
enrojecer[35] VI/VT to redden
enrollar VT (manga, alfombra) to roll up; (hilo, cuerda, cinta) to wind up; **—se con** to become involved with
enronquecer[35] VT to make hoarse; VI to become hoarse
enroscar[30] VT (soga) to coil, to roll up; (tuerca) to screw in; (tapa) to screw on; **—se** (vid) to twine; (serpiente) to coil up
ensacar[30] VT to sack
ensalada F salad
ensalzar[47] VT to extol
ensanchar VT to widen; **—se** (una calle) to widen; (una falda) to flare
ensanche M (de una calle) widening; (de una ciudad) expansion
ensangrentado ADJ gory, bloody
ensangrentar VT to smear blood on; **—se** to get covered with blood
ensartar VT (cuentas) to string; (aguja) to thread; (con un pincho) to pierce; (historias) to rattle off
ensayar VT (probar) to try out; (intentar) to try; (analizar un metal) to assay; (practicar una

obra teatral) to rehearse
ensayo M (intento) trial, attempt; (de teatro) rehearsal; (obra literaria) essay; (nuclear) testing; (de un metal) assay; **— clínico** clinical trial; **— general** dress rehearsal; **por — y error** by trial and error
enseguida ADV at once, immediately
ensenada F cove
enseña F ensign, flag
enseñanza F teaching, education; **—s** teachings
enseñar VT (mostrar) to show; (instruir) to teach; **— a** to teach how to
enseres M PL household utensils
ensillar VT to saddle, to saddle up
ensimismarse VI to lose oneself in thought
ensoberbecer[35] VT to make haughty; **—se** to become haughty
ensombrecer[35] VT (oscurecer) to make shadowy; (entristecer) to sadden
ensoñación F dream
ensordecedor ADJ deafening
ensordecer[35] VT to deafen
ensortijar VT to curl
ensuciar VT to dirty, to sully; **—se** (mancharse) to get dirty; (defecar) to soil oneself
ensueño M reverie, dream
entablar VT (relaciones) to establish; (un conflicto) to start; (una conversación) to strike up; (una demanda) to file; (una pelea) to pick
entablillar VT to splint
entallar VT to take in
entarimar VT to floor with planks
ente M (ser) entity; (excéntrico) weirdo; (agencia) agency
enteco ADJ sickly
entender[2] VT (comprender) to understand; (oír) to hear; **— de** to know about; **—se con** (comunicar) to communicate with; (llevarse bien) to get along with; **dar a —** to intimate; **yo me entiendo** I know what I'm doing; **se entiende** of course
entendido -da ADJ (comprendido) understood; (experto) expert; **tengo — que** I understand that; **caridad mal entendida** misguided charity; MF expert
entendimiento M understanding
enterado ADJ informed; **darse por —** to acknowledge; **estar — de** to be privy to
enterar VT to inform; **—se [de]** to find out [about]; **recién me entero** I just found out; **para que te enteres** just so you know
entereza F fortitude
enternecedor ADJ touching
enternecer[35] VT to touch; **—se** to be touched
entero ADJ (completo) entire, whole; (número) whole; **se mantuvo — durante el funeral** he held himself together during the funeral; M integer, whole number
enterramiento M (de un cable) burying; (de un difunto) burial
enterrar[1] VT (cable, muerto) to bury; (balón) to dunk
entibiar VT to make lukewarm; **—se** to become lukewarm
entidad F entity; **de —** significant; **— bancaria** banking institution
entienda, entiende *ver* entender
entierro M burial, funeral
entintar VT to stain with ink
entoldar VT to cover with an awning
entomología F entomology
entonación F intonation
entonar VT to sing; VI to sing in tune; **— con** to go well with; **—se** to get tipsy
entonces ADV then; **desde —** ever since; **hasta —** until then; **el — presidente** the then president; CONJ (así que) so
entornado ADJ half-open
entornar VT (una puerta) to leave ajar; (los ojos) to close partially
entorno M (lo que rodea) surroundings; (medio ambiente, informático) environment; **— de trabajo** work environment
entorpecer[35] VT (los sentidos) to dull; (el paso) to hinder; **—se** to become sluggish
entorpecimiento M (de los sentidos) dullness; (del paso) hindrance
entrada F (sitio por donde se entra, de un actor) entrance; (acción de entrar, artículo de diccionario) entry; (asistentes a un espectáculo) gate; (oportunidad para actuar) opening; (billete, derecho, precio de entrar) admission; (llegada) arrival; (primer plato) appetizer; (pago inicial) down payment; (tiempo en béisbol) inning; **—s** cash receipts; **— de coches** driveway; **— de datos** data input; **— por partida doble** double entry; **de —** from the start
entramado M lattice
entrante ADJ (alcalde) incoming; (año) next; M recess
entrañable ADJ (amistad) close; (persona) endearing
entrañas F PL (intestinos) entrails, *fam* guts; (sentimientos) heart, core; **— de la tierra** bowels of the earth; **de mis —** of my own flesh and blood
entrar VI (ir hacia adentro) to go in; (comenzar el día de trabajo) to come in; (caber) to fit; **dejar —** to let in; **hacer — en razón** to bring to reason; **— a medicina** to go into medicine; **— en calor** to warm up; **— en coma** to go into a coma; **— en/a un cuarto** to enter a room; **— en materia** to get to the meat of a matter; **— en vigencia/vigor** to go into effect; **me entró miedo** I became afraid; **me entró sueño** I got sleepy; **no sé**

cómo —le a esa chica I don't know how to approach that girl; **la física no me entra** I can't learn physics; **no entra entre mis favoritos** it is not included among my favorites; **la semana que entra** next week; **este vestido no me entra** this dress doesn't fit me; **seis entra dos veces en doce** six goes into twelve two times; **hazle —** show him in; VT (datos) to enter, to input

entre PREP (dos) between; (muchos) among; **— vaso y vaso** between glasses; **— dientes** under one's breath

entreabierto ADJ ajar, half-open

entreabrir[74] VT (puerta) to crack open; (los ojos) to half-open

entreacto M intermission

entrecano ADJ graying

entrecejo M space between the eyebrows

entrecortado ADJ (voz) faltering; (respiración) irregular

entrecortarse VI to falter

entrecruzar[47] VT to interlace; **—se** to cross

entredicho LOC ADV **en —** in doubt

entrega F (de un paquete) delivery; (de un manuscrito) submission; (al vicio) surrender; (de una novela) installment; (de revista) issue; **a la —** on delivery; **por —s** serial; **— a domicilio** home delivery; **— de premios** presentation of awards; **— el mismo día** same-day delivery; **— gratuita** free delivery; **— inicial** down payment

entregar[40] VT (un paquete) to deliver; (a un rehén, prisionero) to hand over; (a un delincuente) to turn in; (a una hija en matrimonio) to give; (premios) to hand out, to present; (tarea escolar) to hand in; (el coche) to trade in; **—se [a]** (la policía) to surrender [to]; (a una misión) to dedicate oneself to

entrelazar[47] VT to intertwine

entremés M (obra de teatro) interlude; (comida) hors d'oeuvre

entremeter VT to insert; **—se en** (meterse) to get mixed up in; (inmiscuirse) to meddle in

entremetido -da ADJ meddlesome, nosy; MF meddler, busybody

entremezclar VT to intermingle

entrenador -ora MF trainer, coach; **— en jefe** head coach

entrenamiento M training

entrenar VI/VT to train

entrepierna F (del cuerpo) crotch; (de pantalón) inseam

entrepiso M mezzanine

entresacar[30] VT (seleccionar) to cull; (adelgazar) to thin

entresuelo M (de hotel) mezzanine; (de cine) balcony

entretanto ADV meanwhile

entretejer VT (el pelo, una tela) to weave; (una historia) to weave together

entretener[58] VT (hacer atrasar) to delay; (distraer) to distract; (divertir) to entertain; **—se** (divertirse) to amuse oneself; (detenerse) to delay

entretenido ADJ entertaining

entretenimiento M entertainment, amusement

entrever[72, 74] VT (apenas) to catch a glimpse of; (a lo lejos) to make out

entreverar VT to mix, to intersperse; **—se** to meddle

entrevía F gauge

entrevista F interview; **— de salida** exit interview

entrevistar VT to interview; **—se con** to have an interview with

entristecer[35] VT to sadden; **—se** to become sad

entrometerse VI to meddle, to interfere

entrometido -da ADJ meddlesome, nosy; MF meddler, busybody

entronque M (ferroviario) junction; (parentesco) relationship

entropía F entropy

entumecido ADJ (dedo, diente) numb; (músculo) stiff

entumecimiento M (de los dedos, dientes) numbness; (de los músculos) stiffness

enturbiar VT (el agua) to muddy; (una decisión) to muddle; (el juicio, la alegría) to cloud; **—se** (agua) to get muddy; (alegría) to be marred

entusiasmado ADJ enthusiastic, excited

entusiasmar VT to excite; **—se** to be excited

entusiasmo M enthusiasm, excitement

entusiasta MF enthusiast; ADJ enthusiastic

enumerar VT to enumerate

enunciado M utterance

enunciar VT (palabras) to enunciate; (una teoría) to articulate, to enunciate

envainar VT to sheathe

envalentonar VT to embolden, to make bold; **—se** to become bold

envanecer[35] VT to make vain; **—se** to become vain

envarado ADJ stiff, staid

envaramiento M stiffness

envasar VT to package; **— al vacío** to vacuum-pack

envase M packaging

envejecer[35] VT to make old; **ese maquillaje te envejece** that makeup makes you look older; VI to grow old, to age

envejecimiento M aging

envenenamiento M poisoning

envenenar VT to poison

envergadura F (de un avión) wingspan; (de un ave) wingspread; (de un evento, proyecto) importance

envés M SG back
enviado -da MF (político) envoy; (periodístico) correspondent
enviar[28] VT to send; **— por fax** to fax
enviciar VT to corrupt; **—se con** to get hooked on
envidia F envy
envidiable ADJ enviable
envidiar VT to envy
envidioso ADJ envious, jealous
envilecer[35] VT to debase
envío M (acción) shipping; (mercancía) shipment; (manuscrito) submission; **— de anotación** touchdown pass; **— rápido** express delivery
envite M bet
envoltorio M (cosa envuelta) bundle; (envoltura) wrapper
envoltura F wrapping, wrapper; **— de plástico transparente** shrinkwrap
envolver[6, 74] VT (involucrar) to involve; (cubrir) to wrap; (atrapar) to entangle; (rodear) to surround; **—se** to become involved
envuelto, envuelva, envuelve *ver* envolver
enyesar VT (enlucir con yeso) to plaster; (escayolar) to put in a cast
enzima MF enzyme
épica F epic
epicentro M epicenter
épico ADJ epic
epidemia F epidemic
epidémico ADJ epidemic
epidermis F epidermis
epifanía F epiphany
epiglotis F epiglottis
epilepsia F epilepsy
epiléptico ADJ epileptic
epílogo M epilogue
episódico ADJ episodic
episodio M episode
epitafio M epitaph
epítome M epitome
época F (momento) time, period; (período histórico) age; (temporada) season; (período geológico) epoch
epopeya F epic poem
equidad F equity
equidistante ADJ equidistant
equilibrado ADJ balanced; M balancing
equilibrar VT to balance; **— un presupuesto** to balance a budget
equilibrio M equilibrium, balance; **perder el —** to lose one's balance; **hacer —s** to do a balancing act
equino ADJ & M equine
equinoccio M equinox
equipaje M baggage, luggage
equipamiento M equipment
equipar VT to equip, to outfit
equiparar VT to equate
equipo M (materiales) equipment; (grupo) team; **— de vida** life-support system; **— deportivo** sweatsuit; **— de esquí** ski gear
equitación F (arte) horsemanship; (actividad) riding
equitativo ADJ equitable
equivalente ADJ equivalent
equivaler[60] VI to be equivalent; **lo que equivale a decir** which amounts to saying
equivocación F mistake
equivocado ADJ mistaken, wrong; **estar —** to be wrong/mistaken
equivocar[30] VT to mistake; **—se** to be mistaken, to make a mistake, to miscalculate; **—se de sala** to choose the wrong room; **si no me equivoco** unless I'm mistaken; **me equivoqué de baño** I went into the wrong bathroom
equívoco ADJ (ambiguo) equivocal; (moralmente dudoso) questionable; M misunderstanding
era F (período) era, age; (lugar donde se trilla) threshing floor; (parcela) plot
era, eras *ver* ser
erario M treasury
erecto ADJ erect; (postura) upright
eres *ver* ser
ergonomía F ergonomics
ergonómico ADJ ergonomic
erguido ADJ erect, upright
erguir[13] VT to lift, to raise; **—se** to rise
erial M uncultivated land
erigir[46] VT (construir) to erect; (fundar) to found; **—se en** to set oneself up as
Eritrea F Eritrea
eritreo -a ADJ & MF Eritrean
erizado ADJ bristly; **— de** bristling with
erizar[47] VT to set on end; **—se** to bristle
erizo M hedgehog; **— de mar** sea urchin; **ser un —** to be a grouch
ermitaño -ña MF (persona) hermit; M (cangrejo) hermit crab
erógeno ADJ erogenous
erosión F erosion
erradicación F eradication
erradicar[30] VT to eradicate, to root out
errado ADJ erroneous, in error
errante ADJ wandering
errar[21] VT to miss; **— el cálculo** to miscalculate; VI (estar equivocado) to be mistaken; (vagar) to roam, to rove, to wander
errata F misprint, typographical error
erático ADJ erratic
erróneo ADJ erroneous
error M error, mistake; **— de hecho** factual error; **— de imprenta** misprint; **— no forzado** unforced error; **— tipográfico** typo

eructar VI to belch, to burp
eructo M belch, burp
erudición F erudition, learning, scholarship
erudito -ta ADJ (persona) erudite; (obra) scholarly, learned; MF scholar
erupción F eruption; **hacer —** to erupt
es *ver* ser
esbelto ADJ slender
esbozar[47] VT to outline; **— una sonrisa** to give a hint of a smile
esbozo M sketch, outline; **— de una sonrisa** hint of a smile
escabechar VT to pickle
escabroso ADJ (agreste) rugged; (espinoso) thorny; (sórdido) lurid, sordid
escabullirse[16] VI (ladrones) to slip away, to steal away; (lagartijas) to scurry away/off; **— de** to wriggle out of
escafandra F (para el agua) scuba gear; (para el espacio) spacesuit
escala F (escalera, escalafón) ladder; (serie de grados, notas, serie ascendente) scale; (parada) stopover; **— de sueldos** salary range, wage scale; **hacer — en** to stop over at; **— salarial** wage scale, pay scale; **a — nacional** nationwide; **a/de gran —** large-scale; **sin —s** nonstop
escalada F (de una montaña) climb; (de violencia) escalation
escalador -ora MF climber
escalar VT (subir) to scale, to climb; (cambiar de tamaño) scale
escaldadura F scald
escaldar VT (la piel) to scald; (las verduras) to blanch; **—se** to get scalded
escalera F (en un edificio) stairs, staircase; (portátil) ladder; (de naipes) straight; **— mecánica** escalator; **— de caracol** spiral/winding staircase; **— de color** straight flush; **— de incendios** fire escape; **— real** royal flush
escalfar VT to poach
escalinata F grand staircase
escalofriante ADJ chilling, hair-raising
escalofrío M chill; **—s** the shivers
escalón M (peldaño) step, stair; (de escalera de mano, de escalafón) rung; (terraza) rung; (formación militar) echelon
escalonar VT (distribuir) to stagger; (aterrazar) to terrace
escalope M scallop
escama F (de animal) scale; (de piel, corteza) flake
escamar VT to scale
escamoso ADJ (animal) scaly; (piel) flaky
escamotear VT (esconder) to palm; (robar) to snatch; (eludir) to shirk
escampar VI to clear up
escandalizar[47] VT (chocar) to scandalize; (causar escándalo) to cause a scandal; **—se** to be shocked
escándalo M (suceso vergonzoso) scandal; (riña) uproar
escandaloso ADJ (chocante) scandalous, shocking; (ruidoso) raucous
escandir VT *lit* to scan
escaneado M scanning
escanear VT to scan
escáner M scanner; **— color** color scanner
escaño M seat in parliament
escapada F (escape) escape
escapar VI (de un lugar, una situación) to escape; (de alguien, de una responsabilidad) to run away; **—se** (persona) to escape; (gas) to leak; **se me escapó una sonrisa** I inadvertently smiled; **Matilde se me está escapando de las manos** Matilde is getting out of hand
escaparate M shop window
escapatoria F (de un lugar) escape, way out; (legal) loophole
escape M (fantasía, escapatoria) escape; (de coche) exhaust; (de gas, agua) leak
escápula F scapula
escarabajo M beetle
escaramuza F skirmish
escaramuzar[47] VI to skirmish
escarbar VI/VT to dig, to scratch; **— en los archivos** to dig around in the files; **—se los dientes** to pick one's teeth
escarcha F frost
escarchar VI to frost
escardar VT to weed
escarlata ADJ INV & M (color) scarlet; F (enfermedad) scarlet fever
escarlatina F scarlet fever
escarmentar[1] VI to learn one's lesson; VT to teach a lesson
escarmiento M lesson; **que te sirva de —** let that be a lesson to you
escarnecer[35] VT to deride
escarnio M derision
escarpa F steep slope
escarpado ADJ steep, precipitous; M steep slope
escasear VI to be scarce
escasez F (falta) shortage; (carestía) scarcity, want
escaso ADJ sparse, scarce; **una docena escasa** a scant dozen; **— de** short on; **— de personal** short-handed
escatimar VT to skimp on; **no — gastos** to spare no expense
escena F (fragmento de una obra de teatro, episodio) scene; (escenario) stage; **montar una —** to make a scene; **en —** on stage; **poner en —** to stage; **entrar en —** to go on stage
escenario M stage
escénico ADJ **pánico —** stage fright

escenificación F staging
escepticismo M skepticism
escéptico -ca ADJ skeptical; MF skeptic
escisión F split
esclarecer[35] VT to elucidate
esclavitud F slavery
esclavizar[47] VT to enslave
esclavo -va MF slave
esclerosis F sclerosis; **— múltiple** multiple sclerosis
esclusa F (de un canal) lock; (de una presa) floodgate, sluice gate
escoba F broom
escobilla F whisk broom
escocer[34] VI to sting
escocés -esa ADJ Scottish; **[cuadros] escoceses** plaid; MF Scot; M (whisky) Scotch; (lengua) Scots
Escocia F Scotland
escoger[45] VT to choose
escolar MF pupil; ADJ **año —** school year
escoliosis F scoliosis
escollo M (arrecife) reef; (obstáculo) obstacle
escolta F (policial) escort; MF (persona) escort; (baloncesto) shooting guard
escoltar VT to escort
escombros M PL rubble, debris
esconder VT to hide; VI **—se** to hide
escondidas LOC ADV **a —** on the sly; **entrar a —** to sneak in; **meter algo a —** to sneak something in; **jugar a las —** to play hide and seek
escondite M (en un juego) hiding place; (de ladrón) hideout; (de cazador) blind; **jugar al —** to play hide and seek
escondrijo M hiding place
escopeta F shotgun
escoplo M chisel
escora F listing
escorar VI to list
escorbuto M scurvy
escoria F (de metales) slag; (de la sociedad) scum, dregs
escorpión M scorpion
escotado ADJ low-cut
escote M (parte del vestido) neckline; (parte del cuerpo) cleavage; **pagar a —** to go Dutch
escotilla F hatch
escozor M smarting sensation; **— vaginal** vaginal itching
escribiente MF clerk
escribir[74] VI/VT to write; **¿cómo se escribe?** how do you spell it? **— a máquina** to type
escrito ADJ written; **— a máquina** typewritten; **no —** unwritten; **por —** in writing; M document
escrito *ver* escribir
escritor -ora MF writer, author
escritorio M (mueble) desk; (oficina) office
escritura F (acción de escribir) writing; (certificado de propiedad) deed; **— de traspaso** conveyance; **— de venta** bill of sale
escrúpulo M scruple, qualm; **sin —s** unscrupulous
escrupuloso ADJ scrupulous
escrutar VT (a una persona) to scrutinize; (el horizonte) to scan; (votos) to count
escrutinio M (examen) scrutiny; (recuento) vote count
escuadra F (de buques, soldados) squadron; (instrumento) square
escuadrilla F (de aviones) flight of aircraft; (de buques) squadron
escuadrón M squadron; **— de la muerte** death squad
escualidez F (delgadez) skinniness; (suciedad) squalor
escuálido ADJ (sucio) squalid; (delgado) thin
escuchar VT to listen to; (oír) to hear; VI to listen; **— a hurtadillas** to eavesdrop
escudar VT to shield
escudo M (arma defensiva) shield; (moneda de Portugal) escudo; **— de armas** coat of arms
escudriñar VT (a una persona) to scrutinize, to peer at; (el horizonte) to scan
escuela F school; **— industrial** trade school; **— normal** school of education; **— pública** public school; **— primaria** elementary school; **— secundaria** secondary school; **tener —** to have good technique
escueto ADJ (explicación) succinct; (verdad) simple
esculpir VI/VT to sculpture, to sculpt
escultor -ora MF sculptor
escultura F sculpture
escupir VI/VT to spit
escupitajo M spit
escurridizo ADJ (acera) slippery; (ladrón) elusive, slippery
escurrir VI/VT (platos, verduras) to drain; (ropa) to wring out; **—se** to slink away
ese ADJ DEM that, those; **esa chica se llama Matilde** that girl is called Matilde; **esas ciudades son antiguas** those cities are old; PRON that one, those; **ese es el mayor** that one is the oldest; **esos son mis hijos** those are my children
esencia F essence
esencial ADJ essential; **lo —** the gist, the bottom line, the name of the game
esfera F (cuerpo sólido) sphere; (espacio, ámbito) realm, sphere; (de reloj) face, dial; **— de influencia** sphere of influence
esférico ADJ spherical; M soccer ball
esfínter M sphincter
esforzado ADJ valiant
esforzarse[49] VI to try hard, to exert oneself; **—**

por to strive to, to make an effort to
esfuerzo M effort
esfumar VT to tone down; **—se** to vanish, to fizzle out
esgrima F fencing; **practicar —** to fence
esgrimir VT (armas) to brandish, to wield; (argumentos) to employ
eslabón M chain link; **— perdido** missing link
eslabonar VT to link
eslavo -va ADJ Slavic; MF Slav
eslogan M slogan
eslovaco ADJ & MF Slovakian; M (lengua) Slovakian
Eslovaquia F Slovakia
Eslovenia F Slovenia
esloveno -na ADJ & MF Slovene; M (lengua) Slovene
esmaltar VT to enamel
esmalte M enamel; **— de uñas** nail polish
esmeradamente ADV carefully
esmerado ADJ careful, painstaking
esmeralda F emerald
esmerarse VI to take pains
esmerilado ADJ frosted; M frosting
esmerilar VT to frost
esmero M care
esmirriado ADJ scrawny
esmoquin M tuxedo
esnifar VT to snort
esnob M snob
esnórquel M snorkel
eso PRON DEM that; **— es verdad** that's true; **— sí** granted; **a — de las tres** at about three o'clock; **de —, nada** no way! yeah, right! **en — llega y me dice** at that moment he arrives and says to me; **y — que le dije que viniese temprano** even when I told him to come early
esófago M esophagus
esotérico ADJ esoteric
espaciado M pitch, spacing; **— de palabras** word spacing
espacial ADJ spatial; **nave —** spaceship
espaciar VT to space; **—se** to space out
espacio M (capacidad) space, room; (superficie) expanse; (separación entre líneas) space, spacing; (en un formulario) blank space; (porción de tiempo) span; **— aéreo** aerospace; **— entre caracteres** letterspacing; **— exterior** outer space; **— noticioso** newscast; **a doble —** double-spaced; **a un —** single-spaced; **por — de una semana** for a week
espacioso ADJ spacious, roomy
espada F sword; **—s** (palo de naipes) swords; **— de doble filo** double-edged sword; **estar entre la — y la pared** to be between a rock and a hard place
espalda F back; **a —s de alguien** behind someone's back; **caerse de —s** to fall on one's back; **nadar [de] —** to do the backstroke; **tener las —s anchas** to take a lot of abuse; **volver las —s** to turn one's back
espaldar M chair back
espantadizo ADJ easily scared
espantado ADJ frightened
espantajo M scarecrow
espantar VT to frighten, to scare; (ahuyentar) to frighten away, to scare away; **—se** to get scared; M SG **espantapájaros** scarecrow
espanto M fright, dread; **estás hecho un —** you look a sight; **estoy curado de —** nothing surprises me anymore
espantoso ADJ frightful, dreadful
España F Spain
español -ola ADJ Spanish; MF Spaniard; M (lengua) Spanish
esparadrapo M surgical tape
esparcimiento M (recreo) relaxation; (reparto) spreading
esparcir[33] VT to scatter, to spread; **—se** to amuse oneself
espárrago M asparagus
espasmo M spasm, jerk
espasmódico ADJ spasmodic, jerky
espástico ADJ spastic
espátula F spatula
especia F spice
especial ADJ & M special; **en —** in particular, especially
especialidad F specialty, specialization
especialista MF specialist
especialización F specialization
especializar[47] VT to specialize; **—se en** to specialize in, to major in
especialmente ADV (de forma particular) specially; **esto lo hice — para ti** I made this specially for you; (en especial) especially; **este tipo es — bueno** this kind is especially good
especie F (clase) kind; (categoría biológica) species; **—s en peligro de extinción** endangered species; **pagar en —** to pay in kind; **una — de** a kind of
especiero M spice rack
especificar[30] VT to specify
específico ADJ & M specific
espécimen M specimen
espectacular ADJ spectacular
espectáculo M (escándalo) spectacle; (actuación pública) show; (vista) sight; **dar el —** to make a spectacle of oneself
espectador -ora MF (de un espectáculo) spectator; (de un suceso) onlooker
espectro M (fantasma) specter; (de la luz, de un antibiótico) spectrum
especulación F speculation
especulador -ora MF speculator

especular VT to speculate; ADJ mirror; **imagen** — mirror image
especulativo ADJ speculative
espejismo M (en el desierto) mirage; (ilusión) illusion
espejo M mirror; — **de cuerpo entero** full-length mirror; — **retrovisor** rearview mirror
espeluznante ADJ hair-raising
espeluznar VT to terrify; —**se** to be terrified
espera F (acción de esperar) wait; (aplazamiento) extension; **estar en** — **de** to be waiting for
esperanza F hope; — **de vida** life expectancy; **con una** — **de voto del 12,5%** expected to get 12.5% of the vote
esperanzado ADJ hopeful
esperanzador ADJ hopeful
esperanzar[47] VT to give hope to
esperar VT (tener esperanza) to hope; (estar embarazada, anticipar) to expect; (aguardar) to wait for; VI to wait; **como era de** — not surprisingly; **era de** — it was to be expected; **espera sentado** don't hold your breath; **estoy esperando un milagro** I'm hoping for a miracle; **todavía espera confirmación** it still awaits confirmation
esperma MF sperm
espermicida M spermicide
esperpento M fright, grotesque person or thing
espesar VT to thicken
espeso ADJ (pelo, sopa, niebla) thick; (cejas) bushy
espesor M thickness
espesura F (espesor) thickness; (lugar poblado de matorrales) thicket
espetar VT (decir bruscamente) to blurt out; (pinchar) to skewer
espeto, espetón M spit
espía MF spy
espiar[28] VI to spy; VT to spy on
espichar VI *fam* to croak, to bite the dust
espiga F spike
espigar[40] VT to glean; VI to grow spikes; —**se** to grow tall
espina F (de planta) thorn; (de pez) fish bone; — **dorsal** spinal column; **me quedé con la** — I was left wondering
espinaca F spinach
espinal ADJ spinal
espinazo M spine, backbone
espinilla F (en la pierna) shin; (de animal) shank; (acné, comedón) blackhead
espino M thorny shrub
espinoso ADJ thorny
espionaje M espionage
espiración F expiration
espiral ADJ & F spiral
espirar VI/VT to exhale, to breathe out, to expire
espíritu M (ánima, fantasma, intención de una ley) spirit; (alma) soul; — **fuerte** free spirit; — **deportivo** sportsmanship; — **emprendedor** can-do attitude, entrepreneurship; — **Santo** Holy Spirit
espiritual ADJ & M spiritual
espiritualidad F spirituality
espita F spigot
espléndido ADJ (estupendo) splendid; (dispendioso) lavish
esplendor M splendor
esplendoroso ADJ magnificent
espliego M lavender
espolear VT to spur
espoleta F bomb fuse
espolón M (de gallo, planta, estímulo) spur; (de buque) ram
espolvorear VT to dust, to sprinkle
esponja F (animal, utensilio) sponge; (borracho) souse
esponjado ADJ spongy
esponjar VT to make spongy; —**se** to become spongy
esponjoso ADJ spongy
esponsales M PL betrothal
espontaneidad F spontaneity
espontáneo ADJ spontaneous
espora F spore
esposar VT to handcuff
esposo -sa M husband; F wife; **esposas** handcuffs
espuela F spur
espulgar[40] VT to delouse
espuma F (de cerveza) froth; (de jabón) suds, lather; (de la boca) foam; (de colchón) foam rubber; (de mar) foam, spray; **echar** — **por la boca** to foam at the mouth; **hacer** — to make suds
espumar VT (quitar la espuma) to skim; (formar espuma) to foam
espumarajo M foam; **echar** —**s por la boca** to foam at the mouth
espumillón M tinsel
espumoso ADJ foamy
esputo M sputum
esquela F note; — **mortuoria** death notice
esquelético ADJ skeletal
esqueleto M (huesos) skeleton; (armazón) framework; **mover el** — (bailar) to dance; (moverse) to move
esquema M outline; **romperle los** —**s a alguien** (planes) to ruin one's plans; (conceptos) to shatter one's preconceptions
esquí M (tabla) ski; (deporte) skiing; — **acuático** (tabla) water ski; (deporte) waterskiing; **hacer** — **acuático** to water-ski
esquiar[28] VI to ski
esquila F (cencerro) cowbell; (acción de esquilar) shearing
esquilador -ora MF sheep shearer

esquilar VT to shear, to clip
esquileo M shearing
esquimal ADJ & MF Eskimo; M (lengua) Eskimo
esquina F corner; **en cada —** everywhere
esquinero ADJ **mesa esquinera** corner table; M cornerback
esquirol M strikebreaker
esquivar VT (a una persona) to avoid; (un golpe) to dodge
esquivo ADV (tímido) shy, coy; (huraño) aloof; (reservado) elusive; (indirecto) evasive
esquizofrenia F schizophrenia
estabilidad F stability
estabilización F stabilization
estabilizar[47] VT to stabilize
estable ADJ (mesa) stable; (precio) firm; (huésped) long-term
establecer[35] VT to establish; (averiguar) to ascertain; **— una cita** to set up an appointment; **—se** to settle
establecimiento M establishment
establezca, establezco *ver* establecer
establishment M establishment
establo M stable
estaca F (con punta) stake; (gruesa) club
estacada F stockade; **dejar en la —** to leave in the lurch
estacar[30] VT (atar) to stake; (delimitar) to stake off
estación F (de tren, autobús, radio) station; (del año) season; **— bípeda** bipedal stance; **— de bomberos** fire station; **— de esquí** ski resort; **— de servicio** gas/filling station; **— de trabajo** workstation; **— espacial** space station
estacional ADJ seasonal
estacionamiento M (acción) parking; (lugar) parking lot
estacionar VT (tropas) to station; (un vehículo) to park; **—se** (un coche) to park; (precios) to level off
estacionario ADJ stationary
estadía F stay
estadio M (recinto deportivo) stadium; (fase) stage
estadista M statesman; F stateswoman
estadística F (ciencia) statistics; **—s** (datos numéricos) statistics
estado M (situación, unidad política) state; **— civil** marital status; **— de cuenta** bank statement; **— de alarma** state of emergency; **— de ánimo** state of mind; **— de excepción** martial law; **— de guerra** state of war; **— de sitio** state of siege; **— mayor** chiefs of staff; **— policíaco** police state; **de — sólido** solid state; **en — interesante** expecting; **en — vegetativo** in a vegetative state, brain-dead
Estados Unidos M PL/SG United States
estadounidense ADJ & MF American
estafa F swindle, scam, racket
estafador -ora MF swindler, racketeer
estafar VT to swindle
estalactita F stalactite
estalagmita F stalagmite
estallar VI (una bomba) to explode; (un globo) to burst; (una guerra) to break out; (una persona) to snap; **— de risa** to burst out laughing; **— en una carcajada** to burst out laughing; **hacer —** to set off
estallido M (explosión) explosion; (ruido) bang, report
estampa F (de revista) illustration; (imagen) image; (apariencia) appearance; **de buena —** good-looking; **la viva — de la madre** the spitting image of her mother; **la viva — de la desolación** the very picture of desolation
estampado ADJ printed; M (tela) print; (acción) printing
estampar VT (en tela, papel) to print; (con un molde, en metal) to stamp; **—le un beso a alguien** to plant a kiss on someone
estampida F stampede
estampido M bang
estampilla F stamp
estampillar VT to stamp
estancado ADJ stagnant
estancamiento M stagnation (también económico)
estancar[30] VT to stem; to dam; to block; **—se** to stagnate
estancia F (estadía) stay; (habitación) hall; (hacienda) RP cattle ranch
estanco ADJ waterproof; M government store
estándar ADJ & M standard
estandarización F standardization
estandarizar[47] VT to standardize
estandarte M standard, banner
estanque M pond
estante M (tabla) shelf; (mueble) bookcase
estantería F (mueble) bookcase; (de biblioteca) stack
estañar VT to tin-plate
estaño M tin
estar[63] VI to be; **— a tres kilómetros de aquí** to be three kilometers from here; **— bien** to be all right; **— mal/enfermo del corazón** to have heart trouble; **— de más** to be unnecessary; **— para** to be about to; **— por** (a favor de) to be in favor of; (a punto de) to be about to; **— trabajando duro** to be working hard; **¿a cuántos estamos?** what day of the month is it? **ahí está** that's it; **¿está Alice?** is Alice there? **están muy buenos tus zapatos nuevos** your new shoes are nice; **estate tranquilo** don't worry; **no —** to be out; **cuarto de —** living room
estatal ADJ **compañía —** state-run company
estático ADJ static

estatua F statue
estatura F (importancia) stature; (altura física) height
estatutario ADJ statutory
estatuto M (ley) statute; (de una sociedad) bylaw; **— de quiebras** bankruptcy law
este ADJ DEM this, these; **esta chica se llama Hilary** this girl is called Hilary; **estas ciudades son antiguas** these cities are old; PRON DEM this one, these; **— es el mayor** this one is the oldest; **estos son mis hijos** these are my children; M & ADJ east; **hacia el —** eastward
estela F (de una embarcación) wake; (de humo, polvo) trail; **dejar una —** to leave a trail
estelar ADJ stellar
estenotipista MF court reporter
estentóreo ADJ booming
estepa F steppe
estera F mat
estercolar VT to fertilize with manure
estercolero M dunghill
estéreo ADJ & M stereo; **en —** in stereo
estereotipo M stereotype
estéril ADJ (gasa, esfuerzo) sterile; (mujer) barren
esterilidad F sterility
esterilizar[47] VT to sterilize
esternón M sternum, breastbone
esteroide M steroid; **— anabólico** anabolic steroid
estertor M death rattle
estética F aesthetics
estético ADJ aesthetic
estetoscopio M stethoscope
estibador M stevedore, longshoreman
estibar VT to stow
estiércol M manure
estigma M stigma
estigmatizar[47] VT to stigmatize
estilarse VI to be in style; **eso no se estila aquí** that's not done here
estilística F stylistics
estilístico ADJ stylistic
estilo M (literario, estético, caligráfico) style; (de natación) stroke; **— de vida** lifestyle; **— espalda** backstroke; **— indirecto** reported speech; **— libre** freestyle; **— mariposa** butterfly stroke; **— pecho** breaststroke; **— perrito** dog paddle; **cosas por el —** things like that
estima F esteem, regard
estimación F (cálculo) estimate; (estima) estimation
estimado ADJ esteemed; **— Sr.** Dear Sir
estimar VT (apreciar) to esteem; (determinar el valor) to estimate; (opinar) to think
estimulación F stimulation
estimulante ADJ stimulating; M stimulant
estimular VT (despertar, excitar) to stimulate; (alentar) to encourage
estímulo M stimulus
estío M *lit* summer
estipendio M stipend
estipulación F stipulation
estipular VT to stipulate
estirado ADJ stuck-up
estirar VT (alargar) to stretch; **— el cuello** to crane one's neck; **— la pata** *fam* to kick the bucket; (crecer) to grow; **—se** to stretch
estirón M growth spurt; **pegar un —** to have a growth spurt
estirpe F lineage
estival ADJ **vacaciones —es** summer vacation
esto PRON DEM this; **— es** that is to say; **a todo —** meanwhile; **en —** at this point
estocada F thrust; **lanzar una —** to thrust
estofa F type; **de baja —** low-class
estofado M stew
estofar VT to stew
estoico-ca ADJ & MF stoic
estolón M runner
estómago M stomach
Estonia F Estonia
estonio-nia ADJ & MF Estonian; M (lengua) Estonian
estopa F tow
estorbar VT (obstaculizar) to hinder, to impede; (molestar) to be a nuisance
estorbo M (obstáculo) hindrance, impediment; (molestia) nuisance
estornino M starling
estornudar VI to sneeze
estornudo M sneeze
estoy *ver* estar
estrado M bench
estrafalario ADJ bizarre, outlandish
estragar[40] VT (físicamente) to devastate; (moralmente) to corrupt
estrago M havoc; **hacer —s** to wreak havoc
estrangular VT to strangle
estratagema F stratagem
estrategia F strategy; (de negocios, deportes) game plan; **— de salida** exit strategy
estratégico ADJ strategic
estrato M stratum, layer; **— social** social class
estratosfera F stratosphere
estrechamente ADV closely
estrechamiento M constriction
estrechar VT (angostar) to narrow; (abrazar) to embrace; **la estrechó en sus brazos** he held her in his arms; **—se** to get narrower; **—se la mano** to shake hands
estrechez F (cualidad de estrecho) narrowness; (acción de estrechar) narrowing; (aprietos) dire straits
estrecho ADJ narrow; **la falda le quedaba estrecha** the skirt was too tight for her; M

strait
estrella F star; **— binaria** binary star; **— de cine** movie star; **— de mar** starfish; **— fugaz** shooting star, falling star; **ver las —s** to see stars
estrellado ADJ (como una estrella) starlike; (cubierto de estrellas) starry
estrellar VT (aplastar) to smash; (romper) to crack; **—se** (avión) to crash; (intento) to fail; **—se contra** to smash into
estremecer[35] VT to make shudder; **el terremoto estremeció París** the earthquake rocked Paris; **—se** to shudder
estremecimiento M shudder
estrenar VT (un vestido) to wear for the first time; (una película, obra de teatro) to debut; (una bicicleta) to try out for the first time; (un título) to use for the first time; **—se** to debut
estreno M (de una película) premiere; (de un objeto) first use; (de una actividad) debut
estreñido ADJ (constipado) constipated; (antipático) uptight
estreñimiento M constipation
estreñir[11] VT to constipate; **—se** to become constipated
estrépito M racket, clatter; **causar —** to clatter
estrepitoso ADJ noisy
estrés M stress
estresante ADJ stressful, high-pressure
estresar VT to stress [out]
estría F (en la piel) stretch mark; (en una columna) flute; (en mármol) striation
estriado ADJ (piel) covered with stretch marks; (columna) fluted; (piedra) streaked
estriar[28] VT to flute; **—se** to get stretch marks
estribación F spur
estribar VI **— en** (apoyarse en) to lean on; (radicar en) to lie in
estribillo M refrain
estribo M (de silla, oído) stirrup; (de coche) running board; **perder los —s** to fly off the handle
estribor M starboard
estricnina F strychnine
estricto ADJ strict
estridente ADJ strident
estrofa F verse, stanza
estrógeno M estrogen
estropajo M scrubber; **tengo la boca que es un —** my mouth is as dry as a bone
estropajoso ADJ sinewy
estropear VT to ruin
estructura F structure
estructuración F structuring
estructural ADJ structural
estructurar VT to structure
estruendo M din, racket
estruendoso ADJ thunderous
estrujamiento M (para romper) crushing; (para sacar jugo) squeezing
estrujar VT (aplastar) to crush; (apretar) to squeeze
estrujón M squeeze
estuario M estuary
estucar[30] VT to stucco
estuche M (para joyas) jewelry box; (para pastillas) pill box; (para lentes) glasses case
estuco M stucco
estudiantado M student body
estudiante MF student
estudiantil ADJ **vida —** student life
estudiar VI/VT to study
estudio M (acción de estudiar, investigación, habitación) study; (taller de artista) studio; (apartamento pequeño) studio apartment; **en —** under study; **— del impacto ambiental** environmental impact study
estudioso -sa ADJ studious; MF scholar
estufa F (para calentar) heater, stove; (para cocinar) stove
estupefaciente ADJ & M narcotic
estupefacto ADJ stunned, speechless
estupendo ADJ stupendous, terrific; **me la pasé — en la casa de Hilary** I had a great time at Hilary's house
estupidez F stupidity; **estupideces** nonsense
estúpido ADJ stupid
estupor M stupor
estupro M statutory rape
estuve, estuviera, estuviese *ver* estar
etanol M ethanol
etapa F stage; **por —s** by stages
etcétera CONJ et cetera, and so forth
éter M ether
eternidad F eternity
eternizarse[47] VI to drag on
eterno ADJ eternal, everlasting
ética F ethics
ético ADJ ethical
etimología F etymology
etíope ADJ & MF Ethiopian
Etiopía F Ethiopía
etiqueta F (de comportamiento) etiquette; (en una lata, botella) label; (en una prenda) tag; **— adhesiva** sticker; **— de identificación** name tag; **— de precio** price tag; **nos trataron con —** they treated us very formally; **vestirse de —** to dress formally
etiquetar VT (latas, botellas, personas) to label; (prendas) to tag
etnicidad F ethnicity
étnico ADJ ethnic
etnografía F ethnography
etnología F ethnology
eucalipto M eucalyptus
eufemismo M euphemism
euforia F euphoria
eunuco M eunuch

euro M euro
Europa F Europe
europeo -a ADJ & MF European
euskera M Basque [language]
eutanasia F euthanasia
evacuación F (de un lugar) evacuation; (del vientre) bowel movement; (de agua) drainage
evacuar VT (un lugar, a una persona) to evacuate; (el vientre) to void; (agua) to drain; VI to defecate
evadir VT to evade; **—se** to escape
evaluación F evaluation; **— del rendimiento** performance review
evaluar[26] VT (analizar) to evaluate, to assess; (tasar) to estimate; (calificar) to test
evangélico ADJ evangelical
evangelio M gospel
evaporación F evaporation
evaporar VT to evaporate; **—se** to vanish
evasión F (fiscal) evasion; (de prisioneros, de la realidad) escape; **— de capitales** capital flight; **— de impuestos** tax evasion
evasiva F **salirse con —s** to beat around the bush
evasivo ADJ evasive
evasor -ora MF evader
evento M event
eventual ADJ (posible) possible; (temporal) temporary
evidencia F evidence; **dejar/poner en — a alguien** to show someone up; **quedar/ponerse en —** to become apparent
evidenciar VT to make evident; **—se** to become evident
evidente ADJ evident, obvious
evidentemente ADV & INTERJ obviously
evitar VT (eludir) to avoid; (ahorrar) to spare
evocación F evocation
evocar[30] VT (una memoria) to evoke; (a los espíritus) to conjure up
evolución F evolution
evolucionar VI to evolve
evolutivo ADJ evolutionary
ex MF *fam* ex
exacerbar VT (intensificar) to exacerbate; (irritar) to aggravate
exactamente ADV & INTERJ exactly, precisely; **llegaron — a las tres** they arrived exactly at three
exactitud F accuracy, precision
exacto ADJ exact, precise, accurate; INTERJ exactly
exageración F exaggeration
exagerado ADJ exaggerated; **Jorge es un —** Jorge always exaggerates
exagerar VI/VT to exaggerate
exaltación F (elogio) praise; (excitación) excitement
exaltar VT to exalt; **—se** to get excited
examen M (inspección) examination; (prueba) examination, test, exam; **— de ingreso** entrance examination; **— dérmico de alergias** scratch test; **— final** final examination; **— físico** physical examination; **— médico** medical exam, checkup; **dar un —** to take a test; **poner un —** to give a test
examinar VT (inspeccionar) to examine; (someter a un examen) to test
exasperar VT to exasperate, to aggravate
excavación F (geológica) excavation; (arqueológica) dig
excavador -ora MF (persona) excavator; F (aparato) excavator, earthmover
excavar VT to excavate, to dig
excedente ADJ & M surplus
exceder VT (sobrepasar) to exceed; (superar) to surpass; **— de** to go beyond
excelencia F excellence; **por —** par excellence
excelente ADJ excellent, great
excentricidad F eccentricity
excéntrico ADJ eccentric
excepción F exception; **a — de** with the exception of
excepcional ADJ exceptional
excepto ADV & PREP except
exceptuar[26] VT to except
excesivo ADJ excessive
exceso M excess; **— de costos** overrun; **— de equipaje** excess baggage; **beber en —** to drink to excess; **comer en —** to overeat
excitación F (de músculos) excitement; (sexual) arousal
excitante ADJ stimulating
excitar VT (un nervio) to excite; (impulso sexual) to arouse; **—se** (sexualmente) to get aroused; (átomos) to be excited
exclamación F exclamation
exclamar VT to exclaim
excluir[19] VT to exclude
exclusión F exclusion
exclusivo ADJ exclusive
excomulgar[40] VT to excommunicate
excrecencia F excrescence
excreción F excretion
excremento M excrement
excretar VT to excrete
excursión F excursion, outing
excusa F excuse
excusable ADJ excusable
excusado M *Méx* toilet
excusar VT to excuse
exención F exemption
exento ADJ exempt; **— de impuestos** tax-exempt
exequias F PL funeral rites
exfoliación F exfoliation
exhalar VI/VT (aire) to exhale, to breathe out; (un olor) to give off; **— un suspiro** to sigh

exhaustivo ADJ exhaustive, thorough
exhausto ADJ exhausted
exhibición F (manifestación) exhibition; (despliegue) display
exhibicionismo M exhibitionism
exhibir VT (fotos) to exhibit; (mercancías) to display; (el carnet de identitad) to show; **—se** to show off; **le gusta exhibirse en traje de baño** she likes to show off in her bathing suit; **esa película ya no se exhibe** that movie is not showing anymore
exhortar VT to exhort, to urge
exhumación F exhumation
exigencia F demand
exigente ADJ demanding, exacting
exigir[46] VT to demand; **exigen a alguien que sepa inglés** they require someone who knows English
exiguo ADJ meager; **exigua mayoría** scant majority
exiliado -da MF exile
exiliar VT to exile
exilio M exile
eximido ADJ exempt; **— por la cláusula del abuelo** grandfathered
eximio ADJ illustrious
eximir VT (de impuestos) to exempt; (de sospecha) to clear; (de una responsabilidad) to excuse
existencia F existence; **complicarle la — a alguien** to cause someone trouble; **la lucha por la —** the fight for survival; **—s** stock on hand; **en —** in stock, on hand
existencial ADJ existential
existente ADJ extant, existing
existir VI to exist
éxito M success; (musical) hit; **— de taquilla** blockbuster; **tener —** to be successful; **tiene — con las mujeres** he's popular with women
exitoso ADJ successful
éxodo M exodus
exonerar VT to exonerate
exorbitante ADJ exorbitant
exorcisar VT to exorcise
exorcismo M exorcism
exótico ADJ exotic
expandir VT (dilatar) to expand, to spread; (propagar) to disseminate; **—se** to expand, to spread
expansión F (crecimiento) expansion; (diversión) relaxation
expansivo ADJ (que crece) expansive; (efusivo) effusive
expatriado -da MF expatriate
expatriar VT to expatriate, to exile
expectación F anticipation
expectativa F (esperanza) expectation; (posibilidad) prospect; **estar a la — de algo** to be on pins and needles; **— de vida** life expectancy
expectorante M expectorant
expectorar VI/VT to expectorate, to cough up
expedición F (viaje) expedition; (de documentos) issuing; (de mercancías) delivery
expedicionario -ria ADJ expeditionary; MF member of an expedition
expedidor -ora ADJ shipping; MF shipper
expediente M (administrativo) file, dossier; (policial, académico, médico) record
expedir[9] VT (enviar) to dispatch; (emitir) to issue
expeler VT to expel
expendedor -ora MF vendor; **— automático** vending machine
experiencia F experience
experimentación F experimentation
experimentado ADJ experienced
experimental ADJ experimental
experimentar VI (hacer experimentos) to experiment; VT (sufrir, tener experiencia) to experience
experimento M experiment
experto -ta ADJ & MF expert; **— en computación** wizard, *fam* techie
expiación F atonement
expiar[28] VT to atone for
expirar VI to expire
explanada F (terreno junto al mar) esplanade; (terreno nivelado) leveled area
explayarse VI to become extended; **— sobre** to enlarge upon
explicable ADJ explainable, explicable
explicación F explanation
explicar[30] VT to explain; **—se** to make oneself clear; **no me explico por qué** I can't figure out why
explicativo ADJ explanatory
explícito ADJ explicit
exploración F exploration
explorador -ora ADJ exploring; MF (expedicionario) explorer; (militar) scout
explorar VI/VT to explore; (con fines diagnósticos) to scan; (con fines militares) to scout
exploratorio ADJ exploratory
explosión F explosion; **hacer —** to explode
explosivo ADJ & M explosive
explotación F exploitation
explotar VT (sacar provecho) to exploit; (hacer explosión) to explode
expondrá, expondría *ver* exponer
exponente M exponent
exponer[56, 74] VT (al sol, al peligro) to expose; (al público) to exhibit, to display; (explicar) to state, to set forth; **—se al peligro** to expose oneself to danger

exponga, expongo *ver* exponer
exportación F (acción) exportation, export; (cosa) export
exportador -ora ADJ exporting; MF exporter
exportar VI/VT to export
exposición F (feria) exposition; (de arte) exhibition; (explicación) explanation; (al sol, a una influencia, al peligro) exposure
expresar VT to express
expresión F expression; **valga la —** so to speak
expresividad F expressiveness
expresivo ADJ expressive
expreso ADJ (explícito) express; (rápido) fast; M express train; **café —** espresso
exprimidor M juicer
exprimir VT (naranjas) to squeeze; (zumo) to squeeze out
expropiar VT to expropriate
expuesto ADJ exposed; **lo —** what has been said
expuesto *ver* exponer
expulsar VT to expel; (de un bar) to throw out; (de un partido) to eject
expulsión F expulsion
expuse, expusiera, expusiese *ver* exponer
exquisito -ta ADJ (arte) exquisite; (comida) delicious
extasiado ADJ rapt
extasiarse[28] VI to be enraptured
éxtasis M ecstasy (también droga)
extender[2] VT (el brazo, radio de acción, gratitud) to extend; (un tapete, una masa, un idioma) to spread; (un cheque) to draw up; **—se** to extend; **la fiesta se extendió hasta las 3** the party lasted until 3 o'clock
extendido ADJ (brazos) outstretched; (costumbre) widespread
extensión F (del antebrazo, de significado, telefónica) extension; (de terreno) expanse; (de un texto) length; (eléctrica) extension cord; **por —** by extension; **tener mucha —** to be widespread
extensivo ADJ extensive; **hacer —** to extend
extenso ADJ (calendario, plan, grupo) extensive; (narración, programa de radio) extended
extenuado ADJ exhausted
exterior ADJ (de fuera) exterior, outer; (mundo) outside; (política) foreign; M (parte de afuera) exterior, outside; (aspecto) outward appearance; (fútbol americano) end; **en —es** on location
exteriorizar[47] VT to externalize
exterminación F extermination
exterminar VT to exterminate
exterminio M extermination
externo ADJ external
extienda, extiende *ver* extender
extinción F extinction
extinguidor M fire extinguisher
extinguir[44] VT (un fuego) to extinguish, to put out; (una especie) to make extinct, to wipe out; **—se** (animal, volcán) to go extinct
extinto ADJ extinct
extintor M fire extinguisher
extirpación F removal
extirpar VT to remove
extorsión F extortion
extorsionar VT to extort money from
extorsionista MF racketeer
extra ADJ extra; **horas —s** overtime; MF (actor) extra; M (cosa accesoria) extra; F (pago extraordinario) bonus
extrabursátil ADJ over-the-counter
extracción F extraction
extracto M (resumen) abstract; (de café) extract
extradición F extradition
extraditar VT to extradite
extraer[59] VT (esencia) to extract; (minerales) to mine; (un diente) to pull
extraiga, extraigo, extraje, extrajera, extrajese *ver* extraer
extrajudicial ADJ out-of-court
extramarital ADJ extramarital
extranjero -ra ADJ foreign; MF foreigner; **en el —** abroad
extrañar VT (sorprender) to surprise; (echar de menos) to miss; **no es de — que** it's no wonder that; **no me extraña** it doesn't surprise me; **—se** to be surprised
extrañeza F surprise
extraño -ña ADJ (persona, costumbre) strange; (partícula) foreign; MF stranger
extraoficial ADJ unofficial
extraordinario ADJ extraordinary
extrapolar VI/VT to extrapolate
extrasensorial ADJ extrasensory
extraterrestre ADJ & M alien, extraterrestrial
extravagancia F (cualidad de extravagante) extravagance; (comportamiento extravagante) outrageous behavior
extravagante ADJ flamboyant, outrageous
extraviar[28] VT (perder) to misplace; (confundir) to lead astray; **—se** to lose one's way, to get lost
extravío M loss
extrayendo *ver* extraer
extremadamente ADV extremely
extremado ADJ extreme
extremar VT to maximize
extremidad F extremity
extremo ADJ (máximo, mínimo, extraordinario) extreme; (más lejano) farthest; **con — cuidado** with utmost care; M (punto más alejado) extreme; (de una región) end; **llegar al — de** to go so far as to; **— Oriente** Far East; **extrema izquierda** far left; F **extrema unción** last rites
extrovertido -da ADJ extroverted; MF extrovert
exuberante ADJ (vegetación, jóvenes)

exuberant; (mujer) voluptuous
exudar VI/VT to exude
exultante ADJ exhilarated, exultant
exultar VI to exult
eyacular VI/VT to ejaculate
eyectar VT to eject

Ff

fábrica F factory, plant; (de acero, textiles) mill
fabricación F manufacture, manufacturing
fabricante MF manufacturer; (de coches) maker
fabricar[10] VT (producir) to manufacture, to make; (construir) to build; (inventar) to concoct, to fabricate
fabril ADJ manufacturing
fábula F (relato) fable; (mentira) falsehood
fabuloso ADJ (imaginario) imaginary; (magnífico) awesome, fabulous
facción F faction; **facciones** facial features
faceta F facet
facha F **estaba hecho una —** he was a sight
fachada F facade
facial ADJ facial
fácil ADJ (sencillo) easy; (promiscuo) easy, loose; **— de entender** self-explanatory; **— de usar** user-friendly
facilidad F ease; (habilidad) facility, knack
facilitar VT (hacer más fácil) to facilitate; (proporcionar) to furnish
facsímil M fax
factible ADJ feasible
fáctico ADJ factual
factor M factor; **—es de riesgo** risk factors
factoría F trading post
factura F bill, invoice; **— detallada** itemized invoice
facturable ADJ billable
facturación F billing
facturar VT (importe) to invoice; (equipaje) to check
facultad F (habilidad) faculty; (autoridad) authority; (división de una universidad) college; **— de odontología** dental school
facundia F gift of gab
faena F (trabajo corporal) chore; (labor) task; (molestia) nuisance
fagot M bassoon
fairway M fairway
faisán M pheasant
faja F (cinta) sash; (prenda interior) girdle; (de tierra) ribbon, strip
fajar VT (ceñir) to gird; (envolver) to wrap up; (golpear) to thrash
fajo M (de dinero) wad; (de papel, paja) sheaf
falacia F fallacy
falaz ADJ fallacious
falda F (prenda de vestir) skirt (también mujeres); (de una montaña) slope
faldón M (de una camisa) tail, shirttail; (de un saco) coattail
falible ADJ fallible
falla F (en un argumento) flaw; (en un motor) miss; (de una máquina) failure; (geológica) fault; **las Fallas** Valencian holiday
fallar VI (no funcionar) to fail; (un motor) to miss; VI/VT (un juez) to find, to rule
fallecer[35] VI to pass away, to decease
fallecimiento M passing, decease
fallo M (de un programa) bug, glitch; (de la memoria) lapse; (de un juez) ruling, finding
falsear VT to falsify
falsedad F (dicho falso) falsehood; (condición de falso) falseness
falsificación F (de dinero) counterfeit; (de un documento) forgery
falsificar[30] VT (documento) to falsify, to fake; (dinero) to counterfeit; (una firma) to forge; (libros de contabilidad) to cook
falso ADJ (dato) false, untrue; (sentimientos) fake, phony; (dinero) counterfeit; (promesa) hollow; (amigo) faithless, two-faced; (excusa) made-up; **falsa alarma** false alarm; **jurar en —** to perjure oneself; **paso en —** a false step; **salida en —** false start
falta F (defecto) fault; (carencia) lack, want; (ausencia) absence, miss; (jugada ilícita) foul; (de ortografía) mistake; **— de aire** shortness of breath, breathlessness; **— de pago** default; **— de respeto** disrespect; **— personal** (baloncesto) personal foul; **— de pie** foot fault; **a — de** for want of, in the absence of; **cometer —** to commit a foul; **hacer —** to be necessary; **me haces —** I miss you; **sin —** without fail
faltar VI (ausentarse) to be absent; (no haber) to be lacking; **— a la palabra** to break a promise; **— a la verdad** to misstate oneself; **—le el respeto a** to disrespect; **— poco para las cinco** to be almost five o'clock; **me falta tiempo** I don't have enough time; **¡no faltaba más!** (con indignación) that's the last straw! (no hay de qué) don't mention it! (no te molestes) I wouldn't hear of it
falto ADJ lacking; **— de esperanza** devoid of hope
fama F (condición de conocido) fame; (reputación) reputation; **de — mundial** world-famous
famélico ADJ ravenous
familia F family; **— nuclear** nuclear family; **en —** in the family; **jefe de —** head of household; **la señora de Juan tuvo —** John's wife had a baby

familiar ADJ (muy conocido) familiar; (de familia) familial; **tamaño —** family-size; **coche —** family car; **vida —** family life; MF relative; **—es** next of kin
familiaridad F familiarity
familiarizar[47] VT to familiarize, to acquaint; **—se** to acquaint oneself, to become familiar with
famoso ADJ famous
fanático -ca ADJ fanatic; MF fanatic, zealot; (de deportes) freak
fanatismo M fanaticism
fanega F bushel
fanfarria F fanfare
fanfarrón -ona MF braggart, show-off; ADJ blustering
fanfarronear VI to bluster
fanfarronería F bluster, swagger
fango M mire
fangoso ADJ miry
fantasear VI to fantasize
fantasía F (imaginación) imagination; (imagen) fantasy; **de —** fake, artificial
fantasioso ADJ (niño) imaginative; (idea) fanciful
fantasma M ghost, phantom
fantasmagórico ADJ ghostly
fantástico ADJ fantastic
farándula F show business
fardo M (paquete) bundle; (de heno, algodón) bale
farfolla F husk
farfulla F jabber
farfullar VI to jabber
faringe F pharynx
faríngeo ADJ pharyngeal
farmacéutico -ca ADJ pharmaceutical; MF pharmacist, druggist
farmacia F pharmacy, drugstore
fármaco M medicine, pharmaceutical
farmacología F pharmacology
faro M (torre) lighthouse; (luz de alerta) beacon; (luz del coche) light; **— delantero** headlight
farol M (portátil) lantern; (del alumbrado público) street lamp, streetlight; (con pie de hierro) lamppost; (jactancia, envite) bluff; **darse —** to show off, to put on airs
farra F spree; **ir de —** to go on a spree
farsa F (engaño) sham, hoax; (obra teatral, imitación ridícula) farce, mockery
farsante MF fraud, fake
fascículo M installment
fascinación F fascination
fascinante ADJ fascinating, riveting
fascinar VI/VT to fascinate
fascismo M fascism
fascista ADJ & MF fascist
fase F phase
fastidiado ADJ irked
fastidiar VT to irk
fastidio M annoyance
fastidioso ADJ annoying, wearisome
fatal ADJ (mortal) fatal; (terrible) terrible; **mujer —** femme fatale; ADV very badly; **me fue — en el examen** I did very poorly on the exam
fatalidad F (desgracia) misfortune; (destino) destiny
fatídico ADJ ill-fated
fatiga F fatigue, exhaustion; **— ocular** eye strain; **—s** hardships
fatigado ADJ tired, weary
fatigar[40] VT to tire out
fatigoso ADJ (cansado) tiring; (aburrido) tiresome
fauces F PL jaws
faul M foul
fauna F fauna
favor M favor; **a — de** in favor of; **por —** please
favorable ADJ favorable
favorecer[35] VT to favor
favorezca, favorezco *ver* favorecer
favoritismo M favoritism
favorito -ta ADJ favorite; MF favorite; (en una elección) front-runner; (de la maestra) pet
fax M fax
faxear VT to fax
faz F face
FBI M FBI
fe F faith; **— de bautismo** baptismal certificate; **— de erratas** list of errors; **— de nacimiento** birth certificate; **buena —** good faith; **de buena —** in good faith; **dar — de** to vouch for
fealdad F ugliness
febrero M February
febril ADJ (con fiebre) feverish; (actividad) feverish, hectic
fecal ADJ fecal
fecha F date; **— de vencimiento** date due, due date
fechado ADJ dated
fechar VT to date
fechoría F misdeed
fecundación F fertilization
fecundar VT (un huevo) to fertilize; (una hembra) to impregnate
fecundo ADJ fertile
federación F federation
federal ADJ federal
felicidad F happiness; **¡—es!** congratulations
felicitación F congratulation; **¡felicitaciones!** congratulations!
felicitar VT to congratulate
feligrés -esa MF parishioner; **feligreses** congregation
felino ADJ feline; M cat
feliz ADJ happy

felizmente ADV happily
felpa F plush
felpudo M doormat
femenino ADJ (como una mujer, relativo al género gramatical) feminine; (de la mujer) female
feminidad F femininity
feminismo F feminism
feminista MF feminist
fémur M femur
fenómeno M phenomenon
feo ADJ (cara) ugly, homely; (dentadura) bad; (accidente) nasty
féretro M coffin
feria F (mercado) market; (exposición) fair; (espectáculo) carnival; (celebración) holiday
feriante MF trader at fairs, stallholder
fermentación F fermentation
fermentar VT (leche) to ferment; (cerveza) to brew
fermento M ferment
ferocidad F ferocity
feroz ADJ ferocious, fierce
férreo ADJ (puente) iron; (disciplina) harsh
ferretería F (tienda) hardware store; (artículos) hardware
ferrocarril M railroad, railway
ferroviario-ria ADJ railroad; MF railroad employee
ferry M ferryboat
fértil ADJ fertile
fertilidad F fertility
fertilización F fertilization
fertilizante M fertilizer
fertilizar[47] VT to fertilize
ferviente ADJ fervent
fervor M fervor, zeal
fervoroso ADJ zealous
festejar VT to celebrate
festejo M celebration
festín M feast; **darse un —** to treat oneself
festival M festival
festividad F festivity
festivo ADJ festive, celebratory; **día —** holiday
festón M scallop
festonear VT to scallop
fetal ADJ fetal
fetiche M fetish
fétido ADJ foul-smelling
feto M fetus
feudal ADJ feudal
feudo M manor
fiabilidad F reliability
fiable ADJ reliable
fiador-ora MF guarantor, voucher; (prestamista) backer; (de un preso) bondsman
fiambre M (carne) cold cut; (cadáver) *fam* stiff
fianza F (de un préstamo) security, guaranty; (de un preso) bail
fiar[28] VT (garantizar) to vouch for; **—se de** to trust
fiasco M fiasco
fibra F fiber; **— de vidrio** fiberglass; **— óptica** optical fiber
fibrosis F fibrosis; **— cística** cystic fibrosis
fibroso ADJ fibrous
ficción F fiction
ficha F (de teléfono) token; (de dominó) domino; (de damas) checker; (en poker, ruleta) chip; (tarjeta) index card; MF (delincuente) delinquent, criminal
fichar VT to open a file on; VI to punch in
fichero M (de computadora) file; (archivador) filing cabinet; **— de datos** data file
ficticio ADJ (no real) fictitious; (novelesco) fictional
fidedigno ADJ trustworthy
fideicomisario-ria MF trustee
fideicomiso M trusteeship
fidelidad F (de un amante) fidelity, faithfulness; (de una traducción) closeness; (a la bandera) allegiance
fideo M noodle
fiduciario-ria ADJ & MF fiduciary
fiebre F fever; **— aftosa** foot-and-mouth disease; **— amarilla** yellow fever; **— de candilejas** stage fright; **— del oro** gold rush; **— reumática** rheumatic fever; **— tifoidea** typhoid fever; **tener —** to run a fever
fiel ADJ (leal) faithful; (exacto) true, accurate; M pointer on a scale; **los —es** the congregation
fieltro M (tela) felt; (sombrero) felt hat
fiera F beast; **ponerse hecho una —** to go berserk
fiereza F ferocity
fiero ADJ (salvaje) fierce; (muy grande) huge
fiesta F (festejo) party; (día feriado) holiday; **aguar una —** to ruin a party
fiestero-ra ADJ fond of parties; MF merrymaker, party animal
figura F figure
figurado ADJ figurative
figurar VI (aparecer) to appear, to figure; (lucirse) to show off; **—se** to imagine; **¡figúrate!** imagine!
figurativo ADJ figurative
figurín M fashion plate
figurón M dummy
fijación F fixing; **— de precios** pricing
fijador M hairspray
fijar VT (un cartel) to fix, to fasten; (una fecha) to set; (precios) to peg; **—se en** (notar) to notice; (prestar atención) to pay attention to, to focus on
fijo ADJ (sujeto, incambiado) fixed; (inmóvil) fixed, stationary; (firme) firm; (definitivo) definite; (permanente) permanent

fila F (uno detrás del otro) row, file; (hombro a hombro) rank; (de espera) line; (de documentos) queue; **— india** single file; **cerrar —s** to close ranks; **romper —s** to break ranks
filamento M filament
filantropía F philanthropy
filarmónica F philharmonic
filarmónico ADJ philharmonic
fildear VT to field
fildeo M fielding
filete M (de carne) fillet; (de un plato) rim
filetear VT to fillet
filiación F (membresía) affiliation; (datos personales) personal information; (lazo de parentesco) filiation; **— política** political affiliation
filial ADJ filial; F affiliate, subsidiary
filibusterismo M filibustering
filigrana F filigree
Filipinas F Philippines
filipino -na ADJ & MF Filipino, Filipina
filme M film, movie
filmación F filming, shooting
filmar VT to film, to shoot
filo M (de una navaja) cutting edge; (biológico) phylum; **de doble —** two-edged; **al — de las dos** at around two o'clock
filón M seam, vein, pocket
filoso ADJ sharp
filosofía F philosophy
filosófico ADJ philosophical
filósofo -fa MF philosopher
filtración F (purificación) filtration; (pérdida) leak; (percolación) seepage
filtrar VT (purificar) to filter; (perder) to leak; (clasificar) to screen; **—se** (gotear) to leak through; (percolarse) to seep
filtro M filter; **— de aire** air filter; **— de amor** love potion
fin M (conclusión, objetivo) end; **— de año** New Year's Eve; **el — del mundo** (lugar apartado) boondocks; **— de semana** weekend; **— de siglo** turn of the century; **al —** at last; **al — y al cabo** at any rate; **a — de que** so that; **a — de mes** toward the end of the month; **de — de año** year-end; **en —** in conclusion; **poner — a** to put an end to; **por —** at last, finally; **sin —** (ilimitado) myriad; (continuo) endless
finado ADJ late
final ADJ final, last; F (deportiva) final; M (de una historia) ending; (de un terreno) end; (de una carrera) finish; (de una filmación) wrap
finalidad F objective, purpose
finalista MF finalist
finalización F completion
finalizar[47] VT to finish; **— una sesión** lo log off/out
finalmente ADV at last, finally
financiación F (para una compra) financing; (para un proyecto) funding
financiamiento M (para una compra) financing; (para un proyecto científico) funding; **— por el propietario** owner financing
financiar VT (una compra) to finance; (un proyecto) to underwrite, *fam* to bankroll
financiero -ra ADJ financial; MF financier
finanza F finance; **—s** finances
finca F (inmueble) property; (granja) farm, country estate
finés -esa MF Finn; M (lengua) Finnish; ADJ Finnish
fineza F (atención) courtesy; (suavidad) smoothness
fingir[46] VI/VT (sorpresa) to feign; (un ataque al corazón) to fake; **fingió que la quería** he pretended to love her
finiquito M settlement
finito ADJ finite
finlandés -esa MF Finn; M (lengua) Finnish; ADJ Finnish
Finlandia F Finland
fino ADJ (vino, arena, pelo, metal) fine; (sentidos) keen, sharp; (medias) sheer; (hielo, alambre, voz) thin; (modales) smooth, refined
finta F fake, juke
firma F (compañía) firm; (rúbrica) signature; **— consultora** consulting firm
firmamento M sky
firmante MF signer
firmar VI/VT (documento, carta) to sign; (contrato) to enter
firme ADJ (estructura) firm; (control) tight; (colores) fast; (amarras) secure; (mano) steady, sure; (resistencia) stiff; (apoyo, resistencia) strong, staunch, steadfast; **mantenerse —** to stand one's ground; **¡—s!** attention!
firmemente ADV firmly
firmeza F (de una estructura) firmness; (de la mano) steadiness; (de la resistencia) stiffness; (del apoyo) strength; **con —** firmly
fiscal ADJ fiscal; MF public prosecutor, district attorney
fiscalía F prosecution
fiscalización F (de comportamiento) supervision; (de gastos) oversight
fiscalizar[47] VT (comportamiento) to supervise; (gastos) to oversee
fisgar[40] VI to snoop
fisgón -ona ADJ snooping; MF snoop
fisgonear VI to snoop
físico -ca ADJ physical; MF (persona) physicist; M (cuerpo) physique; F physics
fisiología F physiology
fisiológico ADJ physiological

fisioterapia F physical therapy
fisonomía F features
fístula F fistula
fisura F fissure
fiyano ADJ Fijian
Fiyi M Fiji
flácido, fláccido ADJ (sin firmeza) limp, flaccid; (gordo) flabby
flaco ADJ thin, skinny; **su lado —** his weakness
flacura F thinness
flagrante ADJ gross; **en — delito** in the act
flamante ADJ brand-new
flamear VI (llamear) to flame; (ondear) to flap
flamenco-ca ADJ Flemish; MF Flemish person; M (lengua) Flemish; (ave) flamingo; (baile) flamenco
flamígero ADJ flaming
flan M caramel custard
flanco M (de un animal, ejército) flank; (de un neumático) sidewall
flanquear VT to flank
flaquear VI (intención) to waver; (salud) to wane
flaqueza F weakness
flash M (noticias, visión, memoria digital) flash; (lámpara) flashbulb, flash
flashback M flashback
flatulencia F flatulence
flauta F flute; **— dulce** recorder
flautín M piccolo
flecha F arrow
flechar VT to wound with an arrow
flechazo M (herida) wound from an arrow; (enamoramiento) love at first sight
fleco M (de una alfombra) fringe; (de pelo) bangs
flema F phlegm
flequillo M bangs
fletamento M charter
fletar VT to charter
flete M (contratación) charter; (envío) transport; (precio de transporte) freight
flexibilidad F (ductilidad) flexibility; (libertad) latitude
flexible ADJ (material) flexible; (cuerpo humano) limber, supple; (opinión) pliant, pliable
flojear VT to slacken
flojedad F laxity, looseness; (debilidad) weakness
flojera F (debilidad) weakness; (pereza) laziness
flojo ADJ (suelto) loose, slack; (holgazán) lazy; (inferior) crummy; (débil) weak; (sin fundamento) flimsy
floppy M floppy disk
flor F flower, blossom, bloom; (cumplido) compliment; **— de la edad** prime of life; **— de Pascua** poinsettia; **— y nata** the cream of the crop; **a — de** flush with; **en —** in bloom
flora F flora (también bacteriana); **— intestinal** intestinal flora
floración F blooming, blossoming
floral ADJ flowery
floreado ADJ flowery
florear VT (adornar con flores) to decorate with flowers; (adornar) to adorn
florecer[35] VI (echar flores) to flower, to bloom; (prosperar) to flourish, to thrive
floreciente ADJ (próspero) flourishing, prosperous; (florecido) blooming
florecimiento M flourishing
floreo M flourish
florería F florist's shop
florero M flower vase
florete M fencing foil
florido ADJ flowery
florista MF florist
floritura F flourish
flota F fleet
flotador M (para nadar) float; (de un avión) pontoon; ADJ floating
flotante ADJ floating, buoyant
flotar VI (estar suspendido, variar en valor) to float; (moverse en la superficie) to drift; (ir por el aire) to waft
flote M flotation; **a —** afloat; **poner a —** to set afloat
fluctuación F fluctuation; (amplitud de variación) range
fluctuar[26] VI to fluctuate
fluidez F (cualidad de fluido) fluency; (cualidad de diluido) thinness
fluido ADJ (que fluye) fluid, flowing; (no vacilante) fluent; M fluid
fluir[19] VI to flow
flujo M (de agua) flow; (vaginal) discharge; (de datos) streaming; **— continuo de datos de audio** audio streaming; **— continuo de datos de vídeo** video streaming; **— de caja** cash flow; **— de trabajo** work flow
flúor M (elemento gaseoso) fluorine; (sal) fluoride
fluorescente ADJ fluorescent
fluoruro M fluoride
fluvial ADJ **transporte —** river transportation
fluyente ADJ flowing
FMI [Fondo Monetario Internacional] M IMF
fobia F phobia
foca F seal
foco M (punto central) focus; (bombilla) bulb; (lámpara potente) spotlight
fofo ADJ mushy
fogata F (fuego abierto) bonfire; (en un campamento) campfire
fogonazo M flash
fogoso ADJ fiery, spirited
folclor, folclore M folklore
folclórico/folklórico ADJ folkloric; **cuento —** folktale

foliculitis F folliculitis
folículo M follicle
folio M folio
folíolo M leaflet
follaje M foliage
folleto M pamphlet, brochure
follón M (confusión) mess; (alboroto) ruckus
fomentar VT (estudio) to promote; (amistad) to foster; (discordia) to foment; (apoyo) to drum up
fomento M encouragement
fonda F inn
fondear VI to anchor
fondillos M PL seat of pants
fondista MF (posadero) innkeeper; (corredor) long-distance runner
fondo M (parte más profunda) bottom; (parte posterior) rear; (del mar) bed; (de un cuadro, foto) background; (de dinero) fund; (de una biblioteca) holdings; (de un jardín) backyard; **— común** pool; **— de contingencia** contingency fund; **— especulativo** hedge fund; **— físico** endurance; **— musical** background music; **— mutuo** mutual fund; **—s** funds; **—s administrados** managed funds; **— sin comisión de entrada** no-load fund; **a —** in depth; **carrera de —** long-distance race; **de cuatro en —** four abreast; **de —** (exhaustivo) in depth; (subyacente) underlying; **sin —** bottomless; **tocar —** to hit rock bottom
fonética F phonetics
fonético ADJ phonetic
fonógrafo M phonograph
fonología F phonology
fontanería F plumbing
fontanero -ra MF plumber
footing M jogging
forajido -da MF outlaw
foráneo ADJ foreign; **influencia foránea** outside influence
forastero -ra MF stranger, outsider
forcejear VI to struggle
forcejeo M struggle
fórceps M PL forceps
forense ADJ forensic; MF forensic scientist
forestal ADJ forest; **división —** forestry division
forja F (fogón) forge; (acción de forjar) forging; (taller) blacksmith's shop
forjado ADJ wrought
forjar VT (metales, un acuerdo) to forge; (un acuerdo) to hammer out; (un documento) to frame
forma F (figura) form, shape; (manera) manner; **— de pago** mode of payment; **— de pensar** mind-set; **ponerse en —** to get in shape; **no hay —** no way; **dar — a** to shape
formación F formation
formal ADJ (que atañe a la forma) formal, serious; (fiable) reliable
formaldehído M formaldehyde
formalidad F (convencionalidad) formality; (fiabilidad) reliability
formalismo M formality
formalizar[47] VT to make official; **—se** to settle down
formar VT (crear) to form; (reunir tropas) to muster; (entrenar) to train; **—se** (montañas) to form; (estudiantes) to be educated
formatear VT to format
formateo M formatting
formativo ADJ formative
formato M format; **— de archivo/fichero** file format; **— de texto enriquecido** rich text format
formidable ADJ formidable
formón M wood chisel
fórmula F formula
formulación F (acción de formular) formulation; (fórmula) formula; (redacción) wording
formular VT to formulate; (un plan, una pregunta) to frame; (un documento) to word
formulario M form
fornicar[30] VI to fornicate
fornido ADJ stout, sturdy
foro M forum; (de un escenario) back
forrado ADJ (con un forro) lined; (bien provisto) flush
forraje M forage, fodder
forrajear VI to forage
forrar VT (un saco) to line; **—se** to line one's pockets
forro M lining; (de un libro) jacket
fortalecer[35] VT to fortify, to strengthen
fortalecimiento M strengthening
fortaleza F (construcción) fortress, fort; (fuerza) fortitude
fortificación F fortification
fortificar[30] VT to fortify
fortuito ADJ fortuitous, accidental
fortuna F fortune; **por —** fortunately; **probar —** to try one's luck; **hacer —** to become rich
forúnculo M boil
forzar[49] VT to force, to coerce; **— la entrada** to break into
forzoso ADJ (por la fuerza) forcible; (inevitable) necessary; (aterrizaje) forced
fosa F (sepultura) grave; (de la nariz) cavity; (en el fondo del mar) trench
fosfato M phosphate
fósforo M (sustancia) phosphorus; (cerilla) match
fósil ADJ & M fossil
foso M (de un castillo) moat; (de un taller, teatro) pit
foto F snapshot, photo

fotocopia F photocopy
fotocopiadora F photocopier
fotocopiar VI/VT to photocopy
fotoeléctrico ADJ photoelectric
fotogénico ADJ photogenic
fotografía F (foto) photograph; (arte) photography; **— digital** digital photography
fotografiar[28] VT to photograph
fotógrafo -fa MF photographer
fotón M photon
fotosíntesis F photosynthesis
foul M foul
frac M tails
fracasar VI (un proyecto) to fail; (de una película) to bomb; (una embarcación) to break up
fracaso M (de un proyecto) failure; (de una película) flop, bomb
fracción F fraction
fractura F fracture, break; **— fina** hairline fracture
fracturar VT to fracture, to break; **se fracturó la cadera** she broke her hip
fragancia F fragrance
fragante ADJ fragrant; **en —** in the act
fragata F frigate
frágil ADJ (delicado) delicate; (quebradizo) fragile, brittle; (una paz) tenuous
fragilidad F (condición de quebradizo) brittleness, delicacy; (debilidad) frailty
fragmentación F fragmentation
fragmento M fragment; (de metal, piedra) scrap; (de una conversación) snatch; (de un texto) extract, excerpt
fragoso ADJ rugged
fragua F (fogón) forge; (taller) blacksmith's shop
fraguar[25] VT to forge; (una trama) to hatch; VI (cemento, yeso) to set
fraile M friar
frambuesa F raspberry
frambueso M raspberry bush
francamente ADV **—, me horroriza** frankly / to be honest, it horrifies me; **lo pasaban — bien** they were doing pretty well; **—, es ridículo** it is simply ridiculous
francés -esa ADJ French; M (lengua) French; (hombre) Frenchman; F (mujer) Frenchwoman
Francia F France
franco ADJ (sincero) frank, candid; (exento) free; **una franca mayoría** a clear majority; **un tratado — -americano** a Franco-American treaty
francotirador -ora MF sniper
franela F flannel
franja F ribbon
franquear VT (una frontera) to cross; (una carta) to frank; **—se** to be frank
franqueo M postage
franqueza F (personal) frankness; (institucional) openness
franquicia F (concesión) franchise; (exención) exemption
frasco M (recipiente de vidrio) flask; (de medicina, perfume) bottle; (de mermelada) jar
frase F phrase
frasear VI/VT to phrase
fraternal ADJ fraternal, brotherly
fraternidad F fraternity
fraternizar[47] VI fraternize
fraterno ADJ fraternal
fraude M fraud
fraudulento ADJ fraudulent
frazada F blanket
frecuencia F frequency; **con —** frequently
frecuentar VT to frequent; (una tienda) to patronize
frecuente ADJ frequent
fregadero M sink
fregado M scrubbing
fregar[41] VT to scour, to scrub
fregona F (persona) scrubwoman, drudge; (utensilio) mop
freír[10, 74] VI/VT to fry
frenar VT (un coche) to brake; (la inmigración) to restrain; (los impulsos) to bridle; VI to brake, to apply the brakes
frenesí M frenzy; (de actividad) flurry
frenético ADJ frantic
freno M (de coche) brake; (de caballo) bit; (contra el contrabando) curb
frente F forehead; **el sudor de la —** the sweat of one's brow; M (parte delantera, zona de combate, zona meteorológica) front; (de un edificio) face; **— a** (ante) in the face of; (al otro lado) facing; **— a —** face to face; **de —** head-on; **en — de** in front of; **hacer —** to face; **pasar al —** to come to the fore
fresa F (fruta) strawberry; (herramienta) mill
fresadora F milling machine
fresar VT to mill
fresco ADJ (reciente, descansado, insolente) fresh; (frío) cool, brisk; (poco abrigado) light; (no cocinado) raw; (pintura) wet; M (frío) coolness; (pintura) fresco
frescor M (de verduras) freshness; (del aire) coolness
frescura F (de verduras, de carácter) freshness; (del tiempo) coolness; (comentario) impudent remark
fresno M ash tree
friabilidad F looseness
frialdad F coldness, coolness
fricción F friction, rubbing
friccionar VT to rub
friega F rubbing, massage
frigorífico M (electrodoméstico) refrigerator;

(cámara) refrigeration chamber
frijol M bean
frío ADJ (de temperatura, de temperamento) cold; (helado) frigid; M cold; **tener —** to be cold
friolento ADJ sensitive to cold
friolera F **la — de $50,000** a trifling $50,000
fritada F dish of fried food
frito ADJ fried; M dish of fried food
fritura F (acción de freír) frying; (comida frita) dish of fried food
frivolidad F frivolity
frívolo ADJ frivolous
fronda F foliage
frondoso ADJ leafy
frontal ADJ (ataque) frontal; (colisión) head-on
frontera F frontier, border
fronterizo ADJ frontier
frontón M (juego) jai alai; (pista) jai alai court
frotación F rubbing
frotar VI/VT to rub
frote M rub
frotis M smear
fructífero ADJ fruitful
fructificar[30] VI to bear fruit
fructosa F fructose
frugal ADJ frugal
frunce M (volante) ruffle; (defecto) pucker
fruncir[33] VT to gather; **— el ceño** to frown, to knit one's brow; **— los labios** to purse one's lips
fruslería F trifle
frustración F frustration
frustrar VT (los planes) to frustrate, to thwart, to foil; (las esperanzas) to shatter, to dash; **—se** to fail, to miscarry
fruta F fruit
frutero -era MF fruit vendor; M fruit dish
fruto M fruit; **—s del mar** seafood
fue *ver* ser, ir
fuego M fire; (para un cigarro) light; **— antiaéreo** antiartillery fire; **—s artificiales** fireworks; **abrir el —** to begin to fire; **alto el —** cease-fire; **bajo —** under fire; **arma de —** firearm; **entre dos —s** between a rock and a hard place; **hacer —** to fire; **prender/poner/pegar — a** to set fire to
fuelle M bellows
fuel-oil M fuel oil
fuente F (surtidor) fountain; (manantial, referencia) spring; (caracteres de imprenta) font; **de buena —** from the horse's mouth
fuera ADV (en el exterior) outside; (tenis) out; **— de** outside of; **— de borda** outboard; **— de combate** out of commission; **— de juego** (fútbol) offside; **— de límites** (golf) out of bounds; **— de línea** offline; **— de serie** one of a kind; **— de servicio** out of service; INTERJ out!
fuera, fuéramos *ver* ser, ir
fuero M (jurisdicción) jurisdiction; (privilegio) privilege, charter
fuerte ADJ (hombre, bebida) strong; (ruido) loud; (cuero) tough; (personalidad) forceful; (estantería) sturdy; (plato) hearty; M (castillo) fort; (talento especial) strong point; ADV (tirar) strongly; (respirar) heavily; (gritar) loud; **soplar —** to bluster; **pisar —** to stomp; **atar —** to tie tight
fuerza F (de una máquina) force; (de una persona, animal) strength; **— aérea** air force; **— bruta** brute force; **— de la naturaleza** force of nature; **— de tarea** task force; **— de voluntad** willpower; **—s armadas** armed forces; **a — de** by dint of; **con —** strongly; **hacer —** to press on; **por la —** by force; **sacar — de flaqueza** to pull oneself together
fuerza, fuerce *ver* forzar
fuese, fuésemos *ver* ser, ir
fuga F (escape) escape, flight; (de la cárcel) jailbreak; (de gas) leak; (de capitales) drain, flight
fugarse[40] VI to flee, to escape; **— con el dinero** to abscond with the money
fugaz ADJ fleeting
fugitivo -va ADJ fugitive; MF fugitive
fui, fuimos *ver* ser, ir
fulano -na MF so-and-so; **—, zutano y mengano** Tom, Dick, and Harry
fulgor M radiance
fulgurar VI to flash
full M full house
fullero -ra MF (tramposo) cheat; (en naipes) card sharp
fulminante M cap; ADJ devastating
fulminar VT to strike with lightning; to thunder; **lo fulminó con la mirada** she gave him a withering look
fumadero M crackhouse
fumador -ora MF smoker
fumar VI/VT to smoke; **—se mucho dinero** to blow a lot of money
fumigar[40] VT to fumigate, to fog
función F (uso) function; (representación) performance; (cargo) office; **— de búsqueda** search function
funcional ADJ functional; **una casa —** a practical/livable house
funcionamiento M operation, working
funcionar VI to function, to work; (motor) to run
funcionario -ria MF government employee, official; **— de préstamos** loan officer
funda F (de un mueble) cover; (de una almohada) pillowcase, slip; (de navaja) sheath
fundación F foundation

fundador -ora MF founder
fundamental ADJ (básico) fundamental; (importante) crucial
fundamentalmente ADV fundamentally, mainly
fundamentar VT to base, to support; **—se en/sobre** to be based on, to be supported by
fundamento M foundation, basis; **—s** fundamentals
fundar VT (un instituto) to found, to establish; (un argumento) to base
fundición F (fábrica) foundry; (acción de fundirse) fusing
fundido ADJ molten; M (en cinematografía) fade-in/fade-out
fundidor -ora MF foundry worker
fundir VT (combinar) to fuse; (derretir) to melt; (moldear) to mold; **—se** (combinarse) to fuse; (romperse una bombilla) to burn out
fúnebre ADJ (relativo a funerales) funeral; (lúgubre) funereal
funeral ADJ & M funeral
funerario -ria ADJ funeral; F funeral parlor; MF funeral director
funesto ADJ ill-fated, unlucky
fungible ADJ fungible
fungicida M fungicide
funicular M cable car
funky ADJ funky
furgón M (vagón) boxcar; (camioneta de policía) police van; **— blindado** armored vehicle; **— de cola** caboose
furia F fury
furibundo ADJ furious, livid
furioso ADJ (persona) furious; (tempestad) fierce
furor M fury; **hacer —** to be all the rage
furtivo ADJ furtive, stealthy
fuselaje M fuselage
fusible M electric fuse
fusil M rifle
fusilamiento M execution by firing squad
fusilar VT to execute with firearms
fusión F (de hielo) melting; (nuclear) fusion; (empresarial) merger; (de documentos digitales) merge; **fusiones y adquisiciones** mergers and acquisitions
fusionar VT (metales) to fuse; (compañías, documentos digitales) to merge
fusta F crop
fustigar[40] VT (golpear) to lash, to whip; (criticar) to lash out at
fútbol M soccer; **— americano** football
futbolista MF soccer player
fútil ADJ futile, trivial
futilidad F triviality
futuro ADJ future; M future; **—s** futures

Gg

gabán M overcoat
gabardina F trench coat
gabinete M (ministerial) cabinet; (administrativo) office
Gabón M Gabon/Gabun
gabonés -esa ADJ & MF Gabonese
gacela F gazelle
gaceta F gazette
gacetilla F short news item
gachas F PL **— de avena** oatmeal
gacho ADJ (orejas) drooping; (cabeza) bowed; (ojos) lowered
gafar VT to jinx
gafas F PL glasses
gafe M jinx
gaffe M gaffe, faux pas
gag M gag
gaita F bagpipe
gaje M **—s del oficio** occupational hazards
gajo M (de planta) branch; (de naranja) section
gala F (cena) banquet; **—s** finery; **hacer — de** to boast of, to flaunt; **vestirse de —** to dress up
galán M (pretendiente) gallant, suitor; (en cine) leading man
galante ADJ gallant
galantear VT to court
galanteo M courting
galantería F (caballerosidad) gallantry; (cumplido) compliment
galardón M award
galaxia F galaxy
galera F galley (también prueba de imprenta); *RP* top hat
galerada F galley proof
galería F (salón) gallery; (pasillo) corridor; (tiendas) mall, gallery; (de coro) loft; (subterráneo) tunnel; **—s** *Esp* department store
Gales M Wales
galés -esa ADJ & MF Welsh
galgo M greyhound
Galicia F Galicia
gallardete M pennant
gallardía F (elegancia) elegance; (valentía) bravery
gallardo ADJ (elegante) elegant; (valiente) brave
gallego -ga ADJ Galician; M (lengua) Galician; MF Galician
gallera F cockpit
galleta F (salada) cracker; (dulce) cookie
gallina F (pollo) chicken; (hembra adulta) hen; MF coward; **— ciega** blind man's bluff; **la — de los huevos de oro** the goose that laid the

golden egg
gallinero M (de gallinas) chicken coop; (de teatro) gallery; **alborotar el —** to raise a ruckus
gallito ADJ cocksure, cocky; M braggart
gallo M cock, rooster; (de la voz) break; **tener —s en la garganta** to have a frog in one's throat; **en menos que canta un —** before you can say Jack Robinson
galón M (de líquido) gallon; (de tela) stripe
galopar VI/VT to gallop
galope M gallop; **al —** at a gallop
galvanizar[47] VT to galvanize
gama F gamut, range
gamba F large shrimp
gamberro -rra MF (rebelde, pandillero) punk, hoodlum; *Esp* (en fútbol) hooligan
Gambia F Gambia
gambiano -na ADJ & MF Gambian
gamo M buck
gamuza F (animal) chamois (también piel); (piel de venado) buckskin, deerskin; (piel de vaca) suede
gana F urge; **con —s** with a vengeance; **de buena —** willingly; **tener —s de** to feel like; **tengo —s [de ir al baño]** I have to go [to the bathroom]; **no me da la —** I just don't feel like it
ganadería F (cría) cattle breeding; (ganado) livestock
ganadero -ra M cattleman; F cattlewoman; ADJ **industria ganadera** cattle industry
ganado M livestock; **— ovino** sheep; **— porcino** swine; **— vacuno** cattle
ganador -ora MF winner; ADJ winning
ganancia F profit, gain, return; **—s** (recaudación de un evento) proceeds; (de un juego) winnings; (de un negocio) earnings; **—s pre-impositivas** before-tax earnings
ganapán M (obrero) menial worker; (trabajo) bread and butter
ganar VI/VT (una guerra, la lotería) to win; (kilos, eficacia) to gain; VT (un sueldo) to earn; (tiempo, espacio) to save; (tierra) to reclaim; **dejarse — por algo** to give in to something; **nos ganaron el partido** they beat us; **—se la vida** to make a living
ganchillo M crochet
gancho M hook (también en boxeo, baloncesto); (rama) snag; (para sujetar) clip; (atractivo) lure; **echar a uno el —** to hook someone; **tener —** to be attractive
gandul -la MF loafer
ganga F bargain, steal
gangoso ADJ twangy
gangrena F gangrene
gangrenarse VI to gangrene
gángster M gangster
ganguear VI to twang
ganso M (animal) goose; (macho) gander; (tonto) *fam* ding-a-ling
ganzúa F picklock
gañido M yelp
gañir[17] VI to yelp
garabatear VI/VT to scribble
garabato M scribble; **hacer —s** to scribble
garaje M garage
garante MF voucher
garantía F (de producto) guarantee, warranty; (de promesa) security, guaranty; (de un derecho) guarantee; (comercial) backing; **— de devolución de dinero** money-back guarantee; **— de préstamo** loan guarantee
garantizar[47] VT (producto) to guarantee, to warranty; (promesa) to warrant
garañón M stud, horse
garbanzo M chickpea
garbo M grace
garboso ADJ graceful
garfio M hook
garganta F (faringe) throat; (cuello) neck; (valle estrecho) gorge
gárgara F gargle; **hacer —s** to gargle
gargarismo M gargle
garita F sentry box
garito M gambling house
garra F (de ave) claw; (de león) paw with claws; **caer en las —s de alguien** to fall into someone's clutches
garrafa F decanter
garrapata F tick
garrapatear VI/VT to scribble
garrapiñar VT to candy
garrocha F pole
garrote M club
garrucha F pulley
gárrulo ADJ garrulous
garza F heron
gas M gas; **—es** (de motor) fumes; (de intestino) gas; **— ionizado** plasma; **— lacrimógeno** tear gas; **— mostaza** mustard gas; **— natural** natural gas; **— nervioso** nerve gas; **a todo —** at full speed
gasa F (tela) gauze; (para heridas) dressing
gaseosa F soda, soft drink
gaseoso ADJ gaseous
gasoducto M pipeline
gasolina F gasoline, gas
gasolinera F gas station
gastado ADJ (neumático) smooth; (ropa) worn-out, shabby
gastador -ora ADJ extravagant, wasteful; MF spendthrift
gastar VT (dinero, tiempo) to spend; (energía) to expend; (neumáticos, ropa) to wear out, to use up; **— una broma** to play a trick; **—se** to wear out
gasto M (desembolso) expense, expenditure;

(desgaste) wear; **—s de desplazamiento** travel costs; **—s del hogar** household expenses; **—s de subsistencia** living expenses; **—s de viaje** travel expenses; **—s menores** incidentals

gástrico ADJ gastric

gastritis F gastritis

gastroenteritis F gastroenteritis

gastrointestinal ADJ gastrointestinal

gastronomía F gastronomy

gatas LOC ADV **a —** on all fours

gatear VI to creep, to crawl

gatillo M (de arma de fuego) trigger; (de dentista) forceps

gatito M kitten

gato M (felino) cat; (aparato para levantar) jack; **— montés** wildcat, mountain lion; **aquí hay — encerrado** I smell a rat; **a gatas** on all fours; **dar — por liebre** to sell someone a pig in a poke

gaucho M gaucho

gaveta F small drawer

gavilán M hawk

gavilla F (de maíz) sheaf; (de maleantes) gang

gaviota F seagull

gayola F *fam* big house

gazmoñería F prudery

gazmoño -ña MF prude; ADJ prudish

gaznate M gullet

gazpacho M *Esp* gazpacho

geco M gecko

géiser M geyser

gel M gel

gelatina F gelatin

gélido ADJ frigid

gema F gem, jewel

gemelo -la ADJ & MF identical twin; **—s** (mellizos) identical twins; (binoculares) binoculars, opera glasses; (botón) studs

gemido M (de dolor) moan, groan; (de queja) whine

gemir[9] VI (gruñir) to moan, to groan; (lloriquear) to whine

gen, gene M gene; **— recesivo** recessive gene

genealogía F genealogy

generación F generation

generador M generator

general ADJ & MF general; **por lo —** generally

generalidad F generality

generalización F (de un concepto) generalization; (de una moda) spreading

generalizar[47] VI/VT to generalize; **—se** to become widespread

generalmente ADV generally, usually

generar VT generate

genérico ADJ generic

género M (clase) kind; (gramatical) gender; (tela) material; (literario) genre; (biológico) genus; **— humano** human race; **—s** dry goods

generosidad F generosity

generoso ADJ generous

genética F genetics

genético ADJ genetic

genial ADJ brilliant

genio MF (persona inteligente) genius; M (inteligencia) genius, brilliance; (temperamento) temperament, nature; (mal humor) temper; **de mal —** mean; **de buen —** good-natured

geniudo ADJ quick-tempered

genocidio M genocide

genoma M genome

gente F people; **— de campo** country folk; **— de color** persons of color; **— en obra** men at work; **— joven** young people; **— menuda** small fry; **buena —** good person

gentil ADJ (cortés) gracious; (no judío) gentile; MF gentile

gentileza F graciousness

gentío M crowd

gentuza F rabble, riffraff

genuino ADJ genuine

geocéntrico ADJ geocentric

geoestacionario ADJ geostationary

geofísica F geophysics

geografía F geography

geográfico ADJ geographical

geología F geology

geológico ADJ geological

geometría F geometry

geométrico ADJ geometric

geopolítico ADJ geopolitical

Georgia F Georgia

georgiano -na ADJ & MF Georgian

geotérmico ADJ geothermal

geranio M geranium

gerencia F management

gerente MF manager

geriatría F geriatrics

geriátrico ADJ geriatric

germánico ADJ Germanic

germen M germ

germinar VI to germinate, to sprout

gerundio M gerund, present participle

gestación F gestation

gesticular VI (con ademanes) to gesture; (con movimientos exagerados) to gesticulate

gestión F (acción) step, measure; (dirección empresarial, digital) management; (administración política) administration; **—es** negotiations; **— de datos** data management; **hacer gestiones para** to take steps to

gestionar VT (negociar) to negotiate; (administrar) to administer, to manage

gesto M (con la cara) face; (con las manos) gesture; **hacerle —s a alguien** to make

faces at someone
gestor -ora MF agent
Ghana F Ghana
ghanés -esa ADJ & MF Ghanaian
giba F hump, hunch
gibón M gibbon
Gibraltar M Gibraltar
gibraltareño -ña ADJ & MF Gibraltarian
giga F jig
gigabyte M gigabyte
gigahercio M gigahertz
gigante ADJ giant, gigantic; MF giant
gigantesco ADJ gigantic
gimnasia F gymnastics
gimnasio M gymnasium, gym
gimotear VI to whimper
gimoteo M whimper
ginebra F gin
ginecología F gynecology
ginecólogo -ga MF gynecologist
gingivitis F gingivitis
gira F tour
girar VI/VT (una llave, un volante, un coche, a la derecha) to turn; VI (un trompo, un disco) to revolve, to spin, to whirl; VT (dinero) to wire
girasol M sunflower
giratorio ADJ rotary, revolving
giro M (movimiento circular) rotation, spin; (cambio de dirección) turn; (expresión) turn of phrase; (monetario) draft, remittance; — **de cheques sin fondos** check kiting; — **postal** money order
giroscopio M gyroscope
gitano -na ADJ & MF gypsy
glacial ADJ glacial, bitter
glaciar M glacier
gladiador M gladiator
glamoroso ADJ glamorous
glamour M glamour
glándula F gland; —**s sudoríparas** sweat glands
glandular ADJ glandular
glaseado M (de torta) glaze; ADJ (papel) glossy
glasear VT to glaze
glaucoma M glaucoma
glicerina F glycerin
global ADJ (mundial) global; (de conjunto) blanket, overall
globalización F globalization
globo M (esfera) globe; (de árbol de Navidad) ball; (lleno de gas) balloon; (en tenis) lob; — **ocular** eyeball; — **terráqueo** globe
globulina F globulin
glóbulo M globule; — **rojo** red cell; — **blanco** white cell
gloria F glory
glorieta F (pérgola) arbor; (rotonda) traffic circle
glorificar[30] VT to glorify
glorioso M glorious
glosa F gloss
glosar VT to gloss
glosario M glossary
glotal ADJ glottal
glótico ADJ glottal
glotis F glottis
glotón -ona ADJ gluttonous; MF glutton
glotonería F gluttony
glucosa F glucose
gluglutear VI to gobble
gluten M gluten
gobernabilidad F governability
gobernación F (acción de gobernar) governing; (entidad gubernamental) government
gobernador -ora ADJ governing; MF governor
gobernante ADJ governing; MF ruler
gobernar[1] VI/VT to govern, to rule; (un buque) to steer
gobierno M government
goce M enjoyment
gofre M waffle
gol M goal; — **de campo** (fútbol americano) field goal; — **del empate** (fútbol) equalizer; — **en contra** (fútbol) own goal
goleador -ora MF (artillero) shooter; (máximo anotador) top scorer
goleta F schooner
golf M golf
golfo -fa M (mar) gulf; (sinvergüenza) rascal
gollería F delicacy
golondrina F swallow
golosina F sweet, goody, tidbit
goloso ADJ sweet-toothed
golpazo M bang, whack
golpe M (físico) blow, knock, whack; (emocional) blow; (estafa) sting; (robo) holdup; (golf) stroke; (de viento) buffet; (con el codo) jab; (con los nudillos) rap; — **bajo** low blow; — **cortado** (tenis) backspin, slice; — **cruzado** (tenis) crosscourt shot; — **de aproximación** (golf) approach shot; — **de calor** heat stroke; — **de derecha** (tenis) forehand; — **de estado** coup; — **de gracia** coup de grâce; — **de penalidad** (golf) penalty stroke; — **de sol** sunstroke; **de** — suddenly; **de un** — all at once
golpear VI/VT (pegar) to strike, to hit; (llamar) to knock, to rap; (dar una paliza) to beat, to batter; (patear) to kick; (codear) to jab
golpecito M tap
golpetear VI (dedos) to tap; (lluvia) to patter; (motor) to knock; (algo suelto) to rattle
golpeteo M (con los dedos) tap; (de lluvia) patter; (de un motor) knock; (de algo suelto) rattle
goma F (chicle) gum; (caucho) rubber; (neumático) tire; (en béisbol) home; — **de borrar** eraser; — **de mascar** chewing gum;

— **elástica** rubber band; —**espuma** foam
gomero M rubber tree
gomoso ADJ slimy
gónada F gonad
góndola F gondola
gong M gong
gonorrea F gonorrhea
gordinflón ADJ *pey* fatso
gordito ADJ chubby
gordo ADJ fat; **se armó la gorda** all hell broke loose; **hacer la vista gorda** to turn a blind eye
gordura F (cualidad) fatness; (sebo) fat
gorgojo M weevil
gorila M (primate) gorilla; (portero) bouncer; (guardaespaldas) bodyguard
gorjear VI (ave) to warble, to chirp, to twitter; (niño) to gurgle
gorjeo M (de ave) warble, twitter, chirp; (de niño) gurgle
gorra F cap; **de** — at someone else's expense; **vivir de** — to sponge
gorrino M piglet
gorrión M sparrow
gorro M cap
gorrón M sponge, sponger
gorronear VI/VT to mooch, to freeload
gospel M gospel
gota F (de líquido) drop; (de sudor) bead; (enfermedad) gout; — **a** — drop by drop; —**s oftálmicas** eyedrops; **ser dos** —**s de agua** to be like two peas in a pod; **sudar la** — **gorda** (transpirar) to sweat profusely; (trabajar) to work hard
gotear VI (caer gota a gota) to drip; (rápidamente) to dribble, to trickle; (salirse) to leak; (llover) to sprinkle
goteo M drip (también intravenoso); (rápido) dribble, trickle
gotera F leak
gotero M dropper
gótico ADJ Gothic; M (lengua) Gothic
gourmet ADJ & MF gourmet
gozar[47] VT to enjoy; — **de** to enjoy
gozne M hinge
gozo M pleasure, enjoyment
gozoso ADJ enjoyable
grabación F recording
grabado M (en piedra) engraving; (con ácido) etching
grabador -ora MF (persona) engraver; F (aparato) tape recorder; (empresa) recording company
grabar VI/VT (en piedra) to engrave; (con ácido) to etch; (en cinta magnetográfica) to record, to tape; (en computadora) to write; — **en la memoria** to etch/imprint on one's memory
gracejo M wit
gracia F (garbo, desenvoltura) grace, gracefulness; (humor) humor; (monería) antic; (favor) favor; (indulto) pardon; **¡—s!** thanks! thank you! —**s a Dios** thank God; **caer en** — to please; **dar** —**s** to say the blessing; **dar las** —**s** to thank; **hacer** — to amuse; **tener** — to be funny
grácil ADJ supple, graceful
gracioso ADJ (chistoso) amusing, funny; (gentil) gracious
grada F step, bleachers
gradación F gradation
graderías F PL bleachers
grado M (de temperatura, de parentesco, de un ángulo, de universidad) degree; (militar) rank; (de alcohol) proof; **de buen** — willingly; **en alto** — to a great extent; **en mayor o menor** — to some extent; **quemadura de primer** — first-degree burn
graduación F (de una escuela) graduation, commencement; (militar) military rank; (de alcohol) proof; (de un lente óptico) correction
graduado -da MF graduate
gradual ADJ gradual
graduar[26] VT (ajustar) to adjust; (regular) to calibrate; —**se** to graduate, to get a degree
graffiti M graffiti
grafiar[28] VT to graph
gráfica F (arte) graphics; (representación) graph, chart; — **de pastel** pie graph
graficar[30] VT to chart
gráfico -ca ADJ graphic; **acento** — written accent; M (representación) graph, chart; MF (empleado) printer
grafito M graphite
grama F lawn
gramática F grammar
gramatical ADJ grammatical
gramo M gram
grana ADJ & F scarlet
granada F (fruta) pomegranate; (proyectil) grenade; — **de mano** hand grenade
Granada F Grenada
granadino -na ADJ & MF Grenadian
granado M pomegranate tree; ADJ notable
granate M garnet
Gran Bretaña F Great Britain
grande ADJ (de tamaño) large, big; (de importancia) great; **un gran poeta** a great poet; **divertirse en** — to have a whale of a time; **a** —**s alturas** at high altitudes; **de gran alcance** far-reaching; **de/a gran escala** large-scale; **en gran parte** in large measure, largely; **gran almacén** department store
grandeza F greatness; **delirios de** — delusions of grandeur
grandiosidad F grandeur
grandioso ADJ grandiose, grand

granero M (edificio) granary, grain barn; (recipiente) bin, crib; **el — de América** the breadbasket of America
granito M granite
granizada F hailstorm
granizar[47] VI to hail
granizo M hail
granja F farm
granjearse VI to win for oneself
granjero -ra MF farmer
grano M (de una foto, arena, semilla) grain; (cereal) cereal, grain; (barrito) pimple; **— de café** coffee bean; **ir al —** to come to the point
granuja MF ragamuffin
granular VT to granulate; **—se** to become granulated
granuloso ADJ granular
grapa F (para sujetar madera) clamp; (para sujetar papel) staple
grapadora F stapler
grasa F (aceite) grease; (animal) fat
grasiento ADJ greasy
graso ADJ (cutis) oily; (leche) fatty; (pelo) greasy
grasoso ADJ greasy
gratificación F bonus
gratificar[30] VT to gratify
gratis ADJ INV & ADV free
gratitud F gratitude, thankfulness
grato ADJ pleasant
gratuito ADJ (gratis) free; (arbitrario) wanton, gratuitous
grava F gravel
gravamen M (impuesto) tax, assessment; (carga sobre una propiedad) lien, encumbrance
gravar VT (con un impuesto) to tax, to assess; (con una carga) to encumber
grave ADJ (enfermedad, decisión) grave, serious; (sonido) low, deep; (injuria) grievous; (personalidad) earnest
gravedad F (fuerza de atracción) gravity; (de una situación) seriousness; (de una tormenta) severity; (de la voz) depth; (de una personalidad) earnestness
gravemente ADV (herido) seriously; (enfermo) seriously, gravely
gravitación F gravitation
gravitatorio ADJ gravitational
gravoso ADJ burdensome
graznar VI (cuervo) to caw, to croak; (pato) to quack; (ganso) to honk
graznido M (de cuervo) caw, croak; (de pato) quack; (de ganso) honk
Grecia F Greece
greda F clay
green M green
gregario ADJ gregarious
gremial ADJ **acuerdo —** union agreement
gremio M (conjunto de personas) trade; (asociación histórica) guild; (sindicato) trade union
greña F mop of hair
grey F flock, fold
griego -ga ADJ & MF Greek
grieta F crevice, crack
grifo M faucet, spigot, tap
grillete M fetter, shackle
grillo M (insecto) cricket; **—s** (grilletes) shackles
grima F uneasiness; **dar —** (disgustar) to be upsetting; (asquear) to be disgusting
gringo -ga ADJ & MF *pey* American
gripe, gripa F flu, influenza; **— asiática** Asiatic flu
gris ADJ & M gray
grisáceo ADJ grayish
gritar VI/VT (vociferar) to shout, to yell; (chillar) to scream
gritería F shouting
grito M (voz alta) shout, cry; (chillido) scream; **el último —** the last word; **estar en un —** to be in agony; **pedir a —s** to clamor for; **poner el — en el cielo** to hit the ceiling
grosella F currant
grosellero M currant
grosería F (cualidad) rudeness; (hecho, dicho) profanity, something rude
grosero ADJ (descortés) rude, ill-mannered, boorish; (vulgar) vulgar, profane; (sin arte) coarse, unrefined
grosor M thickness
grotesco ADJ grotesque
grúa F (máquina) crane; (guinche, remolcadora) wrecker, tow truck
grueso -sa ADJ (persona) thick-set, heavy; (tabla) thick; (palabra, arena) coarse; M (grosor) thickness; (mayoría) majority; F gross
grulla F crane
grumo M lump
grumoso ADJ lumpy
gruñido M (de perro) growl, snarl; (de cerdo) grunt; (humano) grumble
gruñir[17] VI (el cerdo) to grunt; (el perro) to growl, to snarl; (el ser humano) to grumble
gruñón -ona ADJ grumpy; MF grumpy person
grupa F rump; **volver —s** to turn around
grupo M group; **— de apoyo** support group; **— de presión** lobby; **— étnico** ethnicity; **— paritario** peer group; **— sanguíneo** blood type; **— de usuarios** user group
gruta F grotto, cavern
guacal M crate
guacamole M *Méx* guacamole
guacho M (cría de ave) chick; *Am* (animal huérfano) orphan
guadaña F scythe
guagua F (fruslería) trifle; *Carib* bus; *Chile* baby; LOC ADV **de —** for nothing, free
guaje -ja MF urchin

guano M guano, bird dung
guantada F slap
guante M glove (también en deporte); **arrojar el —** to challenge; **echarle el — a alguien** to capture someone; **te queda como un —** it fits you like a glove
guantelete M gauntlet
guantera F glove compartment
guapetón-ona MF *fam* fox
guapo ADJ (hombre) good-looking, handsome; (mujer) good-looking, pretty; (valiente) brave; **¡hola —!** hey, good-looking!
guarapo M cane syrup
guarda MF (guardián) guard; F (almacenamiento) storage
guardameta MF (fútbol) goalkeeper
guardar VT (almacenar) to keep, to store; (observar) to observe; (datos) to save; (proteger) to guard; **— como** to save as; **— rencor** to hold a grudge; **— un secreto** to keep a secret; **—se de** to guard against; M SG **guardabarros** fender; M SG **guardacostas** Coast Guard cutter; MF SG **guardaespaldas** bodyguard; M SG **guardafangos** fender; M SG **guardapelo** locket; M SG **guardarropa** (armario, ropa) wardrobe; (en un local) cloakroom; MF SG **guardabosque[s]** forest ranger, forester; MF SG **guardafrenos** brake operator; MF SG **guardagujas** switch operator; MF SG **guardameta** goalie
guardería F nursery, day-care center
guardia MF (vigilante) guard; (en baloncesto) point guard; **— civil** civil guard; F (vigilancia) guard; **bajar la —** to let down one's guard; **de —** (militar) on duty, on watch; (médico) on call; **en —** en garde; **hacer/montar —** to stand guard
guardián-ana MF guardian, keeper
guarecerse[35] VT to take shelter
guarida F den, lair
guarismo M cipher
guarnecer[35] VT (un plato) to garnish; (un vestido) to trim; (una fortaleza) to man, to garrison
guarnición F (de tropas) garrison; (de comida) trimmings; **guarniciones** harness
guarro ADJ filthy; M pig
guasa LOC ADV **de/a —** in jest, as a joke
guasón-ona MF joker
guata F padding
Guatemala F Guatemala
guatemalteco-ca ADJ & MF Guatemalan
guau INTERJ woof
guay ADJ *Esp* cool, great
guayaba F guava
guayabera F tropical pleated shirt
gubernamental ADJ governmental
gubernativo ADJ governmental
gubia F gouge
guedeja F shock of hair
guepardo M cheetah
guerra F war, warfare; **dar —** to aggravate; **en pie de —** at war; **— fría** cold war
guerrear VI to war
guerrero-ra MF warrior; **operación guerrera** war operation; **espíritu —** warrior spirit
guerrilla F guerrilla army
guerrillero-ra MF guerrilla
gueto M ghetto
guía MF (persona) guide, leader; F (cosa o animal) guide; **— para padres** parenting guide; **— telefónica** telephone directory
guiar[28] VT to guide, to lead; **—se por** to follow
guijarro M pebble
guinche M *Am* (grúa) winch; (remolque) tow truck
guinda F cherry
guindilla F *Esp* small hot pepper
Guinea F Guinea
guineano-na ADJ & MF Guinean
guingán M gingham
guiñada F wink
guiñapo M rag
guiñar VI/VT to wink
guiño M wink
guión M (ortografía) hyphen; (libreto) script, screenplay
guionista MF screenwriter
guirnalda F garland; (de Navidad) tinsel
guisa F **a — de** by way of
guisado M stew, hash
guisante M pea
guisar VI/VT (cocer) to cook; (en olla) to stew
guiso M stew, casserole
guitarra F guitar
gula F gluttony
gusano M worm; **— de seda** silkworm
gustar VT (agradar) to be pleasing to; **ella me gusta** I like her; **le gustan los perros** he likes dogs; **no me gustan las fiestas** I dislike parties; **te guste o no te guste** whether you like it or not; **cuando gustes** whenever you want; **— de** (preferir) to be fond of; (saborear) to taste
gusto M (sentido, sabor, sentido estético) taste; (agrado) pleasure; (preferencia personal) like; **a —** at ease; **a mi —** to my liking; **dar —** to be a pleasure; **darle el — a alguien** to humor someone; **darse el —** to indulge oneself; **de mal —** in bad taste; **el — es mío** the pleasure is mine; **estar a —** to be comfortable; **mucho —** nice to meet you; **por —** for fun; **tener el — de** to have the pleasure of; **tomarle el — a una cosa** to become fond of something
gustoso ADJ (que gusta de) fond of; (agradable) pleasant; ADV willingly

Guyana F Guyana
guyanés -esa ADJ & MF Guyanese

Hh

ha, has *ver* haber
haba F (frijol) bean; (frijol verde) lima bean
habano M cigar
haber[68] V AUX to have; **— comido cuatro veces en un día** to have eaten four times in a day; **habérselas con** (un problema) to grapple with; (una persona) to have it out with; **ha de llegar mañana** he is to arrive tomorrow; **hay** there is, there are; **hay viento** it is windy; **hubo un problema** there was a problem; **había gente** there were people; **hay que** it is necessary to; **no hay de qué** don't mention it; **no hay forma** no way; **no hay problema** no problem; **¿qué hay?** what's up? **todo lo habido y por haber** everything possible; M (hacienda) assets; (columna en una cuenta) credit; **—es** earnings
habichuela F bean; **— verde** string bean
hábil ADJ adept, able; **día —** workday
habilidad F ability, skill
habilidoso ADJ deft, skillful
habilitar VT (equipar) to outfit; (autorizar) to authorize
habitación F (vivienda) dwelling; (cuarto) room
habitante MF (de un país, región) inhabitant; (de un barrio) resident
habitar VT to inhabit
hábitat M habitat
hábito M habit (también vestimenta religiosa); **—s de compra** buying habits
habitual ADJ habitual, usual
habituar[26] VT to accustom; **—se** to get used to
habla F (lenguaje) speech; (variedad local) dialect; **— infantil** baby talk; **al —** in communication with; **quedarse sin —** to be left speechless
hablador ADJ talkative
habladurías F idle talk, gossip
hablante ADJ speaking; **castellano—** Castilian-speaking; MF speaker; **castellano—** Castilian speaker
hablar VI/VT to talk; **— de política** to talk about politics; **— hasta por los codos** to talk one's head off; **— no cuesta nada** talk is cheap; **— por teléfono** to talk on the phone; **— solo / para sí** to talk to oneself; to speak; **— francés** to speak French; **— sin rodeos** to speak one's mind; **— por señas** to use sign language; **hablando mal y pronto** pardon my French; **no —se** not to be on speaking terms; **no me hagas —** don't get me started on it; **hablando en serio, ¿qué es lo que quieres?** seriously, what do you want?
hablilla F malicious tale
habrá, habría *ver* haber
hacedor -ora MF maker
hacendado -da MF landowner
hacendoso ADJ industrious, diligent
hacer[54, 74] VT (crear) to do, to make; (causar) to make; (resolver) to do; (decir) to go; **la vaca hace 'mu'** the cow goes moo; **— clic** to click; **— economías** to scrimp; **— frío/calor/viento** to be cold/hot/windy; **— una oferta** make an offer; **— un pastel** to make a cake; **— un crucigrama** to do a crossword puzzle; **— un gol** to score a goal; **me hizo llorar** he made me cry; **hace mucho tiempo** a long time ago; **hace poco** a short while ago; **hizo como si estuvieras presente** he acted as if you were here; **a lo hecho, pecho** you've got to face the music; **la hiciste buena** you've really screwed up; **¿qué le vamos a hacer?** that's life; **¿qué se hizo de Juan?** whatever became of Juan? **haz el trabajo** do the work; **hecho a pedido** built to order; **—se rico** to become rich; **—se el tonto** to play the fool; **—se el listo** to pull a stunt; **—se pasar por el jefe** to pose as the boss; **—se a un lado** to step aside; **—se amigo de** to befriend; **—se a la oscuridad** to get used to the dark; **—se cargo** to take over; **—se [del] rogar** to play hard to get
hacha F (grande) ax[e]; (pequeña) hatchet
hachís M hashish
hacia PREP (en dirección a) toward; (aproximadamente) about; **— abajo** downward; **— adelante** forward; **— adentro** inward; **— afuera** outward; **— arriba** upward; **— atrás** backward; **— el este** eastward; **— la izquierda** to the left; **dar —** to face
hacienda F (bienes) estate; (establecimiento agropecuario) ranch; (impositiva) Internal Revenue Service
hacina F shock
hacinar VT (liar) to shock; (atestar) to crowd in
hada F fairy
hado M fate
haga, hago *ver* hacer
Haití M Haiti
haitiano -na ADJ & MF Haitian
halagar[40] VT to flatter, to compliment
halago M flattery, compliment
halagüeño ADJ (palabras) flattering; (perspectiva) promising
halcón M falcon
hálito M breath
halitosis F halitosis

hallar VT to find; **—se** to be; **—se en un aprieto** to be in a pickle; **—se mal de salud** to be in a bad way
hallazgo M finding; **ese documento fue un — sensacional** that document was a real find
halo M halo
halógeno ADJ & M halogen
halterofilia F weight training, weightlifting
hamaca F hammock
hambre F (deseo de comer) hunger; (hambruna) famine; **tener —** to be hungry; **pasar —** to go hungry; **morirse de —** to starve
hambrear VI/VT to starve
hambriento ADJ (con hambre) hungry; (famélico) famished, starving
hambruna F famine
hamburguesa F hamburger
hampa F underworld
hámster M hamster
hándicap M handicap
handicapar VT to handicap
hangar M hangar
hará, haría *ver* hacer
haragán -ana ADJ indolent; MF loafer
haraganear VI to loaf
haraganería F laziness
harapiento ADJ ragged, tattered
harapo M rag, tatter
hardware M hardware
harén M harem
harina F (fina) flour; (gruesa) meal; **— de avena** oat flour; **— de maíz** cornmeal; **es — de otro costal** that's another kettle of fish
hartar VT to satiate; **—se** (de comida) to have one's fill; (de aburrimiento) to get fed up
hartazgo M surfeit, excess
harto ADJ (satisfecho) full; **estar —** to be fed up; **ese asunto me tiene —** I'm sick and tired of the whole business
hasta PREP (temporal) till, until; (espacial) [up] to; **— ahora** to date / so far; **— cierto punto** to a certain extent; **— luego** good-bye, see you later; **— pronto** see you later; **caminó — la esquina** he walked to the corner; **lo llenó — el borde** he filled it up to brim; **estar — la coronilla** to be fed up; ADV even; **— mi madre lo notó** even my mother noticed it; **— que** until
hastiado ADJ jaded
hastial M gable
hastiar[28] VT to cloy, to tire; **—se** to grow weary of
hastío M tedium
hato M (envoltorio) bundle; (rebaño) herd
hay *ver* haber
haya F beech
haya, hayamos *ver* haber
hayuco M beechnut
haz[1] M (de leña) bundle; (de luz) beam; (de flechas) sheaf
haz[2] *ver* hacer
hazaña F deed, exploit, feat
hazmerreír M laughingstock
he VT IMPERSONAL **he aquí la lista** here's the list
he, hemos *ver* haber
hebilla F buckle
hebra F (de hilo) thread; (vegetal) fiber
hebreo -a ADJ & MF Hebrew
heces F PL (de vino, café) dregs; (excremento) feces
hechicería F enchantment
hechicero -ra ADJ bewitching; M sorcerer; F sorceress
hechizar[47] VT (embrujar) to bewitch, to enchant; (fascinar) to enthrall
hechizo M charm, spell
hecho M fact; **los —s de la noche del 17** the events of the night of the 17th; **de —** in fact
hecho *ver* hacer
hechura F cut
hectárea F hectare
heder[2] VI to stink, to reek
hediondez F stench
hediondo ADJ stinking, smelly
hedonismo M hedonism
hedor M stink, stench
hegemonía F hegemony
helada F (frente frío) freeze; (escarcha) frost
heladera F refrigerator
heladería F ice-cream parlor
helado ADJ (muy frío) frozen, freezing; (con hielo) icy; M ice cream
helar[1] VI/VT to freeze
helecho M fern
hélice F (espiral) helix; (de avión) propeller; (de barco) screw, propeller
helicóptero M helicopter
helio M helium
hematoma M hematoma
hembra F (de animal) female; (de venado) doe; (de ballena, foca) cow; (de ave) hen
hemisferio M hemisphere (también cerebral)
hemofilia F hemophilia
hemoglobina F hemoglobin
hemorragia F hemorrhage; **— cerebral** cerebral hemorrhage; **— vaginal** vaginal bleeding
hemorroide F hemorrhoid
henchir[9] VT to swell
hender[2] VI/VT to cleave, to split
hendido ADJ cleft, split
hendidura F (quebradura) crack; (geológica) fissure
henil M hayloft
heno M hay; **fiebre de —** hay fever
hepatitis F hepatitis
heraldo M herald

herbicida M weedkiller, herbicide
herbívoro ADJ herbivorous; M herbivore
herboso ADJ grassy
heredad F homestead
heredar VI/VT (recibir) to inherit; (dar) to bequeath
heredero -ra M heir; F heiress; **—s y cesionarios** heirs and assigns
hereditario ADJ hereditary
hereje MF heretic
herejía F heresy
herencia F (económica) inheritance; (cultural) heritage; (genética) heredity
herida F (lastimadura) injury; (abierta) wound; **— de bala** gunshot wound; **— perforada** puncture wound; **respirar por la —** to reopen an old wound
herido ADJ (lastimado) injured; (con herida abierta) wounded
herir[8] VI/VT (lastimar) to injure; (con herida abierta) to wound; (sentimientos) to hurt
hermafrodita MF hermaphrodite
hermanastro -tra M stepbrother; F stepsister
hermandad F (de hombres) brotherhood; (de mujeres) sisterhood
hermanito -ta M little brother; F little sister
hermano -na MF sibling; M brother (también religioso); **— mayor** older brother; **— menor** younger brother; F sister (también religiosa); **— mayor** older sister; **— menor** younger sister
herméticamente ADV tight, tightly
hermético ADJ hermetic, airtight; (a prueba de agua) watertight; (que no revela secretos) secretive
hermosear VT to beautify
hermoso ADJ beautiful, lovely
hermosura F beauty
hernia F hernia
héroe M hero
heroico ADJ heroic
heroína F (droga) heroin; (personaje) heroine
heroísmo M heroism
herpes M (erupción) herpes; (en la boca) cold sore; **— febril** fever blister
herradura F horseshoe
herraje M ironwork
herramienta F tool
herrar[1] VT (un caballo) to shoe; (una vaca) to brand
herrería F blacksmith's shop
herrero -ra MF blacksmith
herrumbre F rust
hervidero M swarm
hervidor M kettle
hervir[8] VI/VT to boil; **— a fuego lento** to simmer; **— de** to be swarming with; **me hervía la sangre** I was seething
hervor M boiling; **levantar el —** to come to a boil
heterodoxo ADJ unorthodox
heterogéneo ADJ heterogeneous
heterosexual ADJ heterosexual; *fam* straight
hexágono M hexagon
hiato M hiatus
hibernar VI to hibernate
hibridación F hybridization
híbrido ADJ & M hybrid
hice, hiciera *ver* hacer
hidalgo M nobleman
hidalguía F (nobleza) nobility; (generosidad) generosity
hidrato M hydrate
hidráulico ADJ hydraulic
hidroavión M hydroplane, seaplane
hidrocarburo M hydrocarbon
hidroeléctrico ADJ hydroelectric
hidrofobia F hydrophobia
hidrógeno M hydrogen
hiedra F ivy
hiel F gall
hielo M ice; **— seco** dry ice; **romper el —** to break the ice
hiena F hyena
hierba F (pasto) grass; (especia) herb; (marihuana) *fam* weed; **—buena** mint; **mala —** weed; **y otras —s** and so on
hierro M iron (también de golf); **— corrugado** corrugated iron; **— forjado** wrought iron; **— fundido** cast iron; **—s** handcuffs
hígado M liver; **malos —s** ill will
higiene F hygiene
higiénico ADJ hygienic
higienista MF hygienist
higo M fig; **me importa un —** I couldn't care less
higuera F fig tree
hijastro -tra M stepson; F stepdaughter
hijo -ja M son; **— de su madre** *fam* son of a gun; **John Smith** — John Smith Jr.; **sin —s** childless; F daughter
hilachas F loose threads
hilado M spinning
hilandería F (fábrica) spinning mill; (técnica) spinning
hilandero -ra MF spinner
hilar VI/VT to spin; **— fino** to split hairs
hilaridad F mirth
hilera F row, line
hilo M (para coser) thread; (para tejer, hilar) yarn; (alambre) filament; **— de agua** trickle; **— de pensamiento** train of thought; **— de perlas** string of pearls; **— de voz** thin voice; **— dental** floss; **al —** in a row; **mover —s** to pull strings; **seguir el — de** to keep track of; **pender de un —** to be hanging by a thread; **perder el —** to lose track
hilván M basting

hilvanar VT to baste, to tack
himen M hymen
himno M (religioso) hymn; (patriótico) anthem
hincapié M emphasis; **hacer —** to emphasize
hincar[30] VT **— los dientes en** to sink one's teeth into; **—se** to kneel
hincha MF (aficionado) supporter; F (antipatía) *Esp* grudge
hinchado ADJ (inflamado) swollen, bloated; (exagerado) inflated
hinchar VT (un río) to swell; (un globo) to blow up; **— por el equipo de Uruguay** to pull for the Uruguayan team; **—se** (cuerpo) to swell; (pulmones) to inflate; (mejillas) to bulge; (de orgullo) to puff up; (el pan) to rise
hinchazón F swelling
hindi M Hindi
hindú ADJ & MF Hindu
hinojos LOC ADV **de —** on one's knees
hipar VI hiccup
hiperactivo ADJ hyperactive, overactive
hiperdocumento M hyperdocument
hiperenlace M hyperlink
hipermedia M hypermedia
hipermercado M superstore
hipermétrope ADJ farsighted
hipersensible ADJ (a la luz) hypersensitive; (a la crítica) touchy
hipertensión F hypertension, high blood pressure
hiperventilar VI to hyperventilate
hipervínculo M hyperlink
hipnosis F hypnosis
hipnoterapia F hypnotherapy
hipnotizar VI/VT to hypnotize, to mesmerize
hipo M (espasmo) hiccup; (sollozo) sob; **tengo —** I have the hiccups
hipoalérgico ADJ hypoallergenic
hipocondríaco -ca, hipocondriaco -ca ADJ & MF hypochondriac
hipocresía F hypocrisy
hipócrita ADJ hypocritical, two-faced; MF hypocrite
hipódromo M racetrack
hipogloso M halibut
hipoglucemia F hypoglycemia
hipopótamo M hippopotamus
hipoteca F mortgage; **— con tasa de interés ajustable** adjustable-rate mortgage; **— de tasa fija** fixed-rate mortgage
hipotecar[30] VT to mortgage
hipotecario ADJ **banco —** mortgage bank
hipótesis F hypothesis
hipotiroidismo M hypothyroidism
hiriente ADJ (comentario) catty, hurtful
hirviente ADJ boiling
hisopo M swab
hispánico -ca ADJ Hispanic
hispano -na ADJ Hispanic, Spanish-speaking; MF (por su lengua) Spanish-speaking person; (por su etnia) Hispanic
Hispanoamérica F Spanish America
hispanoamericano ADJ Spanish-American
histamina F histamine
histerectomía F hysterectomy
histérico ADJ hysterical
historia F (el pasado, estudio del pasado) history; (relato) story; **— clínica** case history, medical history; **dejarse de —s** to stop fooling around; **esa es otra —** that's another story; **la — se repite** history repeats itself; **pasar a la —** to be a thing of the past
historiador -ora MF historian
historial M record; **— de crédito** credit history
histórico ADJ (de importancia histórica) historic; (pertinente a la historia) historical
historietas F PL funnies
histrionismo M histrionics
hito M landmark, milestone; **de — en —** fixedly; **marcar un —** to be a milestone
hobby M hobby
hocicar[30] VI/VT (un cerdo) to root; (un caballo) to nose
hocico M snout, muzzle
hockey M hockey
hogaño ADV *lit* nowadays
hogar M (lumbre) hearth, fireplace; (casa, asilo) home
hogareño ADJ domestic; **persona hogareña** homebody
hoguera F bonfire, campfire
hoja F (de planta) leaf; (de mesa plegable) flap; (de papel) sheet; (de libro) page; (de navaja) blade; **— clínica** medical chart; **— de afeitar** razor blade; **— de depósito** deposit slip; **— de ejercicios** worksheet; **— de metal** foil; **echar —s** to leaf; **— de servicio** record; F **—lata** tin plate
hojaldre M puff pastry
hojarasca F fallen leaves
hojear VT to page through, to flip through, to browse
hojuela F flake; **—s de maíz** cornflakes
hola INTERJ hello, hi
Holanda F Holland
holandés -esa ADJ Dutch; M (hombre) Dutchman; (lengua) Dutch; F Dutchwoman
holding M holding company
holgado ADJ (vida) comfortable; (pantalón) loose-fitting, baggy; (cuarto) roomy
holganza F (haraganería) idleness; (diversión) leisure
holgar[42] VI to loaf; **huelga decir** it is needless to say
holgazán -ana ADJ lazy, idle; MF idler, loafer, slouch
holgazanear VI to idle, to loaf
holgazanería F laziness

holgura F (de movimiento) ease; (financiera) comfort; (de la ropa) looseness
holístico ADJ holistic
hollejo M skin
hollín M soot, smut
holocausto M holocaust
hombre M man; **— anuncio** sandwich man; **— de bien** man of good will; **— de familia** family man; **— de las cavernas** caveman; **— de la calle** man on the street; **— de negocios** businessman; **— del saco** bogeyman; **— de paja** straw man; **— lobo** werewolf; **— orquesta** one-man band; **— rana** frogman; **es bien —** he's a real he-man; INTERJ come on!
hombrera F shoulder pad
hombro M shoulder; **encogerse de —s** to shrug; **cargar al —** to shoulder; **en/a —s** piggyback; **poner el —** to lend a hand
hombruno ADJ mannish
home M home
homenaje M homage, tribute
homeopatía F homeopathy
homeopático ADJ homeopathic
homicida MF murderer
homicidio M homicide, murder; **— culposo/involuntario** manslaughter; **— sin premeditación** manslaughter
homofobia F homophobia
homofóbico ADJ homophobic
homogeneizar[47] VT to homogenize
homogéneo ADJ homogeneous
homólogo -ga MF counterpart
homóplato M shoulder blade
homosexual ADJ homosexual; *fam* gay
honda F sling, slingshot
hondo ADJ deep; M hollow
hondonada F hollow, dell
hondura F depth; **meterse en —s** to get in over one's head
Honduras F Honduras
hondureño -ña ADJ & MF Honduran
honestidad F (castidad) chastity, modesty; (honradez) honesty
honesto ADJ (casto) chaste, modest; (honrado) honest, straightforward
hongo M (seta) mushroom; (moho) fungus; **aburrirse como un —** to be bored stiff
honor M honor; **con —es** with honors; **tener el — de** to have the honor of; **hacerle los —es a** to be appreciative of
honorable ADJ honorable
honorario ADJ honorary; M PL fee
honra F honor
honradez F honesty
honrado ADJ honest
honrar VT (respetar) to honor; (dignificar) to do credit to
honroso ADJ honorable
hora F hour; **— de dormir** bedtime; **— oficial** standard time; **— punta** rush hour; **—s extra[s]** overtime; **a esta —** at this time; **¿a qué —?** at what time? **a todas —s** at all hours; **a última —** at the last minute; **decir la —** to tell time; **en —** on time; **es — de** it is time to; **es — de que me vaya** it's time for me to go; **kilómetros por —** kilometers per hour; **no ver la — de** to be dying to; **por —** by the hour; **¿qué — es?** what time is it? **ya era —** it was about time
horadar VT to bore
horario M (agenda) schedule, timetable; (manecilla del reloj) hour hand; **— de trabajo** work schedule
horca F (cadalso) gallows; (tridente) pitchfork; **— de ajos** string of garlic
horcajadas LOC ADV **a —** astraddle, astride
horda F horde
horizontal ADJ horizontal
horizonte M (del cielo) horizon; (de una ciudad) skyline
horma F (de zapato) shoe last; (de queso) wheel
hormiga F ant; **— blanca** termite
hormigón M concrete
hormigonera F cement mixer
hormiguear VI (moverse en grandes cantidades) to swarm; (dar sensación de hormigueo) to tingle
hormigueo M tingle
hormiguero M anthill
hormona F hormone; **— del crecimiento** growth hormone
hornada F batch
horneado M baking
hornear VI/VT to bake
hornilla F burner
horno M (industrial) furnace; (doméstico) oven; (para cerámica) kiln; **— de microondas** microwave oven; **alto —** blast furnace; **el — no está para bollos** it's not a good time; **recién salido del —** brand-new
horóscopo M horoscope
horquilla F (para el pelo) hairpin; (horca) pitchfork
horrendo ADJ (asesinato) horrific, ghastly; (vestido) hideous, ghastly
horrible ADJ horrible
horripilante ADJ gruesome, hair-raising
horror M (miedo, repulsión) horror; (monstruosidad) abomination; (espectáculo) sight; **tenerle — a** to be scared of
horrorizar[47] VT to horrify, to shock, to appall
horroroso ADJ appalling, awful
hortaliza F vegetable; **—s** produce
hortera ADJ tacky, uncool, cheesy
horticultura F horticulture
hosco ADJ sullen, surly
hospedaje M lodging

hospedar VT to lodge, to accommodate; **—se** to lodge, to room
hospicio M (para peregrinos) hospice; (para huérfanos) orphanage
hospital M hospital
hospitalario ADJ hospitable
hospitalidad F hospitality
hostal M hostel
hostería F inn, hostelry
hostia F (oblea) host, wafer; (golpe) whack
hostigamiento M harassment
hostigar[40] VT to harass, to harry
hostil ADJ hostile
hostilidad F hostility
hotel M hotel
hotelero -ra MF hotel keeper
hoy ADV today; **— [en] día** nowadays; **de — en adelante** from now on; **— por —** at present
hoya F river basin
hoyo M hole (también de golf); (muy profundo) pit; **— en uno** (golf) hole in one
hoyuelo M dimple
hoz F sickle
hozar[47] VI to root
HTML M HTML
hube, hubiera, hubo *ver* haber
hucha F piggy bank
hueco ADJ (vacío) hollow; (vanidoso) vain, affected; **palabras huecas** empty words; M (entre los dientes) gap; (cavidad) hollow; (de ascensor) shaft
huelga F strike, work stoppage; **— de hambre** hunger strike; **declararse en —** to strike; **en —** on strike
huelguista MF striker
huella F (rastro) trace, trail; (de pie) footprint, track; (de rueda) track; **— dactilar/digital** fingerprint; **seguir las —s de alguien** to follow in someone's footsteps
huérfano -na ADJ & MF orphan
huerta F (de verduras) large vegetable garden; (de árboles frutales) large orchard; **la — valenciana** the farming region of Valencia
huerto M (de verduras) vegetable garden; (de árboles frutales) orchard
hueso M (de animal) bone; (de fruta) stone, pit; **calado hasta los —s** soaked to the bone; **la sin —** the tongue; **no dejarle un — sano a alguien** to break someone's bones; **un — duro de roer** a hard pill to swallow
huésped MF (invitado) guest; (anfitrión) host (también de parásitos)
hueste F host
huesudo ADJ bony
hueva F spawn
huevo M egg; **— de Pascua** Easter egg; **— duro** hard-boiled egg; **— estrellado/frito** fried egg; **— pasado por agua** soft-boiled egg; **—s revueltos** scrambled eggs; **ir pisando —s** to walk on eggshells
huida F flight
huir[19] VI to flee, to fly
hule M oilcloth
hulla F soft coal; **— blanca** hydroelectric power
humanidad F (cualidad y condición) humanity; (conjunto de los seres humanos) humankind; **—es** humanities
humanismo M humanism
humanitario ADJ (organización, ayuda) humanitarian; (generoso) humane
humano ADJ (del hombre) human; (generoso) humane; M human
humareda F cloud of smoke
humeante ADJ (hoguera) smoking; (sopa) steaming
humear VI (echar humo) to give off smoke; (echar vapor) to give off steam
humedad F (del aire) humidity; (de un paño) dampness; (en la tierra) moisture; (en una pared) moisture stain
humedal M wetland
humedecer[35] VT (sello, ojo) to moisten; (paño) to dampen; **se le humedecieron los ojos** his eyes grew teary
húmedo ADJ (trapo) damp; (aire) humid; (tierra) moist; (tiempo) wet, soggy
humero M flue, funnel
humidificar[30] VT to humidify
humildad F (actitud) humility; (condición) lowliness
humilde ADJ (actitud) humble; (condición) low, lowly, mean
humillación F humiliation
humillar VT (insultar) to humiliate; (disminuir) to humble; **—se** to grovel
humo M (de combustión) smoke; (de gases tóxicos) fume; (de agua) vapor, steam; **—s** conceitedness; **bajarle los —s a alguien** to cut someone down to size; **echar —** to put out smoke; **estar que echa —** to be fuming; **hacerse —** to vanish into thin air
humor M (actitud risueña) humor; (estado de ánimo) mood
humorada F witty remark
humorismo M (humor) humor; (profesión) comedy
humorista MF comedian
humorístico ADJ humorous
humoso ADJ smoky
hundimiento M (acción de hundirse) sinking; (hoyo) sinkhole
hundir VT (hacer naufragar) to sink, to scuttle; (arruinar) to destroy; (enterrar) to bury; **—se** (barco) to sink; (empresa, edificio, precios) to collapse; (tierra) to subside; (sol) to go down
húngaro -ra MF Hungarian
Hungría F Hungary
huracán M hurricane

huraño ADJ sullen, unsociable
hurgar[40] VI (en una bolsa) to rummage; (en la basura) to scavenge; **—se las narices** to pick one's nose
hurón M ferret
huronear VI to ferret out
hurra INTERJ hurrah
hurtadillas LOC ADV **a —** stealthily
hurtar VT to steal, to swipe; **— el cuerpo** to dodge; **—se** to hide
hurto M (robo) theft, larceny; (robo en tiendas) shoplifting; **— con escalo** break-in
husky M (perro) husky
husmear VT (un pedazo de carne) to sniff at; (a un delincuente) to smell out; (peligro) to smell; (en los asuntos ajenos) to nose around, to poke around
husmeo M sniff
huso M spindle; **— horario** time zone
huy INTERJ (de sorpresa) wow; (de pena) oh
huya, huye, huyendo, huyera, huyese *ver* huir

Ii

ba, ibas *ver* ir
bérico ADJ Iberian
beroamericano-na ADJ Ibero-American
buprofeno M ibuprofen
ceberg M iceberg
ctericia F jaundice
ctérico ADJ jaundiced
D [investigación y desarrollo] F R&D
da F outward journey; **—s y venidas** comings and goings
dea F (reflexión) idea, thought; (intuición) inkling
deal ADJ & M ideal
dealismo M idealism
dealista ADJ idealistic; MF idealist
dear VT (un método) to devise, to think out, to plan; (un plan) to conceive; (una solución) to engineer; (un complot) to hatch
dem PRON & ADV ditto
déntico ADJ identical
dentidad F identity
dentificación F identification
dentificar[30] VT to identify
deología F ideology
deológico ADJ ideological
dilio M idyll
dioma M language
diosincrasia F idiosyncrasy
diota ADJ idiotic, lamebrained; MF *fam* idiot
diotez F idiocy
do[1] ADJ out of it
ido[2] *ver* ir
idolatrar VT to idolize
idolatría F idolatry
ídolo M idol
idóneo ADJ (calificado) expert; (ideal) ideal
iglesia F church
iglú M igloo
ignición F ignition
ignifugar[40] VT to fireproof
ignorancia F ignorance
ignorante ADJ ignorant, uneducated; MF ignoramus
ignorar VT (no saber) to be unaware of; (hacer caso omiso de) to ignore, to disregard; (despreciar) to shrug off, to discount
igual ADJ (idéntico) equal; (semejante) same, alike; (derecho) even; **me da —** it's all the same to me; **al — que** just like; M equal sign
igualar VT (alisar) to level; (ser igual a) to equal; (hacer iguales) to equalize; (compararse con) to match
igualdad F equality
igualmente ADV (de manera igual) equally; **quedaron — sorprendidos** they were similarly surprised; **¡que te vaya bien! —** I hope things go well for you! likewise
ijada F loin
ijar M loin
ilegal ADJ illegal, unlawful, lawless
ilegítimo ADJ illegitimate
ileso ADJ unharmed, unhurt
ilícito ADJ illicit
ilimitado ADJ (crédito) unlimited; (energía) boundless; (horizonte) limitless
iluminación F (luz) illumination, lighting; (moral, académica) enlightenment
iluminado ADJ lit
iluminar VT (con luz) to illuminate, to brighten; (con conocimiento) to enlighten; **—se** to light up
ilusión F (idea o imagen falsa) illusion; (deseo) dream, fond hope; (entusiasmo) thrill; **— óptica** optical illusion; **me da —** I'm looking forward to
ilusionado ADJ excited
iluso ADJ naive
ilusorio ADJ illusory
ilustración F illustration; **la —** the Enlightenment
ilustrador-ora MF illustrator
ilustrar VT (dibujar) illustrate; (educar) to enlighten
ilustre ADJ illustrious
imagen F (representación, reputación) image; (foto, televisión) picture; (unidad de película fotográfica) frame; **— especular** mirror image; **la — del tacto** the soul of tact; **— por resonancia magnética** magnetic resonance imaging; **imágenes por**

ultrasonido ultrasound imaging
imaginable ADJ conceivable
imaginación F imagination
imaginar VT (crear una imagen mental) to imagine, to picture; (idear) to dream up
imaginario ADJ imaginary
imaginativo ADJ imaginative
imán M magnet
imantar VT to magnetize
imbatible ADJ unbeatable
imbécil ADJ idiotic
imbuir[19] VT to imbue
imitación F imitation
imitador-ora MF (copión) imitator; (mímico) mimic; **un — de Elvis** an Elvis impersonator
imitar VT (copiar) to imitate; (hacer mímica) to mimic; (representar a un personaje) to impersonate
impaciencia F impatience
impaciente ADJ impatient; *fam* antsy
impactar VI/VT to impact
impacto M impact
impagado ADJ unpaid
impala M impala
impar ADJ odd, uneven
imparcial ADJ (sin prejuicios) impartial, unbiased, neutral; (justo) evenhanded; (apartidario) nonpartisan
imparcialidad F impartiality
impartir VT to impart
impasible ADJ impassive
impasse M impasse
impávido ADJ undaunted
impeachment M impeachment
impecable ADJ (perfecto) flawless; (limpio) spick and span
impedimento M (obstáculo) impediment, hindrance; (incapacidad) handicap
impedir[9] VT to impede, to prevent, to hinder; (acceso) to bar
impeler VT (empujar) to impel; (inducir) to drive
impenetrable ADJ impenetrable
impensable ADJ unthinkable
imperante ADJ prevailing
imperar VI to prevail
imperativo ADJ & M imperative
imperceptible ADJ imperceptible
imperdible ADJ that shouldn't be missed; **una película** — a must-see movie; M safety pin
imperecedero ADJ undying
imperfecto ADJ & M imperfect
imperial ADJ imperial
imperialismo M imperialism
impericia F lack of skill
imperio M (organización política) empire; (gobierno) rule; **— industrial** manufacturing empire
imperioso ADJ (mandón) imperious; (necesario) imperative
impermeabilizar[47] VT to waterproof
impermeable ADJ (al agua) waterproof; (a la crítica) impervious; M raincoat, slicker
impersonal ADJ impersonal
impertinencia F (actitud) impertinence, impudence; (réplica) backtalk
impertinente ADJ impertinent, impudent
impétigo M impetigo
ímpetu M impetus
impetuoso ADJ impetuous, brash
impida, impide, impidiendo, impidiera, impidiese *ver* impedir
impío ADJ godless
implacable ADJ implacable, relentless
implantación F (de un diente) implantation; (de una costumbre, sistema) establishment, introduction
implantar VT to implant
implante M implant; **— dental** dental implant
implementación F implementation
implementar VT to implement
implemento M implement
implicación F (lógica) implication; (en un delito) involvement
implicar[30] VT (involucrar) to implicate, to involve; (conllevar) to entail
implícitamente ADV implicitly, by implication
implícito ADJ implicit
implorar VI/VT to implore
impondrá, impondría *ver* imponer
imponente ADJ (impresionante) imposing; (espantoso) forbidding
imponer[56, 74] VT to impose, to force upon; (gravar) to assess; **—se** to get one's way
imponible ADJ taxable
impopular ADJ unpopular
importación F import
importancia F importance
importante ADJ (persona) important; (cantidad) substantial; (tema, asunto) weighty; (suceso, ocasión) momentous
importar VI (ser importante) to matter; **me importa un comino** I don't give a hoot; **no importa** it makes no difference; VT (introducir productos) to import
importe M amount
importunar VT to besiege
importuno ADJ inopportune
imposibilidad F impossibility
imposibilitar VT to make impossible
imposible ADJ impossible
imposición F (de ideas) imposition; (de impuestos) assessment
impositivo ADJ **sistema** — tax system
impostor-ora MF impostor, fraud
impotencia F impotence
impotente ADJ (sin poder) powerless; (sin libido) impotent

impreciso ADJ inaccurate
impredecible ADJ unpredictable
impregnar VT to impregnate
impremeditado ADJ unpremeditated
imprenta F (arte, oficio) printing; (máquina) press, printing press
imprescindible ADJ indispensable
impresión F (efecto en el ánimo) impression; (acción de imprimir) printing; (huella) imprint
impresionante ADJ (logro) impressive, imposing; (edificio) grand, imposing; (panorama) breathtaking
impresionar VT to impress; **—se** to be overwhelmed; **para —** for show
impreso M printed matter
impresor-ora MF (persona) printer; F (aparato) printer; **impresora de burbuja** bubble-jet printer; **impresora de inyección de tinta** ink-jet printer; **impresora en serie** serial printer; **impresora gráfica** plotter; **impresora láser** laser printer; **impresora local** local printer
imprevisible ADJ unpredictable
imprevisto ADJ unforeseen; M unforeseen event
imprimir[74] VI/VT (producir un impreso) to print; (marcar con presión) to imprint
improbable ADJ improbable, unlikely
improductivo ADJ unproductive
impromptu M impromptu
impropio ADJ (inadecuado) unbecoming; (atípico) atypical
improvisación F improvisation, role-playing
improvisado ADJ impromptu
improvisando ADV ad lib
improvisar VI/VT to improvise
improviso LOC ADV **de —** all of a sudden
imprudencia F (actitud) recklessness; (acción) reckless act
imprudente ADJ unwise, ill-advised
impublicable ADJ unprintable
impúdico ADJ immodest
impuesto M tax, duty; **—a la herencia** inheritance tax; **—s atrasados** back taxes; **— de tasa única** flat tax; **— de sucesión** inheritance tax; **—s** taxation; **— sobre ingresos** income tax; **— sobre las donaciones** gift tax; **— sobre las ventas** sales tax; **— sobre rentas** income tax
impuesto *ver* imponer
impugnar VT to contest, to dispute
impulsar VT (empujar) to propel, to drive; (estimular) to boost
impulsivo ADJ impulsive
impulso M (estímulo) boost; (deseo espontáneo) impulse, urge
impune ADJ unpunished
impunidad F impunity
impureza F impurity
impuro ADJ (sustancia) impure; (pensamiento) impure, unclean
impuse, impusiera, impusiese *ver* imponer
inacabado ADJ unfinished
inaccesible ADJ inaccessible
inaceptable ADJ (inadmisible) unacceptable; (insuficiente) inadequate
inacostumbrado ADJ unwonted
inactividad F inactivity
inactivo ADJ inactive
inadaptado-da ADJ maladjusted; MF misfit
inadecuado ADJ unsuitable
inadmisible ADJ (comportamiento) unacceptable; (pruebas) inadmissible
inadvertido ADJ unnoticed, unobserved
inagotable ADJ (recursos) inexhaustible; (optimismo) unfailing
inaguantable ADJ unbearable
inalámbrico ADJ cordless, wireless
inalterable ADJ unalterable, unchangeable
inalterado ADJ unchanged
inamovible ADJ immovable
inanición F starvation
inanimado ADJ inanimate
inapetencia F lack of appetite
inapreciable ADJ (invalorable) invaluable; (muy pequeño) too small to be seen
inapropiado ADJ unsuitable
inasequible ADJ inaccessible
inaudible ADJ inaudible
inaudito ADJ (historia, situación) unheard-of, unprecedented; (sufrimiento) untold
inauguración F (de un gobierno) inauguration; (de un monumento) dedication
inaugurar VT (un gobierno) to inaugurate; (un monumento) to dedicate
inca ADJ & MF Inca
incalculable ADJ untold
incandescencia F glow
incandescente ADJ incandescent, glowing
incansable ADJ untiring, tireless
incapacidad F inability
incapacitar VT to disable, to incapacitate
incapaz ADJ incapable
incautación F seizure
incauto ADJ unwary
incendiar VT to set fire to; VI/VT to burn; **—se** to catch fire, to burn down
incendiario-ria ADJ incendiary; MF arsonist
incendio M fire, blaze, conflagration; **— doloso** arson; **— forestal** forest fire
incentivo M incentive, inducement
incertidumbre F uncertainty, suspense
incesante ADJ incessant, ceaseless
incesto M incest
incestuoso ADJ incestuous
incidencia F incidence
incidental ADJ incidental

incidente M incident
incidir VI — **en un asunto** to affect/influence a situation
incienso M incense
incierto ADJ uncertain
incinerar VT to incinerate
incipiente ADJ incipient
incisión F incision
incisivo ADJ incisive; M incisor
incitar VT to incite, to whip up
incivilizado ADJ uncivilized
inclemencia F **las —s del tiempo** foul weather
inclemente ADJ inclement, foul
inclinación F (tendencia) inclination, bent, disposition; (acción de inclinar) tilting; (posición inclinada) tilt; (de un techo) slant; (del terreno) slope; (de opinión) bias
inclinar VT (ladear) to tilt; (bajar) to hang; **— la cabeza** to hang one's head; **—se** (doblarse en la cintura) to bend over; (tener tendencia a) to tend; (hacer una reverencia) to bow
incluido ADJ included; **con todo —** all-inclusive
incluir[19] VT (incorporar) to include; (abarcar) to include, to comprise; **incluyéndote a ti, somos cuatro** including you, there are four of us
inclusión F inclusion; **con — de** including
inclusive ADV even
inclusivo ADJ inclusive
incluso ADV even
incluya, incluye, incluyendo, incluyera, incluyese *ver* incluir
incobrable ADJ noncollectible, uncollectable
incógnita F unknown [quantity]
incógnito LOC ADV **de —** incognito
incoherente ADJ incoherent
incoloro ADJ colorless
incomestible ADJ inedible
incomformista ADJ & MF nonconformist
incomible ADJ inedible
incomodar VT to inconvenience
incomodidad F uneasiness
incómodo ADJ (silla) uncomfortable; (situación) awkward, inconvenient; (baúl) cumbersome; (silencio) uneasy; (que siente molestia) ill at ease
incomparable ADJ incomparable, peerless
incompatible ADJ incompatible
incompetente ADJ incompetent
incompleto ADJ incomplete
incomprensible ADJ incomprehensible
incomunicación F disconnect, miscommunication
inconcebible ADJ inconceivable
inconcluso ADJ unfinished
incondicional ADJ unconditional, unqualified
inconexo ADJ disconnected
inconformista MF nonconformist
inconfundible ADJ unmistakable
inconsciente ADJ (sin sentido) unconscious, senseless; (ignorante) unaware, oblivious
inconsecuencia F inconsistency
inconsecuente ADJ inconsistent
inconsolable ADJ heartbroken
inconstancia F inconstancy
inconstante ADJ inconstant, changeable
inconstitucional ADJ unconstitutional
incontable ADJ countless
incontenible ADJ uncontrollable
incontinente ADJ incontinent
incontrolable ADJ uncontrollable
incontrovertible ADJ incontrovertible
inconveniencia F inconvenience
inconveniente ADJ improper; M inconvenience, downside
incorporación F (inclusión) inclusion; (asimilación) incorporation
incorporado ADJ built-in
incorporar VT (incluir) to include; (asimilar) to incorporate; (agregar) to build into; **—se** (erguirse) to sit up
incorrectamente ADV incorrectly, wrongly
incorrecto ADJ incorrect, wrong
incorregible ADJ incorrigible
incredulidad F disbelief
incrédulo ADJ incredulous
increíble ADJ (inverosímil) incredible, unbelievable; (extraordinario) amazing
incrementar VT to augment
incremento M increment, increase
incriminar VT to incriminate
incrustación F inlay
incrustado ADJ (en piedra) embedded; (joyas) inlaid
incrustar VT (piedra) to embed; (oro) to inlay; **—se en** to become embedded in
incubadora F incubator
incuestionable ADJ unquestionable
inculcar[30] VT to inculcate, to instill
inculto ADJ (sin modales) uncultured, unrefined; (sin instrucción) uneducated
incumbencia F **no es de tu —** it's none of your business
incumplimiento M (de contrato) breach; (de deberes) nonperformance; (de deudas) default; (de metas) failure to accomplish; (de promesas) failure to keep
incumplir VT (contratos) to breach; (deberes) to fail to perform; (deudas) to default on; (metas) to fail to accomplish; (promesas) to renegue on, to fail to keep
incurable ADJ incurable
incurrir VI — **en** (una deuda, un gasto) to incur; (un error) to fall into
incursión F raid, foray
incursionar VI to foray
indagación F investigation, probe

indagar[40] VI/VT to investigate, to inquire into
indebido ADJ improper
indecencia F indecency
indecente ADJ indecent
indecible ADJ unspeakable
indecisión F indecision
indeciso ADJ (que no ha decidido) undecided; (que suele vacilar) wishy-washy
indecoroso ADJ improper
indefendible ADJ indefensible
indefenso ADJ defenseless
indefinible ADJ indefinable
indefinido ADJ (plazo) indefinite; (silueta) undefined
indeleble ADJ indelible
indelicado ADJ indelicate
indemnización F (resarcimiento) indemnity; (de guerra) reparation; (de un pleito) recovery; **— por despido** severance pay
indemnizar[47] VT to indemnify
independencia F independence; (de un individuo) self-reliance
independiente ADJ independent
indescriptible ADJ indescribable
indeseable ADJ undesirable, unwelcome
indestructible ADJ indestructible
indeterminado ADJ indeterminate, undetermined
indexación F indexing
indexar VT to index
India F India
indicación F (señal) indication; (instrucción) instruction; **indicaciones** directions
indicador M pointer, indicator; **— clave** key indicator; **—es anticipados** leading indicators
indicar[30] VT (señalar) to indicate, to point out; (registrar) to read, to register; (mostrar) to show
indicativo ADJ & M indicative
índice M (lista alfabética) index; (tabla de materias) table of contents; (dedo) index finger; **— de confianza del consumidor** consumer confidence index; **— de mortalidad** mortality rate; **— de precios al consumidor** consumer price index
indicio M clue, sign
Indico M **Océano —** Indian Ocean
indiferencia F indifference; (frialdad) coolness
indiferente ADJ (apático) indifferent, unconcerned; (frío) cool; (sin entusiasmo) lukewarm; (no conmovido) unmoved; **esa chica me es —** I don't care about that girl
indígena ADJ indigenous; MF native
indigente ADJ destitute, indigent
indigestión F indigestion
indignación F indignation
indignado ADJ indignant
indignar VT to make indignant; **—se** to become indignant
indigno ADJ unworthy
índigo M indigo
indio-dia ADJ & MF Indian
indirecta F hint
indirecto ADJ (estilo, consecuencia) indirect; (ruta) roundabout
indisciplinado ADJ unruly
indiscreción F indiscretion
indiscreto ADJ indiscreet
indiscutible ADJ unquestionable
indispensable ADJ indispensable
indisponer[56, 74] VT to indispose; **—se** to become indisposed
indispuesto ADJ (disgustado) upset; (enfermo) indisposed
indistinto ADJ indistinct, vague
individual ADJ (derechos) individual; (habitación) single; **—es** singles
individualidad F individuality
individualismo M individualism
individualista ADJ & MF individualist
individuo ADJ & M individual
indivisible ADJ indivisible
indiviso ADJ undivided
indocumentado-da ADJ (carta) undocumented; (persona) without identity papers; MF illegal immigrant
índole F type
indolencia F indolence
indolente ADJ indolent
indoloro ADJ painless
indomable ADJ indomitable
indomado ADJ unbroken
Indonesia F Indonesia
indonesio-sia ADJ & MF Indonesian
inducción F induction
inducir[38] VT to induce, to prompt
indudable ADJ undeniable; unquestionable
indudablemente ADV undoubtedly
indulgencia F indulgence
indulgente ADJ indulgent, lenient
indultar VT to pardon
indulto M pardon
indumentaria F apparel
industria F industry, trade; **— petrolera** oil industry
industrial ADJ industrial; MF industrialist
industrialización F industrialization
industrioso ADJ industrious
inédito ADJ unpublished
inefable ADJ ineffable
ineficaz ADJ ineffective, ineffectual
ineficiente ADJ inefficient
inelegible ADJ ineligible
ineludible ADJ inescapable, unavoidable
inempleable ADJ unemployable
inepto ADJ inept
inequívoco ADJ unequivocal

inercia F inertia
inerte ADJ inert
inescrutable ADJ inscrutable
inesperado ADJ unexpected
inestabilidad F instability
inestable ADJ (personalidad, estructura) unstable; (andar) unsteady
inestimable ADJ inestimable, invaluable
inevitable ADJ (conclusión) inevitable; (accidente) unavoidable
inexacto ADJ inaccurate
inexcusable ADJ inexcusable
inexistente ADJ nonexistent
inexorable ADJ inexorable
inexperto ADJ (trabajador) inexperienced, unskilled; (ojo) untrained
inexplicable ADJ inexplicable
inexpresivo ADJ inexpressive, wooden
infalible ADJ (a toda prueba) infallible, foolproof; (confiable) unfailing
infame ADJ infamous
infamia F infamy
infancia F childhood
infante -ta MF (hijo -ja del rey) infante -ta; M (soldado) infantryman
infantería F infantry; **— de marina** marine corps
infantil ADJ (como niño) childlike; (aniñado) childish, infantile
infarto M infarction, heart attack; **— cardíaco** heart attack; **— cerebral** stroke, cerebral infarction; **— del miocardio** myocardial infarction
infección F infection; **— del tracto urinario** urinary tract infection; **— respiratoria alta** upper respiratory infection
infeccioso ADJ infectious
infectar VT to infect; **—se** to become infected
infecto ADJ foul, repugnant
infelicidad F misery
infeliz ADJ unhappy, wretched, miserable; MF poor wretch
inferencia F inference
inferior ADJ (en calidad) inferior, subpar; (en posición) lower
inferioridad F inferiority
inferir[8] VT to infer
infernal ADJ (calor) infernal; (ruido) unholy
infertilidad F infertility
infestación F infestation
infestar VT to infest
infiel ADJ unfaithful, faithless, untrue
infierno M (bíblico) hell; (lugar caliente) inferno; **en el quinto —** in the middle of nowhere
infinidad F infinity; **una — de** a large number of
infinitivo ADJ & M infinitive
infinito ADJ infinite; M infinity
inflación F inflation; **— básica** core inflation
inflado ADJ bloated; M pumping up
inflamable ADJ flammable
inflamación F inflammation
inflamar VT to inflame; **—se** to become inflamed
inflar VT (neumáticos) to inflate, to pump up; (globos) to blow up; (precios) to balloon
inflexible ADJ (rígido) inflexible; (testarudo) unbending, adamant
infligir[46] VT to inflict
influencia F influence, pull, clout; (sobre las masas) sway
influir[19] VI **— en/sobre** to influence; (las masas) to sway
influjo M influence
influya, influye, influyendo, influyera, influyese *ver* influir
influyente ADJ influential
infomercial M infomercial
información F information; (periodística) story
informal ADJ (no formal) informal, casual; (poco fiable) unreliable
informante MF (para un estudio) informant; (de la policía) informer
informar VT (enterar) to inform, to appraise; (un militar) to debrief; (un periodista) to report; (un abogado) to advise; **—se** to become informed
informática F computer science, information technology
informático -ca ADJ computing; MF computer specialist
informativo ADJ informative; M (televisión, radio) news program
informatizar[47] VT to computerize
informe M (de noticias) report; (militar) debriefing; **— de crédito** credit report; **—s de guía** information; ADJ shapeless
infortunio M misfortune
infracción F (de reglamentos) infraction, infringement; (de contrato) breach; (de tránsito) violation; (en deportes) penalty
infractor -ora MF lawbreaker
infraestructura F infrastructure
infrarrojo ADJ & M infrared
infrascrito -ta MF undersigned
infravalorado ADJ underrated, undervalued
infringir[46] VT to infringe, to breach, to violate
infructuoso ADJ fruitless, unsuccessful
ínfulas F PL airs; **darse —** to put on airs
infundado ADJ groundless, unfounded
infundir VT to infuse, to imbue
infusionar VT to steep
ingeniar VT to contrive; **ingeniárselas para** to contrive to
ingeniería F engineering; **— genética** genetic engineering; **— química** chemical engineering

ingeniero -ra MF engineer; **— civil** civil engineer; **— electricista** electrical engineer; **— en computación** computer engineer; **— informático** computer engineer
ingenio M (mental) ingenuity, cleverness; (verbal) wit; (artefacto) artifact; **— de azúcar** (refinería) sugar refinery, sugar mill; (plantación) sugar plantation
ingeniosidad F ingenuity
ingenioso ADJ ingenious, resourceful
ingenuidad F ingenuousness, naïveté
ingenuo -nua ADJ (inocente) naive, ingenuous; (crédulo) gullible; MF dupe
ingerir VI/VT to ingest
ingestión F ingestion
ingle F groin
inglés -esa ADJ English; M Englishman; (lengua) English; F Englishwoman
ingobernable ADJ unruly
ingratitud F ingratitude
ingrato -ta ADJ thankless, ungrateful; MF ingrate
ingrávido ADJ weightless
ingrediente M ingredient; **ese libro tiene todos los —s de un éxito** that book has all the makings of a best seller
ingresar VT (datos) to input; (dinero en una cuenta) to deposit; VI (a un hospital) to be admitted; (a un sistema) to log in
ingreso M (permiso para entrar) entrance, entry; (depósito bancario) deposit; (renta) income; **—s** (de una firma) earnings; (del estado) revenue; **— bruto** gross income; **— neto ajustado** adjusted net income; **—s discrecionales** discretionary income; **—s disponibles** disposable income
inhábil ADJ unskilled
inhabilidad F inability
inhabilitar VT to disqualify
inhalación F inhalation; **— de humo** smoke inhalation
inhalar VI/VT to breathe in, to inhale
inherente ADJ inherent
inhibición F inhibition
inhibidor ADJ inhibiting; M inhibitor
inhibir VT to inhibit
inhospitalario ADJ inhospitable
inhóspito ADJ inhospitable
inhumano ADJ inhuman
iniciación M initiation, induction
inicial ADJ initial; (pago) up-front; F (letra) initial; (béisbol) first base
inicialista MF first baseman
inicializar[47] VT to initialize
inicialmente ADV initially
iniciar VT (conversaciones) to initiate; (en un grupo) to induct; (software) to launch; (computadora) to boot up; (negociaciones) to enter
iniciativa F initiative
inicio M beginning, start
inimitable ADJ inimitable
ininflamable ADJ fireproof
ininteligible ADJ unintelligible
ininterrumpido ADJ unbroken, uninterrupted
injerencia F interference
injertar VT to graft
injerto M graft; **— óseo** bone graft
injugable ADJ unplayable
injuria F (insulto) insult, verbal abuse; (daño) damage
injuriar VT to insult, to abuse verbally
injurioso ADJ insulting, injurious, verbally abusive
injustamente ADV unjustly, unfairly, wrongly
injusticia F (desigualdad) injustice; (acto injusto) wrong; (error judicial) miscarriage of justice
injustificable ADJ unjustifiable
injustificado ADJ uncalled-for, unwarranted
injusto ADJ unjust, unfair
inmaculado ADJ immaculate, spotless
inmaduro ADJ immature
inmanejable ADJ unmanageable
inmaterial ADJ immaterial
inmediaciones F PL vicinity
inmediato ADJ immediate, instant; **de —** at once
inmensidad F immensity, vastness
inmenso ADJ immense, vast
inmerso ADJ (en agua) submerged; (en el trabajo) absorbed; (en un tema, una situación) immersed
inmerecido ADJ unearned
inmigración F immigration
inmigrante ADJ & MF immigrant
inmigrar VI to immigrate
inminente ADJ imminent, impending
inmiscuir[19] VI to mix; **—se** to meddle
inmodestia F immodesty
inmodesto ADJ immodest
inmoral ADJ immoral
inmoralidad F immorality
inmortal ADJ & MF immortal
inmortalidad F immortality
inmóvil ADJ motionless, immobile
inmovilizar[47] VT (impedir los movimientos) to immobilize; (contra el suelo) to pin
inmueble M building
inmune ADJ immune
inmunidad F immunity
inmunodeficiencia F immunodeficiency
inmutable ADJ unchangeable, immutable
innato ADJ innate, inborn
innecesario ADJ unnecessary, needless
innegable ADJ undeniable
innoble ADJ ignoble
innocuo ADJ innocuous, harmless

innovación F innovation
innovador-ora ADJ innovating, innovative; MF innovator
innovar VI to innovate; VT to modernize
innumerable ADJ innumerable, countless
inocencia F innocence
inocente ADJ innocent, guiltless; MF dupe
inocuo ADJ innocuous, harmless
inodoro ADJ odorless; M toilet, commode
inofensivo ADJ inoffensive, harmless
inolvidable ADJ unforgettable
inoperable ADJ inoperable
inoportuno ADJ inopportune, untimely
inorgánico ADJ inorganic
inoxidable ADJ rustproof
inquietante ADJ distressing, worrisome
inquietar VT to worry
inquieto ADJ (movedizo) restless; (preocupado) uneasy
inquietud F (intranquilidad) restlessness; (preocupación) alarm, concern
inquilino-na MF (de un apartamento) tenant, renter; (de una pensión) lodger
inquina F spite
inquirir[4] VI/VT to inquire
inquisición F inquisition
inquisitivo ADJ inquisitive
insaciable ADJ insatiable
insalubre ADJ unhealthy, unsanitary
insatisfactorio ADJ unsatisfactory
insatisfecho ADJ dissatisfied, unhappy
inscribir[74] VT (grabar) to inscribe; (matricular) to register, to enroll; **—se** to register, to enroll
inscripción F (grabado) inscription; (matriculación) registration, enrollment
insecticida M insecticide
insectívoro ADJ insectivorous
insecto M insect
inseguridad F insecurity; **la — urbana** the lack of safety in cities / the city
inseguro ADJ (personalidad) insecure; (vehículo) unsafe; (andar) unsteady; (computadora) vulnerable to hacking
inseminación F insemination
insensato-ta ADJ foolish; MF fool
insensibilizar[47] VT to desensitize
insensible ADJ (cruel) insensitive, callous; (imperturbable) unfeeling, thick-skinned; (entumecido) numb
inseparable ADJ inseparable
inserción F insertion
insertar VT to insert
inservible ADJ useless
insidioso ADJ insidious
insigne ADJ famous
insignia F insignia, badge
insignificante ADJ insignificant, unimportant
insincero ADJ insincere
insinuación F (sugerencia) insinuation; (comentario sexual) innuendo
insinuante ADJ suggestive
insinuar[26] VT to insinuate, to suggest; **—se** to insinuate oneself
insípido ADJ insipid, flavorless
insistencia F (machaconería, testarudez) insistence; (perseverancia) persistence
insistente ADJ (testarudo, repetitivo) insistent; (perseverante) persistent
insistir VI/VT (repetir) to insist; (perseverar) to persist; **— en** to insist on; **— sobre** to harp on
insolación F (por sol) sunstroke; (por calor) heatstroke
insolencia F (falta de respeto) insolence; (comentario) smart remark
insolente ADJ insolent, sassy
insólito ADJ (situación) unusual; (accidente) freak, freakish
insoluble ADJ insoluble
insolvente ADJ insolvent
insomne ADJ wakeful, unable to sleep
insomnio M insomnia
insoportable ADJ (persona, conducta) unbearable, impossible; (dolor) excruciating, unbearable
insospechado ADJ unsuspected
insostenible ADJ untenable
inspección F (revisación) inspection; (encuesta) canvass
inspeccionar VT to inspect, to survey
inspector-ora MF inspector
inspiración F (idea) inspiration; (inhalación) inhalation
inspirar VI/VT to inspire; VI to inhale, to breathe in
instalación F (de programas, fontanería) installation; (de aparatos electrónicos) setup; **instalaciones** fixtures
instalar VT (programas, fontanería) to install; (aparatos electrónicos) to set up; **—se** to take up residence
instancia LOC ADV **a —s de** at the request of
instantánea F snapshot
instantáneo ADJ instantaneous
instante M instant; **al —** right away
instar VT to enjoin
instauración F establishment
instigador-ra MF instigator
instigar[40] VT to instigate, to abet
instintivo ADJ instinctive
instinto M instinct; **— suicida** death wish
institución F institution; **— benéfica** charity
institucional ADJ institutional
instituir[19] VT to institute
instituto M (institución, agencia) institute; (escuela secundaria) high school
institutriz F governess
instrucción F instruction, schooling

instructivo ADJ instructive
instructor-ora MF instructor
instruir[19] VT to instruct, to school
instrumental ADJ instrumental
instrumentar VT (un plan) to implement; (música) to do the instrumentation for
instrumento M instrument; **— de cuerda** string instrument; **— de metal** brass instrument; **— de percusión** percussion instrument; **— de viento** wind instrument; **—s quirúrgicos** surgical instruments
insubordinado ADJ insubordinate
insuficiencia F (incapacidad) insufficiency; (falla de los órganos) failure; **— cardíaca congestiva** congestive heart failure; **— coronaria** coronary failure; **— renal** kidney failure, renal failure; **— respiratoria** respiratory failure
insuficiente ADJ insufficient, inadequate
insufrible ADJ insufferable
insulina F insulin
insulso ADJ bland
insultar VT to insult
insulto M insult, put-down
insuperable ADJ (resultado) insuperable; (obstáculo) insurmountable
insurgente ADJ & MF insurgent
insurrección F insurrection
insurrecto-ta ADJ rebellious; MF rebel
intachable ADJ blameless
intacto ADJ intact, unbroken
intangible ADJ intangible
integración F (de razas) integration; (de elementos) incorporation
integral ADJ (parte) integral; ADJ (harina) whole-grain
integrante ADJ integral
integrar VT (crear) to form; (ser miembro de) to be a member of
integridad F integrity
íntegro ADJ (objeto) whole; (texto) unabridged; (comportamiento) upright
intelecto M intellect
intelectual ADJ & MF intellectual
inteligencia F intelligence (también militar); (persona) mind; **— artificial** artificial intelligence
inteligente ADJ intelligent, bright, smart
inteligible ADJ intelligible
intemperie LOC ADV **a la —** exposed to the weather
intención F intention, intent
intencional ADJ intentional
intendente MF (civil) administrator; (militar) quartermaster general
intensidad F intensity
intensificar[30] VT to intensify; **—se** (frío) to intensify; (violencia) to escalate
intensivo ADJ intensive
intenso ADJ (actividad) intense; (debate) fierce; (calor) severe
intentar VI/VT to try; VT to attempt
intento M (tentativa) try, attempt; (propósito) intention
interacción F interaction
interactivo ADJ interactive
interactuar[26] VI to interact
intercalación F insertion
intercalar VT to insert
intercambiador M interchange
intercambiar VI/VT to exchange
intercambio M exchange
interceder VI to intercede
interceptación F interception (también en fútbol americano)
interceptar VT intercept (también en fútbol americano)
intercesión F intercession
intercesor-ora MF advocate
interés M (intelectual, financiero) interest; (preocupación) concern; (participación comercial) stake; **— compuesto** compound interest; **— mutuo** mutual interest; **intereses ocultos** hidden agenda
interesado ADJ (atento) interested; (preocupado) concerned; (egoísta) self-serving
interesante ADJ interesting
interesar VT to interest; **—se por** to become interested in
interestatal ADJ interstate
interestelar ADJ interstellar
interface MF interface
interfaz MF interface; **— digital de instrumentos musicales** musical instrument digital interface
interferencia F (en los negocios ajenos) interference; (en una transmisión) interference, static; **— externa** outside interference
interferir[8] VT to jam; VI to interfere
interferón M interferon
ínterin M interim; **en el —** meanwhile
interino ADJ acting, interim
interior ADJ (habitación) inside; (mundo, vida) inner; (zona geográfica) inland; (mercado, comercio) domestic; M (parte) inside part, interior; **el — de la caja** the inside of the box; (de un país) the country, the provinces; **una ciudad del —** a provincial town
interiorizar[47] VT to internalize
interjección F interjection
interlineal ADJ interlinear
interlock M interlock
interlocutor-ora MF interlocutor
interludio M interlude
intermediario-ria M middleman; MF (mensajero) go-between; ADJ intermediary

intermediarista MF second baseman
intermedio -a ADJ intermediate; M intermission; **por — de** through; F (béisbol) second base
interminable ADJ interminable, unending, endless
intermitente ADJ intermittent; M turn signal
internación F inpatient care
internacional ADJ international
internado -da M (escuela) boarding school; (práctica) internship; MF (alumno) boarding student; (en un hospital) patient
internalizar[47] VT to internalize
internar VT (en una cárcel) to intern; (en un hospital) to admit, to hospitalize; (en un hospital psiquiátrico) to commit
internauta MF Internet user
internet M Internet, web; **— inalámbrico** wireless Internet; **— móvil** mobile Internet
internista MF internist
interno -na ADJ (correo) internal; (mercado) domestic; MF (persona que vive internada) inmate; (residente médico) intern
interpersonal ADJ interpersonal
interponer[56,74] VT to interpose; **—se** to intervene
interpretación F (de un texto) interpretation; (artística) performance, rendition
interpretar VT (ideas) to interpret; (música) to perform; (intenciones) to construe
intérprete MF (traductor, explicador) interpreter; (músico) artist, performer
interracial ADJ interracial
interrelacionado ADJ interrelated
interrogación F interrogation
interrogador -ora MF questioner; ADJ questioning
interrogar[40] VI/VT (la policía) to interrogate; (con intensidad) to grill; (a un testigo) to question, to cross-examine
interrogativo ADJ interrogative
interrogatorio M interrogation, questioning
interrumpir VI/VT (cortar) to interrupt; VT (servicios) to disrupt, to cut off; (producción de un modelo) to discontinue; (en una conversación) to intrude, to cut in; (software) to abort
interrupción F interruption; (en una conversación) intrusion; (de producción) stoppage; (software) abort
interruptor M switch
intersección F intersection
intersticio M interstice
intervalo M (período) interval; (en el teatro) intermission, interlude
intervención F intervention; **— de teléfono** wiretap
intervendrá, intervendría, intervenga, intervengo *ver* intervenir
intervenir[61] VI to intervene; **— un teléfono** to wiretap
interventor -ora ADJ controlling, intervening; MF (en las elecciones) observer; (en lo fiscal) auditor
intervine, interviniendo, interviniera, interviniese *ver* intervenir
interviú F interview
intestino ADJ & M intestine; **— delgado** small intestine; **— grueso** large intestine; **—s** bowels
intimar VI to become friendly
intimidad F intimacy
intimidar VT (una persona) to intimidate; (una tarea) to daunt
íntimo ADJ intimate, close
intitular VT to entitle; **—se** to be entitled
intolerable ADJ intolerable
intolerancia F intolerance, bigotry; **— a la lactosa** lactose intolerance
intolerante ADJ intolerant, narrow-minded
intoxicación F intoxication, poisoning; **— con plomo** lead poisoning; **— por alimentos** food poisoning
intoxicar[30] VT to poison, to intoxicate
intransigente ADJ intransigent, uncompromising
intransitivo ADJ intransitive
intravenoso ADJ IV [intravenous]
intrepidez F fearlessness
intrépido ADJ (sin miedo) intrepid, fearless; (aventurero) adventurous
intriga F intrigue
intrigante MF schemer; ADJ scheming
intrigar[40] VI/VT to intrigue, to scheme
intrincado ADJ intricate
intrínseco ADJ intrinsic
introducción F introduction
introducir[38] VT (incorporar) to introduce; (colocar) to put in, to insert
introduzca, introduzco *ver* introducir
introspección F introspection
introvertido -da ADJ introverted; MF introvert
intrusión F intrusion
intrusivo ADJ intrusive
intruso -sa ADJ intruding; MF intruder
intubación F intubation
intuición F intuition
intuir[19] VT to sense
intuitivo ADJ intuitive
inundación F flood
inundar VI/VT (de agua, de pedidos) to inundate, to flood; (de regalos) to shower
inusitado ADJ unusual
inútil ADJ (medida) useless, pointless; (esfuerzo) futile; (persona) worthless, good-for-nothing
inutilidad F uselessness; (de un esfuerzo) futility
inutilizar[47] VT to render useless, to put out of

commission
invadir VI/VT to invade
invalidar VT to render invalid
inválido -da ADJ (discapacitado) invalid; (nulo) void; MF invalid
invalorable ADJ priceless, invaluable
invariable ADJ invariable
invasión F invasion
invasivo ADJ invasive
invasor -ora MF invader; ADJ invading
invencible ADJ invincible
invención F invention (también mentira); (mental) construct
inventar VT (un dispositivo) to invent; (una historia) to fabricate, to make up
inventariar[28] VT to inventory
inventario M inventory
inventiva F ingenuity
inventivo ADJ inventive
invento M invention
inventor -ora MF inventor
invernadero M greenhouse, hothouse; **efecto —** greenhouse effect
invernal ADJ wintry
invernar[1] VI to winter
inverosímil ADJ unlikely, farfetched
inversión F (trasposición) inversion; (financiera) investment
inversionista MF investor
inverso ADJ inverse, reverse; **a la inversa** the other way around
inversor -ora MF investor
invertir[8] VT (dar vuelta) to invert, to reverse; VI/VT (dinero) to invest
investidura F inauguration, investment
investigación F (policial) investigation, inquiry; (científica) research
investigador -ora MF investigator; (científico) researcher
investigar[40] VI/VT (policía) to investigate, to look into; (científico) to research
investir[9] VI/VT to invest; **— de un cargo** to induct into office
invicto ADJ unbeaten
invierno M winter
invierta, invierte, invirtiendo, invirtiera, invirtiese, invirtió *ver* invertir
invisible ADJ (no visible) invisible; (oculto) unseen
invitación F invitation
invitado -da MF guest
invitar VI/VT to invite
invocación F invocation
invocar[30] VT (razones, argumentos) to invoke; (espíritus) to conjure
involucrar VT (implicar) to implicate; (consistir de) to involve
involuntario ADJ (automático) involuntary; (accidental) inadvertent
inyección F (en medicina) injection, shot; (en coches) fuel injection
inyectado ADJ **— de sangre** bloodshot
inyectar VT to inject
ion, ión M ion
ionizar[47] VT to ionize
ir[64] VI to go; **— a caballo** to ride horseback; **— a pie** to walk; **— [a] por** to fetch; **— aprendiendo** to learn gradually; **— corriendo** to run; **— de mal en peor** to go from bad to worse; **— en coche** to drive/ride in a car; **— tirando** to scrape along; **no me va ni me viene** it's all the same to me; **¿cómo te va?** how are you? **los platos no van aquí** the plates don't belong here; **¡vaya!** well now! **¡vaya a saber uno!** go figure! **¡vamos!** let's go! come on! **¡vaya hombre!** what a man! **¡ve a freír espárragos!** take a hike! **va por dos años que me casé** it's going on two years since I got married; **voy a comer** I'm going to eat; **va y se come un hongo venenoso** she goes and eats a poisonous mushroom; **en lo que va del año** since the beginning of the year; **ya van siete veces que me lo dice** that makes seven times that she's told me; **voy a ir de rojo** I'm going dressed in red; **para que no vayas a creer** lest you should think; **no vayas a caerte** don't fall; **¡qué va!** no way! **—se** to go away, to leave; **—se a la quiebra** to go broke; **—se a las manos** to come to blows; **—se a pique** to founder; **—se de vacaciones** to take a vacation
ira F ire, wrath
Irak M Iraq
Irán M Iran
iraní ADJ & MF Iranian
iraquí ADJ & MF Iraqi
irascible ADJ irascible, quick-tempered
iridiscente ADJ iridescent
iris M iris
Irlanda F Ireland
irlandés -esa MF Irish; ADJ Irish
IRM [imagen por resonancia magnética] F MRI
ironía F irony
irónico ADJ ironic, wry
irracional ADJ irrational, unreasonable
irradiar VT to radiate, to irradiate
irreal ADJ unreal
irreconocible ADJ unrecognizable
irrecuperable ADJ irretrievable
irreflexivo ADJ thoughtless
irrefutable ADJ irrefutable
irregular ADJ (situación) irregular; (borde, filo) ragged; (pulso) unsteady; (superficie) rough, uneven; (comportamiento) erratic, haphazard
irregularidad F irregularity

irremediable ADJ hopeless
irremplazable ADJ irreplaceable
irreparable ADJ irreparable
irreprochable ADJ irreproachable, flawless
irresistible ADJ irresistible
irrespetuoso ADJ disrespectful
irresponsabilidad F irresponsibility
irresponsable ADJ irresponsible
irreverente ADJ irreverent
irreversible ADJ irreversible
irrevocable ADJ irrevocable
irrigación F irrigation
irrigar[40] VI/VT to irrigate
irritable ADJ irritable
irritación F irritation
irritante ADJ (molesto) irritating, grating; (agresivo) abrasive
irritar VI/VT to irritate, to aggravate
irrumpir VI to burst into
isla F island, isle; **—s Fiyi** Fiji Islands; **—s Malvinas** Falkland Islands; **—s Marshall** Marshall Islands; **—s Salomón** Solomon Islands; **—s Vírgenes** Virgin Islands
islam, Islam M Islam
islámico ADJ Islamic
islamismo M Islam
islandés -esa MF Icelander; ADJ Icelandic
Islandia F Iceland
isleño -ña MF islander
isobara F isobar
isométrico ADJ isometric
isótopo M isotope
Israel M Israel
israelí ADJ & MF Israeli
istmo M isthmus
Italia F Italy
italiano -na ADJ & MF Italian
itálico ADJ italic; F **itálica** italics
ítem M item
itinerante ADJ itinerant
itinerario M itinerary
IVA [impuesto al valor añadido/agregado] M sales tax, VAT
izar[47] VT to hoist, to raise
izquierda F left (también política); (mano) left hand; **a la —** to the left
izquierdista ADJ & MF leftist
izquierdo ADJ left

Jj

jab M jab
jabalí M [wild] boar
jabalina F javelin
jabón M soap
jabonera F soap dish
jabonoso ADJ soapy
jaca F nag
jacinto M hyacinth
jactancia F boastfulness
jactancioso ADJ boastful, blustering
jactarse VI to boast, to brag
jacuzzi M Jacuzzi™, hot tub
jade M jade
jadear VI to pant, to gasp
jadeo M panting, gasping
jaez M harness
jaguar M jaguar
jalar VI/VT to pull, to tug
jalea F jelly
jaleo M (lío) mess; (barahúnda) ruckus
jam M jam session
Jamaica F Jamaica
jamaicano -na ADJ & MF Jamaican
jamaiquino -na ADJ & MF Jamaican
jamás ADV never
jamelgo M hack
jamón M ham
Japón M Japan
japonés -esa ADJ & MF Japanese
jaque M check; **— mate** checkmate; **tener a uno en —** *fam* to have someone by the short hairs
jaqueca F migraine
jarabe M syrup; **— de ipecacuana** ipecac syrup
jarana F revelry; **ir de —** to paint the town red
jarcia F rigging
jardín M (de flores) garden; (de césped) yard; (béisbol) outfield; **— de niños** kindergarten; **— infantil** nursery
jardinero -ra MF (de oficio) gardener; (en béisbol) outfielder
jarra F (cántaro) jug, pitcher; (taza) mug; **en —s** akimbo
jarro M pitcher, jug
jarrón M vase
jaspe M (piedra silícea) jasper; (mármol) veined marble
jaula F cage, coop
jauría F pack
jazmín M jasmine
jazz M jazz
jeans M PL jeans
jefatura F headquarters
jefe MF, **jefa** F (laboral) boss; (militar) commander; (departamental) chair, head; (policial) chief; **— del estado mayor** chief of staff; **— de departamento** department head
jején M gnat
jengibre M ginger
jerarquía F hierarchy
jerez M sherry
jerga F jargon, slang

jerigonza F (sinsentido) gibberish, gobbledygook; (juego lingüístico) pig Latin
jeringa F syringe
jeringar[40] VT to annoy
jeroglífico ADJ & M hieroglyphic
jersey M sweater
jesuita ADJ & M Jesuit
Jesús INTERJ God bless you! gesundheit!
jeta F (hocico) snout; (cara) mug
jet-set M jet set
jilguero M goldfinch
jinete M rider
jinetear VI to ride horseback
jingle M jingle
jirafa F giraffe
jobar INTERJ holy cow! holy Moses! holy mackerel!
jóckey M jockey
jocoso ADJ jocular
jofaina F basin
jogging M jogging
jolgorio M rumpus
jonrón M home run
Jordania F Jordan
jordano -na ADJ & MF Jordanian
jornada F (día laboral) workday; (coloquio) colloquium
jornal M daily wage
jornalero -ra MF day laborer
joroba F hump
jorobado -da ADJ & MF hunchback
jorobar VT (molestar) to hassle; (estropear) to gum up
jota F jay; **no saber ni —** to know zilch
joven ADJ young; MF young person
jovial ADJ jolly
joya F jewel; (persona apreciada) gem; **—s** jewelry
joyería F jewelry store, jeweler's
joyero -ra MF jeweler
joystick M joystick
juanete M bunion
jubilación F (retiro) retirement; (pagos) pension; **— anticipada** early retirement
jubilado ADJ retired; MF retiree
jubilar VT to pension, to retire; **—se** to retire
jubileo M jubilee
júbilo M glee
jubiloso ADJ jubilant, joyous
judaísmo M Judaism
judicial ADJ judicial
judío -ía ADJ Jewish; MF Jew; F bean; **judía blanca** navy bean; **judía pinta** pinto bean; **judía verde** green bean
juego M (actividad recreativa) play; (deporte) game; (conjunto de piezas) set; (muebles) suite; **— de apuestas** gambling; **— de damas** checkers; **— ofimático** office suite; **— de palabras** pun, play on words; **—s Olímpicos** Olympic Games; **estar en —** to be at stake; **hacer —** to match
juerga F binge; **irse de —** to go on a binge, to party
juerguista MF merrymaker
jueves M Thursday
juez MF, **jueza** F (en un tribunal) judge; (en deportes) referee; **— de paz** justice of the peace; **— de línea** linesman; **— de silla** judge, umpire
jugada F play, move; **— de tres puntos** three-point play
jugador -ora MF (deportista) player; (apostador) gambler
jugar[43] VI to play; (apostar) to gamble; **— a la baraja / a los naipes** to play cards; **— con fuego** to play with fire; **— en casa** to play a home game; **— limpio** to play fair; **—se** to risk
jugarreta F bad turn
jugo M juice
jugoso ADJ juicy
juguete M plaything, toy
juguetear VI to toy with, to fiddle with
juguetón -ona ADJ playful
juicio M (criterio) judgment; (proceso) trial; **— por quiebra** bankruptcy proceedings; **perder el —** to lose one's mind; **a mi —** in my estimation
juicioso ADJ sensible, judicious
juke-box M jukebox
julio M July
jumbo ADJ jumbo; M jumbo jet
jumper M jumper
junco M (planta) rush, reed; (barco chino) junk
jungla F jungle
junio M June
junta F (reunión) meeting; (concejo) council; (juntura) joint; (pieza de motor) gasket; **— directiva** board of directors
juntar VT (tubos) to attach; (flores) to gather, to pick; (ganado) to round up, to wrangle; **— polvo** to gather dust; **— valor** to muster courage; **—se** (acumularse) to gather; (asociarse) to band together; (reunirse) to come together
junto ADJ together; LOC ADV **— a** next to; **— con** together with
juntura F (lugar) juncture; (articulación) joint
jurado -da MF (individuo) juror; M (grupo) jury
juramentar VI/VT to swear in; **—se** to be sworn in
juramento M oath; **— hipocrático** Hippocratic oath
jurar VI/VT to swear, to vow; **— en falso** to perjure oneself; **— la bandera** to pledge allegiance to the flag
jurídico ADJ legal
jurisdicción F jurisdiction

jurisprudencia F (doctrina) jurisprudence; (derecho) law
justa F joust, tilt
justamente ADV (exactamente) precisely; (con justicia) fairly
justicia F justice
justificación F justification
justificar[30] VT to justify
justo ADJ (ecuánime) just; (equitativo) equitable; (pío) righteous, upright; ADV exactly, right; **— después de** right after; **— en ese momento** exactly at that moment
juvenil ADJ (inmaduro) juvenile; (de apariencia joven) youthful
juventud F youth
juzgado M court
juzgar[40] VI/VT to judge, to pass judgment [on]; **— mal** to misjudge

Kk

kaki M khaki
kart M go-cart
kayak M kayak
Kazajstán M Kazakhstan
kazako -ka ADJ & MF Kazak[h]
Kenia F Kenya
keniata ADJ & MF Kenyan
kermés F bazaar
keroseno M kerosene
ketchup M catsup, ketchup
kg *ver* kilogramo
kilo M kilo
kilobyte M kilobyte
kilogramo M kilogram
kilometraje M mileage
kilómetro M kilometer
kilovatio M kilowatt; F **—-hora** kilowatt-hour
Kirguistán M Kyrgyzstan
Kiribati M Kiribati
kosher ADJ kosher
Kuwait M Kuwait
kuwaití ADJ & MF Kuwaiti

Ll

la ART DEF F the; **— del sombrero verde** the one with the green hat, that one with the green hat; PRON PERS it, her; PRON REL **— que** she who, the one that
laberinto M labyrinth, maze
labia F gift of gab
labial ADJ labial
labihendido N harelipped
labio M lip; **—s agrietados** chapped lips; **— leporino** cleft lip, harelip; **con — leporino** harelipped
labor F (trabajo) labor; (tarea) task; (manualidad) handiwork
laboral ADJ work-related; **legislación —** labor legislation
laboratorio M laboratory
laborioso ADJ (trabajoso) laborious; (trabajador) hardworking
laborterapia F occupational therapy
labrado ADJ carved
labrador -ora MF (persona) farmhand; M (perro) labrador
labranza F plowing
labrar VT to till; **—se una carrera** to carve out a career
laca F lacquer
lacar[30] VT to lacquer
lacayo M lackey, flunky
laciar VT *RP* to straighten
lacio ADJ straight
lacónico ADJ (persona) laconic; (comentario) terse
lacra F (física) scar; (moral) blight
lacre M sealing wax
lacrimógeno ADJ tear-producing
lactancia F lactation; **— materna** breast-feeding
lactar VT to nurse
lácteo ADJ (como la leche) milky; (hecho de leche) dairy
lactosa F lactose
LAD [lipoproteína de alta densidad] F HDL
ladeado ADJ (torcido) awry, askew; (asimétrico) lopsided
ladear VT (una superficie) to tilt; (la cabeza) to cock; (un avión) to bank; (ignorar) to snub, to ignore; **—se** to tilt, to lean
ladeo M tilt
ladera F hillside
ladilla F crab louse
ladillo M sidebar
ladino ADJ artful
lado M side; **— a —** side by side; **al —** nearby; **¡a un —!** gangway! **de —** sideways; **hacerse a un —** to move over
ladrar VI (perro) to bark; VI/VT (persona) to snap [at]
ladrido M bark, barking
ladrillo M brick
ladrón -ona MF (de casas) burglar; (con violencia) robber; (con astucia) thief; (de tiendas) shoplifter
lagartija F (animal) lizard; (ejercicio) push-up
lagarto M alligator; **— varano** monitor lizard

lago M lake
lágrima F tear, teardrop
lagrimear VI to weep
laguna F (de agua) lagoon; (de la memoria, conocimiento) gap; (legal) loophole
laico -ca MF layperson; ADJ lay
laja F slab
lamentable ADJ (desafortunado) lamentable, regrettable; (ruinoso) woeful
lamentablemente ADV unfortunately
lamentación F lamentation
lamentar VT (una acción) to lament, to regret; (una muerte) to grieve; **—se** to lament, to wail
lamento M lament, lamentation
lamer VT (pasar la lengua) to lick; (rozar) to lap
lamida F lick
lámina F (de vidrio, metal) sheet; (de metal) plate; (grabado) print
laminar VT to laminate
lámpara F lamp
lamparilla F night-light
lampiño ADJ (sin pelo) hairless; (sin barba) beardless
lana F wool; **— de acero** steel wool
lanar ADJ wool-bearing
lance M incident
lancear VT to lance, to spear
lanceta F lancet, lance
lancha F launch, boat; **— a motor** motorboat
langosta F (crustáceo) lobster; (insecto) locust
langostino M prawn
languidecer[35] VI to languish, to wilt
languidez F languor
lánguido ADJ languid, listless
lanilla F flannel
lanolina F lanolin
lanudo ADJ wooly, shaggy
lanza F lance, spear; **romper una — por alguien** to stick one's neck out for someone
lanzadera F shuttle
lanzador -ora MF (beisbol) pitcher
lanzamiento M (de un cohete, producto) launch; (de suministros) drop; (de una roca grande) heave; (de una pelota, en béisbol) pitch; (en tenis) toss
lanzar[47] VT (un cohete) to launch; (un producto) to launch, to roll out; (una pelota) to throw; (una bala) to fire; (algo pesado) to heave; (lodo) to sling; VI/VT (vomitar) to puke; **—se** to launch forth/out; **— un tiro libre** to shoot a free throw; M SG **—llamas** flamethrower
lanzazo M thrust with a lance
Laos M Laos
laosiano -na ADJ & MF Laotian
lápida F (piedra) stone tablet; (de sepultura) gravestone, tombstone
lapidar VT to stone
lapidario ADJ & M lapidary
lápiz M pencil; **— de color** crayon; **— de labios** lipstick
lapso M lapse, span
lapsus M lapse, slip of the tongue
laptop M laptop
laquear VT to lacquer
largar[40] VT (soltar) to cough up; **—se** *fam* to scram, to buzz off, to shove off
largo ADJ (camino, cuento) long; (discurso) lengthy; **de — alcance** long-range; **¡— de aquí!** scram! M **—metraje** feature film; **a la larga** in the long run; **a lo —** lengthwise; M length
larguero M crossbar
largueza F generosity
larguirucho ADJ lanky
largura F length
laringe F larynx
laringitis F laryngitis
larva F larva
láser M laser
lástima F pity; **¡qué —!** what a shame!
lastimadura F hurt
lastimar VT (herir) to hurt; (insultar) to hurt one's feelings; **—se** to get hurt
lastimoso ADJ pitiful
lastrar VT to ballast
lastre M ballast
lata F (envase) tin can, can; (con tapa) canister; (pesadez) bore; **dar la —** to be a nuisance
latente ADJ latent, dormant
lateral ADJ lateral, side
látex M latex
latido M (individual) beat, throb; (colectivo) beating; (del corazón) heartbeat
latifundio M large estate
latigazo M (golpe) lash; (chasquido) crack of a whip
látigo M whip
latín M Latin
latino -na ADJ (relativo a los hispanos) Latino; (relativo a la lengua latina) Latin; M Latino; F Latina
Latinoamérica F Latin America
latinoamericano ADJ Latin American
latir VI to beat, to throb
latitud F latitude (también flexibilidad)
latón M brass
latrocinio M larceny
laudable ADJ laudable
laurel M laurel; **dormirse sobre los —es** to rest on one's laurels
lava F lava
lavable ADJ washable
lavabo M (retrete) lavatory, toilet; (recipiente) sink
lavadero M laundry; **— automático** Laundromat™
lavado M wash, washing; **— de cerebro**

brainwashing; **— de dinero** money laundering; **— en seco** dry cleaning
lavadora F washing machine
lavanda F lavender
lavandera F washerwoman
lavandería F laundry
lavar VI/VT to wash; (ropa) to launder; **—se** to wash up; **—se las manos** to wash one's hands; M SG **lavaplatos/lavavajillas** dishwasher
lavativa F enema
lavatorio M washroom
laxante M laxative
laxitud F laxity
laxo ADJ lax
lazada F bowknot
lazar[47] VT to lasso
lazarillo M (persona) guide for the blind; (perro) guide dog
lazo M (soga) lasso, rope; (vuelta) loop; (nudo corredizo) noose; (relación) tie, bond
LBD [lipoproteína de baja densidad] F LDL
le PRON PERS **— dije** I told you/him/her; **— vi** *Esp* I saw him/you; **se — murió el perro** his/her dog died on him/her
leal ADJ loyal, trusty
lealtad F loyalty, allegiance; **— de marca** brand loyalty
lección F lesson, assignment; **darle una — a alguien** to teach someone a lesson
lechada F whitewash
leche F (de vaca) milk; **— desnatada** skim milk; **— en polvo** powdered milk; **— entera** whole milk; **— homogeneizada** homogenized milk; **— malteada** malted milk; **mala —** nasty disposition; **ir a toda —** to barrel along; **ese tío es la —** that guy's a case; **es un mala —** *fam* he's a nasty creep
lechería F dairy
lechero -ra ADJ dairy; M milkman; F milkmaid
lecho M bed (también de río)
lechón M suckling pig
lechoso ADJ milky
lechuga F lettuce
lechuza F screech owl, barn owl
lector -ora MF reader; **— de código de barras** bar code reader; M **— de tarjetas** card reader
lectura F (acción) reading; (material) reading matter
leer[18] VI/VT to read
legación F legation
legado M legacy, bequest
legajo M file
legal ADJ legal, lawful
legalidad F (conjunto de normas) law; (cualidad de legal) legality
legalización F (de un documento) authentication; (de una actividad) legalization; **— de una validación testamentaria** probate
legalizar[47] VT to legalize
legar[40] VT to will, to bequeath
legendario ADJ legendary
leggings M PL leggings
legible ADJ (descifrable) legible; (fácil de leer) readable
legión F legion
legionario M legionnaire
legionelosis F legionnaire's disease
legislación F legislation
legislador -ora MF legislator, lawmaker
legislar VI/VT to legislate
legislativo ADJ legislative
legislatura F legislature
legitimidad F legitimacy
legítimo ADJ legitimate, lawful, rightful
lego -ga MF layperson; ADJ lay
legua F league
legumbre F legume
leído ADJ well-read
lejanía F distance
lejano ADJ (distancia) distant, faraway; (parentesco) remote
lejía F (producto de limpieza) bleach; (de sosa) lye
lejos ADV far away, far; **a lo —** in the distance; **— de** far from; **desde —** from afar
lelo ADJ silly
lema M (frase típica) motto; (propaganda política) slogan
lencería F lingerie
lengua F (órgano) tongue; (idioma) language; **— materna** mother tongue
lenguado M sole
lenguaje M language (también en informática); **— compilador** compiler language; **— corporal** body language; **— [de] máquina** machine language; **— de programación** programming language; **— de signos** sign language; **— ensamblador** assembly language
lenguaraz ADJ gossipy
lengüeta F (de un instrumento de viento) reed; (de un zapato) tongue
lengüetazo M lick
lentamente ADV slowly
lente MF lens; **— filtrador** filter lens; **—s** eyeglasses; **—s de contacto** contact lenses; **—s negros/oscuros** sunglasses, shades
lenteja F lentil
lentitud F slowness
lento ADJ (despacioso) slow; (tonto) dull; (letárgico) sluggish; ADV slowly
leña F firewood
leñador -ora MF woodcutter, lumberjack
leñera F woodshed
leño M log
leñoso ADJ woody

león M lion; **— marino** sea lion
León M Leon
leona F lioness
leonés ADJ Leonese
leopardo M leopard
lepra F leprosy
lerdo ADJ slow
lesbiano -na ADJ lesbian; F lesbian
lesión F injury, lesion; **— ocular** eye injury
lesionar VT to injure; **—se** to get injured
Lesotho M Lesotho
letal ADJ lethal
letárgico ADJ lethargic
letargo M lethargy
letón -ona ADJ & MF Latvian
Letonia F Latvia
letra F (del alfabeto) letter; (caligrafía) handwriting; (de una canción) lyrics, words; **— bastardilla/cursiva** italics; **— chica** fine print; **— de cambio** bill of exchange; **— de imprenta** block letter; **— manuscrita** longhand; **sin —s** uneducated
letrado ADJ learned, literate
letrero M sign
letrina F latrine
leucemia F leukemia
leudar VI to rise; VT to leaven
leva F (de tropas) levy; (de motor) cam
levadura F leaven, yeast
levantamiento M (revuelta) uprising; (suspensión) suspension; **— de pesas** weight-lifting
levantar VT (la mano) to raise; (una caja) to lift; (un interruptor) to switch; (del piso) to pick up; (perdices) to flush; (a un dormido) to wake up, to rouse; (un edificio) to put up; **— el campamento** to break camp; **— falso testimonio** to bear false witness; **— la mesa** to clear the table; **— la sesión** to adjourn the meeting; **— vuelo** to take flight; **—se** (de la cama) to get up, to rise, to arise; (de una silla) to stand up, to get up; (un edificio) to go up
levar VT **— anclas** to weigh anchor
leve ADJ (brisa) light; (resfrío) mild; (problema) slight
levedad F (de una brisa) lightness; (de un resfrío) mildness
levemente ADV lightly
léxico M lexicon, dictionary; ADJ lexical
lexicografía F lexicography
ley F law, statute; **— de prescripción** statute of limitations; **— de [los] rendimientos decrecientes** law of diminishing returns; **— marcial** martial law; **de buena —** of good quality
leyenda F (mitología) legend; (texto que acompaña una figura) caption
leyendo, leyera, leyese, leyeron *ver* leer
liar[28] VT (paquetes) to bundle; (cigarros) to roll; **—se** to get involved
libanés -esa ADJ & MF Lebanese
Líbano M Lebanon
libelo M libel
libélula F dragonfly
liberación F (de un país ocupado) liberation; (de pecados) deliverance; (de presos) release
liberal ADJ & MF liberal
liberalidad F liberality
liberalismo M liberalism
liberalización F liberalization
liberar VT (de un deber) to relieve; (a un pueblo) to liberate; (del sufrimiento) to deliver; (a un preso) to free, to release
Liberia F Liberia
liberiano -na ADJ & MF Liberian
líbero M sweeper
libertad F liberty, freedom; **— condicional** parole; **— de expresión** free speech; **poner en —** to set free; **poner en — bajo fianza** to let out on bail; **poner en — condicional** to parole
libertador -ora MF liberator
libertar VT to liberate
libertinaje M licentiousness
libertino -na MF libertine
Libia F Libya
libidinoso ADJ libidinous
libido F libido
libio -bia ADJ & MF Libyan
libra F pound (también moneda)
librar VT (a un preso) to free, to set free; (de una obligación) to release; (un cheque) to write; (una letra de cambio) to draft; (una guerra) to wage; **—se de** to get rid of
libre ADJ (persona) free; (asiento) vacant; (camino) clear; (traducción) loose; (de una obligación) exempt; **— albedrío** free will; **— cambio/comercio** free trade; **— de cargos** toll-free; **— de gravámenes** free and clear; **— de intereses** interest-free; **— de impuestos** duty-free, tax-free; **— de virus** virus-free; **— pensador** freethinker
librería F bookstore
librero -ra MF bookseller
libresco ADJ bookish
libreta F small notebook; **— de direcciones** address book
libreto M libretto
libro M book; **— de bolsa** pocket book; **— de cocina** cookbook; **— de texto** textbook; **— electrónico** e-book; **— en rústica** paperback; **— mayor** ledger
licencia F (carnet de conducir, libertad poética) license; (permiso) leave; (permiso para ausentarse) leave of absence; **— de sitio** site license; **— por maternidad** maternity leave
licenciado -da MF college graduate

licenciar VT to discharge; **—se** to graduate from college
licenciatura F bachelor's degree
licencioso ADJ licentious
liceo M high school
licitación F bid
lícito ADJ lawful, permissible
licor M liqueur, cordial
licuadora F blender
líder MF leader
liderar VT to head up
liderar VT to lead
liderazgo M (de una organización, condición de líder) leadership; (en una competencia) lead
lidiar VI/VT to contend, to grapple
liebre F hare; **levantar la —** to let the cat out of the bag
Liechtenstein M Liechtenstein
liechtensteiniano-na MF Liechtensteiner
lienzo M canvas
liftado M top spin
lifting M face-lift
liga F (alianza, grupo deportivo) league; (cinta elástica) garter; **— mayor** major league
ligado M slur
ligadura F ligature
ligamento M ligament
ligar[40] VT (atar) to bind; (conectar notas) to slur; VI (conquistar sexualmente) to score; **—se** to bind; **—se las trompas** to have one's tubes tied
ligeramente ADV lightly
ligereza F (de peso) lightness; (de temperamento) levity
ligero ADJ (poco pesado) light; (rápido) swift; (pequeño) slight; **a la ligera** lightly
liguero M garter belt
lija F sandpaper
lijar VI/VT to sandpaper, to sand
lila ADJ & MF lilac
lima F (fruta) lime; (árbol) lime tree; **— de uñas** nail file
limar VI/VT to file
limero M lime tree
limitación F (restricción) limitation; (defecto) shortcoming
limitar VT (restringir) to limit; (gastos) to curb; **—se a** to limit oneself to
límite M (restricción) limit; (de una región) boundary; (de la paciencia) bounds; **— de edad** age limit; **— de tiempo** time limit; **— de velocidad** speed limit
limítrofe ADJ bordering
limo M slime
limón M lemon
limonada F lemonade
limonero M lemon tree
limosna F alms, handout
limpiador M cleanser
limpiar VI/VT to clean; VT (una superficie) to wipe; (la piel) to cleanse; (un camino, una pantalla de computadora, la reputación) to clear; (animales) to dress; (zapatos) to shine; (un derrame) to mop up, to wipe up; (dejar sin dinero) to clean out; M SG **limpiaparabrisas** windshield wiper; M SG **limpiavidrios** squeegee
límpido ADJ limpid
limpieza F (pulcritud) cleanliness, neatness; (operación militar) mop-up; **— étnica** ethnic cleansing
limpio ADJ (casa) clean, neat; (piel, conciencia) clear; (juego) fair; (sin dinero) broke; **pasar en —** to make a clean copy
limusina F limousine
linaje M lineage, ancestry
linaza F linseed
lince M (animal) lynx; (persona astuta) sly fox; **con ojos de —** sharp-eyed
linchar VT to lynch
lindante ADJ neighboring
lindar VI to border, to adjoin
linde MF boundary
lindero ADJ adjoining; M boundary
lindo ADJ pretty; **un día —** a nice day; **de lo —** a lot
línea F (raya, cola) line; (en béisbol) line drive; **— aérea** airline; **— de banda** (fútbol) sideline; **— de conducta** course of action; **— de crédito** credit line; **— de fondo** baseline; **— de golpeo** line of scrimmage; **— de meta** goal line; **— de montaje** assembly line; **— ofensiva** offensive line; **batear una —** to line out; **en —** online
lineal ADJ linear
linfa F lymph
linfocito M lymphocyte
linfoma M lymphoma
lingüista MF linguist
lingüística F linguistics
lingüístico ADJ linguistic
linimento M liniment
lino M (tela) linen; (fibra) flax
linóleo M linoleum
linterna F (a pilas, de bolsillo) flashlight; (de un faro) lantern
lío M (bulto) bundle; (enredo, molestia) mess, hassle; (amorío) affair, fling; **armar un —** to raise a ruckus; **meterse en un —** to get oneself into a mess
liofilizar VI/VT to freeze-dry
liposucción F liposuction
liquidación F (ajuste de cuentas, de bienes) settlement, liquidation; (rebaja) sale, clearance sale; (pago completo) payment in full
liquidar VT (bienes, mercancías) to liquidate, to sell off; (una cuenta, herencia) to settle; (a

una persona) *fam* to waste, to off, to whack
liquidez F liquidity
líquido ADJ & M liquid; **— amniótico** amniotic fluid
lira F (moneda) lira
lírica F lyric poetry
lírico ADJ lyric, lyrical
lirio M iris, lily; **— de los valles** lily of the valley
lirismo M lyricism
lisiado ADJ (descapacitado) handicapped; (lesionado) injured
lisiar VT to handicap
liso ADJ (neumático) bald; (camino) even, smooth; (terreno) flat; (pelo) straight; **azul —** solid blue
lisonja F flattery
lisonjear VI/VT to flatter
lisonjero -ra MF flatterer; ADJ flattering
lista F (de palabras) list; (de miembros) roster; (de alumnos) roll; (banda) stripe; (de precios) schedule, list; **— de control** checklist; **— de correo** mailing list; **— de espera** waiting list; **— negra** blacklist; **pasar —** to call the roll
listado ADJ striped; M listing, printout
listo ADJ (preparado) ready, set; (inteligente) clever, smart; **hacerse el —** to pull a stunt
listón M (tabla) board; (en salto de altura) crossbar
lisura F smoothness
litera F (cama en el tren, barco) berth; (cama superpuesta) bunk bed
literal ADJ literal
literario ADJ literary
literato -ta MF writer
literatura F literature
litigante MF litigant
litigio M (pleito) lawsuit; (acción de litigar) litigation
litio M lithium
litoral ADJ seaside; M seaboard, seacoast
litro M liter
Lituania F Lithuania
lituano -na ADJ & MF Lithuanian
liviano ADJ (leve) light; (promiscuo) promiscuous
lívido ADJ livid
living M living room
llaga F sore
llama F (fuego) flame; (animal) llama
llamada F (de teléfono, a la acción) call; (grito) hail; (nota al pie) footnote; **— de cobro revertido / por cobrar** collect call
llamado M (acción de convocar) call; (petición) appeal
llamador M knocker
llamamiento M (conversación) call; (exhortación) appeal; **hacer un —** to appeal
llamar VT (un nombre, una huelga, por teléfono) to call; (a la puerta) to knock; (gritar) to hail; **— la atención** to call attention; **me llamo Juan** my name is Juan
llamarada F blaze, flare
llamativo ADJ (impactante) striking, bold; (chabacano) gaudy, flashy
llameante ADJ flaming
llamear VI to flare, to flame
llana F trowel
llano ADJ (sencillo) plain; (liso) flat, smooth, level; (de poca profundidad) shallow; M plain
llanta F (reborde metálico) rim; (neumático) tire
llanto M crying, weeping
llanura F plain, prairie
llave F (para puertas) key; (de armas de fuego) lock; (en lucha libre) lock, hold; (grifo) faucet, tap; (interruptor) light switch; (de gas) cock; **— de tuercas** wrench; **— inglesa** pipe wrench; **— maestra** master key
llavero M key ring
llegada F arrival
llegar[40] VI (arribar) to arrive, to get there/here; (alcanzar) to reach; **— a las manos** to come to blows; **— a ser** to become; **— a un acuerdo** to strike a deal; **— a un arreglo** to cut a deal; **— tarde** to be late
llenar VT (un recipiente) to fill; (un formulario) to fill out; **— el tanque** to tank up, to gas up; **—se** to fill up; **—se de** to get filled with; **—se de oro** to make a killing
lleno ADJ full; **— de** full of; **de —** totally; M **un — completo** a full house
llevadero ADJ bearable
llevar VT (transportar) to carry, to take; (transportar en coche) to drive; (tener puesto) to wear; (contener) to hold; (inducir) to lead, to drive; **— a cabo** to carry out; **— la cuenta** to keep score; **— la ventaja** to have an advantage; **— los libros** to keep the books; **— un mes aquí** to have been here one month; **le llevo dos años a mi hermano** I'm two years older than my brother; **llevo las de perder** the odds are against me; **—se** to carry away, to take away; **—se bien con** to get along with
llorar VI (con ruido) to cry, to bawl; (con lágrimas) to weep; VT (una pérdida) to lament; (una muerte) to mourn
lloriquear VI to whimper
lloriqueo M whimper
llorón -ona ADJ weeping; MF crybaby, whiner
lloroso ADJ tearful, weeping
llovedizo ADJ **agua llovediza** rainwater
llover[6] VI/VT to rain; **— a cántaros** to rain cats and dogs; **llueva o truene** rain or shine
lloviznа F drizzle
lloviznar VI to drizzle, to mist
lluvia F (precipitación) rain; (de preguntas,

críticas) barrage; (de protestas, flechas, piedras) volley; (de golpes, chispas) shower; **— ácida** acid rain; **— de ideas** brainstorming; **— torrencial** driving rain

lluvioso ADJ rainy

lo PRON PERS **— bueno** the good thing; **— de la protesta** the matter of the protest; **— que quiero** what I want; **sé — bueno que eres** I know how good you are; **yo — vi** I saw it/him/you

loable ADJ laudable, praiseworthy

loar VT to laud

lobato M wolf cub

lobbista, lobista MF lobbyist

lobby M lobby

lobezno M wolf cub

lobo M wolf

lobotomía F lobotomy

lóbrego ADJ gloomy

lóbulo M lobe

local ADJ local; M premises

localidad F (pueblo) town, locality; (en un teatro) seat

localización F location

localizar[47] VT (encontrar) to locate; (limitar) to localize

loción F lotion

loco-ca ADJ insane, mad, crazy; **— de remate** stark raving mad; MF lunatic, insane person; M madman

locomotora F locomotive, train engine

locuaz ADJ garrulous, loquacious

locura F madness, insanity

locutor-ora MF radio announcer

lodazal M quagmire

lodo M mud

lodoso ADJ muddy

logaritmo M logarithm

logia F lodge

lógica F logic

lógicamente ADV logically

lógico ADJ (razonado) logical; (bien fundado) sound

logística F logistics

lograr VT to achieve, to accomplish; **logré convencerle** I managed to / succeeded in convincing him

logro M (lo conseguido) accomplishment, achievement; (hazaña) feat

loma F knoll

lombriz F (de tierra) earthworm; (de estómago) tapeworm

lomo M (de animal) back ridge; (corte de carne) loin

lona F canvas

longaniza F cured sausage

longevidad F longevity

longevo ADJ long-lived

longitud F (distancia angular) longitude; (largo) length; **— de onda** wavelength

lonja F (mercado) commodity exchange; (tajada) slice of meat

loquería F *fam* booby hatch, funny farm

loquero-ra MF (psiquiatra) *fam* shrink; M (manicomio) *fam* funny farm

lord M lord

loro M parrot

losa F (lápida) slab; (baldosa) flagstone

lote M lot

lotería F lottery

loza F (basta) crockery; (fina) china

lozanía F freshness, bloom

lozano ADJ fresh, blooming

LSD MF LSD

lubina F bass

lubricante ADJ & M lubricant

lubricar[30] VI/VT to lubricate

lucero M morning star; **— del alba** morning star

lucha F (pugna, contienda) struggle; (pelea) fight; **— libre** wrestling

luchador-ora MF fighter; (en lucha libre) wrestler

luchar VI/VT (contra un enemigo) to fight; (con un problema) to struggle; (en lucha libre) to wrestle; **— por** to strive for

lucidez F lucidity

lúcido ADJ lucid, clear-headed

luciérnaga F firefly, glowworm

lucio M pike

lucir[39] VI (mostrarse) to look; (favorecer, sentar bien) to look good on, to suit; VT (llevar) to model, to sport; (alardear de) to flaunt; **—se** (sobresalir) to excel; (ostentar) to show off

lucrativo ADJ lucrative, profitable

lucro M **sin fines de —** not for profit

luctuoso ADJ sad, mournful, dismal

luego ADV afterward, then, next; **— de** after; **desde —** of course; **hasta —** so long

lugar M place; **— común** platitude; **— de nacimiento** birthplace, place of birth; **— de trabajo** workplace; **dar — a** to give rise to; **no hay —** there's no room; **en — de** instead of

lúgubre ADJ mournful, gloomy

lujo M luxury; **darse un —** to indulge oneself; **con — de detalles** in great detail

lujoso ADJ (ropa) luxurious; (hotel) plush

lujuria F lust

lujurioso ADJ lustful

lumbago M lumbago

lumbar ADJ lumbar

lumbre F (fuego) fire; (luz) light

luminosidad F brilliance, luminosity

luminoso ADJ luminous

luna F (satélite) moon; (espejo) large mirror; **— de miel** honeymoon; **estar en la —** to be distracted; **— llena** full moon

lunar ADJ lunar; M (en la piel) mole; (en una tela) polka dot
lunático -ca ADJ & MF lunatic
lunes M Monday
lupa F magnifying glass
lúpulo M hops
lupus M lupus
lustrar VT to shine, to polish
lustre M luster, shine
lustroso ADJ (revista) glossy; (pelo) shiny, sleek
luto M mourning
luxación F dislocation
Luxemburgo M Luxembourg
luxemburgués -esa MF Luxembourger; ADJ Luxembourgian
luz F light (también aparato); (del sol) sunshine; (abertura) aperture; **— trasera** taillight; **— verde** green light; **dar a —** to give birth; **sacar a —** to disclose

Mm

macabro ADJ grim
macanudo ADJ cool
Macao M Macao
macarrones M PL macaroni
Macedonia F Macedonia
macedonio -nia ADJ & MF Macedonian
maceta F flower pot
machacar[30] VT (aplastar) to pound, to crush; (insistir) to harp on; (en baloncesto) to dunk
machacón ADJ persistent
machetazo M hack with a machete
machete M machete
machismo M [male] chauvinism
macho M (animal masculino) male; (mulo) he-mule; (varón) man; (hombre muy varonil) he-man; **— cabrío** he-goat; **— y hembra** hook and eye; ADJ (masculino) male; (fuerte) strong; INTERJ man!
machote ADJ butch
machucar[30] VT to bruise
macilento ADJ pale
macizo ADJ massive; M plateau
Madagascar M Madagascar
madeja F skein
madera F wood (también en golf); (árboles maderables) timber; (para construcción) lumber; **— contrachapada** plywood; **— flotante** driftwood; **— noble** hardwood; **—s** woodwinds; **tocar —** to knock on wood
maderaje M woodwork
madero M trunk
madrastra F stepmother
madre F mother; **— de alquiler** surrogate mother; **— patria** mother country; **—perla** mother-of-pearl; **— política** mother-in-law; **—selva** honeysuckle; **ciento y la —** everybody and their dog
madriguera F burrow, hole
madrileño -ña ADJ & MF [person] from Madrid
madrina F godmother
madrugada F early morning hours; **a las dos de la —** at two in the morning
madrugador -ra ADJ & MF early bird
madrugar VI to get up early; **— con gripe** to wake up with a cold
maduración F (animales, personas) maturation, maturing; (frutos) ripening; (vino) aging
madurar VI to mature, to grow up
madurez F (de persona) maturity; (de fruta) ripeness
maduro ADJ (persona) mature; (fruta) ripe
maestría F master's degree; **— en administración de empresas** master of business administration
maestro -tra MF (docente) [school]teacher; (artesano) master; (director) maestro
mafia F mafia
mafioso -sa MF mafioso
magia F magic
mágico ADJ magic, magical
magisterio M (actividad) teaching; (conjunto de los maestros) teachers; (profesión) teaching profession
magistrado -da MF magistrate
magistral ADJ masterful, masterly
magma M magma
magnánimo ADJ magnanimous
magnate MF magnate, tycoon
magnesia F magnesia
magnesio M magnesium
magnético ADJ magnetic
magnetismo M magnetism
magnetizar[47] VT to magnetize
magnificar[30] VT to magnify
magnificencia F magnificence
magnífico ADJ (palacio) magnificent; (día) glorious
magnitud F magnitude
magno ADJ great
magnolia F magnolia
magnolio M magnolia tree
mago M magician, wizard
magro ADJ lean
magulladura F bruise, contusion
magullar VI/VT (machucar) to bruise; (mutilar) to mangle
mahonesa F mayonnaise
maicena® F cornstarch
maíz M corn, maize
maizal M cornfield
majadería F stupidity

majadero ADJ stupid
majar VT to pound
majestad F majesty
majestuoso ADJ majestic, stately
majo ADJ (atractivo) good-looking; (agradable) charming
mal M (maldad) evil; (enfermedad) malady, affliction; (daño) harm; **— de altura** altitude sickness; **— de ojo** evil eye; ADV wrong, badly; **— aconsejado** misguided; **— adquirido** ill-gotten; **— hablado** foulmouthed; **hablar — de alguien** to speak ill of someone; **hacer —** to do wrong; **lo hice mal** I did it badly
malabarista MF juggler
malandanza F misfortune
malaria F malaria
Malasia F Malaysia
malasio-sia ADJ & MF Malaysian
Malawi M Malawi
malawiano-na ADJ & MF Malawian
malbaratar VT to undersell
malcontento ADJ discontented
malcriado ADJ spoiled
malcriar VT to spoil
maldad F evil, wickedness
maldecir[51] VI/VT to curse
maldición F curse
maldito ADJ accursed
Maldivas F PL Maldives
maldivo-va ADJ & MF Maldivian
maleable ADJ malleable
maleante MF gangster, hoodlum
malear VT to corrupt
maleducado ADJ ill-mannered, ill-bred
maleficio M evil spell
maléfico ADJ evil
malentendido M misunderstanding
malestar M (de estómago) upset; (físico) discomfort; (espiritual) malaise; (social) unrest
maleta F suitcase, bag; **hacer la —** to pack one's suitcase
maletero M car trunk
maletín M briefcase
malévolo ADJ (persona) malevolent; (comentario) snide
maleza F (en el monte) underbrush, scrub; (en un jardín) weeds
malformación F malformation
malgache ADJ & MF Madagascan
malgastar VI/VT to waste, to throw away
malgasto M waste
malhechor-ora MF evildoer, criminal
malhumorado ADJ grumpy, ill-humored
Mali, Malí M Mali
malí ADJ & MF Malian
malicia F malice
malicioso ADJ malicious, spiteful
malignidad F malignancy
maligno ADJ (persona) vicious, evil; (tumor) malignant
malinterpretar VI/VT to misunderstand
malla F (de armadura) mail; (de metal) mesh
malo ADJ bad; (calidad, letra) poor; (enfermo) ill; **mal estado** disrepair; **mal humor** bad mood; **mala fama** ill repute; **mala fe** bad faith; **mala hierba** weed; **mala pasada** bad turn; **mala racha** slump; **mala suerte** bad luck
malograr VT to spoil, to ruin; **—se** to fail, to miscarry
malpagar[40] VI/VT to underpay
malparto M miscarriage
malsano ADJ unhealthy, unwholesome
malta F malt
Malta F Malta
maltés-esa ADJ & MF Maltese
maltratar VT to mistreat, to abuse
maltrato M mistreatment, abuse
maltrecho ADJ battered
malvado ADJ wicked, evil
malvavisco M marshmallow
malversación F misuse, misappropriation
malversar VT to misuse, to embezzle
mamá F mama, mamma, mom
mamado ADJ drunk
mamar VI (un bebé) to suckle, to nurse; VI/VT to suck
mamario ADJ mammary
mamarracho M sight
mami F mommy
mamífero ADJ mammalian, mammal; M mammal
mamografía F mammography
mampara F partition
mamut M mammoth
manada F (de ballenas) pod; (de vacas) herd; (de lobos) pack
manantial M (naciente) spring; (fuente inagotable) wellspring
manar VI to stream out
mancha F (marca) stain, spot; (de tinta) blot; (cosa borrosa) blur; (aceitosa) smear, smudge; (menoscabo) tinge; (en la piel) blemish
manchado ADJ spotted
manchar VI/VT (ensuciar) to spot; (menoscabar) to stain, to blemish
manchón M large spot
mancilla F blemish
mancillar VT to defile, to sully
manco ADJ one-armed
mancuerna F dumbbell
mandado M errand
mandamás M *fam* big enchilada, big kahuna
mandamiento M commandment
mandante MF principal
mandar VI/VT (dar órdenes) to command, to

order; (enviar) to send; **— buscar a** to send for; **— decir** to send word; **¿quién manda?** who's in charge? **—se hacer un traje** to have a suit made; **¿mande?** (hola) hello; (perdón) excuse me? what?

mandarina F tangerine

mandatario -ria MF (mediante contrato) agent; (abogado) attorney; (de estado) head of state

mandato M (orden) command, order; (cargo político) term, mandate

mandíbula F (quijada) jaw; (hueso) jawbone

mandil M apron

mandioca F manioc

mando M (de un estado) rule; (de un aparato) control; **— a distancia** remote control

mandolina F mandolin

mandón -ona ADJ bossy, domineering; MF bossy person, control freak

mandonear VI/VT to domineer, to boss around

manea F hobble

manear VT to hobble

manecilla F clock hand

manejable ADJ manageable

manejar VT (un vehículo) to drive, to steer; (un negocio) to run, to manage; (una máquina) to operate

manejo M (de un negocio) running, management; (de asuntos) handling; (de una máquina) operation

manera F manner, way; **a — de** like; **de alguna —** somehow; **de cualquier —** anyway; **de ninguna —** on no account; **de — que** so that

manga F (de una camisa) sleeve; (de una nave) beam; (de agua) hose; (tenis) set; **— de viento** windsock; **en —s de camisa** in shirtsleeves; **ser de — ancha** to be broad-minded; **sacar algo de la —** to pull something out of a hat

manganeso M manganese

mangle M mangrove

mango M (agarradera) handle, grip; (fruta, árbol) mango

mangosta F mongoose

manguera F hose

manguito M muff

maní M peanut

manía F (moda, estado patológico) mania; (hábito) bad habit; (tic) tic

maníaco -ca ADJ maniacal; MF maniac

maníaco-depresivo ADJ manic-depressive

maniatar VT to tie the hands; (manear) to hobble

maniático ADJ (que tiene manías) crotchety; (melindroso) fastidious

manicomio M *pey* insane asylum

manicura F manicure

manicurar VT to manicure

manido ADJ hackneyed

manifestación F (muestra) manifestation; (protesta) demonstration

manifestante MF demonstrator

manifestar[1] VI/VT to manifest, to show; (expresar) to air; (protestar en público) to demonstrate; (declarar) to state

manifiesta, manifieste *ver* manifestar

manifiesto ADJ & M manifest; **poner de —** to underscore; M (dogma) manifesto; **— de vuelo** manifest

manija F handle

maniobra F (militar) maneuver; (para llamar la atención) stunt; **— de Heimlich** Heimlich maneuver

maniobrar VI/VT to maneuver

manipulación F (de la opinión pública) manipulation; (de alimentos) handling

manipular VT (influir) to manipulate; (tocar con las manos) to handle

maniquí M (muñeco) mannequin; MF (modelo) model

manivela F crank

manjar M delicacy

mano F hand (también de naipes); (de pintura) coat; (fútbol) handball; **— a —** one on one; **— de obra** workforce; **—s a la obra** let's get to work; **—s de mantequilla** butterfingers; **a —** (presente) at hand; (con la mano) by hand; **a — armada** at gunpoint; **dar una —** to lend a hand; **dar una — de pintura** to put on a coat of paint; **darle una — a alguien** to lend someone a hand; **darse la —** (saludo) to shake hands; (señal de afecto) to hold hands; **de primera —** firsthand; **de segunda —** secondhand; **estar a — con alguien** to be even with someone; **hecho a —** handmade; **poner las —s en el fuego por alguien** to go out on a limb for someone; **quedar a —** to break even; **se le fue la —** he got carried away; **ser —** to lead [in a card game]; **tener buena — con/para algo** to have a knack for something; **tomarse de la —** to hold hands

manojo M (de monedas) handful; (de llaves) bunch

manómetro M pressure gauge

manopla F (guante) mitten; (en béisbol) glove

manosear VT to feel, to finger

manoseo M feel, grope

manotazo M swat; **tirarle un — a alguien** to take a swipe at someone

manotear VI to swat at

mansalva LOC ADV **a —** at will

mansedumbre F gentleness, meekness

mansión F mansion

manso ADJ (humilde) meek; (domesticado) tame; (apacible) gentle

manta F (gruesa) blanket, cover; (liviana) throw

manteca F lard, shortening; *RP* butter; **— de cacao** cocoa butter

mantecoso ADJ rich, buttery

mantel M tablecloth
mantendrá, mantendría *ver* mantener
mantener[58] VT (conservar, sostener) to maintain; (dejar prolongadamente) to keep; (alimentar, costear a alguien) to provide for; (apoyar a lo largo del tiempo) to sustain; **— a flote** to buoy up; **— el orden público** to keep the peace; **— en secreto** to keep under wraps; **— en suspenso** to keep in suspense; **— la calma** to remain calm; **—se** (quedarse) to remain; (ganarse la vida) to support oneself; **—se al corriente** to keep abreast; **—se al tanto** to stay informed; **—se en contacto** to keep in touch; **—se firme** to stand pat, to stick to one's guns
mantenga, mantengo *ver* mantener
mantenimiento M maintenance, upkeep
mantequera F (platillo) butter dish; (aparato para hacer mantequilla) churn
mantequilla F butter; **— de maní** peanut butter
mantiene, mantienes *ver* mantener
mantilla F mantilla
manto M mantle (también geológico); (de juez) robe
mantón M shawl
mantra M mantra
mantuve, mantuviera, mantuviese *ver* mantener
manual ADJ & M manual
manubrio M handlebar
manufactura F manufacture
manufacturar VT to manufacture
manufacturero -ra ADJ manufacturing; MF manufacturer
manuscrito ADJ written by hand; M manuscript
manutención F maintenance
manzana F (fruta) apple; (de ciudad) block; **— de la discordia** bone of contention
manzanar M apple orchard
manzano M apple tree
maña F (destreza) skill, knack; (artimaña) cunning
mañana F (división del día) morning; (futuro) tomorrow; ADV tomorrow; **— por la —** tomorrow morning
mañanero -ra MF early bird
mañoso ADJ tricky
mapa M map; **— de memoria** memory map; **— en relieve** relief map
mapache M raccoon
maple M maple
maqueta F mock-up
maquillaje M makeup
maquillar[se] VI/VT to put on makeup
máquina F (aparato) machine; (motor) engine; **— de búsqueda** search engine; **— de coser** sewing machine; **— de escribir** typewriter; **— de lavar** washing machine; **— de vapor** steam engine; **— expendedora** vending machine; **— fotográfica** camera
maquinación F scheming, plotting
maquinador -ora MF schemer
maquinal ADJ automatic
maquinar VI/VT to plot, to scheme
maquinaria F (aparato) machinery, apparatus; (del gobierno) machine
maquinilla F clipper; **— de afeitar** razor
maquinista M (de locomotora) locomotive engineer; (obrero) machinist
mar MF sea; **— de fondo** undercurrent; **llover a mares** to rain cats and dogs; **en alta —** on the high seas; **un — de cosas** a lot of things; **hacerse a la —** to put to sea
maraca F maraca
maraña F (de hilos) tangle, snarl; (de pelo) mat
marañón M cashew
maratón M marathon
maravilla F (portento) wonder, marvel; (flor) marigold; **a las mil —s** wonderfully
maravillar VT to amaze; **—se** to be amazed, to marvel
maravilloso ADJ marvelous, wonderful
marca F (récord) record; (de ganado) brand; (de producto) brand, brand name, label; (de coche) make; **— comercial** name brand; **— de nacimiento** birthmark; **— de fábrica** trademark; **— genérica** generic brand; **— registrada** registered trademark; **de —** name-brand
marcadamente ADV sharply
marcado ADJ (acento) thick; (contraste) sharp, stark; (descenso) steep; (parecido) strong
marcador M (lapicero) marker; (en deporte) scoreboard; **— de libros** bookmark; **— genético** genetic marker; **¿cómo va el —?** what's the score?
marcar[30] VT (una respuesta) to mark; (ganado) to brand; (el ritmo) to beat; (la hora) to say; (un tanto) to score; (medida) to read, to show; (un número telefónico) to dial; **— para seleccionar** to highlight; **— un gol** to score a goal
marcha F (caminata, pieza musical) march; (partida) leaving; (progreso) course; (modo de andar) gait; (cambio en un coche) gear; (animación) nightlife; **— atrás** reverse; **ponerse en —** to get going; **puesta en —** beginning; **sobre la —** as you go
marchante MF (vendedor) art dealer; (cliente) customer
marchar VI (soldado) to march; (máquina, vehículo) to run; **—se** to go away
marchista MF walker
marchitar VT to wither; **—se** to wither, to shrivel up
marchito ADJ withered, shriveled up
marcial ADJ martial

marco M (de un cuadro, de una puerta, de referencia) frame; (moneda) mark
marea F tide; **— baja** low tide; **— alta** high tide
mareado ADJ (en un barco) seasick; (en un coche) carsick; (de alegría) giddy; (con vértigo) dizzy, lightheaded
marear VT (dar vértigo) to make dizzy; (en un barco) to make seasick; **—se** (tener vértigo) to get dizzy; (en un barco) to get seasick
marejada F tidal wave
maremoto M tidal wave
mareo M (en un barco) seasickness; (en un vehículo) motion sickness; (vértigo) dizziness
marfil M ivory
marfileño -ña ADJ & MF Ivorian
margarina F margarine
margarita F daisy; **echar —s a los cerdos** to cast pearls before swine
margen M (de un papel) margin; (de la sociedad) fringe; MF (de un río) bank; **— de error** margin of error; **— de ganancia** profit margin, markup; **— de seguridad** margin of safety; **al —** on the outside
marginación F (de un grupo) marginalization; (de un individuo) isolation; **hay cierta — entre entre los colegas** there is a certain distance among the colleagues; **la — de ciertos grupos minoritarios** the marginalization of certain minorities
marginado -da ADJ & MF outcast
marginal ADJ marginal
marginar VT to marginalize
mariachi M mariachi
marido M husband
mariguana, marihuana F marijuana; *fam* pot
marimba F marimba
marina F navy; **— mercante** merchant marine
marinar VT to marinate
marinero -ra ADJ (buque) seaworthy; (nación) seafaring; MF sailor
marino -na ADJ marine; MF sailor; (oficial) naval officer
marioneta F marionette
mariposa F (insecto) butterfly (también en natación); (tuerca) wing nut; **— nocturna** moth
mariquita F ladybug
mariscal M marshal; **— de campo** (militar) field marshal; (fútbol americano) quarterback
mariscos M PL shellfish
marítimo ADJ maritime
marketing M marketing
marmita F pot
mármol M marble
marmóreo ADJ marble
marmota F groundhog
maroma F rope
marqués M marquis
marquesa F marquise
marrano M hog
marrón ADJ brown
marroquí ADJ & MF Moroccan
Marruecos M Morocco
marshalés -esa ADJ & MF Marshallese
marsopa F porpoise
martes M Tuesday
martillar VI/VT to hammer
martillo M hammer (también hueso del oído, pieza de revólver); (de juez) gavel; **— neumático** jackhammer
martinete M (martillo grande) pile driver; (pieza de piano) piano hammer
martini M martini
mártir MF martyr
martirio M martyrdom
martirizar[47] VT to martyr, to torment
marxismo M Marxism
marzo M March
mas CONJ but
más ADJ more; PREP plus; ADV more; (más tiempo) longer; **— allá de** beyond; **— bien** rather; **— de tres** more than three; **— o menos** more or less; **— que nada** primarily; **— que nunca** more than ever; **— que tú** more than you; **a lo —** at best; **a — tardar** at the latest; **de —** extra; **el — allá** the hereafter; **es de lo — simpático** he's really nice; **es —** furthermore; **está de —** it is superfluous; **otro —** yet another; **por — que** no matter how much; **y — todavía** and then some
masa F mass; (de agua) body; (de harina) batter; (para amasar) dough; **en —** en masse, in large numbers; **las —s** the masses; **— de hojaldre** puff pastry
masacrar VT to massacre, to slaughter
masacre M massacre
masaje M massage
masajear VT to massage
masajista M masseur; F masseuse
mascar[30] VI/VT (chicle) to chew; (con ruido) to crunch
máscara F mask; **— de gas** gas mask
mascarada F masquerade
mascota F (animal doméstico) pet; (emblema de un equipo) mascot
masculino ADJ (como un hombre, género gramatical) masculine; (del hombre) male
mascullar VI/VT to mumble
masilla F putty
masivo ADJ massive
masón M mason
masonería F masonry
masoquismo M masochism
mastectomía F mastectomy
máster M master; **— en administración de empresas** master of business administration
masticar[30] VT to chew

mástil M (en un barco) mast; (para una bandera) flagpole, flagstaff
mastín M mastiff
masturbarse VI to masturbate
mata F bush; **— de pelo** head of hair
matadero M slaughterhouse
matador ADJ horrendous; M bullfighter
matanza F slaughter, killing
matar VT to kill; (animales) to butcher, to slaughter; **— a tiros** to gun down; **— de hambre** to starve; VT **matasellar** to cancel a stamp; M SG **matamoscas** flyswatter; M SG **matasellos** postmark; M SG **matasanos** quack [doctor]
mate M (en ajedrez) checkmate; (planta, bebida) mate; ADJ (pintura) flat; **hacer un —** (baloncesto) to dunk the ball
matemática, matemáticas F mathematics
matemático -ca ADJ mathematical; (exacto) precise; MF mathematician
materia F (sustancia) matter; (tema de estudio) school subject; (tema) topic; **— extraña** extraneous matter; **— fecal** fecal matter; **— gris** gray matter; **— prima** raw material
material ADJ (necesidades) material; (autor) real; M material
materialismo M materialism
maternal ADJ (instinto) maternal; (amor) motherly
maternidad F (relacionado con el nacimiento) maternity; (estado de ser madre) motherhood
materno ADJ maternal
matiné M matinee
matiz M (de un color) tint, shade, hue; (de ironía) tinge; (de sentido) nuance
matizar[47] VT (mezclar colores) to blend, to tinge; (moderar) to qualify
matón -ona MF (persona que intimida a los pequeños) bully; (pandillero, peleador) thug
matorral M (mata) thicket; (región) bush
matraz M flask
matriarca F matriarch
matrícula F (alumnado) enrollment, matriculation; (de un coche) registration; (placa) license plate; (costo de la universidad) tuition fees
matriculación F matriculation
matricular VT to matriculate, to enroll
matrilineal ADJ matrilineal
matrimonial ADJ marital
matrimonio M (estado civil) matrimony, marriage; (pareja) married couple
matriz F (en matemáticas) matrix; (bidimensional) array; (útero) womb; (plantilla) stencil; **casa —** main office
matrona ADJ frumpy, matronly; F matron
matutino ADJ of the morning
maullar VI to mew
maullido M mew
mauriciano -na ADJ & MF Mauritian
Mauricio M Mauritius
Mauritania F Mauritania
mauritano -na MF Mauritanian
maxilar M jawbone
máxima F maxim
maximizar VT to maximize
máximo ADJ & M maximum; (autoridad) ultimate; (cuidado) utmost; **— histórico** all-time high
maya ADJ & MF Maya, Mayan
mayo M (mes) May; (palo) maypole
mayonesa F mayonnaise
mayor ADJ (de tamaño) greater, larger; (de edad) older, elder; (rango, clave) major; **al por —** wholesale; **dedo —** middle finger; **el — número de votos** the most votes; M (adulto) adult
mayoral M boss
mayordomo M butler
mayoreo M wholesale
mayoría F majority; **— de edad** legal age, majority; **en su —** largely
mayorista MF wholesale dealer
mayoritario ADJ majority
mayúsculo -la ADJ (letra) capital; (problema) major; F capital letter
mazmorra F dungeon
mazo M mallet
mazorca F (con maíz) ear of corn; (sin maíz) corncob
me PRON PERS **él — vio** he saw me; **él — habló** he talked to me; **se — murió el perro** my dog died on me
mecánico -ca ADJ mechanical; MF mechanic; F mechanics
mecanismo M mechanism; **— de seguridad** safety device
mecanografía F typewriting
mecanografiar[28] VI/VT to type
mecanógrafo -fa MF typist
mecedora F rocking chair, rocker
mecenas MF SG/PL patron, sponsor
mecenazgo M patronage
mecer[32] VI/VT (cuna) to rock; (columpio) to swing
mecha F (de una vela) wick; (de explosivos) fuse; (de pelo) lock; **—s** (en el pelo) highlights
mechar VT (rellenar con tocino) to lard; (robar) to shoplift
mechero -ra MF shoplifter; M burner; **— Bunsen** Bunsen burner
mechón M lock, strand
medalla F medal
médano M dune
media F (hasta el muslo) stocking; (hasta la cintura) pantyhose; (calcetín) sock; (promedio) mean; M PL (medios de comunicación) media

mediación F mediation
mediador -ora MF mediator
mediados LOC ADV **a — de mayo** in mid-May
mediana F median
mediano ADJ (intermedio en tamaño) medium; (intermedio en calidad) average; **de tamaño —** middle-sized; **de mediana edad** middle-aged
medianoche F midnight
mediante PREP by means of
mediar VI (en un asunto) to mediate, to intervene; (tiempo) to intervene; **mediaba febrero** it was mid-February
medible ADJ measurable
medicación F medication
medicamento M medicine, drug
medicar VT to medicate; **—se** to self-medicate
medicina F medicine; **— defensiva** defensive medicine; **— familiar** family practice
medición F (de una cantidad) measurement; (de un terreno) survey
médico -ca MF doctor, physician; **— forense** coroner, medical examiner; **— general** general practitioner; **— tratante** attending physician; ADJ medical
medida F (dimensión) measure; (acto de medir) measurement; **— cautelar** restraining order; **— para áridos** dry measure; **a — que** as; **en la — en que** to the extent that; **hacer a la —** to make to measure; **hecho a la —** made-to-measure; **tomar —s** to take measures; **tomarle las —s a alguien** to measure someone
medidor M gauge, meter
medieval ADJ medieval
medio ADJ (la mitad) half; **— pastel** half a cake; (promedio) average; **el ciudadano —** the average man; **—día** (hora) noon, midday; (hora de comer) lunch hour, noon hour; (punto cardinal) south; (territorio) the south; **— hermano** half-brother; **a media asta** at half-mast; **a — camino** halfway; **clase media** middle class; **el americano —** the average American; **media hora** half an hour; **mi media naranja** my better half; **temperatura media** mean temperature; **— tiempo** (fútbol) halftime; **de — tiempo** part-time; **media volea** (tenis) half-volley; **hacer una cosa a medias** to do something halfway; **ir a medias** to go halves; M (centro) middle; (ambiente) medium; **—s** means, resources; **— ambiente** environment; **—s de comunicación** media; **— de transporte** means of transport; **en [el] — de** in the middle of; **en — de la calle** in the middle of the street; **meterse de por —** to intervene; **por — de** by means of; **por todos los —s** by all possible means; ADV half; **a — derretir** half-melted
medioambiental ADJ environmental
mediocre ADJ mediocre; (actuación) lackluster
mediocridad F mediocrity
medir[9] VI/VT to measure; VT (consecuencias) to gauge; (terreno) to survey; **— a pasos** to step off; **—se** to be moderate
meditación F meditation
meditar VI to meditate, to ponder
mediterráneo ADJ Mediterranean
médium MF medium, psychic
medroso ADJ fearful
médula F marrow, pith; **— espinal** spinal cord; **— ósea** bone marrow
medusa F jellyfish, man-of-war
megabyte M megabyte
megáfono M megaphone
megahercio, megahertz M megahertz
megalomanía F megalomania
mejilla F cheek
mejor ADJ better; **el —** the best; **en el — de los casos** at best; **te deseo lo —** I wish you the best; ADV better; **a lo —** maybe; **tanto —** so much the better
mejora F improvement
mejoramiento M improvement
mejorar VT to improve, to improve upon; (software, aparato) to upgrade; (las posibilidades de uno) to better; VI (ventas) to pick up; **—se** to get better/well
mejoría F improvement
melancolía F melancholy, gloom
melancólico ADJ melancholy, gloomy
melanoma M melanoma
melaza F molasses
melena F mane
melindre M affectation
melindroso ADJ affected, finicky
mella F notch; **hacer —** to make a dent
mellar VT to notch
mellizo -za ADJ & MF twin
melocotón M peach
melocotonero M peach tree
melodía F melody
melódico ADJ (agradable al oído) melodious; (relativo a la melodía) melodic
melodioso ADJ melodious
melodrama M melodrama
melómano -na ADJ music-loving; MF music lover
melón M melon, cantaloupe
membrana F (en un órgano) membrane; (en las patas de los patos) web
membrete M letterhead
membrillo M (fruta) quince; (árbol) quince tree
membrudo ADJ stout
memorable ADJ memorable
memorándum M memorandum
memoria F (facultad de recordar, recuerdo) memory; (obra autobiográfica) memoir;

(actas) proceedings; **— de acceso directo** random access memory [RAM]; **— de caché** cache memory; **— de ROM** read-only memory; **— de sólo lectura** read-only memory [ROM]; **— expandida** expanded memory; **— intermedia** buffer; **— residente** internal memory; **de —** by heart; **hacer —** to try to remember/recollect

memorial M memorial

memorizar[47] VI/VT to memorize

mención F mention

mencionar VT to mention

mendigar[40] VI to beg

mendigo -ga MF beggar

mendrugo M large crumb

menear VT (las caderas) to wiggle, to wriggle, to shake; (la cola) to wag

meneo M (de las caderas) wiggle; (de la cola) wag

menesteroso ADJ needy, destitute

mengua F diminution, waning

menguante ADJ waning

menguar[25] VI (luna) to wane; (energía) to flag; (provisiones) to dwindle

meningitis F meningitis

menjurje M concoction

menopausia F menopause

menor ADJ (de tamaño) smaller; (de cantidad) lesser, smaller; (de edad) younger; (de importancia, en música) minor; **el —** (de tamaño) the smallest; (de cantidad) the least, the smallest; (de edad) the youngest; MF **— de edad** minor; **al por —** retail

menos ADV (no contables) less; (contables) fewer; **— de** less than, fewer than; **— de lo que se esperaba** less than expected, fewer than expected; **— mal** just as well; **a — que** unless; **al —** at least; **dar de —** to shortchange; **echar de —** to miss; **lo —** the least; **no es para —** there is good reason; **por lo —** at least; **signo de —** minus sign; **venir a —** to decline; **el que trabaja —** the one who works the least; **no puede — que hacerlo** he cannot help doing it; **tienes — que yo** you have less than I; **trabaja — que yo** she works less than I; PREP (salvo) except, but; **las cinco — cuarto** quarter to five; ADJ & PRON less, least; **— agua** less water; **— problemas** fewer problems; M minus

menoscabar VT to impair, to undermine

menoscabo M impairment

menospreciar VI/VT (despreciar) to despise; VT (burlarse de) to belittle, to demean

menosprecio M contempt

mensaje M message; **— de error** error message; **— de texto** text message

mensajería F carrier; **— instantánea** instant messaging

mensajero -ra MF messenger, courier

menstruación F menstruation

menstruar VI to menstruate

mensual ADJ monthly

mensualidad F (recibida) monthly allowance; (pagada) monthly installment

mensuario ADJ monthly

mensurable ADJ measurable

menta F mint, peppermint; **— verde** spearmint

mental ADJ mental

mentalidad F mentality

mente F mind

mentecato -ta ADJ foolish, simple; MF simpleton

mentir[8] VI to lie

mentira F lie, falsehood

mentirilla F fib, white lie

mentiroso -sa ADJ lying; MF liar

mentón M chin

mentor -ora MF mentor

menú M menu (también de computadoras); **— abatible** pull-down menu; **— del día** daily special; **— de inicio** start menu; **— emergente** pop-up menu

menudeo LOC ADV **al —** retail

menudo ADJ (pequeño) small; (insignificante) insignificant; **a —** often, frequently; **dinero —** small change; **— perro** that's some dog; M (entrañas) entrails

meñique ADJ & M little finger, *fam* pinkie; **dedo —** little finger

meollo M (médula) marrow; (parte sustancial de un asunto) marrow, pith, core; (seso) brain

mequetrefe M runt, pipsqueak

mercachifle M peddler, huckster

mercadear VT to market

mercadeo M merchandising; **— de nicho** niche marketing

mercader M merchant

mercadería F merchandise

mercado M market, marketplace; **— alcista** bull market; **— bajista** bear market; **— de divisas** currency exchange; **— de prueba** test market; **— de pulgas** flea market; **— de valores** stock market; **— extrabursátil** aftermarket; **— libre** free market; **— negro** black market; **— secundario** aftermarket

mercadotecnia F marketing

mercancía F merchandise, goods

mercante ADJ merchant

mercantil ADJ mercantile

merced LOC ADV **— a** thanks to; **a [la] — de** at the mercy of

mercenario -ria ADJ & MF mercenary

mercería F notions store

mercurio M mercury, quicksilver

merecedor ADJ deserving

merecer[35] VT to deserve, to merit

merecido M deserved punishment, due

merendar[1] VI to have a snack

merendero M picnic area

merezca, merezco *ver* merecer
meridiano ADJ & M meridian
meridional ADJ southern; MF southerner
merienda F afternoon snack
mérito M merit
meritorio ADJ meritorious, worthy
merluza F hake
merma F decrease
mermar VI/VT to decrease, to dwindle
mermelada F (de fresa, pera) jam; (de cítricos) marmalade
mero ADJ mere; **la mera idea** the very idea; M grouper
merodear VI to loiter
mes M month
mesa F (mueble) table; (consejo) board; (formación geológica) mesa; **— de noche** nightstand; **levantar la —** to clear the table; **poner la —** to set the table
mesada F monthly allowance
mesero -ra M waiter; F waitress
meseta F plateau
mesón M inn, lodge
mesonero -ra MF innkeeper
mestizo -za ADJ (perros) mongrel; MF (mezcla de europeo e india) mestizo; (perro de raza mezclada) mongrel
mesura F moderation
mesurado ADJ (persona, opinión) moderate; (respuesta) measured
meta F (objetivo) goal; (en una carrera) finish line
metabólico ADJ metabolic
metabolismo M metabolism
metafísica F metaphysics
metafísico ADJ metaphysical
metáfora F metaphor
metafórico ADJ metaphorical
metal M metal; **— precioso** precious metal
metálico ADJ metallic; M cash
metalurgia F metallurgy
metamorfosis F metamorphosis
metano M methane
metástasis F metastasis
metastatizar VI to metastasize
meteorito M meteorite
meteoro M meteor
meteorología F meteorology
meteorológico ADJ meteorological; **parte —** weather report
meteorólogo -ga M weatherman; F weatherwoman
meter VT (en una bolsa) to put [into], to stick [into]; (un lío) to force [into]; (invertir) to invest; **— el estómago** to suck in one's stomach; **— la pata** to make a mistake; **— miedo** to scare; **— ruido** to make noise; **— un gol** to score a goal; **—se** to meddle; **—se a bailar** to begin to dance; **—se con** to mess with; **—se en camisa de once varas** to get oneself into a fix
metódico ADJ methodical
método M method
metodología F methodology
metralleta F portable machine gun
métrico ADJ metric
metro M (medida, ritmo poético) meter; (cinta de medir) measuring tape; (tren subterráneo) subway, metro
metrónomo M metronome
metrópoli F metropolis
metropolitano ADJ metropolitan; M subway
mexicano -na ADJ & MF Mexican
México M Mexico
mezcla F (de ingredientes) mixture, mix; (en albañilería) mortar; (de café, especias) blend
mezclador -ora MF (persona) mixer; F (aparato) mixer
mezclar VT (ingredientes) to mix, to blend; (naipes) to shuffle; (números) to scramble; **—se** (combinarse) to mix; (tener trato con) to mingle; (entrometerse) to meddle
mezcolanza F hodgepodge
mezquindad F (crueldad) meanness; (tacañería) stinginess
mezquino ADJ (cruel) mean, mean-spirited, petty; (insignificante) small, petty; (tacaño) tight, stingy
mezquita F mosque
mi ADJ POS my
mí PRON PERS me; **es para —** it's for me; **me vio a —** he saw me; **me la dio a —** he gave it to me
miau M meow
mico M long-tailed monkey
micra F micron
micro M (autobús) bus; (micrófono) microphone
microbio M microbe, germ
microbiología F microbiology
microcirujía F microsurgery
microcomputadora F microcomputer
microeconomía F microeconomics
microficha F microfiche
microfilm M microfilm
micrófono M microphone
Micronesia F Micronesia
micronesio -sia ADJ & MF Micronesian
microonda F microwave; M SG **—s** microwave oven
microordenador M microcomputer
microorganismo M microorganism
microprocesador M microprocessor
microscópico ADJ microscopic
microscopio M microscope; **— electrónico** electron microscope
mida, mide, midiendo, midiera, midiese *ver* medir
miedo M fear; **— al escenario** stage fright;

tener — to be afraid
miedoso ADJ fearful
miel F honey
miembro M (integrante) member; (extremidad) limb
mienta, miente *ver* mentir
mientras CONJ (durante) while, as; (siempre y cuando) as long as; — **que** while; — **tanto** meanwhile; ADV in the meantime
miércoles M Wednesday
mies F grain; —**es** fields of grain
miga F crumb; **hacer buenas** —**s** to get along well
migaja F crumb
migración F migration
migrante ADJ migrant
migraña F migraine
migrar VI to migrate
migratorio ADJ migratory
mil NUM thousand; — **millones** billion; **llegamos a las** — **y quinientas** we got there very late
milagro M miracle, wonder
milagroso ADJ miraculous
milano M kite
milenio M millennium
milicia F militia
miligramo M milligram
mililitro M milliliter
milímetro M millimeter
militancia F (actitud) militance; (actitud) militancy
militante ADJ & MF militant
militar ADJ military; MF soldier; VI to militate
milla F mile
millaje M mileage
millar M thousand
millón M million
millonario -ria MF millionaire
millonésimo ADJ & M millionth
mimar VT to pamper, to spoil, to coddle
mimbre M wicker
mímico ADJ mimic; F mimicry
mimo M (trato cariñoso) caressing, cuddling; MF (actor) mime
mimoso ADJ cuddly
mina F (yacimiento) mine; (explosivo) [land] mine; (de un lápiz) lead; (fuente) storehouse
minado M mining
minar VT (sembrar minas) to mine; (socavar) to undermine; VI (cavar) to burrow
mineral M mineral; (de oro) ore; ADJ mineral
minería F mining
minero -ra MF miner; ADJ mining
mingitorio M urinal
miniatura F miniature
mini-break M (tenis) mini-break
minicomputadora F minicomputer
minifalda F miniskirt
minifundio M subsistence farm
minimizar[47] VT (gastos) to minimize; (a una persona) to belittle; VI (un incidente) to play down
mínimo ADJ (cantidad) least; (tamaño) smallest; M minimum; **como** — at least; **en lo más** — at all
minino M kitty
miniordenador M minicomputer
ministerial ADJ cabinet, ministerial
ministerio M (religioso) ministry; (gubernamental) ministry, department
ministro -tra MF minister, secretary; — **de justicia** attorney general
minoría F minority
minoridad F minority
minorista MF retailer
minoritario ADJ minority
mintiendo, mintiera, mintiese, mintió *ver* mentir
minucioso ADJ (detalle) minute; (trabajo) thorough; (persona) fastidious
minúsculo ADJ (tamaño) small, minuscule; (cantidad) negligible; **letra minúscula** lowercase letter
minusvalía F disability
minusválido -da ADJ disabled; MF disabled person
minutas F (honorarios) lawyers' fees; (actas) minutes
minutero M minute hand
minuto M minute
mío ADJ & PRON mine; **este libro es** — this book is mine; **un amigo** — a friend of mine
miope ADJ shortsighted, nearsighted
miopía F nearsightedness, myopia
mira F (dispositivo de arma) gun sight; (intención) intention; **con** —**s a** with a view to
mirada F gaze, look; — **asesina** dirty look; — **de soslayo** side glance; — **fija** stare
mirador M vantage point, overlook
miramiento M consideration
mirar VI/VT to look [at]; (un partido, televisión) to watch; — **de soslayo** to look askance [at]; — **fijamente** to stare [at]; **¡mira [tú]!** you don't say!
miríada F myriad
mirilla F peephole
mirlo M blackbird
mirón M (curioso) onlooker; (erótico) voyeur
mirto M myrtle
misa F mass
misantropía F misanthropy
misántropo -pa MF misanthrope
misceláneo ADJ miscellaneous
miserable ADJ (vil, pobre) wretched, unhappy; (insignificante) paltry; (tacaño) miserly
miseria F (desgracia) misery; (pobreza) poverty,

squalor; (cantidad despreciable) trifle
misericordia F mercy
misericordioso ADJ merciful, gracious
mísero ADJ miserable
misil M missile; **— balístico** ballistic missile; **— crucero** cruise missile
misión F mission (también religiosa)
misionero -ra MF missionary
mismo ADJ same; **ese — día** that very day; **se nombró a sí —** he named himself; **lo —** the same thing; **me da lo —** it's all the same to me; **yo —** I myself
misoginia F misogyny
misterio M mystery
misterioso ADJ mysterious
místico -ca ADJ mystical; MF mystic
mitad F half; **por la —** in half; **en la — de** in the middle of; **a — de[l] camino** midway
mítico ADJ mythic, mythical
mitigar[40] VT to mitigate
mitin M political meeting
mito M myth
mitocondria F mitochondria
mitología F mythology
mitológico ADJ mythological
mixto ADJ mixed; **escuela mixta** coed school
mobiliario M furniture
mocasín M (zapatilla, culebra) moccasin; (zapato sin cordones) loafer
mochar VT to chop off
mochila F backpack, knapsack
moción F motion
moco M (interno) mucus
moda F fashion; **de —** fashionable, in style; **ponerse de —** to catch on
modales M PL manners
modalidad F form, variant; **ganó oro en la — de espalda** she won gold in the backstroke; **la — italiana es más conocida** the Italian form is better known
Moldavia F Moldova
modelar VI/VT to model
modelo ADJ & MF model
módem M modem
moderación F moderation, restraint
moderado -da ADJ (posición política) moderate; (invierno) mild; (precio) reasonable; (respuesta) measured; (clima) temperate; MF moderate
moderar VT (restringir) to moderate, to restrain; (presidir) to moderate
modernidad F (actualidad) modern age; (actualidad) modern world
modernismo M (cualidad de moderno) modernity, modernness; (tendencia artística) modernism
modernización F modernization
moderno ADJ modern
modestia F modesty
modesto ADJ modest
módico ADJ moderate, reasonable
modificación F modification
modificar[30] VT to modify
modismo M idiom
modista MF dressmaker
modo M (manera) mode, manner, way; (categoría gramatical) mood; (de computadora/ordenador) mode; **— a prueba de fallos/errores** safe mode; **— de ahorro** power-save mode; **— de dormir** sleep mode; **— de entrega** mode of delivery; **— de reescritura** overwrite mode; **a — de** by way of; **del mismo —** in like manner, similarly; **de ningún —** by no means; **de — que** so that; **de otro —** otherwise; **de ningún —** not at all; **de todos —s** anyway; **en cierto —** in a way; **ni —** no dice; **no hay —** no way
modorra F drowsiness
modulación F modulation
modular VT to modulate
módulo M (componente) module; (unidad) unit
mofa F jeer, ridicule
mofarse VI **— de** to make fun of, to scoff at
mofeta F skunk
moflete M fat cheek, jowl
mohair M mohair
mohín M grimace
moho M mold, mildew
mohoso ADJ moldy
mojado -da ADJ wet
mojadura F wetting
mojar VT (humedecer) to wet; (sumergir) to dip; **—se** to get wet
mojigatería F prudery
mojigato -ta ADJ prudish; MF prude
mojo M dip
mojón M landmark
molar ADJ molar
moldavo -va ADJ & MF Moldovan
molde M (norma) mold, cast; (tortera) cake pan; (patrón) pattern; (de imprenta) die; **letras de —** block letters
moldeado M molding
moldear VT to mold, to cast
moldura F molding
mole F mass
molécula F molecule
molecular ADJ molecular
moler[6] VI/VT to mill, to grind; **— a palos** to beat thoroughly
molestar VT to bother, to pester; **no te molestes** don't bother
molestia F bother, nuisance; **no te tomes la —** don't go to the trouble
molesto ADJ (que molesta) bothersome, irksome; (que está molesto) uneasy, uncomfortable
molibdeno M molybdenum

molienda F grinding
molinero -ra MF miller
molinete M (puerta) turnstile; (juguete) pinwheel
molinillo M mill, grinder
molino M mill; **— de viento** windmill
mollete M muffin
molusco M mollusk
momentáneo ADJ momentary
momento M (tiempo) moment; (impulso) momentum; **al —** immediately; **a cada —** continually; **en todo —** all the time; **no veo el —** I can't wait
momia F mummy
Mónaco M Monaco
monada F (acción graciosa) antic; (persona atractiva) *fam* peach
monarca MF monarch
monarquía F monarchy
monárquico -ca MF monarchist; ADJ monarchical
monasterio M monastery
mondar VT to pare; **—se los dientes** to pick one's teeth; M SG **mondadientes** toothpick
moneda F (dinero metálico) coin; (divisa) currency; **— corriente** common currency; **— de curso legal** legal tender; **— falsa** counterfeit money
monegasco -ca ADJ & MF Monegasque
monería F antic
monetario ADJ monetary
mongol -la ADJ & MF Mongolian
Mongolia F Mongolia
mongoloide ADJ mongoloid
monigote M puppet
monitor -ora M (aparato) monitor; **— [a] color** color monitor; MF (persona) monitor
monitorear VT to monitor
monitoreo M monitoring
monitorización F monitoring; **— fetal** fetal monitoring
monja F nun
monje M monk
mono -na MF (simio) monkey; **— araña** spider monkey; M (mimo) mimic; (prenda de trabajo) overalls, coverall; (síndrome de abstinencia) withdrawal symptoms; **dormir la mona** to sleep it off; ADJ cute
monogamia F monogamy
monokini M topless swimsuit
monólogo M monologue, monolog
mononucleosis F mononucleosis
monopatín M (tabla) skateboard; (con manillar) scooter; (de nieve) snowboard
monopolio M monopoly
monopolizar[47] VT (un producto) to monopolize; (un mercado) to corner
monotonía F monotony
monótono ADJ monotonous
monseñor M monsignor
monserga F nonsense
monstruo M (ser imaginario, persona perversa) monster; (persona grotesca) freak; ADJ INV monstrous
monstruosidad F monstrosity
monstruoso ADJ monstrous
monta F mount; **de poca —** of little value
montaje M (de un aparato) assembly, set up; (de una película) editing
montante M (total) total; (ventana de puerta) transom; (columna) upright
montaña F mountain; **— rusa** roller coaster
montañés -esa ADJ mountain; MF mountain dweller
montañismo M mountaineering
montañoso ADJ mountainous
montar VT (ir a caballo, en bicicleta) to ride; (un aparato) to assemble; (una película) to edit; (subirse al caballo) to mount, to get on; **— en cólera** to fly into a rage; **— una escena** to make a scene; **—se a caballo** to mount a horse
montaraz ADJ coarse
monte M (montaña) mount; (zona agreste) wilderness; **— de piedad** pawnshop
montés ADJ (salvaje) wild; (de la montaña) of the mountains
montículo M mound; (béisbol) pitcher's mound
monto M amount; **— debido** amount due; **— pagado** amount paid
montón M (pila) pile, heap; (de papel) stack; (de nieve) drift; (de flores) basketful; (de gente) bunch; **a montones** in abundance; **del —** run-of-the-mill
montura F (animal) mount; (silla) saddle; (armazón de gafas) frame, rim
monumental ADJ monumental
monumento M monument
moño M (de pelo) bun; (adorno) bow
mopa F mop
moquearse VI to become snotty
moquillo M distemper
MOR [movimientos oculares rápidos] M PL REM
mora F (fruta) blackberry, mulberry; (tardanza) delay, delinquency; **en —** in default, past due
morada F dwelling, abode
morado ADJ purple; **ojo —** black eye
morador -ora MF dweller
moral ADJ moral; F (principios éticos) morals; (estado de ánimo) morale; M mulberry tree
moraleja F moral
moralidad F morality
moralista MF moralist
moralizar[47] VI/VT to moralize
morar VI to dwell, to abide
mórbido ADJ morbid
morbilidad F (predisposición a la enfermedad)

morbidity
morbosidad F (que produce enfermedad) morbidity
morboso ADJ (mórbido) morbid; (atractivo) sexy
morcilla F blood sausage
mordacidad F sharpness
mordaz ADJ (comentario) cutting, sharp; (persona) sharp-tongued
mordaza F (de la boca) gag; (de un torno) vise jaw
mordedor ADJ biting, snappy
mordedura F bite
morder[6] VI/VT to bite; **—se la lengua** to bite one's tongue
mordida F (mordisco) bite; (soborno) bribe, kickback
mordiscar[30] VI/VT to nibble; to nip
mordisco M nibble, nip
mordisquear VI/VT to nip; to nibble
mordisqueo M nibble
moreno ADJ (piel) dark, dark-skinned, swarthy; (pelo) dark, brunette
moretón M bruise
morfina F morphine
morgue F morgue
moribundo ADJ dying, moribund
morir[7, 74] VI (persona, animal) to die; (calle) to end; **—se de envidia** to eat one's heart out; **—se de hambre** to starve; **—se de miedo** to die of fear; **—se de risa** to die laughing; **—se por algo** to crave something; **—se por alguien** to be crazy about someone
morisco ADJ Moorish
moro -ra ADJ Moorish; MF Moor; **—s y cristianos** (personas) Moors and Christians; (plato) beans and rice; **no hay —s en la costa** the coast is clear
morocho ADJ dark-haired, brunet, brunette
moroso ADJ delinquent, deadbeat
morrear VI to make out
morriña F homesickness
morro M (monte) knoll; (caradura) gall, nerve; (de un avión) nose; (de animal) snout
morrón M bell pepper
morsa F walrus
mortaja F shroud
mortal ADJ mortal, deadly; MF mortal
mortalidad F mortality
mortandad F death toll
mortecino ADJ fading
mortero M mortar
mortífero ADJ deadly
mortificación F mortification, chagrin
mortificar[30] VT to mortify, to chagrin
mortuorio ADJ mortuary; **casa mortuaria** funeral home
mosaico M mosaic
mosca F (insecto) fly; (dinero) dough; **—muerta** hypocrite; **no se oía volar una —** you could have heard a pin drop
mosquear VT (crear desconfianza) to cause distrust; (hacer enfadar) to enrage; **—se** (desconfiar) to distrust; (enfadarse) to become enraged
mosquitero M (pantalla de ventana) window screen; (red) mosquito net
mosquito M mosquito
mostacho M mustache, moustache
mostaza F mustard
mostrador M counter
mostrar[5] VT to show; **—se reticente** to appear reticent
mostrenco ADJ stray
mota F speck, speckle
mote M nickname
moteado ADJ speckled, spotted
motear VT to speck, to speckle
motejar VI **— de** to brand as
motel M motel
motín M (en un barco) mutiny; (de prisioneros) riot
motivación F motivation
motivar VT (impulsar) to motivate; (causar) to cause
motivo M (causa) motive, reason; (figura repetida) motif, theme; **con — de** on the occasion of
moto F bike, motorcycle
motocicleta F motorcycle
motociclista MF biker, motorcyclist
motor ADJ of motion; M motor, engine; **— de reacción** jet engine; **— de búsqueda** search engine; **— de combustión interna** internal combustion engine; **— fuera de borda** outboard engine
motriz ADJ **fuerza —** motive power
movedizo ADJ restless
mover[6] VT to move; **— palancas** to pull strings; **—se** to move, to budge
movible ADJ movable
movido ADJ (vida, fiesta) eventful; (foto) blurred; **— por gas** powered by gas
móvil M (motivo) motive; (teléfono) mobile telephone; (adorno, juguete) mobile; ADJ (que se mueve) mobile; (que puede ser movido) movable; **un blanco —** a moving target
movilidad F mobility
movilización F mobilization
movilizar[47] VI/VT to mobilize
movimiento M (cambio de posición) movement, motion; (organización, pieza de reloj) movement; (comercial) traffic; **—s oculares rápidos** REM [rapid eye movements]; **los rojos tienen poco —** the red ones don't sell well; **un cuerpo en —** a moving body

Mozambique M Mozambique
mozambiqueño-ña ADJ & MF Mozambican
mozárabe ADJ Mozarabic
mozo-za ADJ young; **en mis años —s** in my youth; M (joven) young man; (sirviente) servant; F (joven) young woman; (sirvienta) servant; **— de cordel** porter; **buen —** handsome man
mucama F chambermaid
muchacho-cha M boy, youngster; F (chica) girl; (de servicio) maid
muchedumbre F crowd, throng
mucho ADJ a lot of; (cosas contables) many; (cosas incontables, en oraciones interrogativas y/o negativas) much; **¿tienes — tiempo?** do you have much time? **no tenemos — tiempo** we don't have much time; **tenemos —s problemas** we have many problems; ADV much; (demasiado) too much; **hace — que no lo veo** I haven't seen him for a long time; **ni con —** not by a long shot; **ni — menos** not by any means; **por — que** no matter how much; PRON a lot, many; (en preguntas y oraciones negativas) much; **¿había —s?** were there many?
mucoso ADJ mucous
muda F (de ropa, voz) change; (de plumas, piel de serpiente) molt
mudable ADJ fickle
mudanza F move
mudar VT (condiciones, clima) to change; (el pelo) to shed; (la piel, plumas) to molt; **—se [de casa]** to move [house]; **—se de ropa** to change clothes
mudez F dumbness, muteness
mudo-da ADJ (incapaz de hablar) mute, dumb; (por emoción) speechless; (película) silent; MF mute
mueble M piece of furniture; **—s** furniture
mueblería F (tienda) furniture store; (fábrica) furniture factory
mueca F grimace; **hacer —s** to grimace
muela F (diente) molar tooth; (piedra) grindstone; **— del juicio** wisdom tooth; **— impactada** impacted molar
muelle M (para embarcaciones) wharf, pier; (resorte) spring; **— en espiral** coil; **— real** mainspring
muera, muere *ver* morir
muérdago M mistletoe
muerte F death; **— cerebral** brain death; **— súbita** (fútbol) sudden death; (tenis) tie-break; **dar —** to kill; **sus clases son la —** his classes are unbearable; **de mala —** disreputable
muerto ADJ dead, lifeless; **— de cansancio** dead tired; **— de hambre** famished; **estoy — de sed** I'm parched; **echarle el — a uno** to pass the buck; **ni —** not in a million years
muerto *ver* morir
muesca F notch, indentation
muestra F (ejemplo) sample (también en computadoras); (señal) sign, token; **— de orina** urine specimen; **dar —s de impaciencia** to show impatience
muestra, muestre *ver* mostrar
muestrear VT to sample (también para computadoras)
muestreo M sampling
mueva, mueve *ver* mover
mugido M moo, lowing
mugir[46] VI to moo, to low
mugre F dirt, grime, crud
mugriento ADJ grimy, dirty
mujer F (género) woman; (esposa) wife; **— de negocios** businesswoman; **— de la vida** prostitute
mujeriego ADJ womanizing; M womanizer, *fam* player
mula *ver* mulo
mulato-ta ADJ & MF mulatto
muleta F crutch
muletilla F cliché
mullido ADJ fluffy
mullir[16] VT to fluff
mulo-la MF mule (también en el tráfico de drogas)
multa F fine, penalty; (de tránsito) ticket
multar VT to fine; (en tránsito) to ticket
multianual ADJ multiyear
multicultural ADJ multicultural
multilateral ADJ multilateral
multimedia M & ADJ INV multimedia
multipantalla ADJ multiscreen
múltiple ADJ multiple
multiplicación F multiplication
multiplicar[30] VI/VT to multiply; **—se** to breed
multiplicidad F multiplicity
múltiplo M multiple
multitarea F multitasking
multitud F multitude, throng
mundano ADJ mundane, worldly
mundial ADJ global, worldwide; **la guerra —** the world war
mundo M world; **todo el —** everybody; **tener — to be worldly; el tercer —** the third world; **el — al revés** the world upside-down
munición F ammunition, munition
municipal ADJ municipal; **servicios —es** city services
municipalidad F municipality
municipio M municipality; (ayuntamiento) city hall
muñeca F (juguete) doll; (articulación del brazo) wrist; **— de trapo** ragdoll
muñeco M (juguete) boy doll; (de ventrílocuo) dummy; **— de nieve** snowman
muñón M stump

mural ADJ & M mural
muralla F wall
murciélago M bat
muriendo, muriera, muriese *ver* morir
murmullo M (voz baja) murmur; (ruido de agua) babble
murmuración F gossip
murmurar VI/VT (voz) to murmur; VI (agua) to babble
muro M wall; **— de contención** retaining wall
murria F the blues; **tener —** to have the blues
musa F muse
musaraña F shrew
muscular ADJ muscular
músculo M muscle
musculoso ADJ muscular
muselina F muslin
museo M museum
musgo M moss
musgoso ADJ mossy
música F music; **— de cámara** chamber music; **— folclórica** folk music; **— incidental** incidental music
musical ADJ & M musical
músico -ca ADJ musical; MF musician
musitar VI to mutter
muslo M thigh
mustio ADJ (triste) sad, humble; (marchito) limp; (deslucido) faded
musulmán -ana ADJ & MF Muslim, Moslem
mutación F mutation
mutante ADJ & MF mutant
mutilar VT to mutilate, to mangle; (a un ser vivo) to maim, to mutilate; (una estatua) to deface
mutuo ADJ mutual
muy ADV very; **estás — grande para eso** you're too big for that
Myanmar M Myanmar

Nn

nabo M turnip
nácar M mother-of-pearl
nacarado ADJ pearly
nacer[35] VI (un bebé) to be born; (una calle) to begin; **— de** (río) to spring from; **— de nuevo** to have a new lease on life
naciente ADJ (tendencia) incipient; (sol) rising; M (de río) origin
nacimiento M (alumbramiento) birth; (pesebre) nativity scene; (naciente) origin [of a river]; **— del pelo** hairline
nación F nation
nacional ADJ & MF national
nacionalidad F nationality
nacionalismo M nationalism
nacionalista ADJ & MF nationalist
nacionalizar[47] VT to nationalize
nada PRON nothing; *fam* squat, zilch; **— del otro mundo** nothing special; **— en absoluto** nothing at all; **como si —** as if nothing had happened; **de —** you are welcome, don't mention it; **no es por —, pero** I hope you don't mind my saying this, but; **no sirve para —** it's useless; **no tener — que ver con** to have nothing to do with; **no tengo — de dinero** I don't have any money; **para —** in the least; **quedar en la —** to fall through; **salir de la —** to come out of nowhere; ADV not at all; **no me gusta [para] —** I don't like it at all; (tenis) **quince a —** forty love; F (existencial) nothingness
nadador -ora MF swimmer
nadar VI/VT to swim; **— en la abundancia** to be in the lap of luxury
nadería F trifle, nothing
nadie PRON nobody; **— más** no one else; **no vi a — en el parque** I didn't see anyone in the park; **un don —** a nobody
nafta F gasoline
nailon M nylon
naipe M playing card
nalgada F smack on the bottom
nalgas F PL buttocks
Namibia F Namibia
namibio -bia ADJ & MF Namibian
nana F (canción de cuna) lullaby; (lastimadura) boo-boo; (niñera) babysitter
nanosegundo M nanosecond
nanotecnología F nanotechnology
napalm M napalm
napias F PL *fam* snout
naranja F (fruta) orange; ADJ INV & M (color) orange; **— de ombligo** navel orange; **mi media —** my better half
naranjal M orange grove
naranjo M orange tree
narcisismo M narcissism
narciso M narcissus, daffodil
narcolepsia F narcolepsy
narcótico ADJ & M narcotic
narcotizar[47] VT to drug
narcotraficante MF drug trafficker
narcotráfico M drug trafficking
nariz F nose; **— chata** pug nose; **sonarse la —** to blow one's nose; F PL **narices** nostrils; **se dio de narices contra la ventana** he bumped his nose on the window; **estoy hasta las narices** I've had it up to here
narración F narration
narrador -ora MF narrator
narrar VT to narrate, to recount
narrativa F narrative

narrativo ADJ narrative
NASA F NASA
nasal ADJ nasal
nata F skin of boiled milk; *Esp* cream
natación F swimming
natal ADJ (relativo al nacimiento) natal; (suelo) native; **mi ciudad** — my hometown
natalidad F birth rate
natilla[s] F SG/PL custard
nativo -va ADJ & MF native
nato ADJ **es un músico** — he's a born musician
natural ADJ (no artificial) natural; (nacido en un lugar) native; (nacido fuera del matrimonio) illegitimate; (sin afectación) unaffected; M nature; **al** — unprocessed
naturaleza F nature; — **muerta** still life
naturalidad F naturalness
naturalista MF naturalist
naturalización F naturalization
naturalizar[47] VT to naturalize; —**se** to become naturalized
naturalmente ADV (de forma natural) naturally; (desde luego) of course
naufragar[40] VI (un barco) to shipwreck; (una empresa) to fail
naufragio M shipwreck
náufrago -ga MF shipwrecked person
Nauru M Nauru
nauruano -na ADJ & MF Nauruan
náusea F nausea; —**s** morning sickness; **dar** —**s** to nauseate; **hasta la** — ad nauseam; **tener** —**s** to be nauseated, to be sick to one's stomach
nauseabundo ADJ nauseating
nauseoso ADJ (que siente náuseas) nauseous, queasy; (que provoca náuseas) nauseating
náutica F navigation
náutico ADJ nautical
navaja F (de explorador) jackknife, pocketknife; (de barbero) razor
navajazo M (golpe) stab with a jackknife; (herida) stab wound
naval ADJ naval
navarro ADJ & MF Navarrese
nave F (embarcación) vessel; (parte de una catedral) nave; — **espacial** spaceship
navegable ADJ navigable
navegación F (de mar, río) navigation; (deportiva) boating; (en internet) surfing, browsing
navegador M browser; — **web** web browser
navegante MF navigator; ADJ navigating
navegar[40] VI/VT (buque) to navigate; (barco a vela) to sail; (en internet) to browse, to surf
Navidad F Christmas
navideño ADJ **fiesta navideña** Christmas party
navío M ship
nazi MF Nazi
neblina F mist
neblinoso ADJ misty
nebulosidad F cloudiness
nebuloso ADJ (poco claro) nebulous; (que tiene niebla) foggy
necesario ADJ necessary
neceser M toiletry bag
necesidad F (urgencia, sensación de falta) need; (cosa necesaria) necessity; **hacer sus** —**es** to relieve oneself; **de primera** — indispensable; **por** — out of necessity
necesitado ADJ needy
necesitar VT to need
necio -cia ADJ asinine, foolish
necrología F necrology
necrosis F necrosis
néctar M nectar
nectarina F nectarine
nefasto ADJ unholy
nefritis F nephritis
negación F (partícula gramatical) negation; (rechazo) denial
negar[41] VT (decir que no es verdad) to deny; (no consentir) to refuse; (no reconocer) to disavow; —**se [a]** to refuse [to]
negativa F (rechazo verbal) denial; (falta de cooperación) refusal
negativo ADJ negative; **signo** — minus sign; M [photographic] negative
negligencia F (falta de atención) negligence, neglect; (médica) malpractice
negligente ADJ negligent, neglectful
negociación F negotiation; — **laboral** collective bargaining
negociador -ora MF negotiator; ADJ negotiating
negociante MF businessperson
negociar VI/VT (acordar) to negotiate; (comerciar) to trade
negocio M (tienda, actividad comercial) business; (transacción) business deal, business transaction; — **de ventas por correo** mail-order business; — **principal** core business; **hombre de** —**s** businessman; **mujer de** —**s** businesswoman; **hacer** — to make a profit
negrear VI to appear black; VT to blacken
negrilla F boldface
negritas F PL boldface type
negro -ra ADJ black (también café sin leche); (futuro) bleak; **pasarlas negras** to undergo hardships; F (nota) quarter-note; MF (persona) person of color, black person
negrura F blackness
negruzco ADJ blackish
némesis F nemesis
nene -na M baby boy; F baby girl
nenúfar M water lily
neologismo M neologism

neón M neon
neonatal ADJ neonatal
neozelandés -esa MF New Zealander
Nepal M Nepal
nepalés -esa ADJ & MF Nepali
nepalí ADJ & MF Nepalese
nepotismo M nepotism
nervado ADJ veined
nervio M nerve; **— pellizcado** pinched nerve; **— pinzado** pinched nerve; **perder los —s** to lose one's cool; **tener los —s de punta** to be on edge
nerviosismo M nervousness
nervioso ADJ (relativo a los nervios) nervous; (inquieto) nervous, jumpy
nervudo ADJ sinewy, wiry
neto ADJ (mejoría) distinct; (ganancia) net
neumático M tire; ADJ pneumatic
neural ADJ neural
neuralgia F neuralgia
neurastenia F neurasthenia
neurocirugía F neurosurgery
neurocirujano -na MF neurosurgeon
neurólogo -ga MF neurologist
neurona F neuron, nerve cell
neurosis F neurosis
neurótico -ca ADJ & MF neurotic
neurotransmisor M neurotransmitter
neutral ADJ neutral
neutralidad F neutrality
neutralizar[47] VT to neutralize
neutro ADJ neutral; (género) neuter
neutrón M neutron
nevada F snowfall
nevado ADJ snowy
nevar[1] VI to snow
nevera F icebox, refrigerator
nevisca F snow flurry
ni CONJ & ADV **— con mucho** not by a long shot; **— hablar** forget it; **— habló conmigo** he didn't even talk to me; **— idea** [it] beats me; **— modo** no way; **— que esto fuera un hotel** it's not like this is a hotel; **— siquiera** not even; **— soñar** fat chance; **— trabaja — estudia** he neither works nor studies; **— una palabra** not a word; **no tiene amigos — enemigos** he has no friends nor enemies; **no es rico — mucho menos** he's not even close to being rich
Nicaragua F Nicaragua
nicaragüense ADJ & MF Nicaraguan
nicho M niche, recess
nicotina F nicotine
nidada F (huevos) nest of eggs; (crías) hatch, brood
nido M nest
niebla F fog
niega, niegue *ver* negar
nieto -ta M grandson; F granddaughter; **—s** grandchildren
nieve F snow (también droga en polvo)
Níger M Niger
Nigeria F Nigeria
nigeriano -na ADJ & MF Nigerian
nigerino -na ADJ & MF Nigerien
nigua F chigger
nihilismo M nihilism
nilón M nylon
nimio ADJ insignificant
ninguno ADJ & PRON **no tengo —** I have none / I don't have any; **ningún amigo mío** no friend of mine; **no tengo ningún libro** I don't have any books; **— de los dos** neither one; **de ningún modo** in no way
niñera F (ocasional) babysitter; (permanente) nanny
niñería F childish act
niñez F (infancia) childhood; (de niño) boyhood; (de niña) girlhood
niño -ña M child, kid, boy; F child, kid, girl; **niña del ojo** pupil [of the eye]; ADJ childish
níquel M nickel
niquelado ADJ nickel-plated
níspero M loquat
nitidez F sharpness
nítido ADJ sharp
nitrato M nitrate
nitrógeno M nitrogen
nitroglicerina F nitroglycerine
nivel M level (también herramienta); (grado jerárquico) echelon; **— de cobertura** coverage level; **— de mar** sea level; **— de vida** standard of living; **a —** straight; **a — de** level with
nivelar VT (emparejar) to level; (aplanar) to grade
níveo ADJ snowy
no ADV no; **— quiero** I don't want to; **— acreditado** unlicensed; **— afiliado** unaffiliated; **— ajustado** unadjusted; **— autorizado** unauthorized; **— comercial** noncommercial; **— confirmado** unconfirmed; **— conforme** nonconforming; **— declarado** undeclared; **— disponible** unavailable; **— divulgado** undisclosed; **— esencial** nonessential; **— especificado** unspecified; **— ético** unethical; **— gubernamental** nongovernmental; **— negociable** nonnegotiable; **— reembolsable** nonrefundable; **— relacionado** unrelated; **— residente** nonresident; **— restringido** unrestricted; **— solicitado** unsolicited; **— tributable** nontaxable; **— bien llegaron** no sooner had they arrived; **— sólo** not only; **— sea que** lest; **a — ser que** unless
noble ADJ noble; M nobleman; F noblewoman
nobleza F nobility

nocaut M knockout
noche F (período sin luz) night; (horas de la noche) nighttime; **—buena** Christmas Eve; **—vieja** New Year's Eve; **— y día** day and night; **de —** at night; **de la — a la mañana** overnight; **esta —** tonight; **por la —** at night
noción F notion; **no tener ni —** to have no clue
nocivo ADJ harmful, noxious
nocturno ADJ (que actúa de noche) nocturnal; (que sucede todas las noches) nightly
nodo M node
nodriza F wet nurse
nódulo M node
nogal M walnut tree
nómada MF nomad
ningunear VT to dismiss
nomás ADV *Am* **aquí —** close by; **así —** just like that; **entre —** come right in
nombramiento M (civil) appointment; (militar) commission
nombrar VT (a un funcionario) to name, to appoint; (a un oficial militar) to commission
nombre M name; **— completo** full name; **— de acceso** login name; **— de pila** first name; **— de soltera** maiden name; **— del usuario** username; **en — de** on behalf of; **eso no tiene —** that's unheard of; **hacerse un —** to make a name for oneself
nomenclatura F nomenclature
nomeolvides M SG forget-me-not
nómina F payroll
nominación F nomination
nominal ADJ nominal
nominar VT to nominate
non ADJ odd; M odd number
nopal M prickly pear
noquear VT to knock out
norcoreano -na ADJ & MF North Korean
nordeste ADJ & M northeast
nórdico ADJ Nordic
noreste ADJ & M northeast
norma F norm, standard; **—s industriales** industry standards
normal ADJ (estándar, común) normal, standard; F (escuela) teacher's college; (línea) perpendicular line
normalidad F normalcy, normality; **con toda —** normally; **todo volvió a la —** everything returned to normal
normalizar[47] VT to normalize
normalmente ADV normally, usually
normativa F norm
noroeste ADJ & M northwest
norte ADJ & M north
norteamericano -na ADJ & MF (de América del Norte) North American; (de EEUU) American
norteño -ña ADJ northern; MF northerner
Noruega F Norway
noruego -ga ADJ & MF Norwegian; M (lengua) Norwegian
nos PRON us; **él — vio** he saw us; **— dio el libro** he gave us the book, he gave the book to us
nosotros -as PRON we; **para —** for us
nostalgia F nostalgia
nostálgico ADJ nostalgic
nota F (musical) note; (anotación) annotation; (calificación) grade, mark; **— al pie de página** footnote; **de —** of note; **exagerar la —** to overdo something
notable ADJ notable, noteworthy, remarkable
notablemente ADV (destacadamente) notably; (visiblemente) noticeably
notación F notation
notar VT (percibir) to note, to notice; (señalar) to note
notariar VT to notarize
notario -ria MF notary
noticia F piece of news; **—s** news; **tener —s de alguien** to hear from someone
noticiario M newscast, news bulletin
noticiero M newscast
notificación F (informe) notification; (policial) summons; **— de despido** pink slip
notificar[30] VT to notify
notorio ADJ (conocido públicamente) well-known; (evidente) obvious
novato -ta MF (profesional) novice; (policía, atleta) rookie
novecientos NUM nine hundred
novedad F novelty; **—es** news; **sin —** all's well
novedoso ADJ novel
novela F novel; **— policial** detective novel
novelesco ADJ fictional
novelista MF novelist
noveno ADJ ninth
noventa NUM ninety
noviazgo M engagement
novicio -cia MF novice
noviembre M November
novillo -lla M steer; **hacer —s** to play hooky; F heifer
novio -via M (comprometido) fiancé; (no formal) boyfriend; (de boda) bridegroom; F (comprometida) fiancée; (no formal) girlfriend; (de boda) bride
novocaína F novocaine
nubarrón M thunderhead
nube F (atmosférica) cloud; (de humo) billow; **poner por las —s** to praise to the skies; **está en las —s** his head is in the clouds; **los precios están por las —s** prices have gone through the roof
nublado ADJ (cielo) cloudy, overcast; (los ojos, de emoción) misty; (los ojos, por falta de sueño) bleary
nublar VT to blur; **—se** (el cielo) to become overcast; (los ojos) to cloud over
nubosidad F (de un concepto) nebulousness;

(del cielo) cloudiness
nuboso ADJ cloudy
nuca F nape
nuclear ADJ nuclear
núcleo M (de célula, átomo) nucleus; (de reactor) core; (de sistema operativo) kernel
nudillo M knuckle
nudismo M nudism
nudista ADJ & MF nudist
nudo M knot (también en la madera, medida de velocidad); (de una obra teatral) turning point; (en el pelo) tangle; (en plantas) node; (en la garganta) lump; **— corredizo** slipknot; **— de rizo** square knot
nudoso ADJ knotty, gnarled
nuera F daughter-in-law
nuestro ADJ POS our; **— hijo** our son; PRON ours; **esto es —** this is ours
nuevamente ADV again
nueve NUM nine
nuevo ADJ new; **de —** again; **¿qué hay de —?** what's new?
nuez F walnut; **— de Adán** Adam's apple; **— moscada** nutmeg
nulidad F (legal) nullity; (persona) nonentity
nulo ADJ null and void, invalid
numeral ADJ & M numeral
numerar VT to number
numérico ADJ numerical
número M (dígito) number; (en un espectáculo) act; (de una revista) issue; (cifra) figure; **— de serie** serial number
numeroso ADJ numerous
nunca ADV never, not ever; **no viene —** he never comes, he doesn't ever come; **más que —** more than ever; **casi —** hardly ever; **peor que —** worse than ever
nupcial ADJ nuptial, bridal
nupcias F PL nuptials
nutria F otter
nutrición F nutrition
nutrido ADJ **el congreso tuvo una nutrida concurrencia** the conference was well attended
nutriente M nutrient
nutrir VT to nourish
nutritivo ADJ nutritious, nourishing

Ñ ñ

ñandú M rhea
ñato ADJ *Am* pug-nosed
ñoño ADJ bland
ñu M gnu

O o

o CONJ or; **— se casa — lo mato** either he gets married or I'll kill him; **— sea** that is
oasis M oasis
obedecer[35] VI/VT to obey; **esto obedece a que** this is due to the fact that
obedezca, obedezco *ver* obedecer
obediencia F obedience
obediente ADJ obedient
obertura F musical overture
obesidad F obesity
obeso ADJ obese
obispo M bishop
obituario M obituary
objeción F objection
objetable ADJ objectionable
objetar VI/VT to object, to take exception [to]
objetividad F objectivity
objetivo ADJ objective; M (lente) objective; (meta) aim, objective
objeto M object
oblea F wafer
oblicuo ADJ (inclinado) oblique; (sesgado) biased
obligación F (deber) obligation, duty; (deuda) obligation; (título financiero) bond
obligado ADJ (forzado) forced; (obligatorio) compulsory, obligatory; **me vi — a comprar otro coche** I was forced / had to buy another car
obligar[40] VT to force, to compel, to oblige; **—se [a]** to obligate oneself [to]
obligatorio ADJ obligatory, compulsory
oboe M oboe
obra F (artística, literaria, de construcción) work; (lugar de construcción) construction site; **— maestra** masterpiece; **en —s** under construction
obrar VI to act; **obra en nuestro poder** we acknowledge receipt of
obrero -ra MF worker; ADJ working
obscenidad F obscenity; **—es** filth
obsceno ADJ obscene
obscuridad *ver* oscuridad
obsequiar VT to present, to give; **me obsequió perfume** he gave me perfume
obsequio M gift
obsequioso ADJ obsequious
observación F (mirada) observation; (comentario) remark
observador -ora MF observer; ADJ observant
observancia F observance
observar VI/VT (mirar) to observe; (hacer un comentario) to remark, to observe
observatorio M observatory

obsesión F obsession
obsesionado ADJ obsessed
obsesionar VT to obsess; **—se con** to obsess over, to be obsessed with
obsesivo-compulsivo ADJ obsessive-compulsive
obstaculizar VT to impede
obstáculo M (impedimento) obstacle, hindrance, impediment; (en carreras) hurdle
obstante LOC PREP **no — tu oposición** notwithstanding your opposition; LOC ADV **no —, voy a ir** nevertheless, I am going to go
obstar VT to preclude
obstetra MF obstetrician
obstetricia F obstetrics
obstinación F obstinacy
obstinado ADJ obstinate, bullheaded
obstinarse VI to be obstinate
obstrucción F (de justicia, de un caño) obstruction, blockage; (del intestino) obstruction, occlusion; **— intestinal** intestinal obstruction
obstruir[19] VT (un movimiento, procedimiento) to obstruct, to block; (un aparato) to jam; VI **—se** to get jammed
obtención F acquisition
obtendrá, obtendría *ver* obtener
obtener[58] VT (bienes) to obtain, to get; (permiso) to secure; (con dificultad) to procure
obtenga, obtengo, obtiene, obtienes *ver* obtener
obturador M (de una cámara fotográfica) shutter; (de un coche) choke
obtuve, obtuviera, obtuviese *ver* obtener
obviamente ADV obviously
obviar VT to obviate, to circumvent
obvio ADJ obvious
ocasión F (vez, instancia) occasion; (oportunidad) opportunity; (ganga) bargain; **de —** reduced
ocasional ADJ occasional
ocasionar VT to occasion, to cause
ocaso M sunset, twilight
occidental ADJ occidental, western; MF westerner
occidente M west
oceánico ADJ oceanic
océano M ocean
oceanografía F oceanography
ocelote M ocelot
ochenta NUM eighty
ocho NUM eight
ochocientos NUM eight hundred
ocio M (diversión) leisure; (inacción) idleness
ociosidad F idleness
ocioso ADJ (inactivo) idle; (no usado) unused
oclusión F occlusion
octágono M octagon
octano M octane
octava F octave
octavilla F tract
octavo ADJ & M eighth
octeto M byte
octógono M octagon
octubre M October
ocular M eyepiece; ADJ **infección —** eye infection
oculista MF oculist, eye doctor
ocultar VT to conceal; (información) to withhold
ocultismo M the occult
oculto ADJ (invisible) unseen; (sobrenatural) occult; (escondido) hidden, under wraps
ocupación F (trabajo) occupation; (capacidad) occupancy
ocupado ADJ (persona, teléfono) busy; (asiento, aseo) occupied
ocupante MF occupant
ocupar VT (usar) to occupy; (contratar) to employ; **—se de** to take care of, to address
ocurrencia F witticism, quip
ocurrente ADJ witty
ocurrir VI to occur
oda F ode
odiar VI/VT to hate
odio M hatred, hate
odioso ADJ (tarea) odious; (persona) hateful, obnoxious
odontología F dentistry
odre M wineskin
OEA [Organización de Estados Americanos] F OAS
oeste ADJ & M west
ofender VI/VT to offend; **—se** to get offended, to take offense
ofensa F offense
ofensiva F (militar) offensive; (deportiva) offense; (fútbol americano) offensive series
ofensivo ADJ offensive, obnoxious
oferta F (oportunidad) offer; (rebaja) special offer; **— de apertura** opening bid; **en —** on sale; **— de prueba** trial offer; **— pública inicial** initial public offering
offset M offset
oficial -la ADJ official; MF (militar) officer; (obrero calificado) skilled worker; **— general** high-ranking officer
oficialismo M party in power
oficialista ADJ in power
oficiar VI to officiate; **— de** to serve as
oficina F (despacho) office; (dependencia gubernamental) bureau; **— central** home office, headquarters; **— en el hogar** home office
oficinista MF office worker
oficio M (actividad laboral) trade, craft; (comunicación oficial) official communication; **tiene mucho —** he knows

his stuff; **buenos —s** good offices
oficioso ADJ (entrometido) officious; (no oficial) unofficial, off-the-record
ofrecer[35] VT (un regalo) to offer; (en una subasta) to bid; (una cena) to give; **—resistencia** to put up resistance; **¿qué se le ofrece a usted?** how can I help you?
ofrecimiento M (acción de ofrecer) offering; (oferta) offer
ofrenda F offering
oftalmólogo -ga MF ophthalmologist
ofuscar[30] VT to bewilder
ogro M ogre
ohmio M ohm
oído M (facultad) hearing; (órgano) inner ear; (musical) ear; **— medio** middle ear; **al —** confidentially; **de —** by ear
oiga, oigo *ver* oír
oír[55] VI/VT (percibir) to hear; (atender) to listen; **— decir que** to hear that; **— hablar de** to hear about; **— misa** to attend mass; **¡oye!** listen! hey!
ojal M buttonhole
ojalá INTERJ **— estuviera aquí** I wish he were here; **— que venga** I hope that he comes
ojeada F glimpse
ojear VT to glimpse
ojera F dark circle under the eye
ojeriza F animosity
ojeroso ADJ with dark circles under the eyes
ojiva F (arco) pointed arch; (explosivo) warhead
ojo M (órgano, centro de huracán, instinto, yema de patata) eye; **¡—!** careful! look out! **a — de buen cubero** as a rule of thumb; **a —s vistas** clearly; **me costó un — de la cara** it cost me an arm and a leg; **¿no tienes —s en la cara?** are you blind? **dichosos los —s que te ven** you're a sight for sore eyes; **— de buey** porthole; **— de la cerradura** keyhole; **— de lince** eagle-eye; **— morado** black eye; **— por —** an eye for an eye
ola F wave; (de un olor) waft; (de protesta) storm
oleada F wave, surge
oleaje M swell, surge
óleo M oil painting
oleoducto M oil pipeline
oleoso ADJ oily
oler[22] VI/VT to smell (también sospechar); **— a** to smell of
olfatear VI/VT to scent, to sniff
olfateo M sniff, sniffing
olfato M (facultad) sense of smell; (instinto) nose
olfatorio ADJ olfactory
olimpíada F Olympiad; **—s** Olympic Games
olímpico ADJ Olympian
oliva F olive
olivar M olive grove
olivo M olive tree
olla F pot; **— de grillos** snake pit; **— podrida** stew of mixed vegetables and meat
olmo M elm
olor M smell, odor
oloroso ADJ odorous
olvidadizo ADJ forgetful
olvidar VI/VT to forget; **—se [de]** to forget; **se me olvidó algo** I forgot something
olvido M oblivion; **caer en el —** to be forgotten; **echar al —** to cast into oblivion; **tus —s** your forgetfulness
Omán M Oman
omaní ADJ & MF Omani
ombligo M navel
OMC [Organización Mundial del Comercio] F WTO
omisión F omission; **por —** by default
omiso ADJ **hacer caso — [de]** to ignore
omitir VT (eliminar) to omit, to leave out; (no notar) to overlook
ómnibus M bus
omnipotente ADJ omnipotent
omnisciencia F omniscience
omnisciente ADJ omniscient
omnívoro ADJ omnivorous
omóplato M scapula
OMS [Organización Mundial de la Salud] F WHO
once NUM eleven
oncología F oncology
onda F wave; **— corta** shortwave; **— expansiva** shock wave; **— sonora** sound wave; **agarrarle la — a algo** to get in the swing of things; **captar la —** to get the drift
ondeado ADJ wavy
ondeante ADJ flying
ondear VI to wave
ondulación F ripple, ruffle, roll
ondulado ADJ (pelo) wavy; (paisaje) rolling
ondulante ADJ undulating
ondular VI to undulate; VI/VT to wave
ónix M onyx
omnipotencia F omnipotence
onomatopeya F onomatopoeia
ONU [Organización de las Naciones Unidas] F UN
onza F ounce
opacar[30] VT (oscurecer) to dull; (eclipsar) to overshadow
opaco ADJ (no transparente) opaque; (no brillante) dull
ópalo M opal
opción F option; **opciones** stock options; **— de venta** put option
opcional ADJ optional
OPEP [Organización de Países Exportadores de Petróleo] F OPEC
ópera F (composición) opera; (teatro) opera house
operable ADJ operable

operación F operation
operador-ora M (en matemáticas) operator; MF (de teléfono) operator
operar VI/VT (usar maquinaria) to operate; VT (intervenir quirúrgicamente) to operate on; (llevar a cabo) to carry out; VI (hacer cuentas) to do mathematical operations
operario-ria MF operator, operative
operativo ADJ (que funciona) operative; (vigente) in effect; M *Am* — **policial** police operation
opiáceo M opiate
opinar VI/VT to hold an opinion, to think
opinión F opinion, view, feeling; **cambiar de** — to change one's mind
opio M opium
oponente MF (en un debate) opponent; (en una película) costar
oponer[56, 74] VT to oppose; —**se** to conflict; —**se a** to oppose, to be against
oponga, opongo *ver* oponer
oporto M port wine
oportunidad F (chance) opportunity, chance; (pretexto) opening; (fútbol americano) down
oportunista ADJ & MF opportunistic
oportuno ADJ (conveniente) opportune, timely; (adecuado) appropriate
oposición F opposition; **oposiciones** competitive examinations
opositor-ora MF opponent
opresión F oppression
opresivo ADJ oppressive
opresor-ora MF oppressor
oprimir VT (al pueblo) to oppress; (un botón) to press; (un enlace digital) to click
optar VI to choose; — **por** to choose
optativo ADJ optional
óptico-ca ADJ optical; MF optician; F optics
optimismo M optimism
optimista ADJ optimistic; MF optimist
optimizar VT to optimize
óptimo ADJ optimal
optometría F optometry
optometrista MF optometrist
opuesto ADJ opposite, contrary; **se mostró** — **al casamiento** he was against the marriage; **dos fuerzas opuestas** two opposing forces; **lo** — the opposite; **dirección opuesta** the opposite/reverse direction
opulencia F opulence
opulento ADJ (decoración) opulent; (sociedad) affluent
opuse, opusiera, opusiese *ver* oponer
oración F (frase) sentence; (plegaria) prayer
oráculo M oracle
orador-ora MF orator, speaker
oral ADJ oral
orangután M orangutan
orar VI/VT to pray
oratoria F oratory
oratorio M oratory
órbita F (de los cuerpos celestes) orbit; (de los ojos) eye socket
orbitador M orbiter
orbital ADJ orbital
orbitar VI/VT to orbit
orca F killer whale
orden M (limpieza, secuencia) order; — **ascendente** ascending order; — **de clasificación** sort order; — **del día** order of the day; **perturbar el** — **público** to disturb the peace; **sin** — **ni concierto** haphazard; F (mando) command, order; (grupo religioso) order; — **de cateo** warrant; — **de compra** purchase order; — **judicial** court order; **a sus órdenes** at your service
ordenación F (arreglo) ordering, organization; (de un cura) ordination; (informatización) computerization
ordenado ADJ orderly, neat
ordenador M *Esp* computer; — **de mano** palmtop; — **de sobremesa** desktop computer; — **digital** digital computer; — **portátil** laptop computer; — **torre** tower computer
ordenamiento M (arreglo) ordering, putting in order; (conjunto de leyes) legal code; — **territorial** land use
ordenanza F ordinance; MF orderly
ordenar VT (arreglar) to sort, to put in order; (mandar) to order, to command; (conferir órdenes religiosos) to ordain; —**se** to become ordained
ordeñar VT to milk
ordeño M milking
ordinal ADJ ordinal
ordinariez F vulgarity
ordinario ADJ (corriente) ordinary; (vulgar) vulgar
orear VT to air out
orégano M oregano
oreja F [outer] ear; (de un martillo) claw; (en un utensilio) flap; **aguzar la** — to prick up one's ears; **sonreír de** — **a** — to smile from ear to ear; **estar hasta las** —**s en algo** to be up to one's neck in something
orejera F earmuff
orfanato M orphanage
orfebre MF (con oro) goldsmith; (con plata) silversmith
orgánico ADJ organic
organigrama M organizational chart, flow chart
organismo M organism
organista MF organist
organización F organization
organizado ADJ organized
organizador-ora MF organizer

organizar[47] VT (una reunión, evento) to organize; (un ataque) to stage; (una fiesta) to give, to throw
organizativo ADJ organizational, organizing
órgano M organ
orgía F orgy
orgullo M pride; **es mi —** she's my pride and joy
orgulloso ADJ proud
orientación F (vocacional, psicológica) orientation, guidance; (de velas) trim; (de estudios) track; (de un objeto) lie; (del terreno) lay; **— horizontal** landscape; **— vertical** portrait
orientado ADJ oriented; **— al cliente** customer-oriented
oriental ADJ oriental, eastern; MF oriental
orientar VT to orient; **—se** to get one's bearings
oriente M Orient, east
orificio M orifice
origen M origin; (de un problema, conflicto) source; (antecedentes familiares) birth
original ADJ original; M (de una pintura) original; (de una cinta magnética) master
originalidad F originality
originar VT to originate, to give rise to; **—se** to originate, to arise
originario ADJ (original) original; **— de** (de cierto origen) coming from, native of
orilla F (de un lago, mar) shore, bank; (de una cama) edge; (de una prenda) hem
orillar VT (una calle) to border; (una prenda) to hem
orín M rust; M PL **orines** urine
orina F urine
orinal M chamber pot
orinar VI/VT to urinate
oriundo ADJ **ser — de** (persona) to hail from; (cosa) to originate in
orla F (de un uniforme) trimming; (de una alfombra) fringe
orlar VT to fringe
orlón™ M Orlon™
ornamentación F ornamentation
ornamental ADJ ornamental
ornamentar VT to ornament, to embellish
ornamento M ornament
ornar VT to adorn
ornitología F ornithology
oro M gold; **— blanco** white gold; **— en lingotes** gold bullion; **— negro** black gold; **— puro** solid gold; **prometer el — y el moro** to promise the moon
orondo ADJ self-satisfied
oropel M tinsel
oropéndola F oriole
orquesta F orchestra
orquestar VT to orchestrate
orquídea F orchid
ortiga F nettle
ortodoncia F orthodontics
ortodoxo ADJ orthodox
ortografía F orthography, spelling
oruga F caterpillar
orujo M rape
orzuelo M sty
osadía F boldness, daring
osado ADJ bold, daring
osamenta F skeleton
osar VI/VT to dare
oscilación F oscillation
oscilar VI to oscillate, to seesaw; **— entre** to range between
oscurecer VI (ponerse oscuro) to get dark; VT (poner oscuro) to darken; (volver poco inteligible, ocultar) to obscure; **—se** to get darker
oscuridad F (lugar sin luz) dark, darkness; (condición de oscuro) darkness; (falta de claridad conceptual, anonimato) obscurity
oscuro ADJ (sin luz) dark; (turbio) murky; (poco claro, poco conocido) obscure; **lentes —s** dark glasses; **gris —** dark gray; **a oscuras** in the dark
óseo ADJ bony
osezno M bear cub
osificarse VI to ossify
ósmosis F osmosis
oso -sa M bear; F she-bear; **— blanco/polar** polar bear; **— hormiguero** anteater
ostentación F ostentation, show, display; **hacer — de** to flaunt
ostentar VI/VT to display, to show off, to flaunt
ostentoso ADJ ostentatious, showy
osteoartritis F osteoarthritis
osteoporosis F osteoporosis
ostión M large oyster
ostra F oyster
OTAN [Organización del Tratado del Atlántico Norte] F NATO
otero M hillock
otitis F otitis; **— externa** swimmer's ear
otoñal ADJ autumnal
otoño M autumn, fall
otorgamiento M grant
otorgar[40] VT (permiso) to grant, to concede; (premio) to award
otro ADJ (uno adicional) another; (uno diferente) other; **otra vez** again; **otra cosa** something else; **— más** another one; **al — día** the next day; **de — modo** otherwise; **en otra parte** somewhere else; **la otra cara de la moneda** the flip side; **por otra parte** on the other hand; PRON (uno más) another one; (una persona diferente) someone else; (una cosa diferente) something else
out ADV & M out; **— forzado** force out
ovación F ovation, acclaim
oval ADJ oval

ovalado ADJ oval
óvalo M oval
ovárico ADJ ovarian
ovario M ovary
oveja F (ovino) sheep; (hembra) ewe
ovejero M sheepdog
overoles M PL overalls
ovillar VT to ball; **—se** to curl up into a ball
ovillo M ball of yarn; **hacerse un —** to curl up
OVNI [objeto volador no identificado] M UFO
ovoide N egg-shaped
ovulación F ovulation
ovular VI to ovulate
óvulo M egg
oxidación F oxidation, rusting
oxidado ADJ oxidized, rusty
oxidar VI/VT to oxidize, to rust
óxido M (compuesto químico) oxide; (herrumbre) rust
oxígeno M oxygen
oye, oyendo, oyera, oyese *ver* oír
oyente MF (que oye) listener, hearer; (alumno no oficial) auditor
ozono M ozone

Pp

pabellón M (puesto de feria) pavilion; (parte de un edificio) wing; (bandera) flag; (sección de hospital) ward; **— de la oreja** outer ear
pabilo M wick
paca F bale
pacana F (fruto) pecan; (árbol) pecan tree
pacer[35] VI to pasture, to graze; VT to crop, to graze
paciencia F patience; **con —** patiently; **tener —** to be patient
paciente ADJ & MF patient; **— ambulatorio -ria** outpatient; **— externo -na** outpatient; **— de alto riesgo** high-risk patient
pacificación F pacification
pacificar[30] VT to pacify
pacífico ADJ peaceful; M **Océano Pacífico** Pacific Ocean
pacifismo M pacifism
pactar VT (hacer un pacto) to make a pact / an agreement; (decidir de común acuerdo) to agree; VI **— con el diablo** to sell one's soul to the devil
pacto M pact, covenant
paddock M (de caballos) paddock; (de coches) pit
padecer[35] VI/VT to suffer; **— de cáncer** to suffer from cancer
padecimiento M suffering
padezca, padezco *ver* padecer
padrastro M (marido de la madre) stepfather; (uñero) hangnail
padre M father; **—s** parents, folks; **— de familia** male head of the household; **—nuestro** the Lord's Prayer; **John Smith, —** John Smith Sr.; **ser —** to become a father; ADJ **un lío —** a real mess
padrino M (de bautizo) godfather; (de boda) best man; (en un duelo) second
paella F paella
paga F (salario) pay; (para un niño) allowance; **— de tiempo y medio** time-and-a-half pay; **— por mérito** merit pay
pagadero ADJ payable, due
pagado ADJ paid; **— de sí mismo** self-satisfied
pagador -ora MF payer
paganismo M paganism
pagano -na ADJ & MF pagan
pagar[40] VT (cuentas, deudas) to pay; (préstamo) to pay off; (mercancías) to pay for; **—se de** to be proud of; **— el pato** to be left holding the bag; **pagan justos por pecadores** the just pay for the sins of others; **— a plazos** to pay in installments; **— al contado** to pay cash; **— con la misma moneda** to pay in kind; **— en especie** to pay in kind
pagaré M promissory note
página F page; **— de estilo** stylesheet; **— web** web page
paginar VT to paginate
pago M payment; **— en efectivo** cash payment; ADJ paid
paila F large pan
país M country; **— de origen** country of origin; **— en desarrollo** developing country; **— exportador de petróleo** oil-exporting country
paisaje M landscape, scenery
paisajismo M landscape architecture
paisano -na M countryman; F countrywoman
paja F straw (también para beber de un vaso); **a humo de —s** thoughtlessly; **por un quítame allá esas —s** for a trifle
pajar M hayloft
pájaro M bird; **— carpintero** woodpecker; **— pinto** cautious person; **un — francés** a French guy
paje M page
pajizo ADJ straw-colored
pajonal M *Am* grassland
pala F (para cavar) shovel; (para recoger basura) dustpan; (de hélice, remo) blade; (de zapato) upper; (para remar, de ping-pong) paddle; **— mecánica** power shovel; **lo tuvimos que recoger con —** he was exhausted
palabra F (unidad léxica) word; (facultad) speech; **— clave** key word; **—s mayores** a big deal; **cuatro —s** a few words; **cumplir**

con la — to keep one's word; **dejar con la — en la boca** to cut someone off in midsentence; **en pocas —s** in a nutshell; **faltar a la** — to break a promise; **la última** — the final say; **ni una** — not a word; **no dijo** — he didn't breathe a word; **un hombre de** — a man of his word; **tener la** — to have the floor; **tomar la** — to take the floor; **traducción — por** — word-for-word translation; **tragarse/comerse las propias —s** to eat one's words

palabrero M verbiage

palabrero ADJ long-winded

palabrota F curse word, four-letter word; **—s** profanity

palacio M palace

paladar M palate; **— hendido** cleft palate; **— óseo** hard palate

paladear VT to relish

paladín M champion, crusader

palanca F (para levantar algo) lever; (para abrir algo) crowbar; (fuerza) leverage; **— de cambios** gearshift lever; **— de juegos** joystick; **— del regulador** throttle lever; **hacer** — to use leverage

palangana F basin

Paláu M Palau

palco M box

palenque M fence

paleontología F paleontology

Palestina F Palestine

palestino -na MF Palestinian; ADJ Palestinian

paleta F (de pintor) palette; (de albañil) trowel; (de ping-pong, para mezclar, batir) paddle; (hélice) blade; (de caramelo) lollipop, sucker; (de helado) Popsicle™

paletilla F shoulder

paleto -ta MF hayseed, hick

paliar VT to alleviate

paliativo M palliative

palidecer[35] VI to turn pale

palidez F pallor, paleness

pálido ADJ pallid, pale

palillo M (de dientes) toothpick; (de tambor) drumstick; (para comida china) chopstick; **tocar todos los —s** to try everything

palique M chitchat

paliza F beating, whipping; **dar una** — to beat, to whip

palma F (árbol) palm [tree]; (hoja) palm leaf; (de la mano) palm [of the hand]; **batir —s** to clap; **llevarse la** — to take the prize; **conocer como la — de la mano** to know like the back of one's hand

palmada F (en la espalda) slap; (aplauso) clap; (en el trasero) spank; **dar una** — (en la espalda) to slap; (en el trasero) to spank

palmear VT to slap on the back

palmera F palm tree

palmípedo M web-footed bird

palmo M span; **— a —** inch by inch

palmotear VT to slap on the back

palo M (de madera) stick; (de barco) mast; (de naipes) suit; (fútbol) goalpost; **—s** (fútbol americano) goalposts; **— de golf** golf club; **— de escoba** broomstick; **dar —s** to hit with a stick; **de tal — tal astilla** a chip off the old block

paloma F dove, pigeon

palomar M pigeon loft

palomilla F wing nut

palomita F (béisbol) fly ball; **—s** popcorn; **hacer** — to pop corn

palote M rolling pin

palpable ADJ palpable

palpar VT to feel

palpitación F palpitation

palpitante ADJ palpitating; **una cuestión** — a burning question

palpitar VI to palpitate

palta F *Am* avocado

paludismo M malaria

pampa F *Am* prairie

pamplinas F PL baloney, hogwash

pan M bread; (pieza) loaf of bread; **— comido** piece of cake, cinch; **— de cada día** everyday occurrence; **— rallado/molido** bread crumbs; **al —, — y al vino, vino** to call a spade a spade; **contigo, — y cebolla** love is all we need; **ganarse el** — to make a living

pana F corduroy

panacea F panacea, magic bullet

panadería F bakery

panadero -ra MF baker

panal M honeycomb

Panamá M Panama

panameño -ña ADJ & MF Panamanian

panamericano ADJ Pan-American

panceta F *RP* bacon

páncreas M SG pancreas

panda M panda bear

pandearse VT to buckle, to sag

pandemia F pandemic

pandémico M pandemic

pandeo M sag

pandereta F tambourine

pandilla F gang, band

panecillo M roll

panegírico M eulogy

panel M panel; **— de control** control panel

panera F breadbasket

panfleto M pamphlet

pánico ADJ & M panic

panoja F ear of corn

panorama M (paisaje) panorama; (horizonte) outlook

panorámico ADJ panoramic

panqueque M pancake

pantaletas F PL panties
pantalla F (de lámpara) lampshade; (para películas) screen; (de monitor) screen, display; (para actividades ilícitas) cover, front; **la — grande** the silver screen; **— dividida** split screen; **— táctil** touchscreen, touch-sensitive display
pantalón M pants, trousers; **— corto** shorts; **pantalones** pants, trousers; **llevar bien puestos los pantalones** to be master in one's own home
pantano M swamp, marsh
pantanoso ADJ swampy, marshy
panteón M vault
pantera F panther
pantomima F mime, pantomime
pantorrilla F calf
pantufla F slipper
panty M pantyhose
panza F paunch, belly
panzudo ADJ potbellied
pañal M diaper; **estar en —es** to be in its infancy
paño M (de tela) cloth; (de lana) woolen cloth; (para limpiar) rag; **— higiénico** sanitary napkin; **— mortuorio** pall; **— de manos** towel; **— de cocina** dishcloth; **— de mesa** tablecloth; **ella es mi — de lágrimas** I always cry on her shoulder; **—s menores** underwear
pañuelo M (de nariz) handkerchief; (de cuello) scarf
papa M pope; F *Am* potato; **no saber ni —** not to know a thing; **—s fritas** French fries
papá M papa, dad
papacito M (padre) daddy; (hombre apuesto) hunk
papada F double chin
papado M papacy
papagayo M parrot
papaíto M daddy
papal ADJ papal
papar VT to eat; MF SG **papamoscas** (pájaro) flycatcher; (tonto) half-wit; MF SG **papanatas** twerp
paparruchas F PL baloney, bull
papaya F papaya
papel M (para escribir) paper; (dramático) role, part; **— aluminio** aluminum foil; **— carbón** carbon paper; **— cuadriculado** graph paper; **— de cartas** stationery; **— de estaño** tinfoil; **— de estraza** brown paper; **— de lija** sandpaper; **— de seda** tissue paper; **— encerado** wax paper; **— higiénico** toilet paper; **— moneda** paper money; **— tisú** tissue paper; **desempeñar un —** to play a role; **en el —** on paper; **hacer buen —** to cut a good figure
papeleo M paperwork
papelera F (fábrica) paper factory; (cubo) wastepaper basket
papelería F stationery store
papeleta F (para escribir) slip of paper; (para votar) ballot
paperas F PL mumps
papito M daddy
páprika F paprika
papú ADJ & MF Papua New Guinean
paquete M (envuelto) package; (atado) bundle; (programas de ordenador) package; **— de programas de productividad** office suite; **— turístico** package tour
Paquistán M Pakistan
paquistano -na ADJ & MF Pakistani
par ADJ even; M (de cosas idénticas) pair; (de cosas diferentes) couple; (título nobiliario) peer; (en golf) par; **a la —** at par; **sin —** peerless; **de — en —** wide-open
para PREP in order to, for; **lo hice — ganar dinero** I did it in order to earn money; **demasiado — mí** too much for me; **trabajo — mi padre** I work for my father; **— ser perro es inteligente** for a dog he's smart; **— mi sorpresa** to my surprise; **voy — Madrid** I'm going to Madrid; **— las dos** by two o'clock; **— atrás** backwards; **— empezar** for starters; **— llevar** to go; **¿— qué?** what for? **— que** so that, so as to; **— siempre** forever; **— su información** FYI [for your information]; **habla — sí** he talks to himself; **— mis adentros** to myself; **— morirse de risa** hilarious; **no es — tanto** it's no big deal; **sin qué ni — qué** without rhyme or reason
parabién M congratulations; **dar el —** to congratulate
parada F (acción de parar) stop; (de perro de caza) point; (de taxis) stand; (militar) parade; (relevo de guardia) changing of the guard; (de balón) parry; (en fútbol americano) tackle
paradero M whereabouts
paradigma M paradigm
parado ADJ (inmóvil) stationary; (sin trabajo) unemployed, idle; **salir bien —** to come out on top
paradoja F paradox
paradójico ADJ paradoxical
parafernalia F paraphernalia
parafina F paraffin
parafrasear VI/VT to paraphrase
paráfrasis F paraphrase
paraguas M SG umbrella
Paraguay M Paraguay
paraguayo -ya ADJ & MF Paraguayan
paraíso M paradise
paraje M spot
paralelo -la ADJ & M parallel; F parallel line; **hacer —s** to draw parallels; **barras**

paralelas parallel bars
parálisis F (inmovilidad física, espiritual) paralysis; (condición médica) paralysis, palsy; **— cerebral** cerebral palsy
paralítico -ca ADJ & MF paralytic
paralización F (de tránsito) gridlock; (del cuerpo) paralysis
paralizar[47] VT (movimiento) to paralyze; (negociaciones) to stall; **—se** to gridlock
paramédico -ca ADJ & MF paramedic
parámetro M parameter
paramilitar ADJ & MF paramilitary
páramo M cold highland, moor
parangón M comparison; **sin —** incomparable
parangonar VT to compare
paraninfo M auditorium
paranoia F paranoia
paranoico -ca ADJ & MF paranoid
paranormal ADJ paranormal
parapléjico -ca MF paraplegic
parapsicología F parapsychology
parar VI/VT (detener) to stop; (motor) to stall; VT (un pase de pelota) to block; (un golpe) to parry; **— de hacer algo** to stop doing something; **y para de contar** and that's it; **— en seco** to stop short; **ir a —** to end up; **habló sin —** he talked nonstop; **—se** (detenerse) to stop; (erguirse) *Am* to stand up; **—se a pensar** to stop to think; M SG **parabrisas** windshield; M SG **paracaídas** parachute; M SG **paracaídas dorado** golden parachute; M **paracaidismo** parachuting; M SG **parachoques** bumper; M SG **pararrayos** lightning rod; M **parasol** parasol; MF **paracaidista** parachutist
parasítico ADJ parasitic
parásito M parasite
parcela F parcel, plot
parcelación F subdivision
parcelar VT to parcel [out]
parche M (para remendar, informático) patch; (de tambor) drumhead; (médico) Band-aid®; **— de ojo** eye patch
parcial ADJ partial
pardillo M linnet
pardo ADJ (color) gray-brown; (mulato) mulatto
pareado M couplet
parear VT to match
parecer[35] VI to seem; **— que** to seem like, to look like; **¿qué te parece?** what do you think? **—se a** to resemble, to look like; M (opinión) opinion; (aspecto) appearance; **al —** apparently; **a mi —** to my mind / way of thinking; **del mismo —** like-minded
parecido ADJ alike, similar; **bien —** good-looking; M similarity, resemblance
pared F wall; **poner a alguien contra la —** to corner; **subirse por las —es** to be furious; **de — a —** wall-to-wall; **reloj de —** wall clock
paredón M execution wall
pareja F (de personas) couple; (de cosas) [matching] pair; (compañero) partner
parejo ADJ (hermanos) alike; (carrera) even; (dientes) straight; **correr [al] —** to go hand in hand
parental ADJ parental
parentela F kin
parentesco M kinship, relation
paréntesis M parenthesis
parezca, parezco *ver* parecer
pargo M red snapper
paria MF pariah, outcast
paridad F parity
pariente MF, **parienta** F relative, relation; **— consanguíneo** blood relative
parir VI/VT to give birth [to]
parlamentar VI to parley
parlamentario -ria ADJ parliamentary; MF member of parliament
parlamento M (en una obra de teatro) speech; (negociación) parley; (cuerpo legislativo) parliament
parlanchín ADJ talkative; MF chatterbox
parlotear VI to chatter, to rattle on
parloteo M chatter
paro M (huelga breve) stoppage; (falta de trabajo) unemployment; (ave) tit; **— cardiaco** cardiac arrest; **— laboral** work stoppage
parodia F parody
parodiar VT to parody
parpadear VI (un ojo, pantalla) to blink; (una vela) to flicker; (una estrella) to twinkle
parpadeo M (del ojo) blink; (de una vela) flicker; (de una estrella) twinkle; (de una pantalla) blinking
párpado M eyelid
parque M park; **— automotor** fleet of cars; **— de atracciones** amusement park; **— zoológico** zoo
parra F grapevine
párrafo M paragraph; **echar un — con** to have a chat with
parral M grape arbor
parranda F binge, spree; **andar de —** to go out partying
parrandear VI to revel
parrandero -ra MF party animal
parrilla F (sobre el fuego) grill; (en el horno) broiler; (de calles) grid; (de coche) grille
parrillada F barbecue dish
párroco M parish priest
parroquia F (distrito) parish; (iglesia) parish church
parroquial ADJ parochial
parroquiano -na MF (de iglesia) parishioner; (de tienda) regular
parte F (sección) part; (lugar) place; (papel en

una obra teatral) lines; (persona legal) party; — **integrante** built-in part; — **interesada** interested party; —**s pudendas** private parts, *fam* privates; **a otra** — somewhere else; **a** —**s iguales** fifty-fifty; **de un tiempo a esta** — for some time; **de** — **de** on behalf of; **de** — **a** — completely; **echar a mala** — to take amiss; **en** — partly; **en gran** — in large measure; **en otra** — elsewhere; **en/por todas** —**s** everywhere; **formar** — **de** to be part of; **ir por** —**s** to proceed by steps; **la mayor** — **de** most of; **la** — **del león** the lion's share; **no está en ninguna** — it's nowhere to be found; **no va a ninguna** — it's going nowhere; **por otra** — on the other hand; **tomar** — **en** to take part in; M report; **dar** — to report; **dar** — **de enfermo** to call in sick; **dar** — **de un crimen** to report a crime

partera F midwife

partición F (of a country) partition; (of a cell) division

participación F (en un proyecto) participation, involvement; (en un negocio) interest; — **de nacimiento** birth announcement

participante MF (en un grupo) participant; (en una carrera) entrant; (en un concurso) contestant

participar VI to participate; VT to announce; — **de/en** to participate in, to share in

partícipe MF participant

participio M participle

partícula F particle

particular ADJ (específico) particular; (poco usual) peculiar; (privado) private; **en** — in particular; **clases** —**es** private lessons; M (detalle) particular; (asunto) matter; MF private citizen

partida F (fondos) appropriation; (grupo de personas) party; (cantidad de mercancía) parcel, lot; (de ajedrez) game; (acción de partir) departure; — **de nacimiento** birth record; **jugar una mala** — to play a mean trick; **por** — **doble** double-entry

partidario -ria MF (de una medida) supporter, advocate; (de un partido político) partisan

partidista ADJ & MF partisan

partido M (grupo político) party; (de golf) round; (de tenis, fútbol) game, match; **es un buen** — he's a good match; **sacar** — **de** to take advantage of; **tomar** — to take sides; **¿cómo va el** —**?** what's the score? ADJ split, cleft

partir VT (dividir) to divide; (repartir) to share; (quebrar) to break; **eso me parte por el eje** that screws me up; **que te parta un rayo** go jump in the lake; VI (salir) to depart, to leave; **a** — **de entonces** since then; **a** — **del lunes** starting Monday; —**se de risa** to die of laughter

partisano -na MF partisan

partitura F musical score

parto M childbirth, delivery; — **prematuro** premature birth; **estar en trabajo de** — to be in labor

parvulario M kindergarten, nursery

párvulo -la MF nursery school child

pasa F raisin

pasable ADJ passable

pasada F (acción de pasar) passing; (con una máquina) pass; **una mala** — a mean trick; **de** — by the way

pasadizo M secret passage

pasado M past; ADJ (anterior) past; (demasiado maduro) overripe; — **mañana** day after tomorrow; **el año** — last year; **el** — **mes de septiembre** last September

pasador M (de un cierre) pin; (de la puerta) latch

pasaje M (sitio por donde se pasa, fragmento de texto) passage; (billete) ticket; (precio de un viaje) fare; (conjunto de los pasajeros) passengers

pasajero -ra ADJ fleeting, transitory; MF (en un coche, tren) passenger; (en un taxi) fare

pasante M (tenis) passing shot; MF (compañía) intern

pasaporte M passport

pasar VI (no querer jugar, ir de un lado a otro, seguir su proceso, transcurrir) to pass; (ocurrir) to happen; — **a ser** to become; — **de moda** to go out of style; — **hambre** to go hungry; — **por** to pass by; — **por alto** to pass over; — **una tarjeta por un lector** to swipe a card; —**le por la cabeza a alguien** to occur to someone; **pasan de los 80 años** they're over 80 years old; **te pasaste de la casa** you missed the house; —**se** to spoil; —**se de la raya** to cross the line; —**se de sol** to get too much sun; —**se de listo** to outsmart oneself; **se me pasó ir a buscarte** I totally forgot to pick you up; **me la paso bien** I have a good time; VT (la sal, una prueba, la plancha, una pelota) to pass; (un sofocón) to endure; (una tarde) to spend; — **las de Caín** to go through hell; — **en limpio** to make a new copy; — **por alto** to overlook; — **los 50 kmh** to exceed 50 kmh; — **revista** to pass in review; **nos pasó un Volvo** a Volvo passed us; **no lo paso** I can't stand him; M **tienen un buen** — they have a comfortable life; M **pasamano** (de barco) guard rail, gangway; (de escalera) banister, railing; M **pasatiempo** pastime

pasarela F (en un barco) gangplank; (en un desfile de modas) runway

Pascua F (fiesta cristiana) Easter; (fiesta judía) Passover; — **Florida / de Resurrección** Easter Sunday; — **de Navidad** Christmas

pase M (deporte) pass; **— cruzado** cross; **— de anotación** touchdown pass; **— de cabeza** header; **— pantalla** screen pass
pasear VI (a pie) to take a walk; (en bici, a caballo) to go on a ride; (en coche) to go for a drive, to go on a ride; **—se** to parade, to take a walk; **—se a caballo** to go horseback riding; VT (un perro) to walk a dog
paseo M (a pie) walk, stroll; (a caballo, en bicicleta) ride; (en coche) drive, ride; (calle donde se pasea) mall; (recreativo) outing; **irse a —** to go jump in a lake; **dar un —** (a pie) to take a walk; (a caballo, en bicicleta) to go on a ride; (en coche) to go on a drive
pasillo M (de un teatro) aisle; (de un edificio) hallway, corridor; (para vuelo aéreo) corridor; **— de dobles** alley
pasión F passion
pasivo ADJ passive; **voz pasiva** passive voice; M (en un negocio) liabilities; (de una cuenta) debit side
pasmado ADJ astounded
pasmar VT to astound, to stun; **—se** to be astounded, to be stunned
pasmo M astonishment
pasmoso ADJ astonishing, stunning
paso M (acción de pasar, lugar donde pasar) pass; (de pie, de danza, distancia, de un proceso) step; (velocidad) pace; (de caballerías) walk; (de tornillo) pitch; (de coche) wheelbase; **— elevado** overpass; **— a nivel** grade crossing; **— de tortuga** snail's pace; **— a —** step by step; **dar —** (dejar pasar) to let pass; (dejar actuar) to make possible; **dar —s** to take steps; **hacer —s** to travel; **de —** by the way, in passing; **estar de —** to be passing through; **marcar el —** to set the pace; **al — que** while; **salir del —** to get out of a difficulty; **dicho sea de —** incidentally; **a cada —** at every turn; **— del tiempo** passage of time; **abrir — para** to make way for; **abrirse —** to plow through, to press through; ADJ dried
pasta F (de almidón) paste; (de harina) dough; (de fideos) pasta; (de libro) hard cover, binding; (dinero) *fam* dough; **de buena —** of good disposition; **— dentífrica/dental** toothpaste
pastar VI/VT to pasture, to graze
pastel M (torta) cake; (tarta) pie; (pintura, cuadro) pastel; **— de cumpleaños** birthday cake; **— de limón** lemon pie; **— de carne** meat pie; **descubrir el —** to spill the beans; ADJ pastel
pastelería F (establecimiento) pastry shop; (conjunto de pasteles) pastry
pastelero -ra M pastry cook
pasterizar, pasteurizar[9] VT to pasteurize
pastilla F (de medicina) tablet, pill; (para la tos) drop; (de jabón) bar
pastizal M grassland
pasto M (terreno) pasture, grassland; (hierba) grass; **ser — de** to be a victim of
pastor -ora MF (de ovejas) shepherd; (sacerdote protestante) pastor, minister; M **— alemán** German shepherd
pastoral ADJ pastoral; F pastoral letter
pastoril ADJ pastoral
pastoso ADJ pasty
pastura F feed
pat M putt
pata F (de animal, mueble) foot, leg; (de pollo) drumstick; (de un enchufe) pin; **— palmada** webfoot; **— de gallo** crow's feet; **en cuatro —s** on all fours; **a [la] — coja** skipping on one leg; **estirar la —** *fam* to kick the bucket; **mala —** bad luck; **metedura de —** faux pas; **meter la —** to slip up; **—s arriba** upside down; ADJ **patihendido** cloven-hoofed; **patitieso** dumbfounded; **patizambo** (hacia adentro) knock-kneed; (hacia afuera) bow-legged
patada F kick (también en deportes); **libros a —s** tons of books; **en dos —s** in a jiffy; **dar —s** to kick; **echar a —s** to kick out; **— lateral** (fútbol americano) onside kick
patalear VI (en el aire) to kick; (en el suelo) to stamp
pataleo M (en el aire) kick; (en el suelo) stamp
pataleta F fit; **tener una —** to throw a fit
patán M boor
patata F *Esp* potato; **—s fritas** French fries; **— caliente** hot potato
pateador M kicker
patear VT (algo, a alguien) to kick; (el suelo) to stamp; VI to tramp around; VI/VT (en golf) to putt; VI to kick; **— al arco** to shoot at goal
patentar VT to patent
patente ADJ & F patent; **se hizo — su ignorancia** he betrayed his ignorance; **— en trámite** patent pending
paternal ADJ (del padre) paternal; (como un padre) fatherly
paternidad F paternity, fatherhood; **prueba de —** paternity test
paterno ADJ paternal
patético ADJ moving
patetismo M pathos
patíbulo M gallows scaffold, gallows
patilla F (de gafas) arm; **—s** (de pelo) sideburns
patín M (tabla) skate; (de trineo) runner; **— de ruedas** roller skate; **— de cuchilla / de hielo** ice skate
patinaje M skating
patinar VI (una persona) to skate; (un coche sobre hielo) to skid; (un embrague) to slip; (en un examen) to blank out
patinazo M (de embrague) slip; (de coche) skid
patio M (de casa) patio, courtyard; (de escuela)

playground
pato M (ave) duck; (macho) drake; **pagar el —** to take the rap
patochada F blunder
patógeno M pathogen
patología F pathology
patológico ADJ pathological
patoso ADJ clumsy
patotero -ra MF *Am* hooligan
patraña F tall tale
patria F fatherland, homeland
patriarca M patriarch
patriarcal ADJ patriarchal
patrimonial ADJ inherited, patrimonial
patrimonio M patrimony; **— cultural** cultural heritage; **— neto** net worth; **— personal** personal assets
patriota MF patriot
patriótico ADJ patriotic
patriotismo M patriotism
patrocinador -ora MF sponsor
patrocinar VT to sponsor
patrocinio M sponsorship; **— empresarial** corporate backing
patrón -ona MF (protector) patron; (jefe) employer; (de navío) skipper; M (dueño de pensión) landlord; (de costura) pattern; (punto de referencia) yardstick, standard; (de planta) stock; (de un parásito) host; **— de oro** gold standard; F (dueña de pensión) landlady
patronal ADJ management; **asociación —** employers' association; F management
patronato M board of trustees
patrono -na MF patron
patrulla F (grupo de policías o soldados) patrol, squad; (coche) squad car
patrullar VI/VT to patrol
patrullero -ra M patrol car, squad car; MF patrol officer
pausa F (musical) pause, rest; **trabajar con —** to work slowly; **hacer —** to pause
pauta F guideline
pavimentar VT to pave
pavimento M pavement
pavo M turkey; **— real** peacock; ADJ silly
pavón M peacock
pavonearse VI to strut, to swagger
pavoneo M strut, swagger
pavor M dread
pavoroso ADJ frightful
payasada F clownish act or remark; **—s** antics, horseplay
payasear VI to clown around, to horse around
payaso M (de circo) clown; (persona poco seria) buffoon; **hacer el —** to clown around
paz F peace; **estamos en —** we are even; **[que] en — descanse** may she rest in peace; **hacer las paces** to make up; **dejar en —** to leave alone
PC M PC
peaje M (tasa) toll; (cabina donde se paga) tollbooth
peatón -ona MF pedestrian
peca F freckle
pecado M sin; **— mortal** mortal sin
pecador -ora MF sinner; ADJ sinful
pecaminoso ADJ sinful
pecar[30] VI to sin; **— contra** to transgress against; **— de bueno** to be too good; **— de generoso** to be generous to a fault; **— de oscuro** to be exceedingly unclear
pecera F (pequeña) fish tank, fishbowl; (grande) aquarium
pechera F (de camisa) front; (de delantal) bib
pecho M (parte del cuerpo) chest; (mama) breast; **dar el —** to nurse; **nadar —** to do the breaststroke; **tomar a —[s]** to take to heart; **sacar —** to puff out one's chest
pechuga F breast
pechugona ADJ buxom
pecio M flotsam and jetsam
pecoso ADJ freckled
pectoral ADJ & M pectoral
peculado M embezzlement
peculiar ADJ peculiar
peculiaridad F peculiarity
pedagogía F pedagogy, education
pedagógico ADJ pedagogical, teaching
pedagogo -ga MF pedagogue
pedal M pedal
pedalear VI/VT to pedal
pedante ADJ pedantic; MF pedant
pedazo M piece; **— de idiota** absolute idiot; **él es un — de pan** he's a saint; **hacer —s** to tear to pieces; **caerse a —s** to fall to pieces; **— por —** piece by piece
pederasta M pederast, pedophile
pedófilo -la MF pedophile
pederastia F pederasty
pedernal M flint
pedestal M pedestal
pedestre ADJ pedestrian
pediatra MF pediatrician
pediatría F pediatrics
pedido M (comercial) order; (petición) request; **hacer un —** to place an order; **— fijo** standing order; **— pendiente** back order; **— urgente** rush order
pedigrí M pedigree
pedigüeño -ña MF mooch, moocher; ADJ **no seas —** stop mooching
pedir[9] VT (requerir) to ask for, to request; (exigir) to demand; (encargar) to order, to requisition; **— limosna** to beg; **— prestado** to borrow; **— socorro** to cry for help; **— un deseo** to make a wish; **— que** to ask/pray that; **— la mano de una mujer** to ask a woman's hand in marriage; **— por alguien**

to ask to speak to someone
pedofilia F pedophilia
pedrada F **dar una —** to hit with a stone; **matar a —s** to stone to death
pedregal M rocky ground
pedregoso ADJ stony
pedrería F precious stones
pedrusco M boulder
pedúnculo M stem
pega F snag
pegadizo ADJ catchy
pegado ADJ (adherido) stuck; (contiguo) adjoining, contiguous; **quedarse —** to get an electric shock; **— al televisor** glued to the television
pegajoso ADJ sticky, tacky
pegamento M glue
pegar[40] VT (con el puño) to hit, to strike; (algo con pegamento) to stick, to glue; (botones) to sew on; **— con** to match; **— contra** to touch; **— un cuadrangular** to hit a homerun; **— un grito** to yell; **— un sencillo** to hit a single; **— un susto** to give a scare; **— un salto** to jump; **—le a la bola** to hit the ball; **—le un tiro a alguien** to shoot someone; **—se** (adherir) to stick together, to cling; (contagiarse) to be contagious; **—se a** to latch onto; **no — un ojo** not to sleep a wink
pegote M glob
pegotear VT to gum up
peinado M (estilo) coiffure, hairdo; (acción) combing
peinador-ora MF hairdresser
peinar VT to comb (también registrar); (en una peluquería) to style; **— a contrapelo** to rub the wrong way
peine M comb
pelada F bald spot
pelado ADJ (sin pelo) hairless; (pobre) poor; (sin cáscara) peeled; (sin árboles) treeless; (sin plumas) plucked; (sin dinero) broke
pelador M peeler
pelaje M coat, fur
pelar VT (el pelo) to cut the hair of; (las plumas) to pluck the feathers from; (frutas, verduras, huevo) to peel; (a un jugador) to fleece; **duro de —** hard to deal with; **el agua está que pela** the water is really hot; **—se** to peel; M SG **pelagatos** nobody
peldaño M step, stair
pelea F (de palabra) fight, quarrel; (de obra) fight, scrape; (de boxeo) fight; **— a puñetazos** fistfight; **— de perros** dogfight
pelear VI (con palabras) to fight, to quarrel; (con obras) to fight, to scuffle; **—se con alguien** to have a fight with someone
pelechar VI (perder la piel) to shed; (mejorar) to get better
pelele M (persona sin carácter) wimp; (muñeca) straw doll
peletería F (tienda) fur store; (comercio) fur trade
pelícano M pelican
película F film (también membrana); (obra cinematográfica) motion picture, film, movie; **de —** extraordinary; **dar una —** to show a film; **— muda** silent film
peligrar VI to be in danger
peligro M danger, peril; **ese muchacho es un —** that boy is dangerous; **en —** in danger; **poner en —** to imperil/endanger/jeopardize
peligroso ADJ dangerous, perilous
pellejo M (piel de animal) hide, pelt; (odre) wineskin; **salvar el —** to save one's skin; **ser todo —** to be skin and bones; **jugarse el —** to risk one's life
pellizcar[30] VT to pinch
pellizco M pinching
pelma MF jerk
pelo M (de persona) hair; (de animal) fur; (de alfombra) pile; **con —s y señales** with every possible detail; **de medio —** low-class; **eso me viene al —** that suits me perfectly; **montar en —** to ride bareback; **ni un —** not at all; **no tener —s en la lengua** not to mince words; **se le ponen los —s de punta** his hair stands on end; **se salvó por un —** he was saved by the skin of his teeth; **tomarle el — a alguien** to tease someone, to pull someone's leg; **traído de los —s** far-fetched; ADJ **pelirrojo** redheaded
pelón ADJ bald
pelota F (objeto) ball; (juego) ballgame; **— vasca** jai-alai; **pasar la —** (dar el balón) to pass the ball; (dar la responsabilidad) to pass the buck
pelotear VI to rally
peloteo M rally
pelotera F brawl
pelotero-ra MF (jugador de béisbol) baseball player; (juego para niños) ball pit
pelotón M (pelota grande) large ball; (de tierra seca) clod; (de ciclistas) pack; (de soldados) platoon; (de fusilamiento) firing squad
peltre M pewter
peluca F wig
peludo ADJ (persona) hairy; (animal) furry; (perro) shaggy
peluquería F (para hombres) barbershop; (para mujeres) salon
peluquero-ra MF (de hombres) barber; (de mujeres) hairdresser
peluquín M toupee
pelusa F (de tela, ropa) lint, fluff; (de melocotón, de la piel) fuzz; (de plantas) hair; (de polvo) dust bunny
pelvis F pelvis
pena F (castigo) penalty; (tristeza) sorrow; (vergüenza) embarrassment; **— de muerte**

death penalty, capital punishment; **—s** hardships; **a duras —s** with great difficulty; **me da —** it grieves me; **hecho una —** looking like a mess; **¡qué —!** what a shame! **sería una — perder** it would be a shame to lose; **so — de** on pain of; **valer la —** to be worthwhile

penacho M (de plumas) tuft, crest; (de humo) plume

penal ADJ penal; M penitentiary

penalidad F (penuria) hardship; (castigo) penalty

penalizar[*7] VT to penalize

penalti, penalty M penalty kick

penar VI to suffer; VT to punish

penco M plug, nag

pendencia F wrangle, fight

pendenciero ADJ quarrelsome

pender VI to hang, to dangle

pendiente F slope, incline; M *Esp* earring; ADJ (aretes) dangling; (negocio) pending, unfinished; (pago) outstanding; **quedo — de tu llamada** I look forward to your call

pendón M banner

péndulo M pendulum

pene M penis

penetración F penetration

penetrante ADJ (mirada, sonido) penetrating, piercing; (frío) biting; (comentario) cutting; (inteligencia) keen

penetrar VT (pasar al interior) to penetrate, to pierce; (comprender) to comprehend

penicilina F penicillin

península F peninsula

peninsular ADJ peninsular

penitencia F (religiosa) penance; (castigo) detention; **¡estás en —!** you're grounded!

penitenciaría F penitentiary

penitente ADJ & MF penitent

penoso ADJ (triste) painful, grievous; (difícil) trying; (que da vergüenza) embarrassing

pensador -ora MF thinker; ADJ reflective

pensamiento M (facultad, acción, efecto) thought; (flor) pansy

pensante ADJ thinking

pensar[1] VI/VT to think; **— en** to think about/over; **— hacer algo** to intend to do something; **eso da que —** that seems questionable; **no lo pienses dos veces** don't think twice

pensativo ADJ pensive, thoughtful

pensión F (asignación periódica) pension, allowance; (comidas) board; (hostal) boardinghouse; **— completa** room and board; **tener en —** to have as a boarder

pensionado M boarding school

pensionar VT to pension

pensionista MF (que vive en una pensión) boarder; (que cobra una pensión) pensioner

pentágono M pentagon

pentagrama M musical staff

penthouse M penthouse

penúltimo ADJ next to the last, penultimate

penumbra F semi-darkness, dimness

penuria F (escasez) shortage; (pobreza) poverty

peña F boulder; **— folclórica** folklore club

peñasco M crag

peñascoso ADJ craggy

peñón M crag

peón -ona MF (obrero) unskilled laborer, farmhand; **— caminero** road worker; M (en ajedrez) pawn; (en damas) piece

peonada F gang of laborers

peonaje M gang of laborers

peonza F toy top

peor ADJ worse, worst; **este libro es —** this book is worse; **el — libro** the worst book; ADV worse; **trabaja —** he works worse; **— que** worse than; **— que nunca** worse than ever; **en el — de los casos** if worst comes to worst; **lo —** the worst [thing]; **tanto —** so much the worse

pepa F **es un viva la —** it's bedlam

pepino M cucumber

pepita F (simiente) seed; (tumor de gallina) pip; (masa de oro) nugget

pequeñez F (cualidad de pequeño) smallness; (cosa insignificante) trifle

pequeño -ña ADJ (de poco tamaño) small, little; (de corta edad) young; (de poca importancia) trivial

pera F pear; **pedirle —s al olmo** to ask the impossible

peral M pear tree

perca F perch; **— americana** black bass

percal M percale

percance M accident, mishap

percatarse VI (darse cuenta) to realize; (notar) to notice

percebe M barnacle

percepción F perception

perceptible ADJ perceptible, noticeable

perceptivo ADJ perceptive

percha F (para el armario) clothes hanger; (palo para colgar cosas) peg; (palo para aves) perch; (perchero) coat rack

perchero M coat rack

percibir VT (experimentar) to perceive, to sense; (recibir) to collect

percudir VT to make grimy; **—se** to get grimy

percusión F percussion

percutor M firing pin

perdedor -ora MF loser

perder[2] VT (dejar de tener algo, extraviar) to lose, to mislay, to misplace; (echar a perder) to spoil, to ruin; (ser derrotado) to lose; (no aprovechar) to waste; (no llegar a tiempo, no disfrutar) to miss; **— el conocimiento** to

lose consciousness; — **el tiempo** to waste time; — **los estribos** to fly off the handle; — **hojas** to shed leaves; — **pie** to lose one's footing; — **terreno** to lose ground; **echarse a** — to spoil; **el vaso pierde agua** the glass leaks water; **llevo las de** — the odds are against me; —**se** (extraviarse) to lose one's way, to get lost; (apartarse del buen camino) to go astray, to stray; **se han perdido las llaves** the keys have gotten lost; —**se de vista** to disappear; —**[se] una oportunidad** to pass up / miss an opportunity; — **el balón** (fútbol americano) to fumble; (fútbol) to lose the ball

perdición F perdition, damnation

pérdida F (acción de perder, cosa perdida) loss; (de dinero dado en prenda) forfeiture; **entrar en** — to nosedive; — **de tiempo** waste of time; — **de balón** (fútbol americano) fumble, turnover; (fútbol) loss of ball possession; —**s cubiertas** covered losses; —**s totales** total loss

perdido-da ADJ (extraviado) lost, missing; (aislado) isolated; (promiscuo) promiscuous; **un borracho** — an utter drunkard; **estar** — **por alguien** to be crazy about someone; M degenerate

perdigón M (pollo de perdiz) young partridge; (bolita de plomo) birdshot, buckshot

perdiz F partridge

perdón M (privado) forgiveness; (oficial) pardon; **con** — **de los presentes** present company excepted; **no tener** — to be unforgivable; INTERJ excuse me

perdonar VT (en privado) to forgive; (oficialmente) to pardon

perdurable ADJ lasting

perdurar VI to last

perecedero ADJ perishable

perecer[35] VI to perish

peregrinación F pilgrimage

peregrinar VI to go on a pilgrimage

peregrino-na MF pilgrim; ADJ far-fetched

perejil M parsley

perenne ADJ perennial

pereza F laziness, idleness, sloth

perezoso ADJ lazy, idle; M (animal) sloth

perfección F perfection; **a la** — to perfection, perfectly

perfeccionamiento M perfecting

perfeccionar VT to perfect

perfeccionista MF perfectionist

perfectamente ADV perfectly; **tú hablas español** — you speak Spanish quite well

perfecto ADJ perfect, flawless; **es un** — **tarado** he's an utter idiot; **es un** — **desconocido** he's a complete stranger

perfil M profile; **de** — from the side

perfilar VT to outline; —**se** (marcarse) to be outlined; (definirse) to become clear

perforación F (de una superficie) perforation; (de un pozo) drilling; (de la piel) piercing

perforar VT (agujerear) to perforate; (buscar petróleo) to drill

perfumar VT to perfume, to scent

perfume M perfume, scent

perfumería F perfumery

pergamino M parchment

pérgola F arbor

pericia F expertness, know-how

perico M (loro) parakeet; (cocaína) *fam* snow

periferia F periphery, fringe

periférico ADJ & M peripheral

perilla F (adorno, remate) knob; (pelo de barbilla) goatee; **me viene de** —**s** it's exactly what I need

perímetro M perimeter

periódico M newspaper; — **mensual** monthly periodical; ADJ periodic

periodismo M journalism

periodista MF journalist

periodístico ADJ journalistic

período M period (también menstruación); (de materia radiactiva) half-life; — **de prueba** (para un trabajo) probationary period; (para una mercancía) trial period; — **glaciar** ice age

peripecia F vicissitude

peripuesto ADJ dressed up, dolled up, decked out

periquito M parakeet

periscopio M periscope

perista MF fence

perito-ta ADJ expert, practiced; MF technician

peritonitis F peritonitis

perjudicar[30] VT to harm

perjudicial ADJ harmful, detrimental

perjuicio M harm

perjurar VT to swear; VI to commit perjury; —**se** to commit perjury

perjurio M perjury

perla F (de nácar) pearl; (persona) gem; (de sudor) bead; (de sabiduría) nugget; (frase inoportuna) blooper; **me viene de** —**s** it suits me perfectly

perlado ADJ pearly

permanecer[35] VI to remain, to stay

permanencia F (carácter de permanente) permanence; (acción de permanecer) stay

permanente ADJ permanent

permanezca, permanezco *ver* permanecer

permeable ADJ permeable

permear VT to permeate

permisible ADJ permissible

permisivo ADJ permissive

permiso M (para ir al baño) permission; (para faltar al servicio militar) furlough; (para faltar al trabajo) leave; (para casarse,

conducir) license, permit; **— de trabajo** work permit; **con —** excuse me
permitir VT (dar permiso) to permit, to allow; (posibilitar) to enable; **—se** (una libertad) to take the liberty of; (un lujo) to allow oneself; **¿me permite?** may I?
permuta F exchange
permutación F permutation
permutar VT to exchange
pernetas LOC ADV **en —** barelegged
pernicioso ADJ pernicious
pernicorto ADJ short-legged
perno M bolt, pin
pero CONJ but; ADV **muy — muy lindo** very, very pretty; M objection; **no hay — que valga** there are no buts about it
perogrullada F platitude
perorar VI to hold forth
perorata F lecture
peróxido M peroxide
perpendicular ADJ perpendicular
perpetrar VT to perpetrate
perpetuar[26] VT to perpetuate
perpetuo ADJ perpetual
perplejidad F perplexity, bewilderment
perplejo ADJ perplexed, bewildered; VT **dejar —** to perplex
perrera F (lugar donde guardar perros) pound; (rabieta) tantrum
perrero-ra MF dogcatcher; ADJ dog-loving
perro M dog; **— caliente** hot dog; **— callejero** stray dog; **— cobrador** retriever; **— de caza** hunting dog; **— de lanas** poodle; **— esquimal** husky; **— faldero** lapdog; **— guía** guide dog; **— guardián** watchdog, guard dog; **— pastor** sheepdog; **— policía** police dog; ADJ miserable; **en la perra vida** never
perruno ADJ canine
persa ADJ & MF Persian; M (lengua) Persian
persecución F (religiosa) persecution; (policial) pursuit, chase
perseguidor-ora MF (que sigue) pursuer; (que acosa) persecutor
perseguir[12] VT (seguir para alcanzar) to pursue, to chase; (seguir para encontrar) to track down; (acosar) to hound; (tratar de destruir) to persecute
perseverancia F perseverance
perseverar VI to persevere
Persia F Persia
persiana F blind, shade
persiga, persigo, persigue, persiguiendo, persiguiera, persiguiese *ver* perseguir
persistencia F persistence
persistente ADJ persistent
persistir VI to persist
persona F person; **— influyente** player; **— legal** legal entity; **en —** in person; **— mayor** adult
personaje M (persona importante) personage; (de obra literaria) character; **es todo un —** he's quite a character
personal ADJ personal; M personnel, staff
personalidad F personality
personalmente ADV personally
personificar[30] VT to personify, to embody
perspectiva F (punto de vista, distancia, técnica de dibujo) perspective; (panorama) view, vista; (posibilidad) prospect; **tener en —** to have planned
perspicacia F insight, sharpness
perspicaz ADJ perspicacious, perceptive
persuadir VT to persuade
persuasión F persuasion
persuasivo ADJ persuasive
pertenecer[35] VI to belong
perteneciente ADJ belonging
pertenencias F PL belongings
pertenezca, pertenezco *ver* pertenecer
pértiga F pole
pertinente ADJ pertinent, relevant
pertrechos M PL military supplies
perturbación F disturbance
perturbar VT to perturb, to disturb
Perú M Peru
peruano-na ADJ & MF Peruvian
perversidad F (distorsión) perversity; (maldad) wickedness
perversión F perversion
perverso ADJ (distorsionante) perverse; (malvado) wicked
pervertido-da MF pervert
pervertir[8] VT (enviciar) to pervert; (distorsionar) to distort; **—se** to become perverted
pesa F (para pesar) weight; (para hacer ejercicio) dumbbell; **—s y medidas** weights and measures
pesadez F (cualidad de pesado) heaviness; (tedio) tiresomeness; (persona pesada) tiresome person
pesadilla F nightmare
pesado-da ADJ (que pesa mucho, difícil de digerir) heavy; (aburrido) tiresome; (robusto) heavy-set; (tardo) slow; MF bore, pest
pesadumbre F grief, sorrow
pésame M condolence, expression of sympathy
pesar VT (apenar) to sadden; (medir el peso de) to weigh; (recaer sobre) to weight down; VI (tener peso, importancia) to weigh; M grief, sorrow; LOC ADV **a — de** in spite of
pesaroso ADJ (triste) sad; (arrepentido) repentant
pesca F (acción de pescar) fishing; (lo pescado) catch; **ir de —** to go fishing
pescadería F fish market
pescado M fish

pescador -ora MF fisherman
pescar[30] VI/VT (capturar peces) to fish; (sacar del agua, coger, comprender, sorprender, pillar) to catch; (obtener) to land, to nail
pescozón M blow to the back of the head
pescuezo M neck
pesebre M (para pienso) manger, crib; (belén) nativity scene
peseta F peseta
pesimismo M pessimism
pesimista MF pessimist
pésimo ADJ dismal, wretched
peso M (fuerza, importancia) weight; (cosa opresiva) burden; (cosa pesada) load; **vender al —** to sell by weight; **levantar en —** to lift off the ground
pesquería F fishery
pesquero ADJ fishing; M fishing boat
pesquisa F inquiry
pestaña F (del ojo) eyelash; (en costura) fringe; (de papel, texto) tab; **quemarse las —s** to burn the midnight oil
pestañear VI to blink; **sin —** unflinchingly
pestañeo M blink
peste F (enfermedad) plague; (persona molesta) pest; (hedor) stench; **— bubónica** bubonic plague; **— negra** black death; **hablar —s de alguien** to speak badly of someone
pestilencia F pestilence
pestillo M deadbolt, latch
petaca F (para tabaco) tobacco pouch; (para whisky) flask
pétalo M petal
petardear VI to backfire
petardeo M backfire
petate M bundle; **liar el —** to pack up and go
petición F petition, request
peticionar VT to petition
petirrojo M robin
pétreo ADJ stony
petróleo M petroleum, oil; **— crudo** crude oil
petrolero -ra ADJ oil, petroleum; **plataforma —** oil rig; M oil tanker; F oil company
petrolífero ADJ (que contiene petróleo) oil-bearing; (que produce petróleo) oil-producing; (relativo al petróleo) oil
petulancia F smugness
petulante ADJ smug
petunia F petunia
peyorativo ADJ pejorative
peyote M peyote
pez M fish; **— dorado** goldfish; **— espada** swordfish; **— gordo** *fam* fat cat, big shot; **— vela** sailfish; **— volador** flying fish; **como — en el agua** perfectly at ease; F pitch
pezón M nipple
pezuña F hoof
phishing M phishing
piadoso ADJ pious, saintly
piafar VI to stamp
pianista MF pianist, piano player
piano M piano; **— de cola** grand piano; **— vertical** upright piano
pianola F player piano
piar[28] VI to peep, to chirp
pica F (lanza) pike; (palo de baraja) spade
picada F (de insecto) bite; (de avión) nosedive; **caer en —** to dive
picadillo M meat [and vegetable] hash
picado ADJ (mar) rough, choppy; (carne) chopped; (de viruela) poked; M (de avión) nosedive; **caer en —** to dive
picador M picador; ADJ stinging
picadora F grinder; **— de carne** meat grinder
picadura F (de serpiente) bite; (de insecto) sting, bite
picante ADJ (especia) spicy, hot; (queso) sharp; (obsceno) risqué; M (especia fuerte) strong seasoning; (cualidad) spiciness
picar[30] VI/VT (un pez) to bite; (un ave) to peck; (comer en pequeñas cantidades) to nibble; VT (tomates) to chop up; (carne) to mince; (una vaca) to goad, to poke; (la curiosidad) to pique; (con espuelas) to spur; VI (una comida picante) to sting; (el sol) to burn; (la piel) to itch, to smart; (un avión) to dive; **— alto** to aim high; **—se** to spoil; **se pica el mar** the sea is getting rough; **se me picó un diente** I got a cavity; M SG **picapleitos** *pey* shyster; M **picaporte** latch
picardía F mischief
picaresco ADJ picaresque
pícaro -ra MF rogue, rascal; ADJ roguish, mischievous
picazón F (en la piel) itch; (en la garganta) tickle; **provoca —** it causes itching
picea F spruce
pichi M jumper
pichón M (paloma) pigeon; (cría de ave) chick
picnic M picnic
pico M (de ave) beak, bill; (de montaña) peak; (herramienta) pick; (de tetera) spout; **cuarenta y —** forty-odd; **cerrar el —** to shut one's mouth; **tener el — de oro** to be very eloquent
pícolo M piccolo
picotazo M peck
picotear VI/VT (aves) to peck; (personas) to nibble
pictórico ADJ pictorial
pida, pide, pidiendo, pidiera, pidiese *ver* pedir
pídola F leapfrog
pie M (del cuerpo, de calcetín, de cama, medida) foot; (de foto) caption; (de copa) stem; (de lámpara) stand; (de página) bottom; (para un actor) cue; (de árbol) trunk; (de mueble) leg; **— de atleta** athlete's foot; **— de autor**

byline; — **de imprenta** printer's mark; — **zambo** clubfoot; **a** — on foot; **un soldado de a** — a footsoldier; — **de banco** silly remark; **a** — **juntillas** firmly; **al** — **de la letra** to the letter; **caer de** — to have good luck; **con un** — **en el estribo** with one foot out of the door; **dar** — (a una crítica) to give rise to; (a un actor) to cue; **de/en** — standing; **en** — **de guerra** (enojado) on the warpath; (belicoso) on a war footing; **estar de** — to be standing; **estar en** — **de igualdad con** to be on a par with; **esto no tiene ni** —**s ni cabeza** I can't make heads or tails of this; **ir a** — to walk; **perder** — to lose one's footing; **ponerse de** — to stand up

piedad F (cualidad de pío) piety; (misericordia) mercy; **tener** — to show mercy

piedra F stone; — **angular** cornerstone, keystone; — **caliza** limestone; — **de afilar** whetstone; — **de toque** touchstone; — **pómez** pumice; — **preciosa** gemstone; **ser** — **de escándalo** to be an object of scandal

piel F (humana) skin; (animal) hide, pelt; (para confección) fur; — **de gallina** goosebumps; — **de naranja** cellulite

piensa, piense *ver* pensar

pienso M feed; **ni por** — no way

pierda, pierde *ver* perder

pierna F leg; — **de ternera** leg of lamb; **dormir a** — **suelta** to sleep like a log

pieza F (de artillería, de tela, de música, de teatro) piece; (habitación) room; — **de repuesto** replacement part; **de una** — astonished; **menuda** — a piece of work

pífano M fife

pifia F goof, miscue

pifiar VT to goof up, to miscue

pigmento M pigment

pigmeo -a MF pygmy

pijama M pajamas

pila F (recipiente) basin; (bautismal) baptismal font; (cúmulo) pile, heap, stack; (generador) battery; — **atómica** atomic reactor

pilar M pillar

píldora F pill; —**s para dormir** sleeping pills

pillaje M pillage, plunder

pillar VT (saquear) to pillage, to plunder; (atrapar, coger) to catch; (en un juego infantil) to tag

pillo -lla ADJ (travieso) naughty; (taimado) sly; MF (adulto) scoundrel; (niño) scamp

pilluelo -la MF urchin

pilón M (fuente) large basin; (soporte) pylon

pilotar, pilotear VT to pilot, to fly

pilote M pile, stilt

piloto MF (conductor) pilot; (llama pequeña de gas) pilot light; — **automático** autopilot; — **de pruebas** test pilot

pimentar VT to pepper

pimentero M pepper shaker

pimentón M paprika

pimienta F pepper; — **blanca** white pepper; — **de cayena** red pepper; — **negra** black pepper

pimiento M pepper, bell pepper; — **verde** green pepper

pimpollo M (de rosa) rosebud; (de vid) shoot

PIN M PIN

pináculo M pinnacle

pinar M pine grove

pincel M artist's brush

pincelada F stroke; **dar las últimas** —**s** to put on the final touches

pinchadura F flat tire

pinchar VT (perforar) to prick, to puncture; (apuñalar) to poke; (inyectar) to inject; (intervenir un teléfono) to wiretap; (provocar) to needle; VI to have a flat; **ni corta ni pincha** he doesn't count; M SG **pinchadiscos** disk jockey, DJ

pinchazo M (acción de pinchar) puncture, prick; (neumático) flat tire; (puñalada) stab; (de teléfono) wiretap

pincho M (palo afilado) spike; (de rotisería) spit

pingajo M (harapo) tatter; (harapiento) person dressed in rags

ping-pong M ping-pong

pingüe ADJ abundant

pingüino M penguin

pino M (árbol) pine; (ejercicio) handstand; **en el quinto** — in the boondocks

pinta F (mancha) dot; (aspecto) looks; (medida de líquidos) pint

pintada F grafitti

pintado ADJ (animales, plantas) colorful; **ese traje te queda** — you look great in that suit

pintar VT (colorear) to paint; (describir) to depict; **este marcador no pinta** this marker won't write; **no** — **nada** to count for nothing; **las cosas no pintaban bien** things did not look well; —**se** to put on makeup

pintarrajear VT to daub, to smear with paint; —**se** to put on too much makeup

pinto ADJ paint, dapple[d]

pintor -ora MF painter; — **de brocha gorda** house painter

pintoresco ADJ picturesque, colorful

pintorrear VT to smear with paint

pintura F (acción de pintar, obra) painting; (sustancia) paint; — **al óleo** oil painting; — **en aerosol** spray paint; — **fresca** wet paint

pinza F (de cangrejo) claw; (de médico) clamp; (de vestido) dart; (instrumento) clothespin; —**s** tweezers

piña F (fruto del pino) pinecone; (ananás) pineapple; (bomba) hand grenade

piñata F piñata

piñón M (semilla del pino) pine nut; (rueda del engranaje) pinion; (de bicicleta) sprocket
pío ADJ pious; INTERJ peep; **ni —** not a word
piojo M louse; **como —s en costura** like sardines
piojoso ADJ lousy
pionero -ra MF pioneer
pipa F (para fumar) pipe; (semilla) sunflower seed; **pasarlo —** to have a great time
pipí M pee; **hacer —** *fam* to pee
pipiolo -la MF novice
pique M (rivalidad) rivalry; (desavenencia) falling-out; **echar a —** to sink; **irse a —** to capsize
piquete M picket (también de huelga)
piquetear M to picket
piragua F dugout canoe
pirámide F pyramid
pirata MF pirate; **— informático -ca** hacker
piratear VT to pirate
piratería F piracy
piromanía F pyromania
pirómano -na MF pyromaniac
piropo M compliment
pirotecnia F pyrotechnics
pirulí M sucker, lollipop
pisada F (paso) footstep; (huella) footprint; **seguir las —s de** to follow in the footsteps of
pisar VT (oprimir con el pie) to step on, to tread on; (apisonar) to mash; **jamás pisó una plaza de toros** he never set foot in a bullring; **ir pisando huevos** to walk on eggshells; VI to step on; **— fuerte** to throw one's weight around; M SG **pisapapeles** paperweight
piscifactoría F fishery, fish farm
piscina F swimming pool
piso M (suelo) floor; (planta) story; (vivienda) apartment; **de — a techo** from the ground up
pisotear VT to tramp on, to trample, to stomp on
pisotón M stamp; **dar un —** to stamp, to step on
pista F (rastro) track, scent; (noticia) clue; (de aterrizaje) runway; (de circo) arena, ring; (de patinaje) skating ring; (de tenis) court; (de baile) floor; (de carreras) track, racetrack; **seguir la —** to track; **— para bicicletas** bike lane
pistola F (revólver) pistol; (para pintura) gun
pistolera F holster
pistolero MF gunner; M gunman; F gun woman
pistón M (válvula) piston; (explosivo) cap
pitada F drag, puff
pitar VI to toot, to whistle; VI/VT (rechiflar) to boo
pitazo M honk
pitido M (silbido) whistle, toot; (en deportes) whistle
pitillo M cigarette
pito M whistle; **entre —s y flautas** when all is said and done; **¿qué —s toca?** what's his role here?
pitón M (serpiente) python; (punta de cuerno) tip of a bull's horn
pituitario ADJ pituitary
pivot MF *Am* (baloncesto) center
pivotar VI to pivot
pivote M pivot; **— central** kingpin
píxel M pixel
pizarra F (roca) slate; (pizarrón) blackboard, chalkboard
pizarrón M blackboard, chalkboard
pizca F (de sal) pinch, dash; (de evidencia) shred; (de verdad) grain; (de suciedad) speck; **no entiendo ni —** I don't understand a bit/jot
pizza F pizza
placa F (fotográfica) plate; (de policía) badge; (condecoración, sarro) plaque; (de coche) license plate; (de computadora/ordenador) board, card; **— lógica** logic board; **— madre** motherboard
placaje M tackle
placar[30] VI/VT to tackle
placebo M placebo
placenta F placenta, afterbirth
placentero ADJ pleasant
placer[36] M pleasure, enjoyment; VT *lit* to please
plácido ADJ placid
plaf INTERJ plop
plaga F (enfermedad) plague; (persona, insecto) pest
plagar[40] VT to infest; **—se de** to become infested with
plagio M plagiarism
plan M plan; **— de estudios** curriculum; **— de juego** game plan; **— de salud administrado** managed care; **se vistió en — de vampiresa** she was dressed to kill
plana F newspaper page; **— mayor** top brass; **enmendar la — a uno** to correct a person's mistakes
plancha F (electrodoméstico) iron; (lámina) metal plate; (parrilla) griddle; **hacer la —** to float; **tirarse una —** to fall flat on one's face
planchado M ironing
planchar VT to iron, to press; **me dejó planchado** it left me speechless
plancton M plankton
planeador M glider
planeamiento M planning
planear VI/VT to plan; VI (volar) to glide, to plane; VT (madera) to plane
planeo M gliding
planeta M planet
planetario M planetarium
planificación F organization, planning; **—**

familiar family planning; **— para contingencias** contingency planning
planificador M planner, scheduler; **— de rutas** trip planner
planificar[30] VI/VT to plan
planilla F (de sueldos) payroll; (digital) worksheet; *Am* **— de cálculo** spreadsheet
plano ADJ flat, even; M (superficie) plane; (de un edificio) plan; (de calles) map; **— inclinado** inclined plane; **caer de —** to fall flat; **de —** flatly; **primer —** foreground
planta F (vegetal) plant; (del pie) sole; **— baja** ground floor
plantación F plantation
plantar VT (una planta, cruz) to plant; (a un novio) to dump; (a un colega) to make wait; **—se** to stand firm, to refuse to move; **— una bofetada a alguien** to give someone a slap; **dejar plantado** to stand up
planteamiento M (enfoque) approach; (exposición) presentation; **es un — poco provechoso** it is not a very beneficial approach
plantear VT (presentar) to present; **me planteó sus planes** she explained her plans to me; (provocar) to give rise to; **eso plantea un problema** that gives rise to a problem; **—se** to occur to; **¿te has planteado lo que pasa si te quedas sin trabajo?** have you thought about what will happen if you become unemployed?
plantel M (personal) staff; (almáciga) nursery
plantilla F (pieza suelta) insole; (patrón para calcar) pattern, stencil; (digital) template
plantío M grove
plasma M plasma (también de pantalla)
plasmar VT (captar) to capture; (dar forma plástica o sensible) to mold, to shape; **—se** to materialize
plasta ADJ tiresome; F (cosa informe) lump; (persona) bore
plástico ADJ & M plastic
plata F (metal, color, objeto de plata) silver; *Am* (dinero) money; **hablar en —** to speak in plain language
plataforma F platform (también política y digital); **— de lanzamiento** launching pad; **— petrolífera** oil rig; **— continental** continental shelf
platanar M banana grove
plátano M (fruta) banana; (para cocinar) plantain; (bananero) banana tree; (árbol ornamental) plane tree
platea F main floor of a theater
plateado ADJ & M (color) silver; M (acción de platear) silver-plating
platear VT to silver-plate
platero -ra MF silversmith
plática F chat
platicar[30] VI to chat
platija F flounder
platillo M (plato pequeño) saucer; (instrumento musical) cymbal; **— volador** flying saucer
platino M platinum
plato M (recipiente) plate; (comida) dish; (béisbol) home plate; **— fuerte** main dish/course; **— hondo** bowl; **— sopero** soup dish
plausible ADJ plausible
playa F beach
playboy M playboy
plaza F (espacio amplio) plaza, public square; (puesto de trabajo) job; **de cuatro —s** four-seater; **— de toros** bullring; **— mayor** main square
plazo M term; **a corto —** short-term; **a largo —** long-term, long-range; **a — fijo** fixed-term; **a —s** on credit; **cumplir un —** to meet a deadline
plazoleta F court
plazuela F court
pleamar M high tide
plebe F rabble
plebeyo -ya ADJ & MF plebeian
plegable ADJ folding
plegadera F paper folder
plegadizo ADJ folding
plegar[41] VT to fold; **—se [a]** (ceder) to yield [to]; (unirse) to join
pleitesía F compliance
pleito M (pelea) dispute; (demanda judicial) litigation, lawsuit; **poner —** to sue
plenamente ADV fully
plenario ADJ & M plenary
plenitud F **— de la vida** prime of life
pleno ADJ complete; **en — día** in broad daylight; **en — invierno** in the dead of winter; **en — rostro** right on the face; **en — verano** in midsummer; **en plena vista** in plain sight; M full session
pliego M leaflet
pliegue M (en papel) fold; (en tela) pleat
plomada F plumb
plomería F plumbing
plomero -ra MF plumber
plomizo ADJ leaden
plomo M (metal, color) lead; (pesa) lead weight; (perdigón) shot; **a —** plumb; **caer a —** to fall vertically; **sin —** unleaded; ADJ INV tiresome
pluma F (de ave) feather, quill; (para escribir) pen; **— fuente** fountain pen
plumaje M plumage
plumero M dust mop, duster
plumífero ADJ feathery
plumón M down
plural ADJ & M plural
pluralidad F plurality
pluriempleo M moonlighting
pluscuamperfecto ADJ & N pluperfect

plutonio M plutonium
pluvial ADJ **aguas —es** rainwater
pluviómetro M rain gauge
PNB [producto nacional bruto] M GNP
población F (conjunto de personas) population; (acción de poblar) settlement; (pueblo) town
poblado M hamlet
poblador -ora MF settler
poblar[5] VT (habitar) to populate; (colonizar) to settle; **—se de** to become covered with
pobre ADJ poor; MF **los —s** the poor
pobrecito -ta MF poor thing
pobreza F (miseria) poverty; (escasez) scarcity
pocilga F pigsty, pigpen
pocillo M cup
poción F potion
poco ADJ (no mucho) little; **poca paciencia** little patience; **al — rato** after a little while; (no muchos) few; **—s pasajeros** few passengers; **al — tiempo** shortly; **a los —s meses** after a few months; **de pocas luces** stupid; **en pocas palabras** in a nutshell; ADV little; **trabaja —** he works little; **— caritativo** not very charitable; **— conocido** little known; **— a —** little by little; **— más o menos** about; **hace —** a short while ago; **por — me caigo** I almost fell; **tener en —** to hold in low esteem; PRON a little, a bit; **un —** a little bit, a little while; **como —** at least; **unos —s** a few
poda F trim
podadera F pruning hook
podar VT to prune, to trim
poder[69] VI to be able to; **no puedo llegar antes de las cinco** I can't get there before five; **¿puedo sentarme?** may I be seated? **puede que venga** she may come; **a más no —** to the utmost; **no puedo más** I can't go on; **nadie puede con ella** nobody can deal with her; **no puede menos que venir** he can't help but come; **no puede menos que hacerlo** he cannot help doing it; M (fuerza) power; (escrito que da autoridad) proxy, power of attorney; **— ejecutivo** executive branch; **— judicial** judiciary branch; **— legislativo** legislative branch; **por —** by proxy
poderío M power, might
poderoso ADJ powerful, mighty
podiatra MF podiatrist
podiatría F podiatry
podio M podium
podólogo -ga MF podiatrist
podrá, podría *ver* poder
podredumbre F rot
podrido ADJ rotten
podrir *ver* pudrir
poema M poem
poesía F (género lírico) poetry; (poema) poem
poeta MF, **poetisa** F poet
poética F poetics
poético ADJ poetic
polaco -ca ADJ Polish; M (lengua) Polish; MF Pole
polaina F legging
polar ADJ polar
polaridad F polarity
polarización F polarization
polca F polka
polea F pulley
polémica F polemic, controversy
polémico ADJ polemic
polen M pollen
poli MF cop; F *fam* cops
policía F (en conjunto) police; (mujer) policewoman; M policeman; MF police officer
policíaco ADJ police
policial ADJ police; **parte —** police report
poliéster M polyester
poliestireno M Styrofoam™
poligamia F polygamy
políglota ADJ & MF polyglot
polígrafo M polygraph
poliinsaturado ADJ polyunsaturated
polilla F moth
polímero M polymer
polinizar[47] VT to pollinate
polio F polio
pólipo M polyp
política F (actividad relativa al gobierno) politics; (conjunto de orientaciones) policy; **— exterior** foreign policy
político -ca ADJ (relativo a la política) political; (diplomático) politic; MF politician
poliuretano M polyurethane
póliza F policy; **— de seguros** insurance policy
polizón -ona MF stowaway
polizonte M *pey* cop
polla F pullet
pollada F brood
pollera F (mujer) woman who raises and sells chickens; (falda) *Am* skirt
pollo M (cría de ave) young chicken; (carne) chicken
polo M (punto geográfico) pole; (juego) polo; **— acuático** water polo; **— de atención** focus of attention; **— Norte** North Pole
Polonia F Poland
poltrona F easy chair
polvareda F cloud of dust; **levantar una —** (causar escándalo) to raise a ruckus; (causar una nube de polvo) to kick up the dust
polvera F compact
polvo M (suciedad) dust; (partículas) powder; **— de hornear** baking powder; **juntar —** to gather dust; **limpio de — y paja** net
pólvora F gunpowder
polvoriento ADJ dusty

polvorín M (almacén de pólvora) magazine; (situación explosiva) powder keg
pomada F salve
pomelo M grapefruit
pómez F pumice
pomo M doorknob
pompa F (boato) pomp; (burbuja) soap bubble; **—s fúnebres** funeral ceremony
pomposo ADJ pompous
pómulo M cheekbone
pon *ver* poner
ponchado M (béisbol) strikeout
ponchar VT (un neumático) to puncture; **— a alguien** (en béisbol) to strike someone out; **—se** (un neumático) to become punctured; (en béisbol) to strike out
ponche M (bebida) punch; (en béisbol) strikeout
ponchera F punch bowl
poncho M poncho
ponderación F (acción de ponderar) pondering; (valor relativo) weighting
ponderar VT (considerar) to ponder, to consider; (exagerar) to exaggerate; (ajustar valores) to weight
pondrá, pondría *ver* poner
ponencia F presentation
poner[56, 74] VT to put, to place; (la mesa, un reloj) to set; (huevos) to lay; (azúcar) to add; (un examen) to give; (el televisor) to turn on; (un pleito) to file; **— a alguien a hacer algo** to assign someone to do something; **— en claro** to clarify; **— en limpio** to recopy, to make a clean copy; **— nombre a un niño** to name a child; **— sangre** to give a transfusion; **cada uno pone mil pesetas** each person contributes a thousand pesetas; **pongamos que** let us suppose that; **¿qué pone ahí?** what does it say there? **—se** (volverse) to become; (el sol) to set; (ropa) to put on; **—se a** to begin to; **—se al corriente** to become informed; **—se de acuerdo** to come to an agreement; **—se de pie** to stand up; **—se por delante en el marcador** (deporte) to take the lead
póney M pony
ponga, pongo *ver* poner
poniente M (oeste) west; (viento del oeste) west wind
pontón M pontoon
ponzoña F poison
ponzoñoso ADJ poisonous
pool M pool
popa F poop, stern
populacho M mob
popular ADJ (conocido y citado) popular; (del pueblo) folk
popularidad F popularity
populoso ADJ populous
popurrí M (de perfume) potpourri; (musical) medley
poquito *ver* poco
por PREP **— barco** by boat; **— casualidad** by chance; **— Dios** by God; **— etapas** by stages; **— las buenas o — las malas** by hook or by crook; **— litro** by the liter; **¿— qué?** why? for what reason? **multiplicar —** to multiply by; **lo agarró — la garganta** he grabbed him by the throat; **mi amor — ella** my love for her; **— poco tiempo** for a short time; **— primera vez** for the first time; **— vía de argumento** for the sake of argument; **— ejemplo** for instance; **— el momento** for the time being; **hazlo — mí** do it for my sake; **trabaja — mí** work on my behalf; **no me gustan — su olor** I don't like them because of their smell; **lo supe — él** I found out through him; **pasé — Londres** I passed through London; **un viaje — la costa** a trip along the coast; **— lo que cuentas** from what you're telling me; **— adelantado** in advance; **— escrito** in writing; **— la mañana** in the morning; **— lo general** in general; **— rachas** in spurts; **está — Badajoz** it's near Badajoz; **— fin** at last; **— el mes de marzo** around the month of March; **— ciento** percent; **— consiguiente** consequently; **— escrito** in writing; **— poco se muere** he almost died; **está — hacer** it is yet to be done; **él está — hacerlo** (a favor de) he is in favor of doing it; (a punto de) he is about to do it; **recibir — esposa** to take as a wife; **tener —** to consider, to think of as
porcelana F porcelain, china
porcentaje M percentage; **— de bateo** (béisbol) batting average
porche M porch, stoop
porcino ADJ **ganado —** swine; M pig
porción F (parte) portion, share; (de alimento) helping
pordiosear VT to panhandle
pordiosero -ra MF panhandler
porfía F obstinacy
porfiado ADJ willful
porfiar[28] VT to insist
pormenor M detail
pormenorizar[47] VT to detail, to go into detail about
porno M porn
pornografía F pornography
pornográfico ADJ pornographic
poro M pore
poroso ADJ porous
poroto M *Am* bean
porque CONJ because
porqué M reason; **el — de su tristeza** the reason for his sadness
porquería F (suciedad) filth; (acción despreciable) dirty trick; (cosa de mala

calidad) crud; (comida de mala calidad) junk food

porra F club, cudgel

porrista MF cheerleader

portada F (de un libro) title page; (de una revista) front cover

portador -ora MF (de enfermedad) carrier; (de cheque) bearer; **— del féretro** pallbearer

portal M portal, doorway; **— de videos/vídeos** video portal

portar VT to carry; **—se** to behave; **—se mal** to misbehave; M SG **portaaviones** aircraft carrier; M SG **portaequipajes** luggage bin; M **portaestandarte** standard-bearer; M **portafolio** briefcase; M SG **portalámparas** socket; M SG **portaligas** garter belt; M SG **portamonedas** coin purse; M **portaobjeto** slide; M SG **portapapeles** clipboard; MF **portavoz** spokesperson

portátil ADJ portable

portazo M slam; **dar un —** to slam the door

porte M (envío) freight; (por correo) postage; (aspecto) bearing, carriage; (capacidad de carga) capacity; (tamaño) size; **— de armas** the carrying of arms; **enviar — pagado** to send prepaid

portear VT to carry

portentoso ADJ portentous

porteño -ña MF (de Buenos Aires) person from Buenos Aires; (de un puerto) person from a port city; ADJ (de Buenos Aires) from Buenos Aires; (de un puerto) from a port city

portería F (de un edificio) entrance area; (en fútbol) goal

portero -ra MF (de un edificio) doorkeeper, superintendent; (en fútbol) goalkeeper; M **— automático** intercom

portón M gate

portuario ADJ harbor, port; **trabajador —** dockworker

Portugal M Portugal

portugués -esa ADJ & MF Portuguese; M (lengua) Portuguese

porvenir M future

pos LOC PREP **en — de** after

posada F inn, lodge

posaderas F PL *fam* rear end

posadero -ra MF innkeeper

posar VT (la mano, los ojos) to rest; VI (en el suelo) to sit down; (como modelo) to pose; **—se** (partículas) to settle; (mariposa) to alight; (pájaro) to perch

posdata F postscript

pose F pose

poseedor -ora MF possessor

poseer[18] VT to possess

poseído ADJ possessed

posesión F possession

posesivo ADJ & M possessive

poseyendo, poseyera, poseyese, poseyó *ver* poseer

posfechar VT to postdate

posguerra F postwar period

posibilidad F possibility

posibilitar VT (hacer posible) to make possible; (permitir) to allow, to permit

posible ADJ possible; **hacer lo —** to do one's best; **es —** it's possible

posición F (ubicación) position; (opinión) stance; (rango) standing; **— de negociación** bargaining position; **— fetal** fetal position

posicionamiento M (acción de posicionar, también de productos) placement, positioning; (actitud política) position, stance

posicionarse VI to position oneself

positivo ADJ & M positive

poso M (de vino) dregs; (de café) grounds

posparto M postpartum

posponer[36, 74] VT (aplazar) to postpone, to defer, to put off; (relegar) to put after

posta F (relevo) relay; (perdigón) buckshot

postal ADJ postal; F postcard

poste M (palo) post; (en fútbol) upright, goalpost

póster M poster

postergar[40] VT (para un ascenso) to pass over; (posponer) to postpone

posteridad F posterity; **eso quedará para la —** that will remain for all eternity

posterior ADJ (espacial) back, rear; (anatómico) posterior; (temporal) later; **nuestro divorcio fue — a la compra del negocio** our divorce came after we purchased the business

posterioridad LOC ADV **con —** later, subsequently

posteriormente ADV (atrás) in the back; (después) afterward[s]; **vocal pronunciada —** vowel pronounced in the back [of the mouth]

postigo M shutter

postizo ADJ false; **familia postiza** adoptive family; M hairpiece

postnasal ADJ postnasal

postrado ADJ prostrate, prone

postrar VT to prostrate

postre M dessert; **a la —** at last

postulado M postulate

postulante MF candidate

postular VT to postulate

póstumo ADJ posthumous

postura F posture (también opinión)

potable ADJ drinkable, potable

potasio M potassium

pote M (cilíndrico) jar; (panzudo) jug

potear VI/VT to putt

potencia F (sexual) potency; (de una fuerza, nación) power; **es un asesino en —** he's a potential murderer; **— naval** sea power; **de**

alta — high-powered; **segunda** — the second power
potencial ADJ & M potential
potenciar VT (a una persona) to empower; (proyectos, relaciones) to promote, to support
potentado -da MF potentate
potente ADJ potent, powerful
potranco -ca M colt; F filly
potrero M pasture; *Am* cattle ranch, stock farm
potro M (caballo) colt; (en gimnasia) vaulting horse; — **de tormento** rack
pozo M (de agua, petróleo) well; (hoyo profundo) pit; (minero) mine shaft; **sacar del** — to rescue; — **negro** sink; — **sin fondo** bottomless pit; — **séptico** septic tank
práctica F (repetición, costumbre) practice; (destreza) skill; **en la** — in practice; **poner en** — to put into practice; — **comercial desleal** deceptive practice
prácticamente ADV (casi) practically, virtually; (de forma práctica) practically; (en la práctica) in practice
practicante ADJ practicing; MF (que practica) practitioner; (asistente de médico) physician's assistant
practicar[30] VI/VT (una habilidad) to practice; (un agujero) to make
práctico ADJ (sencillo) practical; (adiestrado) skillful; M — **de puerto** harbor pilot
pradera F prairie, grassland
prado M meadow, pasture
pragmático ADJ pragmatic
preadolescente ADJ & MF preteen, preadolescent
preámbulo M preamble
preaprobado ADJ preapproved
precalentamiento M warmup
precanceroso ADJ precancerous
precario ADJ precarious, *fam* touch-and-go
precaución F precaution
precaverse VT to take precautions
precavido ADJ cautious
precedencia F precedence
precedente ADJ preceding; M precedent; **sin** — unprecedented; **sentar** — to set a precedent
preceder VI/VT to precede
precepto M precept
preciado ADJ (estimado) prized; (valioso) valuable
preciarse VI — **de** to be proud of
precintar VT to seal
precinto M seal
precio M price; **poner** — **a** to put a price on; **no tener** — to be priceless; — **de compra** purchase price; — **de lista** list price; — **de mercado** market price; — **de referencia** bench price; — **justo en el mercado** fair market price; — **sugerido** suggested retail price; — **sugerido por el fabricante** manufacturer's suggested retail price; — **vigente** going price
preciosista ADJ precious
precioso ADJ (metal, piedra, objeto de gran valor) precious; (muy bonito) beautiful, adorable
precipicio M precipice, cliff
precipitación F precipitation (también atolondramiento)
precipitado ADJ precipitate, hasty, rash; M precipitate
precipitar VI to precipitate; VT to hurl; —**se** (apresurarse) to be hasty; (arrojarse) to plunge, to plummet; (depositarse) to precipitate; (adelantarse) to come to a head
precisamente ADV precisely, exactly, just; — **de eso te quería hablar** that is just what I wanted to talk to you about; (de hecho) as a matter of fact; —**, se alojó en este hotel** as a matter of fact he stayed in this hotel
precisar VT (determinar) to determine precisely; (necesitar) to need
precisión F precision, accuracy; **precisiones** clarifications
preciso ADJ precise, accurate; **es** — **que vengas** you must come; **en este** — **instante** at this very moment
precoz ADJ (niño) precocious; (diagnóstico) early
precursor -ora MF precursor, forerunner
predecesor -ora MF predecessor
predecir[53, 74] VT to predict, to foretell
predestinar VT to predestine
predeterminado ADJ predetermined
predicación F preaching
predicado ADJ & M predicate
predicador -ora MF preacher
predicar[30] VI/VT to preach
predicción F prediction
predilección F predilection
predilecto ADJ favorite, pet
predio M piece of land
predisponer[56, 74] VT to predispose
predisposición F predisposition
predominante ADJ predominant, prevailing
predominar VI to predominate
predominio M predominance
preeclampsia F preeclampsia
preeminente ADJ foremost
preempacado ADJ prepacked
preescolar ADJ nursery; MF nursery school child
preestablecido ADJ preset
preestreno M preview
preexistente ADJ preexisting
prefacio M preface
preferencia F preference; (en el tráfico) right of way; **de** — predominantly
preferente ADJ (tratamiento) preferential;

(acciones) preferred
preferible ADJ preferable
preferido ADJ preferred, favorite
preferir[8] VT to prefer
prefiera, prefiere *ver* preferir
prefijar VT to prefix
prefijo M prefix
prefiriendo, prefiriera, prefiriese *ver* preferir
pregonar VT (noticias) to make public; (mercancías) to hawk
pregrabado ADJ prerecorded
pregunta F question; **hacer una —** to ask a question; **—s frecuentes** frequently asked questions
preguntar VI/VT to ask, to inquire; **— por** (pedir información) to inquire about; (pedir para hablar) to ask for; **—se** to wonder
preguntón ADJ inquisitive
prehistórico ADJ prehistoric
prejuicio M prejudice, bias
prejuzgar[40] VT to prejudge
preliminar ADJ & M preliminary
preludiar VT to prelude
preludio M prelude
prematrimonial ADJ premarital
prematuro ADJ (bebé) premature; (muerte) untimely
premeditado ADJ premeditated
premenstrual ADJ premenstrual
premiar VT to reward; **las obras premiadas** the award-winning works
première M premiere
premio M (galardón) prize, award; (de la moneda) appreciation; **Juan Pérez, — nacional de poesía** Juan Pérez, winner of the national poetry award; **— gordo** jackpot
premisa F premise
premonición F premonition
prenatal ADJ prenatal
prenda F (fianza) pawn, pledge; (de vestir) article of clothing, garment; **dejar en —** to pawn; **en — de** as a token of
prendar VT to charm; **—se de** to fall in love with
prendedor M brooch, pin
prender VT (agarrar) to grab; (sujetar) to clasp; (enganchar) to fasten; (detener) to arrest; (arraigar) to take root; (encender) to turn on, to switch on; **— fuego** to set on fire; **la vacuna no prendió** the vaccination didn't take
prensa F press; **tener mala —** to have bad press
prensar VT to press
prensil ADJ prehensile
prenupcial ADJ prenuptial
preñada ADJ pregnant
preñar VT to impregnate
preñez F pregnancy
preocupación F worry, concern
preocupado ADJ worried, concerned, anxious
preocupante ADJ worrisome
preocupar VT to worry, to concern; **—se de** to worry about; **—se por** to be concerned about
preocupón -ona MF worrywart
preparación F preparation
preparado ADJ ready; M preparation
preparar VT to prepare; **—se** to get ready, to brace oneself; **— el cuerpo de un difunto** to embalm a body
preparativo ADJ preparatory; M preparation
preparatorio ADJ preparatory; **escuela preparatoria** preparatory school
preponderancia F preponderance
preponderante ADJ preponderant
preponderar VI to predominate
preposición F preposition
prepucio M foreskin
prerrequisito M prerequisite
prerrogativa F prerogative
presa F (animal de caza) prey, quarry; (dique) dam
presagiar VT to forebode
presagio M omen, sign
présbita, présbite ADV & MF farsighted
prescindible ADJ dispensable
prescindir VI **— de** to dispense with, to do without
prescribir[74] VT to prescribe
prescripción F prescription
presencia F presence; **— de ánimo** presence of mind
presenciar VT to witness
presentable ADJ presentable
presentación F (de un tema) presentation; (de una persona) introduction
presentador -ora MF (de programa de televisión) host; (de noticiero) anchor
presentar VT (una idea) to present; (a una persona) to introduce; (la declaración de impuestos, una demanda) to file; (un informe) to submit; (documentos) to produce; (una queja) to lodge; (una renuncia) to tender; **—se** (aparecer) to appear; (hacerse conocer) to introduce oneself
presente ADJ present; M (tiempo) present; (regalo) present, gift; **al —** at the present time; **tener —** to bear in mind; **en el — [contrato]** herein; **por la — [carta]** hereby
presentimiento M presentiment, foreboding, hunch
presentir[8] VT to have a presentiment of
preservación F (protección) preservation; (ahorro) conservation
preservar VT (proteger) to preserve; (ahorrar) to conserve
presidencia F presidency
presidencial ADJ presidential

presidente MF, **presidenta** F (de un país) president; (de una reunión, junta) chair
presidiario -ria MF prisoner
presidio M prison
presidir VI to preside; VT to preside over
presilla F loop
presión F pressure; **— atmosférica** atmospheric pressure; **— arterial** blood pressure; **— arterial alta** high blood pressure, hypertension; **— de aire** air pressure
presionar VT (un botón) to press; (al gobierno) to lobby
preso -sa MF prisoner, inmate
prestación F provision; **prestaciones** benefits
prestador -ora MF lender
prestamista MF (de dinero) lender; (en un montepío) pawnbroker
préstamo M loan; **— convencional** conventional loan; **— garantizado** guaranteed loan
prestar VT to loan, to lend; **— ayuda** to give help; **— atención** to pay attention; **— juramento** to take an oath; **— servicio** to render service
prestatario -ria MF borrower
prestidigitación F sleight of hand
prestigio M prestige
prestigioso ADJ prestigious
presumido ADJ conceited, presumptuous
presumir VT (suponer) to presume; VI (ostentar) to show off; **— de valiente** to boast of one's valor
presunción F presumption
presuntamente ADV allegedly
presunto ADJ (dueño, autor de una obra) presumed; (autor de un crimen) alleged; **— heredero** heir apparent
presuntuoso ADJ presumptuous
presuponer[56, 74] VT to presuppose
presupuestación F budgeting
presupuestario ADJ budget, budgetary
presupuesto M (de gastos e ingresos) budget; (de costos) estimate; **— equilibrado** balanced budget
presuroso ADJ hasty
pretencioso ADJ pretentious
pretender VI (sostener) to claim, to purport; **— ser** to claim to be; **— al trono** to pretend to the throne; VT (intentar) to attempt
pretendiente MF, **pretendienta** F (al trono) pretender; (a un puesto) aspirant; M (de una mujer) suitor, admirer
pretensión F pretension
pretérito ADJ past; M past tense; **— perfecto** present perfect
pretexto M pretext, pretense; **so — de** under pretense of
pretil M railing
pretina F waistband
prevalecer[35] VI to prevail
prevaleciente ADJ prevalent
prevé, prevea, preveía *ver* prever
prevención F (protección) prevention; (recelo) caution
prevenido ADJ forewarned
prevenir[61] VT (precaver) to prevent; (prever) to foresee; (advertir) to warn; **— contra** to protect oneself against
preventivo ADJ preventive, precautionary
prever[72, 74] VT to foresee, to anticipate
previamente ADV previously
previo ADJ previous, prior; **— examen de salud** after undergoing a health examination
previsible ADJ foreseeable
previsión F foresight, anticipation
previsto *ver* prever
previsualización F previewing
prieto ADJ swarthy
prima F (cuota de seguro) premium; (recargo) surcharge; (pago extraordinario) bonus
primario ADJ primary
primate M primate
primavera F spring
primaveral ADJ springlike
primero ADJ & ADV first; **primer ministro** prime minister; **primer piso** second floor; **primer plano** foreground; **primera base** (posición) first base; (jugador) first baseman; **primera enseñanza** primary education; **primera persona** first person; **primer tiempo** first half; **—s auxilios** first aid; **a primera vista** at first sight; **de primer grado** first degree; **de primera** top-notch; **de primera mano** firsthand; **por primera vez** for the first time; **— del mes** first of the month; **Juan llegó —** Juan arrived first; F (marcha) first gear; (clase en un avión) first class
primicia F (fruto primero) first fruit; (noticia) scoop
primitivo ADJ primitive
primo -ma MF (hijo de tío) cousin; (persona incauta) sucker, dupe; **— hermano** first cousin; **— segundo** second cousin; ADJ prime
primogénito -ta ADJ & MF firstborn
primogenitura F birthright
primor M (esmero) care; (cosa fina) lovely thing
primordial ADJ primordial
primoroso ADJ exquisite
princesa F princess
principal ADJ principal, main; **la causa — de muerte** the leading cause of death; **el dormitorio —** the master bedroom
principalmente ADV mainly, principally
príncipe M prince
principesco ADJ princely

principiante MF beginner; ADJ beginning
principiar VT to commence
principio M (fundamento, regla de conducta) principle, tenet; (hecho de empezar, tiempo, lugar) beginning, start; **a —s de** toward the beginning of; **— activo** active ingredient; **al —** at the beginning, at first; **de — a fin** from beginning to end; **desde el —** from the beginning; **en —** in principle
pringar[40] VT (ensuciar) to get greasy; (mojar) to dip
pringoso ADJ greasy
pringue MF grease
prioridad F (autoridad, preferencia) priority, precedence; (en el tráfico) right of way
prioritario ADJ having priority, most important
prisa F haste, hurry; **a toda —** at full speed; **correr —** to be urgent; **darse —** to hurry; **las —s comienzan a la una** the rush starts at one; **tener —** to be in a hurry; **sin —** leisurely
prisión F prison; **— perpetua** life in prison
prisionero -ra MF prisoner; **— de guerra** prisoner of war
prisma M prism
prismáticos M PL binoculars
privacidad F privacy
privación F privation; **pasar privaciones** to suffer want
privado ADJ private; **en —** in private
privar VT to deprive; **—se de** to deprive oneself of
privativo ADJ exclusive
privatización F privatization
privatizar[47] VT to privatize
privilegiado ADJ privileged
privilegiar VT to favor, to give a privilege to
privilegio M privilege
pro M advantage; **en — de** in favor of; **en — y en contra** for and against
proa F prow, bow
proaborto ADJ INV pro-choice
probabilidad F (chance) likelihood; (en estadística) probability; **tienes pocas —es de ganar** you have little chance of winning; **¿qué —es tiene?** what are her odds?
probable ADJ probable, likely; **lo más — es que haya venido** in all likelihood he came
probador M dressing room
probar[5] VT (alimento, bebida) to taste, to try, to sample; (una hipótesis) to prove; (una guitarra) to try out; (un coche) to test-drive; **—se un vestido** to try on a dress; **— fortuna** to try one's luck; **prueba a venir más temprano** try to come earlier; **no — bocado** not to eat a bite
probatorio ADJ probationary
probeta F test tube
problema M problem; **él sólo da —s** he's nothing but trouble
problemático -ca ADJ problematic; F problems
procedencia F origin
procedente ADJ **— de** from
proceder VI to proceed; **— de** to come from; **— a** to proceed to; **— contra** to take action against
procedimiento M procedure; **—s** proceedings
procesable ADJ actionable
procesado -da MF accused; M processing
procesador ADJ processing; M processor; **— de textos** word processor
procesamiento M prosecution; **— de datos** data processing; **— de textos** word processing
procesar VT to prosecute, to try
procesión F procession; **la — va por dentro** he doesn't let it show
proceso M (etapas) process; (juicio) trial, legal proceedings
proclama F proclamation
proclamación F proclamation
proclamar VT to proclaim; **—se campeón** to be proclaimed winner
proclive ADJ prone
procrear VI/VT to procreate
proctología F proctology
procurador -ora MF attorney
procurar VT (intentar) to endeavor; (obtener) to procure, to obtain
prodigar[40] VT to lavish; **—se** to be lavish
prodigio M prodigy
prodigioso ADJ prodigious
pródigo -ga ADJ (derrochador) prodigal; (muy generoso) lavish; MF spendthrift
producción F (acción de producir) production; (cantidad producida) production, yield; **— masiva** mass production
producir[38] VT (efectos, mercancías, películas) to produce; (fruta, resultados) to yield, to bear; **—se** to happen
productividad F productivity
productivo ADJ (rendidor) productive; (exitoso) successful
producto M product; **— interno bruto** gross national product
productor -ora MF producer; ADJ **un país — de petróleo** an oil-producing country
produje, produjera, produjese *ver* producir
pro-elección ADJ INV pro-choice
proeza F exploit
profanación F desecration
profanar VT to profane, to desecrate
profano ADJ profane
profecía F prophecy
proferir[8] VT to utter
profesar VT to profess
profesión F profession
profesional ADJ & MF professional; **— de la**

salud health care provider
profesionista MF *México* professional
profesor -ora MF (universitario) professor; (de enseñanza secundaria) teacher; (de tenis) instructor
profesorado M faculty
profeta MF prophet
profético ADJ prophetic
profetizar[47] VI/VT to prophesy
profilaxis F prevention
prófugo -ga ADJ & MF fugitive
profundidad F (del mar, de comprensión, de un armario) depth; (sabiduría) profundity
profundizar[47] VT to deepen; VI to go into deeply
profundo ADJ (idea, comentario, razonamiento) profound; (mar, pozo, armario, voz) deep
profuso ADJ profuse
progesterona F progesterone
programa M (de boxeo) card; (de televisión) show, program; (de un curso) syllabus; (de un congreso) program; **— antivirus** antivirus program, antivirus software; **— de protección contra virus** virus protection software; **— de instalación** setup program, install program; **— instalador** setup program, install program; **— para recuperar datos borrados** undelete utility; **—s almacenados en circuitos integrados** firmware
programable ADJ programmable
programación F programming
programador -ora MF programmer
programar VT (una computadora) to program; (un evento) to schedule
progresar VT to progress, to advance
progresión F progression
progresista ADJ & MF progressive
progresivo -va ADJ & MF progressive
progreso M progress
prohibición F prohibition, ban
prohibido ADJ forbidden; **prohibida la entrada** no admittance; **— el paso** no trespassing
prohibir[29] VT to prohibit, to ban; **se prohíbe fumar** no smoking
prohijar VT to adopt
prójimo -ma MF fellow human
prole F offspring
proletariado M proletariat
proletario -ria ADJ & MF proletarian
proliferación F proliferation, spread
prolífico ADJ prolific
prolijo ADJ (verboso) wordy; (esmerado) overly careful
prologar[40] VT to preface
prólogo M prologue, foreword, preface
prolongación F prolongation
prolongado ADJ extended
prolongar[40] VT to prolong; **—se** to wear on
promediar VT to average
promedio M average, mean; **de/en —** on average; **— de carreras limpias permitidas** earned run average
promesa F promise; **romper una —** to break a promise; **una joven —** a promising young player
prometedor ADJ promising
prometer VT to promise; VI to show promise
prometido -da ADJ engaged; M fiancé; F fiancée
prominente ADJ prominent
promiscuo ADJ promiscuous
promisorio ADJ promissory; **un futuro —** a promising future
promoción F (oferta comercial) promotion; (conjunto de personas) class
promocional ADJ promotional
promocionar VT to promote, to publicize
promontorio M promontory
promotor -ora MF (de un producto) promoter; (de bienes inmuebles) developer
promover[6] VT (ideas, producto, a un alumno) to promote; (la paz, una causa) to foster, to further
promulgación F enactment
promulgar[40] VT to promulgate, to enact
pronombre M pronoun
pronominal ADJ pronominal
pronosticar[30] VT to forecast
pronóstico M (del tiempo, de la economía) forecast; (de una enfermedad) prognosis
prontitud F promptness, dispatch
pronto ADJ (rápido) quick; (listo) ready; ADV soon, promptly; **de —** suddenly; **¡hasta —!** see you soon! **tan — como** as soon as
pronunciación F pronunciation
pronunciado ADJ pronounced
pronunciamiento M declaration, pronouncement
pronunciar VT (un sonido, una sentencia) to pronounce; (un discurso) to make, to deliver; **—se** (acusarse) to be pronounced; (expresarse) to declare one's opinion
propagación F propagation, spread
propaganda F (de ideas) propaganda; (de mercancías) advertising, publicity; **hacer —** to advertise
propagar[40] VT to propagate
propalar VT to spread
propano M propane
propasarse VI to go too far
propensión F propensity
propenso ADJ prone
propiciar VT to favor
propicio ADJ propitious, auspicious
propiedad F (cualidad, pertenencia, finca) property; (derecho de dueño) ownership; (corrección) precision; **— mayoritaria**

majority ownership; — **privada** private property; —**es** estate; —**es colindantes** adjoining properties

propietario-ria M (de una tienda) proprietor, owner; (de un apartamento) landlord; F (de una tienda) owner; (de un apartamento) landlady; — **ausente** absentee landlord

propina F tip, gratuity; **dar [una]** — to tip

propinar VT — **una paliza** to give a beating

propio ADJ (correcto) proper; **el significado** — the proper meaning; (típico) like; **no es** — **de él quejarse así** it's not like him to complain like that; (conveniente) appropriate; **una expresión propia** an appropriate expression; (que le pertenece) own; **su** — **hijo** his own son; **un hijo** — a son of his own; **por tu** — **bien** for your own good; (mismo) same; **al** — **tiempo** at the same time

propondrá, propondría *ver* proponer

proponente MF proponent

proponer[56, 74] VT to propose; —**se** to set out to

proponga, propongo *ver* proponer

proporción F proportion, ratio; **proporciones** dimensions

proporcional ADJ proportional, proportionate

proporcionar VT (ajustar a proporción) to proportion; (brindar) to furnish, to provide

proposición F (lógica) proposition; (de matrimonio) proposal; **proposiciones deshonestas** indecent proposals

propósito M purpose, intent; **a** — (adecuado) apropos; (voluntariamente) on purpose, intentionally, deliberately; (además) by the way, incidentally; **a** — **de** apropos of

propuesta F proposal

propuesto *ver* proponer

propugnar VT to urge

propulsar VT to propel

propulsión F propulsion; — **a chorro** jet propulsion

propulsor-ora ADJ propelling; MF promoter

propuse, propusiera, propusiese *ver* proponer

prorratear VT to prorate

prórroga F (plazo) extension of time; (de un préstamo) renewal; (fútbol americano) overtime; (fútbol) extra time

prorrogar[40] VT (un pago) to put off, to defer; (un plazo) to extend; (un préstamo) to renew

prorrumpir VI to burst; — **en llanto** to burst into tears; — **en carcajadas** to burst out laughing

prosa F prose

prosaico ADJ prosaic

proscribir[74] VT to banish, to disenfranchise

proscripción F banishment

proseguir[12] VI to proceed

prosódico ADJ prosodic

prospectar VT to prospect

prospector-ora MF prospector

prosperar VI to prosper, to flourish, to thrive

prosperidad F prosperity

próspero ADJ prosperous

próstata F prostate [gland]

prostitución F prostitution

prostituir[19] VT to prostitute

prostituto-ta MF prostitute

protagonista MF protagonist

protagonizar[47] VT to star in

protección F protection; — **al consumidor** consumer protection; — **contra copias** copy protection; — **contra grabación** write protection; — **contra lectura** read protect; — **por contraseña** password protection

proteccionista ADJ & MF protectionist

protector-ora ADJ protective; MF protector; — **de pantalla** screen saver; — **de tensión** surge protector; — **sobrecargas de voltaje** surge protector; — **solar** sunblock

protectorado M protectorate

proteger[45] VT (a alguien vulnerable) to protect; (a un artista) to sponsor; — **contra grabación** to write-protect

protegido-da MF protégé[e]; — **por contraseña** password protected

proteína F protein

prótesis F prosthesis; — **de cadera** hip prosthesis

protesta F protest

protestante MF Protestant

protestar VI/VT to protest

protocolo M protocol

protón M proton

protoplasma M protoplasm

prototipo M prototype

protozoario M protozoan

protuberancia F protuberance, bulge, bump

protuberante ADJ bulging

provecho M (beneficio) benefit; (eructo) burp; **¡buen** —**!** bon appétit! **sacar** — **[de]** to benefit [from], to profit [from]

provechoso ADJ beneficial, advantageous

proveedor-ora MF (de un servicio) provider; (de un producto) supplier, vendor; — **de acceso** access provider; — **de acceso a internet** Internet access provider

proveer[18, 74] VT to provide; — **de** to provide with; —**se de** to provide oneself with

provenga, provengo *ver* provenir

proveniente ADJ — **de** coming from

provenir[61] VI to arise; — **de** to stem from

proverbio M proverb

providencia F providence

providencial ADJ providential

provincia F province

provincial ADJ provincial

provinciano-na ADJ & MF provincial

provine, proviniendo, proviniera,

proviniese, provino *ver* provenir
provisión F provision, supply, store
provisional ADJ temporary, provisional
provisorio ADJ temporary
provocación F provocation
provocar[30] VT (ira) to provoke; (sexualmente) to excite; (un incendio) to start; (una respuesta) to elicit
provocativo ADJ provocative
proximidad F proximity, nearness; **en las —es** in the vicinity
próximo ADJ (posterior) next; (cercano) near, nearby; **el lunes — pasado** last Monday; **de próxima aparición** forthcoming
proyección F projection
proyectar VT (un plan) to project; (una película) to screen; (una sombra) to cast; **—se** to overhang, to jut
proyectil M projectile
proyecto M (idea) project; (arquitectónico) plan; **— de ley** bill
proyector M (para películas) projector; (en el teatro) spotlight
prudencia F prudence
prudente ADJ prudent
prueba F (de imprenta, argumento irrefutable) proof; (argumento parcial) evidence; (intento, dificultad) trial, test; (examen) test, examination; (de ropa) fitting; **— beta** beta test; **— de detección** screening test; **— de doble incógnita** double-blind test; **— de embarazo** pregnancy test; **— de esfuerzo** stress test; **— de esfuerzo máximo** exercise electrocardiogram; **— de fuego** trial by fire; **— de ingresos** means test; **— de paternidad** paternity test; **— de Rorschach** Rorschach test; **a —** on approval; **a — de fallos** foolproof; **a — de incendio** fireproof; **poner a —** to put to the test
prueba, pruebe *ver* probar
psicoanálisis M psychoanalysis
psicodélico ADJ & M psychedelic
psicología F psychology
psicológico ADJ psychological
psicólogo -ga MF psychologist
psicópata MF psychopath
psicosis F psychosis
psicosomático ADJ psychosomatic
psicoterapia F psychotherapy
psicótico ADJ psychotic
psiquiatra MF psychiatrist
psiquiatría F psychiatry
psíquico ADJ psychic
psoriasis F psoriasis
púa F (con punta aguda) spike; (de alambre) barb; (de guitarra) pick; (de erizo) quill; (de tridente) prong
puaf, puaj INTERJ yuck, ugh
pubertad F puberty
publicación F publication
publicar[30] VT to publish; (revelar) to divulge
publicidad F publicity, advertising; **— de cebo y anzuelo** bait-and-switch advertising; **— engañosa** false advertising; **— exterior** outdoor advertising; **hacer —** to advertise
publicitario -ria MF advertising agent; ADJ publicity
público ADJ public; M (testigo) public; (en un espectáculo) audience; **en —** in public
publirreportaje M infomercial
puchero M (vasija) pot; (guiso) stew; (gesto) pout; **hacer —s** to pout
puck M puck
pude, pudiendo, pudiera, pudiese *ver* poder
pudiente ADJ wealthy
pudín M pudding
pudor M (sexual) modesty; (emocional) reserve
pudrir[74] VI to rot
pueblerino ADJ provincial
pueblo M (población) town; (nación) people, folk
pueda, puede *ver* poder
puente M bridge (también dental, de gafas, de nariz); (fin de semana) long weekend; **— aéreo** (regular) shuttle; (de emergencia) airlift; **— cardiopulmonar** cardiopulmonary bypass, coronary bypass; **— colgante** suspension bridge; **— levadizo** drawbridge
puénting M bungee jumping
pueril ADJ childish
puerta F (de casa) door; (de aeropuerto, de ciudad) gate; (entrada) entrance; **— de acceso** gateway; **vender de — en —** to sell door to door; **dar a alguien con la — en las narices** to slam the door in someone's face; **llamar a la —** to knock on the door; **— trasera** back door; **a — cerrada** behind closed doors
puerto M port (también en informática); **— de acceso** gateway; **— de entrada** port of entry; **— de ratón** mouse port; **— paralelo** parallel port; **— serie/serial** serial port; **— USB** USB port; **llegar a buen —** to bring to a satisfactory conclusion
puertorriqueño -ña ADJ & MF Puerto Rican
pues CONJ (puesto que) since, for; ADV (entonces) then; **— bien** well then, now
puesta F **— al día** update; **— del sol** sunset, setting of the sun; **— en marcha** (de un proyecto) setting in motion; (de un coche) starting; **— en libertad** freeing
puestero -ra MF vendor, seller
puesto ADJ **bien —** (casa) well-appointed; (persona) well made-up; **llevar —** to have on; M (posición) place; (de venta) booth, stand; (de trabajo) post, position; **— de socorros** first-aid station; **quedarse con lo —** to be

left with only the clothes on one's back; CONJ — **que** since
puesto *ver* poner
pugilato M boxing
pugilista MF boxer, prizefighter
pugna F struggle; **estar en — con** to be in conflict with
pugnaz ADJ feisty
puja F (del viento) push; (en una subasta) bid
pujanza F vigor
pujar VI (para dar a luz) to push; (en una subasta) to bid; **— por** to strive to
pujo M contraction
pulcritud F neatness
pulcro ADJ neat
pulga F flea; **tener malas —s** to be ill-tempered
pulgada F inch
pulgar M thumb
pulido ADJ polished; M polishing
pulimento M (de modales) refinement; (de metales) buffing; (polvo para pulir) scouring powder
pulir VT (metal, un discurso) to polish; (madera) to sand
pulla F taunt, dig
pulmón M lung; **— de acero** iron lung
pulmonar ADJ pulmonary; **capacidad —** lung capacity
pulmonía F pneumonia
pulpa F pulp
púlpito M pulpit
pulpo M octopus
pulque M *Méx* pulque
pulquería F *Méx* pulque bar
pulsación F (de corazón) pulse; (de ratón de computadora) click; (de tecla) keystroke
pulsar VT (una tecla) to press; (cuerdas de guitarra) to pluck; (la opinión pública) to gauge; **— y arrastrar** to click and drag
púlsar M pulsar
pulsera F (alhaja) bracelet; (de reloj) watchband; **reloj de —** wristwatch
pulso M (pulsación) pulse; (firmeza de mano) steadiness; **echar un —** to arm-wrestle; **tomar el —** to take the pulse; **a —** with great effort
pulular VI to swarm, to teem with
pulverizar[47] VT to pulverize
puma F mountain lion, cougar, puma
puna F cold, arid tableland of the Andes
punitivo ADJ punitive
punk ADJ & M punk
punkero -ra MF punk
punta F (de cuchillo) point; (de la lengua, de un lápiz) tip; (de calcetín) toe; **— de lanza** spearhead; **una — de** a bunch of; **a — de cuchillo** at knifepoint; **— de flecha** arrowhead; **de —** on end; **iba caminando de —s** he was tiptoeing; **sacar — a un lápiz** to sharpen a pencil; **en la — de la lengua** on the tip of the tongue; **me pone los nervios de —** it makes me nervous; M **—pié** kick; ADJ **puntiagudo** sharp, pointed
puntada F stitch, prick
puntal M (de un edificio) prop; (de la economía) mainstay
puntear VT (una guitarra) to pluck; (un mapa) to make dots on; (una lista) to check off
puntería F aim; **tener buena —** to be a good shot
puntero M pointer
puntilla F point lace; **de —s** on tiptoe
punto M (puntuación) period; (de cinturón) notch; (marca, signo) point, dot; (anotación, tema, lugar) point; (puntada) stitch; **— álgido** fever pitch; **— culminante** (de una carrera) peak; (de una historia) climax; (de negociaciones) critical stage; **— de apoyo** foothold; **— de condensación** dewpoint; **— de congelación** freezing point; **— de ebullición** boiling point; **— de juego** game point; **— de manga** set point; **— de origen** point of origin; **— de partida** point of departure; **— de partido** match-point; **— de referencia** point of reference, benchmark; **— de vista** viewpoint, point of view; **— extra** (fútbol americano) point after touchdown; **— muerto** (en un negocio) stalemate, deadlock; (en un coche) neutral; **— y coma** semicolon; **al —** at once; **a —** ready; **a — de** on the point/verge of; **cogerle el —** to figure out; **dos —s** colon; **el — medio** the halfway mark; **en —** on the dot; **hacer —** to knit; **hasta cierto —** to a certain extent; **poner los —s sobre las íes** to dot one's i's and cross one's t's
puntuación F punctuation
puntual ADJ (en hora) punctual, prompt; (específico) specific
puntualidad F punctuality
puntualizar[47] VT to point out
puntuar[26] VT to punctuate
punzada F (de dolor) stab; (de remordimiento, hambre) pang, twinge
punzante ADJ sharp, piercing
punzar[47] VT to prick
punzón M (en papel) hole punch; (en cuero) awl
puñado M handful; **a —s** by the handful
puñal M dagger
puñalada F stab; **coser a —s** to stab to death
puñetazo M punch, slug; **dar un —** to punch; **dar un — en la mesa** to bang on the table
puño M (mano cerrada) fist; (en una manga) cuff; (de espada) handle; **arreglarlo con los —s** to duke it out; **de mi — y letra** by my own hand
pupa F *Esp* boo-boo

pupila F pupil
pupilo -la MF ward
pupitre M school desk
puré M purée; **— de patatas/papas** mashed potatoes; **hacer —** to smash
pureza F purity
purga F (política) purge; (medicinal) purgative
purgación F atonement
purgante ADJ & M purgative, laxative
purgar[40] VT (el vientre, a un rival) to purge; (frenos) to bleed; (pecados) to atone for
purgatorio M purgatory
purificar[30] VT to purify
purista ADJ & MF purist
puritano ADJ puritanical
puro ADJ pure; **lo hizo de — bueno** he did it out of sheer kindness; **a pura fuerza** by sheer force; **la pura verdad** the plain truth; **son puras mentiras** that's a lot of bull; **de purasangre** thoroughbred; M cigar
púrpura ADJ & M purple
pus M pus
puse, pusiera, pusiese *ver* poner
putrefacto ADJ putrid, decayed
putter M putter

Qq

Qatar M Qatar
quásar M quasar
que PRON REL that; (con antecedente no humano) which; (con antecedente humano) who, whom; **el/la —** the one that; **lo — tú dices** what you say; **vino la suegra, lo — complicó la visita** the mother-in-law came, which complicated the visit; CONJ that; **no creo — haya tiempo** I don't think [that] there's time; **estoy — me muero** I feel like I'm about to die; **Carlos es más alto — Luis** Carlos is taller than Luis; **más/menos —** more/less than; **déjalo aquí — lo voy a necesitar después** leave it here because I will need it later; **por mucho —** no matter how much; **a — gana** I bet he'll win; **— yo sepa** as far as I know
qué ADJ INTERR & PRON what, which; **¿— libro vas a usar?** what/which book are you going to use? **¿— dices?** what are you saying? **no sé — dijo** I don't know what he said; **¡— bonito!** how beautiful! **¡— de gente!** what a lot of people! **¿y eso —?** so what! **no hay de —** don't mention it; **¿— sé yo?** what do I know? **¿— tal?** how are you? **¡— más da!** what's the difference! **¡— va!** *fam* oh yeah? yeah right! **¡a mí —!** so what!
quebrada F (valle) ravine; (arroyo) creek
quebradizo ADJ breakable, brittle
quebrado ADJ (roto) broken; (rajado) cracked; (sin dinero) broke; M fraction
quebrantar VT (una casa, la salud) to weaken; (la ley) to violate
quebranto M weakening
quebrar[1] VT (romper) to break; (rajar) to crack; VI (irse a la bancarrota) to go bankrupt, to go under, to fail; **—se** to break [up]; **se quebró la muñeca** he broke his wrist; **—se uno la cabeza** to rack one's brain
queda F **toque de —** curfew
quedar VI (permanecer) to remain; (no haberse terminado) to be left; **queda leche en el vaso** there's milk in the glass; (estar ubicado) to be located; **la iglesia queda en la esquina** the church is located on the corner; (sentar bien la ropa) to suit; **— bien** to come out well; **— en** to agree to; **—se** to remain, to stay; **—se con una cosa** (comprar) to take/buy something; (llevarse) to take something
quehacer M chore, errand
queja F (protesta) complaint; (oficial) grievance
quejarse VI (protestar) to complain; (protestar ruidosamente) to gripe, to squawk; (protestar incesantemente) to whine
quejica ADJ whiny; MF nag, whiner
quejido M (de tono grave) moan, groan; (de tono agudo) squawk
quejoso ADJ whiny
quema F burning
quemado -da MF burn victim
quemador M burner
quemadura F (lugar quemado) burn; (sensación) burning; (enfermedad de plantas) blight
quemar VT to burn (también cedés); **—se** (un edificio) to burn up/down; (al sol) to sunburn
quemazón F burning sensation
quepa, quepamos *ver* caber
querella F lawsuit
querellante MF plaintiff
querellarse VI to file suit
querer[70] VI/VT (desear) to want; (amar) to love; **como quieras** as you please; **cuando quieras** whenever you want; **no quiso hacerlo** he refused to do it; **quiere llover** it is about to rain; **sin —** unwillingly; **— decir** to mean; **lo quiero mucho** I want it badly
querido -da ADJ beloved, dear; MF (enamorado) sweetheart; (como tratamiento) dear, darling
queroseno M kerosene
querrá, querría *ver* querer
quesería F dairy, cheese factory
queso M cheese; **— crema / de untar** cream cheese; **— suizo** swiss cheese
quiche M quiche
quicio M hinge; **sacar a uno de —** to drive someone up the wall

quiebra F bankruptcy (también moral); (de un mercado) crash; (de un comercio) failure; — **bancaria** bank failure
quiebra, quiebre *ver* quebrar
quiebre M break
quien PRON REL who, whom; **Juan, — recién cumplió cuarenta años** Juan, who just turned forty; — **hizo eso** whoever did that; **a — corresponda** to whom it may concern; —**quiera** whoever; **de —** whose; **con —** with whom
quién PRON INTERR & PRON who; **¿— es?** who is it? **no sé — entró** I don't know who came in; **¿a — se lo diste?** who did you give it to? to whom did you give it?
quiera, quiere *ver* querer
quieto ADJ still
quietud F stillness
quijada F jaw
quilate M carat
quilla F keel
química F chemistry
químico-ca ADJ chemical; MF chemist
quimioterapia F chemotherapy
quince NUM fifteen (también en tenis)
quincena F (de cosas) group of fifteen; (de días) two-week period
quincenal ADV biweekly
quincha F thatch
quinchar VT to thatch
quinesiología F kinesiology
quingombó M okra
quinientos NUM five hundred
quinina F quinine
quinqué M oil lamp
quinta F (casa) villa; (reclutamiento) draft
quinto ADJ, ADV, & M fifth
quiosco M kiosk, newsstand
quiquiriquí INTERJ cock-a-doodle-doo
quirófano M surgery, operating room
quiropráctico-ca ADJ chiropractic; MF chiropractor; F chiropractic
quirúrgico ADJ surgical
quise, quisiera, quisiese *ver* querer
quisquilloso ADJ particular, fussy
quiste M cyst
quitar VT (una mancha) to remove; (una prenda de vestir) to take off; (despojar de) to take away; M SG **quitaesmalte** nail polish remover; M SG **quitanieves** snowplow; M SG **quitamanchas** spot remover; VI —**se** to take off; —**se a alguien de encima** to get rid of someone; **quítate de ahí** move over
quite M **salir al — de** to go to the rescue of
quizá, quizás ADV perhaps, maybe

Rr

rabadilla F (coxis) tailbone; (de un ave) rump
rábano M radish; **me importa un —** I couldn't care less
rabia F (enfermedad) rabies; (enojo) rage; **me tiene —** he hates me; **dar —** to anger
rabiar VI to rage, to fume; **guapa a —** drop-dead beautiful
rabieta F tantrum
rabino-na MF rabbi
rabioso ADJ (hidrofóbico, apasionado) rabid, mad; (enojado) mad, furious
rabo M (cola) tail; (cabo) stem; **mirar con el — del ojo** to look out of the corner of one's eye; **con el — entre las piernas** with his tail between his legs
rabón ADJ bobtail
racha F (de suerte) streak; (de viento) gust
racial ADJ racial
racimo M (de plátanos, personas) bunch; (de uvas) cluster
raciocinio M reasoning
ración F (de guerra) ration, allowance; (de comida) portion
racional ADJ rational (también número)
racionalizado ADJ (justificado) rationalized; (reestructurado) streamlined
racionalizar[47] VT (una acción) to rationalize; (un negocio) to streamline
racionamiento M rationing
racionar VT to ration
racismo M racism
racista ADJ & MF racist
radar M radar
radiación F radiation
radiactivo ADJ radioactive
radiador M radiator
radial ADJ radial
radiante ADJ radiant
radiar VT (calor) to radiate; (por radio) to broadcast
radical ADJ (extremo) radical; (células) root; M (en química) radical; (en gramática) root
radicalismo M radicalism
radicar[30] VI to be located; — **en** to lie in; —**se** to take up residence
radio M (hueso, segmento de un círculo) radius; (elemento radiactivo) radium; F (aparato, difusión) radio; (emisora) radio station; — **de acción** sphere of influence
radiodifusión F broadcasting
radiodifusora F radio station
radioescucha MF radio listener
radiofónico ADJ radio

radiografía F x-ray
radiografiar[28] VT (hacer rayos x) to x-ray; (examinar con cuidado) to examine carefully
radiología F radiology
radiólogo -ga MF radiologist
radiotelescopio M radio telescope
radioterapia F radiation therapy
radiotransmisor M radio transmitter
radón M radon
raer[52] VI/VT to scrape [off]; (un artículo de ropa) to wear out
ráfaga F (de viento) gust, blast; (de luz) flash; (de ametralladora) burst
raído ADJ threadbare
raigón M stump
raíz F root; **— cuadrada** square root; **a — de** due to; **arrancar de —** to uproot; **cortar de —** to nip in the bud; **echar raíces** to take root
raja F (de melón) slice; (de falda) slit; (de leña) stick
rajadura F (en piedra, metal) crack; (en tela) rent, rip
rajar VT (una piedra) to crack; (un tronco) to split; **—se** (partir) to split open; (acobardarse) to chicken out, to blink; ADV **a rajatabla** strictly
ralea F ilk
ralear VI to thin out
ralentización F (de la economía) slump; (de un motor) idle
rallador M grater
rallar VT to grate, to shred
ralo ADJ sparse, thin
RAM M RAM
rama F branch, limb; (delgada) twig; **andarse por las —s** to beat around the bush; **algodón en —** raw cotton
ramaje M foliage
ramal M (de soga) strand; (de vía férrea) branch, spur
ramificarse[30] VI to divide into branches, to branch off
ramillete M bouquet, bunch, spray
ramo M (de flores) bouquet; (de una ciencia) branch; (de una actividad) line; **— de olivo** olive branch
rampa F ramp
ramplón ADJ vulgar
rana F frog
ranchero -ra MF rancher; **música ranchera** Mexican country music
rancho M (comida para soldados) mess; (comida mala) swill; (finca) ranch; (choza) hut; **hacer — aparte** to keep to oneself
rancio ADJ rancid; **de — abolengo** of ancient lineage
rango M (militar) rank; (categoría) standing
ranilla F frog [of a hoof]
ránking M (tenis) ranking
ranura F (corte) groove; (para insertar monedas, cartas) slot; **— para accesorios** accessory slot, expansion slot
rapar VT (pelo) to shave off; (cabeza) to shave
rapaz ADJ (animal) predatory; (destructivo) rapacious
rape M **cortar al —** to crop
rapé M snuff
rapear VI to rap
rápidamente ADV (con mucha velocidad) fast; (en poco tiempo) quickly
rapidez F (de un coche) speed; (de un movimiento) rapidity, quickness
rápido ADJ (con mucha velocidad) fast; (en poco tiempo) quick; M **—s** rapids; ADV (con mucha velocidad) fast; (en poco tiempo) quickly
rapiña F pillage
raptar VT to kidnap, to abduct
rapto M (secuestro) abduction, kidnapping; (arrebato) fit
raqueta F racket (también de tenis)
raquítico ADJ feeble, sickly
raramente ADV seldom, rarely
rareza F (escasez) rarity; (cosa rara) oddity; (cualidad de extraño) strangeness
raro ADJ (infrecuente) rare; (extraño) strange, funny; **rara vez** seldom, rarely; **sentirse —** to feel funny; **gas —** rare gas; **tierra rara** rare earth
ras LOC ADV **a — de la tierra** low to the ground
rascar[30] VT to scratch; M SG **rascacielos** skyscraper
rasgado ADJ **ojos —s** slit eyes
rasgadura F tear, rip
rasgar[40] VT to tear, to rip
rasgo M (propiedad) trait, feature; **a grandes —s** in broad strokes
rasgón M tear
rasguñar VT to scratch
rasguño M scratch
raso ADJ (superficie) smooth; (cucharada) level; **al —** in the open air; M satin
raspado M scrape
raspador M scraper
raspadura F scrape
raspar VT to scrape
raspón M scrape
rastra F harrow; **a —s** dragging, pulling
rastrear VT (a un animal) to trail, to track, to trace; (un terreno) to search
rastreo M sweep, search
rastrero ADJ (planta) creeping; (persona) contemptible
rastrillar VT to rake
rastrillo M rake
rastro M (huella) track, trail; (olor) scent; (mercado) flea market; **ni —s** no trace
rastrojo M stubble

rasurado M shave
rasurador -ora MF razor
rasurar VT to shave
rata F rat
ratear VT to pilfer
ratería F petty larceny, pilferage
ratero -ra MF pickpocket
ratificación F ratification
ratificar[30] VT to ratify
rato M while; **—s perdidos** leisure hours; **a cada —** frequently; **a —s** from time to time; **pasar el —** to kill time; **pasar un buen —** (divertirse) to have a pleasant time; (permanecer) to spend a long time; **un largo —** a great while
ratón M mouse (también de computadora); **— almizclero** muskrat; **— en serie** serial mouse
ratonera F mousetrap
raudal LOC ADV **a —es** in great quantities
raudo ADJ swift
raya F (línea) line; (linde) boundary; (lista) stripe; (en el pelo) part; (en un pantalón) crease; (de ortografía) dash; (en un zapato) scuff; (pez marino) stingray; **tener a —** to hold in check; **pasarse de la —** to be out of line, to cross the line
rayado ADJ (papel) lined; (vestido) striped; **hablaba como disco —** he talked like a broken record
rayar VT (papel) to rule, to make lines on; (disco, espejo) to scratch; (zapatos) to scuff; **— el alba** to dawn; **— en** to border on
rayo M (de luz) ray, beam, streak; (de relámpago) flash of lightning; (de rueda) spoke; (de esperanza) ray, flicker; **— láser** laser beam; **—s infrarrojos** infrared rays; **—s X** x-rays
rayón M rayon
raza F (de personas) race; (de animal) breed
razón F (facultad) reason; (proporción) ratio; **— social** company name; **a — de** at the rate of; **¡con —!** no wonder! **entrar en —** to listen to reason; **te doy la —** I admit you're right; **perder la —** to lose one's mind; **tener —** to be right
razonable ADJ reasonable
razonamiento M reasoning
razonar VI (pensar) to reason; (arguir) to argue
reabastecer[35] VT to replenish
reabrir[74] VT to reopen
reacción F reaction; **— en cadena** chain reaction; **— nuclear** nuclear reaction
reaccionar VI to react
reaccionario ADJ & MF reactionary
reacio ADJ averse, reluctant
reacondicionar VT to rebuild
reactivo M reagent
reactor M reactor; **— nuclear** nuclear reactor
readaptación F readjustment
readaptar VT to readjust
reafirmar VT to reaffirm; **—se** to reassert
reagrupar VT to regroup
reajustar VT to readjust
reajuste M readjustment
real ADJ (verdadero) real, actual; (del rey) royal; M fairground
realce M **dar —** to enhance
realeza F royalty
realidad F reality, actuality; **en —** really, actually; **en — no es abogado** he's not really a lawyer; **— virtual** virtual reality
realismo M realism
realista ADJ (auténtico) realistic; (partidario del rey) royalist; MF (no idealista) realist; (partidario del rey) royalist
realización F (de un sueño) realization, fulfillment; (de una tarea) completion; (de una película) production
realizador -ora MF (director) director; (productor) producer
realizar[47] VT (un sueño) to realize, to fulfill; (película) to produce
realmente ADV really
realzar[47] VT (mejorar) to enhance; (destacar) to accentuate; (intensificar) to heighten
reanimación F resuscitation; **— cardiopulmonar** cardiopulmonary resuscitation
reanimar VT (devolver fuerzas) to revive; (dar ánimos) to rally
reanudación F renewal; **— del juego** (fútbol) restart of play
reanudar VT (una amistad) to renew; (una reunión) to resume; (un partido del fútbol) to restart
reaparecer[35] VI to reappear
reasumir VT to resume
reata F lariat, lasso
reavivar VT to revive
rebaja F markdown, price cut; **con —** at a discount, on sale; **de —s** cut-rate
rebajado N on sale, reduced
rebajar VT (precios) to cut, to lower, to slash; (una bebida) to water down; (una crítica) to tone down; VI/VT (los cambios) to downshift; **—se** to lower oneself; **—se a** to stoop to
rebanada F slice
rebanar VT to slice
rebaño M flock, fold
rebasar VT (un coche) to overtake; (un límite) to exceed
rebatir VT to refute
rebato M alarm
rebelarse VI to rebel, to revolt
rebelde ADJ (niño) rebellious; (pelo) unruly; MF rebel
rebeldía F rebelliousness, defiance; (no comparecencia) default

rebelión F rebellion
rebenque M whip
rebobinar VT to rewind
reborde M edge
rebosante ADJ (de líquido) brimming, overflowing; (de salud) flush, glowing; **— de alegría** overjoyed
rebosar VI (líquido) to overflow, to brim over; (de alegría) to bubble over; (de salud) to glow
rebotar VI/VT (en baloncesto) to rebound, to bounce; (chocar) to bounce; (cambiar de dirección una bala) to ricochet; (cambiar de dirección una pelota) to carom
rebote M (en baloncesto) rebound, bounce; (de bala) ricochet
rebotear VI (en baloncesto) to rebound
rebozar[47] VT to cover with batter; **—se** to muffle up
rebozo M shawl; **sin —** frankly
rebullir[16] VI to stir
rebuscado ADJ (estilo) overly elaborate; (persona) affected
rebuscar[30] VT (espigar) to glean; VI **— en** (la memoria) to search through; (un cajón) to rummage in
rebuznar VI to bray
rebuzno M bray, braying
recabar VT to raise
recado M (mensaje) message; (quehacer) errand; **— de escribir** writing materials
recaer[52] VI to relapse; **— sobre** to fall to
recaída F relapse
recalar VI to make a stop at
recalcar[30] VT to accentuate
recalcitrante ADJ obstinate
recalentar[1] VT (volver a calentar) to warm over; (calentar en exceso) to overheat
recamar VT to embroider
recámara F (de un arma de fuego) chamber; *Méx* (dormitorio) bedroom
recapitular VI/VT to recapitulate, to sum up
recargado ADJ busy
recargar[40] VT to overload, to burden
recargo M (emocional) burden; (de precio) surcharge, premium; **— por mora** late fee
recatado ADJ (cauteloso) cautious; (modesto) modest
recato M (cautela) caution; (modestia) modesty
recaudación F collection, levy; **— de fondos** fundraising
recaudador -ora MF tax collector
recaudar VT (impuestos) to collect, to levy; (fondos) to raise; **— en bruto** to gross; **— fondos** to raise funds; **lo recaudado** proceeds
recaudo M **estar a buen —** to be in a safe place
rección F government
recelar VT to suspect; **— de** to be suspicious of
recelo M misgivings
receloso ADJ mistrustful
recepción F reception
receptáculo M receptacle, holder
receptor M receiver (también en fútbol americano); (en béisbol) catcher; **— abierto** wide receiver; **— cerrado** tight end
recesión F recession
receta F (de cocina) recipe; (de médico) prescription
recetar VT to prescribe
rechazar[47] VT (una propuesta, un plan) to reject; (un ataque) to repel, to repulse; (una invitación) to decline, to turn down, to refuse; (una acusación) to deny; (a un amante) to spurn, to reject
rechazo M (de un amante) rejection; (de un ataque) repulse; (de una oferta) refusal; (de una acusación) denial
rechifla F whistling, booing
rechiflar VT to whistle, to boo
rechinamiento M (de una puerta) creaking, squeaking; (de los dientes) grinding
rechinante ADJ squeaky
rechinar VI (una puerta) to squeak, to creak; VI/VT (los dientes) to grind; **eso me rechina** that grates on my nerves
rechoncho ADJ plump, chubby, roly-poly
recibidor -ora MF receiver; M reception room
recibimiento M reception
recibir VT (premio) to receive, to get; (visitas) to receive, to welcome; (una noticia trágica) to take; **— noticias de** to hear from; **—se** to graduate; **—se de médico** to graduate from medical school
recibo M receipt; **de —** acceptable; **al — de** upon receipt of; **acusar —** to acknowledge receipt; **acuse de —** acknowledgment of receipt
reciclaje M recycling
reciclar VI/VT to recycle
recidiva F relapse
recién ADV recently; **— casado** newlywed; **— comprado** brand-new; **— llegado** newly arrived; **— nacido** newborn; **— me entero** it's news to me
reciente ADJ recent
recinto M enclosure
recio ADJ strong, rugged
recipiente M container
recíproco ADJ reciprocal
recitación F recitation
recital M recital
recitar VT to recite, to speak
reclamación F (protesta) protest; (demanda) claim
reclamante MF claimant
reclamar VT (protestar) to protest; (demandar) to claim; VI (aves) to call
reclamo M (reclamación) claim; (queja) complaint; (voz de animal) call, cry;

(dispositivo) bird call; (señuelo) decoy
reclinar VT to lean; **—se** to recline
recluir[19] VT to confine; **—se** to be a recluse
recluso -sa MF (preso) inmate; (ermitaño) recluse
recluta F recruitment; MF (voluntario) recruit; (forzoso) conscript
reclutamiento M (voluntario) recruitment; (forzoso) conscription
reclutar VT (voluntariamente) to recruit; (por la fuerza) to draft, to conscript
recobrar VI to recover, to recuperate; VT to recover, to regain
recodo M bend, turn
recoger[45] VT (el cabello) to gather; (un cuarto) to tidy up; (citas en un texto) to collect; (la mesa) to clear; (polvo) to sweep up; (a un desamparado) to shelter; (los frutos del campo) to glean; **—se** (retirarse) to retire, to withdraw; (acumularse) to gather
recogida F (del cabello) gathering; (de un cuarto) tidying up; (de la mesa) clearing; (de un desamparado) sheltering
recogido ADJ (apartado) secluded; (tranquilo) peaceful, quiet
recogimiento M (aislamiento) seclusion; (meditación) meditation
recolección F (de frutos, datos) collecting, gathering; (de carga) pickup; (cosecha) harvest
recolectar VT to gather, to forage
recomendable ADJ advisable
recomendación F recommendation
recomendar[1] VT to recommend
recomienda, recomiende *ver* recomendar
recompensa F recompense, reward
recompensar VT to recompense, to reward
reconcentrar VI to concentrate intensely; **—se** to concentrate, to become absorbed in thought
reconciliación F reconciliation
reconciliar VT to reconcile
recóndito ADJ remote
reconfortante ADJ heartwarming, comforting
reconfortar VT to comfort
reconocer[35] VT (identificar) to recognize; (admitir) to admit, to acknowledge; (explorar) to reconnoiter
reconocible ADJ recognizable
reconocimiento M (identificación) recognition; (admisión, agradecimiento) acknowledgment; (exploración) scouting; **— de habla** speech recognition; **— de voz** voice recognition; **— visual** visual recognition; **hacer un —** to reconnoiter
reconozca, reconozco *ver* reconocer
reconsiderar VT to reconsider
reconstrucción F reconstruction
reconstruir[19] VT to reconstruct, to rebuild
reconstruya, reconstruye, reconstruyendo, reconstruyera, reconstruyese *ver* reconstruir
recopilación F collection, compilation
recopilar VT to compile
récord M record
recordar[5] VT (acordarse) to remember, to recollect, to recall; (hacer acordar) to remind
recordatorio M reminder
recorrer VT (andar una distancia) to cover; (examinar) to go over, to look over
recorrido M (ruta) run, route; (distancia) distance
recortado ADJ jagged
recortar VT (pelo, hilos, presupuesto) to trim; (uñas, periódicos) to clip; (una película) to shorten; **—se** to be outlined
recorte M (de pelos, hilos) trimming; (de uñas, periódicos) clipping; (de sueldo, de gastos) cut; (de recursos) cutback; (sobrante) trimming; **— salarial** pay cut
recostar[5] VT (sobre) to lay; (contra) to lean; **—se** to recline
recoveco M (en un camino) turn; (rincón) cranny
recreación F recreation
recrear VT to entertain; **—se** to amuse oneself
recreativo ADJ recreational; **actividades recreativas** leisure activities; **sala recreativa** game room
recreo M (recreación) recreation, relaxation; (tiempo de descanso) recess; (lugar de juego) playground
recriminar VT to recriminate
recrudecer[35] VI to flare up
recrudecimiento M flareup
recta F (de una pista) straight; (en béisbol) fastball; **— final** final stretch
rectangular ADJ rectangular
rectángulo M rectangle
rectificar[30] VT to rectify
rectitud F uprightness, righteousness
recto ADJ (no curvo) straight; (honrado) upright, righteous; (estricto) strict; **todo —** straight ahead; M rectum
rector -ora MF university president, chancellor
recua F herd
recubrir[74] VT to cover; **— con pintura** to coat with paint
recuento M account; **— sanguíneo** blood count
recuerda, recuerde *ver* recordar
recuerdo M (acción de recordar, cosa recordada) memory, recollection; (objeto que hace recordar) souvenir, token; **—s** regards; **dale —s a tu hermana** say hi to your sister
recular VI (retroceder) to move backward; (retroceder en un coche) to back up; (retroceder ante un desafío) to back down

recuperación F (salarial, de salud) recovery; (de datos, documentos guardados) retrieval; (de objetos, datos, documentos perdidos) recovery
recuperar VT (una cosa perdida) to recover; (datos, documentos guardados) to retrieve; (tiempo perdido) to make up for; (dinero perdido) to recoup; **—se** to recuperate
recurrente ADJ MF (que reclama) complainant; ADJ (repetitivo) recurring, recurrent
recurrir VT to appeal; **— a** to resort to, to have recourse to
recurso M (acción de recurrir) recourse; (reclamación) appeal; **—s** resources; **—s humanos** HR [human resources]; **—s naturales** natural resources
recusar VT (a una persona) to reject; (a un juez) to challenge
red F (para pescar, de tenis) net; (malla tejida) mesh; (de conexiones, para computadora) network; (para engañar) snare; (internet) World Wide Web, Internet; **— [de área] local** local area network
redacción F (ensayo) composition; (acción de redactar) drafting; (en un periódico) editorial department
redactar VT (un ensayo) to draft; (trabajo escolar) to compose
redactor-ora MF editor
redada F (de peces) catch, haul; (policial) raid
redar VT to throw a net
redecilla F hairnet
redención F redemption
redil M sheepfold, sheep pen; **volver al —** to come back into the fold
redimir VT (a un pecador) to redeem; (a un esclavo) to set free
rédito M (de ahorros) interest; (de acciones) yield
redituar[26] VT to yield
redoblar VT (esfuerzos) to double; VI/VT (un tambor) to roll
redoble M drumroll
redoma F flask
redonda F whole note; **a la —** all around
redondear VT (una figura) to make round; (una cifra) to round up
redondel M ring
redondez F roundness
redondo ADJ round; **en —** all around; **caer —** to collapse; **salir —** to turn out perfect
reducción F reduction, cutback; **— de sueldo** cut in salary; **hacer — de personal** to cut back on personnel
reducidor-ora MF *Am* fence
reducir[38] VT (una cantidad) to reduce; (un hueso) to set; (actividades) to curtail, to cut down on; (costos) to cut; (personal) to downsize, to cut back on; **—se a** to boil down to
reduje, redujera, redujese *ver* reducir
redundante ADJ redundant
reduzca, reduzco *ver* reducir
reedificar[30] VT to rebuild
reelección F reelection
reelegir[14] VT reelect
reembolsar VT to reimburse, to refund
reembolso M reimbursement, refund
reemplazable ADJ replaceable
reemplazar[47] VT to replace
reemplazo M replacement, substitute
reencarnación F reincarnation
reescribir[74] VT to rewrite
reestructuración F restructuring
reexpedir[9] VT to forward
referencia F reference
referéndum M referendum
referente LOC ADV **— a** relative to
referir[8] VT (narrar) to narrate; **—se a** to refer to
refiera, refiere *ver* referir
refinación F refinement
refinado ADJ refined, genteel
refinamiento M refinement
refinanciar VI/VT to refinance
refinar VT to refine
refinería F refinery
refiriendo, refiriera, refiriese *ver* referir
reflector M (en una bicicleta) reflector; (en deportes) floodlight; (militar, policial) searchlight
reflejar VT (luz) to reflect; (imagen) to mirror; **—se** to be reflected
reflejo M (luz) reflection; (movimiento) reflex; **—s** frosting; ADJ reflex
reflexión F reflection
reflexionar VI to reflect; **— sobre** to think over
reflexivo ADJ (gramatical) reflexive; (pensativo) thoughtful
reflujo M (de agua) ebb; (gástrico) reflux
reforma F (política) reform; (religiosa) reformation
reformador-ora MF reformer
reformar VT (un gobierno, a un delincuente) to reform; (ropa) to make alterations in; **—se** to mend one's ways
reformatorio M reformatory
reformista MF reformer
reforzado ADJ reinforced; M reinforcement
reforzar[49] VT (una construcción) to reinforce; (las defensas) to beef up; (un argumento) to bolster, to buttress
refracción F refraction
refractario ADJ refractory
refrán M proverb, saying
refrenar VT (un caballo) to rein in; (emociones) to restrain, to check
refrendar VT (una sentencia) to uphold; (un documento) to countersign, to endorse
refrendario-ria MF endorser

refrendo M endorsement
refrescante ADJ refreshing
refrescar[30] VT to refresh (también pantalla de computadora); (el tiempo) to get cool; **—se** to cool off
refresco M (bebida) soft drink; (comida ligera) refreshment
refriega F fray, scuffle
refrigeración F refrigeration
refrigerador ADJ refrigerating; M refrigerator
refrigerante ADJ cooling; M coolant
refrigerar VT to cool, to refrigerate
refrigerio M refreshment
refrito ADJ (comida) refried; M (obra) rerun
refuerzo M (acción de reforzar) reinforcement; (de tela) backing; (de una vacuna) booster
refugiado -da MF refugee
refugiar VT to shelter; **—se** to take shelter
refugio M refuge, shelter; **— antiaéreo** bomb shelter; **— fiscal** tax shelter
refulgente ADJ resplendent
refundir VT to recast
refunfuñar VI to grumble, to mutter
refunfuño M grumbling, muttering
refunfuñón -ona ADJ grouchy, grumpy; MF grouch
refutar VT to refute
regadera F watering can
regadío M (tierra irrigada) irrigated land; (riego) irrigation
regalar VT (dar como presente) to give as a gift; (vender barato, donar) to give away; (agasajar) to regale
regaliz M licorice
regalo M (presente) present, gift; (para los sentidos) treat, delight
regañar VI (un perro) to snarl; VT (a un niño) to scold, to go off on; (constantemente) to nag; LOC ADV **a regañadientes** reluctantly
regaño M scolding, reprimand
regañón -ona ADJ nagging, scolding; MF scold
regar[41] VT (campos) to irrigate; (flores) to water
regate M dribble
regatear VI (precios) to haggle, to bargain; (fútbol) to dribble
regateo M bargaining
regazo M lap
regeneración F regeneration; **— audible** audible feedback
regente MF, **regenta** F regent; F regent's wife; ADJ ruling
reggae M reggae
régimen M (gobierno) regime; (dieta) diet; **— de vida** lifestyle
regimiento M regiment
regio ADJ (propio del rey) regal; (excelente) swell
región F region
regional ADJ regional
regir[14] VT to govern (también en sintaxis); VI to be in force; **—se por** to be guided by
registrador -ora MF (empleado) recorder, registrar; M **— de vuelo** flight recorder
registrar VT (examinar) to search; (dejar constancia) to record, to register; (inscribir) to log; **— al desnudo** to strip-search
registro M (de la voz, lingüístico) register; (de nacimientos) record, register; (del equipaje) search; (de un órgano) stop; (en la computadora) log; **— al desnudo** strip search
regla F (norma) rule; (utensilio para medir) ruler; (menstruación) period; **en —** in order; **por — general** as a general rule
reglamentación F (acción de reglamentar) regulation; (conjunto de reglas) regulations
reglamento M regulations; **—s y disposiciones administrativas** rules and regulations
regocijar VT to gladden; **—se** to rejoice
regocijo M joy, rejoicing
regodearse VI (en la desgracia propia) to wallow; (en la desgracia ajena) to gloat
regodeo M (en la desgracia propia) wallowing; (en la desgracia ajena) gloating
regordete ADJ plump
regresar VI to return
regreso M return; **estar de —** to be back
reguero M trail; **correr como un — de pólvora** to spread like wildfire
regulación F (acción de regular) regulation; (de una máquina) adjustment
regulador M regulator, governor, throttle; **— de voltaje** dimmer
regular VT (reglamentar) to regulate; (ajustar una máquina) to adjust; ADJ regular; **una paliza —** quite a beating; ADV so-so
regularidad F regularity
regularizar[47] VT (reglamentar) to regulate; (formalizar) to formalize; **—se** to become regular
regurgitar VI/VT to regurgitate
rehabilitación F rehabilitation
rehabilitador ADJ remedial
rehabilitar VT to rehabilitate
rehacer[54, 74] VT to remake; **—se** to recover
rehén MF hostage
rehuir[19] VT (a una persona) to shun; (responsabilidades) to shirk
rehusar[26] VT to refuse; **—se a** to refuse to
reimpresión F reprint
reina F queen
reinado M reign
reinante ADJ (política, opinión) prevailing; (monarca) ruling
reinar VI to reign
reincidencia F (episodio) relapse; (cualidad) recidivism
reincidir VI to relapse

reiniciar VT to reboot, to reset
reino M (territorio de un rey) kingdom, realm; (período de reinado) reign; (división biológica) kingdom; (ámbito) realm
reinserción F reinsertion; **— laboral** reemployment
reinstaurar VT to reinstate
reintegrar VT to rebate; **—se a** to return to
reintegro M rebate
reinvertir VI/VT to reinvest, to roll over
reír[10] VI to laugh; **—se de** to laugh at
reiterar VT to reiterate
reivindicación F (demanda) demand; (rehabilitación) vindication; (responsabilidad) responsibility; **la — del atentado** the responsibility for the act
reivindicar[30] VT (vengar) to vindicate; (responsabilizarse) to take responsibility, to claim
reja F (enrejado) grate, grating; (pieza de arado) plowshare; **entre —s** behind bars
rejilla F (para equipaje) luggage rack; (de coche) grille
rejuvenecer[35] VT to rejuvenate; VI to become rejuvenated
relación F (conocido) relation, connection; (trato) relationship, involvement; (relato) account, report; (lista) list; **relaciones** (conocidos) connections; (trato) dealings; **relaciones públicas** public relations; **con — a** in relation to
relacionado ADJ related, germane
relacionar VT to relate, to connect; **—se con** to relate to
relajación F relaxation
relajamiento M relaxation
relajante ADJ (actividad) relaxing; (droga) sedative; M **— muscular** muscle relaxant
relajar VT to relax; **—se** (abandonarse moralmente) to become lax; (tranquilizarse) to chill [out], to relax
relajo M (aflojamiento) relaxation; (desorden) mess
relamerse VI to lick one's lips
relámpago M lightning
relampaguear VI (el cielo) to lightning; (los ojos, cosa reluciente) to flash
relampagueo M flash of lightning
relatar VT to relate, to recount
relatividad F relativity
relativo ADJ relative; **— a** relative to
relato M (informe) account; (cuento) story, tale
relé M relay
relegar[40] VT to relegate
relevancia F importance
relevante ADJ important
relevar VT (a un trabajador, guardia) to relieve
relevista MF (atletismo) relay runner; (béisbol) reliever; **— de cierre** (béisbol) closer
relevo M (soldado) relief; **carrera de —s** relay race
relicario M reliquary, locket
relieve M relief; **de —** (mapa) relief; (persona) prominent; **poner de —** to emphasize; **letras en —** raised letters
religión F religion
religioso -sa ADJ religious; M monk; F nun
relinchar VI to neigh
relincho M neigh
reliquia F relic
rellenado M filling
rellenar VT (un vaso) to refill, to replenish; (un tanque de gasolina) to fill, to fill up; (un formulario) to fill out; (un hueco) to fill in; (una almohada) to stuff
relleno ADJ (un pimiento) stuffed; (la cara) full, round; (la figura, el cuerpo) plump; M (de comida) stuffing, dressing; (de un colchón) padding
reloj M (de pared) clock; (de muñeca, bolsillo) watch; (de horno) timer; **— de pulsera** wristwatch; **— de sol** sundial; **— despertador** alarm clock; **contra —** against the clock; **como un —** regularly, like clockwork
relojería F (tienda) watch shop; (actividad) clock-making
relojero -ra MF watchmaker
reluciente ADJ shining
relucir[39] VI to shine; **sacar a —** to bring up
relumbrar VI to glare
relumbre M glare
REM M REM
remachar VT (una victoria, un clavo) to clinch; (un remache) to rivet
remache M (acción de remachar) riveting; (clavo) clinching; (tachuela, clavija) rivet
remanente M remainder
remar VI/VT to row, to paddle
remarcado VT mark-up
rematador -ora MF auctioneer
rematar VT (acabar) to finish; (matar) to finish off; (perfeccionar) to give the finishing touches to; (subastar) to auction; VI (patear un balón) to take a shot
remate M (de una obra) finishing touch; (tiro) shot; (subasta) auction; (tenis) smash; **— de un chiste** punch line; **loco de —** stark raving mad
remedador -ora MF mimic
remedar VT to mimic, to ape, to mock
remediar VT to remedy
remedio M remedy, cure; **sin —** unavoidable; **no tiene —** it can't be helped; **no tengo más —** I can't help it; **el — es peor que la enfermedad** the remedy is worse than the disease
remedo M mockery

remendar[1] VT (ropa) to mend, to patch; (calcetines) to darn; (zapatos) to repair
remendón -ona MF cobbler
remero -ra MF rower
remesa F (de mercancías) shipment; (de dinero) remittance
remiendo M (de ropa) patch; (de zapatos) repair
remilgado ADJ fussy, prim
remilgo M fussiness, primness
reminiscencia F reminiscence
remisión F remission
remitente MF sender
remitir VT (enviar) to remit; (dirigir a otra parte de un texto) to refer; **—se** (ceder) to yield; **a las pruebas me remito** the evidence speaks for itself
remo M (pala) oar, paddle; (deporte) rowing
remodelación F (de una casa) remodeling; (de una ciudad) redevelopment, renewal; (de una organización) reorganization
remodelar VI/VT to remodel
remojar VT to soak
remojo M soaking; **poner en —** to soak
remojón M soaking
remolacha F beet
remolcador M tugboat
remolcar[30] VT to tow
remolino M (de viento) whirlwind; (de agua) whirlpool, eddy; (de pelo) cowlick; (juguete) pinwheel; **— de gente** throng, crowd
remolón -ona ADJ dallying; MF dallier
remolonear VI to dally
remolque M (acción de remolcar) tow; (vehículo remolcado) towed vehicle; (vehículo que remolca) tow truck; (caravana de camión) trailer; **llevar a —** to tow
remontada F (deporte) comeback
remontar VT (una cometa) to fly; (una pendiente, un río) to go up; **—se** to rise; **el globo se remonta** the balloon goes up; **el coche se remonta a los años 20** the car dates from the '20s; **para comprenderlo, debemos remontarnos a su juventud** in order to understand him, we must go back to his youth
remorder[6] VT to gnaw at
remordimiento M remorse
remoto ADJ remote, distant; **no tiene la más remota idea** he doesn't have the slightest idea
remover[6] VT (un cargo, un obstáculo) to remove; (un asunto problemático) to stir up
remuneración F remuneration, compensation
remunerar VT remunerate, compensate
remunerado ADJ gainful
renacentista ADJ Renaissance
renacer[35] VI to be reborn
renacimiento M (resurgimiento) revival; (período histórico) Renaissance
renacuajo M (cría de rana) tadpole; (hombre esmirriado) shrimp
renal ADJ renal
rencilla F quarrel
rencor M rancor; **guardar —** to bear a grudge
rencoroso ADJ resentful
rendición F surrender
rendido ADJ exhausted
rendija F crack
rendimiento M (lo rendido) yield, output; (productividad) performance; **— previo** past performance
rendir[9] VT (someter) to subdue; (producir) to yield; (fatigar) to fatigue; **— homenaje** to pay homage; **— cuentas a** to answer to; VI (obtener buenos resultados) to perform well; **—se** (darse por vencido) to surrender, to give in; (fatigarse) to become fatigued
renegado -da MF renegade
renegar[41] VT (negar) to deny insistently; (repudiar) to renounce; **— de** to gripe about
renegociar VI/VT to renegotiate
renglón M line; **a — seguido** immediately following
rengo ADJ lame
renguear VI to limp
renguera F limp
reno M reindeer
renombrado ADJ renowned
renombre M renown; **de —** of note
renovable ADJ renewable
renovación F renewal; **— urbana** urban renewal
renovador -ora ADJ (artista) innovating; (baño) refreshing; MF innovator
renovar[5] VT (un edificio) to renovate; (ataques, temores) to renew
renquear VT to limp
renta F (de una persona) income; (de un gobierno) revenue; (alquiler) rent; **— anual** annuity; **—s internas** internal revenue; **vivir de la —** to live on the interest
rentabilidad F profitability; **cuentas y depósitos de alta —** high-return accounts and deposits
rentable ADJ (negocio, inversión) profitable; (idea) viable
renuencia F reluctance
renuente ADJ reluctant, loath; **ser — a** to be loath to
renueva, renueve *ver* renovar
renuevo M sprout
renuncia F (dimisión) resignation; (a un derecho) waiver; (a una herencia) renunciation
renunciar VI **— a** (un cargo) to resign; (la ciudadanía) to renounce; (un derecho) to relinquish, to waive
reñido ADJ contested

reñir[11] VI (discutir) to quarrel, to bicker, to argue; (pelear) to fight, to scuffle; (rezongar) to scold
reo -a MF defendant, accused
reojo M **mirar de —** to look out of the corner of one's eye
reorganización F reorganization
reorganizar[47] VT to reorganize, to regroup
repaginar VT to repaginate
repantigarse[40] VI to lounge
reparación F (compensación) reparation, redress; (arreglo) repair
reparador -ra ADJ refreshing; M serviceman; F service woman
reparar VT (arreglar) to repair; (compensar) to redress; **— en** to notice
reparo M **no tener —s en** to have no qualms about; **sin —s** freely; **hacer —s** to object
repartición F distribution
repartir VT (tierras, un botín) to distribute; (volantes) to hand out; (periódicos) to deliver; (naipes) to deal; (días libres) to space out
reparto M (de tierras) distribution; (de periódicos) delivery; (de naipes) dealing; (ruta de entrega) route; (lista de actores) cast; **— proporcional** apportionment
repasar VT (una lección) to review, to go over again; (en la memoria) to retrace; (leer por encima) to skim
repaso M review
repelente ADJ repellent
repeler VT to repel, to repulse
repente M **de —** suddenly
repentinamente ADV suddenly
repentino ADJ sudden
repercusión F repercussion
repercutir VI to have repercussions
repertorio M repertoire
repetición F (reiteración) repetition; (en tenis) let
repetido ADJ repeated; **repetidas veces** repeatedly
repetir[9] VI/VT (reiterar) to repeat; VI (eructar) to belch; (tomar una segunda ración) to have seconds; **— como loro** to parrot; **—se** to recur
repicar[30] VI/VT to ring
repique M ringing, ring
repiquetear VI/VT to ring
repiqueteo M ringing
repisa F shelf
repita, repitiendo, repitiera, repitiese, repito *ver* repetir
replegar[41] VT to fold; **—se** to retreat
repleto ADJ replete
réplica F (contestación) reply, comeback; (copia) replica; (temblor secundario) aftershock
replicación F replication
replicar[30] VI/VT (responder) to reply, to rejoin; (reproducirse) to replicate
repliegue M (pliegue marcado) crease; (retirada) retreat
repollo M cabbage
reponer[56, 74] VT (reemplazar) to replace; (restituir) to restore; (replicar) to reply; (una obra de teatro) to revive; (una película) to show again; **—se** to recover one's health
reportaje M feature story
reportar VT (beneficios) to yield; VI (en una organización) to answer to; **—se enfermo** to call in sick
reportero -ra MF reporter
reposado ADJ quiet, calm
reposar VI to repose, to rest; **dejar —** to let steep; M SG **reposacabezas** headrest; M SG **reposapiés** footrest
reposición F (reemplazo) replacement; (de una obra de teatro) revival
reposo M (descanso) repose, rest; (sosiego) calm
repostería F (establecimiento) pastry shop; (actividad) baking
repostero -ra MF pastry cook
reprender VT to reprimand, to scold, to rebuke
reprensión F rebuke
represa F (dique) dam; (reservorio de agua) reservoir
represalia F reprisal
represar VT to dam
representación F (interpretación) representation; (delegación) delegation; (de un papel) portrayal; (de una obra de teatro) performance
representante MF (legislativo) representative; (comercial) agent
representar VT (una imagen) to represent, to depict; (una obra de teatro) to perform; (un personaje) to portray; **tiene treinta años, pero no los representa** he's thirty years old, but he doesn't look it; **tu presencia representa mucho para mí** your presence means a lot to me
representativo ADJ representative
represión F (psicológica) repression; (política) repression, suppression, crackdown
represivo ADJ repressive
reprimenda F reprimand, rebuke
reprimido ADJ repressed, pent-up
reprimir VT (impulsos) to repress; (una tendencia) to check; (enemigos políticos) to suppress, to crack down on; (una rebelión) to quell
reprobación F reproof
reprobar[5] VT to reprove; VI/VT (no aprobar un examen) to flunk, to fail
reprochar VT to reproach, to rebuke
reproche M reproach, rebuke
reproducción F reproduction
reproducir[38] VI/VT to reproduce; **—se** to

reproduce, to breed
reproductor -ora ADJ breeding; **aparato —** VCR; MF breeding animal
reproduje, reprodujera, reprodujese, reproduzca, reproduzco *ver* reproducir
reptar VI to crawl
reptil M reptile
república F republic
republicano -na ADJ & MF republican; (del Partido Republicano) Republican
repudiar VT (a la sociedad) to repudiate; (a un hijo) to disown; (una herencia) to renounce
repuesto M spare part; **de —** spare
repugnancia F repugnance, disgust, revulsion
repugnante ADJ repugnant, disgusting, loathsome
repugnar VI to be repugnant; VT to disgust, to cloy
repulir VT to polish up
repulsa F rebuff, repulse
repulsar VT to repulse
repulsivo ADJ repulsive, creepy
repuntar VI to rally
reputación F reputation
reputado ADJ reputable
requemar VT to burn
requerimiento M request
requerir[8] VT to require
requesón M cottage cheese
requiebros M PL advances
requisa F requisition
requisar VT (interceptar, incautar) to commandeer, to requisition; (registrar) to search
requisito M requirement, requisite
res F animal; **— lanar** sheep; **— vacuna** cow
resabio M (dejillo) aftertaste; (vicio) bad habit
resaca F (de mar) undertow; (malestar físico) hangover
resaltar VI (sobresalir) to stand out; (poner de relieve) to highlight
resarcir[33] VT to compensate for
resbaladizo ADJ slippery, slick
resbalar VI (deslizar) to slip; (ser/estar resbaladizo) to be slippery; **—se** to slip
resbalón M slip; **darse un —** to slip
resbaloso ADJ (que resbala) slippery; *Méx fam* (inmoral) sleazy
rescatar VT (a un secuestrado) to ransom; (a una persona en peligro) to rescue
rescate M (para un secuestrado) ransom; (de una persona en peligro) rescue
rescindir VT to rescind
rescoldo M embers
resecar[30] VT to dry; **—se** to dry out
reseco ADJ dried-up, parched
resentido ADJ resentful
resentimiento M resentment, grudge; **guardar —** to hold a grudge, to have hard feelings
resentirse[8] VI to hurt, to suffer; **— de** to resent
reseña F book review
reseñar VT to review
reserva F (de provisiones, de oro, de jugadores, del ejército) reserve; (de localidades, de hotel, de indios) reservation; (de animales) preserve; **sin —s** without reservations; **tener —s** to have reservations
reservación F *Am* reservation
reservado ADJ (distante) aloof; (discreto) reserved
reservar VT to reserve; **me reservo mi opinión** I'll spare you my opinion
resfriado M common cold; **estoy —** I've got a cold
resfriarse VI to catch cold
resfrío M cold, head cold
resguardar VT to shelter; **—se de** to seek shelter from
resguardo M (abrigo) shelter; (comprobante) deposit slip
residencia F residence
residencial ADJ (para vivir) residential; (en las afueras) suburban
residente ADJ & MF resident
residir VI to reside
residuo M residue
resignación F resignation
resignarse VI to resign oneself
resina F resin
resistencia F (fuerza opuesta) resistance; (de la calefacción) element; (aguante) endurance, stamina
resistente ADJ resistant, tough
resistir VT (una tentación) to resist; (un ataque) to withstand; **—se a un arresto** to resist arrest; VI to resist, to hold [up]
resollar[5] VI (por enfermedad) to wheeze; (después de un esfuerzo) to pant; (por alivio) to sigh
resolución F (acción de resolver) resolution; (ánimo) determination, resolve; **— óptica** optical resolution
resolver[6, 74] VT (decidir) to decide; (solucionar) to solve; **—se a** to resolve to
resonancia F resonance
resonar[5] VI (sonidos) to resound, to boom; (una polémica) to resonate
resoplar VI (con enfado) to huff and puff; (un caballo) to snort
resoplido M (con enojo) puff; (de caballo) snort
resorte M spring
respaldar VT to back, to stand behind
respaldo M (parte de una silla) back; (apoyo) support, backing; **— automático** automatic backup; **— de archivos** backup; **— global** global backup
respectivo ADJ respective

respecto LOC ADV — **a/de** with respect to, concerning; **a ese** — on that score; **con** — **a** with regard to, regarding, vis-à-vis
respetable ADJ respectable
respetar VT to respect
respeto M respect, regard; **con todo** — with all due respect; **faltar el/al** — to slight, to disregard
respetuoso ADJ respectful
respingado M upturned
respingar[40] VI (dar respingos) to buck; (asustarse) to shy away
respingo M (salto) buck; (susto) start
respiración F respiration, breathing; — **boca a boca** mouth-to-mouth resuscitation
respirar VI/VT (inhalar y exhalar) to breathe; (sentir alivio) to breathe easy; **dejar** — to give a breather
respiratorio ADJ respiratory
respiro M (acto de respirar) breathing; (descanso) respite; **dame un** — I need a break
resplandecer[35] VI (brillar) to glare; (de felicidad) to glow
resplandeciente ADJ resplendent, radiant
resplandor M brilliance, radiance
responder VI (reaccionar) to respond; VT (contestar) to answer; (corresponder) to correspond
respondón ADJ saucy
responsabilidad F (obligación de aceptar consecuencias) responsibility; (obligación de informar) accountability
responsabilizar VT to hold liable, to hold responsible
responsable ADJ (que debe aceptar las consecuencias) responsible; (obligado legalmente) liable; (que tiene que informar) accountable
respuesta F response, answer
resquebrajadura F crack
resquebrajar VI to crack
resquicio M (rendija) crack; (laguna legal) loophole
resta F subtraction
restablecer[35] VT (un servicio) to reestablish; (una costumbre) to revive; —**se** to recover
restador-ora MF receiver
restante ADJ remaining
restañar VT to stanch/staunch
restar VT (sustraer) to subtract; (quitar) to take away from; (quedar) to remain; — **importancia a** to make light of
restauración F restoration
restaurante M restaurant
restaurar VT (el gobierno) to restore; (muebles) to refurbish
restitución F restitution
restituir[19] VT to pay back, to give back
resto M (lo demás) rest; (sobrante) remainder; (tenis) return of service; —**s** (de un edificio) remains; (de una comida) leftovers; **echar el** — to go all out
restorán M restaurant
restregar[41] VT to scrub, to scour
restricción F restriction
restringir[46] VT to restrict, to constrain
resucitación F resuscitation, revival
resucitar VT to resuscitate, to revive
resuello M (por enfermedad) wheeze; (por fatiga) panting
resuelto ADJ (de carácter decidido) resolute, strong-willed; (de actitud decidida) resolved
resuelto, resuelva, resuelve *ver* resolver
resulta LOC ADV **de** —**s** as a result
resultado M (de una operación matemática) result; (de un suceso) outcome; (de un partido) score; — **final** (fútbol) final score; —**s científicos** findings; —**s electorales** returns; **como** — as a result; **dar buen** — to pan out; **dar por** — to result in
resultante ADJ resulting, consequent
resultar VI to result; — **de** to result from; **resulta que** it turns out that; **resultó ser un idiota** he turned out to be an idiot, he proved to be an idiot
resumen M summary, abstract; **en** — in sum, in brief
resumir VT to summarize, to sum up; —**se a** to be condensed to, to boil down to
resurgimiento M revival
resurgir[46] VI to arise again
resurrección F resurrection
retablo M altarpiece
retaguardia F rear guard
retal M remnant
retama F broom
retar VT to challenge
retardar VI/VT to retard
retardo M lag
retazo M remnant
retén M (aparato) retainer; (de vigilancia) checkpoint
retención F retention; — **de líquido** fluid retention; — **impositiva** tax withholding
retendrá, retendría *ver* retener
retener[58] VT (una pelota, la atención) to hold; (salarios, fondos) to garnish, to withhold
retenga, retengo *ver* retener
retina F retina
retintín M (en los oídos) ringing; (de cascabeles) jingle
retirada F (de tropas) retreat, withdrawal; (de un diplomático, producto) recall
retirar VT (apartar) to move away; (dinero) to withdraw; (algo dicho) to take back, withdraw; (un producto) to recall; —**se** (para dormir, de un empleo, de la carrera militar)

to retire; (un ejército) to retreat, to pull back
retiro M (refugio) retreat; (jubilación) retirement; (de fondos) withdrawal; **— de deuda** debt retirement
reto M challenge
retocar[30] VT to retouch, to touch up
retomar VT to take up again
retoñar VI to sprout
retoño M sprout, shoot, bud
retoque M retouching
retorcer[34] VT (una toalla mojada) to wring out; (la muñeca) to wrench, to twist; **—se** (de dolor) to writhe; (de inquietud) to squirm
retorcido ADJ (persona) devious; (rama) gnarled
retorcimiento M (de dolor) writhing; (de inquietud) squirming
retórica F rhetoric
retornar VT to return
retorno M (de un viajero) return (también en un teclado); (de una costumbre, moda) revival; **— de línea automático** word wrap
retozar[47] VI (en juegos infantiles) to frolic, to romp; (en juegos eróticos) to cavort
retozo M frolic, romp
retractarse VI to take back one's words
retraer[59] VT (las garras) to retract; **—se** to withdraw
retraído ADJ shy
retraimiento M shyness
retrasado ADJ (falto de desarrollo) backward; (deficiente mental) retarded
retrasar VT (atrasar) to delay; (un reloj) to set back; **—se** to fall behind
retraso M delay, lag
retratar VT (describir) to portray; (pintar un retrato) to paint a portrait
retrato M (pintura) portrait; (descripción) portrayal
retreta F retreat
retrete M lavatory
retribución F (acción de retribuir) remuneration; (pago) salary
retro ADJ retro
retroactivo ADJ retroactive
retroalimentación F feedback
retroceder VI (recular) to step back; (por miedo) to recoil, to shrink back; (en un coche) to back up; (al mecanografiar) to backspace; (dar marcha atrás) to backtrack; (tropas) to retreat, to fall back; (una inundación) to recede
retroceso M (pérdida) step back; (de un arma de fuego) recoil; (económico) recession; (en un teclado) backspace
retrogradismo M backwardness
retrógrado ADJ backward
retroiluminación F backlighting
retroiluminado ADJ backlit
retroproyector M overhead projector
retrovirus M retrovirus
retrucar[30] VT to counter
retruécano M play on words
retumbar VI to rumble, to roll
retumbo M rumble
retuve, retuviera, retuviese *ver* retener
reubicar[30] VT to relocate
reuma M rheumatism
reumatismo M rheumatism
reumatoide ADJ rheumatoid
reunificación F reunification
reunión F (de negocios) meeting; (informal) get-together; (de ex-alumnos) reunion
reunir[27] VT (juntar) to gather; (convocar) to reunite, to bring together; (coleccionar) to collect; (juntar coraje) to muster; (juntar dinero) to raise; **—se** (formal) to meet; (informal) to get together; (un gentío) to gather
revancha F (venganza) revenge; (en deportes) return game
revelación F revelation
revelado M film development
revelador ADJ revealing
revelar VT (un secreto) to reveal; (película) to develop; (un escándalo) to expose; (información) to disclose; **—se** to show oneself
revendedor -ora MF (de mercadería) middleman; (de entradas) scalper
revender VT (vender de nuevo) to resell; (entradas) to scalp
reventar[1] VI/VT (estallar) to burst, to bust; (morir) to die; (fastidiar) to annoy
reventón M (acción de reventar) bursting; (de un neumático) blowout
reverberar VI to reverberate
reverdecer[35] VI (ponerse verde de nuevo) to become green again; (renovarse) to gain new strength
reverencia F (adoración) reverence; (gesto) bow
reverenciar VT to revere
reverendo -da ADJ & MF reverend
reverente ADJ reverent
reverso M reverse
revertir[8] VI to revert; **— en beneficio de** to be of benefit to
revés M (lado opuesto) reverse; (en tenis) backhand; (contratiempo) setback, downturn; **al —** (con lo de adelante hacia atrás) backwards; (con lo de arriba hacia abajo) upside down; (con lo de adentro hacia afuera) inside out; **dar vuelta al —** to turn inside out
revestimiento M overlay; (de piso) flooring; (de pared exterior) siding; (de pared interior) paneling
revestir[9] VT (un camino) to surface; (una pared) to cover; (conllevar) to be marked by
revisar VT (examinar) to review, to go over; (un

coche) to service
revisión F (de un libro) review; (de una película vieja) revival; (médica, mecánica) checkup
revisor-ora MF (en un tren, autobús) conductor; (de un texto) proofreader
revista F (inspección) inspection; (de tropas) muster; (publicación) magazine, journal, periodical; (espectáculo) revival; **— de historietas** comic book; **— electrónica** e-zine; **pasar —** to pass in review
revistar VT to inspect
revitalizar VT to revitalize
revivir VI/VT to revive
revocación F (de un derecho, de un fallo) revocation; (de una ley) repeal
revocar[30] VT (un fallo) to reverse; (una ley) to repeal; (una pared) to plaster
revolcar[31] VT (derribar) to knock over; **—se** (cerdos) to wallow; (niños) to roll around
revolear VT to roll
revolotear VI to flutter, to flit
revoltijo M (de cosas) jumble; (de pelo) muss
revoltoso-sa ADJ unruly, disorderly; MF troublemaker
revolución F (cambio radical) revolution; (giro) revolution, turn; **revoluciones por minuto** revolutions per minute
revolucionario-ria ADJ revolutionary, earthshaking; MF revolutionary
revolver[6, 74] VT (remover) to stir up; (registrar) to rummage in; (desordenar) to mess up; (huevos) to scramble; (ensalada) to toss; **eso me revuelve el estómago** that makes my stomach turn; **—se en la cama** to toss and turn in bed
revólver M revolver, pistol
revuelo M stir, commotion
revuelta F revolt
revuelto ADJ (el mar) rough; (el ánimo) restless; (el pelo) disheveled; **huevos —s** scrambled eggs
rey M king; **los —es Magos** the Wise Men
reyerta F melee, squabble
rezagarse[40] VI to straggle behind, to lag behind
rezar[47] VI/VT (a Dios) to pray; (un letrero) to say
rezo M prayer
rezongar[40] VI/VT (murmurar) to grumble; (quejarse) to gripe
rezongón-ona ADJ grumpy; MF grouch
rezumar VT to ooze
ría, ríe *ver* reír
riachuelo M brook
riada F flash flood
ribazo M steep bank
ribera F shore, bank; (de río) riverbank
ribereño ADJ on the bank
ribete M (de uniforme) trimming; (de alfombra) binding; (de ropa) piping; (de mosaico) border; **tener —s de** to have hints of
ribetear VT (un uniforme) to trim; (una alfombra) to bind; (un diseño) to border
ricacho ADJ very rich
rico ADJ (persona) rich, wealthy, affluent; (suelo) rich; (adorno) exquisite; (manjar) delicious; (niño) cute
ridiculizar[47] VT to ridicule, to deride
ridículo ADJ (sin sentido) ridiculous; (absurdo, risible) ludicrous; **hacer el —** to act the fool; **poner en —** to ridicule; **ponerse en —** to make a spectacle of oneself
riego M irrigation
riel M rail
rienda F rein; **dar — suelta** to give a free hand
riendo, riera, rieron, riese *ver* reír
riesgo M risk; **— ocupacional** occupational hazard/risk; **en —** at risk; **correr un —** to run a risk
rifa F raffle
rifar VT to raffle
rifirrafe M free-for-all
rifle M rifle
rigidez F rigidity
rígido ADJ rigid
rigor M (exactitud) rigor; (dureza) harshness; **en —** in reality; **de —** indispensable
riguroso ADJ (estricto) rigorous; (duro) harsh
rima F rhyme
rimar VI/VT to rhyme
rimbombante ADJ grandiose
rímel M mascara
rin M rim
rincón M (ángulo) corner; (lugar retirado) nook, alcove
rinconera F (estantería) corner cupboard; (mesa) corner table
rinda, rinde, rindiendo, rindiera, rindiese *ver* rendir
ring M boxing ring
ringlera F row
rinoceronte M rhinoceros
rinoplastia F rhinoplasty, *fam* nose job
rinovirus M rhinovirus
riña F (discusión) quarrel; (pelea) scrap, fight, spat
riñón M (órgano) kidney; (región lumbar) lower back
río M river; **— abajo** downstream
rió *ver* reír
ripio M rubble
riqueza F wealth; **—s** riches
risa F (carcajada) laugh; (acción, sonido de reír) laughter; **reventar/desternillarse de —** to burst with laughter; **morirse de —** to die laughing; **¡qué —!** what a joke!
risco M crag, bluff
risible ADJ laughable
risita F (burlona) snicker; (ahogada) chuckle
risotada F guffaw, gale of laughter

ristra F string
risueño ADJ (sonriente) smiling; (alegre) cheerful
rítmico ADJ rhythmical
ritmo M rhythm; **— cardíaco** heart rate; **— de vida** pace of life
rito M rite
ritual ADJ & M ritual
rival ADJ & MF rival
rivalidad F rivalry; **— entre hemanos** sibling rivalry
rivalizar[47] VI to rival; **— con** to compete with
rizado ADJ curly; M curling
rizar[47] VT (pelo) to curl, to crimp; (agua) to ripple
rizo M (en el pelo) curl, ringlet; (en el agua) ripple, ruffle; (pirueta de avión) loop
robar VT (a una persona) to rob; (un objeto, dinero) to steal; **—se una base** to steal a base
roble M oak tree
robledal M oak grove
robo M (violento) robbery; (furtivo) theft; **— a mano armada** armed robbery, holdup; **— con allanamiento** burglary; **— de base** base steal; **— de identidad** identity theft
robot M robot
robótica F robotics
robusto ADJ (fuerte) robust; (grueso) stout, stocky; (sólido) sturdy
roca F rock
roce M (de una bala) graze; (de dos superficies) rub, rubbing; (con la ley, la policía) brush
rociada F (acción de rociar) sprinkling, spraying; (de insultos) volley
rociar[28] VI/VT (con agua) to spray, to sprinkle; (con jugo, aliño) to baste
rocín M nag
rocío M (del alba) dew; (en aerosol) spray, mist
rock M rock
rocoso ADJ rocky
rodada F (superficial) track; (profunda) rut
rodadura F rolling
rodaja F flat round slice
rodaje M (de un coche) running; (de una película) shoot
rodante ADJ rolling
rodar[5] VI (girar) to roll; (caer) to tumble down; (vagar) to roam; (filmar) to shoot
rodear VT (cercar) to surround; (cubrir) to wrap around; (evitar) to go around
rodeo M (desvío) detour; (modo de expresarse) circumlocution; (espectáculo) rodeo
rodilla F knee; **de —s** on one's knees; **hincarse de —s** to kneel down
rodillo M (para pintar) roller; (para cocinar) rolling pin; (para caminos) road roller
rododendro M rhododendron
roedor M rodent
roer[73] VI/VT to gnaw
rogar[42] VT to pray, to beg, to beseech; **hacerse [del] —** to play hard to get; **se ruega no molestar** please do not disturb
rojez F redness
rojizo ADJ reddish
rojo ADJ & M red; **al — vivo** red-hot
rol M role
roletazo M ground ball; **lo sacaron con un —** he grounded out
rollizo ADJ plump; M log
rollo M (de papel, de película, de grasa) roll; (de árbol) log; (de cuerda) reel; (de tela) bolt; (discurso aburrido) long story; (mentira) lie; (lío) mess, hassle; (relación amorosa) affair; (manuscrito) scroll; (de alambre) coil; **dar el —** to hassle
ROM M ROM
romance ADJ Romance; M (lengua románica) Romance language; (español) Spanish language; (relación amorosa) romance; (composición métrica) ballad; **en buen —** in plain language
románico ADJ (arte) Romanesque; (lengua) Romance
romano -na ADJ & MF Roman
romanticismo M (corriente literaria) romanticism; (sentimentalismo) romance
romántico -ca ADJ & MF romantic
rombo M diamond
romería F pilgrimage
romero -ra MF (persona) pilgrim; M rosemary
romo ADJ (sin punta) blunt; (sin filo) dull
romper[74] VI/VT (un jarrón) to break; VT (relaciones) to sever; **— a** to start to; **— con** to break up with; **— el alba** to dawn; **— filas** to break ranks; **— un contrato** to break a contract; **rompió las aguas / la fuente** her water broke; **de rompe y rasga** coarse; M SG **rompecabezas** jigsaw puzzle; M SG **rompehuelgas** strikebreaker; M SG **rompeolas** breakwater
rompible ADJ breakable
rompientes M PL surf
rompimiento M (con el pasado) break; (de una promesa) breach
rompope M *Méx* eggnog
ron M rum
roncar[30] VI to snore
roncha F (de sarampión) spot; (de mosquito) bite
ronco ADJ hoarse, raspy
ronda F (de policía) patrol, beat; (de niños) circle; (de bebidas, de negociaciones, de golf) round
rondar VT (patrullar) to patrol; (acercarse) to hang around; (cantar serenatas) to serenade; **rondaba los cuarenta** she was around forty years old
ronquera F hoarseness
ronquido M snore

ronronear VI to purr
ronroneo M purr
ronzal M halter
roña F (enfermedad de plantas) scab; (sarna) mange; MF (tacaño) skinflint
roñoso ADJ (planta) scabby; (animal) mangy; (persona) stingy
ropa F clothing, clothes; **— blanca** linens; **— vieja** stew made from leftover meat
ropaje M apparel
ropería F checkroom
ropero M (armario) wardrobe; (cuarto) closet
roque M castle
rorro M baby
rosa F (flor) rose; (marca) blemish; **— de los vientos** mariner's compass; ADJ INV (rosado) rose-colored, pink
rosado ADJ (saludable) rosy; (de color de rosa) rose-colored, pink; M rosé wine
rosal M rosebush
rosario M rosary
rosbif M roast beef
rosca F (de tornillo) screw; (pan) ring-shaped roll; **pasarse de —** to go off the deep end
roséola F roseola
rostro M (cara) face; (morro) nerve
rotación F rotation
rotar VI/VT to rotate
rotativo ADJ (movimiento) rotary; (cultivos) rotating; M newspaper
rotatorio ADJ rotary
roto ADJ (averiado) broken; (cansado) exhausted; (ropa, voz) ragged
roto *ver* romper
rotor M rotor
rótula F kneecap
rotular VT to label
rótulo M (título) title; (etiqueta) label
rotundo ADJ resounding; **una negativa rotunda** a categorical denial
rotura F (de un aparato) break; (de un órgano, tubo) rupture; **— de servicio** (tenis) service break
roturar VT to plow
round M (en boxeo) round
rozadura F chafing
rozamiento M friction
rozar[47] VT (herir levemente) to graze; (arañar) to scrape; (irritar) to rub, to chafe; (limpiar un terreno) to clear; **—se con alguien** to have dealings with someone; **rozaba en los cuarenta** she was almost forty years old
Ruanda F Rwanda
ruandés -esa ADJ & MF Rwandan
rubéola/rubeola F rubella
rubí M (piedra preciosa) ruby; (en un reloj) jewel
rubicundo ADJ (permanente) ruddy; (temporal) flush
rubio -a ADJ & MF blond
rubor M (de la piel) blush, flush; (de las mejillas) bloom, glow
ruborizarse[47] VI to blush
rúbrica F (trazo) flourish; (título) title
rucio ADJ gray
rudeza F rudeness, coarseness
rudo ADJ rude, coarse; **— golpe** hard blow
rueca F spinning wheel
rueda F (de coche) wheel; (de personas) circle; (rodaja) slice; **— de prensa** news conference; **ir sobre —s** to be smooth sailing
ruedo M (de un circo) ring; (de vestido) hem
ruego M (plegaria) prayer; (petición) plea, entreaty
rufián M (matón) ruffian
rugby M rugby
rugido M roar
rugir[46] VI (animal) to roar; (estómago) to growl
rugoso ADJ rough
ruibarbo M rhubarb
ruido M noise; **— de fondo** background noise; **mucho — y pocas nueces** much ado about nothing
ruidoso ADJ noisy, loud
ruin ADJ (persona, cosa) vile; (animal) puny
ruina F (destrucción) destruction; (edificio derruido, estado de pobreza) ruin; (persona) wreck; (perjuicio) downfall; **en —s** in ruins
ruindad F (actitud) vileness; (acto) vile act
ruinoso ADJ ruinous
ruiseñor M nightingale
rulero M *RP* roller, curler
ruleta F roulette
rulo M roller, curler
Rumania F Romania, Rumania
rumano -na ADJ & MF Romanian, Rumanian
rumba F rumba
rumbear VI (dirigirse a) to head in a certain direction; (bailar) to dance the rumba
rumbo M course, route; **— a** toward
rumiar VI (meditar, comer el rumen) to ruminate; (reflexionar) to ruminate, to mull over, to brood over
rumor M rumor
runrún M (rumor) rumor; (sonido sordo) humming
ruptura F (de relaciones) break; (de órganos internos) rupture
rural ADJ rural
Rusia F Russia
ruso -sa ADJ & MF (persona) Russian; M (lengua) Russian
rústico ADJ (rural) rustic, rural; (tosco) coarse; **en rústica** paperback
ruta F (itinerario) route; (carretera) highway; (en informática) path
rutina F routine

Ss

sábado M Saturday
sábalo M shad
sábana F bed sheet
sabana F savannah
sabañón M chilblain
saber[71] VI/VT to know; (tener sabor) to taste; — **nadar** to know how to swim; **supo la verdad** he found out the truth; **las vacaciones me han sabido a poco** my vacation was too short; — **a ciencia cierta** to know for sure; — **de biología** to know all about biology; **a** — namely; **hacer** — to let know; **para que sepas** for your information; **sabérselas todas** to know the ropes; **vaya a** — who knows? **no sabe un comino** he doesn't know squat; — **a** to taste like; **sabe bien** it tastes good; M knowledge, learning; **a mi leal** — **y entender** as far as I know; M SG **sabelotodo** know-it-all
sabiduría F wisdom
sabiendas LOC ADV **a** — knowingly
sabiondo -da ADJ & MF wise guy; know-it-all
sabio -bia ADJ wise, sage; MF (estudioso) scholar; (sabedor) sage, wise person
sable M saber
sabor M taste, flavor
saborear VT to savor, to relish
sabotaje M sabotage
sabotear VT to sabotage
sabrá, sabría *ver* saber
sabroso ADJ (comida) savory, tasty; (cuento) juicy
sabueso M (perro) bloodhound; (detective) sleuth
sacador -ora MF (en deportes) server
sacar[30] VT (cosas de la maleta, a pasear) to take out; (manchas, dinero del banco) to get out; (los zapatos) to take off; (malas notas, carnet de conducir) to get; (una copia) to make; (una foto) to take; (una conclusión) to draw; (la lengua, la cabeza por la ventana) to stick out; (una pelota de tenis) to serve; (una asignatura escolar) *Esp* to pass; — **ampollas** to blister; — **brillo** to polish up; — **provecho [de]** to benefit [from]; — **a bailar** to ask to dance; — **a colación** to broach; — **a luz** to divulge; — **de un apuro** to bail out; **me saca de quicio** he gets my goat, he gets on my nerves; — **el cuerpo** to dodge; — **el mejor partido de** to make the best of; —**le el jugo a algo** to make the most of; — **en limpio** to deduce; —**se el sombrero** *Am* to take off one's hat; **¡sáquese de allí!** *Am* get out of there! — **punta** to sharpen; — **a alguien** (béisbol) to get someone out; M SG **sacabocados** punch; M SG **sacacorchos** corkscrew; M SG **sacamuelas** quack dentist; M SG **sacapuntas** pencil sharpener
sacarina F saccharine
sacarosa F sucrose
sacerdocio M priesthood
sacerdote M priest
saciar VT to satiate; —**se** to be satiated
saco M (bolsa) sack; (chaqueta) blazer, sport coat; (aparato de boxeo) punching bag; (parte de órgano interno) sac; — **de dormir** sleeping bag; — **de noche** overnight bag; **echar en** — **roto** to waste one's effort
sacramento M sacrament
sacrificar[30] VT (en un rito religioso) to sacrifice; (una mascota) to put to sleep
sacrificio M sacrifice (también en béisbol)
sacrilegio M sacrilege
sacrílego ADJ sacrilegious
sacristán M sexton
sacro M sacrum
sacudida F (sacudón) shake, jolt; (de terremoto) tremor; (de la cabeza) toss; (eléctrica) shock
sacudir VT (sarandear) to shake; (las alfombras) to beat; (el polvo) to dust; **ir sacudiéndose** to rattle along, to jolt along; —**se de alguien** to get rid of someone
sádico ADJ sadistic
sadismo M sadism
saeta F arrow
safari M safari
sagaz ADJ shrewd, astute
sagrado ADJ sacred, holy; **Sagradas Escrituras** Holy Scripture
sahumar VT to perfume with incense
sahumerio M burning of incense
sainete M one-act farce; **esa familia es un** — that family is a complete mess
sal F (mineral) salt; (gracia) wit; — **de Epsom** Epsom salt; — **gorda** cooking salt; — **yodada** iodized salt; — **de mesa** table salt; **dar** — to spice up; — **y pimienta** (condimentos) salt and pepper; (gracia) life, spark
sal *ver* salir
sala F (de estar) parlor, living room; (grande) hall, large room; — **de justicia** courtroom; — **de clase** classroom; — **de chat** chat room; — **de cuidados intensivos** intensive care unit; — **de espera** waiting room; — **de directorio** boardroom; — **de lectura** reading room; — **de operaciones** operating room; — **de recuperación** recovery room
salado ADJ (con sal) salty, savory; (gracioso) witty; *Am* (caro) expensive; M (acción) salting
salamandra F salamander
salar VT to salt; —**se** to become salty

salarial ADJ salary, wage
salario M pay, wages; **— base** base pay; **— bruto** gross pay; **— de subsistencia** living wage; **— mínimo** minimum wage
salchicha F sausage
saldar VT to settle
saldo M (resultado final) balance; (venta especial) sale; **—s** (restos) remnants; **— pendiente** balance due
saldrá, saldría *ver* salir
salegar[40] VT to give salt to; M salt lick
salero M (dispensador) salt cellar, salt shaker; (gracia) charm
saleroso ADJ charming
salga, salgo *ver* salir
salida F (partida) departure; (puerta) exit, way out; (comienzo de una carrera) start; (militar) sally; (eléctrica, de computadora) output; (de una crisis) way out; **este artículo tiene mucha —** this article sells well; **dar la —** to start a race; **— del sol** sunrise; **— de emergencia** emergency exit; **— en falso** false start
saliente ADJ (roca) salient, projecting; (gobierno) outgoing; M salient, projection, overhang
salina F salt mine
salino ADJ saline
salir[57] VI (del interior al exterior, para divertirse) to go out; (de un país) to depart, to leave; (del trabajo) to quit; (de un programa de computadora) to exit, to quit; (manchas de tinta) to come out; (un anillo del dedo) to come off; (el sol) to rise; (una publicación) to appear; (flores) to sprout; **— a bolsa** to go public; **trabajando no se puede — de pobre** you can't work your way out of poverty; **salió a su madre** she takes after her mother; **— a la luz** to surface; **— adelante** to overcome difficulties; **— bien** to turn out well; **— con** to date; **— ganando** to come out ahead; **— mal** to go wrong; **¿a cuánto sale?** how much is it? **no me sale ser amable con él** I can't bring myself to be nice to him; **—se** (gotear) to leak; (rebosar) to overflow; (proyectarse) to stick out
salitre F saltpeter
saliva F saliva
salmón M salmon
salmonela F salmonella
salmuera F brine
salobre ADJ salty
salomonense ADJ & MF Solomon Islander
salón M (de estar) living room, parlor; (de conferencias) hall; **— de belleza** beauty salon; **— de clase** classroom; **— de exposición y ventas** showroom; **— de exhibición** exhibition hall; **— de té** tearoom
salpicadero M dashboard
salpicadura F spatter, splash, splatter
salpicar[30] VI/VT (humedecer) to sprinkle, to spatter, to splash; (adornar) to punctuate; (dispersar) to intersperse
salpicón M meat salad
salpimentar[1] VT to salt and pepper
salsa F (blanca) sauce; (picante) salsa; **en su —** in her element; **— tártara** tartar sauce; **— de soya** soy sauce; **— de tomate** ketchup
saltar VI/VT (brincar) to jump, to leap; (una cerca) to jump over, to vault; (un renglón) to skip; (una ley) to ignore; VI (los fusibles) to trip; **— a la vista** to be obvious; **— sobre** to pounce on; **se le saltaron los ojos** his eyes bugged out; **se le saltó un botón** one of his buttons popped off; **se me saltaban las lágrimas** it brought tears to my eyes; M SG **saltamontes** grasshopper
salteador -ora MF bandit
saltear VT to stir-fry
salto M jump, leap; **— alto** high jump; **— con esquí** ski jump; **— con pértiga** pole vault; **— de agua** waterfall; **— de cama** dressing gown; **— de línea** return; **— de línea forzado** hard return; **— de línea suave** soft return; **— de longitud** broad jump; **— de página** page break; **— de página forzado** forced page break, hard page break; **— de página suave/automático** soft page break; **— del ángel** swan dive; **— mortal** somersault; **— triple** triple jump; **a — de mata** from hand to mouth; **dar un —** (saltar) to jump; (el corazón) to skip a beat
saltón ADJ (que salta) jumping; (que resalta) bulging; M grasshopper
salubridad F sanitation
salud F health; **— mental** mental health; **— pública** public health; **curarse en —** to take precautions; INTERJ cheers!
saludable ADJ healthy, healthful
saludar VT (decir hola) to greet; (dar la bienvenida) to salute, to hail; (en el ejército) to salute; (hacer un gesto amistoso con la mano) to wave
saludo M (hola) greeting, salutation; (gesto) wave; (militar) salute; **retirar el — a alguien** to stop speaking to someone; **—s** best wishes, regards
salva F salvo
salvación F salvation
salvado M (harina) bran; (béisbol) save
salvador -ora MF savior; ADJ saving
salvadoreño -ña ADJ & MF Salvador[i]an
salvaguarda F safeguard
salvaguardar VT to safeguard
salvajada F (acción) savage act; (comentario) savage remark
salvaje ADJ (feroz) savage; (no domesticado)

wild; MF savage
salvajismo M savagery
salvamento M (de gente) rescue; (de bienes, propiedades) salvage; (béisbol) save
salvar VT (la vida, el alma) to save; (de un peligro) to rescue; (propiedad) to salvage; (un obstáculo) to clear; (un camino difícil) to negotiate; **— el pellejo** to save one's skin; **el puente salva el río** the bridge spans the river; **—se** to pull through; **—se por poco** to have a narrow escape; **sálvese quien pueda** every man for himself; M SG **salvapantallas** screen saver; M SG **salvavidas** (aparato) life preserver, life jacket; MF (persona) lifeguard
salvia F sage
salvo ADJ safe; **a —** safe; M **—conducto** safe-conduct; PREP save, except; **— en caso de desastre** barring a disaster
Samoa F Samoa
samoano -na ADJ & MF Samoan
sanar VI/VT to heal; M **sanalotodo** cure-all
sanatorio M (para convalecientes) sanatorium; (para enfermos) hospital
sanción F sanction
sancionar VT to sanction
sandalia F sandal
sandez F (acción) stupidity, foolishness; (dicho) foolish remark
sandía F watermelon
saneamiento M sanitation
sanear VT to drain
sangrar VI/VT to bleed; VT (un árbol) to tap; (un párrafo) to indent
sangre F blood; **— fría** coolness under pressure; **a — fría** in cold blood; **hacerse mala —** to get upset; **eso lo llevo en la —** that's in my blood; **de — caliente** warm-blooded; **— azul** blue blood; **sudar —** to sweat bullets; **de pura —** thoroughbred; **chupar la — a alguien** to be a parasite on someone
sangría F (bebida) wine punch; (acción de sangrar) bleeding; (espacio tipográfico) indentation; (pérdida) drain
sangriento ADJ (manchado de sangre, que provoca pérdida de sangre) bloody; (sanguinario) bloodthirsty
sanguijuela F leech
sanguinario ADJ bloody, vicious
sanguíneo ADJ blood; **grupo —** blood group
sanidad F public health
sanitario -ria ADJ sanitary; M **—s** bathroom fittings; MF public health worker
sanmarinense ADJ & MF San Marinese
sanmarinés -esa ADJ & MF San Marinese
sano ADJ (persona) healthy; (juicio) sound; (dieta) healthful; (vaso) unbroken; **— y salvo** safe and sound; **en su — juicio** of sound mind
sánscrito M Sanskrit
sanseacabó INTERJ **te quedas y —** you're staying and that's that
santalucense ADJ & MF St. Lucian
santiamén LOC ADV **en un —** in a jiffy, lickety-split
santidad F sanctity, holiness
santificar[30] VT to sanctify
santiguarse[25] VI to cross oneself
santo -ta ADJ saintly, holy; **esperar todo el — día** to wait the whole blessed day; MF saint; **día del —** saint's day; **quedarse para vestir —s** to be a spinster; **¿a — de qué?** for what reason? **¡por todos los —s!** my goodness!
santotomense ADJ & MF São Tomean
santuario M sanctuary
santurrón -ona ADJ & MF goody-goody
saña F fury
sañudo ADJ furious
sapo M toad (también hombre feo); **echar —s y culebras** to swear, to curse; **sentirse como un — de otro pozo** to feel like a fish out of water
saque M (tenis) service, serve; **— de inicio** (fútbol) kickoff; **— de banda** throw-in; **— de esquina** corner kick; **— de meta** goal kick; **— de puerta** goal kick; **— inicial** kick-off; **— ganador** ace; **— y volea** (tenis) serve and volley
saquear VT to sack, to plunder, to pillage
saqueo M sacking, plundering, pillaging
sarampión M measles; **— alemán** rubella
sarape M *Méx* serape
sarcasmo M sarcasm
sarcástico ADJ sarcastic
sarcófago M sarcophagus
sarcoma M sarcoma
sardina F sardine
sardo -da ADJ & MF Sardinian
sardónico ADJ sardonic
sargento -ta MF sergeant; F battle-ax[e]
sarmentoso ADJ gnarled
sarmiento M vine
sarna F mange
sarnoso ADJ mangy
sarpullido M rash
sarro M tartar, plaque
sarta F string; **una — de mentiras** a pack of lies; **una — de idiotas** a bunch of idiots
sartén F frying pan, skillet
sastre -tra MF tailor
sastrería F tailor shop
satánico ADJ satanic
satélite M satellite; **— artificial** man-made satellite
satén M satin
sátira F satire
satírico ADJ satirical
satirizar[47] VT to satirize

satisfacción F satisfaction
satisfacer[54, 74] VT (un deseo) to satisfy; (una deuda) to pay; **—se** to be satisfied
satisfactorio ADJ (aceptable) satisfactory; (exitoso) successful
satisfaga, satisfago, satisfará, satisfaría *ver* satisfacer
satisfecho ADJ contented, satisfied
satisfecho, satisfice, satisficiera, satisficiese *ver* satisfacer
saturar VT (una solución) to saturate; (un mercado) to glut; (líneas de teléfono) to overload
sauce M willow; **— llorón** weeping willow
saudí, saudita ADJ & MF Saudi Arabian
savia F sap
saxofón M saxophone
sazón F season; **a la —** at that time; **en —** ripe
sazonar VT (condimentar) to season, to flavor; (madurar) to ripen
scooter M scooter
scout MF scout
se PRON PERS **— coronó a sí mismo** he crowned himself; **— lavó la cara** he washed his face; **— besaron** they kissed each other; **— habla español** Spanish is spoken; **— lo puede combatir** it can be fought
sé *ver* saber
sea, seas *ver* ser
sebo M tallow, fat
seborrea F seborrhea
secador M hair dryer
secadora F clothes dryer
secante ADJ drying
secar[30] VT (la ropa) to dry; (las manos) to dry off; **—se** (planta) to dry up; (río) to run dry; (madera) to season
sección F (militar) platoon; (de un almacén) department; (un texto) section
seccionar VT to section
seco ADJ (ropa) dry; (río) dried-up; (planta) withered; (respuesta) curt, brief; **en —** on dry land; **parar en —** to stop short; **quedar —** to fall dead; **estar —** to be broke; **lavar en —** to dry-clean; **a secas** plain
secreción F secretion
secretar VT to secrete
secretaría F secretariat
secretariado M (profesión) secretarial profession; (secretaría) secretariat; (conjunto de secretarias) secretarial pool
secretario -ria MF secretary; **— general** secretary general
secretear VI to whisper
secreto ADJ (oculto) secret; (policía) undercover; M (cosa oculta) secret; (condición de oculto) secrecy; **— a voces** open secret; **en —** in secret; **— bancario** account holder confidentiality
secta F sect
sector M sector
sectorial ADJ sectorial
secuaz M henchman
secuela F consequence; **—s** aftermath
secuencia F (de acontecimientos) sequence; (de datos) string
secuenciar VT to sequence
secuestrador -ora MF kidnapper
secuestrar VT (a una persona) to kidnap, to abduct; (una propiedad) to seize; (un avión) to hijack
secuestro M (de una persona) kidnapping; (de propiedad) seizure; (de un avión) hijacking
secular ADJ secular
secundar VT (apoyar) to second; (imitar) to imitate; (seguir) to follow suit
secundaria F secondary school
secundario ADJ secondary
sed F thirst; **tener —** to be thirsty
seda F silk; **como una —** (suave) soft as silk; (afable) sweet-tempered
sedación F sedation
sedán M sedan
sedante ADJ & M sedative
sedar VT to sedate
sedativo ADJ & M sedative
sede F (gubernamental) seat; (religiosa) see; **— central** headquarters
sedentario ADJ sedentary
sedería F (conjunto de artículos de seda) silk goods; (tienda de sedas) silk shop
sedero -ra MF (que vende) silk dealer; (que fabrica) silk weaver; ADJ **industria sedera** silk industry
sedición F sedition
sediento ADJ thirsty; **estar — de** to thirst for
sedimento M sediment
sedoso ADJ silken, silky
seducción F seduction
seducir[38] VT (corromper) to seduce; (atraer) to entice; (persuadir con argucias) to lure
seductivo ADJ alluring
seductor -ora ADJ alluring; M seducer; F seductress
sefardí ADJ Sephardic; MF Sephardi; M (variedad del español) Sephardi
sefardita ADJ & MF Sephardi
segador -ora MF (persona) mower, reaper; F (máquina) mower, reaper
segar[41] VT (hierba) to mow; (mies) to reap
seglar ADJ secular; M layman; F laywoman
segmento M segment
segregar[40] VT (separar) to segregate; (producir secreciones) to secrete
seguido ADJ in a row; **dos horas seguidas** two hours in a row; ADV straight through; **trabajaron —** they worked continuously
seguidor -ora MF follower

seguimiento M (persecución) pursuit; (atención continuada) follow-up
seguir[12] VT (camino, instrucciones) to follow; (estudios) to pursue; (progreso de un avión) to track; **sigue trabajando** he keeps on working, he continues to work; **sigue allí** he is still there; **de lo anterior se sigue que** from the preceding it follows that; **— los pasos de** to follow in the footsteps of; **—le la corriente a alguien** to play along with someone; **— el tren** to keep up; **— el hilo de** to keep track of; **— la pista de** to trail
según PREP according to; **— se mire** depending on how you see it; **— pasa el tiempo** as time goes by; **— tus instrucciones** per your instructions; CONJ as; **— se informa** reportedly; **lo haré — me digas** I will do it as you tell me to
segundero M second hand
segundo -da ADJ & ADV second; MF second in command; **— tiempo** (fútbol) second half; **— servicio** (tenis) second serve; **segunda base** (posición en béisbol) second base; M (jugador) second baseman; **segunda hipoteca** second mortgage; **segunda intención** ulterior motive; **de segunda mano** secondhand, preowned; **de segunda** second-rate
segundón -ona MF (hijo) second-born child; (persona mediocre) also-ran
seguramente ADV certainly, surely; **lenta pero —** slowly but surely
seguridad F (contra el delito) security; (contra accidentes) safety; **— en sí mismo** self-confidence; **— social** social security
seguro ADJ (a prueba de delincuentes) secure; (que no ofrece o siente duda) sure, certain; (libre de peligro) safe; (firme) stable; **es — que** it is certain that; **su — servidor** yours truly; **— de sí mismo** self-assured; M (contrato contra riesgos) insurance; (dispositivo) safety device, restraint; **— contra accidentes** accident insurance; **— contra daños a terceros** liability insurance; **— contra incendios** fire insurance; **— contra inundaciones** flood insurance; **— contra todo riesgo** comprehensive insurance; **— de discapacidad** disability insurance; **— de vida** life insurance; **— de vida a término** term life insurance; **— de vida permanente** whole life insurance; **— médico** health insurance; **en —** in safety; **sobre —** without risk
seis NUM six
selección F selection, choice; **— de texto** highlighting; **— natural** natural selection; **— nacional** national team
seleccionado M **— nacional** national team
seleccionar VT to select, to choose
selectivo ADJ selective
selecto ADJ select, choice
sellar VT (poner sello) to stamp; (precintar) to seal
sello M (de correo) stamp; (de documento oficial) seal; (instrumento) seal, stamp; (de discos) label; **— de goma** rubber stamp; **— fiscal** revenue stamp
selva F (templada o fría) forest; (tropical) jungle; **— virgen** virgin forest
semáforo M traffic light
semana F week; **entre —** during the week
semanal ADJ weekly
semanario M weekly publication
semántica F semantics
semblante M countenance
semblanza F biographical sketch
sembrado M sown ground
sembradora F planting machine
sembrar[1] VT (plantar) to sow, to plant; (esparcir) to scatter; (minas) to lay; (pánico, alegría) to spread
semejante ADJ similar, like; **— afirmación** such a statement; **un tipo —** such a guy; M fellow human being
semejanza F resemblance, similarity; **a — de** in the manner of
semejar VT to resemble
semental ADJ stud; M stud, stallion
semestral ADJ biannual
semestre M semester
semianual ADJ biannual
semicírculo M semicircle
semiconductor M semiconductor
semifinal ADJ & F semifinal
semilla F seed
semillero M seedbed; **— de vicios** hotbed of vice
seminario M (religioso) seminary; (universitario) seminar
semítico ADJ Semitic
senado M senate
senador -ora MF senator
sencillez F simplicity; **con —** simply
sencillo ADJ (no complicado, humilde) simple; (fácil) easy, simple; (sin adornos) plain; (no afectado) straightforward; M (béisbol) single
senda F (construida) path, pathway; (natural) track, trail
sendero M (construido) path, pathway; (natural) track, trail
sendos ADJ **tenían — sombreros** each one had a hat
Senegal M Senegal
senegalés -esa ADJ & MF Senegalese
senil ADJ senile
senilidad F senility
seno M (pecho) breast; (hueco) sinus; (útero)

womb; (en matemática) sine; **— de la familia** bosom of the family

sensación F (física) sensation; (mental) feeling, impression; **tengo la — de que** I have the feeling that; **fue la — de la fiesta** she was the life of the party

sensacional ADJ sensational

sensatez F common sense

sensato ADJ sensible, level-headed

sensibilidad F (modo de pensar) sensibility; (percepción) sensitiveness

sensibilizar[47] VT to sensitize

sensible ADJ (que siente) sensitive; (notable) perceptible; **tengo el brazo muy — por el accidente** my arm is very tender because of the accident; **Juana es muy — en estas ocasiones** Juana is very emotional on these occasions

sensiblería F sentimentality

sensiblero ADJ sentimental, mushy

sensitivo ADJ sensitive

sensor M sensor

sensorial ADJ sensory

sensual ADJ (carnal) sensual; (de los sentidos) sensuous

sensualidad F sensuality

sentada F (acto de sentarse) sitting; (protesta) sit-in; **de una —** at one sitting

sentado ADJ **dar por —** to take for granted

sentar[1] VT to seat; **— bien** to agree with; **me sentó muy mal lo que dijo** what he said did not sit well with me; **este peinado te sienta** this hairdo becomes you; **no te sienta ese traje** that suit does not fit you; **— precedente** to set a precedent; **—se** to sit down

sentencia F (dicho) maxim; (fallo) ruling; (condena) sentence; (indemnización) award

sentenciar VT (condenar) to sentence; (fallar) to rule

sentido ADJ heartfelt; M (facultad) sense; (significado) meaning; (dirección) way; **— común** common sense; **— de la vista** sense of sight; **— del gusto** sense of taste; **— del humor** sense of humor; **— del oído** sense of hearing; **— del olfato** sense of smell; **— del tacto** sense of touch; **aguzar el —** to prick up one's ears; **de un solo —** one-way; **de dos —s** two-way; **dejar sin —** to render unconscious; **en cierto —** in a sense; **perder el —** to faint; **quedar —** to have one's feelings hurt; **sin —** meaningless; **tener —** to make sense

sentimental ADJ sentimental

sentimentalismo M sentimentality

sentimiento M feeling, sentiment

sentir[8] VT (percibir) to feel; (oír) to hear; (lamentar) to regret; **—se** to feel; **—se capaz de** to feel up to; **—se de los pies** to have pains in the feet

seña F (gesto) sign; (rasgo) trait; (marca) mark; **—s** name and address; **por más —s** as an additional proof; **—s de vida** life signs; **hablar por —s** to use sign language; **hacer —s** to signal

señal F (de tráfico, de violencia, de vida, de la cruz) sign; (de violencia) mark; (de radio) signal; (pago anticipado) deposit; **en — de** in token of

señalar VT (marcar, señalar) to mark; (mostrar, mencionar) to point out; (fijar) to fix; **—se** to distinguish oneself

señor M (título) Mr.; (forma de tratamiento) sir; (dueño) *lit* master, lord; **el Señor** the Lord; **un gran —** a great man

señora F (dama) lady; (forma de tratamiento) madam, ma'am; (título) Mrs., Ms.; (esposa) wife

señorear VI to dominate

señoría F lordship; **su —** Your Honor

señorial ADJ lordly

señorío M (dominio) dominion; (dignidad) lordship

señorita F miss; **toda una —** quite a young lady

señorito M (joven) master; (dandi) dandy

señuelo M decoy, lure

sepa, sepamos *ver* saber

separación F separation

separado ADJ (apartado) separate; (estado civil) separated; **por —** separately

separar VT (apartar) to separate; (clasificar) to sort out; (despedir de un cargo) to remove; **—se** to separate, to part company

separata F offprint, reprint

septentrional ADJ northern

septicemia F blood poisoning

septiembre, setiembre M September

séptimo ADJ & M seventh

sepulcro M tomb

sepultar VT to bury, to inter

sepultura F (acción) burial; (lugar) grave, tomb; **dar —** to bury

sepulturero -ra MF gravedigger

sequedad F dryness

sequía F drought

séquito M retinue, entourage

ser[65] VI to be; **— de Valencia** to be from Valencia; **— de madera** to be made of wood; **a no — que** unless; **así es** that's right; **érase una vez** once upon a time; **es decir** that is to say; **es de esperar** it is to be expected; **es más** what's more; **la boda es hoy** the wedding takes place today; **son las nueve** it is nine o'clock; **somos cuatro** there are four of us; V AUX to be; **fue elegido presidente** he was elected president; M (entidad viviente) being; (esencia) essence; (existencia) existence; **un — humano** a human being

serbio -bia ADJ Serbian; MF (persona) Serb, Serbian; M (lengua) Serbian
serenar VI to quiet; **—se** (el alma) to become serene, to calm down; (el tiempo) to clear up
serenata F serenade; **dar —** to serenade
serenidad F serenity, peace of mind
sereno ADJ (mar, alma) serene; (cielo) clear; **al —** in the night air; M night watchman
serie F series; **— de instrucciones** (en un programa de computadora) macro; **en —** serial; **— ofensiva** offensive series
seriedad F seriousness, earnestness
serio ADJ (problema) serious; (persona) earnest, serious; **en —** seriously
sermón M (prédica) sermon; (reprimenda) lecture
sermonear VI/VT (predicar) to preach; (reprender) to lecture
serpentear VI to wind, to meander
serpiente F snake
serrado ADJ serrated
serranía F mountainous region
serrano -na M mountain man; F mountain woman; ADJ **zona serrana** mountain region
serrín M sawdust
serrucho M handsaw
servicial ADJ helpful
servicio M (también en tenis) service; (sirvientes) servants; (para un comensal) place setting; (aseo) restroom, facilities; **— a la habitación** room service; **— de ayuda al usuario** helpdesk; **— de contestador** answering service; **— de entrega** delivery service; **— directo** ace; **— militar** military service; **a su —** at your service; **de — pesado** heavy-duty; **estar en —** to be in commission; **poner en —** to commission, to put into service
servidor -ora MF (persona) servant; **un —** yours truly; **su seguro —** yours truly; M (ordenador) server; **— remoto** remote server
servidumbre F servitude
servil ADJ (personalidad) servile; (trabajo) menial
servilleta F napkin
servir[9] VI to serve; **— de** to serve as; **— para** to be used for; **para —le** at your service; **no — para nada** to be of no use; **¿en qué le puedo —?** how can I help you? **—se de** to make use of; **sírvase usted hacerlo** please do it
sésamo M sesame; **¡ábrete —!** open sesame!
sesenta NUM sixty
sesgado ADJ biased
sesgar[40] VT (una tela) to cut on the bias; (una opinión) to slant; (las estadísticas) to skew
sesgo M (en la tela) bias; (de los ojos, de orientación) slant; **al —** obliquely
sesión F (reunión, período) session; (de fotografía) sitting; (de una película) showing; **— de ejercicio** workout
seso M brain; **de poco —** foolish; **devanarse los —s** to rack one's brain
sestear VI to take a nap
sesudo ADJ (persona) brainy; (explicación) intelligent; (testarudo) *Méx* stubborn
set M set
seta F mushroom
setenta NUM seventy
seto M hedge
sétter M setter
seudónimo M pseudonym, pen name
severidad F severity, harshness
severo ADJ severe, stern, harsh
sevillano -na ADJ & MF Sevillian; F PL Sevillian dances
sexar VT to sex
sexismo M sexism
sexista MF sexist
sexo M (género) sex; **el bello —** the fair sex
sexto ADV, ADJ & M sixth
sexual ADJ sexual
sexualidad F sexuality
sexy ADJ sexy
Seychelles F PL Seychelles
SFA [Sistema de frenos antibloqueo] M ABS
shock M shock
short, shorts M shorts
si CONJ if; **yo voy — tú vas** I'm going if you're going; **no sé — viene o no** I don't know whether she's coming or not; **¡— ya te lo dije!** but I already told you! **— bien** although; **por — acaso** just in case; **— Dios quiere** God willing; **— no me equivoco** unless I'm mistaken
sí ADV yes; *fam* yeah; **¿—?** really? **— que fui** I did go; **creo que —** I think so; M consent; **me dio el —** she said yes; PRON himself, herself, itself, oneself, themselves; **de por —** in itself; **estar sobre —** to be on the alert; **volver en —** to come to; **pagado de —** self-satisfied; **estar fuera de —** to be beside oneself; **hablar para —** to talk to oneself; **dio todo de —** she gave her all; **cada cual para —** every man for himself
sicario M hitman
sicomoro M sycamore
SIDA [síndrome de inmunodeficiencia adquirida] M AIDS
siderurgia F steel industry
sidra F cider
siega F (de la hierba) mowing; (de las mieses) reaping
siembra F (acción de sembrar) sowing; (época) sowing time
siempre ADV always; **— nos has apoyado** you've always been very supportive of us; **desde —** since forever; **para/por —** forever;

por — **jamás** forevermore; — **que** (en cualquier momento) whenever; (con tal que) provided that; — **y cuando** provided that; **como** — as usual; **hoy no eres el mismo de** — you're not yourself today

sien F temple

sienta, siente *ver* sentar, sentir

sierpe F *lit* serpent

sierra F (herramienta) saw; (cordillera) small mountain range; — **de cadena** chainsaw

siesta F siesta, afternoon nap; **dormir la** — to take an afternoon nap

siete NUM seven

sífilis F syphilis

sifón M (para líquidos) siphon; (tubo) trap

siga, sigamos *ver* seguir

sigilo M stealth

sigla F acronym

siglo M century

signatario -ria MF signer

significación F (sentido) meaning; (importancia) significance

significado M meaning, sense

significar[30] VT to mean, to signify

significativo ADJ significant, meaningful

signo M sign; — **de admiración** exclamation point; — **de igual** equal sign; — **de interrogación** question mark; — **de más** plus sign; — **de menos** minus sign; — **de multiplicación** multiplication sign; — **s vitales** vital signs

sigo, siguiendo *ver* seguir

siguiente ADJ following; **al día** — the next day

siguiera, siguiese *ver* seguir

sílaba F syllable

silbar VI (soplar aire) to whistle; (rechiflar) to hiss

silbato M whistle (también en fútbol)

silbido M whistle

silenciador M (de arma) silencer; (de coche) muffler

silenciar VT to silence

silencio M silence, quiet; **guardar** — to keep quiet

silenciosamente ADV quietly

silencioso ADJ silent, quiet

silicio M silicon

silla F chair; (de montar) saddle; — **de ruedas** wheelchair; — **eléctrica** electric chair; — **plegadiza** folding chair

sillín M saddle, seat

sillón M (mueble) armchair

silo M silo

silogismo M syllogism

silueta F silhouette

siluro M catfish

silvestre ADJ wild

silvicultura F forestry

sima F chasm

simbiosis F symbiosis

simbólico ADJ symbolic

simbolismo M symbolism

simbolizar[47] VT to symbolize

símbolo M symbol; — **de status** status symbol; — **sexual** sex symbol

simetría F symmetry

simétrico ADJ symmetrical

simiente F seed

símil M simile

similar ADJ similar

similitud F resemblance, similarity

simio M ape

simpatía F friendliness; **no le tengo mucha** — I don't like him much

simpático ADJ (amistoso) nice, friendly, congenial; (sistema nervioso) sympathetic

simpatizante ADJ supporting, sympathizing; MF supporter, sympathizer

simpatizar[47] VI (con alguien) to like; (con una idea) to be sympathetic toward

simple ADJ (no complicado) simple; (mero) mere; (tonto) simpleminded

simplemente ADV simply, merely

simpleza F (sencillez) simplicity; (estupidez) stupidity

simplicidad F simplicity

simplificar[30] VT to simplify

simplista ADJ (intepretación) simplistic; (explicación) glib, simplistic

simplón -ona ADJ simpleminded; MF simpleton

simposio M symposium

simulación F simulation

simulacro M — **de batalla** mock battle; — **de incendio** fire drill

simulador -ora MF simulator; M — **de vuelo** flight simulator

simular VT to simulate, to feign

simultanear VI perform simultaneously

simultáneo ADJ simultaneous

sin PREP without; — **aliento** out of breath; — **amueblar** unfurnished; — **azúcar** sugar-free; — **comentarios** no comment; — **compromiso** without obligation; — **condiciones** unconditionally, with no strings attached; — **culpa** no-fault; — **declarar** unreported; — **derecho** nonvoting; — **duda** without doubt, undoubtedly; — **embargo** nevertheless; — **escrúpulos** unscrupulous; — **excepciones** across the board; — **falta** without fail; — **garantía** unsecured; — **intereses** interest-free; — **lujos** no-frills; — **marcar** unmarked; — **peligro** safely; — **percances** safely; — **problemas** trouble-free; — **receta** over-the-counter; — **restricciones** open-ended; — **riesgo** risk-free; — **seguro médico** uninsured; — **sentido** meaningless

sinagoga F synagogue

sincerarse VI to clear the air, to come clean
sinceridad F sincerity
sincero ADJ (personalidad) sincere; (opinión) candid; (agradecimiento) heartfelt, wholehearted
sincrónico ADJ (proceso) synchronous; (enfoque lingüístico) synchronic
sincronización F timing
sincronizar[47] VT to synchronize
sindical ADJ (relativo al síndico) trustee; (relativo al sindicato) union; **dirigente —** union leader
sindicar[30] VT to unionize, to syndicate
sindicato M (de trabajadores) syndicate, trade union, labor union; (de bancos) syndicate
síndico -ca MF receiver, trustee
síndrome M syndrome; **— de abstinencia** withdrawal symptoms; **— de choque tóxico** toxic shock syndrome; **— de Down** Down's syndrome; **— de muerte infantil súbita** crib death, sudden infant death syndrome
sinergia F synergy
sinfín M **un — de cosas** a lot of things
sinfonía F symphony
Singapur M Singapore
singapurense ADJ & MF Singaporean
singular ADJ (número) singular; (excepcional) unique
siniestro ADJ sinister; M disaster
sinnúmero M myriad
sino CONJ but; **no vino — que llamó** she didn't come but instead called; **no tengo dos — tres** I have not two but three; **no es — madera** it's only wood
sinónimo ADJ synonymous; M synonym
sinopsis F synopsis
sinrazón F injustice
sinsabor M trouble
sinsonte M mockingbird
sintamos *ver* sentir
sintaxis F syntax
síntesis F synthesis; **— de habla** speech synthesis; **— de habla** voice synthesis
sintético ADJ (producto) synthetic; (fibras) man-made
sintetizador M synthesizer
sintetizar[47] VT to synthesize
sintiendo, sintiera, sintiese *ver* sentir
síntoma M symptom
sintonía F tuning; **en —** on the same wavelength
sintonizador M tuner
sintonizar[47] VT (una emisora) to tune in; (un sintonizador) to fine-tune; **los dos sintonizan bien** the two are on the same wavelength
sinuoso ADJ (camino) sinuous, winding; (comportamiento) devious
sinusitis F sinusitis
sinvergüenza MF creep
siquiera ADV at least; **dame — unos días** give me a few days at least; **ni —** not even
sirena F (ninfa, bocina) siren; (mitad mujer, mitad pez) mermaid
Siria F Syria
sirio -ria ADJ & MF Syrian
sirve, sirviendo, sirviera, sirviese *ver* servir
sirviente MF, **sirvienta** F servant
sisar VT to pilfer, to swipe
sisear VI to hiss
siseo M hiss, hissing
sísmico ADJ seismic
sistema M system; **— binario** binary system; **— de asistencia de salud** health care system; **— de cifrado** encryption system; **— de reconocimiento óptico de caracteres** optical character recognition; **— experto** expert system; **— inmune** immune system; **— mundial de posicionamiento** global positioning system; **— nervioso central** central nervous system; **— operativo** operating system; **— solar** solar system
sistemático ADJ systematic
sistematizar[47] VI/VT to systematize
sistémico ADJ systemic
sistólico ADJ systolic
sitial M **— de honor** seat of honor
sitiar VT to besiege
sitio M (espacio vacío) room; (ubicación) place, site; (asedio) siege; **no hay —** there's no room; **esto no está en su —** this is out of place; **— web** website; **poner — a** to lay siege to; **poner a alguien en su —** to put someone in his place
sito ADJ situated
situación F (circunstancia) situation; (legal, financiera, social) status
situado ADJ situated; **estar —** to be located
situar[26] VT to locate, to place; **—se** to be located
sketch M sketch, skit
slalom M slalom
smog M smog
smoking M dinner jacket
so PREP **— pena de** under penalty of; **— pretexto de** under the pretext of; INTERJ whoa; ADV **— tonto** you stupid idiot!
sobaco M armpit
sobar VT (la masa) to knead; (a una persona) to fondle; (un traje) to wear out
soberanía F sovereignty
soberano -na ADJ & MF sovereign
soberbia F pride, haughtiness
soberbio ADJ (orgulloso) proud, haughty; (magnífico) magnificent
sobornar VT to bribe
soborno M (acción) bribery; (mordida) bribe, *fam* payola
sobra F surplus; **—s** leftovers, leavings; **de —**

sabes you know full well; **está de —** it is superfluous; **las piezas de —** spare parts
sobrado ADJ more than enough
sobrante ADJ leftover, remaining; surplus
sobrar VI (dinero, libros) to be left over, to remain; (personas) to be in the way
sobre PREP (encima de) above, over; (en contacto con) on, upon; (acerca de) about; **un préstamo — su coche** a loan on his car; **— todo** above all, especially; **— las 9:30** at about 9:30; **marchar — Madrid** to march toward Madrid; M (para cartas) envelope; (de sopa) packet; **— manila** manila envelope; **irse al —** to hit the sack
sobreactuar[26] VI to ham it up
sobrealimentador M supercharger
sobrecalificado ADJ overqualified
sobrecarga F overload; **— de voltaje** power surge; **— sensorial** sensory overload
sobrecargar[40] VT to overload
sobrecogedor ADJ awesome
sobrecoger[45] VI/VT to awe; **—se** to be in awe; **—se de pánico** to be panic-stricken
sobrecogimiento M awe
sobrecompensar VI to overcompensate
sobrecorrección F overcorrection
sobredosis F overdose
sobreendeudado N debt-ridden
sobreentenderse[2] VI to be understood
sobreentendido ADJ understood; M assumption
sobreestimar VT to overestimate
sobreexcitado ADJ overexcited, wired
sobreexcitar VT to overexcite
sobreextendido ADJ overextended
sobregirar VT to overdraw
sobregiro M overdraft
sobrehumano ADJ superhuman
sobrellevar VT to bear, to endure
sobremanera ADV beyond measure
sobremesa F after-dinner conversation
sobrenadar VI to float
sobrenatural ADJ supernatural
sobrenombre M nickname
sobrepasar VT to exceed
sobrepeso M overweight
sobreponerse[56, 74] VT to superimpose; VI **— a** (valer más que) to outweigh; (recuperarse) to get over
sobreproteger[45] VT to overprotect, to smother
sobrepujar VT to surpass
sobresaliente ADJ outstanding; MF understudy
sobresalir[57] VI (ser notable) to stand out; (estar en un plano más saliente) to project, to jut out; (ser excelente) to excel
sobresaltar VT to startle, frighten; **—se** to be startled, to start
sobresalto M start, scare
sobrestante M foreman
sobresueldo M extra pay
sobretasa F surtax
sobretodo M overcoat
sobrevenir[61] VI to happen unexpectedly
sobrevivencia F survival
sobreviviente MF survivor; ADJ surviving
sobrevivir VI/VT to survive
sobriedad F sobriety
sobrino -na M nephew; F niece; **— nieto** great-nephew; **sobrina nieta** great-niece
sobrio ADJ sober
socarrar VT to singe
socarrón ADJ sarcastic
socarronería F sarcasm
socavar VT (excavar por debajo) to dig under; (debilitar) to undermine, to undercut
socavón M sinkhole; shaft, tunnel
sociable ADJ sociable, gregarious
social ADJ social
socialismo M socialism
socialista ADJ & MF socialist
socializar[47] VT to socialize
sociedad F (grupo humano) society; (firma) company, partnership; **— anónima** corporation; **— de consumo** consumer society; **alta —** high society
socio -cia MF (de una firma) partner; (de un club) member; **— minoritario** minority partner; **— principal** senior partner; **— comercial** trading partner
socioeconómico ADJ socioeconomic
sociología F sociology
sociópata MF sociopath
socorrer VT to help
socorro INTERJ & M help; **acudir al — de** to go to the rescue of; **pedir —** to cry out for help
soda F soda
sodio M sodium
sodomía F sodomy
soez ADJ vulgar
sofá M sofa, couch; **— -cama** sleeper, sofa bed
sofisma M fallacy
sofisticado ADJ sophisticated
sofocante ADJ suffocating, oppressive
sofocar[30] VI/VT (ahogar) to suffocate; (una rebelión) to quash, to quell, to suppress; (un incendio) to put out
sofoco M suffocation
softball M softball
software M software; **— de fuente abierta** open source software
soga F rope; **estar con la — al cuello** to have a rope around one's neck
sois *ver* ser
soja F (planta) soy; (semilla) soybean
sojuzgar[40] VT to subjugate, to subdue
sol M sun; **de — a —** from sunrise to sunset; **hace —** it is sunny; **tomar el —** to sunbathe; **ella es un —** she's a gem; **arrimarse al —**

que más calienta to know which side one's bread is buttered on
solamente ADV only, solely
solana F sunny place
solapa F lapel
solapado ADJ underhanded
solar M (terreno) lot; (casa ancestral) manor; ADJ solar
solaz M *lit* recreation
soldado -da MF soldier; **— raso** private; **— de línea** regular soldier
soldador M soldering iron
soldadura F (acción de adherir con estaño) soldering; (resultado) solder; (acción de adherir sin estaño) welding; (resultado) weld; **— autógena** arc welding
soldar[5] VI/VT (con estaño) to solder; (sin estaño) to weld; **—se** to mend
soleado ADJ sunny
solear VT to put in the sun; **—se** to sun oneself
soledad F solitude, loneliness
solemne ADJ solemn; **— disparate** downright foolishness
solemnidad F solemnity
solenoide M solenoid
soler[6, 73] VI **suelo levantarme a las siete** I usually get up at seven; **solía acostarme tarde** I used to go to bed late; **no suele importarle** he usually doesn't mind
solferino ADJ reddish-purple
solicitante MF applicant
solicitar VT (permiso) to request; (un puesto, una beca) to apply for
solícito ADJ solicitous
solicitud F (para beca, puesto) application; (de información, permiso) request; **— de préstamo** loan application; **a — de** at the request of
solidaridad F solidarity
solidario ADJ supportive, sympathetic
solidez F solidity
solidificar[30] VT to solidify
sólido ADJ (materia) solid; (mueble) sturdy; (argumento) strong; M solid
solista MF soloist
solitario -ria ADJ solitary; MF (persona) recluse; M (juego de cartas, brillante) solitaire; F tapeworm
sollozar[47] VI to sob
sollozo M sob
solo ADJ (desamparado) lonely, lonesome; (no acompañado) alone; **tengo un — coche** I have only one car; **a solas** alone; **habla solo** he talks to himself; **ni una sola palabra** not a single word; ADV just, only; **— quiero saber** I just/only want to know; M solo
solomillo M sirloin
solsticio M solstice
soltar[5] VT (a un prisionero) to let go, to release; (el vientre) to loosen; (una carcajada) to let out; (bombas) to drop; (un disparate) to say; **— amarras** to cast off; **— el hervor** to come to a boil; **— tacos** to swear; **—se** to loosen up; **—se el pelo** to kick up one's heels
soltero -ra ADJ single, unmarried; M bachelor; F unmarried woman
solterón -ona M old bachelor; F *pey* spinster
soltura F ease; **hablar con —** to speak fluently
soluble ADJ soluble
solución F solution; **— salina** saline solution
solucionar VT to solve
solventar VT to settle
solvente ADJ & M solvent
somalí ADJ & MF Somalian
Somalia F Somalia
sombra F (de una figura) shadow; (protección del sol) shade; (para ojos) eye shadow; **hacer —** to overshadow; **dar —** to shade; **no fiarse ni de su propia —** to be scared of one's own shadow; **a la —** in the shade; **sin — de duda** without a shadow of a doubt
sombreado ADJ (protegido del sol) shady; (oscuro) shadowy
sombrear VT to shade
sombrerería F millinery
sombrerero -ra MF milliner
sombrero M hat; **— de copa** top hat; **— hongo** derby
sombrilla F parasol
sombrío ADJ (oscuro) dark; (triste) somber, gloomy
somero ADJ (agua) shallow; (discusión) superficial
someter VT (proponer algo) to submit; (poner bajo dominio) to subject; **—se a** to undergo
sometimiento M (propuesta) submission; (dominio) subjection
somnífero M sleeping pill
somnolencia F drowsiness, sleepiness
somnoliento ADJ drowsy
somos *ver* ser
son M sound; LOC ADV **al — de** to the sound of; **venimos en — de paz** we come in peace
son *ver* ser
sonaja F rattle
sonajero M rattle
sonámbulo -la MF sleepwalker
sonar[5] VI (hacer un sonido) to sound; (mencionarse) to be mentioned; (ser familiar) to sound familiar; **— a** to sound like; VT (bocina) to sound; (tambor) to beat; (campana, timbre) to ring; **—se la nariz / los mocos** to blow one's nose; **suena que** it is rumored that; M sonar
sonda F (de médico) catheter; (cohete) probe; **— de alimentación** feeding tube; **tirar una —** to sound
sondear VT (medir la oportunidad) to sound, to

fathom; (investigar la opinión) to sound out
sondeo M survey
soneto M sonnet
sonido M sound
sonoridad F (de la voz) sonority; (de un instrumento) tone; (de un sonido lingüístico) voicing
sonoro ADJ sonorous
sonreír[10] VI to smile
sonriente ADJ smiling
sonrisa F smile
sonrojarse VI to blush
sonrojo M blush, flush
sonrosado ADJ rosy
sonsacar[30] VT to extract
soñador -ora MF dreamer
soñar[5] VI/VT to dream; **—con** to dream of; **—despierto** to daydream; **—que** to dream that; **ni —** *fam* fat chance
soñoliento ADJ sleepy
sopa F (líquido) soup; (pan mojado) sop; **estar hecho una —** to be sopping wet; **—crema** cream soup
sopapo M smack
sopera F soup tureen
sopesar VT to weigh
sopetón LOC ADV **de —** all of a sudden
soplador -ora MF blower
soplar VI/VT (el viento) to blow; (la sopa) to blow on; (en un examen) to whisper the answers
soplete M blowtorch
soplo M breath, puff; **en un —** in a jiffy; **—cardíaco** heart murmur
soplón -ona MF informer, snitch, stool pigeon
sopor M lethargy
soportar VT (un peso) to support, to bear; (una molestia, a una persona) to stand, to bear; (un programa de computadora) to support
soporte M (de un peso, de un programa) support; (de una bicicleta) kickstand; **—técnico** technical support
soprano M (voz) soprano; F (cantante) soprano
sorber VI/VT to sip; **—se los mocos** to sniffle
sorbete M sherbet
sorbo M sip; **de un —** in one gulp
sordera F deafness
sórdido ADJ sordid, tawdry, sleazy
sordina F mute
sordo -da ADJ (persona) deaf; (dolor) dull; (sonido) dull, muffled; **hacer oídos —s** to turn a deaf ear; MF deaf person; **hacerse el —** to pretend not to hear
sordomudo -da ADJ deaf and dumb; MF deaf-mute
sorna F irony
sorprendente ADJ surprising, startling
sorprendentemente ADV surprisingly
sorprender VT to surprise; **—se** to be surprised
sorpresa F surprise; **— de cumpleaños** party favor; **para mi —** to my surprise; **pillar por —** to catch by surprise
sortear VT (elegir al azar) to draw lots, to raffle; (esquivar) to dodge
sorteo M drawing, raffle
sortija F (anillo) ring; (de pelo) ringlet
sortilegio M spell, charm
SOS M SOS
sosa F soda
sosegado ADJ composed, sedate
sosegar[41] VT to calm, to quiet; **—se** to quiet down, to compose oneself
sosiego M quiet, calm
soslayo LOC ADV **de —** oblique, slanting; **mirar de —** to look out of the corner of one's eye
soso ADJ (comida) tasteless, insipid; (persona) dull
sospecha F suspicion
sospechar VT to suspect
sospechoso -sa ADJ suspicious; MF suspect
sostén M (apoyo, sustento) support, prop; (persona que sostiene) supporter, provider; (prenda) brassiere; **— de la familia** breadwinner
sostendrá, sostendría *ver* sostener
sostener[58] VT (una nota musical) to hold, to sustain; (una familia) to support; (un peso) to support, to hold; (una opinión) to claim, to uphold
sostenga, sostengo *ver* sostener
sostenible ADJ sustainable
sostenido ADJ sustained; M sharp
sostiene, sostienes, sostuve, sostuviera, sostuviese *ver* sostener
sota F jack, knave
sótano M cellar, basement
soto M thicket
soy *ver* ser
soya F (semilla) soybean; (planta) soy
squash M squash
Sr. M Mr.
Sra. F (casada) Mrs.; (sin indicación de estado civil) Ms.
S.R.C. [se ruega contestar] LOC RSVP
status M status
stop M stop sign
su ADJ POS (de él) his; (de ella) her; (de usted, ustedes) your; (de ellos, ellas) their
suave ADJ (pelo, piel) soft; (tiempo, droga) mild; (brisa, persona, animal) gentle; (coñac) smooth; **hablan —** they speak gently
suavemente ADV lightly, gently
suavidad F (de pelo, piel) softness; (de coñac) smoothness; (de tiempo, droga) mildness; (de brisa, persona, animal) gentleness
suavizante M fabric softener
suavizar[47] VT to soften
suazi ADJ & MF Swazi
Suazilandia F Swaziland

subalterno -na ADJ & MF subordinate
subarrendar VI/VT to sublet
subasta F auction
subastador -ora MF auctioneer
subastar VT to sell at auction, to auction
subcomité M subcommittee
subconsciente ADJ subconscious
subcontratar VT to subcontract, to contract out, to farm out
subdesarrollado ADJ underdeveloped
súbdito -ta MF subject
subdividir VT subdivide
subdivisión F subdivision
subempleado ADJ underemployed
subestimar VT to underestimate
subgerente MF assistant manager
subida F (de precios, de río) rise; (de montaña) climb; (de drogas) high; (cuesta) slope; **—s y bajadas** ups and downs
subido ADJ (color) bright; **— de tono** risqué
subíndice M subscript
subir VI (los precios) to rise, to go up; (la marea) to surge; (a un tren) to board; (a un autobús, coche) to get into; VT (algo del sótano) to bring up; (una montaña) to climb; (precios) to raise; **— a la red** to upload; **—se** to ride up; **el vino se me sube a la cabeza** wine goes to my head; M **subibaja** seesaw
súbitamente ADV suddenly
súbito ADJ sudden
subjetividad F subjectivity
subjetivo ADJ subjective
subjuntivo ADJ & M subjunctive
sublevación F revolt
sublevar VT (instigar) to incite to rebellion; (indignar) to infuriate; **—se** to revolt
sublime ADJ sublime
submarino ADJ underwater; M submarine
suboficial M noncomissioned officer
subordinado -da ADJ & MF subordinate
subordinar VT to subordinate
subproducto M by-product
subproletariado M underclass
subrayado ADJ underlined; M underscore, underlining
subrayar VT (con una línea) to underline, to underscore; (enfatizar) to emphasize, to underscore
subrepticio ADJ surreptitious
subrutina F subroutine
subsanar VT (una deficiencia) to remedy; (un error) to correct
subsecretario -ia MF undersecretary; **— de justicia** solicitor general
subsidiar VT to subsidize
subsidiario ADJ subsidiary
subsidio M subsidy
subsiguiente ADJ subsequent
subsistencia F survival
subsistir VI to subsist, to survive
subteniente MF second lieutenant
subterfugio M subterfuge
subterráneo ADJ subterranean, underground; M subway
subtítulo M (de un capítulo, película) subtitle; (pie de foto) caption
subtotal M subtotal
suburbano -na ADJ of shantytowns; MF shantytown resident
suburbio M shantytown
subvaluar[26] VT to underestimate
subvención F subsidy
subvencionar VT to subsidize
subversivo ADJ subversive
subyacente ADJ underlying
subyacer[37] VI to underlie
subyugar[40] VT (dominar) to subjugate; (hechizar) to charm
succión F suction
sucedáneo -a ADJ & MF substitute
suceder VI to happen, to occur; **— al trono** to succeed to the throne; VT to succeed
sucesión F (herencia, secuencia) succession; (heredero) descendant
sucesivo ADJ successive; **en lo —** in the future
suceso M (evento) event, occurrence; (incidente) incident
sucesor -ora MF successor
suciedad F (porquería) dirt, filth; (cualidad de sucio) filthiness
sucinto ADJ concise
sucio ADJ (baño, ropa) dirty, filthy; (trabajo, chiste) dirty; (conciencia) guilty; **blanco —** off-white; **este traje es —** this suit gets dirty easily
sucumbir VI to succumb
sucursal F branch, subsidiary
sudadera F sweatshirt
sudado ADJ sweaty
Sudáfrica F South Africa
sudafricano -na ADJ & MF South African
Sudamérica F South America
sudamericano -na ADJ & MF South American
Sudán M Sudan
sudanés -esa ADJ & MF Sudanese
sudar VT to sweat; **— la gota gorda** to sweat blood
sudeste ADJ southeast, southeastern; M southeast
sudoeste ADJ southwest, southwestern; M southwest
sudor M sweat
sudoración F sweating
sudoroso ADJ sweaty
Suecia F Sweden
sueco -ca ADJ Swedish; M (lengua) Swedish; MF Swede; **hacerse el —** to pretend not to understand

suegro -a M father-in-law; F mother-in-law
suela F (de zapato) sole; (pez) flounder
suela, suele *ver* soler
sueldo M salary
suelo M (tierra) soil, ground; (piso) floor; **arrastrar por el —** to drag; **por los —s** at rock-bottom
suelta, suelte *ver* soltar
suelto ADJ (no atado) loose, unattached; (flojo) loose; (libre) free; M loose change
suena, suene *ver* sonar
sueña, sueñe *ver* soñar
sueño M (acto de dormir) sleep; (acto de soñar) dream; (ganas de dormir) sleepiness; **en —s** dreaming; **conciliar el —** to get to sleep; **tener —** to be sleepy; **ni en —[s]** never; **perder el —** to lose sleep; **— profundo** sound sleep; **estar en el séptimo —** to be deeply asleep
suero M serum; **— de leche** buttermilk; **— fisiológico** saline solution
suerte F (destino) fate; (fortuna) luck; (clase) kind; **de —** in luck; **dejar a su —** to leave to his own devices; **echar —s** to cast lots; **mala —** (desgracia) bad luck; (lo siento) too bad; **tener —** to be lucky; **tentar a la —** to court danger; **tocarle algo en — a alguien** to be one's lot
suertudo -da ADJ lucky; MF lucky devil
suéter M sweater
suficiencia F adequacy; **¡tiene una —!** she's so arrogant!
suficiente ADJ (adecuado) sufficient, adequate; (arrogante) smug; M (calificación mínima) lowest passing grade; PRON enough; **ser —** to be enough; **tiempo más que —** ample time
sufijo M suffix
sufragar[40] VT to defray; **— los gastos** to meet the expenses
sufragio M suffrage
sufrido ADJ (madre) long-suffering; (tela) durable
sufrimiento M suffering
sufrir VI/VT (pasar apremios) to suffer; VT (soportar) to stand; (una lesión) to sustain; (un cambio) to undergo; (una pena) to grieve; **— de** to suffer from; **— de los pies** to have foot pains
sugerencia F suggestion
sugerir[8] VT to suggest
sugestión F suggestion
sugiere, sugirió, sugiriendo, sugiriera, sugiriese *ver* sugerir
suicida MF suicide [victim]
suicidarse VI to commit suicide
suicidio M suicide
suite F suite
Suiza F Switzerland
suizo -za ADJ & MF Swiss; M sweet roll
sujeción LOC ADV **con — a** subject to
sujetar VT (fijar) to attach; (unir) to hold; (someter) to subdue, to hold down; **—se** to hold on; M SG **sujetalibros** bookend; M SG **sujetapapeles** paper clip
sujeto ADJ held by; **— a** subject to; M (de oración, de experimento) subject; (individuo) individual
sulfato M sulfate
sulfurarse VI to hit the roof
sulfúrico ADJ sulfuric
sulfuro M sulfide
suma F (resultado aritmético) sum; (operación aritmética) addition; (cantidad) amount, sum; **en —** in sum
sumadora F adding machine
sumamente ADV extremely
sumar VT to add, to add up; **—se a** to join
sumario M brief; ADJ summary
sumergible ADJ waterproof
sumergir[46] VT to submerge, to dip; **—se** to dive; **—se en** to immerse oneself in
sumidero M (socavón) sinkhole; (desagüe) drain
suministrar VT to furnish, to supply with
suministro M provision, supply; **— de energía** power supply; **—s** supplies, provisions
sumir VT to immerse
sumisión F submission
sumiso ADJ submissive
súmmum M ultimate, acme; **el — de la moda** the cat's meow
sumo ADJ utmost, paramount; **a lo —** at the most
suntuoso ADJ sumptuous, luxurious
supe, supiera, supiese *ver* saber
súper ADJ & ADV super; F (gasolina) high-octane gasoline; M (supermercado) supermarket
superabundancia F overabundance, glut
superación F (de expectativas) surpassing; (de límites) exceeding; (de un récord) breaking; (de una dificultad) overcoming
superar VT (las expectativas) to surpass; (un límite) to exceed; (una dificultad) to overcome, to surmount; (una prueba) to pass; (a un rival) to outdo; **—se** to improve oneself
superávit M surplus
supercomputadora F supercomputer
superdirecta F overdrive
superdotado ADJ gifted
superego M superego
superestrella F superstar
superficial ADJ (conocimiento, herida, persona) superficial; (persona) shallow
superficialidad F shallowness
superficie F (parte exterior) surface; (de una figura geométrica) area
superfluo ADJ superfluous
superíndice M superscript

superintendente MF superintendent
superior ADJ (mejor) superior; (más alto) higher; (más grande, intenso) greater; MF superior
superioridad F superiority
superlativo ADJ & M superlative
supermercado M supermarket
superordenador M supercomputer
superponer[56, 74] VT to superimpose
superpotencia F superpower
superproducción F overproduction
supersónico ADJ supersonic
superstición F superstition
supersticioso ADJ superstitious
supervisar VT to supervise
supervisión F supervision
supervisor -ora MF supervisor
supervivencia F survival; **la — del más apto** the survival of the fittest
superviviente ADJ surviving; MF survivor
superyó M superego
supino ADJ supine
suplantar VT to supplant
suplementar VT to supplement
suplementario ADJ supplemental
suplemento M supplement
suplente ADJ & MF substitute
súplica F entreaty, plea
suplicar[30] VT to plead, to beseech
suplicio M ordeal
suplir VT (sustituir) to substitute for; (compensar) to make up for
supondrá, supondría *ver* suponer
suponer[56, 74] VT (dar por sentado) to suppose, to presume, to surmise; (implicar) to involve; **es de — que ya esté preparado** presumably he's already prepared
suponga, supongo *ver* suponer
suposición F supposition, surmise
supositorio M suppository
supremacía F supremacy
supremo ADJ supreme
supresión F (de una idea) suppression; (de una palabra) deletion
suprimir VT (una idea) to suppress; (la esclavitud) to abolish; (una palabra) to delete
supuestamente ADV supposedly, allegedly
supuesto ADJ (hipotético) supposed; (alegado) alleged, ostensible; **dar por —** to assume; **por —** of course; M supposition, assumption
supuesto *ver* suponer
supuración F discharge
supurante ADJ festering, running
supurar VI to fester, to discharge
supuse, supusiera, supusiese *ver* suponer
sur ADJ & M south; **hacia el —** southward; **rumbo al —** southward
surcar[30] VT to plow
surco M (en la tierra) furrow; (en un camino) rut; (en un disco) groove; (en el rostro) wrinkle
surcoreano -na ADJ & MF South Korean
sureño -ña ADJ southern; MF southerner
sureste ADJ southeast, southeastern; M southeast
surfear VI/VT to surf (también en el internet)
surfing M surfing; **hacer —** to surf
surgimiento M rise
surgir[46] VI (situación) to arise; (manantial) to rise; (problema) to emerge, to crop up
Surinam M Surinam, Suriname
surinamés -esa ADJ & MF Surinamer
surmenage M burnout
suroeste ADJ southwest, southwestern; M southwest
surrealismo M surrealism
surrealista ADJ surreal, surrealistic; MF surrealist
surtido M stock, assortment; ADJ assorted
surtidor M (bomba) pump; (chorro, pieza de carburador) jet
surtir VT to provide; **— efecto** to produce the desired effect; **— un pedido** to fill an order
susceptible ADJ susceptible
suscitar VT to stir up
suscribir[74] VT (una opinión) to subscribe to, to endorse; (un seguro) to underwrite; **—se a** to subscribe to
suscripción F subscription
suscriptor -ora MF (de un revista) subscriber; (en el mercado de acciones) underwriter
susodicho ADJ above-mentioned
suspender VT (colgar) to suspend, to hang; (interrumpir) to suspend, to stop; (cancelar) to cancel; (castigar) to suspend; VI/VT (no aprobar) to fail, to flunk
suspense M suspense
suspensión F suspension
suspenso ADJ hanging; **quedarse —** to freeze; M (en un examen) failure; (en una película) suspense; **en —** in suspense
suspensorio M jock [strap]
suspicaz ADJ suspicious
suspirar VT to sigh; **— por** to yearn for
suspiro M sigh
sustancia F substance; **— peligrosa** hazardous substance
sustancial ADJ substantial
sustancioso ADJ substantial
sustantivo M noun; ADJ substantive
sustentable ADJ sustainable
sustentar VT to sustain
sustento M (alimento) sustenance; (apoyo) support; **ganarse el —** to earn a living
sustitución F substitution; **— protésica de la cadera** hip replacement
sustituible ADJ replaceable
sustituir[19] VI/VT to substitute for, to replace; **Juan sustituyó a María** John substituted

for Mary; **sustituí la leche por agua** I replaced the milk with water

sustituto -ta MF substitute

sustituya, sustituye, sustituyendo, sustituyera, sustituyese *ver* sustituir

susto M scare, fright

sustracción F subtraction

sustraer[59] VT to take away; **—se a** to avoid

susurrar VI/VT (una persona, el viento) to whisper; (agua) to murmur, to ripple; (hojas) to rustle

susurro M (de una persona, del viento) whisper; (del agua) murmur; (de las hojas) rustle

sutil ADJ subtle

sutileza F (delicadeza) subtlety; (fineza excesiva) nicety, quibble

sutilizar[47] VT to quibble over

sutura F suture

suyo ADJ & PRON POS (de él) his; (de ella) her; (de usted, de ustedes) your; (de ellos, de ellas) their; PRON (de él) his; (de ella) hers; (de usted, de ustedes) yours; (de ellos, de ellas) theirs; **salirse con la suya** to get one's own way; **hacer de las suyas** to be up to one's tricks; **los —s** his/her/your/their family

swing M swing

Tt

tabaco M tobacco

tábano M horsefly

tabaquismo M smoking

taberna F tavern, saloon

tabernero -ra MF bartender

tabicar[30] VT to partition

tabique M partition

tabla F (madera) board, plank; (teatro) stage; (pliegue) pleat; (gráfica) table, chart; **— de surf** surfboard; **— de planchar** ironing board; **—s** (escenario) stage; **—s de la ley** the tables of the law; **—s de multiplicar** multiplication tables; **— periódica** periodic table; **— de contenidos** table of contents; **— de cortar** cutting board; **hacer —s** to tie

tablado M stage

tablero M (para juegos de mesa) board; (de instrumentos) panel, instrument panel; (de coche) dashboard; (pizarra) blackboard; (para noticias) bulletin board; **— de mando** control panel

tableta F (de aspirina) tablet; (de chocolate) bar

tablilla F (de arcilla) tablet; (de cama) slat; (para fracturas) splint

tabloide M tabloid

tablón M plank

tabú M taboo

tabulador M tab

tabular VT (en una tabla, planilla) to tabulate, to chart; (en la computadora) to tab

taburete M stool, footstool

TAC [tomografía axial computarizada] F CAT scan

tacañería F stinginess, tightness

tacaño -ña ADJ stingy, miserly; MF miser, penny-pincher

tacha F (mancha visible) blemish; (al honor) blot

tachado M strikethrough

tachar VT (borrar) to cross out, to delete; (acusar) to accuse of

tachón M crossing out

tachonar VT to stud

tachuela F tack, thumbtack

tácito ADJ tacit

taciturno ADJ taciturn

taco M (de artillería) wad; (palo de billar) billiard cue; (comida ligera) snack; (palabrota) swear word; (comida) *Méx* taco; **—s** (en el zapato) cleats; **soltar —s** *Esp* to swear

tacómetro M tachometer

tacón M heel

taconear VI to click one's heels

taconeo M clicking

táctica F tactic

táctil ADJ tactile

tacto M (acción de tocar) touch; (sentido) sense of touch; (diplomacia) tact; **con mucho —** gently

TAE [tasa anual equivalente] F APR

tahúr -ura MF gambler

tailandés -esa ADJ & MF Thai, Thailander

Tailandia F Thailand

taimado ADJ sly, devious

Taiwán M Taiwan

taiwanés -esa ADJ & MF Taiwanese

tajada F (de pan, jamón) slice; (de carne) slab; **sacar —** to take one's cut

tajante ADJ (inequívoco) unequivocal; (cortante) sharp

tajar VT to slice

tajear VI/VT to slash

tajo M (corte) slash, hack; (cañón) gorge; (separación) gap

tal ADJ such; **— cual** just so; **— vez** perhaps; **un — García** a certain García; **a — grado** to such an extent; **de — palo — astilla** a chip off the old block; **en — caso** in such a case; CONJ **— como** like, just as; **con — [de] que** provided that; ADV **¿qué —?** how is it going? PRON **y —** and so on; **como si —** as if nothing had happened

taladrar VT to bore, to drill

taladro M drill

talante M temperament

talar VT (un árbol) to chop down; (un bosque) to

lumber
talco M talcum
talento M talent
talentoso ADJ talented, gifted
talismán M charm
talla F (altura) height; (moral, intelectual) stature; (de ropa) size; (de madera) carving
tallado M carving
tallar VT (piedra) to carve; (madera) to whittle, to carve; (naipes) to deal
tallarín M noodle
talle M (cintura) waist, waistline; **tiene buen —** she has a good figure; **corto de —** short-waisted
taller M (para trabajo manual, enseñanza artística, congresos) workshop; (de artista plástico) studio; (de mecánico) garage, shop
tallo M stalk, stem
talón M (de pie, calcetín) heel; (de cheque) stub; **— de Aquiles** Achilles' heel; **girar sobre los talones** to turn on one's heels; **pisarle los talones a alguien** to be hot on someone's heels
talonario M checkbook
talonear VI to walk briskly
tamal M tamale
tamaño M size; **de — mediano** medium-sized; **de — natural** life-sized; ADJ such a big, so big a; **tamaña injusticia** such a big injustice
tambalearse VI (un borracho) to stagger; (un boxeador) to reel; (un viejo) to dodder; (un objeto) to wobble
tambaleo M stagger
también ADV also, too, as well; **este — me gusta** I like this one too, I like this one as well, I also like this one
tambor M (instrumento musical, pieza de máquina) drum; (músico) drummer; (cilindro) cylinder; **a — batiente** with fanfare
tamborilear VI to drum, to tap
tamborilero -ra MF drummer
tamiz M sieve
tamizar[47] VT to sift
tampoco CONJ either; **no lo hizo —** he did not do it either; **ni yo —** me either/neither
tampón M tampon
tan ADV **es — rica** she is so rich; **— alto como Juan** as tall as Juan; **— pronto como** as soon as; **es — idiota** he's such an idiot; **vecinos — simpáticos** such nice neighbors
tanda F (de personas) group; (de galletas) batch; (de ejercicios) set
tándem M tandem
tanga F thong
tangente ADJ & F tangent; **salirse por la —** (irse de tema) to go off on a tangent; (evadir) to beat around the bush
tangerina F tangerine
tangible ADJ tangible
tango M tango
tanque M tank
tantán M African drum
tantear VT (calcular) to estimate roughly; (averiguar) to sound out, to feel out; (apuntar) to score; (palpar) to grope
tanteo M (cálculo) estimate; (número de tantos) score; **al —** approximately
tanto ADJ, PRON, & ADV **lloró — que se le enrojecieron los ojos** he cried so much his eyes got red; **yo tengo — como tú** I have as much as you do; **me quiere —** he loves me so; **no te quiero —** I don't love you that much; **a cada —s pasos** every so many steps; **cuarenta y —s** forty-odd; **a — el kilo** at so much per kilo; **el — por ciento** at such and such a percentage; **estar al —** to be in the know; **no es para —** it's not such a big deal; **— da** it's all the same; **— como** as much as; **— en la ciudad como en el campo** both in the city and in the country; **entre/mientras —** meanwhile; **mantenerse al —** to stay informed; **otros —s** just so many more; **por lo —** therefore; **a las tantas** until late at night; M (en los deportes) point
Tanzania F Tanzania
tanzano -na ADJ & MF Tanzanian
tañer[15] VT *lit* (una guitarra) to play; VI (una campana) to ring, to toll
tañido M (de guitarra) twang; (de campanas) toll
tapa F (de botella) cap; (de libro) cover; (de coche) hood; (de olla, bote) lid, top; *Esp* (comida) bar snack
tapadera F (de recipiente) lid; (de un fraude) cover
tapado ADJ stuffy
tapar VT (una olla) to cover; (una salida) to block; (un caño) to plug up, to stop up; (encubrir) to cover up for; M SG **tapacubos** hubcap; M SG **tapajuntas** flashing; M SG **taparrabos** loincloth
tapete M runner
tapia F garden wall
tapiar VT to board up
tapicería F (para paredes) tapestry; (para muebles) upholstery; (tienda de textiles de decoración) tapestry shop; (arte) tapestry making; (tienda de textiles para muebles) upholstery shop
tapioca F tapioca
tapir M tapir
tapiz M (para pared) tapestry, wall hanging; (para muebles) upholstery
tapizar[47] VT to upholster
tapón M (de botella) stopper; (de lavabo) plug; (de corcho) cork; (en baloncesto) block; **— de oído** earplug; **tapones** (en el zapato de fútbol) cleats

taponar VT (baloncesto) to block
taponazo M pop of a cork
taquigrafía F shorthand
taquígrafo -fa MF stenographer
taquilla F ticket office, box office
tarambana MF knucklehead
tarántula F tarantula
tararear VI/VT to hum
tarareo M hum, humming
tarascada F (mordedura) snap, bite; (réplica) rude answer
tardanza F lateness
tardar VI to take time; **¿cuánto tarda el trámite de divorcio?** how long does it take to get divorced? — **se** to take a long time; **tu padre se tarda** your father is taking a long time; **a más** — at the latest
tarde F (después del almuerzo) afternoon; (hacia el anochecer) evening; **buenas** — **s** good afternoon; ADV late; **ya es** — it is late; — **o temprano** sooner o later; **más** — later on; **llegar** — to be late
tardío ADJ late
tardo ADJ *lit* slow
tarea F (trabajo) task, chore; (escolar) homework
tarifa F (impuesto) tariff; (lista de precios) list of prices; (de transporte) fare; (precio estipulado) rate
tarima F platform
tarjeta F card (también dispositivo de computadora); — **amarilla** yellow card; — **bancaria** bank card; — **comercial** business card; — **de circuito integrado** smart card; — **de sonido** sound card; — **gráfica** graphics card; — **inteligente** smart card; — **postal** postcard; — **de cobro automático /** — **de débito** debit card; — **de crédito** credit card; — **de Navidad** Christmas card; — **roja** red card; **marcar** — to punch in
tarro M jar
tarta F tart, pie
tartajear VI to stutter
tartamudear VI to stutter, to stammer
tartamudeo M stammer, stutter
tartamudez F stuttering
tartamudo -da MF stutterer, stammerer; ADJ stuttering, stammering
tártaro M tartar
tartera F round baking pan
tarugo M (trozo de madera) piece of wood; (tonto) blockhead
tasa F (índice) rate; (impuesto) tax; — **de desempleo** unemployment rate; — **de interés** interest rate; — **de mortalidad** death rate; — **de natalidad** birth rate; — **de ocupación** occupancy rate; — **de paro** unemployment rate; — **prima** prime rate
tasación F valuation, appraisal
tasajo M jerky
tasar VT to appraise, to assess
tatarabuelo -la M great-great-grandfather; F great-great-grandmother
tataranieto -ta M great-great-grandson; F great-great-granddaughter
tatuaje M tattoo
tatuar[26] VT to tattoo
tauromaquia F bullfighting
taxi M taxi, taxicab
taxidermia F taxidermy
taxista MF taxi driver, cab driver
taxonomía F taxonomy
Tayikistán M Tajikistan
tayiko -ka ADJ & MF Tajik
taza F (de té, café) cup; (del inodoro) bowl
tazón M (para beber) mug; (para comer) bowl
té M (bebida) tea; (fiesta) tea party
te PRON PERS you; **yo** — **amo** I love you; — **digo mañana** I'll tell you tomorrow; **no** — **mires en el espejo** don't look at yourself in the mirror
teatral ADJ theatrical
teatro M theater; — **de títeres** puppet show; **no hagas** — don't make such a production
techado M (techo) roof; (acción de techar) roofing
techar VT to roof
techo M (exterior) roof; (interior) ceiling; — **de cristal** glass ceiling
techumbre F roof
tecla F key; — **de alt** alt key; — **de alternativa gráfica** alt gr key; — **de borrado** delete key; — **de cambio** shift key; — **de comando** command key; — **de control** control key; — **de escape** escape key; — **de fin** end key; — **de función** function key; — **de mayúsculas** shift key; — **de ordenación** sort key; — **de reinicio** reset key; — **de retorno** return key; — **de retroceso** backspace key, return key; — **de tabulación** tab key; — **fin** end key; **dar uno en la** — to hit the nail on the head
teclado M keyboard; — **numérico** keypad
teclear VT (pulsar las teclas) to key in, to type; (hacer ruido) to click
tecleo M keying in, clicking
técnica F (método) technique; (tecnología) technology
técnico -ca ADJ technical; MF (en mecánica) technician; (de fútbol) coach
tecnología F technology; — **de punta** cutting-edge technology
tecnológico ADJ technological
tectónica F tectonics
tedio M boredom
tedioso ADJ tedious
tee M tee
teja F (de cerámica) tile; (de madera u otros materiales) shingle

tejado M roof
tejar M tile factory; VT to cover with tiles
tejedor -ora MF weaver
tejer VI/VT (cesta, tela) to weave; (suéter) to knit; M **tejemaneje** (fraude) hanky-panky; (actividad) goings-on
tejido M (tela) textile, fabric; (de células) tissue; (acción de hilar) weaving; (acción y efecto de tejer) knitting
tejo M disk
tejón M badger
tela F (paño) cloth, fabric; (lienzo para pintar) canvas; (de araña) web; (dinero) money; — **adhesiva** adhesive tape; — **de cebolla** onion skin; **en** — hardbound; **poner en** — **de juicio** to call into question
telar M loom
telaraña F cobweb, spider's web
tele F TV
telebobo -ba MF couch potato
telecomunicación F telecommunication
teleconferencia F teleconference
teledifusión F telecast
teledirección F remote guidance
teleférico M cable car
telefonazo M buzz, ring
telefonear VI/VT to telephone, to phone
telefónico ADJ **llamada telefónica** telephone call
telefonista MF telephone operator
teléfono M (aparato) telephone, phone; (número) telephone number
telegrafiar[28] VI/VT to telegraph, to wire
telegráfico ADJ telegraphic
telégrafo M telegraph
telegrama M telegram
telemarketing M telemarketing
telemercadeo M telemarketing
telémetro M range finder
telenovela F soap opera
teleobjetivo M zoom lens
telepatía F telepathy
telescopio M telescope
telespectador -ora MF viewer
telesquí M ski lift
teletipo M Teletype™
teletrabajo M telecommuting
televidente MF television viewer
televisar VT to televise
televisión F television; — **de alta definición** high-definition television
televisivo ADJ (apto para la televisión) televisable; (relativo a la televisión) television
televisor M television set; — **a/en color** color television
telón M theater curtain; — **de acero** iron curtain
tema M (de una obra literaria, musical) theme; (de conversación) topic, subject; (de un CD) song, track
temario M agenda
temático ADJ thematic
temblar[1] VI (la mano, la tierra) to tremble; (la voz) to shake, to quaver; (de frío) to shiver; (de miedo) to shudder; (la luz) to flicker
temblequear VI to dodder
temblón ADJ trembling
temblor M (acción de temblar) trembling; (de tierra) tremor; (de una llama) flicker; (de la voz) quaver; (de frío) shiver; (de miedo) shudder; — **de tierra** earthquake
tembloroso ADJ (mano) shaky; (llama) flickering; (voz) quavering; (de miedo) shuddering; (de frío) shivering
temer VI/VT to fear, to be afraid [of]; — **por** to fear for; **mucho me temo que** I fear that
temerario ADJ rash, reckless
temeridad F temerity, recklessness
temeroso ADJ fearful
temible ADJ dreadful, dread
temor M fear
témpano M (bloque de hielo) block of ice; (persona fría) cold fish
temperamento M temperament, disposition
temperancia F temperance
temperatura F temperature
tempestad F tempest, storm; **una** — **en un vaso de agua** a tempest in a teapot
tempestuoso ADJ tempestuous, stormy
templado ADJ (clima) moderate, temperate; (ánimo) serene; (actitud) moderate
templanza F temperance
templar VT (moderar, dar fuerza) to temper; (calentar) to warm up; (una guitarra) to tune
temple M (dureza) temper; (coraje) mettle; **de mal** — in a bad mood
templo M temple
temporada F season (también de fútbol); — **baja** off-season; — **de caza** hunting season
temporal ADJ (relativo al tiempo) temporal; (secular) worldly; (no permanente) temporary; M storm; **capear el** — to weather the storm
tempranero -ra ADJ early rising; MF early riser
temprano ADJ & ADV early
tenacidad F tenacity
tenaz ADJ tenacious
tenazas F PL (de cangrejo) pincers; (de mecánico) pliers; (de dentista) forceps; (para hielo) tongs
tendedero M clothesline
tendencia F tendency; (orientación) orientation; (de la moda) trend; **de** — **mayoritaria** mainstream; — **a la baja** downturn; — **al alza** upturn, upward trend
tender[2] VT (un mantel) to spread out; (la ropa) to hang out; (la mano) to extend; (un cable) to lay; (una trampa) to set; VI — **a** to tend to;

—**se** to stretch out
tendero -ra MF (de una tienda) storekeeper; (de una tienda de comestibles) grocer
tendido M (de cables) laying; (de ropa mojada) hanging out; (conjunto de cables) cables
tendinitis F tendonitis
tendón M tendon, sinew; — **de Aquiles** Achilles' tendon
tendrá, tendría *ver* tener
tenebroso ADJ (oscuro) dark; (sombrío) gloomy
tenedor -ora M table fork; MF holder, payee; — **de libros** bookkeeper
teneduría F — **de libros** bookkeeping
tener[58] VT to have; **tiene el pelo castaño** she has brown hair, her hair is brown; — **en cuenta** to bear in mind; — **en mucho** to esteem highly; — **por** to consider; — **que** to have to; — **ganas** to feel like; **tengo escrita la carta** I have the letter written; — **éxito** to be successful; — **miedo** to be afraid; — **sueño** to be sleepy; — **frío** to be cold; — **hambre** to be hungry; **tiene cinco años** she is five years old; —**se** to stand straight; **no** — **más remedio** to have no other choice; — **que ver con** to have to do with
tenería F tannery
tenga, tengo *ver* tener
tenia F tapeworm
teniente MF lieutenant
tenis M (juego) tennis; M PL (zapatos) sneakers, tennis shoes
tenista MF tennis player
tenor M (voz, estilo) tenor; (tono) tone, tenor; ADJ **saxofón** — tenor saxophone
tensión F tension
tenso ADJ (nervioso) tense; (extendido) taut
tentación F temptation
tentáculo M tentacle
tentador ADJ tempting
tentar[1] VT to tempt; — **a la suerte** to court danger; — **por todos los medios** to try everything
tentativa F attempt, try
tentativo ADJ tentative
tentempié M snack
tenue ADJ (tela) delicate; (luz) tenuous, dim, faint; (sonido) feeble
tenuidad F faintness, softness
teñir[11] VT (de color) to dye; (de emoción) to tinge
teología F theology
teológico ADJ theological
teólogo -ga MF theologian
teoría F theory; **en** — in theory
teórico ADJ theoretical
tepe M sod
tequila M tequila
terabyte M terabyte
terapeuta MF therapist
terapéutico ADJ therapeutic
terapia F (médica) therapy; (psicológica, marital) counseling; — **de electroshock** shock therapy; — **electroconvulsiva** shock therapy; — **hormonal** hormone therapy; — **ocupacional** occupational therapy
tercero ADJ third; **tercera base** third base; **tercera persona** third person; **tercera edad** old age; **tercer mundo** third world; M (en un contrato) third party; (en béisbol) third baseman
terciar VI/VT to arbitrate
tercio M third
terciopelo M velvet
terco ADJ obstinate, stubborn
tergiversación F distortion, misrepresentation
tergiversar VT (palabras) to distort; (datos) to skew
termal ADJ thermal
térmico ADJ heat, thermal
terminación F (de un proyecto) termination, completion; (de una palabra, cuento) ending; (de un piso) finish
terminal ADJ terminal; MF (de aeropuerto, de omnibus) terminal; M (de computadora, eléctrica) terminal
terminante ADJ (negativa) flat; (prohibición) absolute
terminar VI/VT (completar) to finish, to conclude; VI (tener como final) to end; — **por** to end up; **no termino de entender** I still can't understand; **terminó con las ratas** he got rid of the rats; **sin** — unfinished
término M (final) end; (período de tiempo) period; (límite) boundary; (palabra) term; — **medio** medium; **a** — (trabajo) with a deadline; (embarazo) full-term; **en primer** — first of all; **en** —**s generales** in general terms; **en último** — as a last resort; **estar en buenos** —**s** to be on good terms; **por** — **medio** on average; **poner** — to end
terminología F terminology
termita F termite
termo M thermos
termodinámico ADJ thermodynamic
termómetro M thermometer
termonuclear ADJ thermonuclear
termostato M thermostat
ternero -ra MF (animal) calf; F (carne) veal
terneza F tenderness
terno M three-piece suit
ternura F tenderness
terquedad F obstinacy, stubbornness
terraplén M embankment
terrateniente MF landholder
terraza F (terreno) terrace; (de casa) veranda; (delante de un bar) deck; (azotea) flat roof
terremoto M earthquake
terrenal ADJ earthly
terreno M (campo) piece of land, tract of land;

(lote) lot; (formación geológica) terrain; (campo científico) field; — **de juego parejo** level playing field; **ganarle — a alguien** to gain on someone; **perder —** to lose ground; **tantear el —** to put out feelers; **todo —** with four-wheel drive

terrestre ADJ terrestrial, earthly

terrible ADJ terrible, awful

terrier M terrier

territorio M territory

terrón M (de tierra) clod; (de azúcar) lump

terror M terror, dread

terrorismo M terrorism

terrorista ADJ & MF terrorist

terso ADJ (liso) smooth; (pulido) polished

tersura F smoothness

tertulia F social gathering

tesis F thesis; — **doctoral** dissertation

tesón M determination

tesonero ADJ determined

tesorería F treasury

tesorero -ra MF treasurer

tesoro M (riqueza) treasure; (tesorería) treasury

test M test

testaferro M straw man

testamentaria F (gestiones) execution; (bienes) estate

testamento M testament, will

testarudez F stubbornness

testarudo ADJ stubborn, headstrong

testículo M testicle

testificar[30] VI to testify

testigo MF witness; — **de cargo** witness for the prosecution; — **ocular** eyewitness; M proof

testimoniar VI to give testimony

testimonio M testimony, proof, evidence; **levantar falso —** to bear false witness; **en — de su amor** as a testament to his love

testosterona F testosterone

teta F teat

tétanos M SG tetanus, lockjaw

tetera F teapot, teakettle

tetilla F nipple

tetina F nipple

tetraciclina F tetracycline

tetraplégico -ca ADJ & MF quadriplegic

tétrico ADJ gloomy

teutónico ADJ Teutonic

textear VT to text

textil ADJ & M textile

texto M (algo escrito) text; (libro escolar) textbook; — **listo para cámara** camera-ready copy

textual ADJ verbatim

textura F texture

tez F complexion

ti PRON PERS you; **para —** for you; **te lo doy a —** I give it to you

tía F (pariente) aunt; *fam* (mujer) woman, chick; — **abuela** great-aunt

tibieza F (poco fervor, afecto) lukewarmness; (calor) warmth

tibio ADJ (ni caliente ni frío) tepid, lukewarm; (templado) warm

tiburón M shark

tic M twitch, tic

tictac M **hacer —** to tick

tiempo M (cronológico) time; (climático) weather; (gramatical) tense; (de un partido de cuatro tiempos) quarter; (de un partido de dos tiempos) half; — **compartido** timeshare; — **completo** full-time; — **de descuento** extra time; — **extra** overtime; — **libre** leisure hours, free time; — **parcial** part-time; — **pretérito** past tense; — **real** real time; — **suplementario** (fútbol americano) overtime; (fútbol) extra time; — **y medio** time and a half; **a —** on time; **al mismo —** at the same time; **antes de —** ahead of time; **a su —** in due course; **a un —** at the same time; **con —** in advance; **de medio —** half-time; **en aquel —** back then; **en mis —s** in my day; **hace buen —** the weather is nice; **hace mucho —** a long time ago; **mal —** rough weather; **motor de dos —s** two-stroke motor; **perder el —** to goof off, to waste time; **tener — de sobra** to have time to spare; **todo el —** all the time; **tomar el —** to clock

tienda F (de venta) store; (de campaña) tent; — **minorista** retail store; — **virtual** online store

tienda, tiende *ver* tender

tiene, tienes *ver* tener

tientas LOC ADV **a —** blindly; **andar a —** to feel one's way

tiento M care; **coger el —** to get the hang of something

tierno ADJ (fácil de cortar) tender; (joven) young; (cariñoso) affectionate

tierra F (planeta) earth; (superficie) land; (país) country; (suelo) soil; — **adentro** inland; — **s altas** highlands; — **s bajas** lowlands; — **batida** clay; — **de cultivo** farmland; — **de nadie** no-man's-land; — **firme** mainland; — **s raras** rare earths; **bajo —** underground; **caer a —** to fall to the ground; **dar en — con alguien** to overthrow someone; **echar por —** to knock down; **por —** overland

tieso ADJ stiff; **quedarse —** *fam* to kick the bucket

tiesto M flowerpot

tiesura F stiffness

tifoideo -a ADJ & F typhoid

tifón M typhoon

tifus M (causado por salmonella) typhoid fever; (causado por rickettsia) typhus

tigre M tiger

tijera[s] F SG/PL (instrumento para cortar) scissors; (patada de fútbol) scissor kick
tijereta F scissor kick
tijeretada F snip
tijeretazo M snip
tijeretear VT to snip
tildar VT to brand
tilde F (en la ñ) tilde; (en las vocales) accent [mark]
tilín M *fam* ding-a-ling
timador M confidence man
timbrar VT to stamp
timbrazo M ring
timbre M (aparato) buzzer, doorbell; (cualidad de la voz) timbre; (sello) stamp; (impuesto) stamp tax; (insignia heráldica) crest
timidez F timidity, shyness
tímido ADJ timid, shy, bashful
timo M confidence game, scam; **— en pirámide** Ponzi scheme
timón M helm, rudder
timonear VT to steer
timonel M pilot
timorato ADJ timorous, faint-hearted
tímpano M eardrum
tina F (bañera) tub; (de tintorero) vat
tinaja F large earthen jar
tinglado M (armazón) shed; (plataforma) platform
tinieblas F PL darkness; **en —** in the dark
tinitus M tinnitus
tino M (buen juicio) good judgment; (puntería) marksmanship
tinta F ink; **medias —s** wishy-washiness
tinte M (sustancia) dye, stain; (matiz) tint
tintero M inkwell; **eso se me quedó en el —** I never got to that
tintín M clink
tintinear VI to tinkle, to clink
tintineo M tinkle, tinkling
tinto ADJ red
tintorería F dry cleaner
tintorero -ra MF dry cleaner
tintura F (en medicina) tincture; (tinte) dye, tint
tiñoso ADJ scabby
tío -a M (hermano de la madre o el padre) uncle; **— abuelo** great-uncle; (tipo) guy; F (hermana de la madre o el padre) aunt; (tipa) woman, gal
tíovivo M merry-go-round
tipear, tipiar VI/VT to type
típico ADJ typical
tiple M treble
tipo -pa M (especie, imprenta) type; (tío) *fam* guy, dude; *Am* rate of interest; **— de cambio** rate of exchange; **— de interés** interest rate; **— de letra** typeface, font; **— de letra por omisión** base font; **un buen —** (hombre guapo) a good-looking fellow; (buena persona) a regular guy; **tiene buen —** he's good looking; F (tía) *pey* woman, broad
tipografía F printing
tipología F typology
tira F (de papel, tocino, tela) strip; (de cuero, zapato) strap; **— cómica** comic strip
tirada F (de una pelota) throw; (de una publicación) issue, print run; (distancia) stretch; **de una —** all at once
tirador -ora MF (persona que dispara) shooter; M (tirachinas) slingshot; (pomo de la puerta) knob
tiranía F tyranny
tiránico ADJ tyrannical
tirano -na ADJ tyrannical; MF tyrant
tirante ADJ (cable) taut; (relaciones) strained; M (de caballería) trace; (de vestido) strap; (apoyo) brace, strut; **—s** suspenders
tirantez F tension, strain
tirar VT (pelota) to throw, to toss, to pitch; (derechos, dinero) to throw away; (una bala) to shoot; (una moneda) to flip, to toss; (dados) to cast; (una cuerda) to pull, to tug; VI/VT (en baloncesto) to shoot; VI **— a puerta** to shoot at goal; **—se** (echarse) to lie down; (en fútbol) to fake a foul; **— al suelo** to throw down; **— a** to tend toward; **— abajo** to knock over; **— de** to tug at; **— la cadena** to flush; **— la casa por la ventana** to live it up; **— la chancleta** to kick up one's heels; **—se solo** to go it alone; **tirárselas de** to pretend to be; **no me tira la política** I'm not attracted to politics; **el coche tira a un lado** the car pulls to one side; **ir tirando** to get along; **trabajar con él es un constante tira y afloja** working with him is a roller-coaster; M **tirabuzón** (sacacorchos) corkscrew; (espiral) coil; M SG **tirachinas** slingshot
tiritar VI (de frío) to shiver; (de miedo) to shudder
tiro M (lanzamiento) throw; (disparo) shot; (deporte) shooting; (de cocaína) hit; (de dados) roll; (de caballos) team; (de chimenea) draft; (fútbol) shot; **— al arco** archery; **— al blanco** target practice; **— de esquina** corner kick; **— de penalidad** penalty kick; **— en suspensión** jump shot; **— libre** (baloncesto) free throw; (fútbol) free kick; **errar el —** to miss the mark; **matar a —s** to gun down; **ni a —s** absolutely not; **pegarle un — a alguien** to shoot someone; **me salió el — por la culata** the plan backfired on me
tiroides ADJ & M thyroid
tirón M (tironeo) jerk, tug, pull; (atracción fuerte, lesión de un músculo) pull; **de un —** all at once; **un — de orejas** a slap on the wrist
tironear VI/VT to jerk, to tug at

tirotear VI to shoot; **—se** to exchange shots
tiroteo M (tiros) shooting, gunfire; (entre bandos) shootout
tirria F dislike; **tenerle — a una persona** to have a strong dislike for someone
tisana F herbal tea
tísico ADJ consumptive
tisis F consumption
titánico ADJ titanic
titanio M titanium
títere M (marioneta) puppet; (persona) puppet, dupe; **—s** puppet show; **no dejar — con cabeza** to leave no one standing
titilación F flicker
titilar VI to flicker, to twinkle
titileo M twinkle
titubear VI (vacilar) to hesitate, to waver; (oscilar) to totter, to dodder
titubeo M hesitation
titular VT to entitle; **—se** to graduate; ADJ permanent; M (de periódico) headline; MF (de cargo) incumbent
titularidad F tenure
título M (de una obra, persona, liga) title; (derecho) claim, legal right; (universitario) degree, diploma; **— de propiedad** title deed; **—s de crédito** credits; **a — de** by way of
tiza F chalk
tiznado ADJ sooty
tiznar VT to smear with soot
tizne M soot
tizón M (leña) burning log; (parásito) smut
TNT M TNT
toalla F towel; **tirar la —** to throw in the towel
toallero M towel rack
tobillo M ankle
tobogán M slide
tocado M headdress; ADJ touched
tocador M (mueble) dressing table, vanity table; (habitación) *lit* boudoir
tocante a PREP concerning
tocar[30] VT (con los dedos) to touch; (un instrumento musical) to play; (una campana) to ring; (un timbre) to buzz; (a la puerta) to knock; (la bocina) to honk, to blast; (una alarma) to sound; (mencionar) to touch upon; **— en** to stop over in; **—le a uno** to be one's turn; **— fondo** to hit bottom; **— la pelota** (béisbol) bunt; M SG **tocadiscos** record player
tocayo -ya MF namesake
tocino M bacon
tocón M stump
todavía ADV still, as yet, yet; **— está aquí** she's still here; **¿— no has comido?** have you not eaten yet? **— no ha llegado** she still has not arrived, as yet she has not arrived; **me dio — más** she gave me even more
todo ADJ all; (cada uno) every, each; **— hombre** every man; **—s los días** every day; **a — correr** at top speed; **a toda costa** at all costs; **a toda marcha** in high gear; **a toda vela** under full sail; **a toda velocidad** at full speed; **a — volumen** at full blast; **de — corazón** wholeheartedly; **de —s modos** still, anyway, all the same; **del —** entirely; **en — caso** in any case, at any rate, in any event; **es — un personaje** he's quite a character; **por — lados** everywhere; **— el día** all day; **— el tiempo** all the time; **— el mundo** everyone; **todas las noches** nightly; **toda la noche** all through the night; **toda clase de** all sorts of; **en/por todas partes** everywhere, far and wide; **con toda el alma** from the bottom of one's heart; **con toda sinceridad** in all earnestness; PRON **de una vez por todas** once and for all; **— se vale** anything goes; **—s** everybody; **—s juntos** all together; ADV **— derecho** straight ahead; **— lo contrario** quite the opposite; **— recto** straight ahead; **— sucio** all dirty; **— o nada** all or nothing; **ante —** first of all; **así y —** in spite of that; **con —** in spite of that; **del —** completely; **sobre —** especially; M whole; **—poderoso** almighty; **el — es más que la suma de las partes** the whole is more than the sum of its parts
toga F (de catedrático) gown; (de juez) robe
Togo M Togo
togolés -esa ADJ & MF Togolese
toldería F Indian village
toldo M awning, canopy
tolerancia F tolerance
tolerante ADJ tolerant, broad-minded
tolerar VT to tolerate; **no lo puedo —** I can't stand it
tolete M oarlock
toma F (de una ciudad) taking; (cinematográfica) take; (de juramento) administration; (de teléfono) jack; **— de agua** faucet; **— de corriente** electric outlet; **— de poder** takeover; **— y daca** give-and-take
tomar VT (una pastilla) to take; (un juramento) to administer; (un vestido) to take in; (a un empleado) to hire; (una bebida) to drink; **— a pecho** to take to heart; **— asiento** to take a seat; **— desprevenido** to take by surprise; **— el sol** to sunbathe; **—lo a mal** to take the wrong way; **— el pelo a** to make fun of, to kid, to pull someone's leg; **— medidas** to take action; **— posesión** to take possession; **— una decisión** to make a decision; **—le las medidas a alguien** to measure someone for clothes; **—se de la mano** to hold hands; **—se la molestia** to bother to
tomate M tomato
tomillo M thyme

tomo M volume
tomografía F scan; **— axial computarizada** CAT scan; **— cerebral** brain scan
ton LOC ADV **sin — ni son** for no reason
tonada F tune
tonel M (barril) barrel; (persona) *pey* fatso
tonelada F ton
tóner M toner
Tonga F Tonga
tongano-na ADJ & MF Tongan
tongo M setup
tonicidad F tone; **— muscular** muscle tone
tónico-ca ADJ & M tonic; F (tono) tone; (agua) tonic [water]
tono M (al hablar) tone; (musical) pitch; (intervalo musical) step; **— de ocupado** busy signal; **— menor** minor key; **— muscular** muscle tone; **a —** on key; **bajar el —** to lower the volume; **darse —** to put on airs; **de buen —** in good taste; **fuera de —** out of place; **subido de —** risqué
tontear VI to fool around
tontería F (cualidad de tonto) stupidity; (hecho o dicho tonto) foolishness, nonsense
tonto-ta ADJ (ingenuo) foolish; (de poca inteligencia) stupid, dumb; **a tontas y a locas** haphazardly; MF (persona ingenua) fool; (persona de poca inteligencia) *fam* dummy, blockhead, dimwit; **— de capirote** dunce; **hacer[se] el —** to play the fool
topacio M topaz
topar VT to butt; **—se con** to bump into
tope M (de precios) ceiling, cap; (de tren) bumper; (de puerta) doorstop; **a —** a lot; **hasta el —** to the maximum; **estar hasta el —** to be completely full
topetazo M butt
tópico M (lugar común) cliché; (tema) topic; ADJ topical
topless ADJ topless
topo M mole (también espía)
toque M (con la mano) touch; (de campana) ringing; (de tambor) beat; (de trompeta) blare; (de pintura) dab; **— de queda** curfew; **— de pelota** (béisbol) bunt; **dar los últimos —s** to put the finishing touches; **dar —s** to dab; **un — femenino** a woman's touch
toquetear VI/VT to finger
toqueteo M feel
tórax M thorax
torbellino M whirlwind
torcedura F twist, sprain, strain
torcer[34] VT (el cuello) to twist; (una articulación) to sprain, to strain; (tergiversar) to distort; **—le el pescuezo a alguien** to wring someone's neck; VI (un río) to bend
torcido ADJ crooked, bent
tordo M thrush
torear VT (lidiar) to fight a bull; (provocar) to provoke
torero-ra MF bullfighter
tormenta F storm; **— de arena** sandstorm; **— eléctrica** electrical storm
tormento M torment
tormentoso ADJ stormy
tornadizo ADJ changeable
tornado M tornado, twister
tornar VI (regresar) to return; VT (cambiar) to turn; **— a hacer algo** to do something again
tornasolado ADJ iridescent
tornear VT to turn on a lathe
torneo M tournament
tornillo M screw; **— de banco** vise; **faltarle a uno un —** to have a screw loose
torniquete M (eje giratorio) turnstile; (contra hemorragia) tourniquet
torno M (para levantar cosas pesadas) hoist, winch; (para cerámica) lathe, pottery wheel; **en — [a]** around
toro M bull; **coger/agarrar el — por los cuernos** to take the bull by the horns
toronja F grapefruit
torpe ADJ (poco habilidoso) clumsy, awkward; (lento) slow, sluggish
torpedear VT to torpedo
torpedero-ra MF (en béisbol) shortstop; M (barco) torpedo boat; (avión) torpedo plane
torpedo M torpedo
torpeza F (falta de habilidad) clumsiness; (lentitud) slowness, sluggishness
torpor M torpor
torrar VT to roast
torre F (de castillo) tower; (de buque de guerra) turret; (en ajedrez) castle; **— de control** control tower; **— de marfil** ivory tower; **— de perforación** oil derrick; **— de vigilancia** watchtower
torrencial ADJ torrential
torrente M torrent; **— de lágrimas** flood of tears; **— sanguíneo** bloodstream
torreón M large tower
torreta F turret
tórrido ADJ torrid
torsión F torsion
torso M torso
torta F (postre) cake; (bofetada) slap
tortícolis F kink
tortilla F (de huevo) omelet; (de harina) *Méx* tortilla; **se dio vuelta la —** the tables have turned
tórtola F turtledove
tortuga F tortoise, turtle; **— marina** sea turtle; **a paso de —** at a snail's pace
tortuoso ADJ (camino) tortuous; (carácter) devious
tortura F torture
torturante ADJ torturous

torturar VT to torture
torvo ADJ fierce
tos F cough; **— ferina** whooping cough
tosco ADJ coarse, crude
toser VI to cough
tosquedad F coarseness, crudeness
tostada F toast
tostado ADJ (pan) toasted; (café) roasted; M (acción de tostar pan) toasting; (color, bronceado) tan; (acción de tostar café) roasting
tostador-ora MF toaster
tostar[5] VT (pan) to toast; (piel) to tan; (café) to roast
total ADJ & M total; **en —** all together; **—, a mí no me importa** anyway, I don't care
totalidad F **la — del dinero** all the money; **en su —** as a whole
totalitario ADJ totalitarian
totalmente ADV totally, perfectly
tour M tour
tóxico ADJ toxic
toxina F toxin
traba F (estorbo) hindrance; (de caballo) hobble
trabajador-ora ADJ (esforzado) hardworking; (proletario) working; MF worker
trabajar VI/VT to work; **— un taxi** to drive a taxi; VI (una tienda) to be open; **— duro** to work hard; **— horas extras** to work overtime
trabajo M (actividad) work; (acción de trabajar) working; (empleo) job; (informe académico) paper; **— manual** manual labor; **da mucho —** it's a lot of work; **sin —** unemployed
trabajoso ADJ laborious
trabar VT (una puerta) to jam; (un caballo) to hobble; (a un boxeador) to clinch; (una salsa) to thicken; (negociaciones) to impede; **— amistad con alguien** to strike up a friendship with someone; **— batalla** to join battle; **— conversación** to strike up a conversation; M SG **trabalenguas** tongue twister
tracción F traction
tractocamión M tractor-trailer
tractor M tractor
tradición F tradition
tradicional ADJ traditional
traducción F translation
traducir[38] VI/VT to translate
traductor-ora MF translator
traduje, tradujera, tradujese, traduzca, traduzco *ver* traducir
traer[59] VT (venir con) to bring; (llevar puesto) to have on; (contener) to feature; **— a colación** to bring up; **— a mal a alguien** to mistreat someone; **este niño se las trae** this child is something else; **¿qué te traes entre manos?** what are you up to? **—se secretos** to have secrets
tráfago M bustle
traficante MF dealer
traficar[30] VI to traffic, to trade
tráfico M traffic
tragar[40] VI/VT (ingerir) to swallow; (comer) *fam* to stuff one's face; (consumir gasolina) to guzzle; (aguantar) to stand; (hacer desaparecer) to engulf; **—se algo** to swallow [accidentally]; **no me lo trago** I don't buy that; M **tragaluz** skylight; M/F SG **tragamonedas/tragaperras** slot machine
tragedia F tragedy
trágico ADJ tragic
trago M (lo tragado) swallow; (bebida alcohólica) shot, slug; **a —s** (beber) in sips; (poco a poco) little by little; **echar/tomar un —** to take a drink; **pasar un mal —** to suffer a difficulty
traición F (política) treason; (personal) betrayal; (acto desleal) treachery; **a —** by treachery
traicionar VT to double-cross
traicionero ADJ treacherous
traidor-ora ADJ treacherous; MF (político) traitor; (personal) betrayer
traiga, traigo *ver* traer
trailer M trailer
traílla F leash
traje M (conjunto) suit; (de fiesta) gown; **— de baño** swimsuit
traje, trajera, trajese *ver* traer
trajeado ADJ **bien —** well-dressed
trajín M hustle and bustle
trajinar VI to rush around
trama F (argumento) plot; (intriga) scheme; (conjunto de hilos) woof
tramador-ora MF plotter
tramar VT (con hilos) to weave; (intrigar) to plot, to scheme
tramitación F processing
tramitar VT to take steps to obtain
trámite M procedure, paperwork
tramo M (de carretera) stretch; (de puente) span; (de hielo) patch; (de escalera) flight
tramoyista MF stagehand
trampa F (de caza) trap, snare; (engaño) trick; **— de arena** (golf) sand trap; **hacer —** to cheat, to trick; **tender una —** to set a trap
trampear VI to cheat
trampilla F trapdoor
trampolín M (de piscina) springboard; (de circo) trampoline
tramposo-sa ADJ deceitful; MF cheat
tranca F crossbar
trance M (momento difícil) pass, difficult moment; (estado mental) trance; **el último —** the last moment of life; **a todo —** at any cost
tranco M stride; **a —s** hurriedly; **en dos —s** in a jiffy

tranquera F wooden fence
tranquilidad F tranquillity, calm, quiet
tranquilizante M tranquilizer
tranquilizar[47] VT to quiet, to calm down; **—se** to calm down, to wind down
tranquilo ADJ (silencioso) quiet, peaceful; (apacible) calm, cool; (despreocupado) calm, at ease; (no excitable) sedate, laid-back; (sin olas) smooth, tranquil
transacción F transaction; **— comercial** business transaction; **transacciones** trading; **transacciones a precio de mercado** arm's-length transactions
transar VI to compromise
transatlántico ADJ transatlantic; M transatlantic liner
transbordar VI to transfer
transbordo M transfer
transcribir[74] VT to transcribe
transcripción F transcript
transcultural ADJ cross-cultural
transcurrir VI to elapse
transcurso M passing, passage; **en el — de un año** in the course of a year
transeúnte MF passerby, transient
transferencia F transfer; **— electrónica** wire transfer
transferible ADJ transferable
transferir[8] VT to transfer (también en computadora)
transformación F transformation
transformador M transformer
transformar VT to transform
transfusión F transfusion; **dar una — de sangre** to give a transfusion
transgénico ADV genetically modified
transgredir[73] VT to transgress
transgresión F transgression
transgresor -ora MF lawbreaker
transición F transition
transigir[46] VI to compromise
transistor M transistor
transitable ADJ passable
transitar VI/VT to travel
transitivo ADJ transitive
tránsito M (acción de viajar) transit, passage; (tráfico) traffic; **de/en —** in transit
transitorio ADJ transitory
transmisible ADJ communicable
transmisión F transmission; **— automática** automatic transmission; **— por la web** webcast
transmisor M transmitter; ADJ transmitting
transmitir VI/VT (enviar) to transmit; (una enfermedad) to communicate; (por radio o televisión) to broadcast; **— por la web** to webcast
transnacional ADJ transnational
transparencia F (visual) transparency; (institucional) openness
transparente ADJ transparent
transpiración F perspiration, sweating
transpirar VI/VT to transpire, to perspire
transportación F transportation, transport
transportar VT (mercancías, gente) to transport; (mercancías) to ship, to haul
transporte M (acción) transport, transportation; (vehículo de transporte) transport [vessel]; **— de locura** fit of madness; **— público** mass transit
transportista MF teamster, trucker
transversal ADJ transverse; F transversal
transverso ADJ transverse
tranvía M (transporte urbano) streetcar, trolley; (tren de cercanías) local train
trapacería F racket
trapacero -ra MF racketeer
trapeador M mop
trapear VI/VT *Am* to mop
trapecio M trapeze
trapezoide ADJ & M trapezoid
trapiche M sugar mill
trapisonda F trick
trapo M rag; **—s** *fam* duds; **a todo —** at full speed; **tratar a alguien como un —** to treat someone like dirt; **—s sucios** dirty laundry
tráquea F trachea, windpipe
traqueotomía F tracheotomy
traquetear VI (hacer sonido) to rattle, to clatter; (llevar a todos lados) to drag from place to place
traqueteo M rattle, clatter
tras PREP (temporal) after; (espacial) after, behind, in back of; **correr —** to run after; **día — día** day after day; **una vez — otra** time after time
trascendencia F (concepto filosófico) transcendence; (importancia) importance
trascendental ADJ (que sobrepasa la realidad) transcendental; (importante) important
trascendente ADJ (que sobrepasa la realidad) transcendental; (importante) important
trascender VT (sobrepasar) to transcend; VI (surgir) to emerge; (extender) to extend
trasegar[41] VT (vino) to pour from one container to another; (objetos) to move around; (papeles) to shuffle
trasero ADJ (punto, asiento) rear, back; (pata) hind; M (de persona) *fam* rear, rear end, bottom
traslación F transfer
trasladar VT (a un empleado) to transfer; (una reunión) to postpone; **—se** to travel
traslado M transfer
traslapo M overlap
trasnochar VI to stay up late
traspapelar VT to mislay, to misplace; **—se** to become mislaid

traspasar VT (pasar por) to transfix; (ir más allá de) to go beyond; (pasar un límite) to transgress, to cross over; (una propiedad) to transfer
traspaso M transfer
traspié M stumble, slip; **dar un —** to stumble
trasplantar VT to transplant
trasplante M transplant
trasponer[56, 74] VT to transpose
trasquilar VT (una oveja) to shear; (a una persona) to fleece
trastabillar VI to stumble
trastazo M bump
traste M (de guitarra) fret, stop; (trasero) buttocks; **dar al — con** to destroy; **irse al —** to go down the drain
trasto M piece of junk; **—s** stuff
trastocar[30] VT to disrupt
trastornar VT (alterar psíquicamente) to disturb; (alterar el funcionamiento) to disrupt; **—se** to go crazy
trastorno M (molestia) trouble; (patología) disorder; **— bipolar** bipolar disorder; **— de Asperger** Asperger's syndrome; **— de déficit de atención** attention deficit disorder; **— de la alimentación** eating disorder; **— de la personalidad** personality disorder; **— de personalidad múltiple** multiple personality disorder; **— del sueño** sleep disorder
trasudar VI/VT to perspire
trata F trade; **— de blancas** white slave trade
tratable ADJ (curable) treatable; (amistoso) approachable
tratado M (acuerdo) treaty; (libro) treatise
tratamiento M (acción de tratar) treatment; (fórmula de cortesía) form of address; **— de canal** root canal; **— de convalecencia** aftercare; **— de residuos** waste treatment; **— de textos** *Esp* word processing; **— postoperatorio** aftercare
tratante MF dealer, trader
tratar VT (una enfermedad, a un paciente, un asunto) to treat; VI (intentar) to try; **— como** to treat like; **— con** to have dealings with; **— de** to try to, to attempt; **— sobre** to be about; **lo trató de imbécil** she called him an idiot; **—le a uno de** to address someone as; **— en** to deal in; **—se con** to have to do with; **—se de** to be a question of, to be about
trato M (acuerdo) treatment; (acción de tratar) dealings; (convenio) deal; (comercio) trade; (modales) manners; **¡— hecho!** it's a deal! **tener buen —** to have good manners; **cerrar un —** to strike a bargain
trauma M trauma
traumático ADJ traumatic
traumatismo M trauma
través LOC ADV **a/al — de** through, across; **a — de las declaraciones** throughout the declarations; **de —** across; **mirar de —** to look askance [at]
travesaño M crossbar (también en fútbol)
travesía F crossing, sea voyage, passage
travesura F mischief, prank; **—s** naughtiness; **hacer —s** to play pranks
traviesa F railway tie
travieso ADJ mischievous, naughty
trayecto M course, route
trayectoria F (de proyectil) trajectory, path; (profesional) career, track record
trayendo *ver* traer
traza F (huella) trace; (aspecto) appearance; **tiene —s de no acabar nunca** it looks as if it will never end
trazado M (de ciudad) layout; (de edificio) blueprint; (de un plan) outline
trazador M **— gráfico** plotter
trazar[47] VT (un dibujo) to trace, to sketch; (un plan) to outline; (un edificio) to blueprint; **— el curso** to plot a course
trazo M stroke
trébol M clover
trece NUM thirteen
trecho M stretch; **a —s** at intervals; **de — en —** at intervals
tregua F (de guerra) truce; (descanso) lull, respite
treinta NUM thirty (también en tenis)
treintañero -ra MF thirtysomething
tremendo ADJ (extraordinario) tremendous; (terrible) terrible
trementina F turpentine
tremolar VI (bandera) to flutter; (voz) to trill
trémolo M quaver
trémulo ADJ tremulous, trembling
tren M train; **— de aterrizaje** landing gear; **— de carga / de mercancías** freight train; **— de cercanías** local train; **— de vida** lifestyle; **— expreso** express train; **a todo —** at top speed; **perder el —** to miss the boat; **seguir el —** to keep up
trenza F braid
trenzar[47] VT to braid
trepador -ora ADJ (planta) climbing; (ciclista) climber; MF social climber; F climbing plant
trepar VI to climb
trepidar VI to tremble
tres NUM three
trescientos NUM three hundred
treta F trick, wile
triaje M triage
triangular ADJ triangular
triángulo M triangle; **— recto** right triangle
tribu F tribe
tribulación F tribulation
tribuna F (de orador) rostrum; (para el público) grandstand

tribunal M (sala del juez) court, courtroom; (cuerpo de jueces) panel of judges
tributable ADJ taxable
tributar VT to pay tribute with; VI to pay taxes
tributario ADJ & M tributary
tributo M (pago obligatorio) tribute; (impuesto) tax
triceps M triceps
triciclo M tricycle
tridimensional ADJ three-dimensional
trifulca F fight
trigo M wheat
trigueño ADJ (tez) swarthy; (pelo) dark-blond
trillado ADJ trite
trilladora F threshing machine
trillar VT to thresh
trillizo -za ADJ & MF triplet
trilogía F trilogy
trimestral ADJ quarterly
trimestre M quarter
trinar VI to trill; **está que trina** she is furious
trinchante M carving knife
trinchar VT to carve
trinche M pitchfork
trinchera F (fosa) trench; (gabardina) trench coat
trinchero M carving table
trineo M sleigh, sled
trinitense ADJ & MF Trinidadian
trino M trill
trinquete M ratchet
trío M trio
tripas F PL guts; **hacer de — corazón** to pluck up one's courage
triple ADJ triple; M (también en béisbol) triple; (baloncesto) three-point basket
triplicar[30] VT to triple, to treble
trípode M tripod
triptongo M triphthong
tripulación F crew
tripulante MF crew member
tripular VT to man
triquiñuela F caper
triquitraque M firecracker
triscar[30] VI to frisk
triste ADJ sad, sorrowful
tristeza F sadness, sorrow
tristón ADJ glum
tritón M newt
trituradora F (para desechos) garbage disposal unit; (para papel) paper shredder
triturar VI/VT (documentos) to shred; (granos) to grind
triunfador -ora MF winner; ADJ triumphant
triunfal ADJ triumphal
triunfante ADJ triumphant
triunfar VT to triumph
triunfo M triumph
trivial ADJ trivial, commonplace, trite
trizas F PL **hacer —** to tear into shreds
trocar[31] VT (transformar) to change into; (cambiar una cosa por otra) to exchange
trocear VT to divide into pieces
trocha F trail
trofeo M trophy
troje M granary
trola F whopper
trole M trolley
trolebús M trolley bus
tromba F waterspout; **salir en —** to storm out
trombón M trombone
trombosis F thrombosis; **— coronaria** coronary thrombosis
trompa F (de elefante) trunk; (instrumento musical) horn; **— de Eustaquio** eustachian tube; **— de Falopio** fallopian tube
trompada F blow with the fist
trompeta F trumpet
trompetazo M trumpet blast
trompetear VI to trumpet
trompo M spinning top
tronada F thunderstorm
tronar[5] VI to thunder
tronchar VT to chop off
tronco M (de árbol) trunk, log; (del cuerpo) trunk, torso; **— del encéfalo** brain stem; **dormir como un —** to sleep like a log
tronera F (de buque) gun port; (de mesa de billar) pocket
trono M throne (también wáter)
tropa F (en el ejército) troop; (oficiales) rank and file; **—s de asalto** storm troops; **—s de choque** shock troops
tropel LOC ADV **en —** in droves
tropezar[48] VI to stumble, to trip; **—[se] con alguien** to run into someone; **— con algo** to come across something
tropezón M stumble, trip; **salir a tropezones** to stumble out; **darse un —** to stumble
tropical ADJ tropical
trópico M tropic
tropiezo M stumble
troquel M die
trotar VI to trot, to jog
trote M trot; **al —** at a trot; **no estoy para estos —s** I'm too old for this
troza F log
trozar[47] VT to cut up
trozo M (de roca, madera, torta) piece; (de un texto) section; (de carbón) lump; (de carne) slab
trucha F trout
truco M clever trick
truculento ADJ gruesome
trueno M thunder
trueque M (intercambio) exchange; (transacción sin dinero) bartering
truhán -ana MF scoundrel

truja F cigarette
trust M trust
tu ADJ POS your
tú PRON PERS you
tuba F tuba
tuberculosis F tuberculosis
tubería F (tubo) pipe; (conjunto de tubos) piping
tubo M (cilindro hueco) tube; (de agua, órgano) pipe; (digestivo) tract; **— de ensayo** test tube; **— de escape** tailpipe; **— digestivo** gastrointestinal tract
tubular ADJ tubular
tuerca F nut
tuerto ADJ one-eyed
tuétano M marrow; **hasta los —s** through and through
tufillo M whiff
tufo M (humo) fumes; (hedor) stench
tugurio M hovel; **—s** slums
tulipán M tulip
tullido -da ADJ crippled; MF *pey* cripple
tullir VT to cripple; **—se** to become crippled
tumba F (panteón) tomb; (sepultura) grave; **soy una —** my lips are sealed
tumbar VT to knock down, to flatten; **—se** to lie down, to stretch out
tumbo M tumble, somersault; **dar —s** (persona) to stagger; (coche) to bump along
tumor M tumor; **— cerebral** brain tumor; **— maligno** malignancy
tumorectomía F lumpectomy
tumulto M (alboroto) tumult, uproar; (muchedumbre) mob
tumultuoso ADJ tumultuous
tuna F (fruta) prickly pear; *Esp* (grupo de cantantes) minstrel group
tunante -ta MF scamp
tunda F thrashing
túnel M tunnel
tunesino -na ADJ & MF Tunisian
Túnez M Tunisia
tungsteno M tungsten
túnica F tunic; **— de laboratorio** lab gown
tupido ADJ dense, compact
tupir VT (hacer tupido) to compact; (cubrir) to cover; **—se** to stuff oneself
turba F (muchedumbre) mob; (carbón fósil) peat
turbación F confusion
turbamulta F throng
turbante M turban
turbar VT to disturb; **—se** to become disturbed
turbina F turbine
turbio ADJ (pasado, secreto) dark; (agua, materia) murky
turbocompresor M turbocharger
turborreactor M turbojet
turbulencia F turbulence
turbulento ADJ turbulent
turco -ca ADJ Turkish; MF Turk; M (lengua) Turkish
turcomano -na ADJ & MF Turkmen
turismo M (actividad) tourism; (conjunto de turistas) tourists; **hacer —** to go sightseeing
turista MF tourist
turístico ADJ (relativo al turismo) tourist; **atracción turística** tourist attraction; **clase turística** coach class
Turkmenistán M Turkmenistan
turnarse VI to take turns
turno M (vuelta) turn; (de trabajo) shift; (en béisbol) at bat
turquesa F turquoise
Turquía F Turkey
turrón M nougat
tutear VT to address as "tú"
tutela F guardianship
tutelar VT to have charge of
tutor -ora MF (de un menor) guardian; M (de planta) prop
tutorial M tutorial
Tuvalu M Tuvalu
tuvaluano -na ADJ & MF Tuvaluan
tuve, tuviera, tuviese *ver* tener
tuyo ADJ & PRON POS your, yours; **el amigo —** your friend; **esto es —** this is yours
tweed M tweed

Uu

u CONJ or
ubicación F location
ubicar[30] VT (situar) to locate; (identificar) to place; **—se** to be located
ubicuo ADJ ubiquitous
ubre F udder
UCP [unidad central de proceso] F CPU
Ucrania F Ukraine
ucraniano -na ADJ & MF Ukrainian
UE [Unión Europea] F EU
ufanarse VI to glory [in], to be proud [of]
ufano ADJ proud
Uganda F Uganda
ugandés -esa ADJ & MF Ugandan
ujier M bailiff
úlcera F (lesión superficial) sore; (en el estómago) ulcer; (en la boca) canker, canker sore
ulcerar VI to ulcerate
ulceroso ADJ ulcerous
ulterior ADJ ulterior
últimamente ADV of late
ultimar VT to finalize
ultimátum M ultimatum
último ADJ (palabra, capítulo) last, final;

(destino) ultimate; (más reciente) latest; **estar en las últimas** to be on one's last legs; **la última palabra** the last word; **en los —s tiempos** lately; **en última instancia** ultimately; **a última hora** at the last moment; **por —** finally

ultrajante ADJ outrageous

ultrajar VT to outrage

ultraje M outrage, indignity

ultraligero M ultralight

ultramar LOC ADV **de —** overseas

ultramoderno ADJ ultramodern

ultrasonido M ultrasound

ultratumba LOC ADV **de —** from beyond the grave

ultravioleta ADJ & M ultraviolet

ulular VI (viento) to howl; (búho) to hoot

ululato M (viento) howling; (búho) hooting

umbral M threshold, doorstep; **— de rentabilidad** breakeven point

umbrío ADJ shady

un, uno, una ART INDEF a, an; **un hombre** a man; **un actor** an actor; **una mujer** a woman; **una manzana** an apple; NUM one; **de a —** one at a time; **es la una** it is one o'clock; PRON one; **uno por uno** one by one; **—s** some; **unos cuantos** some; **uno tiene que cuidarse** you've got to take care of yourself; **yo tengo uno** I have one; **uno tras otro** one after the other; **uno más** (tenis) let; **uno al lado del otro** side by side; **los unos a los otros / el uno al otro** one another / each other

unánime ADJ unanimous

unanimidad F unanimity

uncir[33] VT (a un buey) to yoke; (a un carro) to hitch

ungüento M ointment, salve

único ADJ (solo) only; **una única vez** a single time; (extraordinario) unique; **eres —** you're one of a kind

unidad F (indivisibilidad) unity; (ejemplar) unit; (fracción militar) unit, outfit; (de computadora) drive; **— central de proceso/procesamiento** central processing unit; **— de cuidado coronario** coronary care unit; **— de cuidados intensivos** intensive care unit; **— de disco duro** hard disk drive; **— de disquete** diskette drive; **— monetaria** currency unit

unido ADJ united; **una familia unida** a close-knit family

unificar[30] VT to unify

uniformar VT (estandarizar) to standardize; (dar uniformes) to furnish with uniforms

uniforme ADJ & M uniform

uniformidad F uniformity

unilateral ADJ unilateral

unión F (acción de unir, cosas unidas) union; (lugar en que se unen dos cosas) junction; (indivisibilidad) unity

unir VT (una nación) to unite; (dos construcciones) to join; (cinta magnética, genes) to splice; (caños) to couple; VI/VT (con lazos) to bind

unisex ADJ INV unisex

unísono ADJ unison; **al —** in unison

unitario ADJ (partidario de la unidad) unitarian; (que tiene unidad) unitary

universal ADJ universal

universidad F (de enseñanza e investigación) university; (de enseñanza) college

universitario -ria ADJ university; (relativo a los deportes) collegiate; MF college student

universo M universe

untar VT (la piel con crema) to oil; (el pan con mantequilla) to spread on; (la cara con pintura) to smear; **—le la mano a alguien** to grease someone's palm

untuoso ADJ (graso) oily; (zalamero) slick, unctuous

uña F (de dedo) fingernail; (de gato) claw; **— encarnada** hangnail; **como — y carne** thick as thieves; **con —s y dientes** tooth and nail

uñero M hangnail

uranio M uranium

urbanidad F refinement, polish

urbanismo M (modo de vida) urbanism; (planificación) city planning

urbanización F development

urbanizar[47] VT to build up

urbano ADJ (relativo a la ciudad) urban; (refinado) suave; **autobús —** city bus

urbe F metropolis

urdimbre F warp

urdir VT (una tela) to weave; (una historia) to concoct; (un plan) to devise, to work out

uretra F urethra

urgencia F (prisa) urgency; (crisis médica) emergency; **con —** urgently; **—s** emergency room

urgente ADJ urgent, pressing

urgir[46] VT to urge; VI to be urgent

úrico ADJ uric

urinario ADJ urinary; M urinal

URL M URL

urna F (para cenizas) urn; (electoral) ballot box; **acudir a las —s** to go to the polls

urólogo -ga MF urologist

urraca F (ave) magpie; (persona acaparadora) packrat

urticaria F hives

Uruguay M Uruguay

uruguayo -ya ADJ & MF Uruguayan

usado ADJ (utilizado) used; (desgastado) worn

usar VT (emplear) to use; (ponerse) to wear; **—se** to be in use; **sin —** unused

USB M USB
uso M (empleo) use; (costumbre) usage, custom; **al — de la época** according to the custom of the time
usted PRON PERS you; **—es** you, you all, y'all
usual ADJ usual
usuario -ria MF (de un servicio) user; (en una biblioteca) borrower
usufructo M enjoyment
usufructuar[26] VT to enjoy the use of
usura F usury
usurero -ra MF usurer, loan shark
usurpar VT to encroach upon, to usurp
utensilio M utensil
uterino ADJ uterine
útero M uterus, womb
útil ADJ useful, helpful; M PL **—es** utensils
utilidad F usefulness, utility
utilitario ADJ utilitarian
utilización F use, utilization
utilizar[47] VT (emplear) to utilize; (explotar) to use
utopía F utopia
uva F grape
úvula F uvula
uvular ADJ uvular
Uzbekistán M Uzbekistan
uzbeko -ka ADJ & MF Uzbek

Vv

va, vamos *ver* ir
vaca F cow; **— marina** sea cow
vacación F vacation; **de vacaciones** on vacation
vacante ADJ vacant; F vacancy, opening
vaciar[28] VT (una botella) to empty; (una naranja) to hollow out; (una estatua) to cast; (una computadora) to dump
vacilación F hesitation
vacilante ADJ (dudoso) vacillating, hesitating; (temblroso) shaky
vacilar VI to vacillate, to hesitate, to waver; **— [con]** *fam* to make fun [of]
vacío ADJ (envase) empty; (casa) vacant; (comentarios) idle; (expresión) blank; M (condición) emptiness; (lugar) void; (espacio sin aire) vacuum; **envasado al —** vacuum-packed; **hacer el —** to give the cold shoulder
vacuna F (inoculación) vaccine; (enfermedad) cowpox
vacunación F vaccination
vacunar VI/VT to vaccinate
vacuno ADJ bovine
vadear VT to ford
vado M ford, crossing
vagabundear VI to wander idly
vagabundo -da ADJ vagabond, vagrant; MF (pordiosero) tramp, bum; (trabajador errante) drifter, transient; (en la playa) beachcomber
vagancia F vagrancy
vagar[40] VI to wander, to roam
vagina F vagina
vaginal ADJ vaginal
vaginitis F vaginitis
vago -ga ADJ (idea) vague; (silueta) shadowy; (impresión) faint, vague; (persona) lazy; MF vagrant, tramp
vagón M railway car; **— restaurante** dining car
vaguedad F faintness
vahído M dizzy spell
vaho M steam
vaina F (de una espada) sheath; (de legumbres) pod, shell; (molestia) nuisance; (cosa mal recordada) thing
vainilla F vanilla
vaivén M swaying, swinging; **vaivenes** ups and downs
vajilla F tableware, dishes; **— de barro** earthenware; **— de porcelana** chinaware
vale M voucher; INTERJ oh well, OK
valedero ADJ valid
valenciano -na ADJ & MF Valencian
valentía F courage, valor, bravery
valentón -ona ADJ cocky; MF cocky person
valer[60] VT (tener un determinado valor) to be worth; VI (ser válido) to be valid; (estar permitido) to be allowed; (ser de utilidad) to be useful; **— la pena** to be worthwhile; **— más que** to outweigh; **—se de** to avail oneself of; **—se por sí mismo** to be self-sufficient; **¿cuánto vale?** how much is it? **hacer — los derechos** to assert one's rights; **hacerse —** to stand up for oneself; **le valió una paliza** that earned him a beating; **más vale solo que mal acompañado** better alone than in poor company; **no hay pero que valga** no buts about it; **más vale tarde que nunca** better late than never; **no vale ni un comino** it's not worth a hoot; **no vale** that's not fair; **¡vale!** OK! **¡válgame Dios!** gracious! **todo vale** anything goes
valeroso ADJ valorous, brave
valga, valgo *ver* valer
valía F worth
validez F validity
válido ADJ (entrada, cupón) valid; (cheque) good; (argumento) solid
valiente ADJ valiant, brave, courageous
valija F (para viajes) valise, suitcase; (para el correo) pouch
valioso ADJ valuable

valla F (en un jardín) fence; (en carreras) hurdle
vallar VT to fence
valle M valley, vale
valor M (precio) value, worth; (valentía) valor, mettle; **—contable** book value; **—es** securities; **—es en cartera** holdings; **—nominal** face value, par value; **—es respaldados por hipoteca** mortgage-backed securities; **armarse de —** to muster up one's courage
valoración F valuation
valorar VT (apreciar) to value; (determinar el valor) to appraise; (aumentar el valor) to make more valuable
valorizar[47] VT to make more valuable; **—se** to become more valuable
vals M waltz
valsar VI to waltz
valuación F valuation, appraisal
valuar[26] VT to appraise
valva F valve
válvula F valve; **— reguladora de aceleración** throttle
vampiresa F vamp
vampiro M vampire
vanagloria F boastfulness
vanagloriarse VI to boast
vanaglorioso ADJ boastful
vándalo -la MF vandal
vanguardia F vanguard; **a la —** at the forefront
vanidad F vanity, conceit
vanidoso ADJ vain
vano ADJ vain; **en —** in vain
Vanuatu M Vanuatu
vanuatuense ADJ & MF Vanuatuan
vapor M (de agua) vapor, steam; (buque) steamship; **—es** fumes; **cocer al —** to steam; **echar —** to give off steam
vapulear VT to thrash
vapuleo M thrashing
vaquería F cowshed
vaqueriza F cowshed
vaquero -ra M cowboy; **—s** blue jeans; F cowgirl; ADJ **botas vaqueras** cowboy boots
vaqueta F cowhide
vaquilla F heifer
vara F (rama) stick; (palo) rod
varadero M dry dock
varar VT to beach, to strand; VI to run aground
varear VT to whip with a stick
variable ADJ variable, changeable; F variable
variación F variation
variado ADJ varied
variante F variant
variar[28] VI/VT to vary
varicela F chicken pox
vários, varices F PL varicose veins
varicoso ADJ varicose
variedad F variety, assortment
varilla F (palo delgado) small rod; (para azotar) switch; (de paraguas) rib
vario ADJ varied; **—s** various, several
variopinto ADJ variegated
varita F wand
varón M male [person]
varonil ADJ (masculino) manly; (hombruno) mannish
vasco -ca ADJ & MF Basque; M (lengua) Basque
vascuence ADJ Basque; M (lengua) Basque
vascular ADJ vascular
vasectomía F vasectomy
vaselina F Vaseline™
vasija F vessel
vaso M (de vidrio) glass; (de papel, plástico) cup; (corto y grueso) tumbler; (sanguíneo) vessel; **— de precipitado** beaker
vástago M (de planta) shoot, sprout; (de persona) offspring; (de motor) rod
vasto ADJ vast
vataje M wattage
vaticinar VT to foretell
vaticinio M prediction
vatio M watt
vaya, vayamos, ve *ver* ir
vea, veamos *ver* ver
vecindad F (cercanía) vicinity; (barrio) neighborhood
vecindario M neighborhood
vecino -na MF (cercano, contiguo) neighbor; (residente de una zona) resident; ADJ neighboring
vector M vector
vedar VT to prohibit
vega F fertile plain
vegan ADJ & MF vegan
vegetación F vegetation
vegetal ADJ vegetable; M vegetable, plant
vegetar VI to vegetate
vegetariano -na ADJ & MF vegetarian
vehemencia F vehemence
vehemente ADJ vehement
vehículo M vehicle
veía, veíamos *ver* ver
veinte NUM twenty
veintena F (aproximadamente) group of [about] twenty; (exactamente) score
veinticinco NUM twenty-five
veintiuno NUM twenty-one; M (juego de naipes) blackjack
vejancón -ona M codger; F old woman
vejar VT to humiliate
vejestorio -ria M codger; F old woman
vejete M codger
vejez F old age
vejiga F (órgano) bladder; (ampolla) blister
vela F (período de vigilancia) vigil, watch; (de cera) candle; (de un navío) sail; **a toda —** under full sail; **en —** without sleep; **hacerse**

a la — to set sail
velada F (noche) evening; (fiesta) evening party
velador M nightstand
velar VI (no dormir) to keep vigil, to stay awake; (cubrir con velo) to veil; (exponer a la luz una película fotográfica) to expose; — **por** to look after
velatorio M wake
veleidoso ADJ fickle
velero M sailboat; ADJ swift-sailing
veleta F weathervane; MF fickle person
vello M (del cuerpo) body hair; (de frutas) fuzz
vellón M fleece
velloso ADJ fuzzy
velludo ADJ hairy
velo M veil; — **del paladar** soft palate
velocidad F velocity, speed; — **de transferencia** transfer rate; **a toda** — at full speed
velocímetro M speedometer
velorio M wake
veloz ADJ swift, fast
ven *ver* venir
vena F (vaso sanguíneo, veta) vein; (estado de ánimo) mood; (de locura) streak; **estar en** — to be in the mood, to be inspired
venado M (animal) deer; (macho) stag; (carne) venison
vencedor-ora ADJ winning; MF winner, victor
vencer[32] VT (a un enemigo) to conquer, to vanquish; (a un equipo) to defeat, to beat; (obstáculos) to overcome; (en valor, inteligencia) to surpass; VI —**se** (un plazo) to expire; (un colchón) to cave in
vencido ADJ (derrotado) defeated; (a pagar) due, overdue, past due; **darse por** — to give up, to surrender
vencimiento M (de una deuda) maturity; (de un contrato) expiration
venda F (para una herida) bandage; (sobre los ojos) blindfold
vendaje M bandage; — **quirúrgico** surgical dressing
vendar VT (una herida) to bandage; (los ojos) to blindfold
vendaval M gale
vendedor-ora MF vendor, seller, salesperson; — **mayorista** wholesaler
vender VI/VT (comercializar) to sell; (traicionar) to betray; —**se a** to go over to; **se vende** for sale
vendetta F vendetta
vendible ADJ marketable
vendimia F vintage
vendrá, vendría *ver* venir
veneciana F venetian blind
veneno M (sustancia dañina) poison; (ponzoña de víbora) venom
venenoso ADJ (planta) poisonous; (víbora) venomous
venerable ADJ venerable
veneración F veneration, reverence
venerar VT (a una persona) to venerate, to revere; (a Dios) to worship
venezolano-na ADJ & MF Venezuelan
Venezuela F Venezuela
venga, vengamos *ver* venir
vengador-ora ADJ avenging; MF avenger
venganza F vengeance, revenge, payback
vengar[40] VT to avenge; —**se de** to retaliate for, to avenge, to take revenge
vengativo ADJ vindictive, vengeful
venida F coming
venidero ADJ forthcoming
venir[61] VI to come; — **a colación** to come up [in conversation]; — **al caso / a cuento** to be relevant; — **bien** to be convenient; —**le a uno bien** to be suitable to someone; —**se abajo** to collapse; **¿a qué viene eso?** what is the point of that? **el año que viene** next year; **lo mejor está por** — the best is yet to come; **no me vengas con excusas** no excuses; **venga lo que venga** come what may
venta F sale; — **al por mayor** wholesale; — **al por menor** retail; — **de liquidación** fire sale; **en** — for sale; **poner a la** — to put up for sale
ventaja F (también en tenis) advantage; (en una carrera) head start; — **al resto** ad out; — **al saque** ad in; — **al servicio** ad in
ventajoso ADJ advantageous
ventana F window (también digital); **tirar por la** — to throw out the window
ventanal M large window
ventanilla F [de coche, avión] window; (de la nariz) nostril
ventarrón M gale, high wind
ventear VI to sniff the wind
ventilación F (aireado) ventilation; (hueco para el aire) vent
ventilado ADJ airy
ventilador M (abertura) ventilator; (aparato) electrical fan
ventilar VT to ventilate, to air out; (una cuestión) to air
ventisca F blizzard
ventisquero M (lugar ventoso) place prone to blizzards; (lugar nevado) snowfield
ventolera F gust of wind; **darle a uno la** — **de** to take a notion to
ventosear VI to break wind
ventoso ADJ windy, breezy
ventrículo M ventricle
venturoso ADJ fortunate; **futuro** — bright future
veo *ver* ver
ver[72, 74] VI/VT (un paisaje) to see; (televisión,

espectáculos) to watch; (un programa de computadora) to view; **a —** let's see; **eso aún está por —se** that is still to be seen; **no lo puedo —** I can't stand him; **no veo la hora de terminar** I'm dying / I can't wait to finish; **no tener nada que — con** not to have anything to do with; **te veo preocupado** you look worried; **a mi modo de —** in my opinion; **—se obligado a** to be obliged to; **vérselas con algo** to confront something; **vérselas negras** to have a hard time

vera LOC ADV **a la —** beside

veracidad F truthfulness

veranear VI to spend the summer

veraneo M summer vacation

veraniego ADJ summer

verano M summer

veras LOC ADV **de —** really; **¿de —?** oh really? oh yeah?

veraz ADJ truthful

verbal ADJ verbal

verbena F carnival

verbo M verb

verborrágico ADJ long-winded

verboso ADJ verbose, wordy

verdad F truth; **¿—?** really? **— a medias** half-truth; **de —** indeed; **una pistola de —** a real pistol; **faltar a la —** to fib

verdaderamente ADV really, truly

verdadero ADJ true, real

verde ADJ green (también inmaduro, sin experiencia, ecologista); (chiste) off-color; **— oliva** olive-green; **ponerse —** to stuff oneself; M green; **poner — a alguien** to run someone down

verdear VI/VT to turn green

verdín M scum

verdor M greenness

verdoso ADJ greenish

verdugo M executioner, hangman

verdugón M welt

verdulero -ra MF vegetable vendor

verdura F (hortaliza) vegetable; (verdor) *lit* verdure; **—s** produce

vereda F (en el campo) path; (para peatones) *Am* sidewalk; **entrar en —** to toe the line

veredicto M verdict

verga F yard

vergonzoso ADJ (que da vergüenza) shameful, disgraceful; (que siente vergüenza) sheepish, bashful

vergüenza F (humillación) shame; (incomodidad) embarrassment; (escándalo) disgrace; **tener —** to be ashamed; **tener — ajena** to cringe; **es una —** it's a shame; **me dan — mis dientes** I'm embarrassed about my teeth; **me da — decírtelo** I'm embarrassed to tell you

vericueto M twists and turns

verídico ADJ truthful, true

verificación F verification, cross-check

verificar[30] VT to verify, to check; **—se** to take place

verja F grate

vermú M vermouth

vernáculo ADJ & M vernacular

verruga F wart

versado ADJ versed

versalillas F PL small caps

versalitas F PL small caps

versar VI **— sobre** to deal [with], to treat

versátil ADJ versatile

versículo M Bible verse

versión F (de un texto) version; (traducción) translation; (de una canción) rendition; **— beta** beta version; **— impresa** printout; **— original** original [of a film]

verso M line [of poetry]; **— libre** free verse; **— suelto/blanco** blank verse

versus PREP versus

vértebra F vertebra

vertebrado ADJ & M vertebrate

vertebral ADJ spinal

vertedero M dump, landfill

verter[2] VT (echar líquido) to pour; (vaciar) to pour out; (derramar) to spill; **— en** to empty into; **—se** to spill

vertical ADJ (en ángulo recto) vertical; (erguido) upright; (empinado) sheer

vertido M (acción) dumping; (lo vertido) waste; **— de petróleo** oil spill

vertiente F (pendiente) slope; (cuenca) watershed; ADJ flowing

vertiginoso ADJ dizzy, giddy

vértigo M (falta de equilibrio) vertigo; (frenesí) hectic pace

vertigoso ADJ dizzy, giddy

vesícula F gall bladder

vestíbulo M (de un edificio) vestibule, lobby; (de una casa) hallway

vestido M dress; **— de noche** evening gown; **— de novia** bridal dress

vestidura F attire

vestigio M vestige, trace, remnant

vestimenta F attire, dress; (estrafalaria) getup

vestir[9] VT to dress, to clothe; **—se** to get dressed; **—se de gala** to dress up

vestuario M (ropa) wardrobe; (en el teatro) costumes; (lugar para vestirse) changing room

veta F (de minerales) vein, seam; (de madera) grain; (de humor) strain

vetar VT to veto

veteado ADJ veined

veterano -na ADJ & MF veteran

veterinario -ria MF veterinarian; ADJ veterinary; F veterinary medicine

veto M veto
vetusto ADJ ancient
vez F time; **a la —** at the same time; **a su —** in turn; **a veces** sometimes; **cada — más** more and more; **cada — que** whenever; **de — en cuando** from time to time; **de una —** (por entero) all at once; (por fin) one and for all; **de una — por todas** once and for all; **en — de** instead of, in lieu of; **por primera —** for the first time; **otra —** again; **una — [que]** once; **una — tras otra** over and over; **una y otra —** over and over again; **raras veces** seldom; **hacer las veces de** to take the place of
vía F (camino) road; (de ferrocarril) track; (medio de acceso) avenue; **— de transmisión local** local bus; **— Láctea** Milky Way; **— navegable** waterway; **— respiratoria** airway; **—s urinarias** urinary tract; **por — de** by means of; **en —s de** in the process of; PREP via
viabilidad F viability
viable ADJ viable
viaducto M tunnel
viajante MF traveler; **— de comercio** ; M traveling salesman; F saleswoman
viajar VI (por tierra, aire) to travel, to journey; (por mar) to voyage; (con drogas) to trip
viaje M (por tierra, aire) trip, journey; (por mar) voyage; (en coche, caballo) ride; (por efecto de las drogas) trip; **— de ida y vuelta** round trip; **buen —** have a nice trip; **de —** out of town
viajero -ra MF traveler
viandante MF passerby
viático M (de viaje) per diem; (religioso) last rites
víbora F viper; **— de cascabel** rattlesnake
vibración F (de una cuerda) vibration; (de la lengua) trill
vibrador M vibrator
vibrante ADJ vibrating
vibrar VI/VT to vibrate
vicegobernador -ora MF lieutenant governor
vicepresidente MF, **vicepresidenta** F vice president
vicerrector -ora MF provost
viceversa ADV vice versa
viciado ADJ (aire) stale; (costumbre) stuffy; (corrupto) foul
viciar VT (estropear) to foul; (corromper) to corrupt
vicio M (mala costumbre) vice, bad habit; **de —** unjustifiably; **quitarse el — de** to wean oneself of
vicioso ADJ (persona) dissolute; (gasto) unjustifiable; (gramática) faulty
vicisitud F vicissitude
víctima F (de un crimen) victim; (en un accidente) casualty, victim
victimizar[47] VT to victimize
victoria F victory
victorioso ADJ victorious
vid F vine, grapevine
vida F life; **— media** half-life; **— mía** sweetheart; **— nocturna** nightlife; **— sentimental** love life; **así es la —** that's life; **de toda la —** lifelong; **de — o muerte** life-and-death; **en la — voy a hacer eso** I would never do that; **esto es —** this is the life; **ganarse la —** to earn a living; **sin —** lifeless
vidente MF seer; ADJ seeing
vídeo, video M (aparato) VCR; (técnica) video; (cinta) videocassette
videocámara F camcorder
videocasete F videocassette
videoclip M videoclip
videoconferencia F videoconference
videoconsola F video console
videojuego M video game
vidriado M glaze; ADJ glazed
vidriar VT to glaze
vidriera F show window
vidriero -ra MF glazier, glassmaker
vidrio M (sustancia) glass; (en una ventana) pane; **pagar los —s rotos** to be left holding the bag
vidrioso ADJ glassy
vieira F scallop
viejo -ja ADJ old; (chiste) stale; M (anciano) old man; (padre) father; **— amigo** longtime friend; **— verde** dirty old man; **los —s** the old folks; F (anciana) old woman; (madre) mother
viento M wind; **hace —** it is windy; **a los cuatro —s** in all directions
vientre M (abdomen) abdomen; (barriga) belly; (útero) womb
viernes M Friday
Vietnam M Vietnam
vietnamita ADJ & MF INV Vietnamese
viga F (de madera) beam, rafter; (de metal) girder
vigencia F **entrar en —** to go into effect; **estar en —** to be in force
vigente ADJ effective, in force
vigésimo NUM twentieth
vigía F lookout, reef; MF lookout
vigilancia F (cuidado) vigilance; (en una tienda) surveillance
vigilante ADJ vigilant; M watchman; F watchwoman
vigilar VI/VT to keep watch [over]; VT to keep an eye on; (policía) to stake out
vigilia F vigil, watch
vigor M vigor; **en —** in force; **entrar en —** to become effective
vigorizar[47] VT to invigorate

vigoroso ADJ vigorous
VIH [virus de inmunodeficiencia humana] M HIV
vil ADJ vile, base, low
vileza F villainy, baseness
vilipendiar VT to revile
villa F (aldea) village; (casa) country house
villancico M Christmas carol
villanía F villainy
villano -na ADJ villainous; MF villain
vilo LOC ADV **en —** (en el aire) suspended; (en ascuas) in suspense
vinagre M vinegar
vinculación F connection
vincular VT to link (también para páginas web); **—se** to link up
vínculo M link, tie; (en la web) link
vindicar[30] VT to vindicate
vine, viniendo, viniera, viniese *ver* venir
vinilo M vinyl
vino M wine; **— blanco** white wine; **— espumoso** sparkling wine; **— rosado** rosé wine; **— tinto** red wine
viña F vineyard
viñatero -ra MF winegrower
viñedo M vineyard
viola F viola
violación F (de la ley) violation, infringement; (sexual) rape
violado ADJ & M violet
violar VT (una ley) to violate, to break; (una mujer) to rape, to ravish; (una promesa) to breach; (una cerradura) to pick; (derechos) to infringe upon; (mandamientos) to trespass against
violencia F violence; **— doméstica** domestic violence
violentar VT (a una persona) to manhandle; (una casa) to break into; **—se** to get mortified
violento ADJ (deporte, tratamiento) violent, rough; (marido) abusive; (entrada) forcible; (ataque) vicious
violeta ADJ & M violet
violín M (para música clásica) violin; (para música folclórica) fiddle
violinista MF violinist
violonchelo M cello
VIP M VIP
virada F veer
viraje M swerve
viral ADJ viral
virar VI/VT (vehículo) to swerve, to veer; VI (barco) to tack
virgen ADJ & MF virgin; ADJ (cassette) blank; (selva) undisturbed
virginal ADJ virginal
viril ADJ virile, manly
virilidad F virility, manliness
virología F virology
virreinato M viceroyalty
virrey M viceroy
virtual ADJ virtual
virtud F (moral) virtue; (práctica) asset
virtuosismo M virtuosity
virtuoso -sa ADJ (moral) virtuous; ADJ & MF (artístico) virtuoso
viruela F smallpox
virulento ADJ virulent
virus M virus (también de computadoras); **— de inmunodeficiencia humana** human immunodeficiency virus
viruta F wood shaving
visa F visa
visado M visa
visar VT to endorse
visceral ADJ visceral
viscoso ADJ viscous
visera F visor
visibilidad F visibility
visible ADJ visible
visigodo -da ADJ Visigothic; MF Visigoth
visillo M window shade
visión F (capacidad de ver, lo visto) vision; (persona fea) sight; **— en túnel** tunnel vision
visionario -ria ADJ & MF visionary
visita F (acción de visitar) visit; (persona) visitor, caller; (a un edificio) tour; (en una página web) hit; **— de médico** house call
visitación F visitation
visitador -ora MF visitor, caller; (inspector) inspector; (vendedor de medicamentos) pharmaceutical sales representative
visitante MF caller, visitor; ADJ visiting (también en fútbol)
visitar VT (a un amigo, país) to visit; (a un paciente) to make a house call
vislumbrar VT to make out
viso M slip
visón M mink
víspera LOC ADV **en —s de** on the eve of
vista F (panorama) view, vista; (visión) eyesight; **a la —** in sight; **— cansada** eye strain; **a primera —** at first sight; **a simple —** with the naked eye; **bajar la —** to lower one's eyes; **conocer de —** to know by sight; **con —s a** with a view to; **en — de** considering; **hacer la — gorda** to look the other way; **¡hasta la —!** good-bye; **perder de —** to lose sight of; **tener a la —** to have before one's eyes; **tener — a** to look out on
vistazo M glance, glimpse, look; **dar/echar un — a** to glance over
visto ADJ **bien —** well thought of; **mal —** looked down upon; **— que** whereas; M **— bueno** approval; **dar el —bueno** to approve
visto *ver* ver
vistoso ADJ showy
visual ADJ visual

visualizador M display
visualizar[47] VT (en la imaginación) to visualize; (en pantalla) to display
vital ADJ vital; **fuerzas —es** life force
vitalicio ADJ life, for life; M lifetime pension
vitalidad F vitality
vitamina F vitamin
viticultor -ora MF winegrower
vítor M cheer
vitorear VI/VT to cheer
vitral M stained-glass window
vitrina F (ventana) shop window; (armario) showcase
vituperación F vituperation
vituperar VT to revile
vituperio M vituperation
viudo -da M widower; F widow; **viuda negra** black widow spider
vivacidad F vivacity
vivaracho ADJ vivacious
vivaz ADJ vivacious, lively
víveres M PL provisions
vivero M nursery
viveza F (vivacidad) liveliness; (inteligencia) cleverness
vívido ADJ vivid
vivienda F (casa) dwelling; (alojamiento) housing; **— unifamiliar** single-family home
viviente ADJ living
vivir VI/VT to live; **vive una vida normal** he leads a normal life; **vivieron felices y comieron perdices** they lived happily ever after; **¡viva!** hurrah! **¡viva el rey!** long live the king!
vivisección F vivisection
vivo ADJ (viviente) alive, living; (ágil) lively; (vistoso, intenso) vivid; (listo) clever; **en —** before a live audience; **en — y en directo** live; **de viva voz** by word of mouth
vocablo M word
vocabulario M vocabulary
vocación F (profesional) vocation, calling; (religioso) call
vocal ADJ (de la voz) vocal; (no consonántico) vowel; F vowel; MF member
vocálico ADJ vocalic
vocear VI/VT (gritar) to cry out; (anunciar) to page
vocerío M clamor
vocero -ra MF spokesperson
vociferante ADJ vociferous
vociferar VI to clamor
vodevil M vaudeville
vodka M vodka
volado ADJ (drogado) high; (escrito arriba) superscript
volador ADJ flying
volante ADJ flying; M (en un vestido) ruffle, frill; (en un coche) steering wheel; (en un motor) flywheel; (folleto) leaflet, handbill
volar[5] VI/VT to fly; **— por su cuenta** to fly solo; **ir volando** to hurry; VT (un puente) to blow up; VI (hojas) to blow; **—se** (hacer explosión) to blow up; (enojarse) to lose one's temper; (irse volando) to fly away
volátil ADJ volatile
volcada F **hacer una —** (baloncesto) to dunk the ball
volcán M volcano
volcánico ADJ volcanic
volcar[31] VT (voltear) to tip over, to knock over; (derramar) to spill; (vaciar) to empty; VI to roll over; **—se** (un coche) to tip over, to overturn; (en baloncesto) to dunk
volea F (en vóleibol) volley; (en béisbol) fly ball; (en tenis) volley
volear VI/VT to volley
voleibol, vóleibol M volleyball
volición F volition
volqueta F *Am* dump truck
volquete M dump truck
voltaje M voltage
voltear VT (una lámpara) to knock over, to turn over; (la cara) to turn away
voltereta F somersault, tumble; **dar una —** to somersault; **dar —s** to tumble
voltio M volt
voluble ADJ (malhumorado) moody; (mercado de valores) volatile
volumen M volume
voluminoso ADJ voluminous, bulky
voluntad F will; **a —** at will; **buena —** good will, willingness; **mala —** ill will; **por su propia —** of his own volition
voluntario -ria ADJ voluntary; MF volunteer
voluntarioso ADJ (bien dispuesto) willing; (testarudo) willful
voluptuoso ADJ voluptuous
voluta F scroll; **—s de humo** spirals of smoke
volver[6, 74] VI (regresar al punto de partida) to return, to come back; (ir de nuevo) to return, to go back, to go again; **— a comer** to eat again; **— del revés** to turn inside out; **— en sí** to regain consciousness; **—se** (regresar) to go back; (ponerse) to become; **—se contra** to turn against; **—se atrás** to turn back; **—se hacia** to go toward; **—se loco** to go crazy; VT (la cara) to turn away; (la página) to turn; **— las espaldas** to turn one's back
vomitar VI/VT to vomit, to throw up
vómito M vomit
voraz ADJ voracious, ravenous
vórtice M vortex
vos PRON *fam RP, Am Central* you
vosotros -as PRON PERS *Esp* you, you guys; (sur de EEUU) you all, y'all
votación F voting

votante MF voter
votar VI (emitir el voto) to vote; VT (elegir) to vote for; (aprobar) to vote into law; **— a/por** to vote for; **— a favor** to vote in favor; **— en contra** to vote against; **— es un deber importante** voting is an important duty
voto M (opinión) vote; (promesa) vow; **— de confianza** vote of confidence
voy *ver* ir
voz F (sonido, aptitud, voto) voice; (en un diccionario) headword; **a — en cuello** at the top of one's lungs; **alzar la —** to raise one's voice; **correr la —** to be rumored; **en — alta** aloud; **en — baja** quietly, softly; **a voces** shouting; **dar voces** to shout
vozarrón M loud voice
vudú M voodoo
vuela, vuele *ver* volar
vuelco M **dar un —** to overturn, to turn over; **todo daría un —** everything would change radically; **me dio un — el corazón** my heart skipped a beat
vuelo M (en avión) flight; (de una falda) flare; **al —** on the fly; **de alto —** prestigious; **levantar/alzar el —** to fly away
vuelta F (movimiento circular) turn; (regreso, devolución) return; (carrera ciclista) tour; (en una pista) lap; (curva) twist; (de un collar) loop; (en deportes) round; (dinero) change; **— de tuerca** unforeseen event; **a la — de la esquina** around the corner; **a — de correo** by return mail; **dar —** to turn upside down; **dar — al revés** to turn inside out; **dar — a una página / una llave** to turn a page / a key; **dar —s** to spin; **dar —s en la cama** to toss and turn; **dar — a algo** to turn something upside down; **dar la —** to turn around; **dar una —** to take a walk, to take a spin; **darse —** to roll over; **estar de —** (de regreso) to be back; (desencantado) to be jaded; **me da —s la cabeza** my head is spinning; **no tiene — de hoja** there are no two ways about it
vuelto M *Am* change
vuelto, vuelva, vuelve *ver* volver
vuestro ADJ POS *Esp* **— hermano** your brother; **un amigo —** a friend of yours; PRON **el —** yours
vulgar ADJ (común) ordinary; (tosco) vulgar
vulgaridad F vulgarity
vulgo M common people
vulnerable ADJ vulnerable

Ww

wafle M waffle
waflera F waffle iron
wáter M toilet
web F web, Internet, World Wide Web
whisky M whisk[e]y; **— escocés** scotch
wifi [fidelidad inalámbrica] F Wi-Fi™
windsurf M windsurfing
wok M wok

Xx

xenofobia F xenophobia
xilofón, xilófono M xylophone

Yy

y CONJ and
ya ADV (desde antes) already; (ahora) now; (pronto) soon; **¡—!** enough! **— era hora** it was about time; **¡— lo creo!** I should say so! **— no** no longer; **— que** since; **— sea que** whether; **— te arreglo** I'll fix you; **— verás** mark my words; **— voy** I am coming
yacer[37] VI to lie
yacimiento M (de minerales) deposit; (de petróleo) field
yanqui ADJ & MF *pey* American
yapa F freebie
yarda F yard (también en fútbol americano)
yate M yacht
yegua F mare
yelmo M helmet
yema F (de huevo) egg yolk; (de una planta) bud, shoot; **— de huevo** egg yolk; **— del dedo** fingertip
Yemen M Yemen
yemení ADJ & MF Yemeni
yen M yen
yendo *ver* ir
yerba *ver* hierba
yermo ADJ (estéril) barren; (desolado) bleak, stark
yerno M son-in-law
yesca F tinder
yeso M (mineral) gypsum; (en construcción, medicina) plaster [of Paris]; (escayola) cast
Yibuti M Djibouti
yibutiano -na ADJ & MF Djiboutian
yo PRON PERS I; M (ego) ego
yodo M iodine
yoduro M iodide
yoga M yoga
yogur M yogurt

yo-yo M yo-yo
yuan M yuan
yuca F (ornamental) yucca; (comestible) manioc
yudo M judo
yugo M yoke
Yugoslavia F Yugoslavia
yugoslavo -va ADJ & MF Yugoslavian
yugular ADJ & F jugular
yunque M anvil
yunta F yoke
yuppie MF yuppie
yuxtaponer[56, 74] VT juxtapose

Zz

zacate M grass (también en tenis)
zafar VT to release; **—se** (soltarse) to slip off; (no cumplir) to cop out; **—se de un aprieto** to squirm out of a difficulty
zafio ADJ boorish
zafiro M sapphire
zafra F [sugar] harvest
zaga LOC ADV **a la —** behind; F **ir a la —** to be behind; **quedar a la —** to fall behind
zaguán M vestibule, hall
zaino ADJ chestnut-colored
zalamería F (tacto) smoothness; (lisonja) flattery
zalamero -ra MF flatterer; ADJ (empalagoso) smooth, unctuous; (lisonjero) flattering
Zambia F Zambia
zambiano -na ADJ & MF Zambian
zambo ADJ knock-kneed
zambullida F dive, plunge
zambullir[16] VT to plunge, to dip; **—se** to dive, to plunge
zanahoria F carrot
zanca F leg of a wading bird
zancada F stride; **dar —s** to stride
zancadilla F intentional tripping; **hacer una —** to trip
zanco M stilt
zancudo ADJ long-legged, lanky; M *Am* mosquito
zángano M drone (también holgazán)
zangolotear VI/VT to jiggle
zangoloteo M jiggle
zanja F ditch, trench
zanjar VT to settle
zapapico M pickax[e]
zapata F brake shoe
zapatear VI to tap the feet in dancing
zapateo M tapping with the feet in dance
zapatería F shoe store
zapatero -ra MF (fabricante) shoemaker; (vendedor) shoe dealer; (remendón) cobbler
zapatilla F (pantufla) slipper; (de vestir) pump; **—s** sneakers
zapato M shoe; **—s con tacos** (fútbol americano) cleats; **—s con tapones** (fútbol) cleats; **—s del mismo par** matching shoes
zar M czar
zarandear VT to jiggle; **—se** to flop around
zarandeo M jiggle
zarcillo M (arete) earring; (de planta) tendril
zarigüeya F opossum
zarpa F claw
zarpar VI to sail, to set sail
zarpazo M blow with a claw; **dar —s** to claw
zarza F bramble, briar
zarzamora F blackberry
zepelín M blimp, zeppelin
zigoto M zygote
zigzag M zigzag
zigzaguear VI to zigzag, to weave one's way
Zimbabue M Zimbabwe
zimbabuo -bua ADJ & MF Zimbabwean
zirconio M zirconium
zócalo M baseboard; *Méx* main square
zodíaco M zodiac
zombi M zombie
zona F (área) zone; (culebrilla) shingles; **— de anotación/ensayo** (fútbol americano) end zone; **— de calentamiento** (béisbol) bullpen; **— de strike** (béisbol) strike zone; **— gris** gray area; **— tampón** buffer zone
zonificación F zoning
zonzo ADJ silly, foolish
zoo M zoo
zoología F zoology
zoológico ADJ zoological; M zoo
zoom M (de cámara fotográfica) zoom lens; (de computadora) zoom
zopenco -ca MF dolt, numbskull
zorrillo M skunk
zorro -a MF (animal) fox; F (hembra) vixen; ADJ (astuto) foxy, cunning
zorzal M thrush
zozobra F anxiety, worry
zozobrar VI to founder
zueco M clog
zumbar VI (hacer sonidos los insectos) to buzz, to drone, to hum; (hacer ruido las máquinas) to whir, to whiz; (tintinear los oídos) to ring; (dar golpe) to sock
zumbido M (sonido de insectos) buzz, drone, hum; (sonido de máquina) whir, whiz; (sonido en los oídos) ring
zumo M fruit juice
zurcido M (remiendo) darn; (acción de remendar) darning
zurcir[33] VT to darn
zurdo -da ADJ left-handed, southpaw; MF *fam* southpaw

Inglés–Español · English–Spanish

Lista de abreviaturas / List of Abbreviations

adj	adjetivo	adjective
adv	adverbio, adverbial	adverb, adverbial
Am	América	America
art	artículo	article
Carib	Caribe	Caribbean
conj	conjunción	conjunction
def	definido	definite
dem	demostrativo	demonstrative
f	femenino	feminine
fam	familiar	familiar
indef	indefinido	indefinite
interj	interjección	interjection
interr	interrogativo	interrogative
inv	invariable	invariable
lit	literario	literary
loc	locución	locution
m	masculino	masculine
Mex	México	Mexico
n	sustantivo	noun
num	numeral	numeral
pej, pey	peyorativo	pejorative
pl	plural	plural
poss	posesivo	possessive
prep	preposición, preposicional	preposition, prepositional
pron	pronombre	pronoun
rel	relativo	relative
RP	Río de la Plata	River Plate
sg	singular	singular
Sp	España, español	Spain, Spanish
v aux	verbo auxiliar	auxiliary verb
vi	verbo intransitivo	intransitive verb
vt	verbo transitivo	transitive verb
vulg	vulgar	vulgar

Pronunciación inglesa

I. VOCALES

Símbolo fonético	*Ortografía inglesa*	*Explicación*
[i]	see, pea	como la *i* en hilo
[ɪ]	bit	el sonido más aproximado es la *i* en *virtud*, pero la [ɪ] inglesa es más abierta, tirando a *e*
[e]	late, they	equivale aproximadamente a *ei*
[ɛ]	set	semejante a la *e* de *perro*, pero más abierta
[ɝ]	work, bird	como la *u* de *cud* (ver abajo) pero articulada simultáneamente con una *r*
[æ]	sat	sonido intermedio entre *e* y *a*
[ɑ]	hot	como la vocal de *pan*
[ɔ]	saw, laud	sonido intermedio entre *a* y *o*
[o]	low, mode	equivale aproximadamente a *ou*
[ʊ]	book, pull	como la *u* de *turrón*, pero más abierta
[u]	June, moon	como la *u* de *uno*
[ʌ]	cud	una *e* muy relajada
[ə]	adept	una *e* muy relajada y átona
[ɚ]	teacher	una *e* átona relajada articulada simultáneamente con una *r*

II. DIPTONGOS

Símbolo fonético	*Ortografía inglesa*	*Explicación*
[aɪ]	pie, aisle	como *ai* en *aire*
[aʊ]	now, foul	como *au* en *causa*
[ɔɪ]	boy	como *oy* en *hoy*
[ju]	use	como *iu* en *ciudad*

III. CONSONANTES

Símbolo fonético	*Ortografía inglesa*	*Explicación*
[b]	bat	semejante a la *b* española
[d]	day	semejante a la *d* española, pero articulada en los alvéolos y con más tensión
[f]	fun, photo	como la *f* española

[g]	go	como la *g* de *goma*, pero con más tensión
[h]	hat	muy suave como la *j* de los dialectos caribeños del español
[j]	year	como la *i* del diptongo de *hielo*
[k]	cat, kill	como la *c* de *carro*, pero seguida de aspiración en posición inicial de sílaba (sobre todo tónica)
[l]	let	como la *l* de *lado*
[ɫ]	ball	como la *l* final catalana
[m]	much	como la *m* española
[n]	no	como la *n* española
[p]	pea	como la *p* española, pero seguida de aspiración en posición inicial de sílaba (sobre todo tónica)
[r]	red	no tiene equivalente en español; se pronuncia con la punta de la lengua enrollada hacia arriba, sin tocar el paladar
[s]	sea	como la *s* hispanoamericana (no la castellana)
[t]	tea	como la *t* española pero articulada en los alvéolos y seguida de aspiración en posición inicial de sílaba (sobre todo tónica)
[v]	very	se articula con los dientes incisivos superiores colocados en el labio inferior
[w]	weed	equivale a la *u* del diptongo de *fui*
[z]	zero, rose	como la *s* de *mismo* cuando se sonoriza, pero aun más sonora
[ɒ]	latter, ladder	como la *r* de *para*
[θ]	thin	como la *z* del español castellano en *zagal*
[ð]	this	como la *d* de *cada*
[ʃ]	sheet, machine, notation	una *s* muy palatal como en francés *chapeau* o italiano *lasciare*
[ʒ]	measure, beige	como la *ll* argentina en *valle*, cuando es sonora
[tʃ]	church	como la *ch* de *charla*
[ʤ]	judge	como la *y* de *inyectar*
[n̩]	eaten, button	representa la *n* silábica, articulada sin la vocal anterior
[ŋ]	ring	como la *n* española en *mango* y *banco*
[l̩]	rental	representa la *l* silábica, articulada como la *l* final catalana
[hw]	where	combinación de los sonidos [h] y [w] arriba descritos

Notas sobre gramática inglesa

El sustantivo

Género. En la gramática inglesa el género solo desempeña un papel importante en el sistema pronominal, p. ej. **he runs** 'él corre', **she runs** 'ella corre', **I see him** 'lo veo', **I see her** 'la veo'. En los sustantivos que designan a personas, se emplean varios métodos para distinguir entre los sexos, v. gr. el agregado de un sufijo, como en **actor** 'actor', **actress** 'actriz', el agregado de una palabra, como en **baby boy** 'niño', **baby girl** 'niña', **she-bear** 'osa', **male nurse** 'enfermero', o el uso de palabras completamente distintas, como en **uncle** 'tío', **aunt** 'tía'.

Número. Generalmente se forma el plural añadiendo **-s** al singular: **paper, papers** 'papel, papeles', **book, books** 'libro, libros', **chief, chiefs** 'jefe, jefes'.

Los sustantivos que terminan en **-ss, -x, -sh, -z** y **-o** añaden **-es** para formar el plural: **kiss, kisses** 'beso, besos', **box, boxes** 'caja, cajas', **dish, dishes** 'plato, platos', **buzz, buzzes** 'zumbido, zumbidos', **hero, heroes** 'héroe, héroes' (excepción: **piano, pianos**). Esto vale también para **-ch** cuando se pronuncia [č], como en **arch, arches** 'arco, arcos', pero no cuando se pronuncia [k], como en **monarch, monarchs** 'monarca, monarcas'.

Los sustantivos que terminan en **-fe,** y ciertos sustantivos que terminan en **-f,** cambian estas letras en **v** y añaden **-es** en el plural: **leaf, leaves** 'hoja, hojas', **life, lives** 'vida, vidas', **wife, wives** 'esposa, esposas', **knife, knives** 'cuchillo, cuchillos' (pero **reef, reefs** 'arrecife, arrecifes').

Para formar el plural de los sustantivos terminados en **-y** precedida de consonante se cambia la **-y** en **-ies: fly, flies** 'mosca, moscas', **family, families** 'familia, familias'. En cambio, los sustantivos terminados en **-y** precedida de vocal forman el plural añadiendo **-s** al singular: **day, days** 'día, días'.

Ciertos sustantivos forman el plural de una manera irregular: **man, men** 'hombre, hombres', **woman, women** 'mujer, mujeres', **mouse, mice** 'ratón, ratones', **louse, lice** 'piojo, piojos', **goose, geese** 'ganso, gansos', **tooth, teeth** 'diente, dientes', **foot, feet** 'pie, pies', **ox, oxen** 'buey, bueyes'.

Ciertos sustantivos que terminan en **-is** forman el plural cambiando la **i** de la terminación en **e: axis, axes** 'eje, ejes', **crisis, crises** 'crisis' (sg., pl.).

El adjetivo

El adjetivo inglés es invariable en cuanto a género y número. Normalmente se coloca delante del sustantivo: **an interesting woman** 'una mujer interesante', **a large man** 'un hombre grande', **beautiful birds** 'aves hermosas'.

Los comparativos y superlativos. Aunque no hay una regla general, por lo común los adjetivos monosílabos, los adjetivos acentuados en la última sílaba y algunos bisílabos comunes forman el comparativo de aumento y el superlativo añadiendo **-er** y **-est**

(como **tall**). Los demás adjetivos van precedidos de **more** (para el comparativo) y **most** (para el superlativo) (como **careful**). Nótese que (1) si la palabra termina en **-e** muda, se añaden **-r** y **-st** en vez de **-er** y **-est** (ver **wise**), (2) los adjetivos terminados en **-y** cambian esta letra en **i** (ver **happy**), (3) los adjetivos terminados en consonante (menos **r**) precedida de vocal doblan la consonante (ver **fat**):

Positivo	*Comparativo*	*Superlativo*
tall alto	**taller** más alto	**the tallest** el más alto
careful cuidadoso	**more careful** más cuidadoso	**the most careful** el más cuidadoso
wise sabio	**wiser** más sabio	**the wisest** el más sabio
happy feliz	**happier** más feliz	**the happiest** el más feliz
fat gordo	**fatter** más gordo	**the fattest** el más gordo

Los adjetivos siguientes forman el comparativo y el superlativo de una manera irregular:

good	**better**	**best**
bad, ill	**worse**	**worst**
much	**more**	**most**

El adverbio

Muchos adverbios se forman añadiendo **-ly** al adjetivo: **courteous** 'cortés', **courteously** 'cortésmente', **bold** 'atrevido', **boldly** 'atrevidamente'. Existen las irregularidades ortográficas siguientes en la formación de los adverbios que terminan en **-ly:** (1) los adjetivos terminados en **-ble** cambian la **-e** en **-y: possible, possibly,** (2) los terminados en **-ic** añaden **-ally: poetic, poetically,** (3) los terminados en **-ll** añaden solo **-y: full, fully,** (4) los terminados en **-ue** pierden la **-e** final: **true, truly,** (5) los terminados en **-y** cambian la **-y** en **i: happy, happily.**

La mayor parte de los adverbios forman el comparativo y el superlativo con los adverbios **more** 'más' y **most** 'el/la más'. Asimismo los adverbios monosílabos añaden **-er** y **-est:**

Positivo	*Comparativo*	*Superlativo*
boldly	**more boldly**	**most boldly**
generously	**more generously**	**most generously**
soon	**sooner**	**soonest**
early	**earlier**	**earliest**
late	**later**	**latest**
fast	**faster**	**fastest**

Los adverbios siguientes forman el comparativo y el superlativo de una manera irregular:

well	**better**	**best**
badly	**worse**	**worst**
little	**less**	**least**
far	**farther, further**	**farthest, furthest**

Sufijos comunes del inglés

-dom a partir de bases nominales, forma sustantivos con los sentidos de dominio, jurisdicción, estado, condición: **kingdom** 'reino' (**king** 'rey'), **martyrdom** 'martirio' (**martyr** 'mártir'), **freedom** 'libertad' (**free** 'libre')

-ee a partir de verbos, forma sustantivos indicando a la persona que recibe una acción: **addressee** 'destinatario' (**to address** 'dirigir'), **employee** 'empleado' (**to employ** 'emplear').

-eer a partir de bases diversas, forma sustantivos que denotan oficio u ocupación: **auctioneer** 'subastador' (**to auction** 'subastar'), **puppeteer** 'titiritero' (**puppet** 'títere')

-en *a.* forma adjetivos que denotan la sustancia de que está hecha una cosa: **golden** 'dorado' (**gold** 'oro'), **wooden** 'de madera' (**wood** 'madera')
b. forma verbos a partir de adjetivos: **to whiten** 'blanquear' (**white** 'blanco'), **to darken** 'oscurecer' (**dark** 'oscuro')

-er *a.* forma sustantivos a partir de verbos para indicar agente: **player** 'jugador' (**to play** 'jugar'), **speaker** 'hablante' (**to speak** 'hablar'), **baker** 'panadero' (**to bake** 'hornear')
b. forma sustantivos a partir de sustantivos para denominar al residente de un lugar: **New Yorker** 'neoyorquino' (**New York** 'Nueva York'), **islander** 'isleño' (**island** 'isla')

-ess se usa para formar el género femenino de ciertos sustantivos: **princess** 'princesa' (**prince** 'príncipe'), **countess** 'condesa' (**count** 'conde')

-fold indica el número de veces que se repite algo: **twofold** 'dos veces' (**two** 'dos'), **hundredfold** 'cien veces' (**hundred** 'cien')

-ful *a.* forma adjetivos a partir de sustantivos para indicar la presencia de una cualidad: **hopeful** 'esperanzado' (**hope** 'esperanza'), **careful** 'cuidadoso' (**care** 'cuidado'), **willful** 'voluntarioso' (**will** 'voluntad')
b. forma adjetivos a partir de verbos para indicar tendencia: **forgetful** 'olvidadizo' (**to forget** 'olvidar')

c. forma sustantivos a partir de sustantivos indicando la capacidad: **handful** 'puñado' (**hand** 'mano'), **spoonful** 'cucharada' (**spoon** 'cuchara')

-hood forma abstractos a partir de sustantivos concretos: **motherhood** 'maternidad' (**mother** 'madre'), **childhood** 'niñez' (**child** 'niño'), **likelihood** 'probabilidad' (**likely** 'probable')

-ing *a.* forma adjetivos a partir de verbos: **running water** 'agua corriente' (**to run** 'correr'), **drinking water** 'agua potable' (**to drink** 'beber'), **waiting room** 'sala de espera' (**to wait** 'esperar'), **washing machine** 'máquina lavadora' (**to wash** 'lavar')

b. se usa para formar sustantivos que expresan la acción de un verbo: **understanding** 'entendimiento' (**to understand** 'entender'), **supplying** 'abastecimiento' (**to supply** 'abastecer')

c. se usa para formar sustantivos que denominan una cosa que desempeña una acción: **clothing** 'ropa' (**to clothe** 'vestir'), **covering** 'cobertura' (**to cover** 'cubrir')

-ish forma adjetivos a partir de sustantivos indicando semejanza o atenuación: **boyish** 'como un niño' (**boy** 'niño'), **womanish** 'como mujer, mujeril' (**woman** 'mujer'), **whitish** 'blancuzco' (**white** 'blanco')

-less se agrega a sustantivos para indicar falta de algo: **childless** 'sin hijos' (**child** 'hijo'), **penniless** 'sin dinero' (**penny** 'centavo'), **endless** 'interminable, sin fin' (**end** 'fin')

-like se añade a sustantivos para indicar semejanza: **lifelike** 'que parece vivo' (**life** 'vida'), **childlike** 'infantil' (**child** 'niño'), **tigerlike** 'como un tigre' (**tiger** 'tigre')

-ly *a.* se añade a adjetivos para formar adverbios: **slowly** 'lentamente' (**slow** 'lento'), **happily** 'felizmente' (**feliz** 'happy')

b. deriva adjetivos a partir de sustantivos indicando una cualidad: **motherly** 'maternal' (**mother** 'madre'), **gentlemanly** 'caballeroso' (**gentleman** 'caballero'), **friendly** 'amistoso' (**friend** 'amigo')

c. deriva adjetivos o adverbios de tiempo a partir de sustantivos: **daily** 'diario', 'diariamente' (**day** 'día'), **weekly** 'semanal', 'semanalmente' (**week** 'semana')

-ness forma nombres de cualidades a partir de adjetivos: **goodness** 'bondad' (**good** 'bueno'), **darkness** 'oscuridad' (**dark** 'oscuro'), **foolishness** 'tontería' (**fool** 'tonto')

-ship se emplea para derivar sustantivos a partir de sustantivos y verbos para denotar

a. cualidades abstractas: **friendship** 'amistad' (**friend** 'amigo')

b. arte o destreza: **horsemanship** 'equitación' (**horseman** 'jinete')

c. dignidad, oficio, cargo o título: **professorship** 'cátedra' (**professor** 'catedrático'), **lordship** 'señoría' (**lord** 'señor')

d. la duración de una acción: **courtship** 'cortejo' (**to court** 'cortejar')

-some se añade a verbos para formar adjetivos que expresan tendencia excesiva: **tiresome** 'aburrido' (**to tire** 'aburrir'), **quarrelsome** 'pendenciero' (**to quarrel** 'discutir')

-th es el sufijo que forma números ordinales a partir de los cardinales: **fifth** 'quinto' (**five** 'cinco'), **tenth** 'décimo' (**ten** 'diez')

-ward se añade a sustantivos y adverbios para indicar movimiento hacia un lugar: **homeward** 'hacia casa' (**home** 'casa'), **downward** 'hacia abajo' (**down** 'abajo')

-wise, -ways se añaden a sustantivos para indicar dirección o posición: **edgewise** 'de lado' (**edge** 'borde'), **lengthwise** 'a lo largo' (**length** 'largo'), **sideways** 'de lado' (**side** 'lado')

-y

a. es un sufijo diminutivo: **doggy** 'perrito' (**dog** 'perro'), **Johnny** 'Juanito' (**John** 'Juan')

b. se añade a sustantivos para formar adjetivos que indican abundancia: **rocky** 'rocoso' (**rock** 'roca'), **rainy** 'lluvioso' (**rain** 'lluvia'), **hairy** 'peludo' (**hair** 'pelo'), **angry** 'enojado' (**anger** 'enojo')

c. se añade a sustantivos para formar adjetivos que expresan semejanza: **rosy** 'rosado' (**rose** 'rosa')

Verbos irregulares de la lengua inglesa

Se denominan verbos irregulares los que no forman el pretérito o el participio pasivo con la adición de **-d** o **-ed** al presente. Obsérvese que en ciertos verbos (aquí señalados con asterisco) coexiste la forma regular al lado de la irregular. Las formas poco usadas aparecen entre paréntesis.

Presente	*Pretérito*	*Participio pasivo*
*abide	(abode)	abided
am, is, are	was, were	been
arise	arose	arisen
*awake	awoke	awoken

Presente	*Pretérito*	*Participio pasivo*
bear	bore	borne
beat	beat	beaten
become	became	become
befall	befell	befallen
beget	begat	begotten
begin	began	begun
behold	beheld	beheld
bend	bent	bent
*beseech	(besought)	(besought)
beset	beset	beset
bet	bet	bet
bid 'ofrecer'	bid	bid
bid 'mandar'	bade	bidden
bind	bound	bound
bite	bit	bitten, bit
bleed	bled	bled
blow	blew	blown
break	broke	broken
breed	bred	bred
bring	brought	brought
build	built	built
*burn	burnt	burnt
burst	burst	burst
buy	bought	bought
cast	cast	cast
catch	caught	caught
choose	chose	chosen
cling	clung	clung
*clothe	(clad)	(clad)
come	came	come
cost	cost	cost
creep	crept	crept
cut	cut	cut
deal	dealt	dealt
dig	dug	dug
*dive	dove	dived
do	did	done
draw	drew	drawn
*dream	dreamt	dreamt
drink	drank	drunk
drive	drove	driven
*dwell	dwelt	dwelt
eat	ate	eaten
fall	fell	fallen

Verbos irregulares

Presente	*Pretérito*	*Participio pasivo*
feed	fed	fed
feel	felt	felt
fight	fought	fought
find	found	found
*fit	fit	fit
flee	fled	fled
fling	flung	flung
fly	flew	flown
forbear	(forbore)	(forborne)
forbid	forbade	forbidden
foresee	foresaw	foreseen
foretell	foretold	foretold
forget	forgot	forgotten
forgive	forgave	forgiven
forsake	forsook	forsaken
freeze	froze	frozen
get	got	got, gotten
give	gave	given
go	went	gone
grind	ground	ground
grow	grew	grown
hang[1]	hung	hung
have, has	had	had
hear	heard	heard
*hew	hewed	hewn
hide	hid	hidden, hid
hit	hit	hit
hold	held	held
hurt	hurt	hurt
keep	kept	kept
*kneel	knelt	knelt
*knit	knit	knit
know	knew	known
lay	laid	laid
lead	led	led
*lean	(leant)	(leant)
*leap	leapt	leapt
*learn	(learnt)	(learnt)
leave	left	left
lend	lent	lent
let	let	let

1. Es regular cuando significa 'ahorcar'.

Presente	*Pretérito*	*Participio pasivo*
lie[2]	lay	lain
*light	lit	lit
lose	lost	lost
make	made	made
mean	meant	meant
meet	met	met
mistake	mistook	mistaken
*mow	mowed	mown
pay	paid	paid
*plead	pled	pled
put	put	put
quit	quit	quit
read [rid]	read [rɛd]	read [rɛd]
rend	rent	rent
*rid	rid	rid
ride	rode	ridden
ring	rang	rung
rise	rose	risen
run	ran	run
*saw	sawed	sawn
say	said	said
see	saw	seen
seek	sought	sought
sell	sold	sold
send	sent	sent
set	set	set
*sew	sewed	sewn
shake	shook	shaken
*shave	shaved	shaven
*shear	sheared	shorn
shed	shed	shed
shine[3]	shone	shone
shoe	shod	shod
shoot	shot	shot
*show	showed	shown
shrink	shrank (shrunk)	shrunk (shrunken)
shut	shut	shut
sing	sang	sung
sink	sank	sunk
sit	sat	sat
slay	slew	slain

2. Es regular cuando significa 'mentir'.
3. Suele ser regular cuando es transitivo, en el sentido 'pulir, dar brillo'.

Presente	*Pretérito*	*Participio pasivo*
sleep	slept	slept
slide	slid	slid
sling	slung	slung
slink	slunk	slunk
slit	slit	slit
*smell	(smelt)	(smelt)
smite	smote	smitten
*sow	sowed	sown
speak	spoke	spoken
*speed	sped	sped
*spell	(spelt)	(spelt)
spend	spent	spent
*spill	(spilt)	(spilt)
spin	spun	spun
spit	spat, spit	spat, spit
split	split	split
*spoil	(spoilt)	(spoilt)
spread	spread	spread
spring	sprang, sprung	sprung
stand	stood	stood
*stave	(stove)	(stove)
steal	stole	stolen
stick	stuck	stuck
sting	stung	stung
stink	stank	stunk
*strew	strewed	strewn
stride	strode	stridden
strike	struck	struck, stricken
string	strung	strung
*strive	strove	striven
swear	swore	sworn
*sweat	sweat	sweat
sweep	swept	swept
*swell	swelled	swollen
swim	swam	swum
swing	swung	swung
take	took	taken
teach	taught	taught
tear	tore	torn
tell	told	told
think	thought	thought
throw	threw	thrown
thrust	thrust	thrust
tread	trod	trodden

Presente	*Pretérito*	*Participio pasivo*
understand	understood	understood
undertake	undertook	undertaken
undo	undid	undone
uphold	upheld	upheld
upset	upset	upset
*wake	woke	woken
wear	wore	worn
weave	wove	woven
*wed	wed	wed
weep	wept	wept
*wet	wet	wet
win	won	won
wind	wound	wound
withdraw	withdrew	withdrawn
withhold	withheld	withheld
withstand	withstood	withstood
wring	wrung	wrung
write	wrote	written

Aa

a [ə, e] INDEF ART un *m*, una *f*; **what — fool!** ¡qué tonto! **such — fool** tan tonto; **I'm — teacher / Catholic** soy maestro / católico

AA [Alcoholics Anonymous] [éé] N AA *f*

aback [əbǽk] ADV **to be taken —** estar desconcertado

abandon [əbǽndən] VT abandonar; N **with wild —** desenfrenadamente

abandonment [əbǽndənmənt] N abandono *m*, desamparo *m*

abashed [əbǽʃt] ADJ humillado, avergonzado

abate [əbét] VI/VT (trend, payments) disminuir, mitigar[se]; (storm) calmarse, atenuarse

abbey [ǽbi] N abadía *f*

abbot [ǽbət] N abad *m*

abbreviate [əbríviet] VT abreviar

abbreviation [əbriviéʃən] N (act of abbreviating) abreviación *f*; (short form) abreviatura *f*

abdicate [ǽbdɪket] VI/VT abdicar

abdomen [ǽbdəmən] N abdomen *m*, vientre *m*

abdominal [æbdɑ́mənl] ADJ abdominal; **— distension** distensión abdominal *f*

abduct [æbdʌ́kt] VT secuestrar, raptar

abduction [æbdʌ́kʃən] N secuestro *m*, rapto *m*

aberration [æbəréʃən] N anomalía *f*, aberración *f*

abet [əbét] VT instigar

abeyance [əbéəns] ADV LOC **in —** pendiente, en suspenso

abhor [əbhɔ́r] VT aborrecer

abhorrence [əbhɔ́rəns] N aborrecimiento *m*

abhorrent [əbhɔ́rənt] ADJ aborrecible

abide [əbáɪd] VT (tolerate) soportar; VI (dwell) morar, permanecer; **to — by** acatar, atenerse a

ability [əbílɪdɪ] N (skill) habilidad *f*; (aptitude) capacidad *f*

abject [æbʤɛ́kt] ADJ abyecto; **in — poverty** en extrema miseria

ablaze [əblɛ́z] ADV en llamas

able [ébəl] ADJ hábil, capaz; **— -bodied** de cuerpo sano; **to be — to** (be capable of) poder; (have an acquired skill) saber

abnegate [ǽbnɪget] VT renunciar

abnormal [æbnɔ́rməl] ADJ anormal

aboard [əbɔ́rd] ADV a bordo; **all —!** (train) ¡viajeros al tren! (ship) ¡pasajeros a bordo! **to go —** embarcarse, abordar

abode [əbód] N morada *f*

abode [əbód] *see* abide

abolish [əbɑ́lɪʃ] VT abolir, suprimir

abolition [æbəlíʃən] N abolición *f*

abominable [əbɑ́mənəbəl] ADJ abominable

abomination [əbɑmənéʃən] N (action, thing) abominación *f*; (condition, vice) horror *m*

aboriginal [æbəríʤənəl] ADJ aborigen

aborigine [æbəríʤəni] N aborigen *mf*; **Australian —** aborigen australiano -na *mf*

abort [əbɔ́rt] VT (fetus) abortar; VI/VT (mission) suspender; (software) interrumpir; N (software) interrupción *f*

abortion [əbɔ́rʃən] N aborto *m*

abortionist [əbɔ́rʃənɪst] N abortador -ora *mf*, abortero -ra *mf*

abortive [əbɔ́rtɪv] ADJ frustrado

abound [əbáʊnd] VI abundar; **to — with** abundar en

about [əbáʊt] PREP (concerning) acerca de, tocante a; (near, surrounding) alrededor de, por; **to be — one's business** atender a su negocio; ADV más o menos, alrededor de; **at — ten o'clock** a eso de las diez, sobre las diez; **to be — to do something** estar por / para hacer algo, estar a punto de hacer algo; **I'm all — transparency** insisto en la transparencia

above [əbʌ́v] PREP **you could see the towers — the buildings** se veían las torres sobre los edificios; **everyone — five years of age** todos los de más de cinco años; **he's — me in the company** es mi superior en la compañía; **to be — suspicion** estar libre de toda sospecha; **I thought you were — such things** no pensaba que te rebajarías a eso; ADV **the apartment —** el apartamento de arriba; **books of fifty pages and —** libros de cincuenta páginas y más; **the remark quoted —** la observación anteriormente citada; **— all** sobre todo; **— -mentioned** susodicho, ya mencionado

abrasion [əbréʒən] N abrasión *f*

abrasive [əbréɪsɪv] ADJ (material) abrasivo; (person, tone) irritante

abreast [əbrést] ADV al lado; **to keep —** mantenerse al corriente; **four —** de cuatro en fondo

abridge [əbríʤ] VT abreviar

abroad [əbrɔ́d] ADV en el extranjero; **to go —** ir al extranjero

abrupt [əbrʌ́pt] ADJ abrupto

ABS [antilock braking system] [ébíés] N SFA *m*

abscess [ǽbsɛs] N absceso *m*

abscond [æbskɑ́nd] VI fugarse

absence [ǽbsəns] N (nonpresence) ausencia *f*; (lack) falta *f*; **in the — of** a falta de

absent [ǽbsənt] ADJ ausente; **— -minded** distraído, despistado; **to be — from school** faltar a la escuela

absentee [æbsəntí] N ausente *mf*; **— landlord** propietario -ria ausente *mf*

absenteeism [æbsəntíɪzəm] N ausentismo *m*

absolute [æbsəlút] ADJ (ruler, certainty)

absoluto; (prohibition) terminante
absolutely [æbsəlútlɪ] ADV absolutamente; — **not** en absoluto; INTERJ —! ¡sí, señor! ¡claro!
absolve [æbzɑ́lv] VT absolver
absorb [əbzɔ́rb] VT (liquid) absorber; (shock) amortiguar; (people, information) asimilar; **he is —ed in his work** está absorto en su trabajo
absorption [əbzɔ́rpʃən] N absorción *f*
abstain [æbstén] VI abstenerse; — **from** abstenerse de
abstention [æbsténʃən] N abstención *f*
abstinence [ǽbstənəns] N abstinencia *f*
abstract [ǽbstrækt] ADJ abstracto; N (summary) resumen *m*, extracto *m*; **in the** — en abstracto
abstraction [æbstrǽkʃən] N abstracción *f*
absurd [əbsɜ́rd] ADJ absurdo, disparatado
absurdity [əbsɜ́rdɪdɪ] N (quality) absurdo *m*; (action) disparate *m*
abundance [əbʌ́ndəns] N abundancia *f*
abundant [əbʌ́ndənt] ADJ abundante
abuse[1] [əbjús] N (of privileges) abuso *m*; (of authority) abuso *m*, desmán *m*; (physical) maltrato *m*; (verbal) injuria *f*
abuse[2] [əbjúz] VT (privileges) abusar de; (physically) maltratar; (verbally) injuriar
abusive [əbjúsɪv] ADJ (physically) violento; (verbally) injurioso
abysmal [əbízməł] ADJ abismal; — **results** resultados desastrosos *m pl*
abyss [əbís] N abismo *m*
A/C [air conditioning] [ésí] N aire acondicionado *m*
academic [ækədɑ́mɪk] ADJ (university) académico; (school) escolar; N profesor -ora universitario -ria *mf*
academy [əkǽdəmi] N academia *f*
accede [æksíd] VI acceder; **to — to** acceder a
accelerate [æksɛ́ləret] VI/VT acelerar
acceleration [æksɛ̀ləréʃən] N aceleración *f*
accelerator [æksɛ́ləreɪdə˙] N acelerador *m*
accent[1] [ǽksɛnt] N (pronunciation) acento *m*; (written) tilde *f*, acento escrito/ortográfico *m*
accent[2] [æksɛ́nt] VT (syllable) acentuar
accentuate [æksɛ́ntʃuet] VT (differences, facts, syllables) acentuar, recalcar; (beauty) realzar
accept [æksɛ́pt] VT aceptar
acceptable [æksɛ́ptəbəł] ADJ aceptable
acceptance [æksɛ́ptəns] N (action) aceptación *f*; (approval) aprobación *f*
access [ǽksɛs] N acceso *m*; — **code** código de acceso *m*; — **provider** proveedor -ora de acceso *mf*; — **denied** acceso denegado *m*; VT acceder a
accessibility [æksɛsəbílɪdɪ] N accesibilidad *f*
accessible [æksɛ́səbəł] ADJ accesible
accessory [æksɛ́səri] ADJ accesorio; N (to clothes, to gadgets) accesorio *m*; (to a crime) cómplice *mf*; — **slot** ranura para accesorios *f*
accident [ǽksɪdənt] N accidente *m*; (mishap) percance *m*; — **insurance** seguro contra accidentes *m*; **by** — por casualidad
accidental [æksɪdɛ́ntł] ADJ (injury) accidental; (discovery, meeting) casual, fortuito
acclaim [əklém] VT aclamar; N aclamación *f*, ovación *f*
acclamation [æklæméʃən] N aclamación *f*
acclimate [ǽkləmet] VI/VT (to physical conditions) aclimatar[se]; (to an ambience) acostumbrar[se]
accolade [ǽkəled] N elogio *m*
accommodate [əkɑ́mədet] VT (adjust) tener en cuenta; (lodge) hospedar, alojar; (contain) tener capacidad para; VI **to — oneself** adaptarse
accommodation [əkɑmədéʃən] N (adjustment) acomodación *f*, adaptación *f*; —**s** (lodging) alojamiento *m*; (facilities) comodidades *f pl*
accompaniment [əkʌ́mpənɪmənt] N acompañamiento *m*
accompanist [əkʌ́mpənɪst] N acompañante *mf*
accompany [əkʌ́mpəni] VI/VT acompañar
accomplice [əkʌ́mplɪs] N cómplice *mf*
accomplish [əkʌ́mplɪʃ] VT (objective) lograr; (mission) completar
accomplished [əkʌ́mplɪʃt] ADJ (actor, athlete) consumado; (musician) talentoso
accomplishment [əkʌ́mplɪʃmənt] N (achievement) logro *m*; (skill) habilidad *f*; (completion) realización *f*
accord [əkɔ́rd] N acuerdo *m*, convenio *m*; **of one's own** — voluntariamente; VT otorgar, conceder
accordance [əkɔ́rdn̩s] ADV LOC **in — with** de acuerdo con, de conformidad con
according to [əkɔ́rdɪŋ] ADV LOC según
accordingly [əkɔ́rdɪŋlɪ] ADV (therefore) por consiguiente; (correspondingly) como corresponde
accordion [əkɔ́rdɪən] N acordeón *m*
accost [əkɔ́st] VT abordar
account [əkáʊnt] N (bill) cuenta *f*; (story) relato *m*, relación *f*; — **manager** administrador -ora de cuentas *mf*; —**s payable** cuentas por/a pagar *f pl*; —**s receivable** cuentas por/a cobrar *f pl*; **to open [close] an** — abrir [cerrar] una cuenta; **on — of** a causa de, debido a; **on my** — por mí; **on one's own** — por cuenta propia; **on no** — de ninguna manera; **of no** — de ningún valor; **to take into** — tener en cuenta; VI **to — for** dar cuenta de; **how do you — for that?** ¿cómo se explica eso?
accountability [əkaʊntəbílɪdɪ] N responsabilidad *f*
accountable [əkáʊntəbəł] ADJ responsable
accountant [əkáʊntn̩t] N *Am* contador -ra *mf*; *Sp*

contable *mf*

accounting [əkáʊntɪŋ] N contabilidad *f*; **— firm** empresa de contadores públicos *f*; **— period** ejercicio contable *m*

accredit [əkrédɪt] VT acreditar

acculturate [əkʌ́ltʃəret] VI/VT aculturar[se]

accumulate [əkjúmjəlet] VI/VT acumular[se]

accumulation [əkjumjəléʃən] N acumulación *f*

accuracy [ǽkjə-əsi] N (of measure, instrument) precisión *f*, exactitud *f*; (of a translation) fidelidad *f*

accurate [ǽkjə-ɪt] ADJ (measure, instrument) preciso, exacto; (translation) fiel

accursed [əkɝ́-sɪd] ADJ maldito

accusation [ǽkjuzéʃən] N acusación *f*

accuse [əkjúz] VT acusar

accused [əkjúzd] ADJ acusado; N acusado -da *mf*, reo -a *mf*, procesado -da *mf*

accuser [əkjúzɚ] N acusador -ra *mf*

accustom [əkʌ́stəm] VT acostumbrar, habituar; **to — oneself** acostumbrarse, habituarse; **to be —ed to** tener la costumbre de, estar acostumbrado a

AC/DC [alternating current / direct current] [ésidísi] ADJ alterna y continua

ace [es] N (cards, athlete, aviator) as *m*; (tennis) saque ganador *m*, servicio directo *m*; VT (a test) sacarse la máxima nota en

acetaminophen [əsɛdəmínəfən] N acetaminofén *m*

acetone [ǽsətoʊn] N acetona *f*

ache [ek] N dolor *m*; **—s and pains** achaques *m pl*; VT doler; **my stomach —s** me duele el estómago

achieve [ətʃív] VT (a goal) conseguir, lograr; (a level) alcanzar

achievement [ətʃívmənt] N (attainment) consecución *f*; (success) logro *m*, realización *f*

Achilles tendon [əkɪliz tɛ́ndən] N tendón de Aquiles *m*

aching [ékɪŋ] ADJ doliente, dolorido

achy [éki] ADJ dolorido

acid [ǽsɪd] ADJ ácido; N ácido *m*; (hallucinogen) LSD *m*; **— rain** lluvia ácida *f*; **— test** prueba de fuego *f*

acidic [əsídɪk] ADJ ácido

acidity [əsídɪdi] N acidez *f*

acknowledge [ǽknálɪdʒ] VT (merits) reconocer; (faults) admitir, reconocer; (help) agradecer; **to — receipt** acusar recibo

acknowledgment [ǽknálɪdʒmənt] N (of merits) reconocimiento *m*; (of merits, faults) reconocimiento *m*, admisión *f*; (gratefulness) agradecimiento *m*; **— of receipt** acuse de recibo *m*

acme [ǽkmi] N súmmum *m*

acne [ǽkni] N acné *m*

acorn [ékɔrn] N bellota *f*

acoustics [əkústɪks] N acústica *f*

acquaint [əkwént] VT informar, familiarizar; **to — oneself with** informarse de, familiarizarse con; **to be —ed with** (a person, city, country) conocer; (a piece of news) estar enterado de

acquaintance [əkwéntn̩s] N (with facts) conocimiento *m*; (a person) conocido -a *mf*

acquiesce [ǽkwiés] VT asentir, condescender; (unwillingly) consentir

acquiescence [ǽkwiésəns] N asentimiento *m*, consentimiento *m*, condescendencia *f*

acquire [əkwáɪr] VT (knowledge, skill, purchase) adquirir; (fortune, information) obtener; (disease) contraer

acquisition [ǽkwəzíʃən] N (knowledge, skill, purchase) adquisición *f*; (fortune, information) obtención *f*

acquisitive [əkwízɪdɪv] ADJ codicioso

acquit [əkwít] VT absolver

acquittal [əkwídl] N absolución *f*

acre [ékə-] N acre [0.405 hectares] *m*

acrid [ǽkrɪd] ADJ acre

acrimony [ǽkrəmoni] N acritud *f*

acrobat [ǽkrəbæt] N acróbata *mf*

acrobatic [ǽkrəbǽdɪk] ADJ acrobático; N **—s** acrobacia *f*

acronym [ǽkrənɪm] N acrónimo *m*, sigla *f*

acrophobia [ǽkrəfóbiə] N acrofobia *f*

across [əkrɔ́s] PREP **to lay one stick — the other** poner dos palos cruzados; **there's a bridge — that river** hay un puente sobre ese río; **he came — his old love letters** encontró sus viejas cartas de amor; **the library is — the street** la biblioteca está al otro lado de la calle; **— the board** de manera uniforme, sin excepciones; ADV **cut the boards —** corta los tablones a lo ancho; **five hundred miles —** de quinientas millas de ancho; **the meaning doesn't come —** el significado no se entiende

acrylic [əkrílɪk] ADJ & N acrílico *m*

act [ǽkt] N (deed, part of play) acto *m*; (part of show) número *m*; (law) ley *f*, decreto *m*; **— of God** caso de fuerza mayor *m*; VI (behave) actuar, comportarse; (take measures) obrar; (play a part, chemical process) actuar; (represent) representar; (function) funcionar; **to — up** (child) portarse mal; (car) funcionar mal; **to — out** (event) representar; (feelings) exteriorizar

acting [ǽktɪŋ] N actuación *f*; (in a drama) representación *f*; ADJ (interim) interino; (substitute) suplente

action [ǽkʃən] N (practical measure, plot of a play) acción *f*; (deed) acto *m*; (functioning) funcionamiento *m*; **to take —** tomar medidas

actionable [ǽkʃənəbəl] ADJ accionable, procesable

activate [ǽktɪvet] VT activar

active [æktɪv] ADJ activo
activism [æktɪvɪzəm] N activismo *m*
activist [æktɪvɪst] N activista *mf*
activity [æktívɪdɪ] N actividad *f*
actor [æktɚ] N actor *m*
actress [æktrɪs] N actriz *f*
actual [æktʃuəł] ADJ verdadero, real
actually [æktʃuəli] ADV en realidad, efectivamente
actuary [æktʃueri] N actuario -ria *mf*
acuity [əkjúɪdɪ] N agudeza *f*
acumen [ǽkjəmən] N perspicacia *f*, agudeza *f*
acupuncture [ǽkjʊpʌŋktʃɚ] N acupuntura *f*
acupuncturist [ǽkjʊpʌ́ŋktʃə-ɪst] N acupuntor -ora *mf*
acute [əkjút] ADJ (pain, illness) agudo; (observation) perspicaz, penetrante
AD [édí] ADV d.C.
ad [æd] N anuncio publicitario *m*; **— in** (tennis) ventaja al saque *f*, ventaja al servicio *f*; **— out** (tennis) ventaja al resto *f*; **— lib** ADJ improvisado; ADV improvisando; **to — lib** VI improvisar
adamant [ǽdəmənt] ADJ inflexible, firme
Adam's apple [ǽdəmz æpəł] N nuez de Adán *f*
adapt [ədǽpt] VT adaptar; VI **to —** to adaptar[se] a, acomodar[se] a
adaptation [ædəptéʃən] N adaptación *f*
adapter [ədǽptɚ] N adaptador *m*
add [æd] VT añadir, agregar; (find sum) sumar; **—ed cost** costo adicional *m*; **to — to** aumentar; **to — up** (find sum) sumar; (make sense) cuadrar; N **—-on** accesorio *m*
addict [ǽdɪkt] N adicto -ta *mf*
addicted [ədíktɪd] ADJ adicto
addiction [ədíkʃən] N adicción *f*
addition [ədíʃən] N (of numbers) suma *f*; (to a collection, staff) adición *f*, adquisición *f*; (to a building) anexo *m*; **in — [to]** además [de]
additional [ədíʃənəł] ADJ adicional
additive [ǽdɪtɪv] N aditivo *m*
address[1] [ədrés] N (street) dirección *f*, domicilio *m*; (speech) discurso *m*; **— book** libreta de direcciones *f*; **form of —** tratamiento *m*
address[2] [ədrés] VT (write the address) dirigir; (speak to) dirigirse a; (deal with) ocuparse de
addressee [ædresí] N destinatario -ria *mf*
adduce [ədús] VT aducir
adept [ədépt] ADJ hábil
adequacy [ǽdɪkwəsi] N suficiencia *f*
adequate [ǽdɪkwɪt] ADJ (sufficient) suficiente; (acceptable) aceptable
adhere [ædhír] VI adherirse; **to — to** adherirse a
adherence [ædhírəns] N adhesión *f*
adhesion [ædhíʒən] N (thing or tissue that adheres) adherencia *f*; (act of sticking together) adhesión *f*
adhesive [ædhísɪv] ADJ adhesivo; **— tape** cinta adhesiva *f*
adjacent [əʤésənt] ADJ adyacente
adjective [ǽʤɪktɪv] ADJ & N adjetivo *m*
adjoin [əʤɔ́ɪn] VT lindar con, colindar con; **—ing** colindante; VI estar contiguo a
adjourn [əʤɝ́n] VT **to — the meeting** levantar la sesión; **meeting —ed** se levanta la sesión
adjournment [əʤɝ́nmənt] N levantamiento de la sesión *m*
adjudge [əʤʌ́ʤ] VT (declare) declarar; (deem) calificar
adjudicate [əʤúɪdɪket] VI arbitrar; VT declarar
adjunct [ǽʤʌŋkt] ADJ adjunto; N agregado -da *mf*
adjust [əʤʌ́st] VT (fix) ajustar, graduar; (adapt a machine) regular; **—ed net income** ingreso neto ajustado *m*; VI ajustarse, adaptarse
adjustable [əʤʌ́stəbəł] ADJ ajustable; **—-rate mortgage** hipoteca con tasa de interés ajustable *f*
adjustment [əʤʌ́stmənt] N ajuste *m*; (to a machine) regulación *f*
administer [ædmínɪstɚ] VT (a business) administrar, gestionar; (a punishment) aplicar; (an oath) tomar[le]
administration [ædmɪnɪstréʃən] N administración *f*; (period in power) gestión *f*; (of punishment) aplicación *f*; (of an oath) toma *f*
administrative [ædmínɪstrəɪv] ADJ administrativo
administrator [ædmínɪstrəɚ] N administrador -ra *mf*; (civil) intendente *mf*
admirable [ǽdmərəbəł] ADJ admirable
admiral [ǽdmərəł] N almirante *m*
admiration [ædməréʃən] N admiración *f*
admire [ædmáɪr] VT admirar
admirer [ædmáɪrɚ] N admirador -ora *mf*; (suitor) pretendiente *mf*
admissible [ædmísəbəł] ADJ admisible
admission [ædmíʃən] N (acceptance) admisión *f*; (access, ticket price) entrada *f*; (confession) confesión *f*
admit [ædmít] VT (allow entry) admitir; (to a hospital) internar; (acknowledge) reconocer, admitir
admittance [ædmítns] N entrada *f*; **no —** prohibida la entrada
admonish [ædmánɪʃ] VT amonestar
admonition [ædməníʃən] N (warning) advertencia *f*; (reproof) amonestación *f*
adobe [ədóbi] N (mud) adobe *m*; (house) casa de adobe *f*
adolescence [ædl̩ésəns] N adolescencia *f*
adolescent [ædl̩ésənt] ADJ & N adolescente *mf*
adopt [ədápt] VT (child, custom) adoptar; (suggestion) aprobar
adoption [ədápʃən] N (of a child, custom) adopción *f*; (of a suggestion) aprobación *f*
adoptive [ədáptɪv] ADJ adoptivo

adorable [ədɔ́rəbəł] ADJ adorable, precioso
adoration [æ̀dəréʃən] N adoración *f*
adore [ədɔ́r] VT adorar; **I — playing tennis** me encanta jugar al tenis
adorn [ədɔ́rn] VT adornar, ornar
adornment [ədɔ́rnmənt] N adorno *m*
adrenal [ədríni] ADJ suprarrenal
adrenaline [ədrénəlɪn] N adrenalina *f*
adrift [ədrɪ́ft] ADJ & ADV a la deriva
adult [ədʌ́łt] ADJ & N adulto -ta *mf*
adulterate [ədʌ́łtəret] VT adulterar
adulterer [ədʌ́łtərə-] N adúltero -ra *mf*
adultery [ədʌ́łtəri] N adulterio *m*
advance [ædvǽns] VI (move forward) avanzar; (make progress) avanzar, progresar; (bring forward) adelantar; VT (promote) promover; (propose) proponer; (pay beforehand) adelantar, anticipar; N (movement) avance *m*; (progress) adelanto *m*; (loan) adelanto *m*, anticipo *m*; **—s** (sexual) requiebros *m pl*; **in —** por adelantado, con anticipación
advanced [ædvǽnst] ADJ (idea, stage) avanzado; (country) adelantado
advancement [ædvǽnsmənt] N (movement) avance *m*; (rank) ascenso *m*; (knowledge) progreso *m*
advantage [ædvǽntɪʤ] N ventaja *f* (also tennis); **it would be to your —** te convendría; **to take — of** aprovecharse de
advantageous [ædvæntéʤəs] ADJ ventajoso, provechoso
advent [ǽdvent] N advenimiento *m*
adventure [ædvéntʃə-] N aventura *f*
adventurer [ædvéntʃərə-] N aventurero -ra *mf*
adventuresome [ædvéntʃə-səm] ADJ atrevido, osado
adventurous [ædvéntʃə-əs] ADJ (seeking adventure) aventurero, intrépido; (daring) atrevido, audaz
adverb [ǽdvɜ-b] N adverbio *m*
adversary [ǽdvə-sɛri] N adversario -ria *mf*
adverse [ædvɜ́-s] ADJ adverso
adversity [ædvɜ́-sɪdi] N adversidad *f*
advertise [ǽdvə-taɪz] VT anunciar, hacer publicidad/propaganda para; VI hacer propaganda/publicidad; **to — for a cook** poner un anuncio buscando cocinero
advertisement [ædvə-táɪzmənt] N anuncio publicitario *m*, aviso *m*
advertiser [ǽdvə-taɪzə-] N anunciante *mf*
advertising [ǽdvə-taɪzɪŋ] N publicidad *f*; **— agency** agencia de publicidad *f*; **— campaign** campaña publicitaria *f*; **— agent** agente publicitario -ria *mf*
advice [ædváɪs] N consejo *m*; (expert) asesoramiento *m*
advisable [ædváɪzəbəł] ADJ aconsejable, recomendable
advise [ædváɪz] VI/VT (counsel) aconsejar, advertir; VT (inform) avisar, informar; (expertly) asesorar
adviser, advisor [ædváɪzə-] N consejero -ra *mf*, asesor -ora *mf*
advocacy [ǽdvəkəsi] N defensa *f*
advocate[1] [ǽdvəkɪt] N (promoter) partidario -ria *mf*; (defender) defensor -ora *mf*, intercesor -ora *mf*; (lawyer) abogado -da *mf*
advocate[2] [ǽdvəket] VT abogar por, defender
aerial [érial] ADJ aéreo; N antena *f*
aerobic [ɛróbɪk] ADJ (exercise) aeróbico; (air-breathing) aerobio; N **—s** aeróbic *m*
aerodynamic [ɛrodaɪnǽmɪk] ADJ aerodinámico; N **—s** aerodinámica *f*
aeronautics [ɛrənɔ́ɪdɪks] N aeronáutica *f*
aerosol [érəsał] N aerosol *m*
aerospace [érospes] N espacio aéreo *m*; ADJ aeroespacial
aesthetic [ɛsθɛ́ɪdɪk] ADJ estético; N **—s** estética *f*
affable [ǽfəbəł] ADJ afable
affair [əfɛ́r] N (social) acontecimiento social *m*; (business) asunto *m*, negocio *m*; (love) aventura amorosa *f*, affaire *m*
affect [əfɛ́kt] VT (have effect on) afectar; (move) conmover; (feign) fingir
affectation [æ̀fɛktéʃən] N afectación *f*, melindre *m*
affected [əfɛ́ktɪd] ADJ (moved) afectado, conmovido; (feigned) fingido, artificioso, melindroso
affection [əfɛ́kʃən] N afecto *m*, cariño *m*
affectionate [əfɛ́kʃənɪt] ADJ afectuoso, cariñoso
affidavit [æ̀fɪdɛ́vɪt] N declaración jurada *f*
affiliate[1] [əfɪ́łiet] VT afiliar; VI afiliarse, asociarse
affiliate[2] [əfɪ́łiɪt] N filial *f*
affiliation [əfɪ̀łiéʃən] N (relation) afiliación *f*; (membership) filiación *f*; **political —** filiación política *f*
affinity [əfɪ́nɪdi] N afinidad *f*
affirm [əfɜ́-m] VT afirmar
affirmation [æ̀fə-méʃən] N afirmación *f*
affirmative [əfɜ́-məɪv] ADJ afirmativo; **— action** discriminación positiva *f*; N **reply in the —** dar una respuesta afirmativa
affix[1] [əfíks] VT fijar; **to — one's signature** poner su firma, firmar
affix[2] [ǽfɪks] N afijo *m*
afflict [əflíkt] VT aquejar; **to be —ed with** padecer de, sufrir de
affliction [əflíkʃən] N (misery) aflicción *f*; (ailment) achaque *m*, mal *m*
affluent [ǽfluənt] ADJ (society) opulento; (person) rico
afford [əfɔ́rd] VT **I cannot — a car** no me alcanza el dinero para un coche; **he cannot — to waste time** no puede darse el lujo de perder tiempo; **I cannot — the risk** no me puedo permitir ese riesgo; **we will — you every opportunity** se te darán todas las

oportunidades
affordable [əfɔ́rdəbəl] ADJ asequible
affront [əfrʌ́nt] N afrenta *f*
Afghan, Afghani [ǽfgæn/æfgǽni] ADJ & N afgano -na *mf*
Afghanistan [æfgǽnɪstæn] N Afganistán *m*
afire [əfáɪr] ADJ & ADV en llamas
afloat [əflót] ADJ & ADV flotando, a flote
afraid [əfréd] ADJ asustado; **to be — [of]** temer, tener miedo [a]
afresh [əfréʃ] ADV de nuevo, desde el principio
Africa [ǽfrɪkə] N África *f*
African [ǽfrɪkən] ADJ & N africano -na *mf*
African American [ǽfrɪkənəmérɪkən] ADJ & N afroamericano -na *mf*
after [ǽftɚ] PREP (temporal) después de, tras; (spatial) detrás de; **— all** después de todo; ADV después; CONJ después [de] que
afterbirth [ǽftɚbɝθ] N placenta *f*
aftercare [ǽftɚkɛr] N (post-illness) tratamiento de convalecencia *m*; (postoperative) tratamiento post-operatorio *m*
after-hours [ǽftɚ áʊrz] ADV después de horas hábiles
afterlife [ǽftɚlaɪf] N el más allá *m*
aftermarket [ǽftɚmɑrkɪt] ADJ de mercado secundario; N (for merchandise) mercado secundario *m*; (for stocks) mercado extrabursátil *m*
aftermath [ǽftɚmæθ] N secuelas *f pl*
afternoon [æftɚnún] N tarde *f*; INTERJ **good —!** ¡buenas tardes!
aftershave [ǽftɚʃev] N loción para después del afeitado *f*
aftershock [ǽftɚʃɑk] N réplica *f*
aftertaste [ǽftɚtest] N (in the mouth) dejo *m*; (bad memory) resabio *m*
aftertax profit [ǽftɚtæksprǽfɪt] N ganancia neta *f*
afterthought [ǽftɚθɔt] N **it was just an —** se nos ocurrió después
afterward, afterwards [ǽftɚwɚd[z]] ADV después, posteriormente
again [əgén] ADV otra vez, de nuevo; **— and —** repetidas veces; **to fall —** volver a caerse
against [əgénst] PREP contra; **— the grain** a contrapelo; **— all odds** a pesar de todo
age [eʤ] N (of a person) edad *f*; (era) era *f*, época *f*; **— of consent** edad de consentimiento sexual *f*; **— discrimination** discriminación por edad *f*; **— limit** límite de edad *m*; **old —** vejez *f*; **of —** mayor de edad; **to come of —** llegar a la mayoría de edad; **under —** menor de edad; VI/VT envejecer
aged[1] [eʤd] ADJ (wine) añejo; **— forty** de cuarenta años
aged[2] [éʤɪd] ADJ anciano
ageless [éʤɪlɪs] ADJ (everlasting) eterno; (not showing age) siempre joven; (classic) clásico
agency [éʤənsi] N agencia *f*; **through the — of** por mediación de
agenda [əʤéndə] N orden del día *m*, agenda *f*
agent [éʤənt] N agente *mf*; (commercial) representante *mf*, gestor -ora *mf*; (legal) apoderado -da *mf*
aggrandize [əgrǽndaɪz] VT engrandecer
aggravate [ǽgrəvet] VT (worsen) exacerbar, agravar; (annoy) irritar, exasperar, exacerbar
aggregate [ǽgrɪgɪt] N conjunto *m*; (rock) agregado *m*; ADJ total, global
aggression [əgrɛ́ʃən] N (attack) agresión *f*; (propensity to violence) agresividad *f*
aggressive [əgrɛ́sɪv] ADJ (violent) agresivo; (dynamic) emprendedor
aggressiveness [əgrɛ́sɪvnɪs] N agresividad *f*
aggressor [əgrɛ́sɚ] N agresor -ra *mf*
aghast [əgǽst] ADJ horrorizado
agile [ǽʤəl] ADJ ágil
agility [əʤɪ́lɪɾi] N agilidad *f*
aging [éʤɪŋ] N (of a person) envejecimiento *m*; (of wine) maduración *f*
agitate [ǽʤɪtet] VT (shake) agitar; (perturb) turbar; (campaign) alborotar
agitation [æʤɪtéʃən] N agitación *f*
agitator [ǽʤɪtɚ] N agitador -ra *mf*
agnostic [ægnɑ́stɪk] ADJ & N agnóstico -ca *mf*
ago [əgó] ADV **many years —** hace muchos años; **long —** hace mucho tiempo
agog [əgɑ́g] ADJ planchado, boquiabierto
agonize [ǽgənaɪz] VI sufrir angustiosamente; **to — over** atormentarse por
agony [ǽgəni] N (pain) dolor *m*, tormento *m*; (anguish) angustia *f*
agoraphobia [ægəəfóbiə] N agorafobia *f*
agrarian [əgrɛ́riən] ADJ agrario
agree [əgrí] VI (be in agreement) estar de acuerdo; (in grammar, mathematics) concordar; (color, food) sentarle bien; **to — upon** acordar, convenir, pactar; **they —d to meet the next day** quedaron en reunirse al día siguiente, acordaron reunirse al día siguiente; **the two sides —d to a truce** los dos bandos pactaron una tregua
agreeable [əgríəbəl] ADJ (nice) agradable; (willing) conforme
agreement [əgrímənt] N (concord, document) acuerdo *m*, concertación *f*, convenio *m*; (grammatical) concordancia *f*; **to be in —** estar de acuerdo; **to come to an —** ponerse de acuerdo, pactar
agricultural [ǽgrɪkʌ́ltʃəɚl] ADJ (related to crops) agrícola; (related to crops and cattle) agropecuario
agriculture [ǽgrɪkʌ́ltʃɚ] N agricultura *f*
aground [əgráʊnd] ADV **to run —** encallar, varar
ahead [əhɛ́d] ADV delante; **— of time** adelantado, con antelación; **to go —** ir

adelante, adelantarse; **to get —** prosperar; **our team is —** nuestro equipo va primero; **the years —** los años venideros

aid [ed] N (help) asistencia *f*; (assistant) ayudante *mf*; VT ayudar; **to — and abet** instigar

aide [ed] N (high-ranking) asesor -ora *mf*; (low-ranking) ayudante *mf*

AIDS [acquired immune deficiency syndrome] [edz] N SIDA *m*

ail [eɫ] VI/VT **what —s you?** ¿qué tienes? ¿qué te aflige? **he's —ing** está enfermo

aileron [éləran] N alerón *m*

ailing [éliŋ] ADJ (person) achacoso, enfermizo; (economy) debilitado

ailment [eɫmənt] N achaque *m*, dolencia *f*

aim [em] N (with a weapon) puntería *f*; (objective) objetivo *m*; VT (a weapon) apuntar; (a question, blow) dirigir; **to — to please** tratar de agradar

aimless [émlɪs] ADJ (purposeless) sin propósito; (directionless) sin rumbo

air [ɛr] N aire *m*; **—bag** airbag *m*, bolsa de aire *f*; **—brake** freno neumático *m*; **to — condition** poner aire condicionado; **— conditioner** acondicionador de aire *m*; **— conditioning** aire acondicionado *m*, climatización *f*; **—craft** aeronave *f*; **—craft carrier** portaaviones *m sg*; **—field** aeródromo *m*; **— force** fuerza aérea *f*; **—head** cabeza de chorlito *mf*; **—lift** puente aéreo *m*; **—line** línea aérea *f*, areolínea *f*; **— mail** correo aéreo *m*; **—plane** avión *m*; **— piracy** piratería aérea *f*; **—port** aeropuerto *m*; **— power** fuerza aérea *f*; **— pressure** presión de aire *f*; **— raid** ataque aéreo *m*; **— rifle** escopeta de aire comprimido *f*; **—ship** dirigible *m*; **— strike** bombardeo aéreo *m*; **—strip** pista de aterrizaje *f*; **— -to-** aire-aire; **— traffic control** control del tráfico aéreo *m*; **—way** conducto de aire *m*, vía respiratoria *f*; **up in the —** en el aire, incierto; **in the open —** al aire libre; **to be on the —** estar en el aire, emitirse; **to put on —s** presumir, darse ínfulas; **to vanish into thin —** evaporarse; VT (an opinion) manifestar; **to —lift** aerotransportar; **to — out** orear, ventilar; ADJ aéreo; **—borne** (troops) aerotransportado; (particles) transportado por el aire; **— conditioned** con aire acondicionado, climatizado; **—tight** hermético

aisle [aɪɫ] N pasillo *m*; (of a church) nave lateral *f*

ajar [əʤár] ADJ entornado, entreabierto

aka [ékéé] ADV (also called) también conocido como; (in police usage) alias

akin [əkín] ADJ (related) emparentado; (similar) semejante

à la mode [ɑlɑmód] ADV con helado

alarm [əlárm] N (warning) alarma *f*; (worry) inquietud *f*; **— clock** despertador *m*; **to sound an —** tocar a rebato; VT (worry) alarmar; (frighten) asustar

alarming [əlármɪŋ] ADJ alarmante

Albania [æɫbéniə] N Albania *f*

Albanian [æɫbéniən] ADJ & N albanés -esa *mf*

albatross [æɫbətrɑs] N albatros *m*

albinism [æɫbɪnɪzəm] N albinismo *m*

albino [æɫbáɪno] N albino -na *mf*

album [æɫbəm] N álbum *m*

alcohol [æɫkəhɔɫ] N alcohol *m*

alcoholic [æɫkəhɔ́lɪk] ADJ & N alcohólico -ca *mf*

alcoholism [æɫkəhɔlɪzəm] N alcoholismo *m*

alcove [æɫkov] N rincón *m*

ale [eɫ] N cerveza inglesa *f*

alert [əlɜ́ɫt] ADJ (vigilant) alerta; (awake) despierto; **to be —** (on guard) estar alerta; (lively) ser despierto; N alerta *f*; VT alertar, avisar

alfalfa [æɫfǽɫfə] N alfalfa *f*

algae [æɫʤi] N algas *f pl*

algebra [æɫʤəbrə] N álgebra *f*

Algeria [æɫʤíriə] N Argelia *f*

Algerian [æɫʤíriən] ADJ & N argelino -na *mf*

algorithm [æɫgərɪðəm] N algoritmo *m*

alias [éliəs] N alias *m sg*

alibi [æləbɪ] N coartada *f*

alien [éliən] N (visitor from space) extraterrestre *mf*; (foreigner) extranjero -ra *mf*; ADJ ajeno

alienate [éliənet] VT (people) alienar, alejar; (property) enajenar

alight [əláɪt] VI (rider) apearse; (bird, insect) posarse

align [əláɪn] VI/VT alinear[se]

alignment [əláɪnmənt] N alineación *f*

alike [əláɪk] ADJ parecido, igual; **to be —** parecerse, ser iguales; ADV del mismo modo

alimentary [æləmɪ́ntəri] ADJ alimenticio; **— canal** canal alimentario *m*

alimony [æləmoni] N pensión alimenticia *f*

alive [əláɪv] ADJ (living) vivo; **— with** lleno de; **the symphony came — under his direction** la sinfonía cobró vida bajo su dirección

alkali [æɫkəlaɪ] N álcali *m*

alkaline [æɫkəlɪn] ADJ alcalino

all [ɔɫ] ADJ todo; **— the time** todo el tiempo; N todo *m*; **to give one's —** dar todo de sí; PRON todo; **is that —?** ¿eso es todo? **— or nothing** todo o nada; ADV completamente, todo; **— at once** (uninterrupted) de una vez; (sudden) de repente; **— -inclusive** con todo incluido; **— -time high** máximo histórico *m*; **— told** en conjunto; **he's — dirty** está todo sucio; **it is — over** se acabó; **not at —** de ninguna manera; **nothing at —** nada en absoluto; **once [and] for —** de una vez por todas; **she's — right** está bien; INTERJ **— right** bueno

allay [əléˈ] VT (fear, doubt) calmar, disipar; (anger) aplacar
allegation [æləɡéʃən] N acusación *f*
allege [əléʤˈ] VT (state) afirmar; (claim) alegar
alleged [əléʤˈd] ADJ (event) supuesto; (perpetrator) presunto
allegedly [əléʤɪdlɪ] ADV supuestamente, presuntamente
allegiance [əlíʤəns] N lealtad *f*, fidelidad *f*; **to pledge — to the flag** jurar la bandera
allegory [æləɡɔ·ri] N alegoría *f*
allergen [æl·ə·ʤɪn] N alergeno/alérgeno *m*
allergic [əlɜ·ʤɪk] ADJ alérgico
allergist [æl·ə·ʤɪst] N alergólogo -ga *mf*
allergy [æl·ə·ʤi] N alergia *f*
alleviate [əlíviet] VT (suffering) aliviar; (hunger) paliar
alley [æli] N callejón *m*; (tennis) pasillo de dobles *m*; **right up her —** ideal para ella
alliance [əláɪəns] N alianza *f*
allied [əláɪd, æláɪd] ADJ aliado
alligator [æligeɪˈ·ə·] N caimán *m*; *Am* lagarto *m*
alliterate [əlíɪˈ·ə·ret] VI hacer aliteración
allocate [æloˈket] VT asignar
allot [ə·lát] VT asignar
allotment [ə·lát·mənt] N asignación *f*, cuota *f*
allow [ə·láʊ] VI/VT (permit) permitir; (make possible) posibilitar; (admit) admitir; **to — for** tener en cuenta
allowable [ə·láʊ·ə·bə·l] ADJ admisible, permisible
allowance [ə·láʊ·əns] N (regular payment) asignación *f*, pensión *f*; (monthly payment) mensualidad *f*; (for a child) paga *f*, mesada *f*; (payment for a particular purpose) pago *m*; (food) ración *f*; **to make — for** tener en cuenta
alloy[1] [æ·lɔɪ] N aleación *f*
alloy[2] [ə·lɔɪ] VT alear
allude [ə·lúd] VI aludir; **to — to** aludir a
allure [ə·lúr] VI/VT seducir, atraer; N atractivo *m*
alluring [ə·lúrɪŋ] ADJ seductivo, atractivo
allusion [ə·lúʒən] N alusión *f*
ally[1] [æ·laɪ] N aliado -da *mf*
ally[2] [ə·láɪ] VT **to — oneself with** aliarse con
almanac [ɔ́l·mə·næk] N almanaque *m*
almighty [ɔl·máɪˈɪ·di] ADJ todopoderoso
almond [ɔ́m·ənd] N almendra *f*; **— tree** almendro *m*
almost [ɔ́l·most] ADV casi; **I — fell down** por poco me caigo
alms [ɔmz] N limosna *f*
aloe vera [æ·lo·ví·rə] N áloe *m*
alone [ə·lón] ADJ solo; **— among his contemporaries** único entre sus contemporáneos; ADV solo, solamente; **she — knew that** solo ella sabía eso; **all —** a solas; **to leave —** no tocar, dejar en paz
along [ə·lɔ́ŋ] PREP **he was walking — the street** andaba por la calle; **all — the coast** a lo largo de toda la costa; **— with** junto con; **all —** desde el principio; **to carry — with oneself** llevar consigo; **to go — with** acceder a, conformarse con; **to get — with** llevarse bien con
alongside [ə·lɔ́ŋ·sáɪd] PREP al lado de; **— the boat** al lado del bote; ADV al lado, al costado; **the dog ran —** el perro corría al costado
aloof [ə·lúf] ADJ reservado, esquivo; ADV apartado
aloud [ə·láʊd] ADV en voz alta
alphabet [æ·lfə·bet] N alfabeto *m*, abecedario *m*
alphanumeric [æl·fə·nu·mé·rɪk] ADJ alfanumérico
alpine [æl·paɪn] ADJ alpino
already [ɔ·ɹé·di] ADV ya
also [ɔ́l·so] ADV también, además; **—-ran** (horse, candidate) caballo/candidato vencido *m*
alt [æˈt] *see* alternate[1]
altar [ɔ́l·tə·] N altar *m*; **—piece** retablo *m*
alter [ɔ́l·tə·] VI/VT (change) alterar; (neuter) capar, castrar
alteration [ɔ·l·tə·ré·ʃən] N (change) alteración *f*, cambio *m*; **—s** arreglos *m pl*, reformas *f pl*
altercation [ɔ·l·tə·ké·ʃən] N altercado *m*
alternate[1] [ɔ́l·tə·nɪt] ADJ alternativo, alterno; **— route** ruta alternativa *f*; **— spelling** ortografía alterna *f*; **he visits us on — Mondays** nos visita un lunes sí y otro no; **alt key** tecla de alt *f*; **alt gr key** tecla de alternativa gráfica *f*; N suplente *mf*
alternate[2] [ɔ́l·tə·net] VI/VT alternar
alternation [ɔ·l·tə·né·ʃən] N alternancia *f*
alternative [ɔ·lɜ́·tə·nə·ɪv] ADJ alternativo; **— minimum tax** contribución alternativa mínima *f*; N alternativa *f*
alternator [ɔ́l·tə·ne·ɪˈ·ə·] N alternador *m*
although [ɔ·ɪðóˈ] CONJ aunque, si bien
altimeter [æˈl·tí·mɪˈ·ə·] N altímetro *m*
altitude [æˈl·tɪtud] N altura *f*, altitud *f*; **— sickness** mal de altura *m*
alto [ǽl·to] N contralto *mf*; ADJ alto
altogether [ɔ·l·tə·gé·ðə·] ADV (completely) completamente; (all included) en total
altruism [ǽl·tɪu·ɪzəm] N altruismo *m*
aluminum [ə·lú·mə·nəm] N aluminio *m*; **— foil** papel de aluminio *m*
always [ɔ́l·wez] ADV siempre
Alzheimer's disease [ɔ́l·tsha·ɪmə·z dɪziz] N enfermedad de Alzheimer *f*
a.m. [éém] ADV de la mañana
am [æm] *see* be
amalgamate [ə·mǽl·gə·met] VI/VT (metals) amalgamar[se]; (companies) fusionar[se]
amass [ə·mǽs] VT acumular, amasar
amateur [æ·mə·tʃɚ] ADJ amateur; N amateur *mf*; aficionado -da *mf*
amaze [ə·méz] VT maravillar, asombrar
amazement [ə·méz·mənt] N asombro *m*
amazing [ə·méz·ɪŋ] ADJ asombroso, increíble

Amazon [ǽməzɑn] N (region) Amazonia *f*; (river) Amazonas *m sg*
ambassador [æmbǽsədə˞] N embajador -ora *mf*
amber [ǽmbə˞] N ámbar *m*; ADJ (quality) ambarino; (material) de ámbar; (color) [de] color ámbar
ambidextrous [æmbɪdékstrəs] ADJ ambidiestro
ambience, ambiance [ǽmbiəns] N ambiente *m*
ambient [ǽmbiənt] ADJ ambiental; — **temperature** temperatura ambiente *f*
ambiguity [æmbɪgjúɪdɪ] N ambigüedad *f*
ambiguous [æmbígjuəs] ADJ ambiguo
ambition [æmbíʃən] N ambición *f*, aspiración *f*
ambitious [æmbíʃəs] ADJ ambicioso
ambivalent [æmbívələnt] ADJ ambivalente
amble [ǽmbəl] VI deambular
ambulance [ǽmbjələns] N ambulancia *f*
ambulatory [ǽmbjələtɔri] ADJ ambulatorio
ambush [ǽmbʊʃ] N emboscada *f*, celada *f*; **to lie in** — tender una emboscada; VT emboscar
ameliorate [əmíliəret] VI/VT mejorar
amen [ɑ́mén] INTERJ amén
amenable [əménəbəl] ADJ bien dispuesto
amend [əménd] VT enmendar; **to make —s [for]** compensar [por]
amendment [əméndmənt] N enmienda *f*
amenities [əménɪdiz] N PL comodidades *f pl*
America [əmérɪkə] N América *f*
American [əmérɪkən] ADJ & N (continental) americano -na *mf*; (USA) americano -na *mf*, norteamericano -na *mf*, estadounidense *mf*
amethyst [ǽməθɪst] N amatista *f*
amiable [émiəbəl] ADJ amable
amicable [ǽmɪkəbəl] ADJ amistoso, amigable
amid [əmíd] PREP en medio de, entre
amino acid [əmínoǽsɪd] N aminoácido *m*
amiss [əmís] ADV **something is** — algo anda mal
ammonia [əmónjə] N amoníaco *m*
ammunition [æmjənílən] N munición *f*
amnesia [æmníʒə] N amnesia *f*
amnesty [ǽmnɪsti] N amnistía *f*
amniocentesis [æmnioɪsɪntísɪs] N amniocentesis *f*
amniotic [æmniɑ́dɪk] ADJ amniótico; — **fluid** líquido amniótico *m*
amoeba [əmíbə] N ameba *f*
among [əmʌ́ŋ] PREP entre
amoral [emɔ́rəl] ADJ amoral
amorous [ǽmərəs] ADJ (sexually aroused) excitado; (in love) enamorado
amorphous [əmɔ́rfəs] ADJ amorfo
amortization [æmə˞ɪzéʃən] N amortización *f*
amortize [ǽmə˞taɪz] VT amortizar
amount [əmáʊnt] N (of a substance) cantidad *f*; (of money) suma *f*, importe *m*; — **due** cantidad debida *f*, monto debido *m*; — **paid** cantidad pagada *f*, monto pagado *m*; — **payable** cantidad a pagar *f*; VI (add up to) ascender [a]; **that —s to stealing** eso equivale a robar
ampere [æmpír] N amperio *m*
amphetamine [æmfɛ́dəmin] N anfetamina *f*
amphibian [æmfíbiən] N anfibio *m*
amphibious [æmfíbiəs] ADJ anfibio
amphitheater [ǽmfəθiətə˞] N anfiteatro *m*
ampicillin [æmpɪsílɪn] N ampicilina *f*
ample [ǽmpəl] ADJ (in quantity) suficiente; (in size) amplio
amplifier [ǽmpləfaɪə˞] N amplificador *m*
amplify [ǽmpləfaɪ] VT (an explanation) ampliar; (a sound) amplificar
amplitude [ǽmplɪtud] N amplitud *f*
amputate [ǽmpjətet] VT amputar
amuck, amok [əmʌ́k] ADV **to run** — (kill people) perpetrar un ataque homicida; (go crazy) volverse loco
amulet [ǽmjəlɪt] N amuleto *m*
amuse [əmjúz] VT (make laugh) divertir; (help pass time) entretener; **to — oneself** divertirse, entretenerse
amusement [əmjúzmənt] N diversión *f*, entretenimiento *m*
amusing [əmjúzɪŋ] ADJ (entertaining) divertido; (funny) gracioso, chistoso
amygdala [əmígdələ] N amígdala *f*
an [ən, æn] INDEF ART un *m*, una *f*
anabolic [ænəbɑ́lɪk] ADJ anabólico; — **steroid** esteroide anabólico *m*
anachronism [ənǽkrənɪzəm] N anacronismo *m*
anaerobic [ænəróbɪk] ADJ anaerobio
anal [énl] ADJ anal; (neurotic) rígido, neurótico
analgesic [ænlʤízɪk] N & ADJ analgésico *m*
analogical [ænəlɑ́ʤɪkəl] ADJ analógico
analogous [ənǽləgəs] ADJ análogo
analogue, analog [ǽnəlɔg] ADJ analógico; — **device** dispositivo analógico *m*
analogy [ənǽləʤi] N analogía *f*
analysis [ənǽlɪsɪs] N análisis *m*
analyst [ǽnəlɪst] N analista *mf*
analytic, analytical [ænəlídɪk[əl]] ADJ (approach) analítico; (person) analítico, analista
analyze [ǽnəlaɪz] VT analizar
anarchist [ǽnə˞kɪst] N anarquista *mf*
anarchy [ǽnə˞ki] N anarquía *f*
anathema [ənǽθəmə] N anatema *m*
anatomical [ænətɑ́mɪkəl] ADJ anatómico
anatomy [ənǽbəmi] N anatomía *f*
ancestor [ǽnsɛstə˞] N antepasado -da *mf*, ascendiente *mf*
ancestral [ænsɛ́strəl] ADJ ancestral, de los antepasados; — **home** casa solariega *f*
ancestry [ǽnsɛstri] N linaje *m*, ascendencia *f*, abolengo *m*
anchor [ǽŋkə˞] N ancla *f*; —**man** presentador *m*; —**woman** presentadora *f*; **to drop** — anclar, echar anclas; VT (a boat) anclar; (an

argument) basar; VI echar anclas, fondear
anchovy [æntʃovi] N anchoa *f*
ancient [éɪnʃənt] ADJ antiguo; *pej* vetusto
and [ænd] CONJ y; (before i, hi) e; — **so forth** etcétera, y así sucesivamente
Andalusia [ændəlúʒə] N Andalucía *f*
Andalusian [ændəlúʒən] ADJ & N andaluz -za *mf*
Andes [ǽndiz] N Andes *m pl*
Andorra [ændɔ́rə] N Andorra *f*
Andorran [ændɔ́rən] ADJ & N andorrano -na *mf*
androgynous [ændrɑ́dʒənəs] ADJ andrógino
anecdote [ǽnɪkdot] N anécdota *f*
anemia [ənímiə] N anemia *f*
anemic [ənímɪk] ADJ anémico
anesthesia [ænɪsθíʒə] N anestesia *f*
anesthesiologist [ænəsθiziɑ́lədʒɪst] N anestesiólogo -ga *mf*, anestesista *mf*
anesthesiology [ænɪsθiziɑ́lədʒi] N anestesiología *f*
anesthetic [ænɪsθɛ́tɪk] ADJ anestésico; N (substance) anestesia *f*
anesthetize [ənɛ́sθətaɪz] VT anestesiar
aneurysm [ǽnjərtɪzəm] N aneurisma *m*
anew [ənú] ADV de nuevo, otra vez
angel [éndʒəł] N ángel *m*
angelic [ændʒɛ́lɪk] ADJ angélico, angelical
anger [ǽngɚ] N enojo *m*, enfado *m*; VT enojar, enfadar
angina pectoris [ændʒáɪnəpɛ́ktə-ɪs] N angina de pecho *f*
angiocardiography [ændʒiokɑrdɪɑ́grəfi] N angiocardiografía *f*
angiogram [ǽndʒiogræm] N angiograma *m*
angioplasty [ǽndʒiəplæsti] N angioplastia *f*; — **balloon** balón de angioplastia *m*
angle [ǽngəł] N (geometrical) ángulo *m*; (point of view) punto de vista *m*, perspectiva *f*; VI pescar
Anglo-Saxon [ǽŋglosǽksən] ADJ & N anglosajón -ona *mf*
Angola [æŋgólə] N Angola *f*
Angolan [æŋgólən] ADJ & N angolano -na *mf*, angoleño -ña *mf*
angry [ǽŋgri] ADJ enojado, enfadado
angst [ɑ́ŋkst] N angustia *f*
anguish [ǽŋgwɪʃ] N angustia *f*, ansia *f*, congoja *f*
angular [ǽŋgjəlɚ] ADJ angular; (face) anguloso
animal [ǽnəməł] ADJ & N animal *m*; — **rights** derechos de los animales *m pl*
animate[1] [ǽnəmɪt] ADJ animado
animate[2] [ǽnəmet] VT (enliven) animar; (encourage) alentar; —**d cartoon** dibujo animado *m*
animation [ænəméʃən] N animación *f*
animosity [ænəmɑ́sɪDi] N animosidad *f*, ojeriza *f*, encono *m*
anise [ǽnɪs] N anís *m*
ankle [ǽŋkəł] N tobillo *m*
annals [ǽnlz] N anales *m pl*
annex[1] [ǽnɛks] N anexo *m*
annex[2] [ənɛ́ks] VT anexar
annexation [ænɛkséʃən] N anexión *f*
annihilate [ənáɪəlet] VT aniquilar
anniversary [ænəvɝ́səri] N aniversario *m*
annotate [ǽnətet] VT anotar
annotation [ænətéʃən] N (action, result) anotación *f*; (result) nota *f*
announce [ənáʊns] VT (make known) anunciar, dar a conocer; (declare) anunciar
announcement [ənáʊnsmənt] N (of an engagement, birth, candidacy) anuncio *m*; (of a conference or competition) convocatoria *f*
announcer [ənáʊnsɚ] N anunciador -ra *mf*; (on radio) locutor -ora *mf*
annoy [ənɔ́ɪ] VI/VT fastidiar, contrariar
annoyance [ənɔ́ɪəns] N fastidio *m*, contrariedad *f*
annual [ǽnjuəł] ADJ anual; N (book) anuario *m*; (plant) planta anual *f*
annuity [ənjúɪDi] N anualidad *f*, renta anual *f*
annul [ənʌ́ł] VT anular
annulment [ənʌ́łmənt] N anulación *f*
anomalous [ənɑ́mələs] ADJ anómalo
anomaly [ənɑ́məli] N anomalía *f*
anonymous [ənɑ́nəməs] ADJ anónimo
anorak [ǽnəræk] N anorak *m*
anorexia [ænərɛ́ksiə] N anorexia *f*
anorexic [ænərɛ́ksɪk] ADJ anoréxico
another [ənʌ́ðɚ] ADJ otro; — **day** otro día; PRON otro; **I want** — quiero otro; **one** — el uno al otro, los unos a los otros
answer [ǽnsɚ] N (to a question) respuesta *f*, contestación *f*; (to a problem) solución *f*; VI contestar, responder; **to** — **for** ser responsable de/por; VT contestar
answering [ǽnsɚɪŋ] ADJ — **machine** contestador automático *m*; — **service** servicio telefónico contratado *m*, servicio de contestador *m*
ant [ænt] N hormiga *f*; —**eater** oso hormiguero *m*; —**hill** hormiguero *m*
antacid [æntǽsɪd] N & ADJ antiácido *m*
antagonism [æntǽgənɪzəm] N antagonismo *m*
antagonist [æntǽgənɪst] N antagonista *mf*
antagonize [æntǽgənaɪz] VT antagonizar
antarctic [æntɑ́rktɪk] ADJ antártico
Antarctica [æntɑ́rktɪka] N Antártida *f*
antecedent [æntəsídnt] ADJ & N antecedente *m*
antelope [ǽntəlop] N antílope *m*
antenna [ænténə] N antena *f*
anterior [æntíriɚ] ADJ anterior
anthem [ǽnθəm] N himno *m*
anthology [ænθɑ́lədʒi] N antología *f*
anthracite [ǽnθrəsaɪt] N antracita *f*
anthrax [ǽnθræks] N ántrax *m*
anthropologist [ænθrəpɑ́lədʒɪst] N antropólogo -ga *mf*
anthropology [ænθrəpɑ́lədʒi] N antropología *f*

anthropomorphize [ænθrəpəmɔ́rfaɪz] VI/VT antropomorfizar
antiabortion [æntiəbɔ́rʃən] ADJ antiaborto *inv*
antiaircraft [æntiérkræft] ADJ antiaéreo
antiallergic [æntiələ́ʤɪk] ADJ antialérgico
antibacterial [æntibæktíriəł] ADJ antibacteriano
antiballistic [æntibəlístɪk] ADJ antibalístico
antibiotic [æntɪbaɪáɪDɪk] N & ADJ antibiótico *m*
antibody [ǽntɪbɑDi] N anticuerpo *m*
anticancer [æntikǽnsə˞] ADJ anticanceroso *f*
anticipate [æntísəpet] VI/VT (foresee) prever; (jump the gun) anticiparse [a]
anticipation [æntisəpéʃən] N previsión *f*; **with great —** con gran expectación
anticlimactic [æntikləmǽktɪk] ADJ decepcionante
anticoagulant [æntikoǽgjələnt] ADJ & N anticoagulante *m*
anticonvulsant [æntikənvʌ́łsənt] ADJ & N anticonvulsivo *m*
antics [ǽntɪks] N payasadas *f pl*, monerías *f pl*, monadas *f pl*
antidepressant [æntidɪprésənt] ADJ & N antidepresivo *m*
antidiarrheal [æntidaɪəríəł] ADJ & N antidiarreico *m*
antidiuretic [æntidaɪərɛ́DɪK] ADJ & N antidiurético *m*
antidote [ǽntɪdot] N antídoto *m*
antifreeze [ǽntɪfriz] N anticongelante *m*
antigen [ǽntɪʤən] N antígeno *m*
anti-glare [æntiglér] ADJ antireflejante
Antigua and Barbuda [æntígəændbɑrbúDə] N Antigua y Barbuda *f*
Antiguan [æntígən] ADJ & N antiguano -ana *mf*
antihistamine [æntihístəmin] N & ADJ antihistamínico *m*
anti-inflammatory [æntɪɪnflǽmətɔri] ADJ & N antiinflamatorio *m*
antilock [ǽntɪlɑk] ADJ antibloqueo; **— brakes** frenos antibloqueo *mpl*
antimony [ǽntəmoni] N antimonio *m*
antioxidant [æntiǽksɪDənt] N antioxidante *m*
antipathy [æntípəθi] N antipatía *f*
antiperspirant [æntipɝ́spə˞ənt] N antitranspirante *m*
antipsychotic [æntisaɪkɑ́DɪK] ADJ & N antipsicótico *m*
antiquated [ǽntɪkwɛDɪd] ADJ (custom) anticuado; (word) desusado
antique [æntík] ADJ antiguo; N antigüedad *f*
antiquity [æntíkwɪDi] N antigüedad *f*
anti-Semitism [æntisémɪtɪzəm] N antisemitismo *m*
antiseptic [æntisɛ́ptɪk] ADJ & N antiséptico *m*
antisocial [æntisóʃəł] ADJ antisocial
antispasmodic [æntispæzmɑ́DɪK] ADJ & N antiespasmódico *m*
antithesis [æntíθəsɪs] N antítesis *f*
antitoxin [æntitɑ́ksɪn] N antitoxina *f*
antitrust [æntitrást] ADJ antimonopolio, antitrust
antiviral [æntiváɪrəł] ADJ & N antiviral *m*
antivirus [æntivaɪrəs] ADJ antivirus
antler [ǽntlə˞] N asta *f*, cuerno *m*
antonym [ǽntənɪm] N antónimo *m*
antsy [ǽntsi] ADJ (impatient) impaciente; (anxious) ansioso
anvil [ǽnvəł] N yunque *m*
anxiety [æŋzáɪIDi] N ansiedad *f*, angustia *f*
anxious [ǽŋkʃəs] ADJ (worried) ansioso, preocupado; (desirous) ansioso, deseoso
any [éni] ADJ & PRON cualquier[a], cualesquier[a], alguno; **— woman** cualquier mujer, una mujer cualquiera; **— houses** unas casas cualesquiera; *lit* cualesquiera casas; **in — case** en todo caso; **do you have — money?** ¿tienes dinero? **I don't have —** no tengo; **do you like — of these?** ¿te gusta alguno de estos?
anybody [éníbɑDi] PRON alguien, cualquiera; **— could do that** cualquiera podría hacer eso; **is — here?** ¿hay alguien aquí? **he does not know —** no conoce a nadie
anyhow [éníhaU] ADV de todos modos, en todo caso
anymore [énimɔ́r] ADV **he doesn't work —** ya no trabaja, no trabaja más
anyone [éníwʌn] PRON alguien, cualquiera; **— could do that** cualquiera podría hacer eso; **is — here?** ¿hay alguien aquí? **he does not know —** no conoce a nadie
anyplace [éniples] ADV en cualquier parte/lugar; **you can buy it —** se puede comprar en cualquier lugar; **he's not going —** no va a ninguna parte
anything [éniθɪŋ] PRON cualquier cosa, algo; **— is fine** cualquier cosa me viene bien; **— you wish** todo lo que quieras; **do you have — for a cough?** ¿tienes algo para la tos? **I don't know —** no sé nada
anytime [énitaɪm] ADV en cualquier momento
anyway [éníwe] ADV de todos modos, de cualquier manera, en todo caso
anywhere [énihwɛr] ADV en cualquier parte / lugar; **you can buy it —** se puede comprar en cualquier lugar; **he's not going —** no va a ninguna parte
aorta [eɔ́rDə] N aorta *f*
apart [əpárt] ADV **they are three miles —** están a tres millas de distancia; **they kept him — from the group** lo apartaron del grupo; **each factor viewed —** cada factor visto por separado; **to take —** desarmar, desmontar; **to tear —** despedazar, hacer pedazos; **to tell —** distinguir
apartment [əpártmənt] N apartamento *m*; *Sp*

piso *m*
apathetic [æpəθɛ́dɪk] ADJ apático
apathy [ǽpəθi] N apatía *f*, abulia *f*
ape [ep] N simio *m*; VT remedar
aperture [ǽpə-tʃə-] N abertura *f*; (of a pipe) luz *f*
apex [épɛks] N (of tongue) ápice *m*; (of a mountain) cumbre *f*
aphasia [əfézə] N afasia *f*
apiece [əpís] ADV cada uno
apnea [ǽpniə] N apnea *f*
apocalypse [əpɑ́kəlɪps] N apocalipsis *mf*
apogee [ǽpəʤi] N apogeo *m*
apologetic [əpɑlə́ʤɛ́dɪk] ADJ lleno de disculpas
apologize [əpɑ́lə́ʤaɪz] VI disculparse
apology [əpɑ́lə́ʤi] N (expression of regret) disculpa[s] *f* [*pl*]; (justification) apología *f*
apoplexy [ǽpəplɛksi] N apoplejía *f*
apostle [əpɑ́səł] N apóstol *m*
apostrophe [əpɑ́strəfi] N (punctuation) apóstrofo *m*; (invocation) apóstrofe *m*
app [æp] N (computer software) aplicación *f*
appall [əpɑ́ł] VT horrorizar
appalling [əpɑ́lɪŋ] ADJ horroroso
apparatus [æpərǽdəs] N (single) aparato *m*; (group) maquinaria *f*
apparel [əpǽrəł] N indumentaria *f*, ropa *f*; (fine) ropaje *m*
apparent [əpǽrənt] ADJ (visible) visible; (clear) obvio, evidente; (seeming) aparente
apparition [æpərɪ́ʃən] N aparición *f*, fantasma *m*
appeal [əpíł] N (legal) apelación *f*, recurso *m*; (request) llamamiento *m*, llamado *m*; (attraction) atractivo *m*; VT apelar, recurrir [contra]; VI **to — to** atraer
appear [əpír] VI (show up) aparecer[se]; (seem) parecer, aparentar; (be published) salir; (come before a judge) comparecer
appearance [əpírəns] N (looks) apariencia *f*, traza *f*, estampa *f*; (act of appearing) aparición *f*; (coming before a judge) comparecencia *f*
appease [əpíz] VT aplacar, apaciguar
appeasement [əpízmənt] N aplacamiento *m*, apaciguamiento *m*
appellate [əpɛ́lɪt] N — **court** tribunal de apelaciones *m*
append [əpɛ́nd] VT adjuntar
appendage [əpɛ́ndɪʤ] N apéndice *m*
appendectomy [æpɪndɛ́ktəmi] N apendicectomía *f*
appendicitis [əpɛndəsáɪdɪs] N apendicitis *f*
appendix [əpɛ́ndɪks] N apéndice *m*
appetite [ǽpɪtaɪt] N apetito *m*
appetizer [ǽpɪtaɪzə-] N aperitivo *m*
appetizing [ǽpɪtaɪzɪŋ] ADJ apetecible, apetitoso
applaud [əplɔ́d] VI/VT aplaudir
applause [əplɔ́z] N aplauso[s] *m* [*pl*]
apple [ǽpəł] N manzana *f*; — **grove** manzanar *m*; — **of my eye** niña de mis ojos *f*; —**sauce** compota de manzana *f*; — **tree** manzano *m*; **Adam's** — nuez de Adán *f*
appliance [əpláɪəns] N aparato *m*; (electric) aparato electrodoméstico *m*, electrodoméstico *m*
applicable [ǽplɪkəbəł] ADJ aplicable
applicant [ǽplɪkənt] N aspirante *mf*, solicitante *mf*
application [æplɪkéʃən] N (act of applying, computer software) aplicación *f*; (form) solicitud *f*, formulario *f*
applicator [ǽplɪkeɪə-] N aplicador *m*
apply [əpláɪ] VT aplicar; **to — for** solicitar, pedir; **are you —ing for the scholarship?** ¿te presentas para la beca? ¿estás solicitando la beca? **to — oneself** aplicarse, dedicarse
appoint [əpɔ́ɪnt] VT (designate) nombrar, designar; (furnish) amueblar, equipar; **a well —ed house** una casa bien amueblada
appointee [əpɔɪntí] N persona nombrada *f*
appointment [əpɔ́ɪntmənt] N (designation) nombramiento *m*, designación *f*; (engagement) cita *f*; **doctor's —** cita/hora con el médico *f*; **—s** mobiliario *m sg*, accesorios *m pl*
apportion [əpɔ́rʃən] VT repartir proporcionalmente
apportionment [əpɔ́rʃənmənt] N reparto proporcional *m*
appraisal [əprézəł] N (of a property) tasación *f*, valuación *f*; (of a situation) evaluación *f*
appraise [əpréz] VT (a property) avaluar, valorar, tasar; (a situation) evaluar
appreciable [əpríʃəbəł] ADJ apreciable
appreciate [əpríʃiet] VT (value) apreciar, estimar; (recognize) darse cuenta, percibir; (thank) agradecer; **to — in value** apreciarse
appreciation [əpriʃiéʃən] N (esteem) aprecio *m*; (thanks) agradecimiento *m*; (monetary value) apreciación *f*, alza *f*
apprehend [æprɪhénd] VT (arrest) aprehender; (understand) comprender
apprehension [æprɪhénʃən] N (arrest) aprehensión *f*; (worry) aprensión *f*
apprehensive [æprɪhénsɪv] ADJ aprensivo
apprentice [əprɛ́ntɪs] N aprendiz -iza *mf*; VT poner de aprendiz
apprenticeship [əprɛ́ntɪsʃɪp] N aprendizaje *m*
apprise [əpráɪz] VT informar
approach [əprɔ́tʃ] N (act of approaching) aproximación *f*; (method) enfoque *m*, acercamiento *m*; (means of access) acceso *m*, entrada *f*; — **shot** golpe de aproximación *m*; VI (go nearer) acercarse, aproximarse; (in golf) aprochar; VT (a problem) abordar, enfocar; **to — someone about a problem** plantearle a alguien un problema
approachable [əprɔ́tʃəbəł] ADJ tratable
approbation [æprəbéʃən] N aprobación *f*
appropriate[1] [əpróprɪt] ADJ apropiado,

adecuado

appropriate[2] [əpropriet] VT apropiarse; (funds) asignar

appropriation [əpropriéʃən] N (act of seizing) apropiación *f*; (assignment of funds) asignación *f*; (assigned funds) partida *f*

approval [əprúvəł] N aprobación *f*; **on —** a prueba

approve [əprúv] VI/VT aprobar

approximate[1] [əpráksəmɪt] ADJ aproximado

approximate[2] [əpráksəmet] VT aproximarse a

approximately [əpráksəmɪtlı] ADV aproximadamente

APR [annual percentage rate] [épíár] N TAE *f*

apricot [æprɪkɑt] N albaricoque *m*; *Am* damasco *m*; *Mex* chabacano *m*

April [éprəł] N abril *m*

apron [éprən] N (for a cook) delantal *m*; (for a workman) mandil *m*

apropos [æprəpó] ADV a propósito; ADJ oportuno, pertinente; **— of** a propósito de

apt [æpt] ADJ (prone, able) capaz; (suited) pertinente; **is he — to be at home?** ¿estará en casa?

aptitude [æptɪtud] N aptitud *f*, capacidad *f*

aquamarine [ɑkwəmərín] N aguamarina *f*

aquarium [əkwériəm] N (tank) acuario *m*, pecera *f*; (building) acuario *m*

aquatic [əkwɑ́dɪk] ADJ acuático

aqueduct [ǽkwɪdʌkt] N acueducto *m*

Arab [ǽrəb] ADJ & N árabe *mf*

Arabic [ǽrəbɪk] ADJ árabe, arábigo; N (language) árabe *m*

arable [ǽrəbəł] ADJ cultivable

Aragonese [ærəgəníz] ADJ & N aragonés -esa *mf*

arbiter [ɑ́rbɪdə-] N árbitro -ra *mf*

arbitrariness [ɑ́rbɪtrərɪnɪs] N arbitrariedad *f*

arbitrary [ɑ́rbɪtrerı] ADJ arbitrario; **— action** arbitrariedad *f*

arbitrate [ɑ́rbɪtret] VI/VT (mediate) arbitrar [en], terciar [en]; (submit to mediation) someter al arbitraje

arbitration [ɑrbɪtréʃən] N arbitraje *m*

arbitrator [ɑ́rbɪtredə-] N árbitro -tra *mf*

arbor [ɑ́rbə-] N pérgola *f*, glorieta *f*

arboreal [ɑrbɔ́riəł] ADJ arbóreo

arc [ɑrk] N arco *m*

arcade [ɑrkéd] N (series of arcs) arcada *f*; (shops) galería *f*; (video game center) sala de juegos electrónicos *f*

arcane [ɑrkén] ADJ arcano

arch [ɑrtʃ] N arco *m*; (curved roof) bóveda *f*; **—way** arcada *f*; VI/VT arquear[se]

archaeological [ɑrkiəlɑ́dʒɪkəł] ADJ arqueológico

archaeology, archeology [ɑrkiɑ́lədʒi] N arqueología *f*

archaic [ɑrkéɪk] ADJ arcaico

archaism [ɑ́rkeɪzəm] N arcaísmo *m*

archbishop [ɑrtʃbíʃəp] N arzobispo *m*

archenemy [ɑ́rtʃénəmi] N archienemigo -ga *mf*

archer [ɑ́rtʃə-] N arquero -ra *mf*

archery [ɑ́rtʃəri] N tiro al arco *m*

archetype [ɑ́rkɪtaɪp] N arquetipo *m*

archipelago [ɑrkəpéləgo] N archipiélago *m*

architect [ɑ́rkɪtɛkt] N arquitecto -ta *mf*; (creator) artífice *mf*

architectural [ɑrkɪtɛ́ktʃə-əł] ADJ arquitectónico

architecture [ɑ́rkɪtɛktʃə-] N arquitectura *f*

archive [ɑ́rkaɪv] N archivo *m*

arctic [ɑ́rktɪk] ADJ ártico

ardent [ɑ́rdnt] ADJ ardiente

ardor [ɑ́rdə-] N ardor *m*, fervor *m*

arduous [ɑ́rdʒuəs] ADJ arduo

are [ɑr] *see* be

area [ériə] N (space) área *f*; (region) zona *f*; (of a geometric figure) superficie *f*, área *f*

arena [ərínə] N (for sports) estadio *m*; (in a circus) pista *f*

Argentina [ɑrdʒəntínə] N Argentina *f*

Argentinian [ɑrdʒəntíniən] ADJ & N argentino -na *mf*

argon [ɑ́rgɑn] N argón *m*

argue [ɑ́rgju] VT (reason) argüir, argumentar; VI (bicker) discutir, reñir

argument [ɑ́rgjəmənt] N (reason) argumento *m*; (altercation) disputa *f*, discusión *f*

arid [ǽrɪd] ADJ árido

arise [əráɪz] VI (get up) levantarse; (appear) surgir; (result) provenir, resultar

arisen [ərízən] *see* arise

aristocracy [ærɪstɑ́krəsi] N aristocracia *f*

aristocrat [ərístəkræt] N aristócrata *mf*

aristocratic [ərɪstəkrǽdɪk] ADJ aristocrático

arithmetic[1] [əríθmətɪk] N aritmética *f*

arithmetic[2] [ærɪθmɛ́dɪk] ADJ aritmético

ark [ɑrk] N arca *f*; **Noah's —** arca de Noé *f*

arm [ɑrm] N brazo *m*; **—chair** sillón *m*, butaca *f*; **—pit** sobaco *m*, axila *f*; **—rest** (in a car) apoyabrazos *m sg*; (on a sofa) brazo *m*; **— in —** del brazo; **at —'s length** a distancia; **—'s-length transactions** transacciones a precio de mercado *f pl*; **with open —s** con los brazos abiertos; **—s** armas *f pl*; VT armar; **—ed forces** fuerzas armadas *f pl*; **—ed robbery** robo a mano armada *m*

armada [ɑrmɑ́də] N armada *f*, flota *f*

armament [ɑ́rməmənt] N armamento *m*

Armenia [ɑrmíniə] N Armenia *f*

Armenian [ɑrmíniən] ADJ & N armenio -nia *mf*

armful [ɑ́rmfuł] N brazada *f*

armistice [ɑ́rmɪstɪs] N armisticio *m*

armoire [ɑrmwɑ́r] N armario *m*

armor [ɑ́rmə-] N (of a knight) armadura *f*; (on a vehicle) blindaje *m*; (on insects) coraza *f*; VT (a car) blindar; (a tank) acorazar

armored [ɑ́rmə-d] ADJ (van) blindado; (tank) acorazado

armory [ɑ́rməri] N armería *f*
army [ɑ́rmi] N ejército *m*; (multitude) muchedumbre *f*
aroma [ərómə] N aroma *m*
aromatic [ærəmǽɪk] ADJ aromático
arose [əróz] *see* arise
around [ərɑ́ʊnd] ADV **there were books all —** había libros por todos lados; **there is a supermarket — here** hay un supermercado por aquí; **it was the only farm for miles —** era la única granja en millas a la redonda; **the tree is forty centimeters —** el árbol tiene cuarenta centímetros de circunferencia; **I'll show you —** te enseño el lugar; **the wheels turned —** las ruedas giraban; **turn —** date la vuelta; **she finally came —** al final la convencimos; **he hasn't been —** no ha estado por aquí; **— five o'clock** a eso de las cinco; PREP **a ribbon — her wrist** una cinta alrededor de su muñeca; **tie a string — your finger** átate un hilo al dedo; **stay — the house** quédate cerca de la casa; **we drove — the block** dimos vuelta a la manzana; **he wandered — the park** deambuló por el parque; **the church — the corner** la iglesia a la vuelta de la esquina; **a town with mountains — it** un pueblo rodeado de montañas; **motion — its axis** movimiento en torno a su eje; **—-the-clock** veinticuatro horas al día; **we walked — town** dimos una vuelta por el pueblo
arouse [ərɑ́ʊz] VI despertar; VT (suspicion) despertar; (sexual response) excitar
arraign [ərén] VT hacer comparecer ante un juez
arrange [ərénʤ] VT arreglar
arrangement [ərénʤmənt] N (array) arreglo *m*; (placement) disposición *f*; (agreement) acuerdo *m*; **to make —s [for]** hacer arreglos [para]
array [əré] N (arrangement) abanico *m*, selección *f*; (placement of troops) orden *m*, formación *f*; (attire) gala *f*; (in software) vector *m*; VT (troops) formar; (attire) ataviar
arrears [ərírz] ADV LOC **in —** atrasado; N atrasos *m pl*
arrest [ərést] N arresto *m*, detención *f*; VI/VT arrestar, detener
arrhythmia [əríðmiə] N arritmia *f*
arrival [ərɑ́ɪvəł] N llegada *f*; *lit* arribo *m*; **the new —s** los recién llegados
arrive [ərɑ́ɪv] VI llegar; *lit* arribar
arrogance [ǽrəgəns] N arrogancia *f*
arrogant [ǽrəgənt] ADJ arrogante
arrow [ǽro] N flecha *f*; *lit* saeta *f*; **—head** punta de flecha *f*
arsenal [ɑ́rsən|] N arsenal *m*
arsenic [ɑ́rsənɪk] N arsénico *m*
arson [ɑ́rsən] N incendio doloso *m*
art [ɑrt] N arte *m* [sg] *f* [*pl*]; (works) obras *f pl*; (skill) destreza *f*; **fine —s** bellas artes *f pl*; **master of —s** maestría en humanidades *f*; **— deco** art déco *m*
arterial [ɑrtíriəł] ADJ arterial
arteriosclerosis [ɑrtiriosklərósɪs] N arteriosclerosis *f*
artery [ɑ́rʊəri] N arteria *f*
artful [ɑ́rtfəł] ADJ (aesthetic) artístico; (deceitful) artero, astuto
arthritis [ɑrθráɪdɪs] N artritis *f*
arthroscopic [ɑrθrəskɑ́pɪk] ADJ artroscópico
arthroscopy [ɑ́rθrəskɑpi] N artroscopia *f*
artichoke [ɑ́rʊɪtʃok] N alcachofa *f*
article [ɑ́rʊɪkəł] N artículo *m*; **— of clothing** prenda de vestir *f*
articulate[1] [ɑrtíkjəlɪt] ADJ (clear) claro; (eloquent) elocuente; **he's very —** se expresa muy bien
articulate[2] [ɑrtíkjəlet] VI/VT (pronounce, join) articular; (express) enunciar
articulation [ɑrtɪkjəléʃən] N articulación *f*
artifact [ɑ́rʊəfækt] N artefacto *m*, ingenio *m*
artifice [ɑ́rʊəfɪs] N artificio *m*
artificial [ɑrʊəfíʃəł] ADJ artificial; (affected) afectado; **— insemination** inseminación artificial *f*; **— intelligence** inteligencia artificial *f*
artillery [ɑrtíləri] N artillería *f*
artisan [ɑ́rʊɪzən] N artesano -na *mf*, artífice *mf*
artist [ɑ́rʊɪst] N (painter, sculptor) artista *mf*; (performer) intérprete *mf*
artistic [ɑrtístɪk] ADJ artístico
Aruba [ərúbə] N Aruba *f*
as [æz] CONJ **— for me** en lo que a mí respecta; **— if** como si; **— is** en la condición en que está; **— it were** por decirlo así; **— of** a partir de; **— per** según; **— the illness worsened** a medida que empeoraba la enfermedad; **— yet** hasta ahora, todavía; **the same —** lo mismo que; **it broke — I was using it** se rompió cuando lo usaba; **she knitted — we talked** tejía mientras conversábamos; **he played — never before** jugó como nunca; PREP **— a child, I always felt loved** de niño, siempre me sentí querido; **— a teacher, I must be tough** como maestro, tengo que ser estricto; ADV tan, tanto; **— large —** tan grande como; **— long — you wish** todo el tiempo que quieras; **— much —** tanto como; **— well** también; **it's not — important** no es tan importante
ASAP [as soon as possible] [ésæp] ADV lo antes posible
asbestos [æzbéstəs] N asbesto *m*, amianto *m*
ascend [əsénd] VI ascender; **—ing order** orden ascendente *m*
ascent [əsént] N ascenso *m*
ascertain [æsə-tén] VT averiguar, establecer

ascetic [əséɾɪk] ADJ ascético; N asceta *mf*
ascorbic [əskórbɪk] ADJ ascórbico
ascribe [əskráɪb] VT atribuir, imputar
aseptic [əséptɪk] ADJ aséptico
asexual [esékʃuəł] ADJ asexual
ash [æʃ] N (residue, remains) ceniza *f*; (species of tree) fresno *m*; **—tray** cenicero *m*; **— Wednesday** miércoles de ceniza *m*
ashamed [əʃémd] ADJ avergonzado; **to be —** tener vergüenza, avergonzarse
ashen [æʃən] ADJ ceniciento
ashore [əʃór] ADV (movement) a tierra; (location) en tierra; **to go —** desembarcar
Asia [éʒə] N Asia *f*
Asian [éʒən] ADJ & N asiático -ca *mf*
Asiatic [eʒiǽɾɪk] ADJ **— flu** gripe asiática *f*
aside [əsáɪd] ADV **all kidding —** bromas aparte; **his father took him —** su padre lo llamó aparte; **he threw his coat —** tiró su saco a un lado; PREP **— from** aparte de, además de; N (theater) aparte *m*
asinine [ǽsənaɪn] ADJ necio
ask [æsk] VT (inquire) preguntar; (request) pedir; **to — a question** hacer una pregunta; **to — about** preguntar por; **to — for** pedir; **to — for someone** pedir para hablar con alguien; **to — a woman's hand in marriage** pedir la mano de una mujer; **to — out** invitar a salir; **what's your —ing price?** ¿cuánto pides? **you —ed for it** te lo has buscado
askance [əskǽns] ADV **to look —** (obliquely) mirar de soslayo/través/reojo; (suspiciously) mirar con recelo
askew [əskjú] ADJ ladeado, torcido
asleep [əslíp] ADJ dormido; **to fall —** dormirse; **my arm is —** se me ha dormido/entumecido el brazo
asparagus [əspǽrəgəs] N espárrago *m*
aspartame [ǽspə·tem] N aspartamo *m*
aspect [ǽspɛkt] N aspecto *m*
aspen [ǽspɪn] N álamo temblón *m*
Asperger's disorder [ǽspə·gə·zdɪsɔ́ɾdə·] N trastorno de Asperger *m*
asphalt [ǽsfɑłt] N asfalto *m*
asphyxia [æsfíksiə] N asfixia *f*
aspiration [æspəréʃən] N aspiración *f*
aspire [əspáɪr] VI aspirar
aspirin [ǽspɪrɪn] N aspirina *f*
ass [æs] N asno *m*, burro *m*, borrico *m*
assail [əséł] VT (physically) asaltar, atacar; (verbally) atacar
assailant [əséłənt] N atacante *mf*, agresor -ora *mf*
assassin [əsǽsɪn] N asesino -na *mf*
assassinate [əsǽsənet] VT asesinar
assassination [əsæsənéʃən] N asesinato *m*
assault [əsɑ́łt] N asalto *m*, agresión *f*; **— rifle** rifle de asalto *m*; **— and battery** agresión con lesiones *f*; VT asaltar, agredir; (sexually) violar
assay[1] [æsé] VT (situation) examinar, analizar; (metal) ensayar
assay[2] [ǽse] N ensayo *m*
assemble [əsɛ́mbəł] VI/VT (call together) reunir[se], congregar[se]; VT (put together) armar, montar
assembly [əsɛ́mbli] N (meeting) asamblea *f*, reunión *f*; (putting together) montaje *m*, armado *m*; **— language** lenguaje ensamblador *m*; **— line** cadena de producción *f*, línea de montaje *f*
assent [əsɛ́nt] N asentimiento *m*; VI asentir
assert [əsɜ́·t] VT (declare) aseverar, afirmar; **to — one's rights** hacer valer los derechos de uno; **to — oneself** obrar con firmeza
assertion [əsɜ́·ʃən] N (declaration) aseveración *f*, afirmación *f*, aserto *m*; **an — of ownership** una afirmación de los derechos de propiedad
assess [əsɛ́s] VT (evaluate for tax purposes) tasar; (impose tax) gravar, imponer; (measure performance) evaluar
assessment [əsɛ́smənt] N (estimate) avalúo *m*, tasación *f*; (tax) imposición *f*, gravamen *m*; (testing) evaluación *f*
asset [ǽset] N (useful thing) ventaja *f*; (useful quality) virtud *f*; **—s** activo *m*, bienes *m pl*; (on balance sheet) haber *m*, activo *m*; **personal —s** bienes muebles *m pl*; **real —s** bienes inmuebles *m pl*
assiduous [əsíʤuəs] ADJ (constant) asiduo; (industrious) diligente
assign [əsáɪn] VT (allot) asignar; (appoint, designate) designar; (transfer property) ceder
assignment [əsáɪnmənt] N (act of assigning) asignación *f*; (task) encargo *m*, encomienda *f*; (mission) misión *f*; (transfer of property) cesión [de bienes] *f*; (homework) tarea *f*; (lesson) lección *f*
assimilate [əsímələt] VI/VT asimilar[se]
assist [əsíst] VI/VT ayudar, asistir; N (in sports) asistencia *f*
assistance [əsístəns] N ayuda *f*, asistencia *f*
assistant [əsístənt] N ayudante *mf*, asistente -ta *mf*; ADJ auxiliar; **— manager** subgerente *mf*
assistantship [əsístəntshɪp] N ayudantía *f*
associate[1] [əsóʃɪɪt] ADJ asociado; N (acquaintance) compañero -ra *mf*; (co-worker) colega *mf*; (employee) empleado -da *mf*
associate[2] [əsóʃiet] VI/VT asociar[se]; **to be —d with** asociarse con
association [əsosiéʃən] N asociación *f*
assonance [ǽsənəns] N asonancia *f*
assorted [əsɔ́ɾdɪd] ADJ variado, surtido
assortment [əsɔ́ɾtmənt] N (act of assorting) clasificación *f*; (selection of wares) surtido *m*; (selection of tools, etc.) colección *f*
assume [əsúm] VT (responsibility, role) asumir;

(right) arrogarse; (suppose) dar por sentado, suponer; **—d name** alias *m*

assumption [əsʌ́mpʃən] N (premise) suposición *f*, supuesto *m*; (unstated belief) sobreentendido *m*; (seizure) toma *f*; (acceptance of duties) asunción *f*

assurance [əʃúrəns] N (promise) promesa *f*, palabra *f*; (reassurance) palabras de apoyo *f pl*; (certainty) certeza *f*; (confidence) confianza *f*

assure [əʃúr] VT (give confidence) asegurar; (encourage) infundir confianza

assuredly [əʃúrɪdlɪ] ADV seguramente, sin duda

asterisk [ǽstərɪsk] N asterisco *m*

asteroid [ǽstərɔɪd] N asteroide *m*

asthma [ǽzmə] N asma *m*

asthmatic [æzmǽdɪk] ADJ asmático

astigmatism [əstígmətɪzəm] N astigmatismo *m*

astonish [əstɑ́nɪʃ] VT asombrar, pasmar

astonishing [əstɑ́nɪʃɪŋ] ADJ asombroso, pasmoso

astonishment [əstɑ́nɪʃmənt] M asombro *m*, pasmo *m*

astound [əstáʊnd] VT pasmar, asombrar

astraddle [əstrǽdl] ADV a horcajadas

astray [əstré] ADV **to go —** perderse, extraviarse; **to lead —** (seduce) llevar por mal camino, seducir; (perplex) confundir

astride [əstráɪd] ADV a horcajadas

astringent [əstrínʤənt] ADJ & N astringente *m*

astrology [əstrɑ́ləʤi] N astrología *f*

astronaut [ǽstrənɔt] M astronauta *mf*

astronautics [æstrənɔ́dɪks] N astronáutica *f*

astronomer [əstrɑ́nəmə-] N astrónomo -ma *mf*

astronomic [æstrənɑ́mɪk] ADJ astronómico

astronomical [æstrənɑ́mɪkəl] ADJ astronómico

astronomy [əstrɑ́nəmi] N astronomía *f*

astrophysics [æstrofízɪks] N astrofísica *f*

Asturian [æstúriən] ADJ & N asturiano -na *mf*

Asturias [æstúriəs] N Asturias *f sg*

astute [əstút] ADJ astuto, sagaz

asylum [əsáɪləm] N asilo *m*

asymmetric, asymmetrical [esɪmétrɪk[əl]] ADJ; asimétrico

asymptomatic [esɪmptəmǽdɪk] ADJ asintomático

at [æt] PREP **— the end of the story** al final de la historia; **— five o'clock** a las cinco; **— high altitude** a grandes alturas; **— last** por fin, al fin; **— once** enseguida; **— the table** a/en la mesa; **— five dollars a kilo** a cinco dólares el kilo; **— Easter** en Pascua; **— home** en casa; **— war** en guerra; **wait — the door** espera en la puerta; **he is — peace with himself** está en paz consigo mismo; **the children are — play** los niños están jugando; **look — that** mira eso; **amazed —** pasmado por; **he laughed — me** se rió de mí

ate [et] *see* eat

atheism [éθiɪzəm] N ateísmo *m*

atheist [éθiɪst] N ateo -a *mf*

athlete [ǽθlit] N deportista *mf*; (track and field) atleta *mf*; **—'s foot** pie de atleta *m*

athletic [æθlédɪk] ADJ deportivo; (concerning track and field; well-built) atlético

athletics [æθlédɪks] N deporte *m*; (track and field) atletismo *m*

Atlantic [ætlǽntɪk] ADJ atlántico; **— Ocean** Océano Atlántico *m*

atlas [ǽtləs] N atlas *m*

ATM [automatic teller machine] [étiém] N cajero automático *m*

atmosphere [ǽtməsfɪr] N (air) atmósfera *f*; (mood) ambiente *m*

atmospheric [ætməsfírɪk] ADJ atmosférico

atom [ǽdəm] N átomo *m*; **— bomb** bomba atómica *f*

atomic [ətɑ́mɪk] ADJ atómico; **— age** era atómica *f*; **— energy** energía atómica *f*; **— number** número atómico *m*; **— weight** peso atómico *m*

atomize [ǽdəmaɪz] VT atomizar

atomizer [ǽdəmaɪzə-] N atomizador *m*

atone [ətón] VI **to — for** expiar, purgar

atonement [ətónmənt] N expiación *f*, purgación *f*

atop [ətɑ́p] PREP encima de

atrium [étriəm] N (of office building, hotel) vestíbulo *m*, patio central *m*; (of church) atrio *m*

atrocious [ətrɔ́jəs] ADJ atroz

atrocity [ətrɑ́sɪdi] N atrocidad *f*, barbaridad *f*

atrophy [ǽtrəfi] N atrofia *f*; VI/VT atrofiar[se]

attach [ətǽtʃ] VI/VT (pipe, cable) unir[se], juntar; (paper) sujetar; (wages) retener; (significance) atribuir; (an electronic file) adjuntar; **to be —ed to someone** estar apegado a alguien

attaché [ætæʃé] N agregado -da *mf*

attachment [ətǽtʃmənt] N (act of attaching) unión *f*; (pipe, cable) conexión *f*; (of wages) retención *f*; (significance) atribución *f*; (to an e-mail) adjunto *m*; (affection) apego *m*, cariño *m*; (accessory) accesorio *m*

attack [ətǽk] N ataque *m*, acometida *f*; VI/VT atacar, acometer

attain [ətén] VT (rank) alcanzar; (ambition) lograr *m*, realizar *f*; VI (age) llegar a

attainment [əténmənt] N (rank) alcance *m*; (ambition) logro *m*, realización *f*

attempt [ətémpt] N tentativa *f*, intento *m*; (murder) atentado *m*; VT tratar [de], intentar

attend [ətɛ́nd] VT (meeting) asistir a, acudir a; VI **to — to** (a sick person) atender, cuidar; (a speaker) prestar atención; **—ing physician** médico -ca tratante *mf*

attendance [ətɛ́ndəns] N asistencia *f*

attendant [ətɛ́ndənt] N (at a gas station) encargado -da *mf*; (servant) sirviente -ta *mf*; ADJ concomitante

attention [ətén͡ʃən] N atención *f*; (courtesy) atenciones *f pl*; — **deficit disorder** trastorno de déficit de atención *m*; **to pay** — prestar atención; **to pay** — **to** atender a; **to call** — llamar la atención; INTERJ —**!** ¡firmes!
attentive [əténtɪv] ADJ (focused) atento; (courteous) cortés
attenuate [əténjuet] VT atenuar
attest [ətést] VT (bear witness to) atestiguar; (manifest) demostrar; VI certificar, dar fe, atestar
attic [ǽdɪk] N desván *m*, altillo *m*
attire [ətáɪr] N atavío *m*, vestidura *f*; VT ataviar
attitude [ǽdɪtud] N (mental) actitud *f*; (physical) postura *f*; (insolence) insolencia *f*, descaro *m*
attorney [ətɔ́-ni] N abogado -da *mf*, mandatario -ria *mf*; — **General** Ministro -tra de Justicia *mf*
attract [ətrǽkt] VT atraer; **to** — **attention** llamar la atención
attraction [ətrǽkʃən] N (act, power) atracción *f*; (charm) atractivo *m*; (of customers) captación *f*
attractive [ətrǽktɪv] ADJ atractivo; (beautiful) atractivo, agraciado
attractiveness [ətrǽktɪvnɪs] N atractivo *m*
attribute[1] [ǽtrəbjut] N atributo *m*
attribute[2] [ətríbjut] VT atribuir
attribution [ætrəbjúʃən] N atribución *f*
attrition [ətríʃən] N (wearing out) desgaste *m*; (casualties) bajas *f pl*; **war of** — guerra de agotamiento *f*
atypical [etípɪkəł] ADJ atípico
auburn [ɔ́bə-n] N & ADJ castaño rojizo *m*
auction [ɔ́kʃən] N subasta *f*, remate *m*; — **house** casa de subastas *f*; VI/VT subastar, rematar
auctioneer [ɔ̀kʃənír] N subastador -ra *mf*, rematador -ra *mf*
audacious [ɔdéʃəs] ADJ audaz, atrevido
audacity [ɔdǽsɪdɪ] N audacia *f*, desfachatez *f*, atrevimiento *m*
audible [ɔ́dəbəł] ADJ audible; — **feedback** regeneración audible *f*
audience [ɔ́dɪəns] N público *m*, auditorio *m*; (TV, radio) audiencia *f*
audio [ɔ́dɪo] ADJ de audio; — **book** audiolibro *m*; — **frequency** audiofrecuencia *f*; —**visual** audiovisual; —**visuals** audiovisuales *m pl*; N audio *m*
audiology [ɔdɪáləd͡ʒi] N audiología *f*
audit [ɔ́dɪt] VI/VT (class) asistir de oyente; (accounts) auditar; N auditoría *f*; — **cycle** ciclo de auditoría *m*
auditing [ɔ́dɪtɪŋ] N auditoría *f*
audition [ɔdíʃən] N audición *f*; VI dar una audición [para]
auditor [ɔ́dɪdə-] N (of accounts) auditor -ora *mf*, contralor -ora *mf*; (of a class) oyente *mf*
auditorium [ɔdɪtɔ́riəm] N auditorio *m*, paraninfo *m*
auditory [ɔ́dɪtɔri] ADJ auditivo
augment [ɔgmént] VT incrementar, aumentar
August [ɔ́gəst] N agosto *m*
aunt [ænt] N tía *f*
aura [ɔ́rə] N aura *f*
aurora [ərɔ́rə] N aurora *f*; — **borealis** aurora boreal *f*
auspices [ɔ́spɪsɪz] N auspicios *m pl*
auspicious [ɔspíʃəs] ADJ propicio
austere [ɔstír] ADJ austero
austerity [ɔstérɪdɪ] N austeridad *f*
Australia [ɔstréljə] N Australia *f*
Australian [ɔstréljən] ADJ & N australiano -na *mf*
Austria [ɔ́strɪə] N Austria *f*
Austrian [ɔ́strɪən] ADJ & N austríaco -ca *mf*
authentic [ɔθéntɪk] ADJ auténtico
authenticate [ɔθéntɪket] VT autenticar
authentication [ɔθɛntɪkéʃən] N legalización *f*
authenticity [ɔθɛntísɪdɪ] N autenticidad *f*
author [ɔ́θə-] N (professional) escritor -ra *mf*; (creator) autor -ora *mf*
authoritarian [əθɔrɪtériən] ADJ autoritario
authoritative [əθɔ́rɪtɛdɪv] ADJ (official) autorizado; (dictatorial) autoritario
authority [əθɔ́rɪdɪ] N autoridad *f*; (permission) autorización *f*; **to have on good** — saber de buena fuente; **it's not within your** — no está dentro de tus facultades
authorization [ɔθə-ɪzéʃən] N autorización *f*
authorize [ɔ́θəraɪz] VT autorizar, habilitar
autism [ɔ́tɪzəm] N autismo *m*
autistic [ɔtístɪk] ADJ autista
auto [ɔ́do] *see* automobile, automatic
autobiography [ɔdobaɪáɡrəfi] N autobiografía *f*
autocrat [ɔ́dɔkræt] N autócrata *mf*
autograph [ɔ́dɔɡræf] N autógrafo *m*
autoimmune [ɔdoɪmjún] ADJ autoinmune
automated [ɔ́dəmedɪd] ADJ automatizado
automatic [ɔdəmǽdɪk] ADJ automático; (response) maquinal; — **backup** (copy) copia de respaldo automático *f*; (process) respaldo automático *m*; — **pilot** piloto automático *m*; — **transmission** transmisión automática *f*
automation [ɔdəméʃən] N automatización *f*
automobile [ɔ́dəməbił] N automóvil *m*
automotive [ɔdəmóʊɪv] ADJ (sport) automovilístico; (industry) automotor, automotriz
autonomic [ɔdənámɪk] ADJ autonómico
autonomous [tánəməs] ADJ autónomo
autonomy [tánəmi] N autonomía *f*
autopilot [ɔ́dopaɪlət] N piloto automático *m*
autopsy [ɔ́tɑpsi] N autopsia *f*
autumn [ɔ́dəm] N otoño *m*
autumnal [ɔtámnəł] ADJ otoñal
auxiliary [ɔgzíləri] ADJ & N auxiliar *mf*
avail [əvéł] VI/VT servir; **to** — **oneself of**

aprovecharse de; N utilidad *f*; **of no —** de ninguna utilidad; **to no —** en vano

availability [əveləbílɪdi] N (of a person, taxicab, funds) disponibilidad *f*; (of merchandise) existencias *f pl*

available [əvéləbəł] ADJ disponible, asequible

avalanche [ǽvəlænʧ] N avalancha *f*, alud *m*

avarice [ǽvərɪs] N avaricia *f*

avaricious [æ̀vəríʃəs] ADJ avaro, avariento

avatar [ǽvətɑr] N avatar *m*

avenge [əvénʤ] VT vengar

avenger [əvénʤə˞] N vengador -ra *mf*

avenue [ǽvənu] N avenida *f*; (means of access) vía *f*

aver [əvɝ́] VT afirmar

average [ǽvrɪʤ] N promedio *m*; **on —** de promedio; ADJ medio, mediano; **just —** (person) del montón; (thing) nada del otro mundo; VT promediar; **he —s 20 miles an hour** hace un promedio de 20 millas por hora

averse [əvɝ́s] ADJ reacio; **he's not — to a glass of wine** no se opone a una copa de vino

aversion [əvɝ́ʒən] N aversión *f*

avert [əvɝ́t] VT (eyes) desviar, apartar; (danger) evitar

aviation [eviéʃən] N aviación *f*

aviator [évieɪdə˞] N aviador -ra *mf*

avid [ǽvɪd] ADJ ávido

avocado [æ̀vəkɑ́do] N aguacate *m*; *Am* palta *f*

avocation [æ̀vəkéʃən] N pasatiempo *m*

avoid [əvɔ́ɪd] VI/VT (stay away from) evitar; (dodge) esquivar

avow [əváʊ] VT confesar

avowal [əváʊəł] N confesión *f*

avuncular [əvʌ́ŋkjələ˞] ADJ propio de un tío; **— attitude** actitud paternal y amistosa

await [əwét] VT aguardar

awake [əwék] ADJ despierto; VI/VT despertar[se]

awaken [əwékən] VI/VT despertar[se]

award [əwɔ́rd] N premio *m*, galardón *m*; (judicial) adjudicación *f*; VT otorgar, adjudicar

aware [əwɛ́r] ADJ consciente, enterado; **I'm — of that** eso me consta

awareness [əwɛ́rnɪs] N conciencia *f*

away [əwé] ADV **far —** lejos; **— from his family** lejos de su familia; **she looked —** apartó la vista; **she's —** no está; **he's been painting — all day** se ha pasado todo el día pintando; **right —** ahora mismo, ahorita; **ten miles —** a diez millas de distancia; **to give —** regalar; **to go —** irse; **to take —** quitar; **to blow —** (destroy) [hacer] volar; (astonish) dejar atónito

awe [ɔ] N sobrecogimiento *m*; **to be in —** sobrecogerse; VT sobrecoger

awesome [ɔ́səm] ADJ (awe-inspiring) sobrecogedor; (impressive) fabuloso

awestruck [ɔ́strʌk] ADJ pasmado

awful [ɔ́fəł] ADJ terrible, horroroso; ADV espantoso

awhile [əhwáɪł] ADV un rato

awkward [ɔ́kwə˞d] ADJ (clumsy) torpe, desmañado; (embarrassing) embarazoso; (unwieldy) incómodo

awl [ɔł] N punzón *m*

awning [ɔ́nɪŋ] N toldo *m*

awoke [əwɔ́k] *see* wake

awoken [əwɔ́kn̩] *see* wake

awry [əráɪ] ADJ (clothes) mal puesto; (hat) ladeado; **my plans went —** mis planes fracasaron rotundamente

ax, axe [æks] N hacha *f*; VT eliminar

axis [ǽksɪs] N eje *m*

axle [ǽksəł] N eje *m*

Azerbaijan [æ̀zə˞baɪʤɑ́n] N Azerbaiyán *m*

Azerbaijani, Azerbaijanian [æ̀zə˞baɪʤɑ́ni[ən]] ADJ & N azerbaijano -na *mf*, azerbaiyano -na *mf*

Aztec [ǽztɛk] ADJ & N azteca *mf*

azure [ǽʒə˞] ADJ [azul] celeste; N azul celeste *m*

Bb

babble [bǽbəł] N (baby talk) balbuceo *m*; (chatter) parloteo *m*; (murmur) murmullo *m*; VI (to talk like a baby) balbucear; (to chatter) parlotear; (to murmur) murmurar

baboon [bæbún] N babuino *m*

baby [bébi] N bebé *mf*; **who's the — in your family?** ¿quién es el menor/benjamín en tu familia? **— blue** celeste *m*; **— boomer** persona nacida entre 1946 y 1965 *f*; **— carriage** cochecito de bebé *m*; **— food** comida para bebés *f*; **— girl** nena *f*; **— sister** hermanita *f*; **— sitter** niñera *f*; **— talk** habla infantil *f*; **— tooth** diente de leche *m*; **to —sit** cuidar niños; **she had a —** dio a luz; VT mimar

baccalaureate [bæ̀kəlɔ́rɪət] N bachillerato *m*

bachelor [bǽʧələ˞] N soltero *m*; **—'s degree** licenciatura *f*; **— of Arts** (degree) licenciatura en filosofía y letras *f*; (person) licenciado -da en filosofía y letras *mf*

bacillus [bəsíləs] N bacilo *m*

back [bæk] N (human body part) espalda *f*; (animal body part) lomo *m*; (opposite side) dorso *m*; (of chair) respaldo *m*, espaldar *m*; **—ache** dolor de espalda *m*; **—bone** columna vertebral *f*, espinazo *m*; **—pack** mochila *f*; **behind one's —** a espaldas de uno; **he has no —bone** no tiene carácter; **in — of** detrás de, tras; **in the — of the house** atrás de la casa; **to fall on one's —** caer de espaldas; **to**

turn one's — volver las espaldas; ADJ **— charges** cargos atrasados *m pl*; **— door** puerta trasera *f*; **— issues** números atrasados *m pl*; **— order** pedido pendiente *m*; **— taxes** impuestos atrasados *m pl*; **on the — burner** en suspenso; **— -and-forth movement** movimiento de vaivén *m*; VT respaldar, apoyar; VI dar marcha atrás; **to — down** echarse [para] atrás, recular; **to — up** (in a car) dar marcha atrás; (a file) hacer una copia de seguridad de; ADV (look) atrás / para atrás; (fall) de espaldas; **to — off** echarse atrás; **— and forth** de aquí para allá; **he ran — to the house** volvió corriendo a la casa; **he's — from work** está de vuelta del trabajo

backbite [bǽkbaɪt] VI/VT difamar

back date [bǽk det] VT antedatar

backer [bǽkɚ] N (financial) fiador -ra *mf*; (political) partidario -ria *mf*

backfire [bǽkfaɪr] VI (automobile) petardear, hacer detonaciones; (plan) ser contraproducente; N petardeo *m*

backgammon [bǽkgæmən] N backgammon *m*

background [bǽkgraʊnd] N (of a picture) fondo *m*; (experience) antecedentes *m pl*; (software) **— application** aplicación de fondo *f*; **— noise** ruido de fondo *m*; **I have a — in computers** tengo conocimientos de informática; **I know what goes on in the —** sé lo que pasa entre bastidores; **a humble —** orígenes humildes *m pl*

backhand [bǽkhænd] N revés *m*

backing [bǽkɪŋ] N (support) respaldo *m*, apoyo *m*; (guarantee) garantía *f*; (fabric) refuerzo *m*

backlash [bǽklæʃ] N reacción violenta *f*

backlighting [bǽklaɪdɪŋ] N retroiluminación *f*

backlit [bǽklɪt] ADJ retroiluminado

backlog [bǽklɑg] N atraso *m*

backpack [bǽkpɑk] N mochila *f*; VI viajar con mochila

backseat [bǽksɪt] N asiento trasero *m*

backslash [bǽkslæʃ] N barra invertida *f*

backslide [bǽkslaɪd] VI volver a las andadas, reincidir

backspace [bǽkspes] N (action) retroceso *m*; (key) tecla de retroceso *f*; VI apretar la tecla de retroceso

backspin [bǽkspɪn] N efecto *m*, cortado *m*

backstage [bǽkstéʤ] ADV entre bastidores

backtrack [bǽktræk] VI retroceder, dar marcha atrás

backup [bǽkʌp] N (support) respaldo *m*; (copy) copia de seguridad *f*

backward [bǽkwɚd] ADV hacia atrás, para atrás; **— search** búsqueda hacia atrás *f*; **to go —** recular; ADJ (underdeveloped) atrasado; (reactionary) retrógrado

backwardness [bǽkwɚdnɪs] N (underdevelopment) atraso *m*; (conservatism) retrogradismo *m*; (timidity) timidez *f*

backyard [bǽkjɑrd] N patio trasero *m*

bacon [békən] N tocino *m*, *Sp* beicon *m*

bacteria [bæktíriə] N bacteria[s] *f* [*pl*]

bacterial [bæktíriəl] ADJ bacteriano

bacteriology [bæktiriáləʤi] N bacteriología *f*

bad [bæd] ADJ malo; (man) perverso; (teeth) feo; (drug) dañoso; (flood) grave; (fruit) podrido; **— blood** enemistad *f*; **— check** cheque sin fondos *m*; **— debt** deuda incobrable *f*; **— faith** mala fe *f*; **to go from — to worse** ir de mal en peor; **he has a — heart** está enfermo del corazón; **to look —** tener mal aspecto; *fam* quedar mal; ADV mal; **not —** no está nada mal; **too —** ¡qué pena! VT **to —mouth** difamar [a]

bade [bed] *see* bid

badge [bæʤ] N insignia *f*, chapa *f*

badger [bǽʤɚ] N tejón *m*; VT acosar

badly [bǽdli] ADV (do) mal; (want) mucho; (hurt) gravemente

baffle [bǽfəl] VT (confuse) confundir; (frustrate) desconcertar; N deflector *m*

bag [bæg] N bolsa *f*, bolso *m*; (suitcase) maleta *f*; (under eyes) ojera *f*; **— lady** vagabunda *f*; **—pipe** gaita *f*; VT (groceries) empacar, embolsar; (prey) cazar

baggage [bǽgɪʤ] N (suitcases) equipaje *m*; (impediments) bagaje *m*; **— car** vagón de equipajes *m*; **— check** contraseña de equipajes *f*; **— claim** recogida de equipaje *f*; **— tag** etiqueta *f*; **— inspection** revisión de equipaje *f*

baggy [bǽgi] ADJ flojo, holgado

Bahamas [bəhɑ́məz] N Bahamas *f pl*

Bahamian [bəhémiən] ADJ & N bahameño -ña *mf*

Bahrain [bɑrén] N Bahréin *m*

Bahraini [bɑréni] ADJ & N bahreiní *mf*

bail [bel] N fianza *f*; **—out** rescate financiero *m*; **to let out on —** poner en libertad bajo fianza; VT pagar la fianza; **to — someone out** pagarle la fianza a alguien; **to — someone out of a predicament** sacar a alguien de un apuro; **to — out water** achicar, vaciar; VI **to — out** (of a plane) tirarse con paracaídas de un avión; (of a situation) abandonar

bailiff [bélɪf] N ujier *mf*

bait [bet] N cebo *m*; VT (prepare hook) cebar; (attract customers) seducir; (harass) acosar; **— and switch advertising** publicidad de cebo y anzuelo *f*

bake [bek] VI/VT (in an oven) hornear; (in the sun) calcinar, abrasar; **I'm baking in this heat** me estoy asando, me muero de calor

baker [békɚ] N panadero -ra *mf*; **—'s dozen** la docena del fraile *f*

bakery [békəri] N panadería *f*

baking [békɪŋ] N (act of baking) horneado *m*; (activity) repostería *f*; **— powder** polvo de hornear *m*; **— soda** bicarbonato de sodio *m*
balance [bǽləns] N (instrument) balanza *f*; (equilibrium) equilibrio *m*; (debit, credit) saldo *m*, balance *m*; **— due** saldo pendiente *m*; **— sheet** balance *m*; **— of payments** balanza de pagos *f*; **— of trade** balanza comercial *f*; **to lose one's —** perder el equilibrio; VT equilibrar, hacer equilibrio con; **to — the risks with the benefits** sopesar los riesgos y los beneficios; VI (accounts) cuadrar; **—ed budget** presupuesto equilibrado *m*; **to — a budget** equilibrar un presupuesto
balanced [bǽlənst] ADJ equilibrado
balancing [bǽlənsɪŋ] N equilibrado *m*
balcony [bǽtkəni] N balcón *m*; (in a theater) palco *m*, entresuelo *m*
bald [bɔld] ADJ (person) calvo, pelón; (mountain) pelón; (tire) liso; **— eagle** águila americana de cabeza blanca *f*; **—headed** calvo; **— spot** calva *f*; **he went —** se quedó calvo
baldness [bɔ́ldnɪs] N calvicie *f*
bale [beɪl] N paca *f*, fardo *m*; VT empacar, enfardar
balk [bɔk] VI oponerse, rehusarse a
ball [bɔl] N (tennis, baseball, golf) pelota *f*, bola *f*; (baseball, opposite of strike) bola *f*; (basketball, football, soccer) balón *m*; (billiards) bola *f*; (of string, thread) ovillo *m*; (cannon) bala [de cañón] *f*; (dance) baile *m*; **— and chain** grillete *m*; **— bearing** cojinete de bolas *m*; **— game** juego de pelota *m*; (baseball) partido de béisbol *m*; **—park estimate** cifra aproximada *f*; VT ovillar
ballad [bǽləd] N balada *f*; (historical) romance *m*
ballast [bǽləst] N lastre *m*; (railroad) balasto *m*; VT lastrar
ballerina [bǽlərínə] N bailarina de ballet *f*
ballet [bǽlé] N ballet *m*
ballistic [bəlístɪk] ADJ balístico; **— missile** misil balístico *m*; N **—s** balística *f*
balloon [bəlún] N globo *m*; **— mortgage** hipoteca con pago final mayor *f*; VI (travel in a balloon) pasear en globo; VI/VT (grow) inflar[se]
ballot [bǽlət] N (system of voting) votación *f*; (paper) papeleta *f*; *Mex* boleta *f*; **— box** urna *f*
balm [bɑm] N bálsamo *m*
balmy [bɑ́mi] ADJ templado
baloney [bəlóni] N pamplinas *f pl*, paparruchas *f pl*
balsa [bɔ́lsə] N (wood) madera balsa *f*; (raft) balsa *f*
balsam [bɔ́lsəm] N (resin) bálsamo *m*; (tree) especie de abeto *m*
bamboo [bǽmbú] N bambú *m*
ban [bǽn] N prohibición *f*; (church) excomunión *f*; VT prohibir
banal [bén] ADJ banal
banana [bənǽnə] N plátano *m*, banana *f*; **— grove** platanar *m*; **— split** banana split *m*; **— tree** plátano *m*, banano *m*
band [bǽnd] N (group) banda *f*, pandilla *f*; (group of musicians) banda *f*, conjunto *m*; (cloth) banda *f*; (ribbon) cinta *f*; (leather) tira *f*; **to join the —wagon** subirse al carro/tren; **—width** amplitud de banda *f*; VI/VT **to — together** unirse, juntarse
bandage [bǽndɪʤ] N venda *f*, vendaje *m*; VT vendar
Band-aid® [bǽnded] N Curita® *f*, parche *m*
bandit [bǽndɪt] N bandido -da *mf*, bandolero -ra *mf*, salteador -ora *mf*
bang [bæŋ] N (blow) golpe *m*, golpazo *m*; (sound) estampido *m*, estallido *m*; **—s** fleco *m*, flequillo *m*; **I get a — out of seeing my grandkids** me emociona ver a mis nietos; VI/VT (hit) golpear; (make noise) hacer estrépito
Bangladesh [bæŋgləděʃ] N Bangladesh *m*
Bangladeshi [bæŋgləděʃi] ADJ & N bangladeshí *mf*, banglades*í* *mf*, bengalés -esa
banish [bǽnɪʃ] VT desterrar
banishment [bǽnɪʃmənt] N destierro *m*, proscripción *f*
banister [bǽnɪstə-] N barandal *m*, pasamano[s] *m*, balaustrada *f*
banjo [bǽnʤo] N banjo *m*
bank [bæŋk] N (financial institution) banco *m*; (in gambling) banca *f*; (of a body of water) orilla *f*, ribera *f*, margen *m*; (slope) escarpa *f*; **— card** tarjeta bancaria *f*; **— account** cuenta bancaria *f*; **— check** cheque de caja *m*; **— failure** quiebra bancaria *f*; **—note** billete *m*; **— statement** estado de cuenta *m*; **— vault** cámara *f*; ADJ bancario, de banco; VT (money) depositar en un banco; VI (snow, sand) amontonar; (airplane) ladear; **to — on** contar con; **to —roll** financiar
banker [bǽŋkə-] N (bank owner) banquero -ra *mf*; (bank employee) bancario -ria *mf*
banking [bǽŋkɪŋ] N (activity) actividad bancaria *f*; (industry) banca *f*; ADJ bancario, de banco
bankrupt [bǽŋkrʌpt] ADJ en bancarrota, en quiebra; VT arruinar, quebrar
bankruptcy [bǽŋkrʌptsi] N bancarrota *f*, quiebra *f*; **— law** estatuto de quiebras *m*; **— proceedings** juicio por quiebra *m*; **to go into —** declararse en quiebra
banner [bǽnə-] N estandarte *m*, pendón *m*; ADJ sobresaliente
banquet [bǽŋkwɪt] N banquete *m*, gala *f*
baptism [bǽptɪzəm] N (sacrament) bautismo *m*; (action) bautizo *m*
baptize [bǽptaɪz] VT bautizar
bar [bɑr] N (of iron, sand, soap, of a tavern) barra *f*; (of chocolate) barra *f*, tableta *f*; (vertical

rod) barrote *m*; (obstacle) barrera *f*, obstáculo *m*; (in music) compás *m*; (saloon) bar *m*; **—bell** barra para pesas *f*; **—code** código de barras *m*; **—code reader** lector de código de barras *m*; **— graph** gráfica de barras *f*; **—keeper/tender** tabernero -ra *mf*, cantinero -ra *mf*; **—room** bar *m*; **—room brawl** pelea de borrachos *f*; **behind —s** tras las rejas; **to be admitted to the —** recibirse de abogado; VT (door, exit) atrancar; (access) impedir; (from membership) excluir; **— none** sin excepción; **—ring a disaster** salvo en caso de desastre

barb [bɑrb] N púa *f*; **—ed wire** alambre de púas *m*; *Sp* alambre de espino *m*

Barbadian [bɑrbéɒiən] ADJ & N barbadense *mf*

Barbados [bɑrbéɒos] N Barbados *m*

barbarian [bɑrbéríən] ADJ & N bárbaro -ra *mf*

barbaric [bɑrbǽrɪk] ADJ bárbaro

barbarous [bárbə-əs] ADJ bárbaro

barbecue [bárbɪkju] N (meat dish) barbacoa *f*, asado *m*, parrillada *f*; **— sauce** adobo de barbacoa *m*; VI/VT asar con adobo

barber [bárbə-] N peluquero *m*, barbero *m*; **—shop** peluquería *f*, barbería *f*

barbiturate [bɑrbítʃə-ɪt] N barbitúrico *m*

bard [bɑrd] N bardo *m*

bare [bɛr] ADJ (legs, walls) desnudo; (pantry) vacío; **—back** a pelo; **—bones** básico; **—faced** descarado; **—foot** descalzo; **the — necessities** lo imprescindible; **—headed** con la cabeza descubierta; **—legged** con las piernas desnudas; **— majority** escasa mayoría *f*; **to lay —** poner al descubierto; **with his — hands** con las propias manos

barely [bérli] ADV apenas

bargain [bárgɪn] N (agreement) trato *m*; (inexpensive purchase) ganga *f*, ocasión *f*; **— basement** sección de ofertas *f*; **into the —** por añadidura; **to strike a —** cerrar un trato; VI (haggle) regatear; (expect) contar con

bargaining [bárgənɪŋ] N (haggling) regateo *m*; (negotiation) negociación *f*; **—ing position** posición de negociación *f*

barge [bɑrʤ] N barcaza *f*; VI **to — into a room** irrumpir en un cuarto

baritone [bǽrɪton] N & ADJ barítono *m*

barium [bǽriəm] N bario *m*

bark [bɑrk] N (of a dog) ladrido *m*; (on a tree) corteza *f*; VI/VT ladrar

barley [bárli] N cebada *f*

barn [bɑrn] N (for animals) establo *m*; (for grain) granero *m*; **— owl** lechuza *f*; **—yard** corral *m*

barnacle [bárnəkəł] N percebe *m*

barometer [bəráɒmɪdə-] N barómetro *m*

baron [bǽrən] N barón *m*

baroque [bərók] ADJ & N barroco *m*

barracks [bǽrəks] N cuartel *m*

barracuda [bærəkúdə] N barracuda *f*

barrage [bəráʒ] N (of artillery fire) barrera de fuego *f*; (of questions) lluvia *f*, aluvión *m*

barrel [bǽrəł] N barril *m*, tonel *m*; (gun) cañón *m*, caño *m*; **he's a — of laughs** es un payaso; **he is scraping the bottom of the —** está desesperado; VI **to — along** ir disparado

barren [bǽrən] ADJ (land) árido, yermo; (female) estéril

barrette [bərét] N broche *m*

barricade [bærɪkéd] N barricada *f*; VT cerrar con barricadas; VI atrincherarse

barrier [bǽriə-] N barrera *f*; **— reef** barrera de coral *f*

barrio [bário] N barrio hispano *m*

barter [bárdə-] VI hacer trueque; VT trocar; N trueque *m*

bartering [bárdə-ɪŋ] N trueque *m*

basal cell carcinoma [bésəłsełkɑrsɪnómə] N carcinoma de célula basal *m*

basalt [bésɔłt] N basalto *m*

base [bes] N base *f*; **—ball** béisbol *m*; **—ball player** beisbolista *m*, pelotero -ra *mf*; **—board** zócalo *m*; ADJ bajo, vil; (metal) de baja ley; **— font** tipo de letra por omisión *m*; **—line** línea de fondo *f*; **— on balls** base por bolas *f*; **— pay** salario base *m*; **—s loaded** bases llenas *f pl*; **— steal** robo de base *m*; VI/VT basar, fundamentar; **to be —d on** fundamentarse en; **the general is —d in Berlin** el general está estacionado en Berlín

baseless [bésłɪs] ADJ sin fundamento

basement [bésmənt] N sótano *m*

baseness [bésnɪs] N bajeza *f*, vileza *f*

bash [bæʃ] VT golpear; N (party) fiesta *f*

bashful [bǽʃfəł] ADJ tímido, vergonzoso

bashfulness [bǽʃfəłnɪs] N timidez *f*

basic [bésɪk] ADJ básico

basin [bésɪn] N (bowl) palangana *f*, jofaina *f*; (of a fountain) pilón *m*; (geographical formation) cuenca *f*; (pond) estanque *m*

basis [bésɪs] N fundamento *m*, base *f*; **on the — of** en base a, con base en; **on a regular —** regularmente

bask [bæsk] VI (in the sun) asolearse; (in praise) deleitarse

basket [bǽskɪt] N canasta *f*, cesta *f*, cesto *m*; (in basketball) canasta *f*; **—ball** (game) baloncesto *m*, básquetbol *m*, básquet *m*; (ball) balón de baloncesto *m*; **— case** (crazy person) chiflado -da *mf*; (helpless person) caso perdido *m*; **to make a —** (in basketball) encestar

basketful [bǽskɪtfʌł] N (contents of a basket) canasto *m*; (large amount) montón *m*

basketry [bǽskɪtri] N cestería *f*

Basque [bæsk] ADJ & N (person) vasco -ca *mf*; (language) vascuence *m*, vasco *m*, euskera *m*

bass[1] [bes] N (voice, bass guitar) bajo *m*; (double bass) contrabajo *m*; **— clef** clave de fa *f*; **—**

drum bombo *m*; **— horn** tuba *f*

bass[2] [bæs] (marine fish) lubina *f*; (freshwater fish) perca *f*

bassist [bésɪst] N bajista *mf*

bassoon [bæsún] N fagot *m*

bastard [bǽstə-d] N & ADJ bastardo -da *mf*

baste [best] VT (fabric) hilvanar; (meat) rociar

bat [bæt] N (baseball, cricket) bate *m*; (animal) murciélago *m*; VT golpear; **he is at —** está al bate; **it was his first at- —** fue su primer turno; VI (baseball) batear; **not to — an eye** no pestañear

batch [bætʃ] N (of cookies) hornada *f*; (of cement, files) tanda *f*; (of data) colección *f*

bath [bæθ] N baño *m*; **—robe** bata [de baño] *f*; *Sp* albornoz *m*; **—room** (in a house) baño *m*, cuarto de baño *m*; (public) *Sp* aseo *m*; *Am* servicio *m*, baño *m*; **—tub** bañera *f*

bathe [beð] VI/VT bañar[se]; **bathing suit** traje de baño *m*

bather [béðə-] N bañista *mf*

baton [bətán] N batuta *f*

battalion [bətǽljən] N batallón *m*

batter [bǽtə-] N (in baking) pasta *f*, masa *f*; (in baseball) bateador -ora *mf*; **—'s box** caja de bateo *f*; VT golpear

battery [bǽtəri] N (of car, artillery, in baseball) batería *f*; (of electronic devices) pila *f*; (of tests) serie *f*; (assault) asalto *m*

batting [bǽdɪŋ] N bateo *m*; **— average** porcentaje de bateo *m*

battle [bǽdl] N batalla *f*; **—-ax[e]** (weapon) hacha de guerra *f*; (woman) *pej* sargenta *f*; **— cry** grito de guerra *m*; **—field** campo de batalla *m*; **—ship** acorazado *m*; VI batallar; **to — cancer** luchar contra el cáncer

bawl [bɔł] VI berrear; **to — somebody out** echarle la bronca a uno

bay [be] N (body of water) bahía *f*; (howl) aullido *m*; **— leaf** hoja de laurel *f*; **— window** ventana saliente *f*; **to hold at —** tener a raya; ADJ bayo; VI aullar

bayonet [beənét] N bayoneta *f*

bazaar [bəzár] N (market place) bazar *m*; (benefit) kermés *f*

bazooka [bəzúka] N bazuca *f*

be [bi] VI ser, estar; **I am from Uruguay** soy de Uruguay; **there were four of us** éramos cuatro; **he is a doctor** es médico; **it's her** es ella; **sugar is sweet** el azúcar es dulce; **London is in England** Londres está en Inglaterra; **this water is cold** esta agua está fría; **the windows were open** las ventanas estaban abiertas; **there is a problem** hay un problema; **to — cold/warm/hungry/right / in a hurry** tener frío/calor/hambre/razón/prisa; **to be cold/hot/windy** hacer frío/calor/viento

beach [bitʃ] N playa *f*; **—comber** vagabundo -da *mf*; **—head** cabeza de playa *f*; VT varar, encallar

beacon [bíkən] N faro *m*

bead [bid] N (of glass) cuenta *f*; (of sweat) gota *f*, perla *f*; **to get a — on somebody** apuntarle a alguien; VT (string) enhebrar/ensartar cuentas; (decorate) adornar con cuentas

beagle [bígəł] N beagle *m*

beak [bik] N pico *m*

beaker [bíkə-] N vaso de precipitados *m*

beam [bim] N (of light) rayo *m*, haz *m*; (of a building) viga *f*; (of a ship) manga *f*; (of a scale) brazo *m*; **broad in the —** ancho de caderas; VI/VT (light, radio) emitir; (smile) estar radiante

bean [bin] N judía *f*, habichuela *f*; *Sp* alubia *f*; *Am* frijol *m*, *Am* poroto *m*; **Lima —** haba *f*; **—stalk** tallo de habas / frijol *m*; **Jack and the —stalk** Juanito y las habichuelas; **I don't know —s about that** no sé ni papa / ni jota de eso

bear [bɛr] N oso *m*; **— hug** abrazo fuerte *m*; **— market** mercado bajista *m*; VT (hold up, tolerate) soportar, aguantar; (suffer) sobrellevar; (have a child) dar a luz; (produce young) parir; (produce fruit) producir; **to — down** (mash) apretar; (push) pujar; **to — a grudge** guardar rencor; **to — in mind** tener en cuenta; **to — oneself with dignity** portarse con dignidad; **to — out** confirmar; **to — testimony** dar testimonio; **to — interest** devengar interés; **to — gifts** traer regalos; **to — a resemblance** parecerse; **to — the cost of something** asumir el costo de algo; **it doesn't — repeating** no merece repetirse

bearable [bɛ́rəbəł] ADJ llevadero, soportable

beard [bird] N (on a man) barba *f*; (of wheat) aristas *f pl*

bearded [bírdɪd] ADJ barbado, barbudo

bearer [bɛ́rə-] N portador -ora *mf*

bearing [bɛ́rɪŋ] N porte *m*; **to lose one's —s** perder el rumbo, desorientarse; **it has no — on our situation** no tiene relación con nuestra situación

bearish [bɛ́rɪʃ] ADJ (of bears) osuno; (of stock market) bajista

beast [bist] N bestia *f*

beat [bit] VT (wings, eggs) batir; (a person) golpear; (a drum) tocar; (an opponent) vencer; (tempo) marcar; VI (heart) latir; (drum) sonar; **to — around the bush** andarse por las ramas; **to — off** rechazar; **to — up** dar una paliza; **—s me!** ¡ni idea! N (blow) golpe *m*; (drum) toque *m*; (heart) latido *m*; (tempo) compás *m*; (policeman's territory) ronda *f*; ADJ cansado

beaten [bítn] ADJ (mixed) batido; (defeated) vencido; **— path** camino trillado *m*

beaten [bítn̩] *see* beat

beater [bíDə˞] N batidor *m*

beating [bíDɪŋ] N (whipping) paliza *f*; (pulsation) latido *m*

beau [bo] N pretendiente *m*

beautiful [bjúːdəfəl] ADJ hermoso; **— people** jet set *m*

beautify [bjúːdəfaɪ] VT embellecer, hermosear

beauty [bjúːDɪ] N belleza *f*, hermosura *f*; (woman) beldad *f*; **— contest/pageant** concurso/certamen de belleza *m*; **— parlor** salón de belleza *m*

beaver [bíva˞] N castor *m*

became [bikém] *see* become

because [bɪkɔ́z] CONJ porque; **— of** por, a causa de, debido a

beckon [békən] VT llamar por señas

become [bɪkám] VT (turn into) convertirse en; **the water became ice** el agua se convirtió en hielo; **he became a doctor** llegó a ser médico; (suit) sentar bien; **that suit —s you** ese traje te luce bien; VI (change emotional or physical condition) ponerse; **she became ill** se puso enferma; (undergo a drastic change) volverse; **he became crazy** se volvió loco; **to — angry** enojarse; **to — frightened** asustarse; **to — old** envejecer; **what has — of him?** ¿qué ha sido de él?

becoming [bɪkámɪŋ] ADJ (appropriate) propio; **that dress is — to you** te sienta bien ese vestido

bed [bɛd] N (furniture) cama *f*; *lit* lecho *m*; (of a river) cauce *m*; (of the sea) fondo *m*; (in a garden) cuadro *m*; **—bug** chinche *mf*; **—clothes** ropa de cama *f*; **—pan** cuña *f*, chata *f*; **—ridden** postrado en cama; **—rest** reposo *m*; **—rock** lecho de roca *m*; **—room** alcoba *f*, dormitorio *m*; *Mex* recámara *f*; **at the —side** al lado de la cama; **—side table** mesita de noche *f*; **—side manner** manera de tratar a los pacientes *f*; **—sore** llaga *f*; **—spread** colcha *f*; **—spring** resorte del colchón *m*; **—time** hora de dormir *f*; **—wetting** enuresis nocturna *f*; **to go to —** acostarse; **to put to —** acostar

bedding [bɛ́Dɪŋ] N ropa de cama *f*

bee [bi] N (insect) abeja *f*; (social gathering) tertulia *f*; **to have a — in one's bonnet** tener una idea metida en la cabeza; **—hive** colmena *f*; **— sting** picadura de abeja *f*

beech [bitʃ] N haya *f*; **—nut** hayuco *m*

beef [bif] N (meat) carne de vaca/res *f*; (complaint) queja *f*; **— jerky** cecina *f*; **—steak** bistec *m*; VI quejarse; **to — up** reforzar

been [bɪn] *see* be

beep [bip] N pitazo *m*; VI/VT (alarm) sonar; (horn) tocar

beeper [bípə˞] N buscapersonas *m sg*

beer [bir] N cerveza *f*

beet [bit] N remolacha *f*

beetle [bídl̩] N escarabajo *m*

befall [bɪfɔ́ł] VT acontecerle a

befallen [bɪfɔ́lən] *see* befall

befell [bɪfɛ́ł] *see* befall

befit [bɪfɪ́t] VT convenir

before [bɪfɔ́r] ADV (temporal) antes, con anterioridad; (spatial) delante; PREP (temporal) antes de; (spatial) delante de; *lit* ante; CONJ antes [de] que, antes de; **— beginning** antes de que comiences, antes de comenzar; **—-tax earnings** ganancias pre-impositivas *f pl*

beforehand [bɪfɔ́rhænd] ADV de antemano, con anterioridad

befriend [bɪfrɛ́nd] VT hacerse amigo de

beg [bɛg] VI (ask for alms) mendigar, pedir limosna; VI/VT (implore) rogar; **to — for mercy** pedir misericordia; **she —ged me to do it** me rogó que lo hiciera; **to — the question** dar por sentado lo mismo que se arguye

began [bɪgǽn] *see* begin

begat [bɪgǽt] *see* beget

beget [bɪgɛ́t] VT engendrar

beggar [bɛ́gə˞] N mendigo -ga *mf*

begin [bɪgín] VI/VT comenzar, empezar; **the ten dollars won't — to cover the expense** los diez dólares ni siquiera cubren los gastos

beginner [bɪgínə˞] N principiante *mf*

beginning [bɪgínɪŋ] N principio *m*; (temporal only) comienzo *m*; **— with** comenzando con/por; **at the —** al/por el principio

begotten [bɪgátn̩] *see* beget

begrudge [bɪgrʌ́dʒ] VT aceptar de mala gana

begun [bɪgán] *see* begin

behalf [bɪhǽf] PREP LOC **on — of** (in place of) por, en nombre de, de parte de; (in favor of) a favor de

behave [bɪhév] VI portarse, comportarse; **— yourself!** ¡pórtate bien!

behavior [bɪhévjə˞] N comportamiento *m*, conducta *f*

behavioral [bɪhévjərəł] ADJ conductual, relativo a la conducta / al comportamiento

behead [bɪhɛ́d] VT decapitar, descabezar

beheld [bɪhɛ́łd] *see* behold

behind [bɪháɪnd] ADV detrás; (in payments, schedule) atrasado; **he fell — his competitors** quedó a la zaga de sus competidores; **an hour —** una hora de retraso; **from —** desde atrás; **to fall —** atrasarse; **to leave something —** dejar atrás algo; PREP detrás de, tras; **we're all — you** todos te apoyamos; **who's — this evil plot?** ¿quién está detrás de este plan macabro? **— one's back** a espaldas de uno; N trasero *m*

behold [bɪhółd] VT contemplar; **— the future**

king! ¡he aquí el futuro rey!

behoove [bɪhúv] VI **it behooves [one]** le corresponde [a uno]

beige [beʒ] ADJ & N beige *m*

being [bíɪŋ] N ser *m*; **for the time —** por ahora

Belarus [bɛlərús] N Bielorrusia *f*

belated [bɪlépɪtɪd] ADJ atrasado, tardío

belch [bɛltʃ] VI eructar, repetir; N eructo *m*

belfry [bɛ́lfrɪ] N campanario *m*

Belgian [bɛ́lʤən] ADJ & N belga *mf*

Belgium [bɛ́lʤəm] N Bélgica *f*

belief [bɪlíf] N creencia *f*; (strong opinion) convicción *f*

believable [bɪlívəbəł] ADJ creíble

believe [bɪlív] VI/VT creer

believer [bɪlívɚ] N creyente *mf*; (proponent) partidario -ria *mf*

belittle [bɪlídł] VT (a person) menospreciar, disminuir; (a situation) minimizar

belittling [bɪlídłɪŋ] N menosprecio *m*, disminución *f*

Belize [bəlíz] N Belice *m*

Belizean [bəlíziən] ADJ & N beliceño -ña *mf*

bell [bɛł] N campana *f*; (small) campanilla *f*; **—boy/hop** botones *m sg*; **— curve** curva de campana *f*; **—flower** campanilla *f*, campánula *f*; **— jar** campana de cristal *f*; **— pepper** pimiento *m*, morrón *m*; **— tower** campanario *m*; **with all the —s and whistles** con todos los accesorios

bellicose [bɛ́lɪkos] ADJ belicoso

belligerent [bəlíʤəənt] ADJ & N beligerante *mf*

bellow [bɛ́lo] VI/VT bramar, berrear; N bramido *m*; **—s** fuelle *m*

belly [bɛ́lɪ] N barriga *f*, vientre *m*, panza *f*; **—ache** dolor de barriga *m*; **— button** ombligo *m*; **— dance** danza del vientre *f*; **— laugh** carcajada *f*

belong [bɪlɔ́ŋ] VI (ownership) pertenecer; **this car —s to me** este coche me pertenece; (correspondence) corresponder; **this key —s to this door** esta llave corresponde a esta puerta; (placement) ir; **this —s on the shelf** esto va en el estante

belongings [bɪlɔ́ŋɪŋz] N pertenencias *f pl*

beloved [bɪlʌ́vɪd] ADJ querido; N amado -da *mf*

below [bɪló] ADV abajo; **five — [zero]** cinco bajo cero; PREP bajo, debajo de, abajo de

belt [bɛłt] N (for the waist) cinturón *m*, cinto *m*; (for a machine) correa *f*; (region) zona *f*; **— line** cintura *f*; VT pegar; **to — out a song** cantar una canción a voz en cuello

bemoan [bɪmón] VT lamentarse de, quejarse de

bench [bɛntʃ] N banco *m*; (without a back) banqueta *f*; (in sports) banco *m*, banquillo *m*; (in court) estrado *m*; **—mark** (upper limit) cota *f*; (parameter) punto de referencia *m*; **— price** precio de referencia *m*; **opinion of the —** opinión del tribunal *f*

bend [bɛnd] VI/VT (make curved) doblar[se]; (force) someter; **to — over** inclinarse; **to — over backward** desvivirse; **to — the rules** hacer una excepción; N (road) curva *f*, recodo *m*; **—s** enfermedad de los buzos *f*

bending [bɛ́ndɪŋ] N doblado *m*

beneath [bɪníθ] ADV abajo; PREP debajo de, bajo; (in rank) inferior a; **— contempt** totalmente despreciable; **that's — me** no es digno de mí

benediction [bɛnɪdíkʃən] N bendición *f*

benefactor [bɛ́nəfæktɚ] N benefactor -ora *mf*; *lit* bienhechor -ora *mf*

beneficent [bənɛ́fɪsənt] ADJ benéfico

beneficial [bɛnəfíʃəł] ADJ beneficioso

beneficiary [bɛnəfíʃɪɛrɪ] N beneficiario -ria *mf*

benefit [bɛ́nəfɪt] N beneficio *m*, provecho *m*; **— performance** función de beneficencia *f*; VI/VT beneficiar[se], sacar provecho

benevolence [bənɛ́vələns] N benevolencia *f*

benevolent [bənɛ́vələnt] ADJ benévolo

benign [bɪnáɪn] ADJ benigno

Benin [bɛnín] N Benín *m*

Beninese [bɛnɪníz] ADJ & N beninés -esa *mf*

bent [bɛnt] N inclinación *f*; **to be — on** estar resuelto a

bent [bɛnt] *see* bend

benzine [bɛ́nzɪn] N bencina *f*

bequeath [bɪkwíð] VT legar, heredar

bequest [bɪkwɛ́st] N legado *m*

berate [bɪrét] VT reprender

bereaved [bɪrívd] ADJ de luto

beret [bəré] N boina *f*

berry [bɛ́rɪ] N baya *f*

berserk [bɚ́rzɚ́k] ADJ fuera de sí; **he went —** se puso hecho una fiera, se enfureció

berth [bɚθ] N litera *f*; **to give a wide — to** mantener una distancia prudencial de

beseech [bɪsítʃ] VT suplicar, rogar

beset [bɪsɛ́t] VT (attack) acosar; (surround) rodear

beside [bɪsáɪd] PREP al lado de; **sit down — me** siéntate a mi lado; **to be — oneself** estar fuera de sí; **that is — the point** eso no viene al caso; ADV al lado

besides [bɪsáɪdz] ADV además; **they have a table but not much —** tienen una mesa pero poca cosa más; PREP además de, aparte de

besiege [bɪsíʤ] VT (lay siege) sitiar, cercar; (importune) importunar, asediar

best [best] ADJ mejor; **—-case scenario** la mejor situación; **— man** padrino de boda *m*; **— seller** bestseller *m*; **she's the —** ella es la mejor; ADV mejor; **at —** a lo más, en el mejor de los casos; N **the — is still to come** lo mejor está por venir; **to do one's —** hacer lo mejor posible; **to get the — of a person** ganarle a una persona; **to make the — of** sacar el mejor partido de; VT vencer

bestial [béstʃəł] ADJ bestial
bestow [bɪstó] VT conferir; **to — gifts upon** dar regalos a
bet [bɛt] N apuesta *f*; VI/VT apostar; **to — on** apostar por
beta [béɪdə] N **— blocker** betabloqueador *m*, betabloqueante *m*; **— test** prueba beta *f*; **— version** versión beta *f*
betray [bɪtré] VT (a person) traicionar; (a secret) revelar; (a feeling) traslucir, delatar; **to — one's ignorance** hacer patente su ignorancia
betrayal [bɪtréəł] N traición *f*
betrayer [bɪtréə-] N traidor -ra *mf*
betrothal [bɪtróðəł] N esponsales *f pl*
better [béɪdə-] ADJ mejor; **— half** media naranja *f*; **the — part of a year** la mayor parte de un año; ADV mejor; **he lives — than a mile away** vive a más de una milla; **so much the —** tanto mejor; **— -off** en mejor posición económica; **to be — off** estar mejor así; **to change for the —** cambiar para bien; **to get —** mejorar[se], aliviarse; VT mejorar; **to — oneself** mejorarse, mejorar de situación; N **the — of the two** el/la mejor de los dos
better, bettor [béɪdə-] N apostador -ra *mf*
between [bɪtwín] PREP entre; ADV en medio
bevel [bévəł] N bisel *m*; VT biselar
beverage [bévrɪʤ] N bebida *f*
bevy [bévi] N (of birds, people) bandada *f*; (of deer) manada *f*
beware [bɪwér] VI cuidarse [de]; **— of the dog** cuidado con el perro
bewilder [bɪwíłdə-] VT dejar perplejo, aturdir; **to be —ed** estar perplejo
bewilderment [bɪwíłdə-mənt] N perplejidad *f*, aturdimiento *m*
bewitch [bɪwítʃ] VT hechizar, embrujar
beyond [bɪjánd] ADV más allá; PREP más allá de; **— my reach** fuera de mi alcance; N **the great —** el más allá
Bhutan [butǽn] N Bután *m*
Bhutanese [butníz] ADJ & N butanés -esa *mf*
biannual [baɪǽnjuəł] ADJ bianual, semestral, semianual
bias [báɪəs] N (prejudice) prejuicio *m*; (in fabric) sesgo *m*; ADJ sesgado, oblicuo; VT predisponer; **—ed** parcial
bib [bɪb] N babero *m*; (of an apron) pechera *f*
Bible [báɪbəł] N Biblia *f*
biblical [bíbłɪkəł] ADJ bíblico
bibliography [bɪbliógrəfi] N bibliografía *f*
bicarbonate [baɪkárbənɪt] N bicarbonato *m*
bicep, biceps [báɪsɛp[s]] N bíceps *m sg*
bicker [bíkə-] VI reñir
bicuspid [baɪkáspɪd] ADJ bicúspide
bicycle [báɪsɪkəł] N bicicleta *f*; VI andar en bicicleta
bid [bɪd] N (in an auction, contest) licitación *f*, puja *f*; (in card games) apuesta *f*; (attempt) tentativa *f*; VI/VT (offer) pujar; (command) mandar; (invite) rogar; (enter a bid in cards) apostar; **to — good-bye** despedirse; **to — up** pujar el precio
bidden [bídn] *see* bid
bidding [bídɪŋ] N (in auction) puja *f*; **at someone's —** por orden de alguien; **to do someone's —** cumplir con los deseos de alguien
bide [baɪd] VI/VT **to — one's time** esperar una oportunidad
biennium [baɪéniəm] N bienio *m*
bifurcate [báɪfə-ket] VI/VT bifurcar[se]
big [bɪg] ADJ grande; **— Bang Theory** Teoría del Big Bang *f*; **— brother** hermano mayor *m*; **— bucks** mucha plata *f*; **— business** el gran capital *m*; **— deal** asunto importante *m*; **— deal!** ¡no es para tanto! **— Dipper** Osa Mayor *f*; **— enchilada** *fam* mandamás *m*, *fam* pez gordo *m*; **— -headed** cabezón, cabezudo; **— -hearted** magnánimo; **— house** *fam* gayola *f*; **— kahuna** *fam* mandamás *m*, *fam* pez gordo *m*; **— name** personalidad prominente *f*; **— picture** panorama general *m*; **— shot** *fam* pez gordo *m*; **— sister** hermana mayor *f*; **— -ticket** caro; **—wig** *fam* pez gordo *m*; **— with child** embarazada; **jazz was — in the 1920s** el jazz era popular en los años veinte; **she's a — deal** es una persona importante; ADV **she wants to go —time** se muere por ir; **to talk —** jactarse, fanfarronear; *Am* lucirse; **to go over —** tener éxito; **to be — on** ser entusiasta de
bigamy [bígəmi] N bigamia *f*
bigot [bígət] N intolerante *mf*
bigotry [bígətri] N intolerancia *f*
bike [baɪk] N (bicycle) bici *f*; (motorcycle) moto *f*
biker [báɪkə-] N (bicyclist) ciclista *mf*; (motorcyclist) motociclista *mf*
bikini [bɪkíni] N bikini *m*
bilateral [baɪlǽdə-əł] ADJ bilateral
bile [baɪł] N (secretion) bilis *f*; (ill temper) mal genio *m*; **— duct** conducto biliar *m*
bilingual [baɪlíŋgwəł] ADJ & N bilingüe *mf*
bilingualism [baɪlíŋgwəlzəm] N bilingüismo *m*
bill [bɪł] N (statement) factura *f*; (in a restaurant) cuenta *f*; (poster) cartel *m*; (bank note) billete *m*; (for movies, theater) programa *m*; (of a bird) pico *m*; (legislative) proyecto de ley *m*; **—board** cartelera *f*; **—fold** cartera *f*, billetera *f*; **— of exchange** letra de cambio *f*; **— of lading** conocimiento de embarque *m*; **— of rights** declaración de derechos *f*; **— of sale** escritura de venta *f*; VT cobrar, mandar la factura a
billable [bíłəbəł] ADJ facturable
billiards [bílja-dz] N billar *m*

billing [bílɪŋ] N (theater) orden de importancia en espectáculos *m*; (business) facturación *f*; — **cycle** ciclo de facturación *m*
billion [bíljən] NUM mil millones *m pl*
billow [bílo] N (of smoke) nube *f*; (of water) ola *f*; VI ondular, hacer olas
bimonthly [baɪmánθli] ADV bimestral
bin [bɪn] N (for clothes, food) cajón *m*, recipiente *m*; (on an airplane) portaequipajes *m sg*; (for coal) carbonera *f*; (for grain) granero *m*
binary [báɪnɛrɪ] ADJ binario; — **star** estrella binaria *f*
bind [baɪnd] VI/VT (unite) unir; (connect) ligar; (tie) atar; (put a cover on a book) encuadernar; (press tightly) apretar; (oblige by contract) obligar
binding [báɪndɪŋ] N (of a book) encuadernación *f*; (on a rug) ribete *m*; ADJ obligatorio
binge [bɪnʤ] N (alcoholic) juerga *f*, parranda *f*; (food) comilona *f*; VI (on alcohol) emborracharse; (on food) atiborrarse
bingo [bíŋgo] N bingo *m*
binoculars [bənákjələ-z] N gemelos *m pl*, prismáticos *m pl*
binomial [baɪnómiəł] N binomio *m*; ADJ binomial
biochemistry [baɪokémɪstri] N bioquímica *f*
biodegradable [baɪodɪgrédəbəł] ADJ biodegradable
bioengineering [baɪoɛnʤənírɪŋ] N bioingeniería *f*
biofeedback [baɪofídbæk] N biofeedback *m*, retroalimentación biológica *f*
biography [baɪágrəfi] N biografía *f*
biological [baɪəlóʤɪkəł] ADJ biológico
biologist [baɪáləʤɪst] N biólogo -ga *mf*
biology [baɪáləʤi] N biología *f*
biopsy [báɪapsi] N biopsia *f*
biorhythm [báɪorɪðəm] N biorritmo *m*
biotechnology [baɪotɛknáləʤi] N biotecnología *f*
bipartisan [baɪpárdɪzən] ADJ bipartidista
bipolar [baɪpólə-] ADJ bipolar; — **disorder** trastorno bipolar *m*
birch [bɝtʃ] N abedul *m*
bird [bɝd] N ave *f*; (small) pájaro *m*; — **of prey** ave de rapiña *f*; — **seed** alpiste *m*; **odd** — persona peculiar *f*
birth [bɝθ] N (act of being born) nacimiento *m*; (act of giving birth) parto *m*; (lineage) linaje *m*; (origin) origen *m*; — **canal** canal de parto *m*; — **certificate** certificado de nacimiento *m*, fe/acta de nacimiento *f*; — **control** (policy) control de la natalidad *m*; (devices) anticonceptivos *m pl*; —**day** cumpleaños *m sg*; **in his / her** —**day suit** como Dios lo/la trajo al mundo; —**mark** antojo *m*, marca de nacimento *f*; —**place** lugar de nacimiento *m*; —**rate** natalidad *f*, tasa de natalidad *f*; —**right** derechos de nacimiento *m pl*; (of oldest child) primogenitura *f*; **to give** — dar a luz, parir, alumbrar; **by** — de nacimiento
biscuit [bískɪt] N panecillo *m*
bisect [báɪsɛkt] VT bisecar
bishop [bíʃəp] N obispo *m*; (in chess) alfil *m*
bison [báɪsən] N bisonte *m*, búfalo *m*
bit [bɪt] N (small piece) pedacito *m*, trocito *m*; (some) poquito *m*; (of a bridle) bocado *m*, freno *m*; (of a drill) broca *f*, barrena *f*; (computer) bit *m*; **I don't care a** — no me importa en absoluto
bit [bɪt] *see* bite
bitch [bɪtʃ] N perra *f*
bite [baɪt] VI/VT morder; (be duped) dejarse engañar; (insect, fish, snake) picar; **to** — **off** arrancar de un mordisco; N (act, wound) mordedura *f*, dentellada *f*; (morsel, small meal) bocado *m*, bocadito *m*; (of an insect) picadura *f*, roncha *f*
bitten [bɪtn̩] *see* bite
bitter [bídə-] ADJ (taste) amargo; (cold) glacial; (enemy) acérrimo; (person) resentido; —**sweet** dulceamargo, agridulce; **to fight to the** — **end** luchar hasta morir; N —**s** cerveza amarga *f*
bitterness [bídə-nɪs] N (taste) amargor *m*; (feelings) amargura *f*; (anger) rencor *m*, resentimiento *m*
biweekly [baɪwíkli] ADV (every two weeks) quincenal; (twice a week) bisemanal
bizarre [bɪzár] ADJ (event) extraño; (appearance) estrafalario
blab [blæb] VI parlotear; VT descubrir el pastel
black [blæk] ADJ (color, ethnicity) negro; (night) oscuro; —-**and-blue** lleno de moretones, amoratado; N negro -a *mf*; — **bean** frijol negro *m*; —**berry** zarzamora *f*, mora *f*; —**bird** mirlo *m*; —**board** pizarrón *m*, pizarra *f*; — **death** peste negra *f*; — **eye** ojo amoratado/morado *m*; —**head** espinilla *f*; — **hole** agujero negro *m*; —**jack** (weapon) cachiporra *f*; (card game) black-jack *m*, veintiuno *m*; —**list** lista negra *f*; — **magic** magia negra *f*; —**mail** chantaje *m*; — **mark** mancha *f*; — **market** mercado negro *m*; —**out** apagón *m*; — **pepper** pimienta negra *f*; — **pudding** morcilla *f*; — **sheep** oveja negra *f*; —**smith** herrero *m*; —**smith's shop** herrería *f*, forja *f*; —**top** asfalto *m*; — **widow spider** viuda negra *f*; **to put down in** — **and white** poner por escrito; VI **to** — **out** (faint) desmayarse, perder el conocimiento; VT **to** —**mail** chantajear
blacken [blǽkən] VT ennegrecer, negrear; VI (sky) oscurecerse
blackness [blǽknɪs] N negrura *f*
bladder [blǽdə-] N vejiga *f*
blade [bled] N (of a knife) hoja *f*; (of grass) brizna

f; (of an oar) pala *f*, paleta *f*; (of a propeller) aspa *f*

blame [blem] VT culpar, echar la culpa a, achacar la culpa a; **to be to —** tener la culpa; N (responsibility) culpa *f*; (reproof) reproche *m*

blameless [blémlɪs] ADJ intachable

blanch [blæntʃ] VI palidecer; VT (whiten) blanquear; (scald) escaldar

bland [blænd] ADJ insulso

blank [blæŋk] ADJ (not written on) en blanco; (not recorded on) virgen; (unadorned, expressionless) vacío; (confused) desconcertado; **— cartridge** cartucho de fogueo *m*; **— check** cheque en blanco *m*; **— verse** verso blanco *m*; N (place to be filled in on a form) espacio [en blanco] *m*; (gap) vacío *m*; VI **to — out** quedarse en blanco

blanket [blǽŋkɪt] N manta *f*, frazada *f*; *Am* cobija *f*; ADJ global; VT cubrir

blare [blɛr] VI hacer un ruido estruendoso; N estruendo *m*; (of a trumpet) toque *m*

blaspheme [blæsfím] VI/VT blasfemar [contra]

blasphemy [blǽsfəmi] N blasfemia *f*

blast [blæst] N (of wind) ráfaga *f*; (of criticism) lluvia *f*; (of a trumpet) trompetazo *m*; (explosive charge) carga *f*; (explosion) explosión *f*; **— furnace** alto horno *m*; **—off** despegue *m*; **we had a —** lo pasamos bomba; **at full —** a todo volumen; VI/VT (blow a horn) pitar, tocar; (shatter) volar; (criticize) criticar duramente; (blow hard) azotar; **to — off** despegar

blatant [blétnt] ADJ descarado

blaze [blez] N (flame) llamarada *f*; (fire) incendio *m*; (glow) resplandor *m*; (mark) señal *f*; **— of anger** arranque de ira *m*; VI (burn) arder; (shine) resplandecer; **to — a trail** marcar una senda

blazer [blézɚ] N blazer *m*, saco *m*

bleach [blitʃ] VI/VT (intentional) blanquear[se]; (accidental) desteñir[se]; N blanqueador *m*; *Sp* lejía *f*

bleachers [blítʃɚz] N gradas *f pl*

bleak [blik] ADJ (terrain) yermo, desolado; (winter) crudo; (wind) helado; (future) negro

bleary [blíri] ADJ nublado

bleat [blit] N balido *m*; VI balar

bled [blɛd] *see* bleed

bleed [blid] VI (lose blood) sangrar; (run, as in colors) correrse, desteñir[se]; **my heart —s for the poor** los pobres me dan lástima; VT (let blood) desangrar; (extort) extorsionar; (clean brakes) purgar

blemish [blémɪʃ] N mancha *f*, tacha *f*; VT manchar

blend [blɛnd] VI/VT (tea, paint) mezclar, entremezclar; (sea and sky) fundirse; (voices) armonizar; N mezcla *f*

blender [bléndɚ] N licuadora *f*

bless [blɛs] VT bendecir; INTERJ **— you!** ¡salud! ¡Jesús!

blessed[1] [blɛ́sɪd] ADJ (beatified) beato; (happy) bienaventurado, feliz; **— event** feliz acontecimiento *m*; **the whole — day** todo el santo día; **not a — drop of rain** ni una bendita gota de agua

blessed[2] [blɛst] ADJ **— with** dotado de

blessing [blɛ́sɪŋ] N bendición *f*; **to say the —** dar gracias

blew [blu] *see* blow

blight [blaɪt] N (plant disease) quemadura *f*, añublo *m*; (scourge) lacra *f*; VT (cause to wither) marchitar; (ruin) arruinar

blimp [blɪmp] N zepelín *m*

blind [blaɪnd] ADJ ciego; **— alley** callejón sin salida *m*; **— date** cita a ciegas *f*; **—fold** venda para los ojos *f*; **to —fold** vendar los ojos a; **— man's bluff** juego de la gallina ciega *m*; **— spot** ángulo muerto *m*; **to fly —** volar a ciegas; **to go —** quedarse ciego; N (shade) persiana *f*; (hunter's hiding place) escondite *m*; VT (make blind) cegar; (darken) oscurecer

blinder [bláɪndɚ] N anteojera *f*

blindly [bláɪndli] ADV a ciegas

blindness [bláɪndnɪs] N ceguera *f*

blink [blɪŋk] VI/VT (move eyelids) pestañear, parpadear; (go on and off, as of a light) parpadear; (ignore) pasar por alto; (flee a challenge) rajarse; N parpadeo *m*, pestañeo *m*; **on the —** averiado

blinker [blíŋkɚ] N intermitente *m*

blinking [blíŋkɪŋ] N parpadeo *m*

blip [blɪp] N (on radar) punto *m*; (moment) bache *m*

bliss [blɪs] N dicha *f*, felicidad absoluta *f*

blister [blístɚ] N ampolla *f*; (small) vejiga *f*; VT sacar ampollas; VI ampollarse

blitz [blɪts] N ataque relámpago *m*

blizzard [blízɚd] N ventisca *f*

bloat [blot] VI hinchar[se], abotagar[se]

bloated [blóʊɪd] ADJ hinchado, inflado

blob [blɑb] N pedazo de algo sin forma *m*

block [blɑk] N (piece of stone, cement) bloque *m*; (piece of wood) trozo de madera *m*; (toy) cubo *m*; (in sports) bloqueo *m*; (in basketball) tapón *m*; (length from one street to the next) cuadra *f*; (square block) manzana *f*; (obstacle) obstáculo *m*; (group of tickets) sección *f*; **—buster** éxito de taquilla *m*; **—head** tarugo -ga *mf*, alcornoque *m*; VT (obstruct, also in sports) bloquear, tapar; (in basketball) taponar; (stop a pass) parar; **to — out** (an essay) esbozar, bosquejar; (the sun) ocultar

blockade [blɑkéd] N bloqueo *m*; VT bloquear

blockage [blɑ́kɪʤ] N obstrucción *f*

blocking [blɑ́kɪŋ] N bloqueo *m*

blog [blɑg] N blog *m*; VI bloguear; **—ging** blogueo *m*

blogger [blágɚ] N bloguero -ra *mf*
blond [blɑnd] ADJ & N rubio -a *mf*
blood [blʌd] N sangre *f*; **—bank** banco de sangre *m*; **—bath** carnicería *f*, baño de sangre *m*; **—count** recuento sanguíneo *m*; **— group** grupo sanguíneo *m*; **—hound** sabueso *m*; **—plasma** plasma sanguíneo *m*; **— poisoning** septicemia *f*; **— pressure** presión arterial *f*; **— relative** pariente consanguíneo *mf*; **—shed** derramamiento de sangre *m*; **—shot** inyectado de sangre; **—thirsty** sanguinario, sangriento; **— type** grupo sanguíneo *m*; **— vessel** vaso sanguíneo *m*; **in cold —** a sangre fría
bloody [blʌ́dɪ] ADJ (violent) sangriento; (smeared) ensangrentado
bloom [blum] N (flower) flor *f*; (flowering) floración *f*; (youthfulness) lozanía *f*; (flush) rubor *m*; **in —** en flor; VI florecer
blooming [blúmɪŋ] ADJ (flowering) floreciente; (thriving) lozano
blooper [blúpɚ] N perla *f*
blossom [blɑ́səm] N (flower) flor *f*; VI florecer
blot [blɑt] N (on paper) mancha *f*, borrón *m*; (on honor) tacha *f*; VI/VT manchar[se], emborronar[se]; **to — out** (obscure) borrar, tachar
blotch [blɑtʃ] VT borronear, manchar, cubrir con manchas; N mancha *f*, borrón *m*
blouse [blɑʊs] N blusa *f*
blow [blo] VI (wind) soplar; (leaf) volar; (siren) sonar; (horse) resoplar; VT (play a horn) sonar; **to — a fuse** quemar un fusible; **to — away** (amaze) dejar atónito; (carry away on the wind) llevarse el viento; **to — down** tirar abajo; **to —-dry** secar con secador; **to — off** (ignore) ignorar; **to — one's nose** sonarse las narices / la nariz; **to — on the soup** soplar la sopa; **to — one's brains out** levantarse la tapa de los sesos; **to — out** reventar[se]; **to — over** (knock down) derribar; (dissipate) disiparse; **to — up** (a balloon) inflar, hinchar; (a bridge) volar; **this party —s** esta fiesta es pésima; N (stroke, shock) golpe *m*; (wind) tempestad *f*; (breath) soplo *m*; **—out** (tire failure) reventón *m*; (party) fiestón *m*; **—pipe** cerbatana *f*; **—torch** soplete *m*; **—up** (fight) pelea *f*, riña *f*; (photo) ampliación *f*; **to come to —s** irse a las manos
blower [blóɚ] N (artisan) soplador *m*; (machine) aventadora *f*
blown [blon] *see* blow
blue [blu] ADJ azul; (sad) triste, melancólico; (from cold) amoratado; N azul *m*; **—bell** campanilla *f*; **—berry** arándano *m*; **—bird** pájaro azul *m*; **—blood** sangre azul *f*; **— book** lista de precios de mercado *f*; **—-chip** de primera línea; **—-collar** de clase obrera; **—jay** arrendajo *m*; **— jeans** vaqueros *m pl*; **—print** (of a building) cianotipo *m*; (of a project) plan *m*, trazado *m*; **—-ribbon** distinguido; **— whale** ballena azul *f*; **light —** [azul] celeste *m*; **the —s** (sadness) melancolía *f*, murria *f*; (genre of music) blues *m pl*; VI ponerse azul, azulear; VT azular, teñir de azul; **to —print** trazar
bluff [blʌf] N (cliff) acantilado *m*, risco *m*; (false boast) bluff *m*; (in poker) farol *m*; VT hacer un bluff; **to call a —** poner en evidencia
bluffer [blʌ́fɚ] N bluff *m*
bluing [blúɪŋ] N añil *m*
bluish [blúɪʃ] ADJ azulado
blunder [blʌ́ndɚ] N disparate *m*, patochada *f*; VI meter la pata; **to — upon/into** tropezar con
blunt [blʌnt] ADJ (not sharp) romo; (rounded) contundente; (frank) directo, franco; VT despuntar
blur [blɝ] VT (to obscure) emborronar, desvanecer; (to make vision blurry) nublar; VI empañarse, nublarse; N [indistinct sight] mancha *f*; **it's a — in my mind** sólo tengo un recuerdo vago de eso
blurred [blɝd] ADJ borroso
blurry [blɝ́i] ADJ borroso
blurt [blɝt] VT **to — [out]** espetar
blush [blʌʃ] VI sonrojarse, ponerse colorado, ruborizarse; N (act of blushing) sonrojo *m*; (effect of blushing) rubor *m*; **at first —** a primera vista
bluster [blʌ́stɚ] VI (blow hard) soplar fuerte, rugir; (boast) fanfarronear; N (sound of wind) ventarrón *m*; (attitude) fanfarronería *f*
blustering [blʌ́stɚɪŋ] ADJ fanfarrón, jactancioso; **— wind** ventarrón *m*
BM [bowel movement] [bíɛm] N defecación *f*
boa constrictor [bóəkənstríktɚ] N boa *f*
boar [bɔr] N jabalí *m*
board [bɔrd] N (wood) tabla *f*, listón *m*; (for a game) tablero *m*; (meals) pensión *f*; (for bulletins) cartelera *f*; **— of directors** junta directiva *f*; **—ing school** pensionado *m*, internado *m*; **—inghouse** pensión *f*; **— of trustees** patronato *m*; **—room** sala de directorio *f*; **on —** a bordo; **to go by the —** irse por la borda; VI (lodge) alojarse; **to — up** tapiar, cerrar con tablas; VT (boat, plane, train) abordar; (provide lodging) alojar
boarder [bɔ́rdɚ] N pensionista *mf*
boast [bost] N alarde *m*; VI jactarse, vanagloriarse, blasonar; VT **the town —s two new schools** el pueblo ostenta dos escuelas nuevas
boastful [bóstfəł] ADJ jactancioso, vanglorioso
boastfulness [bóstfəłnɪs] N jactancia *f*, vanagloria *f*
boat [bot] N (any water vessel) embarcación *f*; (open and small) bote *m*, lancha *f*; (closed, larger) barco *m*; **—house** cobertizo para

botes *m*; **—man** barquero *m*, botero *m*

boating [bóʊɪŋ] N navegación *f*; **to go —** navegar

bob [bɑb] N (horsetail) cola cortada *f*; (of the head) sacudida *f*; (haircut) melena corta *f*; (of a pendulum) pesa *f*, plomada *f*; **—tail** rabón *m*; VI sacudirse; (a ship) cabecear; VT **to — one's hair** cortarse el pelo en melena

bobbin [bɑ́bɪn] N carrete *m*, bobina *f*

bobcat [bɑ́bkæt] N lince rojo *m*

bode [boʊd] VI **that doesn't — well** eso no augura nada bueno

bodice [bɑ́dɪs] N corpiño *m*

bodily [bɑ́dɪli] ADJ corporal; **— harm** daño físico *m*

body [bɑ́di] N (of a person, animal, wine, fabric) cuerpo *m*; (torso) tronco *m*; (corpse) cuerpo *m*, cadáver *m*; (of a text, army, etc.) parte principal *f*; (of water) masa *f*; (of a car) carrocería *f*; (of an airplane) fuselaje *m*; **— armor** armadura corporal *f*, armadura de cuerpo *f*; **— bag** bolsa para cadáveres *f*; **—-building** culturismo *m*; **— count** número de muertos *m*; **—guard** guardaespaldas *m sg*; **— language** lenguaje corporal *m*; **— temperature** temperatura *f*; **— shop** taller de carrocería *m*; VT **to —search** cachear

bog [bɑg] N pantano *m*; VI hundir[se]; **to get —ged down** atascarse

bogey [bógi] N (golf) bogey *m*

bogeyman [búgimæn] N coco *m*; *RP* cuco *m*

bogus [bógəs] ADJ falso, fraudulento; **— company** compañía fantasma *f*

Bohemian [bohímiən] ADJ & N bohemio -a *mf*

boil [bɔɪl] VI/VT (water) hervir; (eggs) cocer; (ocean) bullir; (angry person) echar chispas; **to — down to** reducirse a; **to — over** derramarse; N (inflammation) forúnculo *m*, divieso *m*; (act of boiling) hervor *m*; **—ing point** punto de ebullición *m*; **to come to a —** soltar/romper el hervor

boiler [bɔ́ɪlɚ] N caldera *f*

boisterous [bɔ́ɪstɚəs] ADJ bullicioso

bold [boʊld] ADJ (not fearful) atrevido, osado; (unconventional) audaz; (visually striking) llamativo; **—-faced** descarado; **—face type** negrita *f*, negrilla *m*

boldness [bóʊldnɪs] N (courage) atrevimiento *m*, osadía *f*; (unconventional attitude) audacia *f*

Bolivia [bəlíviə] N Bolivia *f*

Bolivian [bəlíviən] ADJ & N boliviano -na *mf*

bolster [bóʊlstɚ] N cojín cilíndrico *m*; VT reforzar; **to — someone's courage** alentar a alguien

bolt [boʊt] N (door lock) pestillo *m*, cerrojo *m*; (crossbar) aldaba *f*; (pin) perno *m*, tornillo grande *m*; (of cloth) rollo *m*; **it came as a — from the blue** cayó como bomba; VT (fasten) atornillar; (lock door) cerrar con tranca, atrancar; (devour) engullir; (break with) romper con; VI echarse a correr

bomb [bɑm] N bomba *f*; **—shell** bomba *f*; **— shelter** refugio antiaéreo *m*; VT (attack with bombs) bombardear; VI (fail) fracasar

bombard [bɑmbɑ́rd] VT bombardear

bombardier [bɑmbɚ-dír] N bombardero -ra *mf*

bombardment [bɑmbɑ́rdmənt] N bombardeo *m*

bombastic [bɑmbǽstɪk] ADJ grandilocuente, ampuloso

bomber [bɑ́mɚ] N bombardero *m*, avión de bombardeo *m*

bombing [bɑ́mɪŋ] N (from airplanes) bombardeo *m*; (terrorist) atentado *m*

bona fide [bónəfaɪd] ADJ genuino; **— offer** oferta seria *f*

bonbon [bɑ́nbɑn] N caramelo *m*; (chocolate) bombón *m*

bond [bɑnd] N (tie) lazo *m*; (fetter) cadenas *f pl*; (financial instrument) bono *m*, obligación *f*; (adhesion) adherencia *f*; (chemical) enlace *m*; VI/VT (stick to) adherirse; (connect) establecer vínculos

bondage [bɑ́ndɪʤ] N servidumbre *f*, esclavitud *f*

bonded [bɑ́ndɪd] ADJ afianzado

bonding [bɑ́ndɪŋ] N (mother-child) lazos afectivos *m pl*; (male) compenetración *f*

bondsman [bɑ́ndzmən] N fiador *m*

bone [bon] N hueso *m*; (of fish) espina *f*; **— china** porcelana fina *f*; **— graft** injerto óseo *m*; **—head** estúpido -da *mf*; **— marrow** médula ósea *f*; **—yard** cementerio *m*; **— of contention** manzana de la discordia *f*; **to make no —s about it** no andarse con rodeos; VT deshuesar; (fish) quitar las espinas; **to — up on something** estudiar algo

bonfire [bɑ́nfaɪr] N hoguera *f*, fogata *f*

bonnet [bɑ́nɪt] N gorro *m*

bonus [bónəs] N (extra salary) gratificación *f*, prima *f*; (at Christmas) aguinaldo *m*

bony [bóni] ADJ (with large bones) huesudo; (made of bones) óseo

boo [bu] VI/VT abuchear, rechiflar; INTERJ ¡bu! N rechifla *f*, abucheo *m*

boo-boo [búbu] N (minor injury) lastimadura *f*; *Sp fam* pupa *f*; *Am* nana *f*; **to make a —** meter la pata

booby [búbi] N (fool) bobo -a *mf*; (bird) bobo *m*; **— hatch** *fam* loquería *f*; **— prize** premio al peor competidor *m*; **— trap** trampa explosiva *f*

booger [búgɚ] N moco [seco] *m*

book [bʊk] N libro *m*; **—binding** encuadernación *f*; **—case** estante *m*, estantería *f*, biblioteca *f*; **—end** sujetalibros *m sg*; **—keeper** tenedor -ra de libros *mf*; *Sp* contable *mf*; **—keeping** teneduría de libros *f*, contabilidad *f*; **—mark** marcador de libros

m; **—mobile** biblioteca móvil *f*; **— review** reseña *f*; **—seller** librero -ra *mf*; **—shelf** estante *m*; **—store** librería *f*; **— value** valor contable *m*; **by the —** siguiendo las reglas; **on the —s** registrado en los libros; **to keep —s** llevar los libros; VT (reserve) reservar; (hire) contratar; (record charges against) fichar

bookish [búkɪʃ] ADJ (person) estudioso; (allusion) libresco

booklet [búklɪt] N cartilla *f*

boom [bum] VI (resound) resonar; (prosper) prosperar; N (noise) explosión *f*; (increase) auge *m*

boon [bun] N (blessing) bendición *f*; (favor) favor *m*

boondocks [búndɑks] ADV LOC **[out] in the —** *fam* en los quintos infiernos, en el quinto pino

boondoggle [búndɑgəł] N despilfarro *m*

boor [bur] N patán -ana *mf*

boorish [búrɪʃ] ADJ grosero, zafio

boost [bust] VT (to shove) empujar [desde abajo o detrás]; (to promote) estimular, impulsar; N (shove) empujón [desde abajo] *m*; (aid) estímulo *m*, impulso *m*; **— in prices** alza de precios *f*

booster [bústə-] N (person) animador -ra *mf*; (rocket) acelerador *m*; (electronic device) amplificador *m*; (vaccination) refuerzo *m*

boot [but] N (shoe) bota *f*; (trunk of a car) cajuela *f*; (clamp for cars) cepo *m*; **—black** limpiabotas *m sg*; **— disk** disco de iniciación *m*; **—legger** contrabandista de licores *m*; **—able diskette** disquete de iniciación *f*; **to give the —** poner de patitas en la calle; **to —** por añadidura; VT dar una patada a; **to — [out]** echar a patadas; **to — up** (a computer) iniciar

booth [buθ] N (telephone) cabina *f*; (sales) puesto *m*; (ticket) taquilla *f*

booty [búɪ] N (loot) botín *m*; (buttocks) trasero *m*

booze [buz] N *fam* bebercio *m*, bebida alcohólica *f*

borax [bɔ́ræks] N bórax *m*

border [bɔ́rdə-] N (line between countries) frontera *f*; (edge, brink) borde *m*; (bed of flowers) ariete *m*; (design) ribete *m*; **— control** control fronterizo *m*; **— patrol officer** carabinero -ra *mf*; ADJ **—line** (on a border) fronterizo; (not up to standards) dudoso; VI/VT (make a design) ribetear; **to — on** colindar con; **it —s on madness** raya en la locura

bordering [bɔ́rdə-ɪŋ] ADJ limítrofe

bore [bɔr] N (hole) agujero *m*; (of a gun, cylinder) calibre *m*; (uninteresting person) aburrido -da *mf*, pesado -da *mf*; (uninteresting thing) lata *f*; VT (make a hole) taladrar, horadar; (fail to interest) aburrir

bore [bɔr] *see* bear

bored [bɔrd] ADJ aburrido; **I'm —** estoy aburrido

boredom [bɔ́rdəm] N aburrimiento *m*, tedio *m*

boric acid [bɔ́rɪk ǽsɪd] N ácido bórico *m*

boring [bɔ́rɪŋ] ADJ aburrido; **he's —** es aburrido

born [bɔrn] ADJ nacido; **he's a — dancer** es un bailarín nato; **she's a — liar** es una mentirosa de nacimiento; **to be —** nacer

borne [bɔrn] *see* bear

boron [bɔ́rɑn] N boro *m*

borrow [báro] VT pedir prestado; **I —ed money from Fred** le pedí dinero prestado a Fred; **may I — your car?** ¿me prestas tu coche? **I —ed these books from the library** saqué estos libros de la biblioteca

borrower [bároə-] N (of money) prestatario -ria *mf*; (of library books) usuario -ria *mf*

Bosnia and Herzegovina [bázniənhə-tsəgəvínə] N Bosnia-Herzegovina *f*

Bosnian [bázniən] ADJ & N bosnio -nia *mf*

bosom [búzəm] N pecho *m*, seno *m*; **in the — of the family** en el seno de la familia; **— buddy** amigo íntimo *m*

boss [bɔs] N jefe -fa *mf*; (on a plantation) mayoral *m*, capataz *m*; (political) dirigente *m*; (mafia) capo *m*; VT **to — around** mandonear

bossy [bɔ́si] ADJ mandón

botanical [bətǽnɪkəł] ADJ botánico

botany [bátnɪ] N botánica *f*

botch [bátʃ] VT chapucear, estropear; N chapucería *f*, chapuza *f*

both [boθ] ADJ & PRON ambos, los dos

bother [bɑ́ðə-] VT molestar, fastidiar; VI molestarse, tomarse la molestia; N molestia *f*

bothersome [bɑ́ðə-səm] ADJ (activity) molesto, enojoso; (person) enfadoso, molesto

botox [bɔ́tɑks] N bótox *m*

Botswana [bɑtswɑ́nə] N Botsuana *f*

bottle [bɑ́dł] N botella *f*; (for medicine, perfume) frasco *m*; **—neck** atascadero *m*, embotellamiento *m*; **— top** chapa de botella *f*; VT embotellar; **to — up** atascar, embotellar

bottom [bɑ́dəm] N (of a hole) fondo *m*; (of a pile, page, bed) pie *m*; (lower part) base *f*, parte de abajo *f*; (buttocks) trasero *m*; **to be at the — of the class** ser el último de la clase; **to hit —** tocar fondo; **who is at the — of all this?** ¿quién está detrás de todo esto? ADJ de abajo; **— line** (business) balance final *m*; (essential element) lo esencial; VI **to — out** tocar fondo

bottomless [bɑ́dəmlɪs] ADJ sin fondo; **— supply** recursos ilimitados *m pl*; **— accusation** acusación infundada *f*; **he's a — pit** es un barril sin fondo

botulism [bátʃəlɪzəm] N botulismo *m*

boudoir [búdwɑr] N tocador *m*

bough [bɑʊ] N rama *f*

bought [bɔt] *see* buy

bouillon [búljɑn] N caldo *m*

boulder [bóʊldə˞] N peña *f*, pedrusco *m*

boulevard [búləvɑrd] N bulevar *m*

bounce [baʊns] N (of a ball) bote *m*, rebote *m*; (vitality) vitalidad *f*; VT echar, botar; **to — a check** rebotar un cheque; VI rebotar; **to — back** recuperarse

bouncer [baʊnsə˞] N gorila *m*

bound [baʊnd] N (jump) salto *m*; **—s** límite *m*, confín *m*; ADJ (tied up) atado; (confined) confinado; (obliged) obligado; (as a book) encuadernado; **to be — for** ir rumbo a; **to be — up in one's work** estar absorto en su trabajo; **it is — to happen** es seguro que pasará; **I am — to do it** estoy resuelto a hacerlo; VI (jump) saltar; (be contiguous) lindar

bound [baʊnd] *see* bind

boundary [báʊndri] N (of a country, city) límite *m*, término *m*; (of a property) linde *mf*, lindero *m*

boundless [báʊndlɪs] ADJ ilimitado, sin límites

bountiful [báʊntəfəł] ADJ abundante

bounty [báʊnti] N (abundance) abundancia *f*; (reward) recompensa *f*

bouquet [buké] N (of flowers, large) ramo *m*; (of flowers, small) ramillete *m*; (of wine) aroma *m*, bouquet *m*

bourgeois [burʒwɑ́] ADJ & N burgués -sa *mf*

bourgeoisie [burʒwɑzí] N burguesía *f*

bout [baʊt] N [sports] encuentro *m*; **a — of flu** una gripe

boutique [butík] N boutique *f*

bovine [bóvaɪn] ADJ vacuno

bow[1] [baʊ] N (gesture) reverencia *f*; (prow) proa *f*; VI (bend at the waist) hacer una reverencia; (yield) someterse; **to — out** retirarse; VT inclinar

bow[2] [bo] N (for arrows, violin) arco *m*; (curve) curva *f*; (decoration) moño *m*; **—knot** lazada *f*; **—string** cuerda de arco *f*; ADJ **—-legged** patizambo; VI/VT (bend) arquear[se]; (play a violin with a bow) tocar con arco

bowel [báʊəł] N **—s** intestinos *m pl*; **—s of the earth** entrañas de la tierra *f pl*; **— movement** evacuación del vientre *f*

bower [báʊə˞] N enramada *f*

bowl [boł] N (container) bol *m*, tazón *m*; (dish) plato hondo *m*; (depression) cuenco *m*; (of a toilet) taza *f*; (of a pipe) cazoleta *f*; VT **to — over** apabullar, deslumbrar

bowling [bólɪŋ] N boliche *m*, bowling *m*; **let's go —** vamos al boliche; **— alley** boliche *m*, bolera *f*

box [bɑks] N caja *f*; (for jewelry) estuche *m*; (in the theater) palco de teatro *m*; (for the jury) tribuna *f*; (on a page) cuadro *m*; (in soccer) área de penales *f*; **— car** vagón de carga *m*; **— office** taquilla *f*; **— seat** asiento de palco *m*; VT (put in a box) meter en una caja; (hit) abofetear; (engage in sport) boxear

boxer [bɑ́ksə˞] N (fighter) boxeador -ra *mf*, pugilista *mf*; (breed of dog) bóxer *m*; **— shorts** calzoncillo[s] *m*

boxing [bɑ́ksɪŋ] N boxeo *m*, pugilato *m*; **— glove** guante de boxeo *m*; **— ring** ring *m*, cuadrilátero *m*

boy [bɔɪ] N (baby) niño *m*; (young man) muchacho *m*, chico *m*; **— scout** boy scout *m*; **—friend** novio *m*

boycott [bɔ́ɪkat] VT boicotear; N boicoteo *m*, boicot *m*

boyhood [bɔ́ɪhʊd] N niñez *f*, juventud *f*

boyish [bɔ́ɪɪʃ] ADJ de muchacho

brace [bres] N (in construction) tirante *m*; (pair) par *m*; (printed character) corchete *m*; (of a carpenter) berbiquí *m*; **—s** (for teeth) aparato ortodóntico *m*; (for a leg) aparato ortopédico *m*; VT (against a shock) agarrarse; (support) asegurar

bracelet [bréslɪt] N brazalete *m*, pulsera *f*

bracket [brǽkɪt] N (support) soporte *m*, sostén *m*; (typographic sign) paréntesis recto *m*, corchete *m*; (division) banda *f*; VT (fix with brackets) fijar con soportes; (write in brackets) colocar entre paréntesis rectos; (associate) agrupar

brag [bræg] VI jactarse [de], hacer alarde [de]

braggart [brǽgə˞t] ADJ & N fanfarrón -na *mf*

braid [bred] N trenza *f*; VT trenzar

brain [bren] N cerebro *m*; (food) seso *m*; **she blew out his —s** le levantó la tapa de los sesos; **he's short on —s** es corto de inteligencia; **he is the — s in this operation** él es el cerebro en esta operación; **to rack one's —s** devanarse los sesos, romperse la cabeza; **— death** muerte cerebral *f*; **— drain** fuga de cerebros *f*; **— scan** tomografía cerebral *f*; **— trust** grupo de expertos *m*; **— stem** tronco del encéfalo *m*; **—storming** lluvia de ideas *f*; **— tumor** tumor cerebral *m*; VT **to — someone** romperle la crisma a alguien; **to —wash** lavarle el cerebro a; ADJ **— -dead** clínicamente muerto, en estado vegetativo

brainy [bréni] ADJ sesudo

brake [brek] N freno *m*; **— drum** tambor del freno *m*; **— fluid** líquido para frenos *m*; **—man** guardafrenos *m sg*; **— shoe** zapata *f*; **to apply the —s** frenar; VI/VT frenar

bramble [brǽmbəł] N zarza *f*

bran [bræn] N salvado *m*; (for birds) afrecho *m*

branch [brǽntʃ] N (of a plant, of a family) rama *f*; (of a train track) ramal *m*; (of antlers) brazo *m*; (of a science) ramo *m*; (of a business) sucursal *f*; (of the armed forces) arma *f*; (in a computer program) bifurcación *f*; (of a river) tributario *m*; VI/VT ramificar[se]

brand [brænd] N (make, mark) marca *f*; (of

humor, etc.) tipo *m*; (mark of disgrace) estigma *m*; **— awareness** conciencia de marca *f*; **— loyalty** lealtad de marca *f*; **— name** marca *f*; ADJ **—-new** flamante, recién comprado; VT (burn) herrar, marcar; (stigmatize) estigmatizar; **to — as** tildar de, tachar de

brandish [brǽndɪʃ] VT blandir, esgrimir

brandy [brǽndi] N (fine) brandy *m*; (cheap) aguardiente *m*

brash [bræʃ] ADJ (impudent) descarado; (impetuous) impetuoso

brass [bræs] N (metal) latón *m*; (attitude) descaro *m*; (high-ranking officers) la plana mayor; **— instrument** instrumento de metal *m*; **to get down to — tacks** ir al grano; ADJ de latón

brassiere [brəzír] N sostén *m*

brat [bræt] N mocoso -sa *mf*

bravado [brəvɑ́dɒ] N alarde *m*

brave [brev] ADJ valiente, gallardo; N guerrero indio *m*; VT desafiar

bravery [brévəri] N valentía *f*, gallardía *f*

brawl [brɔł] N reyerta *f*, riña *f*, pelotera *f*; VI reñir

bray [bre] N rebuzno *m*; VI rebuznar

brazen [brézən] ADJ (impudent) descarado; (made of brass) de latón

brazier [bréʒɚ] N brasero *m*

Brazil [brəzíł] N Brasil *m*

Brazilian [brəzíljən] ADJ & N brasileño -ña *mf*, brasilero -ra *mf*

breach [britʃ] N (opening) brecha *f*; (infraction) infracción *f*; (severance) ruptura *f*; **— of contract** incumplimiento de contrato *m*; **— of faith** abuso de confianza *m*; VT (make an opening) abrir una brecha en; (violate a law) violar, infringir

bread [bred] N pan *m*; **—basket** panera *f*; **— box** panera *f*; **—winner** sostén de la familia *m*; ADJ **—-and-butter** básico; VT empanar

breadth [brɛdθ] N anchura *f*, ancho *m*; (size) extensión *f*; (perspective) amplitud *f*

break [brek] VI (fracture) romperse; (pause) parar; VT (a record) batir; (a code) descifrar; (a law) violar; (news) dar, divulgar; (a bone) fracturar; (a horse) domar, desbravar; (a habit) quitar[se]; (a contract, promise) romper; (one's spirit) quebrar, doblegar; (one's heart) desgarrar; (cause to go bankrupt) arruinar; **to — a ten-dollar bill** conseguir cambio para un billete de diez dólares; **to — away** escaparse; **to — down** (a person) descomponerse; (a car) averiarse; (resistance) vencer; (continuity) interrumpir; **to — even** quedar a mano; **to — into** violentar; **to — loose** liberarse; **to — out** (war) estallar; (one's face) brotarse; (from prison) escaparse; **to — up** (into pieces) quebrarse; (a relationship) romper con; N (weather) cambio *m*; (from work) descanso *m*; (with tradition) quiebre *m*, rompimiento *m*; (of a bone) fractura *f*; (from prison) fuga *f*; (opportunity) oportunidad *f*; **—-in** hurto con escalo *m*; **—down** (analysis) análisis *m*; (automotive) avería *f*; (nervous) colapso *m*; **—down of charges** desglose de cargos *m*; **—even point** umbral de rentabilidad *m*; **— point** (in tennis) bola de break *f*, bola de ruptura *f*; **—through** adelanto *m*; (military) penetración *f*; **—water** rompeolas *m sg*; **lucky —** golpe de suerte *m*

breakable [brékəbəł] ADJ quebradizo, rompible

breaker [brékɚ] N rompiente *f*

breakfast [brékfəst] N desayuno *m*; VI desayunar

breast [brɛst] N (of a woman) seno *m*, pecho *m*; (of a bird) pechuga *f*; **—bone** esternón *m*; **— cancer** cáncer de mama *m*; **—-feeding** lactancia materna *f*; **—stroke** (estilo de natación) pecho *m*; VI/VT **to — -feed** amamantar, dar de mamar

breath [brɛθ] N aliento *m*; *lit* hálito *m*; (current of air) soplo *m*; **in the same —** al mismo tiempo; **out of —** sin aliento; **to catch one's —** recobrar el aliento; **to hold one's —** aguantar la respiración; **to take a —** inhalar; **to take a deep —** respirar hondo; **under one's —** entre dientes, por lo bajo; ADJ **—taking** impresionante

breathe [brið] VI/VT respirar; **to — in** inspirar, aspirar; **to — into** infundir; **to — out** exhalar, espirar; **he did not — a word** no dijo palabra

breathing [bríðɪŋ] N respiración *f*

breathless [bréθlɪs] ADJ sin aliento

breathlessness [bréθlɪsnɪs] N falta de aire *f*

bred [bred] *see* breed

breed [brid] VT (mate) criar; (bring up) educar; (give rise to) engendrar; VI reproducirse, multiplicarse; N (species) raza *f*; (type) clase *f*

breeder [bríɒɚ] N (person who breeds) criador -ora *mf*; (animal used for breeding) [animal] reproductor *m*

breeding [bríɒɪŋ] N (of animals) cría *f*; (of people) educación *f*, modales *m pl*

breeze [briz] N brisa *f*

breezy [brízi] ADJ (windy) ventoso; (jaunty) ameno

brevity [brévɪɒɪ] N brevedad *f*

brew [bru] VT (coffee) hacer; (mischief) fomentar, tramar; (beer) fabricar; VI (storm) armarse una tormenta; **let the tea —** deja reposar el té; N (mixture) mezcla *f*; (beer) cerveza *f*

brewery [brúɚi] N cervecera *f*, fábrica de cerveza *f*

briar [bráɪɚ] N zarza *f*

bribe [braɪb] N soborno *m*, cohecho *m*; *Mex* mordida *f*; VT sobornar

bribery [bráıbəri] N soborno *m*
brick [brɪk] N ladrillo *m*; **—bat** (piece of brick) pedazo de ladrillo *m*; (insult) insulto *m*; **—layer** albañil *m*; **—laying** albañilería *f*; VT (adorn with bricks) revestir de ladrillo; (pave with bricks) enladrillar
bridal [bráıdl] ADJ nupcial; **— dress** vestido de novia *m*
bride [braıd] N novia *f*; **—groom** novio *m*; **—smaid** dama de honor *f*
bridge [brɪʤ] N puente *m*; (of the nose) caballete *m*; (card game) bridge *m*; VT (a river) tender un puente sobre; (a gap) llenar, salvar
bridle [bráıdl] N (harness) brida *f*; (restraint) freno *m*; VT (put on a bridle) poner una brida; (restrain) frenar; VI (be insulted) ofenderse
brief [brif] ADJ (short) breve, escueto; (concise) conciso, escueto; (curt) seco; N sumario *m*, resumen *m*; (report) expediente *m*; **—case** portafolio[s] *m sg*, maletín *m*; **—s** calzoncillos *m pl*; **in —** en suma; VT informar
briefing [brífɪŋ] N reunión para dar instrucciones *f*
brigade [brɪgéd] N brigada *f*
bright [braıt] ADJ (shining) brillante; (full of light) iluminado; (smart) inteligente; (promising) venturoso, prometedor; (radiant) radiante; (colorful) subido
brighten [bráıtn] VT (a room) iluminar; VI **to — up** (person) animar[se]; (sky) despejarse
brightness [bráıtnıs] N (light) claridad *f*; (cheerfulness) viveza *f*; (intelligence) inteligencia *f*
brilliance [bríljəns] N (of hair, of a historical period) brillantez *f*; (of intellect) genio *m*
brilliant [bríljənt] ADJ (shining) brillante; (intelligent) genial; (splendid) espléndido; N brillante *m*, diamante *m*
brim [brɪm] N borde *m*; (of a hat) ala *f*; **to fill to the —** llenar hasta el borde; **to be filled to the —** estar de bote en bote; VI **to — over** rebosar; **to be —ming with** estar rebosante de
brine [braın] N salmuera *f*
bring [brɪŋ] VT traer; (cause) ocasionar, causar; **to — about** producir, ocasionar; **to — down** (kill) bajar; (depress) deprimir; **to — forth** (give birth) dar a luz; (produce) producir; **to — to a stop** parar; **to — a session to a close** clausurar una sesión; **to — together** reunir, juntar; **to — oneself to do something** poder hacer algo; **to — a good price** redituar una buena ganancia; **to — up** (raise children) criar, educar; (mention) mencionar
brink [brɪŋk] N borde *m*; **on the — of** al borde de
brisk [brɪsk] ADJ (walk) rápido; (weather) fresco; (trading) activo
bristle [brɪsəł] N cerda *f*; VI erizar[se]; **to — with** estar erizado de
bristly [brísli] ADJ (with bristles) erizado, cerdoso; (irascible) irascible
Britain [brítn] N Gran Bretaña *f*
British [brítıʃ] ADJ británico
brittle [brídl] ADJ quebradizo, frágil
brittleness [bríd]nıs] N fragilidad *f*
broach [brotʃ] VT sacar a colación
broad [brɔd] ADJ (wide) ancho; (vast) vasto; (ample) amplio; **—band** banda ancha *f*; **—cast** emisión *f*; (on TV) transmisión por televisión *f*; **—cast station** emisora *f*; **— hint** insinuación clara *f*; **— jump** salto de longitud *m*; **— -minded** tolerante; **—side** andanada *f*; **— spectrum antibiotic** antibiótico de amplio espectro *m*; **in — daylight** en pleno día; N *pej* tipa *f*; VT **to —cast** (communicate electronically) transmitir, emitir, radiar
broadcasting [brɔ́dkæstɪŋ] N (radio) radiodifusión *f*; (TV) transmisión por televisión *f*
brocade [brokéd] N brocado *m*
broccoli [brákəli] N brócoli *m*, brécol *m*
brochure [broʃúr] N folleto *m*
broil [brɔıł] VI/VT asar[se] [a la parrilla]
broiler [brɔ́ılə-] N (oven) parrilla *f*; (chicken) pollo [para asar] *m*
broke [brok] ADJ **to be —** estar limpio, estar pelado; **to go —** irse a la quiebra
broke [brok] *see* break
broken [brókən] ADJ (fragmented) roto, quebrado; (tamed) domado; (not functioning) descompuesto; (not continuous) interrumpido; **— -down** averiado, descompuesto; **— English** inglés chapurrado/chapurreado *m*; **—hearted** deshecho, con el corazón destrozado
broken [brókən] *see* break
broker [brókə-] N (intermediary) agente *mf*; (stock salesperson) corredor -ora de bolsa *mf*
brokerage [brókə-ıʤ] N correduría *f*
bromide [brómaıd] N bromuro *m*
bromine [brómin] N bromo *m*
bronchial [bráŋkiəł] ADJ bronquial; **— tube** bronquio *m*
bronchitis [braŋkáıdıs] N bronquitis *f*
bronco [bráŋko] N caballo no domado *m*
bronze [brɑnz] N bronce *m*; VT broncear
brooch [brutʃ] N broche *m*, prendedor *m*
brood [brud] N pollada *f*, nidada *f*; VI/VT empollar; **to — over** rumiar
brook [brʊk] N riachuelo *m*, cañada *f*; VT tolerar
broom [brum] N (tool) escoba *f*; (plant) retama *f*; **—stick** palo de escoba *m*
broth [brɔθ] N caldo *m*
brothel [bráθəł] N burdel *m*
brother [bráðə-] N hermano *m*; **— -in-law**

cuñado *m*; **oh —!** ¡caray!

brotherhood [bráðə·hʊd] N hermandad *f*

brotherly [bráðə·li] ADJ fraternal

brought [brɔt] *see* bring

brow [braʊ] N (eyebrow) ceja *f*; (ridge of eye) arco superciliar *m*; (forehead) frente *f*

brown [braʊn] ADJ (skin) moreno; (eyes, shoes, clothes) café, marrón; (hair) castaño; (dun) pardo; (tanned) bronceado; **— bear** oso pardo *m*; **— rice** arroz integral *m*; **— sugar** azúcar moreno -na *mf*; VI/VT (food) dorar[se]; N (color) café *m*, castaño *m*, moreno *m*, pardo *m*

brownie [bráʊni] N bizcocho de chocolate *m*; **— points** méritos *m pl*

browse [braʊz] VT (a book) hojear; VI (grass) pacer, pastar; (Internet) navegar

browser [bráʊzə·] N navegador *m*

browsing [bráʊzɪŋ] N navegación *f*

bruise [bruz] N (on skin) moretón *m*, cardenal *m*, contusión *f*; (on fruit) magulladura *f*, cardenal *m*; VI/VT magullar[se], machucar[se]

brunch [brʌntʃ] N brunch *m*, desayuno tardío *m*

Brunei [brunáɪ] N Brunéi *m*

Bruneian [brunáɪən] ADJ & N bruneano -na *mf*

brunette, brunet [brunɛ́t] ADJ & N moreno -na *mf*, morocho -cha *mf*; *Cuba* trigueño -ña *mf*

brunt [brʌnt] N impacto *m*

brush [brʌʃ] N (for teeth, clothes) cepillo *m*; (for paint, shaving) brocha *f*; (artist's) pincel *m*; (vegetation) maleza *f*; (contact) roce *m*; **—-off** despedida brusca *f*; **—wood** (dead) broza *f*; (live) maleza *f*; VT (clean with a brush) cepillar; (touch lightly) rozar; **to — aside** echar a un lado; **to — up on** repasar; **to — off** (clean) quitar con cepillo; (reject) despedir bruscamente a alguien

brusque [brʌsk] ADJ brusco

Brussels sprouts [brʌsəɫspraʊts] N coles de Bruselas *f pl*, repollitos de Bruselas *m pl*

brutal [brúdl̩] ADJ brutal

brutality [brutǽlɪɾi] N brutalidad *f*

brute [brut] N (animal) bestia *f*; (person) bruto -ta *mf*; ADJ bruto

bubble [bʌ́bəɫ] N burbuja *f*; (in soap) pompa *f*; (in boiling water) borbollón *m*; (illusion) encanto *m*; **— bath** baño de burbujas *m*; **—gum** chicle de globo *m*; **—-jet printer** impresora de burbuja *f*; VI (make bubbles) borbotar, borbollar; (boil) bullir, hervir; **to — over with joy** rebosar de alegría

bubonic plague [bubɑ́nɪkpléɡ] N plaga bubónica *f*

buck [bʌk] N (deer) gamo *m*; (male of other animals) macho *m*; (leap of horse) respingo *m*; **— private** soldado raso *m*; **—shot** posta *f*, perdigón *m*; **—skin** gamuza *f*; **—wheat** trigo sarraceno *m*; **to pass the —** echarle el muerto a uno; ADJ **—toothed** de dientes salidos; VI (horse) respingar, corcovear; **to — a trend** oponerse; **to — up** cobrar ánimo

bucket [bʌ́kɪt] N cubo *m*, balde *m*; (of a loader) cuchara *f*; **— seat** asiento delantero individual *m*

buckle [bʌ́kəɫ] N (clasp) hebilla *f*; (kink in a board) torcedura *f*; VT (to clasp) abrocharse; (to bend) torcerse, pandearse; **to — down** esforzarse; **to — up** abrocharse

bud [bʌd] N botón *m*, retoño *m*; VI (make buds) echar retoños

Buddhism [bʊ́dɪzəm] N budismo *m*

Buddhist [bʊ́dɪst] ADJ & N budista *mf*

buddy [bʌ́di] N camarada *mf*

budge [bʌʤ] VI moverse

budget [bʌ́ʤɪt] N presupuesto *m*; VT (money) presupuestar; (time, personal resources) administrar; **— cycle** ciclo presupuestario *m*; **— deficit** déficit presupuestario *m*

budgetary [bʌ́ʤɪtɛri] ADJ presupuestario

budgeting [bʌ́ʤɪdɪŋ] N presupuestación *f*

buff [bʌf] N (leather) gamuza *f*; (tan color) color beige *m*; (wheel for polishing) pulidor *m*; (devotee) aficionado *m*; **in the —** en cueros; ADJ (beige) de color beige; (muscular) musculoso; VT pulir

buffalo [bʌ́fəlo] N bisonte *m*, búfalo *m*; **— wings** alitas *f pl*

buffer [bʌ́fə·] N (in a computer) memoria intermedia *f*; (shock absorber) amortiguador *m*; (polishing device) pulidor -ra *mf*; **— zone** zona tampón *f*

buffet[1] [bʌ́fɪt] N (blow) golpe *m*, puñetazo *m*; (shock) azote *m*; VT (hit) golpear; (hit repeatedly) azotar

buffet[2] [bəfé] N (cabinet) aparador *m*; (meal) buffet *m*

buffoon [bəfún] N payaso -a *mf*, bufón -ona *mf*

bug [bʌg] N bicho *m*; (disease-causing) microbio *m*, virus *m*; (for eavesdropping) micrófono oculto *m*; (in a computer program) fallo *m*, bicho *m*; VT (bother) molestar; (install microphones) colocar micrófonos ocultos; **his eyes —ged out** se le saltaron los ojos

buggy [bʌ́gi] N (cart) calesa *f*; (baby carriage) cochecillo *m*

bugle [bjúɡəɫ] N clarín *m*; VI tocar el clarín

build [bɪɫd] VT (construct) construir, edificar; (manufacture) fabricar; **to — into** incorporar; **to — up** (make stronger) fortalecer; (accumulate) acumular; (enhance) desarrollar; (urbanize) urbanizar; N **—-up** (of military forces) concentración *f*; (of substance) acumulación *f*; (of anticipation) aumento *m*; N (of human body) complexión *f*

builder [bɪ́ɫdə·] N contratista *mf*, constructor -ora *mf*

building [bɪ́ɫdɪŋ] N (thing built) edificio *m*; (act of building) construcción *f*, edificación *f*;

(unit in a housing complex) bloque *m*; **—block** (solid mass) bloque [de construcción] *m*; (toy) cubo *m*; (essential element) elemento fundamental *m*

built [bɪłt] ADJ **—-in** (furniture appliance) empotrado; (feature) incorporado; **—-in part** parte integrante *f*; **—-to-order** hecho a pedido; **—-up** urbanizado

built [bɪłt] *see* build

bulb [bʌłb] N (plant) bulbo *m*; (light) bombilla *f*; *Am* foco *m*

bulbous [bʌ́łbəs] ADJ bulboso

Bulgaria [bʌłgériə] N Bulgaria *f*

Bulgarian [bʌłgériən] ADJ & N búlgaro -ra *mf*

bulge [bʌłʤ] N bulto *m*, protuberancia *f*; VI abultar, hincharse

bulgy [bʌ́łʤi] ADJ abultado

bulimia [bjulímiə] N bulimia *f*

bulk [bʌłk] N (mass) cantidad *f*, volumen *m*; (greater part) mayor parte *f*; **— storage** almacenamiento masivo *m*; **in —** a granel; VI **to — up** echar músculos

bulky [bʌ́łki] ADJ voluminoso

bull [bʊł] N toro *m*; **—dog** bulldog *m*; **—dozer** bulldozer *m*; **—fight** corrida de toros *f*; **—fighter** torero *m*; **—fighting** tauromaquia *f*; **—frog** rana grande *f*; **— market** mercado alcista *m*; **—pen** (baseball) zona de calentamiento *f*; **—'s eye** diana *f*; **to hit the —'s-eye** dar en el blanco; ADJ **—headed** terco, obstinado

bullet [bʊ́lɪt] N bala *f*; ADJ **—proof** antibalas *inv*, antibalístico

bulletin [bʊ́lɪtn] N boletín *m*; **— board** tablero *m*, cartelera *f*

bullion [bʊ́ljən] N oro en lingotes *m*

bully [bʊ́li] N matón -ona *mf*, bravucón -ona *mf*; VT intimidar

bulwark [bʊ́łwə-k] N baluarte *m*

bum [bʌm] N (lazy person) holgazán -ana *mf*; (hobo) vagabundo -da *mf*; (sports fan) fanático -ca *mf*; ADJ falso; VI **to — around** holgazanear; VT **to — something from someone** gorronearle algo a alguien

bumblebee [bʌ́mbəłbi] N abejorro *m*, abejón *m*

bump [bʌmp] VT chocar; **to — along** ir dando tumbos; **to — off** despachar; **to — into** toparse con; N (blow) choque *m*, trastazo *m*; (lump) protuberancia *f*; (lump on a person) chichón *m*

bumper [bʌ́mpə-] N parachoques *m sg*, tope *m*; **— car** coche de choque *m*, autito chocador *m*; **— crop** cosecha abundante *f*; **—-to-traffic** caravana de autos *f*; **— sticker** autoadhesivo *m*

bumpy [bʌ́mpi] ADJ bacheado, lleno de baches

bun [bʌn] N (bread) bollo *m*; (in hair) moño *m*

bunch [bʌntʃ] N (of things) manojo *m*; (of people) montón *m*, grupo *m*; (of grapes, bananas) racimo *m*; (of flowers) ramillete *m*; VI/VT juntar[se], agrupar[se]

bundle [bʌ́ndł] N (of things) paquete *m*, fardo *m*, envoltorio *m*; (of clothes) lío *m*, atado *m*; (of belongings) hato *m*, petate *m*; (of firewood) haz *m*; VT (tie together) liar, atar; **to — up** abrigarse; **to — off** despachar

bungalow [bʌ́ŋgəlo] N bungaló *m*

bungee jumping [bʌ́nʤiʤʌ́mpɪŋ] N bungee *m*, puénting *m*

bungle [bʌ́ŋgəł] VT estropear; VI chapucear

bunion [bʌ́njən] N juanete *m*

bunk [bʌŋk] N (place to sleep) litera *f*; (nonsense) tonterías *f pl*; **— bed** litera *f*; VI dormir en una litera

bunker [bʌ́ŋkə-] N búnker *m*

bunny [bʌ́ni] N conejito *m*

bunt [bʌnt] N (baseball) toque de pelota *m*; VT tocar la pelota

buoy [bʊ́i] N boya *f*; VI boyar; **to — up** mantener a flote, animar

buoyant [bɔ́ɪənt] ADJ (floating) boyante, flotante; (optimistic) optimista

burden [bɝ́dn] N (load) carga *f*; (responsibility) peso *m*; **— of proof** peso de la prueba *m*; VT (heavily) recargar; (oppressively) agobiar

burdensome [bɝ́dnsəm] ADJ agobiante, gravoso

bureau [bjʊ́ro] N (government department) oficina *f*, agencia *f*; (chest of drawers) cómoda *f*

bureaucracy [bjʊrʊ́krəsi] N burocracia *f*

bureaucrat [bjʊ́rəkræt] N burócrata *mf*

burglar [bɝ́glə-] N ladrón -ona *mf*; **— alarm** alarma antirrobo *f*; **— proof** a prueba de robos

burglary [bɝ́gləri] N robo con allanamiento *m*

burial [bɛ́riəł] N entierro *m*, enterramiento *m*; **— ground** enterramiento *m*; **— place** lugar de sepultura *m*

Burkina Faso [bə-kínəfʌ́so] N Burkina Faso *m*

burlap [bɝ́læp] N arpillera *f*

burlesque [bə-łɛ́sk] ADJ burlesco; N espectáculo de variedades *m*

burly [bɝ́li] ADJ corpulento

Burma [bə-mə] N Birmania *f*

Burmese [bə-míz] ADJ & N birmano -na *mf*

burn [bɝn] VI/VT quemar[se], abrasar[se]; (a house) incendiar[se]; (a CD) quemar; (food) quemar[se], requemar[se]; **he got —ed in the transaction** lo estafaron en el negocio; **the bulb is still —ing** la bombilla sigue prendida; **the iodine —ed his skin** el yodo le quemó la piel; VI (with heat, passion) arder, abrasar; **my skin —s** me arde la piel; **he's —ing with desire** arde en deseos; **to — down** incendiarse; **to — off** (fog) disiparse; **to — out** (bulb) fundirse; (worker) agotarse; **to — up** quemarse completamente; N quemadura *f*; **—out** surmenage *m*

burner [bɝ́nɚ] N (person or thing that burns something) quemador -ra *mf*; (on stove) hornilla *f*; **Bunsen** — mechero Bunsen *m*
burning [bɝ́nɪŋ] ADJ (desire) ardiente, abrasador; (question) urgente; N (caused by acid) ardor *m*; (caused by fire) quemadura *f*
burnish [bɝ́nɪʃ] VT bruñir
burnt [bɝrnt] *see* burn
burp [bɝp] N eructo *m*; VI eructar, repetir
burr, bur [bɝ] N abrojo *m*
burrow [bɝ́o] N madriguera *f*; VI (dig) hacer madrigueras; (live) vivir en una madriguera
bursitis [bɝsáɪdɪs] N bursitis *f*
burst [bɝst] VI reventar[se]; **to — into a room** irrumpir en un cuarto; **to — into tears** romper en llanto; **to — out** salir disparado; **to — with laughter** estallar/reventar de risa; N (of activity) explosión *f*; (of laughter) carcajada *f*; (of machine-gun fire) ráfaga *f*; (of speed) aceleración *f*
Burundi [bʊrúndi] N Burundi *m*
Burundian [bʊrúndiən] ADJ & N burundés -esa *mf*
bury [bɛ́ri] VT (body, treasure) enterrar; (body) sepultar; **to be buried in thought** estar absorto/meditabundo
bus [bʌs] N autobús *m*, ómnibus *m*; *Mex* camión *m*; *RP* colectivo *m*; *Chile* micro *m*; *Cuba* guagua *f*; (in a computer) bus *m*; VT transportar en autobús
bush [bʊʃ] N (plant) arbusto *m*, mata *f*; (region) matorral *m*; **to beat around the —** andarse por las ramas
bushed [bʊʃt] ADJ fatigado
bushel [bʊ́ʃəl] N fanega *f*
bushing [bʊ́ʃɪŋ] N buje *m*, cojinete *m*
bushy [bʊ́ʃi] ADJ (whiskers) espeso; (plants) poblado de arbustos
business [bíznɪs] N (trade, store) negocio *m*; (occupation) ocupación *f*; (commercial activity) comercio *m*; **— acumen** buen sentido para los negocios *m*; **— agreement** convenio comercial *m*; **— card** tarjeta comercial *f*; **— day** día hábil *m*; **— group** grupo empresarial *m*; **— hours** horas hábiles *f pl*, horario de atención al público *m*; **— is booming** el negocio florece; **—like** (efficient) eficiente; (cold) impersonal; **—man** hombre de negocios *m*, negociante *m*; **— suit** traje *m*; **— transaction** negocio *m*, transacción comercial *f*; **—woman** mujer de negocios *f*, negociante *f*; **I'm tired of the whole —** este asunto me tiene harto; **I mean —** hablo en serio; **to do —** with comerciar con; **he has no — doing it** no tiene derecho a hacerlo; **it's none of your —** no es asunto tuyo; **mind your own —** no te metas en lo que no te importa
bust [bʌst] N (statue, body part) busto *m*; VI/VT (burst, hit, break) reventar; (force into bankruptcy) hacer quebrar; (lower in rank) degradar
bustle [bʌ́səl] N (noise) bullicio *m*; (movement) ajetreo *m*, tráfago *m*; VI (move busily) ajetrear[se]; (be crowded) bullir
busy [bízi] ADJ ocupado, atareado; (overdecorated) recargado; **—body** entrometido -da *mf*; **— signal** señal de ocupado *f*; VI **to — oneself** ocuparse
but [bʌt] CONJ (on the contrary) pero; (excepting) sino; PREP menos; **any day — today** cualquier día menos hoy; **he's nothing — trouble** sólo da problemas; ADV **— for you** si no fuera por ti
butane [bjúten] N butano *m*
butch [bʊtʃ] ADJ machote
butcher [bʊ́tʃɚ] N carnicero -ra *mf*; **—'s shop** carnicería *f*; VT (cattle) matar; (people) masacrar; (performance) estropear
butchery [bʊ́tʃəri] N carnicería *f*
butler [bʌ́tlɚ] N mayordomo *m*
butt [bʌt] N; (of a rifle) culata *f*; (of a cigarette) colilla *f*; (blow with head) topetazo *m*, cabezada *f*, cabezazo *m*; **the — of ridicule** el blanco de las burlas; VT embestir, topar; **to — in** entrometerse; **to — into a conversation** meter baza; *Am* meter la cuchara
butter [bʌ́dɚ] N mantequilla *f*; **—cup** botón de oro *m*; **— dish** mantequera *f*; **—fingers** manos de mantequilla *mf sg*; **—milk** suero de leche *m*; **—scotch** dulce de azúcar y mantequilla *m*; VT (bread) untar con mantequilla; (a cakepan) enmantecar
butterfly [bʌ́dɚflaɪ] N mariposa *f*; **— stroke** estilo mariposa *m*
buttery [bʌ́dɚi] ADJ mantecoso
buttocks [bʌ́dəks] N nalgas *f pl*, asentaderas *f pl*, cachas *f pl*
button [bʌ́tn] N botón *m*; **—hole** ojal *m*; VI/VT abotonar[se]; VI **to —hole** hacer ojales; VT **to —hole someone** detener a alguien
buttress [bʌ́trɪs] N apoyo *m*, sostén *m*; (of a building) contrafuerte *m*; VT apoyar, reforzar
buy [baɪ] VT comprar; **to — on credit** comprar a crédito; **to — in installments** comprar a plazos; **to — off** sobornar; **to — out** comprar la parte de; **to — up** acaparar; **I don't — that** no me lo trago; N (purchase) compra *f*; (bargain) ganga *f*
buyer [báiɚ] N comprador -ra *mf*
buying [báɪɪŋ] N **— frenzy** frenesí de compras *m*; **— habits** hábitos de compras *m pl*
buzz [bʌz] N zumbido *m*; (feeling of intoxication) borrachera *f*; (phone call) telefonazo *m*; **—word** palabra de moda *f*; **— saw** sierra circular *f*; VI (insect, ears) zumbar; (group) murmurar; VT hacer zumbar; **to — the bell** tocar el timbre; **to give someone a —**

pegarle/echarle un telefonazo a alguien; **to — off** largarse

buzzard [bázə·d] N buitre *m*

buzzer [bázə·] N timbre *m*, chicharra *f*

by [baɪ] PREP por; **— and —** a la larga; **— chance** por casualidad; **— dint of** a fuerza de; **— far** con mucho; **— night** de noche; **— the way** a propósito; **— the liter** por litro; **— this time tomorrow** mañana a esta hora; **— two o'clock** para las dos; **we drove — the church** pasamos por la iglesia; **a 4 — 3 room** un cuarto de 4 por 3; **multiply 2 — 2** multiplica 2 por 2; **we live — the church** vivimos al lado de la iglesia; **she had a son — him** tuvo un hijo con él; **piece — piece** pedazo a/por pedazo; ADV **the factory is close —** la fábrica está cerca; **the bus drove —** pasó el autobús

bye-bye [báɪbáɪ] INTERJ ¡adiós! ¡chaucito!

bygones [báɪgɔnz] N **let — be —** lo pasado pisado

bylaw [báɪlɔ] N estatuto *m*

by-line [báɪlaɪn] N pie de autor *m*

bypass [báɪpæs] VT evitar; N desvío *m*; **— operation** bypass *m*

by-product [báɪprɑ·dəkt] N subproducto *m*; (chemical) derivado *m*

bystander [báɪstændə·] N persona presente *f*

byte [baɪt] N byte *m*, octeto *m*

Cc

cab [kæb] N (of a truck) cabina *f*; (taxi) taxi *m*; **— driver** taxista *mf*

cabaret [kæbəréˈ] N cabaret *m*

cabbage [kǽbɪʤ] N col *f*, repollo *m*, berza *f*

cabin [kǽbɪn] N (hut) cabaña *f*; (in an airplane) cabina *f*; (in a ship) camarote *m*

cabinet [kǽbnɪt] N (for dishes) armario *m*; (for medicines) botiquín *m*; (for display) vitrina *f*; (of ministers) gabinete *m*; **—level appointment** nombramiento ministerial *m*; **—maker** ebanista *mf*

cable [kébəł] N cable *m*; (on ships) amarra *f*; (telegram) telegrama *m*; **— car** funicular *m*, teleférico *m*; **— television** televisión por cable *f*, cablevisión *f*; VI/VT telegrafiar

caboose [kəbús] N furgón de cola *m*

cache [kæʃ] N (of weapons) alijo *m*; (in a computer) caché *m*; **— memory** memoria de caché *f*

cachet [kæʃéˈ] N caché *m*

cackle [kǽkəł] VI (hen) cacarear; (people) parlotear; N (hen) cacareo *m*; (people) parloteo *m*

cacophony [kəkɑ́fəni] N cacofonía *f*

cactus [kǽktəs] N cacto *m*, cactus *m*

cad [kæd] N *pej* canalla *mf*

cadaver [kədǽvə·] N cadáver *m*

caddie [kǽDi] N caddy *m*, caddie *m*

cadence [kédn̩s] N cadencia *f*

cadet [kədétˈ] N cadete *mf*

cadmium [kǽdmiəm] N cadmio *m*

café [kæfé] N (coffee only) café *m*; (coffee and food) cafetería *f*

cafeteria [kæftíriə] N cafetería *f*

caffeine [kæfín] N cafeína *f*

cage [keʤ] N jaula *f*; VT enjaular

cahoots [kəhúts] ADV LOC **in —** arreglados

cajole [kəʤół] VI/VT engatusar, persuadir con halagos

cake [kek] N pastel *m*, torta *f*; (sponge) bizcocho *m*; (soap) pastilla *f*; **a piece of —** pan comido; **to take the —** ser el colmo; VI/VT apelmazar[se]

calamine [kǽləmaɪn] N calamina *f*

calamity [kəlǽmɪDi] N calamidad *f*

calcium [kǽlsiəm] N calcio *m*

calculate [kǽłkjəlet] VI/VT calcular; **his actions were —d to fool us** con sus acciones trataba de engañarnos

calculating [kǽłkjəleDɪŋ] ADJ calculador

calculation [kæłkjəléʃən] N cálculo *m*

calculator [kǽłkjəleDə·] calculadora *f*

calculus [kǽłkjələs] N cálculo *m*

calendar [kǽlɪndə·] N calendario *m*; **— year** año civil *m*

calf [kæf] N (of leg) pantorrilla *f*, canilla *f*; (animal) ternero -ra *mf*, becerro -rra *mf*; **— skin** piel de becerro *f*

caliber [kǽləbə·] N calibre *m*

calibrate [kǽləbret] VT calibrar, graduar

calico [kǽlɪko] N calicó *m*

caliper [kǽləpə·] N (on brakes) calibrador *m*; (for measuring) calibre *m*

call [kɔł] VT (summon, by telephone, a name, a strike) llamar; (cry out) gritar; (a meeting) convocar; **she —ed me a liar** me llamó mentiroso; **— me back** llámame tú, devuélveme la llamada; VI/VT (birds) reclamar; **to — roll** pasar lista; VI (call out) gritar; **to — a meeting to order** abrir la sesión; **to — at a port** hacer escala en un puerto; **to — for** pedir; **to — off** cancelar; **to — on** (visit) visitar; (depend on) acudir a; **to — together** convocar; **to — up** llamar por teléfono; N (by telephone) llamada *f*; (summons) llamamiento *m*, llamado *m*; (to the ministry) vocación *f*; (for conference papers) convocatoria *f*; (device for calling birds) reclamo *m*; **to be on —** estar de guardia; **there's no — for panic** no hay motivo de alarma; **it's your —** tú decides; **within —** al alcance de la voz

caller [kɔ́lə˞] N visita *f*, visitante *mf*; (by telephone) persona que llama *f*; **— ID** identificador de llamadas *m*
calligraphy [kəlígrəfi] N caligrafía *f*
calling [kɔ́lɪŋ] N vocación *f*
callous [kǽləs] ADJ (having calluses) calloso; (insensitive) insensible
callus [kǽləs] N callo *m*
calm [kɑm] ADJ tranquilo, reposado, calmo; N calma *f*, tranquilidad *f*, sosiego *m*; VT calmar, tranquilizar, sosegar; **to — down** calmar[se]
calmness [kɑ́mnɪs] N calma *f*, tranquilidad *f*
calorie [kǽlə˞ri] N caloría *f*
calumny [kǽləmni] N calumnia *f*
cam [kæm] N leva *f*
Cambodia [kæmbóʊdiə] N Camboya *f*
Cambodian [kæmbóʊdiən] ADJ & N camboyano -na *mf*
camcorder [kǽmkɔ̀rdə˞] N videocámara *f*
came [kem] *see* come
camel [kǽməł] N camello *m*
cameo [kǽmio] N camafeo *m*; **— appearance** actuación especial *f*
camera [kǽmrə] N cámara *f*, cámara fotográfica *f*; **—man** cámara *m*, camarógrafo *m*; **—-ready copy** texto listo para cámara *f*; **—woman** cámara *f*, camarógrafa *f*
Cameroon [kæmərún] N Camerún *m*
Cameroonian [kæmərúniən] ADJ & N camerunés -esa *mf*
camouflage [kǽməflɑʒ] N camuflaje *m*; VT camuflar
camp [kæmp] N (campsite) campamento *m*; (faction) bando *m*; **—fire** fogata *f*, hoguera *f*; **—ground** campamento *m*, cámping *m*; **—site** campamento *m*; VI/VT acampar
campaign [kæmpén] N campaña *f*; VI hacer campaña
camper [kǽmpə˞] N acampante *mf*, campista *mf*
camphor [kǽmfə˞] N alcanfor *m*
camping [kǽmpɪŋ] N cámping *m*, acampada *f*; **let's go —** vamos de camping / de acampada
campus [kǽmpəs] N campus *m*
can [kæn] N lata *f*, bote *m*; **— of worms** caja de Pandora *f*; **— opener** abrelatas *m sg*; VT enlatar; V AUX **— you come tomorrow?** ¿puedes venir mañana? **— you see me?** ¿me ves? **I — ride a bicycle** sé andar en bicicleta; **a —-do attitude** un espíritu emprendedor
Canada [kǽnədə] N Canadá *m*
Canadian [kənéɪdiən] ADJ & N canadiense *mf*
canal [kənǽł] N canal *m*
canary [kənéri] N canario *m*; **Canary Islands** Islas Canarias *f pl*
Canary Islands [kənériáɪlənz] N Islas Canarias *f pl*
cancel [kǽnsəł] VT cancelar; (a stamp) matasellar; (an order) anular
cancellation [kænsəléʃən] N (of a flight, performance) cancelación *f*; (of an order) anulación *f*
cancer [kǽnsə˞] N cáncer *m*; **— patient** canceroso -sa *mf*; ADJ **—-causing** cancerígeno
cancerous [kǽnsə˞əs] ADJ canceroso
candelabrum, candelabra [kændəlɑ́brəm -brə] N candelabro *m*
candid [kǽndɪd] ADJ franco, sincero
candidacy [kǽndɪdəsi] N candidatura *f*
candidate [kǽndɪdɪt] N (for office) candidato -ta *mf*; (for a job) aspirante *mf*, postulante *mf*
candle [kǽndł] N vela *f*, candela *f*; (on the altar) cirio *m*; **—stick** candelero *m*
candor [kǽndə˞] N franqueza *f*
candy [kǽndi] N dulce *m*, caramelo *m*, confite *m*; (with chocolate) bombón *m*; **— store** bombonería *f*; VT confitar, acaramelar; (nuts) garapiñar; VI (syrup) cristalizarse
cane [ken] N (sugar) caña *f*; (walking) bastón *m*; **— chair** silla de mimbre *f*
canine [kéɪnaɪn] ADJ canino, perruno; N (dog) can *m*, perro *m*; (tooth) canino *m*
canister [kǽnɪstə˞] N lata *f*
canker [kæŋkə˞] N úlcera *f*
cannery [kǽnəri] N fábrica de conservas *f*
cannibal [kǽnəbəł] N caníbal *m*
cannon [kǽnən] N cañón *m*; **— fodder** carne de cañón *f*
canny [kǽni] ADJ sagaz, astuto
canoe [kənú] N canoa *f*
canon [kǽnən] N (rule, melody, body of works) canon *m*; (priest) canónigo *m*
canopy [kǽnəpi] N (of a bed) dosel *m*; (of a building) toldo *m*
cantaloupe [kǽntłop] N melón *m*
canteen [kæntín] N (snack bar) cantina *f*; (container) cantimplora *f*
canvas [kǽnvəs] N (fabric) lona *f*; (for painting) lienzo *m*
canvass [kǽnvəs] VI/VT (poll) encuestar; (solicit votes) solicitar votos en; (solicit sales) buscar pedidos comerciales en; N solicitud *f*
canyon [kǽnjən] N cañón *m*
cap [kæp] N (head covering without visor) gorro *m*; (head covering with visor) gorra *f*; (of a bottle) tapa *f*; (of a pen) capucha *f*, contera *f*; (limit) tope *m*; (for capgun) fulminante *m*, pistón *m*; VT (to cover, put a cap on) tapar; (to complete) rematar; (to limit) limitar
capability [kepəbílɪdi] N capacidad *f*
capable [képəbəł] ADJ capaz
capacious [kəpéʃəs] ADJ amplio
capacity [kəpǽsɪdi] N capacidad *f*
cape [kep] N (clothing) capa *f*; (promontory) cabo *m*
caper [képə˞] N (skipping) cabriola *f*; (prank) treta *f*, triquiñuela *f*; (crime) delito *m*; (food) alcaparra *f*; VI retozar

Cape Verde [kepvɝ́d] N Cabo Verde *m*
Cape Verdean [kepvɝ́diən] ADJ & N caboverdiano -na *mf*
capillary [kǽpəlɛri] N & ADJ [vaso] capilar *m*
capital [kǽpɪdl] N (city) capital *f*; (wealth) capital *m*; (of a column) capitel *m*; (letter) mayúscula *f*; **to make — of** sacar partido de, aprovecharse de; ADJ (city) capital; (financial) de capital; **— gains** ganancias en bienes de capital *f pl*; **— investment** inversión de capital *f*; **— punishment** pena de muerte *f*
capitalism [kǽpɪdlɪzəm] N capitalismo *m*
capitalist [kǽpɪdlɪst] N capitalista *mf*
capitalistic [kæpɪdlístɪk] ADJ capitalista
capitalization [kæpɪdlɪzéʃən] N capitalización *f*
capitalize [kǽpɪdlaɪz] VT (finance) capitalizar; (write) escribir con mayúscula; **to — on** sacar provecho de
capitol [kǽpɪdl] N capitolio *m*
capitulate [kəpítʃəlet] VI capitular
cappuccino [kæpətʃíno] N capuchino *m*
caprice [kəprís] N capricho *m*
capricious [kəpríʃəs] ADJ caprichoso
capsize [kǽpsaɪz] VI/VT volcar[se]
capsule [kǽpsəł] N cápsula *f*
captain [kǽptɪn] N capitán *m*; VT capitanear
caption [kǽpʃən] N (with illustration) pie *m*; (subtitle) subtítulo *m*
captivate [kǽptəvet] VT cautivar
captive [kǽptɪv] ADJ & N cautivo -va *mf*; **— animals** animales en cautiverio *m pl*
captivity [kæptívɪdɪ] N cautiverio *m*
captor [kǽptə-] N captor -ra *mf*
capture [kǽptʃə-] VT (apprehend, record data) capturar; (give expression to) plasmar; (attract) cautivar; (conquer) tomar; N captura *f*
car [kɑr] N (automobile) coche *m*, automóvil *m*; *Am* carro *m*, auto *m*; (railroad) vagón *m*, coche *m*; (elevator) cabina *f*; *Am* elevador *m*; **— bomb** coche bomba *m*; **—fare** pasaje *m*; **—jacking** secuestro de vehículo *m*; **—load** carga de un coche *f*; **—port** cochera *f*; **— wash** túnel de lavado *m*; ADJ **—sick** mareado; **to get —sick** marearse en el coche
caramel [kǽrəməł] N caramelo *m*
carat [kǽrət] N quilate *m*
caravan [kǽrəvæn] N caravana *f*
carbohydrate [kɑrbəháɪdret] N carbohidrato *m*, hidrato de carbono *m*
carbon [kárbən] N carbono *m*; **— copy** copia en papel carbón *f*; **— dioxide** dióxido de carbono *m*; **— monoxide** monóxido de carbono *m*; **— paper** papel carbón *m*
carburetor [kárbərɛdə-] N carburador *m*
carcass [kárkəs] N (of an animal) cuerpo muerto *m*; (of a ship) casco *m*
carcinogen [kɑrsínəʤən] N cancerígeno *m*, carcinógeno *m*
carcinoma [kɑrsənómə] N carcinoma *m*
card [kɑrd] N (piece of stiff paper) tarjeta *f*; (for games) naipe *m*, carta *f*; (for boxing events) programa *m*; (for textiles) carda *f*; (witty person) gracioso -sa *mf*; (in a computer) tarjeta *f*, placa *f*; **—board** (thick) cartón *m*; (thin) cartulina *f*; **— reader** lector de tarjetas *m*; **— sharp** fullero -ra *mf*; **pack of —s** baraja *f*; **to play —s** jugar a la baraja, jugar a los naipes; **he's holding all the —s** tiene todas las ventajas; VT (comb) cardar; (ask for identification) pedir identificación
cardiac [kárdɪæk] ADJ cardiaco, cardíaco
cardinal [kárdnəł] ADJ (number, main) cardinal; (colored red) rojo, bermellón; N (bishop, bird) cardenal *m*
cardioangiogram [kɑrdioǽnʤiəgræm] N cardioangiograma *m*
cardiogram [kárdiogræm] N cardiograma *m*
cardiologist [kɑrdiáləʤɪst] N cardiólogo -ga *mf*
cardiology [kɑrdiáləʤi] N cardiología *f*
cardiopulmonary [kɑrdiopʊ́łmənɛri] ADJ cardiopulmonar; **— bypass** puente cardiopulmonar *m*
cardiovascular [kɑrdiovǽskjələ-] ADJ cardiovascular
care [kɛr] N (worry) preocupación *f*; (attention) cuidado *m*, atención *f*, tiento *m*; (extreme attention) esmero *m*, primor *m*; **—giver** cuidador -ra de enfermos *mf*; **—taker** (of a house) casero -ra *mf*; **to be under the — of** estar al cuidado de; **to take — of** cuidar de, atender; ADJ **—free** despreocupado; VI (be concerned) importarle a uno; **to — about** interesarle a uno, importarle a uno; **to — for** (look after) cuidar de; (love) tenerle cariño a; **to — to** tener ganas de; **I couldn't — less** me importa un rábano; **what does he —?** ¿a él qué le importa? **would you — for a drink?** ¿te puedo ofrecer algo?
careen [kərín] VI ladearse a toda velocidad
career [kərír] N carrera *f*, trayectoria *f*
careful [kérfəł] ADJ (cautious) cuidadoso, cauteloso; (painstaking) esmerado; **to be —** tener cuidado
carefully [kérfəli] ADV (safely) con cuidado; (painstakingly) esmeradamente
carefulness [kérfəlnɪs] N cuidado *m*
careless [kérlɪs] ADJ descuidado
caress [kərés] N caricia *f*; VT acariciar
cargo [kárgo] N cargamento *m*
Caribbean [kærəbíən] N Caribe *m*; ADJ caribeño
caricature [kǽrɪkətʃə-] N caricatura *f*; VT caricaturizar
caries [kériz] N caries *f*
carnage [kárnɪʤ] N carnicería *f*
carnal [kárnł] ADJ carnal
carnation [karnéʃən] N (flower) clavel *m*; (color) rosado *m*

carnival [kárnəvəł] N carnaval *m*; (traveling) feria *f*
carnivorous [kɑrnívə-əs] ADJ carnívoro, carnicero
carol [kǽrəł] N villancico *m*; VI cantar villancicos
carom [kǽrəm] N carambola *f*; VI rebotar
carotid artery [kəráɪdɪdárdəri] N [arteria] carótida *f*
carouse [kəráʊz] VI andar de parranda
carp [kɑrp] N carpa *f*; VI (complain) quejarse
carpenter [kárpəntə-] N carpintero -ra *mf*
carpentry [kárpəntri] N carpintería *f*
carpet [kárpɪt] N alfombra *f*; **—bagger** político -ca oportunista *mf*; VT alfombrar
carriage [kǽrɪʤ] N (wheeled vehicle) carruaje *m*, coche *m*; (posture) porte *m*
carrier [kǽriə-] N (one who carries) portador -ra *mf*; (postal worker) cartero -ra *mf*; (transport company) mensajería *f*
carrion [kǽriən] N carroña *f*
carrot [kǽrət] N zanahoria *f*
carry [kǽri] VT llevar; **do you — Italian wine?** ¿venden vino italiano? **the bill carried** se aprobó el proyecto de ley; **you — yourself well** te comportas bien; **he can't — a tune** no puede seguir una tonada; **this suitcase will — a lot** esta maleta es espaciosa; **to — away** llevarse; **he got carried away** se le fue la mano; **to — on** continuar; **to — out** (complete) llevar a cabo, ejecutar; (take out) sacar; N **—-on** maleta de mano *f*
cart [kɑrt] N (also golf) carro *m*; VT acarrear
cartilage [kárdlɪʤ] N cartílago *m*
carton [kártn̩] N caja de cartón *f*
cartoon [kɑrtún] N (drawing) caricatura *f*; (strip) tira cómica *f*; (film) dibujo animado *m*
cartoonist [kɑrtúnɪst] N caricaturista *mf*
cartridge [kártrɪʤ] N cartucho *m*; **— belt** cartuchera *f*, canana *f*
carve [kɑrv] VI/VT (a piece of wood) tallar; (a turkey) trinchar; **to — out a career** labrarse una carrera
carving [kárvɪŋ] N (action) tallado *m*; (figure) talla *f*; **— knife** trinchante *m*
cascade [kæskéd] N cascada *f*
case [kes] N caso *m*; (box) caja *f*; (of a pillow) funda *f*; **— history** historia clínica *f*; **in — [that]** en caso de [que]; **in — it rains** por si llueve; **in any —** en todo caso; **just in —** por si acaso; **get off my —!** ¡déjame en paz! **—-sensitive** sensible a la diferencia entre mayúsculas y minúsculas
cash [kæʃ] N efectivo *m*; **— advance** anticipo en efectivo *m*; **— and carry** al contado y sin entrega a domicilio; **— flow** corriente en efectivo *f*; **— on delivery** entrega contra reembolso *f*; **— payment** pago en efectivo *m*; **— register** caja registradora *f*; **to pay —** pagar al contado; VT cobrar
cashew [kǽʃu] N marañón *m*, castaña de cajú *f*, *Sp* anacardo *m*
cashier [kæʃír] N cajero -ra *mf*; **—'s check** cheque de caja *m*
casino [kəsíno] N casino *m*
cask [kæsk] N tonel grande *m*
casket [kǽskɪt] N ataúd *m*
casserole [kǽsərоł] N (container) cazuela *f*; (food) guiso *m*
cassette [kəsét] N cassette *mf*, casete *mf*
cast [kæst] VT (throw) tirar, echar; (form an object) moldear, vaciar; (give out dramatic roles) repartir papeles; **to — a ballot** votar; **to — about** buscar; **to — a glance** echar un vistazo; **to — aside** desechar; **to — doubt** poner en duda; **to — light on** aclarar; **to — lots** echar suertes; **to — off** (a ship) soltar amarras; (something rejected) deshacerse de; **to — out** exiliar; **to be — down** estar abatido; N (form) molde *m*; (in theater) reparto *m*, elenco *m*; (for broken bones) yeso; **to put in a —** enyesar; **— iron** hierro fundido *m*
castanet [kǽstənɛt] N castañuela *f*
caste [kæst] N casta *f*
castigate [kǽstɪget] VT (criticize) criticar, reprender; (punish) castigar
Castile [kæstíł] N Castilla *f*
Castilian [kæstíljən] N & ADJ castellano -na *mf*; **— speaker** castellanohablante *mf*; ADJ **— speaking** castellanohablante
casting [kǽstɪŋ] N (throwing) tiro *m*; (piece of metal) pieza fundida *f*; (selection of actors) cásting *m*
castle [kǽsəł] N castillo *m*; (chess piece) torre *f*, roque *m*
castor oil [kǽstə-ɔɪł] N aceite de ricino *m*
castrate [kǽstret] VT castrar; (animals) capar
casual [kǽʒuəł] ADJ (informal) informal; (offhand) al pasar
casualty [kǽʒuəłti] N (of war) baja *f*; (in an accident) víctima *f*
cat [kæt] N (domestic) gato -ta *mf*; (others) felino *m*; **—'s meow** súmmum *m*; **—fish** siluro *m*
Catalan [kǽdlæn] ADJ & N catalán -ana *mf*; (language) catalán *m*
catalog, catalogue [kǽdlɔg] N catálogo *m*; VT catalogar
Catalonia [kædlóniə] N Cataluña *f*
Catalonian [kædlóniən] ADJ catalán
catalyst [kǽdlɪst] N catalizador *m*
cataract [kǽbərækt] N catarata *f*
catastrophe [kətǽstrəfi] N catástrofe *f*
catatonia [kæbətóniə] N catatonia *f*
catch [kætʃ] VT (a criminal, ball) atrapar; *Sp*, *Cuba* coger; (a fish) pescar, capturar; (someone in an act) pillar; (a bus) agarrar; (what someone said) comprender, agarrar; **to — a glimpse of** vislumbrar; **to — cold**

resfriarse; **to — fire** prenderse fuego; **to — on** (understand) caer en cuenta; (become popular) ponerse de moda; **to — oneself** contenerse; **to — one's eye** llamarle a uno la atención; **to — sight of** avistar; **to — unawares** sorprender; **to — up** (with a person) alcanzar; (on work) ponerse al día, actualizarse; VI (get entangled) enredarse; (snap into place) agarrar; N (act of catching prey, quantity caught) captura *f*, redada *f*, pesca *f*; (prey) presa *f*; (device) pestillo *m*; (act of catching a ball) atrapada *f*; **—phrase** eslogan *m*; **— twenty-two** paradoja *f*; **he is a good —** es un buen partido; **to play —** jugar a la pelota; **what's the —?** ¿cuál es la treta?

catcher [kǽtʃə-] N (baseball) receptor -ora *mf*

catching [kǽtʃɪŋ] ADJ contagioso

catchy [kǽtʃi] ADJ pegadizo

catechism [kǽɒɪkɪzəm] N catecismo *m*

category [kǽɒɪgəri] N categoría *f*

cater [kéɪə-] VI/VT abastecer de alimentos [banquetes, fiestas, etc.]; **to — to** atender a

caterpillar [kǽɒəpɪlə-] N (insect) oruga *f*; (tractor) tractor oruga *m*, caterpillar *m*

cathedral [kəθídrəł] N catedral *f*

catheter [kǽθɪɒə-] N catéter *m*, sonda *f*

catheterization [kæθəɒə-ɪzéʃən] N cateterización *f*

catheterize [kǽθəɒə-aɪz] VT cateterizar

cathode [kǽθod] N cátodo *m*; **— rays** rayos catódicos *m pl*

Catholic [kǽθlɪk] N & ADJ católico -ca *mf*

Catholicism [kəθɑ́lɪsɪzəm] N catolicismo *m*

CAT [computerized axial tomography] scan [kǽtskæn] N TAC *f*

catsup [kǽtʃəp] N cátsup *m*, ketchup *m*, salsa de tomate *f*

cattle [kǽdł] N ganado [vacuno] *m*; **—breeding** ganadería *f*; **—man** ganadero *m*; **— rustler** cuatrero *m*; **— rustling** abigeato *m*

catty [kǽɒi] ADJ malicioso

caught [kɔt] *see* catch

cauliflower [kɔ́lɪflaʊə-] N coliflor *f*

cause [kɔz] N causa *f*, causante *f*; **— for celebration** motivo de celebración *m*; **the democratic —** la causa democrática *f*; **without —** sin motivo; VT (make happen) causar, ocasionar; (motivate) motivar; **to — to flee** hacer huir; **the heat —d her to faint** el calor la hizo desmayar

caustic [kɔ́stɪk] ADJ cáustico

cauterize [kɔ́ɒəraɪz] VT cauterizar

caution [kɔ́ʃən] N (prudence) cautela *f*, recato *m*; (warning) advertencia *f*; **—!** ¡cuidado! ¡atención! VT advertir; **to — against** desaconsejar

cautious [kɔ́ʃəs] ADJ cauto, cauteloso, precavido

cava [kɑ́və] N (wine) cava *f*

cavalier [kǽvəlír] N caballero *m*, galán *m*; ADJ (disdainful) desdeñoso; (overly casual) displicente

cavalry [kǽvəłri] N caballería *f*

cave [kev] N cueva *f*, caverna *f*; **—man** hombre de las cavernas *m*; VI **to — in** (yield) ceder; (collapse) derrumbarse, desplomarse

cavern [kǽvə-n] N caverna *f*, gruta *f*

cavity [kǽvɪɒi] N cavidad *f*; (in a tooth) caries *f*; (nasal) fosa *f*

cavort [kəvɔ́rt] VI cabriolar, retozar

caw [kɔ] N graznido *m*; VI graznar

CD [compact disc] [sídí] N CD *m*, disco compacto *m*; **— player** reproductor de discos compactos *m*; **—-ROM** CD-ROM *m*

cease [sis] VI cesar; VT interrumpir; N **—-fire** alto el fuego *m*; *Am* cese el fuego *m*

ceaseless [sísłɪs] ADJ incesante

cedar [sídə-] N cedro *m*

cede [sid] VT ceder

ceiling [sílɪŋ] N techo *m*, cielo raso *m*; (cap) tope *m*; (sky) altura máxima *f*

celebrate [séləbret] VI/VT celebrar, festejar

celebrated [séləbreɒɪd] ADJ célebre

celebration [seləbréʃən] N (action) celebración *f*, festejo *m*; (festivities) fiesta *f*

celebratory [səlébrətori] ADJ festivo

celebrity [səlébrɪɒi] N celebridad *f*

celery [séləri] N apio *m*

celestial [saléstʃəł] ADJ celeste; (heavenly) celestial; **— body** astro *m*

celibate [séləbɪt] ADJ célibe

cell [sɛł] N (room) celda *f*; (structural) célula *f*; **— biology** citología *f*

cellar [sélə-] N sótano *m*; (for wine) bodega *f*, cava *f*

cello [tʃélo] N violonchelo *m*

cellophane [séləfen] N celofán *m*

cellular [séljələ-] ADJ celular; **— phone** celular *m*; *Sp* móvil *m*

cellulite [séljəlaɪt] N celulitis *f*

celluloid [séljəɔɪd] N celuloide *m*

cellulose [séljəlos] N celulosa *f*

cement [sɪmɛ́nt] N cemento *m*; (glue) adhesivo *m*; **— mixer** hormigonera *f*; VI/VT cementar

cemetery [sémɪtɛri] N cementerio *m*

censor [sénsə-] N censor -ora *mf*; VT censurar

censorship [sénsə-ʃɪp] N censura *f*

censure [sénʃə-] N censura *f*; VT censurar

census [sénsəs] N censo *m*; **to take a —** censar

cent [sɛnt] N centavo *m*, céntimo *m*

centennial [sɛnténiəł] ADJ & N centenario *m*

center [séntə-] N centro *m*; (in basketball) centro *m*, *Am* pivot *m*; **— forward** (soccer) ariete *mf*; **— of gravity** centro de gravedad *m*; VI/VT centrar[se]

centigrade [séntɪgred] ADJ centígrado

centimeter [séntəmɪɒə-] N centímetro *m*

centipede [séntəpid] N ciempiés *m*

central [séntrəł] ADJ central; (downtown) céntrico; N central de teléfonos *f*; **— heating** calefacción central *f*; **— nervous system** sistema nervioso central *m*; **— processing unit** unidad central de proceso/procesamiento *f*

Central [séntrəł] ADJ **— African Republic** República Centroafricana *f*; **— America** Centroamérica *f*; **— American** centroamericano

centralize [séntrəlaɪz] VI/VT centralizar[se]; **to be/become —d** centralizarse

centrifugal [sɛntrífəgəł] ADJ centrífugo

centripetal [sɛntrípɪdł] ADJ centrípeto

century [séntʃəri] N siglo *m*

CEO [chief executive officer] [sííó] N *Am* director -ora general *mf*, *Sp* consejero -ra, delegado -da *mf*

ceramic [sərǽmɪk] ADJ cerámico; N **—s** cerámica *f*

cereal [síriəł] N (breakfast food) cereal *m*; (the grain itself) grano *m*; ADJ cereal

cerebral [sərí́brəł] ADJ cerebral; **— concussion** conmoción cerebral *f*; **— cortex** corteza cerebral *f*; **— embolism** embolia cerebral *f*; **— hemorrhage** hemorragia cerebral *f*; **— palsy** parálisis cerebral *f*

ceremonial [sɛrəmóniəł] ADJ & N ceremonial *m*

ceremonious [sɛrəmóniəs] ADJ ceremonioso

ceremony [sérəmoni] N ceremonia *f*

certain [sɝ́tn̩] ADJ seguro; **— people** determinadas personas *f pl*; **— rules are inviolable** ciertas/determinadas reglas son inviolables; **death and taxes are —** lo único seguro son los impuestos y la muerte; **he's — to come** seguro que viene; **it is — that it rained** seguro que llovió

certainly [sɝ́tn̩li] ADV seguramente, sin duda; **she — gets her way** no cabe duda de que se sale con la suya; INTERJ ¡cómo no!

certainty [sɝ́tn̩ti] N certeza *f*, certidumbre *f*

certificate [sɚ́tífɪkɪt] N certificado *m*; **— of baptism** fe de bautismo *f*; **— of deposit** certificado de depósito *m*

certification [sɚ́dəfɪkéʃən] N certificación *f*

certify [sɝ́dəfaɪ] VT certificar; **certified check** cheque certificado *m*; **certified mail** correo certificado *m*; **certified public accountant** contador -ora público -ca *mf*

cervical [sɝ́vɪkəł] ADJ cervical

cervix [sɝ́vɪks] N (neck) cerviz *f*; (uterine) cérvix *m*, cuello uterino *m*

cesarean section [sɪzérɪənsékʃən] N cesárea *f*

cessation [sɛséʃən] N cese *m*

cesspool [sésputł] N pozo séptico *m*, fosa séptica *f*

Chad [tʃæd] N Chad *m*

Chadian [tʃǽdɪən] ADJ & N chadiano -na *mf*

chafe [tʃef] VI/VT rozar[se]; N rozadura *f*

chaff [tʃæf] N ahechaduras *f pl*

chagrin [ʃəgrín] N mortificación *f*; VT mortificar

chain [tʃen] N cadena *f*; **— reaction** reacción en cadena *f*; **— saw** sierra *f*; **— smoker** persona que fuma como una chimenea *f*; **— store** tienda de cadena *f*; VI/VT encadenar[se]

chair [tʃɛr] N silla *f*; (academic) cátedra *f*; (of a meeting) presidente -ta *mf*; (of a department) jefe -fa *mf*; **—man** presidente *m*, director *m*, jefe *m*; **—manship** dirección *f*; **—person** presidente -ta *mf*, jefe -fa *mf*; **—woman** presidenta *f*, jefa *f*

chalk [tʃɔk] N (substance) caliza *f*; (piece) tiza *f*; **—board** pizarrón *m*, pizarra *f*, tablero *m*; VT marcar con tiza; **to — up** (attribute) atribuir; (score) marcar

chalky [tʃɔ́ki] ADJ de/con/como tiza

challenge [tʃǽlɪnʤ] N desafío *m*, reto *m*; (of a jury) recusación *f*; VT (defy) desafiar, retar; (take exception) cuestionar, disputar; (recuse) recusar; **to be vertically —d** ser muy bajito

chamber [tʃémbə-] N (legislative) cámara *f*; (in a palace) aposento *m*; (of a cannon) recámara *f*; **—maid** camarera *f*, mucama *f*; **— music** música de cámara *f*; **— of commerce** cámara de comercio *f*; **— pot** orinal *m*; **—s** (of a judge) despacho *m*

chameleon [kəmílɪjən] N camaleón *m*

chamois [ʃǽmi] N gamuza *f*

champagne [ʃæmpén] N champán *m*, champaña *mf*

champion [tʃǽmpɪən] N campeón -ona *mf*; (of a cause) defensor -ora *mf*, paladín *m*; VT defender

championship [tʃǽmpɪənʃɪp] N campeonato *m*

chance [tʃæns] N (opportunity) oportunidad *f*; (probability) probabilidad *f*; (unpredictable element) casualidad *f*, azar *m*; **by —** por casualidad; **game of —** juego de azar *m*; **to take a —** correr riesgo, arriesgarse; ADJ casual; VI arriesgarse; **we —d to meet him at the bar** nos encontramos con él en el bar por casualidad

chancellor [tʃǽnsələ-] N (chief minister) canciller *m*; (of a university) rector -ora de universidad *mf*

chandelier [ʃændəlír] N araña de luces *f*

change [tʃenʤ] VT cambiar; **to — clothes** cambiarse de ropa; **to — into** transformar[se] en; **to — trains** cambiar de tren; N cambio *m*; (money returned) vuelta *f*; *Am* vuelto *m*; (fresh clothes) muda de ropa *f*; **— of heart** cambio de opinión *m*; **— over** (tennis) cambio de lado *m*; **—-up** (baseball) cambio *m*, cambio de velocidad *m*

changeable [tʃéinʤəbəł] ADJ (variable) cambiante, variable; (fickle) inconstante, tornadizo; **— silk** seda tornasolada *f*

channel [tʃǽnł] N canal *m*; (bed of stream) cauce *m*; VT canalizar, encauzar

chant [tʃænt] N (plain song) canto llano *m*; (hymn) cántico *m*; (repeated slogan) cantinela *f*; VI/VT (sing) cantar; (repeat a slogan) corear
chaos [kéɑs] N caos *m*
chaotic [keɑ́ɒɪk] ADJ caótico
chap [tʃæp] VI/VT cuartear[se], agrietar[se]; **—ped lips** labios agrietados *m pl*; **—stick®** crema para los labios *f*; N (fellow) tipo *m*
chaparral [ʃæpərǽl] N chaparral *m*
chapel [tʃǽpəɫ] N capilla *f*
chaperon, chaperone [ʃǽpəron] N chaperón -ona *f*; VI ir de chaperón -ona
chaplain [tʃǽplɪn] N capellán *m*
chapter [tʃǽptɚ] N capítulo *m*
char [tʃɑr] VI/VT (reduce to ashes) carbonizar[se]; (scorch) chamuscar[se]
character [kǽrɪktɚ] N carácter *m*; (of a novel) personaje *m*; **— actor** actor de carácter *m*; **Chinese —s** caracteres chinos *m pl*; **he's quite a —** es todo un personaje; **that's out of — for him** eso no es característico de él
characteristic [kærɪktərístɪk] ADJ característico; N característica *f*; (genetic) carácter *m*
characterization [kærɪktɚɪzéʃən] N caracterización *f*
characterize [kǽrɪktərɪaɪz] VT (describe) caracterizar; (attribute) calificar
charade [ʃəréd] N farsa *f*; **—s** charada *f*
charcoal [tʃɑ́rkoɫ] N carbón de leña *m*; **— drawing** dibujo al carbón *m*
charge [tʃɑrʤ] VT (demand money) cobrar; (load) cargar; (buy on credit) cargar a cuenta; (attack) embestir; (in basketball) cargar; **to — off a loss** restar una pérdida; **to — someone with a task** encargarle a alguien una tarea; **to — with murder** acusar de homicidio; N (mission) misión *f*, encargo *m*; (accusation) cargo *m*, acusación *f*; (charge in account) cargo *m*, débito *m*; (explosives, electricity) carga *f*; (attack) embestida *f*; **— account** cuenta de crédito *f*; **— card** tarjeta de crédito *f*; **there will be a — for delivery** se cobra entrega a domicilio; **to be in — of** estar a cargo de; **under my —** a mi cargo
charger [tʃɑ́rʤɚ] N (for a battery) cargador *m*; (horse) corcel *m*
chariot [tʃǽrɪət] N carro de guerra *m*
charisma [kərízmə] N carisma *m*
charitable [tʃǽrɪtəbəɫ] ADJ caritativo
charity [tʃǽrɪtɪ] N (virtue, aid to the poor) caridad *f*; (institution) institución benéfica *f*, institución de beneficencia *f*; **to give to —** dar dinero a las instituciones benéficas; **to live on —** vivir de la caridad
charlatan [ʃɑ́rləɫən] N charlatán -ana *mf*
charm [tʃɑrm] N (attractiveness) encanto *m*, saleroso *m*; (trinket) dije *m*; (spell) sortilegio *m*, hechizo *m*; (amulet) talismán *m*, amuleto *m*; VT (delight) encantar; (influence) hechizar, subyugar
charming [tʃɑ́rmɪŋ] ADJ encantador, saleroso; *Sp* majo
chart [tʃɑrt] N (table) tabla *f*; (graph) gráfica *f*; (marine map) carta *f*; (of musical hits) lista de éxitos *f*; VT (in a table) tabular; (in a graph) graficar; (a region) cartografiar; **to — a course** trazar una ruta
charter [tʃɑ́rtɚ] N (of a city) fuero *m*; (of an organization) estatuto *m*; (document granting rights) constitución *f*, carta *f*; (hire) flete *m*; **— flight** [vuelo] chárter *m*; **— member** socio -cia fundador -ora *mf*; VT (a corporation) aprobar los estatutos; (a flight) fletar
chase [tʃes] VT (hunt) cazar; (follow rapidly) perseguir; **to — after** correr tras; **to — away** ahuyentar; N caza *f*, persecución *f*
chasm [kǽzəm] N sima *f*
chassis [tʃǽsɪ] N chasis *m*, bastidor *m*
chaste [tʃest] ADJ casto, honesto
chastise [tʃǽstaɪz] VT (punish) castigar; (criticize) criticar
chastisement [tʃǽstáɪzmənt] N (punishment) castigo *m*; (criticism) crítica *f*
chastity [tʃǽstɪɒɪ] N castidad *f*, honestidad *f*
chat [tʃæt] N charla *f*; *Mex* plática *f*; **— room** sala de chat *f*; VI charlar; *Mex* platicar; VI chatear
chattel [tʃǽdɫ] N (movable property) bien mueble *m*; (slave) esclavo -va *mf*
chatter [tʃǽɒɚ] VI (jabber) cotorrear, parlotear; VT (click rapidly) castañetear; N (of speech) cotorreo *m*, parloteo *m*; (of teeth) castañeteo *m*; **—box** charlatán -ana *mf*, cotorra *f*
chauffeur [ʃofɚ] N chófer *m*
chauvinism [ʃóvənɪzəm] N (nationalist) chovinismo *m*; (sexist) machismo *m*
cheap [tʃip] ADJ (economical) barato; (stingy) avaro; **life is — there** la vida no vale nada allí; **talk is —** hablar no cuesta nada; **to feel —** sentirse despreciable; N **— shot** golpe bajo *m*; **—skate** tacaño -ña *mf*
cheapen [tʃípən] VI/VT (lower in price) abaratar[se]; VT (lower in esteem) desvalorizar
cheapness [tʃípnɪs] N (low price) baratura *f*; (stinginess) avaricia *f*
cheat [tʃit] N tramposo -sa *mf*, fullero -ra *mf*; VT engañar; **to — at cards** hacer trampa en/a las cartas, trampear; **to — on a test** copiar; **to — on one's spouse** engañar a la pareja de uno
check [tʃek] VT (stop) refrenar; (restrain) reprimir; (leave luggage) facturar; (leave a coat) dejar; (verify) comprobar, verificar; *Am* chequear; *Mex* checar; (in chess) dar jaque; **to — against** cotejar con; **to — into a hotel** registrarse; **to — into something** averiguar algo; **to — off** puntear; **to — out a book** sacar [prestado] un libro; **to — up on**

controlar; **that —s out** lo hemos comprobado; N (bank) cheque *m*; (means of restraint) control *m*; (ticket) ficha *f*; (mark) marca *f*; (in a restaurant) cuenta *f*; (in fabric) cuadro *m*; (checked fabric) tela a cuadros *f*; (examination) comprobación *f*; (in chess) jaque *m*; **—book** chequera *f*, talonario *m*; **—ing account** cuenta corriente *f*; **— kiting** giro de cheques sin fondos *m*; **—list** lista de control *f*; **—mate** jaque mate *m*; **—out counter** caja *f*; **—point** control *m*, retén *m*; **—room** guardarropa *m*; **— stub** talón *m*; **—up** examen físico *m*

checker [tʃékə˞] N (on a fabric) cuadro *m*; (on a checkerboard) casilla *f*; (game piece) ficha *f*; (cashier) cajero -ra *mf*; (person who checks) verificador -ora *mf*; **—board** tablero *m*; **—ed cloth** tela a cuadros *f*; **—ed past** pasado oscuro *m*; **—s** juego de damas *m*; VT cuadricular

cheek [tʃik] N (on face) mejilla *f*; *Am* cachete *m*; (impudence) descaro *m*; (of buttocks) nalga *f*; **—bone** pómulo *m*

cheer [tʃɪr] N (shout) viva *m*, vítor *m*; (applause) aplausos *m pl*; (encouragement) ánimo *m*; (joy) alegría *f*; **—leader** animador -ora *mf*; *Am* porrista *mf*; INTERJ **—s!** ¡salud! VI/VT vitorear; **to — on** dar ánimo; **to — up** animar[se]

cheerful [tʃɪrfəɫ] ADJ (person) risueño, alegre; (room) alegre

cheerfulness [tʃɪrfəɫnɪs] N alegría *f*

cheerless [tʃírlɪs] ADJ triste, sombrío

cheese [tʃiz] N queso *m*; **—burger** hamburguesa con queso *f*; **—cake** tarta de queso *f*

cheesy [tʃízi] ADJ (of cheese) de queso; (cheap) barato; (uncool) *Sp* hortera

cheetah [tʃíːə] N guepardo *m*

chef [ʃɛf] N chef *mf*

chemical [kémɪkəɫ] ADJ químico; **— engineering** ingeniería química *f*; **— warfare** guerra química *f*; N producto químico *m*

chemist [kémɪst] N químico -ca *f*

chemistry [kémɪstri] N química *f*

chemotheraphy [kimoθérəpi] N quimioterapia *f*

cherish [tʃérɪʃ] VT apreciar; **I — the memory of him** tengo muy buenos recuerdos de él

cherry [tʃéri] N cereza *f*; **— tree** cerezo *m*

chess [tʃɛs] N ajedrez *m*; **—board** tablero de ajedrez *m*

chest [tʃɛst] N (body part) pecho *m*; (box) arca *f*; **— of drawers** cómoda *f*

chestnut [tʃésnʌt] N castaña *f*; **— tree** castaño *m*; ADJ castaño; (horse) zaino

chew [tʃu] VT (food) masticar; (nonfood) mascar; **—ing gum** goma de mascar *f*; *Am* chicle *m*; **to — a hole** hacer un agujero a mordiscones; **to — out** reprender; **to — over** meditar sobre; **to — up** romper a mordiscones; N mascada *f*, bocado *m*

chewy [tʃúi] ADJ correoso

chic [ʃik] ADJ & N chic *m*

chick [tʃɪk] N (young chicken) pollito *m*; (young bird) pichón *m*; (young woman) *fam* chavala *f*, tía *f*; **—pea** garbanzo *m*

chicken [tʃíkɪn] N gallina *f*; (flesh) pollo *m*; **— coop** gallinero *m*; **—-hearted** cobarde; **— pox** varicela *f*

chicory [tʃíkəri] N achicoria *f*

chide [tʃaɪd] VT regañar

chief [tʃif] N jefe *m*; (of a tribe) cacique *m*; **— of staff** (military) jefe del estado mayor *m*; (of a division) secretario -ria general *mf*; ADJ principal; **— justice** presidente de la Suprema Corte de los Estados Unidos *m*

chieftain [tʃíftən] N cacique *m*

chiffon [ʃɪfán] N chifón *m*

chigger [tʃígə˞] N nigua *f*

chilblain [tʃíɫblen] N sabañón *m*

child [tʃaɪɫd] N (young person) niño -ña *mf*; (offspring) hijo -ja *mf*; **—birth** parto *m*, alumbramiento *m*; **—like** infantil, aniñado; **—proof** a prueba de niños; **—'s play** cosa de niños *f*; **to be with —** estar embarazada; ADJ **of —bearing age** en edad de procrear

childhood [tʃáɪɫdhʊd] N niñez *f*, infancia *f*

childish [tʃáɪɫdɪʃ] ADJ infantil, pueril

childless [tʃáɪɫdlɪs] ADJ sin hijos

Chile [tʃíli] N Chile *m*

Chilean [tʃíliən] ADJ & N chileno -na *mf*

chili, chile [tʃíli] N (pepper) chile *m*, ají *m*; (meat dish) chile con carne *m*

chill [tʃɪɫ] N (coldness) frío *m*; (fear, cold with shivering) escalofrío *m*; **it had a —ing effect on the group** le cayó al grupo como un baldazo de agua fría; VI/VT enfriar[se]; **to — out** tranquilizarse, relajarse

chilly [tʃíli] ADJ frío

chime [tʃaɪm] N (sound) repique *m*; (instrument) carillón *m*, carrillón *m*; VI repicar; VT tañer; **to — in** intervenir [en una conversación]

chimney [tʃímni] N chimenea *f*

chimpanzee [tʃɪmpənzí] N chimpancé *m*

chin [tʃɪn] N barbilla *f*, mentón *m*

china [tʃáɪnə] N (material) porcelana *f*, china *f*; (dishes) vajilla de porcelana *f*, china *f*; **—ware** vajilla de porcelana *f*

China [tʃáɪnə] N China *f*

Chinese [tʃaɪnízˌ] ADJ chino; N (inhabitant of China) chino -na *mf*; (language) chino *m*

chink [tʃɪŋk] N grieta *f*

chip [tʃɪp] N (of wood) astilla *f*; (in glass) desportilladura *f*; (in gambling) ficha *f*; (in computers) chip *m*; **he's a — off the old block** de tal palo, tal astilla; **he has a — on his shoulder** guarda resentimientos; VI/VT (wood) astillar[se]; (glass, plaster)

desportillarse, desconchar[se]; (paint) descascarar[se]; (in golf) chipear; **to — in** contribuir; **to — a tooth** romperse un diente
chipmunk [tʃípmʌŋk] N ardilla listada *f*
chiropractic [kaɪrəprǽktɪk] ADJ quiropráctico; N quiropráctica *f*
chiropractor [káɪrəpræktɚ] N quiropráctico -ca *mf*
chirp [tʃɝp] N pío *m*, gorjeo *m*; VI/VT piar, gorjear
chisel [tʃízəl] N escoplo *m*; (for stone) cincel *m*; (for wood) formón *m*; VT cincelar; (swindle) estafar
chiseler [tʃízlɚ] N estafador -ra *mf*
chit-chat [tʃíttʃæt] N palique *m*; VI charlar
chivalrous [ʃívərəs] ADJ (of knights) caballeresco; (courteous to women) caballeroso
chivalry [ʃívəri] N caballerosidad *f*
chloride [klóraɪd] N cloruro *m*
chlorine [klórin] N cloro *m*
chloroform [klórəfɔrm] N cloroformo *m*
chlorophyl, chlorophyll [klórəfɪl] N clorofila *f*
chocolate [tʃáklɪt] N chocolate *m*; (bar) chocolatina *f*; **— pot** chocolatera *f*
choice [tʃɔɪs] N (act of selecting, thing selected) selección *f*; (alternative) opción *f*; **to have no other —** no tener más remedio; ADJ selecto
choir [kwaɪr] N coro *m*
choke [tʃok] VI/VT (suffocate) ahogar[se]; (strangle) estrangular[se]; (on food) atragantarse, atorarse; (obstruct) tapar[se]; VI (in sports) bloquearse; **I'm all —d up** estoy muy conmovido; **to — back/down** contener; N (act of choking on something) atragantamiento *m*; (act of choking someone) estrangulación *f*; (device in cars) obturador *m*; (in sports) bloqueo *m*
cholera [kálərə] N cólera *m*
choleric [kálərɪk] ADJ colérico
cholesterol [kəlɛ́stərɔl] N colesterol *m*
choose [tʃuz] VI/VT elegir, seleccionar, escoger; **to — to** optar por
choosy [tʃúzi] ADJ quisquilloso
chop [tʃɑp] VI/VT cortar; **to — down** talar; **to — off** mochar, tronchar; **to — up** picar; N (act of chopping) golpe *m*; (cut of meat) chuleta *f*; **—s** morro *m*; **—stick** palillo *m*
choppy [tʃápi] ADJ picado, agitado
choral [kɔ́rəl] ADJ coral
chord [kɔrd] N (mathematical) cuerda *f*; (musical) acorde *m*; **it struck a — with me** me conmovió
chore [tʃɔr] N tarea *f*, faena *f*, quehacer *m*; **it's such a —** es un trabajo horrible
choreography [kɔriágrəfi] N coreografía *f*
chorus [kɔ́rəs] N coro *m*
chose [tʃoz] *see* choose
chosen [tʃózən] ADJ **my — profession** la profesión de mi preferencia; **the — one** el elegido, la elegida
chosen [tʃózən] *see* choose
christen [krísən] VT bautizar
Christendom [krísəndəm] N cristianismo *m*
christening [krísənɪŋ] N bautizo *m*, bautismo *m*
Christian [krístʃən] ADJ & N cristiano -na *mf*; **— name** nombre de pila *m*
Christianity [krɪstʃiǽnɪdi] N cristianismo *m*
Christmas [krísməs] N Navidad *f*, Pascua de Navidad *f*; **— card** tarjeta de Navidad *f*; **— Eve** Nochebuena *f*; **— gift** regalo de Navidad *m*; **— tree** árbol de Navidad *m*; ADJ navideño
chrome [krom] N cromo *m*; ADJ cromado
chromium [krómiəm] N cromo *m*
chromosome [króməsom] N cromosoma *m*
chronic [kránɪk] ADJ crónico
chronicle [kránɪkəl] N crónica *f*; VT registrar
chronicler [kránɪklɚ] N cronista *mf*
chronological [krɑnl̩ádʒɪkəl] ADJ cronológico
chronology [krənálədʒi] N cronología *f*
chronometer [krənámɪdɚ] N cronómetro *m*
chrysalis [krísəlɪs] N crisálida *f*
chrysanthemum [krɪsǽnθəməm] N crisantemo *m*
chubby [tʃábi] ADJ rechoncho, gordito
chuck [tʃʌk] N (cut of meat) paletilla *f*; VT (to throw) lanzar; (to discard) tirar, botar
chuckle [tʃʌ́kəl] N risita *f*; VI reírse levemente
chum [tʃʌm] N compinche *mf*
chunk [tʃʌŋk] N trozo *m*, pedazo *m*; **a — of cash** un montón de plata
church [tʃɝtʃ] N iglesia *f*; **—man** clérigo *m*
churn [tʃɝn] N mantequera *f*; VI/VT (make butter) batir; (agitate) agitar, revolver
CIA [Central Intelligence Agency] [síáié] N CIA *f*
cicada [sɪkéɪdə] N chicharra *f*
cider [sáɪdɚ] N (alcoholic) sidra *f*; (non-alcoholic) *Am* jugo de manzana *m*; *Sp* zumo de manzana *m*
cigar [sɪgár] N puro *m*, habano *m*; **— store** tabaquería *f*; **close, but no —** bien, pero te quedaste corto
cigarette [sɪgərét] N cigarrillo *m*; *Sp* pitillo *m*; *Am* cigarro *m*; **— case** cigarrera *f*; *Sp* pitillera *f*; **— holder** boquilla *f*; **— lighter** encendedor *m*
cinch [sɪntʃ] N (for a saddle) cincha *f*; (something easy) pan comido *m*; (favorite) favorito -ta *mf*; VT cinchar
cinder [síndɚ] N ceniza *f*, rescoldo *m*
cinema [sínəmə] N cine *m*
cinematography [sɪnəmətágrəfi] N cinematografía *f*
cinnamon [sínəmən] N canela *f*; **— tree** canelo *f*
cipher [sáɪfɚ] N cifra *f*, guarismo *m*; VI/VT cifrar[se]
circle [sɝ́kəl] N círculo *m*; (literary) ámbito *m*,

círculo *m*; VT (draw a circle) encerrar en un círculo; VI (go around) dar una vuelta

circuit [sɜ́·kɪt] N circuito *m*; — **board** circuito impreso *m*; — **breaker** cortacircuitos *m sg*

circuitry [sɜ́·kɪtrɪ] N circuitería *f*

circular [sɜ́·kjələ·] ADJ circular; — **saw** sierra circular *f*; N circular *f*

circulate [sɜ́·kjəlet] VI circular; VT (distribute) poner en circulación

circulation [sɜ·kjəléʃən] N circulación *f*

circulatory [sɜ́·kjələtɔrɪ] ADJ circulatorio; — **system** aparato circulatorio *m*

circumcise [sɜ́·kəmsaɪz] VT circuncidar

circumference [sə·kámfə·əns] N circunferencia *f*

circumlocution [sɜ·kəmlokjúʃən] N circunlocución *f*, rodeo *m*

circumscribe [sɜ·kəmskráɪb] VT circunscribir

circumspect [sɜ́·kəmspɛkt] ADJ circunspecto

circumstance [sɜ́·kəmstəns] N circunstancia *f*; —**s** condiciones financieras *f pl*

circumstantial [sɜ·kəmstǽnʃəł] ADJ circunstancial; — **evidence** pruebas circunstanciales *f pl*

circumvent [sɜ·kəmvɛ́nt] VT evitar, obviar

circus [sɜ́·kəs] N circo *m*

cirrhosis [sɪróʊsɪs] N cirrosis *f*

cirrus [sírəs] N cirro *m*

cistern [sístə·n] N cisterna *f*, aljibe *m*

citadel [sídədɛł] N ciudadela *f*

citation [saɪtéʃən] N (summons) citación *f*; (quote, quotation) cita *f*; (commendation for bravery) mención *f*

cite [saɪt] VT (quote, summon) citar; (comment on) mencionar

citizen [sídɪzən] N (of a nation) ciudadano -na *mf*; (of a city or region) habitante *mf*

citizenship [sídɪzənʃɪp] N ciudadanía *f*

citrus [sítrəs] ADJ & N cítrico *m*

city [sídɪ] N ciudad *f*; — **council** concejo *m*; — **hall** ayuntamiento *m*, alcaldía *f*; — **planning** urbanismo *m*; ADJ municipal, urbano

civic [sívɪk] ADJ cívico; N —**s** educación cívica *f*

civil [sívəł] ADJ (civilian) civil; (polite) cortés; — **disobedience** desobediencia civil *f*; — **engineer** ingeniero -ra civil *mf*; — **rights** derechos civiles *m pl*; — **service** administración pública *f*; — **war** guerra civil *f*

civilian [sɪvíljən] ADJ & N civil *mf*

civility [sɪvílɪtɪ] N civilidad *f*, cortesía *f*

civilization [sɪvəlɪzéʃən] N civilización *f*

civilize [sívəlaɪz] VT civilizar

clad [klæd] ADJ vestido

claim [klem] VT (demand) reclamar, reivindicar; (assert) sostener, pretender; **to — to be** pretender ser; **to — responsibility** atribuirse la responsabilidad; **to — a mine** denunciar una mina; N (demand) reclamación *f*, reclamo *m*; (assertion) afirmación *f*; (right) derecho *m*, título *m*; (on insurance) demanda *f*, denuncia *f*

claimant [klémənt] N demandante *mf*, reclamante *mf*; (to the throne) pretendiente *mf*

clairvoyant [klɛrvɔ́ɪənt] ADJ & N clarividente *mf*

clam [klæm] N almeja *f*; VI **to — up** callarse

clamber [klǽmbə·] VI/VT (climb with effort) trepar con dificultad; (climb on all fours) subir gateando

clammy [klǽmɪ] ADJ frío y húmedo

clamor [klǽmə·] N clamor *m*, vocerío *m*; VI clamar, vociferar

clamorous [klǽmə·əs] ADJ clamoroso

clamp [klæmp] N (support) grapa *f*; (vice) tornillo *m*; (wrap-around) abrazadera *f*; (medical) pinza *f*; VT sujetar; **to — down on** reprimir

clan [klæn] N clan *m*

clandestine [klændéstɪn] ADJ clandestino

clang [klæŋ] VI sonar; N sonido metálico *m*

clap [klæp] N (tap) palmada *f*; (blow) golpe seco *m*; — **of thunder** trueno *m*; VT (on the back) palmear; (in approval) aplaudir; (a book) cerrar de golpe

clapper [klǽpə·] N badajo *m*

clarification [klærəfɪkéʃən] N aclaración *f*

clarify [klǽrəfaɪ] VT aclarar, clarificar

clarinet [klærənɛ́t] N clarinete *m*

clarity [klǽrɪtɪ] N claridad *f*

clash [klæʃ] N (noise) estruendo metálico *m*; (collision) choque *m*; (conflict) conflicto *m*, enfrentamiento *m*; VI/VT (collide) chocar; (oppose, fight) enfrentarse a; (not go with) no combinar, no pegar

clasp [klæsp] N (fastener) broche *m*, cierre *m*; (grip) apretón *m*; VT (fasten) abrochar; (grip) apretar; (embrace) abrazar, prender

class [klæs] N clase *f*; (graduation class) promoción *f*, graduación *f*; **in a — by itself** único; —**mate** compañero -ra de clase *mf*, condiscípulo -la *mf*; —**room** salón de clase *m*, aula *f*; — **struggle** lucha de clases *f*; VI/VT clasificar[se]

classic [klǽsɪk] ADJ & N clásico -ca *mf*

classical [klǽsɪkəł] ADJ clásico

classicism [klǽsɪsɪzəm] N clasicismo *m*

classification [klæsəfɪkéʃən] N clasificación *f*

classify [klǽsəfaɪ] VT clasificar; **classified ad** anuncio clasificado *m*

classy [klǽsɪ] ADJ elegante

clatter [klǽdə·] N (noise) estrépito *m*; (movement) traqueteo *m*; VI (make noise) causar estrépito; (move) traquetear

clause [klɔz] N cláusula *f*

claustrophobia [klɔstrəfóbiə] N claustrofobia *f*

claustrophobic [klɔstrəfóbɪk] ADJ claustrofóbico

clavicle [klǽvɪkəł] N clavícula *f*

claw [klɔ] N (of a bear) garra *f*, zarpa *f*; (of a cat) uña *f*; (of a crab) pinza *f*; (of a hammer) orejas *f pl*; VI/VT arañar; **they —ed their way through** se abrieron paso con las uñas

clay [kle] N arcilla *f*; (for ceramics) greda *f*; (in tennis) tierra batida *f*

clean [klin] ADJ limpio; (free from impurities, not ornate) puro; (honorable) decente; —-**cut** (person) acicalado; (concept) bien definido; — **joke** broma inocente *f*; —-**shaven** afeitado; **he has a — record** no tiene antecedentes; **you'd better come —** deberías confesar; VI/VT limpiar; **he —ed me out** me limpió, me desvalijó; **to — up** (a room) limpiar, asear; (a document) pasar en limpio; (get rich) forrarse; N **—up** limpieza *f*

cleaner [klínɚ] N limpiador -ra *mf*; **—s** tintorería *f*

cleanliness [klénlɪnɪs] N limpieza *f*; (personal) aseo *m*

cleanse [klɛnz] VT limpiar

cleanser [klénzɚ] N limpiador *m*

clear [klɪr] ADJ claro; (skin, conscience) limpio; (sky) despejado; (path) libre; —-**cut** (clearly defined) bien definido; (obvious) claro; —-**headed** lúcido; — **profit** ganancia neta *f*; **to keep — of someone** evitar a alguien; **to pass — through** pasar de lado a lado; N **to be in the —** estar libre de culpa; VT (the mind, confusion, voice) aclarar[se]; (a road, one's reputation, computer screen) limpiar; (of criminal charges) absolver; (of suspicion) eximir; (liquid) clarificar; (a legislative bill, plan) aprobar, obtener autorización para; (land for farming) desmontar; (a hurdle) salvar; (a net gain) sacar; **to — the air** sincerarse; **to — the table** levantar la mesa; **to — up** (a mystery) aclarar[se]; (the sky) despejar[se]

clearance [klírəns] N (space) espacio libre *m*; (vertical) margen de altura *m*; (permission) autorización *f*; — **sale** liquidación *f*

clearing [klírɪŋ] N (terrain) claro *m*; (of checks) compensación *f*; — **house** banco de compensación *m*

cleats [klɪts] N (projection) tacos *m pl*, tapones *m pl*; (shoes) zapatos con tacos *m pl*

cleavage [klívɪʤ] N (cut) hendidura *f*; (in dress) escote *m*

cleave [kliv] VT hender[se]; **to — to** adherirse a

cleaver [klívɚ] N cuchilla *f*

clef [klɛf] N clave *f*

cleft [kleft] N hendidura *f*; ADJ hendido, partido; — **lip** labio leporino *m*; — **palate** paladar hendido *m*

clemency [klémənsi] N clemencia *f*

clench [klɛntʃ] VT agarrar, asir; (teeth, fist) apretar

clergy [klɝʤi] N clero *m*, clerecía *f*; **—man** clérigo *m*, pastor *m*; **—woman** pastora *f*

clerical [klérɪkəł] ADJ (of the clergy) clerical, eclesiástico; (of office personnel) de oficina; — **error** error de copia *m*; — **work** trabajo de escritorio *m*

clerk [klɝk] N (sales) dependiente -ta *mf*; (office) empleado -da de oficina *mf*; (court) escribiente *mf*, actuario -ria *mf*; VI trabajar como actuario -ria

clever [klévɚ] ADJ (ingenious) ingenioso; (smart) listo, vivo; (dexterous) habilidoso

cleverness [klévɚnɪs] N (ingenuity) ingenio *m*; (intelligence) inteligencia *f*, viveza *f*; (dexterity) habilidad *f*

cliché [kliʃé] N cliché *m*, muletilla *f*; *Sp* tópico *m*

click [klɪk] N (sound) clic *m*, chasquido *m*; (sound of heels) taconeo *m*; (on a computer) clic *m*, pulsación *f*; VI chascar; (on a computer) hacer clic, oprimir, pulsar; (heels) taconear; VT chascar, chasquear; — **and drag** pulsar y arrastrar

clickable image [klíkəbəłímɪʤ] N imagen en donde se puede pulsar *f*

client [kláɪənt] N (of professional or store) cliente -ta *mf*; (of social service) beneficiario -ria *mf*

clientele [klaɪəntɛ́ł] N clientela *f*

cliff [klɪf] N precipicio *m*, despeñadero *m*; (by the sea) acantilado *m*

climate [kláɪmɪt] N clima *m*

climatic [klaɪmǽɾɪk] ADJ climático

climax [kláɪmæks] N clímax *m*, punto culminante *m*; VI culminar, alcanzar el clímax

climb [klaɪm] N (ascent) subida *f*; (in alpinism) escalada *f*; VI/VT (ascend) subir; (ascend with effort) trepar[se] [a], encaramar[se] [a]; VT (a mountain, wall) escalar; **to — down** bajar

climber [kláɪmɚ] N (in alpinism) escalador -ora *mf*; (plant) trepadora *f*

clinch [klɪntʃ] VT (resolve) rematar; (hammer down) remachar; (hug, in boxing) trabar; (secure) sujetar; (finalize) cerrar; N (nail) remache *m*; (embrace) abrazo *m*; (in boxing) clinch *m*

cling [klɪŋ] VI (to stick to) pegarse; (to hold onto) aferrarse

clinic [klínɪk] N clínica *f*; (workshop) taller *m*

clinical [klínɪkəł] ADJ clínico; — **trial** ensayo clínico *m*

clink [klɪŋk] N tintín *m*; VI tintinear

clip [klɪp] VT (cut) cortar; (trim) recortar; (shear) esquilar; (shorten) acortar; (hit) tocar; (fasten) abrochar; (attach paper) sujetar con un clip; N (fastener) gancho *m*; (for paper) clip *m*; (of cartridge) cargador *m*; (brooch) broche *m*; **—board** portapapeles *m sg*

clipper [klípɚ] N (shearer) esquilador -ra *mf*; **—s** (scissors) tijeras *f pl*; (hair trimmer)

maquinilla *f*
clipping [klípɪŋ] N recorte *m*
clique [klɪk] N (political) camarilla *f*; (in school) pandilla *f*
cloak [klok] N capa *f*; (military) capote *m*; **—room** guardarropa *m*; VT (put a cloak on) vestirse con una capa; (hide) encubrir
clock [klɑk] N reloj *m*; **— -making** relojería *f*; **— radio** radio reloj *f*; **—work** maquinaria de reloj *f*; **like —work** con precisión, sin falta; VT **you swim and I'll — you** tú nadas y yo te tomo el tiempo; **the police —ed him at 90 mph** la policía lo pescó haciendo noventa millas por hora
clockwise [klákwaɪz] ADV en el sentido de las manecillas de reloj
clod [klɑd] N (piece of dirt) terrón *m*, pelotón *m*; (dolt) tonto -ta *mf*, necio -cia *mf*
clog [klɑg] VI/VT obstruir[se], tapar[se]; N (shoe) zueco *m*; **— dance** baile zapateado *m*
cloister [klɔ́ɪstə-] N claustro *m*; (monastery) monasterio *m*; VT enclaustrar
clone [klon] N clon *m*; VT clonar
cloning [klónɪŋ] N clonaje *m*, clonación *f*
close[1] [kloz] VI/VT cerrar[se]; VT (a hole) tapar; **to — an account** cerrar una cuenta; **to — a meeting** levantar una sesión; **to — down a store** clausurar una tienda; **to — in upon** (oppress) oprimir; (approach) cercar a uno; **to — out** liquidar; N fin *m*; (act of closing) cierre *m*; **at the —** al cierre
close[2] [klos] ADJ (near) cercano; (dense) tupido; (intimate) íntimo, entrañable; **— attention** mucha atención *f*; **— by** cercano, *Am* aquí nomás; **— -fought** reñido; **— -knit** muy unido; **— translation** traducción fiel *f*; **at — range** de cerca; **that was a — call** nos salvamos por poco; N **—up** primer plano *m*; ADV cerca
closed [klozd] ADJ cerrado; **— circuit** circuito cerrado *m*; **— -minded** cerrado; **— -mindedness** cerrazón *f*
closely [klósli] ADV (examine) de cerca; (resemble) mucho; (study) detenidamente; (work) estrechamente
closeness [klósnɪs] N (of location) cercanía *f*; (of friendship) intimidad *f*; (correctness) fidelidad *f*
closer [klózə-] N (baseball) relevista de cierre *mf*, cerrador -ora *mf*
closet [klázɪt] N ropero *m*, armario *m*; VI enclaustrarse; ADJ a escondidas
closure [klóʒə-] N (conclusion) cierre *m*; (sense of completeness) clausura *f*
clot [klɑt] VI/VT coagular[se]; N coágulo *m*, cuajarón *m*
cloth [klɔθ] N tela *f*, tejido *m*; (wool) paño *m*; ADJ de tela; **— bound** encuadernado en tela; **man of the —** clérigo *m*
clothe [kloð] VT vestir; N **—s** ropa *f*; **—sline** tendedero *m*; **—spin** pinza *f*
clothier [klóðjə-] N comerciante en ropa o paño *mf*
clothing [klóðɪŋ] N ropa *f*
clotting [klάɒɪŋ] N coagulación *f*
cloud [klaʊd] N nube *f*; **—burst** chaparrón *m*, aguacero *m*; VT nublar, anublar; (make indistinct, place under suspicion) enturbiar; **to — up** nublarse, anublarse; **to be on — nine** estar en el séptimo cielo; **under a —** bajo sospecha
cloudiness [kláʊɒɪnɪs] N nebulosidad *f*, nubosidad *f*
cloudless [kláʊdlɪs] ADJ despejado
cloudy [kláʊɒɪ] ADJ nublado; *Sp* nuboso; (gloomy) sombrío
clout [klaʊt] N influencia *f*
clove [klov] N clavo *m*; **— of garlic** diente de ajo *m*
cloven [klóvən] ADJ hendido; **— -hoofed** patihendido
clover [klóvə-] N trébol *m*; **—leaf** trébol *m*; **to be in —** vivir en el lujo
clown [klaʊn] N payaso *m*; VI payasear, bufonear
cloy [klɔɪ] VI/VT (to satiate) hastiar; (to be too sweet for) repugnar
club [klʌb] N (society, nightclub) club *m*; (stick) porra *f*, garrote *m*; (suit of cards) basto *m*; **—foot** pie zambo *m*; **—house** casa de club *f*; VT aporrear
cluck [klʌk] VI cloquear; N cloqueo *m*
clue [klu] N pista *f*, indicio *m*; **to have no —** no tener ni noción
clueless [klúlɪs] ADJ (absent-minded) despistado; (uninformed) en ayunas
clump [klʌmp] N (of bushes) matorral *m*; (of trees) arboleda *f*; VI/VT apiñar[se]
clumsiness [klʌ́mzɪnɪs] N torpeza *f*
clumsy [klʌ́mzi] ADJ torpe, desmañado, chambón; *Sp* patoso
clung [klʌŋ] *see* cling
clunker [klʌ́ŋkə-] N cacharro *m*
cluster [klʌ́stə-] N grupo *m*; (of grapes) racimo *m*; VI/VT agrupar[se], arracimar[se]
clutch [klʌtʃ] N (in a car) embrague *m*; **— pedal** pedal del embrague *m*; **to step on the —** pisar el embrague; **—es** garras *f pl*; VT (seize) asir; (hold) apretar
clutter [klʌ́ɒə-] N desparramo *m*, desorden *m*, confusión *f*; VT **books —ed her desk** tenía libros desparramados por todo el escritorio
coach [kotʃ] N (carriage) coche *m*, carruaje *m*, carroza *f*; (bus) autobús *m*; (in sports) entrenador -ra *mf*; (in soccer) técnico -ca *mf*, director -ora técnico -ca *mf*; (in air travel) clase turista *f*; (tutor) profesor -ra particular *mf*; **—man** cochero *m*; VI/VT entrenar
coagulant [koǽgjələnt] ADJ & N coagulante *m*

coagulate [koǽgəlet] VI/VT coagular[se]
coagulation [koǽgəléʃən] N coagulación *f*
coal [koł] N carbón *m*; — **bin** carbonera *f*; — **tar** alquitrán *m*
coalition [kəəlíʃən] N coalición *f*
coarse [kɔrs] ADJ (fabric) burdo, basto; (sand) grueso; (manners, language) grosero, tosco, rudo
coarseness [kórsnɪs] N (fabric) bastedad *f*; (language, manners) tosquedad *f*, rudeza *f*; (of a joke) chocarrería *f*
coast [kost] N costa *f*; — **Guard** Guardia Costera *f*; —**line** costa *f*; ADJ & ADV —**-to-**— de costa a costa; VI (on a sled) deslizar[se]; (in a car, on a bike) tirarse por una bajada; **he —ed through medical school** la Facultad de Medicina le resultó muy fácil
coastal [kóstl] ADJ costero
coat [kot] N abrigo *m*; (of paint) capa *f*, mano *f*; (on animals) pelaje *m*; — **of arms** escudo de armas *m*, blasón *m*; — **rack** percha *f*, perchero *m*; —**tail** faldón *m*; VT cubrir; (with paint) recubrir, dar una mano a; (with grease) engrasar; (with soap) enjabonar; (with sugar) bañar
coax [koks] VT persuadir con halagos, engatusar
coaxial cable [koǽksiəłkébəł] N cable coaxial *m*
cob [kɑb] N mazorca *f*, panoja *f*; —**web** telaraña *f*
cobalt [kóbɔłt] N cobalto *m*
cobbler [kɑ́blɚ] N (person who repairs shoes) zapatero -ra *mf*, remendón -ona *mf*; (dessert) budín de bizcocho y fruta *m*
cobblestone [kɑ́bəłston] N adoquín *m*
cobra [kóbrə] N cobra *f*
cocaine [kokén] N cocaína *f*
coccyx [kɑ́ksɪks] N cóccix *m*
cock [kɑk] N (rooster) gallo *m*; (male bird) macho de ave de corral *m*; (faucet) llave *f*; (gun part) martillo *m*; —**fight** riña de gallos *f*; —**pit** (for cockfights) gallera *f*; (in an airplane) cabina *f*; —**scomb** cresta de gallo *f*; ADJ —**sure** gallito; VT (a gun) amartillar; (one's head) ladear
cock-a-doodle-doo [kɑ́ədudl̩dú] INTERJ quiquiriquí
cockatoo [kɑ́kətu] N cacatúa *f*
cocker spaniel [kɑ́kɚspǽnjəł] N cócker *m*
cockroach [kɑ́krotʃ] N cucaracha *f*
cocktail [kɑ́ktełł] N cóctel *m*; — **party** cóctel *m*
cocky [kɑ́ki] ADJ gallito, valentón
cocoa [kóko] N (powder) cacao *m*; (drink) chocolate *m*
coconut [kɑ́kənʌt] N coco *m*
cocoon [kəkún] N capullo *m*
cod [kɑd] N *Sp* abadejo *m*; *Am* bacalao *m*; —**-liver oil** aceite de hígado de bacalao *m*
coddle [kɑ́dl̩] VT mimar
code [kod] N código *m*; — **switching** alternancia de códigos *f*; VT codificar
codeine [kódin] N codeína *f*
codger [kɑ́ʤɚ] N vejete *m*, vejancón *m*
codify [kɑ́dəfaɪ] VT codificar
coding [kódɪŋ] N codificación *f*
coed [kóɛd] ADJ mixto; N alumna universitaria *f*
coefficient [koəfíʃənt] N coeficiente *m*
coerce [koɝ́s] VT forzar, obligar
coercion [koɝ́ʒən] N coacción *f*
coexist [koɪgzíst] VI coexistir, convivir
coexistence [koɪgzístəns] N coexistencia *f*, convivencia *f*
coffee [kɔ́fi] N café *m*; (with a little milk) cortado *m*; — **bean** grano de café *m*; — **break** descanso para tomar el café *m*; — **bush** cafeto *m*; — **maker** máquina de café *f*, cafetera *f*; —**pot** cafetera *f*; — **shop** (for coffee) café *m*; (for coffee and light meals) cafetería *f*; — **table** mesa baja *f*
coffer [kɔ́fɚ] N cofre *m*
coffin [kɔ́fɪn] N ataúd *m*, féretro *m*
cog [kɑg] N diente *m*; —**wheel** rueda dentada *f*
cogent [kóʤənt] ADJ convincente
cognac [kónjæk] N coñac *m*
cognate [kɑ́gnet] ADJ & N cognado *m*
cognitive [kɑ́gnɪdɪv] ADJ cognitivo
cohabitate [kohǽbɪtet] VI cohabitar, convivir
cohabitation [kohæ̀bɪtéʃən] N cohabitación *f*, convivencia *f*
coherent [kohírənt] ADJ coherente; (sticking together) cohesivo
cohesion [kohíʒən] N cohesión *f*
coiffure [kwafjúr] N peinado *m*
coil [kɔɪł] VI/VT arrollar[se], enrollar[se]; (snake) enroscar[se]; N (roll) rollo *m*; (spiral) tirabuzón *m*; (electric) bobina *f*; — **spring** muelle en espiral *m*
coin [kɔɪn] N moneda *f*; ADJ —**-operated** de monedas; VT acuñar (also words)
coinage [kɔ́ɪnɪʤ] N acuñación *f* (also of words)
coincide [koɪnsáɪd] VI coincidir
coincidence [koínsɪdəns] N coincidencia *f*, casualidad *f*
coitus [kóɪtəs] N coito *m*
coke [kok] N (coal) cok *m*, coque *m*; (cocaine) *fam* coca *f*
cola [kólə] N gaseosa *f*
colander [kɑ́ləndɚ] N colador *m*
cold [kołd] ADJ frío; — **cream** cold cream *m*; — **cuts** fiambres *m pl*; — **fish** *fam* témpano *m*; — **snap** ola de frío *f*; — **sore** herpes *m sg*; — **war** guerra fría *f*; **to be** — tener frío; **to be out** — quedar seco; **it is** — **today** hace frío hoy; **he gave me the** — **shoulder** me hizo el vacío; **he quit** — **turkey** dejó de un día para otro; **he got** — **feet** se acobardó; N frío *m*; (illness) resfrío *m*, resfriado *m*, catarro *m*; **to catch a** — resfriarse
coldness [kɔ́łdnɪs] N frialdad *f*
colic [kɑ́lɪk] N cólico *m*

colicky [káliki] ADJ que sufre de cólico
coliseum [kɑlɪsíəm] N coliseo *m*
collaborate [kəlǽbəret] VI colaborar
collaboration [kəlæ̀bəréʃən] N colaboración *f*
collaborator [kəlǽbəreɚ] N colaborador -ora *mf*
collage [kəlɑ́ʒ] N collage *m*
collagen [kɑ́lədʒən] N colágeno *m*
collapse [kəlǽps] VI (fold into sections) plegarse; (cave in) hundirse, derrumbarse; (fail) fracasar; (faint) desmayarse; (empty of air, decline in value) colapsar[se]; N (falling in) derrumbe *m*, derrumbamiento *m*, desplome *m*; (breakdown) colapso *m*
collar [kɑ́lɚ] N (for restraining dogs, necklace) collar *m*; (of a shirt) cuello *m*; **—bone** clavícula *f*; VT acollarar; (grab by the neck) agarrar por el cuello; **I was —ed by the boss** el jefe me agarró de charla
collate [kɔ́let] VT (put in order) colacionar; (compare) cotejar
collateral [kəlǽdəəɫ] ADJ (on the side) colateral; (auxiliary) subsidiario; N garantía subsidiaria *f*; **— damage** daño colateral *m*
colleague [kɑ́lig] N colega *mf*
collect [kəlɛ́kt] VT (gather) recoger; (build a collection) coleccionar; (receive taxes) recaudar; VI/VT (receive payment) cobrar, percibir; (assemble) reunir[se]; (accumulate) acumular[se]; **to — oneself** calmarse; N **— call** llamada de cobro revertido *f*, llamada por/a cobrar *f*; **— on delivery** pago contra reembolso *m*
collection [kəlɛ́kʃən] N (set of collectibles, clothes) colección *f*; (for charity) colecta *f*; (of taxes) recaudación *f*, cobranza *f*, cobro *m*; (of data, fruit) recolección *f*; (of texts) recopilación *f*; (of water) captación *f*
collective [kəlɛ́ktɪv] ADJ colectivo; **— bargaining** convenio colectivo *m*; N colectivo *m*, colectividad *f*
collector [kəlɛ́ktɚ] N (of taxes) recaudador -ora *mf*; (of collectibles) coleccionista *mf*; (of other things) colector -ora *mf*
college [kɑ́lɪʤ] N (institution) universidad *f*; (university division) facultad *f*; (association) colegio *m*; **let's give it the old — try** esforcémonos al máximo
collegial [kəlíʤəɫ] ADJ cooperador
collegiate [kəlíʤɪt] ADJ universitario
collide [kəlɑ́ɪd] VI/VT chocar
collie [kɑ́li] N collie *m*
collision [kəlíʒən] N colisión *f*, choque *m*
colloid [kɑ́lɔɪd] N coloide *m*
colloquial [kəlókwiəɫ] ADJ coloquial; **— expression** frase familiar *f*
colloquium [kəlókwiəm] N coloquio *m*, jornada *f*
collusion [kəlúʒən] N confabulación *f*
cologne [kəlón] N colonia *f*
Colombia [kəlámbiə] N Colombia *f*
Colombian [kəlámbiən] ADJ & N colombiano -na *mf*
colon[1] [kólən] N (punctuation) dos puntos *m pl*; (bowels) colon *m*
colon[2] [kəlón] (currency of El Salvador and Costa Rica) colón *m*
colonel [kɚ́nɫ] N coronel *m*
colonial [kəlóniəɫ] ADJ colonial
colonist [kɑ́lənɪst] N (settler) colono *m*; (colonizer) colonizador -ra *mf*
colonization [kɑ̀lənɪzéʃən] N colonización *f*
colonize [kɑ́lənaɪz] VT colonizar
colonoscopy [kolənɑ́skəpi] N colonoscopia *f*
colony [kɑ́ləni] N colonia *f*
color [kɑ́lɚ] N color *m*; (colorfulness) colorido *m*; **— blindness** ceguera cromática *f*; **— monitor** monitor [a] color *m*; **— scanner** escáner color *m*; **the —s** la bandera; **he showed his true —s** se mostró tal cual era; **persons of —** gente de color *f*; **a — TV** un televisor en/a color; ADJ **—-blind** daltónico; **—fast** de colores firmes; VT (give color) colorear; (make colorful) dar colorido; (influence) influir; (blush) ruborizarse
colorectal cancer [kolərɛ́ktɫkǽnsɚ] N cáncer de colon *m*
colored [kɑ́lɚd] ADJ coloreado; (biased) sesgado
colorful [kɑ́lɚfəɫ] ADJ (full of color) colorido; (animals, plants) pintado; (eccentric) pintoresco
coloring [kɑ́lərɪŋ] N (tone) colorido *m*; (action) coloración *f*; (substance) colorante *m*
colorless [kɑ́lərɪs] ADJ (without color) incoloro; (bleached) descolorido
colossal [kəlɑ́səɫ] ADJ colosal
colostomy [kəlɑ́stəmi] N colostomía *f*
colt [koɫt] N potro *m*
column [kɑ́ləm] N columna *f*
columnist [kɑ́ləmnɪst] N columnista *mf*
coma [kómə] N coma *m*
comatose [kómətos] ADJ comatoso
comb [kom] N (for hair) peine *m*; (of a rooster) cresta *f*; (for wool) carda *f*; (for horses) almohaza *f*; (of honey) panal *m*; VT (hair) peinar; (wool) cardar; (search an area) peinar, batir; **to — one's hair** peinarse
combat[1] [kɑ́mbæt] N combate *m*
combat[2] [kəmbǽt] VI/VT combatir
combatant [kɑ́mbətnt] ADJ & N combatiente *mf*
combative [kəmbǽtɪv] ADJ combativo
combination [kɑmbənéʃən] N combinación *f*; **— lock** cerradura de combinación *f*
combine[1] [kəmbáɪn] VI/VT combinar[se]
combine[2] [kɑ́mbaɪn] N cosechadora *f*
combo [kɑ́mbo] N combo *m*
combustible [kəmbɑ́stəbəɫ] ADJ & N combustible *m*
combustion [kəmbɑ́stʃən] N combustión *f*

come [kʌm] VI venir; **an idea came to me** se me ocurrió una idea; **Christmas is coming** llega la Navidad; **milk —s from cows** la leche se saca de las vacas; **no harm will — to you** no te va a pasar nada; **the dress —s to her knees** el vestido le llega a las rodillas; **to — about** suceder; **to — across** (find) encontrar; (make an impression) parecer; **to — along** (accompany) acompañar; (appear) surgir; **how's your paper coming along?** ¿cómo va tu trabajo? **to — again** volver, volver a venir; **to — back** volver; **to make a —back** resurgir; (in sports) recuperarse; **to — down with a cold** cogerse un resfriado; **to — downstairs** bajar; **to — from** ser de; **to — in** entrar; **to — out** salir; **to — over** venir para acá; **to — to** volver en sí; **to — together** (meet) juntarse, unirse; (reach agreement) ponerse de acuerdo; **to — up** subir; **your name came up** tu nombre vino a colación; **to — up short** quedarse corto; N **—back** (reply) réplica *f*; (in sports) remontada *f*, recuperación *f*

comedian [kəmídiən] N cómico -ca *mf*, comediante *mf*

comedy [kámədi] N (genre) comedia *f*; (profession) humorismo *m*

comet [kámɪt] N cometa *m*

comfort [kámfə·t] VT reconfortar; N (feeling of ease) comodidad *f*, confort *m*, holgura *f*; (solace) consuelo *m*

comfortable [kámfə·bəbəł] ADJ cómodo, confortable; **— life** vida holgada/desahogada *f*

comforter [kámfə·bə·] N edredón *m*

comic [kámɪk] ADJ cómico, chistoso, gracioso; **— book** revista de historietas *f*, cómic *m*; **—s** tiras cómicas *f pl*, historietas *f pl*; **— strip** tira cómica *f*

comical [kámɪkəł] ADJ cómico, gracioso

coming [kámɪŋ] N venida *f*; **— of Christ** advenimiento de Cristo *m*; **— from** proveniente de, originario de; **—s and goings** idas y venidas *f pl*; ADJ que viene, próximo

comma [kámə] N coma *f*

command [kəmǽnd] VT (order) mandar; (have authority over) comandar; **to — respect** inspirar respeto, imponerse; N (order) mandato *m*, orden *f*; (post) comandancia *f*; (dominance) dominio *m*; (on a computer) comando *m*; **— key** tecla de comando *f*; **he has a good — of English** domina bien el inglés; **to be in — of** estar al mando de; **to be under the — of** estar al mando de; **at your —** a sus órdenes

commandeer [kɑməndír] VT apoderarse de; (for the military) requisar

commander [kəmǽndə·] N (leader) jefe -fa *mf*; (army officer) comandante *mf*; (navy officer) capitán -ana de fragata *mf*; **— in chief** comandante en jefe *mf*

commandment [kəmǽndmənt] N mandamiento *m*

commemorate [kəmémərət] VT conmemorar

commemoration [kɑmɛmərəféjən] N conmemoración *f*

commence [kəméns] VI/VT comenzar, principiar

commencement [kəméns̄mənt] N (beginning) comienzo *m*; (graduation) graduación *f*, colación *f*

commend [kəménd] VT (praise) alabar; (entrust) encomendar

commendation [kɑməndéfən] N (praise) alabanza *f*; (mention) mención de honor *f*

commensurate [kəménsə·ɪt] ADJ proporcional, acorde

comment [kámɛnt] N comentario *m*; **no —** sin comentarios; VI/VT comentar

commentary [kámənterɪ] N comentario *m*

commentator [kámənteɪbə·] N (person who comments) comentador -ra *mf*; (talking head) comentarista *mf*

commerce [kámə·s] N comercio *m*

commercial [kəmə́·ʃəł] ADJ comercial; N (on radio or television) anuncio *m*

commercialize [kəmə́·ʃəlaɪz] VT comercializar

commiserate [kəmízəret] VI/VT compadecerse de

commiseration [kəmɪzəréfən] N conmiseración *f*

commissary [kámɪsɛri] N economato *m*

commission [kəmíʃən] N (act, committee, payment) comisión *f*; (of a broker) corretaje *m*; (charge) encargo *m*; (mission) misión *f*; (title) nombramiento *m*; **to be in —** estar en servicio; **to be out of —** estar fuera de servicio; **to put out of —** (object) inutilizar; (person) retirar de servicio; VT (authorize) comisionar; (order) encargar; (appoint) nombrar; (get ready) poner en servicio; **—ed officer** oficial *m*

commissioner [kəmíʃənə·] N comisario -ria *mf*

commit [kəmít] VT (perpetrate) cometer; (entrust) encargar; (direct) destinar; **to — an error** cometer un error; **to — a foul** cometer/hacer falta; **to — oneself to** comprometerse a/con; **to — to an asylum** internar; **to — to memory** aprender de memoria

commitment [kəmítmənt] N compromiso *m*

committed [kəmíɪdɪd] ADJ (to a cause) comprometido

committee [kəmíɪdi] N comité *m*, comisión *f*

commode [kəmód] N wáter *m*, inodoro *m*

commodity [kəmádɪti] N (product) mercancía *f*, artículo *m*, producto *m*; (raw material)

materia prima *f*

common [kɑ́mən] ADJ (shared, frequent) común; (general) general; (vulgar) ordinario; (unremarkable) simple; **— cold** resfriado *m*; **— denominator** denominador común *m*; **— law** derecho consuetudinario *m*; **— sense** sentido común *m*, sensatez *f*; **— soldier** soldado raso *m*; **— stock** acciones ordinarias *f pl*; **—wealth** (state) estado *m*; (republic) república *f*; ADJ **—place** trivial; N **—s** (land) ejido *m*

commotion [kəmóʃən] N conmoción *f*, revuelo *m*

communal [kəmjúnl̩] ADJ comunitario

commune[1] [kəmjún] VI (communicate) comunicarse, departir; (take communion) comulgar

commune[2] [kɑ́mjun] N comuna *f*

communicable [kəmjúnɪkəbəł] ADJ comunicable; (disease) transmisible

communicate [kəmjúnɪket] VI/VT comunicar[se]; (disease) transmitir[se]

communication [kəmjunɪkéʃən] N comunicación *f*

communicative [kəmjúnɪkətɪv] ADJ comunicativo

communion [kəmjúnjən] N comunión *f*

communiqué [kəmjunɪké] N comunicado *m*

communism [kɑ́mjənɪzəm] N comunismo *m*

communist [kɑ́mjənɪst] N & ADJ comunista *mf*

community [kəmjúnɪdi] N comunidad *f*, colectividad *f*; **— spirit** espíritu comunitario *m*

commute [kəmjút] VT (reduce a sentence) conmutar; VI viajar diariamente al trabajo

commuter [kəmjúdɚ] N persona que viaja diariamente al trabajo *f*

Comoros [kɑ́məroz] N Comoras *f pl*

compact[1] [kɑ́mpækt, kəmpǽkt] ADJ compacto; (dense) tupido, apretado; (concise) conciso; (make denser) tupir

compact[2] [kɑ́mpækt] N (agreement) pacto *m*; (case for powder) polvera *f*; **— disk** disco compacto *m*; VT compactar

compactness [kɑmpǽktnɪs] N densidad *f*; (conciseness) concisión *f*

companion [kəmpǽnjən] N (comrade, partner) compañero -ra *mf*; (caregiver) acompañante *mf*

companionship [kəmpǽnjənʃɪp] N compañía *f*

company [kɑ́mpəni] N compañía *f*; **to keep — with** codearse con, frecuentar

comparable [kɑ́mpərəbəł] ADJ comparable

comparative [kəmpǽrətɪv] ADJ comparativo

compare [kəmpér] VI/VT comparar[se]; **beyond —** incomparable, sin parangón

comparison [kəmpǽrɪsən] N comparación *f*; **in — with** comparado con

compartment [kəmpɑ́rtmənt] N compartimiento *m*

compass [kɑ́mpəs] N (for drawing) compás *m*; (for directions) brújula *f*

compassion [kəmpǽʃən] N compasión *f*

compassionate [kəmpǽʃənɪt] ADJ compasivo

compatibility [kəmpætəbɪ́lɪti] N compatibilidad *f*

compatible [kəmpǽtəbəł] ADJ compatible (also of computers)

compatriot [kəmpétriət] N compatriota *mf*

compel [kəmpɛ́ł] VT (force) obligar; (demand) exigir

compelling [kəmpɛ́lɪŋ] ADJ (argument) convincente; (story) emocionante

compensate [kɑ́mpənset] VT (make up for) compensar, resarcir; (pay) remunerar

compensation [kɑmpənséʃən] N (making up for) compensación *f*; (remuneration) remuneración *f*

compete [kəmpít] VI/VT competir

competence [kɑ́mpɪtəns] N competencia *f*

competent [kɑ́mpɪtənt] ADJ competente

competition [kɑmpɪtíʃən] N competencia *f*; (sports match) competición *f*, contienda *f*

competitive [kəmpɛ́tɪtɪv] ADJ competitivo; **— examination** *Sp* oposición *f*; *Am* concurso *m*; **— sports** deportes de competición *m pl*

competitiveness [kəmpɛ́tɪtɪvnɪs] N competitividad *f*

competitor [kəmpɛ́tɪdɚ] N (business) competidor -ora *mf*; (sports) atleta *mf*

compilation [kɑmpɪléʃən] N recopilación *f*

compile [kəmpáɪł] VT recopilar, compilar

compiler [kəmpáɪlɚ] N compilador *m*; **— language** lenguaje compilador *m*

complacency [kəmplésənsi] N confianza infundada *f*

complacent [kəmplésənt] ADJ confiado

complain [kəmplén] VI quejarse

complainant [kəmplénənt] ADJ & N recurrente *mf*

complaint [kəmplɛ́nt] N queja *f*; (official) reclamo *m*; (civil charge) demanda *f*; (ailment) dolencia *f*

complement[1] [kɑ́mpləmənt] N complemento *m*; (of staff) dotación *f*

complement[2] [kɑ́mpləmɛnt] VT complementar

complementary [kɑmpləméntri] ADJ complementario

complete [kəmplít] ADJ completo, pleno; **a — stranger** un perfecto desconocido; VT completar; **to — a pass** completar un pase

completion [kəmplíʃən] N finalización *f*, terminación *f*; **she brought the project to —** completó el proyecto

complex[1] [kɑ́mplɛ́ks] ADJ complejo

complex[2] [kɑ́mplɛ́ks] N complejo *m*

complexion [kəmplɛ́kʃən] N (skin) cutis *m*; (color) tez *f*; (perspective) cariz *m*

complexity [kəmpléksɪdi] N complejidad *f*
compliance [kəmpláɪəns] N (obedience) conformidad *f*, acatamiento *m*; (polite reverence) pleitesía *f*; **in — with** en conformidad con
complicate [kámplɪket] VT complicar
complicated [kámplɪkeɒɪd] ADJ complicado
complication [kɑmplɪkéʃən] N complicación *f*
complicity [kəmplísɪdi] N complicidad *f*
compliment [kámpləmənt] N cumplido, halago *m*; (on looks) piropo *m*; (from a suitor) galantería *f*; **to pay someone a —** hacerle un cumplido a alguien; **to send one's —s** enviar saludos; VI/VT elogiar, halagar
comply [kəmpláɪ] VI obedecer; **to — with** cumplir con, acatar
component [kəmpónənt] ADJ & N componente *m*
compose [kəmpóz] VI/VT componer; **to — oneself** sosegarse
composed [kəmpózd] ADJ sosegado; **to be — of** estar compuesto de, componerse de, constar de
composer [kəmpózɚ] N compositor -ra *mf*
composite [kəmpázɪt] ADJ compuesto; N amalgama *f*
composition [kɑmpəzíʃən] N (make-up, musical piece) composición *f*; (aggregate material) compuesto *m*; (school essay) composición *f*, redacción *f*
composure [kəmpóʒɚ] N compostura *f*
compound[1] [kámpaʊnd] ADJ & N compuesto *m*; **— fracture** fractura expuesta *f*; **— interest** interés compuesto *m*
compound[2] [kɑmpáʊnd] VT (combine) combinar; (worsen) empeorar
comprehend [kɑmprɪhénd] VT comprender
comprehensible [kɑmprɪhénsəbəł] ADJ comprensible
comprehension [kɑmprɪhénʃən] N comprensión *f*
comprehensive [kɑmprɪhénsɪv] ADJ exhaustivo; **— insurance** seguro contra todo riesgo *m*
compress[1] [kəmprés] VT comprimir; **—ed disk** disco comprimido *m*; **—ed file** archivo comprimido *m*
compress[2] [kámprɛs] N compresa *f*
compression [kəmpréʃən] N compresión *f*
comprise [kəmpráɪz] VT comprender, incluir; **to be —d of** comprender, incluir
compromise [kámprəmaɪz] N (arrangement) arreglo por concesiones mutuas *m*, compromiso *m*; (intermediate thing) cruce *m*, término medio *m*; VI/VT (make agreement) transigir; *Am* transar; (jeopardize) comprometer
comptroller [kəntrólɚ] N controlador -ra *mf*; *Am* contralor -ora *mf*
compulsion [kəmpáłʃən] N (impulse) compulsión *f*, coacción *f*; (coercion) coerción *f*
compulsive [kəmpáłsɪv] ADJ compulsivo
compulsory [kəmpáłsəri] ADJ obligatorio, obligado
computation [kɑmpjʊtéʃən] N cómputo *m*, cálculo *m*
compute [kəmpjút] VI/VT computar, calcular
computer [kəmpjúɚ] N *Am* computadora *f*; *Sp* ordenador *m*; **— engineer** ingeniero -ra en computación *mf*, ingeniero -ra informático -ca *mf*; **— graphics** gráficos por computadora/ordenador *m pl*; **— literacy** (process) alfabetización digital *f*; (result) alfabetismo digital *m*; **— science** informática *f*; **— virus** virus de computadora/ordenador *m*
computerization [kəmpjuɒɚɪzéʃən] N *Sp* ordenación *f*, *Am* computarización *f*
computerize [kəmpjúɒəraɪz] VI/VT informatizar, computarizar
computing [kəmpjúɒɪŋ] N informática *f*; ADJ informático
comrade [kámræd] N camarada *mf*
concave [kánkev] ADJ cóncavo
conceal [kənsíł] VT encubrir, ocultar, disimular
concealment [kənsíłmənt] N encubrimiento *m*, disimulo *m*
concede [kənsíd] VI/VT (recognize) conceder, reconocer; (allow) conceder
conceit [kənsít] N (vanity) vanidad *f*; (literary device) concepto *m*
conceited [kənsíɒɪd] ADJ engreído, presumido
conceivable [kənsívəbəł] ADJ imaginable, concebible
conceive [kənsív] VI/VT concebir; (a plan) concebir, idear
concentrate [kánsəntret] VI/VT concentrar[se]
concentration [kɑnsəntréʃən] N concentración *f*; **— camp** campo de concentración *m*
concept [kánsɛpt] N concepto *m*
conception [kənsépʃən] N concepción *f*
conceptual [kənsépt∫uəł] ADJ conceptual
concern [kənsɝ́n] VT (be of interest) concernir, atañer; (worry) preocupar; **to — oneself with** ocuparse de; **to whom it may —** a quien corresponda; N (interest) interés *m*; (matter) asunto *m*; (worry) preocupación *f*; (company) compañía *f*; **to be of no —** no tener consecuencia
concerned [kənsɝ́nd] ADJ (involved) involucrado; (anxious) preocupado; **as far as I am —** en lo que a mí respecta; **to be — about** preocuparse por
concerning [kənsɝ́nɪŋ] PREP tocante a, respecto a
concert[1] [kánsɚt] N concierto *m*
concert[2] [kənsɝ́t] VT concertar
concession [kənséʃən] N concesión *f*
conciliate [kənsíliet] VI/VT (make compatible)

conciliar; (appease) aplacar
conciliation [kənsɪliéʃən] N conciliación *f*
concise [kənsáɪs] ADJ conciso, sucinto
conciseness [kənsáɪsnɪs] N concisión *f*
conclude [kənklúd] VI/VT concluir
conclusion [kənklúʒən] N conclusión *f*
conclusive [kənklúsɪv] ADJ concluyente
concoct [kənkákt] VT (contrive) fabricar, urdir; (prepare by cooking) preparar
concoction [kənkákʃən] N mejunje *m*
concord [kánkɔrd] N (peace) concordia *f*; (agreement) convenio *m*, acuerdo *m*
concrete[1] [kɑnkrít] ADJ concreto
concrete[2] [kánkrit] N hormigón *m*; (made of concrete) de hormigón
concubine [káŋkjəbaɪn] N concubina *f*
concur [kənkɝ] VI estar de acuerdo
concussion [kənkáʃən] N (brain injury) conmoción cerebral *f*; (shock) concusión *f*
condemn [kəndém] VT condenar; (acquire public ownership) expropiar; (declare unsafe) declarar ruinoso
condemnation [kɑndɛmnéʃən] N condenación *f*, condena *f*
condensation [kɑndɛnséʃən] N condensación *f*; (of a book) compendio *m*
condense [kəndéns] VI/VT condensar[se]
condescend [kɑndəsénd] VI condescender a
condescension [kɑndəsénʃən] N condescendencia *f*
condiment [kándəmənt] N condimento *m*, aliño *m*
condition [kəndíʃən] N condición *f*; **he's got a heart —** sufre del corazón, tiene una afección cardíaca; **he's in good physical —** está en buen estado físico; **the patient is in critical —** el paciente está en estado crítico; **on — that** a condición de que; VT (restrict on a condition, establish a conditioned response) condicionar; (accustom oneself) acostumbrarse
conditional [kəndíʃənl] ADJ & N condicional *m*
conditioning [kəndíʃənɪŋ] N condicionamiento *m*
condolences [kəndóləns ɪz] N pésame *m*, condolencias *f*; **to express one's —** dar las condolencias
condominium [kɑndəmíniəm] N condominio *m*
condone [kəndón] VT tolerar
conducive [kəndúsɪv] ADJ conducente
conduct[1] [kándʌkt] N conducta *f*, comportamiento *m*
conduct[2] [kəndʌ́kt] VI/VT (behave) conducirse, comportarse; (carry out) llevar a cabo; (direct, lead) dirigir; (serve as channel for) conducir
conduction [kəndʌ́kʃən] N conducción *f*
conductor [kəndʌ́ktɚ] N (substance that conducts) conductor *m*; (of an orchestra) director -ora *mf*; (of a train) revisor -ora *mf*
conduit [kánduɪt] N conducto *m*
cone [kon] N cono *m*; (container) cucurucho *m*
confection [kənfɛ́kʃən] N (of clothes) confección *f*; (of candy) confitura *f*
confectionery [kənfɛ́kʃənɛri] N confitería *f*; (shop) dulcería *f*; (candies) dulces *m pl*
confederacy [kənfɛ́dɚəsi] N confederación *f*
confederate[1] [kənfɛ́dɚɪt] ADJ & N confederado -da *mf*
confederate[2] [kənfɛ́dɚet] VI/VT confederar[se]
confederation [kənfɛdɚéʃən] N confederación *f*
confer [kənfɝ] VT (grant) conferir, atribuir; (consult) consultar; (negotiate) conferenciar
conference [kánfərəns] N (consultation) consulta *f*; (professional meeting) congreso *m*; (legislative) asamblea general *f*; (sports league) liga *f*; **— call** llamada en conferencia *f*
confess [kənfɛ́s] VI/VT confesar[se]
confession [kənfɛ́ʃən] N confesión *f*
confessional [kənfɛ́ʃənl] N confesionario *m*
confessor [kənfɛ́sɚ] N confesor *m*
confidant [kánfɪdɑnt] N confidente *mf*
confide [kənfáɪd] VI/VT (entrust) confiar; VI (tell secrets to) hacer confidencias a
confidence [kánfɪdəns] N confianza *f*; (certainty) seguridad *f*; (secret communication) confidencia *f*; **— game** timo *m*; **— man** timador *m*, embaucador *m*; **in —** en confianza
confident [kánfɪdənt] ADJ seguro; **he's a — person** tiene mucha confianza
confidential [kɑnfɪdénʃəl] ADJ confidencial; (secretary, etc.) de confianza
configuration [kənfɪgjəréʃən] N configuración *f* (also for computers)
configure [kənfíɡjɚ] VT configurar
confine[1] [kənfáɪn] VT confinar, recluir; **to — oneself to** limitarse a
confine[2] [kánfaɪn] N confín *m*
confinement [kənfáɪnmənt] N confinamiento *m*
confirm [kənfɝ́m] VT confirmar
confirmation [kɑnfɚméʃən] N confirmación *f*
confiscate [kánfɪsket] VT confiscar
confiscation [kɑnfɪskéʃən] N confiscación *f*
conflagration [kɑnfləɡréʃən] N incendio *m*
conflict[1] [kánflɪkt] N conflicto *m*, contienda *f*; **— of interest** conflicto de intereses *m*
conflict[2] [kənflíkt] VI oponerse
confluence [kánfluəns] N confluencia *f*
conform [kənfɔ́rm] VI/VT conformar[se]
conformity [kənfɔ́rmɪdi] N (agreement) conformidad *f*; (passive acquiescence) conformismo *m*
confound [kənfáʊnd] VT (bewilder) desconcertar; (confuse) confundir; **— it!** *fam* ¡caramba!
confront [kənfrʌ́nt] VT (set face to face, fight)

confrontar; (face up to) enfrentarse a
confrontation [kɑnfrəntéʃən] N confrontación *f*, enfrentamiento *m*
confuse [kənfjúz] VT confundir
confused [kənfjúzd] ADJ (person) confundido; (situation) confuso; **to become —** confundirse
confusing [kənfjúzɪŋ] ADJ confuso
confusion [kənfjúʒən] N confusión *f*
congeal [kənʤíl] VI/VT cuajar[se]
congenial [kənʤínjəl] ADJ agradable, simpático
congenital [kənʤénɪdl] ADJ congénito
congestion [kənʤéstʃən] N congestión *f*
congestive heart failure [kənʤestɪv hárt feljə-] ADJ insuficiencia cardíaca congestiva *f*
conglomeration [kəŋglɑməréʃən] N (unit) conglomeración *f*; (mass) conglomerado *m*
Congo [káŋgo] N Congo *m*
Congolese [kɑŋgəlíz] ADJ & N congoleño -ña *mf*
congratulate [kəŋgrǽtʃəlet] VT felicitar
congratulation [kəŋgrætʃəléʃən] N felicitación *f*, parabién *m*; **—s!** ¡enhorabuena! ¡albricias!
congregate [káŋgrɪget] VI/VT congregar[se]
congregation [kɑŋgrɪgéʃən] N (worshipers) fieles *m pl*, feligreses *m pl*; (act of congregating, committee of cardinals) congregación *f*
congress [káŋgrɪs] N (professional) congreso *m*; (political) asamblea legislativa *f*; (US) congreso *m*; **—man** (US) congresista *m*; **—woman** (US) congresista *f*
congressional [kəŋgréʃənl] ADJ congresual
congruence [kəŋgrúnəs] N congruencia *f*
conifer [kɑ́nəfə-] N conífera *f*
conjecture [kənʤéktʃə-] N conjetura *f*; VI/VT conjeturar
conjugal [kɑ́nʤəgəł] ADJ conyugal
conjugate [kɑ́nʤəget] VI/VT conjugar[se]
conjugation [kɑnʤəgéʃən] N conjugación *f*
conjunction [kənʤʌ́ŋkʃən] N conjunción *f*
conjunctivitis [kənʤʌŋktəvɑ́ɪdɪs] N conjuntivitis *f*
conjure [kɑ́nʤə-] VT invocar; **to — up** evocar; VI hacer hechizos
connect [kənékt] VI/VT conectar[se], enlazar[se]; (buildings, callers) comunicar[se]; (concepts) relacionar[se]; (pipes) acoplar[se]; **—ing rod** biela *f*
connection [kənékʃən] N (act of connecting) conexión *f*, vinculación *f*; (of telephone) comunicación *f*, enganche *m*; (of concepts) relación *f*; (of pipes) acople *m*; (affinity) afinidad *f*; (supplier) contacto *m*; **—s** contactos *m pl*, enchufe *m*
connectivity [kənɛktɪ́vɪdɪ] N conectividad *f*
connive [kənáɪv] VI conspirar
connoisseur [kɑnəsʊ́r] N conocedor -ora *f*
connotation [kɑnətéʃən] N connotación *f*
conquer [káŋkə-] VT (win) conquistar; (overcome) vencer
conqueror [kɑ́ŋkərə-] N conquistador -ora *mf*; (one who overcomes) vencedor -ora *mf*
conquest [kɑ́ŋkwɛst] N conquista *f*
conscience [kɑ́nʃəns] N conciencia *f*
conscientious [kɑnʃiéntʃəs] ADJ concienzudo
conscious [kɑ́nʃəs] ADJ consciente
consciousness [kɑ́nʃəsnɪs] N conciencia *f*; **to lose —** perder el conocimiento
conscript[1] [kənskrípt] VT reclutar
conscript[2] [kɑ́nskrɪpt] N recluta *mf*
conscription [kənskrípʃən] N reclutamiento *m*
consecrate [kɑ́nsɪkret] VT consagrar
consecration [kɑnsɪkréʃən] N consagración *f*
consecutive [kənsékjəɡɪv] ADJ consecutivo
consensus [kənsénsəs] N consenso *m*
consent [kənsɛ́nt] N consentimiento *m*; VI consentir
consequence [kɑ́nsɪkwɛ́ns] N consecuencia *f*; (negative) secuela *f*
consequent [kɑ́nsɪkwənt] ADJ consiguiente, resultante; N (in mathematics) consecuente *m*; (in logic) consiguiente *m*
consequently [kɑ́nsɪkwəntlɪ] ADV por consiguiente, en consecuencia
conservation [kɑnsə-véʃən] N conservación *f*, preservación *f*
conservatism [kənsə́-vətɪzəm] N conservadurismo *m*
conservative [kənsə́-vəɡɪv] ADJ & N conservador -ora *mf*
conservatory [kənsə́-vətɔri] N conservatorio *m*
conserve[1] [kənsə́-v] VT conservar, preservar
conserve[2] [kɑ́nsə-v] N confitura *m*
consider [kənsídə-] VT considerar
considerable [kənsídə-əbəł] ADJ considerable
considerate [kənsídə-ɪt] ADJ considerado
consideration [kənsɪdəréʃən] N consideración *f*; (respect) miramiento *m*; (payment) remuneración *f*
considering [kənsídə-ɪŋ] PREP en vista de, teniendo en cuenta; **she cooks well, —** para ser ella, cocina bien
consign [kənsáɪn] VT consignar
consignee [kɑnsaɪní] N consignatario -ria *mf*
consignment [kənsáɪnmənt] N consignación *f*; **on —** a/en consignación
consist [kənsíst] VI consistir [en]
consistency [kənsístənsɪ] N (adherence to principles) coherencia *f*, consecuencia *f*; (density) consistencia *f*
consistent [kənsístənt] ADJ (adherent to principles) consecuente, coherente; (cohering) consistente
consolation [kɑnsəléʃən] N consuelo *m*, consolación *f*
console[1] [kənsół] VT consolar
console[2] [kɑ́nsołˌ] N consola *f*
consolidate [kənsɑ́lɪdet] VI/VT consolidar[se]

consolidation [kənsɑlɪdéʃən] N consolidación *f*
consonant [kánsənənt] N consonante *f*; ADJ consonante, conforme
consort[1] [kənsɔ́rt] VI **to — with** asociarse con
consort[2] [kánsɔrt] N consorte *mf*
consortium [kənsɔ́rʃiəm] N consorcio *m*
conspicuous [kənspíkjuəs] ADJ evidente
conspiracy [kənspírəsi] N conspiración *f*, conjura *f*
conspirator [kənspírədə·] N conspirador -ora *mf*, conjurado -da *mf*
conspire [kənspáɪr] VI conspirar, conjurar
constable [kánstəbəł] N oficial de policía *mf*; (keeper of fortress) condestable *m*
constancy [kánstənsi] N constancia *f*
constant [kánstənt] ADJ & N constante *f*
constellation [kɑnstəléʃən] N constelación *f*
consternation [kɑnstə·néʃən] N consternación *f*
constipate [kánstəpet] VT estreñir
constipated [kánstəpeɪɪd] ADJ estreñido
constipation [kɑnspépéʃən] N estreñimiento *m*
constituent [kənstítʃuənt] ADJ componente, constitutivo; N (component) componente *m*; (voter) votante *mf*; (part of a sentence) constituyente *m*
constitute [kánstɪtut] VT constituir
constitution [kɑnstɪtúʃən] N constitución *f*
constitutional [kɑnstɪtúʃənł] ADJ constitucional; N caminata *f*
constrain [kənstrén] VT constreñir, restringir
constraint [kənstrént] N constreñimiento *m*
constrict [kənstrík̇t] VT constreñir
constriction [kənstrík̇ʃən] N (action) constricción *f*; (place) estrechamiento *m*
construct[1] [kənstrák̇t] VT construir
construct[2] [kánstrɑkt] N invención *f*
construction [kənstrák̇ʃən] N construcción *f*; **— company** constructora *f*
constructive [kənstrák̇tɪv] ADJ constructivo
construe [kənstrú] VT interpretar
consul [kánsəł] N cónsul *mf*
consulate [kánsəlɪt] N consulado *m*
consult [kənsáłt] VI/VT consultar; VI (serve as a consultant) asesorar
consultant [kənsáłtənt] N asesor -ora *mf*
consultation [kɑnsəłtéʃən] N consulta *f*
consultative [kənsáłtədɪv] ADJ consultivo
consulting [kənsáłtɪŋ] N asesoramiento *m*, consultoría *f*; ADJ consultor; **— firm** firma consultora *f*
consumable [kənsúməbəł] ADJ **— goods** bienes consumibles *m pl*
consume [kənsúm] VI/VT consumir
consumer [kənsúmə·] N consumidor -ora *mf*; **— confidence index** índice de confianza del consumidor *m*; **— credit** crédito al consumidor *m*; **— protection** protección al consumidor *f*
consumerism [kənsúmərɪzəm] N consumismo *m*
consuming [kənsúmɪŋ] ADJ (need) imperioso; (drive) abrasador
consummate[1] [kánsəmet] VT consumar
consummate[2] [kánsəmɪt] ADJ consumado
consumption [kənsʌ́mpʃən] N (using up) consumo *m*; (wasting of the body) consunción *f*; (tuberculosis) tisis *f*
consumptive [kənsʌ́mptɪv] ADJ tísico
contact [kántæ̇kt] N contacto *m*; **— lens** lente de contacto *mf*; VI/VT (touch) tocar; (communicate with) contactar
contagion [kəntéd̊ʒən] N (spread) contagio *m*; (disease spread) enfermedad contagiosa *f*
contagious [kəntéd̊ʒəs] ADJ contagioso
contain [kənténˈ] VI/VT contener
container [kənténə·] N recipiente *m*; (on a ship) contenedor *m*; **—ship** buque portacontenedores *m*
containerize [kənténəraɪz] VT contenedorizar
containment [kənténmənt] N contención *f*
contaminate [kəntǽmənet] VT contaminar
contamination [kəntæ̇mənéʃən] N contaminación *f*
contemplate [kántəmplet] VT (observe) contemplar; (consider) considerar
contemplation [kɑntəmpléʃən] N (observation) contemplación *f*; (consideration) consideración *f*
contemporary [kəntémpərɛri] ADJ contemporáneo
contempt [kəntémpt] N desprecio *m*, menosprecio *m*; **— of court** desacato al tribunal *m*
contemptible [kəntémptəbəł] ADJ despreciable, rastrero
contemptuous [kəntémptʃuəs] ADJ desdeñoso
contend [kənténd] VI (struggle) contender, lidiar; (argue) disputar; VT afirmar
content[1] [kənténtˈ] ADJ (happy) contento; (resigned) conforme; N **to one's heart's —** a discreción
content[2], **contents** [kántɛnt[s]] N contenido *m*
contented [kənténtɪd] ADJ contento, satisfecho
contention [kənténʃən] N (opinion) opinión *f*; **in —** (disputed) en discusión; (still eligible) con posibilidades
contentious [kənténʃəs] ADJ conflictivo
contentment [kənténtmənt] N contento *m*
contest[1] [kántɛst] N (competition) concurso *m*, certamen *m*; (struggle) contienda *f*
contest[2] [kənténst] VT (compete) contender; (dispute) disputar; (challenge) impugnar
contestant [kənténstənt] N concursante *mf*, participante *mf*
context [kántɛkst] N contexto *m*
contiguous [kəntígjuəs] ADJ contiguo, pegado
continent [kántənənt] N (landmass) continente *m*; ADJ (sexually abstinent) continente; (of

bodily functions) capaz de controlar los esfínteres

continental [kɑntɪnénɪtl] ADJ continental

contingency [kəntínʤənsi] N contingencia *f*; — **fund** fondo de contingencia *m*; — **planning** planificación para contingencias *f*

contingent [kəntínʤənt] ADJ & N contingente *m*

continual [kəntínjuəɫ] ADJ continuo

continuance [kəntínjuəns] N continuación *f*; (delay) aplazamiento *m*

continuation [kəntɪnjuéʃən] N continuación *f*

continue [kəntínju] VI/VT continuar

continuing [kəntínjuɪŋ] ADJ continuado; — **education** educación para adultos *f*

continuity [kɑntɪnúɪdɪ] N continuidad *f*

continuous [kəntínjuəs] ADJ (uninterrupted in time) continuo; (uninterrupted in space) ininterrumpido

contortion [kəntórʃən] N contorsión *f*

contour [kántur] N contorno *m*

contra account [kántrə əkɑʊnt] N cuenta de contrapartida *f*

contraband [kántrəbænd] N contrabando *m*

contraception [kɑntrəsépʃən] N anticoncepción *f*

contraceptive [kɑntrəséptɪv] ADJ & N anticonceptivo *m*

contract[1] [kántrækt] N contrato *m*; — **killer** asesino -na a sueldo *mf*; **by** — por contrato

contract[2] [kəntrǽkt] VI/VT contraer[se]; (assign by contract) contratar; **to** — **out** subcontratar

contraction [kəntrǽkʃən] N contracción *f*; (in childbirth) contracción *f*, pujo *m*

contractor [kántrækt͡ə] N contratista *mf*

contractual agreement [kəntrǽktʃuəɫəgrímənt] N acuerdo contractual *m*

contradict [kɑntrədíkt] VI/VT contradecir

contradiction [kɑntrədíkʃən] N contradicción *f*

contradictory [kɑntrədíktəri] ADJ contradictorio

contraption [kəntrǽpʃən] N chisme *m*, coso *m*

contrary [kántrɛri] ADJ contrario, opuesto; (obstinate) testarudo; N lo contrario; **on the** — al contrario

contrast[1] [kántræst] N contraste *m*

contrast[2] [kəntræst] VI/VT contrastar

contravene [kɑntrəvín] VT contravenir

contribute [kəntríbjut] VI contribuir; (to a newspaper) colaborar; VT contribuir con, aportar

contribution [kɑntrəbjúʃən] N (donation, article) contribución *f*; (scientific) aporte *m*, aportación *f*

contributor [kəntríbjət͡ə-] N colaborador -ra *mf*

contrite [kəntráɪt] ADJ contrito

contrivance [kəntráɪvəns] N artefacto *m*

contrive [kəntráɪv] VI/VT ingeniar; **he** — **d to get their money** se las ingenió para sacarles el dinero

contrived [kəntráɪvd] ADJ artificioso

control [kəntróɫ] VI/VT controlar; N control *m*; (of a machine) mando *m*; **who's in** —? ¿quién manda? **under** — bajo control; — **freak** mandón -ona *mf*; — **key** tecla de control/mando *f*; — **panel** panel de control *m*; — **tower** torre de control *f*

controller [kəntróɫə-] N (comptroller) controlador -ora *mf*; *Am* contralor *m*; (device) regulador *m*

controversial [kɑntrəvɜ́ʃəɫ] ADJ controvertido

controversy [kántrəvɜ-si] N controversia *f*, polémica *f*

contusion [kəntúʒən] N contusión *f*, magulladura *f*

conundrum [kənándrəm] N (riddle) adivinanza *f*, acertijo *m*; (mystery) enigma *m*

convalesce [kɑnvəlés] VI convalecer

convalescence [kɑnvəlésəns] N convalecencia *f*

convalescent [kɑnvəlésənt] ADJ & N convaleciente *mf*

convection [kənvékʃən] N convección *f*

convene [kənvín] VT convocar; VI reunirse

convenience [kənvínjəns] N (practicality) conveniencia *f*; (appliance) comodidad *f*; — **store** autoservicio *m*; **at your** — cuando le venga bien

convenient [kənvínjənt] ADJ conveniente, oportuno; (at hand) accesible

convent [kánvɛnt] N convento *m*

convention [kənvénʃən] N (political assembly) convención *f*; (professional assembly) congreso *m*; (pact) convenio *m*; (international agreement, acceptable usage) convención *f*

conventional [kənvénʃənl] ADJ (not original) convencional; (traditional) clásico; — **loan** préstamo convencional *m*

conventioneer [kənvɛnʃəníɪr] N congresista *mf*

converge [kənvɜ́ʤ] VI converger

convergence [kənvɜ́ʤəns] N convergencia *f*

conversant [kənvɜ́sənt] ADJ — **with** versado en

conversation [kɑnvə-séʃən] N conversación *f*; — **piece** tema de conversación *m*

converse [kənvɜ́s] VI conversar

conversion [kənvɜ́ʒən] N conversión *f*

convert[1] [kənvɜ́t] VI/VT convertir[se]

convert[2] [kánvɜ-t] N converso -sa *mf*

converter [kənvɜ́ɾə-] N convertidor *m*

convertible [kənvɜ́ɾəbəɫ] ADJ convertible; (car) descapotable; — **assets** activo convertible *m*; N (car) descapotable *m*

convex [kánveks] ADJ convexo

convey [kənvé] VT (carry) llevar; (transfer) transferir; (transmit) transmitir; (communicate) comunicar

conveyance [kənvéəns] N (vehicle) vehículo *m*; (transfer of property) transferencia *f*; (document) escritura de traspaso *f*

conveyer, conveyor [kənvéə-] N transmisor

-ora *mf*; **— belt** cinta transportadora *f*
convict[1] [kɑ́nvɪkt] N convicto -ta *mf*
convict[2] [kənvíkt] VI/VT declarar culpable
conviction [kənvíkʃən] N (belief) convicción *f*, convencimiento *m*; (act of convicting) declaración de culpabilidad *f*; (on one's record) condena *f*
convince [kənvíns] VT convencer
convincing [kənvínsɪŋ] ADJ convincente, contundente
convocation [kɑnvəkéʃən] N (act) convocación *f*; (group of people) asamblea *f*
convoke [kənvók] VT convocar
convoluted [kɑnvəlúɪɪd] ADJ retorcido
convoy [kɑ́nvɔɪ] N convoy *m*; VT convoyar
convulse [kənvʌ́ls] VI/VT convulsionar[se]
convulsion [kənvʌ́lʃən] N convulsión *f*
coo [ku] VI arrullar; N arrullo *m*
cook [kʊk] N cocinero -ra *mf*; **—book** libro de cocina *m*; VT cocinar, guisar; **to — the books** falsificar los libros de contabilidad; **to — up a plan** urdir un plan; **her —ing is outstanding** cocina muy bien; **now we're —ing!** ahora sí
cookery [kʊ́kəri] N cocina *f*
cookie [kʊ́ki] N (sweet food) galletita dulce *f*; (computer record) archivo cookie *m*
cool [kuł] ADJ (not hot) fresco; (indifferent) frío, indiferente; (calm) tranquilo; (good) excelente; *Carib* chévere; *RP* macanudo; *Sp* guay; **that's not —** eso no se hace; **—ing-off period** tregua *f*; N (cold) fresco *m*; (composure) tranquilidad *f*; VT (make cooler) enfriar; (air condition) refrigerar; **to — off** (get cold) enfriarse; (get cooler) refrescar[se]; (calm down) calmarse
coolant [kʊ́lənt] N refrigerante *m*
cooler [kʊ́lə-] N (room) cámara frigorífica *f*; (container) nevera portátil *f*
coolness [kʊ́łnɪs] N (cold weather) fresco *m*, frescor *m*; (indifference) frialdad *f*, indiferencia *f*
coon [kun] N (raccoon) mapache *m*; **a —'s age** una eternidad
co-op [kóɑp] N cooperativa *f*
coop [kup] N jaula *f*; (for chickens) gallinero *m*; VT enjaular; **to — up** encerrar
cooperate [koɑ́pəret] VI cooperar
cooperation [koɑpəréʃən] N cooperación *f*
cooperative [koɑ́pə-əɪv] ADJ (helpful) cooperativo; (relative to a cooperative) cooperativista; N cooperativa *f*
coordinate[1] [koɔ́rdnɪt] ADJ coordinado; N coordenada *f*; **—s** (clothes) conjunto *m*
coordinate[2] [koɔ́rdnet] VI/VT coordinar
coordinating [koɔ́rdnəɪɪŋ] ADJ coordinador
coordination [koɔrdnéʃən] N coordinación *f*
coordinator [koɔ́rdnəɪə-] N coordinador -ora *mf*
cop [kɑp] N *fam* poli *mf*, polizonte *m*; VI **to — out** zafarse
copayment [kópemənt] N copago *m*
cope [kop] VI **to — with** arreglárselas con; **I cannot — with this** no puedo con esto
copious [kópiəs] ADJ copioso
copper [kɑ́pə-] N cobre *m*; (cop) *fam* poli *mf*; ADJ de cobre
copulate [kɑ́pjəlet] VI copular
copulation [kɑpjəléʃən] N copulación *f*
copy [kɑ́pi] N (reproduction) copia *f*; (specimen, example) ejemplar *m*; (news story) texto *m*; **—cat** copión -ona *mf*; **— machine** copiadora *f*; **— protection** protección contra copias *f*; **—right** copyright *m*, derechos de autor *m pl*; **this material is —righted** reservados todos los derechos; VT copiar; **to —right** registrar los derechos
coquette [kokét] N coqueta *f*
coral [kɔ́rəł] N coral *m*; ADJ (related to coral) coralino; (made of coral) de coral; **— reef** arrecife de coral *m*
cord [kɔrd] N (thread) cuerda *f*; (for shoes) cordón *m*; (firewood measure) medida de leña *f*; **—s** pantalones de pana *m pl*
cordial [kɔ́rʤəł] ADJ cordial; N licor *m*
cordless [kɔ́rdlɪs] ADJ inalámbrico
corduroy [kɔ́rDərɔɪ] N pana *f*; **—s** pantalones de pana *m pl*
core [kor] N (of fruit) corazón *m*; (of a problem) meollo *m*; (of a magnet, reactor) núcleo *m*; **— business** negocio principal *m*; **— inflation** inflación básica *f*; VT despepitar
cork [kɔrk] N (woody material) corcho *m*; (stopper, buoy) tapón *m*; **—screw** sacacorchos *m sg*, tirabuzón *m*; **— tree** alcornoque *m*; VT tapar con un corcho
corn [kɔrn] N (plant) maíz *m*; (painful growth) callo *m*; **—bread** pan de maíz *m*; **—cob** mazorca *f*; *Sp* zuro *m*; **— on the cob** choclo *m*; *Mex* elote *m*; **—ed beef** corned beef *m*; **—field** maizal *m*; *Mex* milpa *f*; **—flakes** copos de maíz *m pl*; **—meal** harina de maíz *f*; **—starch** Maicena™ *f*
corner [kɔ́rnə-] N (angle) ángulo *m*; (of a space) rincón *m*; (of two streets) esquina *f*; **—back** (football) esquinero *m*; **— kick** (soccer) saque/tiro de esquina *m*, córner *m*; **—stone** piedra angular *f*; **— table** mesa rinconera *f*; VT (trap) arrinconar, acorralar; (monopolize) monopolizar; VI doblar, *Sp* girar; **— the market** acaparar el mercado
cornered [kɔ́rnə-d] ADJ (animal) acorralado; (person) arrinconado
cornet [kɔrnét] N corneta *f*
cornice [kɔ́rnɪs] N cornisa *f*
corny [kɔ́rni] ADJ sensiblero; (joke) viejo
corollary [kɔ́rəłeri] N corolario *m*
coronary [kɔ́rənɛri] ADJ coronario; **— bypass** puente cardiopulmonar *m*; **— care unit**

unidad de cuidado coronario *f*; **— failure** insuficiencia coronaria *f*; **— thrombosis** trombosis coronaria *f*

coronation [kɔrənéʃən] N coronación *f*

coroner [kɔ́rənə-] N médico -ca forense *mf*

corporal [kɔ́rpə-əɫ] ADJ corporal; N (rank) cabo *m*

corporate [kɔ́rpərɪt] ADJ corporativo; **— backing** patrocinio empresarial *m*; **— officers** ejecutivos -vas de empresa *mf pl*

corporation [kɔrpəréʃən] N sociedad anónima *f*

corps [kor] N cuerpo *m*

corpse [kɔrps] N cadáver *m*

corpulent [kɔ́rpjələnt] ADJ corpulento

corpus [kɔ́rpəs] N corpus *m*

corpuscle [kɔ́rpəsəɫ] N corpúsculo *m*; (of blood) glóbulo *m*

corral [kərǽɫ] N corral *m*; VT acorralar

correct [kərékt] VT corregir; ADJ correcto; **that is —** es cierto

correction [kərékʃən] N corrección *f*; (for glasses) graduación *f*

correctness [kəréktnɪs] N corrección *f*

corrector [kəréktə-] N corrector -ora *mf*

correlate[1] [kɔ́rəlet] VI/VT correlacionar

correlate[2] [kɔ́rəlɪt] N correlato *m*

correlation [kərəléʃən] N correlación *f*

correspond [kɔrɪspánd] VI (be in agreement) corresponder, responder; (exchange letters) cartearse, escribirse

correspondence [kɔrɪspándəns] N correspondencia *f*

correspondent [kɔrɪspándənt] ADJ correspondiente; N (writer of letters) correspondiente *mf*; (news gatherer) corresponsal *mf*, enviado -da *mf*

corresponding [kɔrɪspándɪŋ] ADJ correspondiente; (secretary) encargado de la correspondencia

corridor [kɔ́rɪdɔr] N corredor *m*, pasillo *m*

corroborate [kərábəret] VT corroborar

corrode [kəród] VI/VT corroer[se]

corrosion [kəróʒən] N corrosión *f*

corrupt [kərápt] ADJ (dishonest) corrupto; (rotten) corrompido; **to become —** corromperse; VT corromper, viciar; **—ed file** archivo corrupto *m*

corruption [kərápʃən] N corrupción *f*

corset [kɔ́rsɪt] N corsé *m*

cortex [kɔ́rtɛks] N córtex *m*, corteza cerebral *f*

corticosteroid [kɔrtɪkostɛ́rɔɪd] N corticoesteroide *m*

cortisone [kɔ́rtɪzon] N cortisona *f*

cosigner [kósaɪnə-] N cosignatario -ria *mf*

cosmetic [kɑzmɛ́dɪk] ADJ & N cosmético *m*; **— surgery** cirugía estética *f*

cosmic [kɑ́zmɪk] ADJ cósmico

cosmology [kɑzmɑ́ləʤi] N cosmología *f*

cosmonaut [kɑ́zmənɔt] N cosmonauta *mf*

cosmopolitan [kɑzməpɑ́lɪtn] ADJ cosmopolita

cosmos [kɑ́zmos] N cosmos *m*

cost [kɔst] N costo *m*; *Sp* coste *m*; **—s** (in court) costas *f pl*; **at —** al coste/costo; **at all —s** a toda costa; **— of living** costo/coste de vida *m*; **to sell at —** vender al costo / al coste; VT costar; **how much does this —?** ¿cuánto vale/cuesta esto? ADJ **— -benefit analysis** análisis costo-beneficio *m*; **— effective** económico

costar [kɔ́stɑr] N coprotagonista *mf*, oponente *mf*

Costa Rica [kɔ́stəríkə] N Costa Rica *f*

Costa Rican [kɔ́stəríkən] ADJ & N costarricense *mf*, costarrigueño -ña *mf*

costly [kɔ́stli] ADJ costoso, caro

costume [kɑ́stum] N (style of clothing) vestimenta *f*; (in the theater) vestuario *m*; (disguise) disfraz *m*; **— jewelry** bisutería *f*

cot [kɑt] N catre *m*

cottage [kɑ́dɪʤ] N (small house) casita *f*; (vacation house) cabaña *f*, chalé *m*; **— cheese** requesón *m*

cotter pin [kɑ́də-pɪn] N chaveta *f*

cotton [kɑtn] N algodón *m*; **— candy** algodón de azúcar *m*; **— gin** desmontadora de algodón *f*; **—seed** semilla de algodón *f*; **—wood** álamo [de Virginia] *m*

couch [kaʊtʃ] N sofá *m*; (psychiatrist's) diván *m*; **— potato** telebobo -ba *mf*; VT expresar

cougar [kúgə-] N puma *f*

cough [kɔf] VI toser; **to — up** (spit) expectorar; (hand over) soltar, largar; N tos *f*; **— drop** pastilla para la tos *f*; **— syrup** jarabe para la tos *m*

could [kʊd] V AUX **I — do it if I wanted** podría hacerlo si quisiera; **— you arrive early?** ¿podrías llegar temprano? **— I leave early?** ¿puedo salir temprano? **you — be right** quizá tengas razón

council [kɑ́ʊnsəɫ] N (religious) concilio *m*; (advisory) consejo *m*, junta *f*; (provincial) diputación *f*; (municipal) concejo *m*; **—man** concejal *m*; **—woman** concejal *f*, concejala *f*

councilor [kɑ́ʊnsələ-] N concejal *mf*

counsel [kɑ́ʊnsəɫ] N (advice) consejo *m*; (lawyer) abogado -da *mf*; VI/VT (give advice) aconsejar

counseling [kɑ́ʊnsəlɪŋ] N (academic) asesoramiento *m*, orientación *f*; (psychological, marriage) terapia *f*

counselor [kɑ́ʊnsələ-] N consejero -ra *mf*; (lawyer) abogado -da *mf*

count [kaʊnt] VI/VT contar; **to — in** incluir; **to — on** contar con; **to — oneself lucky** considerarse dichoso; **to — out** excluir; N (reckoning) cuenta *f*; (charge) cargo *m*; (noble) conde *m*; (in baseball) conteo *m*; **—down** cuenta regresiva *f*

countenance [kɑ́ʊntnəns] N (expression) semblante *m*; (face) cara *f*; VT (tolerate)

tolerar; (approve) aprobar

counter [káʊntɚ] N (in a kitchen) *Sp* encimera *f*; *Am* mostrador *m*; (in a store) mostrador *m*; (in a bar) barra *f*; (in board games) tablero *m*; (counting device) contador *m*; **over the —** sin receta; ADJ contrario, opuesto; ADV **— to** contra; **to run — to** ser contrario a; VT (an argument) retrucar (a blow), devolver; VI/VT (reply) replicar

counteract [kaʊntɚǽkt] VT contrarrestar

counterattack [káʊntɚətæk] N contraataque *m*; VI/VT contraatacar

counterbalance[1] [kaʊntɚbǽləns] VI/VT contrapesar

counterbalance[2] [káʊntɚbæləns] N contrapeso *m*

counterclockwise [kaʊntɚklɑ́kwaɪz] ADV en el sentido opuesto al de las manecillas del reloj

counterculture [káʊntɚkʌltʃɚ] N contracultura *f*

counterespionage [kaʊntɚéspiənɑʒ] N contraespionaje *m*

counterexample [káʊntɚɪgzæmpəɫ] N contraejemplo *m*

counterfeit [káʊntɚfɪt] N falsificación *f*; ADJ falso; **— money** moneda falsa *f*; VT falsificar

countermand[1] [kaʊntɚmǽnd] VT contramandar

countermand[2] [káʊntɚmænd] N contraorden *f*

countermeasure [káʊntɚmɛʒɚ] N contramedida *f*

counteroffer [káʊntɚɔfɚ] N contraoferta *f*

counterpart [káʊntɚpɑrt] N homólogo -ga *mf*

counterproductive [kaʊntɚprədʌ́ktɪv] ADJ contraproducente

counterrevolution [kaʊntɚrɛvəlúʃən] N contrarrevolución *f*

countersign [káʊntɚsaɪn] N contraseña *f*; VT refrendar

countess [káʊntɪs] N condesa *f*

countless [káʊntɪlɪs] ADJ incontables, innumerables

country [kʌ́ntri] N (nation) país *m*; (territory) territorio *m*; (homeland) patria *f*; (rural area) campo *m*; ADJ (of the countryside) rural; (uncouth) rústico; **— club** club campestre *m*; **— code** código de país *m*; **—man** compatriota *m*; **— music** música country *f*; **— of origin** país de origen *m*; **—side** (rural area) campo *m*; (scenery) paisaje *m*; **—woman** compatriota *f*

county [káʊnti] N condado *m*; **— fair** feria [de ganado] *f*; **— seat** capital de condado *f*

coup [ku] N (success) golpe maestro *m*; (putsch) golpe de estado *m*; **— d'état** golpe de estado *m*

coupe [kup] N cupé *m*

couple [kʌ́pəɫ] N (of times, of forces, of people) par *m*; (romantic) pareja *f*; VI/VT (pair up) formar parejas; VT (connect) acoplar; VI (copulate) copular

couplet [kʌ́plɪt] N pareado *m*

coupling [kʌ́plɪŋ] N (mechanical action) acoplamiento *m*, enganche *m*; (device) acople *m*, enganche *m*; (mating) cópula *f*

coupon [kjúpɑn] N cupón *m*

courage [kɝ́ɪdʒ] N valentía *f*, valor *m*, coraje *m*

courageous [kəréɪʤəs] ADJ valiente

courier [kʊ́riɚ] N mensajero -ra *mf*

course [kɔrs] N (of a river, of study, of a disease) curso *m*; (of a road, route) trayecto *m*; (of a ship, plane) derrotero *m*; (progression of time) marcha *f*; (dish) plato *m*; **— of action** línea de conducta *f*, proceder *m*; **in the — of a year** en el transcurso de un año; **in due —** a la larga; INTERJ **of —** claro, por supuesto, naturalmente; VI correr, fluir

court [kɔrt] N (courtyard) patio *m*; (atrium) patio interior *m*; (in sports) cancha *f*, pista *f*; (in a city) plazuela *f*, plazoleta *f*; (lower tribunal) juzgado *m*; (higher tribunal) tribunal *m*; (session) audiencia *f*; (royal residence, retinue) corte *f*; **— -martial** consejo de guerra *m*; **— of law** tribunal de justicia *m*; **— order** orden judicial *f*; **— reporter** estenotipista *mf*; **— room** tribunal *m*; **—yard** patio *m*; **to settle out of —** llegar a un arreglo extrajudicial; **to pay — to** cortejar; VT cortejar, galantear; **to — danger** tentar a la suerte; **to — -martial** someter a consejo de guerra; VI estar de novios

courteous [kɝ́ɪdəs] ADJ cortés

courtesy [kɝ́ɪdɪsi] N (attitude) cortesía *f*; (act) fineza *f*, atención *f*

courtier [kɔ́rdiɚ] N (member of the court) cortesano -na *mf*; (sycophant) adulador -ora *mf*

courtship [kɔ́rtʃɪp] N cortejo *m*

cousin [kʌ́zən] N primo -ma *mf*; **first —** primo -ma hermano -na *mf*

cove [kov] N ensenada *f*

covenant [kʌ́vənənt] N pacto *m*; (religious) alianza *f*

cover [kʌ́vɚ] VI/VT cubrir, recubrir; (with lid, screen) tapar; (replace) sustituir; (include, deal with) comprender; (traverse) recorrer; (sing) hacer una versión; **—ed losses** pérdidas cubiertas *f pl*; **to — up** (wrap up) tapar bien; (hide) ocultar; N (lid) tapa *f*; (book) cubierta *f*, tapa *f*; (blanket) manta *f*; (for appliances, furniture) funda *f*; (front for activity) tapadera *f*, pantalla *f*; (shelter) resguardo *m*, abrigo *m*; **—all** mono *m*; **— charge** entrada *f*; **— girl** modelo de portada *f*; **— letter** carta con anexos *f*, carta de remisión *f*; **— -up** encubrimiento *m*; **to send under separate —** enviar por separado; **to take —** resguardarse; **under —** de incógnito;

under — of dark bajo el manto de la noche
coverage [kávə-ɪʤ] N cobertura *f*; **— level** nivel de cobertura *m*
covert [kovɝt] ADJ encubierto
covet [kávɪt] VT (desire wrongfully) codiciar; (want) ansiar
covetous [kávɪDəs] ADJ codicioso
cow [kaʊ] N (bovine female) vaca *f*; (female of other animals) hembra *f*; **—bell** cencerro *m*, esquila *f*; **—boy** vaquero *m*; **—hide** cuero de vaca *m*, vaqueta *f*; **—lick** remolino *m*; **—pox** vacuna *f*; **—shed** vaquería *f*, vaqueriza *f*; **to have a —** tener una pataleta; VT intimidar
coward [káʊə-d] N cobarde *mf*
cowardice [káʊə-DɪS] N cobardía *f*
cowardly [káʊə-dli] ADJ cobarde
cower [káʊə-] VI achicarse
cowl [kaʊł] N capucha *f*
coy [kɔɪ] ADJ (coquettish) remilgado; (evasive) esquivo
coyote [kaɪóDɪ, káɪot] N coyote *m*
cozy [kózi] ADJ (warm) acogedor; (beneficial) conveniente; VI **to — up to** adular
CPA [certified public accountant] [sípíé] N contador -ora público -ca con licencia *mf*
CPI [consumer price index] [sípíáɪ] N índice de precios al consumidor *m*
CPR [cardiopulmonary resuscitation] [sípíár] N reanimación cardiopulmonar *f*
CPU [central processing unit] [sípíjú] N UCP *f*
crab [kræb] N cangrejo *m*; (mechanism) carro corredizo *m*; (grouch) cascarrabias *mf sg*; **— apple** manzana silvestre *f*; **—s** (parasites) ladillas *f pl*; VI (fish) pescar cangrejos; (complain) quejarse
crack [kræk] VI (single fissure) rajarse; (multiple fissures) resquebrajarse, agrietarse; (psychological breakdown) sufrir un ataque de nervios; (of voice) quebrarse; VT (knuckles) hacer un chasquido con, chascar, chasquear; (nuts) cascar; (jokes) contar; (a prisoner) quebrar; (a case) resolver; (a code) descifrar; (a door) entreabrir; **to — down on** reprimir; **that —s me up** eso me hace desternillar de risa; N (fissure) rajadura *f*, grieta *f*, resquebrajadura *f*; (sound) chasquido *m*; (joke) pulla *f*, chanza *f*; **— cocaine** crack *m*; **—down** represión *f*; **—house** fumadero *m*; **—pot** excéntrico -ca *mf*; **at the — of dawn** al romper el alba; **I'd like a — at the championship** me gustaría poder participar en el campeonato
cracked [krækt] ADJ rajado, quebrado; (crazy) chiflado; **it's not all it's — up to be** no es para tanto
cracker [krákə-] N galleta *f*
crackle [krákəł] N (of paper) crujido *m*; (of fire) crepitación *f*; VI crujir, crepitar
cradle [krédl] N cuna *f*
craft [kræft] N (skill) destreza *f*; (cunning) astucia *f*; (occupation) arte *m*, oficio *m*; (boat) embarcación *f*; **—sman** artesano *m*; **—swoman** artesana *f*; VT fabricar
crafty [kráfti] ADJ astuto, taimado
crag [kræg] N risco *m*, peñasco *m*, peñón *m*
craggy [krági] ADJ peñascoso
cram [kræm] VT (pack in) embutir; VI (study intensely) memorizar; *Sp* empollar; **the bar was —med with people** el bar estaba atestado
cramp [kræmp] N (spasm) calambre *m*; (staple) grapa *f*; VI/VT (to suffer a spasm) acalambrar[se]; VT (to staple) engrapar; **you're —ing my style** me estorbas
cranberry [krænberi] N arándano rojo *m*
crane [kren] N (bird) grulla *f*; (machine) grúa *f*; VT **to — one's neck** estirar el cuello
cranium [kréniəm] N cráneo *m*
crank [kræŋk] N (mechanism) manivela *f*; (grouch) cascarrabias *mf sg*; (overzealous advocate) fanático -ca *mf*; **—case** cárter superior del aceite *m*; **—shaft** cigüeñal *m*; VI/VT arrancar con manivela
cranky [kráŋki] ADJ (irritable) irritable; (eccentric) excéntrico
cranny [kráni] N (crevice) rendija *f*; (corner) recoveco *m*
crash [kræʃ] VI (collide) estrellarse; (market) quebrar; (stay overnight with someone) quedarse a dormir; (hang up, as with a computer) bloquearse, caerse; (sleep) dormir; VT **to — a party** colarse en una fiesta; N (noise) estallido *m*; (collision) choque *m*; (financial collapse) quiebra *f*, colapso *m*; (computer failure) bloqueo *m*, caída *f*; **— landing** aterrizaje forzoso *m*
crass [kræs] ADJ craso
crate [kret] N cajón *m*, guacal *m*; VT poner en cajones
crater [krédə-] N cráter *m*
cravat [krəvæt] N corbata *f*
crave [krev] VT anhelar; **I — chocolate** me muero por un chocolate
craving [krévɪŋ] N antojo *m*
crawl [krɔł] VI (on hands and knees) gatear; (on the belly) arrastrarse, reptar; (proceed slowly) avanzar a paso de tortuga; **to be —ing with** hormiguear de; N (swimming stroke) crol *m*; **traffic is going at a —** el tráfico va a paso de tortuga
crayon [kréɑn] N lápiz de color *m*, Crayola™ *f*
craze [krez] N (fad) moda pasajera *f*; VI/VT enloquecer[se]
craziness [krézɪnɪs] N locura *f*, chifladura *f*
crazy [krézi] ADJ & N loco -ca *mf*; **I'm — about you** estoy loco por ti; **that's —!** ¡qué locura! **to go —** volverse loco, enloquecerse
creak [krik] N (of wooden floor) crujido *m*; (of a

hinge) rechinamiento *m*; VI (a wooden floor) crujir; (a hinge) rechinar

cream [krim] N (milk product) crema *f*; *Sp* nata *f*; (medicament) crema *f*; **— cheese** queso de untar *m*, queso crema *m*; **— of tomato soup** sopa crema de tomate *f*; **the — of the crop** la flor y nata; VT (decream) desnatar; (butter, sugar) batir; (vegetables) preparar con salsa blanca; (defeat) aplastar

creamy [krími] ADJ cremoso

crease [kris] N (in trousers) raya *f*, repliegue *m*; (wrinkle) arruga *f*; VT (trousers) planchar la raya; (wrinkle) arrugar

create [kriét] VI/VT crear

creation [kriéʃən] N creación *f*

creationism [kriéʃənɪzəm] N creacionismo *m*

creative [kriétɪv] ADJ creativo

creativity [kriətívɪdɪ] N creatividad *f*

creator [kriétə-] N creador -ra *mf*

creature [krítʃə-] N (being) ser *m*; (animal) animal *m*; **a — of your imagination** un producto de tu imaginación

credence [krídns] N crédito *m*

credentials [krɪdéntʃəłz] N credenciales *f pl*

credibility [krɛdɪbílɪdɪ] N credibilidad *f*

credible [krédəbəł] ADJ creíble

credit [krédɪt] N crédito *m*; (commendation) reconocimiento *m*; **— approval** aprobación de crédito *f*; **— card** tarjeta de crédito *f*; **— counseling** asesoramiento de crédito *m*; **— line** línea de crédito *f*; **— history** historial de crédito *m*; **— rating** calificación crediticia *f*; **— report** informe de crédito *m*; **—s** créditos *m pl*; **— underwriters** aseguradores de crédito *m pl*; **— union** banco cooperativo *m*; **on —** a crédito; **to give — to** (believe) dar crédito; (ascribe) acreditar; ADJ **—worthy** solvente; VT (believe) creer; (enter as credit) acreditar; (attribute) atribuir; **— an account** abonar/acreditar a una cuenta

creditor [krédɪtə-] N acreedor -ora *mf*

credulous [krédʒələs] ADJ crédulo

creed [krid] N credo *m*

creek [krik] N arroyo *m*, quebrada *f*

creep [krip] VI (crawl on belly) arrastrarse; (crawl on all fours) gatear; (grow upward) trepar; (go slowly) andar a paso de tortuga; **to — up on** acercarse furtivamente a; N (obnoxious person) *pej* persona repulsiva *f*, sinvergüenza *mf*; **that gives me the —s** eso me da asco; *Sp* eso me da grima

creeper [krípə-] N enredadera *f*, planta trepadora *f*

creepy [krípi] ADJ repulsivo

cremate [krímet] VT cremar

Creole [kríoł] ADJ & N criollo -lla *mf*

creosote [kríəsot] N creosota *f*

crepe [krep] N (fabric) crespón *m*; (band of fabric) crespón negro *m*

crept [krɛpt] *see* creep

crescent [krésənt] N media luna *f*; ADJ creciente

crest [krɛst] N (of a wave, rooster) cresta *f*; (of feathers) penacho *m*, copete *m*; (of mountain) cima *f*, cumbre *f*; (of heraldic arms) timbre *m*; **—fallen** alicaído, cabizbajo; VI **the river —ed at two meters above flood level** el río creció hasta dos metros por encima de lo normal

crevice [krévɪs] N grieta *f*

crew [kru] N (for ships, etc.) tripulación *f*; (of workers) cuadrilla *f*; **— member** tripulante *mf*

crib [krɪb] N (bed) cuna *f*; (manger) pesebre *m*; (bin for grain) granero *m*; (cheat notes) hoja para copiar *f*; **— death** síndrome de muerte súbita infantil *m*; VI copiar

cricket [kríkɪt] N (insect) grillo *m*; (game) críquet *m*

crime [kraɪm] N (illegal act) delito *m*; (act of violence against people) crimen *m*; (criminal activity) delincuencia *f*, criminalidad *f*

criminal [krímənəł] ADJ & N delincuente *mf*, malhechor -ora *mf*; (perpetrator of violent crimes) criminal *mf*; **— record** antecedentes delictivos *m pl*

crimp [krɪmp] VT rizar; N rizo *m*

crimson [krímzən] ADJ & N carmesí *m*, carmín *m*

cringe [krɪnʤ] VI **it makes me —** me da vergüenza ajena

cripple [krípəł] N *offensive* tullido -da *mf*; (in the legs) *pey* cojo -ja *mf*; (in the arms) *offensive* manco -ca *mf*; VT tullir

crisis [kráɪsɪs] N crisis *f*

crisp [krɪsp] ADJ (apple, bacon) crocante, crujiente; (weather) fresco y despejado; (hair) crespo; VI/VT volver crujiente

crispy [críspi] ADJ crocante, crujiente

criterion [kraɪtíriən] N criterio *m*

critic [krídɪk] N crítico -ca *mf*

critical [krídɪkəł] ADJ crítico; **— stage** punto culminante *m*

criticism [krídɪsɪzəm] N crítica *f*

criticize [krídɪsaɪz] VT criticar

croak [krok] VI (make the sound of a frog) croar; (make the sound of a crow) graznar; (die) *fam* espichar; N (sound made by frogs) canto de rana *m*; (sound made by crows) graznido *m*

Croatia [kroéʃə] N Croacia *f*

Croatian [kroéʃən] ADJ & N croata *mf*

crochet [kroʃé] N ganchillo *m*, croché *m*, crochet *m*; **— hook** aguja de croché *f*; VI hacer ganchillo, hacer croché

crock [krak] N (pot) vasija *f*; (lies) pamplinas *f pl*

crockery [krákəri] N loza *f*

crocodile [krákədaɪł] N cocodrilo *m*

croissant [krəsánt] N cruasán *m*, croissant *m*

crony [króni] N compinche *mf*, compadre *m*, comadre *f*

cronyism [krónɪzəm] N amiguismo *m*
crook [krʊk] N (criminal) delincuente *mf*; (curve) curva *f*; (hook) gancho *m*; (staff) cayado *m*
crooked [krʊ́kɪd] ADJ (bent) torcido; *Am* chueco; (dishonest) deshonesto
crop [krɑp] N (harvest) cosecha *f*; (group of contemporaries) promoción *f*; (of a bird) buche *m*; (horse whip) fusta *f*; **— rotation** rotación de cultivos *f*; VT (graze) pastar, pacer; (trim) recortar; **to — up** surgir
croquet [kroké] N cróquet *m*
cross [krɔs] N (symbol) cruz *f*; (street intersection) cruce *m*; (soccer) pase cruzado *m*; (act of mixing) cruzamiento *m*; (in boxing) cruzado *m*; **—bar** (soccer) travesaño *m*, larguero *m*; (in gymnastics) barra *f*; (in high jump) listón *m*; (of a door) tranca *f*; **—-check** verificación *f*; **—court shot** golpe cruzado *m*; **—-fertilization** fecundación cruzada *f*; **—piece** cruceta *f*; **—-reference** referencia cruzada *f*; **—road** encrucijada *f*; **— section** corte transversal *m*; **—walk** cruce peatonal *m*, cebra *f*; **—word puzzle** crucigrama *m*; **to bear one's —** cargar la cruz; VI/VT (intersect, form a cross, breed, meet) cruzar[se]; (make sign of the cross) santiguarse; **to —-check** verificar; VT (betray) traicionar; (move to other side) cruzar; **to — examine** interrogar; **to — out** tachar; **to — over** (change allegiance) cambiar de bando; (go to the other side) traspasar; **to —-reference** hacer una referencia cruzada; **you've —ed the line** te pasaste de la raya; ADJ (transverse) transversal; (angry) enojado; **—-country** a campo traviesa; **—-cultural** transcultural; **—-eyed** bizco; **to be —-eyed** bizquear
crossing [krɔ́sɪŋ] N (street or railroad intersection, pedestrian path) cruce *m*; (hybridization, act of mixing) cruzamiento *m*; (of ocean) travesía *f*; (of a border) paso *m*; (of a river) vado *m*
crotch [krɑtʃ] N entrepierna *f*
crotchety [krɑ́tʃɪdɪ] ADJ cascarrabias *inv*
crouch [kraʊtʃ] VI (stoop) agacharse; (prepare to spring) agazaparse
croup [krup] N tos *f*, croup *m*
crow [kro] N (bird) cuervo *m*; (sound of rooster) canto del gallo *m*; **—bar** alzaprima *f*; **—'s-foot** pata de gallo *f*; **to eat —** comerse sus propias palabras; VI cantar; (gloat, brag) jactarse
crowd [kraʊd] N (group of people) muchedumbre *f*, gentío *m*, aglomeración *f*; (at a performance) público *m*; (clique) pandilla *f*; VI (push forward) agolparse; VI/VT (gather in large numbers) apiñar[se], amontonar[se], aglomerar[se]; (gather in a confined space) hacinar[se]
crowded [kráʊdɪd] ADJ **it is — in here** hay demasiada gente aquí; **the restaurant is —** el restaurante está lleno
crown [kraʊn] N corona *f*; (of head) coronilla *f*, crisma *f*; (of a hat) copa *f*; **— jewels** joyas de la corona *f pl*; VT coronar; (hit on head) dar un coscorrón
crucial [krúʃəł] ADJ (element) fundamental; (moment) crucial
crucible [krúsəbəł] N crisol *m*
crucifix [krúsəfɪks] N crucifijo *m*
crucify [krúsəfaɪ] VT crucificar
crud [krʌd] N (filth) mugre *f*; (worthless thing, sickness, despicable person) *fam* porquería *f*
crude [krud] ADJ (vulgar, unpolished) basto, tosco; **— oil** petróleo crudo *m*
cruel [krúəł] ADJ cruel
cruelty [krúəłti] N crueldad *f*
cruise [kruz] VI (take a cruise) tomar un crucero; (patrol) patrullar; **— control** control de crucero *m*; **cruising speed** velocidad de crucero *f*; N crucero *m*; **— missile** misil crucero *m*
cruiser [krúzɚ] N crucero *m*
crumb [krʌm] N (small) miga *f*, migaja *f*; (large) mendrugo *m*; VT (break into crumbs) desmigajar; (remove crumbs) sacar las migas
crumble [krʌ́mbəł] VI/VT (bread) desmigajar[se]; (clods of dirt) desmenuzar[se]; (house) desmoronar[se]
crummy [krʌ́mi] ADJ (place) *fam* de mala muerte; (object) *fam* de porquería; (show) flojo
crumple [krʌ́mpəł] VI/VT (crush) arrugar[se]; VI (collapse) aplastarse
crunch [krʌntʃ] VI/VT (eat noisily) mascar; N (sound) crujido *m*; (shortage) crisis *f*; **—es** abdominales *m pl*
crunchy [krʌ́ntʃi] ADJ crocante, crujiente
crusade [kruséd] N cruzada *f*; VI (engage in a campaign) hacer una campaña
crusader [kruséɚ] N cruzado -da *mf*; **a — for human rights** un paladín de los derechos humanos
crush [krʌʃ] VI/VT aplastar, machacar; (stone) demoler; N (act of crushing) aplastamiento *m*; (crowd) tumulto *m*; (infatuation) enamoramiento *m*; **—ing victory** victoria contundente *f*
crust [krʌst] N (of bread, earth) corteza *f*; (of bread) costra *f*; (of pie) tapa *f*
crusty [krʌ́sti] ADJ (with a crust) costroso; (grouchy) irascible
crutch [krʌtʃ] N muleta *f*
cry [kraɪ] N (shout) grito *m*; (weeping) llanto *m*; (call of a bird) reclamo *m*; **—baby** llorón -ona *mf*; **a far — from** muy distante de, muy lejos de; VI (shout) gritar; (weep) llorar; **to — over spilt milk** hacer como la lechera; **to — for**

attention reclamar atención; **to — for help** pedir socorro; **to — out** vocear
cryogenic [kraɪəʤɛ́nɪk] ADJ criogénico
crystal [krístḷ] N cristal *m*; **— ball** bola de cristal *f*; **— clear** cristalino
crystalline [krístḷɪn] ADJ cristalino
crystallize [krístḷaɪz] VI/VT cristalizar[se]
cub [kʌb] N (lion) cachorro *m*; (bear) osezno *m*; (whale) ballenato *m*; (wolf) lobato *m*, lobezno *m*; **— reporter** reportero -ra novato -ta *mf*
Cuba [kjúbə] N Cuba *f*
Cuban [kjúbən] ADJ & N cubano -na *mf*
cubbyhole [kʌ́bɪhoł] N casilla *f*
cube [kjúb] N cubo *m*; **— root** raíz cúbica *f*; VT (cut) cortar en cubos; (raise to the third power) elevar al cubo
cubic [kjúbɪk] ADJ cúbico
cubicle [kjúbɪkəł] N cubículo *m*
cubism [kjúbɪzəm] N cubismo *m*
cuckold [kʌ́kəłd] N cornudo *m*, cabrón *m*; VT poner los cuernos a
cuckoo [kʊ́ku] N cuclillo *m*, cuco *m*; **— clock** reloj de cucú *m*; ADJ & N chiflado -da *mf*; INTERJ cucú
cucumber [kjúkʌmbɚ] N pepino *m*
cud [kʌd] N **to chew the —** rumiar
cuddle [kʌ́dḷ] VI/VT hacer[se] mimos; N mimo *m*
cuddly [kʌ́dlɪ] ADJ mimoso
cudgel [kʌ́ʤəł] N porra *f*; VT aporrear
cue [kju] N (in theater) pie *m*; (psychological stimulus) estímulo *m*; **— ball** bola blanca *f*; **— stick** taco de billar *m*; VT dar pie, dar la señal
cuff [kʌf] N (of sleeve, glove) puño *m*; (of pants) bajo *m*; (blow) bofetada *f*; **hand—s** esposas *f pl*; VT (in making pants) hacer los bajos; (put on handcuffs) esposar; (hit) abofetear
cuisine [kwɪzín] N cocina *f*
cul-de-sac [kʌ́łdəsæk] N callejón sin salida *m*
culinary [kjúlənɛri, kʌ́lənɛri] ADJ culinario
cull [kʌł] VT (choose) seleccionar, entresacar; (collect) recoger
culminate [kʌ́łmənet] VI/VT culminar
culmination [kʌłmənéʃən] N culminación *f*
culprit [kʌ́łprɪt] N culpable *mf*
cult [kʌłt] N (sect) secta religiosa *f*; (worship) culto *m*
cultivable [kʌ́łtəvəbəł] ADJ cultivable
cultivate [kʌ́łtəvet] VT cultivar
cultivated [kʌ́łtəvɛdɪd] ADJ (land) cultivado; (plant) de cultivo; (person) culto
cultivation [kʌłtəvéʃən] N (tillage) cultivo *m*; (education) cultura *f*
cultivator [kʌ́łtəvɛdɚ] N (person) cultivador -ora *mf*; (implement) cultivadora *f*
cultural [kʌ́łtʃə-əł] ADJ cultural
culture [kʌ́łtʃɚ] N cultura *f*; (microorganisms) cultivo *m*; **— shock** choque cultural *m*; VT (microorganisms) cultivar
cultured [kʌ́łtʃə-d] ADJ (person) culto; (pearl) cultivado, de cultivo
cumbersome [kʌ́mbə-səm] ADJ (bulky) voluminoso; (unwieldy) incómodo
cumulative [kjúmjələɪv] ADJ acumulativo
cumulus [kjúmjləs] N cúmulo *m*
cunning [kʌ́nɪŋ] ADJ (sly) astuto, zorro; N astucia *f*, maña *f*
cup [kʌp] N (with handle) taza *f*, pocillo *m*; (without handle) vaso *m*; (measure) taza *f*; (trophy, brassiere part) copa *f*; **—board** armario *m*, aparador *m*
cur [kɝ] N (dog) perro *m*; (villain) *pej* villano -na *mf*
curable [kjúrəbəł] ADJ curable
curator [kjúrɛdɚ] N conservador -ora *mf*
curb [kɝb] N (of a street) *Sp* bordillo *m*; *Mex* borde *m*; *RP* cordón *m*; (of a well) brocal *m*; (restraint) freno *m*, restricción *f*; VT (emotions) refrenar; (spending) limitar
curd [kɝd] N cuajada *f*; VI/VT cuajar[se], coagular[se]
curdle [kɝ́dḷ] VI/VT cuajar[se], coagular[se]; **my blood —d** se me heló la sangre
cure [kjur] N (healing, preserving meat) cura *f*, curación *f*; (method) tratamiento *m*; VI/VT curar[se]; **— -all** sanalotodo *m*
curfew [kɝ́fju] N toque de queda *m*, queda *f*
curio [kjúrio] N curiosidad *f*
curiosity [kjuriɑ́sɪdi] N curiosidad *f*
curious [kjúriəs] ADJ curioso
curl [kɝł] VI/VT (form ringlets) rizar[se], ensortijar[se]; (coil) enroscar[se]; (smoke) alzarse en espirales; **to — up** ovillar[se]; N (of hair) rizo *m*, bucle *m*; (of smoke) espiral *f*
curler [kɝ́lə-] N *Sp* rulo *m*; *Mex* tubo *m*; *RP* rulero *m*
curly [kɝ́li] ADJ rizado
currant [kɝ́ənt] N (fruit) grosella *f*; (tree) grosellero *m*
currency [kɝ́ənsi] N (money) moneda *f*, divisa *f*; (acceptance) aceptación *f*; **— exchange** mercado de divisas *m*; **— unit** unidad monetaria *f*
current [kɝ́ənt] ADJ (commonly used) corriente; (prevalent) actual; **the — issue of a magazine** el último número de una revista; **— year** año en curso *m*; N (of river, electricity, air) corriente *f*
currently [kɝ́əntlɪ] ADV actualmente
curriculum [kəríkjələm] N plan de estudios *m*, currículo *m*
curry [kɝ́ri] N curry *m*
curse [kɝs] N (ill wish) maldición *f*; (swear word) palabrota *f*; VI/VT (wish ill) maldecir; (swear) decir palabrotas
cursive [kɝ́sɪv] ADJ cursivo; N cursiva *f*
cursor [kɝ́sɚ] N cursor *m*
curt [kɝt] ADJ (abrupt) seco, brusco; (brief) breve
curtail [kɚtét] VT restringir, cercenar

curtain [kɝtn̩] N cortina *f*; (theater) telón *m*; VT ponerle cortinas a
curvature [kɝvətʃʊr] N curvatura *f*; (of the spine) desviación *f*
curve [kɝv] N (also in baseball) curva *f*; **he threw me a —** me agarró desprevenido; VI/VT encorvar[se]; (road) torcer[se], desviar[se]
curved [kɝvd] ADJ curvo
cushion [kʊ́ʃən] N (pad) almohadilla *f*; (emergency resources, pad of air) colchón *m*; (pillow) almohadón *m*; (decorative pillow) cojín *m*; VT (put pads) poner almohadones; (soften a blow) amortiguar
cuspid [kə́spɪd] N colmillo *m*
cuss [kʌs] VI decir palabrotas; N **—word** *fam* palabrota *f*; **strange old —** *fam* bicho raro *m*
custard [kə́stɝd] N flan *m*, natilla[s] *f sg or pl*
custodian [kʌstóʊdiən] N (caretaker) cuidador -ora *mf*; (guardian) custodio -dia *mf*
custody [kə́stədi] N custodia *f*; **to take into —** detener
custom [kə́stəm] N costumbre *f*, uso *m*; **—s** (government department) aduana *f*; (taxes) derechos de aduana *m pl*; **—[s]house** aduana *f*; ADJ **—-built** construido por encargo; **—-made** hecho a medida
customary [kə́stəmeri] ADJ acostumbrado
customer [kə́stəmɚ] N cliente -ta *mf*; **— base** clientela *f*; **— care** atención al cliente *f*; **— rights** derechos del cliente *m pl*; ADJ **—-oriented** orientado al cliente
customize [kə́stəmaɪz] VT adaptar por encargo
cut [kʌt] VI/VT cortar; (shorten) acortar; (harvest) talar; (lower) rebajar; **—!** ¡corte[n]! **to — a deal** llegar a un arreglo; **to — across** (take a shortcut) cortar por; (transcend) trascender; **to — and paste** cortar y pegar; **to — back** reducir; **to — class** faltar a clase; **to — costs** reducir costos; **to — down on** reducir; **to — in** (interrupt) interrumpir; (in traffic) atravesarse; **to — prices** bajar los precios; **may I — in?** ¿me permite? **to — off** (interrupt) interrumpir; (intercept) interceptar; **to — out** omitir; **to be — out for** estar hecho para; **to — up** (divide) trozar; (misbehave) portarse mal; N corte *m*; (in salary) recorte *m*, reducción *f*; (of prices) rebaja *f*; (of a suit) hechura *f*, corte *m*; (insult) desaire *f*; **—back** recorte *m*; **— glass** cristal labrado *m*; **—off date** fecha límite *f*; ADJ **—-and-dried** predeterminado; **—-rate** de rebajas; **—throat** despiadado
cutaneous [kjuténiəs] ADJ cutáneo
cute [kjut] ADJ mono, rico; **to act —** ser afectado, ser melindroso
cuticle [kjúʊɪkəł] N cutícula *f*
cutlery [kə́tləri] N (knives, knife store) cuchillería *f*; (eating utensils) cubiertos *m pl*
cutlet [kə́tlɪt] N filete *m*
cutter [kə́dɚ] N (person) cortador -ora *mf*; (device) cortadora *f*; (sleigh) trineo *m*; **Coast Guard —** guardacostas *m sg*
cutting [kə́dɪŋ] ADJ (sharp) cortante; (cold) penetrante; (sarcastic) mordaz, sarcástico; **— board** tabla de cortar *f*; **— edge** filo *m*; **—-edge technology** tecnología de punta *f*; N (action) cortado *m*
CV [curriculum vitae] [sívi] N currículo *m*, currículum vitae *m*
cyanide [sáɪənaɪd] N cianuro *m*
cybercafe [saɪbɚkafé] N cibercafé *m*
cybernetics [saɪbɚnɛ́dɪks] N cibernética *f*
cyberpunk [sáɪbɚpʌnk] N ciberpunk *m*
cyberspace [sáɪbɚspes] N ciberespacio *m*
cyborg [sáɪbɔrg] N cyborg *m*
cycle [sáɪkəł] N ciclo *m*
cyclical [síklɪkəł] ADJ cíclico
cyclone [sáɪklon] N ciclón *m*
cyclotron [sáɪklətrɑn] N ciclotrón *m*
cylinder [sílɪndɚ] N cilindro *m*; (of a gun) tambor *m*; **— head** culata *f*
cylindrical [sɪlíndrɪkəł] ADJ cilíndrico
cymbal [símbəł] N címbalo *m*, platillo *m*
cynic [sínɪk] N cínico -ca *mf*
cynical [sínɪkəł] ADJ cínico
cynicism [sínɪsɪzəm] N cinismo *m*
cypress [sáɪprɪs] N ciprés *m*
Cypriot, Cypriote [sípriət] ADJ & N chipriota *mf*
Cyprus [sáɪprəs] N Chipre *m*
cyst [sɪst] N quiste *m*
cystic [sístɪk] ADJ cístico; **— fibrosis** fibrosis cística *f*
cytology [saɪtáləʤi] N citología *f*
czar [zɑr] N zar *m*
Czech [tʃɛk] ADJ & N checo -ca *mf*; **— Republic** República Checa *f*

Dd

dab [dæb] VT (pat) dar toques; (apply) aplicar con golpecitos; N toque *m*
dabble [dǽbəł] VI (splash) chapotear; (be interested superficially) ser aficionado a
dachshund [dáksənd] N perro salchicha *m*
dad [dæd] N papá *m*
daddy [dǽdi] N papaíto *m*, papito *m*, papacito *m*
daffodil [dǽfədɪł] N narciso *m*
dagger [dǽgɚ] N daga *f*, puñal *m*
dahlia [dǽljə] N dalia *f*
daily [déli] ADJ diario; **— planner** agenda *f*; **— wage** jornal *m*, salario *m*; N (newspaper) diario *m*
dainty [dénti] ADJ (delicate) delicado, exquisito; (finicky) remilgado
dairy [déri] N (milk) lechería *f*; (cheese) quesería

f; ADJ (industry) lechero; (product) lácteo; N producto lácteo *m*

daisy [dézi] N margarita *f*; **to be pushing up daisies** *fam* estar criando malvas

dale [deɪl] N valle *m*

dally [dǽli] VI (flirt) coquetear; (risk danger) jugar con fuego; (waste time) remolonear

dam [dæm] N presa *f*, represa *f*; VT represar

damage [dǽmɪʤ] N daño *m*, destrozo *m*; **—control** control de daños *m*; **—s** daños y perjuicios *m pl*; **to pay —s** indemnizar *m*; VI/VT dañar[se]

damaging [dǽmɪʤɪŋ] ADJ perjudicial

dame [dem] N (noblewoman) dama *f*; (woman) *pej* tipa *f*

damn [dæm] VT condenar

damnation [dæmnéʃən] N condenación *f*, perdición *f*

damned [dæmd] ADJ condenado

damp [dæmp] ADJ húmedo; N humedad *f*; VT (wet) humedecer; (deaden) amortiguar; (extinguish) apagar

dampen [dǽmpən] VT (wet) humedecer; (deaden) amortiguar; (depress) deprimir

dampness [dǽmpnɪs] N humedad *f*

damsel [dǽmzəl] N damisela *f*

dance [dæns] N (act of dancing, party, activity) baile *m*; (artistic activity, animal courtship movements) danza *f*; **— music** música bailable *f*; VI/VT (at a party) bailar; (in ballet, of animals) danzar; **she —d her way to stardom** llegó al estrellato bailando

dancer [dǽnsə˞] N bailarín -ina *mf*, danzante *mf*

dancercise [dǽnsə˞saɪz] N baile aeróbico *m*

dandelion [dǽndl̩aɪən] N diente de león *m*

dandruff [dǽndrəf] N caspa *f*

dandy [dǽndi] N dandi *m*, señorito *m*; ADJ estupendo

Dane [den] N danés -esa *mf*

danger [dénʤə˞] N peligro *m*

dangerous [dénʤə˞əs] ADJ peligroso

dangle [dǽŋgəl] VI/VT (hang) colgar; (sway) bambolear[se]; **her legs were dangling off the bench** sus piernas pendían del banco

Danish [dénɪʃ] ADJ danés; N bollo dulce *m*

dapple, dappled [dǽpəl[d]] ADJ pinto, moteado

dare [dɛr] VI/VT (be brave) atreverse [a], osar; (challenge) desafiar; **how — you?** ¿cómo te atreves? N desafío *m*; **—devil** temerario -ria *mf*

daring [dérɪŋ] N atrevimiento *m*, osadía *f*; ADJ atrevido, osado, arriesgado

dark [dɑrk] ADJ (in color) oscuro; (of hair) moreno, morocho, trigueño; (gloomy) sombrío, tenebroso; (evil, ignorant) oscuro; (shameful) turbio; **— Ages** [Alta] Edad Media *f*; **—room** cuarto oscuro *m*; **—-skinned** moreno; N oscuridad *f*; **after —** después de que oscurece

darken [dɑ́rkən] VI/VT oscurecer

darkness [dɑ́rknɪs] N (complete) oscuridad *f*, tinieblas *f pl*; (partial) penumbra *f*

darling [dɑ́rlɪŋ] ADJ & N amado -da *mf*, querido -da *mf*; **my —** vida mía, amor mío

darn [dɑrn] VT zurcir, remendar; **—ing needle** aguja de zurcir *f*; N zurcido *m*; **it is not worth a —** no vale un comino; INTERJ ¡caramba! ¡caracoles!

dart [dɑrt] N (missile) dardo *m*; (tuck) pinza *f*; (swift movement) movimiento rápido *m*; **—board** diana *f*; **to play —s** jugar a los dardos; VI disparar; **to — out** salir disparado

dash [dæʃ] VI/VT (of waves, porcelain) estrellar[se]; VT (plans) frustrar; VI (hopes) desplomarse; **to — by** pasar corriendo; **to — off/out** salir disparado; **to — off a letter** escribir de prisa una carta; N (line) raya *f*; (run) corrida *f*; (race) carrera *f*; (small amount) pizca *f*; (splash) salpicadura *f*; **the one-hundred-meter —** la carrera de los cien metros llanos/planos; **—board** tablero *m*, salpicadero *m*

data [déɪtə, dǽtə˞] N datos *m pl*; **—base** base de datos *f*; **—bank** banco de datos *m*; **— encryption** cifrado de datos *m*; **— file** archivo de datos *m*; **— input** entrada de datos *f*; **— management** gestión de datos *f*; **— processing** procesamiento de datos *m*, fichero de datos *m*; **— recovery** recuperación de datos *f*; **— storage** almacenamiento de datos *m*

date [det] N (time) fecha *f*; (appointment) cita *f*; (person) acompañante *mf*; (fruit) dátil *m*; **— due** fecha de vencimiento *f*; **out of —** anticuado; **to —** hasta ahora; **up to —** al día; VI (be dated) estar fechado; (go out socially) salir; VT (write the date) fechar; (show to be old-fashioned) delatar la edad; (go out socially) salir con; **to — from** datar de, remontarse a

dated [déɪtɪd] ADJ (having a date) fechado; (old-fashioned) anticuado

daub [dɔb] VT (smear) embarrar, embadurnar; (apply unskillfully) pintarrajear

daughter [dɔ́tə˞] N hija *f*; **—-in-law** nuera *f*

daunt [dɔnt] VT (intimidate) intimidar; (dishearten) desanimar

dauntless [dɔ́ntlɪs] ADJ intrépido

davenport [dǽvənpɔrt] N sofá grande *m*

dawn [dɔn] N alba *f*, amanecer *m*, aurora *f*; **the — of civilization** los albores de la civilización; VI amanecer, aclarar; **it just —ed on me that** caí en [la] cuenta de que

day [de] N día *m*; **— after tomorrow** pasado mañana *m*; **— before yesterday** anteayer *m*; **—break** amanecer *m*; **at —break** al amanecer; **—care** guardería *f*; **—dream** fantasía *f*; **— laborer** jornalero -ra *mf*;

—light luz del día *f*; **—light saving time** adelanto de la hora en verano *m*; **—time** día *m*; **—time activity** actividad diurna *f*; **—-to-—** día a día; **by —** de día; **by the —** por día; **eight-hour —** jornada de ocho horas *f*; **in my —** en mis tiempos; **in the old —s** antaño; **make my —** dame el gusto; **New Year's —** Año Nuevo *m*; ADJ diurno; VI **to —dream** soñar despierto

daze [dez] VT aturdir; N **to be in a —** estar aturdido

dazzle [dǽzəł] VI/VT deslumbrar

deacidify [diasídɪfaɪ] VT neutralizar la acidez

deacon [díkən] N diácono *m*

deactivate [diǽktɪvet] VI/VT desactivar

deactivation [diæktɪvéʃən] N desactivación *f*

dead [dɛd] ADJ muerto; **he's a — duck** está muerto; **—-end job** puesto sin perspectivas *m*; **— sure** completamente seguro; **— tired** muerto de cansancio; N **— air** aire viciado *m*; **—beat** moroso -sa *mf*; **—bolt** pestillo *m*; **— end** callejón sin salida *m*; **— letter** letra muerta *f*; **—line** fecha límite *f*; **— link** enlace muerto *m*; **—lock** punto muerto *m*; **—pan** de palo; **— ringer** fiel retrato *m*; **—wood** (person) persona inútil *f*; (thing) cosa inútil *f*; **the —** los muertos; **in the — of the night** en el silencio de la noche; **in the — of winter** en pleno invierno; VI **to —lock** trancarse

deaden [dédn̩] VT amortiguar

deadly [dédli] ADJ (enemy) mortal; (poison) letal; (weapon) mortífero; ADV mortalmente; **— dull** sumamente aburrido

deaf [dɛf] ADJ sordo; **—-mute** ADJ & N sordomudo -da *mf*

deafen [défən] VT (make deaf) ensordecer; (deaden) amortiguar

deafening [défənɪŋ] ADJ ensordecedor, atronador

deafness [défnɪs] N sordera *f*

deal [diɨ] VT (cards) dar, repartir; (drugs) vender; (a blow) dar, asestar; **to — in** comerciar en; **biology —s with the study of life** la biología se ocupa del estudio de la vida; **I have to — with all kinds of people** tengo que vérmelas con todo tipo de gente; N (business transaction) trato *m*, negocio *m*; (shady transaction) componenda *f*; (act of dealing cards) reparto *m*; **a great — of** una gran cantidad de; **it's a —** ¡trato hecho! **I got a raw —** me clavaron

dealer [dílə-] N (in cars, antiques) comerciante *mf*; (in drugs, arms) traficante *mf*; (of cards) el/la que reparte *mf*

dealership [dilə-ʃɪp] N concesionario *m*

dealings [dílɪŋz] N trato *m*, relaciones *f pl*; (business) negocios *m pl*

dealt [dɛłt] *see* deal

dean [din] N (of university, professional group) decano -na *mf*; (in church) deán *m*

dear [dir] ADJ (beloved) querido; (expensive) caro; (cherished) apreciado; **— Sir/Madam** Estimado señor / Estimada señora; **my —est wish** mi deseo más ferviente; N **he's such a —!** ¡es un amor! **my —** querido mío *m* / querida mía *f*; ADV caro; **that cost me —** eso me costó caro; **— me!** ¡Dios mío! **oh — !** ¡Dios mío!

dearth [dɜθ] N escasez *f*

death [dɛθ] N muerte *f*; **—bed** lecho de muerte *m*; **— benefits** beneficios por fallecimiento *m*; **— certificate** partida de defunción *f*; **— penalty** pena de muerte *f*; **— rate** tasa de mortalidad *f*; **— row** pabellón de los condenados a muerte *m*; **he's on — row** está condenado a muerte; **— squad** escuadrón de la muerte *m*; **— toll** mortandad *f*; **—trap** trampa mortal *f*; **— wish** instinto suicida *m*; **to put to —** ejecutar; **we have discussed this to —** hemos discutido esto hasta el hartazgo; **I'm sick to — of this job** estoy harto de este trabajo

debacle [dɪbákəł] N debacle *f*

debase [dɪbés] VT degradar, envilecer

debatable [dɪbéɪdəbəł] ADJ discutible

debate [dɪbét] N debate *m*; VI/VT (discuss) debatir, discutir; (weigh a decision) considerar

debilitate [dɪbílɪtet] VT debilitar

debilitating [dɪbílɪteɪdɪŋ] ADJ debilitante

debit [débɪt] N débito *m*, adeudo *m*; (column in an account) debe *m*; (total sum owed) pasivo *m*; **— card** tarjeta de débito *f*; VT adeudar; **to — an account** adeudar una cuenta

debriefing [dibrífɪŋ] N informe *m*

debris [dəbrí] N (ruins) escombros *m pl*; (detritus) detritus *m* [*pl*]

debt [dɛt] N deuda *f*; **— relief** alivio de la deuda *m*; **bad —** cuenta incobrable *f*; **to get into —** endeudarse; ADJ **—-ridden** sobreendeudado

debtor [déɪdɔ-] N deudor -ora *mf*

debug [dibág] VT depurar

debugger [dibágɔ-] N depurador *m*

debugging [dibágɪŋ] N depuración *f*

debunk [dibáŋk] VT (ideas, beliefs) desacreditar; (myths) desmitificar

debut [debjú] N (of a play or film) estreno *m*; (in society) presentación en sociedad *f*; **to make a —** (an actor) debutar; (in society) presentarse en sociedad; VI/VT (a film) estrenar[se]; (a product) lanzar[se] al mercado

decade [déked] N década *f*, decenio *m*

decadence [dékədəns] N decadencia *f*

decadent [dékədənt] ADJ decadente

decaffeinated [dɪkǽfɪneɪdɪd] ADJ descafeinado

decal [díkæł] N calcomanía *f*, autoadhesivo *m*

decalcification [dikælsɪfɪkéʃən] N

descalcificación *f*

decanter [dɪkǽntɚ] N garrafa *f*

decapitate [dɪkǽpɪtet] VT decapitar

decathlon [dɪkǽθlɑn] N decatlón *m*

decay [dɪké] VI/VT (biological matter) descomponer[se]; (teeth) cariar[se]; VI (health) deteriorarse; (radioactive matter) desintegrarse; N (moral) decadencia *f*; (biological) descomposición *f*; (nuclear) desintegración *f*; (tooth) caries *f*

decayed [dɪkéd] ADJ (flesh) putrefacto; (tooth) cariado

decease [dɪsís] N muerte *f*, fallecimiento *m*; VI morir, fallecer

deceased [dɪsíst] ADJ & N difunto -ta *mf*

deceit [dɪsít] N engaño *m*, trampa *f*

deceitful [dɪsítfəl] ADJ tramposo, engañoso

deceive [dɪsív] VI/VT engañar

decelerate [dɪsɛ́ləret] VI desacelerar

December [dɪsɛ́mbɚ] N diciembre *m*

decency [dísənsi] N decencia *f*

decent [dísənt] ADJ decente

decentralization [disɛntrəlɪzéʃən] N descentralización *f*

deception [dɪsépʃən] N engaño *m*

deceptive [dɪséptɪv] ADJ engañoso; **— practice** práctica comercial desleal *f*

decibel [désəbəl] N decibelio *m*

decide [dɪsáɪd] VT (make a decision) decidir; (award victory) fallar; **what —d you to come?** ¿qué te motivó a venir?

decided [dɪsáɪdɪd] ADJ (resolute) decidido; (clear) claro

deciduous [dɪsídʒuəs] ADJ deciduo, caduco; **— tooth** diente de la primera dentición *m*

decimal [désəməl] ADJ decimal

decimate [désəmet] VT diezmar

decipher [dɪsáɪfɚ] VT descifrar

decision [dɪsíʒən] N decisión *f*; (in court) fallo *m*

decisive [dɪsáɪsɪv] ADJ decisivo

deck [dɛk] N (of a boat) cubierta *f*; (of a house) terraza *f*; (of playing cards) baraja *f*; **hit the —!** ¡cuerpo a tierra! VT (knock down) tumbar; (decorate) decorar; **to — oneself out** emperifollarse

declaration [dɛkləréʃən] N declaración *f*, pronunciamiento *m*

declare [dɪklɛ́r] VI/VT declarar, afirmar

decline [dɪkláɪn] N (deterioration) decadencia *f*; (slope) declive *m*; (reduction in prices) baja *f*; VI/VT declinar; (an offer) rechazar; **to — to do something** negarse a hacer algo

decode [dikód] VT descodificar

decompose [dikəmpóz] VI/VT descomponer[se]

decompress [dikəmprɛ́s] VT descomprimir

decongest [dikəndʒɛ́st] VT descongestionar

decongestant [dikəndʒɛ́stənt] N descongestionante *m*

decontaminate [dikəntǽmɪnet] VT descontaminar

decontamination [dikəntæmɪnéʃən] N descontaminación *f*

decorate [dɛ́kəret] VT decorar; (award medals) condecorar

decoration [dɛkəréʃən] N (embellishment) adorno *m*; (interior decorating) decoración *f*; (medal of honor) condecoración *f*

decorative [dɛ́kərətɪv] ADJ decorativo

decorous [dɛ́kərəs] ADJ decoroso

decorum [dɪkɔ́rəm] N decoro *m*

decoy [dɪ́kɔɪ] N (artifact) señuelo *m*, reclamo *m*; (live animal or person) cimbel *m*; VT atraer con señuelo/cimbel

decrease[1] [dɪ́kris] N disminución *f*, merma *f*

decrease[2] [dɪkrís] VI/VT disminuir, mermar

decree [dɪkrí] N decreto *m*; VI/VT decretar

decrepit [dɪkrɛ́pɪt] ADJ decrépito

decrepitude [dɪkrɛ́pɪtud] N decrepitud *f*

decry [dɪkrái] VT condenar

decrypt [dikrípt] VT descifrar

decryption [dikrípʃən] N descifrado *m*, descodificación *f*

dedicate [dɛ́dɪket] VI/VT dedicar[se]; VT (a highway) inaugurar

dedication [dɛdɪkéʃən] N (act of dedicating) dedicación *f*; (in a book) dedicatoria *f*; (of a highway, etc.) inauguración *f*

deduce [dɪdús] VT deducir

deduct [dɪdʌ́kt] VT deducir

deductible [dɪdʌ́ktəbəl] ADJ deducible, desgravable; N deducible *m*

deduction [dɪdʌ́kʃən] N deducción *f*

deed [did] N (action) acción *f*; (exploit) hazaña *f*; (certificate of ownership) escritura *f*

deem [dim] VT considerar

deep [dip] ADJ (extending down) hondo, profundo; (dark) oscuro; (of a voice) grave; **— in debt** cargado de deudas; **— in thought** absorto; **—-sea** de altura; **he's got — pockets** es un ricachón; **he went off the — end with his hobby** se le fue la mano con el pasatiempo; **she went — into the woods** se adentró en el bosque; **ten meters —** de diez metros de profundidad; N **— freeze** congelador *m*; **the —** el piélago, el abismo; ADV **to dive —** bucear en las profundidades; VT **to —-six** hacer desaparecer

deepen [dípən] VI/VT ahondar, profundizar

deer [dir] N ciervo *m*, venado *m*; **—skin** gamuza *f*

deface [dɪfés] VT (disfigure) desfigurar; (smear with paint) pintarrajear; (mutilate) mutilar

defame [dɪfém] VT difamar

default [dɪfɔ́lt] N (negligence) negligencia *f*; (failure to pay) incumplimiento *m*; (failure to appear in court) rebeldía *f*; (computer setting) opción por defecto *f*; **in —** en mora; **by —** por defecto, por omisión; (in sports) por abandono de los contrincantes; VI (on a loan)

incumplir, no pagar; (in a sports match) no comparecer

defeat [dɪfít] VT vencer, derrotar; N derrota *f*

defecate [défɪkeɪt] VI defecar, evacuar

defect[1] [difɛkt] N defecto *m*

defect[2] [dɪfékt] VI desertar

defection [dɪfékʃən] N defección *f*

defective [dɪféktɪv] ADJ defectuoso

defend [dɪfénd] VI/VT defender

defendant [dɪféndənt] N (criminal) acusado -da *mf*, reo -a *mf*; (civil) demandado -da *mf*

defender [dɪféndə˞] N defensor -ora *mf*; (sports) defensa *mf*

defense [dɪféns] N defensa *f*

defenseless [dɪfénslɪs] ADJ indefenso

defensible [dɪfénsəbəł] ADJ defendible

defensive [dɪfénsɪv] ADJ defensivo; **— medicine** medicina defensiva *f*; N **on the —** a la defensiva

defer [dɪfɝ˞] VT (a meeting) diferir, posponer; (a payment) prorrogar; (an appointment) dilatar; (from military service) eximir; **to — to another's opinion** remitirse a la opinión de otro

deference [défə˞əns] N deferencia *f*

deferral [dɪfɝ˞əł] N aplazamiento *m*

defiance [dɪfáɪəns] N (challenge) desafío *m*; (resistance to authority) rebeldía *f*; **in — of** en abierta oposición a

defiant [dɪfáɪənt] ADJ desafiante

defibrillate [difíbrəlet] VT desfibrilar

defibrillation [difɪbrɪléʃən] N desfibrilación *f*

defibrillator [difíbrɪleɪdə˞] N desfibrilador *m*

deficiency [dɪfíʃənsi] N deficiencia *f*

deficient [dɪfíʃənt] ADJ deficiente

deficit [défɪsɪt] N déficit *m*; **— spending** gastos deficitarios *m pl*

defile [dɪfáɪł] VT (violate) mancillar; (desecrate) profanar; (to make dirty) ensuciar

define [dɪfáɪn] VI/VT definir

defining [dɪfáɪnɪŋ] ADJ decisivo

definite [défənɪt] ADJ (clearly defined) definido, determinado; (certain) seguro; **she was — in her demands** ella fue terminante es sus exigencias; **— article** artículo definido *m*

definitely [défənɪtli] ADV sin duda, definitivamente

definition [dɛfənɪ́ʃən] N definición *f*

definitive [dɪfínɪdɪv] ADJ (final) definitivo; (authoritative) de mayor autoridad

deflate [dɪflét] VI/VT desinflar[se]

deflation [dɪfléʃən] N deflación *f*.

deflect [dɪflékt] VI/VT desviar[se]

deforestation [difɔrɪstéʃən] N deforestación *f*

deform [dɪfɔ́rm] VI/VT deformar[se]

deformed [dɪfɔ́rmd] ADJ deforme

deformity [dɪfɔ́rmɪdi] N (body part) deformidad *f*; (act or result of deforming) deformación *f*

defraud [dɪfrɔ́d] VT defraudar

defray [dɪfré] VT sufragar, costear

defrost [difrɔ́st] VI/VT descongelar[se]

deft [dɛft] ADJ diestro, habilidoso

defunct [dɪfáŋkt] ADJ caduco; **the Whig party is now —** el partido de los whigs se disolvió

defuse [difjúz] VT (bomb) desactivar; (situation) distender

defy [dɪfáɪ] VT (challenge) desafiar; (resist) resistir

degenerate[1] [dɪʤénə˞ɪt] ADJ & N degenerado -da *mf*

degenerate[2] [dɪʤénə˞et] VI degenerar[se]

degenerative [dɪʤénə˞ətɪv] ADJ degenerativo; **— joint disease** artrosis *f*, enfermedad degenerativa articular *f*

degradation [dɛgrədéʃən] N degradación *f*

degrade [dɪgréd] VI/VT degradar[se]

degree [dɪgrí] N (stage) grado *m*; (academic) título *m*; **by —s** gradualmente; **to a —** hasta cierto punto; **to get a —** graduarse

dehumanize [dihjúmənaɪz] VI/VT deshumanizar

dehumidifier [dihjumídɪfaɪə˞] N deshumidificador *m*

dehydrate [dihháɪdret] VI/VT deshidratar[se]

deign [den] VI dignarse

deity [díɪɪti] N deidad *f*

déjà vu [deʒɑvú] N deja vu *m*

dejected [dɪʤéktɪd] ADJ abatido, desconsolado

dejection [dɪʤékʃən] N abatimiento *m*, desconsuelo *m*

delay [dɪlé] N demora *f*, retraso *m*; VT demorar, retrasar; VI demorar, retrasarse

delectable [dɪléktəbəł] ADJ delicioso; N delicia *f*

delegate[1] [déɪlɪgɪt] N delegado -da *mf*

delegate[2] [déɪlɪget] VT delegar

delegation [dɛlɪgéʃən] N delegación *f*, representación *f*

delete [dɪlít] VT (omit) suprimir; (cross out) tachar; **— key** tecla de borrado *f*

deleterious [dɛlɪtíriəs] ADJ nocivo

deletion [dɪlíʃən] N supresión *f*

deliberate[1] [dɪlíbə˞ɪt] ADJ (intentional) deliberado; (careful) cuidadoso

deliberate[2] [dɪlíbə˞et] VI/VT deliberar

deliberately [dɪlíbə˞ɪtli] ADV a propósito, deliberadamente

deliberation [dɪlɪbə˞éʃən] N deliberación *f*

delicacy [déɪlɪkəsi] N (fineness, precision, sensitivity) delicadeza *f*; (food) manjar *m*, delicatessen *f pl*, gollería *f*; (breakability) fragilidad *f*

delicate [déɪlɪkɪt] ADJ delicado, tenue; (breakable) frágil; (acute) fino

delicatessen [dɛlɪkətésən] N (store) tienda de fiambres *f*, charcutería *f*; *RP* rotisería *f*; (foods) delicatessen *f pl*

delicious [dɪlíʃəs] ADJ delicioso, rico

delight [dɪláɪt] N (pleasure) deleite *m*, regalo *m*;

(source of pleasure) delicia *f*; VI/VT deleitar[se]

delighted [dɪlάɪdɪd] ADJ encantado; **to be — to** alegrarse de; **I'm — to meet you** me alegro de conocerla; **I'd be — to dance with you** me encantaría bailar contigo

delightful [dɪlάɪtfəł] ADJ encantador

delimit [dɪlímɪt] VT delimitar

delineate [dɪlínɪet] VT delinear

delinquent [dɪlínkwənt] ADJ & N (debtor) moroso -sa *mf*; (wrongdoer) delincuente *mf*; (juvenile) delincuente juvenil *mf*

delirious [dɪlíriəs] ADJ (hysterical) delirante; (happy) contentísimo; **to be —** delirar

delirium [dɪlíriəm] N delirio *m*

deliver [dɪlívə˞] VT (hand over) entregar; (hand out) repartir; (liberate) liberar; (pronounce a speech) pronunciar; (administer a blow) dar; (have a baby) dar a luz; (assist a birth) atender en un parto; **to — the goods** cumplir con lo prometido

deliverance [dɪlívə˞əns] N liberación *f*

delivery [dɪlívəri] N (handing out) entrega *f*, expedición *f*; (things to be delivered) pedido *m*; (birth) parto *m*; (speaking) ejecución *f*, expresión oral *f*; **on —** a la entrega; **— service** servicio de entrega *m*; **— truck** camión de reparto *m*; **to take —** aceptar entrega

dell [dɛł] N hondonada *f*

deltoids [dέłtɔɪdz] N deltoides *m sg*

delude [dɪlúd] VT engañar

deluge [dέljudʒ] N diluvio *m*; VT abrumar

delusion [dɪlúʒən] N (act of deluding, state of being deluded) engaño *m*; **—s of grandeur** delirios de grandeza *m pl*

deluxe [dɪlΛks] ADJ de lujo

demagogue, demagog [déməgɑg] N demagogo -ga *mf*

demand [dɪmǽnd] VT (ask for) exigir; (require) requerir, exigir; N exigencia *f*, reivindicación *f*; **on —** por demanda

demanding [dɪmǽndɪŋ] ADJ exigente

demarcate [dɪmάrket] VT demarcar

demean [dɪmín] VT menospreciar

demeanor [dɪmínə˞] N conducta *f*, comportamiento *m*

demented [dɪméntɪd] ADJ demente

dementia [dɪménʃə] N demencia *f*

demijohn [démidʒɑn] N damajuana *f*

demise [dɪmάɪz] N fallecimiento *m*, desaparición *f*

demo [démo] N demostración *f*

demobilize [dɪmóbəlaɪz] VT desmovilizar

democracy [dɪmάkrəsi] N democracia *f*

democrat [déməkræt] N demócrata *mf*

democratic [dɛməkrǽdɪk] ADJ democrático

democratization [dɪmɑkrədɪzéʃən] N democratización *f*

demographics [dɛməgræfɪks] N demografía *f*

demolish [dɪmάlɪʃ] VT demoler, derrumbar

demon [dímən] N demonio *m*

demonstrate [démənstret] VT (prove) demostrar; (show a product) hacer una demostración; VI manifestar

demonstration [dɛmənstréʃən] N (proof, exhibition) demostración *f*; (protest) manifestación *f*, concentración *f*

demonstrative [dɪmάnstrətɪv] ADJ demostrativo

demonstrator [démənstreɪtə˞] N manifestante *mf*

demoralize [dɪmórəlaɪz] VT desmoralizar

demote [dɪmót] VT degradar, bajar de categoría

den [dɛn] N (of an animal) guarida *f*; (room in a house) cuarto de estar *m*; (cave) cueva *f*; **— of iniquity** antro de perdición *m*

dengue fever [déŋgi fívə˞] N dengue *m*

denial [dɪnάɪəł] N (assertion that an allegation is false) desmentido *m*; (refusal to approve) denegación *f*, negativa *f*; (refusal to recognize) negación *f*; **he is in —** no lo quiere aceptar

denigrate [dénɪgret] VT denigrar

denim [dénɪm] N tela de vaquero *f*

Denmark [dénmɑrk] N Dinamarca *f*

denomination [dɪnɑmənéʃən] N (name, monetary value) denominación *f*; (sect) secta religiosa *f*

denominator [dɪnάmɪneɪtə˞] N denominador *m*

denotation [dinotéʃən] N denotación *f*

denote [dɪnót] VT denotar

denounce [dɪnάʊns] VT denunciar

dense [dɛns] ADJ (compacted) denso, tupido, cerrado; (stupid) *fam* burro, duro de entendederas

density [dénsɪdɪi] N densidad *f*

dent [dɛnt] N abolladura *f*; **to make a — in a task** hacer mella en una tarea; VI/VT abollar[se]

dental [dέntł] ADJ dental; **— care** cuidado dental *m*; **— floss** hilo dental *m*; **— hygienist** higienista dental *mf*; **— implant** implante dental *m*; **— plaque** placa dental *f*; **— school** facultad de odontología *f*

dentifrice [dέntəfrɪs] N dentífrico *m*, pasta dental *f*

dentist [dέntɪst] N dentista *mf*

dentistry [dέntɪstri] N odontología *f*

dentures [dέntʃə˞z] N dientes postizos *m pl*

denunciation [dɪnΛnsiéʃən] N denuncia *f*, acusación *f*

deny [dɪnάɪ] VT (state that something is false) negar, desmentir; (refuse to approve) rechazar; **to — oneself** abstenerse

deodorant [dióʊdə˞ənt] N desodorante *m*

deodorize [dióʊdə˞aɪz] VT desodorizar

deoxidize [diάksɪdaɪz] VT desoxidar

depart [dɪpάrt] VI (leave) salir, partir; (deviate)

desviarse, apartarse; (die) fallecer, dejar de existir

departed [dɪpárɒɪd] ADJ & N difunto -ta *mf*

department [dɪpártmənt] N (of company, school, country) departamento *m*; (of government) ministerio *m*; (of a store) sección *f*; (of knowledge, expertise) especialidad *f*; **— head** jefe -fa de departamento *mf*; **— store** gran almacén *m*

departure [dɪpártʃə˞] N (scheduled) salida *f*; (not scheduled) partida *f*; (deviation) desviación *f*

depend [dɪpénd] VI depender; **to — on** (rely on) contar con; (be conditioned by) depender de; **—ing on the number of guests** dependiendo de la cantidad de invitados

dependable [dɪpéndəbəł] ADJ confiable, fiable

dependence [dɪpéndəns] N dependencia *f*

dependency [dɪpéndənsi] N dependencia *f*

dependent [dɪpéndənt] ADJ dependiente; **success is — on perseverance** el éxito depende de la perseverancia; N familiar a cargo *mf*

depict [dɪpíkt] VT (verbally) describir; (visually) representar

depilate [dépəlet] VT depilar[se]

depilatory [dɪpílə˞tɔri] ADJ & N depilatorio *m*

deplane [dɪplén] VI desembarcar

deplete [dɪplít] VT agotar

depletion [dɪplíʃən] N agotamiento *m*

deplorable [dɪplɔ́rəbəł] ADJ deplorable

deplore [dɪplɔ́r] VT deplorar

deploy [dɪplɔ́ɪ] VT desplegar

deport [dɪpɔ́rt] VT deportar; VI comportarse

deportment [dɪpɔ́rtmənt] N comportamiento *m*, conducta *f*

depose [dɪpóz] VT (overthrow) deponer, derrocar; (testify) declarar; (take testimony) tomar declaración

deposit [dɪpɑ́zɪt] VT (add to an account) depositar; *Sp* ingresar; (place) colocar; N (amount added to an account) depósito *m*; *Sp* ingreso *m*; (of a mineral) yacimiento *m*; (earnest money) señal *f*, anticipo *m*; **— slip** hoja de depósito *f*

deposition [dɛpəzíʃən] N (removal from office) deposición *f*; (testimony) declaración *f*

depositor [dɪpɑ́zɪtə˞] N depositante *mf*

depot [dípo] N (of trains) estación *f*; (of buses) terminal *mf*; (for storage) almacén *m*, depósito *m*; (for military training) cuartel *m*

depraved [dɪprévd] ADJ depravado

deprecate [dépɪket] VT despreciar

depreciate [dɪpríʃiet] VT (currency) depreciar[se]; (goods) desvalorizar[se], amortizar[se]

depreciation [dɪpriʃiéʃən] N (of currency) depreciación *f*; (of goods) amortización *f*

depress [dɪprés] VT deprimir

depressed [dɪprést] ADJ deprimido

depressing [dɪprésɪŋ] ADJ deprimente

depression [dɪpréʃən] N depresión *f*

deprive [dɪpráɪv] VT privar

depth [dɛpθ] N (of hole, feeling) profundidad *f*, hondura *f*; (of the voice) gravedad *f*; **in the —s** en las profundidades; **in —** a fondo; **what is the — of that bookshelf?** ¿cuánto miden estos estantes de fondo? **he has sunk to such —s** ha caído muy bajo; **in the — of the night** bien entrada la noche; **in the — of winter** en lo más crudo del invierno

deputation [dɛpjətéʃən] N delegación *f*

deputy [dépjəɔ̈i] N (elected official) diputado -da *mf*; (substitute) suplente *mf*

derail [diré̞ł] VI/VT descarrilar[se]

deranged [dɪrénʤd] ADJ trastornado, demente

derby [dɝ́bi] N (hat) sombrero hongo *m*; (race) derby *m*

deregulate [dirégjəlet] VT desregular

derelict [dérəlɪkt] ADJ (deserted) abandonado; (negligent) negligente; N (ship) buque abandonado *m*; (person) vagabundo -da *mf*

dereliction [dɛrəlíkʃən] N **— of duties** abandono de funciones *m*

deride [dɪráɪd] VT escarnecer, ridiculizar

derision [dɪríʒən] N escarnio *m*

derivation [dɛrəvéʃən] N derivación *f*

derivative [dɪrívədɪv] ADJ & N derivado *m*

derive [dɪráɪv] VI/VT derivar[se]; **to — pleasure from** disfrutar de

dermabrasion [dɝ́məbreʒən] N abrasión cutánea *f*, dermabrasión *f*

dermatologist [dɝ́mətɑ́ləʤɪst] N dermatólogo -ga *mf*

dermatology [dɝ́mətɑ́ləʤi] N dermatología *f*

derogatory [dɪrɑ́gə˞tɔri] ADJ despectivo

derrick [dérɪk] N torre de perforación *f*

descend [dɪsénd] VI/VT descender; **—ing sort** clasificación descendiente *f*; **to — upon** caer sobre

descendant [dɪsénd̞ənt] ADJ & N descendiente *mf*

descent [dɪsént] N (act of descending, decline) descenso *m*; (slope) bajada *f*; (lineage) descendencia *f*

describe [dɪskráɪb] VT describir

description [dɪskrípʃən] N descripción *f*, caracterización *f*; **of all —s** de todas clases

descriptive [dɪskríptɪv] ADJ descriptivo

desecrate [désɪkret] VT profanar

desecration [dɛsɪkréʃən] N profanación *f*

desegregate [diségrɪget] VI/VT eliminar la segregación racial

deselect [disɪlékt] VT anular [una selección previa]

desensitize [disénsɪtaɪz] VT insensibilizar

desert[1] [dézə˞t] ADJ (barren, empty) desierto; (of the desert) desértico; N desierto *m*

desert[2] [dɪzɝ́t] VI/VT (a person, place)

abandonar; (military service) desertar
deserter [dɪzɝ́-dɚ-] N desertor -ora *mf*
desertion [dɪzɝ́-ʃən] N (of a person or place) abandono *m*; (from the military) deserción *f*
deserve [dɪzɝ́-v] VT merecer
deserving [dɪzɝ́-vɪŋ] ADJ merecedor
desiccate [désɪket] VI/VT desecar[se]
design [dɪzáɪn] VI/VT (prepare a sketch of) diseñar, trazar; (plan) planear, idear; N (model, pattern) diseño *m*; (sketch) esbozo *m*; **he has —s on her** le ha echado el ojo
designate [dézɪgnet] VT designar, denominar; **—d hitter** bateador -ora designado -da *mf*
designation [dɛzɪgnéʃən] N denominación *f*, designación *f*
designer [dɪzáɪnɚ-] N diseñador -ora *mf*; **—drugs** drogas de diseño *f pl*
desirability [dɪzaɪrəbɪ́lɪtɪ] N deseabilidad *f*, conveniencia *f*
desirable [dɪzáɪrəbəł] ADJ deseable
desire [dɪzáɪr] VT desear; **I — your cooperation** requiero tu cooperación; N deseo *m*
desirous [dɪzáɪrəs] ADJ deseoso
desist [dɪsíst] VI desistir
desk [desk] N escritorio *m*; (school) pupitre *m*; **—top computer** *Am* computadora de escritorio *f*, *Sp* ordenador de sobremesa *m*; **—top publishing** edición de sobremesa *f*, autoedición *f*
desolate[1] [désəlɪt] ADJ (barren) desolado
desolate[2] [désəlet] VT desolar, asolar
desolation [dɛsəléʃən] N desolación *f*, asolamiento *m*
despair [dɪspɛ́r] N desesperanza *f*; VI desesperarse, perder la esperanza
despairing [dɪspɛ́rɪŋ] ADJ de desesperación
desperate [déspə-ɪt] ADJ desesperado
desperately [déspə-ɪtlɪ] ADV desesperadamente; **— ill** gravemente enfermo; **he's — looking for funds** está desesperado buscando financiación
desperation [dɛspəréʃən] N desesperación *f*
despicable [dɪspíkəbəł] ADJ despreciable, deleznable
despise [dɪspáɪz] VT despreciar, menospreciar
despite [dɪspáɪt] N despecho *m*; PREP a pesar de
despoil [dɪspɔ́ɪł] VT despojar
despondency [dɪspándənsɪ] N abatimiento *m*, desaliento *m*
despondent [dɪspándənt] ADJ abatido, desalentado
despot [déspət] N déspota *mf*
despotic [dɪspátɪk] ADJ despótico
despotism [déspətɪzəm] N despotismo *m*
dessert [dɪzɝ́t] N postre *m*
destabilize [distébəlaɪz] VT desestabilizar
destination [dɛstənéʃən] N destino *m*
destine [déstɪn] VT destinar; **she's —d for greatness** promete grandes cosas
destiny [déstənɪ] N destino *m*
destitute [déstɪtut] ADJ menesteroso, indigente; **— of** falto de, desprovisto de
destroy [dɪstrɔ́ɪ] VT (demolish) destruir, deshacer; (kill an animal) sacrificar; (ruin a reputation) arruinar
destroyer [dɪstrɔ́ɪə-] N (person who destroys) destructor -ora *mf*; (ship) destructor *m*
destructible [dɪstráktəbəł] ADJ destructible
destruction [dɪstrákʃən] N (act of demolishing) destrucción *f*; (act of killing) matanza *f*; (act of ruining a reputation) ruina *f*
destructive [dɪstráktɪv] ADJ destructivo, destructor
detach [dɪtǽtʃ] VT separar, desprender; (troops) destacar
detachment [dɪtǽtʃmənt] N (physical) separación *f*; (emotional) desapego *m*; (of troops) destacamento *m*; (of the retina) desprendimiento *m*
detail[1] [dítel] N detalle *m*, pormenor *m*; (military) destacamento *m*; **to go into —** detallar, pormenorizar
detail[2] [dɪtél] VT detallar, pormenorizar; (assign duties) destacar
detain [dɪtén] VT detener
detect [dɪtékt] VT detectar
detection [dɪtékʃən] N detección *f*
detective [dɪtéktɪv] N detective *mf*; **— novel** novela policial *f*
detector [dɪtékta-] N detector *m*
detention [dɪténʃən] N (in jail) detención *f*; (in school) castigo *m*
deter [dɪtɝ́] VT (dissuade) disuadir; (prevent) prevenir
detergent [dɪtɝ́-ʤənt] N detergente *m*
deteriorate [dɪtɪ́rɪəret] VI deteriorar[se]
deterioration [dɪtɪrɪəréʃən] N deterioro *m*
determination [dɪtɝ-mənéʃən] N (act of determining) determinación *f*; (resolution) resolución *f*; (persistence) tesón *m*, perseverancia *f*
determine [dɪtɝ́-mɪn] VT determinar; **to — to do something** decidirse a hacer algo
determined [dɪtɝ́-mɪnd] ADJ (resolute) decidido, resuelto; (persistent) tesonero
determiner [dɪtɝ́-rmɪnɚ-] N (grammatical) determinante *m*
determining [dɪtɝ́-rmɪnɪŋ] ADJ determinante
detest [dɪtɛ́st] VT detestar, abominar de
detestable [dɪtɛ́stəbəł] ADJ detestable
dethrone [diθrón] VT destronar
detonate [dɛtṇet] VI/VT detonar
detonation [dɛtṇéʃən] N detonación *f*
detour [dítur] N desvío *m*; VI/VT desviar[se]
detoxification [ditɑksəfɪkéʃən] N destoxificación *f*
detract [dɪtrǽkt] VT distraer; VI **to — from**

disminuir

detrimental [dɛtrəménṭl] ADJ perjudicial

deuce [dus] N (in tennis) deuce *m*, cuarenta iguales

devaluation [divæljuéʃən] N devaluación *f*

devastate [dévəstet] VT devastar, asolar

devastating [dévəstɛdɪŋ] ADJ devastador

develop [dɪvéləp] VI/VT (mature, elaborate) desarrollar[se]; (build houses on) construir, edificar; (treat film) revelar; **she —ed an allergy** le vino una alergia; **—ing country** país en desarrollo *m*

developer [dɪvéləpɚ] N (of computer programs) desarrollador -ora *mf*; (of real estate) promotor -ora *mf*; **a late —** persona de maduración tardía *f*

development [dɪvéləpmənt] N (evolution) desarrollo *m*; (buildings) urbanización *f*, colonia *f*; (of a photograph) revelado *m*

developmental [dɪvèləpménṭl] ADJ relativo al desarrollo

deviate [díviet] VI/VT desviar[se]

deviation [diviéʃən] N desviación *f*

device [dɪváɪs] N (gadget) dispositivo *m*; (literary convention) recurso *m*; (emblem) divisa *f*; **they left me to my own —s** me dejaron que me las arreglara sola

devil [dévəl] N diablo *m*; **lucky —!** ¡suertudo! **what the — are you saying?** ¿qué diablos dices? **—'s advocate** abogado del diablo *m*

devilish [dévəlɪʃ] ADJ (evil) diabólico; (extreme) endiablado, endemoniado

deviltry [dévəltri] N (mischief) diablura *f*; (witchcraft) brujería *f*

devious [díviəs] ADJ (roundabout) sinuoso, tortuoso; (crafty) taimado, retorcido

devise [dɪváɪz] VT idear, urdir

devoid [dɪvɔ́ɪd] ADJ **— of** falto de, desprovisto de

devolution [dɛvəlúʃən] N devolución *f*

devote [dɪvót] VT dedicar; (consecrate) consagrar

devoted [dɪvóʊɪd] ADJ (friend) leal; (parent) dedicado; (worshiper) devoto

devotion [dɪvóʃən] N devoción *f*

devour [dɪváʊr] VT devorar

devout [dɪváʊt] ADJ devoto

dew [du] N rocío *m*; **—drop** gota de rocío *f*; **—point** punto de condensación *m*

dexterity [dɛkstérɪɪdɪ] N destreza *f*

dextrose [dɛ́kstros] N dextrosa *f*

diabetes [daɪəbíɪdiz] N diabetes *f*

diabolic [daɪəbɑ́lɪk] ADJ diabólico

diacritic [daɪəkrídɪk] ADJ & N diacrítico *m*

diagnose [daɪəgnós] VT diagnosticar

diagnosis [daɪəgnósɪs] N diagnóstico *m*, diagnosis *f*

diagnostic [daɪəgnɑ́stɪk] ADJ diagnóstico

diagonal [daɪǽgən] ADJ & N diagonal *f*

diagram [dáɪəgræm] N diagrama *m*

dial [dáɪəl] N (of a watch, clock) esfera *f*; (of radio) dial *m*; **— tone** *Sp* señal de marcar *f*; *Am* tono de discar *m*; VI/VT (a telephone number) *Sp* marcar; *Am* discar

dialect [dáɪəlɛkt] N dialecto *m*

dialectic [daɪəlɛ́ktɪk] ADJ dialéctico; N dialéctica *f*

dialectology [daɪəlɛktɑ́ləʤi] N dialectología *f*

dialogue, dialog [dáɪəlɑg] N diálogo *m*; VI dialogar

dialysis [daɪǽlɪsɪs] N diálisis *f*

diameter [daɪǽmɪdɚ] N diámetro *m*

diamond [dáɪəmənd] N (stone) diamante *m*; (shape) rombo *m*

diaper [dáɪpɚ] N pañal *m*; VT poner pañales

diaphragm [dáɪəfræm] N diafragma *m*

diarrhea [daɪəríə] N diarrea *f*

diary [dáɪəri] N diario *m*

diastolic [daɪəstɑ́lɪk] ADJ diastólico

diatribe [dáɪətraɪb] N diatriba *f*

dice [daɪs] N PL dados *m pl*; VT cortar en cubos; **no —!** (impossibility) no hay forma, *Am* ¡ni modo! (refusal) de ninguna manera

dichotomy [daɪkɑ́dəmi] N dicotomía *f*

dicker [díkɚ] VI regatear

dictate [díktet] VI/VT dictar; N dictado *m*, precepto *m*

dictation [dɪktéʃən] N dictado *m*; **to take —** escribir al dictado

dictator [dɪ́ktɛdɚ] N dictador -ora *mf*

dictatorship [dɪktédɚ-ʃɪp] N dictadura *f*

diction [díkʃən] N dicción *f*

dictionary [dɪ́kʃənɛri] N diccionario *m*

did [dɪd] *see* do

didactic [daɪdǽktɪk] ADJ didáctico

die [daɪ] VI morir[se]; **to — down/away** disminuir; **to — off** irse muriendo; **to — out** morirse, extinguirse; **my car —d** se me murió el coche; N (game piece) dado *m*; (press) molde *m*; (stamp) cuño *m*, troquel *m*; **—hard** intransigente *mf*

diesel [dízəl] N diesel *m*; **— engine** motor diesel *m*

diet [dáɪɪt] N (food) dieta *f*; (controlled intake of food) dieta *f*, régimen *m*; **to be/go on a —** estar a dieta/régimen; **to put on a —** poner a dieta; VI estar a dieta, hacer dieta

dietary [dáɪɪtɛri] ADJ dietético

dietitian [daɪɪtíʃən] N dietista *mf*

differ [dɪ́fɚ] VI diferir; **to — with** disentir, no estar de acuerdo con; **to — from** ser diferente de

difference [dɪ́fɚ-əns] N diferencia *f*; **it makes no —** no importa, da igual

different [dɪ́fɚ-ənt] ADJ diferente, distinto

differential [dɪfərénʃəl] ADJ & N (difference, car part) diferencial *m*; **— equation** diferencial *f*

differentiate [dɪfərénʃiet] VI/VT diferenciar[se], distinguir[se]

differentiation [dɪfərɛnʃiéʃən] N diferenciación *f*

differently [dɪ́fɚ-əntli] ADV de manera

diferente; **the~y act** — no se comportan igual
difficult [dífɪkəłt] ADJ difícil
difficulty [dífɪkəłti] N dificultad *f*; **with —** con dificultad, difícilmente
diffident [dífɪdənt] ADJ tímido
diffuse[1] [dɪfjúz] VI/VT difundir
diffuse[2] [dɪfjús] ADJ difuso
diffusion [dɪfjúʒən] N difusión *f*
dig [dɪg] VI/VT cavar; (by machine) excavar; (superficially) escarbar; **to — in the files** escarbar en los archivos; **to — under** socavar; **to — up** desenterrar; **he dug his heels into the ground** clavó los talones en el suelo; **I — your new shoes** están muy buenos tus zapatos nuevos; N (archaeological site) excavación *f*; (sarcastic remark) pulla *f*; **a — in the ribs** un codazo
digest[1] [dɪʤést] VI/VT digerir
digest[2] [dáɪʤest] N (summary) compendio *m*; (legal) digesto *m*
digestible [dɪʤéstəbəł] ADJ digerible, digestible
digestion [dɪʤéstʃən] N digestión *f*
digestive [dɪʤéstɪv] ADJ digestivo
digit [díʤɪt] N dígito *m*
digital [díʤɪdł] ADJ digital; **— camera** cámara digital *f*; **— computer** *Am* computadora digital *f*, *Sp* ordenador digital *m*; **— photography** fotografía digital *f*
digitalize [díʤɪdłaɪz] VT digitalizar
digitize [díʤɪtaɪz] VT digitalizar
dignified [dígnəfaɪd] ADJ digno
dignitary [dígnɪteri] N dignatario -ria *mf*
dignity [dígnɪdi] N dignidad *f*
digress [dɪgrés] VI divagar
digression [dɪgréʃən] N digresión *f*
dike [daɪk] N dique *m*
dilapidated [dɪłǽpɪdeɪd] ADJ (machine) destartalado; (furniture) desvencijado; (house) derruido, venido abajo
dilate [daɪłet] VI/VT dilatar[se]
dilation [daɪłéʃən] N dilatación *f*
dilemma [dɪłémə] N dilema *m*
dilettante [díłɪtant] N diletante *mf*
diligence [díləʤəns] N diligencia *f*
diligent [díləʤənt] ADJ diligente, hacendoso
dill [dɪł] N eneldo *m*; **— pickle** pepinillo en vinagre con eneldo *m*
dilute [dɪłút] VI/VT diluir[se]; ADJ diluido
dim [dɪm] ADJ (light) tenue; (outline) difuso; (room) oscuro, en penumbras; (person) *fam* de pocas luces; **—wit** *fam* tonto, bobo; VI/VT (make less bright) atenuar; VT (switch to low beam) bajar
dime [daɪm] N moneda de diez centavos *f*; **unskilled workers are a — a dozen** sobran los obreros no cualificados
dimension [dɪméntʃən] N dimensión *f*
diminish [dɪmínɪʃ] VI/VT disminuir, menguar; **the law of —ing returns** la ley de los rendimientos decrecientes
diminution [dɪmənúʃən] N disminución *f*, mengua *f*
diminutive [dɪmínjətɪv] ADJ diminuto; N diminutivo *m*
dimmer [dímə-] N regulador de voltaje *m*
dimness [dímnɪs] N oscuridad *f*, penumbra *f*
dimple [dímpəł] N hoyuelo *m*; VT formar hoyuelos
din [dɪn] N estruendo *m*, estrépito *m*
dine [daɪn] VI cenar; **to — out** cenar afuera
diner [dáɪnə-] N (restaurant) cafetería *f*; (on a train) coche comedor *m*; (person) comensal *mf*
ding-a-ling [díŋəłɪŋ] N (silly person) ganso -sa *mf*; (eccentric person) excéntrico -ca *mf*; (sound) tilín *m*
dingy [dínʤi] ADJ deslucido
dining [dáɪnɪŋ] ADJ **— car** coche comedor *m*; **— room** comedor *m*
dinner [dínə-] N (main meal) comida *f*; (at midday) almuerzo *m*; (in the evening) cena *f*; **— jacket** smoking *m*; **—time** hora de la comida *f*
dinosaur [dáɪnəsɔr] N dinosaurio *m*
dint [dɪnt] ADV LOC **by — of** a fuerza de
dip [dɪp] VT (make wet) mojar; (scoop) sacar; (immerse) sumergir; (immerse in insecticide) bañar; (immerse in sauce, coffee) pringar, mojar; VI (sun) hundirse; (stocks) bajar; (road) hacer una bajada; (airplane) descender súbitamente; N (act of wetting) mojada *f*; (portion of ice-cream) bola *f*, cucharada *f*; (sauce) mojo *m*; (reduction in sales) disminución *f*; (low place in a road) declive *m*; (low place in the land) hondonada *f*; (swim) baño *m*; (airplane maneuver) descenso rápido *m*; (irritating person) *pej* pesado -da *mf*
diphtheria [dɪpθíriə] N difteria *f*
diphthong [dípθɔŋ] N diptongo *m*
diploma [dɪplómə] N diploma *m*
diplomacy [dɪplóməsi] N diplomacia *f*
diplomat [dípləmæt] N diplomático -ca *mf*
diplomatic [dɪpləmǽtɪk] ADJ diplomático
dipper [dípə-] N cucharón *m*, cazo *m*
dire [daɪr] ADJ terrible, espantoso; **— need** necesidad acuciante *f*; **— predictions** predicciones funestas *f pl*; **— situation** situación extrema *f*
direct [dɪrékt] ADJ directo; **— current** corriente continua *f*; **— object** complemento directo *m*; **— quotation** cita textual *f*; ADV directo, directamente; VI/VT dirigir; **he —ed me to leave** me mandó irme
direction [dɪrékʃən] N dirección *f*; **—s** indicaciones *f pl*; **I'm thinking in that —** me inclino por eso
directive [dɪrékɪtɪv] ADJ directivo; N directiva *f*
director [dɪréktə-] N (theater, movies) director

-ra *mf*; (film, TV) realizador -ora *mf*

directory [dɪréktəri] N directorio *m*

dirigible [dərídʒəbəl] ADJ & N dirigible *m*

dirt [dɜ́t] N (filth) suciedad *f*; (foul substance) mugre *f*; (earth) tierra *f*; **—bag** *offensive* porquería *f*; **I've got some — on him** le conozco los trapos sucios; ADJ **— cheap** baratísimo; **—-poor** pobrísimo

dirty [dɜ́-di] ADJ sucio, mugriento; **— joke** chiste verde *m*; **— look** mirada asesina *f*; **— money** dinero sucio *m*; **— shame** pena horrible *f*; **— trick** trampa *f*; **— word** palabrota *f*; *Sp* taco *m*; **— work** trabajo sucio *m*; VI/VT ensuciar; ADV **to talk —** decir cosas obscenas

disability [dɪsəbílɪɪdi] N incapacidad *f*, discapacidad *f*, minusvalía *f*; **— insurance** seguro de discapacidad *m*

disable [dɪsébəl] VT (person) incapacitar; (device) desactivar

disabled [dɪsébəld] ADJ discapacitado, minusválido

disabuse [dɪsəbjúz] VT desengañar

disadvantage [dɪsɪdvǽntɪdʒ] N desventaja *f*; **to be at a —** estar en desventaja

disadvantaged [dɪsɪdvǽntɪdʒd] ADJ carenciado

disagree [dɪsəgrí] VI (differ in opinion) disentir, no estar de acuerdo; (differ) diferir; **pizza —s with me** no me cae bien la pizza

disagreeable [dɪsəgríəbəl] ADJ desagradable

disagreement [dɪsəgrímənt] N (lack of agreement, argument) desacuerdo *m*; (discrepancy) discrepancia *f*

disallow [dɪsəláU] VT desaprobar; (in sports) anular

disappear [dɪsəpír] VI desaparecer

disappearance [dɪsəpírəns] N desaparición *f*

disappoint [dɪsəpɔ́ɪnt] VI/VT decepcionar, desilusionar; **to be —ed** estar desilusionado

disappointing [dɪsəpɔ́ɪntɪŋ] ADJ decepcionante

disappointment [dɪsəpɔ́ɪntmənt] N decepción *f*, desilusión *f*

disapproval [dɪsəprúvəl] N desaprobación *f*

disapprove [dɪsəprúv] VI/VT desaprobar

disarm [dɪsárm] VI/VT desarmar[se]

disarmament [dɪsárməmənt] N desarme *m*

disarray [dɪsəré] VT desordenar; N confusión *f*, desorden *m*; **in —** en desorden

disaster [dɪzǽstə-] N desastre *m*

disastrous [dɪzǽstrəs] ADJ desastroso

disavow [dɪsəváU] VT negar

disband [dɪsbǽnd] VT disolver; VI desbandarse

disbelief [dɪsbɪlíf] N incredulidad *f*

disbelieve [dɪsbɪlív] VI/VT descreer de

disburse [dɪsbɜ́-s] VT desembolsar

disbursement [dɪsbɜ́-smənt] N desembolso *m*

discard[1] [dɪskárd] VT (a card) descartar; (garbage) desechar

discard[2] [dískard] N (card) descarte *m*; (garbage) desecho *m*

discern [dɪsɜ́-n] VT (distinguish mentally) discernir; (perceive) percibir

discernment [dɪsɜ́-nmənt] N discernimiento *m*

discharge[1] [dɪstʃárdʒ] VI/VT (battery, load, firearm) descargar[se]; (obligation) cumplir; (prisoner) poner en libertad, soltar; (odor) despedir; (soldier) dar de baja; (patient) dar de alta; (a debt) pagar; (pus) supurar

discharge[2] [dístʃardʒ] N (of a battery, load, firearm) descarga *f*; (of an obligation) cumplimiento *m*; (of a prisoner) puesta en libertad *f*; (of an odor) emisión *f*; (of a soldier) baja *f*; (of a patient) alta *f*; (of a debt) pago *m*; (of oil) pérdida *f*; (of pus) supuración *f*; (uterine, vaginal) flujo *m*; (from a job) despido *m*

disciple [dɪsáɪpəl] N discípulo -la *mf*

discipline [dísəplɪn] N disciplina *f*; VT disciplinar

disclaimer [dɪsklémə-] N descargo de responsabilidad *m*

disclose [dɪsklóz] VT revelar

disco [dísko] N discoteca *f*

discolor [dɪskʌ́lə-] VI/VT decolorar[se]

discomfort [dɪskʌ́mfə-t] N malestar *m*

disconcert [dɪskənsɜ́-t] VT desconcertar

disconnect [dɪskənɛ́kt] VI/VT desconectar; N desconexión *f*

disconnected [dɪskənɛ́ktɪd] ADJ (broken) desconectado; (incoherent) inconexo

disconsolate [dɪskánsəlɪt] ADJ desconsolado

discontent [dɪskəntɛ́nt] N descontento *m*

discontinue [dɪskəntínju] VT suspender, interrumpir

discontinuous [dɪskəntínjuəs] ADJ discontinuo

discord [dískɔrd] N (lack of concord) discordia *f*, desavenencia *f*; (dissonance) disonancia *f*, discordancia *f*

discotheque [dískotɛk] N discoteca *f*

discount [dískaUnt] VT (deduct from a charge, take into account in advance) descontar; (sell at a reduced price) rebajar; (disregard) ignorar; N descuento *m*; **at a —** con descuento, con rebaja

discourage [dɪskɜ́-ɪdʒ] VT desanimar, desalentar; **to — from** disuadir de

discouragement [dɪskɜ́-ɪdʒmənt] N desánimo *m*, desaliento *m*

discourse[1] [dískɔrs] N (conversation, talk) discurso *m*; (treatise) disertación *f*

discourse[2] [dɪskɔ́rs] VI (talk) discurrir; (treat a subject) disertar

discourteous [dɪskɜ́-ɪdəs] ADJ descortés

discourtesy [dɪskɜ́-ɪdɪsi] N descortesía *f*

discover [dɪskʌ́və-] VT descubrir

discoverer [dɪskʌ́vərə-] N descubridor -ora *mf*

discovery [dɪskʌ́vəri] N descubrimiento *m*

discredit [dɪskrɛ́dɪt] VT (injure the reputation of) desacreditar; (give no credence to) no

creer; N descrédito *m*

discreet [dɪskrít] ADJ discreto

discrepancy [dɪskrépənsi] N discrepancia *f*

discrete [dɪskrít] ADJ (separate) separado; (en matemáticas) discreto

discretion [dɪskréʃən] N discreción *f*; **at your own** — a discreción; **at the judge's** — al arbitrio del juez

discretionary [dɪskréʃəneri] ADJ discrecional; — **income** ingresos discrecionales *m pl*

discriminate [dɪskrímənet] VI/VT distinguir; **to** — **against** discriminar a

discrimination [dɪskrɪmɪnéʃən] N discriminación *f*

discuss [dɪskás] VT discutir

discussion [dɪskáʃən] N discusión *f*

disdain [dɪsdén] N desdén *m*, desprecio *m*; VT (treat with contempt) desdeñar; (think unworthy of a response) no dignarse a

disdainful [dɪsdénfəł] ADJ desdeñoso

disease [dɪzíz] N enfermedad *f*

diseased [dɪzízd] ADJ enfermo

disembark [dɪsɪmbárk] VI/VT desembarcar

disenfranchise [dɪsɪnfréntʃaɪz] VT (politician) proscribir; (minorities) privar de derechos, desheredar

disengage [dɪsɪngéʤ] VI/VT (a clutch) soltar[se]; (from a situation) distanciar[se]

disentangle [dɪsɪntǽŋgəł] VI/VT desenredar[se], desenmarañar[se]

disfavor [dɪsfévɚ] VT mirar con malos ojos; N **to fall into** — (a person) caer en desgracia; (a fashion) caer en desuso

disfigure [dɪsfígjɚ] VT desfigurar

disgrace [dɪsgrés] N (dishonor) deshonra *f*; (shame) vergüenza *f*; **to fall into** — caer en desgracia; VT deshonrar

disgraceful [dɪsgrésfəł] ADJ vergonzoso

disgruntled [dɪsgrántḷd] ADJ descontento, resentido

disguise [dɪsgáɪz] VT disfrazar[se]; N disfraz *m*

disgust [dɪsgást] VT (repel) asquear, repugnar; (displease) disgustar; N asco *m*, repugnancia *f*

disgusted [dɪsgástɪd] ADJ asqueado, repugnado

disgusting [dɪsgástɪŋ] ADJ asqueroso, repugnante

dish [dɪʃ] N (plate, food, quantity) plato *m*; (serving container) fuente *f*; (attractive person) *fam* bombón *m*; **—es** vajilla *f*; **—cloth/towel** paño de cocina *m*, repasador *m*; **—washer** lavaplatos *m sg*, lavavajillas *m sg*; **—water** agua de fregar *f*; VI/VT (serve food) servir; **to** — **out** repartir

dishearten [dɪshártn̩] VT desanimar, descorazonar, desalentar

disheartening [dɪshártn̩ɪŋ] ADJ descorazonador, desalentador

dishevel [dɪʃévəł] VT desgreñar

disheveled [dɪʃévəłd] ADJ (hair) desgreñado, revuelto; (clothes) desaliñado

dishonest [dɪsánɪst] ADJ deshonesto

dishonesty [dɪsánɪsti] N deshonestidad *f*

dishonor [dɪsánɚ] N deshonra *f*; VT deshonrar; (a check) no pagar

dishonorable [dɪsánərəbəł] ADJ deshonroso

disillusion [dɪsɪlúʒən] N desilusión *f*, desencanto *m*; VT desilusionar, desencantar

disinfect [dɪsɪnfékt] VT desinfectar

disinfectant [dɪsɪnféktənt] N desinfectante *m*

disinfection [dɪsɪnfékʃən] N desinfección *f*

disinfestation [dɪsɪnfestéʃən] N desinfestación *f*

disinformation [dɪsɪnfɚméʃən] N desinformación *f*

disinherit [dɪsɪnhérɪt] VT desheredar

disintegrate [dɪsíntɪgret] VI/VT desintegrar[se]

disintegration [dɪsɪntɪgréʃən] N desintegración *f*

disinterested [dɪsíntrɪstɪd] ADJ desinteresado

disjointed [dɪsʤɔ́ɪntɪd] ADJ desarticulado

disk, disc [dɪsk] N disco *m*; (game piece) tejo *m*; (in a computer) disco *m*, disquete *m*; **— brake** freno de disco *m*; **— capacity** capacidad de almacenamiento de disco *f*; **— drive** disquetera *f*; **— jockey** pinchadiscos *mf sg*

diskette [dɪskét] N disquete *m*; **— drive** unidad de disquete *f*

dislike [dɪsláɪk] N aversión *f*, tirria *f*; VT **I — parties** no me gustan las fiestas

dislocate [dɪslóket] VT dislocar, descoyuntar

dislocation [dɪsloké ʃən] N dislocación *f*, luxación *f*

dislodge [dɪsláʤ] VT (force out) desatascar; (displace) desprender

disloyal [dɪslɔ́ɪəł] ADJ desleal

dismal [dízməł] ADJ pésimo; **a — failure** un fracaso rotundo

dismantle [dɪsmǽntḷ] VT (a factory) desmantelar; (a car, watch) desmontar

dismay [dɪsmé] VT (disappoint) consternar; (daunt) desalentar; (alarm) alarmar; N (disappointment) consternación *f*; (loss of courage) desaliento *m*; (alarm) alarma *f*

dismember [dɪsmémbɚ] VT desmembrar

dismiss [dɪsmís] VT (fire a private employee) despedir; (fire a public employee) destituir, cesar; (reject a possibility) desechar, descartar; (discharge from military service) dar de baja; (reject a claim) desestimar; (ignore a person) ningunear; **class —ed!** ¡pueden retirarse!

dismissal [dɪsmísəł] N (firing) destitución *f*, despido *m*; (of a possibility) rechazo *m*; (from military service) baja *f*; (of a claim) desestimación *f*; (of a person) ninguneo *m*

dismount [dɪsmáʊnt] VI (get off a horse) desmontarse, apearse; (take apart) desarmar; N bajada *f*

disobedience [dɪsəbíɒɪəns] N desobediencia *f*

disobedient [dɪsəbídɪənt] ADJ desobediente
disobey [dɪsəbé] VI/VT desobedecer
disorder [dɪsɔ́rdə˞] N (confusion) desorden *m*; (public disturbance) desorden público *m*; (illness) trastorno *m*, desarreglo *m*
disorderly [dɪsɔ́rdə˞li] ADJ (untidy) desordenado; (unruly) revoltoso; **— conduct** alteración del orden público *f*
disorganization [dɪsɔ̀rgənɪzéʃən] N desorganización *f*
disorganized [dɪsɔ́rgənaɪzd] ADJ desorganizado
disown [dɪsón] VT repudiar
disparage [dɪspǽrɪʤ] VT denigrar
disparate [díspə-ɪt] ADJ dispar
dispassionate [dɪspǽʃənɪt] ADJ desapasionado
dispatch [dɪspǽtʃ] VT despachar; N (sending off) envío *m*; (putting to death) ejecución *f*; (news story, official communication) despacho *m*; (promptness) prontitud *f*
dispel [dɪspél] VT disipar
dispensable [dɪspénsəbəł] ADJ prescindible
dispensary [dɪspénsəri] N dispensario *m*
dispensation [dɪspənséʃən] N (relaxation of law) dispensa *f*; (act of handing out) dispensación *f*
dispense [dɪspéns] VT (goods) dispensar; (justice) administrar; **to — from an obligation** eximir de una obligación; **to — with** prescindir de
dispersal [dɪspɝ́-səł] N dispersión *f*
disperse [dɪspɝ́-s] VI/VT dispersar[se]; ADJ disperso
dispersed [dɪspɝ́-st] ADJ disperso
displace [dɪsplés] VT (evict) desalojar; (take up space, remove from office) desplazar; **—d person** (domestic) desplazado -da *mf*; (foreign) expatriado -da *mf*
displacement [dɪsplésmənt] N (of refugees, of a ship) desplazamiento *m*; (of an engine) cilindrada *f*
display [dɪsplé] VT (exhibit) exhibir, exponer; (unfold) desplegar; (flaunt) ostentar; (show on a computer screen) visualizar; N (of wares, etc.) exhibición *f*, despliegue *m*; (advertisement) cartel *m*; (flaunting) ostentación *f*; (computer screen) pantalla *f*, visualizador *m*, display *m*
displease [dɪsplíz] VT contrariar, desagradar, descontentar; VI molestar
displeasure [dɪsplέʒə˞] N disgusto *m*, desagrado *m*
disposable [dɪspózəbəł] ADJ **— income** ingresos disponibles *m pl*
disposal [dɪspózəł] N (arrangement) disposición *f*; (elimination) eliminación *f*
dispose [dɪspóz] VT (give inclination) predisponer; (set in order, make ready) disponer; **to — of** descartar, eliminar
disposition [dɪspəzíʃən] N (attitude) temperamento *m*; (inclination) inclinación *f*, tendencia *f*; (arrangement, disposal) disposición *f*
dispossess [dɪspəzés] VT desposeer
disproportionate [dɪsprəpɔ́rʃənɪt] ADJ desproporcionado
disprove [dɪsprúv] VT refutar
dispute [dɪspjút] N disputa *f*; VT discutir, impugnar
disqualify [dɪskwáləfaɪ] VT (deprive of rights) inhabilitar; (exclude from a sport event) descalificar
disregard [dɪsrɪgárd] VT hacer caso omiso de, ignorar; N (neglect) descuido *m*; (disrespect) falta de respeto *f*
disrepair [dɪsrɪpér] N mal estado *m*; **in —** deteriorado
disreputable [dɪsrépjə̀dəbəł] ADJ (of bad reputation) de mala reputación; (shabby) de mala muerte
disrespect [dɪsrɪspékt] N desacato *m*, falta de respeto *f*; VT faltar el respeto
disrespectful [dɪsrɪspéktfəł] ADJ irrespetuoso
disrobe [dɪsrób] VI/VT desvestir[se]
disrupt [dɪsrʌ́pt] VT (cause disorder) trastornar, trastocar; (interrupt) interrumpir
dissatisfied [dɪssǽdɪsfaɪd] ADJ insatisfecho, disconforme
dissatisfy [dɪssǽdɪsfaɪ] VT no satisfacer
dissect [daɪsékt] VT (cut apart) disecar; (analyze argument) analizar minuciosamente
dissemble [dɪsémbəł] VI/VT (hide) disimular; (feign) fingir
disseminate [dɪsémənet] VT (spread out) diseminar, propagar; (publicize) divulgar
dissemination [dɪsemənéʃən] N (spreading out) diseminación *f*; (publicizing) divulgación *f*
dissension [dɪsénʃən] N disensión *f*, disenso *m*
dissent [dɪsént] VI disentir; N disenso *m*
dissertation [dɪsə-téʃən] N (formal discourse) disertación *f*; (doctoral treatise) tesis de doctorado *f*
dissident [dísɪdənt] N disidente *mf*
dissimilar [dɪssímələ˞] ADJ diferente
dissimulation [dɪsɪmjəléʃən] N disimulo *m*
dissipate [dísəpet] VI/VT disipar[se]
dissipation [dɪsəpéʃən] N disipación *f*
dissolute [dísəlut] ADJ disoluto, vicioso
dissolution [dɪsəlúʃən] N disolución *f*
dissolve [dɪzάłv] VI/VT disolver[se]
dissuade [dɪswéd] VT disuadir
distance [dístəns] N distancia *f*, recorrido *m*; **— learning** educación a distancia *f*; **in the —** a lo lejos, en la lejanía; VT distanciarse de, distanciar
distant [dístənt] ADJ (far away, aloof) distante; (remote) lejano, remoto; **to be — from** distar de
distaste [dɪstést] N aversión *f*

distasteful [dɪstéstfəɫ] ADJ desagradable
distemper [dɪstémpə˞] N moquillo *m*
distend [dɪstɛ́nd] VI/VT distender[se]
distill [dɪstíɫ] VI/VT destilar[se]
distillation [dɪstəléʃən] N destilación *f*
distillery [dɪstíɫəri] N destilería *f*
distinct [dɪstíŋkt] ADJ (different) distinto; (clear) bien delineado, neto
distinction [dɪstíŋkʃən] N (honor) distinción *f*; (differentiation) distinción *f*, diferenciación *f*; **he passed with —** aprobó con sobresaliente
distinctive [dɪstíŋktɪv] ADJ distintivo
distinguish [dɪstíŋgwɪʃ] VI/VT distinguir
distinguished [dɪstíŋgwɪʃt] ADJ distinguido
distinguishing [dɪstíŋgwɪʃɪŋ] ADJ distintivo
distort [dɪstɔ́rt] VT (an object) deformar; (reports, sound) distorsionar
distortion [dɪstɔ́rʃən] N (object) deformación *f*; (image, sound) distorsión *f*; (of a statement) tergiversación *f*
distract [dɪstrǽkt] VT distraer, entretener
distracted [dɪstrǽktɪd] ADJ distraído, disperso
distraction [dɪstrǽkʃən] N distracción *f*; **to drive to —** volver loco
distraught [dɪstrɔ́t] ADJ angustiado
distress [dɪstrɛ́s] N (anxiety) angustia *f*; (pain) dolor *m*, congoja *f*; **to be in —** (a person) estar en apuros; (a ship, plane) estar en peligro; VT (cause anxiety) angustiar, atribular; (cause pain) acongojar, afligir
distressing [dɪstrɛ́sɪŋ] ADJ inquietante
distribute [dɪstríbjut] VT distribuir, repartir
distribution [dɪstrəbjúʃən] N distribución *f*, reparto *m*
distributor [dɪstríbjəɾə˞] N distribuidor *m*
district [dístrɪkt] N distrito *m*, comarca *f*; **— attorney** fiscal de distrito *mf*
District of Columbia [dístrɪktəvkəlámbiə] N Distrito de Columbia *m*
distrust [dɪstrʌ́st] N desconfianza *f*; VT desconfiar de
distrustful [dɪstrʌ́stfəɫ] ADJ desconfiado
disturb [dɪstɝ́b] VI/VT (interrupt, interfere, perplex) perturbar; (trouble) turbar, perturbar, trastornar; (mess up) desarreglar; **do not —** se ruega no molestar
disturbance [dɪstɝ́bəns] N disturbio *m*; (weather) perturbación *f*
disuse [dɪsjús] N desuso *m*; **to fall into —** caer en desuso
ditch [dɪtʃ] N (trench) zanja *f*; (roadside) cuneta *f*; (for irrigation) acequia *f*; VT (make ditches) abrir zanjas; (get rid of) deshacerse de; (crash-land an airplane on water) hacer un amarizaje
dither [díðə˞] VI (hesitate) titubear; N **it threw her into a —** se puso muy nerviosa
ditsy [dítsi] ADJ atolondrado, cabeza de chorlito
ditto [dído] PRON & ADV ídem
diuretic [daɪərɛ́dɪk] ADJ & N diurético *m*
diurnal [daɪɝ́nɫ] ADJ diurno
divan [dɪvǽn] N diván *m*, canapé *m*
dive [daɪv] VI (into water) zambullirse, chapuzar, *Am* tirarse un clavado; (into an activity) zambullirse; (with scuba equipment) bucear; (airplane) bajar en picado -da; (submarine) sumergirse; N (of a person) zambullida *f*, chapuz *m*; (of an airplane) picado -da *mf*; (cheap bar) antro *m*
diver [dáɪvə˞] N saltador -ora *mf*; (high-dive) clavadista *mf*; (scuba) buzo *mf*
diverge [dɪvɝ́dʒ] VI (branch off, differ in opinion) divergir; VI/VT (deviate) desviar
divergence [dɪvɝ́dʒəns] N (separation, difference in opinion) divergencia *f*; (deviation) desviación *f*
diverse [dɪvɝ́s] ADJ (of various kinds) diverso; (different) diferente
diversify [dɪvɝ́səfaɪ] VI/VT diversificar[se]
diversion [dɪvɝ́ʒən] N (entertainment) entretenimiento *m*; (distraction) distracción *f*; (military) diversión *f*; (turning aside) desvío *m*, desviación *f*
diversity [dɪvɝ́sɪdi] N diversidad *f*
divert [dɪvɝ́t] VI/VT (turn aside) desviar, distraer; (distract) entretener
diverticulitis [dɪvə˞tɪkjəláɪdɪs] N diverticulitis *f*
divest [dɪvɛ́st] VT (strip) despojar; (get rid of) deshacerse de
divide [dɪváɪd] VI/VT dividir[se]; (classify) clasificar[se]; N línea divisoria *f*
dividend [dívɪdɛnd] N dividendo *m*
divine [dɪváɪn] ADJ divino; VI/VT adivinar
divinity [dɪvínɪtɪ] N (godhead, state or quality of being divine) divinidad *f*; (theology) teología *f*
division [dɪvíʒən] N división *f*
divorce [dɪvɔ́rs] N divorcio *m*; VI/VT divorciar[se]
divot [dívət] N (golf) chuleta *f*
divulge [dɪvʌ́ɫdʒ] VT divulgar, publicar
dizziness [dízɪnɪs] N mareo *m*
dizzy [dízi] ADJ (person) mareado; (height) vertiguoso; (speed) vertiginoso; **— spell** vahido *m*
DJ [disc jockey] [díʤe] N pinchadiscos *mf sg*
Djibouti [ʤɪbúti] N Yibuti *m*
Djiboutian [jɪbúʃɪən] ADJ & N yibutiano -na *mf*
DNA [deoxyribonucleic acid] [diéné] N ADN *m*
do [du] VI/VT hacer; **to — away with** eliminar; **to — one's hair** arreglarse el pelo; **to — the dishes** lavar los platos; **to — drugs** tomar drogas; **to — in** matar; **to — time** cumplir una condena; **to — well** prosperar; **to — without** prescindir de; **we were —ing 100 kph** íbamos a cien kph; **to have nothing to — with** no tener nada que ver con; **that will —** basta; **that won't —** eso no sirve; **I'm —ing well** estoy bien; **this will have to —**

habrá que conformarse con esto; **—-it-yourself** hágalo usted mismo; V AUX **I feel as you —** pienso igual que tú; **how — you —?** ¿cómo estás? **— you hear me?** ¿me oyes? **yes, I —** sí; **— come again** vuelve por favor; N (hairstyle) peinado *m*; (party) fiesta *f*

DOA [dead on arrival] [díóé] ADJ muerto -ta antes de ingresar al hospital

docile [dásəł] ADJ dócil

dock [dɑk] N (pier) muelle *m*; (for landing) desembarcadero *m*, atracadero *m*; (water between piers) dique *m*, dársena *f*; **— worker** trabajador -ora portuario -ria *mf*; **dry —** dique seco *m*; VI/VT (a boat) atracar; (a space ship) acoplar[se]; (wages) descontar

doctor [dáktə-] N (physician) médico -ca *mf*; (PhD, scholar) doctor -ora *mf*; (expert) especialista *mf*; VT (treat) atender; (cure) curar; (restore) restaurar; (counterfeit) alterar; **I —ed up this recipe** le hice unos retoques a esta receta

doctorate [dáktə-ɪt] N doctorado *m*

doctrine [dáktrɪn] N doctrina *f*

document[1] [dákjəmənt] N documento *m*

document[2] [dákjəmɛnt] VT documentar

documentary [dɑkjəméntəri] N documental *m*

documentation [dɑkjəmɪntéʃən] N documentación *f*

dodder [dádə-] VI (stumble along) tambalearse, titubear; (shake) temblequear

dodge [dɑʤ] VT esquivar, sortear; VI (be evasive) dar rodeos; (move sideways) apartarse, echarse a un lado; N evasiva *f*

doe [do] N cierva *f*; (female of various animals) hembra *f*

dog [dɔg] N perro *m*, perra *f*; **—catcher** perrero -ra *mf*; **— collar** collar de perro *m*; **—fight** (dogs) pelea de perros *f*; (aircraft) combate aéreo *m*; (people) reyerta *f*; **—house** casilla de perro *f*; *Sp* caseta *f*; **to be in the —house** haber caído en desgracia, estar en capilla; **—paddle** natación estilo perrito *m*; **—sled** trineo para perros *m*; **— tag** placa de identificación *f*; **—wood** cornejo *m*; **to go to the —s** venirse abajo; ADJ **— -eared** sobado, muy gastado; **—gone** maldito; VT (follow) seguir la pista de; (harass) hostigar; **to —-paddle** nadar estilo perrito

doggy [dɔ́gi] N perrito -ta *mf*; **— bag** bolsa para las sobras *f*

dogma [dɔ́gmə] N dogma *m*

dogmatic [dɔgmǽɪk] ADJ dogmático

doily [dɔ́ili] N mantelito *m*

doings [dúɪŋz] N actividades *f pl*

dole [dołł] N (alms) limosna *f*; **to be on the —** estar cobrando el seguro de desempleo/paro; **to — out** repartir

doleful [dółfəł] ADJ apesadumbrado, triste

doll [dał] N (toy) muñeco -ca *mf*; (attractive female) muñeca *f*; **—house** casa de muñecas *f*; VI **to get —ed up** emperifollarse, empaquetarse

dollar [dálə-] N dólar *m*; **— diplomacy** diplomacia del dólar *f*; **— sign** signo del dólar *m*

dolly [dáli] N (doll) muñeca *f*; (cart) carretilla *f*

dolphin [dɔ́łfɪn] N (mammal) delfín *m*; (fish) dorado *m*

dolt [dołł] N zopenco -ca *mf*

domain [domén] N dominio *m*

dome [dom] N (roof) cúpula *f*, domo *m*; (head) coco *m*, pelada *f*

domestic [dəméstɪk] ADJ (appliance, pet, chore) doméstico; (devoted to homemaking) hogareño; (home-loving) casero; (of a country) interno, nacional; **— violence** violencia doméstica *f*; N doméstico -ca *mf*

domesticate [dəméstɪket] VI/VT (animals) domesticar; (plants) aclimatar

domicile [dáməsałł] N domicilio *m*

dominant [dámənənt] ADJ dominante

dominate [dámənet] VI/VT dominar; VI señorear

domination [dɑmənéʃən] N (act of dominating) dominación *f*; (rule) dominio *m*

domineer [dɑmənír] VI/VT dominar, mandonear

domineering [dɑmənírɪŋ] ADJ tiránico, mandón

Dominica [dəmínɪkə] N Dominica *f*

Dominican [dəmínɪkən] ADJ & N (of Dominica) dominiqués -esa *mf*; (of the Dominican Republic) dominicano -na *mf*

Dominican Republic [dəmínɪkənrɪpáblɪk] N República Dominicana *f*

dominion [dəmínjən] N dominio *m*, señorío *m*

domino [dámənо] N (game, costume) dominó *m*; (piece) ficha *f*

don [dɑn] N (title, form of address, mafia boss) don *m*; (lecturer) profesor -ora universitario -ria *mf*; VT ponerse, vestirse

donate [dónet] VI/VT donar

donation [donéʃən] N donación *f*

done [dʌn] *see* do

done [dʌn] ADJ terminado, acabado; **when you are —** cuando termines; **to be all — in** estar muerto de cansancio; **the meat is well —** está bien asada la carne; **that sort of thing just isn't —** eso no se hace

donkey [dáŋki] N burro *m*, asno *m*, borrico *m*

donor [dónə-] N donante *mf*, donador -ora *mf*

doodad [dúdæd] N (trinket) chucheria *f*; (device) chisme *m*, coso *m*

doohickey [dúhɪki] N chisme *m*, coso *m*

doom [dum] N perdición *f*; **—sday** día del juicio final *m*; VT condenar; **to be —ed to failure** estar condenado al fracaso

door [dɔr] N puerta *f*; **—bell** timbre *m*;

—**keeper** portero -ra *mf*; —**knob** pomo *m*; —**man** portero *m*; —**mat** felpudo *m*; —**step** umbral *m*; —**way** puerta *f*, portal *m*; **I showed him the** — lo eché; ADJ —**-to-**— de puerta a puerta

dopamine [dópəmin] N dopamina *f*

dope [dop] N (narcotic) droga *f*; (stimulant) estimulante *m*; (information) chismes *m pl*; (moron) *fam* zopenco; VT dopar; **to — oneself up** medicarse en exceso

dork [dɔrk] N *fam* idiotà *mf*, tarambana *mf*

dorky [dɔ́rki] ADJ **that's a — dress** *fam* pareces una tonta con ese vestido

dormant [dɔ́rmənt] ADJ latente

dormitory [dɔ́rmɪtɔri] N residencia estudiantil *f*

DOS [Disk Operating System] [dɑs] N DOS *m*

dose [dos] N dosis *f*; VT dosificar

dossier [dɔ́sie] N expediente *m*

dot [dɑt] N punto *m*; (on a tie) pinta *f*; —**-com** punto com; —**-matrix printer** impresora de matriz de puntos *f*; —**ted eighth note** corchea con puntillo *f*; **on the** — en punto; VT marcar con puntos

dotage [dóʊɪʤ] N chochez *f*, chochera *f*; **to be in one's** — chochear, estar chocho

dote [dot] VI **to** — **on** estar chocho con

double [dábəł] ADJ doble; — **agent** doble agente *mf*; —**-barreled** de doble caño; — **bass** contrabajo *m*; — **bed** cama doble *f*; —**-blind test** prueba de doble incógnita *f*; — **bind** dilema *m*; — **boiler** baño de María *m*; —**-breasted** cruzado; — **chin** papada *f*; — **cross** traición *f*; — **click** doble pulsación *f*; — **dealing** duplicidad *f*; — **entry** entrada por partida doble *f*; — **fault** doble falta *f*; — **indemnity** doble indemnización *f*; — **play** doble matanza *f*; — **sided** de dos caras; — **shift** turno doble *m*; — **standard** trato discriminatorio *m*; — **vision** doble visión *f*; **to do a** — **take** quedar atónito; ADV **to sleep** — dormir de a dos; N (in baseball) doble *m*, doblete *m*; (in tennis) —**s** dobles *m pl*, juego de dobles *m*; VI/VT duplicar[se]; (an effort) redoblar[se]; (fold, be twice as old, challenge a bid) doblar[se]; **to** — **up** (bend over) doblarse; (crowd) amontonarse; **to** —**-check** verificar; **to** —**-click** pulsar dos veces; **to** —**-cross** traicionar; **to** —**-date** salir dos parejas juntas; **to** —**-talk** salirse con evasivas; **this sofa** —**s as a bed** este sofá sirve también de cama

doubt [daʊt] VI/VT dudar; (not trust) desconfiar; N duda *f*; **beyond a** — indudablemente; **in** — en duda; **no** —! ¡sin duda!

doubtful [dáʊtfəł] ADJ dudoso

doubtless [dáʊtlɪs] ADV (certainly) sin duda; (probably) probablemente

dough [do] N pasta *f*, masa *f*; (money) pasta *f*, mosca *f*; —**nut** rosquilla *f*; *Mex* dona *f*; *Sp* donut *m*

douse [daʊs] VI/VT empapar; (a flame) apagar [con agua]

dove [dʌv] N paloma *f*

dove [dov] *see* dive

dowdy [dáʊdi] ADJ (article of clothing) pasado de moda; (person) sin gracia

dowel [dáʊəł] N clavija *f*

down [daʊn] ADV abajo; — **and dirty** sucio; — **and out** tirado; **to be** — **with** estar de acuerdo con; **to come** — **with a cold** caer con gripe, *Sp* cogerse un resfriado; **to fall** — caerse; **to get** — **to work** aplicarse al trabajo; **to go/come** — bajar; **to lie** — acostarse, echarse; **to put someone** — denigrar a alguien; **to turn** — **the volume** bajar el volumen; **to water** — **a drink** rebajar una bebida con agua; **to write** — anotar; **two blocks** — dos calles más abajo; **slow** —! ¡anda más despacio! **the wind died** — amainó el viento; **one** — **and two to go** hicimos uno y nos quedan dos por hacer; **prices are** — han bajado los precios; **the system is** — se cayó el sistema; **they're** — **on me** están mal conmigo; PREP — **the street** calle abajo; ADJ (depressed) abatido; N (turn for the worse) revés *m*; (feathers) plumón *m*; VT (knock, shoot) derribar; (drink quickly) despachar de un solo trago; (defeat) vencer; (football play) oportunidad *f*

downcast [dáʊnkæst] ADJ abatido, cabizbajo

downfall [dáʊnfɔł] N ruina *f*

downgrade [dáʊngred] N declive *m*, pendiente *f*; VT quitarle importancia a

downhill[1] [dáʊnhíł] ADV cuesta abajo; **his health is going** — su salud se deteriora

downhill[2] [dáʊnhɪł] ADJ **a** — **slope** una pendiente; N bajada contra-reloj *f*

download [dáʊnlod] VT descargar; N descarga *f*

down payment [dáʊnpémənt] N entrega inicial *f*, entrada *f*

downplay [dǎʊnple] VT quitar la importancia a

downpour [dáʊnpɔr] N aguacero *m*

downright [dáʊnraɪt] ADJ absoluto; — **foolishness** reverenda tontería *f*; **he was** — **angry** echaba chispas

downshift [dáʊnshɪft] VI rebajar [el cambio]

downside [dáʊnsaɪd] N inconveniente *m*

downsize [dáʊnsaɪz] VI (personnel) hacer reducción; VT (an object or organization) reducir el tamaño de; (one's lifestyle) simplificar *f*; **he got** —**d** perdió el trabajo cuando hicieron reducción de personal

downstairs[1] [dáʊnstérz] ADV abajo; (in the apartment one floor lower) en el piso de abajo

downstairs[2] [dáʊnstɛrz] ADJ de abajo; N planta baja *f*

downstream [dáʊnstrím] ADV río abajo

downtime [dáʊntaɪm] N (of a machine) tiempo

de inactividad *m*; (of a person) horas de ocio *f pl*

down-to-earth [dáʊntə́ɜ·θ] ADJ sensato, práctico

downtown [dáʊntáʊn] ADV (toward) al centro; (in) en el centro; ADJ del centro, céntrico; N centro *m*

downturn [dáʊntɜ·n] N tendencia a la baja *f*

down under [dáʊnándɚ] ADV en/a Australia

downward [dáʊnwɚ·d] ADJ descendente; — **mobility** descenso social *m*; —**s** hacia abajo

downwind [dáʊnwínd] ADV en la dirección del viento

downy [dáʊni] ADJ sedoso, suave

dowry [dáʊri] N dote *f*

doze [doz] VI dormitar; N siesta *f*

dozen [dázən] N docena *f*

drab [dræb] ADJ triste; N pardo *m*

draft [dræft] N (of air) corriente *f*; (drink) trago *m*; (bank) giro *m*; (outline) esbozo *m*; (military) conscripción *f*, quinta *f*; (of a ship) calado *m*; — **beer** cerveza de barril *f*; — **horse** caballo de tiro *m*; —**sman** dibujante *m*; VT (to sketch) esbozar; (to compose) redactar; (to select for military service) conscribir

drag [dræg] VI/VT (haul slowly) arrastrar[se]; (search a body of water) dragar; **don't — me into this** no me metas en esto; **to — -and-drop/release** arrastrar y soltar; **to — on and on** eternizarse; **to — out** estirar; N (dredge) draga *f*; (boring person) pesado -da *mf*; (hassle) lata *f*; (counterforce) resistencia *f*; (on a cigarette) pitada *f*; — **race** carrera de dragsters *f*; — **strip** pista de dragsters *f*

dragon [drǽgən] N dragón *m*; —**fly** libélula *f*

drain [dren] N (channel) desagüe *m*, sumidero *m*; (depletion of resources) sangría *f*, fuga *f*; —**pipe** desaguadero *m*, desagüe *m*; **to go down the —** irse por la borda; VI/VT (empty a sink) desagotar[se], desaguar[se]; (exhaust) agotar[se]; VT (wetlands) drenar, sanear; VI (a battery) descargarse

drainage [drénɪʤ] N (act of draining) desagüe *m*, drenaje *m*; (system for draining) drenaje *m*; — **pipe** tubo de desagüe *m*

drake [drek] N pato [macho] *m*

drama [drámə] N drama *m*

dramatic [drəmǽdɪk] ADJ dramático

dramatically [drəmǽdɪkli] ADV (changing) de forma fundamental, fundamentalmente; (presenting) de manera dramática/teatral

dramatist [drámətɪst] N dramaturgo -ga *mf*

dramatize [drámətaɪz] VI/VT dramatizar

drank [dræŋk] *see* drink

drape [drep] VI (hang in folds) colgar, drapear; VT (cover) cubrir; N cortina *f*

drapery [drépəri] N cortinado *m*, colgadura *f*

drastic [dræstɪk] ADJ drástico

draw [drɔ] VT (a picture) dibujar; (lines, shapes) trazar; (a cart) tirar de; (a curtain) correr; (cards, blood, water, conclusion, strength) sacar; (a crowd) atraer; (comparison, distinction) hacer; (a sword) desenvainar; VI (of a boat) tener calado; (of a fireplace) tirar; (in sports, have the same score) empatar; (receive money) cobrar; (withdraw money) retirar, sacar; **to — aside** apartar[se]; **to — away** separar[se]; **to — a breath** aspirar, tomar aliento; **to — a blank** quedarse en blanco; **to — in** involucrar; **to — lots/ straws** echar a la suerte, sortear; **to — near** acercarse; **to — off** irse, retirarse; **to — on** (be based on) basarse en; (have recourse to) recurrir a; **to — out** (remove) sacar; (prolong) alargar, prolongar; **to — up** (approach) acercar[se]; (write) redactar; (shrink) encoger; N (in sports, tie game) empate *m*; (lot) número sorteado *m*; (attraction) atracción *f*; —**back** inconveniente *m*; —**bridge** puente levadizo *m*

drawer [drɔɚ] N cajón *m*; (small) gaveta *f*; —**s** calzones *m pl*

drawing [drɔ́ɪŋ] N (picture) dibujo *m*; (raffle) sorteo *m*; — **room** sala [de recibo] *f*

drawn [drɔn] ADJ demacrado; —**-out** interminable

drawn [drɔn] *see* draw

dread [dred] N pavor *m*, terror *m*, espanto *m*; VT **I — going to the dentist** me aterra ir al dentista

dreadful [drédfəł] ADJ horrendo, espantoso, temible

dream [drim] N sueño *m* (also aspiration); (reverie) ensueño *m*, ensoñación *f*; (fancy) ilusión *f*; —**land** tierra del ensueño *f*; — **team** equipo de estrellas *m*; — **world** mundo de ensueño *m*; VI/VT soñar; **to — of** soñar con; **I wouldn't — of stealing** no se me ocurriría robar; **to — that** soñar que; **to — up** imaginar; ADJ **a — holiday** unas vacaciones perfectas

dreamer [drímɚ] N (impractical person) soñador -ora *mf*; (visionary) visionario -ria *mf*

dreamt [drɛmt] *see* dream

dreary [dríri] ADJ sombrío, deprimente

dredge [drɛʤ] N draga *f*; VT (a river) dragar; (facts) desenterrar, sacar a luz

dregs [drɛgz] N heces *f pl*, poso *m*; — **of society** escoria de la sociedad *f*

drench [drɛnʧ] VT empapar, calar; —**ed in blood** bañado en sangre

dress [drɛs] N (article of clothing for women) vestido *m*; (attire) ropa *f*; (formal) traje de etiqueta *m*, ropa de etiqueta *f*; (costume) vestimenta *f*; —**maker** modista *mf*; — **rehearsal** ensayo general *m*; — **shirt**

camisa para traje *f*; **what's the — code?** ¿cómo hay que ir vestido? VI/VT vestir; VT (store window) arreglar; (slaughtered animals) limpiar; (salad) aderezar; (hides) adobar; (a wound) vendar; **to — down** (scold) regañar; (wear casual clothes) ponerse ropa informal; **to — up** (wear fine clothes) vestirse de gala; (make more appealing) embellecer

dresser [drésɚ] N cómoda *f*; **she is a good —** se viste con elegancia

dressing [drésɪŋ] N (act, result) vestir *m*; (for salad) aderezo *m*; (for fowl) relleno *m*; (for wounds) gasa *f*, vendaje *m*; **—-down** regaño *m*; **— gown** bata *f*; **— room** (in a theater) camerino *m*; (in a store) probador *m*; **— table** tocador *m*

drew [dru] *see* draw

dribble [dríbəł] VI (trickle) gotear; (drool) babear; VT (a ball) driblar, regatear; (liquid) rociar; N (trickle) goteo *m*; (small quantity) chorrito *m*; (of a ball) drible *m*, regate *m*

dried [draɪd] ADJ seco; **— fig** higo paso/seco *m*; **—-up** (without water) seco; (wizened) arrugado

drift [drɪft] N (direction) deriva *f*; (current) corriente *f*; (meaning) sentido *m*, tenor *m*; (pile) montón *m*, acumulación *f*; **—wood** madera flotante *f*; **do you get my —?** ¿me captas la onda? VI (float) flotar; (be adrift) ir a la deriva; (wander) errar; **he —ed off** se durmió; VI/VT (deviate) desviar[se]; (accumulate) amontonar[se], acumular[se]

drifter [dríftɚ] N (wanderer) vagabundo -da *mf*; (of a worker) itinerante *mf*

drill [drɪł] N (tool) taladro *m*; (dental) fresa *f*; (training) ejercicios *m pl*; (procedure) procedimiento *m*; (rehearsal) simulacro *m*; (cloth) dril *m*; VI/VT (make a hole) taladrar, perforar, barrenar; (train) entrenar[se], adiestrar[se]; VI (train) hacer ejercicios; (practice) practicar; VT hacer practicar

drink [drɪŋk] VI/VT (person) beber; (animal) abrevar; (absorb, take in) absorber; **to — up** apurar el trago; **to — to someone's health** brindar por alguien; N bebida *f* (also alcoholic); (a measure of beverage) trago *m*

drinkable [dríŋkəbəł] ADJ potable

drinking [dríŋkɪŋ] ADJ **— water** agua potable *f*; **he has a — problem** tiene problemas con el alcohol

drip [drɪp] N goteo *m*; (a bore) plasta *mf*; VI gotear

drive [draɪv] VI/VT (a car) conducir, manejar; (an animal) arrear; VI (go in a vehicle) ir en coche; VT (move forth) impulsar, impeler; (convey) llevar [en coche]; (force) forzar; (a nail) clavar; (a ball) tirar, golpear; **to — a hard bargain** regatear mucho; **to — away** ahuyentar; **to — someone mad** volver loco a alguien; **what are you driving at?** ¿qué quieres decir con eso? N (ride) paseo [en coche] *m*; (of an animal) arreo *m*; (urge) impulso *m*; (of a computer) unidad *f*; (military offensive) ofensiva *f*; (road) carretera *f*; (driveway) camino *m*; (campaign) campaña *f*; (energy) empuje *m*; (propulsion system) propulsión *f*; (of a ball) tiro *m*; (in tennis and golf) drive *m*; **—-by shooting** tiroteo desde un coche *m*; **—-in** drive-in *m*, establecimiento en que el cliente es atendido en el coche *m*; **—-in movie theater** autocine *m*; **—way** camino de entrada *m*, entrada de coches *f*; **front wheel —** tracción delantera *f*

drivel [drívəł] N (saliva) baba *f*; (idiocy) tontería *f*; VI babearse

driveling [drívəlɪŋ] ADJ baboso; **he's a — idiot** es un oligofrénico

driven [drívən] *see* drive

driver [dráɪvɚ] N (chauffeur) chofer *mf*, conductor -ra *mf*; (of animals) arriero -ra *mf*; (golf club) driver *m*; (in a computer) controlador *m*

driving [dráɪvɪŋ] ADJ **— force** impulso *m*; **— rain** lluvia torrencial *f*; **— school** autoescuela *f*

drizzle [drízəł] VI lloviznar; N llovizna *f*

drone [dron] N (male bee, idler) zángano *m*; (remote-controlled vehicle) vehículo teledirigido *f*; (drudge) esclavo *m*; (sound) zumbido *m*; VI/VT (make a sound) zumbar; (talk) hablar monótonamente

drool [druł] N baba *f*; VI babearse

droop [drup] VI (sag) colgarse; (flag) languidecer; (wither) marchitarse; **his shoulders —** tiene los hombros caídos; **—ing ears** orejas gachas *f pl*

drop [drap] N (liquid quantity) gota *f*; (descent) caída *f*; (incline) declive *m*; (in value) baja *f*; (in prices) caída *f*; (lozenge) pastilla *f*; (of mail, etc.) buzón *m*, punto de recolección *m*; (of supplies) lanzamiento *m*; **—out** (student) desetor -ora escolar *mf*; (marginalized person) marginado -da *mf*; **— shot** dejada de volea *f*; VI caer; (let fall) dejar caer, descargar; (in golf) dropar; **to — a line** mandar unas líneas; **to — from sight** desaparecer; **to — in** caer de sorpresa; **to — out** (sports) retirarse; (school) abandonar; **why don't you — by?** ¿por qué no pasas por aquí? VI/VT (a course) abandonar; (a curtain) bajar; ADJ **—-dead beautiful** hermosísima

dropper [drápɚ] N gotero *m*

drought [draʊt] N sequía *f*

drove [drov] N tropel *m*

drove [drov] *see* drive

drown [draʊn] VI/VT ahogar[se]

drowning [dráʊnɪŋ] N ahogamiento *m*

drowse [draʊz] VI (be half-asleep) dormitar; (feel drowsy) estar amodorrado
drowsiness [dráʊzɪnɪs] N modorra *f*, somnolencia *f*
drowsy [dráʊzi] ADJ amodorrado, somnoliento; **to become —** amodorrarse
drudge [drʌʤ] N esclavo del trabajo *m*, fregona *f*; VI trabajar como un esclavo
drug [drʌg] N (chemical substance, narcotic) droga *f*; (medicine) medicamento *m*; **—ged** drogado, endrogado; **— abuse** abuso de drogas *m*; **— addict** drogadicto -ta *mf*; **—store** (drugs) farmacia *f*; (non-drug items) droguería *f*; perfumería *f*; **— trafficker** narcotraficante *mf*; VT (stupefy with drugs) drogar; (mix with a drug) adulterar con droga
druggist [drágɪst] N farmacéutico -ca *mf*, droguero -ra *mf*
drum [drʌm] N (musical instrument) tambor *m*; (of ear) tímpano *m*; (receptacle for storing liquids) barril *m*; **—head** parche *m*; **—stick** (music) palillo de tambor *m*; (fowl) pata *f*; VI (play a drum) tocar el tambor; (beat rhythmically) tamborilear; **to — out** expulsar; **to — up** fomentar; **I'm trying to — this idea into his head** le estoy repitiendo esta idea con insistencia
drummer [drámə˞] N (classical) tambor *m*; (folk) tamborilero -ra *mf*; (rock & roll) baterista *mf*
drunk [drʌŋk] ADJ & N borracho -cha *mf*; *fam* mamado -da *mf*; **to get —** emborracharse
drunk [drʌŋk] *see* drink
drunkard [dráŋkə˞d] N borracho -cha *mf*, borrachín -ina *mf*
drunken [dráŋkən] ADJ borracho, embriagado
drunkenness [dráŋkənnɪs] N borrachera *f*, embriaguez *f*
dry [draɪ] ADJ seco; (sober) sobrio; (topic, book) árido, aburrido; **— land** tierra firme *f*; **— cleaner** (business) tintorería *f*; (owner of business) tintorero -ra *mf*; **— cleaning** limpieza en seco *f*; **— county** condado seco *m*; **— wit** humor agudo *m*; **— goods** géneros *m pl*; **— measure** medida para áridos *f*; **— run** prueba *f*; **— ice** hielo seco *m*; **— dock** dique seco *m*, varadero *m*; VI/VT (wet clothes) secar[se]; (leather) resecar[se]; **to — up** secarse, resecarse; **to — out** desintoxicar[se]
dryer [dráɪə˞] N (hair) secador *m*; (clothes) secadora *f*
dryness [dráɪnɪs] N (skin) sequedad *f*; (land, lecture) aridez *f*
dual [dúə˞l] ADJ (function) doble; (ownership) compartido
dub [dʌb] VT (translate a film) doblar; (give a nickname) apodar
dubious [dúbiəs] ADJ dudoso
duchess [dʌ́tʃɪs] N duquesa *f*
duck [dʌk] N (bird) pato *m*; (downward dodge) agachada *f*; VI/VT (plunge under water) hundir[se]; (bend down) agachar[se]; VT (avoid) esquivar
duckling [dʌ́kliŋ] N patito *m*
duct [dʌkt] N conducto *m*; **— tape** cinta aislante *f*
ductile [dʌ́kt!] ADJ dúctil
dud [dʌd] N (disappointing thing) chasco *m*; (useless person) inútil *m*; (unexploded bomb) bomba que no estalla *f*; **—s** (clothes) ropa *f*, *fam* trapos *m pl*; (belongings) pertenencias *f pl*
dude [dud] N (dandy) chulo *m*; (fellow) tipo *m*
due [du] ADJ (payable) pagadero; (immediately owed) vencido; (fitting, rightful) debido; (adequate) suficiente; **— date** fecha de vencimiento *f*; **— diligence** diligencia debida *f*; **in — time/course** a su debido tiempo; **the train is — at two o'clock** se supone que el tren llega a las dos; ADV **— east** hacia el este; N (punishment) merecido *m*; **give Mary her —; she's honest** tienes que reconocer que María es honrada; **—s** cuotas *f pl*
duel [dúə˞l] N duelo *m*; VI/VT batirse en/a duelo [con alguien]
duet [duét] N (played) dúo *m*; (sung) dueto *m*
dug [dʌg] *see* dig
dugout [dʌ́gaʊt] N (canoe) piragua *f*; (underground refuge) trinchera *f*
DUI [driving under the influence] [díjúái] N delito de conducir en estado de ebriedad *m*
duke [duk] N duque *m*; **to put up one's —s** levantar los puños; VT **to — it out** arreglarlo con los puños
dukedom [dúkdəm] N ducado *m*
dull [dʌl] ADJ (lackluster) opaco; (listless, muted) apagado; (boring) aburrido, soso, desanimado; (blunt) romo, desafilado; (sluggish, stupid) lento; (pain) sordo; VI/VT (a knife) desafilar[se]; (color) opacar[se]; (sound, impact) amortiguar[se]; (pain) aliviar[se]; (senses) embotar[se], entorpecer[se]
duly [dúli] ADV debidamente
dumb [dʌm] ADJ (mute) mudo; (dull) tonto; **—bell** (handweight) mancuerna *f*; (stupid person) bobo -ba *mf*; **—founded** patitieso, atónito; VT **to — down** simplificar demasiado
dumbness [dʌ́mnɪs] N (muteness) mudez *f*; (foolishness) estupidez *f*
dummy [dʌ́mi] N (figure) muñeco *m*; (fool) tonto -ta *mf*; (front) hombre de paja *m*; ADJ (fake) falso; **a — president** un títere
dump [dʌmp] VT (unload) descargar; (empty) botar; (transfer computer data) vaciar; (dismiss) echar, despedir; (discard waste) tirar la basura, descargar desechos; (flood a market) hacer dumping; (abandon) plantar; **to — on** (criticize) criticar; (unload problems) descargarse; N (place for waste) vertedero *m*,

basural *m*, basurero *m*; (of weapons) depósito *m*; (act of discarding) vertido *m*; **—truck** camión volteador *m*, volquete *m*, *Am* volqueta *f*; **to be in the —s** estar deprimido, estar depre

dumping [dámpɪŋ] N vertido *m*

dunce [dʌns] N burro -rra *mf*, tonto -ta de capirote *mf*

dune [dun] N duna *f*, médano *m*

dung [dʌŋ] N boñiga *f*, bosta *f*; **—hill** estercolero *m*

dungeon [dándʒən] N mazmorra *f*

dunk [dʌŋk] VT (a donut) remojar; (a basketball) volcar, enterrar; (a person) sumergir

duodenum [duədínəm] N duodeno *m*

dupe [dup] N (gullible person) ingenuo -nua *mf*, inocente *mf*; *Sp* primo -ma *mf*; (manipulated person) títere *m*; VT embaucar

duplex [dúplɛks] N & ADJ dúplex *m*

duplicate[1] [dúplɪkɪt] ADJ & N duplicado *m*; **in —** por duplicado

duplicate[2] [dúplɪket] VT duplicar[se]

duplicity [duplísɪdi] N duplicidad *f*

durability [dʊrəbílɪdi] N durabilidad *f*

durable [dʊ́rəbəł] ADJ (long-lasting) duradero; (serviceable) sufrido

duration [dʊréʃən] N duración *f*

duress [dʊrés] N coacción *f*

during [dʊ́rɪŋ] PREP durante

dusk [dʌsk] N atardecer *m*, anochecer *m*; **at —** al atardecer

dusky [dʌ́ski] ADJ (dark) oscuro; (gloomy) sombrío

dust [dʌst] N polvo *m*; **—pan** pala *f*; **to bite the —** (die) *fam* espichar; (lose) morder el polvo de la derrota; **cloud of —** polvareda *f*; VI/VT (remove dust) quitar/sacudir el polvo [a]; VT (sprinkle with powder) espolvorear; VI (become dusty) empolvarse; **to — off** desempolvar

duster [dʌ́stɚ] N plumero *m*

dusty [dʌ́sti] ADJ polvoriento

Dutch [dʌtʃ] ADJ & N holandés -esa *mf*; (language) holandés *m*; **to go —** pagar a escote

Dutchman [dʌ́tʃmən] N holandés *m*

duty [dúɪ́di] N deber *m*, obligación *f*; (tax on imports) derechos aduaneros *m pl*; (any tax) impuesto *m*; **to be on —** estar de guardia; **to be off —** no estar de guardia; ADJ **—-free** libre de impuestos

DVD [digital versatile disc] [dívidí] N DVD *m*

dwarf [dwɔrf] ADJ & N enano -na *mf*; VT hacer parecer pequeño

dwarfism [dwɔ́rfɪzəm] N enanismo *m*

dwell [dwɛł] VI morar, habitar; **to — on a subject** dilatarse en un asunto

dweller [dwɛ́lɚ] N habitante *mf*, morador -ora *mf*

dwelling [dwɛ́lɪŋ] N vivienda *f*, domicilio *m*

dwelt [dwɛłt] *see* dwell

DWI [driving while intoxicated] [dídábəɫjuáɪ] N delito de conducir en estado de ebriedad *m*

dwindle [dwíndł] VI/VT menguar, mermar

dye [daɪ] N tinte *m*, tintura *f*; VT teñir

dying [dáɪɪŋ] ADJ moribundo

dynamic [daɪnǽmɪk] ADJ dinámico; N dinámica *f*

dynamite [dáínəmaɪt] N dinamita *f*; VT dinamitar; ADJ fabuloso

dynamo [dáínəmo] N dínamo *m*

dynasty [dáínəsti] N dinastía *f*

dysentery [dísəntɛri] N disentería *f*

dysfunction [dɪsfʌ́ŋkʃən] N disfunción *f*

dyslexia [dɪsléksiə] N dislexia *f*

Ee

each [itʃ] ADJ cada; **— person** cada persona; PRON cada uno; **— receives a prize** cada uno recibe un premio; **they looked at — other** se miraron el uno al otro

eager [ígɚ] ADJ (enthusiastic) ansioso; (avid) ávido

eagerness [ígɚnɪs] N (enthusiasm) ansia *f*, afán *m*; (strong desire) avidez *f*

eagle [ígəł] N águila *f*; **—-eye** ojo de lince *m*

eaglet [íglɪt] N aguilucho *m*

ear [ir] N (outer organ) oreja *f*; (inner organ, sense of hearing, musical aptitude) oído *m*; (of corn) mazorca *f*; *Am* elote *m*; **—ache** dolor de oídos *m*; **—drops** gotas para los oídos *f pl*; **—drum** tímpano *m*; **—lobe** lóbulo de la oreja *m*; **— muff** orejera *f*; **—phone** audífono *m*, auricular *m*; **—plug** tapón del oído *m*; **—ring** pendiente *m*, zarcillo *m*, arete *m*; **by —** de oído; **within —shot** al alcance del oído; **he has the — of the governor** el gobernador le presta mucha atención; VT **to —mark** asignar

earful [írfuł] N **I got an —** (scolding) me echó un rapapolvo; (gossip) me dio la lata

early [ɝ́li] ADJ temprano; **— detection** diagnóstico precoz *m*; **— man** hombre primitivo *m*; **— retirement** jubilación anticipada *f*; **— riser/bird** madrugador -ora *mf*, mañanero -ra *mf*; **the — bird gets the worm** al que madruga, Dios lo ayuda

earn [ɝn] VI/VT (money, admiration, etc.) ganar; (salary) cobrar, ganar; (interest) devengar; **—ed run** carrera limpia *f*; **—ed run average** promedio de carreras limpias permitidas *m*; **to — a living** ganarse la vida

earnest [ɝ́nɪst] ADJ (sincere) serio, formal;

(grave) grave; **in —** en serio; **— money** señal *f*; *Mex* enganche *m*
earnestness [ɝ́nɪstnɪs] N (sincerity) seriedad *f*, formalidad *f*; (gravity) gravedad *f*; **in all —** con toda sinceridad
earnings [ɝ́nɪŋz] N (of a person) ingresos *m pl*; (of a business) ganancias *f pl*
earth [ɝθ] N tierra *f*; **—mover** excavadora *f*; **—quake** terremoto *m*, temblor de tierra *m*; **—worm** lombriz *f*; **the —** la Tierra; ADJ **—shaking** revolucionario
earthen [ɝ́θən] ADJ (wall) de tierra; (pot) de barro; **—ware** vajilla de barro *f*, cerámica *f*
earthly [ɝ́θli] ADJ terrenal; **— possessions** bienes terrenales *m pl*; **to be of no — use** no servir para nada
earthy [ɝ́θi] ADJ natural; (person) campechano; (sense of humor, joke) basto; **— smell** olor a tierra *m*
ease [iz] N (facility) facilidad *f*; (unaffectedness) soltura *f*, desparpajo *m*; (comfort) comodidad *f*; (lack of worry) tranquilidad *f*; (fullness of a garment) holgura *f*; **at —** (military) en descanso; (comfortable) tranquilo, a gusto; **a life of —** una vida desahogada; **ill at —** incómodo; VT (make easier) facilitar; VI/VT (relieve pain) aliviar[se]; (release from tension) aflojar[se]; (relieve anxiety) tranquilizar[se]; **to — up** aflojar
easel [ízəł] N caballete *m*
east [ist] N este *m*, oriente *m*; ADJ del este, oriental; ADV **— of here** al este [de aquí]; **to go —** ir al / hacia el este; **back —** en el este
Easter [ístɚ] N Pascua *f*; **— egg** huevo de Pascua *m*; **— Sunday** Domingo de Pascua *m*
eastern [ístɚn] ADJ oriental, del este
eastward [ístwɚd] ADV & ADJ hacia el este
easy [ízi] ADJ (simple) fácil, sencillo; (compliant) fácil; (comfortable) cómodo; (informal) desenvuelto; (unworried) tranquilo; **— chair** poltrona *f*; **—-going** calmoso; **— terms** facilidades de pago *f pl*; **— does it** despacio; **take it —** cálmate; **he's on — street** vive en la abundancia; **within — reach** al alcance de la mano; ADV **go — on me** sea bueno
eat [it] VI/VT comer[se]; VT (costs) absorber; **to — away** corroer, comer; **to — breakfast** desayunar[se]; **to — dinner** (midday) comer; (evening) cenar; **to — lunch** comer, almorzar; **to — one's heart out** morirse de envidia; **to — one's words** tragarse las palabras; **to — supper** cenar; **to — up** comerse todo; **what's —ing you?** ¿qué bicho te picó?
eaten [itn] *see* eat
eating [ídɪŋ] N (act) comer *m*; (food) comida *f*; **— disorder** trastorno de la alimentación *m*; **— utensils** cubiertos *m pl*; **— apples** manzanas para comer *f pl*
eaves [ivz] N PL alero *m*; **to —drop** escuchar furtivamente
e-banking [íbæŋkɪŋ] N banca electrónica *f*
ebb [ɛb] N (flowing back) reflujo *m*; (decay) decadencia *f*; **— tide** reflujo *m*; **to be at a low —** estar en un punto bajo; VI (tide) bajar; (energy) decaer
ebony [ébəni] N ébano *m*
e-book [íbʊk] N libro electrónico *m*
e-business [íbɪznɪs] N comercio electrónico *m*
eccentric [ɛksɛ́ntrɪk] ADJ & N excéntrico -ca *mf*
ecclesiastic [ɪkliziǽstɪk] ADJ & N eclesiástico *m*
echelon [éʃəlɑn] N (military formation) escalón *m*; (rank) nivel *m*, estrato *m*
echo [éko] N eco *m*; VI hacer eco; **the gym —ed with laughter** el gimnasio resonó de risas; VT repetir
echocardiogram [ɛkokárdɪəgræm] N ecocardiograma *m*
eclectic [ɪklɛ́ktɪk] ADJ ecléctico
eclipse [ɪklíps] N eclipse *m*; VT eclipsar
eco-friendly [ikofréndli] ADJ ecológico
ecological [ikəlɑ́ʤɪkəł] ADJ ecológico
ecology [ɪkɑ́ləʤi] N ecología *f*
e-commerce [íkámə·s] N comercio electrónico *m*
economic [ɛkənámɪk] ADJ económico; N **—s** economía *f*
economical [ɛkənámɪkəł] ADJ económico
economist [ɪkɑ́nəmɪst] N economista *mf*
economize [ɪkɑ́nəmaɪz] VI economizar
economy [ɪkɑ́nəmi] N economía *f* (also thrift); ADJ **— car** coche económico *m*; **— class** clase turista *f*
ecosystem [íkosɪstəm] N ecosistema *m*
ecstasy [ɛ́kstəsi] N éxtasis *m* (also drug)
Ecuador [ɛ́kwədɔr] N Ecuador *m*
Ecuadorian [ɛkwədɔ́riən] ADJ & N ecuatoriano -na *mf*
ecumenical [ɛkjəméníkəł] ADJ ecuménico
eczema [égzəmə] N eccema *m*
eddy [ɛ́di] N remolino *m*; VI arremolinarse
edge [ɛʤ] N borde *m*, canto *m*; (of a knife) filo *m*; (of a block) arista *f*; **to be on —** estar nervioso; **her voice has an — to it** tiene la voz penetrante; **a competitive —** una ventaja sobre la competencia; VT (make an edge) hacerle el borde; (sharpen) afilar; (move sideways) meterse de costado; **to — out** ganar por un pelito; **to — up** aproximarse; ADV **—wise** de costado
edgy [ɛ́ʤi] ADJ nervioso
edible [ɛ́dəbəł] ADJ & N comestible *m*
edict [ídɪkt] N edicto *m*, bando *m*
edifice [ɛ́dəfɪs] N edificio *m*
edify [ɛ́dəfaɪ] VT edificar
edit [ɛ́dɪt] VT (revise, correct) corregir; (serve as editor) editar; (revise a film) montar; **to — out** eliminar; N corrección *f*
edition [ɪdíʃən] N edición *f*

editor [ɛ́dɪtə˞] N (director of a publication) redactor -ora *mf*; (compiler, radio or film worker) editor -ora *mf*; (proofreader) corrector -ora *mf*

editorial [ɛ̀dɪtɔ́riəɫ] ADJ editorial; N editorial *f*

editorialize [ɛdɪtɔ́riəlaɪz] VI editorializar

educate [ɛ́ʤəket] VT educar

education [ɛʤəkéʃən] N educación *f*, enseñanza *f*; (academic subject) pedagogía *f*; **school of —** escuela normal *f*

educational [ɛʤəkéʃənɫ] ADJ educativo

educator [ɛ́ʤəkeə˞] N educador -ora *mf*

EEG [electroencephalogram] [íiʤí] N electroencefalograma *m*

eel [iɨ] N anguila *f*

eerie [íri] ADJ misterioso

effect [ɪfɛ́kt] N efecto *m*; **to go into —** entrar en vigencia, ponerse en operación; **in —** vigente, operativo; **I wrote a letter to that —** escribí una carta en ese sentido; **personal —s** efectos personales *m pl*; VT efectuar

effective [ɪfɛ́ktɪv] ADJ efectivo, eficaz; (a law) vigente; **— date** fecha de vigencia *f*

effectively [ɪfɛ́ktɪvli] ADV (well) eficazmente; (in fact) de hecho, en efecto

effectiveness [ɪfɛ́ktɪvnɪs] N efectividad *f*, eficacia *f*

effectual [ɪfɛ́ktʃuəɫ] ADJ eficaz

effeminate [ɪfɛ́mənɪt] ADJ afeminado

efficacy [ɛ́fɪkəsi] N eficacia *f*

efficiency [ɪfíʃənsi] N eficiencia *f*; **— apartment** estudio *m*

efficient [ɪfíʃənt] ADJ eficiente; (motor) económico

effigy [ɛ́fəʤi] N efigie *f*; **to burn in —** quemar en efigie

effort [ɛ́fə˞t] N (exertion) esfuerzo *m*; (work of art) obra *f*; (campaign) campaña *f*

effrontery [ɪfrʌ́ntəri] N descaro *m*

effusive [ɪfjúsɪv] ADJ efusivo

egg [ɛg] N huevo *m*; (female gamete) óvulo *m*; (fellow) tipo *m*; **—beater** batidor de huevos *m*; **—head** empollón -na *mf*; **—nog** rompopo *m*, rompope *m*, ponche de huevo *m*; **—plant** berenjena *f*; **—shell** cáscara de huevo *f*; **— white** clara de huevo *f*; **— yolk** yema de huevo *f*; **to have — on one's face** estar avergonzado, quedar mal; **to lay an —** (of a hen) poner un huevo; (fail) fracasar; **to walk on —shells** ir pisando huevos; ADJ **—-shaped** ovoide; VT **to — on** incitar

ego [ígo] N (self) yo *m*, ego *m*; (vanity) ego *m*; (self-esteem) amor propio *m*; **winning the prize was an — trip for him** ganar el premio le aceitó el ego

egocentric [igosɛ́ntrɪk] ADJ egocéntrico

egotism [ígətɪzəm] N egotismo *m*

Egypt [iʤɪpt] N Egipto *m*

Egyptian [ɪʤípʃən] ADJ & N egipcio -cia *mf*

eight [et] NUM ocho; **— hundred** ochocientos

eighteen [etfín] NUM dieciocho

eighth [etθ] ADJ, N & ADV octavo *m*; **— note** corchea *f*

eighty [éɪti] NUM ochenta

either [íðə˞] ADJ & PRON **— will do** cualquiera de los dos está bien; **choose — suit** elige uno de los dos trajes; **choose —** elige uno [u otro] de los dos; **there were flowers on — side of the road** había flores a ambos lados de la carretera; ADV **if you don't, I won't —** si tú no lo haces, yo tampoco; **I'll go — by bus or by car** voy [o] en autobús o en auto

ejaculate [ɪʤǽkjəlet] VI/VT eyacular; (exclaim) exclamar

eject [ɪʤɛ́kt] VT (throw out) echar, expulsar; VI/VT (throw from a plane) eyectar[se]

ejection [ɪʤɛ́kʃən] N expulsión *f*

EKG [electrocardiogam] [íkéʤí] N electrocardiograma *m*

elaborate[1] [ɪlǽbə˞ɪt] ADJ (ornate) elaborado; (detailed) detallado

elaborate[2] [ɪlǽbə˞et] VI/VT (create) elaborar; (develop) desarrollar

elapse [ɪlǽps] VI transcurrir, pasar

elastic [ɪlǽstɪk] ADJ elástico; N elástico *m*; (rubber band) goma elástica *f*

elasticity [ɪlæstísɪdi] N elasticidad *f*

elated [ɪléɪdɪd] ADJ eufórico

elbow [ɛ́ɫbo] N codo *m*; VI/VT codear, dar codazos; **to — one's way through** abrirse paso a codazos

elder [ɛ́ɫdə˞] ADJ (older) mayor; N (older person) mayor *mf*; (old person) anciano -na *mf*; (in a church) miembro del consejo de una iglesia *m*; **our —s** nuestros mayores *m pl*

elderly [ɛ́ɫdə˞li] ADJ anciano

e-learning [íl˞nɪŋ] N educación en línea *f*

elect [ɪlɛ́kt] ADJ (elected) electo; (chosen by God) elegido; VI/VT elegir

election [ɪlɛ́kʃən] N elección *f*

elector [ɪlɛ́ktə˞] N elector -ora *mf*

electoral [ɪlɛ́ktə˞əɫ] ADJ electoral

electric [ɪlɛ́ktrɪk] ADJ eléctrico; (exciting) electrizante; (excited) electrizado; **— chair** silla eléctrica *f*; **— eel** anguila eléctrica *f*; **— eye** célula fotoeléctrica *f*; **— meter** contador eléctrico *m*; **— storm** tormenta eléctrica *f*

electrical [ɪlɛ́ktrɪkəɫ] ADJ eléctrico; **— engineer** ingeniero -ra electricista *mf*; **— engineering** ingeniería eléctrica *f*; **— tape** cinta aislante *f*

electrician [ɪlɛktríʃən] N electricista *mf*

electricity [ɪlɛktrísɪdi] N electricidad *f*

electrify [ɪlɛ́ktrəfaɪ] VT (apply electricity) electrificar; (thrill) electrizar

electrocardiogram [ɪlɛktrokɑ́rdɪəgræm] N electrocardiograma *m*

electrocute [ɪlɛ́ktrəkjut] VT electrocutar

electrode [ɪlɛ́ktrod] N electrodo *m*

electroencephalogram [ɪlɛktroɛnséfələgræm] N electroencefalograma *m*
electrolysis [ɪlɛktrálɪsɪs] N electrólisis *f*
electromagnet [ɪlɛktromǽgnɪt] N electroimán *m*
electromagnetic [ɪlɛktromægnɛ́dɪk] ADJ electromagnético
electron [ɪlɛ́ktrɑn] N electrón *m*; — **microscope** microscopio electrónico *m*
electronic [ɪlɛktrɑ́nɪk] ADJ electrónico; — **banking** banca electrónica *f*; — **mail** correo electrónico *m*; —**s** electrónica *f*; — **signature** firma electrónica *f*
elegance [élɪgəns] N elegancia *f*, gallardía *f*
elegant [élɪgənt] ADJ elegante, gallardo; (gift) de lujo
element [éləmənt] N elemento *m*; (component part) componente *m*, pieza *f*; (for heating) resistencia *f*; **the —s** los elementos
elemental [eləméntl] ADJ elemental; — **forces** fuerzas de la naturaleza *f pl*
elementary [eləméntri] ADJ elemental; — **school** escuela primaria *f*
elephant [éləfənt] N elefante -ta *mf*
elevate [éləvet] VT elevar
elevation [eləvéʃən] N (action of elevating, elevated place) elevación *f*; (altitude) altura *f*
elevator [éləvedə-] N ascensor *m*; *Am* elevador *m*; (for grain) elevador *m*
eleven [ɪlévən] NUM once
elf [ɛlf] N elfo *m*; (mischievous person) pillo -lla *mf*
elicit [ɪlísɪt] VT provocar; **to — admiration** despertar admiración
eligibility [ɛlɪʤəbílɪti] N elegibilidad *f*
eligible [élɪʤəbəł] ADJ elegible; **an — bachelor** un buen partido; **you are — for a scholarship** tienes derecho a solicitar una beca
eliminate [ɪlímənet] VT eliminar
elimination [ɪlɪmənéʃən] N eliminación *f*
elite [ɪlít] N elite *f*, élite *f*
elitist [ɪlídɪst] ADJ & N elitista *mf*
elk [ɛłk] N alce *m*
elliptical [ɪlíptɪkəł] ADJ elíptico
elm [ɛłm] N olmo *m*
elongate [ɪlɔ́nget] VI/VT alargar[se]
elope [ɪlóp] VI fugarse para casarse a escondidas
eloquence [éləkwəns] N elocuencia *f*
eloquent [éləkwənt] ADJ elocuente
El Salvador [ɛłsǽłvədɔr] N El Salvador *m*
else [ɛls] ADJ & ADV **who — was there?** ¿quién más estaba? **someone —'s son** el hijo de otro; **somebody** — [algún] otro; **or** — si no; **leave town or** — vete del pueblo o sufre las consecuencias / o verás lo que es bueno; **nobody** — nadie más; **nothing** — nada más; **how —?** ¿de qué otra forma? ADV **—where** (location) en otra parte / en otro lado; (movement) a otra parte / a otro sitio
elucidate [ɪlúsɪdet] VI/VT elucidar, dilucidar, esclarecer
elucidation [ɪlusɪdéʃən] N elucidación *f*, dilucidación *f*
elude [ɪlúd] VT eludir
elusive [ɪlúsɪv] ADJ (slippery) escurridizo; (evasive) esquivo; (difficult to understand) difícil de entender
emaciated [ɪméʃɪeɪdɪd] ADJ escuálido, descarnado
e-mail [ímeł] N correo electrónico *m*; — **address** dirección de correo electrónico *f*
emanate [émənet] VI/VT emanar
emanation [ɛmənéʃən] N emanación *f*
emancipate [ɪmǽnsəpet] VT emancipar
emancipation [ɪmæ̀nsəpéʃən] N emancipación *f*
emasculate [ɪmǽskjəlet] VT castrar; (remove testicles) castrar, emascular
embalm [ɪmbɑ́m] VT (the body of a deceased person) preparar; (a mummy) embalsamar
embalming [ɪmbɑ́mɪŋ] N preparación del cuerpo *f*
embankment [ɪmbǽŋkmənt] N terraplén *m*
embargo [ɪmbárgo] N embargo *m*; VT imponer un embargo a/contra
embark [ɪmbárk] VI/VT embarcar[se]
embarrass [ɪmbǽrəs] VT (cause shame) hacerle pasar vergüenza a; (cause discomfit, financial difficulties) poner en aprietos; **—ed** avergonzado, en aprietos; **I'm —ed about my teeth** me dan vergüenza mis dientes; **I'm —ed to tell you** me da vergüenza decírtelo
embarrassing [ɪmbǽrəsɪŋ] ADJ (shameful) vergonzoso, penoso; (hindering) embarazoso
embarrassment [ɪmbǽrəsmənt] N (shame) vergüenza *f*, bochorno *m*, pena *f*; (act of embarrassing) vergüenza *f*; (financial difficulty) aprieto *m*; **he's an — to the company** hace quedar mal a la compañía; **we have an — of riches** nadamos en la abundancia
embassy [émbəsi] N embajada *f*
embattled [ɪmbǽdłd] ADJ hostigado, agobiado
embed [ɪmbéd] VT incrustar
embedded [ɪmbédɪd] ADJ incrustado
embellish [ɪmbélɪʃ] VT adornar, ornamentar
ember [émbə-] N ascua *f*, brasa *f*
embezzle [ɪmbɛ́zəł] VT desfalcar, malversar
embezzlement [ɪmbɛ́zəɪmənt] N desfalco *m*, peculado *m*, malversación *f*
embitter [ɪmbítə-] VT amargar
emblem [émbləm] N emblema *m*, divisa *f*
embody [ɪmbɑ́dɪ] VT (personify) personificar; (to provide with a body) encarnar
embolism [émbəlɪzəm] N embolia *f*
embrace [ɪmbrés] VI/VT (hug, adopt) abrazar[se]; (include) abarcar; N abrazo *m*

embroider [ɪmbróɪdɚ] VI/VT bordar, recamar
embroidery [ɪmbróɪdəri] N bordado *m*
embroil [ɪmbróɪl] VT (involve in a conflict) meter en un lío; (throw into confusion) embrollar
embryo [émbrio] N embrión *m*
embryonic [embriánɪk] ADJ embriónico, embrionario
emerald [émərəld] N esmeralda *f*
emerge [ɪmɝ́dʒ] VI (come into view) emerger; (arise, as a question, problem) surgir
emergency [ɪmɝ́dʒənsi] N emergencia *f*; **— brake** freno de emergencia *m*; **— exit** salida de emergencia *f*; **— room** urgencias *f pl*
emergent [ɪmɝ́dʒənt] ADJ emergente
emerging [ɪmɝ́dʒɪŋ] ADJ emergente
emigrant [émɪgrənt] ADJ & N emigrante *mf*
emigrate [émɪgret] VI emigrar
emigration [emɪgréʃən] N emigración *f*
eminence [émənəns] N eminencia *f*
eminent [émənənt] ADJ eminente
emissary [émɪseri] N emisario -ria *mf*
emission [ɪmíʃən] N emisión *f*
emit [ɪmít] VT (light, sound) emitir; (smells) despedir; (sparks) echar
emoticon [ɪmóʊɪkan] N emoticón *m*, emoticono *m*
emotion [ɪmóʃən] N emoción *f*
emotional [ɪmóʃənl] ADJ (of the emotions) emocional; (arousing or expressing emotions) emotivo; (easily moved) sensible
empathy [émpəθi] N empatía *f*
emperor [émpərɚ] N emperador *m*; **— penguin** pingüino emperador *m*
emphasis [émfəsɪs] N énfasis *m*, hincapié *m*
emphasize [émfəsaɪz] VT enfatizar, hacer hincapié en, subrayar
emphatic [ɪmfǽdɪk] ADJ enfático
emphysema [ɛmfɪsímə] N enfisema *m*
empire [émpaɪr] N imperio *m*
empirical [empírɪkəl] ADJ empírico
employ [ɪmplɔ́ɪ] VT emplear; (hire) emplear, ocupar; N empleo *m*; **to be in someone's —** trabajar a las órdenes de alguien
employee [ɪmplɔ́ɪí] N empleado -da *mf*
employer [ɪmplɔ́ɪɚ] N patrón -na *mf*; **—s'** patronal
employment [ɪmplɔ́ɪmənt] N empleo *m*; (occupation) ocupación *f*; **— bureau** agencia de empleo *f*; **— opportunities** oportunidades laborales *f pl*; **place of —** lugar de trabajo *m*
empower [ɪmpáʊɚ] VT (authorize) autorizar; (give strength) potenciar
empress [émpɪrɪs] N emperatriz *f*
emptiness [émptɪnɪs] N vacío *m*
empty [émpti] ADJ (devoid of content) vacío; (devoid of activity) desocupado; **—-handed** con las manos vacías; VI/VT vaciar[se], volcar[se]; (flow into) desembocar; N **to run on —** (of a car, person) quedarse sin combustible
emulate [émjəlet] VT emular (also computer term)
enable [inébəl] VT permitir
enact [inǽkt] VT (a law) promulgar; (a role) desempeñar
enamel [ɪnǽməl] N esmalte *m*; VT esmaltar
enamor [ɪnǽmɚ] VT enamorar; **to be —ed of** estar enamorado de
encamp [ɪnkǽmp] VI acampar
encephalitis [ɪnsɛfəláɪdɪs] N encefalitis *f*
enchant [ɪntʃǽnt] VT (bewitch) hechizar; (delight) encantar
enchanting [ɪntʃǽntɪŋ] ADJ encantador
enchantment [ɪntʃǽntmənt] N encantamiento *m*, encanto *m*, hechicería *f*
encircle [ɪnsɝ́kəl] VT cercar, ceñir
enclave [ánklev] N enclave *m*
enclose [ɪnklóz] VT (confine someone or something) encerrar; (fence in) cercar; (put in the same envelope) adjuntar, anexar
enclosure [ɪnklóʒɚ] N (wall or fence) cerca *f*; (enclosed area) cercado *m*, recinto *m*; (enclosed document) documento adjunto *m*; (act of enclosing) encierro *m*
encode [ɪŋkód] VT codificar
encoding [ɪŋkóʊɪŋ] N codificación *f*
encompass [ɪnkǽmpəs] VT (include) abarcar, englobar; (surround) circundar
encore [ánkɔr] N bis *m*; INTERJ ¡otra!
encounter [ɪnkáʊntɚ] VI/VT encontrar[se]; **they —ed the enemy army** se enfrentaron con el ejército enemigo; N (meeting, athletic event) encuentro *m*; (battle) enfrentamiento *m*
encourage [ɪnkɝ́ɪdʒ] VT (inspire with confidence) alentar, animar; (promote) fomentar, estimular
encouragement [ɪnkɝ́ɪdʒmənt] N (inspiration) aliento *m*, ánimo *m*; (promotion) estímulo *m*, fomento *m*
encouraging [ɪŋkɝ́ədʒɪŋ] ADJ alentador
encroach [ɪnkrótʃ] VT **to — upon** (liberties) cercenar; (territory) usurpar; (time) quitar
encrypt [ɪnkrípt] VT codificar, cifrar
encryption [ɪŋkrípʃən] N cifrado *m*
encumber [ɪnkámbɚ] VT (block) impedir; (burden) agobiar; (charge an account) gravar
encumbrance [ɪŋkámbrəns] N gravamen *m*
encyclopedia [ɪnsaɪkləpídiə] N enciclopedia *f*
end [ɛnd] N (temporal) fin *m*, término *m*; (limit, boundary) final *m*, extremo *m*; (tip) cabo *m*; (aim) fin *m*; (in football) exterior *m*; **— key** tecla [de] fin *f*; **—-of-life care** cuidado terminal *m*; **— table** mesa pequeña *f*; **— zone** zona de ensayo *f*, zona de anotación *f*; **at the — of the movie** al final de la película; **the north — of town** el barrio norte; **no —**

of things un sinfín de cosas; **at the — of the day** al fin y al cabo; **on —** de punta; **for days on —** día tras día; **to put an — to** poner fin a; VI/VT terminar; (a street) morir; **he —ed his life** puso fin a su vida; **a prayer —s the class** la clase termina con una oración; **a war to — all wars** una guerra que supera a todas las anteriores; ADV **— to —** uno tras otro

endanger [ɪndéndʒə-] VT poner en peligro; **—ed species** especie en peligro de extinción *f*

endear [ɪndír] VI **to — oneself** congraciarse; **his humor —ed him to her** se ganó la simpatía de ella gracias a su humor

endearing [ɪndírɪŋ] ADJ entrañable

endeavor [ɪndévə-] VT (try) tratar de, intentar, procurar; VI (strive) esforzarse por; N esfuerzo *m*

endemic [ɪndémɪk] ADJ endémico

ending [éndɪŋ] N final *m*; (of a story) desenlace *m*; (derivational, inflectional) terminación *f*; (inflectional) desinencia *f*

endless [éndlɪs] ADJ (having no end) interminable; (continuous) sin fin; (infinite) eterno

endocrine [éndəkrɪn] ADJ endocrino

endocrinology [ɛndəkrɪnáləʤi] N endocrinología *f*

endoderm [éndoʤə-m] N endodermo *m*

endorphin [ɪndɔ́rfɪn] N endorfina *f*

endorse [ɪndɔ́rs] VT (sign a check) endosar; (support) respaldar; (authorize a document) refrendar, visar

endorsement [ɪndɔ́rsmənt] N (signature) endoso *m*; (backing) respaldo *m*; (authorization) refrendo *m*

endorser [ɪndɔ́rsə-] N (check signer) endosante *mf*; (supporter) partidario -ria *mf*; (authorizer) refrendario -ria *mf*

endow [ɪndáʊ] VT (grant funds) hacer un legado; (furnish powers) dotar

endowment [ɪndáʊmənt] N (funds granted) legado *m*, dotación *f*; (power) dote *f*; **— annuity** anualidad dotal *f*; **— fund** fondo de un legado *m*

endurance [ɪndʊ́rəns] N (stamina) resistencia *f*; (ability to bear pain) aguante *m*

endure [ɪndʊ́r, ɪndjʊ́r] VT (undergo) sobrellevar, soportar, pasar; VI (live on) durar; (bear up) aguantar

enema [énəmə] N enema *m*, lavativa *f*

enemy [énəmi] N enemigo -ga *mf*

energetic [ɛnə-ʤéɪɪk] ADJ enérgico

energy [éna-ʤi] N energía *f*; **— policy** política energética *f*

enervate [éna-vet] VT enervar, debilitar

enforce [ɪnfɔ́rs] VT hacer cumplir

enforcement [ɪnfɔ́rsmənt] N **the sheriff is responsible for the — of the law** el alguacil es responsable de hacer cumplir la ley

engage [ɪngéʤ] VT (hire) contratar; (attract) captar, atraer; (interlock) engranar; **to — the brake** poner el freno; **to — someone in conversation** trabar conversación con alguien; **to — in battle** trabar batalla; **to be —d in something** estar ocupado en algo; **to be —d to be married** estar comprometido [para casarse], estar prometido

engaged [ɪngéʤd] ADJ comprometido

engagement [ɪngéʤmənt] N (commitment) compromiso *m*; (betrothal) compromiso *m*, noviazgo *m*; (employment) empleo *m*; (battle) batalla *f*; (gear interlocking) engranaje *m*

engender [ɪnʤéndə-] VT engendrar

engine [éndʒɪn] N (machine) máquina *f*; (in a vehicle) motor *m*; (locomotive) locomotora *f*; **— block** bloque del motor *m*

engineer [ɛnʤənír] N ingeniero -ra *mf*; (of locomotive) maquinista *mf*; VT (create) idear; (plot) maquinar

engineering [ɛnʤəníɪŋ] N ingeniería *f*

English [íŋglɪʃ] ADJ inglés; N (spin) efecto *m*; **the —** los ingleses; **—man, —woman** inglés -esa *mf*

engrave [ɪngrév] VI/VT grabar

engraver [ɪngrévə-] N grabador -ora *mf*

engraving [ɪngrévɪŋ] N grabado *m*

engross [ɪngrós] VT absorber

engrossed [ɪngróst] ADJ absorto

engulf [ɪngʌ́lf] VT (swallow) tragar; (overwhelm) abrumar

enhance [ɪnhǽns] VT (intensify) realzar; (improve) mejorar

enigma [ɪnígmə] N enigma *m*

enjoin [ɪnʤɔ́ɪn] VT instar; **to — from** prohibir

enjoy [ɪnʤɔ́ɪ] VI/VT (take pleasure) disfrutar [de], gozar [de]; (benefit from) gozar [de]; **—!** ¡que lo disfrutes! **to — oneself** divertirse; **to — the use of** usufructuar

enjoyable [ɪnʤɔ́ɪəbəł] ADJ (pleasant) agradable, gozoso; (fun) ameno

enjoyment [ɪnʤɔ́ɪmənt] N (act of enjoying) goce *m*, disfrute *m*; (right of use) usufructo *m*; (pleasure) placer *m*, gozo *m*

enlarge [ɪnlárʤ] VI/VT agrandar[se]; VT (blow up a photo) ampliar; VI **to — upon** explayarse sobre, extenderse sobre

enlargement [ɪnlárʤmənt] N (photo, building) ampliación *f*; (act of enlarging) agrandamiento *m*; (temporary swelling) dilatación *f*

enlighten [ɪnláɪtn] VT (morally) iluminar; (intellectually) explicar, ilustrar

enlightenment [ɪnláɪtnmənt] N (moral) iluminación *f*; (intellectual) explicación *f*; **the —** la Ilustración

enlist [ɪnlíst] VI/VT (for the army) alistar[se]; (for a campaign) conseguir el apoyo de

enlistment [ɪnlístmənt] N alistamiento *m*
enliven [ɪnláɪvən] VT animar, avivar
enmity [énmɪdɪ] N enemistad *f*
ennoble [ɪnnóbəɫ] VT ennoblecer
enormous [ɪnɔ́rməs] ADJ enorme, descomunal
enough [ɪnʌ́f] ADJ suficiente; ADV **he's tall —** tiene altura suficiente; N lo suficiente; **we have — to live comfortably** tenemos lo suficiente como para vivir cómodamente; **that is —** con eso basta; **more than —** bastante; INTERJ ¡basta!
enrage [ɪnréʤ] VT enfurecer
enrapture [ɪnrǽptʃə-] VT embelesar
enrich [ɪnrítʃ] VT enriquecer
enrichment [ɪnrítʃmənt] N enriquecimiento *m*
enroll [ɪnróɫ] VI/VT matricular[se], inscribir[se]
enrollment [ɪnróɫmənt] N matrícula *f*, inscripción *f*; **what is your —?** ¿cuántos alumnos tienes matriculados?
ensemble [ɑnsɑ́mbəɫ] N conjunto *m*
ensign [énsɪn] N (naval rank) alférez de fragata *mf*; (flag) enseña *f*; (badge) insignia *f*
enslave [ɪnslév] VT esclavizar
ensnare [ɪnsnér] VT atrapar, coger en una trampa
ensue [ɪnsú] VI (follow) ocurrir después, suceder; (result from) resultar; **the ensuing events** los sucesos subsiguientes
ensure [ɪnʃʊ́r] VT asegurar
entail [ɪntéɫ] VT implicar, conllevar
entangle [ɪntǽŋgəɫ] VT enredar
enter [éntə-] VT (go in) entrar en/a; (join) ingresar en/a; (write) escribir; (put data in a computer) dar entrada a; (put data in account books) asentar; (start negotiations) iniciar; VI/VT (register for a competition) inscribir[se]; VI salir / entrar a escena; **to — into** (make an agreement) concertar; (form part of) figurar en
enterprise [éntə-praɪz] N empresa *f*
enterprising [éntə-praɪzɪŋ] ADJ emprendedor
entertain [ɛntə-tén] VI/VT (amuse) divertir, recrear; (host) invitar; **we — a lot** tenemos invitados muy a menudo; (consider) contemplar; (harbor) abrigar
entertainer [ɛntə-ténə-] N artista *mf*
entertaining [ɛntə-ténɪŋ] ADJ (fun) divertido; (serving as pastime) entretenido; (pleasant) ameno
entertainment [ɛntə-ténmənt] N (source of fun) diversión *f*; (pastime) entretenimiento *m*; (of guests) agasajo *m*
enthrall [ɪnθrɔ́ɫ] VT (captivate) cautivar, hechizar; (make a slave of) esclavizar
enthusiasm [ɪnθúzɪæzəm] N entusiasmo *m*
enthusiast [ɪnθúzɪɪst] N entusiasta *mf*
enthusiastic [ɪnθuziǽstɪk] ADJ entusiasta; **I'm very — about the trip** estoy muy entusiasmado con el viaje
entice [ɪntáɪs] VI/VT (attract) atraer; (lure) tentar; (seduce) seducir
entire [ɪntáɪr] ADJ (unbroken) entero; (complete) completo; **the — crew** toda la tripulación, la tripulación entera
entirety [ɪntáɪrɪdɪ] N totalidad *f*
entitle [ɪntáɪdɪl] VT (give a title) titular, intitular; (give a right) dar derecho
entitlement [ɪntáɪdlmənt] N derecho *m*
entity [éntɪdɪ] N (institution) entidad *f*; (being) ente *m*, ser *m*
entomology [ɛntəmɑ́ləʤi] N entomología *f*
entourage [ɑ́ntʊrɑʤ] N séquito *m*, cortejo *m*
entrails [éntrəɫz] N entrañas *f pl*
entrance[1] [éntrəns] N (act, point of entering) entrada *f*; (permission to enter) ingreso *m*; **— examination** examen de ingreso *m*
entrance[2] [ɪntrǽns] VT embelesar
entrant [éntrənt] N participante *mf*; **—s in the law profession** abogados recién recibidos *m pl*
entrap [ɪntrǽp] VT (ensnare) coger con una trampa; (deceive) embaucar
entreaty [ɪntrí́dɪ] N súplica *f*, ruego *m*
entrench [ɪntrɛ́ntʃ] VI (establish) afianzar[se]; (dig trenches) atrincherar; **a deeply —ed habit** un hábito muy arraigado
entrepreneur [ɑntrəprənʊ́r] N empresario -ria *mf*
entrepreneurship [ɑntrəprənʊ́rʃɪp] N espíritu emprendedor *m*
entropy [éntrəpi] N entropía *f*
entrust [ɪntrʌ́st] VT confiar, encomendar
entry [éntri] N (act, point of entry) entrada *f*; (permission to enter) ingreso *m*; (record) anotación *f*; (contestant) participante *mf*; (dictionary definition) entrada *f*, artículo *m*; (computer) entrada *f*; (in bookkeeping) asiento *m*; **double — accounting** contabilidad por partida doble *f*; ADJ **—-level** que no requiere experiencia
enumerate [ɪnúmərət] VT enumerar
enunciate [ɪnə́nsiət] VI/VT (pronounce) articular; (state a theory) enunciar; (proclaim) proclamar
envelop [ɪnvéləp] VT envolver
envelope [énvələp] N sobre *m*
enviable [énviəbəɫ] ADJ envidiable
envious [énvɪəs] ADJ envidioso
environment [ɪnváɪə-nmənt] N ambiente *m*, medio ambiente *m*; (biological) medio ambiente *m*, ecología *f*; (in computers) entorno *m*; ADJ ambiental; (biological) medioambiental, ecológico
environmental [ɪnvaɪə-nmɛ́ntl] ADJ ambiental; (biological) medioambiental, ecológico; **— impact study** estudio del impacto ambiental *m*
environmentalist [ɪnvaɪə-nmɛ́ntlɪst] N

ecologista *mf*

envisage [ɪnvízɪʤ] VT anticipar, prever

envision [ɪnvíʒən] VT imaginar

envoy [ánvɔɪ] N enviado -da *mf*

envy [énvi] N envidia *f*; VI/VT envidiar

enzyme [énzaɪm] N enzima *f*

ephemeral [ɪfémə·əł] ADJ efímero

epic [épɪk] ADJ épico; N (poem) epopeya *f*; (genre) épica *f*

epicenter [épɪsɛntə·] N epicentro *m*

epidemic [ɛpɪdémɪk] ADJ epidémico; N epidemia *f*

epidermis [ɛpɪdɝ́mɪs] N epidermis *f*

epiglottis [épɪglɑDɪs] N epiglotis *f*

epilepsy [épəlɛpsi] N epilepsia *f*

epileptic [ɛpəléptɪk] ADJ epiléptico

epilogue, epilog [épəlɔg] N epílogo *m*

epiphany [ɪpífəni] N epifanía *f*

episode [épɪsod] N episodio *m*

episodic [ɛpɪsɑ́dɪk] ADJ (sporadic) episódico; (serial) en episodios

epitaph [épɪtæf] N epitafio *m*

epitome [ɪpíməmi] N epítome *m*

epoch [épək] N época *f*; **—-making** trascendental

Epsom salt [épsəmsɔ́łt] N sal de Epsom *f*

equal [íkwəł] ADJ igual; **— rights** igualdad de derechos *f*; **an — contest** una competición pareja; **to be — to a task** ser capaz de cumplir una tarea; N igual *m*; **— sign** signo de igual *m*; VT igualar

equality [ɪkwɑ́lɪDɪ] N igualdad *f*

equalize [íkwəlaɪz] VT igualar; (electronically) ecualizar

equalizer [íkwəlaɪzə·] N (in soccer) gol del empate *m*

equally [íkwəli] ADV igualmente

equate [ɪkwét] VT equiparar

equation [ɪkwéʒən] N ecuación *f*

equator [ɪkwédə·] N ecuador *m*

Equatorial Guinea [ɛkwətɔ́riəłgɪ́ni] N Guinea Ecuatorial *f*

equidistant [ikwɪdístənt] ADJ equidistante

equilibrium [ikwəlíbriəm] N equilibrio *m*

equine [íkwaɪn] ADJ & N equino *m*

equinox [íkwənɑks] N equinoccio *m*

equip [ɪkwíp] VT equipar

equipment [ɪkwípmənt] N (supplies) equipo *m*; (act of equipping) equipamiento *m*

equitable [ékwɪDəbəł] ADJ equitativo, justo

equity [ékwɪDi] N equidad *f*, valor libre de hipoteca de una propiedad *m*; **equities** acciones *f pl*

equivalent [ɪkwívələnt] ADJ & N equivalente *m*

equivocal [ɪkwívəkəł] ADJ equívoco

era [írə] N era *f*

eradicate [ɪrǽDɪket] VT (extirpate) erradicar; (pull up by roots) arrancar

eradication [ɪræDɪkéʃən] N erradicación *f*

erase [ɪrés] VI/VT borrar[se]

eraser [ɪrésə·] N (pencil) goma de borrar *f*; (blackboard) borrador *m*

erasure [ɪréʃə·] N (act of erasing) borrado *m*; (smudge) borrón *m*

erect [ɪrékt] ADJ erecto; (of the body) erguido; VT erigir

ergonomic [ɝgənɑ́mɪk] ADJ ergonómico

ergonomics [ɝgənɑ́mɪks] N ergonomía *f*

Eritrea [ɛrɪtríə] N Eritrea *f*

Eritrean [ɛrɪtríən] ADJ & N eritreo -a *mf*

ermine [ɝ́mɪn] N armiño *m*

erode [ɪród] VI/VT erosionar[se]

erogenous [ɪrɑ́ʤənəs] ADJ erógeno

erosion [ɪróʒən] N erosión *f*

err [ɛr] VI errar

errand [érənd] N mandado *m*, recado *m*; **— boy** mandadero *m*

errant [érənt] ADJ errante

erratic [ɪrǽDɪk] ADJ (unpredictable) irregular, errático; (eccentric) excéntrico; (wandering) errante

erroneous [ɪróniəs] ADJ erróneo, errado

error [érə·] N (also in baseball) error *m*; **to be in —** estar errado; **— message** mensaje de error *m*

erudite [érjədaɪt] ADJ erudito

erudition [ɛrjədíʃən] N erudición *f*

erupt [ɪrápt] VI (volcano) hacer erupción; (angry person) estallar; (pimples) salir

eruption [ɪrápʃən] N erupción *f*

escalate [éskəlet] VI (prices) aumentar; (violence) intensificarse, aumentar

escalator [éskəledə·] N escalera mecánica *f*

escapade [éskəped] N (adventure) aventura *f*; (prank) travesura *f*

escape [ɪskép] N (of gas) escape *m*; (from reality) escape *m*, evasión *f*; (of prisoners) fuga *f*, evasión *f*; (means of escaping) escapatoria *f*; **— key** tecla de escape *f*; VI escapar[se], evadirse; VT (elude) eludir; **his name —s me** no me acuerdo de su nombre

escort[1] [éskɔrt] N (people who accompany) escolta *mf*; (male companion) acompañante *m*; (paid female companion) señorita de compañía *f*

escort[2] [ɪskɔ́rt] VT (protect) escoltar; (accompany) acompañar

escrow [éskro] N **— account** cuenta de depósito en garantía *f*; ADV LOC **in —** en custodia

escudo [ɪskúdo] N escudo *m*

Eskimo [éskəmo] N esquimal *mf*

esophagus [ɪsɑ́fəgəs] N esófago *m*

esoteric [ɛsətérɪk] ADJ esotérico

especial [ɪspéʃəł] ADJ especial

especially [ɪspéʃəli] ADV (above all) especialmente; (mainly) sobre todo; **he's — tired today** hoy está más cansado que de costumbre

espionage [éspiənɑʒ] N espionaje *m*
esplanade [éspləɡnɑd] N explanada *f*
espouse [ispáʊz] VT defender, abrazar
essay[1] [ése] N ensayo *m*
essay[2] [ɛsé] VT ensayar
essence [ésəns] N esencia *f*; **time is of the —** el tiempo apremia
essential [isénʃəł] ADJ esencial
establish [istǽblɪʃ] VT (cause to be accepted, prove the validity of) establecer; (found) fundar
establishment [istǽblɪʃmənt] N (action or fact) establecimiento *m*, conformación *f*; (authority) establishment *m*; (of a custom, system) implantación *f*; (of a regime) instauración *f*
estate [istét] N (piece of land) hacienda *f*; (possessions) bienes *m pl*; (property) propiedades *f pl*; (of a deceased person) testamentaria *f*; **— tax** impuesto de sucesión *m*
esteem [istím] VT (regard highly) estimar; (consider) considerar; N estima *f*
estimate[1] [éstəmet] VT estimar, evaluar; VI hacer una estimación
estimate[2] [éstəmɪt] N (calculation) estimación *f*; (approximate charge) presupuesto *m*
estimation [estəméʃən] N (opinion) juicio *m*; (esteem) estima *f*; (estimate) estimación *f*; **in my —** a mi juicio
Estonia [estóniə] N Estonia *f*
Estonian [estóniən] ADJ & N estonio -nia *mf*
estrange [istréndʒ] VT (alienate) enajenar; **to become —d** separarse
estrogen [éstrəʤən] N estrógeno *m*
estuary [éstʃuɛri] N estuario *m*
et cetera, etc. [etsétrə] ADV etcétera, etc.
etch [etʃ] VI/VT (engrave) grabar; (outline) perfilar[se]
etching [étʃɪŋ] N grabado *m*
eternal [itɝ́nł] ADJ eterno
eternity [itɝ́nɪdi] N eternidad *f*
ethanol [éθənɑł] N etanol *m*
ether [iθɚ] N éter *m*
ethernet [iθənɛt] N ethernet *m*
ethical [éθɪkəł] ADJ ético
ethics [éθɪks] N ética *f*
Ethiopia [iθióupiə] N Etiopía *f*
Ethiopian [iθióupiən] ADJ & N etíope *mf*
ethnic [éθnɪk] ADJ étnico; (dances, clothes) tradicional; **— Chinese** de ascendencia china; **— cleansing** limpieza étnica *f*
ethnicity [eθnísɪdi] N etnicidad *f*; (group) grupo étnico *m*
ethnography [eθnágrəfi] N etnografía *f*
ethnology [eθnáləʤi] N etnología *f*
ethyl alcohol [éθəlǽłkəhɑł] N alcohol etílico *m*
etiquette [étɪkɪt] N etiqueta *f*
etymology [ɛtəmáləʤi] N etimología *f*
EU [European Union] [íjú] N UE *f*
eucalyptus [jukəlíptəs] N eucalipto *m*
eulogy [júləʤi] N (praise) elogio *m*; (at a funeral) panegírico *m*
eunuch [júnək] N eunuco *m*
euphemism [júfəmɪzəm] N eufemismo *m*
euphoria [jufɔ́riə] N euforia *f*
euro [júro] N euro *m*
Europe [júrəp] N Europa *f*
European [jurəpíən] ADJ & N europeo -a *mf*; **— Union** Unión Europea *f*; **— Union budget** presupuesto comunitario *m*
Eustachian tube [justéʃən] N trompa de Eustaquio *f*
euthanasia [juθənéʒə] N eutanasia *f*
evacuate [ɪvǽkjuet] VI/VT (remove due to danger, defecate) evacuar; (empty a building) desalojar
evade [ɪvéd] VT (taxes, responsibilities) evadir, burlar; (questions) eludir
evaluate [ɪvǽljuet] VT (assess) evaluar; (appraise) avaluar, tasar
evaluation [ɪvǽljuéʃən] N evaluación *f*
evangelical [ivəndʒélɪkəł] ADJ evangélico
evaporate [ɪvǽpəret] VI/VT evaporar[se]; VI (vanish) esfumarse
evaporation [ɪvæpəréʃən] N evaporación *f*
evasion [ivéʒən] N (escape) evasión *f*; (subterfuge) evasiva *f*
evasive [ɪvésɪv] ADJ evasivo
eve [iv] N (day before) víspera *f*; (evening) atardecer *m*; **on the — of** en vísperas de
even [ívən] ADJ (flat) plano, llano; (smooth) liso; (parallel) paralelo; (without fluctuation) parejo; (equal) igual; (divisible by two) par; (placid) tranquilo; **—handed** imparcial; **—tempered** apacible; **an — dozen** una docena exacta; **to be — with someone** estar a mano con alguien; **to get — with someone** desquitarse de alguien; ADV (still, yet) aun; (for extreme case) hasta, inclusive, incluso; **— if/though** aun cuando; **— my mother went** hasta mi madre fue; **— so** aun así; **it's — more expensive** es aun más caro; **not —** ni siquiera; VI/VT (make a surface even) nivelar[se]; (make accounts even) emparejar
evening [ívnɪŋ] N tarde *f*; (dusk) atardecer *m*; **— gown** vestido de fiesta *m*, vestido de noche *m*; **— party** velada *f*; **— star** lucero de la tarde *m*; **good —!** ¡buenas noches!
event [ɪvɛ́nt] N (happening) hecho *m*, evento *m*; (of importance) acontecimiento *m*, suceso *m*; **in any —** en todo caso; **in the — of** en caso de
eventful [ɪvɛ́ntfəł] ADJ agitado, movido
eventual [ɪvɛ́ntʃuəł] ADJ (later) posterior; (final) final
eventuality [ɪvɛntʃuǽlɪdi] N eventualidad *f*

eventually [ɪvéntʃuəli] ADV a la larga
ever [évɚ] ADV alguna vez; **—more** para siempre; **— since** desde entonces; **have you — studied French?** ¿alguna vez has estudiado francés? **how did you — do this?** ¿cómo pudiste hacer esto? **for — and —** por/para siempre jamás; **hardly —** casi nunca; **if —** si alguna vez; **more than —** más que nunca; **the best friend I — had** el mejor amigo que he tenido jamás; **for —more** para/por siempre jamás; ADJ **—green** [planta] perenne *f*; **—lasting** eterno
every [évri] ADJ (each) cada; **— child is different** cada niño es diferente; (all) todo[s]; **— once in a while** de vez en cuando; **— other day** cada dos días, un día sí y otro no; **—where** (location) por/en todas partes; (direction) a todas partes; **we go — Friday** vamos todos los viernes; PRON **—body** todos -das *mf pl*, todo el mundo *m*; **— day** todos los días; **—one** todos -das *mf pl*, todo el mundo *m*; **—thing** todo; **you are —thing to me** eres todo para mí; ADJ **—day** (of clothes) de diario, de todos los días; (of occurrences) cotidiano
evict [ɪvíkt] VT desalojar
evidence [évɪDəns] N evidencia *f*; (data in court) prueba *f*; **to be in —** ser evidente; VI/VT evidenciar[se], demostrar[se]
evident [évɪDənt] ADJ evidente
evil [ívəł] ADJ (wicked) malo, malvado; (harmful) maligno; N (force of nature) mal *m*; (human wickedness) maldad *f*; **—doer** malhechor -ora *mf*; **— eye** mal de ojo *m*; **the lesser of two —s** el mal menor
evocation [ɛvəkéʃən] N evocación *f*
evoke [ɪvók] VT (call up) evocar; (elicit) provocar
evolution [ɛvəlúʃən] N evolución *f*
evolutionary [ɛvəlúʃənɛri] ADJ evolutivo
evolve [ɪvɑ́lv] VI/VT desarrollar[se]; VI evolucionar
ewe [ju] N oveja *f*
ex [eks] N ex *mf*
exacerbate [ɪgzæsɚbet] VI/VT exacerbar
exact [ɪgzǽkt] ADJ exacto; VT exigir
exacting [ɪgzǽktɪŋ] ADJ exigente
exactly [ɪgzǽktli] ADV exactamente, precisamente; **he's not — a genius** no es un genio ni mucho menos / no es ningún genio que digamos; **they arrived — at three** llegaron exactamente a las tres
exaggerate [ɪgzǽʤəret] VT exagerar
exalt [ɪgzɔ́łt] VT exaltar
exam [ɪgzǽm] N examen *m*
examination [ɪgzæmənéʃən] N examen *m* (also medical)
examine [ɪgzǽmɪn] VT (inspect) examinar; (analyze) analizar
example [ɪgzǽmpəł] N ejemplo *m*
exasperate [ɪgzǽspəret] VT exasperar
excavate [ékskəvet] VT excavar
excavator [ékskəvedɚ] N (person) excavador -ora *mf*; (machine) excavadora *f*
exceed [ɪksíd] VT (go beyond) exceder, rebasar; (be superior to) superar, sobrepasar
exceeding [ɪksíDɪŋ] N superación *f*
exceedingly [ɪksíDɪŋli] ADV sumamente, extremadamente
excel [ɪksɛ́ł] VI sobresalir, lucirse, descollar
excellence [éksələns] N excelencia *f*
excellent [éksələnt] ADJ excelente
except [ɪksépt] PREP excepto, menos; **all the students — Pam** todos los estudiantes menos Pam; CONJ excepto, salvo; **the cars are identical — that one is older** los coches son idénticos salvo que uno es más viejo; **we would go to the beach, — for the inclement weather** iríamos a la playa si no fuera por el mal tiempo; VT exceptuar
excepting [ɪksépt̬ɪŋ] PREP exceptuando
exception [ɪksépʃən] N excepción *f*; **with the — of** con/a excepción de; **to take —** (object) objetar; (resent) ofenderse
exceptional [ɪksépʃənł] ADJ (unusual) excepcional; (gifted) superdotado; (handicapped) con necesidades especiales
excerpt[1] [éksɚpt] N fragmento *m*
excerpt[2] [éksɚpt, ɪksɚ́pt] VT seleccionar fragmentos
excess [éksɛs] N exceso *m*, hartazgo *m*; **— baggage** exceso de equipaje *m*; **— profits tax** impuesto sobre ganancias excesivas *m*; **— weight** exceso de peso *m*; **in — of twenty pounds** más de veinte libras; **to drink to —** beber en exceso
excessive [ɪksɛ́sɪv] ADJ excesivo, desmedido
exchange [ɪkstʃénʤ] VT (replace with something similar) cambiar; (give mutually) intercambiar; (trade political prisoners, books, CDs) canjear; (barter) permutar; **to — greetings** saludarse; N (replacement) cambio *m*; (interchange) intercambio *m*; (barter) permuta *f*; (of prisoners, books) canje *m*; (for stock trading) bolsa *f*; (for commodity trading) lonja *f*; (telephone) central de teléfonos *f*; **— student** estudiante de intercambio *mf*; **rate of —** tipo de cambio *m*, tasa de cambio *f*
excise [éksaɪz] N impuesto sobre bienes de consumo *m*
excite [ɪksáɪt] VT (agitate, arouse) excitar, alborotar; (enthuse) entusiasmar
excited [ɪksáɪDɪd] ADJ (agitated, aroused) excitado; (enthusiastic) entusiasmado, ilusionado; **to get —** (aroused) excitarse; (enthused) entusiasmarse
excitement [ɪksáɪtmənt] N (arousal) excitación *f*; (enthusiasm) entusiasmo *m*

exciting [ɪksáɪdɪŋ] ADJ (stimulating) excitante; (thrilling) emocionante, apasionante
exclaim [ɪksklém] VI exclamar
exclamation [ɛkskləméʃən] N exclamación *f*; **— point** signo de admiración *m*
exclude [ɪksklúd] VT excluir
exclusion [ɪksklúʒən] N exclusión *f*
exclusive [ɪksklúsɪv] ADJ exclusivo; **— of** sin incluir
excommunicate [ɛkskəmjúnɪket] VT excomulgar
excrement [ékskrəmənt] N excremento *m*
excrescence [ɪkskrésəns] N excrecencia *f*
excrete [ɪkskrít] VI/VT excretar
excretion [ɪkskríʃən] N excreción *f*
excruciating [ɪkskrúʃɪeɪŋ] ADJ insoportable, atroz
excursion [ɪksk*r*ʒən] N excursión *f*
excusable [ɪkskjúzəbəł] ADJ excusable, disculpable
excuse[1] [ɪkskjúz] VT (release from a duty, seek exemption) excusar, eximir; (forgive) disculpar, perdonar; **— me!** (forgive me) disculpe; (let me pass) con permiso; (excuse me?) ¿cómo? ¿perdón? *Mex* ¿mande?
excuse[2] [ɪkskjús] N excusa *f*, disculpa *f*; **it's a poor — for a car** no merece llamarse un coche
executable [ɛgzəkjúdəbəł] ADJ ejecutable
execute [éksɪkjut] VT ejecutar (also computer term); (by firing squad) fusilar
execution [ɛksɪkjúʃən] N ejecución *f*; (by firing squad) fusilamiento *m*; **— wall** paredón *m*
executioner [ɛksɪkjúʃənɚ] N verdugo *mf*
executive [ɪgzékjədɪv] ADJ ejecutivo; N (person) ejecutivo -va *mf*; (branch of government) poder ejecutivo *m*
executor [ɪgzékjədə-] N albacea *mf*
exemplary [ɪgzémpləri] ADJ ejemplar
exemplify [ɪgzémpləfaɪ] VT ejemplificar
exempt [ɪgzémpt] VT eximir, dispensar; ADJ exento, libre
exemption [ɪgzémpʃən] N exención *f*, franquicia *f*
exercise [éksə-saɪz] N ejercicio *m*; **—s** ceremonia *f*; VT ejercer; VI hacer ejercicio; **— electrocardiogram** prueba de esfuerzo máximo *f*; **to be —d about something** estar disgustado por algo
exert [ɪgzɝ́t] VT ejercer; **to — oneself** esforzarse, empeñarse
exertion [ɪgzɝ́ʃən] N (use of powers, faculties) ejercicio *m*; (vigorous action) esfuerzo *m*, empeño *m*
exfoliation [ɪksfoliéʃən] N exfoliación *f*
exhale [ɛkshél] VT exhalar; VI espirar
exhaust [ɪgzɔ́st] VT agotar, desmadejar; (a topic) tratar exhaustivamente; N (from a car) escape *m*
exhausted [ɪgzɔ́stɪd] ADJ rendido, agotado
exhausting [ɪgzɔ́stɪŋ] ADJ agotador
exhaustion [ɪgzɔ́stʃən] N (act or process of exhausting) agotamiento *m*; (weakness, tiredness) fatiga *f*
exhaustive [ɪgzɔ́stɪv] ADJ exhaustivo
exhibit [ɪgzíbɪt] VI/VT (manifest) exhibir; (put on view) exponer; N exposición *f*
exhibition [ɛksəbíʃən] N (manifestation, show of skills) exhibición *f*; (public display of objects) exposición *f*
exhibitionism [ɛksɪbíʃənɪzəm] N exhibicionismo *m*
exhilarated [ɪgzíləreɪdɪd] ADJ exultante
exhort [ɪgzɔ́rt] VT exhortar
exhumation [ɛgzjuméʃən] N exhumación *f*
exile [égzaɪł] N exilio *m*, destierro *m*; (person exiled) exiliado -da *mf*, desterrado -da *mf*; VT exiliar
exist [ɪgzíst] VI existir
existence [ɪgzístəns] N existencia *f*
existential [ɛgzɪsténʃəł] ADJ existencial
existing [ɪgzístɪŋ] ADJ existente
exit [égzɪt] N salida *f*; VI/VT salir [de]; (theater) hacer mutis; **— interview** entrevista de salida *f*; **— strategy** estrategia de salida *f*; VI salir; **he —ed the building** salió del edificio
exodus [éksədəs] N éxodo *m*
exonerate [ɪgzánəret] VT exonerar
exorbitant [ɪgzɔ́rbɪdənt] ADJ exorbitante
exorcise [éksɔ-saɪz] VT exorcisar
exorcism [éksɔ-sɪzəm] N exorcismo *m*
exotic [ɪgzádɪk] ADJ exótico
expand [ɪkspǽnd] VI/VT expandir[se], ampliar[se]; (an equation, an idea) desarrollar[se]; (through heat) dilatar[se]; **—ed memory** memoria expandida *f*
expanse [ɪkspǽns] N extensión *f*
expansion [ɪkspǽnʃən] N expansión *f*; (of an equation, of an idea) desarrollo *m*; (through heat) dilatación *f*; **— slot** ranura para accesorios *f*
expansive [ɪkspǽnsɪv] ADJ expansivo
expatriate[1] [ɛkspétriet] VI/VT expatriar[se]
expatriate[2] [ɛkspétrɪɪt] N expatriado -da *mf*
expect [ɪkspékt] VT esperar; **we — guests** esperamos visita[s]; **I — you to be on time** cuento con que vengas puntualmente; **I'm —ed to work fifty hours a week** tengo que trabajar cincuenta horas por semana; **I — you're tired** estarás cansado; **she's —ing** está embarazada/encinta
expectation [ɛkspektéʃən] N (anticipation) expectación *f*; (expected thing) expectativa *f*; **he has great —s** tiene grandes expectativas
expectorant [ɪkspéktə-ənt] ADJ & N expectorante *m*
expectorate [ɪkspéktəret] VI/VT expectorar
expedient [ɪkspíɪdɪənt] ADJ conveniente,

expeditivo

expedite [ékspɪdaɪt] VT (facilitate) agilizar; (deal with promptly) despachar

expedition [ɛkspɪdíʃən] N expedición *f*

expeditionary [ɛkspɪdíʃənɛri] ADJ expedicionario

expel [ɪkspél] VT (discharge) expeler; (throw out) expulsar

expend [ɪkspénd] VT gastar, agotar

expenditure [ɪkspénditʃə˞] N gasto *m*

expense [ɪkspéns] N gasto *m*; **— account** cuenta de gastos *f*; **they had fun at my —** se divirtieron a mi costa

expensive [ɪkspénsɪv] ADJ caro

experience [ɪkspíriəns] N experiencia *f*; VT experimentar; **—d** experimentado

experiment [ɪkspérəmənt] N experimento *m*; VI experimentar

experimental [ɪkspɛrəménṭl] ADJ experimental

experimentation [ɪkspɛrɪməntéʃən] N experimentación *f*

expert [ékspɜ˞t] N experto -ta *mf*; ADJ experto, idóneo, perito; **— system** sistema experto *m*

expertise [ɛkspɜ˞tíz] N pericia *f*

expiration [ɛkspəréʃən] N (of a contract) vencimiento *m*, caducidad *f*; (breathing out) espiración *f*

expire [ɪkspáɪr] VI (die, terminate) expirar; (breathe out) espirar; (lapse) vencer, caducar

explain [ɪksplén] VT explicar; **he tried to — away his absence** trató de justificar su ausencia

explainable [ɪksplénəbəł] ADJ explicable

explanation [ɛksplənéʃən] N explicación *f*

explanatory [ɪksplǽnətɔri] ADJ explicativo

expletive [ékspləɪtɪv] N palabrota *f*

explicable [ɪksplíkəbəł] ADJ explicable

explicit [ɪksplísɪt] ADJ explícito

explode [ɪksplód] VI/VT estallar, hacer explosión, explotar; VT (a theory) hacer añicos; VI (population) dispararse

exploit[1] [ékspɹɔɪt] N hazaña *f*, proeza *f*

exploit[2] [ɪksplɔ́ɪt] VT explotar

exploitation [ɛksplɔɪtéʃən] N explotación *f*

exploration [ɛkspləréʃən] N exploración *f*

exploratory [ɪksplɔ́rətɔri] ADJ exploratorio

explore [ɪksplɔ́r] VI/VT explorar; (a topic) bucear

explorer [ɪksplɔ́rə˞] N explorador -ora *mf*

explosion [ɪksplóʒən] N explosión *f*, estallido *m*

explosive [ɪksplósɪv] ADJ & N explosivo *m*

exponent [ɪkspónənt] N exponente *m*

export[1] [ɪkspɔ́rt] VI/VT exportar

export[2] [ékspɔrt] N exportación *f*

exportation [ɛkspɔ˞téʃən] N exportación *f*

exporter [ɪkspɔ́rdə˞] N exportador -ora *mf*

exporting [ɪkspɔ́rdɪŋ] N exportación *f*; **— firm** empresa exportadora *f*

expose [ɪkspóz] VT (to lay open to danger, exhibit, subject to light) exponer; (to make known) revelar; (to unmask) desenmascarar

exposition [ɛkspəzíʃən] N exposición *f*

exposure [ɪkspóʒə˞] N (to danger, to light, act of exposing) exposición *f*; (disclosure) revelación *f*; **to die of —** morir de frío

expound [ɪkspáʊnd] VI/VT exponer, explicar

express [ɪksprés] VT expresar; (send by mail) enviar por correo expreso; (squeeze out) exprimir; ADJ (clearly indicated) expreso; **— delivery** envío rápido *m*; **— train** tren expreso *m*; ADV por expreso; N (train) expreso *m*

expression [ɪkspréʃən] N expresión *f*

expressive [ɪksprésɪv] ADJ expresivo

expressiveness [ɪksprésɪvnɪs] N expresividad *f*

expropriate [ɛkspropríet] VT expropiar

expulsion [ɪkspɑ́łʃən] N expulsión *f*

exquisite [ɛkskwízɪt] ADJ exquisito, primoroso; (pain) penetrante

extant [ékstənt] ADJ existente

extemporaneous [ɪkstɛmpəréniəs] ADJ improvisado

extend [ɪksténd] VI/VT extender[se]; (a street) ampliar[se]; **he —ed his hand to her** le tendió la mano

extended [ɪksténdɪd] ADJ (extensive) extenso; (prolonged) prolongado; (folded out) extendido; **— coverage** cobertura extendida *f*; **— care facility** centro de atención médica prolongada *m*

extension [ɪksténʃən] N extensión *f* (also phone line); (of a deadline) prórroga *f*; (addition) anexo *m*, ampliación *f*; **— cord** extensión *f*

extensive [ɪksténsɪv] ADJ extenso; (agriculture) extensivo

extent [ɪksténṭ] N extensión *f*; **to a great —** en alto grado; **to such an — that** a tal grado que; **to the — that you are able** en la medida en que seas capaz; **to a certain —** hasta cierto punto

extenuate [ɪksténjuet] VT atenuar

exterior [ɪkstíria˞] ADJ & N exterior *m*

exterminate [ɪkstɜ˞mənet] VT exterminar

extermination [ɪkstɜ˞mənéʃən] N exterminio *m*, exterminación *f*

external [ɪkstɜ́˞nł] ADJ externo; (concerned with foreign countries) exterior

extinct [ɪkstíŋkt] ADJ extinto

extinguish [ɪkstíŋgwɪʃ] VT apagar, extinguir

extol [ɪkstół] VT ensalzar, enaltecer

extort [ɪkstɔ́rt] VT extorsionar

extortion [ɪkstɔ́rʃən] N extorsión *f*

extra [ékstrə] ADJ de más, adicional; **make some — cakes** haz unos pasteles de más / adicionales / extras; N extra *m* (including newspaper, actor); ADV extra; extrasensorial; (soccer) **— time** tiempo suplementario *m*, tiempo de descuento *m*; ADJ **—marital** extramarital; **—ordinary** extraordinario;

—**sensory** extrasensorial

extract[1] [ékstrækt] N (something extracted) extracto *m*; (passage from a book) fragmento *m*

extract[2] [ɪkstrǽkt] VT extraer; (a secret) sonsacar

extraction [ɪkstrǽkʃən] N extracción *f*

extradite [ékstrədaɪt] VT extraditar

extradition [ɛkstrədíʃən] N extradición *f*

extraneous [ɪkstréniəs] ADJ superfluo

extrapolate [ɪkstrǽpəlet] VI/VT extrapolar

extravagance [ɪkstrǽvəgəns] N (unnecessary expense) despilfarro *m*, derroche *m*; (excess) exceso *m*; (oddity) extravagancia *f*

extravagant [ɪkstrǽvəgənt] ADJ (shopper) gastador, derrochador; (price) exorbitante; (praise, demand) excesivo

extreme [ɪkstrím] ADJ & N extremo *m*; **to go to —s** exagerar, llegar a extremos; **to the —** extremadamente, sumamente

extremely [ɪkstrímli] ADV extremadamente, sumamente; **it's — cold** hace un frío que pela; **she's — intelligent** es inteligentísima

extremity [ɪkstrémɪdɪ] N extremidad *f*

extricate [ékstrɪket] VT sacar; VI **to — oneself from** conseguir salir de

extrovert [ékstrəvɜ·t] N extrovertido -da *mf*

extroverted [ékstrəvɜ·dɪd] ADJ extrovertido

exuberant [ɪgzúbə·ənt] ADJ exuberante

exude [ɪgzúd] VI/VT (liquid) exudar; (cheerfulness, confidence) emanar

exult [ɪgzʌ́lt] VI exultar

eye [aɪ] N ojo *m* (also of hurricane, needle, tools); (look) mirada *f*; **—ball** globo ocular *m*; **—brow** ceja *f*; **— chart** cartilla de examen de vista *f*; **— contact** contacto visual *m*; **—dropper** cuentagotas *m sg*; **— drops** colirio *m*, gotas oftálmicas *f pl*; **—glass** (of a telescope, microscope) ocular *m*; **—glasses** anteojos *m pl*, lentes *m pl*; **— injury** lesión ocular *f*; **—lash** pestaña *f*; **—lid** párpado *m*; **—liner** delineador *m*; **—-opener** revelación *f*; **—piece** ocular *m*; **—sight** vista *f*; **—sore** monstruosidad *f*; **— shadow** sombra para ojos *f*; **— socket** órbita *f*; **— strain** vista cansada *f*; **—tooth** colmillo *m*; **—witness** testigo ocular *mf*; **my —s are bad** tengo mala vista; **in the twinkling of an —** en un abrir y cerrar de ojos; **her dress caught his —** su vestido le llamó la atención; **to keep an — on** cuidar, vigilar; **to see — to —** estar de acuerdo; **in the —s of the law** ante la ley; **to give someone the —** hacerle ojito a alguien; **to have —s for someone** estar prendado de alguien; **to keep one's — open** tener cuidado; VT mirar

eyeful [áɪfʊł] N **we got an —** vimos más que suficiente

e-zine [ízin] N revista electrónica *f*

Ff

fable [fébəł] N fábula *f*

fabric [fǽbrɪk] N tela *f*, tejido *m*; (wool) paño *m*; (of society) estructura *f*; **— softener** suavizante *m*

fabricate [fǽbrɪket] VT (goods) fabricar; (a story) inventar

fabulous [fǽbjələs] ADJ fabuloso

facade [fəsád] N fachada *f*

face [fes] N (of head, coin, cube, facial expression) cara *f*; (of a building) frente *m*; (of a watch) esfera *f*; (of the Earth) faz *f*; **—cloth** toalla para la cara *f*; **—lift** lifting *m*; **— value** valor nominal *m*; **about —!** ¡media vuelta! **left —!** ¡a la izquierda! **on the — of it** aparentemente; **she put on a brave —** se comportó con entereza; **to make —s** hacer muecas; **to lose —** quedar mal; **to save —** quedar bien; **to show one's —** aparecerse; ADJ **—-to-—** cara a cara; ADV **in the — of** ante, frente a; VT (stand opposite to) encarar; (meet defiantly) enfrentar, enfrentarse con, afrontar; (look forward) mirar a/hacia; (to have the front toward) dar a/hacia; (to put on facing) ribetear; **to — down** intimidar; **to — the music** dar la cara; **to — with marble** revestir de mármol

faceless [fésɪlɪs] ADJ (anonymous) anónimo; (without a face) sin cara

facet [fǽsɪt] N faceta *f*

facetious [fəsíʃəs] ADJ gracioso

facial [féʃəł] ADJ facial; N limpieza de cutis *f*

facilitate [fəsílɪtet] VT facilitar

facility [fəsílɪtɪ] N (skill) facilidad *f*; **facilities** (of a building) instalaciones *f pl*; (restroom) aseo *m*, servicio *m*

fact [fǽkt] N hecho *m*; **hard —s** datos concretos *m pl*; **is that a —!** ¡no me digas! **as a matter of —** de hecho; **in —** de hecho; **it's a — of life** así son las cosas

faction [fǽkʃən] N facción *f*

factor [fǽktə·] N factor *m*; VT descomponer en factores; VI **to — in** tener en cuenta

factory [fǽktəri] N fábrica *f*

factual [fǽktʃuəł] ADJ (of facts) fáctico; (based on facts) objetivo; **— error** error de hecho *m*

faculty [fǽkəłti] N (ability) facultad *f*; (in a college) profesorado *m*, cuerpo docente *m*, claustro *m*

fad [fæd] N moda pasajera *f*

fade [fed] VI/VT (cloth) decolorar[se], desteñir[se]; (color) deslavar[se]; VI (strength) disminuir; (lights) apagarse; (feelings, colors) desvanecerse

fail [feɫ] VI (faculties, organs, machinery, structure) fallar; (experiment, plan) fracasar, frustrarse; (health) decaer; (business) quebrar, hacer bancarrota; VI/VT (exam, student) suspender, reprobar; **he —ed to remember their anniversary** no se acordó de su aniversario; **don't — to come** no dejes de venir; **without —** sin falta

failure [féljə˞] N (of a plan, a person) fracaso *m*; (of organs) insuficiencia *f*; (of faculties) deterioro *m*; (of machinery) falla *f*, *Sp* fallo *m* (of business), quiebra *f*, bancarrota *f*; (in an exam) suspenso *m*; (to keep a promise, to reach a goal) incumplimiento *m*; **her — to respond puzzled me** su falta de respuesta me confundió

faint [fent] ADJ (sound) débil; (light) tenue; (image) vago; **to feel —** sentirse mareado; **—-hearted** timorato, cobarde; N desmayo *m*, desfallecimiento *m*; VI desmayarse, desfallecer

faintness [féntnɪs] N (of sound) debilidad *f*; (of light) tenuidad *f*; (of an image) vaguedad *f*

fair [fɛr] ADJ (just) justo; (by the rules) limpio; (large) considerable; (of weather) bueno; (of sky) despejado; (of wind) propicio; (of complexion) blanco; **— market price** precio justo en el mercado *m*; **— play** juego limpio *m*; **— chance of success** buena probabilidad de éxito *f*; **the — sex** el sexo bello; **that's not —!** ¡no vale! ¡no es justo! ADV **to play —** jugar limpio; N feria *f*; **—ground** real de la feria *m*; **—way** calle *f*, fairway *m*

fairly [férli] ADV (justly) justamente; (moderately) medianamente; **— difficult** bastante difícil

fairness [fɛ́rnɪs] N (justice) justicia *f*; (whiteness) blancura *f*

fairy [fɛ́ri] N hada *f*; **— godmother** hada madrina *f*; **—land** país de las hadas *m*; **— tale** cuento de hadas *m*

faith [feθ] N fe *f*; (fidelity) fidelidad *f*; **— healing** curanderismo *m*; **in good —** de buena fe; **to have — in someone** tener confianza en alguien; **to keep —** cumplir con la palabra

faithful [féθfəɫ] ADJ fiel

faithfulness [féθfəɫnɪs] N fidelidad *f*

faithless [féθlɪs] ADJ (disloyal) desleal, falso; (lacking in faith, fidelity) infiel

fake [fek] N (object) objeto falso *m*; (person who fakes) farsante *mf*; ADJ falso; **— pearls** perlas de fantasía *f pl*; N (in sports) amague *m*, finta *f*; VT (render false, counterfeit) falsificar; **to — a foul** tirarse; VI/VT (feign) fingir

falcon [fǽɫkən] N halcón *m*

Falkland Islands [fɔ́kləndáɪləndz] N Islas Malvinas *f pl*

fall [fɔɫ] VI (drop) caer[se]; (slope downward) bajar; (be assigned to) tocar a, recaer sobre; **to — asleep** dormirse; **to — back** retroceder; **to — back on** recurrir a; **to — behind** atrasarse, retrasarse; **to — down** (drop) caerse; (fail) fallar; **to — in with** asociarse con; **to — in love** enamorarse; **to — off** disminuir; **to — out with** reñir con; **to — through** quedar en la nada; **he —s for blondes** se enamora de las rubias; **you — for it** te dejas engañar; N (drop) caída *f*; (of a terrain) declive *m*; (season) otoño *m*; **— guy** cabeza de turco *mf*; **—ing out** desavenencia *f*, pique *m*; **—ing star** estrella fugaz *f*; **—s** catarata *f*, salto de agua *m*

fallacious [fəléʃəs] ADJ falaz

fallacy [fǽləsi] N (false notion) falacia *f*; (false argument) sofisma *m*

fallen [fɔ́lən] *see* fall

fallible [fǽləbəɫ] ADJ falible

Fallopian tubes [fəlópiəntúbz] ADJ trompas de Falopio *f pl*

fallout [fɔ́laʊt] N (particle-settling) precipitación radiactiva *f*; (consequences) repercusiones *f pl*

fallow [fǽlo˞] ADJ baldío, en barbecho; N barbecho *m*; VT dejar en barbecho

false [fɔ́ɫs] ADJ falso; **to bear — witness** jurar en falso; **— advertising** publicidad engañosa *f*; **— alarm** falsa alarma *f*; **— arrest** detención ilegal *f*; **— pretense** estafa *f*; **— start** salida en falso *f*; **— step** paso en falso *m*; **— teeth** dentadura postiza *f*

falsehood [fɔ́ɫshʊd] N falsedad *f*, mentira *f*

falseness [fɔ́ɫsnɪs] N falsedad *f*

falsify [fɔ́ɫsəfaɪ] VT falsificar, falsear

falter [fɔ́ɫtə˞] VI (hesitate) vacilar, entrecortarse; (stutter) titubear

fame [fem] N fama *f*

famed [femd] ADJ afamado

familiar [fəmíljə˞] ADJ (generally known) familiar, conocido; (informal) familiar; (too friendly) confianzudo; (closely personal) íntimo; **to be — with a subject** conocer bien un tema

familiarity [fəmɪljǽrɪdi] N familiaridad *f*

family [fǽmli] N familia *f*; **— doctor** médico general *m*; **— man** hombre de familia *m*; **— name** apellido *m*; **— planning** planificación familiar *f*; **— practice** medicina familiar *f*; **— room** cuarto de estar *m*; **— tree** árbol genealógico *m*; **— values** valores tradicionales *m pl*

famine [fǽmɪn] N (lack of food) hambruna *f*, hambre *f*; (scarcity) escasez *f*

famished [fǽmɪʃt] ADJ hambriento, muerto de hambre; **to be —** morirse de hambre

famous [féməs] ADJ famoso

fan [fæn] N (handheld) abanico *m*; (electrical) ventilador *m*; (for cleaning grain) aventadora *f*; (of sports) aficionado -da *mf*, hincha *mf*; (of a person) admirador -ora *mf*; **— belt** correa

del ventilador *f*; **— mail** correo de admiradores *m*; VT (blow air) abanicar; (enliven) avivar; **to — out** abrirse en abanico

fanatic [fənǽdɪk] ADJ & N fanático -ca *mf*

fanaticism [fənǽdɪsɪzəm] N fanatismo *m*

fanciful [fǽnsɪfəł] ADJ (whimsical) caprichoso; (imaginary) imaginario; (given to fantasy) fantasioso

fancy [fǽnsi] N fantasía *f*; (whim) capricho *m*; **to strike one's —** gustarle a alguien; **to take a — to** aficionarse a; **he took a — to his teacher** se enamoró de su maestra; ADJ (luxurious) de lujo; (elaborate) elaborado; (strange) estrafalario; **— free** despreocupado; **— work** bordado fino *m*; VT imaginar[se]; **he fancies himself an artist** se cree artista; **just — the idea!** ¡figúrate!

fanfare [fǽnfɛr] N fanfarria *f*; **with great —** con bombo y platillo

fang [fæŋ] N colmillo *m*

fantasize [fǽntəsaɪz] VI fantasear

fantastic [fæntǽstɪk] ADJ fantástico

fantasy [fǽntəsi] N fantasía *f*

FAQ [frequently asked questions] [fǽk] N preguntas frecuentes *f pl*

far [far] ADV lejos; **— and away** sin duda; **— and wide** por todas partes; **— away/off** lejos, lejano; **— be it from me to complain** no es mi intención quejarme; **— more money** mucho más dinero; **— off we could see land** a lo lejos divisábamos tierra; **as — as I know** que yo sepa; **as — as I'm concerned** en lo que a mí respecta; **by —** con mucho; **how — do I need to walk?** ¿cuánto tengo que caminar? **how — is the church?** ¿a cuánto queda la iglesia? **so —** hasta ahora; **we talked — into the night** hablamos hasta entrada la noche; **we traveled as — as Chicago** viajamos hasta Chicago; ADJ lejano; **—fetched** (implausible) inverosímil, peregrino; (forced) traído por los cabellos; **—-flung** remoto; **—-off** distante; **—-out** radical, poco convencional; **—-reaching** de gran alcance; **—sighted** (with defective vision) présbita, hipermétrope; (seeing the future) con visión de futuro; **the — corner** la esquina de más allá; **it is a — cry from what you said** dista mucho de lo que dijiste

farce [fɑrs] N farsa *f*

fare [fɛr] N (ticket) billete *m*; (ticket price) pasaje *m*; (price of transport) tarifa *f*; (food) comida *f*; (taxi patron) pasajero -ra *mf*; **—well** despedida *f*; **to bid —well to** despedirse de; **—well!** ¡adiós! VI **I —d well in the course** me fue bien en el curso

farm [fɑrm] N (large) hacienda *f*; (small) granja *f*; **—hand** labrador -ora *mf*, peón *m*; **—house** alquería *f*, caserío *m*; **—land** tierra de cultivo *f*; **— produce** productos agrícolas *m pl*; **—yard** (enclosed) corral *m*; (open) patio *m*; VI/VT cultivar; **to — out** (lease) dar en arriendo; (distribute) repartir; (subcontract) subcontratar

farmer [fɑ́rmə-] N agricultor -ora *mf*; (small) granjero -ra *mf*; (large) hacendado -da *mf*

farming [fɑ́rmɪŋ] N agricultura *f*; ADJ agrícola *mf*

farther [fɑ́rðə-] ADV más lejos; **it's an even — distance** es una distancia mayor todavía; **the concept was extended —** el concepto se extendió más; **— on** más adelante; ADJ más lejano

farthest [fɑ́rðɪst] ADJ el más lejano; ADV lo más lejos

fascinate [fǽsənet] VI/VT fascinar, alucinar

fascinating [fǽsənetɪŋ] ADJ fascinante

fascination [fǽsənéʃən] N fascinación *f*

fascism [fǽʃɪzəm] N fascismo *m*

fascist [fǽʃɪst] N fascista *mf*

fashion [fǽʃən] N (style) moda *f*; (way) manera *f*, modo *m*; **— plate** figurín *m*; **after a —** más o menos; **to be in —** estar de moda; VT hacer; (with metal) forjar; (with putty) moldear; (character) formar

fashionable [fǽʃənəbəł] ADJ de moda

fast [fæst] ADJ (quick) rápido, veloz; (ahead, of a watch) adelantado; (firm, permanent) firme; (closed) atrancado; (loyal) fiel; (dissolute) disipado; **—ball** recta *f*; **— break** contraataque *m*; **— food** comida rápida *f*; **life in the — lane** vida loca *f*; **— money** dinero mal habido *m*; ADV (quickly) rápido, rápidamente; (firmly) firmemente; **— asleep** profundamente dormido; N ayuno *m*; VI ayunar; VI/VT **to —-forward** avanzar

fasten [fǽsən] VT (with buckles, buttons, hooks) abrochar[se], prender; (with ribbon, thread) atar; (door) atrancar

fastener [fǽsənə-] N cierre *m*

fastidious [fæstɪ́dɪəs] ADJ (hard to please) maniático; (painstaking) minucioso

fasting [fǽstɪŋ] N ayuno *m*

fat [fæt] ADJ gordo; **— cat** pez gordo *m*; **— cell** célula adiposa *f*; **— chance** ¡ni soñar! **—head** idiota *mf*; **— job** trabajo lucrativo *m*; **— profits** pingües ganancias *f pl*; **to get —** engordar; N (oily substance) grasa *f*; (animal tissue) gordura *f*, sebo *m*; **the — of the land** la abundancia de la tierra

fatal [fédł] ADJ letal

fatality [fətǽlɪdi] N víctima fatal *f*; **— rate** índice de mortalidad *m*

fate [fet] N (lot) destino *m*, fatalidad *f*, hado *m*; (outcome) suerte *f*; VT destinar

father [fɑ́ðə-] N padre *m*; **— figure** figura paterna *f*; **—-in-law** suegro *m*; **—land** patria *f*; VT engenderar

fatherhood [fɑ́ðɚˌhʊd] N paternidad *f*
fatherly [fɑ́ðɚli] ADV paternal
fathom [fǽðəm] N braza *f*; VT (measure) sondear; (understand) comprender
fatigue [fətíg] N fatiga *f*; **—s** ropa de faena *f*; VI/VT fatigar[se], rendir[se]
fatness [fǽtnɪs] N gordura *f*
fatso [fǽtso] N *pej* gordinflón *m*, tonel *m*
fatten [fǽtn] VT engordar, cebar
fatty [fǽDi] ADJ adiposo, graso; **— acids** ácidos grasos *m pl*; N (insult for fat people) *pej* gordo -da *mf*
faucet [fɔ́sɪt] N grifo *m*, llave *f*
fault [fɔ́łt] N (defect, misdeed) falta *f*; (responsibility) culpa *f*; (geological) falla *f*; **—finder** criticón -ona *mf*; **no-** — sin culpa; **careful to a** — demasiado cuidadoso; **to be at** — ser culpable; **to find — with** criticar a
faultless [fɔ́łtlɪs] ADJ perfecto
faulty [fɔ́łti] ADJ defectuoso; (grammar) vicioso
fauna [fɔ́nə] N fauna *f*
faux pas [fopɑ́] N gaffe *f*, metedura de pata *f*
favor [févɚ] N (kind act, goodwill) favor *m*, gracia *f*; (popularity) popularidad *f*; (party gift) sorpresa *f*; VT (give help, show preference) favorecer; (foster) propiciar; (approve of) estar a favor de; **they are —ed to win** son los favoritos; **she —s her mother** se parece a su madre; **he's out of —** ha caído en desgracia
favorable [févɚəbəł] ADJ favorable
favorite [févɚɪt] ADJ & N preferido -da *mf*, favorito -ta *mf*, predilecto -ta *mf*
favoritism [févɚɪtɪzəm] N favoritismo *m*
fawn [fɔn] N cervatillo *m*; VI **to — over** adular
fax [fæks] N fax *m*, facsímil *m*; VT faxear, enviar por fax
FBI [Federal Bureau of Investigation] [éfbíáɪ] N FBI *m*
fear [fɪr] N miedo *m*, temor *m*; **— of God** temor de Dios *m*; VI/VT (be afraid of) temer, tenerle miedo a; (suspect) temerse; **to — for** temer por
fearful [fɪ́rfəł] ADJ (causing fear) terrible, espantoso; (showing fear) temeroso, miedoso, medroso
fearless [fɪ́rlɪs] ADJ intrépido
fearlessness [fɪ́rlɪsnɪs] N intrepidez *f*
feasible [fízəbəł] ADJ factible
feast [fist] N (party, religious celebration) fiesta *f*; (abundant meal) festín *m*, banquete *m*; VI **to — on** darse un festín de; **to — one's eyes on** deleitarse la vista con
feat [fit] N (heroic act) hazaña *f*; (achievement) logro *m*
feather [fɛ́ðɚ] N pluma *f*; **a — in one's cap** un triunfo personal; **—weight** peso pluma *m*; **birds of a — flock together** Dios los cría y ellos se juntan; VI/VT (grow feathers, cover with feathers) emplumar; (change blade angle) poner horizontal
feature [fítʃɚ] N (characteristic) aspecto *m*, característica *f*; (newspaper article) reportaje *m*; (facial) facción *f*, fisonomía *f*, rasgo *m*; **— article** artículo principal *m*; **— film** largometraje *m*; VT (give prominence to) destacar; (depict) mostrar; **this film —s John Smith** esta película cuenta con la actuación de John Smith; **— that!** ¡imagínate! VI figurar
February [fɛ́bjuɛri] N febrero *m*
fecal [fíkəł] ADJ fecal
feces [físiz] N PL heces *f pl*
fed [fɛd] *see* feed
federal [fɛ́Dɚəłˌłˌłˌ

feign [fen] VI/VT fingir, simular, aparentar
feisty [fáɪsti] ADJ (aggressive) pugnaz, belicoso; (energetic) vivaz
feline [fílaɪn] ADJ felino
fell [fɛł] VT (an animal) derribar; (a tree) talar; N (pelt) piel de animal *f*; **in one — swoop** de un golpe
fell [fɛł] *see* fall
fellow [félo] N (member) miembro *m*; (scholar) becario -ria *mf*; (man or boy) tipo *m*; **— citizen** conciudadano -na *mf*; **— man** prójimo *m*; **— student** compañero -ra de clase *mf*
fellowship [fɛ́loʃɪp] N (friendly relations) amistad *f*; (community of interest) confraternidad *f*; (scholarship) beca *f*
felony [fɛ́ləni] N delito grave *m*
felt [fɛłt] N fieltro *m*; ADJ de fieltro
felt [fɛłt] *see* feel
female [fímeł] N (animal) hembra *f*; (person) mujer *f*; ADJ (animal, fastener) hembra; (person) femenino
feminine [fɛ́mənɪn] ADJ femenino
femininity [fɛ́mənínɪti] N feminidad *f*
feminism [fɛ́mənɪzəm] N feminismo *m*
feminist [fɛ́mɪnɪst] ADJ & N feminista *mf*
femur [fímə-] N fémur *m*
fence [fɛns] N (barrier) cerca *f*, cerco *m*, valla *f*; (person who deals in stolen goods) *Am* reducidor -ora *mf*, *Sp* perista *mf*; (store for stolen goods) tienda de artículos robados *f*; **to be sitting on the —** estar indeciso; VT (enclose) cercar, vallar; **to — in** cercar; **to — off** dividir con una cerca; VI (sport) practicar esgrima
fencing [fɛ́nsɪŋ] N (dealing in stolen goods) tráfico en artículos robados *m*; (barrier) cerca *f*; (construction of barrier) cerco *m*; (sport) esgrima *f*
fender [fɛ́ndə-] N guardabarro[s] *m sg*, guardafango *m*; **— bender** choquecito *m*
ferment[1] [fɝ-mɛnt] N fermento *m*
ferment[2] [fɝ-mɛ́nt] VI/VT fermentar[se]
fermentation [fɝ-mɛntéʃən] N fermentación *f*
fern [fɝ-n] N helecho *m*
ferocious [fəróʃəs] ADJ feroz, fiero
ferocity [fərásɪdi] N ferocidad *f*, fiereza *f*
ferret [fɛ́rɪt] N hurón *m*; VI **to — out** hurgar
Ferris wheel [fɛ́rɪswił] N rueda gigante *f*
ferry [fɛ́ri] N ferry *m*, transbordador *m*; **— boat** ferry *m*; VT transportar de una orilla a otra; VI viajar en ferry
fertile [fɝ-dł] ADJ fértil, fecundo
fertility [fɝ-tílɪdi] N fertilidad *f*
fertilization [fɝ-dɪɪzéʃən] N fertilización *f*, fecundación *f*
fertilize [fɝ-dɪaɪz] VT fertilizar; (female, egg) fecundar; (land) abonar
fertilizer [fɝ-dɪaɪzə-] N fertilizante *m*, abono *m*
fervent [fɝ-vənt] ADJ ferviente
fervor [fɝ-və-] N fervor *m*
fester [fɛ́stə-] VI (form pus) supurar; (rankle) enconarse
festival [fɛ́stəvəł] N festival *m*
festive [fɛ́stɪv] ADJ festivo
festivity [fɛstívɪdi] N festividad *f*
fetal [fídł] ADJ fetal; **— position** posición fetal *f*; **— monitoring** monitorización fetal *f*
fetch [fɛtʃ] VT *Sp* ir a por; *Am* ir a buscar; **the ring — ed a fancy price** nos dieron una buena suma por el anillo; VI/VT (dog) buscar
fetching [fɛ́tʃɪŋ] ADJ atractivo
fetish [fɛ́dɪʃ] N fetiche *m*
fetter [fɛ́də-] N grillete *m*; VT engrillar
fetus [fídəs] N feto *m*
feud [fjud] N enemistad hereditaria *f*; VI pelear
feudal [fjúdł] ADJ feudal
fever [fívə-] N fiebre *f*, calentura *f*; **— blister** herpes febril *m*; **— pitch** punto álgido *m*
feverish [fívə-ɪʃ] ADJ (related to fever) febril; (having a fever) afiebrado, destemplado
few [fju] ADJ & PRON pocos; **— er than expected** menos de los que se esperaba; **a —** unos pocos, algunos; **the —** una minoría
fiancé [fiansé] N novio *m*, prometido *m*; **— e** novia *f*, prometida *f*
fiasco [fiǽsko] N fiasco *m*
fib [fɪb] N mentirilla *f*; VI decir mentirillas
fiber [fáɪbə-] N (textile) fibra *f*; (animal, vegetable) hebra *f*; **— -optic** de fibra óptica; **— glass** fibra de vidrio *f*
fibrous [fáɪbrəs] ADJ fibroso
fickle [fɪ́kł] ADJ veleidoso, mudable
fiction [fɪ́kʃən] N ficción *f*
fictional [fɪ́kʃənł] ADJ novelesco
fictitious [fɪktíʃəs] ADJ ficticio
fiddle [fídł] N violín *m*; VI (play the violin) tocar el violín; **to — around** perder el tiempo; **to — with** juguetear con; **they like to — with the computer** siempre juguetean con la computadora
fidelity [fɪdɛ́lɪdi] N fidelidad *f*; **high —** alta fidelidad *f*
fidget [fídʒɪt] VI estar inquieto; **stop — ing!** ¡deja de moverte!
fiduciary [fɪdúʃiɛri] ADJ & N fiduciario -ria *mf*
field [fiłd] N (land, computers, heraldry, optics) campo *m*; (in sports) campo *m*; *Am* cancha *f*; (of oil) yacimiento *m*; (group of competitors) participantes *mf pl*; (of knowledge) campo *m*, terreno *m*; **— artillery** artillería de campaña *f*; **— day** (day for outdoor activity) día de campo *m*; (for military maneuvers) día de maniobras *m*; (unrestrained enjoyment) festín *m*; **— glasses** binoculares *m pl*; **— goal** gol de campo *m*; **— mouse** ratón de campo *m*; **— trip** (in school) paseo escolar *m*; (in science) viaje de estudio *m*; **— work** trabajo

de campo *m*; VT (a baseball) atrapar, fildear; (questions) contestar

fielding [fíłdɪŋ] N (of questions) contestación *f*; (of baseballs) fildeo *m*

fiend [find] N (devil) demonio *m*, diablo *m*; (fanatic) fanático -ca *mf*

fierce [firs] ADJ (animals) feroz, fiero; (illness) espantoso; (storms, etc.) furioso, espantoso; (competition, debate) intenso, encarnizado; (look) torvo

fierceness [fírsnɪs] N ferocidad *f*, bravura *f*

fiery [fáɪəri] ADJ (passionate) fogoso; (hot, causing burning sensation) ardiente

fife [faɪf] N pífano *m*

fifteen [fíftín] NUM quince

fifth [fɪfθ] ADJ & N quinto *m*; (measure of liquor) tres cuartos de un litro *m pl*

fifty [fífti] NUM cincuenta; ADV **to go —-—** ir a medias; ADJ **a —--— chance** un cincuenta por ciento de probabilidades

fig [fɪg] N higo *m*; **— leaf** hoja de higuera *f*; **— tree** higuera *f*; **it's not worth a —** no vale ni un pepino/pito

fight [faɪt] N (combat) lucha *f*, combate *m*; **the — against AIDS** la lucha contra el SIDA; (argument) pelea *f*, riña *f*; VI/VT (combat) luchar [con], pelear [con]; VI (argue) pelear, reñir; **to — a duel** batirse a duelo; **to — back** (to hold back) contener; (resist) resistir; **to — it out** arreglarlo a los golpes; **to — off** rechazar; **to — one's way through** abrirse camino a la fuerza

fighter [fáɪdɚ] N (boxer) boxeador -ora *mf*; (someone who fights) luchador -ora *mf*; (dog, cock) animal de pelea/riña *m*; **— airplane** avión caza *m*

fighting [fáɪdɪŋ] N (fight) lucha *f*; ADJ combativo; **— chance** posibilidad remota *f*; **— words** palabras incendiarias *f pl*

figurative [fígjəɚəɪv] ADJ (art) figurativo; (language) figurado

figure [fígjɚ] N (number, amount) cifra *f*; (form, bodily shape, representation, dance move, syllogism) figura *f*; (character) personaje *m*; **—head** figurón de proa *m*; **— of speech** figura retórica *f*; **—s** (written symbols) números *m pl*; **— skating** patinaje artístico *m*; **to cut a poor —** dar una mala impresión; VI (appear) figurar; VI/VT (think) imaginar[se], figurar[se]; **to — in** tener en cuenta; **to — on** contar con; **to — out** (solve) resolver; (calculate) calcular; **it —s!** no me extraña, era de esperar; VT calcular

Fijian [fíʤiən] N fijiano -na *mf*

Fiji Islands [fíʤiáłəndz] N Islas Fiji *f pl*

filament [fíləmənt] N filamento *m*

file [faɪł] N (documents) archivo *m*; (for computers) archivo *m*, fichero *m*; (official report) expediente *m*, legajo *m*; (line) fila *f*; (tool) lima *f*; **— compression** compresión de archivos *f*; **— format** formato de archivo/fichero *m*; **—name** nombre de archivo *m*; **— server** servidor *m*; **on —** archivado; **filing cabinet** fichero *m*, archivador *m*; VT (papers) archivar; (news story) entregar; (tax return, claim, etc.) presentar; **to — a suit** entablar una demanda, querellarse; VI (for a job) presentarse; (walk in a line) desfilar; VI/VT (smooth) limar

filial [fíliəł] ADJ filial

filiation [fɪliéʃən] N filiación *f*

filibuster [fíləbʌstɚ] VI/VT practicar obstrucción parlamentaria; N filibusterismo *m*, obstrucción *f*

filigree [fíligri] N filigrana *f*

fill [fɪł] VI/VT (glass, container) llenar[se]; (a hole, a pastry, land) rellenar; **the smell —ed the room** la habitación se llenó del olor; **the airline —ed the position** la compañía aérea llenó el cargo; **the new employee —ed the vacancy** el nuevo empleado ocupó el cargo vacante; VT (a tooth) empastar; (prescription, order) despachar; (a need) satisfacer; VI (sails) hinchar; **to — out** llenar; **to — in** (inform) informar; (fill out a form) llenar; (replace) sustituir; **to — up** llenarse hasta el tope

fillet[1] [fɪlé] N filete *m*; VT filetear

fillet[2] [fílɪt] N cinta *f*

filling [fíłɪŋ] N (act) rellenado *m*; (filler) relleno *m*; (of a tooth) empaste *m*; **— station** estación de servicio *f*, gasolinera *f*

filly [fíłi] N potranca *f*

film [fɪłm] N (video) película *f*, filme *m*; (celluloid) película *f*, cinta *f*; (thin coating) película *f*; **— industry** industria cinematográfica *f*; **—maker** cineasta *mf*; VI/VT filmar, cinematografiar

filming [fíłmɪŋ] N filmación *f*

filter [fíłtɚ] N filtro *m*; VI/VT filtrar[se]

filtering [fíłtɚɪŋ] N filtración *f*

filth [fɪłθ] N (dirt, despicable person) mugre *f*, suciedad *f*; (moral impurity) porquería *f*; (vulgar material) obscenidades *f pl*

filthiness [fíłθɪnɪs] N suciedad *f*

filthy [fíłθi] ADJ (dirty) cochino, mugriento; (vile) puerco, cochino; *Sp* guarro; (obscene) obsceno; **— rich** riquísimo

filtration [fɪłtréʃən] N filtración *f*

fin [fɪn] N aleta *f*

final [fáɪnł] ADJ (result, conclusion) final; (last) último; (conclusive) definitivo; **— score** resultado final *m*; **— stretch** recta final *f*; N (in sports) final *f*; (exam) examen final *m*

finalist [fáɪnłɪst] N finalista *mf*

finalize [fáɪnłaɪz] VT completar, ultimar

finally [fáɪnłi] ADV (at last) finalmente, por fin; (lastly) finalmente, por último

finance [fáɪnæns] N finanza *f*; **—s** finanzas *f pl*; VI/VT (to fund) financiar; (to purchase on credit) comprar financiado
financial [fɪnǽnʃəɫ] ADJ financiero; **— disclosure** divulgación financiera *f*
financier [fɪnænsír] N financiero -ra *mf*
financing [fáɪnænsɪŋ] N financiamiento *m*; *Am* financiación *f*
find [faɪnd] VT hallar, encontrar; (discover) descubrir; (determine innocence or guilt) declarar; VI (determine officially) fallar; **to — fault with** criticar a, censurar a; **to — out** (discover) descubrir; (verify) averiguar; N hallazgo *m*
finding [fáɪndɪŋ] N fallo *m*; **—s** resultados *m pl*
fine [faɪn] ADJ (wine, sand, hair, precious metal) fino; (thread) delgado; (cloth) delicado; (artist, athlete) consumado; (manners) refinado; (good-looking person) atractivo, guapo; (weather) bueno; (distinction) sutil; **— arts** bellas artes *f pl*; **— print** letra pequeña *f*, letra chica *f*; **I'm —** estoy bien; **to feel —** sentirse muy bien de salud; **to have a — time** pasarlo bien; N multa *f*; VT multar; **to — -tune** (a receiver) sintonizar; (an engine) ajustar; (a plan) afinar
finery [fáɪnəri] N galas *f pl*
finesse [fɪnɛ́s] N (subtlety) sutileza *f*; (tact) diplomacia *f*; VI usar artimañas; VT conseguir por artimañas
finger [fíŋgɚ] N dedo *m*; **— food** canapé *m*, aperitivo *m*; **—nail** uña *f*; **—print** huella dactilar/digital *f*; **—tip** punta del dedo *f*; **at one's —tips** al alcance de la mano; **little —** dedo meñique *m*; **middle —** dedo del corazón *m*; **to give someone the —** hacerle un gesto obsceno a alguien; **I'll keep my —s crossed** cruzo los dedos; **to wrap someone around one's —** meterse a alguien en el bolsillo; **I can't put my — on it** no sabría decir lo que es; VT (play a guitar) tañer; (squeal on) delatar
finicky [fíɪnɪki] ADJ melindroso, dengoso
finish [fíɪnɪʃ] VI/VT (end) terminar[se], finalizar[se]; VT (polish) pulir; (varnish) barnizar; (kill) liquidar; **to — off** acabar con, rematar; **to — up** terminar; N (ending) final *m*; (decisive end) fin *m*; (polish, treatment) acabado *m*; (varnish) barniz *m*; (coat of paint) última mano *f*; **— line** meta *f*; **with a rough —** sin pulir
finished [fíɪnɪʃt] ADJ (doomed) acabado; (polished) pulido
finite [fáɪnaɪt] ADJ finito
Finland [fínlənd] N finlandia *f*
Finn [fɪn] N finlandés -esa *mf*, finés -esa *mf*
Finnish [fíɪnɪʃ] ADJ finlandés, finés
fir [fɝ] N abeto *m*
fire [faɪr] N (flame) fuego *m*; (conflagration) incendio *m*; (passion) ardor *m*; (for cigarettes, hearths) lumbre *f*; **— alarm** alarma contra incendios *f*; **—cracker** triquitraque *m*; **— drill** simulacro de incendio *m*; **— department** cuerpo de bomberos *m*; **— engine** coche de bomberos *m*, autobomba *f*; **— escape** escalera de incendios *f*; **— extinguisher** extinguidor [de incendios] *m*, extintor *m*; **— fighter** bombero -ra *mf*; **—fly** luciérnaga *f*; **— hydrant** boca de incendio *f*; **— insurance** seguro contra incendios *m*; **—man** (who extinguishes) bombero *m*; (who stokes) fogonero *m*; **—place** hogar *m*, chimenea *f*; **—proof** ininflamable, a prueba de incendio; **— sale** venta de liquidación *f*; **—side** hogar *m*; **— station** estación de bomberos *f*; **— trap** edificio sin medios de escape en caso de incendio *m*; **—wall** cortafuegos *m sg*; **—wood** leña *f*; **—works** fuegos artificiales *m pl*; **when he finds out, there will be —works** cuando se entere, se va a armar la gorda; **to be on —** estar quemándose; **to catch —** incendiarse, prenderse fuego; **to set —** to prender fuego a, incendiar; **under —** bajo fuego; **to play with —** jugar con fuego; **firing pin** percutor *m*; **firing squad** pelotón de fusilamiento *m*; VT (pottery) cocer; (an employee) despedir; (a projectile) lanzar; **to —proof** hacer incombustible, ignifugar; VI/VT (a gun) disparar; VI **to — up** entusiasmar; **to — off** (gun) disparar; (letter) despachar
firm [fɝm] ADJ (solid, unwavering) firme; (fixed) fijo; (not fluctuating, as prices) estable; VI/VT **to — up** (finalize) concretar; (harden) endurecer; N firma *f*; **—ware** programas almacenados en circuitos integrados *m pl*
firmly [fɝ́mli] ADV con firmeza, firmemente
firmness [fɝ́mnɪs] N firmeza *f*
first [fɝst] ADJ primero; **— aid** primeros auxilios *m pl*; **— base** primera base *f*, inicial *f*; **— baseman** primera base *mf*, inicialista *mf*; **to get to — base** comenzar con éxito; **—born** primogénito -ta *mf*; **— chapter** capítulo primero *m*, primer capítulo *m*; **— class** primera clase *f*; **—-class** de primera clase; **— cousin** primo hermano; **—-degree** (burn) de primer grado; (murder) en primer grado; **— floor** (ground floor) planta baja *f*; **for the — time** por primera vez; **— half** primer tiempo *m*; **—hand** de primera mano; **— lady** primera dama *f*; **— name** nombre de pila *m*; **— person** primera persona *f*; **—-rate** de primera clase; ADV (before anything else) primero; **I'd die —** antes la muerte; **at —** al principio; **— off** al principio; N (first in series) primero -ra *mf*; (low gear) primera *f*
fiscal [fískəɫ] ADJ fiscal; **— period** año fiscal *m*
fish [fɪʃ] N (in water) pez *m*; (out of water)

pescado *m*; **— farm** piscifactoría *f*; **—hook** anzuelo *m*; **— market** pescadería *f*; **— story** patraña *f*; **like a — out of water** como sapo de otro pozo; **neither — nor fowl** ni chicha ni limonada; **I have other — to fry** tengo otras cosas mejores que hacer; VI/VT pescar; **to — out** sacar, rebuscar; **to — for compliments** buscar cumplidos; **to —tail** colear

fisherman [fíʃə·mən] N pescador *m*

fishery [fíʃəri] N (for breeding) piscifactoría *f*; (for fishing) pesquería *f*; (industry) industria pesquera *f*

fishing [fíʃɪŋ] N pesca *f*; **— pole/rod** caña de pescar *f*; **— tackle** aparejos de pescar *m pl*; **to go —** ir de pesca

fishy [fíʃi] ADJ (of smell, taste) a pescado; (suspicious) sospechoso

fissure [fíʃɚ] N fisura *f*

fist [fɪst] N puño *m*; **—fight** pelea a puñetazos *f*

fistula [fístʃələ] N fístula *f*

fit [fɪt] ADJ (suited) apto; (healthy) en buen estado físico; **are you — for driving?** ¿estás en condiciones de manejar? ADV **he didn't see — to greet her** no se dignó a saludarla; N (process of fitting) prueba *f*; (mechanical union) encaje *m*; (attack of a disease) ataque *m*; (sudden outburst) rapto *m*; (of anger, coughing) acceso *m*; **to throw a —** tener una pataleta; **by —s and starts** a trompicones; **that suit is a good —** ese traje le queda bien; VT (be suitable for) adecuarse a; (be in agreement with) cuadrar con, ajustarse a; (measure for clothes) tomarle las medidas a; (make suitable) capacitar, preparar; **to — in with** acomodarse a; **I tried to — you in** traté de incluirte; VI (conform to contours of a person) quedarle bien a alguien; (conform to the contours of a mechanism) encajar

fitness [fítnɪs] N (suitability) aptitud *f*; (health) buen estado físico *m*

fitting [fídɪŋ] ADJ apropiado; N ajuste *m*; (trying on) prueba *f*

five [faɪv] NUM cinco; **— hundred** quinientos

fix [fɪks] VT (repair, arrange) arreglar; (place permanently, determine) fijar; (prepare food) preparar; **to — up** arreglar, aviar; **to get an animal —ed** castrar a un animal; **I was —ing to call** estaba a punto de llamar; **I'll — you!** ¡ya te arreglo! N (predicament) apuro *m*, aprieto *m*; (temporary repair) arreglo provisorio *m*; (narcotic injection) chute *m*; **to get a — on** localizar

fixed [fɪkst] ADJ (stationary) fijo; (arranged in advance) arreglado; **— term** a plazo fijo; **—-rate mortgage** hipoteca de tasa fija *f*

fixture [fíkstʃɚ] N (bath, kitchen component) instalaciones *f pl*; **she's a permanent — in this office** está siempre en la oficina

fizzle [fízəł] VI (fail) fracasar; **to — [out]** (make a noise) apagarse chisporroteando; (interest) esfumarse

flabby [flǽbi] ADJ flácido/fláccido

flaccid [flǽsɪd] ADJ flácido/fláccido

flag [flæg] N (also in golf) bandera *f*; **—pole** mástil *m*; **—staff** mástil *m*; **—stone** losa *f*, baldosa *f*; VT (adorn with flags) embanderar; (mark with flags) marcar con banderas; (for attention) marcar, identificar; **to — [down]** hacer parar; VI (diminish) menguar

flagrant [flégrənt] ADV flagrante

flair [flɛr] N (aptitude) aptitud *f*, facilidad *f*; (style) estilo *m*

flak [flæk] N (antiartillery fire) fuego antiaéreo *m*; (criticism) crítica *f*

flake [flek] N (snow) copo *m*; (small thin piece) escama *f*; (eccentric person) chiflado -da *mf*; VI descascararse

flamboyant [flæmbɔ́ɪənt] ADJ (clothes) llamativo; (behavior) extravagante

flame [flem] N llama *f*; **— thrower** lanzallamas *m sg*; **old —** viejo amor *m*; VI llamear, flamear, encenderse

flaming [flémɪŋ] ADJ (emitting flames) llameante; (like a flame) flamígero; (ardent) ardiente; **— red** rojo encendido

flammable [flǽməbəł] ADJ inflamable

flank [flæŋk] N (of a bastion or army) flanco *m*; (of an animal) ijar *m*; VT flanquear

flannel [flǽnł] N franela *f*, lanilla *f*

flap [flæp] VI (wings) aletear; (flag) flamear; VT (wings) batir; (arms) sacudir; N (of a jacket, pocket) cartera *f*; (of a saddle, table) hoja *f*; (of an airplane) alerón *m*; (action of flapping) aleteo *m*

flare [flɛr] VI (burn unsteadily) llamear; (become wider) ensancharse; **to — up** (fire) avivarse; (activity, illness) recrudecer; VT (a skirt) levantar; (a flame) avivar; (a pipe) abocinar; (signal by flare) señalar con bengala; N (flaring light, burst of flame) llamarada *f*; (signal light) bengala *f*; (sudden emotional outburst) arranque *m*; (outward curvature) vuelo *m*; **—up** recrudecimiento *m*

flash [flæʃ] N (of light) destello *m*, ráfaga *f*; (of explosion) fogonazo *m*; (news, camera, vision, computer memory) flash *m*; **—back** flashback *m*, escena retrospectiva *f*; **—bulb** flash *m*; **— flood** riada *f*; **—light** linterna *f*; **— of hope** rayo de esperanza *m*; **— of lightning** relampagueo *m*, rayo *m*; **in a —** en un instante; VI/VT (shine) destellar [sobre]; (expose oneself) exhibir[se]; VI (gleam) relucir, fulgurar, relampaguear; (appear) aparecer; VT (display) ostentar; **to — by** pasar como un relámpago

flashing [flǽʃɪŋ] ADJ destellante

flashy [flǽʃi] ADJ (colorful) llamativo;

(ostentatious) ostentoso; (tasteless) chillón, de mal gusto

flask [flæsk] N (glass container) frasco *m*; (in a laboratory) matraz *m*, redoma *f*; (for alcoholic beverages) petaca *f*

flat [flæt] ADJ (surface) plano; (land) llano; (skin) liso; (spatial orientation) horizontal, acostado; (city) arrasado, aplastado; (shoes, nose) chato; (tire) desinflado, pinchado; (color) apagado; (beer, tonic water) sin gas; (mood) soso; (paint) mate; (denial) terminante; (photo) sin contraste; (pitch) demasiado grave; (musical note) bemol; **—footed** con pie plano; **— rate** tarifa fija *f*; **— tax** impuesto de tasa única *m*; **trading was —** hubo poco movimiento bursátil; **to be — broke** estar completamente pelado; **to fall —** (of a body) caer de plano/redondo; (of a joke) caer mal; (of a plan) fracasar; N (shoe) zapato sin tacón *m*; (flat tire) desinflado *m*, pinchadura *f*, pinchazo *m*; (wooden box) caja para plantas *f*; (musical note) bemol *m*; **—iron** plancha *f*; ADV **—-out** (directly) absolutamente; (at full speed) a toda velocidad; **in two minutes —** en dos minutos exactos

flatten [flǽtn̩] VI/VT (make flat) achatar[se], aplanar[se]; VT (knock down) tumbar, voltear; (raze) arrasar

flatter [flǽdɚ] VI/VT (manipulate) lisonjear, adular; (praise) halagar; **this picture —s you** esta foto te favorece; **I was —ed by his attentions** me halagaron sus atenciones

flatterer [flǽdɚɚ] N lisonjero -ra *mf*, adulador -ora *mf*

flattering [flǽdɚɪŋ] ADJ (comment) lisonjero, halagüeño; (person) adulón

flattery [flǽdɚri] N lisonja *f*, adulación *f*, halago *m*

flatulence [flǽtʃələns] N flatulencia *f*

flaunt [flɔnt] VI/VT ostentar, lucir[se]

flavor [flévɚ] N (taste, quality) sabor *m*; (flavoring) condimento *m*; VT sazonar

flavorless [flévɚlɪs] ADJ insípido

flaw [flɔ] N (in character, in construction) defecto *m*; (in an argument) falla *f*

flawless [flɔ́lɪs] ADJ (logic) impecable; (behavior) intachable, irreprochable; (appearance) perfecto

flax [flæks] N lino *m*

flea [fli] N pulga *f*; **— collar** collar antipulgas *m*; **— market** *Sp* rastro *m*; *Am* mercado de [las] pulgas *m*

fled [flɛd] *see* flee

flee [fli] VI huir; VT huir de

fleece [flis] N vellón *m*; VT (shear) trasquilar, esquilar; (defraud) estafar; (in card games) pelar, desplumar

fleet [flit] N (of boats, buses) flota *f*; (of cars) parque *m*; ADJ veloz

fleeting [flíDɪŋ] ADJ fugaz, efímero, pasajero

flemish [flémɪʃ] ADJ & N flamenco -ca *mf*

flesh [fleʃ] N carne *f*; (of a fruit) pulpa *f*; **— and blood** carne y hueso; **of my own — and blood** de mi propia sangre; **in the —** en persona; VI/VT **to — out** (a character) dar cuerpo a; (an argument) desarrollar

fleshy [fléʃi] ADJ (succulent) carnoso; (fat) metido en carnes

flew [flu] *see* fly

flexibility [flɛksəbílɪDi] N flexibilidad *f*

flexible [flɛ́ksəbəł] ADJ flexible

flicker [flíkɚ] VI (stars) titilar; (candle) parpadear; N (of light) parpadeo *m*, titilación *f*; (of hope) rayo *m*

flier [fláiɚ] N (one who flies) volador -ora *mf*; (aviator) aviador -ora *mf*; (leaflet) volante *m*

flight [flait] N (act of flying, trip) vuelo *m*; (trajectory) trayectoria *f*; (flock of birds) bandada *f*; (group of military aircraft) escuadrilla *f*; (escape) fuga *f*, huida *f*; **— attendant** auxiliar de vuelo *mf*; **— plan** plan de vuelo *m*; **— school** escuela de aviación *f*; **— recorder** caja negra *f*; **— simulator** simulador de vuelo *m*, registrador de vuelo *m*; **a — of fancy** una fantasía; **— of stairs** tramo de escalera *m*; **to put to —** poner en fuga; **to take —** darse a la fuga

flimsy [flímzi] ADJ (structure, argument) endeble; (excuse) flojo, pobre

flinch [flɪntʃ] VI pestañear

fling [flɪŋ] VT arrojar, lanzar; **she flung herself at the attacker** se le tiró arriba al atacante; **he flung himself into his work** se dedicó de lleno a su trabajo; **he flung open the door** abrió la puerta de golpe; N (act of flinging) lanzamiento *m*; (sexual affair) aventura *f*

flint [flɪnt] N pedernal *m*

flip [flɪp] VT (a coin) tirar; (a switch on) levantar; (a switch off) bajar; (a pancake) dar vuelta; VI (go head over heels) dar una voltereta; (get excited, go crazy) volverse loco; **to — through** hojear; **—-flop** (reversal of opinion) giro de 180 grados *m*; (backward somersault) voltereta para atrás *f*; (slipper) chancleta *f*; **— side** la otra cara de la moneda

flippant [flípənt] ADJ (frivolous) frívolo, displicente; (impudent) impertinente

flipper [flípɚ] N aleta *f*

flirt [flɚt] VI coquetear; N coqueto -ta *mf*

flirtation [flɚtéʃən] N coquetería *f*, coqueteo *m*

flit [flɪt] VI revolotear; **a smile —s across her face** una sonrisa le cruza la cara

float [flot] VI (rest on water, air, fluctuate freely) flotar; (in soup) sobrenadar; (drift) errar, ir a la deriva; **she —ed down the stairs** se

deslizó por la escalera; VT (set afloat) poner a flote; (start a company, scheme) lanzar; (issue shares) emitir; (let fluctuate) dejar flotar; (try out an idea) proponer; N (thing that floats) flotador *m*; (on a line) corcho *m*, boya *f*; (in a parade) carro alegórico *m*, carroza *f*; (with soda) gaseosa con helado *f*

flock [flɑk] N (birds, children) bandada *f*; (sheep) rebaño *m*; (worshipers) grey *f*; (people) muchedumbre *f*; VI acudir en masa, afluir; **to — around someone** rodear a alguien; **to — together** andar juntos

flog [flɑg] VT azotar

flood [flʌd] N inundación *f*; (of tides) creciente *f*; **—gate** (of a dam) compuerta *f*; (of a canal lock) esclusa *f*; **— insurance** seguro contra inundaciones *m*; **—light** reflector *m*; **— of tears** torrente de lágrimas *m*; **the —** el Diluvio Universal; VI/VT inundar[se], anegar[se]; (car) ahogar[se], emborrachar[se]

floor [flɔr] N (surface of a room, vehicle) suelo *m*, piso *m*; (story) piso *m*; (of sea) fondo *m*; (for dancing) pista *f*; (minimum level) mínimo *m*; **to have the —** tener la palabra; VT (knock down) tumbar, derribar; (stun, surprise) asombrar; **— it!** ¡acelera! *Sp* ¡mete caña!

flooring [flɔ́rɪŋ] N revestimiento *m*

flop [flɑp] VI (flail) zarandearse; (fish) dar coletazos; (drop) dejarse caer; (fail) fracasar; **to — down** dejarse caer, desplomarse; **to — over** voltear[se] flojamente; N (failure) fracaso *m*; (sound) ruido sordo *m*

floppy [flɑ́pi] ADJ caído; **— disk** disquete *m*, floppy *m*

flora [flɔ́rə] N flora *f*

florist [flɔ́rɪst] N florista *mf*; **—'s shop** florería *f*

floss [flɔs] N (silk fibers) seda floja *f*; (for embroidery) hilo de seda *m*; (dental) hilo dental *m*; VI/VT pasar hilo dental [por]

flounder [flɑ́ʊndɚ] VI (in mud, etc.) andar/moverse con dificultades; (for an answer) quedarse sin saber qué decir, perder pie; N platija *f*

flour [flaʊr] N harina *f*

flourish [flɝ́ɪʃ] VI (prosper) florecer, prosperar; VT (brandish) blandir; N (ornament, florid language, brandishing) floreo *m*; (of music) floritura *f*; (of a signature) rúbrica *f*; **in full —** en plena eclosión

flow [flo] VI (run) fluir, correr; (issue forth) surgir, brotar; (come and go) circular; (fall loosely) caer; (abound) abundar; (rise) crecer; **to — into** desembocar en, afluir a; N (of liquid) flujo *m*; (of electricity) corriente *f*; (of traffic, blood, air) circulación *f*; **—chart** diagrama de flujo *m*, organigrama *m*; **— of words** torrente de palabras *m*

flower [flɑ́ʊɚ] N flor *f*; (paragon) flor y nata *f*; **in —** en flor; **— bed** *Mex*, *Sp* arriate *m*; *RP* cantero *m*; **—pot** maceta *f*, tiesto *m*; **— vase** florero *m*; VI florecer

flowery [flɑ́ʊə-i] ADJ (of a garden, language) florido; (of a pattern) floreado; (of a fragrance) floral

flowing [flóɪŋ] ADJ (liquid) fluyente; (clothing) suelto

flown [flon] *see* fly

flu [flu] N gripe *f*, *Am* gripa *f*

fluctuate [flʌ́ktʃuet] VI fluctuar

fluctuation [flʌktʃuéʃən] N fluctuación *f*

fluency [flúənsi] N fluidez *f*

fluent [flúənt] ADJ fluido; **he is — in French** habla francés con fluidez/soltura

fluff [flʌf] VT mullir; (blunder) pifiar; N pelusa *f*; (blunder) pifia *f*; **this book is pure —** este libro es insustancial

fluffy [flʌ́fi] ADJ (airy) mullido; (covered with fluff) peludo

fluid [flúɪd] ADJ & N fluido *m*, líquido *m*; **— ounce** onza líquida [29.42 milliliters]*f*; **— retention** retención de líquido *f*

fluke [fluk] N (of whale) aleta *f*; (chance) chiripa *f*; **by a —** por chiripa

flung [flʌŋ] *see* fling

flunk [flʌŋk] VI/VT *Am* reprobar, *Sp* suspender; VI **to — out** *Am* salir reprobado, *Sp* salir suspendido

flunky [flʌ́ŋki] N (lackey, servant) lacayo *m*; (yes-man) adulón *m*

fluorescent [flʊrésənt] ADJ fluorescente; **— light** tubo fluorescente *m*

fluoride [flɔ́raɪd] N (chemical) fluoruro *m*; (dental aid) flúor *m*

fluorine [flɔ́rin] N flúor *m*

flurry [flɝ́i] N (of snow) nevisca *f*; (of activity) frenesí *m*

flush [flʌʃ] N (rosy glow, heat) rubor *m*; (of anger) arranque *m*; (of youth, color) resplandor *m*; (of embarrassment) sonrojo *m*; (in poker) color *m*; **did you hear the — of the toilet?** ¿oíste el sonido de la cisterna? ADJ (well supplied, rich) forrado; (ruddy, reddish) rubicundo; (full) rebosante; **— with** a[l] ras de; **— against** pegado a; VI/VT (make or turn red) sonrojar[se], ruborizar[se]; (activate toilet) tirar la cadena; (rinse) baldear

fluster [flʌ́stɚ] VI/VT agitar[se], poner[se] nervioso

flute [flut] N (musical instrument) flauta *f*; (of a column) estría *f*; VT estriar

flutter [flʌ́ʊə-] VI (wings) aletear; (butterfly) revolotear; (flag) tremolar; (heart) palpitar; VT (agitate) agitar; N (of wings) aleteo *m*; (of excitement) agitación *f*; (of a fly) tremolar *m*; (of the heart) palpitación *f*

flux [flʌks] N flujo *m*; **a state of —** un estado de cambio continuo

fly [flaɪ] VI (through air) volar; (from danger)

huir; (flag) ondear; (kite) remontar; VT (aircraft) pilotar; (air cargo) transportar en avión; **to — away** volarse; **to — into a rage** montar en cólera; **to — off the handle** perder los estribos; **to — open [shut]** abrirse [cerrarse] de un golpe; **to — out of a room** salir disparado de un cuarto; **that idea won't —** esa idea no va a ser aceptada; **he flew the coop** se escapó; N (insect) mosca *f*; (over a zipper) bragueta *f*; **— ball** (in baseball) volea *f*, bombo *m*, elevado *m*, palomita *f*; **—catcher** papamoscas *m sg*; **—swatter** matamoscas *m sg*; **—wheel** volante *m*; **on the —** al vuelo

flying [flάɪɪŋ] ADJ (passing through the air) volador; (fluttering) ondeante; **with — colors** con distinción; **— saucer** platillo volador *m*; N **I hate —** no me gusta viajar en avión

foam [fom] N (suds, padding) espuma *f*; **— rubber** goma espuma *f*; VI hacer espuma; **to — at the mouth** echar espuma por la boca

focus [fókəs] N foco *m*; VI/VT (bring into or be in focus) enfocar[se]; (concentrate) centrarse; **to — on** fijarse en

fodder [fάdɚ] N forraje *m*

foe [fo] N enemigo -ga *mf*

fog [fɑg] N niebla *f*; **to be in a —** estar confundido; **—horn** sirena de niebla *f*; VI/VT (confuse) ofuscar; (spray with insecticide) fumigar; (become faded) velar[se]; **to — up** (window) empañar[se]; (one's sight) nublar[se]; **the airport was —ged in** el aeropuerto estaba cerrado por niebla

foggy [fάgi] ADJ (weather) brumoso, nebuloso; (window) empañado; (confused) confuso; (blurred, as a photograph) borroso

foil [fɔɪl] N (any metal) hoja de metal *f*; (aluminum) papel de aluminio *m*; (on mirrors) azogue *m*; (rapier) florete *m*; (thing contrasted) contraste *m*; VT frustrar

fold [foʊld] VI/VT (sheets) doblar[se]; (paper, folding chairs) plegar[se]; (wings, flag) replegar[se]; (in cards) abandonar; (close a business) cerrar[se]; (end a performance) bajar de cartel; **to — one's arms** cruzarse de brazos; N (pleat, hollow) pliegue *m*; (crease) doblez *m*; (enclosure) redil *m*, aprisco *m*; (sheep) rebaño *m*; (congregation) grey *f*; **to rejoin the —** volver al redil; **three—** tres veces

folder [fóʊldɚ] N (file) carpeta *f*; (instrument for folding) plegadera *f*

folding [fóʊldɪŋ] ADJ plegadizo, plegable; **— chair** silla plegadiza *f*; **— screen** biombo *m*; N doblado *m*

foliage [fóliiʤ] N follaje *m*, fronda *f*, ramaje *m*

folic acid [fólɪkάsɪd] N ácido fólico *m*

folio [fólio] N (page) folio *m*; (book) libro en folio *m*

folk [fok] N (people) gente *f*; (nation) pueblo *m*; ADJ popular; **— dance** baile folclórico/folklórico *m*; **—lore** folclore/folklore *m*; (traditional stories) leyendas tradicionales *f pl*; **— medicine** medicina tradicional *f*; **— music** música folclórica/folklórica *f*; **— song** canción tradicional *f*; **— tale** cuento folclórico/folklórico *m*; **old —s** los viejos; **—s** (relatives) parientes *m pl*; *fam* (parents) padres *m pl*, viejos *m pl*

folkloric [foklɔ́rɪk] ADJ folclórico/folklórico

follicle [fάlɪkəl] N folículo *m*

folliculitis [fəlɪkjəlάɪdɪs] N foliculitis *f*

follow [fάlo] VI/VT seguir; VI (be a consequence) seguirse; (come next) ir a continuación; **to — suit** seguir el ejemplo, secundar; **to — through** llevar a cabo; **to — up [on]** (pursue) obtener más detalles [sobre]; (develop) desarrollar; N **—through** (in sports) acompañamiento *m*, continuación *f*; **— -up** seguimiento *m*

follower [fάloɚ] N seguidor -ora *mf*

following [fάloɪŋ] N seguidores -oras *mf pl*; **the —** lo siguiente; ADJ siguiente

foment [foμέnt] VT fomentar

fond [fɑnd] ADJ **I'm — of cats** soy amigo de los gatos, me encantan los gatos; **I'm — of Chinese food** me gusta la comida china; **I'm — of John** le tengo cariño a Juan; **— hopes** ilusión *f*; **to become — of** encariñarse de

fondle [fάndl] VI/VT acariciar

fondness [fάndnɪs] N (affection) cariño *m*, afecto *m*; (liking or weakness) afición *f*

font [fɑnt] N (of water) pila *f*; (of characters) tipo de letra *m*

food [fud] N comida *f*, alimento *m*; **— chain** cadena alimenticia *f*; **— poisoning** intoxicación por alimentos *f*; **— stamps** cupones para alimentos *m pl*; **—stuff** producto alimenticio *m*; **— for thought** algo para reflexionar

fool [fuł] N (foolish person) tonto -ta *mf*, bobo -ba *mf*, necio -cia *mf*; (jester) bufón *m*; **—proof** (plan) infalible, a prueba de fallos; (device) a prueba de tontos; **to make a — of** hacer quedar como un tonto; **to play the —** hacer el tonto; **I'm a card-playing —** soy loco por los naipes; VI bromear; **to — around** tontear; VT engañar

foolish [fúlɪʃ] ADJ tonto, necio

foolishness [fúlɪʃnɪs] N tontería *f*, bobería *f*, sandez *f*

foot [fut] N pie *m*; (of an animal) pata *f*; **— -and-mouth disease** fiebre aftosa *f*; **—ball** (American) fútbol americano *m*; (soccer) fútbol *m*; (ball) balón [de fútbol] *m*, pelota [de fútbol] *f*; **— fault** falta de pie *f*; **—hill** pie de la montaña *m*; **—hold** punto de apoyo *m*;

—lights candilejas *f pl*; **—man** lacayo *m*; **—note** nota al pie de página *f*, llamada *f*; **—path** senda *f*; **—print** huella *f*, pisada *f*; **—race** carrera a pie *f*; **— soldier** soldado de infantería *m*; **—step** pisada *f*, paso *m*; **—print** huella *f*, pisada *f*; **—stool** taburete *m*; **—wear** calzado *m*; **—work** (in sports) juego de piernas *m*; **to follow in the —steps of** seguir los pasos de; **he has a —hold in the computer business** ha logrado establecerse en el negocio de la informática; **it'll take some pretty fancy —work to get out of this** va a ser difícil zafarse de esto; **on** — a pie; **to put one's — in it** meter la pata; VI **to — it** andar a pie; VT **to — the bill** pagar la cuenta

footing [fʊ́dɪŋ] N (basis) base *f*; (foothold) punto de apoyo *m*; **to be on a friendly — with** tener relaciones amistosas con; **to lose one's** — perder pie

for [fɔr] PREP para, por; **this gift is — John** este regalo es para John; **we're headed — the beach** vamos para la playa; **this is a device — sorting letters** este es un aparato para clasificar cartas; **they gave me enough food — three people** me dieron comida [como] para tres personas; **she's studying — the bar** está estudiando para el examen de abogacía; **the party is planned — Saturday** la fiesta está organizada para el sábado; **he has a good eye — talent** tiene buen ojo para descubrir talento; **he works — IBM** trabaja para IBM; **smoking is bad — your health** fumar es perjudicial para la salud; **he's mature — his age** es maduro para su edad; **I've come — the money** he venido por el dinero; **she asked — you** preguntó por ti; **I walk to work — the exercise** voy al trabajo andando por el ejercicio; **we went to Spain — a month** fuimos a España por un mes; **she did it — the first time** lo hizo por primera vez; **my wife signed — me** mi esposa firmó por mí; **mothers feel love — their children** las madres sienten amor por sus hijos; **they fired him — arriving late** lo echaron por llegar tarde; **run — your life!** ¡corre por tu vida! **she took me — a fool** me tomó por tonto; **thanks — the help** gracias por la ayuda; **I paid ten dollars — the book** pagué diez dólares por el libro; **I'm — gun control** estoy por el control de armas; **— all her intelligence** a pesar de su inteligencia; **that's not — you to decide** a ti no te toca decidir esto; **as — him** en cuanto a él; **it's time — me to go** es hora de que me vaya; **to know — a fact** saber a ciencia cierta; CONJ porque, pues; **I wish to eat, — I'm hungry** quiero comer, pues tengo hambre

forage [fɔ́rɪʤ] N (feed) forraje *m*; (searching) recolección *f*; VI (gather food) forrajear; VT (feed) dar forraje a; (collect) recolectar

foray [fɔ́re] N incursión *f*, correría *f*; VI (explore) incursionar; (maraud) saquear

forbade [fɔrbéd] *see* forbid

forbear [fɔrbɛ́r] VT abstenerse de; VI contenerse

forbid [fə-bíd] VT prohibir

forbidden [fə-bídn̩] ADJ prohibido

forbidden [fɔrbídn̩] *see* forbid

forbidding [fə-bídɪŋ] ADJ (strict) severo; (daunting) imponente

force [fɔ́rs] N fuerza *f*; **— out** (baseball) out forzado *m*; **in —** (effective) en vigor, vigente; (in large numbers) en masa; **armed —s** fuerzas armadas *f pl*; VT (oblige, compel) obligar; (rape, break open) forzar; **she —d a laugh** soltó una risa forzada; **to — upon** imponer; **to — one's way** abrirse paso a la fuerza; **to — out** (from a place) echar a la fuerza; (in baseball) forzar out

forced [fɔ́rst] ADJ forzado, obligado; (of a landing) forzoso; **— page break** salto de página forzado *m*

forceful [fɔ́rsfəł] ADJ (of personality) fuerte; (of arguments) convincente, contundente; (of behavior) enérgico

forceps [fɔ́rsəps] N (in obstetrics) fórceps *m*; (in dentistry) tenazas *f pl*, gatillo *m*

forcible [fɔ́rsəbəł] ADJ (done by force) forzoso; (effective) convincente; **— entry** allanamiento de morada *m*

ford [fɔrd] N vado *m*; VT vadear

fore [fɔr] ADJ delantero; (of a ship) de proa; N **to come to the —** ponerse en evidencia; INTERJ (in golf) ¡cuidado!

forearm [fɔ́rɑrm] N antebrazo *m*

forebear [fɔ́rbɛr] N antepasado -da *mf*

forebode [fɔrbód] VT (foretell) presagiar; (have a presentiment) presentir

foreboding [fɔrbódɪŋ] N (omen) presagio *m*; (presentiment) presentimiento *m*

forecast [fɔ́rkæst] N pronóstico *m*; VI/VT pronosticar

foreclose [fɔrklóz] VI ejecutar una hipoteca

foreclosure [fɔrklóʒə-] N ejecución *f*

forefather [fɔ́rfaðə-] N antepasado *m*

forefront [fɔ́rfrʌnt] ADV LOC **at the —** a la cabeza, a la vanguardia

forego, forgo [fɔrgó] VT abstenerse de

foregone [fɔ́rgɔn] ADJ **it's a — conclusion** eso es de cajón

foreground [fɔ́rgraʊnd] N primer plano *m*

forehand [fɔ́rhænd] N (in tennis) derecha *f*, golpe de derecha *m*

forehead [fɔ́rɪd] N frente *f*

foreign [fɔ́rɪn] ADJ (from another country) extranjero; (not local) foráneo; (alien) ajeno; **— affairs** relaciones exteriores *f pl*; **— aid**

ayuda exterior *f*; — **body** cuerpo extraño *m*; —**-born** nacido en el extranjero; — **currency** divisa *f*; — **debt** deuda exterior *f*; — **exchange** cambio de divisas *m*; — **exchange system** sistema cambiario *m*; — **matter** materia extraña *f*; — **policy** política exterior *f*; — **trade** comercio exterior *m*

foreigner [fɔ́rənə-] N extranjero -ra *mf*

foreman [fɔ́rmən] N (in a factory) capataz *m*, sobrestante *m*; (of a jury) presidente *m*

foremost [fɔ́rmost] ADJ principal, preeminente

forensic [fərénzɪk] ADJ forense

forerunner [fɔ́rrʌnə-] N (precursor) precursor -ora *mf*; (omen) presagio *m*; (harbinger) mensajero -ra *mf*

foresaw [fɔrsɔ́] *see* foresee

foresee [fɔrsí] VT prever, prevenir

foreseeable [fɔrsíəbəł] ADJ previsible

foreseen [fɔrsín] *see* foresee

foresight [fɔ́rsaɪt] N previsión *f*

foreskin [fɔ́rskɪn] N prepucio *m*

forest [fɔ́rɪst] N (temperate) bosque *m*; (tropical) selva *f*; — **fire** incendio forestal *m*; — **ranger** guardabosque[s] *m sg*

forestall [fɔrstɔ́ł] VT bloquear

forester [fɔ́rɪstə-] N (forest ranger) guardabosque[s] *m sg*

forestry [fɔ́rɪstri] N silvicultura *f*; — **division** división forestal *f*

foretell [fɔrtɛ́ł] VT predecir, vaticinar

foretold [fɔrtóld] *see* foretell

forever [fərévə-] ADV para siempre; **I'm — having to pick up after him** siempre tengo que estar juntando sus cosas; **we can't go on like this** — no podemos seguir así por toda la vida

foreword [fɔ́rwə-d] N prólogo *m*

forfeit [fɔ́rfɪt] VT perder; N (fine) multa *f*; (loss) pérdida *f*

forfeiture [fɔ́rfɪtʃə-] N confiscación *f*, pérdida *f*

forgave [fɔrgév] *see* forgive

forge [fɔrʤ] N fragua *f*, forja *f*; VT (plans) fraguar; (metal, agreement) forjar, fraguar; VI/VT (signature, legal document) falsificar; **to — ahead** abrirse paso

forgery [fɔ́rʤəri] N falsificación *f*

forget [fə-gɛ́t] VI/VT olvidar, olvidarse de; **I forgot my keys** se me olvidaron las llaves; **to — oneself** meter la pata; N —**-me-not** nomeolvides *mf*

forgetful [fə-gɛ́tfəł] ADJ olvidadizo; — **of** negligente de

forgetfulness [fə-gɛ́tfəłnɪs] N falta de memoria *f*

forgive [fə-gív] VI/VT perdonar; (a debt) perdonar, disculpar

forgiven [fə-gívən] *see* forgive

forgiveness [fə-gívnɪs] N perdón *m*

forgiving [fə-gívɪŋ] ADJ clemente

forgo [fɔrgó] *see* forego

forgot [fɔrgɑ́t] *see* forget

forgotten [fɔrgɑ́tn] *see* forget

fork [fɔrk] N (for eating) tenedor *m*; (for hay) horca *f*, trinche *m*; (for tuning) diapasón *m*; (in a road) bifurcación *f*; —**lift** montacargas de horquilla *m sg*; VI bifurcarse; **to — over** soltar

forlorn [fərlɔ́rn] ADJ desamparado, abandonado

form [fɔrm] N forma *f*; (type) modalidad *f*; (physical condition) condiciones físicas *f pl*; (document to be filled in) formulario *m*; VI/VT formar[se]

formal [fɔ́rməł] ADJ formal; — **attire** ropa de etiqueta *f*; — **dance** baile de etiqueta *m*

formaldehyde [fɔrmǽlɪDi] N formaldehído *m*

formality [fɔrmǽlɪDi] N (conventionality) formalidad *f*; (rigidity) formalismo *m*; (legal step) trámite *m*

format [fɔ́rmæt] N formato *m*; VT formatear

formation [fɔrméʃən] N formación *f*

formative [fɔ́rmətɪv] ADJ formativo

formatting [fɔ́rmæDɪŋ] N formateo *m*

former [fɔ́rmə-] ADJ **the — capital** la antigua capital; **my — husband** mi ex-marido; **the — president** el ex-presidente; **in — times** antiguamente; PRON aquel [aquella, etc.], ese [esa, etc.]

formerly [fɔ́rmə-li] ADV antes, anteriormente

formidable [fɔ́rmɪDəbəł] ADJ formidable

formula [fɔ́rmjələ] N fórmula *f*, formulación *f*; (for babies) preparado para biberón *m*

formulate [fɔ́rmjəlet] VT formular

formulation [fɔrmjəléʃən] N formulación *f*

fornicate [fɔ́rnɪket] VI fornicar

forsake [fərsɛ́k] VT abandonar, desamparar

forsaken [fərsɛ́kən] *see* forsake

forsook [fərsúk] *see* forsake

fort [fɔrt] N fuerte *m*, fortaleza *f*; **to hold [down] the —** quedar de guardián

forth [fɔrθ] ADV (time) en adelante; (space) hacia adelante; **to go —** irse; **and so —** etcétera, y así sucesivamente

forthcoming [fɔ́rθkʌ́mɪŋ] ADJ (approaching) venidero, próximo; (available) disponible; (frank, friendly) abierto; (soon to be published) de próxima aparición

forthright [fɔ́rθraɪt] ADJ directo

forthwith [fɔrθwíθ] ADV en seguida, al punto

fortification [fɔ́rDəfɪkéʃən] N fortificación *f*

fortify [fɔ́rDəfaɪ] VT (building, body) fortificar; (food) enriquecer; (hair, mind) fortalecer; (argument) reforzar

fortitude [fɔ́rDɪtud] N fortaleza *f*, entereza *f*

fortress [fɔ́rtrɪs] N fortaleza *f*

fortuitous [fɔrtúɪDəs] ADJ (coincidental) fortuito; (lucky) afortunado

fortunate [fɔ́rtʃənɪt] ADJ afortunado

fortunately [fɔ́rtʃənɪtli] ADV afortunadamente

fortune [fɔ́rtʃən] N fortuna *f*; **— teller** adivino -na *mf*; **it cost me a —** me costó un dineral; **to tell someone's —** decirle la buenaventura a alguien
forty [fɔ́rtɪ] NUM cuarenta; **— love** (in tennis) quince a nada
forum [fɔ́rəm] N foro *m*
forward [fɔ́rwə-d] ADJ (toward the front) hacia adelante; (leading, in the front) delantero; (pushy) descarado; ADV adelante, en adelante; **to bring —** presentar; VT reexpedir; N (in sports) delantero -ra *mf*; (in basketball) alero -ra *mf*
fossil [fɑ́sə‡] N fósil *m*; (old fogey) carcamal *m*, carca *mf*; **— fuel** combustible fósil *m*
foster [fɔ́stə-] VT (promote) fomentar, promover; (bring up) criar; **— family** familia de acogida *f*
fought [fɔt] *see* fight
foul [faʊł] ADJ (dirty, illicit) sucio; (disgusting) asqueroso; (of a smell) fétido; (of weather) inclemente; (of winds) adverso; (morally offensive) vil; (of air) viciado; **—mouthed** mal hablado; **the police suspect — play** la policía sospecha que fue un crimen; N (in sports) falta *f*, faul *m*; **— -up** desastre *m*; VT (make dirty) ensuciar; (pollute) viciar; (tarnish) manchar; VI cometer una falta; **to — up** estropear
found [faʊnd] VT (establish) fundar; (build) cimentar
found [faʊnd] *see* find
foundation [faʊndéʃən] N (establishment, institution) fundación *f*; (of a building) cimiento *m*; (of an argument) fundamento *m*; (cosmetic) base *f*
founder [fáʊndə-] N (establisher) fundador -ora *mf*; (smith) fundidor -ora *mf*; VI (sink) zozobrar, irse a pique; (fail) fracasar
foundry [fáʊndrɪ] N fundición *f*
fountain [fáʊntn̩] N fuente *f*; **— pen** pluma fuente *f*
four [fɔr] NUM cuatro; **— hundred** cuatrocientos; **—score** ochenta; N **— -eyes** *fam* cuatro ojos *mf sg*; **— -letter word** palabrota *f*; **—some** grupo de cuatro *m*
fourteen [fɔ́rtín] NUM catorce
fourth [fɔrθ] ADJ cuarto; N cuarta parte *f*; **the Fourth of July** el cuatro de julio
fowl [faʊł] N (domestic) ave de corral *m*; (wild) ave *m*
fox [faks] N zorro *m*, zorra *f*; (crafty person) persona astuta *f*; (attractive person) guapetón -ona *mf*; **—hole** madriguera *f*; (military) trinchera *f*
foxy [fáksi] ADJ (crafty) zorro; (attractive) sexy
foyer [fɔ́ɪə-] N vestíbulo *m*
fraction [frǽkʃən] N fracción *f*, quebrado *m*
fracture [frǽktʃə-] N fractura *f*; VI/VT fracturar[se]
fragile [frǽʤł] ADJ frágil
fragment[1] [frǽgmənt] N fragmento *m*
fragment[2] [frægmɛ́nt] VI/VT fragmentar[se]
fragmentation [frægmənté͡ʃən] N fragmentación *f*
fragrance [frégrəns] N fragancia *f*
fragrant [frégrənt] ADJ fragante
frail [freł] ADJ frágil, débil
frailty [fréłtɪ] N fragilidad *f*, debilidad *f*
frame [frem] N (of a building, airplane, furniture) armazón *m*; (of eyeglasses) montura *f*, armadura *f*; (of a car) chasis *m*; (of a person's body) estatura *f*; (of a picture, door) marco *m*; (for embroidery) bastidor *m*; (on a strip of film) imagen *f*; **— of mind** disposición *f*; **—work** (of a house, structure) armazón *m*; (of reference) marco *m*, esquema *m*; VT (a document) forjar; (a question, plan) formular; (a picture) enmarcar; (a person) tenderle una trampa
franc [fræŋk] N franco *m*
France [fræns] N Francia *f*
franchise [frǽntʃaɪz] N (license) concesión *f*, franquicia *f*; (voting privilege) derecho al voto *m*; VT conceder en franquicia, dar la concesión para
frank [fræŋk] ADJ franco, abierto; VT franquear; N salchicha alemana *f*
frankfurter [frǽŋkfə-tə-] N salchicha alemana *f*
frankness [frǽŋknɪs] N franqueza *f*
frantic [frǽntɪk] ADJ (wild) frenético; (desperate) desesperado
fraternal [frə-tɝ́-nł] ADJ fraternal, fraterno
fraternity [frə-tɝ́-nɪdɪ] N (relationship) fraternidad *f*, confraternidad *f*; (student association) asociación estudiantil *f*
fraternize [frǽtə-naɪz] VI confraternizar, fraternizar
fraud [frɔd] N (deceit) fraude *m*; (impostor) farsante *mf*, impostor -ora *mf*
fraudulent [frɔ́ʤə-lənt] ADJ (of a business, etc.) fraudulento; (of a person) engañoso
fray [fre] N (fight) reyerta *f*, riña *f*; (harsh debate) refriega *f*; VI/VT (rub, wear out) desgastar[se], deshilachar[se]; (strain) crispar[se]
freak [frik] N (anomaly) anomalía *f*; (monster) monstruo *m*, anormal *mf*; (enthusiast) fanático -ca *mf*; (pervert) pervertido -da *mf*; ADJ (unusual) insólito; VI chiflar, flipar; **to — out** chiflar[se], flipar[se]
freakish [fríkɪʃ] ADJ insólito
freckle [frɛ́kəł] N peca *f*; VI/VT cubrir[se] de pecas
freckled [frɛ́kəłd] ADJ pecoso
free [fri] ADJ (having liberty, unrestricted, loose, uncombined chemically, independent) libre; (unobstructed, unoccupied) libre, despejado; (without charge) gratis, gratuito; (generous) generoso; (unstinted) sin límites,

descontrolado; (frank) franco, abierto; **— and clear** libre de gravámenes; **— and easy** despreocupado; **— delivery** entrega gratuita *f*; **— enterprise** empresa libre *f*; **— fall** caída libre *f*; **—-for-all** rifirrafe *m*; **— kick** tiro libre *m*; **—lance** freelance *m*; **— lunch/ride** algo gratis *m*; **— market** mercado libre *m*; **— radical** radical libre *m*; **— speech** libertad de expresión *f*; **— spirit** espíritu fuerte *m*; **—style** estilo libre *m*, crol *m*; **—thinker** libre pensador -ora *mf*; **— throw** tiro libre *m*; **— trade** libre comercio *m*; **— verse** verso libre *m*; **—way** autopista *f*, autovía *f*; **— will** libre albedrío *m*; **to give someone a — hand** dar rienda suelta a alguien; **to set —** poner en libertad; **sugar-** — sin azúcar; ADV libremente; **— lance** por cuenta propia; **for —** gratis; VT (liberate) liberar; (deliver, rid) librar; (untie a knot) desenredar; (drain) desatascar; **to —load** gorronear; **to — up** (time) dejar libre

freebie [fríbi] N yapa *f*

freedom [fríɒəm] N libertad *f*; **— of speech** libertad de expresión *f*; **we all want — from fear** todos queremos vivir libres de miedo; **I want — from having to go to work every day** no quiero tener que ir a trabajar todos los días

freeze [friz] VI/VT (food, water) congelar[se]; (accounts) bloquear[se], congelar[se]; **to —-dry** liofilizar; **he froze to death** murió congelado; **my computer froze up** se me colgó la computadora / el ordenador; VI (of temperature) helar; N (action or state of being frozen) congelación *f*; (cold snap) helada *f*

freezer [frízə˞] N congelador *m*

freezing [frízɪŋ] ADJ helado; **— cold** frío glacial *m*; **— point** punto de congelación *m*

freight [freɪt] N (load) carga *f*; (charge) flete *m*, porte *m*; **— train** tren de carga *m*, tren de mercancías *m*

freighter [fréɪə˞] N buque de carga *m*

French [frɛntʃ] ADJ francés; **— dressing** salsa francesa *f*; **— fries** *Am* papas fritas *f pl*; *Sp* patatas fritas *f pl*; **— horn** corno francés *m*; **—man** francés *m*; **—woman** francesa *f*; N (language) francés; **the —** los franceses

frenzy [frénzi] N frenesí *m*; **he worked himself into a —** se puso histérico

frequency [fríkwənsi] N frecuencia *f*

frequent [fríkwənt] ADJ frecuente; VT frecuentar

frequently [fríkwəntli] ADV con frecuencia, a menudo; **— asked questions** preguntas frecuentes *f pl*

fresh [freʃ] ADJ (pure, cool, not stale, not frozen, not tired) fresco; (new) nuevo; (bold) impertinente, atrevido; (healthy) lozano; **— paint** pintura fresca *f*; **— water** agua dulce *f*; ADV **— out of school** recién salido de la escuela; **we're — out of ideas** se nos acabaron las ideas

freshen [fréʃən] VI/VT refrescar[se]; **to — up** arreglarse, lavarse

freshman [fréʃmən] N (student) estudiante de primer año *mf*; (novice) novato -ta *mf*

freshness [fréʃnɪs] N (of food, of temperature) frescor *m*, frescura *f*; (of skin, flowers, youth) lozanía *f*; (of an idea) originalidad *f*; (impudence) descaro *m*

fret [frɛt] VI/VT (worry) preocupar[se]; (irritate) irritar[se]; N traste *m*

fretful [frɛ́tfəɫ] ADJ ansioso, inquieto

friar [fráɪə˞] N fraile *m*

friction [fríkʃən] N fricción *f*, rozamiento *m*

Friday [fráɪdɛ] N viernes *m*

fried [fraɪd] ADJ frito

friend [frɛnd] N amigo -ga *mf*

friendliness [fréndlɪnɪs] N afabilidad *f*, simpatía *f*

friendly [frɛ́ndli] ADJ amistoso, simpático, amigable; **— advice** consejo de amigo *m*; **user-** — fácil de usar

friendship [fréndʃɪp] N amistad *f*

frigate [fríɡɪt] N fragata *f*

fright [fraɪt] N (fear) espanto *m*, susto *m*; (grotesque thing or person) espantajo *m*, esperpento *m*; **to take —** asustarse

frighten [fráɪtn] VI/VT espantar[se], asustar[se]; **to — away** ahuyentar, espantar

frightened [fráɪtnd] ADJ asustado, espantado; **to get —** espantarse

frightful [fráɪtfəɫ] ADJ espantoso, pavoroso; **we had a — time** lo pasamos horrible; **he's a — flatterer** es un adulón espantoso

frigid [fríʤɪd] ADJ (of weather) gélido; (of personal relations) frío

frill [frɪɫ] N (trimming) volante *m*; (something superfluous) adorno *m*; **no- —s** sin lujos

fringe [frɪnʤ] N (of a rug) fleco *m*, orla *f*; (of a city) periferia *f*; (of a political party) extremo *m*; (of society) margen *m*; **— benefits** prestaciones *f pl*, complementos *m pl*; VT orlar, poner un fleco

Frisbee® [frízbi] N disco volador *m*

frisk [frɪsk] VI/VT (frolic) retozar, triscar; (search) cachear

frisky [fríski] ADJ retozón

fritter [fríɒə˞] VI/VT desmenuzar[se]; VI irse gastando de poco a poco; **to — away** malgastar; N buñuelo *m*, churro *m*

frivolity [frɪvɑ́lɪɒi] N frivolidad *f*

frivolous [frívələs] ADJ frívolo

fro [fro] ADV **to and —** de aquí para allá

frock [frɑk] N (dress) vestido *m*; (habit) hábito *m*

frog [frɑg] N (animal) rana *f*; (fastener) alamar *m*; (of a hoof) ranilla *f*; (French person) *pej* franchute -ta *mf*; **to have a — in one's throat** tener gallos en la garganta; **—man**

hombre rana *m*

frolic [frɑ́lɪk] N retozo *m*; VI retozar

from [frʌm, frəm] PREP desde, de, por; **— here to there** desde aquí hasta allá; **— two to four** de las dos a las cuatro; **— what I can tell** por lo que yo veo; **four hours — now** de aquí a cuatro horas, dentro de cuatro horas; **different — the other one** diferente del otro; **to come — Minnesota** ser de Minesota; **death — starvation** muerte por inanición *f*

front [frʌnt] N frente *m*; (cover for illegal activity) pantalla *f*; **—-runner** favorito -ta *mf*; **—-wheel drive** tracción delantera *f*; **in — of** en frente de, delante de; ADJ delantero; VI/VT (face) dar a; (cover up) servir de pantalla

frontal [frʌ́ntl] ADJ frontal

frontier [frʌntír] N frontera *f*; ADJ fronterizo; **— spirit** espíritu pionero *m*; **— town** pueblo fronterizo *m*

frost [frɔ́st] N helada *f*, escarcha *f*; VI/VT helar, escarchar; VT (a cake) bañar; (glass) esmerilar; (hair) hacer rayitos/reflejos; **—bite** necrosis por congelación *f*

frosting [frɔ́stɪŋ] N (of a cake) baño *m*; (for glass) esmerilado *m*; (of hair) rayos *m pl*, reflejos *m pl*

frosty [frɔ́sti] ADJ (cold, unfriendly) helado; (covered with frost) escarchado

froth [frɔθ] N espuma *f*; VI echar espuma; VT batir

frown [fraʊn] VI fruncir el ceño; **to — on** desaprobar; N ceño *m*

froze [froz] *see* freeze

frozen [frózən] ADJ congelado

frozen [frózən] *see* freeze

fructose [frúktos] N fructosa *f*

frugal [frúgəł] ADJ (economical) económico, ahorrativo; (meager) frugal

fruit [frut] N (food) fruta *f*; (plant part, product of labor) fruto *m*; **—cake** (food) torta de frutas secas *f*; (crazy person) *fam* chiflado -da *mf*

fruitful [frútfəł] ADJ fructífero

fruitless [frútlɪs] ADJ infructuoso

frumpy [frʌ́mpi] ADJ matrona

frustrate [frʌ́stret] VT frustrar; **to get —d** frustrar[se]

frustration [frʌstréʃən] N frustración *f*

fry [fraɪ] VI/VT (cook, also execute by electrocution) freír[se]; **—ing pan** sartén *f*; N (fried potato) papa/patata frita *f*; (gathering with fried food) fiesta con comida frita *f*; (young fish) alevín *m*; **small —** gente menuda *f*

fudge [fʌʤ] N turrón blando de chocolate *m*; VI (cheat) hacer trampa; (avoid an issue) dar rodeos

fuel [fjúəł] N (combustible) combustible *m*, carburante *m*; (topic) tema *m*; **— injection** inyección *f*; **— oil** fuel *m*; VT (a vehicle) llenar el tanque, cargar de combustible; (fire, debate) avivar

fugitive [fjúʤɪDIv] ADJ (fleeing) fugitivo; (transitory) fugaz; N fugitivo -va *mf*, prófugo -ga *mf*

fulfill [fʊłfíł] VT (promise, order) cumplir; (need) satisfacer; **she doesn't feel —ed** no se siente realizada

fulfillment [fʊłfíłmənt] N (of a promise, order) cumplimiento *m*; (of a need) satisfacción *f*; (of a person) realización *f*; (of a dream) culminación *f*

full [fʊł] ADJ (completely filled) lleno; (complete) completo; (a dress) amplio; (a person's figure) relleno; (sated) harto; **—-blooded** de raza; **—-blown** (of disease) declarado; (complete) auténtico; **—-bodied** con cuerpo; **—-fledged** verdadero; **—-grown** adulto; **— house** full *m*; **—-length** (movie) de largometraje; (mirror) de cuerpo entero; **— moon** luna llena *f*; **— name** nombre completo *m*; **—-scale** (model) de tamaño natural; (war) total; (investigation) exhaustivo; **—-service** de servicio completo; **—-size** (bed) de matrimonio; (model) de tamaño natural; **—-term** a término; **— time** tiempo completo *m*, de tiempo completo; **to pay in —** pagar el total de la deuda; ADV **you know — well** sabes perfectamente; **it hit him — in the chest** le pegó en pleno pecho

fully [fʊ́li] ADV (entirely) completamente, plenamente; (at least) al menos

fumble [fʌ́mbəł] N pérdida de balón *f*; VI (search for) buscar a tientas; (move clumsily) andar a tientas; (blunder) meter la pata; (football) perder el balón; **he —d his way into the living room** entró a tientas a la sala

fume [fjum] VI (be angry) rabiar; (emit vapors, smoke) emitir humo; N **—s** gases *m pl*, vapores *m pl*, tufo *m*

fumigate [fjúmɪget] VT fumigar

fun [fʌn] N diversión *f*; **for —** por gusto; **to make — of** burlarse de; **to have —** divertirse; ADJ divertido

function [fʌ́ŋkʃən] N función *f*; **— key** tecla de función *f*; VI (work) funcionar; (serve) oficiar

functional [fʌ́ŋkʃən!] ADJ funcional

fund [fʌnd] N (of money) fondo *m*; (of knowledge) acervo *m*; **—-raising** recaudación de fondos *f*; VT financiar

fundamental [fʌndəméntł] ADJ fundamental; N fundamento *m*

fundamentalism [fʌndəméntłɪzəm] N fundamentalismo *m*

fundamentally [fʌndəméntłi] ADV fundamentalmente

funding [fʌ́ndɪŋ] N financiamiento *m*,

financiación *f*

funeral [fjúnə-ɔł] N funeral *m*, entierro *m*, exequias *f pl*; **— director** director -ora de pompas fúnebres *mf*; **— home** casa de pompas fúnebres *f*, funeraria *f*; **— service** funeral *m*; **it's your —** te estás cavando tu propia tumba; ADJ (march, procession) fúnebre; (pyre) funerario; (expenses) de entierro

funereal [fjuníriəł] ADJ lúgubre

fungible [fʌ́nʤɪbəł] ADJ fungible

fungicide [fʌ́nʤɪsaɪd] N fungicida *m*

fungus [fʌ́ŋgəs] N hongo *m*

funky [fʌ́ŋki] ADJ (of music) funky; (strange) estrafalario, raro; (smelly) hediondo

funnel [fʌ́nł] N (for liquids) embudo *m*; (in a chimney) humero *m*; VT canalizar, encauzar

funny [fʌ́ni] ADJ (amusing) cómico, chistoso, gracioso; (strange) raro; **— farm** *fam* loquero *m*, loquería *f*; **that's not —** eso no tiene gracia; **don't get — with me** no te pases de listo; N **funnies** historietas *f pl*, tiras cómicas *f pl*; ADV raro

fur [fɝ] N (hair) pelo *m*; (coat) pelaje *m*; (hide) piel *f*; **— store** peletería *f*; VT forrar de piel

furious [fjúriəs] ADJ (person) furioso, sañudo, rabioso; (fight, storm) feroz; (activity) febril

furlough [fɝ́lo] N licencia *f*, permiso *m*; VT dar licencia

furnace [fɝ́nɪs] N (for heating) caldera *f*; (in industry) horno *m*

furnish [fɝ́nɪʃ] VT (put in furniture) amueblar; (equip) equipar; (provide) proporcionar, suministrar, facilitar

furniture [fɝ́nɪtʃə-] N muebles *m pl*, mobiliario *m*; **— store** mueblería *f*

furrow [fɝ́o] N surco *m*; VT (soil) arar; (face) fruncir

furry [fɝ́i] ADJ peludo

further [fɝ́ðə-] ADV **we want to go —** queremos ir más lejos; **I refuse to discuss this —** me niego a seguir discutiendo esto; (additionally) [lo que] es más; ADJ (more distant) más lejano; (additional) adicional; VT (promote) promover; ADV **— more** además

furthest [fɝ́ðɪst] ADJ [el] más lejano, [el] más remoto; ADV más lejos

furtive [fɝ́tɪv] ADJ (stealthy) furtivo; (shifty) sospechoso

fury [fjúri] N furia *f*, furor *m*, saña *f*

fuse [fjuz] N (in an explosive) mecha *f*; (in a circuit) fusible *m*; **he has a short —** tiene pocas pulgas; **he blew a —** estalló; VT (to join) fusionar; VI/VT (to merge) fusionar[se]; (to blend metals) fundir[se]

fuselage [fjúsəlɑʒ] N fuselaje *m*

fusion [fjúʒən] N fusión *f*

fuss [fʌs] N (bustle) alboroto *m*, bulla *f*; (uproar) escándalo *m*; (argument) discusión *f*; VI (worry about trifles) preocuparse por naderías; (complain) quejarse

fussiness [fʌ́sɪnɪs] N remilgo *m*, ñoñería *f*

fussy [fʌ́si] ADJ (particular) quisquilloso, remilgado; (whiny) quejica, cargoso

futile [fjúdł] ADJ inútil

futility [fjutíłɪti] N inutilidad *f*

future [fjútʃə-] N futuro *m*, porvenir *m*; **—s** futuros *m pl*; ADJ futuro

fuzz [fʌz] N (fluff) pelusa *f*; (fine hair) vello fino *m*; (on the lip) bozo *m*

fuzzy [fʌ́zi] ADJ (fluffy) cubierto de pelusa; (hairy) velloso; (blurred) borroso; (muddled) confuso

FYI [for your information] [éfwáɪáɪ] ADV para su información

Gg

gab [gæb] VI parlotear, charlar; N parloteo *m*, charla *f*; **gift of —** labia *f*, facundia *f*

gable [gébəł] N hastial *m*; **— roof** tejado de dos aguas *m*; **— window** buhardilla *f*

Gabon, Gabun [gəbɔ́n] N Gabón *m*

Gabonese [gæbənníz] ADJ & N gabonés -esa *mf*

gad [gæd] VI **to — about** callejear

gadget [gǽʤɪt] N coso *m*, chisme *m*

gaffe [gæf] N gaffe *f*, metedura de pata *f*

gag [gæg] VT (stop up mouth, silence) amordazar; (cause to choke) dar arcadas; VI tener arcadas; N (thing stuffed into mouth) mordaza *f*; (joke) gag *m*, burla *f*; **— order** orden de supresión de la libertad de expresión *f*

gaiety [géɪɪti] N alegría *f*; **gaieties** festejos *m pl*

gain [gen] VT ganar; VI **to — on** irse acercando a; VI/VT (watch) adelantar; N (profit, act of gaining) ganancia *f*; (in weight) aumento *m*

gainful [génfəł] ADJ remunerado

gait [get] N marcha *f*, paso *m*

galaxy [gǽləksi] N galaxia *f*

gale [geł] N ventarrón *m*, vendaval *m*; **—-force winds** vientos huracanados *m pl*; **— of laughter** risotada *f*

Galicia [gəlíʃə] N Galicia *f*

Galician [gəlíʃən] ADJ & N gallego -ga *mf*

gall [gɔł] N (bile, bitterness) hiel *f*; (impudence) morro *m*; (of a plant) agalla *f*; **— bladder** vesícula [biliar] *f*; **—nut** agalla *f*; **—stone** cálculo biliar *m*; VT (irritate) irritar

gallant[1] [gǽlənt] ADJ (brave) valiente; (attentive to women) galante

gallant[2] [gəlánt] N galán *m*

gallantry [gǽləntri] N (courage) valentía *f*, bizarría *f*; (chivalrous attention) galantería *f*

gallery [gǽləri] N (art, shopping) galería *f*;

(theater) paraíso *m*, gallinero *m*; (golf) público *m*

galley [gǽli] N (kitchen) cocina *f*; (boat) galera *f*; **— proof** galerada *f*

gallium [gǽliəm] N galio *m*

gallon [gǽlən] N galón [3.7853 liters] *m*

gallop [gǽləp] VI galopar; N galope *m*

gallows [gǽloz] N horca *f*, cadalso *m*

galore [gəlɔ́r] ADV en abundancia

galoshes [gəlɑ́ʃɪz] N chanclos *m pl*

galvanize [gǽlvənaɪz] VT (metals) galvanizar; (a crowd) electrizar

Gambia [gǽmbiə] N Gambia *f*

Gambian [gǽmbiən] ADJ & N gambiano -na *mf*

gamble [gǽmbəɫ] VI jugar; VT jugarse; **I'll — my whole fortune on this venture** voy a jugarme todo en este negocio; **to — away** perder en el juego; N (risk) riesgo *m*; (bet) apuesta *f*

gambler [gǽmblə-] N apostador -ora *mf*, tahúr *m*

gambling [gǽmblɪŋ] N juego [de apuestas] *m*

game [gém] N juego *m*; (match of chess, etc.) partida *f*; (sports match) partido *m*; (wild animals and their meat) caza *f*; **— console** consola de juegos *f*; **— plan** (deporte) plan de juego *m*; (negocios) estrategia *f*; **— point** punto de juego *m*; **— room** sala recreativa *f*; **— show** programa concurso *m*; **to be fair —** ser blanco legítimo; ADJ **I'm — for some tennis** me apunto para jugar al tenis; **he has a — knee** tiene la rodilla lisiada

gamut [gǽmət] N gama *f*

gander [gǽndə-] N ganso [macho] *m*; **to take a — at** echarle un vistazo a

gang [gǽŋ] N (of youths, thieves, etc.) pandilla *f*, gavilla *f*, banda *f*; (group of friends) grupo *m*; **—plank** pasarela *f*; **—way** (passage way) pasillo *m*; (on a ship) pasamano *m*; **—way!** ¡abran cancha! VI **to — up on** conspirar contra, conspirar en masa

gangrene [gǽŋgrin] N gangrena *f*; VI/VT gangrenar[se]

gangster [gǽŋstə-] N gángster *m*, maleante *m*

gap [gæp] N (breach) brecha *f*, hueco *m*; (of memory) laguna *f*; (of time) intervalo *m*; **she has a — between her teeth** tiene los dientes separados; VT espaciar [correctamente]

gape [gep] VI mirar boquiabierto

garage [gərɑ́ʒ] N (for parking) garaje *m*; (for repairing) taller mecánico *m*; **— sale** venta de garaje *f*; VT estacionar en un garaje

garb [gɑrb] N vestimenta *f*, atavío *m*; VT vestir, ataviar

garbage [gárbɪʤ] N basura *f*; **— can** bote de basura *m*; **— disposal unit** trituradora *f*; **—man** basurero *m*; **— truck** camión de la basura *m*; **what a load of —!** ¡qué montón de mentiras!

garden [gárdn̩] N jardín *m*; **— of Eden** jardín del Edén *m*; VI cultivar un jardín

gardener [gárdnə-] N jardinero -ra *mf*

gargle [gárgəɫ] VI hacer gárgaras; VT hacer gárgaras con; N (liquid) gargarismo *m*; (sound) gárgara *f*

garland [gárlənd] N guirnalda *f*

garlic [gárlɪk] N ajo *m*

garment [gármənt] N prenda *f*

garner [gárnə-] VT cosechar

garnet [gárnɪt] N granate *m*

garnish [gárnɪʃ] VT (decorate) decorar; (decorate food) aderezar, guarnecer; (withhold wages) retener; N (decoration) adorno *m*, decoración *f*

garret [gǽrɪt] N desván *m*, buhardilla *f*

garrison [gǽrɪsən] N guarnición *f*; VT guarnecer

garrulous [gǽrələs] ADJ locuaz, gárrulo

garter [gárdə-] N liga *f*; **— belt** liguero *m*, portaligas *m sg*; **— snake** culebra de jaretas *f*; VT sujetar con ligas

gas [gæs] N (vapor) gas *m*; (fuel) gasolina *f*; (flatulence) gases *m pl*; **— chamber** cámara de gas *f*; **— mask** máscara de gas *f*; **— pedal** acelerador *m*; **— station** gasolinera *f*; **to step on the —** acelerar; **we had a —** lo pasamos bomba; VT asfixiar con gas, matar en la cámara de gas; **to — up** llenar el tanque

gaseous [gǽ[əs] ADJ gaseoso

gash [gæʃ] N tajo *m*; VT hacer un tajo en

gasket [gǽskɪt] N junta [de culata] *f*

gasoline [gǽsəlɪn] N gasolina *f*, nafta *f*

gasp [gæsp] N (cry) grito sofocado *m*; (pant) jadeo *m*, boqueada *f*; VI (cry out) dar un grito sofocado; (in surprise) quedar boquiabierto; (for breath) jadear, boquear

gastric [gǽstrɪk] ADJ gástrico; **— ulcer** úlcera gástrica *f*

gastritis [gæstráɪdɪs] N gastritis *f*

gastroenteritis [gæstroɛntərə́ɪdɪs] N gastroenteritis *f*

gastrointestinal [gæstroɪntɛ́stɪn] ADJ gastrointestinal; **— tract** tubo digestivo *m*

gastronomy [gæstrɑ́nəmi] N gastronomía *f*

gate [get] N (to a garden) portón *m*; (to a city) puerta *f*; (at an airport) puerta de embarque *f*; **—way** (entrance, access) puerta [de entrada] *f*; (in computers) portal *m*

gather [gǽðə-] VT (bring together) reunir, allegar; (pick) recolectar; (deduce) deducir, colegir; (sew) fruncir; VI (come together) reunirse; (collect) juntarse; (contract into folds) fruncirse; **to — dust** juntar polvo/tierra; **to — speed** acelerar; N frunce *m*

gathering [gǽðə-ɪŋ] N (meeting) asamblea *f*; (social) tertulia *f*; (assemblage of people) concurrencia *f*, reunión *f*; (act of gathering fruit, etc.) recolección *f*

gaudy [gɔ́di] ADJ (of bright color) chillón; (ostentatious) llamativo

gauge [geʤ] VT (measure) medir; (estimate) estimar; (calibrate) calibrar; N (measurement standard) medida *f*; (caliber) calibre *m*; (measuring device) medidor *m*; (track width) entrevía *f*

gaunt [gɔnt] ADJ demacrado

gauntlet [gɔ́ntlɪt] N (glove) guante *m*; (mailed glove) guantelete *m*; **to throw down the —** retar, desafiar; **to run the —** sufrir acosos

gauze [gɔz] N gasa *f*

gave [gev] *see* give

gavel [gævəł] N martillo *m*

gawk [gɔk] VT mirar boquiabierto

gawky [gɔ́ki] ADJ torpe, desgarbado

gay [ge] ADJ (happy) alegre, festivo; (homosexual) gay, homosexual; N *fam* gay *m*, homosexual *m*

gaze [gez] VI mirar fijamente, contemplar; N mirada fija *f*

gazelle [gəzél] N gacela *f*

gazette [gəzét] N gaceta *f*

gear [gir] N (equipment) equipo *m*; (cog) rueda dentada *f*; (assembly of cogs) engranaje *m*; (transmission speed) marcha *f*, cambio *m*; (personal property) pertenencias *f pl*; **—box** caja de cambios *f*; **—shift lever** palanca de cambios *f*; **to be in —** estar engranado; **to change —s** cambiar de marcha, poner el cambio; **to put into —** engranar; **to put out of —** desengranar; VI **to — up** prepararse

gearing [gírɪŋ] N engranaje *m*

gecko [gékо] N geco *m*

geek [gik] N persona que tiene exagerada pasión por la informática *f*

Geiger counter [gáigə-káʊntə-] N contador Geiger *m*

gel [ʤɛł] VI/VT cuajar[se]

gelatin [ʤélətn̩] N gelatina *f*

gem [ʤɛm] N (precious stone) gema *f*; (valuable person) joya *f*; **—stone** piedra preciosa *f*

gender [ʤéndə-] N género *m*; **— discrimination** discriminación de género *f*; **— gap** diferencias entre los sexos *f pl*; **—-specific** propio de un solo sexo

gene [ʤin] N gen *m*; **— marker** marcador genético *m*; N **— pool** conjunto de genes de una población *m*; **— splicing** empalme genético *m*; **— therapy** terapia genética *f*

genealogy [ʤiniɑ́lə̌ʤi] N genealogía *f*

general [ʤénə-əł] ADJ & N general *mf*; **in —** por lo general; **— practitioner** médico -ca general *mf*

generality [ʤɛnərǽlɪDi] N generalidad *f*

generalization [ʤɛnə-əlɪzéʃən] N generalización *f*

generalize [ʤénə-əlaɪz] VI/VT generalizar

generally [ʤénə-əli] ADV generalmente

generate [ʤénəret] VT generar

generation [ʤɛnəréʃən] N generación *f*; **— gap** brecha generacional *f*, abismo generacional *m*

generator [ʤénərеdə-] N generador *m*

generic [ʤənérɪk] ADJ genérico; **— brand** marca genérica *f*

generosity [ʤɛnərɑ́sɪDi] N generosidad *f*, largueza *f*

generous [ʤénə-əs] ADJ generoso

genetic [ʤənéDɪk] ADJ genético; **— code** código genético *m*; **— engineering** ingeniería genética *f*; **— fingerprinting** identificación genética *f*; **— marker** marcador genético *m*; N **—s** genética *f*

genetically [ʤənéDɪkli] ADV **— modified** transgénico

genial [ʤínjəł] ADJ afable, de buen genio

genital [ʤénɪdł] ADJ genital

genius [ʤínjəs] N genio *m*

genocide [ʤénəsaɪd] N genocidio *m*

genome [ʤínom] N genoma *m*

genre [ʒɑ́nrə] N género *m*

genteel [ʤɛntíł] ADJ refinado

gentile [ʤéntaɪł] ADJ & N gentil *mf*

gentle [ʤéntł] ADJ (kindly) amable; (mild, slow, gradual) suave; (tame) manso

gentleman [ʤéntl̩mən] N caballero *m*

gentlemanly [ʤéntl̩mənli] ADJ caballeroso

gentleness [ʤéntl̩nɪs] N (kindness) amabilidad *f*; (mildness) suavidad *f*; (tameness) mansedumbre *f*

gently [ʤéntli] ADV (smoothly) suavemente; (tactfully) con mucho tacto

genuine [ʤénjuɪn] ADJ genuino

genus [ʤínəs] N género *m*

geocentric [ʤiosɛ́ntrɪk] ADJ geocéntrico

geographical [ʤiəgrǽfɪkəł] ADJ geográfico

geography [ʤiɑ́grəfi] N geografía *f*

geological [ʤiəlɑ́dʤɪkəł] ADJ geológico

geology [ʤiɑ́lə̌ʤi] N geología *f*

geometric [ʤiəmétrɪk] ADJ geométrico

geometry [ʤiɑ́mɪtri] N geometría *f*

geophysics [ʤiofízɪks] N geofísica *f*

geopolitical [ʤiopəlíDɪkəł] ADJ geopolítico

Georgia [ʤɔ́rʤə] N Georgia *f*

Georgian [ʤɔ́rʤən] ADJ & N georgiano -na *mf*

geostationary [ʤiostéʃənɛri] ADJ geoestacionario

geothermal [ʤiоθə́-məł] ADJ geotérmico

geranium [ʤəréniəm] N geranio *m*

geriatric [ʤɛriǽtrɪk] ADJ geriátrico; N **—s** geriatría *f*

germ [ʤɜ-m] N (microorganism) microbio *m*, germen *m*; (bud, embryo, rudiment) germen *m*; **— warfare** guerra biológica *f*

German [ʤɜ́-mən] ADJ & N alemán -na *mf*; **— measles** rubeola, rubéola *f*; **— shepherd** pastor alemán *m*

germane [ʤə-mén] ADJ pertinente, relacionado

Germanic [ʤə-mǽnɪk] ADJ germánico -ca

Germany [ʤɜ́-məni] N Alemania *f*

germinate [ʤɜ́ˑmənet] VI germinar; VT hacer germinar
gerund [ʤérənd] N gerundio *m*
gestate [ʤéstet] VI/VT gestar[se]
gestation [ʤestéʃən] N gestación *f*
gesticulate [ʤestíkjəlet] VI gesticular
gesture [ʤéstʃəˑ] N gesto *m*, ademán *m*; (token) muestra *f*; VI gesticular
gesundheit [gəzúnthaɪt] INTERJ (after a sneeze) ¡salud! *Sp* ¡Jesús!
get [get] VT (receive, earn) recibir; (obtain) obtener; (reach by phone) comunicarse con; (hear, understand) entender; (seize) agarrar; *Sp* coger; (prevail) conseguir, lograr; (affect) afectar; (catch disease) pescar; *Sp* coger; **to — across** comunicar; **to — ahead** prosperar; **to — along [with]** llevarse bien [con]; **to — angry** enojarse; **to — around** (skirt) esquivar, evitar; (go out) salir mucho; **to — away** escapar[se]; **to — away with** quedar impune; **to — back** (return) volver; (recover something) recuperar; **to — back at** vengarse de; **to be —ting on in years** ponerse viejo; **to — by** (go past) pasar; (survive) ir tirando; **to — dark** oscurecer; **to — down** (lower oneself) bajar; (depress) deprimir; (swallow) tragar; **to — down to business / brass tacks** ir al grano; **to — going** ponerse en marcha; **to — in** (enter) entrar; (arrive) llegar; (a vehicle) subir a; **to — it** captar, entender; **to — married** casarse; **to — nowhere** no llegar a ningún lado; **to — off** (dismount, get down) bajar; (not receive punishment) salir impune; (leave work) salir; **to — off on** enloquecerse por; **to — off someone's back** dejar de fastidiar; **to — old** envejecer; **to — on** montarse a; **to — out** (take out) sacar; (exit) salir; **to — over** (recuperate) recuperarse, sobreponerse a; (forgive) olvidar; **to — ready** preparar[se]; **to — rich** enriquecerse; **to — rid of** deshacerse de; **to — sick** enfermarse; **to — somewhere** tener resultado; **to — through** (survive an ordeal) sobrevivir; (reach by phone, be understood) comunicarse; (complete) lograr terminar; **to — to someone** afectar a alguien; **to — together** reunirse; **to — up** (arise) levantarse; (prepare) montar; **I got him to do it** conseguí/logré que lo hiciera; **I have got to do it** tengo que hacerlo; **we got our house painted** nos pintaron la casa; **he got a year in jail** le dieron un año de cárcel; **we — to stay up late in summer** en el verano nos dejan quedarnos despiertos hasta tarde; **that —s my goat** eso me fastidia; N **—away** (ĕscape) escape *m*; (vacation) escapada *f*; **—-together** reunión *f*; **—up** disfraz *m*, atuendo *m*; **from the —-go** desde el principio
geyser [gáɪzəˑ] N géiser *m*
Ghana [gánə] N Ghana *f*
Ghanaian [gániən] ADJ & N ghanés -esa *mf*
ghastly [gǽstli] ADJ (horrible) horrendo, espantoso; (cadaverous) cadavérico
ghetto [gétɒ] N gueto *m*
ghost [gost] N fantasma *m*; **— town** pueblo fantasma *m*; **—writer** colaborador -ora anónimo -ma *mf*; **not a — of a chance** ni la menor posibilidad
ghostly [góstli] ADJ fantasmagórico
ghoul [guł] N fantasma *m*
giant [ʤáɪənt] N & ADJ gigante -ta *mf*
gibberish [ʤíbəˑɪʃ] N jerigonza *f*
gibbon [gíbən] N gibón *m*
Gibraltar [ʤɪbrɔ́łtəˑ] N Gibraltar *m*
Gibraltarian [ʤɪbrɔłtériən] ADJ & N gibraltareño -ña *mf*
giddy [gíɒi] ADJ (dizzy) mareado; (of heights) vertigoso; (of speed) vertiginoso
gift [gɪft] N (thing given, act of giving) regalo *m*, presente *m*; (special ability) don *m*; **— certificate** vale por un regalo *m*; **— tax** impuesto sobre las donaciones *m*; **—-wrap** envolver para regalo; VT regalar
gifted [gíftɪd] ADJ (artist) talentoso; (child) superdotado
gigabyte [gígəbaɪt] N gigabyte *m*
gigahertz [gígəhɜ̃ts] N gigahercio *m*
gigantic [ʤaɪgǽntɪk] ADJ gigantesco, gigante
giggle [gígəł] VI reír tontamente; N risita tonta *f*
gild [gɪłd] VT dorar
gill [gɪł] N agalla *f*
gilt [gɪłt] ADJ & N dorado *m*
gimmick [gímɪk] N treta *f*, estratagema *f*
gin [ʤɪn] N (liquor) ginebra *f*; **— rummy** gin rummy *m*
ginger [ʤíndʒəˑ] N jengibre *m*; **— ale** ginger ale *m*; **—bread** pan de jengibre *m*
gingham [gíŋəm] N guingán *m*
gingivitis [ʤɪnʤəváɪDɪs] N gingivitis *f*
giraffe [ʤərǽf] N jirafa *f*
gird [gɜ̃d] VT ceñir; **to — oneself** prepararse
girder [gɜ̃ˑdəˑ] N viga *f*
girdle [gɜ̃ˑdł] N faja *f*; VT rodear
girl [gɜ̃ˑł] N (female child) niña *f*; (young female) muchacha *f*, joven *f*, chica *f*; (servant) muchacha *f*, chacha *f*; **—friend** novia *f*
girlhood [gɜ̃ˑłhʊd] N niñez *f*
girlish [gɜ̃ˑłɪʃ] ADJ de niña
girth [gɜ̃ˑθ] N (of things) circunferencia *f*; (of persons) contorno *m*; (of horses) cincha *f*; VT cinchar
gist [ʤɪst] N esencia *f*, lo esencial
GI [gastrointestinal] tract [ʤíáɪ] N tubo digestivo *m*
give [gɪv] VT dar; (a gift) regalar; (a party) organizar; (a name) poner; (a donation) donar; **I don't — a hoot** me importa un

comino; VI dar; (yield) ceder; (break) romperse; **to — away** (a gift) regalar, donar; (the bride) entregar; (a secret) revelar; **to — back** devolver; **to — in** (acknowledge defeat) rendirse; **to — off** emitir, despedir, desprender; **to — out** (announce) anunciar; (distribute) repartir; (become exhausted) rendirse; (run out) acabarse; **to — over** entregar; **to — up** (surrender) darse por vencido; (stop) dejar [de]; **we'll work on this two years, — or take a month** vamos a trabajar en esto dos años, un mes más, un mes menos; N elasticidad *f*; **— and take** toma y daca *m*

given [gívən] ADJ (stated, fixed) dado; (bestowed) regalado; **— name** nombre de pila *m*; **— that she's not here** dado que ella no está; **— to** propenso a; N premisa *f*

given [gívən] *see* give

giver [gívɚ] N dador -ora *mf*, donador -ora *mf*

gizmo [gízmo] N coso *m*, chisme *m*

glacial [gléʃəl] ADJ glacial

glacier [gléʃɚ] N glaciar *m*

glad [glæd] ADJ contento; **I'm — to see you** me alegro de verte; **I'd be — to help** sería un placer ayudarte

ladden [glǽdn̩] VT alegrar, regocijar, alborozar

gladiator [glǽdiedɚ] N gladiador *m*

glamorous [glǽmərəs] ADJ glamoroso, encantador

glamour [glǽmɚ] N (charm) glamour *f*, encanto *m*; (excitement) atractivo *m*

glance [glæns] VI echar un vistazo; **to — off** rebotar con efecto; N (look) vistazo *m*; (bounce) rebote oblicuo *m*

gland [glænd] N glándula *f*

glandular [glǽndʒələ] ADJ glandular

glare [glɛr] N (bright light) relumbre *m*; (stare) mirada furiosa *f*; VI (shine) relumbrar; (stare fiercely) lanzar una mirada hostil

glaring [glɛ́rɪŋ] ADJ (blinding) deslumbrante; (obvious) evidente; (hostile) hostil

glass [glæs] N (substance) vidrio *m*; (window pane) vidrio *m*, cristal *m*; (tumbler) vaso [de vidrio] *m*; (mirror) espejo *m*; (glassware) cristalería *f*; (magnifier) lupa *f*; **—blowing** soplado de vidrio *m*; **— ceiling** techo de cristal *m*; **— cutter** cortavidrio *m*; **—es** anteojos *m pl*, lentes *m pl*, gafas *f pl*; **— eye** ojo de vidrio *m*; **—maker** vidriero -ra *mf*; **—ware** cristalería *f*

glassy [glǽsi] ADJ vidrioso

glaucoma [glɔkómə] N glaucoma *m*

glaze [glez] VT (windows) poner vidrios a; (ceramics) vidriar; (food) glasear; (wood) barnizar; VI vidriarse; N (pottery) vidriado *m*, barniz *m*; (food) glaseado *m*

glazier [gléʒɚ] N vidriero -ra *mf*

gleam [glim] N reflejo *m*, brillo *m*; **a — of hope** un rayo de esperanza; VI brillar, relucir

glean [glin] VT (grain) espigar; (information) extraer, deducir

glee [gli] N regocijo *m*, júbilo *m*; **— club** coro *m*

glib [glɪb] ADJ (fluent) de mucha labia; (superficial) simplista, superficial

glide [glaɪd] VI (slide) deslizarse; (fly) planear; N (sliding movement) deslizamiento *m*; (flight) planeo *m*

glider [gláɪdɚ] N planeador *m*

glimmer [glímɚ] N luz trémula *f*; **a — of hope** un destello de esperanza; **the — of an idea** el atisbo de una idea; VI guiñar, emitir una luz trémula

glimpse [glɪmps] N (look) ojeada *f*, vistazo *m*; (hint) atisbo *m*; VT ojear

glint [glɪnt] N destello *m*; VI destellar

listen [glísən] VI brillar, relucir

glitch [glɪtʃ] N fallo *m*, problema técnico *m*

glitter [glítɚ] VI destellar; N (light) destello *m*; (showiness) brillo *m*; (sparkling powder) brillantina *f*

gloat [glot] VI regodearse; N regodeo *m*

glob [glɑb] N pegote *m*

global [glóbəl] ADJ global, mundial; **— backup** respaldo global *m*; **— positioning system** sistema mundial de posicionamiento *m*; **— warming** calentamiento global *m*

globalization [globəlɪzéʃən] N globalización *f*

globe [glob] N globo *m*; (map of the Earth) globo terráqueo *m*

globule [glábjuł] N glóbulo *m*

globulin [glábjəlɪn] N globulina *f*

gloom [glum] N (darkness) oscuridad *f*; (melancholy) melancolía *f*, tristeza *f*

gloomy [glúmi] ADJ (dark, depressing) sombrío, lúgubre, tenebroso; (melancholic) melancólico, deprimido

glorify [glɔ́rəfaɪ] VT glorificar

glorious [glɔ́riəs] ADJ (wonderful) magnífico, excelente; (related to glory) glorioso

glory [glɔ́ri] N gloria *f*; VI **to — in** regocijarse con

gloss [glɔs] N (shine, cosmetic) brillo *m*; (marginal note) glosa *f*; (in a dictionary) acepción *f*; VT (polish) lustrar, dar brillo a; (explain) glosar; **to — over** disfrazar, encubrir

glossary [glɔ́səri] N glosario *m*

glossy [glɔ́si] ADJ lustroso; (paper) glaseado

glottal [glɑdl̩] ADJ (cancer) glótico; (phonetic) glotal

glottis [glɑ́dɪs] N glotis *f*

glove [glʌv] N guante *m*; (baseball) guante *m*, manopla *f*; **— compartment** guantera *f*

glow [glo] N incandescencia *f*; (of cheeks) rubor *m*; (of emotion) calor *m*; VI resplandecer; (of metal) estar al rojo vivo; (of cheeks) ruborizarse; **to — with health** estar rebosante de salud; **—worm** luciérnaga *f*

glowing [glóɪŋ] ADJ (with light) incandescente; (colors) vivo; (with health) rebosante; (report) favorable
glucose [glúkos] N glucosa *f*
glue [glu] N cola *f*, pegamento *m*; VT (put glue on) engomar; (stick together) pegar; (stick wood together) encolar; **she's —d to the television** está pegada al televisor
glum [glʌm] ADJ tristón
glut [glʌt] VI/VT (with food) hartar[se]; VT (with products) saturar; N superabundancia *f*
gluten [glútn̩] N gluten *m*
glutton [glátn̩] N glotón -ona *mf*
gluttonous [gláthəs] ADJ glotón
gluttony [gláthɪ] N glotonería *f*, gula *f*
glycerin [glísə-ɪn] N glicerina *f*
gnarled [nɑrld] ADJ (knotty) nudoso, sarmentoso; (twisted) retorcido
gnash [næʃ] VI/VT rechinar
gnat [næt] N jején *m*
gnaw [nɔ] VI/VT (bite, corrode) roer; (torment) remorder; **to — a hole** hacer un agujero a mordiscos
GNP [gross national product] [ʤíénpí] N PNB *m*
gnu [nu] N ñu *m*
go [go] VI (move) ir; (function) andar, marchar; **—ing price** precio vigente *m*; **to — against** oponerse a; **to — ahead** seguir adelante; **to — all out** dar todo de sí; **to — along** conformarse; **to — around** (circumvent) dar la vuelta a; (circulate) circular; (be sufficient) alcanzar; **to — around with** andar con; **to — away** irse; **to — back** volver; **to — back on one's word** faltar a la palabra; **to — beyond** traspasar; **to — by** (pass) pasar; (be guided by) guiarse por; **to — by another name** usar otro nombre; **to — crazy** enloquecerse; **to — down** (descend) bajar; (fall) caer, estrellarse; (lose) perder; (be accepted) gustar; **to — for it** atreverse; **— for it!** ¡adelante! ¡atrévete! **to — in with** participar; **to — it alone** tirarse solo; **to — off** (explode) estallar; (happen) suceder; (leave) irse; **to — off on** regañar; **to — on** (happen) pasar; (continue) seguir; **to — out** (extinguish) apagarse; (socialize) salir; **to — over** (review) repasar, revisar; (read) leer; (cross) cruzar; **to — through** (suffer) sufrir; (examine) examinar; (be approved) ser aprobado; (spend) gastar; **to — through with** llevar a cabo; **to — to sleep** dormirse; **to — under** (go bankrupt) quebrar; (sink) hundirse; **to — up** (building) levantarse; (prices) subir; **pizza to —** pizza para llevar; **to let —** soltar[se]; **the car went for a good price** el coche se vendió a un buen precio; **he's smart, as dogs —** para ser perro, es inteligente; **that old couch has got to —** hay que deshacerse de ese sofá viejo; **cows — "moo"** las vacas hacen "mu"; **they — straight for the pizza** se van derechito a la pizza; **she's —ing to buy a house** va a comprar una casa; **anything —es** todo vale; **what I say —es** lo que yo digo, vale; **don't — to any trouble** no te molestes; **— figure!** ¡vaya a saber uno! **I've got to — [to the bathroom]** tengo que ir [al baño]; N (energy) energía *f*; (attempt) intento *m*; **—-ahead** visto bueno *m*; **—-between** intermediario -ria *mf*; **—-cart** kart *m*; **in one —** de una vez; **on the —** a las corridas; **at the first —** de primera; **they made a — of it** tuvieron éxito; **it's a —** ¡trato hecho! **from the word —** desde el vamos
goad [god] N aguijada *f*; VT aguijonear
goal [gol] N (objective) meta *f*; (score) gol *m*; **— area** área de penales *f*; **—keeper** portero -ra *mf*, arquero -ra *mf*; **— kick** saque de meta *m*, saque de puerta *m*; **— line** línea de meta *f*; **— post** palo *m*, poste *m*
goalie [góli] N guardameta *mf*
goat [got] N cabra *f*; **—herd** cabrero -ra *mf*; **he gets my —** me saca de quicio
goatee [goti] N perilla *f*
gobble [gábəl] VI/VT (devour) engullir; VI (turkey) gluglutear; **to — up** engullir
gobbledygook [gábəldiguk] N jerigonza *f*
gobbler [gáblə-] N pavo *m*
goblet [gáblɪt] N copa *f*
goblin [gáblɪn] N duende *m*
god, God [gɑd] N dios *m*, Dios *m*; **— bless you!** (blessing) ¡que Dios te bendiga! (after a sneeze) ¡salud! ¡Jesús! **—child** ahijado -da *mf*; **—father** padrino *m*; **—forsaken** de mala muerte; **—-given** divino; **—mother** madrina *f*; **—send** bendición *f*; **— willing** si Dios quiere; **by —** por Dios; **my —!** ¡Dios mío!
goddess [gádɪs] N diosa *f*
godless [gádlɪs] ADJ impío
godly [gádli] ADJ piadoso
goggles [gágəlz] N gafas protectoras *f pl*, antiparras *f pl*
going [góɪŋ] ADJ que marcha bien; **—s-on** tejemanejes *m pl*
goiter [gɔɪdə-] N bocio *m*
gold [gold] N oro *m*; **— bullion** oro en lingotes *m*; **— digger** mujer cazafortunas *f*; **—finch** jilguero *m*; **—fish** pez dorado *m*; **— medal** medalla de oro *f*; **—smith** orfebre *m*; **a heart of —** un corazón de oro
golden [góldən] ADJ (made of gold) de oro, áureo; (of gold color) dorado; **— eagle** águila dorada *f*; **— parachute** paracaídas dorado *m sg*; **— retriever** golden retriever *m*; **— rule** regla de oro *f*
golf [gɑlf] N golf *m*; **— bag** bolsa de golf *f*; **— ball** pelota de golf *f*; **— cart** coche/cochecito

de golf *m*; **— club** (stick) palo de golf *m*; (place) club de golf *m*; **— course** campo de golf *m*

gonad [gónæd] N gónada *f*

gondola [gándələ] N (boat, basket under a balloon) góndola *f*; (cable car) cabina *f*

gone [gɔn] ADJ **my computer is —** desapareció mi computadora; **the candy is all —** se acabaron los dulces

gone [gɔn] *see* go

gong [guŋ] N batintín *m*, gong *m*

gonorrhea [gɑnəríə] N gonorrea *f*

good [gʊd] ADJ bueno; (valid) válido; **— faith** buena fe *f*; **—-for-nothing** inútil, zanguango; **— for two burritos** vale por dos burritos; **—-looking** guapo, apuesto; **—-natured** apacible, bonachón, de buen genio; **—will** buena voluntad *f*; **for —** para siempre; **a — hour** una hora larga; **a — many** muchos; **to have a — time** divertirse; **to make —** cumplir; **to smell —** oler bien; N (moral act, benefit) bien *m*; **for your own —** por tu propio bien; INTERJ ¡bien! **— afternoon** buenas tardes; **—bye** adiós; **— day** buenos días; **— evening** buenas noches; **— morning** buenos días; **— night** buenas noches; N **—s** mercancías *f pl*; **—s and services** bienes y servicios *m pl*; **to deliver the —s** cumplir lo prometido

goodly [gúdli] ADJ (considerable) considerable; (of fine appearance) de buen aspecto

goodness [gʊ́dnɪs] N bondad *f*; (of food) calidad *f*; INTERJ ¡Dios mío!

goody [gʊ́di] N golosina *f*; **—-—** santurrón -ona *mf*; INTERJ ¡qué bien!

goof [guf] VI pifiar; **to — off** perder el tiempo; **to — up** pifiarla; N pifia *f*

goofy [gúfi] ADJ (person) bobalicón; (idea) tonto

goose [gus] N (bird, fool) ganso -sa *mf*; **—berry** (berry) grosella espinosa *f*; (bush) grosellero *m*; **—bumps** carne de gallina *f*; **— egg** cero *m*; VT **to — someone** sorprender a alguien tocándole entre las nalgas

GOP [Grand Old Party] [ʤíópí] N Partido Republicano *m*

gopher [gófɚ] N ardilla de tierra *f*

gore [gɔr] N sangre derramada *f*; VT cornear

gorge [gɔrʤ] N (body part) garganta *f*; (ravine) garganta *f*, tajo *m*; VI **to — one's self [on]** atracarse [de], darse un atracón [de]

gorgeous [gɔ́rʤəs] ADJ (woman, outfit) precioso; (weather) espléndido

gorilla [gərílə] N gorila *mf*; (thug) matón *m*

gory [gɔ́ri] ADJ (of a battle) sangriento; (of a surface) ensangrentado

gospel [gáspəl] N evangelio *m*; (music) gospel *m*; **— truth** pura verdad *f*

gossip [gásəp] N (rumor) chismorreo *m*, murmuración *f*, habladurías *f pl*; (person) chismoso -sa *mf*; (woman) comadre *f*; **a piece of —** un chisme *m*; VI chismear, murmurar

gossipy [gásəpi] ADJ chismoso, lenguaraz

got [gɑt] *see* get

Gothic [gáθɪk] ADJ gótico; N (language) gótico *m*, godo *m*; (style) estilo gótico *m*

gotten [gɑtn] *see* get

gouge [gaʊʤ] N gubia *f*; VT (scoop) sacar con gubia; (overcharge) cobrar de más; **to — someone's eyes out** arrancarle los ojos a alguien

gourd [gɔrd] N calabaza *f*

gourmet [gɔrmé] N & ADJ gourmet *mf*; **— cheese** queso fino *m*

gout [gaʊt] N gota *f*

govern [gávɚn] VI/VT gobernar, regir; VT (in grammar) regir

governability [gʌvɚnəbílɪɪ] N gobernabilidad *f*

governess [gávɚnɪs] N institutriz *f*

governing [gávɚnɪŋ] N gobernación *f*; **— principle** principio rector *m*

government [gávɚnmənt] N gobierno *m*; (in grammar) rección *f*; **— agency** agencia gubernamental *f*; **—-backed** respaldado por el gobierno

governmental [gʌvɚnmɛ́ntl] ADJ gubernamental, gubernativo

governor [gávɚnɚ] N (leader) gobernador -ora *mf*; (of an engine) regulador *m*

gown [gaʊn] N (woman's dress) vestido *m*; (for sleeping) camisón *m*; (in hospital) bata *f*; (for graduation) toga *f*

grab [græb] VT agarrar, prender; **how does that idea — you?** ¿qué te parece esa idea? VI **to — at** tratar de agarrar; N agarrón *m*; **up for —s** a la rebatiña

grace [gres] N gracia *f*; (of movement) garbo *m*; (of expression) donaire *m*; **to say —** dar la oración; **to be in the good —s of someone** gozar del favor de alguien, disfrutar de la gracia de alguien; VT (adorn) adornar; (honor) honrar, agraciar

graceful [grésfəł] ADJ (of movement) grácil, garboso; (of behavior) donoso

gracefulness [grésfəłnɪs] N gracia *f*, donaire *m*

gracious [gréjəs] ADJ (kind) gentil, cortés; (elegant) elegante; (merciful) misericordioso; **—!** ¡válgame Dios!

graciousness [gréjəsnɪs] N gentileza *f*

gradation [gredéʃən] N gradación *f*

grade [gred] N (rank) grado *m*; (category) calidad *f*; (year in school) año *m*, curso *m*; (marks) nota *f*, calificación *f*; (slope) declive *m*; **to make the —** alcanzar el nivel deseado; **— point average** promedio de notas *m*; VT (classify) clasificar; (assign grades) calificar, corregir; (level) nivelar

gradual [grǽʤuəł] ADJ gradual

graduate[1] [grǽʤuɪt] N (advanced student)

estudiante de posgrado *mf*; (degree-holder) graduado -da *mf*, egresado -da *mf*; ADJ de posgrado; **— school** programa de posgrado *m*

graduate[2] [grǽʤuet] VI graduarse, titularse; VT (confer a degree) dar un diploma a; (mark a scale) graduar

graduation [grǽʤuéʃən] N graduación *f*

graffiti [grəfíDi] N grafiti *m*, pintada *f*

graft [græft] N (of plant, tissue) injerto *m*; (corruption) concusión *f*, corrupción *f*; VI/VT injertar[se]

grain [gren] N (cereal, seed) grano *m*, mies *f*; (photographic texture) grano *m*; (of gold) pepita *f*; (of wood, meat, stone) veta *f*; (texture) textura *f*; (small amount) pizca *f*; **against the —** a/al redopelo, a contrapelo

gram [græm] N gramo *m*

grammar [grǽmə-] N gramática *f*

grammatical [grəmǽDɪkəł] ADJ gramatical

granary [grǽnəri] N granero *m*, troje *m*

grand [grænd] ADJ (splendid) grandioso, espléndido; (lofty) elevado; (impressive) impresionante; **—child** nieto -ta *mf*; **—children** nietos *m pl*; **—daughter** nieta *f*; **—father** abuelo *m*; **—fathered** eximido por la cláusula del abuelo; **— jury** jurado de acusación *m*; **—mother** abuela *f*; **—ma** abuelita *f*; **—pa** abuelito *m*; **—parent** abuelo *m*; **—parents** abuelos *m pl*; **— piano** piano de cola *m*; **—son** nieto *m*; **—stand** tribuna *f*; **a — old man** un gran señor; **the — total** el total

grandeur [grǽnʤə-] N grandiosidad *f*

grandiose [grǽndios] ADJ (complex) complejo; (of speech) grandilocuente, rimbombante; (imposing) grandioso

granite [grǽnɪt] N granito *m*

grant [grænt] VT (give) conceder, otorgar, dispensar; (accept) admitir; (transfer) ceder; **to take for —ed** (an assumption) dar por sentado; (a person) no valorar; N (something granted) concesión *f*; (act of granting) concesión *f*, otorgamiento *m*; (subsidy, e.g., for scientists) subvención *f*

granular [grǽnjələ-] ADJ granuloso

granulate [grǽnjəlet] VI/VT granular[se]

grape [grep] N uva *f*; **—fruit** pomelo *m*, toronja *f*; **—vine** vid *f*; (ornamental) parra *f*; **I heard it through the —vine** me lo contó un pajarito

graph [græf] N (curve) gráfica *f*; **— paper** papel cuadriculado *m*; VT grafiar

graphic [gráfɪk] ADJ gráfico; **— design** diseño gráfico *m*; N gráfico *m*; **—s** gráfica *f*; **—s card** tarjeta gráfica *f*

graphite [gráfaɪt] N grafito *m*

grapple [grǽpəł] VI/VT (hold) aferrar; (struggle) luchar, lidiar

grasp [græsp] VT (seize) agarrar, asir, aferrar; (understand) comprender; VI **to — at/for** tratar de agarrar; N (hold) agarre *m*, asidero *m*; (comprehension) comprensión *f*; **within one's —** al alcance; **to have a good — of a subject** dominar una materia

grass [græs] N (plant) hierba *f*; (lawn) césped *m*; (pasture) pasto *m*; (in tennis) césped *m*, hierba *f*; **—hopper** saltamontes *m sg*, saltón *m*; **—land** praderа *f*, pastizal *m*; **— roots** las bases *f pl*

grassy [grǽsi] ADJ herboso

grate [gret] N (of a fireplace) parrilla *f*; (partition, guard) reja *f*, verja *f*; VT (install a grate) enrejar; (mince) rallar; (rub teeth together) crujir, rechinar; VI **to — on** rechinar

grateful [grétfəł] ADJ agradecido

grater [gréDə-] N rallador *m*

gratification [grædəfɪkéʃən] N gratificación *f*

gratify [grǽdəfaɪ] VT complacer, gratificar

grating [gréDɪɪŋ] N reja *f*, enrejado *m*, rejilla *f*; ADJ (discordant) rechinante; (irritating) irritante

gratitude [grǽDɪtud] N gratitud *f*

gratuitous [grətúɪDəs] ADJ gratuito

gratuity [grətúɪDi] N propina *f*

grave [grev] ADJ grave; N fosa *f*, sepultura *f*; **—digger** sepulturero *m*; **—stone** lápida *f*; **—yard** cementerio *m*; **—yard shift** turno de la noche *m*; **to have one foot in the —** *fam* estar por reventar

gravel [grǽvəł] N grava *f*; VT cubrir con grava

gravitation [grævɪtéʃən] N gravitación *f*

gravitational [grævɪtéʃənł] ADJ gravitatorio

gravity [grǽvɪDi] N gravedad *f* (also seriousness)

gravy [grévi] N jugo de carne *m*; **the rest is —** el resto es fácil

gray [gre] ADJ gris; (hair) canoso; (horse) rucio; **— area** zona gris *f*; **—-haired** cano, canoso; **— matter** materia gris *f*; N gris *m*; VI/VT agrisar; (hair) encanecer

grayish [gréɪʃ] ADJ grisáceo

graze [grez] VI/VT (feed) pacer, pastar, apacentar; (brush) rozar; N roce *m*

grease [gris] N grasa *f*; VT engrasar; **to — someone's palm** untarle la mano a alguien, engrasar a alguien

greasy [grísi, grízi] ADJ (covered with grease) grasiento; (impregnated with grease) grasoso; (hair) graso

great [gret] ADJ (large, numerous) grande; (good, excellent, considerable) gran; **—-aunt** tía abuela *f*; **—-grandchild** bisnieto -ta *mf*; **—-grandfather** bisabuelo *m*; **—-grandmother** bisabuela *f*; **—-—-grandchild** tataranieto -ta *mf*; **a — tree blocked the path** un árbol grande bloqueaba el camino; **she's a — friend** es una gran amiga; **a — while** un largo rato;

she's — at tennis juega muy bien al tenis; **a — deal of** mucho; ADV muy bien, excelente; **she did —** le fue muy bien; N **the —s** los/las grandes *mf*; **they occur in —er numbers** son más numerosos; **he's the —est** es el mejor; INTERJ ¡qué bien!

greatly [grétli] ADV **it's — improved** lo han mejorado mucho / está mucho mejor; **we're — interested** estamos muy interesados

greatness [grétnɪs] N grandeza *f*

Greece [gris] N Grecia *f*

greed [grid] N codicia *f*

greedy [gríDɪ] ADJ (covetous) codicioso; (voracious) voraz; (eager) ávido

Greek [grik] ADJ & N griego -ga *mf*; **that's — to me** para mí es chino

green [grin] ADJ (green in color, verdant, unripe, inexperienced, nauseated, environmentally conscious) verde; **—back** dólar *m*; **— bean** *Sp* judía verde *f*; *Mex* ejote *m*; *RP* chaucha *f*; *Carib* habichuela; **— card** tarjeta verde *f*; **—horn** novato -ta *mf*; **—house** invernadero *m*; **—house effect** efecto invernadero *m*; **— light** luz verde *f*; **— pepper** pimiento verde *m*; N (color) verde *m*; (lawn) césped *m*; (pasture) prado *m*; (in golf) green *m*; (commons) ejido *m*; **—s** verduras de hoja verde *f pl*

greenish [gríniʃ] ADJ verdoso

greenness [grínnɪs] N verdor *m*

greet [grit] VT (say hello) saludar; (welcome) dar la bienvenida; (receive) recibir

greeting [gríDɪŋ] N saludo *m*; **— card** tarjeta de felicitación *f*; **—s!** ¡saludos!

gregarious [grigɛ́riəs] ADJ (person) sociable; (animal) gregario

gremlin [grémlɪn] N duende *m*

Grenada [grənédə] N Granada *f*

grenade [grənéd] N granada *f*

Grenadian [grənédiən] ADJ & N granadino -na *mf*

grew [gru] *see* grow

greyhound [gréhaʊnd] N galgo *m*

griddle [gríDl] N plancha *f*

gridlock [gríDlɑk] N paralización *f*; VI paralizarse

grief [grif] N congoja *f*, pesar *m*, pesadumbre *f*; **to come to —** sufrir una desgracia; **to give someone —** meterse con alguien, jorobar a alguien; **good —!** ¡caramba! ADJ **—-stricken** acongojado, desconsolado

grievance [grívəns] N (complaint) queja *f*; (cause for complaint) motivo de queja *m*

grieve [griv] VI estar de duelo; **to — for/over** llorar, lamentar [la muerte de alguien]; **he's grieving over the loss of his dog** lamenta la muerte de su perro; VT **that —s me** eso me apena

grieved [grivd] ADJ apenado

grievous [grívəs] ADJ (painful) doloroso, penoso; (atrocious) grave, atroz; (sorrowful) dolido

grill [grɪł] N (metal grid, restaurant fixture) parrilla *f*; (food) parrillada *f*; VI/VT asar a la parrilla; (interrogate) interrogar

grille [grɪł] N parrilla *f*

grim [grɪm] ADJ (news, situation) desalentador; (war) cruento; (joke) macabro

grimace [grímɪs] N mueca *f*, mohín *m*; VI hacer muecas

grime [graɪm] N mugre *f*, suciedad *f*

grimy [gráimi] ADJ mugriento, sucio; **to make —** percudir; **to get —** percudirse

grin [grɪn] VI sonreír; N sonrisa *f*; **wipe that — off your face** deja de reírte

grind [graɪnd] VI/VT (mill finely) moler; (mill coarsely) triturar; (make shiny) pulir; (rub harshly) rechinar; (study hard) estudiar mucho; *Sp* empollar; **to — to a halt** pararse con un chirrido; N (drudgery) trabajo pesado *m*; (overzealous student) empollón -ona *mf*; **—stone** muela *f*; **the daily —** la lucha diaria; **to keep one's nose to the —stone** matarse trabajando/estudiando

grinder [gráində-] N (for coffee, pepper) molinillo *m*; (for meat) picadora *f*; (for sharpening tools) afilador *m*

grip [grɪp] N (hold) agarre *m*; (control) control *m*; (handle) mango *m*; (on a baseball bat, golf club) agarre *m*, empuñadura *f*; **he had a firm — on the tool** tenía bien agarrada la herramienta; **get a — on yourself** contrólate, cálmate; VT (seize) agarrar, asir; (take hold, interest) atrapar

gripe [graɪp] VI quejarse, rezongar, renegar; N queja *f*

grisly [grízli] ADJ cruento, espantoso

gristle [grísəł] N cartílago *m*

grit [grɪt] N (sand) arena *f*; (pluck) firmeza *f*; **—s** sémola de maíz *f*; VT **to — one's teeth** apretar los dientes

gritty [gríDi] ADJ (sandy) arenoso; (plucky) resuelto

grizzly [grízli] ADJ (grayish) grisáceo; **— bear** oso pardo *m*

groan [gron] N quejido *m*, gemido *m*; VI quejarse, gemir; (creak) crujir

grocer [grósə-] N tendero -ra *mf*; *Mex* abarrotero -ra *mf*; *Carib* bodeguero -ra *mf*; *RP* almacenero -ra *mf*

grocery [grósəri] N tienda de comestibles *f*; *Mex* tienda de abarrotes *f*; *Carib* bodega *f*; *RP* almacén *m*; **groceries** comestibles *m pl*

groin [grɔɪn] N ingle *f*

groom [grum] N (in a wedding) novio *m*; (in a stable) mozo de cuadra *m*, caballerizo *m*; VT (a horse) almohazar; (prepare for a position) preparar; **to — oneself** arreglarse; **well-**

—**ed** bien arreglado

groove [gruv] N (narrow cut) estría *f*, ranura *f*; (on a record, road) surco *m*; (routine) rutina *f*; VT estriar, acanalar

grope [grop] VI (feel one's way) andar a tientas; (search) buscar a tientas; N toqueteo *m*

gross [gros] ADJ (before deductions) bruto; (flagrant) flagrante; (indecent) grosero; (overall) general; (disgusting) asqueroso; — **domestic product** producto interno bruto *m*; — **income** ingreso bruto *m*; — **pay** salario bruto *m*; N gruesa *f*; VT recaudar en bruto; **to** — **out** dar asco, asquear

grotesque [grotésk] ADJ grotesco

grotto [gráɒo] N gruta *f*

grouch [graʊtʃ] N cascarrabias *mf sg*, refunfuñón -ona *mf*, rezongón -ona *mf*; VI refunfuñar

grouchy [gráʊtʃi] ADJ cascarrabias, refunfuñón

ground [graʊnd] N (land, electrical cable) tierra *f*; (soil) suelo *m*; (basis) fundamento *m*; — **ball** (in baseball) roletazo *m*; — **floor** planta baja *f*; —**hog** marmota *f*; —**s** (reason) motivo *m*; (dregs) borra *f*, poso *m*; (tract of land) terreno *m*; **to gain/lose** — ganar/perder terreno; **to stand one's** — ponerse firme; **from the** — **up** de piso a techo; VT (a wire) conectar a tierra; (a ship) hacer encallar; (punish) poner en penitencia; **the 747 was** —**ed** se prohibió volar en el 747

ground [graʊnd] *see* grind

groundless [gráʊndlɪs] ADJ infundado

group [grup] N grupo *m*; — **discount** descuento por grupo *m*; — **therapy** terapia de grupo *f*; VI/VT agrupar[se]

grouper [grúpɚ] N mero *m*

groupie [grúpi] N admiradora *f*

grouping [grúpɪŋ] N agrupamiento *m*

grove [grov] N arboleda *f*, plantío *m*; **orange** — naranjal *m*

grovel [grávəł] VI arrastrarse, humillarse

grow [gro] VI (naturally increase in size) crecer; (increase) aumentar, acrecentarse; (expand) desarrollarse; VT (crops) cultivar; (beard) dejarse crecer; **to** — **old** envejecer; **to** — **up** madurar; **Thai food** — **s on you** la comida tailandesa acaba gustándote

growing [gróɪŋ] N cultivo *m*; — **pains** (physical symptom) dolores del crecimiento *m pl*; (troubles) dificultades iniciales *f pl*; **he's a** — **boy** es un muchacho en crecimiento

growl [graʊł] VI gruñir; (of thunder) retumbar; (of stomach) rugir; N gruñido *m*

grown [gron] ADJ adulto; — **man** hombre hecho y derecho *m*; N —**-up** adulto *m*; ADJ —**-up** para adultos

grown [gron] *see* grow

growth [groθ] N (increase in size) crecimiento *m*; (increase in number) aumento *m*, acrecentamiento *m*; (tumor) bulto *m*; (expansion) desarrollo *m*; — **hormone** hormona del crecimiento *f*; **a** — **industry** una industria en expansión

grudge [grʌʤ] N resentimiento *m*

grueling [grúlɪŋ] ADJ arduo

gruesome [grúsəm] ADJ cruento, truculento

gruff [grʌf] ADJ (manner) bronco; (voice) ronco

grumble [grámbəł] VI/VT refunfuñar, rezongar; N refunfuño *m*, gruñido *m*

grumpy [grámpi] ADJ refunfuñón, gruñón, rezongón

grunt [grʌnt] VI/VT gruñir; N gruñido *m*

guarantee [gærənti] N (promise, pledge) garantía *f*; (guaranty) fianza *f*; VT (promise, pledge) garantizar; (warrant) dar fianza, avalar; —**d loan** préstamo garantizado *m*

guarantor [gærəntɔr] N fiador -ora *mf*

guaranty [gærənti] N (guarantee) garantía *f*; (thing taken as security) fianza *f*; (guarantor) fiador -ora *mf*

guard [gɑrd] VT custodiar; (watch over) vigilar; (protect) proteger; VI **to** — **against** guardarse de; N (person that guards) guardia *mf*, guarda *mf*; (of a machine) dispositivo protector *m*; **to be on** — estar alerta / estar en guardia; — **dog** perro guardián *m*; —**rail** baranda *f*, pasamano *m*

guardian [gárɒiən] N guardián -ana *mf*; (legal) tutor -ora *mf*; — **angel** ángel de la guarda *m*

guardianship [gárɒiənʃɪp] N tutela *f*

Guatemala [gwɑɒəmálə] N Guatemala *f*

Guatemalan [gwɑɒəmálən] ADJ & N guatemalteco -ca *mf*

guava [gwávə] N guayaba *f*

guerrilla [gərílə] N — **army** guerrilla *f*

guess [gɛs] VT (hazard, conjecture) adivinar; (suppose) suponer; N (conjecture) conjetura *f*; (supposition) suposición *f*; **I'll give you three** —**es** te doy tres oportunidades para adivinar

guest [gɛst] N (to a party, function) invitado -da *mf*; (at a restaurant) cliente *mf*; (overnight) huésped *mf*

guffaw [gəfɔ́] N carcajada *f*, risotada *f*

guidance [gáɪdns] N (act of guiding) dirección *f*; (counsel) orientación *f*; (in a missile) teledirección *f*

guide [gaɪd] VT (serve as a guide) guiar; (direct the course of) dirigir; (counsel) orientar; —**d missile** misil guiado *m*; N (person) guía *mf*; (publication, mechanism) guía *f*; —**book** guía *f*; — **dog** perro guía *m*; —**lines** directivas *f pl*, pautas *f pl*, directrices *f pl*

guild [gɪłd] N gremio *m*, corporación *f*

guile [gaɪł] N astucia *f*

guilt [gɪłt] N culpa *f*; — **trip** manipulación por acusaciones falsas *f*

guiltless [gɪ́łtlɪs] ADJ inocente

guilty [gɪ́łti] ADJ culpable; **we find the**

defendant not — hallamos al acusado inocente
Guinea [gíni] N Guinea *f*; — **pig** conejillo de Indias *m*; — **-Bissau** Guinea-Bissau *f*
Guinean [gíniən] ADJ & N guineano -na *mf*
guise [gaɪz] ADV LOC **under the — of** so/bajo pretexto de; **in the — of** a manera de
guitar [gɪtár] N guitarra *f*
gulf [gʌlf] N (body of water) golfo *m*; (abyss, gap) abismo *m*; — **Stream** Corriente del Golfo *f*
gull [gʌł] N (bird) gaviota *f*; (dupe) crédulo -la *mf*; *Sp* primo -ma *mf*
gullet [gálɪt] N gaznate *m*
gullible [gáləbəł] ADJ crédulo, ingenuo
gully [gáli] N barranco *m*, barranca *f*; (gutter) alcantarilla *f*
gulp [gʌłp] VT tragar saliva; N trago *m*
gum [gʌm] N goma *f*; (for chewing) chicle *m*; **—s** encías *f pl*; VT **to — up** (ruin) jorobar; (stick) pegotear
gumption [gámpʃən] N (initiative) iniciativa *f*, arranque *m*; (courage) agallas *f pl*
gun [gʌn] N (firearm) arma de fuego *f*; (revolver) revólver *m*; (rifle) rifle *m*; (shotgun) escopeta *f*; (cannon) cañón *m*; (for painting, nailing) pistola *f*; VT (an engine) acelerar; **—boat** cañonero *m*; **—fire** tiroteo *m*; **—man** pistolero *m*; **—powder** pólvora *f*; **—shot** disparo *m*; **—shot wound** herida de bala *f*; **at —point** a mano armada; **to stick to one's —s** mantenerse firme; **don't jump the —** no te precipites; **to be under the —** estar bajo mucha presión; VT **to — down** matar a tiros; **to — for** andar a la caza de
gung-ho [gáŋhó] ADJ fanático, entusiasta
gunner [gánə-] N (shooting artillery) artillero -ra *mf*; (shooting a machine gun) ametrallador -ora *mf*
gurgle [gɜ́-gəł] VI (water) borbotar; (baby) gorjear; N (of water) borboteo *m*; (of a baby) gorjeo *m*
gush [gʌʃ] VI (liquids) chorrear, brotar; (talk effusively) hablar con efusividad
gust [gʌst] N ráfaga *f*; — **of wind** racha/ráfaga de viento *f*, ventolera *f*; VI soplar en ráfagas
gusto [gásto] N (pleasure) placer *m*; (enthusiasm) entusiasmo *m*
gut [gʌt] N tripa *f*; (belly) barriga *f*; — **feeling** corazonada *f*; **—s** (intestines) entrañas *f pl*; VT (eviscerate) destripar; (destroy the insides of) destrozar el interior de; (strip) desarmar
gutter [gʌ́də-] N (in the street) alcantarilla *f*; (on the roof) canaleta *f*, desagüe *m*; (squalor) miseria *f*
guy [gaɪ] N (man) tipo *m*; *Sp* tío *m*; **you —s** ustedes; *Sp* vosotros/vosotras; — **wire** cable *m*
Guyana [gaɪánə] N Guyana *f*
Guyanese [gaɪəníz] ADJ & N guyanés -esa *mf*
gym [ʤɪm] N gimnasio *m*
gymnasium [ʤɪmnéziəm] N gimnasio *m*
gymnastics [ʤɪmnǽstɪks] N gimnasia *f*
gynecologist [gaɪnəkáləʤɪst] N ginecólogo -ga *mf*
gynecology [gaɪnəkáləʤi] N ginecología *f*
gyp [ʤɪp] VT estafar, timar; N estafa *f*, timo *m*
gypsum [ʤípsəm] N yeso *m*
gypsy [ʤípsi] N & ADJ gitano -na *mf*
gyrate [ʤáɪret] VI girar
gyroscope [ʤáɪrəskop] N giroscopio *m*

Hh

habit [hǽbɪt] N (custom) hábito *m*, costumbre *f*; (clerical dress) hábito *m*; (vice) vicio *m*; **—-forming** adictivo
habitat [hǽbɪtæt] N hábitat *m*
habitual [həbítʃuəł] ADJ habitual
hack [hæk] N (cut) tajo *m*, machetazo *m*; (cough) tos seca *f*; (horse for hire) caballo de alquiler *m*; (nag) jamelgo *m*; (writer) escritor -ora mercenario -ria *mf*; **—saw** sierra para metales *f*; VI/VT tajar, cortar a machetazos; VI toser con tos seca
hacker [hǽkə-] N pirata informático -ca *mf*
had [hæd] *see* have
hag [hæg] N (witch) bruja *f*; (ugly old woman) vieja fea *f*
haggard [hǽgə-d] ADJ demacrado
haggle [hǽgəł] VI regatear
hail [heł] N (precipitation) granizo *m*; (greeting) saludo *m*; (shout) llamada *f*; — **Mary** Ave María *f*; **—storm** granizada *f*; VI (precipitate) granizar; VT (greet) saludar; (call out) llamar; (acclaim) aclamar; **to — from** ser oriundo de
hair [hɛr] N pelo *m*; (of the head only) cabello *m*; (of the body only) vello *m*; (on plants) pelusa *f*; **—brush** cepillo para el cabello *m*; **—cut** corte de pelo *m*; **to get a —cut** cortarse el pelo; **—do** peinado *m*; **—dresser** peluquero -ra *mf*, peinador -ora *mf*; — **follicle** folículo capilar *m*; **—line** nacimiento del pelo *f*; **—line fracture** fractura fina *f*; **—piece** postizo *m*; **—pin** horquilla *f*; **—-raising** horripilante, espeluznante; **—spray** fijador *m*
hairless [hérlɪs] ADJ (deprived of hair) pelado; (growing no hair) lampiño
hairy [héri] ADJ (including head) peludo; (body only) velludo
Haiti [hédi] N Haití *m*
Haitian [héʃən] ADJ & N haitiano -na *mf*
hake [hek] N merluza *f*
half [hæf] N mitad *f*; — **an apple** media

manzana *f*; ADJ medio; **—-baked** (not fully cooked) a medio cocer; (not fully developed) mal concebido; **—-breed** mestizo -za *mf*; **—brother** medio hermano *m*; **—-cocked** mal preparado; **he went off —-cocked** actuó precipitadamente; **—-cooked** a medio cocer; **—-dozen** media docena *f*; **—hearted** desganado; **—-hour** media hora *f*; **—-life** vida media *f*; **—-moon** media luna *f*; **— note** blanca *f*; **—-open** entreabierto, entornado; **— past one** la una y media; **—time** medio tiempo *m*, descanso *m*; **—-truth** verdad a medias *f*; **— volley** media volea *f*; **—way** a medio camino; **—way house** casa de rehabilitación *f*; **—way measures** medidas parciales *f pl*; **—way point** punto medio *m*; **—-wit** *pej* imbécil *mf*, papamoscas *mf*; **at —-mast** a media asta; **to do something —way** hacer algo a medias; **to go halves** ir a medias

halibut [hǽləbət] N hipogloso *m*

halitosis [hǽlɪtóʊsɪs] N halitosis *f*

hall [hɔł] N (corridor) corredor *m*, pasillo *m*; (large room) salón *m*, sala *f*; (building) edificio *m*; **—mark** distintivo *m*; **—way** (corridor) corredor *m*, pasillo *m*; (entrance) zaguán *m*, vestíbulo *m*

Halloween [hæ̀ləwín] N víspera del día de Todos los Santos *f*, noche de brujas *f*

hallucinate [həlúsənet] VI alucinar

hallucination [həlusənéʃən] N alucinación *f*

hallucinogen [həlúsənəʤən] N alucinógeno *m*

halo [hélo] N halo *m*, aureola *f*

halogen [hǽləʤən] ADJ halógeno

halt [hɔłt] N **to come to a —** detenerse; VI/VT parar, detener[se]; **—!** ¡alto!

halter [hɔ́łtə-] N cabestro *m*

halting [hɔ́łtɪŋ] ADJ vacilante

halve [hæv] VT partir por la mitad

ham [hæm] N (meat) jamón *m*; (attention getter) payaso *m*; **—string** (human) ligamento de la corva *m*; (horse) tendón del jarrete *m*; **to — it up** sobreactuar, exagerar

hamburger [hǽmbɜ-gə-] N (meat) carne picada de vaca/res *f*; (sandwich, patty) hamburguesa *f*

hamlet [hǽmlɪt] N aldea *f*, poblado *m*, caserío *m*

hammer [hǽmə-] N martillo *m*; VI/VT martillar, amartillar; **to — out** (an agreement) forjar; (differences) negociar

hammock [hǽmək] N hamaca *f*

hamper [hǽmpə-] N canasto *m*, cesto *m*; VT impedir, embarazar

hamster [hǽmstə-] N hámster *m*

hand [hænd] N mano *f*; (of a clock) aguja *f*, manecilla *f*; (farm helper) peón *m*; **—bag** (purse) bolsa *f*, cartera *f*; (valise) maletín *m*; **—ball** (American game) pelota *f*, frontón *m*; (European game) balonmano *m*; (in soccer) mano *f*; **—bill** volante *m*; **—cuffs** esposas *f pl*; **— grenade** granada de mano *f*, bomba de piña *f*; **—gun** revólver *m*; **— in —** [cogidos] de la mano; **—kerchief** pañuelo *m*; **—out** (notes) repartido *m*, ejemplario *m*; (alms) limosna *f*; **—saw** serrucho *m*; **—shake** apretón de manos *m*; **—stand** pino *m*, paro de manos *m*; **—work** trabajo manual *m*; **—writing** letra *f*; **at —** (within reach) al alcance; (about to happen) cerca; **in —** (under control) bajo control; (available) disponible, en mano; **on —** disponible, a mano; **on the other —** en cambio, por otra parte; **to have one's —s full** estar ocupadísimo; ADJ **—held** de mano; **—made** hecho a mano; **—picked** cuidadosamente seleccionado; **—s-on** práctico; VT entregar, dar; **to —cuff** esposar; **to — down** (a thing) pasar; (a judgment) pronunciar; **to — in** entregar; **to — over** entregar

handful [hǽndfʊł] N manojo *m*, puñado *m*

handicap [hǽndikæp] N (physical disability) impedimento *m*, minusvalía *f*; (mental disability) retardo *m*; (disadvantage) desventaja *f*; (in golf) hándicap *m*; **— race** carrera de hándicap *f*; VT (hinder) perjudicar, handicapar; (injure) lisiar; **physically —ped** minusválido físico

handiwork [hǽndiwɜ-k] N labor *f*

handle [hǽndl] N (straight) mango *m*; (curved) asa *f*; (of a drawer) manija *f*; (of a knife) empuñadura *f*, puño *m*; **—bar** manubrio *m*; VT (manage) manejar; (touch) manipular, tocar; (deal in) comerciar en; **the car —s easily** el coche tiene buena maniobrabilidad

handling [hǽndlɪŋ] N (dealing) manejo *m*; (touching) manipulación *f*; (charge) porte *m*; (of a car) maniobrabilidad *f*; **— charges** cargos de tramitación *m pl*

handsome [hǽnsəm] ADJ guapo, bien parecido; **a — sum** una suma considerable

handy [hǽndi] ADJ (near) a [la] mano; (practical) práctico; (skillful) hábil, diestro; N **—man** hombre habilidoso *m*

hang [hæŋ] VI/VT colgar, suspender; VT (door) colocar; (one's head) inclinar; (a condemned person) ahorcar; VI pender; **— in there!** ¡ánimo! **to — around** quedarse por ahí, rondar; **to — on** (hold tight) agarrarse bien; (persevere) aguantar; (wait) esperar; **to — out** (be outside) estar fuera; (socialize with) andar [con]; **to — over** sobresalir; **to — paper on a wall** empapelar una pared; **to — up** colgar; **sentenced to —** condenado a la horca; N caída *f*; **— glider** ala delta *f*; **—man** verdugo *m*; **—nail** padrastro *m*, uña encarnada *f*, uñero *m*; **—out** sitio frecuentado *m*; **—over** resaca *f*; **—-up** complejo *m*; **to get the — of something** agarrarle la onda a

algo
hangar [hǽŋɚ] N hangar *m*
hanger [hǽŋɚ] N colgadero *m*; (for clothes) percha *f*
hanging [hǽŋɪŋ] N muerte en la horca *f*; **—s** colgaduras *f pl*, tapiz *m*; ADJ colgante
hanky-panky [hǽŋkipǽŋki] N (deceit) tejemaneje *m*; (illicit sexual activity) aventuras *f pl*
haphazard [hæphǽzɚd] ADV a la buena de Dios; ADJ irregular
happen [hǽpən] VI suceder, pasar, acontecer; **I — to know** da la casualidad de que sé; **to — to pass by** acertar a pasar; **to — upon** encontrarse con, toparse con
happening [hǽpənɪŋ] N acontecimiento *m*, suceso *m*
happily [hǽpɪli] ADV (in a state of happiness) felizmente; (luckily) afortunadamente; **they lived — ever after** vivieron felices y comieron perdices
happiness [hǽpɪnɪs] N felicidad *f*, dicha *f*
happy [hǽpi] ADJ (satisfied) feliz, dichoso; (pleased) contento; (lucky) afortunado; **— ending** final feliz *m*; **to be — to** hacer algo de buena gana
harangue [hərǽŋ] N arenga *f*; VT arengar
harass [hərǽs] VT acosar, hostigar
harassment [hərǽsmənt] N acoso *m*, hostigamiento *m*
harbor [hárbɚ] N (for ships) puerto *m*; (refuge) refugio *m*; **— authority** autoridad portuaria; VT (refugees, criminals, suspicions) albergar; (hopes) abrigar
hard [hard] ADJ (firm) duro; (difficult) difícil; (arduous) arduo; **to play —ball** ser despiadado; **—-boiled egg** huevo duro *m*; **— cash** dinero contante y sonante *m*; **— coal** antracita *f*; **— copy** copia en papel *f*, copia impresa *f*; **— core** núcleo resistente *m*; **—-core** radical; **— disk** disco duro *m*; **— disk drive** unidad de disco duro *f*; **— feelings** resentimiento *m*; **— hat** casco *m*; **—headed** testarudo; **—hearted** duro de corazón; **— liquor** bebida alcohólica fuerte *f*; **— luck** mala suerte *f*; **— of hearing** medio sordo; **— page break** salto de página forzado *m*; **— palate** paladar óseo *m*; **—-pressed** en aprietos; **— return** salto de línea forzado *m*; **—ware** (metal articles) ferretería *f*; (computer) hardware *m*; **—ware store** ferretería *f*; **—wood** madera noble *f*; **— water** agua dura *f*; **— winter** invierno crudo *m*; **—-wired** programado; **—-working** trabajador; ADV (fall, push) con fuerza; (work) duro, con ahinco
harden [hárdn] VI/VT (make or become hard) endurecer[se]; (make or become experienced) curtir[se]
hardening [hárdnɪŋ] N endurecimiento *m*
hardly [hárdli] ADV (scarcely) apenas, difícilmente; (at all) en absoluto; **— anyone** casi nadie; **— surprising** nada sorprendente
hardness [hárdnɪs] N dureza *f*
hardship [hárdʃɪp] N penuria *f*, penalidad *f*
hardy [hárdi] ADJ robusto
hare [hɛr] N liebre *f*; **—brained** descabellado; **—lip** labio leporino *m*; **—lipped** con labio leporino, labihendido
harem [hérəm] N harén *m*
harm [harm] N daño *m*, mal *m*, perjuicio *m*; VT (object) dañar; (person) hacer daño; (chances) perjudicar
harmful [hármfəł] ADJ perjudicial, dañino, nocivo
harmless [hármlɪs] ADJ inocuo, inofensivo
harmonic [harmánɪk] ADJ & N armónico *m*
harmonious [harmóniəs] ADJ armonioso
harmonize [hármənaɪz] VI/VT armonizar
harmony [hárməni] N armonía *f*
harness [hárnɪs] N arnés *m*, jaez *m*, guarnición *f*; VT (put on a harness) enjaezar; (utilize) aprovechar
harp [harp] N arpa *f*; VI (play the harp) tocar el arpa; (insist) machacar; **to — on** insistir sobre
harpoon [harpún] N arpón *m*; VT arponear
harpsichord [hárpsɪkɔrd] N clavicémbalo *m*
harrowing [hǽroɪŋ] ADJ angustioso; **— adventure** aventura espeluznante *f*
harry [hǽri] VT acosar, hostigar
harsh [harʃ] ADJ (words) duro; (surface) áspero; (character, discipline) severo, férreo; (winter) crudo, riguroso
harshness [hárʃnɪs] N (of words) dureza *f*; (of a surface) aspereza *f*; (of character, discipline) severidad *f*; (of a winter) rigor *m*
harvest [hárvɪst] N cosecha *f*; (of sugar) zafra *f*; VT cosechar
has [hæz] *see* have
hash [hæʃ] N guisado *m*, picadillo *m*
hashish [hæʃíʃ] N hachís *m*
hassle [hǽsəł] N rollo *m*, lío *m*; VT jorobar
haste [hest] N prisa *f*; **in —** de prisa; **to make —** darse prisa, apresurarse; *Am* apurarse
hasten [hésən] VI apresurarse; *Am* apurarse; VT acelerar, adelantar
hasty [hésti] ADJ apresurado, precipitado, presuroso; *Am* apurado; **to be —** precipitarse, apresurarse
hat [hæt] N sombrero *m*
hatch [hætʃ] VI/VT (chicks) empollar; (plot, scheme) fraguar, maquinar; N (chicks) nidada *f*; (opening) escotilla *f*; **— way** escotilla *f*
hatchet [hǽtʃɪt] N hacha *f*; **— job** crítica feroz *f*; **— man** sicario *m*; **to bury the —** hacer las paces
hate [het] N odio *m*; VI/VT odiar; **I — to admit it** me molesta admitirlo; **I — eating leftovers**

detesto comer restos

hateful [hétfəł] ADJ odioso, aborrecible

hatred [hétrɪd] N odio *m*

haughtiness [hɔ́ɔtinɪs] N altivez *f*, altanería *f*, soberbia *f*

haughty [hɔ́ɔti] ADJ altivo, altanero, soberbio

haul [hɔł] VT (transport) transportar; (drag) arrastrar; (pull) jalar [de], tirar [de]; N (quantity transported) carga *f*; (tug) tirón *m*; (catch of fish) redada *f*; (stolen goods) botín *m*; **long —** distancia larga *f*

haunch [hɔ́ntʃ] N anca *f*

haunt [hɔnt] VI/VT (frequent) frecuentar, rondar; (enchant) embrujar; **that idea —s me** me obsesiona esa idea; **—ed house** casa embrujada *f*; N (of animals, criminals) guarida *f*; (of people socializing) sitio frecuentado *m*

have [hæv] V AUX haber; VT tener; **to — to** tener que; **to — a baby** dar a luz; **to — a look at** echar una mirada a; **to — a suit made** mandarse hacer un traje; **— him come later** dile que venga más tarde; **what did she — on?** ¿qué tenía puesto? **we've been had** nos estaforon

haven [hévən] N abrigo *m*, refugio *m*

havoc [hǽvək] N estrago *m*; **to wreak —** hacer estragos

hawk [hɔk] N gavilán *m*; VT pregonar

hay [he] N heno *m*; **— fever** alergia al polen *f*; **— loft** henil *m*; **—seed** paleto -ta *mf*; **—stack** almiar *m*; **to look for a needle in a —stack** buscar una aguja en un pajar

hazard [hǽzɚd] N (chance) azar *m*; (danger) peligro *m*; VT arriesgar, aventurar

hazardous [hǽzɚdəs] ADJ peligroso; **— substance** sustancia peligrosa *f*

haze [hez] N neblina *f*, calina *f*; VT atormentar [como parte de un rito de iniciación]

hazel [hézəł] N avellano *m*; **—nut** avellana *f*; ADJ de avellano

hazy [hézi] ADJ (weather) brumoso; (idea) confuso, vago

HDL [high density lipoprotein] [étʃdíél] N LAD *f*

he [hi] PRON él; **—-goat** macho cabrío *m*; **— who** el que, quien

head [hɛd] N (of body) cabeza *f*; (of bed) cabecera *f*; (chief) jefe -fa *mf*; **—ache** dolor de cabeza *m*; **— coach** entrenador -ora en jefe *mf*; **— cold** resfrío *m*; **—count** recuento de personas *m*; **—dress** tocado *m*, adorno para la cabeza *m*; **—gear** (hat) sombrero *m*; (helmet) casco *m*; (for a horse) cabezada *f*; **—hunter** cazatalentos *mf sg*; **—land** cabo *m*, promontorio *m*; **—light** faro delantero *m*; **—line** titular *m*; **—long** (head first) de cabeza; (hastily) precipitadamente; **— of hair** cabellera *f*; **— of state** mandatario -ria *mf*; **—phone** audífono *m*, auricular *m*; **—quarters** (military) cuartel general *m*; (police) jefatura *f*; (corporation) oficina central *f*; **—rest** reposacabezas *m sg*; **—set** auriculares *m pl*; **—s or tails** cara o cruz; **I can't make —s or tails of it** esto no tiene ni pies ni cabeza; **— start** ventaja *f*; **—stone** lápida *f*; **—strong** testarudo; **—way** avance *m*; **—word** voz *f*; **to make —way** avanzar, progresar; **it went to his —** se le fue a la cabeza; **to be out of one's —** desvariar; **to come to a —** (a crisis) precipitarse; (an abscess) supurar; **to keep one's —** mantener la calma; VT (lead) encabezar; (steer) dirigir; (in soccer) cabecear; VI dirigirse; **to — up** liderar; **to — off** atajar; ADV **—-on** de frente, frontal

header [hɛ́dɚ] N (in soccer) cabezazo *m*, pase de cabeza *m*; (in text) cabecera *f*, encabezado *m*

heading [hɛ́dɪŋ] N encabezamiento *m*

heal [hił] VT curar; VI (get well) sanar, curarse; (form a scar) cicatrizarse

health [hɛłθ] N salud *f*; **— care** asistencia médica *f*; **— care system** sistema de asistencia de salud *m*; **— care provider** profesional de la salud *mf*; **— food** comida macrobiótica *f*; **— insurance** seguro de salud *m*

healthful [hɛ́łθfəł] ADJ saludable, sano

healthy [hɛ́łθi] ADJ sano, saludable

heap [hip] N montón *m*, pila *f*; VT amontonar, apilar; VI **to — up** amontonarse

hear [hir] VI/VT (perceive) oír; VT (listen) escuchar; **to — about/of someone/something** oír hablar de alguien/algo; **to — from someone** tener noticias de alguien; **I won't — of your leaving** no quiero saber de que te vayas

heard [hɝd] *see* hear

hearer [hírɚ] N oyente *mf*

hearing [hírɪŋ] N (sense) oído *m*; (trial) audiencia *f*; **within —** al alcance del oído; **— aid** audífono *m*; ADJ **—-impaired** sordo

hearsay [hírse] N testimonio de oídas *m*; **by —** de oídas

hearse [hɝs] N coche fúnebre *m*, carroza *f*

heart [hɑrt] N (organ) corazón *m*; (spirit) ánimo *m*; **—ache** angustia *f*; **— attack** ataque cardíaco *m*; **—beat** latido *m*; **I would do it in a —beat** lo haría sin pestañear; **—burn** acidez de estómago *f*; **— disease** enfermedad coronaria *f*; **— murmur** soplo cardíaco *m*; **at —** en realidad, en el fondo; **from the bottom of one's —** de corazón, con toda el alma; **to learn by —** aprender de memoria; **to take —** cobrar ánimo; **to take to —** tomar a pecho; ADJ **—broken** inconsolable; **—felt** sincero, sentido; **my —felt sympathy** mi más sentido pésame; **—-warming** reconfortante

hearten [hártn̩] VT animar
hearth [hɑrθ] N hogar *m*
heartless [hártlɪs] ADJ despiadado, desalmado
hearty [hárdɪ] ADJ (cordial) cordial; (strong) fuerte; **— appetite** apetito saludable *m*; **a — laugh** una risa desbordante; **— meal** una comida abundante
heat [hit] N (warmth) calor *m*; (passion) ardor *m*; (estrus) celo *m*; (source of heat) calefacción *f*; (preliminary race) eliminatoria *f*; **— exchange** equilibrio térmico *m*; **—stroke** insolación *f*; VI/VT calentar[se]; **to — up** acalorarse
heater [híɾə˞] N calentador *m*
heating [híɾɪŋ] N calefacción *f*; **— pad** almohadilla eléctrica *f*
heave [hiv] VT (raise) levantar; (throw) arrojar, lanzar; (sigh) exhalar; (pull) jalar; VI (pant) jadear; (vomit) hacer arcadas; N (throw) lanzamiento *m*; (pull) tirón *m*
heaven [hévən] N cielo *m*
heavenly [hévənli] ADJ celestial; **— bodies** cuerpos celestes *m pl*; **it was —** estuvo divino
heavily [hévəli] ADV (fall) pesadamente; (drink) mucho; **he's breathing —** está jadeando; **he's — indebted** está muy endeudado / tiene muchas deudas
heaviness [hévɪnɪs] N pesadez *f*
heavy [hévi] ADJ (weighty) pesado; (thick) grueso, pesado; (dense) denso; (oppressive) opresivo; **— artillery** artillería pesada *f*; **— breathing** jadeos *m pl*; **— -duty** de servicio pesado; **— -handed** severo, autoritario; **with a — heart** abatido; **— rain** lluvia fuerte *f*; **— schedule** agenda cargada *f*; **—weight** peso pesado *m*; N villano -na *mf*
Hebrew [híbru] N & ADJ hebreo -a *mf*; (language) hebreo *m*
heck [hɛk] INTERJ ¡caramba! **what the — are you doing?** ¿qué demonios haces? **that was a — of a good game** fue un partidazo
hectare [hékt͡ɚ] N hectárea *f*
hectic [hékt͡ɪk] ADJ febril, agitado
hedge [hɛd͡ʒ] N (row of bushes) seto *m*; (precaution) precaución *f*; **— fund** fondo especulativo *m*; **—hog** erizo *m*; VI/VT (a bet) cubrir[se]; VT (a question) evadir
hedonism [híd̩nɪzəm] N hedonismo *m*
heebie-jeebies [híbid͡ʒíbiz] N **it gives me the —** me pone los pelos de punta
heed [hid] VT atender; N atención *f*, cuidado *m*; **to pay — to** prestar atención a
heel [hil] N (of foot or sock) talón *m*; (of shoe) tacón *m*; **to kick up one's —s** tirar la chancleta, soltarse el pelo; VT poner tacón a; VI/VT seguir de cerca
hegemony [hɪd͡ʒɛ́məni] N hegemonía *f*
heifer [héfə˞] N novilla *f*, vaquilla *f*
height [hait] N (of a building, mountain) altura *f*; (of a person) estatura *f*; (utmost point) colmo *m*
heighten [háɪtn̩] VI/VT (increase) aumentar[se]; (intensify) realzar
Heimlich maneuver [háɪmlɪkmənúvə˞] N maniobra de Heimlich *f*
heinous [hénəs] ADJ aborrecible
heir [ɛr] N heredero -ra *mf*; **— apparent** presunto heredero *m*, presunta heredera *f*; **—s and assigns** herederos y cesionarios *m pl*
heiress [érɪs] N heredera *f*
held [hɛld] *see* hold
helicopter [hélɪkɑpt͡ə˞] N helicóptero *m*
helium [híliəm] N helio *m*
helix [hílɪks] N hélice *f*
hell [hɛl] N infierno *m*
hello [hɛló] INTERJ ¡hola! (on the telephone) hola; *Sp* diga; *Mex* bueno
helm [hɛlm] N timón *m*
helmet [hɛ́lmɪt] N (for bikes, etc.) casco *m*; (armor) yelmo *m*
help [hɛlp] N (aid) ayuda *f*; (rescue) auxilio *m*; (remedy) remedio *m*; (employee) empleado -da *mf*; **— desk** servicio de ayuda al usuario *m*; INTERJ ¡auxilio! ¡socorro! VI/VT (aid) ayudar, asistir; (rescue) auxiliar, socorrer; **— yourself** sírvete; **he cannot — it** no puede evitarlo; **he cannot — but come** no puede menos que venir; **may I — you?** ¿en qué le puedo servir?
helper [hɛ́lpə˞] N ayudante *mf*, asistente *mf*
helpful [hɛ́lpfəl] ADJ (useful) útil; (willing to help) servicial
helping [hɛ́lpɪŋ] N porción *f*
helpless [hɛ́lplɪs] ADJ desamparado, desvalido
helplessness [hɛ́lplɪsnɪs] N desamparo *m*, desvalimiento *m*
hem [hɛm] N dobladillo *m*, *Am* ruedo *m*; VT hacer dobladillos en, orillar; **to — in** arrinconar; **to — and haw** vacilar
hematoma [himət͡ómə] N hematoma *m*
hemisphere [hémɪsfɪr] N hemisferio *m*
hemlock [hémlɑk] N cicuta *f*
hemoglobin [híməglobɪn] N hemoglobina *f*
hemophilia [himəfíliə] N hemofilia *f*
hemorrhage [hémərɪd͡ʒ] N hemorragia *f*
hemorrhoids [hémərɔɪdz] N hemorroides *f pl*
hemp [hɛmp] N cáñamo *m*
hen [hɛn] N (chicken) gallina *f*; (female bird) ave hembra *f*; ADJ **—pecked** dominado por su mujer
hence [hɛns] ADV de ahí; **—forth** de aquí en adelante, de hoy en adelante; **a week —** de aquí a una semana
hepatitis [hɛpət͡áɪdɪs] N hepatitis *f*
her [hɜ˞] PRON **I see —** la veo; **I talk to —** le hablo [a ella]; **I went with —** fui con ella; POSS ADJ **this is — dog** este es su perro, este es el perro de ella

herald [hérəld] N heraldo *m*; VT anunciar, proclamar
herb [ɜˑb] N hierba *f*
herbal [ɜ́ˑbəł] ADJ de hierbas; **— tea** tisana *f*
herbicide [hɜ́ˑbɪsaɪd] N herbicida *m*
herbivore [hɜ́ˑbəvɔr] N herbívoro *m*
herbivorous [hɜˑbívərəs] ADJ herbívoro
herd [hɜˑd] N (of animals) manada *f*; (of goats) hato *m*; (of sheep) rebaño *m*; (of horses, donkeys) recua *f*; **the common —** el populacho, la chusma; **—sman** pastor *m*; VT arrear; VI ir en manada
here [hir] ADV aquí, acá; **— it is** aquí está; **—after** en adelante; **the —after** el más allá; **—by** (in writing) por la presente; **I —by pronounce you husband and wife** los declaro marido y mujer; **—in** en el presente; **—'s to you!** ¡a tu salud! **—tofore** hasta ahora; **—with** (hereby) por la presente; (attached) adjunto; **come —!** ¡ven acá! **the — and now** el presente; **that is neither — nor there** eso no viene al caso
hereditary [hərédɪtɛri] ADJ hereditario
heredity [hərédɪti] N herencia *f*
heresy [hérɪsi] N herejía *f*
heretic [hérɪtɪk] N hereje *mf*
heritage [hérɪtɪʤ] N herencia *f*, patrimonio *m*
hermaphrodite [hɜˑmǽfrəDaɪt] N hermafrodita *mf*
hermetic [hɜˑmédɪk] ADJ hermético
hermit [hɜ́ˑmɪt] N ermitaño -ña *mf*; **— crab** ermitaño *m*
hernia [hɜ́ˑniə] N hernia *f*; **—ted** herniado; **—ted disk** hernia de disco *f*
hero [híro] N (brave man) héroe *m*; (main character) protagonista *mf*
heroic [hɪróɪk] ADJ heroico
heroin [hérоɪn] N heroína *f*
heroine [hérоɪn] N heroína *f*
heroism [hérоɪzəm] N heroísmo *m*
heron [hérən] N garza *f*
herpes [hɜ́ˑpiz] N herpes *m*
herring [hérɪŋ] N arenque *m*
hers [hɜˑz] PRON **this book is —** este libro es suyo / de ella; **these things are —** estas cosas son suyas; **— is bigger** el suyo / la suya es más grande; **a friend of —** un amigo suyo / de ella
herself [hɜˑsɛ́łf] PRON ella misma; **she's not — today** hoy no es la misma de siempre; **she was sitting by —** estaba sentada sola; **she — did it** lo hizo sola, lo hizo ella misma; **she talks to —** ella habla para sí, habla consigo misma; **she looked at — in the mirror** se miró en el espejo; **she bought — a house** se compró una casa
hesitant [hézɪtənt] ADJ vacilante
hesitate [hézɪtet] VI (pause) vacilar; (stutter) titubear; (doubt) dudar
hesitating [hézɪteDɪŋ] ADJ vacilante
hesitation [hɛzɪtéʃən] N (pause) vacilación *f*; (stammer) titubeo *m*; (doubt) duda *f*
heterogeneous [hɛDəˑəʤíniəs] ADJ heterogéneo
heterosexual [hɛDərosɛ́kʃuəł] ADJ heterosexual
hexagon [héksəgɑn] N hexágono *m*
hey [he] INTERJ ¡oiga!
heyday [héde] N auge *m*
hi [haɪ] INTERJ hola; **say — to your sister for me** dale recuerdos a tu hermana de mi parte
hiatus [haɪéDəs] N hiato *m*
hibernate [háɪbəˑnet] VI hibernar
hiccup, hiccough [hɪ́kʌp] N hipo *m*; VI hipar, tener hipo
hick [hɪk] N & ADJ paleto -ta *mf*
hickory [hɪ́kəri] N nogal americano *m*
hid, hidden [hɪd, hídn] *see* hide
hidden [hídn] ADJ (out of sight) oculto; (illegal) clandestino; **— agenda** intereses ocultos *m pl*
hide [haɪd] VI/VT ocultar[se], esconder[se]; **— and seek** escondite *m*, escondidas *f pl*; **—out** escondite *m*; N cuero *m*, piel *f*, pellejo *m*
hideous [hídiəs] ADJ horrendo, espantoso
hierarchy [háɪərɑrki] N jerarquía *f*
hieroglyphic [haɪrəglífɪk] ADJ & N jeroglífico *m*
high [haɪ] ADJ alto; (intoxicated) ebrio; (on drugs) volado; **— altitude sickness** enfermedad de altura *f*; **— and dry** (ship) en seco; (person) colgado; **— blood pressure** hipertensión *f*; **—brow** culto; **—-class** de clase; **— contrast** alto contraste *m*; **— definition television** televisión de alta definición *f*; **— density** alta densidad *f*; **—er-up** superior; **—er education** educación superior *f*; **— explosive** explosivo de alta potencia *m*; **— fever** fiebre elevada *f*; **— fidelity** alta fidelidad *f*; **— finance** altas finanzas *f pl*; **—-grade** de calidad superior; **—-handed** arbitrario; **— jump** salto alto *m*; **—lands** tierras altas *f pl*; **—-level** de alto nivel; **—light** lo más destacado; **—lighting** (on a computer) selección de texto *f*; **—lights** (in hair) claritos *m pl*, mechas *f pl*; **—-minded** idealista; **—-octane gasoline** súper *m*; **—-pitched** agudo; **— point** culminación *f*; **—-powered** de alta potencia; **—-pressure** estresante, intenso; **—-priced** caro; **—-quality** de alta calidad; **—-return** de alta rentabilidad; **—-rise** de muchos pisos; **—-risk** de alto riesgo; **—-risk behavior** conducta de alto riesgo *f*; **—-risk patient** paciente con alto riesgo *mf*; **— school** escuela secundaria *f*, colegio *m*; *Sp* instituto *m*; **— seas** alta mar *f*; **—-sounding** altisonante; **—-speed** de alta velocidad; **— spirits** buen ánimo *m*; **—-strung** nervioso; **—-tech** alta tecnología *f*; **— temperature** temperatura máxima *f*; **— tide** pleamar *f*; **—way** carretera

f, ruta *f*; **— wind** ventarrón *m*; **in — gear** a toda marcha; **two feet —** dos pies de altura; **it is — time that** ya era hora de que; **to look — and low** buscar por todas partes; N flash *m*, subida *f*; VT **to —light** (emphasize) destacar, resaltar

highly [háɪli] ADV **— amusing** sumamente divertido; **— paid** muy bien pagado; **— qualified** altamente cualificado; **he spoke — of her** habló muy bien de ella

highness [háɪnɪs] N alteza *f*

hijack [háɪʤæk] VT secuestrar [un vehículo]

hike [haɪk] N caminata *f*; **take a —!** ¡ve a freír espárragos! VI salir a caminar

hilarious [hɪlérɪəs] ADJ graciosísimo, para morirse de risa

hill [hɪł] N (elevated area) colina *f*, cerro *m*; (pile) montón *m*; **—billy** paleto -ta *mf*; **—side** ladera *f*; **—top** cumbre *f*, cima *f*

hillock [hílək] N otero *m*

hilly [híli] ADJ accidentado

hilt [hɪłt] N empuñadura *f*; **to the —** al máximo

him [hɪm] PRON **I see —** lo veo; *Sp* le veo; **I talk to —** le hablo; **I went with —** fui con él

himself [hɪmsélł] PRON él mismo; **he — wrote the letter** él mismo escribió la carta; **he's not — today** hoy no es el mismo de siempre; **he was sitting by —** estaba sentado solo; **he talks to —** él habla para sí, habla consigo mismo; **he looked at — in the mirror** se miró en el espejo; **he bought — a house** se compró una casa

hind [haɪnd] ADJ trasero; **—most** último; **in —sight** a posteriori; N cierva *f*

hinder [híndə-] VT impedir, entorpecer, estorbar

Hindi [híndi] N hindi *m*

hindrance [híndrəns] N obstáculo *m*, impedimento *m*, traba *f*

Hindu [híndu] ADJ & N hindú *mf*

hinge [hɪnʤ] N gozne *m*, quicio *m*; VT engoznar, poner goznes; VI **to — on** depender de

hint [hɪnt] N (clue) indirecta *f*, pista *f*; (trace) dejo *m*; **to take the —** darse por enterado; VT insinuar

hip [hɪp] N cadera *f*; **— replacement** (operation) sustitución protésica de la cadera *f*; (prosthesis) prótesis de cadera *f*

Hippocratic oath [hɪpəkrǽdɪkóθ] N juramento hipocrático *m*

hippopotamus [hɪpəpátəməs] N hipopótamo *m*

hire [haɪr] VT (engage for work) contratar; VI/VT (rent) alquilar[se]; **— and fire** contratar y despedir; **to — out** dar en alquiler, alquilar; N (engagement) contratación *f*; (employee) nuevo -va empleado -da *mf*; (rent) alquiler *m*

his [hɪz] POSS ADJ **this is — dog** éste es su perro / el perro de él; PRON **these things are —** estas cosas son suyas; **— is right here** el suyo / la suya está aquí; **a friend of —** un amigo suyo / una amiga suya

Hispanic [hɪspǽnɪk] ADJ hispánico, hispano; N hispano -na *mf*

hiss [hɪs] VI sisear; (to boo) silbar; N siseo *m*

histamine [hístəmin] N histamina *f*

historian [hɪstɔ́rɪən] N historiador -ra *mf*

historic [hɪstɔ́rɪk] ADJ histórico

historical [hɪstɔ́rɪkəł] ADJ histórico

history [hístəri] N historia *f*

histrionics [hɪstriánɪks] N histrionismo *m*

hit [hɪt] VT (a target) dar en; (a car) chocar con; (a key) pulsar, tocar; (a baseball) batear; **to — a homerun** batear un jonrón, pegar un cuadrangular; **to — it off** llevarse bien desde el principio; **to — the mark** acertar, dar en el blanco; **to — upon an idea** dar con una idea; **to — on a person** tratar de ligar con alguien; N (blow) golpe *m*; (success) éxito *m*; (dose) dosis *f*; **that was a — with me** me encantó; **—man** sicario *m*; **—s** (on a website) visitas *f pl*; ADJ **— -and-run** que se da a la fuga después de atropellar a alguien; **— -or-miss** al azar

hitch [hɪtʃ] VT atar, amarrar; (pants) levantar; (yoke) uncir, enganchar; **to get —ed** casarse; **to —hike** *Sp* hacer autostop; *Am* hacer dedo; N (knot) nudo *m*; (difficulty) dificultad *f*; (period) período *m*

hither [híðə-] ADV acá; **— and thither** acá y allá; **—to** hasta ahora

HIV [human immunodeficiency virus] [étʃáɪví] N VIH *m*

hive [haɪv] N (shelter for bees) colmena *f*; (colony of bees) enjambre *m*; **—s** urticaria *f*

HMO [health maintenance organization] [étʃémó] N organización de mantenimiento de salud *f*

hoard [hɔrd] N reserva *f*; VI/VT acaparar

hoarse [hɔrs] ADJ ronco; (like alcoholics) aguardentoso

hoarseness [hórsnɪs] N ronquera *f*

hoax [hoks] N engaño *m*

hobble [hábəł] VI (limp) cojear; VT (tie to impede walking) manear; (hinder) trabar; N cojera *f*; (rope) traba *f*, manea *f*

hobby [hábi] N hobby *m*

hobo [hóbo] N vagabundo *m*

hockey [háki] N hockey *m*

hodgepodge [háʤpɑʤ] N mezcolanza *f*, batiburrillo *m*

hoe [ho] N azada *f*, azadón *m*; VI/VT limpiar con azadón

hog [hɑg] N puerco *m*, cerdo *m*, marrano *m*; *Am* chancho *m*; **—wash** pamplinas *f pl*; **to live high on the —** vivir en la abundancia; VT acaparar, adueñarse de

hoist [hɔɪst] VT izar; N torno *m*, guinche *m*

hokey [hóki] ADJ sensiblero

hold [hołd] VT (bear) llevar, sujetar; (contain)

contener; (detain) detener; (decide legally, sustain a note) sostener; (opine) opinar; **to — back** detener; **to — down** sujetar; **to — forth** perorar; **to — hands** tomarse de la mano; **to — in place** sujetar; **to — a meeting** celebrar una reunión; **to — someone responsible** hacerle a uno responsable; **to — someone to his word** obligar a uno a cumplir con su palabra; **to — oneself erect** ponerse derecho; **to — one's own** defenderse; **to — one's tongue** callarse, morderse la lengua; **— the pickles on that burger!** una hamburguesa sin pepinillos, por favor; VI (remain fast) aguantar, resistir; (occupy a position) ocupar; (be valid) ser válido; **to — off** mantener[se] a distancia; **to — off doing something** abstenerse de hacer algo; **to — liable** responsabilizar; **to — on** (not let go) agarrar[se], sujetar[se]; (stop) esperar; (persist) persistir; **to — out** aguantar; **to — still** quedarse/estarse quieto; **to — tight** agarrarse; **to — to one's promise** cumplir con la palabra; **to — up** (raise) alzar; (detain) detener; (rob) atracar, asaltar; (persevere) aguantar; **how much does it — ?** ¿Qué capacidad tiene? N (grip) agarro *m*; (thing to grasp) asidero *m*; (dominion) dominio *m*; (wrestling move) llave *f*; (in music) calderón *m*; (of a ship) bodega *f*; **—up** golpe *m*, atraco *m*; **to get — of** agarrar; **to take — of** *Sp* coger, agarrar; **to have a good — on something** agarrarse bien de algo

holder [hóʊldɚ] N (person) tenedor -ora *mf*, poseedor -ora *mf*; (device) receptáculo *m*

holding [hóʊldɪŋ] N propiedad *f*; **— company** holding *m*; **—s** (financial) valores en cartera *m pl*; (of a library) fondos *m pl*

hole [hoʊl] N agujero *m*; (in a wall) boquete *m*; (of an animal) madriguera *f*; (in the ground, in golf) hoyo *m*; **to be in a —** hallarse/estar en un apuro/aprieto; **—in-one** hoyo en uno *m*

holiday [hálɪde] N día de fiesta *m*; **—s** vacaciones *f pl*

holiness [hóʊlinɪs] N santidad *f*

holistic [holístɪk] ADJ holístico

Holland [hálənd] N Holanda *f*

hollow [hálo] ADJ (empty) hueco; (concave) cóncavo; (sunken) hundido; (insincere) falso; N (cavity) hueco *m*, concavidad *f*; (valley) hondonada *f*, hondo *m*; VT **to — out** ahuecar, vaciar

holly [háli] N acebo *m*

holocaust [háləkɔst] N holocausto *m*

holster [hóʊlstɚ] N pistolera *f*, funda de pistola *f*

holy [hóli] ADJ santo, sagrado; **— Bible** Santa Biblia *f*; **— cow/Moses/mackerel!** ¡que increíble! *Sp* ¡jobar! **— Ghost** Espíritu Santo *m*; **— Spirit** Espíritu Santo *m*; **— war** guerra santa *f*; **— water** agua bendita *f*

homage [hámɪʤ] N homenaje *m*; **to pay —** rendir homenaje, honrar

home [hom] N casa *f*, hogar *m*; (for old people, orphans) asilo *m*, hogar *m*; **—boy** amigo del barrio *m*; **— economics** economía doméstica *f*; **— delivery** entrega a domicilio *f*; **— equity loan** préstamo garantizado por el valor residual de la vivienda *m*; **— game** partido en casa *m*; **—land** patria *f*; **—less** sin techo; **— office** (headquarters) oficina central *f*; (at home) oficina en el hogar *f*; **—owner** propietario -ria de vivienda *mf*; **—owners' association** asociación de propietarios de vivienda *f*; **— page** página de inicio *f*; **— plate** goma *f*, plato *m*; **— rule** autonomía *f*; **— run** jonrón *m*, cuadrangular *m*; **at —** en casa; **to be —sick** echar de menos / extrañar [a la familia]; **—sickness** morriña *f*, añoranza *f*; **— stretch** último trecho *m*; **—work** tarea domiciliaria *f*, deber *m*; ADJ doméstico; ADV (direction) a casa; (location) en casa; **to strike —** dar en el blanco; ADJ **—made** casero

homely [hómli] ADJ (ugly) feo; (familiar) familiar, doméstico

homeopathic [homiopǽθɪk] ADJ homeopático

homeopathy [homiápəθi] N homeopatía *f*

homestead [hómstɛd] N heredad *f*, casa de la familia *f*

homeward [hómwə-d] ADV a casa; **— bound** camino a casa

homicide [hámɪsaɪd] N homicidio *m*

homogeneous [homəʤíniəs] ADJ homogéneo

homogenize [həmáɑʤənaɪz] VT homogeneizar

homonym [hámənɪm] N homónimo *m*

homophobia [homəfóbiə] N homofobia *f*

homophobic [homəfóbɪk] ADJ homofóbico

homosexual [homoséksʃuəɫ] ADJ & N homosexual *mf*

Honduran [hɑndúrən] ADJ & N hondureño -ña *mf*

Honduras [hɑndúrəs] N Honduras *f*

hone [hon] VT afilar; **to — one's skills** desarrollar las destrezas; N piedra de afilar *f*

honest [ánɪst] ADJ honrado, honesto; **I'll be — with you** voy a ser franco contigo; **—!** ¡de veras!

honesty [ánɪsti] N (integrity) honradez *f*, honestidad *f*; (sincerity) franqueza *f*

honey [háni] N (sweet substance) miel *f*; (endearment) querido -da *mf*; **—bee** abeja *f*; **—comb** panal *m*; **—suckle** madreselva *f*

honeymoon [hánimun] N luna de miel *f*; VI pasar la luna de miel

honk [hʊŋk] N (of a car) bocinazo *m*, pitazo *m*; (of a goose) graznido *m*; VI/VT (car) tocar la bocina; VI (goose) graznar

honor [ánə-] N (respect, privilege) honor *m*;

(good reputation) honra *f*; **with —s** con honores; **your —** su señoría; VT (revere) honrar; (accept invitation, check) aceptar; **to — a promise** cumplir [con] una promesa

honorable [ánə·əbəł] ADJ honorable

honorary [ánərɛri] ADJ honorario

hood [hʊd] N (of a coat) capucha *f*, caperuza *f*; (of a car) capó *m*; *Am* tapa *f*; VT encapuchar

hoodlum [húdləm] N maleante *mf*, gamberro -rra *mf*

hoof [hʊf] N casco *m*, pezuña *f*; VI **to — it** ir andando

hook [hʊk] N (for lifting) gancho *m*, garfio *m*; (for fishing) anzuelo *m*; **— and eye** alamar *m*, macho y hembra *m*; **by — or by crook** por las buenas o por las malas; **—up** conexión *f*, enganche *m*; VT (snag) enganchar; (a dress) abrochar; **to — up** conectar, enganchar

hooked [hʊkt] ADJ (shaped like a hook) ganchudo; (addicted) enganchado

hooky [húki] N **to play —** hacer novillos

hooligan [húlɪgən] N *Sp* gamberro -rra *mf*, *Am* patotero -ra *mf*

hoop [hup] N (also in basketball) aro *m*

hoot [hut] VI/VT (of owl) ulular; (in derision) abuchear; N (of an owl) ululato *m*; (cry of derision) abucheo *m*; **I don't give a —** no me importa un comino; **it's a —** es para morirse de risa

hop [hɑp] VI saltar, brincar; **to — on** subirse a montar; N (short jump) saltito *m*, brinco *m*; (dance) bailongo *m*; **—s** lúpulo *m*

hope [hop] N esperanza *f*; VI/VT esperar; **to — for** esperar; **to — against —** esperar lo imposible

hopeful [hópfəł] ADJ (having hopes) esperanzado; (giving hopes) esperanzador, alentador

hopefully [hópfəli] ADV **— she'll come** ojalá [que] venga

hopeless [hóplɪs] ADJ (without hope) desesperanzado; (with no solution) irremediable; (unattainable) inalcanzable; **— cause** causa perdida *f*; **it is —** no tiene remedio; **the new secretary is — with numbers** el nuevo secretario es un desastre con los números

hopelessness [hóplɪsnɪs] N desesperanza *f*

horde [hɔrd] N (of people) horda *f*; (of animals) plaga *f*

horizon [həráɪzən] N horizonte *m*

horizontal [hɔrɪzɑ́ntł] ADJ horizontal

hormone [hɔ́rmon] N hormona *f*; **— therapy** terapia hormonal *f*

horn [hɔrn] N (of an animal, substance) cuerno *m*, asta *f*; (of an automobile) bocina *f*, claxon *m*; (musical) corno *m*, trompa *f*; **— of plenty** cuerno de la abundancia *m*; **to toot one's own —** darse autobombo; VI **to — in** entrometerse

hornet [hɔ́rnɪt] N avispón *m*; **—'s nest** avispero *m*

horny [hɔ́rni] ADJ calloso

horoscope [hɔ́rəskop] N horóscopo *m*

horrendous [hɔréndəs] ADJ horrendo

horrible [hɔ́rəbəł] ADJ horrible

horrid [hɔ́rɪd] ADJ horrendo

horrify [hɔ́rəfaɪ] VT horrorizar

horror [hɔ́rə·] N horror *m*

hors d'oeuvre [ɔrdɝv] N entremés *m*

horse [hɔrs] N caballo *m*; **—back** lomo de caballo *m*; **to ride —back** montar a caballo, cabalgar; **—fly** tábano *m*; **—laugh** carcajada *f*; **—man** jinete *m*; **—manship** equitación *f*; **—play** payasadas *f pl*; **—power** caballo de fuerza *m*; **— race** carrera de caballos *f*; **—radish** rábano picante *m*; **— sense** sentido común *m*; **—shoe** herradura *f*; **hold your —s!** ¡para el carro! VI **to — around** payasear

horticulture [hɔ́rɪdɪkəłtʃə·] N horticultura *f*

hose [hoz] N (for legs) medias *f pl*; (for liquids) manguera *f*, manga *f*

hosiery [hóʒəri] N (stockings) medias *f pl*; (shop for stockings) calcetería *f*

hospice [háspɪs] N (inn) hospicio *m*; (hospital) hospital para enfermos terminales *m*

hospitable [haspítəbəł] ADJ hospitalario, acogedor

hospital [háspɪdł] N hospital *m*

hospitality [haspɪtǽlɪti] N hospitalidad *f*

hospitalize [háspɪdḷaɪz] VT internar

host [host] N (also computer) anfitrión *m*; (in a home or hotel, for a parasite) huésped *m*; (on television) presentador -ora *mf*; (army) hueste *f*; (multitude) multitud *f*, cúmulo *m*; (wafer) hostia *f*

hostage [hástɪʤ] N rehén *mf*

hostel [hástł] N hostal *m*

hostelry [hástḷri] N hostería *f*

hostess [hóstɪs] N anfitriona *f*

hostile [hástł] ADJ hostil; **— takeover** compra hostil *f*

hostility [hɑstílɪti] N hostilidad *f*

hot [hɑt] ADJ (at high temperature) caliente; (sweltering) caluroso; (spicy) picante; (sexy) bueno; (stolen) robado; (recent) de último momento; (popular) popular; **— and heavy** apasionado, apasionadamente; **—bed** semillero *m*; **— dog** perro caliente *m*; **—headed** impetuoso, exaltado; **—house** invernadero *m*; **— potato** patata caliente *f*; **— seat** situación embarazosa *f*; **—shot** estrella *f*; **— tub** jacuzzi *m*; **it is — today** hace calor hoy; **— under the collar** enojado; VT **to — -wire** hacerle un puente a

hotel [hotɛ́ł] N hotel *m*; **—keeper** hotelero -ra *mf*

hound [haʊnd] N perro de caza *m*, sabueso *m*; VT

acosar, perseguir

hour [aʊr] N hora *f*; **— hand** horario *m*; **his finest —** su mejor momento *m*

hourly [áʊrli] ADV (on the hour) cada hora; (by the hour) por horas; **— wages** salario por hora *m*

house[1] [haʊs] N (residence) casa *f*; (legislature) cámara legislativa *f*; **— arrest** detención domiciliaria *f*; **—boat** casa flotante *f*; **—cleaning** limpieza de la casa *f*; **—hold** casa *f*, familia *f*; **—keeper** (in a house) ama de llaves *f*; (in a home) encargado -da de limpieza *mf*; **—keeping** mantenimiento del hogar *m*; **—top** techo *m*, tejado *m*; **—wife** ama de casa *f*; **—work** trabajo de casa *m*, quehaceres domésticos *m pl*; **in- —** interno; **on the —** la casa paga; **to keep —** cuidar la casa; **—hold expenses** gastos del hogar *m pl*; **— -to- —** puerta a puerta

house[2] [haʊz] VI/VT alojar

housing [háʊzɪŋ] N (place to live) vivienda *f*; (protective covering) caja *f*

hovel [hávəł] N (hut) choza *f*, cabaña *f*, tugurio *m*; (open shed) cobertizo *m*

hover [hávə-] VI (bird) cernerse; (hang in air) estar suspendido; (linger) rondar; **—craft** aerodeslizador *m*

how [haʊ] ADV cómo; **— about your mom?** ¿y tu mamá? **— beautiful!** ¡qué hermoso! **— come?** ¿por qué? **— early [late, soon]?** ¿cuándo? ¿a qué hora? **— far is it?** ¿a qué distancia está? ¿cuánto dista de aquí? **— long?** ¿cuánto tiempo? **— many?** ¿cuántos? **— much is it?** ¿cuánto vale? **— old are you?** ¿cuántos años tienes? **no matter — much it rains** por mucho que llueva; **he knows — difficult it is** él sabe lo difícil que es

however [haʊévə-] CONJ sin embargo, no obstante; ADV **— you want it** como quieras; **— difficult it may be** por muy difícil que sea; **— much it rains** por mucho que llueva

howl [haʊł] VI aullar; (wind) ulular; (with laughter) reír a carcajadas; N aullido *m*, alarido *m*

HQ [headquarters] [étʃkjú] N oficina central *f*, sede central *f*

HR [human resources] [étʃár] N recursos humanos *m pl*

HTML [HyperText Markup Language] [étʃtíémél] N HTML *m*

hub [hʌb] N (center of wheel) cubo *m*; (center of activity) núcleo *m*; **—cap** tapacubos *m sg*

hubbub [hábʌb] N alboroto *m*, barullo *m*

huckster [hákstə-] N (peddler) vendedor ambulante *m*; (promoter) mercachifle *m*

huddle [hádł] VI/VT (form a group) apiñar[se]; (curl up) acurrucar[se]; (consult) conferenciar; N tropel *m*; (group meeting for consultation) reunión *f*; **to be in a —** estar agrupados; **to get in a —** agruparse

hue [hju] N matiz *m*

huff [hʌf] N **to get into a —** enojarse; VI **to — and puff** resoplar

hug [hʌg] VI/VT abrazar[se]; **to — the coast** costear; N abrazo *m*

huge [hjuʤ] ADJ enorme, fiero

hull [hʌł] N (of a ship, airplane) casco *m*; (of beans, peas) vaina *f*; (of fruits, nuts) cáscara *f*; VT (beans, peas) desvainar; (nuts) cascar

hum [hʌm] VI/VT (person) tararear; (insect, machine) zumbar; (place of activity) hervir; **to — to sleep** arrullar; N (of voice) tarareo *m*; (of insect, machine) zumbido *m*

human [hjúmən] ADJ & N humano *m*; **— being** ser humano *m*; **— immunodeficiency virus** virus de inmunodeficiencia humana *m*

humane [hjumén] ADJ humano, humanitario

humanism [hjúmənɪzəm] N humanismo *m*

humanitarian [hjumænɪtériən] ADJ humanitario

humanity [hjumǽnɪdi] N humanidad *f*; **humanities** humanidades *f pl*

humble [hámbəł] ADJ humilde; VT humillar

humid [hjúmɪd] ADJ húmedo

humidify [hjumídəfaɪ] VT humidificar

humidity [hjumídɪdi] N humedad *f*

humiliate [hjumíliet] VT humillar, vejar

humiliation [hjumìliéjən] N humillación *f*

humility [hjumílɪdi] N humildad *f*

hummingbird [hámɪŋbɚd] N colibrí *m*

humor [hjúmə-] N humor *m*, humorismo *m*; **out of —** de mal humor, malhumorado; VT complacer a

humorous [hjúmə-əs] ADJ gracioso, chistoso

hump [hʌmp] N joroba *f*, giba *f*, corcova *f*; **we're over the —** ya pasamos lo peor; **—back** jorobado -da *mf*; **—back whale** ballena jorobada *f*, yubarta *f*

hunch [hʌntʃ] N presentimiento *m*, corazonada *f*; **—back** (person) jorobado -da *mf*; (hump) corcova *f*; VI encorvar

hundred [hándrɪd] NUM cien[to]; **a — people** cien personas; **a — and fifty people** ciento cincuenta personas; N cien/ciento *m*; **—s** centenares *m pl*, cientos *m pl*

hundredth [hándrɪdθ] ADJ centésimo

hung [hʌŋ] *see* hang 'ahorcar'

Hungarian [hʌŋgériən] ADJ & N húngaro -ra *mf*

Hungary [hʌ́ŋgəri] N Hungría *f*

hunger [hʌ́ŋgə-] N hambre *f*; VI pasar hambre; **to — for** ansiar, anhelar

hungry [hʌ́ŋgri] ADJ hambriento; **to be —** tener hambre; **to go —** pasar hambre

hunk [hʌŋk] N pedazo *m*, cacho *m*; **he's a real —** es un cacho de hombre, es un papacito

hunt [hʌnt] VI/VT (seek prey) cazar; **to — down** dar caza a; **to — for** buscar; N (activity of

hunting) caza *f*; (instance of hunting) cacería *f*; (search) búsqueda *f*

hunter [hʌ́ntɚ] N (who captures game) cazador -ora *mf*; (seeker) buscador -ora *mf*; (dog) perro de caza *m*

hunting [hʌ́ntɪŋ] N caza *f*; **— knife** cuchillo de caza *m*

huntsman [hʌ́ntsmən] N cazador *m*

hurdle [hɝ́dl] N (impediment) obstáculo *m*; (in races) valla *f*; VT saltar

hurl [hɝ́l] VI/VT arrojar, lanzar, precipitar

hurrah [hərɑ́] INTERJ ¡hurra!

hurricane [hɝ́ɪken] N huracán *m*

hurried [hɝ́id] ADJ apresurado; *Am* apurado

hurry [hɝ́i] VI darse prisa, apresurarse; *Am* apurarse; **to — in [out]** entrar [salir] de prisa; **to — up** apresurar[se], dar[se] prisa; *Am* apurar[se]; VT apresurar; *Am* apurar; N prisa *f*; *Am* apuro *m*; **to be in a —** tener prisa; *Am* estar apurado

hurt [hɝt] VI/VT (to injure) lastimar[se], hacer[se] daño; (damage) dañar[se]; (harm) perjudicar[se]; **to — someone's feelings** lastimar/herir a alguien; VI (suffer pain) doler; **my tooth —s** me duele la muela / el diente; N (damage) daño *m*; (wound) herida *f*, lastimadura *f*; ADJ (physically) lastimado, herido; (emotionally) herido; **to get —** lastimarse

hurtful [hɝ́tfəl] ADJ hiriente

husband [hʌ́zbənd] N marido *m*, esposo *m*; VT administrar

hush [hʌʃ] VI/VT aquietar[se], callar[se]; **—!** ¡chitón! ¡silencio! **to — up a scandal** encubrir un escándalo; N silencio *m*; **he gave her — money** compró su silencio

husk [hʌsk] N (shell) cáscara *f*; (pod) vaina *f*; (of corn) *Am* chala *f*; *Sp* farfolla *f*; VT (corn) quitar la chala/farfolla a; (beans, peas) desvainar

husky [hʌ́ski] ADJ (build) ronco; (strong) recio; N (breed of dog) husky *m*, perro esquimal *m*

hustle [hʌ́səl] VI (work energetically) afanarse; (swindle) estafar; VT (hurry along) empujar; N (bustle) ajetreo *m*; (scheme) timo *m*; **— and bustle** ajetreo *m*, trajín *m*

hut [hʌt] N choza *f*, cabaña *f*

hyacinth [háɪəsɪnθ] N jacinto *m*

hybrid [háɪbrɪd] ADJ híbrido

hybridization [haɪbrɪdɪzéʃən] N hibridación *f*

hydrate [háɪdret] N hidrato *m*; VI/VT hidratar[se]

hydraulic [haɪdrɔ́lɪk] ADJ hidráulico

hydrocarbon [háɪdrəkɑrbən] N hidrocarburo *m*

hydroelectric [haɪdroɪléktrɪk] ADJ hidroeléctrico

hydrogen [háɪdrəʤən] N hidrógeno *m*; **— bomb** bomba de hidrógeno *f*; **— peroxide** peróxido de hidrógeno *m*, agua oxigenada *f*

hydrophobia [haɪdrəfóbiə] N hidrofobia *f*

hydroplane [háɪdrəplen] N hidroavión *m*

hyena [haɪínə] N hiena *f*

hygiene [háɪʤin] N higiene *f*

hygienic [haɪʤénɪk] ADJ higiénico

hygienist [haɪʤínɪst] N higienista *mf*

hymen [háɪmən] N himen *m*

hymn [hɪm] N himno *m*

hype [háɪp] N exageración *f*; VT promocionar [exageradamente]

hyper [háɪpɚ] ADJ hiperactivo

hyperactive [haɪpɚ-ǽktɪv] ADJ hiperactivo

hyperbaric chamber [haɪpɚ-bǽrɪk tʃémbɚ] N cámara hiperbárica *f*

hyperdocument [haɪpɚ-dɑ́kjəmənt] N hiperdocumento *m*

hyperlink [háɪpɚ-lɪŋk] N hiperenlace *m*, hipervínculo *m*

hypermedia [haɪpɚ-míDiə] N hipermedia *m*

hypersensitive [haɪpɚ-sénsIDIV] ADJ hipersensible

hypertension [haɪpɚ-ténʃən] N hipertensión *f*, presión arterial alta *f*

hyperventilate [haɪpɚ-véntḷet] VI hiperventilar

hyphen [háɪfən] N guión *m*

hypnosis [hɪpnósɪs] N hipnosis *f*

hypnotherapy [hɪpnoθérəpi] N hipnoterapia *f*

hypnotize [hípnətaɪz] VT hipnotizar

hypoallergenic [haɪpoælə-ʤénɪk] ADJ hipoalérgico

hypochondriac [haɪpokándriæk] N hipocondríaco *mf*, hipocondriaco *mf*

hypocrisy [hɪpɑ́krɪsi] N hipocresía *f*

hypocrite [hípəkrɪt] N hipócrita *mf*

hypocritical [hɪpəkrídɪkəl] ADJ hipócrita, doblado

hypodermic needle [haɪpədɝ́mɪk nídḷ] N aguja hipodérmica *f*

hypoglycemia [haɪpoglaɪsímiə] N hipoglucemia *f*

hypothesis [haɪpɑ́θɪsɪs] N hipótesis *f*

hypothyroidism [haɪpoθáɪrɔIDIZəm] N hipotiroidismo *m*

hysterectomy [hɪstərɛ́ktəmi] N histerectomía *f*

hysterical [hɪstérɪkəl] ADJ (out of control) histérico; (funny) desternillante

Ii

I [aɪ] PRON yo

I-beam [áɪbɪm] N viga doble *f*

Iberian [aɪbíriən] ADJ ibérico

Ibero-American [aɪbiroəmérɪkən] ADJ iberoamericano -na

ibuprofen [aɪbjuprófɪn] N ibuprofeno *m*

ice [aɪs] N hielo *m*; **— age** periodo glaciar *m*; **—berg** iceberg *m*; **—box** nevera *f*;

refrigerador *m*; **— cream** helado *m*; **— cream cone** cucurucho de helado *m*; **—-cream parlor** heladería *f*; **— hockey** hockey sobre hielo *m*; **— skates** patines de cuchilla *m pl*; **— water** agua helada *f*; **to break the —** romper el hielo; **on —** en suspenso; VI/VT (freeze) helar[se]; (cover with ice) cubrir[se] de hielo; VT (cover with icing) bañar; (insure a deal) cerrar; **to —-skate** patinar sobre hielo; **—d tea** té helado *m*

Iceland [áɪslənd] N Islandia *f*

Icelander [áɪsləndə-] N islandés -esa *mf*

Icelandic [aɪsléndɪk] ADJ islandés

icicle [áɪsɪkəl] N carámbano *m*

icing [áɪsɪŋ] N (frosting) baño *m*; (formation of ice) formación de hielo *f*

icon [áɪkɑn] N icono *m*, ícono *m* (also computer term)

ICU [intensive care unit] [áɪsíjú] N unidad de cuidados intensivos *f*

icy [áɪsi] ADJ helado

ID [identification card] [áɪdí] N tarjeta de identidad *m*

idea [aɪdíə] N idea *f*

ideal [aɪdíəl] N ideal *m*; ADJ ideal, idóneo

idealism [aɪdíəlɪzəm] N idealismo *m*

idealist [aɪdíəlɪst] N idealista *mf*

idealistic [aɪdiəlístɪk] ADJ idealista

identical [aɪdéntɪkəl] ADJ idéntico; **— twins** gemelos *m pl*, gemelas *f pl*

identification [aɪdentəfɪkéʃən] N identificación *f*; **— card** tarjeta de identidad *m*, cédula de identidad *f*

identify [aɪdéntəfaɪ] VI/VT identificar[se]

identity [aɪdéntɪdi] N identidad *f*; **— theft** robo de identidad *m*

ideological [aɪdɪəlɑ́dʒɪkəl] ADJ ideológico

ideology [aɪdiɑ́lədʒi] N ideología *f*

idiocy [ídiəsi] N idiotez *f*

idiom [ídiəm] N modismo *m*

idiosyncrasy [idiosínkrəsi] N idiosincrasia *f*

idiot [ídiət] N idiota *mf*

idiotic [idiádɪk] ADJ idiota

idle [áɪdl] ADJ (not active) ocioso; (lazy) perezoso, holgazán; (of a machine, worker) parado; (of an engine) en ralentí; (meaningless) vacío; VI (person) holgazanear; (motor) girar en vacío; VT (cause to be idle) dejar parado/desocupado

idleness [áɪdlɪnɪs] N (inactivity) ociosidad *f*, ocio *m*, holganza *f*; (sloth) pereza *f*

idler [áɪdlə-] N holgazán -ana *mf*, zanguango -ga *mf*

idol [áɪdl] N ídolo *m*

idolatry [aɪdɑ́lətri] N idolatría *f*

idolize [áɪdlaɪz] VT idolatrar

idyll [áɪdl] N idilio *m*

if [ɪf] CONJ si; **— I were you** en tu lugar / yo que tú; **— only I had known** de haber sabido / ojalá hubiera sabido; **he's tall, — a bit stooped** es alto, aunque un poco encorvado; N **—s** condiciones *f pl*; **no —s, ands, or buts** no hay pero que valga

igloo [íglu] N iglú *m*

ignite [ɪgnáɪt] VI/VT encender[se], prender fuego [a]

ignition [ɪgníʃən] N ignición *f*, encendido *m*; **— switch** llave de contacto *f*

ignoble [ɪgnóbəl] ADJ innoble

ignorance [ígnərəns] N ignorancia *f*

ignorant [ígnərənt] ADJ ignorante

ignore [ɪgnɔ́r] VT ignorar

ilk [ɪlk] N ralea *f*, calaña *f*

ill [ɪl] ADJ enfermo, malo; **— fortune** mala suerte *f*; **— nature** mal genio *m*, mala índole *f*; **— repute** mala fama *f*; **— will** mala voluntad *f*; N (sickness) enfermedad *f*; (calamity) calamidad *f*; ADJ **—-advised** imprudente; **— at ease** incómodo; **—-bred** maleducado; **—-fated** fatídico, funesto, desastrado; **—-gotten** mal adquirido; **—-humored** malhumorado; **—-mannered** maleducado, grosero; **—-natured** de mal genio; ADV **we can — afford to stop now** no podemos darnos el lujo de detenernos ahora

illegal [ɪlígəl] ADJ ilegal

illegitimate [ɪlɪdʒídəmɪt] ADJ ilegítimo

illicit [ɪlísɪt] ADJ ilícito

illiteracy [ɪlíʃərəsi] N analfabetismo *m*

illiterate [ɪlíʃərɪt] ADJ & N analfabeto -ta *mf*

illness [íɫnɪs] N enfermedad *f*

illuminate [ɪlúmənet] VI/VT iluminar[se]

illumination [ɪlumənéʃən] N iluminación *f*

illusion [ɪlúʒən] N ilusión *f*

illusory [ɪlúzəri] ADJ ilusorio

illustrate [íləstret] VI/VT ilustrar

illustration [ɪləstréʃən] N ilustración *f*, estampa *f*

illustrator [íləstreɪə-] N ilustrador -ra *mf*, dibujante *mf*

illustrious [ɪlástriəs] ADJ ilustre, eximio

image [ímɪdʒ] N imagen *f*

imagery [ímɪdʒri] N conjunto de imágenes *m*

imaginary [ɪmǽdʒənɛri] ADJ imaginario, fabuloso

imagination [ɪmædʒənéʃən] N imaginación *f*, fantasía *f*

imaginative [ɪmǽdʒənəɪv] ADJ imaginativo, fantasioso

imagine [ɪmǽdʒɪn] VI/VT imaginar[se]; **— that!** ¡figúrate!

imbalance [ɪmbǽləns] N desequilibrio *m*

imbecile [ímbəsəɫ] N imbécil *mf*

imbibe [ɪmbáɪb] VI/VT beber

imbue [ɪmbjú] VT imbuir, infundir

IMF [International Monetary Fund] [áɪéméf] N FMI *m*

imitate [ímɪtet] VT imitar

imitation [ɪmɪtéʃən] N imitación *f*; **— leather**

imitación de cuero *f*

imitator [ímɪtɛɒ-ɹ] N imitador -ora *mf*

immaculate [ɪmǽkjəlɪt] ADJ inmaculado

immaterial [ɪmətíriəł] ADJ inmaterial; **it is — to me** me es indiferente

immature [ɪmətʃúr] ADJ inmaduro

immediate [ɪmíɒɪt] ADJ inmediato

immediately [ɪmíɒɪtli] ADV inmediatamente, enseguida

immense [ɪméns] ADJ inmenso

immensity [ɪménsɪɒi] N inmensidad *f*

immerse [ɪmɝ́s] VT (submerge) sumergir; (absorb) sumir

immersed [ɪmɝ́st] ADJ inmerso

immigrant [ímɪgrənt] ADJ & N inmigrante *mf*

immigrate [ímɪgret] VI inmigrar

immigration [ɪmɪgréʃən] N inmigración *f*

imminent [ímənənt] ADJ inminente

immobile [ɪmóbəł] ADJ inmóvil

immobilize [ɪmóbəlaɪz] VT inmovilizar

immodest [ɪmɑ́ɒɪst] ADJ inmodesto

immodesty [ɪmɑ́ɒɪsti] N inmodestia *f*

immoral [ɪmɔ́rəł] ADJ inmoral

immorality [ɪmɔrǽlɪɒi] N inmoralidad *f*

immortal [ɪmɔ́rdl] ADJ & N inmortal *mf*

immortality [ɪmɔrtǽlɪɒi] N inmortalidad *f*

immovable [ɪmúvəbəł] ADJ inamovible

immune [ɪmjún] ADJ inmune; **— system** sistema inmune *m*

immunity [ɪmjúnɪɒi] N inmunidad *f*

immunodeficiency [ɪmjənodɪfíʃənsi] N inmunodeficiencia *f*

immutable [ɪmjúdəbəł] ADJ inmutable

impact [ímpækt] N impacto *m*; VI/VT repercutir [sobre]; **—ed molar** muela impactada *f*

impair [ɪmpér] VT dañar, deteriorar, menoscabar; **—ed** con las facultades disminuidas

impairment [ɪmpérmənt] N daño *m*, deterioro *m*, menoscabo *m*

impala [ɪmpálə] N impala *m*

impale [ɪmpél] VT empalar

impart [ɪmpárt] VT (bestow knowledge) impartir; (reveal) revelar

impartial [ɪmpárʃəł] ADJ imparcial

impartiality [ɪmpɑrʃiǽlɪɒi] N imparcialidad *f*

impasse [ímpæs] N impasse *m*

impassioned [ɪmpǽʃənd] ADJ apasionado

impassive [ɪmpǽsɪv] ADJ impasible

impatience [ɪmpéʃəns] N impaciencia *f*

impatient [ɪmpéʃənt] ADJ impaciente

impeach [ɪmpítʃ] VT acusar formalmente; **to — a person's honor** poner en tela de juicio el honor de uno

impeachment [ɪmpítʃmənt] N impeachment *m*

impede [ɪmpíd] VT obstaculizar, estorbar, trabar

impediment [ɪmpɛ́dəmənt] N impedimento *m*, obstáculo *m*; (of speech) defecto *m*

impel [ɪmpél] VT impeler

impending [ɪmpéndɪŋ] ADJ inminente

impenetrable [ɪmpénɪtrəbəł] ADJ impenetrable

imperative [ɪmpɛ́rəɒɪv] ADJ (like a command) imperativo; (necessary) imperioso; N (command, grammatical mood) imperativo *m*; (obligation) obligación *f*

imperceptible [ɪmpə-séptəbəł] ADJ imperceptible

imperfect [ɪmpɝ́fɪkt] ADJ & N imperfecto *m*

imperial [ɪmpíriəł] ADJ imperial

imperialism [ɪmpíriəlɪzəm] N imperialismo *m*

imperil [ɪmpérəł] VT poner en peligro

imperious [ɪmpíriəs] ADJ imperioso

impersonal [ɪmpɝ́sənl] ADJ impersonal

impersonate [ɪmpɝ́sənet] VT (assume traits of) hacerse pasar por; (mimic) imitar

impersonator [ɪmpɝ́sənɛɒɚ] N imitador -ora *mf*

impertinence [ɪmpɝ́tn̩əns] N impertinencia *f*

impertinent [ɪmpɝ́tn̩ənt] ADJ impertinente

impervious [ɪmpɝ́viəs] ADJ impermeable; (to reason) refractario

impetigo [ɪmpɪtáɪgo] N impétigo *m*

impetuous [ɪmpétʃuəs] ADJ impetuoso

impetus [ímpəɒəs] N ímpetu *m*, empuje *m*

impious [ímpiəs] ADJ impío

implacable [ɪmplǽkəbəł] ADJ implacable

implant[1] [ɪmplǽnt] VT implantar

implant[2] [ímplænt] N implante *m*

implantation [ɪmplæntéʃən] N implantación *f*

implement[1] [ímpləmənt] N implemento *m*, utensilio *m*

implement[2] [ímpləmɛnt] VT implementar, instrumentar

implementation [ɪmpləmɪntéʃən] N implementación *f*

implicate [ímplɪket] VT implicar, involucrar

implication [ɪmplɪkéʃən] N implicación *f*; **by —** implícitamente

implicit [ɪmplísɪt] ADJ implícito

implore [ɪmplɔ́r] VI/VT implorar

imply [ɪmpláɪ] VT dar a entender

impolite [ɪmpəláɪt] ADJ descortés

import[1] [ɪmpɔ́rt] VT (bring in) importar

import[2] [ímpɔrt] N (act of importing, thing imported) importación *f*; (significance) significado *m*; **—-export company** compañía de importación y exportación *f*

importance [ɪmpɔ́rtn̩s] N importancia *f*, relevancia *f*

important [ɪmpɔ́rtn̩t] ADJ importante, relevante

impose [ɪmpóz] VT imponer; **to — [upon]** abusar [de]

imposing [ɪmpózɪŋ] ADJ imponente, impresionante

imposition [ɪmpəzíʃən] N (act of imposing, burden) imposición *f*; (abuse) abuso *m*

impossibility [ɪmpɑsəbílɪɒi] N imposibilidad *f*

impossible [ɪmpásəbəł] ADJ (not possible) imposible; (unbearable) insoportable; **to make —** imposibilitar
impostor [ɪmpástə˞] N impostor -ora *mf*
impotence [ímpətəns] N impotencia *f*
impotent [ímpətənt] ADJ impotente
impoverish [ɪmpáva˞ɪʃ] VT empobrecer
impregnate [ímprégnet] VT (cause to be permeated) impregnar; (make pregnant) fecundar, preñar
impress [ɪmprés] VT (make a mark by pressing) estampar; VI/VT (affect deeply) impresionar
impression [ɪmpréʃən] N impresión *f*; (feeling) impresión *f*, sensación *f*
impressive [ɪmprésɪv] ADJ impresionante
imprint[1] [ímprɪnt] N (indentation) impresión *f*, marca *f*; (printer's mark) pie de imprenta *m*
imprint[2] [ɪmprínt] VT (impress on) imprimir; (fix firmly in mind) grabar
imprison [ɪmprízən] VT (in jail) encarcelar; (anywhere) apresar
imprisonment [ɪmprízənmənt] N encarcelamiento *m*
improbable [ɪmprúbəbəł] ADJ improbable
impromptu [ɪmprámptu] ADJ improvisado; **he gave the speech —** improvisó el discurso; N impromptu *m*
improper [ɪmprápə˞] ADJ indecoroso, inconveniente
improve [ɪmprúv] VI/VT mejorar[se]; **to — upon** mejorar
improvement [ɪmprúvmənt] N (of a plan) mejora *f*; (in health) mejoría *f*
improvisation [ɪmpravɪzéʃən] N improvisación *f*
improvise [ímprəvaɪz] VI/VT improvisar
imprudent [ɪmprúdn̩t] ADJ imprudente, desatinado
impudence [ímpjədəns] N impertinencia *f*, descaro *m*, desparpajo *m*
impudent [ímpjədənt] ADJ impertinente, descarado
impulse [ímpaɪs] N impulso *m*; **to act on —** obrar impulsivamente
impulsive [ɪmpáɪsɪv] ADJ impulsivo
impunity [ɪmpjúnɪdɪ] N impunidad *f*
impure [ɪmpjúr] ADJ impuro
impurity [ɪmpjúrɪdɪ] N impureza *f*
in [ɪn] PREP en; (in tennis) buena, dentro; **— London** en Londres; **— haste** de prisa; **— the morning** por/en la mañana; **— writing** por escrito; **she was walking — the street** andaba por la calle; **to arrive — London** llegar a Londres; **the books — the box** los libros de la caja; **at two — the morning** a las dos de la mañana; **dressed — white** vestido de blanco; **the tallest — his class** el más alto de su clase; **to come — a week** venir dentro de una semana; ADV adentro, dentro; **is she — or out?** ¿está adentro o afuera? **to be all —** estar rendido; **to be — with someone** estar bien con alguien; **to come —** entrar; **to have it — for someone** tenerle ojeriza a una persona; **to put —** meter; **the doctor is —** el doctor está; **hats are —** los sombreros están de moda; **—field** cuadro interior *m*; N **—patient** paciente internado -da *mf*; **—patient care** internación *f*; **—seam** entrepierna *f*; **—step** empeine *m*; ADJ **the — place to eat** el restaurante de moda; **an — joke** una broma para un grupo selecto
inability [ɪnəbíłɪdɪ] N inhabilidad *f*, incapacidad *f*
inaccessible [ɪnæksésəbəł] ADJ inaccesible, inasequible
inaccurate [ɪnǽkjə˞ɪt] ADJ (not precise) inexacto, impreciso; (wrong) incorrecto
inactive [ɪnǽktɪv] ADJ inactivo
inactivity [ɪnæktívɪdɪ] N inactividad *f*
inadequate [ɪnǽdɪkwɪt] ADJ (insufficient) insuficiente; (unacceptable) inaceptable
inadmissible [ɪnədmísəbəł] ADJ inadmisible
inadvertent [ɪnədvə˞tn̩t] ADJ (unintentional) involuntario; (careless) descuidado, negligente
inadvisable [ɪnədváɪzəbəł] ADJ desaconsejable
inane [ɪnén] ADJ necio
inanimate [ɪnǽnəmɪt] ADJ inanimado
inasmuch as [ɪnəzmátʃæz] CONJ puesto que
inattentive [ɪnəténtɪv] ADJ desatento
inaudible [ɪnɔ́dəbəł] ADJ inaudible
inaugurate [ɪnɔ́gjə˞et] VT (initiate) inaugurar; (induct into office) investir de un cargo
inauguration [ɪnɔgjə˞éʃən] N (initiation) inauguración *f*; (induction) investidura *f*
inboard [ínbɔ˞d] ADJ dentro del casco
inborn [ɪnbɔ́rn] ADJ innato
Inca [íŋkə] ADJ & N inca *mf*
incandescence [ɪŋkændésəns] N incandescencia *f*
incandescent [ɪnkændésənt] ADJ incandescente
incantation [ɪnkæntéʃən] N conjuro *m*
incapable [ɪnképəbəł] ADJ incapaz
incapacitate [ɪnkəpǽsɪtet] VT incapacitar
incarcerate [ɪnkársə˞et] VT encarcelar
incarnation [ɪnkə˞néʃən] N encarnación *f*
incendiary [ɪnséndɪe˞ɪ] ADJ & N incendiario -ria *mf*; **— bomb** bomba incendiaria *f*
incense[1] [ínsəns] N incienso *m*
incense[2] [ɪnséns] VT encolerizar
incentive [ɪnséntɪv] N incentivo *m*, acicate *m*
inception [ɪnsépʃən] N comienzo *m*
incessant [ɪnsésənt] ADJ incesante
incest [ínsɛst] N incesto *m*
incestuous [ɪnséstʃuəs] ADJ incestuoso
inch [ɪntʃ] N pulgada [2.54 centímetros] *f*; **to be within an — of** estar a un punto de; VI avanzar poco a poco

incidence [ínsɪdəns] N incidencia *f*
incident [ínsɪdənt] N incidente *m*, lance *m*; (crime, accident) suceso *m*
incidental [ɪnsɪdéntl] ADJ (happening in accordance with) accesorio; **— music** música incidental *f*; N **—s** gastos menores *m pl*
incidentally [ɪnsɪdéntlɪ] ADV a propósito
incinerate [ɪnsínəret] VT incinerar
incipient [ɪnsípɪənt] ADJ incipiente, naciente
incision [ɪnsíʒən] N incisión *f*
incisive [ɪnsáɪsɪv] ADJ incisivo
incisor [ɪnsáɪzɚ] N (tooth) incisivo *m*
incite [ɪnsáɪt] VT incitar
inclement [ɪnklémənt] ADJ inclemente
inclination [ɪnklənéʃən] N (slope) inclinación *f*; (tendency) afición *f*, inclinación *f*
incline[1] [ɪnkláɪn] VI/VT inclinar[se]
incline[2] [ínklaɪn] N declive *m*, pendiente *f*
include [ɪnklúd] VT incluir
including [ɪnklúdɪŋ] ADJ **it costs a thousand dollars, not — air travel** cuesta mil dólares, sin incluir el vuelo; **that whole week, — Saturday** toda esa semana, incluyendo el sábado / el sábado inclusive; **— you, there are four of us** incluyéndote a ti, somos cuatro
inclusion [ɪnklúʒən] N (acceptance) inclusión *f*; (addition) incorporación *f*
inclusive [ɪnklúsɪv] ADJ inclusivo; **from Monday to Friday —** de lunes a viernes inclusive
incoherent [ɪnkohírənt] ADJ incoherente
income [ínkʌm] N *Sp* renta *f*; *Am* ingreso *m*; **— tax** *Sp* impuesto sobre la renta *m*; *Am* impuesto sobre ingresos *m*; **— tax return** declaración de impuestos sobre la renta / los ingresos *f*
incoming [ínkʌmɪŋ] ADJ entrante
incomparable [ɪnkámpɚəbəł] ADJ incomparable, sin parangón
incompatible [ɪnkəmpǽtəbəł] ADJ incompatible
incompetent [ɪnkámpɪtənt] ADJ incompetente
incomplete [ɪnkəmplít] ADJ incompleto
incomprehensible [ɪnkʌmprɪhénsəbəł] ADJ incomprensible
inconceivable [ɪnkənsívəbəł] ADJ inconcebible
inconclusive [ɪnkənklúsɪv] ADJ no concluyente
inconsiderate [ɪnkənsídɚɪt] ADJ desconsiderado
inconsistency [ɪnkənsístənsi] N (condition) inconsecuencia *f*; (instance) incoherencia *f*
inconsistent [ɪnkənsístənt] ADJ inconsecuente
inconspicuous [ɪnkənspíkjuəs] ADJ poco llamativo; **to be —** pasar inadvertido
inconstancy [ɪnkánstənsi] N inconstancia *f*
inconstant [ɪnkánstənt] ADJ inconstante
incontinent [ɪnkántənənt] ADJ incontinente
incontrovertible [ɪnkɑntrəvɝ́dəbəł] ADJ incontrovertible
inconvenience [ɪnkənvínjəns] N (state of being inconvenient) inconveniencia *f*; (thing that is inconvenient) molestia *f*, inconveniente *m*; VT incomodar, molestar
inconvenient [ɪnkənvínjənt] ADJ (bothersome) incómodo; (untimely) inoportuno
incorporate [ɪnkɔ́rpəret] VI/VT (include) incorporar[se]; (form a corporation) constituir[se] en sociedad
incorporation [ɪŋkɔrpəréʃən] N (inclusion) incorporación *f*; (integration) integración *f*
incorrect [ɪnkərékt] ADJ incorrecto
incorrigible [ɪnkɔ́rɪdʒəbəł] ADJ incorregible
increase[1] [ɪnkrís] VI/VT aumentar[se], incrementar[se]
increase[2] [ínkris] N aumento *m*, incremento *m*
increasingly [ɪnkrísɪŋlɪ] ADV cada vez más
incredible [ɪnkrédəbəł] ADJ increíble
incredulous [ɪnkrédʒələs] ADJ incrédulo
increment [ínkrəmənt] N incremento *m*
incriminate [ɪnkrímənet] VT incriminar
incubator [ɪŋkjəbeɪdɚ] N incubadora *f*
inculcate [ɪnkáłket] VT inculcar
incumbent [ɪnkámbənt] ADJ **a duty — upon me** un deber que me incumbe; N titular *m*
incur [ɪnkɝ́] VT (an expense) incurrir en; (a debt) contraer
incurable [ɪŋkjúrəbəł] ADJ incurable
indebted [ɪndédɪd] ADJ endeudado, en deuda
indebtedness [ɪndédɪdnɪs] N endeudamiento *m*, adeudo *m*
indecency [ɪndísənsi] N indecencia *f*
indecent [ɪndísənt] ADJ indecente; **— exposure** delito de exhibicionismo *m*
indecision [ɪndɪsíʒən] N indecisión *f*
indeed [ɪndíd] ADV de verdad; INTERJ (ironically) ¡no me digas! (sincerely) ¡tienes razón! ¡efectivamente!
indefensible [ɪndɪfénsəbəł] ADJ indefendible
indefinite [ɪndéfənɪt] ADJ indefinido
indelible [ɪndéləbəł] ADJ indeleble
indelicate [ɪndélɪkɪt] ADJ (tactless) indelicado; (offensive) indecoroso
indemnify [ɪndémnəfaɪ] VT indemnizar
indemnity [ɪndémnɪdi] N indemnización *f*
indent [ɪndént] VI/VT sangrar
indentation [ɪndɛntéʃən] N (notch) muesca *f*; (blank space) sangría *f*
independence [ɪndɪpéndəns] N independencia *f*
independent [ɪndɪpéndənt] ADJ independiente, autónomo
indestructible [ɪndɪstráktəbəł] ADJ indestructible
indeterminate [ɪndɪtɝ́mənɪt] ADJ indeterminado
index [índɛks] N índice *m*; **— card** ficha *f*; **— finger** índice *m*; VT (incorporate into an index) poner en el índice; (make the index)

poner/hacer un índice; (adjust wages) indexar
indexing [índe̞ksɪŋ] N índexación *f*
India [índiə] N India *f*
Indian [índiən] ADJ & N indio -a *mf*; **— Ocean** Océano Indico *m*
indicate [índɪket] VT indicar
indication [ɪndɪkéʃən] N indicación *f*
indicative [ɪndíkə̞dɪv] ADJ & N indicativo *m*
indicator [índɪkeɒ-] N indicador *m*
indict [ɪndáɪt] VT acusar
indictment [ɪndáɪtmənt] N acusación *f*
indifference [ɪndífrəns] N indiferencia *f*
indifferent [ɪndífrənt] ADJ indiferente
indigenous [ɪndíʤənəs] ADJ (person) indígena; (plant, animal) autóctono
indigent [índɪʤənt] ADJ & N indigente *mf*
indigestion [ɪndɪʤéstʃən] N indigestión *f*
indignant [ɪndígnənt] ADJ indignado
indignation [ɪndɪgnéʃən] N indignación *f*
indignity [ɪndígnɪɒɪ] N ultraje *m*, afrenta *f*
indigo [índɪgo] N índigo *m*, añil *m*; **— blue** azul añil *m*
indirect [ɪndɪrékt] ADJ indirecto; **— object** complemento/objeto indirecto *m*
indiscreet [ɪndɪskrít] ADJ indiscreto
indiscretion [ɪndɪskréʃən] N indiscreción *f*
indispensable [ɪndɪspénsə̞bə̞l] ADJ indispensable, imprescindible
indispose [ɪndɪspóz] VT indisponer
indisposed [ɪndɪspózd] ADJ indispuesto; **to become —** indisponerse
indistinct [ɪndɪstíŋkt] ADJ indistinto
individual [ɪndə̞vídʒuə̞l] ADJ individual; N individuo *m*, persona *f*; *pej* sujeto *m*, individuo *m*
individualism [ɪndə̞vídʒuə̞lɪzə̞m] N individualismo *m*
individualist [ɪndə̞vídʒuə̞lɪst] N individualista *mf*
individuality [ɪndə̞vɪdʒuæ̞lɪɒɪ] N individualidad *f*
indivisible [ɪndə̞vízə̞bə̞l] ADJ indivisible
indoctrinate [ɪndɑ́ktrɪnet] VT adoctrinar
indolence [índə̞lə̞ns] N indolencia *f*, desidia *f*
indolent [índə̞lə̞nt] ADJ indolente, haragán
indomitable [ɪndɑ́mɪɒə̞bə̞l] ADJ indomable
Indonesia [ɪndə̞níʒə̞] N Indonesia *f*
Indonesian [ɪndə̞níʒə̞n] ADJ & N indonesio -sia *mf*
indoor [índɔr] ADJ interior
indoors [ɪndɔ́rz] ADV dentro; **to go —** entrar, ir para adentro
induce [ɪndús] VT inducir
inducement [ɪndúsmənt] N aliciente *m*, incentivo *m*
induct [ɪndə́kt] VT (initiate) admitir, iniciar; (draft) reclutar
induction [ɪndə́kʃən] N (philosophical, electrical) inducción *f*; (into an organization) admisión *f*, iniciación *f*
indulge [ɪndə́ɫʤ] VT mimar, consentir; VI **to — in** darse a, entregarse a; **to — oneself [in]** darse el gusto [de]
indulgence [ɪndə́ɫʤəns] N (act or state of indulging, religious) indulgencia *f*; (thing indulged in) exceso *m*, lujo *m*
indulgent [ɪndə́ɫʤənt] ADJ indulgente; (toward a child) complaciente
industrial [ɪndə́strɪə̞ɫ] ADJ industrial
industrialist [ɪndə́strɪə̞lɪst] N industrial *mf*
industrialization [ɪndɑstrɪə̞lɪzéʃən] N industrialización *f*
industrious [ɪndə́strɪəs] ADJ (student) aplicado, diligente; (worker) industrioso
industry [índə̞stri] N (manufacturing) industria *f*; (hard work) diligencia *f*; **— standards** normas industriales *f pl*
inebriated [ɪníbrɪeɒɪd] ADJ ebrio
inedible [ɪnéɒə̞bə̞ɫ] ADJ incomestible, incomible
ineffable [ɪnéfə̞bə̞ɫ] ADJ inefable
ineffective [ɪnɪféktɪv] ADJ ineficaz, ineficiente
ineffectual [ɪnɪféktʃuə̞ɫ] ADJ ineficaz
inefficient [ɪnɪfíʃə̞nt] ADJ ineficiente
ineligible [ɪnéɫɪʤə̞bə̞ɫ] ADJ inelegible
inept [ɪnépt] ADJ inepto
inequality [ɪnɪkwɑ́lɪɒɪ] N desigualdad *f*
inert [ɪnɝ́t] ADJ inerte
inertia [ɪnɝ́ʃə] N inercia *f*
inescapable [ɪnɪsképə̞bə̞ɫ] ADJ inevitable, ineludible
inestimable [ɪnéstə̞mə̞bə̞ɫ] ADJ inestimable
inevitable [ɪnévɪɒə̞bə̞ɫ] ADJ inevitable
inexcusable [ɪnɪkskjúzə̞bə̞ɫ] ADJ inexcusable
inexhaustible [ɪnɪgzɔ́stə̞bə̞ɫ] ADJ inagotable
inexorable [ɪnéksə̞ə̞bə̞ɫ] ADJ inexorable
inexpensive [ɪnɪkspénsɪv] ADJ económico, barato
inexperienced [ɪnɪkspírɪə̞nst] ADJ no experimentado, inexperto
inexplicable [ɪnɪksplíkə̞bə̞ɫ] ADJ inexplicable
infallible [ɪnfǽɫə̞bə̞ɫ] ADJ infalible
infamous [ínfə̞məs] ADJ infame, de mala fama
infamy [ínfə̞mi] N infamia *f*
infancy [ínfə̞nsi] N primera infancia *f*
infant [ínfə̞nt] N bebé *mf*
infantile [ínfə̞ntaɪɫ] ADJ infantil
infantry [ínfə̞ntri] N infantería *f*; **—man** infante *m*
infatuated [ɪnfǽtʃueɒɪd] ADJ enamorado
infect [ɪnfékt] VT (cause disease) infectar; (spread a mood) contagiar
infection [ɪnfékʃən] N infección *f*
infectious [ɪnfékʃəs] ADJ (disease) infeccioso, contagioso; (mood) contagioso
infer [ɪnfɝ́] VT inferir, deducir
inference [ínfə̞ə̞ns] N inferencia *f*, deducción *f*
inferior [ɪnfíriə̞] ADJ inferior
inferiority [ɪnfɪriɔ́rɪɒɪ] N inferioridad *f*; **—**

complex complejo de inferioridad *m*
infernal [ɪnfɚ́nl] ADJ infernal
inferno [ɪnfɚ́no] N (fire) incendio *m*; (hot place) infierno *m*
infertility [ɪnfə·tɪ́lɪdɪ] N infertilidad *f*
infest [ɪnfɛ́st] VT infestar, plagar
infestation [ɪnfestéʃən] N infestación *f*
infiltrate [ɪnfɪ́ltret] VI/VT infiltrar[se]; **to — an organization** infiltrarse en una organización
infinite [ɪ́nfənɪt] ADJ & N infinito *m*
infinitive [ɪnfɪ́nɪdɪv] ADJ & N infinitivo *m*
infinity [ɪnfɪ́nɪdɪ] N (large number) infinidad *f*; (space) infinito *m*
infirm [ɪnfɚ́m] ADJ enfermizo, achacoso
infirmary [ɪnfɚ́məri] N enfermería *f*
infirmity [ɪnfɚ́mɪdɪ] N enfermedad *f*, achaque *m*
inflame [ɪnflém] VT (with infection) inflamar[se]; (with passion) enardecer[se]; (with fire) encender[se]
inflammation [ɪnfləméʃən] N inflamación *f*
inflate [ɪnflét] VI/VT (fill with air) inflar[se], hincharse; (exaggerate) exagerar
inflation [ɪnfléʃən] N (rise in prices) inflación *f*; (introduction of air) inflado *m*
inflexible [ɪnflɛ́ksəbəł] ADJ inflexible
inflict [ɪnflɪ́kt] VT (impose on) infligir; **to — a blow** asestar un golpe
influence [ɪ́nfluəns] N influencia *f*, influjo *m*; VT influir en/sobre, incidir en; **— peddling** tráfico de influencias *m*
influential [ɪnfluɛ́nʃəł] ADJ influyente
influenza [ɪnfluɛ́nzə] N gripe *f*
influx [ɪ́nflʌks] N (of fluid, goods) entrada *f*; (of people) afluencia *f*
infomercial [ɪ́nfomɚʃəł] N infomercial *m*, publirreportaje *m*
inform [ɪnfɔ́rm] VI/VT (give knowledge) informar[se]; VT (inspire) inspirar; **to — against/on** delatar a, denunciar a
informal [ɪnfɔ́rməł] ADJ informal
informant [ɪnfɔ́rmənt] N informante *mf*
information [ɪnfə·méʃən] N (news, data, details, act of informing) información *f*; (details) informes *m pl*; **— superhighway** autopista de la información *f*
informative [ɪnfɔ́rmədɪv] ADJ informativo
informer [ɪnfɔ́rmə·] N informante *mf*, delator -ora *mf*, *pej* soplón -ona *mf*
infotainment [ɪ́nfotɛ́nmənt] N entretenimiento informativo *m*
infraction [ɪnfrǽkʃən] N infracción *f*
infrared [ɪ́nfrərɛ́d] ADJ & N infrarrojo *m*
infrastructure [ɪ́nfrəstrʌ́ktʃə·] N infraestructura *f*
infringe [ɪnfrɪ́ndʒ] VT infringir; VI **to — upon** violar
infringement [ɪnfrɪ́ndʒmənt] N infracción *f*, violación *f*
infuriate [ɪnfjúrɪet] VT enfurecer, sublevar
infuse [ɪnfjúz] VT infundir
ingenious [ɪnʤínjəs] ADJ ingenioso
ingenuity [ɪnʤənúɪdɪ] N ingenio *m*, inventiva *f*
ingenuous [ɪnʤénjuəs] ADJ ingenuo *f*
ingenuousness [ɪnʤénjuəsnɪs] N ingenuidad *f*
ingest [ɪnʤɛ́st] VI/VT ingerir
ingrate [ɪ́ngret] N ingrato -ta *mf*
ingratitude [ɪngrǽdɪtud] N ingratitud *f*
ingredient [ɪngrídiənt] N ingrediente *m*
ingrown [ɪ́ngron] ADJ encarnado
inhabit [ɪnhǽbɪt] VT habitar
inhabitant [ɪnhǽbɪtənt] N habitante *mf*
inhale [ɪnhél] VI/VT inhalar, aspirar
inherent [ɪnhɪ́rənt] ADJ inherente
inherit [ɪnhɪ́rɪt] VI/VT heredar
inheritance [ɪnhɛ́rɪdəns] N herencia *f*; **— tax** impuesto a la herencia *m*
inherited [ɪnhɛ́rɪdɪd] ADJ patrimonial
inhibit [ɪnhíbɪt] VT inhibir, cohibir
inhibiting [ɪnhíbɪdɪŋ] ADJ inhibidor
inhibition [ɪnɪbíʃən] N inhibición *f*, cohibición *f*
inhibitor [ɪnhíbɪdɚ] N inhibidor *m*
inhospitable [ɪnhɑspídəbəł] ADJ (person) inhospitalario; (place) inhóspito
inhuman [ɪnhjúmən] ADJ inhumano
inimitable [ɪnímɪdəbəł] ADJ inimitable
initial [ɪníʃəł] ADJ & N inicial *f*; VT firmar las iniciales
initialize [ɪníʃəlaɪz] VT inicializar
initially [ɪníʃəli] ADV al comienzo, inicialmente
initiate [ɪníʃiet] VT iniciar
initiative [ɪníʃəɪv] N iniciativa *f*
inject [ɪnʤɛ́kt] VI/VT inyectar[se], pinchar[se]
injection [ɪnʤɛ́kʃən] N inyección *f*
injunction [ɪnʤʌ́ŋkʃən] N mandato judicial *m*, orden judicial *f*
injure [ɪ́nʤɚ] VI/VT herir[se]; (sports) lesionar[se]
injurious [ɪnʤúriəs] ADJ (harmful) perjudicial; (defamatory) injurioso
injury [ɪ́nʤəri] N herida *f*, lesión *f*; **— time** (soccer) descuento *m*
injustice [ɪnʤʌ́stɪs] N injusticia *f*
ink [ɪŋk] N tinta *f*; VT (mark with ink) entintar; (sign) firmar; **— cartridge** cartucho de tinta *m*; **— -jet printer** impresora de inyección de tinta *f*; **—pad** almohadilla *f*; **—well** tintero *m*
inkling [ɪ́ŋklɪŋ] N idea *f*
inlaid [ɪ́nled] ADJ incrustado; **— work** incrustación *f*
inland [ɪ́nlənd] ADJ interior; ADV tierra adentro
inlay[1] [ɪnlé] VT incrustar
inlay[2] [ɪ́nle] N incrustación *f*
inmate [ɪ́nmet] N (in a prison) preso -sa *mf*, recluso -sa *mf*; (in an asylum) internado -da *mf*; (in a hospital) paciente *mf*
inn [ɪn] N posada *f*, fonda *f*; **—keeper** posadero -ra *mf*, fondista *mf*

innate [ínet] ADJ innato
inner [ínə˞] ADJ (inside) interior; (intimate) íntimo; **— city** zona céntrica empobrecida *f*; **— ear** oído interno *m*; **—most** más recóndito; **— tube** cámara *f*
inning [ínɪŋ] N entrada *f*
innocence [ínəsəns] N (absence of guilt) inocencia *f*; (naiveté) candidez *f*, candor *m*
innocent [ínəsənt] ADJ & N inocente *mf*
innocuous [ɪnɑ́kjuəs] ADJ innocuo, inocuo
innovate [ínəvet] VI innovar
innovating [ínəvɛdɪŋ] ADJ innovador, renovador
innovation [ɪnəvéʃən] N innovación *f*
innovative [ínəvɛdɪV] ADJ innovador
innovator [ínəvedə˞] N innovador -ora *mf*
innuendo [ɪnjuéndo] N insinuación *f*
innumerable [ɪnúmə˞əbəł] ADJ innumerables
inoculate [ɪnɑ́kjəlet] VI/VT inocular[se]
inoffensive [ɪnəfénsɪv] ADJ inofensivo
inoperable [ɪnɑ́pə˞əbəł] ADJ inoperable
inopportune [ɪnɑpə˞tún] ADJ inoportuno
inordinate [ɪnɔ́rdɪnɪt] ADJ desmesurado
inorganic [ɪnɔrgǽnɪk] ADJ inorgánico; **— chemistry** química inorgánica *f*
input [ínput] N (electric, computer) entrada *f*; (opinion) opinión *f*; VT ingresar/entrar datos
inquire [ɪŋkwáɪr] VI/VT inquirir, preguntar; **to — about/after** preguntar por; **to — into** indagar, investigar
inquiry [ínkwəri] N (scientific) investigación *f*; (police) pesquisa *f*; **we made inquiries about hotels** hicimos averiguaciones acerca de hoteles
inquisition [ɪŋkwɪzíʃən] N inquisición *f*
inquisitive [ɪnkwízɪdɪV] ADJ (curious) inquisitivo, curioso; (asking many questions) preguntón
insane [ɪnsén] ADJ demente, loco; **— asylum** manicomio *m*
insanity [ɪnsǽnɪdɪ] N locura *f*, demencia *f*
insatiable [ɪnséʃə˞əbəł] ADJ insaciable
inscribe [ɪnskráɪb] VT (mark) inscribir; (engrave) grabar; (dedicate) dedicar
inscription [ɪnskrípʃən] N (marks, engraving) inscripción *f*; (dedication) dedicatoria *f*
inscrutable [ɪnskrúdə˞əbəł] ADJ inescrutable
insect [ínsɛkt] N insecto *m*
insecticide [ɪnsɛ́ktɪsaɪd] N insecticida *m*
insectivorous [ɪnsɛktívə˞əs] ADJ insectívoro
insecure [ɪnsɪkjúr] ADJ inseguro
insecurity [ɪnsɪkjúrɪdɪ] N inseguridad *f*
insemination [ɪnsɛmɪnéʃən] N inseminación *f*
insensible [ɪnsénsə˞əbəł] ADJ insensible
insensitive [ɪnsénsɪdɪV] ADJ insensible
inseparable [ɪnsépə˞əbəł] ADJ inseparable
insert[1] [ɪnsɝ́t] VT insertar, introducir; (into a text) intercalar
insert[2] [ínsɝt] N encarte *m*
insertion [ɪnsɝ́ʃən] N inserción *f*; (into a text) intercalación *f*
inside[1] [ɪnsáɪd] PREP dentro de; ADV dentro, adentro
inside[2] [ínsaɪd] N interior *m*; **— job** delito cometido por un empleado *m*; **—s** entrañas *f pl*; **— track** pista interior *f*; **to turn — out** volver del revés; **he passed me on the —** me pasó por la derecha; ADJ (interior) interior
insider [ɪnsáɪdə˞] N privilegiado -da *mf*; **— trading** abuso de información privilegiada *m*
insidious [ɪnsídɪəs] ADJ insidioso
insight [ínsaɪt] N (intuition) perspicacia *f*; (discernment) discernimiento *m*
insignia [ɪnsígniə] N insignia *f*
insignificant [ɪnsɪgnɪ́fɪkənt] ADJ insignificante, menudo, nimio
insincere [ɪnsɪnsír] ADJ insincero
insinuate [ɪnsínjuet] VT insinuar
insinuation [ɪnsɪnjuéʃən] N insinuación *f*
insipid [ɪnsípɪd] ADJ insípido, soso
insist [ɪnsíst] VI/VT insistir; **to — on** insistir en
insistence [ɪnsístəns] N insistencia *f*
insistent [ɪnsístənt] ADJ insistente
insole [ínsoł] N plantilla *f*
insolence [ínsə˞ləns] N insolencia *f*
insolent [ínsə˞lənt] ADJ insolente, atrevido
insoluble [ɪnsɑ́ljə˞əbəł] ADJ insoluble
insolvent [ɪnsɑ́łvənt] ADJ insolvente
insomnia [ɪnsɑ́mɪniə] N insomnio *m*
inspect [ɪnspɛ́kt] VT inspeccionar; **to — the troops** pasar revista a la tropa, revistar a la tropa
inspection [ɪnspɛ́kʃən] N inspección *f*; (of troops) revista *f*
inspector [ɪnspɛ́ktə˞] N inspector -ora *mf*
inspiration [ɪnspə˞réʃən] N inspiración *f*
inspire [ɪnspáɪr] VI/VT inspirar
instability [ɪnstə˞bɪ́lɪdɪ] N inestabilidad *f*
install [ɪnstɔ́ł] VT instalar; N **— program** programa instalador *m*
installation [ɪnstəléʃən] N instalación *f*
installment [ɪnstɔ́łmənt] N (payment of debt) cuota *f*; (of a book) entrega *f*, fascículo *m*; **to pay in —s** pagar a plazos
instance [ínstəns] N ejemplo *m*; **for —** por ejemplo; **court of first —** tribunal de primera instancia *m*
instant [ínstənt] N instante *m*; **this —** ahora mismo; ADJ inmediato; **— coffee** café instantáneo *m*; **— messaging** mensajería instantánea *f*
instantaneous [ɪnstənténiəs] ADJ instantáneo
instead [instɛ́d] ADV **— of** en lugar de, en vez de; **she didn't want a desk, so she ordered a chair —** no quería un escritorio, así que pidió una silla en su lugar
instigate [ínstɪget] VT instigar

instigator [ɪnstɪgeɪɚ] N (of a crime) instigador -ora *mf*; (of an event) causante *mf*

instill [ɪnstɪ́ł] VT inculcar

instinct [ɪ́nstɪŋkt] N instinto *m*

instinctive [ɪnstɪ́ŋktɪv] ADJ instintivo

institute [ɪ́nstɪtut] N instituto *m*; VT instituir

institution [ɪnstɪtúʃən] N institución *f*

institutional [ɪnstɪtúʃənəł] ADJ institucional

instruct [ɪnstrʌ́kt] VT (teach) instruir; (command, advise) dar instrucciones; (command) mandar

instruction [ɪnstrʌ́kʃən] N instrucción *f*; **—s** (orders) órdenes *f pl*; (information) instrucciones *f pl*, indicaciones *f pl*

instructive [ɪnstrʌ́ktɪv] ADJ instructivo

instructor [ɪnstrʌ́ktɚ] N (of skills) instructor -ora *mf*; (of knowledge) profesor -ora *mf*

instrument [ɪ́nstrəmənt] N instrumento *m*; **— panel** salpicadero *m*, tablero *m*

instrumental [ɪnstrəmɛ́ntł] ADJ instrumental; **to be — in** ser fundamental para

insubordinate [ɪnsəbɔ́rdnɪt] ADJ insubordinado

insufferable [ɪnsʌ́fɚ·əbəł] ADJ insufrible

insufficiency [ɪnsəfɪ́ʃənsi] N insuficiencia *f*

insufficient [ɪnsəfɪ́ʃənt] ADJ insuficiente

insulate [ɪ́nsəlet] VT aislar

insulation [ɪnsəléʃən] N aislamiento *m*

insulator [ɪ́nsəleɪɚ] N (material) aislante *m*; (device) aislador *m*

insulin [ɪ́nsəlɪn] N insulina *f*; **— shock** choque insulínico *m*

insult[1] [ɪnsʌ́łt] VT insultar, injuriar

insult[2] [ɪ́nsʌłt] N insulto *m*, injuria *f*

insulting [ɪnsʌ́łtɪŋ] ADJ insultante, injurioso

insuperable [ɪnsúpɚ·əbəł] ADJ insuperable

insurable [ɪnʃʊ́rəbəł] ADJ asegurable

insurance [ɪnʃʊ́rəns] N seguro *m*; **— agent** agente de seguros *mf*; **— company** compañía de seguros *f*; **— policy** póliza de seguro *f*

insure [ɪnʃʊ́r] VI/VT asegurar[se]

insurgent [ɪnsɝ́dʒənt] N alzado -da *mf*

insurmountable [ɪnsɚ·máʊntəbəł] ADJ insuperable

insurrection [ɪnsərɛ́kʃən] N insurrección *f*

intact [ɪntʌ́kt] ADJ intacto

intangible [ɪntǽndʒəbəł] ADJ intangible

integer [ɪ́ntɪdʒɚ] N [número] entero *m*

integral [ɪ́ntɪgrəł] ADJ (complete) integral; (forming part of) integrante; **— calculus** cálculo integral *m*; N integral *f*

integrate [ɪ́ntɪgret] VT integrar; VI integrarse a

integration [ɪntɪgréʃən] N integración *f*

integrity [ɪntɛ́grɪdɪ] N integridad *f*

intellect [ɪ́ntłɛkt] N intelecto *m*

intellectual [ɪntłɛ́ktʃuəł] ADJ & N intelectual *mf*

intelligence [ɪntɛ́lɪdʒəns] N inteligencia *f* (also secret information); **— quotient** coeficiente intelectual / de inteligencia *m*

intelligent [ɪntɛ́lɪdʒənt] ADJ inteligente

intelligible [ɪntɛ́lɪdʒəbəł] ADJ inteligible

intend [ɪntɛ́nd] VT pensar; **to — to do something** pensar hacer algo; **a book —ed for children** un libro destinado/dirigido a los niños

intense [ɪntɛ́ns] ADJ intenso

intensify [ɪntɛ́nsɪfaɪ] VI/VT intensificar[se]

intensity [ɪntɛ́nsɪdɪ] N intensidad *f*

intensive [ɪntɛ́nsɪv] ADJ intensivo; **— care unit** sala de cuidados intensivos *f*

intent [ɪntɛ́nt] N intención *f*, propósito *m*; **to/for all —s and purposes** en la práctica; ADJ atento; **— on** resuelto a

intention [ɪntɛ́nʃən] N intención *f*

intentional [ɪntɛ́nʃənəł] ADJ intencional; **— base on balls** base por bolas intencional *f*

intentionally [ɪntɛ́nʃənəli] ADV a propósito

inter [ɪntɝ́] VT sepultar

interact [ɪntɚ·ǽkt] VI interactuar

interaction [ɪntɚ·ǽkʃən] N interacción *f*

interactive [ɪntɚ·ǽktɪv] ADJ interactivo

intercede [ɪntɚ·síd] VI interceder

intercept [ɪntɚ·sépt] VT interceptar

interception [ɪntɚ·sépʃən] N interceptación *f*

intercession [ɪntɚ·séʃən] N intercesión *f*

interchange[1] [ɪ́ntɚ·tʃendʒ] N cambio *m*; (on road) enlace *m*; *Sp* intercambiador *m*

interchange[2] [ɪntɚ·tʃéndʒ] VI/VT cambiar, intercambiar

intercourse [ɪ́ntɚ·kɔrs] N comunicación *f*, trato *m*

interest [ɪ́ntrɪst] N interés *m*; (financial) interés *m*, rédito *m*; (share in a business) participación *f*; **—-bearing** que devenga intereses; **—-free** libre de intereses, sin intereses; **— rate** tasa de interés *f*; **mining —s** los negocios mineros; VT interesar; **may I — you in a cookie?** ¿te puedo ofrecer una galleta?

interested [ɪ́ntrɪstɪd] ADJ interesado; **— party** parte interesada *f*; **to be/become — in** interesarse en/por

interesting [ɪ́ntrɪstɪŋ] ADJ interesante

interface [ɪ́ntɚ·fes] N interface *mf*, interfaz *f*

interfere [ɪntɚ·fír] VI interferir; (meddle) entrometerse; **to — with** interferir en

interference [ɪntɚ·fírəns] N interferencia *f*, injerencia *f*

interferon [ɪntɚ·fɪrɑn] N interferón *m*

interim [ɪ́ntɚ·ɪm] N ínterin *m*; ADJ (person) interino; (decision) provisional

interior [ɪntɪ́riɚ] ADJ & N interior *m*; **— decoration** decoración de interiores *f*; **— design** diseño de interiores *m*

interjection [ɪntɚ·dʒɛ́kʃən] N interjección *f*, exclamación *f*

interlace [ɪntɚ·lés] VI/VT entrelazar[se]

interlinear [ɪntɚlɪ́niɚ] ADJ interlineal

interlock [ɪntɚ·lʌ́k] VI/VT (gears) engranar[se];

(branches, etc.) entrelazar[se]; N interlock *m*
interlocking [ɪntɚˈlɑkɪŋ] ADJ (gears) engranado; (branches) entrelazado
interlude [ˈɪntɚˌlud] N (interval) intervalo *m*; (musical) interludio *m*; (theatrical) entremés *m*
intermediary [ˌɪntɚˈmɪdɪɛrɪ] ADJ intermediario
intermediate [ˌɪntɚˈmɪdɪɪt] ADJ intermedio
interment [ɪnˈtɝmənt] N entierro *m*
interminable [ɪnˈtɝmənəbəɫ] ADJ interminable
intermingle [ˌɪntɚˈmɪŋgəɫ] VI/VT entremezclar[se]
intermission [ˌɪntɚˈmɪʃən] N entreacto *m*, intervalo *m*
intermittent [ˌɪntɚˈmɪtn̩t] ADJ intermitente
intern [ˈɪntɝn] VT internar, confinar; N (prisoner, doctor) interno -na *mf*
internal [ɪnˈtɝn̩] ADJ interno, interior; —- **combustion engine** motor de combustión interna *m*; — **hard disk** disco duro interno *m*; — **revenue** rentas internas *f pl*; — **Revenue Service** Hacienda *f*
internalize [ɪnˈtɝnəlaɪz] VT interiorizar, internalizar
international [ˌɪntɚˈnæʃən̩l] ADJ internacional; — **law** derecho internacional *m*
Internet [ˈɪntɚˌnɛt] N internet *m*, red *f*, web *f*; — **access** acceso a internet *m*; — **access provider** proveedor de acceso a internet *m*; — **banking** banca por internet *f*; — **community** comunidad internauta *f*; — **user** internauta *mf*
internist [ɪnˈtɝnɪst] N internista *mf*
internship [ˈɪntɚˌnʃɪp] N (medical) internado *m*; (student) práctica *f*
interpersonal [ˌɪntɚˈpɝsən̩l] ADJ interpersonal
interpose [ˌɪntɚˈpoz] VI/VT interponer[se]
interpret [ɪnˈtɝprɪt] VI/VT interpretar
interpretation [ɪnˌtɝprɪˈteʃən] N interpretación *f*
interpreter [ɪnˈtɝprɪdɚ] N intérprete *mf*
interracial [ˌɪntɚˈreʃəɫ] ADJ interracial
interrelated [ˌɪntɚrɪˈlɛdɪd] ADJ interrelacionado
interrogate [ɪnˈtɛrəˌget] VI/VT interrogar
interrogation [ɪnˌtɛrəˈgeʃən] N interrogación *f*, interrogatorio *m*
interrogative [ˌɪntərˈɑgədɪv] ADJ interrogativo; N palabra/oración interrogativa *f*
interrupt [ˌɪntərˈʌpt] VI/VT interrumpir
interruption [ˌɪntərˈʌpʃən] N interrupción *f*
intersect [ˌɪntɚˈsɛkt] VI/VT (math) intersecar[se]; (road) cruzar[se]
intersection [ˌɪntɚˈsɛkʃən] N (math) intersección *f*; (street) cruce *m*, intersección *f*
intersperse [ˌɪntɚˈspɝs] VT (scatter) esparcir; (intermingle) entremezclar, entreverar; (spice up) salpicar
interstate [ˈɪntɚˌstet] ADJ interestatal; — **highway** autopista interestatal *f*
interstellar [ˌɪntɚˈstɛɫɚ] ADJ interestelar
interstice [ɪnˈtɝstɪs] N intersticio *m*
intertwine [ˌɪntɚˈtwaɪn] VI/VT entrelazar[se]
interval [ˈɪntɚvəɫ] N intervalo *m*
intervene [ˌɪntɚˈvin] VI intervenir; (mediate) interponerse, mediar
intervening [ˌɪntɚˈvinɪŋ] ADJ interventor
intervention [ˌɪntɚˈvɛnʃən] N intervención *f*; (mediation) mediación *f*
interview [ˈɪntɚˌvju] N entrevista *f*; (for entertainment) *Sp* interviú *f*; VT entrevistar; VI entrevistarse
intestinal [ɪnˈtɛstən̩l] ADJ intestinal; — **flora** flora intestinal *f*; — **obstruction** obstrucción intestinal *f*
intestine [ɪnˈtɛstɪn] ADJ & N intestino *m*; **small** — intestino delgado *m*; **large** — intestino grueso *m*
intimacy [ˈɪntəməsi] N intimidad *f*
intimate[1] [ˈɪntəmɪt] ADJ íntimo, entrañable; (knowledge) profundo
intimate[2] [ˈɪntəmet] VT insinuar, dar a entender
intimation [ˌɪntəˈmeʃən] N insinuación *f*
intimidate [ɪnˈtɪmɪdet] VT intimidar, acobardar
into [ˈɪntu] PREP **she came — the room** entró en/a la habitación; **he put it — the box** lo metió en la caja; **he translated it — German** lo tradujo al alemán; **he ran — a tree** chocó contra un árbol; **it fell — oblivion** cayó en el olvido; **he went — medicine** entró a medicina; **I'm really — pop music** me ha dado por la música pop
intolerable [ɪnˈtɑləɚəbəɫ] ADJ intolerable
intolerance [ɪnˈtɑləɚəns] N intolerancia *f*
intolerant [ɪnˈtɑləɚənt] ADJ intolerante
intonation [ˌɪntəˈneʃən] N entonación *f*
intoxicate [ɪnˈtɑksɪket] VI/VT embriagar (also exhilarate); (poison) intoxicar
intoxication [ɪnˌtɑksɪkˈeʃən] N (drunkenness) embriaguez *f*; (poisoning) intoxicación *f*
intransigent [ɪntrˈænzɪdʒənt] ADJ intransigente
intransitive [ɪntrˈænzɪdɪv] ADJ intransitivo
intrauterine device [ˌɪntrəˈjudɚərɪndɪˈvaɪs] N dispositivo intrauterino *m*
intravenous [ˌɪntrəˈvinəs] ADJ intravenoso; — **feeding** alimentación intravenosa *f*
intrepid [ɪnˈtrɛpɪd] ADJ intrépido
intricate [ˈɪntrɪkɪt] ADJ intrincado
intrigue[1] [ˈɪntrig] VI/VT intrigar
intrigue[2] [ˈɪntrig] N intriga *f*
intrinsic [ɪnˈtrɪnzɪk] ADJ intrínseco
introduce [ˌɪntrəˈdus] VT (put in, bring) introducir; (make acquainted) presentar
introduction [ˌɪntrəˈdʌkʃən] N (of a book) introducción *f*; (of a custom or system) introducción *f*, implantación *f*; (to a person) presentación *f*
introspection [ˌɪntrəˈspɛkʃən] N introspección *f*
introvert [ˈɪntrəˌvɝt] N introvertido -da *mf*
introverted [ˌɪntrəˈvɝdɪd] ADJ introvertido

intrude [ɪntrúd] VI/VT interrumpir; (penetrate, of rock) penetrar
intruder [ɪntrúdɚ] N intruso -sa *mf*
intrusion [ɪntrúʒən] N (interruption) interrupción *f*; (penetration) intrusión *f*
intrusive [ɪntrúsɪv] ADJ (rock) intrusivo; (people) entrometido
intubation [ɪntjubéʃən] N intubación *f*
intuition [ɪntuíʃən] N intuición *f*
intuitive [ɪntúɪdɪv] ADJ intuitivo
inundate [ínəndet] VT inundar
invade [ɪnvéd] VI/VT invadir
invader [ɪnvédɚ] N invasor -ora *mf*
invalid[1] [ínvəlɪd] ADJ & N (infirm) inválido -da *mf*
invalid[2] [ɪnvǽlɪd] ADJ (not valid) nulo
invaluable [ɪnvǽljuəbəɫ] ADJ invalorable, inestimable
invariable [ɪnvériəbəɫ] ADJ invariable
invariably [ɪnvériəbli] ADV siempre
invasion [ɪnvéʒən] N invasión *f*
invasive [ɪnvésɪv] ADJ invasivo
invent [ɪnvént] VT inventar
invention [ɪnvénʃən] N (act of inventing, thing invented) invención *f*, invento *m*; (falsehood) invención *f*
inventive [ɪnvéntɪv] ADJ inventivo
inventor [ɪnvéntɚ] N inventor -ora *mf*
inventory [ínvəntɔri] N inventario *m*; VT inventariar
inverse [ɪnvɝ́s] ADJ & N inverso *m*
inversion [ɪnvɝ́ʒən] N inversión *f*
invert [ɪnvɝ́t] VT invertir
invest [ɪnvést] VI/VT (money) invertir; (a rank upon someone) investir
investigate [ɪnvéstɪget] VI/VT investigar, indagar
investigation [ɪnvestɪgéʃən] N investigación *f*
investigator [ɪnvéstɪgeɪɚ] N investigador -ora *mf*
investment [ɪnvéstmənt] N (of money) inversión *f*; (of rank) investidura *f*; **— broker** corredor -ora de bolsa *mf*
investor [ɪnvéstɚ] N inversionista *mf*, inversor -ora *mf*
invigorate [ɪnvígəret] VT vigorizar
invincible [ɪnvínsəbəɫ] ADJ invencible
invisible [ɪnvízəbəɫ] ADJ invisible
invitation [ɪnvitéʃən] N invitación *f*
invite[1] [ɪnváɪt] VI/VT invitar; **to — trouble** buscarse problemas
invite[2] [ínvaɪt] N *fam* invitación *f*
inviting [ɪnváɪdɪŋ] ADJ atractivo, seductor
in vitro fertilization [ɪnvítrofɝdɪzéʃən] N fertilización in vitro *f*
invocation [ɪnvəkéʃən] N invocación *f*
invoice [ínvɔɪs] N factura *f*; VT facturar
invoke [ɪnvók] VT invocar
involuntary [ɪnvɑ́ləntɛri] ADJ involuntario
involve [ɪnvɑ́ɫv] VT (take, last) suponer; **how much time will this —?** ¿cuánto tiempo supone esto?; (consist of, entail) consistir en, involucrar; **what does your work —?** ¿en qué consiste tu trabajo?; (be in question) ser cuestión de; **national security is —d!** ¡es una cuestión de seguridad nacional!; (implicate) implicar; **they tried to — her** trataron de implicarla; (wrapped up in) estar metido; **he's very —d in the family business** está muy metido en el negocio familiar; (have a liaison) enredarse; **she got —d with a married man** se enredó con un hombre casado
involved [ɪnvɑ́ɫvd] ADJ complicado, enrevesado
involvement [ɪnvɑ́ɫvmənt] N (in a crime) implicación *f*; (in a project) participación *f*; (with a person) relación *f*
inward [ínwɚd] ADV hacia dentro; ADJ interior
iodide [áɪədaɪd] N yoduro *m*
iodine [áɪədaɪn] N yodo *m*
ion [áɪɑn] N ión *m*
ionize [áɪənaɪz] VT ionizar
ipecac syrup [ípɪkæksɪrəp] N jarabe de ipecacuana *m*
IPO [initial public offering] [áɪpíó] N oferta pública inicial *f*
IQ [intelligence quotient] [áɪkjú] N coeficiente de inteligencia *m*
Iran [ɪrán] N Irán *m*
Iranian [ɪréniən] ADJ & N iraní *mf*
Iraq [ɪrǽk] N Irak *m*
Iraqi [ɪrǽki] ADJ & N iraquí *mf*
irascible [ɪrǽsəbəɫ] ADJ irascible
irate [aɪrét] ADJ airado
ire [aɪr] N ira *f*
Ireland [áɪrlənd] N Irlanda *f*
iridescent [ɪrɪdésənt] ADJ iridiscente, tornasolado
iridium [ɪrídɪəm] N iridio *m*
iris [áɪrɪs] N (part of eye) iris *m*; (plant, flower) lirio *m*; (rainbow) arco iris *m*
Irish [áɪrɪʃ] ADJ irlandés; N (language) irlandés *m*; **the —** los irlandeses
irk [ɝ́k] VT fastidiar; **—ed** fastidiado
irksome [ɝ́ksəm] ADJ engorroso, molesto
iron [áɪə·n] N (element, golf club) hierro *m*; (appliance) plancha *f*; **in —s** en grilletes; **— deficiency anemia** anemia por deficiencia de hierro *f*; **—work** herrajes *m pl*; **—works** fundición *f*; ADJ férreo, de hierro; VI/VT planchar; **to — out a difficulty** allanar una dificultad
ironic [aɪrɑ́nɪk] ADJ irónico
ironing [áɪə·nɪŋ] N planchado *m*
irony [áɪrəni] N ironía *f*; (mockery) ironía *f*, sorna *f*
irradiate [ɪréɒɪet] VT irradiar
irrational [ɪrǽʃən!] ADJ irracional

irrefutable [ɪrɪfjúːtəbəl] ADJ irrefutable
irregular [ɪrégjələ-] ADJ irregular
irregularity [ɪregjəlǽrɪtɪ] N irregularidad *f*
irrelevant [ɪréləvənt] ADJ no pertinente; **your age is —** tu edad no viene al caso
irreparable [ɪrépə-əbəl] ADJ irreparable
irreplaceable [ɪrɪpléːsəbəl] ADJ irreemplazable
irreproachable [ɪrɪprótʃəbəl] ADJ irreprochable
irresistible [ɪrɪzístəbəl] ADJ irresistible
irresponsibility [ɪrɪspɑnsəbílɪtɪ] N irresponsabilidad *f*
irresponsible [ɪrɪspɑ́nsəbəl] ADJ irresponsable
irretrievable [ɪrɪtríːvəbəl] ADJ irrecuperable
irreverent [ɪrévə-ənt] ADJ irreverente
irreversible [ɪrɪvə́ː-səbəl] ADJ irreversible
irrevocable [ɪrévəkəbəl] ADJ irrevocable
irrigate [ír̬ɪget] VI/VT (a garden) irrigar, regar; (the eyes) irrigar
irrigation [ɪrɪgéjən] N riego *m*, irrigación *f*; **— ditch** acequia *f*
irritable [ír̬ɪtəbəl] ADJ irritable, colérico
irritate [ír̬ɪtet] VT irritar
irritating [ír̬ɪtetɪŋ] ADJ irritante
irritation [ɪrɪtéjən] N irritación *f*
IRS [Internal Revenue Service] [áɪárés] N Hacienda *f*
is [ɪz] *see* be
Islam [ízlɑm] N islamismo *m*, islam *m*
Islamic [ɪzlɑ́mɪk] ADJ islámico
island [áɪlənd] N isla *f*
islander [áɪləndə-] N isleño -ña *mf*
isle [aɪl] N isla *f*
isobar [áɪsəbɑr] N isobara *f*
isolate [áɪsəlet] VT aislar
isolation [aɪsəléjən] N aislamiento *m*, marginación *f*
isolationism [aɪsəléjənɪzəm] N aislacionismo *m*
isometric [aɪsəmétrɪk] ADJ isométrico
isotope [áɪsətop] N isótopo *m*, isotopo *m*
Israel [ír̬ɪəl] N Israel *m*
Israeli [ɪzréli] ADJ & N israelí *mf*
issue [íʃu] N (of printed matter) tirada *f*; (of stock, bonds) emisión *f*; (copy of a magazine) número *m*, entrega *f*; (of a fluid) flujo *m*; (problem) problema *m*, tema *m*; (progeny) descendencia *f*; **he's got —s** es muy acomplejado; **to take — with** discrepar de; VT (written material) publicar; (a decree) promulgar; (a permit, document) expedir; (shares) emitir; (to flow) brotar; (to come out of) salir de; (to descend from) descender de
isthmus [ísməs] N istmo *m*
it [ɪt] PRON **— all started yesterday** todo empezó ayer; **— is necessary** es necesario; **— is raining** llueve, está lloviendo; **— is said that** se dice que; **— is two o'clock** son las dos; **— was broken** estaba roto; **who is —?** ¿quién es? **if — weren't five o'clock** si no fueran las cinco; **I saw —** lo/la vi; **he talked about —** habló de eso; **what time is — ?** ¿qué hora es? **how is — going?** ¿qué tal? **I don't get —** no entiendo; **you're —!** ¡tú la quedas! / ¡tú la traes!
IT [information technology] [áɪtí] N informática *f*
Italian [ɪtǽljən] ADJ & N italiano -na *mf*
italic [ɪtǽlɪk] ADJ itálico; N **—s** letra bastardilla/cursiva *f*
italicize [ɪtǽlɪsaɪz] VT poner en bastardilla/cursiva
Italy [ídlɪ] N Italia *f*
itch [ɪtʃ] VI/VT picar; **to be —ing to** tener ganas de; N (sensation) comezón *f*, picazón *f*; (longing) ansia *f*
itching [ítʃɪŋ] N comezón *f*, picazón *f*
itchy [ítʃi] ADJ que pica; **it feels —** me pica
item [áɪtəm] N (piece of news) artículo *m*; (topic of gossip) tema de conversación *m*; (unit) ítem *m*; (couple) pareja *f*
itemize [áɪtəmaɪz] VT (list) enumerar; (break down) desglosar; **—d invoice** factura detallada *f*
itinerant [aɪtínə-ənt] ADJ itinerante, ambulante
itinerary [aɪtínərerɪ] N (schedule) itinerario *m*; (guidebook) guía de viajeros *f*
its [ɪts] POSS ADJ su/sus, de él, de ella, de ello
itself [ɪtsélf] PRON **this story wrote —** esta historia se escribió sola; **the bike was standing by —** la bici estaba parada sola; **the dog bit —** el perro se mordió [a sí mismo]; **the fox found — a hole** la zorra se encontró una guarida
IUD [intrauterine device] [áɪjúdí] N DIU *m*
IV [intravenous] [áɪví] ADJ intravenoso
Ivorian [aɪvɔ́ːrɪən] ADJ & N marfileño -ña *mf*
ivory [áɪvrɪ] N marfil *m*; **— tower** torre de marfil *f*
Ivory Coast [áɪvrɪkóst] N Costa de Marfil *f*
ivy [áɪvi] N hiedra *f*

Jj

jab [ʤæb] VI/VT (hit) golpear; (hit with elbow) codear; N (blow) golpe *m*; (blow with elbow) codazo *m*; (in boxing) jab *m*, puñetazo directo *m*
jabber [ʤǽbə-] VI (unintelligibly) farfullar; (incessantly) charlotear; N (unintelligible) farfulla *f*; charloteo *m*
jack [ʤæk] N (tool) gato *m*; (card) sota *f*; (plug-in) hembra *f*, toma *f*; (flag) bandera de proa *f*; **—ass** asno *m*, burro *m* (also person); **—hammer** martillo neumático *m*; **—knife** navaja *f*; **— of all trades** hombre orquesta

m; **—pot** premio gordo *m*; **—rabbit** liebre americana *f*; **you don't know —** no sabes ni un comino; VT **to — up** (a car) alzar con gato; (prices) subir

jackal [ʤǽkəł] N chacal *m*

jacket [ʤǽkɪtˈ] N (clothing) chaqueta *f*; (of a book) forro *m*; (of a potato) piel *f*

jade [ʤed] N jade *m*

jaded [ʤéɒɪd] ADJ (disenchanted) de vuelta; (sated) hastiado

jagged [ʤǽgɪd] ADJ recortado, desigual

jaguar [ʤǽgwɑr] N jaguar *m*

jail [ʤeł] N cárcel *f*; **—break** fuga *f*; VT encarcelar

jailer [ʤélə˙] N carcelero -ra *mf*

jalopy [ʤəlápi] N cacharro *m*

jam [ʤæm] VT (stuff) embutir; (block) atestar; (immobilize) trabar; (make unworkable) obstruir, atascar, atorar; (stop radio signals) interferir; VI (become stuck or unworkable) atascarse; (crowd in) apiñarse; **to — on the brakes** frenar de golpe; **to — one's fingers** pillarse los dedos; N (jelly) mermelada *f*, dulce *m*; (difficult situation) aprieto *m*; (traffic) embotellamiento *m*; **— session** jam *m*

Jamaica [ʤəmékə˙] N Jamaica *f*

Jamaican [ʤəmékən] ADJ & N jamaicano -na *mf*, jamaiquino -na *mf*

janitor [ʤǽnɪɒ˙] N conserje *m*

January [ʤǽnjuɛriˈ] N enero *m*

Japan [ʤəpǽn] N Japón *m*

Japanese [ʤǽpənízˈ] ADJ & N japonés -esa *mf*

jar [ʤɑr] VI/VT (shake) sacudir[se]; (clash) chocar; **to — one's nerves** ponerle a uno los nervios de punta; N (container) tarro *m*, frasco *m*, pote *m*; (large earthen container) tinaja *f*; (collision) choque *m*; (shake) sacudida *f*

jargon [ʤárgən] N jerga *f*

jasmine [ʤǽzmɪn] N jazmín *m*

jasper [ʤǽspə˙] N jaspe *m*

jaundice [ʤɔ́ndɪs] N ictericia *f*

jaundiced [ʤɔ́ndɪst] ADJ ictérico

jaunt [ʤɔnt] N excursión *f*; VI pasear

javelin [ʤǽvlɪn] N jabalina *f*

jaw [ʤɔ] N (of animal) quijada *f*; (of human) mandíbula *f*; (of mammals) fauces *f pl*; **—bone** mandíbula *f*, maxilar *m*

jay [ʤe] N arrendajo *m*

jazz [ʤæz] N jazz *m*; VI **to — up** animar

jealous [ʤéləs] ADJ (possessive) celoso; (envious) envidioso; (protective) protector

jealousy [ʤélə̇si] N celos *m pl*

jeans [ʤinz] N jeans *m pl*, vaqueros *m pl*

jeer [ʤir] VI/VT (mock) mofarse [de], burlarse [de]; (boo) abuchear, befar; N (act of mockery) mofa *f*, burla *f*; (boos) abucheo *m*, befa *f*

jelly [ʤéli] N jalea *f*; **—fish** medusa *f*

jeopardize [ʤépə-daɪz] VT comprometer, poner en peligro

jeopardy [ʤépə-di] ADV LOC **in —** en peligro

jerk [ʤɜ˙k] N (quick pull) tirón *m*; (muscular contraction) espasmo *m*; (idiot) *pej* pelmazo *m*; VI/VT tironear; **to — around** manipular

jerky [ʤɜ́ki] ADJ espasmódico; N tasajo *m*

jersey [ʤɜ́zi] N jersey *m*

jest [ʤɛst] N broma *f*, chanza *f*; **in —** en broma; VI bromear

jester [ʤéstə˙] N bufón *m*

Jesuit [ʤɛ́zuɪt] N jesuita *m*

jet [ʤɛt] N (stream) chorro *m*; (spout) surtidor *m*; (stone) azabache *m*; **— [air]plane** avión a reacción *m*; **— engine** motor a reacción *m*; **— lag** jet lag *m*; **—liner** avión a reacción de pasajero *m*; **— propulsion** propulsión a chorro *f*; **— set** jet *m*, jet-set *m*; **— stream** (of air) corriente en chorro *f*; (of a jet) chorro *m*; ADJ **—-black** negro como el azabache; VI (stream out) salir a chorros; (travel) volar en avión a reacción; VT (spew out) lanzar a chorros; (transport) transportar en avión a reacción

jettison [ʤɛ́ɒɪsən] VT echar por la borda

Jew [ʤu] N judío -a *mf*

jewel [ʤúəł] N (ornament, prized person) joya *f*, alhaja *f*; (stone) gema *f*; (watch jewel) rubí *m*; **— box** joyero *m*

jeweler [ʤúə̇lə˙] N joyero -ra *mf*; **—'s shop** joyería *f*

jewelry [ʤúə̇ri] N joyas *f pl*, alhajas *f pl*; **— box** alhajero *m*; **— store** joyería *f*

Jewish [ʤúɪʃ] ADJ judío

jiffy [ʤɪ́fi] ADV LOC **in a —** en un santiamén

jig [ʤɪg] N (dance) giga *f*; **—saw** sierra de vaivén *f*; **—saw puzzle** rompecabezas *m sg*; VI (dance) bailotear

jiggle [ʤígəł] VI/VT zangolotear[se], zarandear[se]; N zangoloteo *m*, zarandeo *m*

jilt [ʤɪłt] VT dejar plantado

jingle [ʤíŋgəł] VI tintinear; VT agitar; N retintín *m*; (short song) jingle *m*

jinx [ʤɪŋks] N persona que trae mala suerte *f*; VT traer mala suerte

job [ʤɑb] N (task) tarea *f*; (position) trabajo *m*, empleo *m*; (theft) golpe *m*; **to be out of a —** estar sin trabajo; *Sp* estar en [el] paro; **by the —** a destajo; **to do a good —** hacer buen trabajo; VI trabajar a destajo; **on-the-— training** capacitación en el lugar de trabajo *f*

jobber [ʤábə˙] N (day-worker) trabajador -ora a destajo *mf*; (wholesaler) vendedor -ora mayorista *mf*

jobless [ʤábɪlɪs] ADJ sin trabajo; *Sp* en paro

jock [ʤɑk] N deportista *mf*; **— [strap]** suspensorio *m*

jockey [ʤáki] N jockey *m*; VI **to — for position** disputarse la posición

jocular [ʤákjə̇lə˙] ADJ jocoso

jog [ʤɑg] VI (run) correr, trotar; VT (refresh) refrescar; N trote *m*; **to go for a —** salir a correr

jogging [ʤɑ́gɪŋ] N jogging *m*, footing *m*

join [ʤɔɪn] VI/VT juntar[se]; (pipes) acoplar[se], unir[se]; (bones) articular[se]; (a club) asociarse [a]; (the navy, etc.) alistarse [en]

joint [ʤɔɪnt] N (point of contact) juntura *f*, junta *f*; (connection between bones) articulación *f*, coyuntura *f*; (nodule on a plant) nudo *m*; (dive, bar) antro *m*; **out of —** descoyuntado; ADJ (shared) común; **— account** cuenta conjunta *f*; **— action** acción colectiva *f*; **— custody** custodia compartida *f*; **— owner** copropietario -ria *mf*; **— session** sesión plena *f*; **— venture** joint venture *m*

jointly [ʤɔ́ɪntlɪ] ADV conjuntamente

joke [ʤok] N broma *f*, chiste *m*; VI bromear

joker [ʤókɚ] N (person who jokes) bromista *mf*, guasón -ona *mf*; (card) comodín *m*

jokingly [ʤókɪŋlɪ] ADV en broma

jolly [ʤóli] ADJ jovial

jolt [ʤoʊlt] N sacudida *f*; VT sacudir; **to — along** avanzar a los tumbos

Jordan [ʤɔ́rdn̩] N Jordania *f*

Jordanian [ʤɔrdéniən] ADJ & N jordano -na *mf*

jostle [ʤɑ́sət] VI/VT codear[se], dar empujones [a]; N empujón *m*

jot [ʤɑt] VT **to — down** apuntar; N pizca *f*

journal [ʤɝ́n̩] N (diary) diario *m*; (periodical) revista *f*; (logbook) cuaderno de bitácora *m*

journalism [ʤɝ́nəlɪzəm] N periodismo *m*

journalist [ʤɝ́nəlɪst] N periodista *mf*

journalistic [ʤɝnəlístɪk] ADJ periodístico

journey [ʤɝ́ni] N viaje *m*; VI viajar

joust [ʤɑʊst] N justa *f*

jowl [ʤáʊl] N carrillo *m*, moflete *m*

joy [ʤɔɪ] N (delight) alegría *f*, regocijo *m*, alborozo *m*; (source of delight) deleite *m*; **—ride** paseo en coche robado *m*; **—stick** joystick *m*, palanca de mando *f*

joyful [ʤɔ́ɪfəl] ADJ alborozado

joyous [ʤɔ́ɪəs] ADJ jubiloso, alegre

jubilant [ʤúbələnt] ADJ jubiloso

jubilee [ʤubəlí] N jubileo *m*

Judaism [ʤúdɪɪzəm] N judaísmo *m*

judge [ʤʌʤ] N juez -eza *mf*; (in tennis) juez -eza de silla *mf*; **to be a good — of character** saber juzgar a la gente; VI/VT juzgar; (estimate) calcular

judgment [ʤʌ́ʤmənt] N juicio *m*; (in court) fallo *m*; **— day** día del juicio final *m*

judicial [ʤudíʃəl] ADJ judicial

judicious [ʤudíʃəs] ADJ juicioso, sensato

judo [ʤúdo] N judo *m*, yudo *m*

jug [ʤʌg] N (pitcher) jarro *m*, jarra *f*; (storage jar) pote *m*

juggle [ʤʌ́gəl] VI/VT hacer juegos malabares [con], hacer malabarismo [con]; **to — the accounts** manipular las cuentas

juggler [ʤʌ́glɚ] N malabarista *mf*

jugular [ʤʌ́gjəlɚ] N yugular *f*

juice [ʤus] N jugo *m*; (fruit only) *Sp* zumo *m*

juicer [ʤúsɚ] N exprimidor *m*

juicy [ʤúsi] ADJ jugoso; **a — story** un cuento sabroso

juke [ʤuk] N (in sports) amague *m*, finta *f*; **—box** juke-box *m*

July [ʤulái] N julio *m*

jumble [ʤʌ́mbəl] VI/VT revolver[se] *m*; N revoltijo *m*

jumbo [ʤʌ́mbo] ADJ jumbo, gigantesco; **— jet** jumbo *m*

jump [ʤʌmp] VI (spring) saltar; (increase, as temperature, prices) dar un salto; VT (capture in checkers) comer; (ride a horse over barrier) hacer saltar; (mug) asaltar; (cross a river, mountains, etc.) salvar; **to — at** abalanzarse sobre; **to — over** saltar; **to —-start** hacer un puente; **to — the track** descarrilarse; **to — to conclusions** hacer deducciones precipitadas; N salto *m*; (in prices) subida repentina *f*; **—rope** cuerda de saltar *f*; **— shot** tiro en suspensión *m*; **—suit** mono *m*

jumper [ʤʌ́mpɚ] N (person who jumps) saltador -ora *mf*; (dress) jumper *m*; *Sp* pichi *m*; **— cable** puente *m*

jumpy [ʤʌ́mpi] ADJ nervioso, asustadizo

junction [ʤʌ́ŋkʃən] N (act or state of joining) unión *f*; (joining of two rivers) confluencia *f*; (of two railways) empalme *m*, entronque *m*; (of roads) cruce *m*

juncture [ʤʌ́ŋktʃɚ] N (point where joined) juntura *f*; **at this —** en esta coyuntura

June [ʤun] N junio *m*

jungle [ʤʌ́ŋgəl] N selva *f*, jungla *f*; **the law of the —** la ley de la selva

junior [ʤúnjɚ] ADJ (younger) menor; (more recent) más nuevo, de menos antigüedad; **— college** institución para los dos primeros años de la licenciatura *f*; **John Smith Jr.** John Smith, hijo; N estudiante del tercer año *mf*

juniper [ʤúnəpɚ] N enebro *m*

junk [ʤʌŋk] N (useless articles) trastos viejos *m pl*; (metal) chatarra *f*; (Chinese boat) junco *m*; **— dealer** chatarrero -ra *mf*; **— food** comida basura *f*, porquerías *f pl*; **— mail** publicidad por correo *f*; **— e-mail** correo electrónico basura *m*; **—yard** chatarrería *f*; VT desechar, echar a la basura

junkie [ʤʌ́ŋki] N *fam* drogata *mf*, drogota *mf*

jurisdiction [ʤʊrɪsdíkʃən] N jurisdicción *f*

jurisprudence [ʤʊrɪsprúdn̩s] N jurisprudencia *f*

juror [ʤʊ́rɚ] N miembro de un jurado *m*, jurado -da *mf*

jury [ʤʊ́ri] N jurado *m*; **— box** banco de jurado *m*; VT **to —-rig** chapucear

just [ʤʌst] ADJ justo; ADV (exactly) exactamente, precisamente; (only) solo; **— like that** *Am* así nomás; **he — left** acaba de salir; **she is — a little girl** no es más que una niña; **you'll — have to wait** tendrás que esperar; **— barely** apenas; **the meeting is — starting** la reunión apenas comienza; **that is — what I wanted to talk to you about** precisamente de eso te quería hablar

justice [ʤástɪs] N (fairness) justicia *f*; (judge) juez -eza *mf*; **to bring to —** enjuiciar; **the painting doesn't do him —** el retrato no le favorece

justification [ʤʌstəfɪkéʃən] N justificación *f*

justify [ʤástəfaɪ] VT justificar

jut [ʤʌt] VI sobresalir, proyectarse

juvenile [ʤúvənaɪl] ADJ juvenil; **— delinquent** delincuente juvenil *mf*

juxtapose [ʤʌkstəpoz] VT yuxtaponer

Kk

kangaroo [kæŋgərú] N canguro *m*

karat, carat [kǽrət] N quilate *m*

kayak [káɪæk] N kayak *m*

Kazak, Kazakh [kəzǽk] ADJ & N kazako -ka *mf*

Kazakhstan [kəzʌ́kstɑn] N Kazajstán *m*

keel [kiɨ] N quilla *f*; VI/VT volcar[se]; **to — over** (ship) volcar[se]; (person) caer de cabeza, desplomarse

keen [kin] ADJ (edge) afilado; (perception) fino; (mind) agudo, penetrante

keenness [kínnɪs] N (of a blade) lo afilado; (of perception) fineza *f*; (of mind) agudeza *f*

keep [kip] VI (continue) seguir; (not spoil) aguantar; VT (retain) guardar; (maintain) mantener; (employ) tener; (look after) cuidar; **to — a diary** llevar un diario; **to — a secret** guardar un secreto; **to — at it** persistir; **to — away** mantener[se] alejado; **to — back** (stay away) tener a raya; (restrain) contener; **to — bad company** andar en mala compañía; **to — from** (prevent) impedir; (protect) proteger contra; **to — [on] talking** seguir hablando; **to — the door open** mantener la puerta abierta; **to — off the grass** no pisar el césped; **to — up** (perform as well) seguir el tren; (stay informed) mantenerse al tanto; **to — one's hands off** no tocar; **to — someone posted** mantener al corriente a alguien; **to — quiet** estarse callado; **to — to the right** mantenerse a la derecha; **to — track of** (do accounts) llevar la cuenta de; (consider) no perder de vista; **to — watch** vigilar; **he —s a maid** tiene una criada; **she kept me on the phone** me [re]tuvo en el teléfono; N **for —s** (forever) para siempre; (for real) en serio; **—sake** recuerdo *m*

keeper [kípə-] N (of people) guardián *m*; (of things) custodio *m*

keeping [kípɪŋ] N custodia *f*; **in — with** en armonía con

keg [kɛg] N barril *m*

Kegel exercises [kégəł ɛksə-saɪzɪz] N ejercicios de Kegel *m pl*

kennel [kénl] N residencia de perros *f*

Kenya [kénjə] N Kenia *f*

Kenyan [kénjən] ADJ & N keniata *mf*

kept [kɛpt] *see* keep

kernel [kɜ́-nl] N (seed) semilla *f*, grano *m*; (essence) meollo *m*

kerosene [kɛ́rəsin] N queroseno *m*

kestrel [késtrəł] N cernícalo *m*

ketchup [kétʃəp] N salsa de tomate *f*, cátsup *m*

kettle [kédl] N caldera *f*, hervidor *m*; (for tea) tetera *f*; **—drum** tímpano *m*, timbal *m*; **that's another — of fish** es harina de otro costal

key [ki] N (for locks) llave *f*; (secret, book of answers) clave *f*; (for winding) clavija *f*; (on keyboard) tecla *f*; (island) cayo *m*; (music) clave *f*; **—board** teclado *m*; **—hole** ojo de la cerradura *m*; **— indicator** indicador clave *m*; **—note** tónica *f*; **—note address** discurso de apertura *m*; **—pad** teclado numérico *m*; **—ring** llavero *m*; **— signature** armadura *f*; **—stone** piedra angular *f*; **—stroke** pulsación [de la tecla] *f*; **—word** palabra clave *f*; **—word search** búsqueda por palabra clave *f*; **to sing on —** cantar a tono; ADJ clave; VT (scratch) rayar; **to be —ed up** estar sobreexcitado

kg [kíləgræm] *see* kilogram

khaki [kǽki] N kaki *m*, caqui *m*

kick [kɪk] VI/VT (person) patear; (horse) dar coces [a], cocear; VI (gun) dar un culatazo, retroceder; **to — around** (discuss) discutir; (to mistreat) dar por la cabeza; **to — at** dar patadas; **to — out** echar a patadas; **to —start** arrancar; **to — the bucket** estirar la pata; **to — up a lot of dust** levantar una polvareda; **to — a habit** dejar un vicio; N (by a person) patada *f*, puntapié *m*; (by a soccer player) patada *f*; (of a horse) coz *f*; *Am* patada *f*; (of a gun) culatazo *m*; (in the air) pataleo *m*; **this whisky has a —** este whisky es fuerte; **I get a — out of swimming** me encanta nadar; **—back** comisión ilegal *f*; *Mex* mordida *f*; **—off** (football) saque de inicio *m*; (soccer) saque inicial *m*; **—stand** soporte *m*

kid [kɪd] N (young goat) cabrito *m*, chivo *m*; (leather) cabritilla *f*; (child) niño -ña *mf*; (young person) chico -ca *mf*; **— stuff** juego de niños *m*; VI bromear, embromar, tomar el

pelo

kidnap [kídnæp] VT secuestrar, raptar

kidnapper [kídnæpə˞] N secuestrador -ora *mf*

kidnapping [kídnæpɪŋ] N secuestro *m*, rapto *m*

kidney [kídni] N riñón *m*; **— bean** judía *f*; **— failure** insuficiencia renal *f*; **— stone** cálculo renal *m*

kill [kɪł] VI/VT matar; (drink completely) terminar; (turn off) apagar; **that comedian —s me** ese cómico me mata de risa; N (animal killed) caza *f*; (slaughter) matanza *f*; **—joy** aguafiestas *mf sg*

killer [kílə˞] N asesino -na *mf*; **— bee** abeja asesina *f*; **— whale** orca *f*; **a — game** un partidazo

killing [kílɪŋ] N (slaughter) matanza *f*; (murder) asesinato *m*; (animal killed) caza *f*; **to make a —** llenarse de oro

kilo [kílo] N kilo *m*, quilo *m*

kilobyte [kíləbaɪt] N kilobyte *m*

kilogram [kíləgræm] N kilogramo *m*

kilometer [kɪlámɪdə˞] N kilómetro *m*

kilowatt [kíləwɑt] N kilovatio *m*; **—-hour** kilovatio-hora *f*

kin [kɪn] N parentela *f*, parientes *m pl*; **—sman** pariente *m*; **—swoman** parienta *f*; **next of —** deudos *m pl*

kind [kaɪnd] ADJ benevolent) bondadoso, bueno; (words) amable; **to be — to animals** ser cariñoso con los animales; **—hearted** de buen corazón; **— of tired** algo cansado; N clase *f*, tipo *m*, género *m*; **to pay in —** (without money) pagar en especie; (retaliate) pagar con la misma moneda

kindergarten [kíndə˞gɑ˞tn] N jardín infantil / de niños *m*; *Sp* parvulario *m*

kindle [kíndl] VT (fire) prender; (interest) despertar, provocar; VI encenderse

kindling [kíndlɪŋ] N leña ligera *f*, astillas *f pl*

kindly [káɪndli] ADJ bondadoso, bueno; ADV (with kindness) amablemente; (please) por favor; **we thank you —** le agradecemos mucho; **not to take — to criticism** no aceptar de buen grado las críticas

kindness [káɪndnɪs] N (state) bondad *f*, amabilidad *f*; (act) favor *m*

kindred [kíndrɪd] ADJ emparentado; **— spirits** espíritus afines *m pl*, almas gemelas *f pl*

kinesiology [kəniziɑ́ləʤi] N quinesiología *f*

kinesthesia [kɪnɪsθíʒə] N cinestesia *f*

king [kɪŋ] N rey *m* (also in chess, cards); (in checkers) dama *f*; **—fisher** martín pescador *m*; **—pin** (in a mechanism) pivote central *m*; (in bowling) bolo central *m*; (person) figura central *f*; ADJ **—-sized** extra grande

kingdom [kíŋdəm] N reino *m*

kingly [kíŋli] ADJ real

kink [kɪŋk] N (bend) doblez *m*; (pain) tortícolis *f*

kinky [kɪŋki] ADJ crespo

kinship [kínʃɪp] N (family connection) parentesco *m*; (likeness) afinidad *f*

kiosk [kíɑsk] N quiosco *m*

Kiribati [kirəbáɪdi] N Kiribati *m*

kiss [kɪs] VI/VT besar[se]; N beso *m*

kit [kɪt] N (of tools) caja *f*; (of first aid) botiquín *m*; (of sewing notions) costurero *m*

kitchen [kítʃɪn] N cocina *f*; **—ware** utensilios de cocina *m pl*

kite [kaɪt] N (toy) cometa *f*; (bird) milano *m*

kitten [kítn] N gatito *m*

kitty [kíɾi] N (young cat) gatito *m*, minino *m*; (petty cash) caja chica *f*, fondo *m*

kleptomania [klɛptəméniə] N cleptomanía *f*

kleptomaniac [klɛptəméniæk] N cleptómano -na *mf*

knack [næk] N buena mano *f*, maña *f*; **once you get the —** una vez que le agarras la vuelta/ onda

knapsack [nǽpsæk] N mochila *f*

knave [nev] N pícaro *m*; (in cards) sota *f*

knead [nid] VT amasar, sobar

knee [ni] N rodilla *f*; **—cap** rótula *f*; **—-deep** hasta las rodillas; **—-jerk liberal** liberal fanático *m*; **—-jerk reaction** reacción visceral *f*; VT dar un rodillazo

kneel [niɫ] VI arrodillarse

knell [nɛɫ] N doble *m*; VI doblar

knelt [nɛɫt] *see* kneel

knew [nu] *see* know

knickknack [níknæk] N chuchería *f*, baratija *f*

knife [naɪf] N cuchillo *m*; (big) cuchilla *f*; (folding) navaja *f*; (for carving) trinchante *m*; VT acuchillar; **at —point** a punta de cuchillo

knight [naɪt] N caballero *m*; (in chess) caballo *m*; **— errant** caballero andante *m*; VT armar caballero

knighthood [náɪthʊd] N (all knights) caballería *f*; (title) orden de la caballería *f*

knit [nɪt] VI/VT tejer; **to — one's brow** fruncir el entrecejo / el ceño

knitting [nídɪŋ] N tejido *m*; **— needle** aguja de punto *f*

knob [nɑb] N (on a door) pomo *m*, perilla *f*, tirador *m*; (protuberance) protuberancia *f*

knock [nɑk] VI (hit) golpear; (precombust) golpetear; (call at the door) llamar, tocar; VT (criticize) criticar; **to — a hole in the wall** hacer un agujero en la pared a golpes; **to — down** derribar, echar abajo, tumbar; **to — off** (stop working) terminar; (reduce) rebajar; (make fall) tirar; (kill) liquidar; **— it off!** ¡basta! **to — into** golpearse contra; **to — out** noquear; **to — over** voltear, revolcar; N (pounding) golpe *m*, toque *m*; (criticism) crítica *f*; (in a motor) golpeteo *m*; **—out** (boxing) nocaut *m*; (attractive person) bomba *f*; ADJ **—-kneed** patizambo, zambo

knocker [nɑ́kə˞] N llamador *m*, aldaba *f*

knoll [noł] N morro *m*, loma *f*
knot [nɑt] N nudo *m* (also in wood, unit of speed); (of people) grupo *m*; (swelling) chichón *m*; VI/VT anudar[se]
knotty [nɑ́ɒi] ADJ (full of knots) nudoso; (difficult) dificultoso, enredado
know [no] VI/VT (to have knowledge of, to know how to) saber; VT (to be acquainted with, have sexual intercourse with) conocer; (to recognize) reconocer; (distinguish) distinguir; **to — how to swim** saber nadar; **to — of** estar enterado de; N **to be in the —** estar al tanto; **— -how** pericia *f*; **— -it-all** sabelotodo *mf*
knowing [nóɪŋ] ADJ (complicitous) cómplice; (astute) astuto
knowingly [nóɪŋli] ADV a sabiendas
knowledge [nɑ́lɪʤ] N (awareness) conocimiento *m*; (information known) saber *m*, conocimientos *m pl*; **not to my —** no que yo sepa
known [non] ADJ **little —** poco conocido; **well —** bien conocido; **he's — for his cooking** se le conoce por su cocina; **the truth wasn't — until last year** no se supo la verdad hasta el año pasado
known [non] *see* know
knuckle [nɑ́kəł] N nudillo *m*; **—ball** bola de nudillos *f*; **—head** tarambana *mf*; VI **to — down** arremangarse, aplicarse con empeño; **to — under** someterse
Korea [kɔríə] Corea *f*
Korean [kɔríən] ADJ & N coreano -na *mf*
kosher [kóʃə˞] ADJ kosher
Kuwait [kuwét] N Kuwait *m*
Kuwaiti [kuwéɒi] ADJ & N kuwaití *mf*
Kyrgyzstan [kírgistɑn] N Kirguistán *m*

Ll

lab [læb] *see* laboratory
label [lébəł] N (sticker) etiqueta *f*, rótulo *m*; (characterization) calificativo *m*; (brand) marca *f*; (of recording companies) sello *m*; VT etiquetar, rotular
labor [lébə˞] N trabajo *m*, labor *f*; (body of workers) mano de obra *f*; (working class) clase obrera *f*; (uterine contractions) trabajo de parto *m*; **— -intensive** que requiere mucha mano de obra; **— pains** dolores de parto *m pl*; **— union** sindicato *m*; **to be in —** estar de parto; ADJ laboral; VI (work) trabajar; (dedicate oneself) afanarse; **to — under a disadvantage** sufrir una desventaja
laboratory [lǽbrətɔri] N laboratorio *m*
laborer [lébə˞rə˞] N jornalero -ra *mf*; (unskilled) peón -ona *mf*
laborious [ləbɔ́riəs] ADJ (industrious) laborioso; (difficult) trabajoso
labrador [lǽbrədɔr] N (dog) labrador *m*
labyrinth [lǽbə˞ɪnθ] N laberinto *m*
lace [les] N (cloth) encaje *m*; (cord) cordón *m*; VT (to adorn with lace) bordar con encaje; (to insert laces into) poner cordones a; (to spike) echar alcohol; VI atarse
lack [læk] N falta *f*, carencia *f*; VI/VT carecer de, faltarle a uno; **he —s courage** le falta valentía; **—luster** mediocre
lackey [lǽki] N lacayo *m*
lacking [lǽkɪŋ] ADJ (deficient) deficiente; **good bars are — in this town** faltan buenos bares en este pueblo; **— in** falto de, carente de
laconic [ləkɑ́nɪk] ADJ lacónico
lacquer [lǽkə˞] N laca *f*; VT lacar, laquear
lactation [læktéʃən] N lactancia *f*
lactic acid [lǽktɪkǽsɪd] N ácido láctico *m*
lactose [lǽktos] N lactosa *f*; **— intolerance** intolerancia a la lactosa *f*
ladder [lǽdə˞] N escalera *f*
laden [lédn] ADJ cargado
ladle [lédl] N cucharón *m*, cazo *m*; VT servir con cucharón
lady [léɒi] N señora *f*, dama *f*; **—bug** mariquita *f*; **—like** muy fina; **—love** amada *f*; **ladies' room** *Sp* aseo de damas *m*, *Am* servicio de damas *m*
lag [læg] VI (fall behind) quedarse atrás, rezagarse; (flag) disminuir; N retardo *m*, retraso *m*
lagoon [ləgún] N laguna *f*
laid [led] *see* lay
laid-back [ledbǽk] ADJ apacible, tranquilo
lain [len] *see* lie 'estar situado'
lair [lɛr] N guarida *f*
lake [lek] N lago *m*
lamb [læm] N cordero *m*; (yearling) borrego *m*
lame [lem] ADJ cojo; *Am* rengo; **—brained** idiota; **— duck** funcionario -ria cesante *mf*; **— excuse** pretexto tonto *m*; VT dejar cojo
lament [ləmɛ́nt] N lamento *m*; VI lamentar[se]; VT llorar
lamentable [ləmɛ́ntəbəł] ADJ lamentable
lamentation [læməntéʃən] N lamentación *f*, lamento *m*
laminate [lǽmənet] VT laminar
lamp [læmp] N lámpara *f*; (on a street) farol *m*; **—post** farol *m*; **—shade** pantalla *f*
LAN [local area network] [læn] N red [de área] local *f*
lance [læns] N lanza *f*; (lancet) lanceta *f*; VT lancear; (a wound) abrir con una lanceta
lancet [lǽnsɪt] N lanceta *f*
land [lænd] N tierra *f*; (lot) terreno *m*; (country) país *m*, tierra *f*; **—fill** vertedero *m*; **— grant university** universidad con terrenos

concedidos por el estado *f*; **—lady** casera *f*, propietaria *f*; **—lord** casero *m*, propietario *m*; **—mark** (marker) hito *m*, mojón *m*; (historical) hito *m*; **— mine** mina *f*; **—owner** hacendado -da *mf*; **—scape** (terrain) paisaje *m*; (in printing) orientación horizontal *f*; **—scape architecture** paisajismo *m*; **—slide** (mass of land) derrumbe *m*, desprendimiento *m*; (election) victoria aplastante *f*; **— use** ordenamiento territorial *m*; VI/VT (a ship) atracar; (an airplane) aterrizar; **you'll — in jail** terminarás en la cárcel; VT (a fish) *Sp* coger; *Am* pescar; (a job) conseguir

landing [lǽndɪŋ] N (of a ship) desembarco *m*; (of cargo) desembarque *m*; (of an airplane) aterrizaje *m*; (place) desembarcadero *m*; (on stairs) descansillo *m*; **— field** campo de aterrizaje *m*; **— gear** tren de aterrizaje *m*; **— strip** pista de aterrizaje *f*

lane [len] N (country road) sendero *m*; (road division) carril *m*; (for ships) ruta *f*

language [lǽŋgwɪʤ] N lengua *f*, idioma *m*; (faculty of speech, computer code) lenguaje *m*

languid [lǽŋgwɪd] ADJ lánguido

languish [lǽŋgwɪʃ] VI languidecer

languor [lǽŋgɚ] N languidez *f*

lanky [lǽŋki] ADJ larguirucho, zancudo

lanolin [lǽnəlɪn] N lanolina *f*

lantern [lǽntɚn] N farol *m*; (of a lighthouse) faro *m*, linterna *f*

Laos [léɑs] N Laos *m*

Laotian [leóʃən] ADJ & N laosiano -na *mf*

lap [læp] N (part of body) regazo *m*; (part of a race) vuelta *f*; **—dog** perro faldero *m*; **—top computer** *Am* computadora portátil *f*, *Sp* ordenador portátil *m*; **to live in the — of luxury** vivir en la abundancia; VI/VT lamer

lapel [ləpél] N solapa *f*

lapidary [lǽpɪdɛri] ADJ & N lapidario -ria *mf*

lapse [læps] N (period of time) lapso *m*; (linguistic error) lapsus *m*; (defect in memory) fallo *m*; (fall) caída *f*; (termination) caducidad *f*; VI (fall) caer; (decline) decaer; (end) caducar, vencer

larceny [lársəni] N latrocinio *m*, hurto *m*

lard [lɑrd] N manteca *f*; VT enmantecar; (with bacon) mechar

large [lɑrʤ] ADJ grande; **—-scale** a gran escala; **a — company** una gran compañía / una compañía grande; **at —** (not in jail) suelto, libre; N tamaño grande *m*

largely [lárʤli] ADV (in the greatest number) en su mayoría; (to the greatest degree) en gran parte

lariat [lǽriət] N reata *f*

lark [lɑrk] N (bird) alondra *f*; (bit of fun) diversión *f*; **to go on a —** ir de jarana

larva [lárvə] N larva *f*

laryngeal [lərínʤəł] ADJ laríngeo; **— angina** angina laríngea *f*

laryngitis [lærənʤáɪdɪs] N laringitis *f*

larynx [lǽrɪŋks] N laringe *f*

lascivious [ləsíviəs] ADJ lascivo

laser [lézɚ] N láser *m*; **— beam** rayo láser *m*; **— printer** impresora láser *f*

lash [læʃ] N (blow with a whip, tail, etc.) azote *m*, latigazo *m*; (blow of waves) embate *m*; (part of eye) pestaña *f*; VT (whip) azotar; (tie) amarrar; **to — out at** fustigar

lasso [lǽso] N lazo *m*, reata *f*; VT lazar; *Am* enlazar

last [læst] ADJ (in a series) último; (definitive) final; **—-ditch** desesperado; **— minute** de último momento; **— name** apellido *m*; **— night** anoche; **— rites** extrema unción *f*, viático *m*; **— straw** colmo *m*; **— word** última palabra *f*; **— year** el año pasado; **next to the —** penúltimo; ADV último; **to arrive —** ser el último en llegar; **when — seen** cuando se lo vio por última vez; **at —** finalmente; N el último; (of a shoe) horma *f*; VI durar; (live on) perdurar

lasting [lǽstɪŋ] ADJ duradero, perdurable

lastly [lǽstli] ADV por último

latch [lætʃ] N pestillo *m*, picaporte *m*, cierre *m*; VI cerrar con el pestillo; **to — on** agarrarse de; **to — onto** pegarse a

late [let] ADJ (tardy) tardío; (hour) avanzada; (recent) reciente, último; (recently deceased) finado; **— afternoon** atardecer *m*; **—comer** rezagado -da *mf*; **— fee** recargo por mora *m*; ADV tarde; **— in the night** a una hora avanzada de la noche; **— into the night** hasta cualquier hora de la noche; **— in the week** a finales de la semana; **it is —** ya es tarde; **of —** últimamente; **to be —** llegar tarde; **to work —** trabajar hasta tarde; **the train was ten minutes —** el tren llegó con diez minutos de retraso

lately [létli] ADV últimamente

lateness [létnɪs] N tardanza *f*

latent [létnt] ADJ latente

later [léɪdɚ] ADJ posterior; ADV más tarde, con posterioridad; **see you —** hasta luego; **— on** más tarde

lateral [lǽɪdɚəł] ADJ lateral

latest [léɪdɪst] ADV último; **the — fashion** la última moda; **the — news** las últimas novedades; N **at the —** a más tardar

latex [létɛks] N látex *m*

lathe [leð] N torno *m*

lather [lǽðɚ] N (foam) espuma *f*; (sweat) sudor *m*; **he got into a —** se puso histérico; VT enjabonar; VI hacer espuma

Latin [lǽtn] ADJ latino; **— America** América Latina *f*, Latinoamérica *f*; **— American** latinoamericano -na *mf*; N (language) latín *m*

latitude [lǽdɪtud] N latitud *f*; (freedom) flexibilidad *f*
latrine [lətrín] N letrina *f*
latter [lǽdə˞] ADJ último; **in the — days of the Roman Republic** en los últimos días de la República Romana; **toward the — part of the week** a finales de la semana; **the —** este *m*, esta *f*
lattice [lǽdɪs] N enrejado *m*, entramado *m*; (of a window) celosía *f*
Latvia [lǽtviə] N Letonia *f*
Latvian [lǽtviən] ADJ & N letón -ona *mf*
laud [lɔd] VT loar
laudable [lɔ́dəbəł] ADJ laudable, loable
laugh [læf] VI reír[se]; **to — at** reírse de; **to — loudly** reírse a carcajadas; **to — up/in one's sleeve** reírse para sus adentros; **she —ed in his face** se rió en su cara; N risa *f*; **we did it for —s** lo hicimos por diversión
laughable [lǽfəbəł] ADJ risible
laughingstock [lǽfɪŋstɑk] N hazmerreír *m*
laughter [lǽftə˞] N risa *f*
launch [lɔntʃ] VT (a boat) botar; (a rocket, new product) lanzar; (software) iniciar; **to — forth/out** lanzarse; N lancha *f*; (act of launching a boat) botadura *f*; (act of launching a rocket) lanzamiento *m*
launder [lɔ́ndə˞] VI/VT (clothes) lavar; (money) blanquear, lavar; (wash and iron clothes) lavar y planchar
Laundromat™ [lɔ́ndrəmæt] N lavadero automático *m*
laundry [lɔ́ndri] N (business establishment) lavandería *f*, lavadero *m*; (room in house) cuarto de lavado *m*, lavadero *m*; (clothes to be washed) ropa sucia *f*; (washed clothes) ropa limpia *f*
laurel [lɔ́rəł] N laurel *m* (also honor); **to rest on one's —s** dormirse sobre los laureles
lava [lɑ́və] N lava *f*
lavatory [lǽvətɔri] N (basin) lavabo *m*; (bathroom) baño *m*, retrete *m*
lavender [lǽvəndə˞] N espliego *m*, lavanda *f*; ADJ lavanda
lavish [lǽvɪʃ] ADJ (generous) pródigo, espléndido; (abundant) abundante, copioso; VT prodigar; **to — praise upon** colmar de alabanzas a
law [lɔ] N ley *f*; (discipline) derecho *m*, jurisprudencia *f*; (police) policía *f*; **— and order** orden público *m*; **—breaker** infractor -ora *mf*, transgresor -ora *mf*; **—maker** legislador -ora *mf*; **— of diminishing returns** ley de [los] rendimientos decrecientes *f*; **— student** estudiante de derecho *mf*; **—suit** pleito *m*, litigio *m*; **to practice —** ejercer la abogacía; **to take the — into one's hands** hacer justicia por mano propia; ADJ **—-abiding** respetuoso de las leyes
lawful [lɔ́fəł] ADJ (in accordance with the law) legal; (allowed by law) lícito; (recognized by law) legítimo
lawless [lɔ́lɪs] ADJ (anarchic) anárquico; (illegal) ilegal
lawn [lɔn] N césped *m*, grama *f*; **— mower** cortadora de césped *f*
lawyer [lɔ́jə˞] N abogado -da *mf*
lax [læks] ADJ laxo
laxative [lǽksəɾɪv] ADJ & N laxante *m*, purgante *m*
laxity [lǽksɪɾi] N flojedad *f*, laxitud *f*
lay [le] VT colocar; (eggs) poner; (a cable) tender; **to — aside** (abandon) dejar de lado; (save) guardar; **to — a wager** apostar; **to — bare** poner al descubierto; **to — bricks** poner ladrillos; **to — down arms** rendir las armas; **to — down the law** imponerse; **to — hold of** asir, agarrar; **to — into** atacar; **to — off a workman** despedir temporalmente a un obrero; **to — one's head on a pillow** recostar la cabeza sobre una almohada; **to — open** exponer; **to — out a plan** trazar un plan; **to — up** almacenar; **to be laid up** estar en cama; **to — waste to** asolar; N situación *f*, orientación *f*; **—man** (nonexpert) lego *m*; (clergy) laico *m*; **—off** despido temporal de un empleado *m*; **—out** diseño/trazado de página *m*; ADJ lego, laico
lay [le] *see* lie 'estar situado'
layer [léə˞] N capa *f*; (geological) estrato *m*; (hen) gallina ponedora *f*; **— cake** tarta de capas *f*
laziness [lézɪnɪs] N pereza *f*, holgazanería *f*, flojera *f*
lazy [lézi] ADJ perezoso, holgazán, flojo
LBO [leveraged buyout] [éłbíó] N compra apalancada *f*
LDL [low density lipoprotein] [éłdíéł] N LBD *f*
lead[1] [lɛd] N (metal) plomo *m*; (graphite) mina *f*; **— poisoning** intoxicación con plomo *f*
lead[2] [lid] VT (guide) guiar; (guide a horse) llevar de la rienda; (induce, take) llevar, inducir; (be in charge, be first) encabezar, liderar; (direct) dirigir; (be superior to) estar a la cabeza de; **to — a life of ease** llevar una vida fácil; **to — the way** mostrar el camino; VI (provide passage to, result in) llevar a; (be first) estar a la cabeza; **to — astray** llevar por mal camino; N (first position) delantera *f*, primer lugar *m*; (clue) indicio *m*; (most important role) papel principal *m*, liderazgo *m*; **—off** comienzo; **— story** noticia principal *f*; **to take the —** (in sports) ponerse por delante en el marcador
leaden [lɛ́dn̩] ADJ (of lead) de plomo; (color) plomizo; (oppressive, slow) pesado
leader [lídə˞] N (in politics) líder *mf*, caudillo *m*; (in a race) líder *mf*; (in music) director -ora

mf; (as a guide) guía *mf*

leadership [líɒ˞ʃɪp] N dirección *f*, liderazgo *m*

leading [líɒɪŋ] ADJ (most important) principal; (arriving first) delantero; **— indicators** indicadores anticipados *m pl*; **— man** actor principal *m*

leaf [lif] N hoja *f*; VI echar hojas; **to — through a book** hojear un libro

leafless [lífɪlɪs] ADJ sin hojas, deshojado

leaflet [lífɪlɪt] N (small leaf) folíolo *m*; (printed matter) volante *m*; (folded printed matter) pliego *m*

leafy [lífi] ADJ (with foliage) frondoso; (in the form of leaves) de hoja

league [lig] N (alliance) liga *f*; (unit of distance) legua *f*; VI/VT aliar[se]

leak [lik] N (in a roof) gotera *f*; (in a boat, bucket, etc.) agujero *m*; (of information) filtración *f*; (of gas, steam, electricity) escape *m*, fuga *f*; VI (roof) gotear[se]; (boat) hacer agua; (gas) salirse, escaparse; (information) filtrarse; VT revelar información interna confidencial

leaky [líki] ADJ (roof) que tiene goteras; (boat) que hace agua; (gas, electricity) que pierde

lean [lin] VI/VT (incline) inclinar[se]; (support) apoyar[se], reclinar[se], recostar[se]; **to — on** presionar; ADJ magro; **— year** mal año *m*

leap [lip] VI/VT saltar; **to — at a chance** aprovechar una oportunidad; **to — to mind** ocurrírsele a uno; N salto *m*; **—frog** pídola *f*; **— year** año bisiesto *m*

leapt [lɛpt] *see* leap

learn [lɜ˞n] VI/VT aprender; (find out) enterarse de

learned [lɜ́˞nɪd] ADJ erudito, letrado

learner [lɜ́˞nə˞] N estudiante *mf*; (driver) aprendiz -iza *mf*

learning [lɜ́˞nɪŋ] N (result) erudición *f*, saber *m*; (process) aprendizaje *m*; **— disability** problema de aprendizaje *m*

learnt [lɜ˞nt] *see* learn

lease [lis] N (action) arrendamiento *m*; (contract) contrato de arrendamiento *m*; (period) período de arrendamiento *m*; **for —** se arrienda; **to have a new — on life** nacer de nuevo; VI/VT arrendar

leash [liʃ] N traílla *f*, correa *f*

least [list] ADJ **he doesn't have the — chance** no tiene la más mínima posibilidad; **the — amount of money** la menor cantidad de dinero; **— common denominator** mínimo común denominador *m*; ADV menos; **the — important** el/la menos importante; **at —** al menos, por lo menos; N **I received the — of anyone** yo fui el que recibió menos de todos

leather [léðə˞] N cuero *m*; ADJ de cuero; **— strap** correa *f*

leave [liv] VT (a person, thing) dejar; (a place) salir de, irse de; VI salir, partir; **to — off** (stop) parar de; (omit) omitir; **to — out** omitir; **I have two books left** me quedan dos libros; N permiso *m*; **to be on —** estar de licencia; **— of absence** licencia *f*; **to take — of** despedirse de

leaven [lévən] N levadura *f*; VT leudar

leavings [lívɪŋz] N (leftovers) sobras *f pl*; (refuse) desperdicios *m pl*

Lebanese [lɛbəníz] ADJ & N libanés -esa *mf*

Lebanon [lébənɑn] N Líbano *m*

lecherous [létʃə˞əs] ADJ lujurioso

lecture [léktʃə˞] N (presentation) conferencia *f*, disertación *f*; (sermon) sermón *m*; (long-winded speech) perorata *f*; VI (present) dar una conferencia, disertar; VT (scold) sermonear

lecturer [léktʃərə˞] N conferenciante *mf*; (academic rank) profesor -ora *mf*

led [lɛd] *see* lead

LED [light-emitting diode] [éɫídí] N LED *m*

ledge [lɛʤ] N cornisa *f*

ledger [léʤə˞] N libro mayor *m*

leech [litʃ] N sanguijuela *f*

leer [lir] VT (sideways) mirar de soslayo; (lecherously) mirar con lujuria; N (sideways) mirada de soslayo *f*; (lecherous) mirada lujuriosa *f*

leeway [líwe] N margen de maniobra *m*; (of a ship) deriva *f*

left [lɛft] ADJ izquierdo; **—-click** presionar el botón izquierdo del ratón; **—-handed** zurdo; **—-handed compliment** alabanza irónica *f*; **—-handed tool** herramienta para zurdos *f*; **— justification** alineación a la izquierda *f*; **—-wing** de izquierdas; N izquierda *f*; **at / on/to/toward the —** a/hacia la izquierda; **to make a —** doblar/girar a la izquierda

left [lɛft] *see* leave

leftist [léftɪst] N & ADJ izquierdista *mf*

leg [lɛg] N (human) pierna *f*; (animal, furniture) pata *f*; (wading bird) zanca *f*; (of a journey) etapa *f*; **to be on one's last —s** estar en las últimas; **to pull someone's —** tomarle el pelo a alguien; **to stretch one's —s** estirar las piernas

legacy [légəsi] N legado *m*

legal [lígəɫ] ADJ (in accordance with the law) legal; (permitted by law) lícito; (recognized by law) legítimo; (having to do with the law) jurídico; **— age** mayoría de edad *f*; **— code** ordenamiento *m*; **— fees** honorarios del abogado *m pl*; **— holiday** día feriado *m*; **— procedure** procedimiento jurídico *m*; **— tender** moneda de curso legal *f*

legality [lɪgǽlɪɾi] N legalidad *f*

legalization [ligəɫɪzéʃən] N legalización *f*

legalize [lígəɫaɪz] VT legalizar

legation [lɪgéʃən] N legación *f*

legend [léʤənd] N leyenda *f* (also inscription);

(of a map) clave *f*
legendary [léʤəndɛri] ADJ legendario
leggings [légɪŋz] N (ankle to knee) polainas *f pl*; (trousers) leggings *m pl*
legible [léʤəbəł] ADJ legible
legion [líʤən] N legión *f*
legionnaire [liʤənɛ́r] N legionario *m*; **—'s disease** enfermedad del legionario *f*, legionelosis *f*
legislate [léʤɪslet] VI/VT legislar
legislation [lɛʤɪsléʃən] N legislación *f*
legislative [léʤɪslɛɒɪv] ADJ legislativo
legislator [léʤɪsleɒ-] N legislador -ora *mf*
legislature [léʤɪsletʃə-] N legislatura *f*
legitimacy [ləʤíɒməsi] N legitimidad *f*
legitimate [lɪʤíɒmɪt] ADJ legítimo
legitimize [ləʤíɒmaɪz] VT legitimar
legume [légjum] N legumbre *f*
leisure [líʒə-] N ocio *m*, holgura *f*; **— activities** actividades recreativas *f pl*; **— hours** horas de ocio *f pl*, tiempo libre *m*; **to be at —** estar desocupado; **do it at your —** hazlo cuando te convenga
leisurely [líʒə-li] ADJ lento, deliberado; ADV sin prisa
lemon [lémən] N limón *m*; ADJ de limón; **— tree** limonero *m*
lemonade [lɛmənéd] N limonada *f*
lend [lɛnd] VI/VT prestar; **to — a hand** dar una mano
lender [lɛ́ndə-] N (person who lends) prestador -ora *mf*; (professional) prestamista *mf*
length [lɛŋkθ] N (of an object, road) largo *m*, largura *f*, longitud *f*; (of a movie) duración *f*; (of a book) extensión *f*; **at —** (in detail) pormenorizadamente; (finally) finalmente; **by two —s** por dos cuerpos; **two meters in —** dos metros de largo; **to go to any —s** hacer lo imposible
lengthen [lɛ́ŋkθən] VI/VT alargar[se]
lengthwise [lɛ́ŋkθwaɪz] ADV & ADJ a lo largo
lengthy [lɛ́ŋkθi] ADJ largo, prolongado
lenient [líniənt] ADJ indulgente
lens [lɛnz] N lente *m*; (of the eye) cristalino *m*
Lent [lɛnt] N Cuaresma *f*
lent [lɛnt] *see* lend
lentil [lɛ́ntł] N lenteja *f*
Leon [león] N León *m*
Leonese [liənís] ADJ leonés
leopard [lépə-d] N leopardo *m*
leprosy [lépрəsi] N lepra *f*
lesbian [lézbiən] ADJ lesbiano; N lesbiana *f*
lesion [líʒən] N lesión *f*
Lesotho [ləsóto] N Lesoto *m*
less [lɛs] ADJ, ADV & PREP menos; **I have — than you do** tengo menos que tú; **— and —** cada vez menos
lessen [lɛ́sən] VI/VT disminuir, aminorar
lessening [lɛ́sənɪŋ] N disminución *f*
lesser [lɛ́sə-] ADJ menor
lesson [lɛ́sən] N lección *f*
lest [lɛst] CONJ no sea que; **— you should think I'm teasing** para que no vayas a creer que estoy bromeando
let [lɛt] VT (permit) dejar, permitir; (rent) alquilar; **— him come** que venga; **—'s do it** hagámoslo; **to — be** dejar en paz; **to — down** (lower) bajar; (disappoint) decepcionar; **to — go** soltar; **to — in** dejar entrar; **to — know** hacer saber; **to — off** (not punish) dejar ir; (allow to get off) dejar bajar; **to — through** dejar pasar; **to — up** (permit to stand) dejar incorporarse; (cease) disminuir; N (in tennis) repetición *f*; **—down** desilusión *f*; **—up** tregua *f*
lethal [líθəł] ADJ letal
lethargic [ləθárʤɪk] ADJ aletargado, letárgico
lethargy [léθə-ʤi] N letargo *m*; **to fall into a —** aletargarse
letter [lɛ́tə-] N (of alphabet) letra *f*; (missive) carta *f*; **— carrier** cartero -ra *mf*; **—head** membrete *m*; **—head paper** papel membretado *m*; **—-spacing** espacio entre caracteres *m*; **—s** letras *f pl*; **the — of the law** la letra de la ley *f*; **to the —** al pie de la letra; VT grabar
lettuce [lɛ́tɪs] N lechuga *f*
leukemia [lukímiə] N leucemia *f*
levee [lévi] N dique *m*
level [lɛ́vəł] ADJ llano, plano; **—-headed** sensato; **— playing field** terreno de juego parejo *m*; **— with** a nivel de; **a — tablespoon** una cucharada al ras; N nivel *m* (also tool); **on the —** en serio; VT (make level) nivelar, igualar; (to demolish) arrasar, allanar; (to knock down a person) tumbar; (to aim criticism) dirigir; (to aim a gun) apuntar; **to — off** quedar paralelo al suelo; **to — with** hablar en serio con/a
lever [lɛ́və-] N palanca *f*
leverage [lɛ́və-ɪʤ] N (influence) palanca *f*; (physical, financial) apalancamiento *m*
levity [lɛ́vɪdi] N ligereza *f*
levy [lɛ́vi] N (of taxes) recaudación *f*; (of troops) leva *f*; VT (taxes) recaudar; (troops) reclutar, hacer una leva de
lewd [lud] ADJ lascivo
lewdness [lúdnɪs] N lascivia *f*
lexical [lɛ́ksɪkəł] ADJ léxico
lexicography [lɛksɪkágrəfi] N lexicografía *f*
lexicon [lɛ́ksɪkən] N léxico *m*
liability [laɪəbíłɪdi] N (disadvantage) desventaja *f*; (debit) pasivo *m*; (debts) deudas *f pl*; (responsibility) responsabilidad legal *f*; **— insurance** seguro contra daños a terceros *m*; **liabilities** obligaciones *f pl*
liable [láɪəbəł] ADJ responsable; **— to** propenso a; **she's — to get angry** es probable que se

enoje

liaison [liézɑn] N (connection) enlace *m*; (illicit love affair) aventura *f*

liar [láɪə-] N mentiroso -sa *mf*, embustero -ra *mf*

libel [láɪbəł] N libelo *m*, difamación *f*; VT difamar

liberal [líbə-ał] ADJ & N liberal *mf*

liberalism [líbə-əlɪzəm] N liberalismo *m*

liberality [lɪbərǽlɪDi] N (generosity) liberalidad *f*; (tolerance) tolerancia *f*

liberalization [lɪbə-əlɪzéʃən] N liberalización *f*

liberalize [líbə-əlaɪz] VI/VT liberalizar[se]

liberate [líbəret] VT (give freedom to) libertar, liberar; (release from obligation) librar; (give off) desprender

liberation [lɪbəréʃən] N liberación *f*

liberator [líbərerə-] N libertador -ora *mf*

Liberia [laɪbíriə] N Liberia *f*

Liberian [laɪbíriən] ADJ & N liberiano -na *mf*

libertine [líbə-tin] ADJ & N libertino -na *mf*, calavera *m*

liberty [líbə-DI] N libertad *f*; **at —** autorizado

libidinous [lɪbídnəs] ADJ libidinoso

libido [lɪbíDo] N libido *f*

librarian [laɪbrérɪən] N bibliotecario -ria *mf*

library [láɪbrɛri] N biblioteca *f*

libretto [lɪbrɛ́Do] N libreto *m*

Libya [líbjə] N Libia *f*

Libyan [líbjən] ADJ & N libio -bia *mf*

license [láɪsəns] N (permission) permiso *m*; (driver's permit, poetic freedom) licencia *f*; **— plate** placa *f*, matrícula *f*; VT (issue license to) otorgar una licencia; (give permission) autorizar

licensing authority [láɪsənsɪŋ əθɔ́rɪDi] N autoridad para otorgar licencias *f*

licentious [laɪsénʃəs] ADJ licencioso

lick [lɪk] VT (touch with tongue) lamer (also waves); (thrash) dar una paliza; (defeat) derrotar; N lamida *f*, lengüetazo *m*; (blow) golpe *m*; **not to do a — of work** no mover un dedo

lickety-split [lɪkIDisplít] ADV en un santiamén

licking [líkɪŋ] N paliza *f*

licorice [líkə-ɪʃ] N regaliz *m*

lid [lɪd] N (of a container) tapadera *f*, tapa *f*; (of eye) párpado *m*; (on prices) tope *m*

lie [laɪ] N (falsehood) mentira *f*, embuste *m*; (orientation of an object) orientación *f*; **— detector** detector de mentiras *m*; **to give the — to** desmentir; VI mentir; **to — one's way out of a situation** salirse de una situación a mentiras; (be buried) yacer; (to be on a flat surface) estar; (to be situated) estar situado; (be horizontal) tumbarse, acostarse; **he's lying in bed** está acostado en la cama; **to — back** recostarse; **to — down** acostarse, tumbarse; **to — in wait** acechar

Liechtenstein [líktənstaɪn] N Liechtenstein *m*

Liechtensteiner [líktənstaɪnə-] N liechtensteiniano -na *mf*

lien [lin] N gravamen *m*, carga *f*

lieu [lu] ADV LOC **in — of** en vez de

lieutenant [luténənt] N teniente *mf*; **— colonel** teniente coronel *mf*; **— governor** vicegobernador -ora *mf*

life [laɪf] N vida *f*; **—-and-death** de vida o muerte; **—boat** bote de salvamento *m*; **— cycle** ciclo vital *m*; **— expectancy** expectativa de vida *f*; **—guard** salvavidas *mf sg*; **— imprisonment** prisión perpetua *f*; **— insurance** seguro de vida *m*; **— jacket** salvavidas *m sg*; **— of the party** alma de la fiesta *f*; **— preserver** salvavidas *m sg*; **— raft** balsa salvavidas *f*; **— savings** ahorros de toda la vida *m pl*; **—span** duración de la vida *f*; **—style** estilo de vida *m*; **—-support system** (in space) equipo de vida *m*; (in a hospital) máquina corazón-pulmón *f*; **—time** vida *f*; ADJ (relative to life) vital; (for duration of life) vitalicio; ADJ **—like** natural, que parece vivo; **—long** de toda la vida; **—-sized** de tamaño natural

lifeless [láɪflɪs] ADJ (without living things) sin vida; (dead) muerto, sin vida; (fainted) desfallecido; (without liveliness) sin animación

lifer [láɪfə-] N (prisoner) condenado -da a cadena perpetua *mf*; (soldier) militar de carrera *m*

lift [lɪft] VT (hoist) levantar; (steal) robar; (plagiarize) copiar; VI (disperse) disiparse; (go up) elevarse; N (upward force) empuje *m*; (feeling) mejoría de ánimo *f*; (device for lifting) montacargas *m sg*; **to give someone a —** llevar en coche; *Mex* dar un aventón; **—off** despegue *m*

ligament [lígəmənt] N ligamento *m*

ligature [lígətʃə-] N ligadura *f*

light [laɪt] N (luminescence) luz *f*; (device) luz *f*, lámpara *f*; (for traffic) semáforo *m*; (perspective) perspectiva *f*; (for cigarettes) fuego *m*; **—-emitting diode** diodo electroiluminiscente *m*; **—house** faro *m*; **—-year** año luz *m*; ADJ (well-lighted) claro; (of little weight) ligero, leve; (of clothes) fresco; *Am* liviano; **— blue** azul claro *m*; **—-headed** mareado; **—hearted** alegre; **— rain** lluvia fina *f*; **—-skinned** de tez blanca; **— touch** mano delicada *f*; **—weight** de peso ligero; **to make — of** restar importancia a; VI/VT (turn on, ignite) encender[se], prender[se]; (provide light, brighten) iluminar[se]; (land on) posarse en; **to — up** (cigarette) prender, encender; (face) iluminarse; **to — upon** caer sobre

lighten [láɪtn] VI/VT (make / become lighter) aligerar[se], alivianar[se]; (brighten) iluminar[se]; **— up!** ¡no tomes las cosas a la tremenda!

lighter [láɪdə˞] N encendedor *m*
lighting [láɪdɪŋ] N iluminación *f*; (in the street) alumbrado *m*
lightly [láɪtli] ADV (toast) ligeramente; (touch) levemente, suavemente; **I don't take your criticism** — no tomo tus críticas a la ligera
lightness [láɪtnɪs] N (little weight) ligereza *f*, levedad *f*; (brightness) claridad *f*
lightning [láɪtnɪŋ] N relámpago *m*; **— bug** luciérnaga *f*; **— rod** pararrayos *m sg*; **it happened at — speed** pasó como rayo; VI relampaguear
likable [láɪkəbəł] ADJ agradable, simpático
like [laɪk] ADV & PREP como; **to feel — going** tener ganas de ir; **to look — someone** parecerse a alguien; **it looks — rain** parece que va a llover; ADJ semejante, parecido; **in — manner** del mismo modo; **—-minded** del mismo parecer; N **—s** gustos *m pl*, preferencias *f pl*; VT gustarle a uno; **he —s dogs** le gustan los perros; **do whatever you** — haz lo que quieras; CONJ **he talked — he was crazy** hablaba como si estuviera loco; **she came — you predicted she would** vino, tal como tú pronosticaste; **I'm —, "you're crazy"** yo pensé/dije, "estás loco"; INTERJ **he was, —, way too old** era como que demasiado viejo
likelihood [láɪklihʊd] N probabilidad *f*; **in all — he came** lo más probable es que haya venido
likely [láɪkli] ADJ (probable) probable; (believable) creíble; (promising) prometedor; **John is — to win** es probable que gane Juan; ADV probablemente
liken [láɪkən] VT comparar
likeness [láɪknɪs] N (similarity) parecido *m*; (portrait) retrato *m*
likewise [láɪkwaɪz] ADV (the same thing) lo mismo; **we did —** hicimos lo mismo; (similarly) asimismo; (also) también
liking [láɪkɪŋ] N preferencia *f*, gusto *m*
lilac [láɪlɔk] N lila *f*; ADJ lila
lily [líli] N lirio *m*, azucena *f*; ADJ **—-white** (very white) blanquísimo; (pure) puro; (for whites only) exclusivamente para blancos
limb [lɪm] N (branch) rama *f*; (appendage) miembro *m*
limber [límbə˞] ADJ flexible; VT hacer flexible; VI **to — up** estirarse
lime [laɪm] N (mineral) cal *f*; (fruit, color) lima *f*; **—light** candilejas *f pl*; **in the —light** en el candelero; **—stone** piedra caliza *f*; **— tree** limero *m*
limit [límɪt] N límite *m*; **to the —** al máximo; VT limitar
limitation [lɪmɪtéʃən] N limitación *f*
limitless [límɪtlɪs] ADJ ilimitado
limousine [líməzin] N limusina *f*
limp [lɪmp] N cojera *f*, renguera *f*; VI cojear, renguear, renquear; ADJ (body) flácido; (plants) mustio
limpid [límpɪd] ADJ límpido
line [laɪn] N (bus route, telephone connection) línea *f*; (of words) renglón *m*, línea *f*; (row) raya *f*, hilera *f*; (cord) cuerda *f*; (persons waiting) cola *f*, fila *f*; (business) ramo *m*; (wrinkle) arruga *f*; (boundary) límite *m*; **— drive** (baseball) línea *f*; **— of credit** línea de crédito *f*; **— of scrimmage** línea de golpeo *f*; **—s** (in a play) parte *f*; **—sman** juez -eza de línea *mf*; **—up** hilera de personas *f*; (sports) alineación *f*; **drop me a —** escríbeme unas líneas; **out of —** irrespetuoso; **to get in —** hacer cola; VI/VT (border) alinear, bordear; (put in a lining) forrar; **to — up** alinear[se]; ADJ **off-—** fuera de línea; **on-—** en línea
lineage [líniɪʤ] N linaje *m*, estirpe *f*
linear [líniə˞] ADJ lineal
lined [laɪnd] ADJ (with lines) rayado; (with a lining) forrado
linen [línɪn] N (fabric) lino *m*; (bedclothes) ropa blanca *f*
liner [láɪnə˞] N (ocean) transatlántico *m*; (air) avión comercial *m*; (eye) delineador *m*
linger [líŋgə˞] VI (stay) quedarse, demorarse; (persist) persistir; (saunter) rezagarse; (contemplate) detenerse; (delay death) aguantar
lingerie [lɑnʒəréi] N lencería *f*
linguist [líŋgwɪst] N lingüista *mf*
linguistics [lɪŋgwístɪks] N lingüística *f*
liniment [línəmənt] N linimento *m*
lining [láɪnɪŋ] N forro *m*; **every cloud has a silver —** no hay mal que por bien no venga
link [lɪŋk] N (of a chain) eslabón *m*; (bond, tie) vínculo *m*; (rail, radio connection) enlace *m*; (computer) enlace *m*, vínculo *m*; VI/VT enlazar[se], conectar[se]; (on a computer) vincular
linnet [línɪt] N pardillo *m*
linoleum [lɪnóliəm] N linóleo *m*
linseed [línsid] N linaza *f*; **— oil** aceite de linaza *m*
lint [lɪnt] N pelusa *f*
lion [láɪən] N león *m*; **—'s share** la parte del león
lioness [láɪənɪs] N leona *f*
lip [lɪp] N labio *m*; (of a pitcher) borde *m*; **— balm** crema para labios *f*; **—stick** lápiz de labios *m*, carmín *m*; **don't give me no —!** no me contestes; VI **to —read** leer los labios
liposuction [láɪpoʊkʃən] N liposucción *f*
liqueur [lɪkɜ́˞] N licor *m*
liquid [líkwɪd] ADJ líquido; **— assets** activo líquido *m*; **— measure** medida para líquidos *f*; N líquido *m*
liquidate [líkwɪdet] VI/VT liquidar
liquidation [lɪkwɪdéʃən] N liquidación *f*
liquidity [lɪkwídɪti] N liquidez *f*

liquor [lík͡ɚ] N bebida espirituosa *f*
lira [lírə] N lira *f*
lisp [lɪsp] N ceceo *m*; VI cecear
list [lɪst] N (series of items) lista *f*; (of a ship) escora *f*; **— price** precio de lista *m*; **— server** servidor de lista *m*; VT (make a list) hacer una lista de; VI (lean) escorar; **this chair —s for two hundred dollars** esta silla está a doscientos dólares
listen [lísən] VI/VT (hear) escuchar, oír; (heed) escuchar, prestar atención; **to — in** (on radio) sintonizar; (eavesdrop) escuchar a hurtadillas
listener [lísənɚ] N oyente *mf*; **radio —** radioescucha *mf*, oyente *mf*
listing [lístɪŋ] N listado *m*
listless [lístlɪs] ADJ lánguido
lit [lɪt] ADJ (provided with light) iluminado; (tipsy) alegre, alumbrado
lit [lɪt] *see* light
literacy [lídə͡ərəsi] N (action of making literate) alfabetización *f*; (rate) alfabetismo *m*
literal [lídə͡ərəɫ] ADJ literal
literary [lídə͡rɚri] ADJ literario
literate [lídə͡rɪt] ADJ (who can read and write) alfabeto; (erudite) erudito, letrado; **he's barely —** apenas sabe leer y escribir
literature [lídə͡rəʧɚ] N literatura *f*; (handbills) impresos *m pl*, folletos *m pl*; **the scientific —** la literatura científica
lithium [líθiəm] N litio *m*; **—-ion battery** batería de iones de litio *f*
Lithuania [lɪθuéniə] N Lituania *f*
Lithuanian [lɪθuéniən] ADJ & N lituano -na *mf*
litigant [lídɪgənt] N litigante *mf*
litigation [lɪdɪgéʃən] N litigio *m*, pleito *m*
litter [lídɚ] N (young animals) camada *f*, cría *f*; (stretcher) camilla *f*; (straw) cama de paja para animales *f*; (trash) basura *f*; (for cats) arena higiénica *f*; VI/VT (dirty) ensuciar; (strew) esparcir; VI (give birth) parir
little [lídɫ] ADJ (small) pequeño, chico; (not much) poco; **— brother** hermano menor *m*, hermanito *m*; **— finger** [dedo] meñique *m*; **— pig** puerquito *m*; **a — coffee** un poco de café; **a — while** un ratito, un poco; ADV & N poco; **— by —** poco a poco
livable [lívəbəɫ] ADJ funcional
live[1] [lɪv] VI/VT vivir; **to — together** convivir; **to — up to** cumplir; **to — it up** tirar la casa por la ventana; **long — the king!** ¡viva el rey! ADJ **all the —long day** todo el santo día
live[2] [laɪv] ADJ vivo; (ammunition) cargado; **— coal** ascua encendida *f*; **— oak** roble de Virginia *m*; **—stock** ganado *m*, ganadería *f*; **— wire** (electric) cable cargado *m*; (person) persona vivaz *f*; **before a — audience** en vivo; **—-in** con cama; ADV en vivo y en directo
livelihood [láɪvlihʊd] N sustento *m*
liveliness [láɪvlɪnɪs] N viveza *f*, animación *f*
lively [láɪvli] ADJ (party) animado; (person) vivaz, avispado; ADV con animación
liver [lívɚ] N hígado *m*
livid [lívɪd] ADJ (pallid, bluish) lívido; (angry) furibundo
living [lívɪŋ] N (life) vida *f*; **— expenses** gastos de subsistencia *m pl*; **— room** sala *f*, living *m*; **— together** cohabitación *f*; **— wage** salario de subsistencia *m*; **— will** documento de instrucciones previas *m*, documento de voluntad anticipada *m*; **to earn/make a —** ganarse la vida; **the —** los vivos; ADJ vivo, viviente
lizard [lízɚd] N lagartija *f*
llama [lámə] N llama *f*
load [lod] N (supported mass) carga *f*; (weight) peso *m*; (ship cargo) cargamento *m*; **no- — fund** fondo sin comisión de entrada *m*; **—s of** montones de; VI/VT cargar; **to — down** colmar; **to — oneself down** agobiarse
loaf [lof] N hogaza de pan *f*, pan *m*; VI holgar, holgazanear, haraganear
loafer [lófɚ] N (idler) holgazán -ana *mf*, haragán -ana *mf*, gandul -la *mf*; (shoe) mocasín *m*
loan [lon] N préstamo *m*; (to a government) empréstito *m*; **— application** solicitud de préstamo *f*; **— guarantee** garantía de préstamo *f*; **— officer** funcionario -ria de préstamos *mf*; **— shark** usurero -ra *mf*; **—word** préstamo *m*; VI/VT prestar
loath [loθ] ADJ renuente; **to be — to** ser renuente a
loathe [loð] VT aborrecer
loathsome [lóðsəm] ADJ repugnante, abominable
lob [lab] VT tirar por lo alto; N (tennis) globo *m*
lobby [lábi] N (vestibule) vestíbulo *m*; (special interest) grupo de presión *m*, lobby *m*; VI/VT (influence) presionar
lobbyist [lábiɪst] N representante de un grupo de presión *mf*
lobe [lob] N lóbulo *m*
lobotomy [ləbáɾəmi] N lobotomía *f*
lobster [lábstɚ] N langosta *f*
local [lókəɫ] ADJ local; **— bus** (computer) vía de transmisión local *f*; **— printer** impresora local *f*; **— train** tren de cercanías *m*
localize [lókəlaɪz] VT localizar
locate [lóket] VI/VT (establish in a place) situar, ubicar; (find) localizar; VI (settle) radicarse, establecerse
location [lokéʃən] N (position) ubicación *f*, emplazamiento *m*; (finding) localización *f*; **on —** en exteriores
lock [lɑk] N (door) cerradura *f*; (canal) esclusa *f*; (firearms, wrestling) llave *f*; (of hair) mecha *f*, mechón *m*; **—jaw** tétanos *m sg*; **—-out** cierre patronal *m*; **—smith** cerrajero -ra *mf*; **to**

have a — on the award tener asegurado el premio; VI/VT cerrar con llave; (make immovable) trabar[se]; **to — in** encerrar; **to — out** dejar afuera; **to — up** (door) cerrar con llave; (animal) encerrar; (prisoner) encarcelar; (valuables) poner bajo llave

locker [lákɜ·] N (for athletic equipment) casillero *m*; (for frozen food) cámara frigorífica *f*; **— room** vestuario *m*

locket [lákɪt] N relicario *m*, guardapelo *m*

locomotive [lokəmóʊDɪv] N locomotora *f*

locust [lókəst] N langosta *f*; **— tree** algarrobo *m*

lodge [ladʒ] N (of fraternal organization) logia *f*; (cabin) cabaña *f*; (hotel) posada *f*, mesón *m*; VI/VT alojar[se], hospedar[se]; **to — a complaint** presentar una queja

lodger [ládʒɜ·] N inquilino -na *mf*

lodging [ládʒɪŋ] N alojamiento *m*, hospedaje *m*, albergue *m*

loft [lɔft] N (attic) desván *m*; (for choir) coro *m*; (for hay) pajar *m*; VT tirar por lo alto

lofty [lɔ́fti] ADJ elevado, encumbrado

log [lag] N (wood) leño *m*, madero *m*, rollizo *m*; (ship record) cuaderno de bitácora *m*; (record of activity) diario *m*; (on a computer) registro *m*; **— cabin** cabaña de troncos *f*; VI/VT (cut trees) cortar; **—-in name** nombre de acceso *m*; VT (write down) anotar; **to — in** ingresar al sistema; **to — off/out** finalizar una sesión; VT registrar una acción

logarithm [lógərɪðəm] N logaritmo *m*

logic [ládʒɪk] N lógica *f*; **— board** placa lógica *f*

logical [ládʒɪkəl] ADJ lógico

logically [ládʒɪkli] ADV lógicamente

logistics [ləʤístɪks] N logística *f*

loin [lɔɪn] N ijada *f*; (in animals) ijar *m*; (cut of meat) lomo *m*; **—s** entrañas *f pl*

loiter [lɔ́ɪdɜ·] VI (idly) holgazanear; (with ill intent) merodear; **to — behind** rezagarse

loll [lɑl] VI arrellanarse

lollipop [lálipɑp] N *Sp* pirulí *m*; *Mex* paleta *f*; *RP* chupetín *m*

lone [lon] ADJ (solitary) solitario; (only) único

loneliness [lónlɪnɪs] N soledad *f*

lonely [lónli] ADJ solo

lonesome [lónsəm] ADJ solo

long [lɔŋ] ADJ largo; **a — way from home** lejos de casa; **to work — hours** trabajar muchas horas; **— distance** de larga distancia; **— division** división de más de una cifra *f*; **—hand** letra manuscrita *f*; **— johns** calzoncillos largos *m pl*; **— jump** salto largo *m*; **—-lasting** duradero, perdurable; **—-lived** (batteries) duradero; (people) longevo; **—-range** (missiles) de largo alcance; (plans) a largo plazo; **—shoreman** estibador *m*; **—-suffering** sufrido; **—-term** a largo plazo; **—-term care** atención médica a largo plazo *f*; **—time friend** viejo amigo; **— underwear** calzoncillo largo *m*; **—-winded** verborrágico, palabrero; **it's a — shot** es muy improbable; ADV mucho, mucho tiempo; **— ago** hace mucho tiempo; **— before** mucho antes; **— live . . . !** ¡viva . . . ! **all winter —** todo el invierno; **how — did he stay?** ¿cuánto tiempo se quedó? **not for —** no por mucho tiempo; **so —!** ¡hasta luego! **to be — in coming** tardar en venir; **three meters —** tres metros de largo; **will you be —?** ¿tardarás mucho? **the whole day —** todo el santo día; VI **to — for** anhelar

longer [lɔ́ŋgɜ·] ADJ más largo; ADV más; **no —** ya no; **how much —?** ¿hasta cuándo?

longevity [lɑnʤévɪDi] N longevidad *f*

longing [lɔ́ŋɪŋ] N anhelo *m*; ADJ anhelante

longitude [lɑ́nʤɪtud] N longitud *f*

look [lʊk] VI (see) mirar; (seem) parecer; **it —s good on you** te queda bien, te luce; **to — after** atender, cuidar; **to — alike** parecerse; **to — down on someone** despreciar a alguien; **to — for** (search for) buscar; (anticipate) esperar; **I — forward to it** lo espero con ansia, me da mucha ilusión; **to — into** investigar; **she —s her age** aparenta la edad que tiene; **to — out on** dar a, tener vista a; **to — out of** asomarse a; **— out!** ¡cuidado! **to — over** dar un vistazo a; **to — up** (upward) levantar la vista; (in a directory) buscar; **to — up to** admirar; N (gaze) mirada *f*; (examination) vistazo *m*; **—-alike** doble *mf*; **—out** (person) vigía *mf*; (place) mirador *m*, vigía *f*; **to be on the —out** estar alerta; **—s** aspecto *m*, pinta *f*; **good —s** belleza *f*

looking glass [lʊ́kɪŋglæs] N espejo *m*

loom [lum] N telar *m*; VI (appear indistinctly) dibujarse; (threaten) cernerse

loon [lún] N (bird) somorgujo *m*; (person) chiflado -da *mf*

loony [lúni] ADJ chiflado

loop [lup] N (for fastening) presilla *f*; (in a rope) lazo *m*; (of a flight) rizo *m*; (electric) circuito cerrado *m*; (computer programming, ice-skating) bucle *m*; **—hole** escapatoria *f*; **in the —** al corriente, al tanto de lo que pasa; VI (make a loop) hacer un lazo; (curve around) serpentear; (loop the loop) rizar el rizo; VT enlazar

loose [lus] ADJ (free) suelto; (not tight) flojo; (approximate) libre; (unfettered) desatado; (immoral) disoluto; (promiscuous) fácil; **— cannon** mono con una metralleta *m*; **— change** suelto *m*, cambio *m*; **— end** cabo suelto *m*; **—-fitting** holgado; **—-jointed** de articulaciones flexibles; **—-leaf** [de] hojas sueltas; **to let —** soltar; VT desatar, soltar

loosen [lúsən] VI/VT (untie) soltar[se], desatar; (make/become less tight/dense/strict) aflojar[se]

looseness [lúsnɪs] N (of skin) flojedad *f*; (of morals) relajamiento *m*; (of clothing) holgura *f*; (of soil) friabilidad *f*; (of translation) lo libre
loot [lut] N botín *m*; VI/VT saquear
lop [lɑp] VT (cut) cortar; (eliminate) eliminar; VI caer[se]; ADJ **—sided** (leaning to one side) ladeado; (unbalanced) desequilibrado; (listing) escorado
lope [lop] VI correr a pasos largos
loquacious [lokwéʃəs] ADJ locuaz
loquat [lókwɑt] N níspero *m*
lord [lɔrd] N señor *m*; (God) Señor *m*; (British title) lord *m*; **—'s Prayer** Padrenuestro *m*; **my —!** ¡Dios mío! VI **to — it over someone** tratarle a alguien con arrogancia
lordly [lɔ́rdli] ADJ (kingly) señorial; (haughty) altivo
lordship [lɔ́rdʃɪp] N (title) señoría *f*; (power) señorío *m*
lore [lɔr] N saber *m*
lose [luz] VI/VT perder; (a pursuer) dejar atrás; **to — sight of** perder de vista; **to — oneself in thought** ensimismarse
loser [lúzɚ] N perdedor -ora *mf*
loss [lɔs] N (destruction) pérdida *f*; (misplacement) pérdida *f*, extravío *m*; (sports) derrota *f*; **to be at a —** no saber qué hacer; **to sell at a —** vender con pérdida; **—es** bajas *f pl*
lost [lɔst] ADJ perdido; **— cause** caso perdido *m*; **— in thought** absorto; **to get —** perderse, extraviarse
lost [lɔst] *see* lose
lot [lɑt] N (parcel) lote *m*; (fate) suerte *f*, destino *m*; (piece of land) solar *m*, terreno *m*; **the —** todo; **a — of / —s of** mucho[s]; **a — of money** mucho dinero; **by —** al azar; **to draw —s** echar suertes; **to fall to one's —** caerle en suerte a uno; ADV **a — better** mucho mejor
lotion [lóʃən] N loción *f*
lottery [lɑ́dəri] N lotería *f*
loud [laʊd] ADJ (noisy) ruidoso; (strong) fuerte; (ostentatious) chillón; **—speaker** altavoz *m*, altoparlante *m*; **—mouth** bocazas *mf* sg; ADV fuerte, alto
Lou Gehrig's disease [lugérɪgz dɪziz] N enfermedad de Lou Gehrig *f*
lounge [laʊnʤ] VI repantigarse, arrellanarse; N (waiting room) sala de espera *f*; (room in bar) salón *m*; (divan) diván *m*; **— chair** diván *m*
louse [laʊs] N piojo *m*
lousy [láʊzi] ADJ (infested with lice) piojoso; (contemptible) despreciable; (poorly done) pésimo
lout [laʊt] N bruto *m*
lovable [lávəbəɫ] ADJ adorable
love [lʌv] N (affection) amor *m*; (fondness) afición *f*; (in tennis) nada *f*; **— affair** aventura *f*, amorío *m*; **— at first sight** amor a primera vista *m*, flechazo *m*; **— life** vida sentimental *f*; **— seat** confidente *m*; **books were her great —** los libros fueron su gran pasión; **to be in —** estar enamorado; **to fall in — with** enamorarse de; **to make — to** hacerle el amor a; VI/VT amar, querer; **I — to eat apples** me encanta comer manzanas
loveliness [lávlɪnɪs] N (beauty) hermosura *f*; (charm) encanto *m*
lovely [lávli] ADJ (beautiful) hermoso; (charming) encantador; (pleasant) ameno
lover [lávɚ] N (sexually involved) amante *mf*; (in love) enamorado -da *mf*, amante *mf*; (interested in) aficionado -da *mf*
loving [lávɪŋ] ADJ cariñoso, afectuoso
low [lo] ADJ (not high) bajo; (base) vil; (humble) humilde; (downcast) abatido; (deep in pitch) grave; **— beam** luces cortas *f pl*; **—brow** poco culto; **—-budget** de bajo presupuesto; **—-cal** de bajas calorías; **—-cost** de bajo precio; **—down** verdad *f*; **—-end** de baja calidad; **— gear** primera marcha *f*; **—-grade** (inferior) inferior; (low) bajo; **—-income** de bajos ingresos; **—-key** tranquilo; **—land** tierra baja *f*; **—-level** de bajo nivel; **—life** canalla *f*; **— quality** baja calidad *f*; **—-tech** sencillo; **— tide** bajamar *f*, marea baja *f*; **dress with a — neck** vestido escotado *m*; **to be — on something** estar escaso de algo; **to be in — spirits** estar abatido/desanimado; ADV bajo; **to buy —** comprar barato; N (sound of a cow) mugido *m*; VI mugir
lower [lóɚ] VI/VT bajar; (prices) rebajar; (flag, sail) arriar; ADJ más bajo, inferior; **—case** minúscula *f*; **— house** cámara de diputados *f*
lowliness [lólinɪs] N humildad *f*
lowly [lóli] ADJ humilde
loyal [lɔ́ɪəɫ] ADJ leal
loyalty [lɔ́ɪəɫti] N lealtad *f*
LSD [lysergic acid diethylamide] [éɫɛ́sdí] N LSD *m*
lubricant [lúbrɪkənt] ADJ & N lubricante *m*
lubricate [lúbrɪket] VI/VT lubricar
lucid [lúsɪd] ADJ lúcido
lucidity [lusídɪdi] N lucidez *f*
luck [lʌk] N suerte *f*; **in —** de suerte; **to be out of —** estar de mala suerte; VI **to — into** conseguir por un golpe de suerte; **to — out** tener suerte
luckily [lʌ́kəli] ADV afortunadamente
lucky [lʌ́ki] ADJ afortunado; **— charm** amuleto de la suerte *m*; **to be —** tener suerte
lucrative [lúkrəɪv] ADJ lucrativo
ludicrous [lúdɪkrəs] ADJ ridículo
lug [lʌg] VT acarrear
luggage [lʌ́gɪʤ] N equipaje *m*; **— rack** rejilla *f*
lukewarm [lúkwɔ́rm] ADJ (not warm or cold) tibio; (indifferent) indiferente
lull [lʌɫ] VT (put to sleep) arrullar; VI/VT (soothe)

calmar[se]; N (calm) calma *f*, tregua *f*; (sound) arrullo *m*

lullaby [lʌ́ləbaɪ] N canción de cuna *f*, nana *f*

lumbago [lʌmbégo] N lumbago *m*

lumbar [lʌ́mbɚ] ADJ lumbar

lumber [lʌ́mbɚ] N madera *f*; **—jack** leñador *m*; **—man** maderero *m*; **— mill** aserradero *m*; **—yard** almacén de maderas *m*; VI/VT (cut trees) talar; (move heavily) moverse pesadamente; (make a low noise) tronar

luminous [lúmənəs] ADJ luminoso

lump [lʌmp] N (in breast) bulto *m*; (in sauce) grumo *m*; (in throat) nudo *m*; (of coal) trozo *m*; (of food) plasta *f*; (on head) chichón *m*; (of sugar) terrón *m*; **to take one's —s** recibir palos; **— sum** pago global *m*; VT juntar; VI agrumarse

lumpectomy [lʌmpéktəmi] N tumorectomía *f*

lumpy [lʌ́mpi] ADJ grumoso

lunar [lúnɚ] ADJ lunar; **— eclipse** eclipse lunar *m*

lunatic [lúnətɪk] ADJ & N lunático -ca *mf*, loco -ca *mf*; **— fringe** extremistas *mf pl*

lunch [lʌntʃ] N comida *f*, almuerzo *m*; **—time** hora de comer/almorzar *f*; **out to —** (having lunch) almorzando; (crazy) en la luna; VI comer, almorzar

lung [lʌŋ] N pulmón *m*

lunge [lʌnʤ] N arremetida *f*; VI arremeter, abalanzarse; **to — at** arremeter contra, abalanzarse sobre

lupus [lúpəs] N lupus *m*

lurch [lɝtʃ] N tambaleo *m*; **to give a —** tambalearse; **to leave someone in the —** dejar a alguien en la estacada; VI tambalearse, dar barquinazos

lure [lʊr] N (thing that attracts) atractivo *m*, gancho *m*; (in hunting) señuelo *m*; (in fishing) cebo *m*; VT atraer, seducir

lurid [lʊ́rɪd] ADJ (gruesome) sangriento; (shocking) escabroso

lurk [lɝk] VI (lie in wait) estar en acecho, acechar; (move furtively) moverse furtivamente

luscious [lʌ́ʃəs] ADJ (delicious) exquisito, delicioso; (sexy) voluptuoso

lust [lʌst] N (sexual desire) lujuria *f*, lascivia *f*; (craving) deseo *m*, ansia *f*; VI desear; **to — after** codiciar

luster [lʌ́stɚ] N lustre *m*, brillo *m*

lustful [lʌ́stfəł] ADJ lujurioso

lusty [lʌ́sti] ADJ (robust) robusto; (full of lust) lujurioso

Luxembourg [lʌ́ksəmbɝg] N Luxemburgo *m*

Luxembourger [lʌ́ksəmbɝgɚ] N luxemburgués -esa *mf*

Luxembourgian [lʌksəmbɝ́giən] ADJ luxemburgués

luxurious [lʌgʒʊ́riəs] ADJ (characterized by luxury) lujoso; (luxuriant) exuberante

luxury [lʌ́gʒəri] N lujo *m*; **— tax** impuesto suntuario *m*; ADJ de lujo

lye [laɪ] N lejía *f*

lying [láɪɪŋ] ADJ mentiroso

Lyme disease [lʌ́ɪm dɪziz] N enfermedad de Lyme *f*

lymph [lɪmf] N linfa *f*; **— node** nodo linfático *m*

lymphocyte [lɪ́mfəsaɪt] N linfocito *m*

lymphoma [lɪmfóma] N linfoma *m*

lynch [lɪntʃ] VT linchar

lynx [lɪŋks] N lince *m*

lyre [laɪr] N lira *f*

lyric [lɪ́rɪk] N poema lírico *m*; **— poetry** lírica *f*; **—s** letra *f*; ADJ lírico

lyrical [lɪ́rɪkəł] ADJ lírico

lyricism [lɪ́rɪsɪzəm] N lirismo *m*

Mm

ma'am [mæm] N señora *f*

Macao [məkáʊ] N Macao *m*

macaroni [mækəróni] N macarrones *m pl*

Macedonia [mæsɪdóniə] N Macedonia *f*

Macedonian [mæsɪdóniən] ADJ & N macedonio -nia *mf*

machine [məʃín] N máquina *f*; (of government) maquinaria *f*, aparato *m*; **— gun** (not portable) ametralladora *f*; (portable) metralleta *f*; **— language** lenguaje de máquina *m*, lenguaje máquina *m*; ADJ **—-made** hecho a máquina; VT trabajar a máquina

machinery [məʃínəri] N maquinaria *f*

machinist [məʃínɪst] N maquinista *mf*, operario -ria *mf*

mackerel [mækɚəł] N caballa *f*

macro [mákro] N serie de instrucciones *f*

mad [mæd] ADJ (crazy) loco; (angry) rabioso, enojado; (hydrophobic) rabioso; **— cow disease** encefalopatía espongiforme bovina *f*, enfermedad de las vacas locas *f*; **—man** loco *m*; **to be — about someone** estar loco por alguien; **to drive —** enloquecer, volver loco; **to get —** enojarse; **to go —** volverse loco, enloquecerse; **like —** como loco

Madagascan [mæDəgǽskən] ADJ & N malgache *mf*

Madagascar [mæDəgǽskɑr] N Madagascar *m*

madam [mǽDəm] N (title) señora *f*

maddening [mǽdn̩ɪŋ] ADJ enloquecedor

made [med] ADJ **—-to-measure** hecho a la medida; **—-to-order** hecho por encargo; **—-up** (invented) inventado, falso; (wearing makeup) maquillado; **to be — of** ser de; **to have something —** mandar hacer algo; **I'm**

a — man estoy hecho; **to have it —** estar hecho

made [med] *see* make

madness [mǽdnɪs] N (insanity) locura *f*; (anger) rabia *f*

Mafia [máfiə] N mafia *f*

mafioso [mɑfióso] N mafioso *m*

magazine [mǽgəzɪn] N (publication) revista *f*; (room for ammunition) polvorín *m*; (part of gun) cargador *m*

magic [mǽʤɪk] N magia *f*; ADJ mágico; **— bullet** panacea *f*; **— wand** varita mágica *f*

magical [mǽʤɪkəł] ADJ mágico

magician [məʤíʃən] N (person adept at magic) mágico -ca *mf*; (person adept at finances) mago -ga *mf*

magistrate [mǽʤɪstret] N magistrado -da *mf*

magma [mǽgmə] N magma *m*

magnanimous [mægnǽnəməs] ADJ magnánimo

magnate [mǽgnet] N magnate *m*

magnesia [mægníʒə] N magnesia *f*

magnesium [mægníziəm] N magnesio *m*

magnet [mǽgnɪt] N imán *m*

magnetic [mægnɛ́DɪK] ADJ magnético; **— pole** polo magnético *m*; **— resonance imaging** imagen por resonancia magnética *f*; **— tape** cinta magnetofónica *f*

magnetism [mǽgnɪtɪzəm] N magnetismo *m*

magnetize [mǽgnɪtaɪz] VT magnetizar, imantar

magnificence [mægnífɪsəns] N magnificencia *f*

magnificent [mægnífɪsənt] ADJ magnífico

magnify [mǽgnɪfaɪ] VT (to make larger) aumentar; (to make louder) amplificar; (to exaggerate) exagerar, magnificar

magnitude [mǽgnɪtud] N magnitud *f*

magnolia [mægnóljə] N (flower) magnolia *f*; (tree) magnolio *m*

magpie [mǽgpaɪ] N urraca *f* (also hoarder)

mahogany [məhágəni] N caoba *f*

maid [med] N criada *f*, sirvienta *f*; (in hotel) camarera *f*; **— of honor** dama de honor *f*

maiden [médn] N *lit* doncella *f*, virgen *f*; **— voyage** primer viaje *m*; **— name** nombre de soltera *m*

mail [meł] N correo *m*; (electronic) mensaje *m*; (of metal) malla *f*; **—bag** cartera *f*; **—box** buzón *m*; **—man** cartero *m*; **— order** pedido por correo *m*; **— order business** negocio de ventas por correo *m*; VT echar al correo; **—ing list** lista de correo *f*

maim [mem] VT mutilar

main [men] ADJ principal; **— office** oficina central *f*; N (pipe) cañería principal *f*; (sea) alta mar *f*; **—frame** *Sp* ordenador central *m*, *Am* computadora central *f*; **—land** continente *m*; **—spring** muelle real *m*; **—stream** tendencia mayoritaria *f*; **—stream engineering** ingeniería conforme a la corriente dominante *f*; **—stay** pilar *m*, puntal *m*; **— street** calle principal *f*

mainly [ménli] ADV principalmente, fundamentalmente

maintain [mentén] VT (repair, support) mantener; (assert) afirmar

maintenance [méntnəns] N (repairs) mantenimiento *m*; (monetary support) manutención *f*; **— cost** costo de mantenimiento *m*

maize [mez] N maíz *m*

majestic [məʤɛ́stɪk] ADJ majestuoso

majesty [mǽʤɪsti] N majestad *f*; **Your —** Su Majestad

major [méʤɚ] ADJ (greater) mayor, más grande; (large) grande; **— key** mayor *m*; N (military rank) comandante *m*; (field of study) especialidad *f*, carrera *f*; **— league** liga mayor *f*; VI especializarse

majority [məʤɔ́rɪDi] N (greater number) mayoría *f*; (age) mayoría de edad *f*; **— ownership** propiedad mayoritaria *f*; **the —** el grueso

make [mek] VT (do) hacer; (create) fabricar; (cause) causar; (earn) ganar; (a speech) pronunciar; **to — a clean breast of** sacarse del pecho; **to —a decision** tomar una decisión; **to — a living** ganarse la vida; **to — a train** llegar a tiempo para tomar un tren; **to — a turn** girar, doblar; **to — away with** fugarse con; **to — believe** hacer de cuenta que; **to — out** (see) vislumbrar, divisar; (read) descifrar; (kiss) *Sp* morrear; *Am* besuquearse; **to — possible** posibilitar; **to — too much of** exagerar; **to — up** (a story) inventar; (after a quarrel) hacer las paces; (a loss) recuperar; (one's face) maquillarse; (one's mind) decidirse; **to — up for** compensar; **two plus two —s four** dos y dos son cuatro; **what do you — of that?** ¿cómo interpretas eso? **I'll — it up to you** te voy a compensar por eso; **you'll — a good teacher** vas a ser un buen profesor; N (brand) marca *f*; **—-up** (composition) composición *f*; (character) carácter *m*; (cosmetics) maquillaje *m*; ADJ **—shift** provisional

maker [mékɚ] N (creator) creador -ora *mf*, hacedor -ora *mf*; (manufacturer) fabricante *m*

makings [mékɪŋz] N (potential) potencial *m*; (ingredients) ingredientes *m pl*

maladjusted [mæləʤʌ́stɪd] ADJ inadaptado

malady [mǽləDi] N mal *m*

malaise [məléz] N malestar *m*

malaria [məlérə] N malaria *f*, paludismo *m*

Malawi [məlɑ́wi] N Malawi *m*

Malawian [məlɑ́wiən] ADJ & N malawiano -na *mf*

Malaysia [məléʒə] N Malasia *f*

Malaysian [məléʒən] ADJ & N malasio -sia *mf*
malcontent [mǽlkəntɛnt] ADJ & N descontento -ta *mf*
Maldives [mɔ́ldaɪvz] N Maldivas *f pl*
Maldivian [mɔldívɪən] ADJ & N maldivo -va *mf*
male [meɪl] ADJ (animal, plant) macho; (person) varón; (trait) masculino; N (animal, plant) macho *m*; (person) varón *m*
malevolent [məlévələnt] ADJ malévolo
malformation [mǽlfɔrméʃən] N malformación *f*
malfunction [mǽlfʌ́ŋkʃən] N funcionamiento defectuoso *m*; VI funcionar mal
Mali [máli] N Malí *m*
Malian [máliən] ADJ & N malí *mf*
malice [mǽlɪs] N malicia *f*; **with — aforethought** con premeditación y alevosía
malicious [məlíʃəs] ADJ malicioso
malign [məláɪn] VT calumniar, difamar
malignancy [məlígnənsi] N (quality) malignidad *f*; (tumor) tumor maligno *m*
malignant [məlígnənt] ADJ maligno
mall [mɔl] N (closed street) paseo *m*; (enclosed shopping area) galería *f*, centro comercial *m*
mallet [mǽlɪt] N mazo *m*
malnourished [mǽlnɝ́-rɪʃt] ADJ desnutrido
malnutrition [mǽlnutríʃən] N desnutrición *f*
malpractice [mǽlprǽktɪs] N negligencia *f*, mala práctica *f*
malt [mɔlt] N malta *f*; **—ed milk** leche malteada *f*
Malta [mɔ́ltə] N Malta *f*
Maltese [mɔltíz] ADJ & N maltés -esa *mf*
mama, mamma [mámə] N mamá *f*; **—'s boy** nene de mamá *m*
mammal [mǽməl] N mamífero *m*
mammary [mǽməri] ADJ mamario
mammography [mæmógrəfi] N mamografía *f*
mammoth [mǽmoθ] ADJ enorme; N mamut *m*
man [mæn] N hombre *m*; (servant) criado *m*; (in games) pieza *f*, ficha *f*; **— and wife** marido y mujer; **—hunt** persecución *f*; **—kind** humanidad *f*; **—-of-war** (ship) buque de guerra *m*; (jellyfish) medusa *f*; **—power** (for work) mano de obra *f*; **—slaughter** (accidental) homicidio culposo *m*, homicidio involuntario *m*; (unpremeditated) homicidio sin premeditación *m*; **—-to-— defense** defensa al hombre *f*, defensa de asignación *f*, defensa individual *f*; **every — for himself** cada cual para sí; **to a —** unánimamente; ADJ **—-eating** que come carne humana; **—-made** (fiber) sintético; (lake) artificial; INTERJ ¡hombre! VT (a fort) guarnecer; (a ship) tripular; **to —handle** violentar
manage [mǽnɪʤ] VT (succeed in) conseguir, lograr; (direct) dirigir, administrar, gestionar; (maneuver) manejar; VI **to — without help** arreglárselas sin ayuda
manageable [mǽnɪʤəbəl] ADJ manejable; (hair) dócil
managed [mǽnɪʤd] ADJ — **care** plan de salud administrado *m*; **— funds** fondos administrados *m pl*
management [mǽnɪʤmənt] N (act of managing) dirección *f*, gestión *f*; (persons controlling a business) gerencia *f*, patronal *f*, gestión *f*; (area of study) empresariales *f pl*
manager [mǽnɪʤɚ] N (of a store) gerente -ta *mf*; (of a company) director -ora *mf*
mandate [mǽndet] N mandato *m*; VT decretar
mandatory [mǽndətɔri] ADJ obligatorio
mandolin [mǽndəlɪn] N mandolina *f*
mane [men] N (of a lion) melena *f*; (of a horse) crin *f*
maneuver [mənúvɚ] N maniobra *f*; VI/VT maniobrar
manganese [mǽŋgəniz] N manganeso *m*
mange [menʤ] N sarna *f*, roña *f*
manger [ménʤɚ] N pesebre *m*
mangle [mǽŋgəl] VT (mutilate) magullar, mutilar; (ruin) estropear
mango [mǽŋgo] N mango *m*
mangrove [mǽŋgrov] N mangle *m*
mangy [ménʤi] ADJ sarnoso
manhood [mǽnhʊd] N virilidad *f*; (men collectively) hombres *m pl*; (adult age) edad adulta *f*
mania [méniə] N manía *f*
maniac [méniæk] N maníaco -ca *mf*, maniaco -ca *mf*
maniacal [mənáɪəkəl] ADJ maníaco
manic-depressive [mǽnɪkdɪprésɪv] ADJ maniaco-depresivo
manicure [mǽnɪkjʊr] N manicura *f*; VT manicurar
manifest [mǽnəfɛst] ADJ manifiesto; N (list of cargo) manifiesto *m*, hoja de ruta *f*; VT (show) manifestar, poner de manifiesto; (express) declarar
manifestation [mǽnəfɛstéʃən] N manifestación *f*
manifesto [mǽnɪfɛ́stə] N manifiesto *m*
manifold [mǽnəfołd] ADJ diverso; N (on a motor) colector *m*
manila [mənílə] N abacá *m*; **— envelope** sobre manila *m*
manioc [mǽniɑk] N mandioca *f*, yuca *f*
manipulate [mənípjəlet] VT manipular
manipulation [mənɪpjəléʃən] N manipulación *f*
manlike [mǽnlaɪk] ADJ (manly) varonil; (mannish) hombruna; (resembling a human) de hombre
manliness [mǽnlɪnɪs] N virilidad *f*
manly [mǽnli] ADJ varonil, viril
manner [mǽnɚ] N (way) manera *f*, modo *m*, forma *f*; (type) tipo *m*; (outward bearing) aire *m*, además *m*, porte *m*; **—s** modales *m pl*, crianza *f*; **in the — of** a la manera de

mannerism [mǽnərɪzəm] N peculiaridad *f*
mannish [mǽnɪʃ] ADJ hombruno, varonil
manor [mǽnɚ] N feudo *m*, solar *m*; **— house** casa solariega *f*
mansion [mǽnʃən] N mansión *f*
mantel [mǽntl] N repisa de chimenea *f*
mantle [mǽntl] N manto *m*
mantra [mǽntrə] N mantra *f*
manual [mǽnjuəl] ADJ & N manual *m*; **— labor** trabajo manual *m*
manufacture [mænjəfǽktʃɚ] VT fabricar, manufacturar; (clothes, shoes) confeccionar; N fabricación *f*, manufactura *f*; (of clothes, shoes) confección *f*
manufacturer [mænjəfǽktʃərɚ] N fabricante *m*; **—'s suggested retail price** precio sugerido por el fabricante *m*
manufacturing [mænjəfǽktʃɚɪŋ] N fabricación *f*, manufactura *f*; ADJ fabril, manufacturero; **— empire** imperio industrial *m*
manure [mənʊ́r] N estiércol *m*; VT estercolar, abonar
manuscript [mǽnjəskrɪpt] ADJ & N manuscrito *m*
many [mɛ́ni] ADJ muchos; **— apples** muchas manzanas; **— came** vinieron muchos; **— a time** muchas veces; **a great —** muchísimos; **as — as** tantos como; **as — as five** hasta cinco; **how —?** ¿cuántos? **three books too —** tres libros de más; **too —** demasiados
map [mæp] N (geographical) mapa *m*; (of streets) plano *m*; VT trazar un mapa de; **to — out** planear
maple [mépəl] N *Sp* arce *m*; *Am* maple *m*; **— syrup** miel de arce/maple *f*
mar [mɑr] VT estropear
marathon [mǽrəθɑn] N maratón *mf*
marble [mɑ́rbəl] N mármol *m*; (toy) canica *f*, bola *f*; **to play —s** jugar a las canicas; ADJ de mármol, marmóreo
march [mɑrtʃ] N marcha *f*; VI marchar; (leave) marcharse; **to — in** entrar; **to — out** marcharse; VT hacer marchar
March [mɑrtʃ] N marzo *m*
mare [mɛr] N yegua *f*
margarine [mɑ́rʤɚɪn] N margarina *f*
margin [mɑ́rʤɪn] N margen *m*; **— of error** margen de error *m*; **— of safety** margen de seguridad *m*; **on —** comprado en cuenta de margen
marginal [mɑ́rʤənl] ADJ marginal
marginalization [mɑrʤənlɪzéʃən] N marginación *f*
marginalize [mɑ́rʤənlˌaɪz] VT marginar
marigold [mǽrɪgoʊld] N caléndula *f*, maravilla *f*
marijuana, marihuana [mærəwɑ́nə] N marihuana *f*, mariguana *f*
marinate [mǽrənet] VT marinar
marine [mərín] ADJ (of the sea) marino; (maritime) marítimo; **— corps** infantería de marina *f*; N soldado de infantería de marina *m*
marionette [mæriənɛ́t] N marioneta *f*
marital [mǽrɪdl] ADJ conyugal, matrimonial; **— status** estado civil *m*
maritime [mǽrɪtaɪm] ADJ marítimo
mark [mɑrk] N marca *f*, seña *f*; (token) señal *f*; (indication) seña *f*; (grade) nota *f*, calificación *f*; (former German currency) marco *m*; **—down** rebaja de precio *f*; **—sman** tirador *m*; **he's a good —sman** tiene muy buena puntería / muy buen tino; **—-up** (amount above wholesale price) margen de ganancia *m*; **the halfway —** el punto medio, la mitad; **to hit the —** dar en el blanco; **on your —, get set, go!** ¡en sus marcas, listos y ya! ¡en sus marcas, listos, fuera! **to make one's —** distinguirse; **to miss the —** errar el tiro; **easy —** blanco fácil *m*; VT (write on) marcar; (indicate) señalar; (observe) observar, notar; (grade) calificar; **—ed for greatness** destinado a la grandeza; **— my words!** ¡ya verás! **to — down prices** rebajar los precios; **to — off** acotar, deslindar; **to — up prices** subir los precios
marker [mɑ́rkɚ] N marcador *m*
market [mɑ́rkɪt] N mercado *m*; **— analysis** análisis de mercado *m*; **—place** mercado *m*; **— price** precio de mercado *m*; **— share** sector del mercado *m*; **I'm in the — for** estoy buscando; VT comercializar, mercadear
marketable [mɑ́rkɪɚbəl] ADJ vendible
marketing [mɑ́rkɪɚɪŋ] N (field of study) mercadotecnia *f*, marketing *m*; (selling) comercialización *f*
marmalade [mɑ́rməled] N mermelada de naranja *f*
maroon [mərʊ́n] ADJ & N bordó/bordeaux *m*; VT abandonar
marquis [mɑrkí] N marqués *m*
marquise [mɑrkíz] N marquesa *f*
marriage [mǽrɪʤ] N matrimonio *m*; (combination) combinación *f*; **— license** licencia de matrimonio *f*
marriageable [mǽrɪʤəbəl] ADJ casadero
married [mǽrid] ADJ (united in marriage) casado; (relation to marriage) conyugal; **— couple** matrimonio *m*; **to get —** casarse
marrow [mǽro] N (in the bones) médula *f*; (food) tuétano *m*; (essential part) meollo *m*
marry [mǽri] VT (to marry off) casar; (to get married) casarse con; VI casarse
marsh [mɑrʃ] N pantano *m*, ciénaga *f*
marshal [mɑ́rʃəl] N (military) mariscal *m*; (police chief) alguacil *m*; (of a parade) maestro de ceremonia *m*; VT (facts, forces) reunir; (troops) formar
Marshallese [mɑrʃəlíz] ADJ & N marshalés -esa *mf*

Marshall Islands [márʃəlílənʤz] N Islas Marshall *f pl*
marshmallow [márʃmɛlo] N malvavisco *m*
marshy [márʃi] ADJ pantanoso, cenagoso
martial [márʃəł] ADJ marcial; **— arts** artes marciales *f pl*; **— law** ley marcial *f*
martin [mártɪn] N avión *m*
martini [mɑrtíni] N martini *m*
martyr [mártɚ] N mártir *m*; VT martirizar
martyrdom [mártɚdəm] N martirio *m*
marvel [márvəł] N maravilla *f*; VI maravillarse
marvelous [márvələs] ADJ maravilloso
Marxism [márksɪzəm] N marxismo *m*
mascara [mæskǽrə] N rímel *m*
mascot [mǽskɑt] N mascota *f*
masculine [mǽskjəlɪn] ADJ masculino
mash [mæʃ] VT aplastar, pisar; **—ed potatoes** puré de papas/patatas *m*; N (pulpy mass) puré *m*; (food for livestock) afrecho *m*; (malt) malta remojada *f*
mask [mæsk] N máscara *f*, careta *f*; VT enmascarar; **—ed ball** baile de máscaras *m*
masochism [mǽsəkɪzəm] N masoquismo *m*
mason [mésən] N (builder) albañil *m*; (Freemason) masón *m*
masonry [mésənri] N (bricklaying) albañilería *f*; (fraternal order) masonería *f*
masquerade [mæskəréd] N mascarada *f*; VI **to — as** hacerse pasar por
mass [mæs] N masa *f*; (in church) misa *f*; **— communication** comunicación de masas *f*; **— marketing** comercialización masiva *f*; **— media** medios de comunicación [de masas] *m pl*; **— production** fabricación en masa *f*; **— storage** almacenamiento masivo *m*; **— transit** transporte público *m*; **— unemployment** desempleo/paro masivo *m*; **the —es** las masas *f pl*; VI/VT juntar[se] en masa; (troops) concentrar[se]
massacre [mǽsəkɚ] N masacre *m*; VT masacrar
massage [məsɑ́ʒ] N masaje *m*; **— parlor** salón de masajes *m*; VT (give a massage) masajear; (change data) manipular
masseur [məsɝ́] N masajista *m*
masseuse [məsús] N masajista *f*
massive [mǽsɪv] ADJ (severe) masivo; (solid) macizo; (large) enorme
mast [mæst] N mástil *m*, árbol *m*
mastectomy [mæstéktəmi] N mastectomía *f*
master [mǽstɚ] N (person in control) amo -a *mf*, señor -ora *mf*; (owner of slave or animal) amo -a *mf*; (best representative, skilled laborer) maestro *m*; (young boy) señorito *m*; (tape or disk) original *m*; **—'s degree** maestría *f*; ADJ (dominant) dominante; **— bedroom** dormitorio principal *m*; **— key** llave maestra *f*; **—mind** cerebro *m*; **—piece** obra maestra *f*; VT dominar; **to —mind** planificar y dirigir
masterful [mǽstɚfəł] ADJ magistral
masterly [mǽstɚli] ADJ magistral
mastery [mǽstɚri] N dominio *m*
mastiff [mǽstɪf] N mastín *m*, alano *m*
masturbate [mǽstɚbet] VI/VT masturbar[se]
mat [mæt] N (floor covering) estera *f*; (for wiping feet) felpudo *m*; (in gymnastics) colchoneta *f*; (of hair) maraña *f*; VI enmarañarse
match [mætʃ] N (pair) pareja *f*; (chess game) partida *f*; (tennis, golf game) partido *m*; (boxing encounter) combate *m*; (device for fire) fósforo *m*, cerilla *f*; **—ball** bola de partido *f*; **—box** cajita de fósforos *f*; **—maker** casamentero -ra *mf*; **—point** punto de partido *m*; **he has no —** no tiene igual; **he is a good —** es un buen partido; **the hat and coat are a good —** el abrigo y el sombrero hacen juego; VI/VT hacer juego [con]; VI (to correspond) estar de acuerdo; **the colors don't —** los colores no combinan; VT (equal) igualar; (come to correspond) poner de acuerdo; (form pairs) parear
matching [mǽtʃɪŋ] ADJ emparejados; **— colors** colores que combinan *m pl*; **— pair** pareja *f*; **— shoes** zapatos del mismo par *m pl*
matchless [mǽtʃlɪs] ADJ sin par
mate [met] N (one of a pair) pareja *f*; (friend) compañero -ra *mf*; (on a ship) oficial *m*; (in chess) mate *m*; VI/VT aparear[se]
material [mətíriəł] ADJ (made of matter) material; (pertinent) pertinente; N (substance) material *m*; (fabric) tejido *m*, género *m*
materialism [mətíriəlɪzəm] N materialismo *m*
materialize [mətíriəlaɪz] VI/VT materializar[se], plasmarse
maternal [mətɝ́nł] ADJ (motherly) maternal; (on mother's side of family) materno
maternity [mətɝ́nɪDi] N maternidad *f*; **— leave** licencia por maternidad *f*
math [mæθ] N matemática[s] *f* [*pl*]
mathematical [mæθəmǽDɪkəł] ADJ matemático
mathematician [mæθəmətíʃən] N matemático -ca *mf*
mathematics [mæθəmǽDɪks] N matemática[s] *f* [*pl*]
matinee [mætnéi] N matiné *f*
mating [méDɪŋ] N (copulation) cópula *f*; (reproduction) reproducción *f*
matriarch [métriark] N matriarca *f*
matriculate [mətríkjəlet] VI/VT matricular[se]
matriculation [mətrɪkjəléʃən] N matriculación *f*, matrícula *f*
matrilineal [mætrəlíniəł] ADJ matrilineal
matrimony [mǽtrəmoni] N matrimonio *m*
matrix [métrɪks] N matriz *f*
matron [métrən] N (married woman or widow) matrona *f*; (in a hospital) jefa de enfermeras *f*
matter [mǽDɚ] N (substance, pus) materia *f*;

(affair) asunto *m*; (printed) impreso *m*; (reading) material de lectura *m*; **— for complaint** motivo de queja *m*; **a — of two minutes** cosa de dos minutos *f*; **as a — of fact** de hecho, precisamente; **it is of no —** no tiene importancia; **no — what you say** no importa lo que digas; **as a — of course** por rutina; **what is the —?** ¿qué pasa? VI importar; **it doesn't —** no importa

mattress [mǽtrɪs] N colchón *m*

maturation [mætʃəréʃən] N maduración *f*

mature [mətʃúr] ADJ maduro; **a — note** un pagaré vencido/pagadero *m*; **for — audiences** para adultos; VI/VT madurar[se]; (a savings bond) vencer[se]

maturing [mətʃúrɪŋ] N maduración *f*

maturity [mətúrɪdi] N madurez *f*; (of a debt) vencimiento *m*

maul [mɔł] VT atacar, herir gravemente

Mauritania [mɔrɪténiə] N Mauritania *f*

Mauritanian [mɔrɪténiən] ADJ & N mauritano -na *mf*

Mauritian [mɔríʃən] ADJ & N mauriciano -na *mf*

Mauritius [mɔríʃəs] N Mauricio *m*

maverick [mǽvə-ɪk] N cimarrón *m*; (person) inconformista *mf*, cimarrón -ona *mf*

maxim [mǽksɪm] N máxima *f*, sentencia *f*

maximize [mǽksəmaɪz] VT maximizar

maximum [mǽksəməm] ADJ & N máximo *m*

may [me] V AUX — **I sit down?** ¿puedo sentarme? — **you have a merry Christmas** que pases una feliz Navidad; **it — be that** puede ser que; **it — rain** puede [ser] que llueva, tal vez llueva; **she — have been late** puede [ser] que haya llegado tarde; **be that as it —** sea como fuere

May [me] N mayo *m*; **— Day** primero de mayo *m*; **—pole** mayo *m*

Maya [máiə] N & ADJ maya *mf*

Mayan [máiən] N & ADJ maya *mf*

maybe [mébi] ADV quizá[s], tal vez

mayonnaise [méənez] N mayonesa *f*, mahonesa *f*

mayor [méə-] N alcalde *m*

mayoralty [méə-əłti] N alcaldía *f*

maze [mez] N laberinto *m*

MBA [master of business administration] [émbíé] N máster en administración de empresas *m*, maestría en administración de empresas *f*

MD [medicinae doctor] [émdí] N doctor -ora en medicina *mf*

me [mi] PRON **she sees —** me ve; **he talks to —** me habla; **he comes with —** viene conmigo; **he did it for —** lo hizo para mí

meadow [médo] N pradera *f*, prado *m*; **—lark** alondra *f*

meager [mígə-] ADJ escaso, exiguo

meal [mił] N (repast) comida *f*; (flour) harina *f*; **—time** hora de comer *f*

mean [min] ADJ (unkind) cruel; (petty) vil; (humble) humilde; (stingy) mezquino; (difficult) de mal genio; (middle) medio; **—-spirited** mezquino; **I make a — lasagna** me sale muy rica la lasagna; N (average) media *f*, promedio *m*; **—s** medios *m pl*; **the ends justify the —s** el fin justifica los medios; **a man of —s** un hombre adinerado; **by —s of** por medio de; **—s of transport** medios de transporte *m pl*; **—s test** prueba de ingresos *f*; **by all —s** (of course) por supuesto; (using all resources) por todos los medios; **by no —s** de ningún modo; VT (intend) querer, tener intenciones de; (signify) querer decir, significar; **he —s well** tiene buenas intenciones; **winning —s everything to them** lo que más les importa es ganar; **they are meant for each other** son el uno para el otro

meander [miǽndə-] VI (be winding) serpentear; (to wander) vagar

meaning [míníŋ] N (sense) significado *m*, sentido *m*; (purpose) sentido *m*; ADJ **well-—** bien intencionado

meaningful [míníŋfə-ł] ADJ (result, event) significativo, trascendente; (sentence) coherente

meaningless [míníŋlɪs] ADJ sin sentido

meanness [mínnɪs] N (cruelty) crueldad *f*; (pettiness) mezquindad *f*

meant [mɛnt] *see* mean

meantime [míntaɪm] ADV LOC **in the —** mientras tanto

meanwhile [mínhwaɪł] ADV mientras tanto

measles [mízəłz] N sarampión *m*

measurable [mɛ́ʒə-əbə-ł] ADJ medible, mensurable

measure [mɛ́ʒə-] N (dimension) medida *f*; (criterion) criterio *m*; (in musical bar) compás *m*; (bill) proyecto de ley *m*; **beyond —** sobremanera; **dry —** medida de áridos *f*; **in large —** en gran parte; **—s** medidas *f pl*; VI/VT medir; **to — up** compararse con; **measuring tape** cinta de medir *f*, metro *m*

measured [mɛ́ʒə-d] ADJ (rhythmical) acompasado; (moderate) moderado, mesurado

measurement [mɛ́ʒə-mənt] N (act of measuring) medición *f*; (dimension) medida *f*, dimensión *f*

meat [mit] N carne *f*; (essential point) meollo *m*; **—ball** albóndiga *f*; **—loaf** pan/pastel de carne *m*

meaty [mídi] ADJ (with meat) con mucha carne; (substantial) sustancioso

mechanic [mɪkǽnɪk] ADJ & N mecánico *m*; N **—s** mecánica *f*

mechanical [mɪkǽnɪkə-ł] ADJ mecánico

mechanism [mékənɪzəm] N mecanismo *m*
medal [médl] N medalla *f*; VI ganar una medalla
meddle [médl] VI entrometerse, inmiscuirse
meddler [médlə-] N entrometido -da *mf*
meddlesome [médləsəm] ADJ entrometido
media [mídɪə] N (communication) medios *m pl*, media *m pl*, medios de comunicación masiva *m pl*; (cables) cables del ordenador/ de la computadora *m pl*
median [mídɪən] ADJ mediano; N (middle value, line) mediana *f*
mediate [mídɪet] VI/VT mediar
mediation [mìdɪéʃən] N mediación *f*
mediator [mídɪedə-] N mediador -ora *mf*
medical [médɪkəł] ADJ médico; **— chart** hoja clínica *f*; **— exam** examen médico *m*; **— examiner** médico -ca forense *mf*; **— history** historia clínica *f*; **— record** expediente médico *m*; **— school** facultad de medicina *f*
medicate [médɪket] VT medicar
medication [mɛdɪkéʃən] N medicación *f*
medicine [médɪsɪn] N (profession) medicina *f*; (drug) medicamento *m*, fármaco *m*; **— ball** balón medicinal *m*; **— cabinet** botiquín *m*; **— man** curandero *m*
medieval [mɪdívəł] ADJ medieval
mediocre [mìdɪókə-] ADJ mediocre
mediocrity [mìdɪákrɪdɪ] N mediocridad *f*
meditate [médɪtet] VI meditar
meditation [mɛdɪtéʃən] N meditación *f*, recogimiento *m*
Mediterranean [mɛdɪtəréɪniən] ADJ mediterráneo
medium [mídɪəm] N (substance, agency) medio *m*; (person who contacts spirits) médium *mf*; **— of exchange** medio de cambio *m*; ADJ mediano; ADV término medio
medley [médlɪ] N (music) popurrí *m*; (mixture) mezcla *f*
meek [mik] ADJ manso
meekness [míknɪs] N mansedumbre *f*
meet [mit] VT (encounter) encontrarse con; (make acquaintance) conocer; (face in conflict) enfrentar; (satisfy) satisfacer; (pay) pagar; **to — a deadline** cumplir el plazo; **to — expenses** sufragar los gastos; **to — halfway** partir la diferencia; **to — a train** esperar un tren; **I will — you at the station** nos encontramos/vemos en la estación; **have you met my brother?** ¿conoces a mi hermano? **we were met with disapproval** se nos recibió con desaprobación; VI (encounter) encontrarse; (make acquaintance) conocerse; (have a meeting) reunirse; (cross) cruzarse; **to — in battle** trabar batalla; **to — with** (intentional) reunirse con; (unintentional) tropezar con; N encuentro deportivo *m*, competición *f*
meeting [mídɪɪŋ] N reunión *f*, junta *f*; (political) mitin *m*; (crossing of roads) cruce *m*
megabyte [mégəbaɪt] N megabyte *m*
megahertz [mégəhə-tz] N megahertz *m*, megahercio *m*
megalomania [mɛgəloméniə] N megalomanía *f*
megaphone [mégəfon] N megáfono *m*, bocina *f*
melancholy [mélənkəli] N melancolía *f*; ADJ melancólico
melanoma [mɛlənómə] N melanoma *m*
meld [mełd] VT fusionar
melee [méle] N reyerta *f*, tumulto *m*
mellow [mélo] ADJ (soft) dulce, suave; (gentle) tranquilo; VI/VT suavizar[se]
melodic [məlάdɪk] ADJ melódico
melodious [məlódɪəs] ADJ melodioso, melódico
melodrama [mélodrɑmə] N melodrama *m*
melody [méləɪdi] N melodía *f*
melon [mélən] N melón *m*
melt [mɛłt] VI/VT (liquefy) derretir[se]; (dissolve) disolver[se]; **—ing pot** crisol *m*; N **—down** (fusion) catástrofe por fusión nuclear incontrolada *f*; (any developing disaster) catástrofe *f*
member [mémbə-] N miembro *m* (also body part)
membership [mémbə-ʃɪp] N (number) número de miembros/socios *m*; (state) calidad de miembro/socio *f*
membrane [mémbren] N membrana *f*
memento [məménto] N recuerdo *m*
memoir [mémwɑr] N memoria *f*; **—s** memorias *f pl*, autobiografía *f*
memorable [mémə-əbəł] ADJ memorable
memorandum [mɛmərǽndəm] N memorándum *m*
memorial [məmɔ́riəł] N (monument) monumento conmemorativo *m*; (petition) memorial *m*; ADJ conmemorativo
memorize [méməraɪz] VI/VT memorizar
memory [méməri] N (faculty) memoria *f*; (recollection) recuerdo *m*; **— cache** caché de memoria *f*; **— map** mapa de memoria *m*
menace [ménɪs] N amenaza *f*; VI/VT amenazar
mend [mɛnd] VT remendar; **to — matters** enmendar la situación; **to — one's ways** enmendarse, reformarse; VI (sick person) mejorarse; (bones) soldarse; N remiendo *m*; **to be on the —** ir mejorando
menial [míniəł] ADJ (lowly) bajo; (job) servil; N criado -da *mf*
meningitis [mɛnɪnʤáɪdɪs] N meningitis *f*
menopause [ménəpɔz] N menopausia *f*
menstruate [ménstruet] VI menstruar
menstruation [mɛnstruéʃən] N menstruación *f*
mental [mént] ADJ mental; (insane) *fam* chiflado; **— health** salud mental *f*; **— illness** enfermedad mental *f*; **— retardation** retraso mental *m*

mentality [mɛntǽlɪdɪ] N mentalidad *f*
mention [ménʃən] VT mencionar; **don't — it** no hay de qué; N mención *f*
mentor [méntɔr] N mentor -ora *mf*
menu [ménju] N (list of dishes) carta *f*, menú *m*; (computer) menú *m*; **— bar** (computer) barra de menú *f*
meow [mjaʊ] INTERJ miau
mercantile [mɜ́kəntiɫ] ADJ mercantil
mercenary [mɜ́sənɛri] ADJ mercenario
merchandise[1] [mɜ́tʃəndaɪs] N mercancía *f*, mercadería *f*
merchandise[2] [mɜ́tʃəndaɪz] VT comercializar
merchandising [mɜ́tʃəndaɪzɪŋ] N mercadeo *m*, comercialización *f*
merchant [mɜ́tʃənt] N (trader) comerciante *m*, mercader *m*; ADJ mercante; **— marine** marina mercante *f*
merciful [mɜ́sɪfəɫ] ADJ misericordioso
merciless [mɜ́sɪɫɪs] ADJ despiadado
mercury [mɜ́kjəri] N mercurio *m*; (on a mirror) azogue *m*
mercy [mɜ́si] N (compassion) misericordia *f*, clemencia *f*, piedad *f*; **to be at the — of** estar a merced de; **— killing** eutanasia *f*
mere [mir] ADJ mero, simple; **a — trifle** una nonada
merely [mírli] ADV (only) solo, solamente; (simply) simplemente
merge [mɜ́dʒ] VI/VT (forces) unir[se]; (colors) fundir[se]; (companies) fusionar[se]; (data files) fusionar; N fusión *f*
merger [mɜ́dʒə˞] N fusión *f*; **—s and acquisitions** fusiones y adquisiciones *f pl*
meridian [mərídɪən] ADJ & N meridiano *m*
merit [mérɪt] N mérito *m*; **— pay** paga por mérito *f*; **— raise** aumento por mérito *m*; VT merecer
meritorious [mɛrɪtɔ́riəs] ADJ meritorio
mermaid [mɜ́med] N sirena *f*
merriment [mérɪmənt] N alegría *f*, algazara *f*
merry [méri] ADJ alegre; **—-go-round** tiovivo *m*; **—maker** fiestero -ra *mf*, juerguista *mf*; **—making** fiesta *f*, juerga *f*; **to make —** divertirse; INTERJ **— Christmas** Feliz Navidad *f*, Felices Pascuas
mesa [mésə] N mesa *f*
mesh [mɛʃ] N (of metal) malla *f*; (of fiber) red *f*; (of gears) engranaje *m*; VI engranar
mesmerize [mézməraɪz] VI/VT hipnotizar
mess [mɛs] N (state of confusion) desorden *m*, desarreglo *m*; (disorderly person) desordenado -da *mf*, mugriento -ta *mf*; (confused person) desastre *m*; (difficult situation) lío *m*, jaleo *m*; (food for soldiers) rancho *m*; (cafeteria) cantina *f*; **— hall** cantina *f*; **— of fish** plato de pescado *m*; **to make a — of** (a room) ensuciar, desordenar; (a project) estropear; VI/VT **to — around** (waste time) perder el tiempo; (philander) correr detrás de las mujeres; **to — up** (a room) alborotar, desordenar; (clothes, hair) desarreglar; (a project) estropear; **to — with** meterse con
message [mésɪdʒ] N mensaje *m*, recado *m*; **I get the —** ya caí en cuenta
messenger [mɛ́sənʤə˞] N mensajero -ra *mf*
messy [mési] ADJ (chaotic) desordenado; (embarrassing) embarazoso
met [mɛt] *see* meet
metabolic [mɛDəbáɫɪk] ADJ metabólico
metabolism [mətǽbəɫɪzəm] N metabolismo *m*
metal [mɛ́dɫ] N metal *m*; **— detector** detector de metales *m*; ADJ de metal, metálico
metallic [mətǽɫɪk] ADJ metálico
metallurgy [mɛ́dɫə˞ʤi] N metalurgia *f*
metamorphosis [mɛDəmɔ́rfəsɪs] N metamorfosis *f*
metaphor [mɛ́Dəfɔr] N metáfora *f*
metaphysical [mɛDəfízɪkəɫ] ADJ metafísico
metaphysics [mɛDəfízɪks] N metafísica *f*
metastasis [mətǽstəsɪs] N metástasis *f*
metastasize [mətǽstəsaɪz] VI metastatizar
meteor [mídɪɔr] N meteoro *m*; **— shower** lluvia de meteoritos *f*
meteorite [mídɪəraɪt] N meteorito *m*
meteorological [mɪDɪə-əláʤɪkəɫ] ADJ meteorológico
meteorology [mɪDɪəráɫəʤi] N meteorología *f*
meter [mídə˞] N (unit of length) metro *m*; (measuring device) contador *m*, medidor *m*
methane [mɛ́θɛn] N metano *m*
method [mɛ́θəd] N método *m*
methodical [məθǽDɪkəɫ] ADJ metódico
methodology [mɛθədáɫəʤi] N metodología *f*
meticulous [mətíkjələs] ADJ detallista
metric [métrɪk] ADJ métrico
metro [métro] N metro *m*
metronome [métrənom] N metrónomo *m*
metropolis [mətrápəlɪs] N metrópoli *f*, urbe *f*
metropolitan [mɛtrəpáɫɪDən] ADJ metropolitano
mettle [mɛ́dɫ] N temple *m*, valor *m*
mew [mju] N maullido *m*; VI maullar
Mexican [mɛ́ksɪkən] ADJ & N mexicano -na *mf*
Mexico [mɛ́ksɪko] N México *m*
mezzanine [mɛ́zənin] N entrepiso *m*, entresuelo *m*
mickey mouse [míkimáʊs] ADJ poco serio, informal
microbe [máɪkrob] N microbio *m*
microbiology [maɪkrobaɪáɫəʤi] N microbiología *f*
microcomputer [maɪkrokəmpjúDə˞] N *Am* microcomputadora *f*; *Sp* microordenador *m*
microeconomics [maɪkroɛkənámɪks] N microeconomía *f*
microfiche [máɪkrofiʃ] N microficha *f*

microfilm [máikrofɪłm] N microfilme *m*
micromanage [maɪkromǽnɪʤ] VI/VT administrar con excesivo control
micron [máikrɑn] N micrón *m*, micrómetro *m*
Micronesia [maɪkronízə] N Micronesia *f*
Micronesian [maɪkrəníʒən] ADJ & N micronesio -sia *mf*
microorganism [maɪkroórgənɪzəm] N microorganismo *m*
microphone [máikrəfon] N micrófono *m*
microprocessor [maɪkroprásesə˞] N microprocesador *m*
microscope [máikrəskop] N microscopio *m*
microscopic [maɪkrəskɑ́pɪk] ADJ microscópico
microsurgery [maɪkrosə́ʤəri] N microcirujía *f*
microwave [máikrowev] N microonda *f*; **—oven** [horno] microondas *m sg*
mid [mɪd] ADJ medio; **—air** en el aire; **—day** [del] mediodía *m*; **—field player** (soccer) centrocampista *m*; **—life** madurez *f*; **—life crisis** crisis de la edad madura *f*; **—night** [de] medianoche *f*; **—shipman** guardiamarina *m*; **in —stream** (of a river) en medio del río; (of a task) en plena actividad; **—summer** pleno verano *m*; **—term examination** examen a mitad del curso *m*; **—way** a medio camino, a mitad del camino; **—wife** partera *f*, comadre *f*
middle [mídḷ] ADJ (average) medio, mediano; (intermediate) intermedio; (central) central; **—-aged** de mediana edad; **— Ages** Edad Media *f*; **— class** clase media *f*, burguesía *f*; **—-class neighborhood** barrio de clase media; **— ear** oído medio *m*; **— finger** dedo mayor *m*, dedo del corazón *m*; **—man** intermediario *m*, revendedor *m*; **— management** administración intermedia *f*; **— name** segundo nombre *m*; **—-of-the-road** moderado; **—-sized** [de] tamaño mediano; N medio *m*; (waist) cintura *f*; **in the — of** en el medio de; **I'm in the — of something** estoy ocupado haciendo algo; **toward the — of the month** a mediados del mes
midget [mídʒɪt] N enano -na *mf*
MIDI [musical instrument digital interface] [mídi] N interfaz digital de instrumentos musicales *f*
midst [mɪdst] ADV LOC medio *m*, centro *m*; **in the — of** en medio de, entre; **in our —** entre nosotros
mien [min] N porte *m*
might [maɪt] V AUX **it — be that** podría ser que; **he said it — rain tomorrow** dijo que tal vez lloviera mañana; **she — have been late** puede ser que haya llegado tarde; N poder *m*, poderío *m*
mighty [máɪdɪ] ADJ (strong) poderoso, potente; (large) imponente; ADV muy
migraine [máigren] N migraña *f*, jaqueca *f*
migrant [máigrənt] ADJ migratorio, migrante; N trabajador -ora itinerante *mf*, bracero -ra *mf*
migrate [máigret] VI (also computers) migrar
migration [maɪgréʃən] N migración *f*
migratory [máigrətori] ADJ migratorio
mild [maɪłd] ADJ (gentle) suave; (moderate) moderado; (not serious) leve
mildew [mídłdu] N moho *m*
mildness [máɪłdnɪs] N (gentleness) suavidad *f*; (lack of gravity) levedad *f*
mile [maɪł] N milla *f*; **—stone** hito *m*
mileage [mílɪʤ] N (distance, odometer reading) millaje *m*, kilometraje *m*; **this car gets good —** este coche es económico; **what kind of — are you getting?** ¿cuántos kilómetros por litro hace tu coche?
milieu [mɪljú] N ambiente *m*
militance [mílɪtəns] N militancia *f*
militancy [mílɪtənsi] N militancia *f*
militant [mílɪtənt] ADJ & N (fanatic) militante *mf*; (combatant) combatiente *mf*
military [mílɪtəri] ADJ militar; N **the —** (armed forces) el ejército; (military personnel) los militares
militia [məlíʃə] N milicia *f*
milk [mɪłk] N leche *f*; **— chocolate** chocolate con leche *m*; **—maid** lechera *f*; **—man** lechero *m*; **— shake** batido *m*; VT ordeñar; (exploit) exprimir; **he's —ing it for all it's worth** le está sacando todo el jugo
milky [mɪ́łki] ADJ (consistency) lechoso; (product) lácteo; **— Way** Vía Láctea *f*
mill [mɪł] N (building) molino *m*; (factory) fábrica *f*; (for sugar) trapiche *m*, ingenio *m*; (rotating tool) fresa *f*; (small grinder) molinillo *m*; **—stone** muela de molino *f*; **a —stone around your neck** una piedra al cuello; VT (grind grain) moler; (cut wood) aserrar; (cut grooves on coins) acordonar; (machine) fresar; **to — around** dar vueltas
millennium [məlíniəm] N milenio *m*
miller [mílə˞] N (person who mills) molinero -ra *mf*; (machine for milling) fresadora *f*; (moth) mariposa nocturna *f*
milligram [mílɪgræm] N miligramo *m*
milliliter [míləlidə˞] N mililitro *m*
millimeter [míləmidə˞] N milímetro *m*
milliner [mílənə˞] N sombrerero -ra *mf*
millinery [mílənəri] N (shop) sombrerería *f*; (hats) sombreros de señora *m pl*
million [míljən] N millón *m*; **a — dollars** un millón de dólares
millionaire [mɪljənér] N millonario -ria *mf*
millionth [míljənθ] ADJ & N millonésimo *m*
mime [maɪm] N (actor) mimo *m*; (technique, performance) pantomima *f*; VI hacer la mímica
mimic [mímɪk] VT imitar, remedar; N mono -na

mf, remedador -ora *mf*

mince [mɪns] VT picar, desmenuzar; **not to — words** no tener pelos en la lengua; **—meat** picadillo *m*; **I'm going to make —meat of you** te voy a hacer picadillo

mind [maɪnd] N (thinking process) mente *f*; (person of intellect) inteligencia *f*; (opinion) parecer *m*, opinión *f*; **— games** manipulación psicológica *f*; **— over matter** el espíritu sobre la materia; **—-set** actitud *f*, forma de pensar *f*; **to be out of one's —** estar loco; **to bear in —** tener en cuenta; **to change one's —** cambiar de parecer/opinión; **to give someone a piece of one's —** cantarle a alguien las cuarenta; **I have a — to** me dan ganas de; **to make up one's —** decidirse; **to my —** a mi modo de ver; **to speak one's — freely** hablar con toda franqueza; **what do you have in —?** ¿qué tienes en mente? **to call to —** recordar; **to keep one's — on one's work** concentrarse en el trabajo; ADJ **—-altering** alucinógeno; VT (take care of) cuidar; (pay attention to) atender a; (obey) obedecer; **I don't —** no tengo inconveniente en ello; **— what you say** cuidado con lo que dices; **to — one's own business** no meterse en lo ajeno

mindful [máɪndfəł] ADJ atento

mine [maɪn] PRON **this book is —** este libro es mío; **these things are —** estas cosas son mías; **— is bigger** el mío / la mía es más grande; **a friend of —** un amigo mío / una amiga mía; N mina *f* (also explosive device); **—field** campo minado *m*; **— sweeper** dragaminas *m sg*, barreminas *m sg*; VT (plant explosives) minar; (dig out minerals) extraer; (exploit an area for minerals) explotar; VI (lay mines) sembrar minas; (dig a mine) cavar una mina; **to — for** extraer

miner [mánər] N minero -ra *mf*

mineral [mínərəł] ADJ & N mineral *m*; **— rights** derechos mineros *m pl*; **— water** agua mineral *f*

mingle [míŋgəł] VI mezclarse; (sounds) confundirse; VT mezclar

miniature [mínɪətʃɚ] N miniatura *f*; ADJ en miniatura

minicomputer [mɪnɪkəmpjúɾər] N *Am* minicomputadora *f*; *Sp* miniordenador *m*

minimal [mínəməł] ADJ mínimo

minimize [mínəmaɪz] VT minimizar

minimum [mínəməm] ADJ & N mínimo *m*; **— wage** salario mínimo *m*

mining [máɪnɪŋ] N (exploitation of mines) minería *f*; (act of mining) minado *m*; ADJ minero; **open —** minería a cielo abierto *f*

miniskirt [mínɪskɚt] N minifalda *f*

minister [mínɪstɚ] N (official) ministro -tra *mf*; (pastor) pastor -ora *mf*, clérigo *m*; VI **to — to** atender a

ministerial [mɪnɪstíriəł] ADJ ministerial

ministry [mínɪstri] N (government agency) ministerio *m*; (functions of pastor) clerecía *f*

minivan [mínivæn] N camioneta *f*

mink [mɪŋk] N visón *m*

minnow [mínɔ] N pececillo *m*

minor [máɪnɚ] ADJ (smaller) menor, más pequeño; (of secondary importance) menor; **— key** tono menor *m*; **— league** liga menor *f*; N (young person) menor de edad *mf*; (musical interval) tono menor *m*; (subfield) asignatura secundaria *f*; VI tener como segunda especialización

minority [mənɔ́rɪɾɪ] N (smaller part or group) minoría *f*; (state of being underage) minoridad *f*; (member of a minority) miembro de una minoría *m*; ADJ minoritario; **— partner** socio -cia minoritario -ria *mf*

mint [mɪnt] N (flavor) menta *f*, hierbabuena *f*; (candy) pastilla de menta *f*; (money) casa de la moneda *f*; VT acuñar

minus [mánəs] PREP **seven — four** siete menos cuatro; **we came — my brother** vinimos sin mi hermano; N signo de menos *m*; ADJ negativo

minuscule [mínəskjuł] ADJ minúsculo

minute[1] [mínɪt] N minuto *m*; **— hand** minutero *m*; **—s** actas *f pl*

minute[2] [maɪnút] ADJ (small) diminuto; (detailed) detallado, minucioso

miracle [mírəkəł] N milagro *m*

miraculous [mɪrǽkjələs] ADJ milagroso

mirage [mɪráʒ] N espejismo *m*

mire [maɪr] N (mud) cieno *m*, fango *m*; (muddy place) ciénaga *f*; VI/VT (bog down) atascar[se] en el fango; (be or get covered with mud) enlodar[se]

mirror [mírɚ] N espejo *m*; (large) luna *f*; **— image** imagen especular *f*; VT reflejar

mirth [mɜθ] N risa *f*, hilaridad *f*

mirthful [mɜ́θfəł] ADJ risueño

miry [máɪri] ADJ cenagoso, fangoso

misanthropy [mɪsǽnθrəpi] N misantropía *f*

misappropriation [mɪsəpropriéʃən] N malversación *f*

misbehave [mɪsbɪhév] VI portarse mal

miscalculate [mɪskǽłkjəlet] VI/VT (in math) calcular mal; (in situations) equivocarse

miscarriage [mískæɾɪʤ] N aborto espontáneo *m*, malparto *m*; **— of justice** injusticia *f*

miscarry [mɪskǽri] VI (abort) abortar espontáneamente; (fail) malograrse, frustrarse

miscellaneous [mɪsəléniəs] ADJ diverso; (texts) misceláneo; **— expenses** gastos varios *mf*

mischief [místʃɪf] N travesura *f*, diablura *f*, picardía *f*; (serious prank) barrabasada *f*, bellaquería *f*; **this will come to —** va a

suceder una desgracia

mischievous [místʃəvəs] ADJ travieso, pícaro

misconception [mɪskənsépʃən] N concepto erróneo *m*

misconduct[1] [mɪskándʌkt] N (bad behavior) mala conducta *f*; (malfeasance) mala administración *f*

misconduct[2] [mɪskəndʌ́kt] VT administrar mal; **to — oneself** portarse mal

miscue [mɪskjú] N pifia *f*; VI/VT pifiar

misdeed [mɪsdíd] N fechoría *f*

misdemeanor [mɪsdɪmínə˞] N delito menor *m*

miser [máɪzə˞] N avaro -ra *mf*, tacaño -ña *mf*

miserable [mízə-əbəł] ADJ infeliz, desdichado; **a — day** un día asqueroso; **a — failure** un fracaso rotundo

miserly [máɪzə-li] ADJ avariento, tacaño

misery [mízəri] N (wretchedness) desgracia *f*; (poverty) miseria *f*; (unhappiness) infelicidad *f*

misfit [mísfɪt] N inadaptado -da *mf*

misfortune [mɪsfɔ́rtʃən] N desgracia *f*, desdicha *f*, desventura *f*

misgivings [mɪsgívɪŋz] N aprensión *f*, recelo *m*

misguided [mɪsgáɪdɪd] ADJ mal aconsejado, poco feliz

mishap [míshæp] N contratiempo *m*, percance *m*

misinform [mɪsɪnfɔ́rm] VT desinformar, dar información errónea

misjudge [mɪsʤʌ́ʤ] VT juzgar mal

mislay [mɪslé] VT (keys, etc.) extraviar, perder; (a document) traspapelar; (lay wrong) colocar mal

mislead [mɪslíd] VT (in the wrong direction) guiar por mal camino; (into error) engañar, confundir

misleading [mɪslídɪŋ] ADJ engañoso

mismanage [mɪsmǽnɪʤ] VT administrar mal

misogyny [mɪsɑ́ʤəni] N misoginia *f*

misplace [mɪsplés] VT (lose keys, etc.) extraviar; (lose a document) traspapelar; (place wrong) colocar mal; **she —d her trust** confió en la persona equivocada

misprint [mísprɪnt] N errata *f*, error de imprenta *m*

misrepresent [mɪsrɛprɪzɛ́nt] VT distorsionar, tergiversar

misrepresentation [mɪsrɛprɪzɛntéʃən] N distorsión *f*, tergiversación *f*

miss [mɪs] VI (fail to hit) errar; (misfire) fallar; VT (fail to hit) errar, no acertar; (fail to be on time for) perder; (fail to attend) faltar a; (feel absence of) echar de menos; *Am* extrañar; **he just —ed being killed** por poco se mata; N (of a target) tiro errado *m*; (in a motor) falla *f*; (from class) falta *f*; (young woman) señorita *f*; **— Smith** la señorita Smith

misshapen [mɪsʃépən] ADJ deforme

missile [mísəł] N (projectile) proyectil *m*; (guided weapon) misil *m*

missing [mísɪŋ] ADJ (not present) ausente; (lost) perdido; **— link** eslabón perdido *m*; **one book is —** falta un libro

mission [míʃən] N misión *f*; **— statement** declaración de la misión *f*

missionary [míʃənɛri] ADJ & N misionero -ra *mf*

misspell [mɪsspɛ́ł] VT (written) escribir mal; (oral) deletrear mal

misstatement [mɪsstétmənt] N declaración errónea/falsa *f*

misstep [místɛp] N paso en falso *m*

mist [mɪst] N (of water droplets) neblina *f*, bruma *f*; (of perfume) rocío *m*; VI lloviznar; VT rociar

mistake [mɪsté́k] N error *m*, equivocación *f*; (orthographical) falta *f*; **to make a —** equivocarse; VI/VT equivocar[se]; **I — my sister for my mother** confundo a mi hermana con mi madre

mistaken [mɪstékən] ADJ equivocado; **to be —** estar equivocado, equivocarse; **unless I'm —** si no me equivoco

mistaken [mɪstékən] *see* mistake

mister [místə˞] N señor *m*

mistletoe [mísəłto] N muérdago *m*

mistook [mɪstúk] *see* mistake

mistreat [mɪstrít] VT maltratar

mistreatment [mɪstrítmənt] N maltrato *m*

mistress [místrɪs] N (of a household) señora *f*; (employing servants, animal owner) ama *f*; (lover) amante *f*

mistrial [místraɪł] N proceso viciado de nulidad *m*

mistrust [mɪstrʌ́st] N desconfianza *f*; VT desconfiar de

mistrustful [mɪstrʌ́stfəł] ADJ desconfiado, receloso

misty [místi] ADJ (foggy) neblinoso, brumoso; (in tears) nublado; (blurry) empañado

misunderstand [mɪsʌndə-stǽnd] VT comprender mal, malinterpretar

misunderstanding [mɪsʌndə-stǽndɪŋ] N (confusion) malentendido *m*; (failure to understand) equivocación *f*, mala inteligencia *f*; (argument) desavenencia *f*

misuse[1] [mɪsjús] N (of drugs) abuso *m*; (of a word) mal uso *m*; (of funds) malversación *f*

misuse[2] [mɪsjúz] VT (drugs) abusar de; (a friend) maltratar; (a word) emplear mal; (funds) malversar

mite [maɪt] N ácaro *m*; ADV **a — greedy** un poquito codicioso

mitigate [mídɪget] VT mitigar

mitochondria [maɪdokándriə] N mitocondria *f*

mitten [mítn̩] N manopla *f*

mix [mɪks] VI/VT mezclar[se]; **to — up** confundir; N mezcla *f*; (for baking) preparado *m*; **—-up** (confusion) confusión *f*; (fight)

pelea *f*

mixed [mɪkst] ADJ mixto; **— bag** grupo heterogéneo *m*; **— doubles** dobles mixtos *m pl*; **— drink** cóctel *m*; **— -up** confundido

mixer [míksɚ] N (appliance) batidora *f*; (party) fiesta *f*; (soda) refresco *m*; (sound technician) mezclador -ora *mf*; (sound device) mezcladora *f*

mixture [míkstʃɚ] N mezcla *f*

moan [mon] N quejido *m*, gemido *m*; VI gemir, quejarse; VI/VT lamentar

moat [mot] N foso *m*

mob [mɑb] N (disorderly crowd) tumulto *m*, turba *f*; (crowd) muchedumbre *f*, populacho *m*; (mafia) mafia *f*; VT (attack) asaltar; (crowd) atestar

mobile [móbəł] ADJ móvil; (personnel) que tiene movilidad; **— home** casa prefabricada *f*; **— Internet** internet móvil *m*; **— phone** [teléfono] móvil *m*, [teléfono] celular *m*

mobility [mobílɪdɪ] N movilidad *f*

mobilization [mobəlɪzéʃən] N movilización *f*

mobilize [móbəlaɪz] VI/VT movilizar[se]

moccasin [mákəsɪn] N mocasín *m* (also snake)

mock [mɑk] VI (ridicule) burlar[se]; VT (imitate) remedar; ADJ de práctica; **— battle** simulacro de batalla *m*; N **— -up** maqueta *f*, modelo *m*

mockery [mákəri] N (ridicule) burla *f*; (imitation) remedo *m*; (travesty) farsa *f*

mockingbird [mákɪŋbɝd] N sinsonte *m*

mode [mod] N modo *m*; **— of delivery** modo de entrega *m*; **— of payment** forma de pago *f*

model [mɑ́dł] N (guide) modelo *m*; (person) modelo *mf*, maniquí *mf*; ADJ modelo, ejemplar; **— school** escuela modelo *f*; VI/VT modelar; (display clothes) lucir

modem [móɑ́dəm] N módem *m*

moderate[1] [mɑ́də-ɪt] ADJ (not excessive) moderado, mesurado; (person) comedido; (weather) templado; (price) módico; N moderado -da *mf*

moderate[2] [mɑ́dəret] VI/VT moderar[se] (also preside at meetings)

moderation [mɑdəréʃən] N moderación *f*, mesura *f*

modern [mɑ́dɚn] ADJ moderno; **— age** modernidad *f*

modernism [mɑ́dɚ-nɪzəm] N modernismo *m*

modernity [mədɝ́nɪdɪ] N modernismo *m*

modernization [mɑdɚ-nɪzéʃən] N modernización *f*

modernize [mɑ́dɚ-naɪz] VI/VT modernizar[se], innovar

modernness [mɑ́dɚ-nnɪs] N modernismo *m*

modest [mɑ́dɪst] ADJ (humble) modesto; (chaste) recatado, honesto

modesty [mɑ́dɪsti] N (humility) modestia *f*; (chastity) recato *m*, pudor *m*, honestidad *f*

modification [mɑdəfɪkéʃən] N modificación *f*

modify [mɑ́dəfaɪ] VT modificar

modulate [mɑ́ʤəlet] VI/VT modular[se]

modulation [mɑʤəléʃən] N modulación *f*

module [mɑ́ʤul] N módulo *m*

mohair [móhɛr] N mohair *m*

moist [mɔɪst] ADJ húmedo

moisten [mɔ́ɪsən] VI/VT humedecer[se]

moisture [mɔ́ɪstʃɚ] N humedad *f*

moisturizer [mɔ́ɪstʃəráɪzɚ] N [crema] hidrante/humectante *f*

molar [mólɚ] ADJ molar; N muela *f*, molar *m*

molasses [məlǽsɪz] N melaza *f*

mold [mołd] N (form) molde *m*; (fungi) moho *m*; (mettle) temple *m*; VT (shape) moldear, plasmar; (adapt) amoldar; (fuse) fundir; VI/VT (become moldy) enmohecer[se]

molder [mółdɚ] VI/VT descomponerse; (paper) enmohecerse

molding [mółdɪŋ] N (adornment) moldura *f*; (action of molding) moldeado *m*

Moldova [mɔ́łdóvə] N Moldavia *f*

Moldovan [mɔ́łdóvən] ADJ & N moldavo -va *mf*

moldy [mółdi] ADJ mohoso

mole [moł] N (blemish) lunar *m*; (animal, spy) topo *m*; (breakwater) rompeolas *m sg*

molecular [məlékjəlɚ] ADJ molecular

molecule [mɑ́lɪkjuł] N molécula *f*

molest [məlést] VT abusar sexualmente de

mollify [mɑ́ləfaɪ] VT apaciguar, aplacar

mollusk [mɑ́ləsk] N molusco *m*

molt [mołt] VI (birds) mudar la pluma; (snakes) mudar la piel; N muda *f*

molten [mółtn̩] ADJ fundido

molybdenum [məlíbdənəm] N molibdeno *m*

mom [mɑm] N mamá *f*; **— and pop store** tienda familiar *f*

moment [mómənt] N momento *m*; **being a parent has its —s** ser padre/madre tiene sus momentos de recompensa

momentary [mómənterɪ] ADJ momentáneo

momentous [moménəs] ADJ importante, trascendental

momentum [moméntəm] N (in physics) momento *m*; (in politics, sports) empuje *m*

mommy [mámi] N mami *f*

Monaco [mɑ́nəko] N Mónaco *m*

monarch [mɑ́nɑrk] N monarca *mf*

monarchical [mənárkɪkəł] ADJ monárquico

monarchist [mɑ́nə-kɪst] N monárquico -ca *mf*

monarchy [mɑ́nə-ki] N monarquía *f*

monastery [mɑ́nəsterɪ] N monasterio *m*

Monday [mɑ́nde] N lunes *m*

Monegasque [mɑnɪgɑ́sk] ADJ & N monegasco -ca *mf*

monetary [mɑ́nɪterɪ] ADJ monetario

money [mɑ́ni] N dinero *m*; **— -back guarantee** garantía de devolución de dinero *f*; **— belt** faltriquera en forma de cinturón *f*; **—**

changer cambista *mf*; **— laundering** lavado de dinero *m*; **— machine** cajero automático *m*; **— market** mercado de valores *m*; **— market account** cuenta de mercado monetario *f*; **— order** giro postal *m*; **to get one's —'s worth** sacar jugo al dinero; ADJ **— -grubbing** codicioso; **— -making** lucrativo, rentable

moneyed [mánid] ADJ adinerado

Mongolia [maŋgóliə] N Mongolia *f*

Mongolian [maŋgóliən] ADJ & N mongol -ola *mf*

mongoloid [máŋgəlɔɪd] ADJ mongoloide

mongoose [máŋgus] N mangosta *f*

mongrel [máŋgrəł] ADJ & N mestizo *m*

monitor [mánɪtə-] N monitor *m*; (in a school) celador -ora *mf*; **— lizard** varano *m*; VT monitorear

monitoring [mánɪtə-ɪŋ] N monitoreo *m*, monitorización *f*

monk [maŋk] N monje *m*, religioso *m*

monkey [máŋki] N mono *m*, mico *m*; **— bars** jaula de los monos *f*; **— business** (mischief) picardía *f*; (trickery) chanchullo *m*; **— wrench** llave inglesa *f*; **to have a — on one's back** estar adicto; VI **to — around** bobear, payasear; **to — with** bobear con

monogamy [mənágəmi] N monogamia *f*

monologue, monolog [mánəbɡ] N monólogo *m*

mononucleosis [mənonukliósɪs] N mononucleosis *f*

monopolize [mənápəlaɪz] VT monopolizar

monopoly [mənápəli] N monopolio *m*

monotonous [mənátnəs] ADJ monótono

monotony [mənátṇi] N monotonía *f*

monsignor [mənsínjə-] N monseñor *m*

monster [mánstə-] N monstruo *m*; ADJ enorme, monstruo *inv*

monstrosity [mənstrásɪdi] N monstruosidad *f*

monstrous [mánstrəs] ADJ monstruoso

month [mʌnθ] N mes *m*

monthly [mʌ́nθli] ADJ mensual; **— installment** mensualidad *f*; N publicación mensual *f*, mensuario *m*; ADV mensualmente

monument [mánjəmənt] N monumento *m*

monumental [mənjəméntł] ADJ monumental

moo [mu] N mugido *m*; VI mugir

mooch [mutʃ] VI/VT gorronear; N pedigüeño -ña *mf*

mood [mud] N (emotional state) humor *m*, vena *f*, ánimo *m*; (grammatical category) modo *m*; **to be in a good —** estar de buen humor; **to be in the — to** tener ganas de

moody [múdi] ADJ (sullen) malhumorado; (changing) voluble

moon [mun] N luna *f*; **—beam** rayo de luna *m*; **—light** claro de la luna *m*, luz de la luna *f*; **—lighting** pluriempleo *m*; **—shine** bebida alcohólica destilada sin licencia *f*; **once in a blue —** de Pascuas a Ramos

moor [mʊr] VI/VT amarrar; N páramo *m*

Moor [mʊr] N moro -ra *mf*

Moorish [múrɪʃ] ADJ morisco, moro

moose [mus] N alce *m*

moot [mut] ADJ **it became a — point** dejó de tener importancia

mop [map] N (for floors) *Sp* fregona *f*, *Sp* mopa *f*; *Mex* trapeador *m*; (for dust) plumero *m*; (of hair) greña *f*; **— -up** (of an enemy) limpieza *f*; (of a task) remate *m*; VI/VT pasar la mopa [sobre]; *Am* trapear; **to — one's brow** enjugarse la frente; **to — up** (a spill) limpiar; (an enemy) acabar con; (a task) rematar

mope [mop] VI andar abatido

moped [móped] N ciclomotor *m*, scooter *m*

moral [mórəł] ADJ moral; N moraleja *f*; **—s** moral *f*

morale [məráł] N moral *f*

moralist [mórəlɪst] N moralista *mf*

morality [mərǽlɪdi] N moralidad *f*

moralize [mórəlaɪz] VI/VT moralizar

morbid [mórbɪd] ADJ mórbido, morboso

morbidity [mɔrbídɪdi] N (predisposition to illness) morbilidad *f*; (producing illness) morbosidad *f*

more [mɔr] ADJ & ADV más; **— and —** cada vez más; **— or less** más o menos; **there is no —** no hay más; **—over** además

morgue [mɔrg] N depósito de cadáveres *m*, morgue *f*

moribund [mórəbʌnd] ADJ moribundo

morning [mórnɪŋ] N mañana *f*; **— glory** dondiego de día *m*; **— sickness** náuseas *f pl*; **— star** lucero del alba *m*; **good —!** ¡buenos días! **tomorrow —** mañana por la mañana; ADJ de la mañana, matutino

Moroccan [mərákən] ADJ & N marroquí *mf*

Morocco [mərákó] N Marruecos *m*

moron [mórɑn] N imbécil *m*

morphine [mórfin] N morfina *f*

morsel [mórsəł] N bocado *m*

mortal [mórdł] ADJ & N mortal *mf*; **— sin** pecado mortal *m*

mortality [mɔrtǽlɪdi] N (rate) mortalidad *f*; (toll) mortandad *f*

mortar [mórdə-] N (for pounding) mortero *m* (also ballistics); (for bricks) argamasa *f*, mezcla *f*; **—board** birrete *m*

mortgage [mórgɪʤ] N hipoteca *f*; VT hipotecar; ADJ hipotecario; **— -backed securities** valores respaldados por hipoteca *m pl*

mortgagor [mórgɪʤə-] N deudor -ora hipotecario -ria *mf*

mortification [mɔ́rdəfɪkéʃən] N mortificación *f*

mortify [mɔ́rdəfaɪ] VI/VT mortificar[se]

mortuary [mɔ́rtʃʊɛri] N mortuorio *m*

mosaic [mozéɪk] N mosaico *m*

Moslem [mázləm] ADJ & N musulmán -ana *mf*

mosque [mɔsk] N mezquita *f*

mosquito [məskíɒo] N mosquito *m*; **— net** mosquitero *m*
moss [mɔs] N musgo *m*
mossy [mɔ́si] ADJ musgoso
most [most] ADJ **— children are good** la mayoría de los niños son buenos; **— people** la mayoría de la gente; **the — money** más dinero *m*; **the — votes** el mayor número de votos; **for the — part** generalmente; PRON **the — that I can do** lo más que puedo hacer; **we ate the —** comimos más que nadie; **— of the guests are here** ha llegado la mayoría de los invitados; ADV **the — ambitious** el más ambicioso; **a — pleasant day** un día de lo más agradable
mostly [móstli] ADV generalmente
motel [motɛ́ł] N motel *m*
moth [mɔθ] N (pest) polilla *f*; (nocturnal insect) mariposa nocturna *f*; **—ball** bolita de naftalina *f*; **—-eaten** apolillado
mother [máðə-] N madre *f*; **—board** placa madre *f*; **— country** madre patria *f*; **— -in-law** suegra *f*; **—-of-pearl** madreperla *f*; **— tongue** lengua materna *f*; VT mimar a, cuidar de/a
motherhood [máðə-hʊd] N maternidad *f*
motherly [máðə-li] ADJ maternal
motif [motíf] N motivo *m*
motion [móʃən] N (movement) movimiento *m*; (signal) ademán *m*; (proposal) moción *f*; **— picture** película de cine *f*; **—-picture industry** industria cinematográfica *f*; **— sickness** mareo *m*; VI/VT hacer un ademán
motionless [móʃənlɪs] ADJ inmóvil
motivate [mópəvet] VT motivar
motivation [mopəvéʃən] N motivación *f*
motive [mópɪv] N motivo *m*; ADJ motriz
motley [mátli] ADJ abigarrado
motor [mópə-] N motor *m*; **—bike** motocicleta pequeña *f*; **—boat** lancha a motor *f*; **—cycle** motocicleta *f*; **—cyclist** motociclista *mf*; **— home** casa rodante *f*, caravana *f*; **— scooter** scooter *m*; **— vehicle** vehículo motorizado *m*; VI pasear en coche
motorist [mópə-ɪst] N automovilista *mf*
motto [mápo] N lema *f*
mound [maʊnd] N montículo *m*; **burial —** túmulo *m*; **— of laundry** pila de ropa *f*
mount [maʊnt] VI/VT (get on) montar; VI (increase) subir; VT (assemble) armar; N (mountain) monte *m*; (getting on a horse) montar *f*; (animal for riding) montura *f*
mountain [maʊntn] N montaña *f*; **— bike** bicicleta de montaña *f*; **— climber** alpinista *mf*; **— climbing** alpinismo *m*, montañismo *m*; **— goat** cabra montés *f*; **— lion** puma *f*, gato montés *m*; **— range** (large) cordillera *f*; (small) sierra *f*; **—side** ladera [de una montaña] *f*; **—top** cumbre [de una montaña] *f*; ADJ (animal, person) montañés; (thing) de montaña
mountaineer [maʊntn̩ír] N alpinista *mf*
mountainous [máʊntn̩əs] ADJ montañoso
mourn [mɔrn] VI estar de duelo/luto; VT llorar; **to — for** llorar a
mourner [mɔ́rnə-] N doliente *mf*
mournful [mɔ́rnfəł] ADJ lúgubre, triste
mourning [mɔ́rnɪŋ] N luto *m*, duelo *m*; **to be in —** estar de luto/duelo; ADJ de luto
mouse [maʊs] N ratón *m* (also computer); **— pad** alfombrilla [de ratón] *f*; **— port** puerto de ratón *m*; **—trap** ratonera *f*
mouth[1] [maʊθ] N boca *f*; (of a cave) abertura *f*; (of a river) desembocadura *f*; **—piece** (part of a trumpet) boquilla *f*; (spokesman) portavoz *mf*; **—-to-mouth resuscitation** respiración boca a boca *f*; **—wash** enjuague bucal *m*; ADJ **—-watering** delicioso
mouth[2] [maʊð] VT articular silenciosamente una palabra; VI **to — off** contestar
mouthful [máʊθfʊł] N (of food) bocado *m*; (of liquid) bocanada *f*, buche *m*
movable [múvəbəł] ADJ movible, móvil
move [muv] VI (change position) mover[se] (also board games); (change residence) mudar[se] de casa; (sell) venderse; **to — away** (distance oneself) apartarse; (change residence) irse; **to — forward** avanzar; **to — on** seguir adelante; **to — out** mudarse de casa; VT (propose) proponer; (affect emotionally) conmover; N (act of changing position) movimiento *m*; (change of residence) mudanza *f*; (action toward a goal) paso *m*; (play, in games) jugada *f*; **get a — on there!** ¡date prisa! **he made the first —** dio el primer paso
movement [múvmənt] N (motion, part of a watch) movimiento *m*; (of troops) desplazamiento *m*; **to have a bowel —** mover el vientre
mover [múvə-] N compañía de mudanzas *f*; **—s and shakers** la plana mayor
movie [múvi] N película *f*, filme *m*; **—s** cine *m*; **—making** cinematografía *f*
moving [múvɪŋ] ADJ (target) móvil; (car) en movimiento; (company) de mudanzas; (story) conmovedor; **— picture** película *f*; **— van** camión de mudanzas *m*
mow [mo] VT cortar; (harvest) segar
mower [móə-] N (for lawns) cortadora de céspedes *f*, cortacésped *m*; (farm implement) segadora *f*; (farmworker) segador -ora *mf*
mown [mon] *see* mow
Mozambican [mozæmbíkən] ADJ & N mozambiqueño -ña *mf*
Mozambique [mozæmbík] N Mozambique *m*
Mozarabic [mozérəbɪk] ADJ mozárabe
Mr. [místə-] N Sr. *m*

MRI [magnetic resonance imaging] [émáráí] N IRM *f*
Mrs. [mísɪz] N Sra. *f*
Ms. [mɪz] N Sra. *f*
much [mʌtʃ] ADJ & ADV mucho; **— the same** casi lo mismo; **— like the others** muy parecido a los demás; **as — as** tanto como; **how — ?** ¿cuánto? **too —** demasiado; **very —** muchísimo; **to make — of** dar mucha importancia a; **— as I'd like, I won't do it** aunque me gustaría, no lo voy a hacer; **that's not — of a book** ese libro no es gran cosa; **she cried so —** lloró tanto; **they need water, — as they need sun** necesitan agua, del mismo modo que necesitan sol
muck [mʌk] N (manure) estiércol *m*; (mire) cieno *m*, lodo *m*; (filth) porquería *f*
mucous [mjúkəs] ADJ mucoso
mucus [mjúkəs] N mucosidad *f*
mud [mʌd] N lodo *m*, barro *m*; **—slinging** difamación *f*
muddle [mʌdl] VT (confuse) confundir; (make turbid) enturbiar; VI **to — along** ir tirando; **to — through** salir del paso; N (confusion) confusión *f*; (confused situation) embrollo *m*
muddy [mʌ́dɪ] ADJ (path) lodoso, barroso; (shoes) embarrado; (vague) confuso; VT (cover with mud) enlodar, embarrar; (make unclear) enturbiar
muff [mʌf] N manguito *m*; VT estropear
muffin [mʌ́fɪn] N mollete *m*
muffle [mʌ́fəł] VT amortiguar
muffler [mʌ́flə˞] N (scarf) bufanda *f*; (exhaust device) silenciador *m*
mug [mʌg] N (ceramic) tazón *m*; (glass) jarra *f*; (face) jeta *f*; VT atracar
mugger [mʌ́gə˞] N asaltante *mf*; atracador -ora *mf*
muggy [mʌ́gi] ADJ bochornoso
mulatto [muláɾɔ] ADJ & N mulato -ta *mf*
mulberry [mʌ́łbɛɾi] N mora *f*; **— tree** moral *m*
mule [mjuł] N mulo -la *mf* (also in drug trafficking)
mull [mʌł] VI/VT rumiar
multicultural [mʌłtikʌ́ltʃə˞əł] ADJ multicultural
multilateral [mʌłtilǽɾə˞əł] ADJ multilateral
multimedia [mʌłtimídiə] N & ADJ INV multimedia *m*
multiple [mʌ́łtəpəł] N múltiplo *m*; ADJ múltiple; **—-choice** de opción múltiple; **— personality disorder** trastorno de personalidad múltiple *m*; **— sclerosis** esclerosis múltiple *f*
multiplication [mʌłtəplɪkéʃən] N multiplicación *f*; **— sign** signo de multiplicación *m*; **— table** tabla de multiplicar *f*
multiplicity [mʌłtəplísɪdɪ] N multiplicidad *f*
multiply [mʌ́łtəplaɪ] VI/VT multiplicar[se]
multiscreen [mʌ́łtiskrin] ADJ multipantalla
multitasking [mʌ́łtitæskɪŋ] N multitarea *f*
multitude [mʌ́łtɪtud] N multitud *f*
multiuser [mʌłtijúzə˞] N multiusuario -ria *mf*
multi-year [mʌ́ltijír] ADJ multianual
mum [mʌm] ADJ callado; **to keep —** callarse la boca
mumble [mʌ́mbəł] VI/VT mascullar; N refunfuño *m*
mumbo jumbo [mʌ́mboʤʌ́mbo] N jerigonza *f*
mummy [mʌ́mi] N momia *f*
mumps [mʌmps] N paperas *f pl*
munch [mʌntʃ] VT mascar
mundane [mʌndén] ADJ mundano
municipal [mjunísəpəł] ADJ municipal; **— council** concejo *m*
municipality [mjunɪsəpǽlɪdɪ] N municipio *m*, municipalidad *m*
munition [mjuníʃən] N munición *f*
mural [mjʊ́rəł] ADJ & N mural *m*
murder [mɜ́ˑdə˞] N asesinato *m*, homicidio *m*; **to get away with —** salirse con la suya; **that exam was —** ese examen fue matador; VI/VT asesinar
murderer [mɜ́ˑdərə˞] N asesino *mf*, homicida *mf*
murderous [mɜ́ˑdə˞əs] ADJ asesino, homicida
murky [mɜ́ˑki] ADJ (of water, matter) turbio; (of sky) oscuro
murmur [mɜ́ˑmə˞] N (noise) murmullo *m*, susurro *m*; (complaint) queja *f*; VI/VT (make noise) murmurar, susurrar; (complain) quejarse
muscle [mʌ́səł] N músculo *m*; **— relaxant** relajante muscular *m*; **— strain** distensión muscular *f*; **— tone** tonicidad muscular *f*, tono muscular *m*
muscular [mʌ́skjələ˞] ADJ (relative to muscles) muscular; (endowed with muscles) musculoso; **— dystrophy** distrofia muscular *f*
muse [mjuz] VI meditar; VT cavilar; N musa *f*
museum [mjuzíəm] N museo *m*
mushroom [mʌ́ʃrum] N seta *f*, hongo *m*, champiñón *m*
mushy [mʌ́ʃi] ADJ (soft) fofo; (sentimental) sensiblero
music [mjúzɪk] N música *f*; **— stand** atril *m*; **— video** *Am* video musical *m*; *Sp* vídeo musical *m*
musical [mjúzɪkəł] ADJ (pertaining to music) musical; (fond of music) aficionado a la música, melómano; **— comedy** comedia musical *f*
musician [mjuzíʃən] N músico -ca *mf*
muskrat [mʌ́skræt] N ratón almizclero *m*
Muslim [mʌ́zləm] ADJ & N musulmán -ana *mf*
muslin [mʌ́zlɪn] N muselina *f*
muss [mʌs] VT revolver, alborotar; N revoltijo *m*

mussel [másəl] N mejillón *m*
must [mʌst] V AUX **you — arrive before nine** debes llegar antes de las nueve; **you really — eat at that restaurant** tienes que comer en ese restaurante; **you — be his son** debes [de] / has de ser su hijo; **they — have seen me** deben [de] haberme visto
mustache, moustache [mástæʃ] N bigote *m*; (large) mostacho *m*
mustard [mástɚd] N mostaza *f*; **— gas** gas mostaza *m*
muster [mástɚ] VT (troops) formar; (courage) juntar, reunir; VI (assemble for inspection) formar; (come together) reunirse; **to — out** dar de baja; **to — up one's courage** juntar valor; N revista *f*; **to pass —** ser aceptable
musty [másti] ADJ (stale smelling) con olor a encierro/humedad; (antiquated) anticuado
mutant [mjútnt] ADJ & N mutante *mf*
mutation [mjutéʃən] N mutación *f*
mute [mjut] ADJ mudo; N (mute person) mudo -da *mf*; (for musical instruments) sordina *f*
mutilate [mjúdlet] VT mutilar
mutiny [mjútṇi] N motín *m*; VI amotinarse
mutter [mʌ́dɚ] VI/VT refunfuñar, musitar; N refunfuño *m*
mutton [mʌ́tṇ] N carne de cordero *f*
mutual [mjútʃuəl] ADJ mutuo; **— fund** fondo mutuo/mutual *m*
muzzle [mʌ́zəl] N (snout) hocico *m*; (mouthguard) bozal *m*; (gun opening) boca *f*; VT (a dog) abozalar, poner bozal a; (critics) amordazar, silenciar
my [maɪ] POSS ADJ mi; **these are — friends** estos son mis amigos; **oh —!** ¡Dios mío! **— foot!** ¡ni lo pienses!
Myanmar [mjɑnmár] N Myanmar *m*
myocardial infarction [maɪokárdɪəl ɪnfárkʃən] N infarto del miocardio *m*
myopia [maɪópiə] N miopía *f*
myriad [mírɪəd] N miríada *f*, sinfín *m*; **— problems** un sinfín de problemas
myrtle [mɝ́dl] N mirto *m*, arrayán *m*
myself [maɪsɛ́lf] PRON I **— wrote the letters** yo mismo escribí las cartas; **I'm not — today** hoy no soy la misma de siempre; **I was sitting by —** estaba sentado solo; **I talk to —** hablo solo; **I looked at — in the mirror** me miré en el espejo; **I bought — a house** me compré una casa
mysterious [mɪstíriəs] ADJ misterioso
mystery [místəri] N misterio *m*
mystic [místɪk] ADJ & N místico -ca *mf*
mystical [místɪkəl] ADJ místico
myth [miθ] N mito *m*
mythic [míθɪk] ADJ mítico
mythical [míθɪkəl] ADJ mítico
mythological [mɪθəládʒɪkəl] ADJ mitológico
mythology [mɪθálədʒi] N mitología *f*

Nn

nab [næb] VT pescar; *Sp* coger
nag [næg] N (horse) jaca *f*, rocín *m*, penco *m*; (complainer) quejica *mf*; VI/VT regañar, criticar
nail [neɫ] N (for wood) clavo *m*; (of finger, toe) uña *f*; **—-biter** situación angustiante *f*; **— file** lima *f*; **— polish** esmalte para uñas *m*; **to hit the — on the head** dar en el clavo; VT (fasten) clavar; (nab) pescar; *Sp* coger
naive [naív] ADJ ingenuo, cándido, bonachón
naiveté [naivté] N ingenuidad *f*
naked [nékɪd] ADJ desnudo
nakedness [nékɪdnɪs] N desnudez *f*
name [nem] N nombre *m*; **—-brand** marca comercial *f*; **—plate** placa *f*; **—sake** tocayo *m*; **—tag** etiqueta de identificación *f*; **— of the game** lo esencial *m*; **to call someone —s** motejar a alguien; **to make a — for oneself** hacerse un nombre; **what is your —?** ¿cómo te llamas? VT nombrar; **— your price** haz una oferta
nameless [némlɪs] ADJ anónimo
namely [némli] ADV a saber, en concreto
Namibia [nəmíbiə] N Namibia *f*
Namibian [nəmíbiən] ADJ & N namibio -bia *mf*
nanny [nǽni] N niñera *f*
nanosecond [nǽnosekənd] N nanosegundo *m*
nanotechnology [nænotɛknáləʤi] N nanotecnología *f*
nap [næp] N (sleep) siesta *f*; (fibers) pelo *m*; **to take a —** echar/dormir una siesta; VI echar/dormir una siesta
napalm [népɑɫm] N napalm *m*
nape [nep] N nuca *f*
napkin [nǽpkɪn] N servilleta *f*
narcissism [nársɪsɪzəm] N narcisismo *m*
narcissus [nɑrsísəs] N narciso *m*
narcolepsy [nárkəlɛpsi] N narcolepsia *f*
narcotic [nɑrkáɑɪk] ADJ & N narcótico *m*, estupefaciente *m*
narcotrafficking [nɑrkotrǽfɪkɪŋ] N narcotráfico *m*
narrate [nǽret] VI/VT narrar
narration [nǽréʃən] N narración *f*
narrative [nǽrədɪv] ADJ narrativo; N narrativa *f*
narrator [nǽreɪdɚ] N narrador -ora *mf*
narrow [nǽro] ADJ (of little width) estrecho, angosto; (limited in scope) limitado; (intolerant) intolerante; **to have a — escape** salvarse por poco; **— gauge** de vía angosta/estrecha; **—-minded** intolerante; N **—s** desfiladero *m*, estrecho *m*, angostura *f*; VI/VT angostar[se], estrechar[se]; **to — down**

reducir
narrowness [nǽroʊnɪs] N (quality of being narrow) estrechez *f*, angostura *f*
nasal [nézəł] ADJ nasal
nastiness [nǽstɪnɪs] N (filth) suciedad *f*; (stinkiness) asquerosidad *f*; (rudeness, obscenity) grosería *f*
nasturtium [nəstɜ́·ʃəm] N capuchina *f*
nasty [nǽsti] ADJ (mess) sucio; (smell) asqueroso; (comment) hiriente; (accident) feo; (word) grosero; (disposition) malo
natal [nédḷ] ADJ natal
nation [néʃən] N nación *f*; ADJ **—wide** a escala nacional
national [nǽʃənḷ] ADJ nacional; **— park** parque nacional *m*; **— team** seleccionado nacional *m*; N ciudadano -na *mf*, nacional *mf*
nationalism [nǽʃənəlɪzəm] N nacionalismo *m*
nationalist [nǽʃənəlɪst] N & ADJ nacionalista MF
nationality [nǽʃənǽlɪɒɪ] N nacionalidad *f*; **adjective of —** gentilicio *m*
nationalize [nǽʃənəlaɪz] VT nacionalizar
native [néɒɪv] ADJ nativo; **— language** lengua nativa *f*; **— plants** flora nativa *f*; **my — Italy** mi Italia natal *f*; (innate) innato; N (person born in a place) natural *m*; (member of a tribal group) indígena *mf*, nativo -va *mf*; **he's a — of Italy** es oriundo de Italia
nativity [nətívɪɒɪ] N nacimiento *m*; **— scene** pesebre *m*; **the —** la Natividad
NATO [North Atlantic Treaty Organization] [néɒo] N OTAN *f*
natural [nǽtʃə·əł] ADJ natural; (inborn) innato; **— childbirth** parto natural *m*; **— gas** gas natural *m*; **— resources** recursos naturales *m pl*; **— selection** selección natural *f*; N (musical sign) becuadro *m*; **he is a — for that job** tiene aptitud natural para ese puesto
naturalist [nǽtʃə·əlɪst] N naturalista *mf*
naturalization [nǽtʃə·əlɪzéʃən] N naturalización *f*
naturalize [nǽtʃə·əlaɪz] VI/VT naturalizar[se]
naturally [nǽtʃə·əli] ADV (of course) naturalmente; **I have — curly hair** tengo rizos naturales
naturalness [nǽtʃə·əłnɪs] N naturalidad *f*
nature [nétʃə·] N naturaleza *f*; (disposition) genio *m*, natural *m*
naught [nɔt] N (zero) cero *m*; (nothing) nada *f*
naughtiness [nɔ́ɒɪnɪs] N travesuras *f pl*
naughty [nɔ́ɒi] ADJ (child) travieso, pícaro, pillo; **— word** picardía *f*
Nauru [nɑúru] N Nauru *m*
Nauruan [nɑúrʊən] ADJ & N nauruano -na *mf*
nausea [nɔ́ziə] N náuseas *f pl*, mareo *m*
nauseate [nɔ́ziet] VT dar náuseas; **to be —d** tener náuseas
nauseating [nɔ́zieɒɪŋ] ADJ nauseabundo, nauseoso
nauseous [nɔ́ʃəs] ADJ (feeling nausea) mareado, nauseoso; (causing nausea) nauseabundo, nauseoso
nautical [nɔ́ɒɪkəł] ADJ náutico
naval [névəł] ADJ naval; **— officer** oficial de marina *m*
Navarrese [nævəríz] ADJ & N navarro -rra *mf*
nave [nev] N nave *f*
navel [névəł] N ombligo *m*; **— orange** naranja de ombligo *f*
navigable [nǽvɪgəbəł] ADJ navegable
navigate [nǽvɪget] VI/VT navegar
navigation [nævɪgéʃən] N navegación *f*; (science) náutica *f*
navigator [nǽvɪgeɒə·] N navegante *mf*
navy [névi] N marina [de guerra] *f*, armada *f*; **— bean** judía blanca *f*; **— blue** azul marino *m*
nay [ne] N (refusal) no *m*; (negative vote) voto negativo *m*
Nazi [nátsi] N nazi *mf*
near [nir] ADV cerca; **— at hand** cerca, a la mano; **to come/go/draw —** acercarse; PREP cerca de; **— the end of the month** hacia fines del mes; **to be — death** estar a punto de morir; ADJ cercano, próximo; **— East** Cercano Oriente *m*, Oriente Próximo *m*; **—sighted** miope; **I had a — miss** por poco me sucede un accidente; VI/VT acercarse [a]
nearby [nírbáɪ] ADV cerca; ADJ cercano, próximo
nearly [nírli] ADV casi, cerca de; **I — did it** casi lo hago
nearness [nírnɪs] N cercanía *f*, proximidad *f*
neat [nit] ADJ (clean) limpio, pulcro; (ordered) ordenado; (cool) bueno
neatness [nítnɪs] N (cleanness) limpieza *f*, pulcritud *f*; (order) orden *m*
nebulous [nébjələs] ADJ nebuloso
nebulousness [nébjələsnɪs] N nubosidad *f*
necessary [nésɪseri] ADJ (needed) necesario; (involuntary) forzoso
necessitate [nəsésɪtet] VT requerir
necessity [nəsésɪɒi] N necesidad *f*; **out of —** por necesidad
neck [nɛk] N (of a human) cuello *m*; (of an animal) pescuezo *m*; (of clothes) escote *m*; (throat) garganta *f*; **— and —** parejos; **—lace** collar *m*; **—line** escote *m*; **— of land** istmo *m*; **—tie** corbata *f*
necrology [nəkrɑ́łəʤi] N necrología *f*
necrosis [nəkrɔ́sɪs] N necrosis *f*
nectar [nɛ́ktə·] N néctar *m*
nectarine [nɛktərín] N nectarina *f*
need [nid] N (lack) necesidad *f*; (poverty) carencia *f*; **in —** en apretos; **if — be** en caso de necesidad; VT necesitar, precisar; **you — to come at four** tienes que venir a las cuatro
needle [nídḷ] N aguja *f*; **—point** bordado *m*; **—work** (embroidery) bordado *m*; (sewing) costura *f*; VT pinchar

needless [nídlɪs] ADJ innecesario; **— to say** huelga decir
needy [níDi] ADJ necesitado, menesteroso
ne'er-do-well [nérduwɛł] N inútil *mf*
negate [nɪgét] VT negar
negation [nɪgéʃən] N negación *f*
negative [négəDɪv] ADJ negativo; **the search proved —** la búsqueda no dio resultado; N negativa *f*; (photographic) negativo *m*; **this plan has one —** este plan tiene una contra; INTERJ ¡negativo!
neglect [nɪglékt] VT (fail to heed) postergar; (fail to care for) descuidar; (fail to carry out) desatender; **you're —ing your friends** tienes abandonados a tus amigos; **to — to** olvidarse de; N negligencia *f*, descuido *m*
neglectful [nɪgléktfəł] ADJ negligente, descuidado
negligence [néglɪʤəns] N negligencia *f*
negligent [néglɪʤənt] ADJ negligente, descuidado
negligible [néglɪʤəbəł] ADJ despreciable, minúsculo
negotiate [nɪgóʃiet] VI/VT (a contract) negociar, gestionar; (an obstacle) salvar
negotiating [nɪgóʃieDɪŋ] ADJ negociador
negotiation [nɪgoʃiéʃən] N negociación *f*, gestión *f*
negotiator [nɪgóʃieDə·] N negociador -ora *mf*
Negro [nígro] ADJ & N negro -gra *mf*
neigh [ne] N relincho *m*; VI relinchar
neighbor [nébə·] N (person who lives near) vecino -na *mf*; (fellow human) prójimo -ma *mf*; ADJ vecino; VI **to — with** lindar con
neighborhood [nébə·hUd] N vecindario *m*, barrio *m*; **in the — of a hundred dollars** alrededor de cien dólares
neighboring [nébərɪŋ] ADJ vecino, colindante
neither [níðə·] PRON ninguno de los dos, ni [el] uno ni [el] otro; **— of the two** ninguno de los dos; ADJ ninguno de los dos; **— one of us** ninguno de nosotros dos; CONJ ni; **— hot nor cold** ni caliente ni frío; **— will I** yo tampoco
nemesis [némɪsɪs] N némesis *f*
neologism [niáləʤɪzəm] N neologismo *m*
neon [níɑn] N neón *m*
neonatal [nionédł] ADJ neonatal
Nepal [nəpół] N Nepal *m*
Nepali [nəpóli] ADJ & N nepalés -esa *mf*, nepalí *mf*
nephew [néfju] N sobrino *m*
nephritis [nəfráIDɪs] N nefritis *f*
nepotism [népətɪzəm] N nepotismo *m*
nerd [nɝd] N (technological adept) persona aficionada a las computadoras / los ordenadores *f*; (socially inept person) persona socialmente inepta *f*
nerve [nɝv] N (anatomy) nervio *m*; (courage) valor *m*; (impertinence) descaro *m*, morro *m*; **— cell** neurona *f*; **— gas** gas nervioso *m*; **—[w]racking** angustiante; **he gets on my —s** me saca de quicio
nervous [nɝ́vəs] ADJ nervioso; **— breakdown** ataque de nervios *m*
nervousness [nɝ́vəsnɪs] N nerviosismo *m*
nest [nɛst] N nido *m*; (brood) nidada *f*; **— egg** ahorros *m pl*; **— of thieves** guarida de ladrones *f*; VI/VT anidar; (fit together) encajarse
nestle [nésəł] VI acurrucarse; VT apoyar, recostar
net [nɛt] N (fishing, network, tennis) red *f*; (in hair) redecilla *f*; **—work** red *f*; **—working** (social) relaciones profesionales *f pl*; (computer) diseño de redes y comunicaciones *m*; VT (catch a fish) pescar con red; (cover with a net) cubrir con una red; (catch a criminal) atrapar; (hit the tennis net) dar en la red; (make money after expenses) producir/ganar neto; ADJ neto; **— price** precio neto *m*; **— profit** ganancia neta *f*; **— assets** activo neto *m*; **— income** ingreso neto *m*; **— worth** patrimonio neto *m*
Netherlander [néðə·ləndə·] N holandés -esa *mf*
Netherlands [néðə·ləndz] N Países Bajos *m pl*
nettle [nédł] N ortiga *f*
neural [núrəł] ADJ neural
neuralgia [nUræłʤə] N neuralgia *f*
neurasthenia [nUrəsθíniə] N neurastenia *f*
neurologist [nUrálə̇ʤɪst] N neurólogo -ga *mf*
neuron [nÚrɑn] N neurona *f*
neurosis [nUrósɪs] N neurosis *f*
neurosurgeon [núrosɝʤən] N neurocirujano -na *mf*
neurosurgery [nUrosɝʤəri] N neurocirugía *f*
neurotic [nUráDɪk] ADJ & N neurótico -ca *mf*
neurotransmitter [nUrotrǽnzmIDə·] N neurotransmisor *m*
neuter [núDə·] ADJ neutro; VT castrar
neutral [nútrəł] ADJ neutral, imparcial; (of colors) neutro; N punto muerto *m*
neutrality [nutrǽlɪDi] N neutralidad *f*
neutralize [nútrəlaɪz] VI/VT neutralizar[se]
neutron [nútrɑn] N neutrón *m*; **— bomb** bomba de neutrones *f*
never [névə·] ADV nunca, jamás; **— mind** no te preocupes; **this will — do** esto no va a funcionar; **—-ending** interminable
nevertheless [nɛvə·ðəlés] ADV & CONJ sin embargo, no obstante
new [nu] ADJ (not old) nuevo; (fresh) otro; **a — sheet of paper** otra hoja de papel; **— age [music]** [música] nueva era *f*; **—born baby** recién nacido -da *mf*; **—comer** recién llegado -da *mf*; **—fangled** moderno, recién inventado; **—found** nuevo; **— year** año nuevo *m*; **— Year's Eve** fin de año *m*; *Sp* nochevieja *f*
newly [núli] ADV recientemente; **— arrived** recién llegado; **—wed** recién casado

newness [núnɪs] N novedad *f*
news [nuz] N (item) noticias *f pl*; (latest gossip) novedades *f pl*; (newspaper) periódico *m*; **it is — to me** recién me entero; **— broadcast/bulletin** noticiero *m*, noticiario *m*; **—cast** noticiero *m*, noticiario *m*, informativo *m*; **—clipping** recorte de diario *m*; **—letter** boletín informativo *m*; **—paper** periódico *m*, diario *m*; **—print** papel de periódico *m*; **—room** sala de redacción *f*; **—stand** quiosco *m*; **piece of —** noticia *f*; ADJ **—worthy** de interés periodístico
newt [nut] N tritón *m*
New Zealand [nuzílənd] N Nueva Zelanda *f*
New Zealander [nuzílənd͡ɚ] N neozelandés -esa *mf*
next [nɛkst] ADJ (future) próximo, entrante; (following) siguiente; (contiguous) contiguo, de al lado; **—-door** de al lado; **who's —?** ¿quién sigue? ADV después, luego; **— best** segundo en calidad; **when — we meet** cuando nos volvamos a ver; PREP **— of kin** familiares *m pl*; **— to** junto a, al lado de
nibble [nɪbəł] VI/VT (bite) mordiscar, mordisquear; (eat) picotear; (of fish) picar; N (bite) mordisco *m*; (act of nibbling) mordisqueo *m*
Nicaragua [nɪkərágwə] N Nicaragua *f*
Nicaraguan [nɪkərágwən] ADJ & N nicaragüense *mf*
nice [naɪs] ADJ (kind) amable, simpático; (agreeable) *Am* lindo, *Sp* majo; **it's — and hot** está bien calentito
nicety [náɪsɪdi] N (subtlety) sutileza *f*; (detail) detalle *m*
niche [nɪtʃ] N (also environmental) nicho *m*; **— marketing** mercadeo de nicho *m*; **I've found my —** he encontrado mi lugar
nick [nɪk] N (chip) muesca *f*; (cut) corte *m*; **in the — of time** justo a tiempo; VT (chip) hacer muescas; (cut) cortar; **—name** apodo *m*, mote *m*, sobrenombre *m*; **to —name** apodar
nickel [nɪkəł] N (metal) níquel *m*; (coin) moneda de cinco centavos *f*; **—-plated** niquelado
nicotine [níkətin] N nicotina *f*
niece [nis] N sobrina *f*
Niger [náɪd͡ʒɚ] N Níger *m*
Nigeria [naɪd͡ʒíriə] N Nigeria *f*
Nigerian [naɪd͡ʒíriən] ADJ & N nigeriano -na *mf*
Nigerien [naɪd͡ʒíriɛn] ADJ & N nigerino -na *mf*
niggardly [nígɚdli] ADJ mezquino
night [naɪt] N noche *f*; ADJ nocturno, de noche; **—club** club nocturno *m*; **—fall** anochecer *m*, atardecer *m*; **—gown** camisón *m*; **—life** vida nocturna *f*; *Sp* marcha *f*; **—light** lamparilla *f*; **—mare** pesadilla *f*; **— owl** trasnochador -ora *mf*; **— shift** turno de la noche *m*; **—stand** veladora *f*, mesilla de noche *f*; **—time** noche *f*; **— watchman** celador *m*
nightingale [náɪtɪŋɡəł] N ruiseñor *m*
nightly [nátli] ADV todas las noches; ADJ nocturno
nihilism [náiəlɪzəm] N nihilismo *m*
nil [nɪł] ADJ nulo
nimble [nímbəł] ADJ ágil
nincompoop [nɪ́ŋkəmpup] N *fam* tarambana *mf*, bobalicón -ona *mf*
nine [naɪn] NUM nueve; **— hundred** novecientos
nineteen [naɪntín] NUM diecinueve
ninety [náɪnti] NUM noventa
ninth [náɪnθ] ADJ & N noveno *m*
nip [nɪp] VT (pinch) pellizcar; (bite) mordiscar, mordisquear; (cause frostbite) helar; **to — in the bud** cortar de raíz; **to — off** despuntar; VI (drink in sips) dar sorbitos; N (pinch) pellizco *m*; (bite) mordisco *m*; (sip) traguito *m*, sorbito *m*; (cold) frío *m*; **it's going to be — and tuck** va a ser muy reñido
nipple [nípəł] N (on female breast) pezón *m*; (on male breast) tetilla *f*; (on bottle) tetina *f*
nitpick [nítpɪk] VI criticar detalles insignificantes
nitrate [nátret] N nitrato *m*
nitric acid [náɪtrɪkǽsɪd] N ácido nítrico *m*
nitrogen [náɪtrəd͡ʒən] N nitrógeno *m*
nitroglycerin [naɪtroglísəɹɪn] N nitroglicerina *f*
nitty-gritty [nídigríDi] N **to get down to the —** ir al grano
no [no] ADV no; **— longer** ya no; **— man's land** tierra de nadie *f*; **— matter how much** por mucho que; **— one** ninguno, nadie; **— smoking** se prohibe fumar; **—where** (location) en ninguna parte / ningún lado; (direction) a ninguna parte / ningún lado; **he was a —-show** no se presentó; **a —-win situation** una situación insoluble; **there is — more** no hay más; ADJ ningun[o]; **I have — friends** no tengo amigos; **it's a —-brainer** la respuesta es obvia; **— friend of mine will go hungry** ningún amigo mío pasará hambre; **of — use** inútil; N (refusal) no *m*; (negative vote) voto negativo *m*; ADJ **—-frills** básico, sin lujos
nobility [nobɪ́lɪDi] N nobleza *f*, hidalguía *f*
noble [nóbəł] ADJ & N noble *mf*; **—man** hidalgo *m*
nobody [nóbəDi] PRON nadie, ninguno; N don nadie, pelagatos *mf sg*
nocturnal [nɑktɝ́nl] ADJ nocturno
nod [nɑd] VI/VT (signal affirmation) asentir con la cabeza; VI (doze) cabecear, dar cabezadas; **to — off** dormirse; N (as signal) inclinación de cabeza *f*, saludo con la cabeza *m*; (from sleepiness) cabezada *f*
node [nod] N (of cells) nódulo *m*; (in plants) nudo *m*; (in physics) nodo *m*
noise [nɔɪz] N ruido *m*; **— pollution**

contaminación sonora *f*; VI **it is being —d about that** corre el rumor que
noiseless [nɔ́ɪzlɪs] ADJ silencioso
noisy [nɔ́ɪzi] ADJ ruidoso
nomad [nómæd] N nómada *mf*
nomenclature [nómɪnkletʃə-] N nomenclatura *f*
nominal [námənl] ADJ nominal
nominate [námənet] VT nominar
nomination [nɑmənéʃən] N nominación *f*
nominee [nɑməní] N candidato -ta *mf*
nonchalant [nɑnʃəlánt] ADJ despreocupado
noncollectible [nankəléktəbəł] ADJ incobrable
noncommercial [nɑnkəmə́ʃəł] ADJ no comercial
noncommissioned officer [nɑnkəmíʃənd ɔ́fɪsə-] N suboficial *m*
nonconforming [nɑnkənfɔ́rmɪŋ] ADJ no conforme
nonconformist [nɑnkənfɔ́rmɪst] ADJ & N incomformista *mf*
none [nʌn] PRON ninguno; **I want — of that** no me quiero meter en eso; **that is — of your business** no es asunto tuyo; ADV **— too soon** al último momento; **—theless** sin embargo
nonentity [nɑnéntɪdɪ] N nulidad *f*
nonessential [nɑnɪsénʃəł] ADJ no esencial
nonexistent [nɑnɪgzístənt] ADJ inexistente
nonfiction [nɑnfíkʃən] N no ficción *f*
nongovernmental [nangʌvə-nménṭl] ADJ no gubernamental
nonnegotiable [nɑnnɪgóʃəbəł] ADJ no negociable
nonpartisan [nɑnpárdɪzən] ADJ (neutral) imparcial; (not affiliated) sin afiliación política
nonperformance [nɑnpə-fɔ́rməns] N incumplimiento *m*
nonproductive [nɑnprədáktɪv] ADJ improductivo
nonprofit [nɑnpráfɪt] ADJ sin fines de lucro; N organización sin fines de lucro *f*
nonrefundable [nɑnrɪfíndəbəł] ADJ no reembolsable
nonresident [nɑnrézɪdənt] ADJ & N no residente *mf*
nonsense [nánsɛns] N tonterías *f pl*, monsergas *f pl*, estupideces *f pl*; **to talk —** decir barbaridades/disparates
nonstop [nánstáp] ADJ sin escala, directo; ADV sin parar
nontaxable [nɑntǽksəbəł] ADJ no tributable
nonvoting [nɑnvóṭɪŋ] ADJ sin derecho a voto
noodle [núdl] N fideo *m*, tallarín *m*
nook [nʊk] N rincón *m*
noon [nun] N mediodía *m*; **— hour** mediodía *m*, hora de comer; **—time** mediodía *m*
noose [nus] N soga *f*, lazo *m*; **with a — around his neck** con la soga al cuello; VT (catch with a rope) enlazar; (make a loop in) hacer un lazo corredizo en
nope [nop] ADV no
nor [nɔr] CONJ ni; **we have neither eggs — flour** no tenemos ni huevos ni harina
Nordic [nɔ́rdɪk] ADJ nórdico
norm [nɔrm] N norma *f*, normativa *f*
normal [nɔ́rməł] ADJ normal; (perpendicular) normal; **to return to —** volver a la normalidad; (perpendicular line) línea perpendicular *f*
normalcy [nɔ́rmə́łsi] N normalidad *f*
normality [nɔrmǽlɪdɪ] N normalidad *f*
normalize [nɔ́rmə́laɪz] VI/VT normalizar[se]
normally [nɔ́rmə́li] ADV (in a normal way) de manera normal, con toda normalidad *f*; (usually) normalmente
north [nɔrθ] N norte *m*; **—east** noreste, hacia el noreste; **—west** noroeste *m*, hacia el noroeste; ADJ (in the north) norte, norteño; (from the north) del norte; **— America** América del Norte *f*; **— American** norteamericano -na *mf*; **—eastern** del noreste; **— Korea** Corea del Norte *f*; **— Korean** norcoreano -na; **— Pole** Polo Norte *m*; **— wind** cierzo *m*, viento norte *m*; **the — entrance** la entrada norte; ADV al norte, hacia el norte
northern [nɔ́rðə-n] ADJ del norte; (from the north) norteño; (in the north) septentrional; **— lights** aurora boreal *f*
northerner [nɔ́rðə-nə-] N norteño -ña *mf*
northward [nɔ́rθwə-d] ADV hacia el norte
Norway [nɔ́rwe] N Noruega *f*
Norwegian [nɔrwíʤən] ADJ & N noruego -ga *mf*
nose [noz] N nariz *f*; (of an airplane) morro *m*; (of an animal) hocico *m*; (perspicacity) olfato *m*; **—bleed** hemorragia nasal *f*; **—dive** caída en picado *f*; **— job** rinoplastia *f*; **keep your — clean** no te metas en líos; **on the —** exactamente; **to pick one's —** hurgarse las narices; VI/VT (move forward) entrar de punta; (muzzle) hocicar; **to — around** husmear
nostalgia [nɑstǽłʤə] N nostalgia *f*
nostalgic [nɑstǽłʤɪk] ADJ nostálgico
nostrils [nástrəlz] N narices *f pl*, ventanillas de la nariz *f pl*
nosy, nosey [nózi] ADJ entrometido
not [nɑt] ADV no; **I'm — your friend** no soy tu amigo; **— at all** (no way) de ningún modo; (you're welcome) de nada; **— at all sure** nada seguro; **— even a word** ni una palabra
notable [nóʊəbəł] ADJ notable, destacable
notably [nóʊəblɪ] ADV notablemente
notarize [nóʊərɑɪz] VT notariar
notary [nóʊəri] N notario -ria *mf*; **— public** notario -ria público -ca *mf*
notation [notéʃən] N (system of signs) notación

f; (act of writing) anotación *f*; (short note) anotación *f*, apunte *m*

notch [nɑtʃ] N (nick) muesca *f*, mella *f*; (degree) grado *m*; **a — above the rest** mejor que los demás; VT hacer una muesca; **he —ed another win** se anotó otra victoria

note [not] N (written) nota *f*, anotación *f*; (musical) nota *f*; (touch) toque *m*; (financial) pagaré *m*; (currency) billete *m*; **—book** cuaderno *m*; (small) libreta *f*; **—s** apuntes *m pl*; **of —** de renombre / de nota; **to take — of** notar; ADJ **—worthy** notable; VT (notice) notar; (write down) anotar, apuntar

noted [nóʊɪd] ADJ célebre

nothing [nʌ́θɪŋ] PRON nada; (score) cero, nada; N (insignificant person) don nadie *m*; (insignificant thing) nadería *f*; **— to it** no tiene ciencia; ADV **it was — like that** no fue así para nada; **we did it for —** (free) lo hicimos gratis; (fruitlessly) lo hicimos en balde

notice [nóʊɪs] N (information) aviso *m*; (warning) advertencia *f*; (attention) atención *f*; **a week's —** una semana de plazo; **to give —** renunciar; **to take —** hacer caso; VT (perceive) notar, advertir, percatarse [de]; (pay attention to) fijarse [en], reparar [en]

noticeable [nóʊɪsəbəł] ADJ perceptible, apreciable

noticeably [nóʊɪsəbli] ADV notablemente

notification [noʊəfɪkéʃən] N notificación *f*

notify [nóʊəfaɪ] VT notificar

notion [nóʃən] N noción *f*, idea *f*; (whim) capricho *m*; **—s** mercería *f*

notorious [noʊ́ɾɪəs] ADJ de mala fama; **he's a — liar** tiene fama de mentiroso

nougat [núgət] N turrón *m*

noun [naʊn] N sustantivo *m*

nourish [nɝ́ɪʃ] VT (a person) nutrir, alimentar; (a hope) abrigar

nourishing [nɝ́ɪʃɪŋ] ADJ nutritivo

nourishment [nɝ́ɪʃmənt] N (food) alimento *m*; (act of nourishing) alimentación *f*

novel [nɑ́vəł] N novela *f*; ADJ novedoso

novelist [nɑ́vəlɪst] N novelista *mf*

novelty [nɑ́vəlti] N novedad *f*; **the — soon wore off** se pasó la novedad; **novelties** chucherías *f pl*

November [noʊ́mbə·] N noviembre *m*

novice [nɑ́vɪs] N novato -ta *mf*, pipiolo -la *mf*; (religious) novicio -cia *mf*

novocaine [nóʊəken] N novocaína *f*

now [naʊ] ADV ahora; **— and then** de vez en cuando; **— that** ahora que; **he left just —** salió hace poco, recién salió; **—, —, calm down!** bueno, bueno, ¡cálmate!

nowadays [náʊəɑdez] ADV hoy [en] día

noxious [nɑ́kʃəs] ADJ nocivo

nuance [núans] N matiz *m*

nuclear [núkliə·] ADJ nuclear; **— energy** energía nuclear *f*; **— family** familia nuclear *f*; **— fission** fisión nuclear *f*; **— fusion** fusión nuclear *f*; **— physics** física nuclear *f*; **— weapon** arma nuclear *f*

nucleus [núkliəs] N núcleo *m*

nude [nud] ADJ & N desnudo *m*

nudge [nʌʤ] VI/VT codear; N golpe suave con el codo *m*

nugget [nágɪt] N (of gold) pepita *f*; (of chicken) pedacito *m*; (of wisdom) perla *f*

nuisance [núsəns] N molestia *f*; *Sp* pesadez *f*; (legal) perjuicio *m*; **you're such a —!** ¡qué pesado eres tú! **— tax** impuesto de consumo *m*

nuke [nuk] N arma nuclear *f*; VT (bomb) bombardear con armas nucleares; (cook) calentar en microondas

null [nʌł] ADJ nulo; **— and void** nulo

nullify [nɑ́ləfaɪ] VT anular

numb [nʌm] ADJ entumecido; **to get —** entumecerse; VT entumecer

number [nʌ́mbə·] N número *m*; **— one** uno mismo *m*; **—-crunching** procesamiento de datos numéricos complejos *m*; VI (total) ascender a; **I — him among my friends** lo cuento entre mis amigos; VT numerar

numberless [nʌ́mbə·lɪs] ADJ sin número

numbskull, numskull [nʌ́mskʌł] N zopenco -ca *mf*

numeral [nú(m)ə·əł] N número *m*; ADJ numeral

numerical [numéɾɪkəł] ADJ numérico

numerous [nú(m)ə·əs] ADJ numeroso

nun [nʌn] N monja *f*, religiosa *f*

nuptial [nʌ́pʃəł] ADJ nupcial; N **—s** nupcias *f pl*

nurse [nɝ·s] N (for the sick) enfermero -ra *mf*; (for children) niñera *f*; VT (give milk) amamantar, lactar; (tend to a sick person) cuidar; **to — a grudge** guardar rencor; **to — a cup of coffee** tomar una taza de café a sorbitos; **to — a cold** cuidarse durante un resfrío; VI (drink milk) mamar

nursery [nɝ́·sri] N (children's room) cuarto para niños *m*; (day-care center) guardería *f*; (place for growing plants) almáciga *f*, vivero *m*, plantel *m*; **— rhyme** canción infantil *f*, ronda *f*; **— school** preescolar *m*; *Sp* parvulario *m*; *Am* jardín infantil *m*

nursing [nɝ́·sɪŋ] N (profession) enfermería *f*; (care) cuidado *m*; **— home** (for old people) hogar de ancianos *m*; (for sick people) casa de salud *f*

nurture [nɝ́·tʃə·] VT (rear) criar; (feed) nutrir, alimentar; (encourage) fomentar; N (rearing) crianza *f*; (feeding) alimentación *f*

nut [nʌt] N (fruit) fruto seco *m*; (device) tuerca *f*; (person) excéntrico -ca *mf*; **—cracker** cascanueces *m sg*; **—meg** nuez moscada *f*; **—s** ADJ crazy; **—s and bolts** los fundamentos;

—shell cáscara de fruto seco *f*; **in a —shell** en pocas palabras

nutrient [nútriənt] N nutriente *m*

nutrition [nutríʃən] N nutrición *f*, alimentación *f*

nutritious [nutríʃəs] ADJ nutritivo, alimenticio

nylon [náɪlɑn] N nilón *m*, nailon *m*

Oo

oak [ok] N roble *m*, encina *f*; **— grove** robledal *m*

oar [ɔr] N remo *m*; VI/VT remar, bogar; **—lock** tolete *m*

OAS [Organization of the American States] [óéés] N OEA *f*

oasis [oésɪs] N oasis *m*

oat [ot] N avena *f*; **—meal** (flour) harina de avena *f*; (breakfast food) gachas de avena *f pl*; **—s** avena *f*

oath [oθ] N (pledge) juramento *m*; (curse) maldición *f*; (swear word) palabrota *f*; taco *m*; **to take an —** prestar juramento

obedience [obíDiəns] N obediencia *f*

obedient [obíDiənt] ADJ obediente

obese [obís] ADJ obeso

obesity [obísɪDi] N obesidad *f*

obituary [obítʃueri] N nota necrológica *f*, obituario *m*

object[1] [ábʤɪkt] N objeto *m*; (of a verb) complemento *m*

object[2] [əbʤékt] VI/VT objetar

objection [əbʤékʃən] N objeción *f*

objectionable [əbʤékʃənəbəł] ADJ objetable

objective [əbʤéktɪv] ADJ objetivo; N objetivo *m*, finalidad *f*

objectivity [abʤektívɪDi] N objetividad *f*

obligate [ábliget] VT obligar

obligated [ábligeDɪd] ADJ obligado, comprometido

obligation [abligéʃən] N obligación *f*; **under no — to buy** sin compromiso de compra

obligatory [əblígətori] ADJ obligatorio, obligado

oblige [əbláɪʤ] VT (make obliged) obligar; VI/VT (do a favor for) complacer; VI (obey an order) obedecer; **much —d!** ¡muchas gracias! ¡muy agradecido!

obliging [əbláɪʤɪŋ] ADJ complaciente; *Am* comedido

oblique [oblík] ADJ oblicuo

obliterate [əblíDəret] VT (blot out) tachar; (destroy) arrasar, destruir

oblivion [əblíviən] N olvido *m*

oblivious [əblíviəs] ADJ inconsciente; **— to the danger** ajeno al peligro

obnoxious [əbnákʃəs] ADJ (remark, behavior) ofensivo; (person) odioso

oboe [óbo] N oboe *m*

obscene [əbsín] ADJ obsceno; **his salary is —** lo que gana es escandaloso

obscenity [əbsénɪDi] N obscenidad *f*

obscure [əbskjúr] ADJ oscuro; VT oscurecer

obscurity [əbskjúrɪDi] N oscuridad *f*

obsequious [əbsíkwiəs] ADJ obsequioso

observance [əbzɝ́vəns] N observancia *f*

observant [əbzɝ́vənt] ADJ observador

observation [abzə́véʃən] N observación *f*

observatory [əbzɝ́vətɔri] N observatorio *m*

observe [əbzɝ́v] VT observar; (holidays, rituals) guardar

observer [əbzɝ́və·] N observador -ora *mf*; (of elections) interventor -ora *mf*

obsess [əbsés] VI/VT obsesionar[se]; **he's —ing over it** está obsesionado con eso

obsession [əbséʃən] N obsesión *f*

obsessive-compulsive [əbsésɪvkəmpáłsɪv] ADJ obsesivo-compulsivo

obsolescence [absəlésəns] N desuso *m*

obsolete [absəlít] ADJ anticuado, desusado

obstacle [ábstəkəł] N obstáculo *m*

obstetrician [abstətríʃən] N obstetra *mf*

obstetrics [abstétrɪks] N obstetricia *f*

obstinacy [ábstənəsi] N obstinación *f*, terquedad *f*, porfía *f*

obstinate [ábstənɪt] ADJ obstinado, terco, recalcitrante; **to be —** obstinarse

obstruct [əbstrʌ́kt] VI/VT obstruir; (traffic) atascar, obstruir

obstruction [əbstrʌ́kʃən] N obstrucción *f*

obtain [əbtén] VT obtener, procurar; VI prevalecer

obtainable [əbténəbəł] ADJ conseguible

obviate [ábviet] VT obviar

obvious [ábviəs] ADJ obvio, evidente

obviously [ábviəsli] ADV & INTERJ evidentemente, obviamente

occasion [əkéʒən] N (moment) ocasión *f*; (chance) oportunidad *f*, ocasión *f*; (cause) motivo *m*; (event) acontecimiento *m*, ocasión *f*; VT ocasionar

occasional [əkéʒənl] ADJ ocasional

occasionally [əkéʒənłi] ADV de vez en cuando, ocasionalmente

occidental [aksɪdéntł] ADJ & N occidental *mf*

occlusion [əklúʒən] N obstrucción *f*, oclusión *f*

occult [əkʌ́łt] ADJ oculto; N ocultismo *m*, ciencias ocultas *f pl*; VT ocultar

occupancy [ákjəpənsi] N ocupación *f*; **— rate** tasa de ocupación *f*

occupant [ákjəpənt] N ocupante *mf*

occupation [akjəpéʃən] N ocupación *f*

occupational [akjəpéʃənl] ADJ ocupacional; **— hazard/risk** riesgo ocupacional *m*; **— therapy** laborterapia *f*, terapia ocupacional *f*

occupy [ákjəpaɪ] VI/VT ocupar

occur [əkɜ́-] VI ocurrir, suceder; **it —red to me** se me ocurrió
occurrence [əkɜ́-əns] N suceso *m*, acontecimiento *m*
ocean [óʃən] N océano *m*
oceanic [oʃiǽnɪk] ADJ oceánico
oceanography [oʃənágrəfi] N oceanografía *f*
ocelot [ásəlɑt] N ocelote *m*
o'clock [əklɑ́k] ADV **it is one —** es la una; **it is two —** son las dos
octagon [ɑ́ktəgɑn] N octágono *m*, octógono *m*
octane [ɑ́kten] N octano *m*
octave [ɑ́ktɪv] N octava *f*
October [ɑktóbə-] N octubre *m*
octopus [ɑ́ktəpəs] N pulpo *m*
oculist [ɑ́kjəlɪst] N oculista *mf*
OD [overdose] [ódí] N sobredosis *f*; VI tomar una sobredosis
odd [ɑd] ADJ (unusual) extraño; (not even) impar, non; **—ball** excéntrico -ca *mf*; **— change** suelto *m*, cambio *m*; **— job** trabajo ocasional *m*; **— shoe** zapato sin compañero *m*; ADV **thirty-—** treinta y tantos
oddity [ɑ́dɪti] N rareza *f*; (person) excéntrico -ca *mf*
odds [ɑdz] N (probabilities) probabilidades *f pl*; **— and ends** cachivaches *m pl*; **the — are against me** llevo las de perder; **to be at —** estar en desacuerdo; ADJ **—-on favorite** favorito *m*
ode [od] N oda *f*
odious [ódɪəs] ADJ odioso
odor [ódə-] N olor *m*; (bad) hedor *m*
odorless [ódə-lɪs] ADJ inodoro
odorous [ódə-əs] ADJ oloroso
of [av] PREP de; **— course** por supuesto, desde luego; **a quarter — five** las cinco menos cuarto; **doctor — medicine** doctor -ora en medicina *mf*; **the smell — paint** el olor a pintura; **a friend — mine** un amigo mío
off [ɔf] ADV **— and on** de vez en cuando; **— the record** extraoficialmente; **ten cents —** rebaja de diez centavos *f*; **ten miles —** a diez millas de distancia; **to take a day —** tomarse un día libre; ADJ **— chance** posibilidad remota *f*; **—-color** verde; **— season** temporada baja *f*; **— year** de producción decreciente; **our deal is —** se canceló nuestro plan; **prices are —** los precios han caído; **you're — by a mile** estás equivocadísimo; **he's a little —** está tocadito; **with his hat —** sin el sombrero; **the electricity is —** está apagada la electricidad; **to be — to war** haberse ido a la guerra; **to be well —** tener mucho dinero; PREP **— course** fuera de curso; **he drove — the road** se salió de la carretera; **I bought it — a gypsy** se lo compré a un gitano; **he's — playing golf** se fue a jugar al golf; VT liquidar
off-duty [ɔfdúɒi] ADJ **to be —** no estar de turno
offend [əfénd] VI/VT (insult) ofender, afrentar; (affect disagreeably) desagradar
offender [əféndə-] N delincuente *mf*
offense[1] [əféns] N (sin, insult) ofensa *f*; (misdemeanor) delito *m*; **no — was meant** no te lo tomes a mal
offense[2] [áfens] (in sports) ofensiva *f*
offensive [əfénsɪv] ADJ ofensivo; **— line** línea ofensiva *f*; **— series** serie ofensiva *f*, ataque *m*; N ofensiva *f*
offer [ɔ́fə-] VT ofrecer; **to — to** ofrecerse a; N oferta *f*; **make an —** hacer una oferta
offering [ɔ́fə-ɪŋ] N (thing given in worship) ofrenda *f*; (thing presented for sale) oferta *f*; (action of offering) ofrecimiento *m*
offhand [ɔ́fhǽnd] ADV **he remarked —** mencionó al descuido; ADJ **an — remark** un comentario descuidado
office [ɔ́fɪs] N (function) cargo *m*, función *f*; (place) oficina *f*, despacho *m*; (headquarters) oficinas *f pl*; **— boy** mandadero de oficina *m*; **— building** edificio para oficinas *m*; **— suite** (furniture) juego ofimático *m*; (rooms) suite *f*; (software) paquete de programas de productividad *m*; **through the —s of** por la intervención de
officer [ɔ́fɪsə-] N (military) oficial *m*; (police) agente de policía *mf*; (of an organization) directivo -va *mf*
official [əfíʃəl] ADJ oficial; N funcionario -ria *mf*
officiate [əfíʃiet] VI oficiar; (in sports) arbitrar
officious [əfíʃəs] ADJ oficioso
off-key [ɔfkí] ADJ desafinado
off-limits [ɔflímɪts] ADJ vedado, de acceso prohibido
off-line [ɔfláɪn] ADV fuera de línea
off-season [ɔ́fsizən] N temporada baja *f*; ADJ de temporada baja
offset[1] [ɔ́fset] N offset *m*
offset[2] [ɔfsét, ɔ́fsét] VT compensar
offshore [ɔf[ɔ́r] ADJ & ADV cerca de la costa; **— account** cuenta en un paraíso fiscal *f*; **— drilling** explotación petrolífera en el fondo del mar *f*
offside [ɔ́fsáɪd] ADV fuera de juego
offspring [ɔ́fsprɪŋ] N prole *m*
offstage [ɔ́fstédʒ] ADV & ADJ entre bastidores, fuera de escena
off-the-record [ɔ́fθə-rékə-d] ADJ oficioso
often [ɔ́fən] ADV a menudo; **how —?** ¿con qué frecuencia? ¿cada cuánto?
ogre [ógə-] N ogro *m*
oh [o] INTERJ **— no!** ¡ay no! **— really?** ¿de veras? **— well** está bien, vale; **— yeah?** (not true) ¡qué va! (really?) ¿de veras?
ohm [om] N ohmio *m*
oil [ɔɪl] N (for cars, cooking) aceite *m*; (crude)

petróleo *m*; **—can** alcuza *f*, aceitera *f*; **—cloth** hule *m*, tela de hule *f*; **— factory** aceitera *f*; **— field** campo petrolífero *m*; **— industry** industria petrolera *f*; **— lamp** quinqué *m*; **— painting** pintura al óleo *f*, óleo *m*; **— pan** cárter *m*; **— pipeline** oleoducto *m*; **— rig** plataforma petrolífera *f*; **— slick** mancha de petróleo *f*; **— spill** vertido de petróleo *m*; **— tanker** barco petrolero *m*; **— well** pozo de petróleo *m*; ADJ **—-bearing** petrolífero; **—-exporting** exportador de petróleo; **—-producing** petrolífero; VT (apply oil) aceitar; (bribe) untar

oily [ɔ́ɪli] ADJ (food) aceitoso; (liquid) oleoso; (hair) graso; (person) untuoso

oink [ɔ́ɪŋk] VI gruñir; N gruñido *m*

ointment [ɔ́ɪntmənt] N ungüento *m*

OK/okay [oké] ADJ bueno; **he's an — guy** es un buen tipo; **his work is just —** su trabajo no es nada del otro mundo; ADV bien; **it's —** (fine) está bien; (adequate) es regular; N **to give one's —** dar el visto bueno; VT dar el visto bueno, aprobar; INTERJ bien, *Sp* vale

okra [ókrə] N quingombó *m*

old [ołd] ADJ viejo; (objects only) antiguo; (wine) añejo; **— age** vejez *f*, ancianidad *f*; **—-boy network** red favoritista entre hombres *f*; **—-fashioned** (unfashionable) pasado de moda; (antiquated) anticuado; (morally prudish) chapado a la antigua; **— fogey** carcamal *m*, carca *m*; **— hat** pasado de moda; **— maid** solterona *f*; **—-time** antiguo, viejo; **—-timer** (longtime member) miembro de la vieja guardia *m*; (oldster) viejo *m*; **— wives' tale** superstición *f*; **— world** viejo mundo *m*; **days of —** antaño; **how — are you?** ¿cuántos años tienes? **— man** (husband) marido *m*; (father) *fam* viejo *m*; **I'm not — enough to drive** soy muy joven para conducir; **to be an — hand at** ser ducho en

olden [ółdn] ADJ **in — days** antaño

oldie [ółdi] N viejo éxito *m*

oleander [óliændə-] N adelfa *f*

olfactory [ɔłfǽktəri] ADJ olfatorio

olive [álɪv] N (tree) olivo *m*; (fruit) aceituna *f*, oliva *f*; **— branch** ramo de olivo *m*; **— grove** olivar *m*; **— oil** aceite de oliva *m*; **— wood** madera de olivo *m*; ADJ verde oliva

Olympiad [olímpiæd] N Olimpiada *f*, Olimpíada *f*

Olympic [olímpɪk] ADJ olímpico; **— Games** Olimpiadas *f pl*, Olimpíadas *f pl*, Juegos Olímpicos *m pl*

Oman [omán] N Omán *m*

Omani [ománi] ADJ & N omaní *mf*

omelet [ámlɪt] N tortilla francesa *f*

omen [ómən] N agüero *m*, presagio *m*

ominous [ámənəs] ADJ (threatening) amenazador; (like an omen) agorero

omission [omíʃən] N omisión *f*

omit [omít] VT omitir

omnipotence [amnípətəns] N omnipotencia *f*

omnipotent [amnípətənt] ADJ omnipotente

omniscience [amníʃəns] N omnisciencia *f*

omniscient [amníʃənt] ADJ omnisciente

omnivorous [amnívərəs] ADJ omnívoro

on [an] PREP en, sobre, encima de; **— the table** en / sobre / encima de la mesa; **— all sides** por todos lados; **— arriving** al llegar; **—-board** a bordo; **— call** de guardia; **— credit** al fiado; **— drugs** drogado; **— horseback** a caballo; **— Monday** el lunes; **— purpose** a propósito; **—-screen** en la pantalla; **— the house** la casa paga; **— time** a tiempo; **a book — stamps** un libro sobre sellos; **do you have any cigarettes — you?** ¿tienes cigarros? **drunk — beer** borracho de cerveza; **to talk — the phone** hablar por teléfono; ADJ **—line** en línea; **—line banking** banca en línea *f*; **—line help** ayuda en línea *f*; ADV **— and —** dale que dale; **his hat is —** lleva puesto el sombrero; **the light is —** está encendida la luz; **there's a war —** estamos en guerra; **you're —** (broadcasting) estás en el aire; (acceptance) te acepto la propuesta

once [wʌns] ADV (in the past, a single time) una vez; (if ever) si alguna vez; **— and for all** una vez por todas, definitivamente; **— in a while** de vez en cuando; **— upon a time** érase una vez; **at —** de inmediato, enseguida; **just this —** sólo por esta vez; **cousin — removed** primo -ma segundo -da *mf*; CONJ una vez que, cuando; N una vez; **—-over** vistazo *m*

oncology [ankáləʤi] N oncología *f*

one [wʌn] NUM uno; **— book** un libro; **— hundred** cien; **— hundred and one** ciento uno; **— thousand** mil; **—-armed** manco; **—-armed bandit** tragaperras *mf sg*; **—-eyed** tuerto; **— John Smith** un tal John Smith; **—-man band** hombre orquesta *m*; **— on —** mano a mano; **—-sided fight** pelea desigual *f*; **—-upmanship** competitividad *f*; **—-way street** calle de sentido único *f*; **his — chance** su única oportunidad; **the — and only** el único; **this is — smart dog** es un perro muy listo; N & PRON uno *m*; **— at a time** de a uno; **— by —** uno por uno; **love — another** amaos los unos a los otros; **the — who** el/la que; **the green —** el verde; **this —** este/esta

oneself [wʌnsɛ́łf] PRON **to be —** ser uno mismo; **to sit by —** estar sentado solo; **to talk to —** hablar para sí; **to look at — in the mirror** mirarse en el espejo; **to buy — a house** comprarse una casa

ongoing [ángoɪŋ] ADJ continuo

onion [ánjən] N cebolla *f*; **— patch** cebollar *m*

onlooker [ánlʊkɚ] N espectador -ora *mf*, mirón -ona *mf*
only [ónli] ADJ único; ADV solo, solamente; **I — just caught the train** por poco pierdo el tren; CONJ solo que, pero
onomatopoeia [ɑnəmɑdəpíə] N onomatopeya *f*
onset [ánsɛt] N comienzo *m*
on-side kick [ɔ́nsaɪd kík] N patada lateral *f*
onto [ántu] PREP en, sobre, encima de; **she got — the plane late** subió tarde al avión; **he dropped it — the table** lo dejó caer en la mesa; **I'm — your plot** conozco tu plan
onward [ánwɚd] ADV hacia adelante
onyx [ánɪks] N ónix *m*
oops [ups] INTERJ ¡huy!
ooze [uz] VI/VT rezumar[se]; N cieno *m*
opal [ópəł] N ópalo *m*
opaque [opék] ADJ opaco
OPEC [Organization of Petroleum Exporting Countries] [ópɛk] N OPEP *f*
open [ópən] VI/VT abrir[se]; **to — into** comunicarse con; **to — one's way** abrirse paso; **to — onto** dar a; **to — up** abrirse; ADJ abierto; **— and shut** claro, evidente; **— code** código abierto *m*; **— door policy** política de acceso libre *f*; **—-ended** sin restricciones; **—-heart surgery** cirujía de corazón abierto *f*; **—-minded** de amplias miras; **—-mouthed** boquiabierto; **— question** cuestión discutible *f*; **— season** temporada de caza *f*; **— source software** software de fuente abierta *m*; **— to criticism** expuesto a la crítica; N (outdoors) aire libre *m*; (tournament) abierto *m*
opener [ópənɚ] N abridor *m*; (in sports) primer partido *m*; **for —s** para empezar
opening [ópənɪŋ] N (open space) abertura *f*; (act of making or becoming open, ceremony) apertura *f*; (beginning) comienzo *m*; (clearing) claro *m*; (vacancy) vacante *m*, apertura *f*; (pretext) oportunidad *f*; **— bid** oferta de apertura *f*; **— ceremony** ceremonia de apertura *f*; **— night** estreno *m*; **at the —** a/en la apertura
openness [ópənnɪs] N franqueza *f*, transparencia *f*, apertura *f*
opera [ápərə] N ópera *f*; **— glasses** gemelos *m pl*; **— house** ópera *f*
operable [ápəəbəł] ADJ operable
operate [ápəret] VI (function) funcionar; (intervene surgically) operar; **to — on a person** operar a una persona; VT (run a machine) manejar; (administrate) dirigir; (make function) accionar
operating [ápərɛdɪŋ] N **— costs** costos de operación *m pl*; **— room** sala de operaciones *f*, quirófano *m*; **— system** sistema operativo *m*
operation [apəréʃən] N (surgical intervention, mission, math function) operación *f*; (function) funcionamiento *m*; (use of a machine) manejo *m*; **to be in —** (law) estar vigente; (machine) estar funcionando
operative [ápəəɹɪv] ADJ (law) vigente; (contract provision) pertinente; (word) clave, operativo; N (machine worker) operario -ria *mf*; (spy) agente *mf*
operator [ápərɛdɚ] N (telephone, math) operador -ora *mf*; (machine) operario -ria *mf*; (stock) especulador -ora *mf*; **he's a smooth —** es un astuto
ophthalmologist [afθəłmáləʤɪst] N oftalmólogo -ga *mf*
opiate [ópiət] N opiáceo *m*
opinion [əpínjən] N opinión *f*
opium [ópiəm] N opio *m*
opossum [əpásəm] N zarigüeya *f*
opponent [əpónənt] N opositor -ora *mf*, contrincante *mf*, adversario -ria *mf*, oponente *mf*
opportune [ɑpəɚtún] ADJ oportuno
opportunistic [ɑpəɚtunístɪk] ADJ oportunista, aprovechado
opportunity [ɑpəɚtúnɪdi] N oportunidad *f*, ocasión *f*
oppose [əpóz] VI/VT oponer[se]
opposing [əpózɪŋ] ADJ opuesto, contrario; **— thumb** pulgar oponible *m*
opposite [ápəzɪt] ADJ (contrary) opuesto, contrario; **— to** frente a; PREP frente a, en frente de; N contrario *m*, opuesto *m*; ADV en frente
opposition [ɑpəzíʃən] N oposición *f*; **they met with little —** encontraron poca resistencia
oppress [əprés] VT oprimir
oppression [əpréʃən] N opresión *f*
oppressive [əprésɪv] ADJ (regime) opresivo; (heat) bochornoso, sofocante
oppressor [əprésɚ] N opresor -ora *mf*
optic [áptɪk] ADJ óptico; N **—s** óptica *f*
optical [áptɪkəł] ADJ óptico; **— character recognition** sistema de reconocimiento óptico de caracteres *m*; **— fiber** fibra óptica *f*; **— illusion** ilusión óptica *f*; **— resolution** resolución óptica *f*
optician [ɑptíʃən] N óptico -ca *mf*
optimal [áptəməł] ADJ óptimo
optimism [áptəmɪzəm] N optimismo *m*
optimist [áptəmɪst] N optimista *mf*
optimistic [ɑptəmístɪk] ADJ optimista
optimize [áptəmaɪz] VT optimizar
option [ápʃən] N opción *f* (also financial); (feature) extra *m*; **to leave one's —s open** no descartar posibilidades
optional [ápʃənł] ADJ opcional, optativo
optometrist [ɑptámɪtrɪst] N optometrista *mf*
optometry [ɑptámɪtri] N optometría *f*
opulence [ápjələns] N opulencia *f*

opulent [ápjələnt] ADJ opulento
or [ɔr] CONJ o; **seven — eight** siete u ocho
OR [operating room] [óár] N quirófano *m*, sala de operaciones *f*
oracle [ɔ́rəkəł] N oráculo *m*
oral [ɔ́rəł] ADJ oral; (hygiene) bucal
orange [ɔ́rɪnʤ] N naranja *f*; **— blossom** azahar *m*; **— grove** naranjal *m*; **— tree** naranjo *m*; ADJ & N anaranjado *m*
orangutan [ərǽŋətæn] N orangután *m*
orator [ɔ́rədə-] N orador -ora *mf*
oratory [ɔ́rətɔri] N (skill in speaking) oratoria *f*; (place for prayer) oratorio *m*
orbit [ɔ́rbɪt] N órbita *f*; VI/VT orbitar
orbital [ɔ́rbɪdl] ADJ orbital
orbiter [ɔ́rbɪdə-] N orbitador *m*
orchard [ɔ́rʧə-d] N huerto *m*; (large) huerta *f*
orchestra [ɔ́rkɪstrə] N orquesta *f*
orchestrate [ɔ́rkɪstret] VT orquestar
orchid [ɔ́rkɪd] N orquídea *f*
ordain [ɔrdén] VT (as minister) ordenar; (with an edict) decretar
ordeal [ɔrdíł] N suplicio *m*, tortura *f*; **— by fire** ordalía de fuego *f*
order [ɔ́rdə-] N (command) orden *f*, mandato *m*; (request, commission) pedido *m*; (sequence, obedience to law) orden *m*; **holy —s** órdenes sagradas *f pl*; **an apology is in —** corresponde una disculpa; **in — to** para; **in working —** en buen estado; **in — that** para que, a fin de que; **on —** encargado; **out of —** no funciona; **to put in —** ordenar; VI/VT (command, arrange) ordenar, mandar; (place an order) pedir
ordering [ɔ́rdə-ɪŋ] N (putting in order) ordenación *f*, ordenamiento *m*
orderly [ɔ́rdə-li] ADJ ordenado; N (military) ordenanza *m*; (hospital) camillero *m*
ordinal [ɔ́rdn̩əł] ADJ ordinal
ordinance [ɔ́rdn̩əns] N ordenanza *f*
ordinary [ɔ́rdn̩eri] ADJ común, corriente, ordinario; **do it the — way** hazlo de la forma habitual
ordination [ɔrdn̩éʃən] N ordenación *f*
ore [ɔr] N mineral *m*
oregano [ərégəno] N orégano *m*
organ [ɔ́rgən] N órgano *m* (also musical instrument)
organic [ɔrgǽnɪk] ADJ orgánico; **— chemistry** química orgánica *f*
organism [ɔ́rgənɪzəm] N organismo *m*
organist [ɔ́rgənɪst] N organista *mf*
organization [ɔrgənɪzéʃən] N organización *f*, planificación *f*
organizational [ɔrgənɪzéʃənl] ADJ organizativo; **— chart** organigrama *m*
organize [ɔ́rgənaɪz] VI/VT organizar[se]
organized [ɔ́rgənaɪzd] ADJ organizado
organizer [ɔ́rgənaɪzə-] N organizador -ora *mf*
organizing [ɔ́rgənaɪzɪŋ] ADJ organizativo
orgy [ɔ́rʤi] N orgía *f*
orient[1] [ɔ́riənt] N oriente *m*
orient[2] [ɔ́rient] VT orientar
oriental [ɔriéntł] ADJ & N oriental *mf*
orientate [ɔ́riɛntet] VT orientar
orientation [ɔriɛntéʃən] N (guidance) orientación *f*; (tendency, leaning) tendencia *f*
orifice [ɔ́rəfɪs] N orificio *m*
origin [ɔ́rəʤɪn] N origen *m*, procedencia *f*; (of a river) naciente *f*, nacimiento *m*
original [əríʤənl] ADJ original, originario; N original *m*
originality [ərɪʤənǽlɪdi] N originalidad *f*
originate [əríʤənet] VI/VT originar[se]
oriole [ɔ́rioł] N oropéndola *f*
Orlon™ [ɔ́rlɑn] N orlón *m*
ornament[1] [ɔ́rnəmənt] N adorno *m*, ornamento *m*
ornament[2] [ɔ́rnəmɛnt] VT adornar, ornamentar
ornamental [ɔrnəméntł] ADJ ornamental
ornamentation [ɔrnəmɪntéʃən] N ornamentación *f*
ornate [ɔrnét] ADJ adornado en exceso; **— style** estilo rebuscado *m*
ornithology [ɔrnəθáləʤi] N ornitología *f*
orphan [ɔ́rfən] ADJ & N huérfano -na *mf*; VT dejar huérfano a
orphanage [ɔ́rfənɪʤ] N orfanato *m*, hospicio *m*
orthodontics [ɔrθədántɪks] N ortodoncia *f*
orthodox [ɔ́rθədɑks] ADJ ortodoxo
orthography [ɔrθágrəfi] N ortografía *f*
oscillate [ásəlet] VI oscilar; VT hacer oscilar
oscillation [asəléʃən] N oscilación *f*
osmosis [azmósɪs] N ósmosis *f*
osprey [áspre] N águila pescadora *f*
ossify [ásəfaɪ] VI osificarse
ostensible [asténsəbəł] ADJ supuesto
ostentation [astɪntéʃən] N ostentación *f*
ostentatious [astɪntéʃəs] ADJ ostentoso
osteoarthritis [astioɑrθráɪdɪs] N osteoartritis *f*
osteoporosis [astiopərósɪs] N osteoporosis *f*
ostracize [ástrəsaɪz] VT aislar
ostrich [ástrɪʧ] N avestruz *m*
OTC [over-the-counter] [ótísí] ADJ extrabursátil
other [áðə-] ADJ, PRON, & N otro -tra *mf*; **— than Bob** salvo Bob; **every — day** cada dos días, un día sí y otro no; **—wise** de otro modo; **—worldly** fantástico
otter [ádə-] N nutria *f*
ouch [aʊʧ] INTERJ ¡ay!
ought [ɔt] V AUX **you — to sit down** deberías sentarte; **we — to get up early** deberíamos levantarnos más temprano
ounce [aʊns] N onza *f*
our [aʊr] POSS ADJ nuestro
ours [aʊrz] ADJ nuestro; **this book is —** este libro es nuestro; **these things are —** estas

cosas son nuestras; PRON el nuestro / la nuestra; **— is bigger** el nuestro / la nuestra es más grande; **a friend of —** un amigo nuestro

ourselves [aʊrsɛ́lvz] PRON **we made the cake — nosotros mismos hicimos la torta; we were sitting by —** estábamos sentados solos; **we look at — in the mirror** nos miramos en el espejo; **we bought — a house** nos compramos una casa

oust [aʊst] VT echar, expulsar

out [aʊt] ADV (outside) fuera; ADJ (turned off, extinguished) apagado; (tennis) fuera; (baseball) out; **— -of-date** pasado de moda, anticuado; N (way out) escape *m*; (baseball) out *m*; PREP **she ran — the door** salió corriendo por la puerta; **they locked me —** me dejaron fuera; **— -and- — criminal** criminal empedernido *m*; **— -and- — refusal** una negativa rotunda; **— of bounds** (golf) fuera de límites; **— of commission/order** fuera de servicio; **— of fashion** pasado de moda; **— of fear** por miedo; **he's really — of it** está ido, está despistado; **— of joint** dislocado; **— of money** sin dinero; **— of print/stock** agotado; **— of touch with** desconectado de; **— of tune** desentonado; **— of work** desempleado; **— to lunch** *fam* chiflado; **made — of** hecho de; **miniskirts are on the way —** las minifaldas se están dejando de usar; **I had it — with him** me peleé con él; **you were —** no estabas; **before the week is —** antes de que termine la semana; **the book is just —** acaba de publicarse el libro; **the secret is —** se ha divulgado el secreto; **we had some, but now we're —** teníamos, pero se nos acabó; **I'm — $10** perdí $10; INTERJ ¡fuera! VT (expel) expulsar; (expose) descubrir; VI **the truth will —** se descubrirá la verdad

outage [áʊdɪʤ] N apagón *m*

outbreak [áʊtbrek] N (of pimples) erupción *f*; (of war) comienzo *m*; (of disease) brote *m*

outburst [áʊtbɜ·st] N (emotional) arrebato *m*; (of tears) ataque *m*; (of violence) motín *m*, explosión *f*

outcast [áʊtkæst] ADJ & N marginado -da *mf*

outcome [áʊtkʌm] N resultado *m*, desenlace *m*

outcry [áʊtkraɪ] N clamor *m*, protesta *f*

outdated [aʊtdéɪdɪd] ADJ anticuado

outdo [aʊtdú] VT superar

outdoor [áʊtdɔr] ADJ al aire libre; **— advertising** publicidad exterior *f*

outdoors [aʊtdɔ́rz] ADV al aire libre, afuera

outer [áʊdɚ] ADJ exterior; **— ear** oído externo *m*; **— space** espacio exterior *m*

outfield [áʊtfild] N jardín *m*

outfielder [áʊtfíldɚ] N jardinero -ra *mf*

outfit [áʊtfɪt] N (gear) equipo *m*; (clothes) conjunto *m*; (soldiers) unidad *f*; VI/VT equipar, habilitar

outfox [aʊtfɑ́ks] VT ser más listo que

outgoing[1] [áʊtgoɪŋ] ADJ (leaving) saliente

outgoing[2] [aʊtgóɪŋ] ADJ (extrovert) extrovertido

outgrow [aʊtgró] VT **she will — her clothes** la ropa le quedará pequeña; **she will — her epilepsy** la epilepsia se le irá con la edad

outing [áʊdɪŋ] N excursión *f*, paseo *m*

outlandish [aʊtlǽndɪʃ] ADJ estrafalario

outlast [aʊtlǽst] VT (last longer than) durar más que; (live longer than) sobrevivir a

outlaw [áʊtlɔ] N bandido -da *mf*, forajido -da *mf*; VT prohibir

outlay[1] [áʊtle] N gasto *m*, desembolso *m*

outlay[2] [aʊtlé] VT gastar, desembolsar

outlet [áʊtlɪt] N (exit) salida *f*; (stream) desagüe *m*, emisario *m*; (store) tienda *f*; (electric connection) toma de corriente *f*; **she needs an — for her talent** necesita canalizar su talento

outline [áʊtlaɪn] N (abstract) bosquejo *m*, esbozo *m*, trazado *m*; (boundary) contorno *m*; VT (summarize) bosquejar, esbozar; (draw) delinear; (plan) trazar

outlook [áʊtlʊk] N perspectiva *f*, panorama *m*

outlying [áʊtlaɪɪŋ] ADJ (marginal) periférico; (distant) remoto

outpatient [áʊtpeʃənt] N paciente ambulatorio -ria *mf*, paciente externo -na *mf*

output [áʊtpʊt] N (production) rendimiento *m*; (computer information) salida *f*; **— device** dispositivo de salida *m*

outrage [áʊtreʤ] N (offense) ultraje *m*, agravio *m*, atropello *m*; (indignation) indignación *f*; VT (offend) ultrajar, agraviar; (enrage) indignar

outrageous [aʊtréʤəs] ADJ (offensive) ultrajante; (exorbitant) exorbitante; (extravagant) extravagante

outreach[1] [áʊtritʃ] N extensión *f*

outreach[2] [aʊtrítʃ] VT exceder

outright[1] [aʊtráɪt] ADV completamente; **he bought it —** lo compró al contado; **he rejected it —** lo rechazó categóricamente

outright[2] [áʊtraɪt] ADJ **— denial** negativa rotunda *f*; **— lie** mentira descarada *f*

outset [áʊtsɛt] N comienzo *m*, principio *m*

outshine [aʊtʃáɪn] VT eclipsar

outside[1] [aʊtsáɪd] ADV fuera, afuera; PREP fuera de

outside[2] [áʊtsaɪd] ADJ (external) exterior; (foreign) foráneo; N exterior *m*; **— chance** posibilidad remota *f*; **— interference** interferencia externa *f*; **in a week, at the —** en una semana, a lo sumo; **to close on the —** cerrar por fuera

outsider [aʊtsáɪdɚ] N forastero -ra *mf*

outskirts [áʊtskɜ·ts] N alrededores *m pl*, afueras

f pl

outsourcing [áʊtsɔrsɪŋ] N contratación externa *f*

outspoken [aʊtspókən] ADJ franco

outstanding [aʊtstǽndɪŋ] ADJ (excellent) sobresaliente, destacado; (pending) pendiente

outstretched [aʊtstrétʃt] ADJ extendido

outward [áʊtwərd] ADJ exterior, externo; **— appearances** apariencias *f pl*; ADV hacia fuera; **— bound** que sale

outweigh [aʊtwé] VT (weigh more) pesar más que; (be more important) sobreponerse a, valer más que

outwit [aʊtwít] VT ser más listo que

oval [óvəł] ADJ oval, ovalado; N óvalo *m*

ovarian [ovériən] ADJ ovárico

ovary [óvəri] N ovario *m*

ovation [ovéʃən] N ovación *f*

oven [ávən] N horno *m*

over [óvər] PREP **— here** acá; **— in Japan** allá en Japón; **— many years** durante muchos años; **— the counter** (medicine) sin receta; (stocks) extrabursátil; **— the sea** al otro lado del mar; **— the hill** viejo; **— there** allá; **an umbrella — his head** un paraguas sobre la cabeza; **I heard it — the radio** lo oí por la radio; **he jumped — the fence** saltó por encima de la cerca; **he is — her in the hierarchy** él está por encima de ella en la jerarquía; **not — one year** no más de un año; **he hit him — the head with a rock** le golpeó en la cabeza con una piedra; **all — the city** por toda la ciudad; **I'm — it** (recovered) me he recuperado; (no longer interested) ya no me interesa; ADV **— again** de nuevo, otra vez; **— against** en contraste con; **— and —** una y otra vez; **—generous** demasiado generoso; **do it —** hazlo de nuevo, hazlo otra vez; **the world —** por todo el mundo; **it is — with** se acabó; INTERJ **— and out** cambio y fuera

overachiever [ovərətʃívər] N (bookish) empollón -ona *mf*; (successful) persona muy exitosa *f*

overactive [ovərǽktɪv] ADJ hiperactivo, demasiado activo

overall [óvərɔł] ADJ global, total; N **—s** mono *m*, overol *m*

overbearing [ovərbérɪŋ] ADJ mandón -ona, dominante

overboard [óvərbɔrd] ADV (into the water) al agua; **she went — on her project** se le fue la mano con su proyecto

overcast [óvərkæst] ADJ nublado, encapotado; **to become —** nublarse, encapotarse

overcharge[1] [ovərtʃárdʒ] VI/VT cobrar demasiado, cobrar de más

overcharge[2] [óvərtʃardʒ] N cobro excesivo *m*

overcoat [óvərkot] N sobretodo *m*, gabán *m*

overcome [ovərkʌ́m] VI/VT (to get the better of) superar; (to overwhelm) embargar; **to be — by weariness** estar agobiado

overcompensate [ovərkámpɪnset] VI sobrecompensar

overcorrection [ovərkərékʃən] N sobrecorrección *f*

overdose [óvərdos] N sobredosis *f*; VI tomar una sobredosis

overdraft [óvərdræft] N sobregiro *m*, descubierto *m*

overdraw [ovərdrɔ́] VI/VT sobregirar[se]

overdrawn [ovərdrɔ́n] ADJ en descubierto, sobregirado

overdrive [óvərdraɪv] N superdirecta *f*

overdue [ovərdú] ADJ (borrowed item) atrasado; (bill) vencido

overeat [ovərít] VI comer en exceso

overestimate [ovəréstɪmet] VT sobreestimar

overexcite [ovərɪksáɪt] VT sobreexcitar

overextended [ovərɪksténdɪd] ADJ sobreextendido

overflow[1] [ovərflǒ] VI desbordar, rebosar

overflow[2] [óvərflo] N desborde *m*

overgrown [ovərgrón] ADJ cubierto, crecido; **— boy** muchacho demasiado crecido para su edad *m*

overhang[1] [ovərhǽŋ] VI (jut) proyectarse; (hang over) estar suspendido

overhang[2] [óvərhæŋ] N saliente *m*

overhaul[1] [óvərhɔł] VT revisar

overhaul[2] [óvərhɔł] N revisión *f*

overhead[1] [óvərhɛd] N gastos generales *m pl*; ADJ elevado; **— projector** retroproyector *m*

overhead[2] [ovərhɛ́d] ADV en lo alto

overhear [ovərhír] VT oír por casualidad

overjoyed [ovərdʒɔ́ɪd] ADJ rebosante de alegría

overkill [óvərkɪł] N exageración *f*

overland [óvərlænd] ADV & ADJ por tierra

overlap[1] [ovərlǽp] VI/VT solapar[se], superponer[se]

overlap[2] [óvərlæp] N traslapo *m*

overlay[1] [ovərlé] VT cubrir; (with gold, etc.) incrustar

overlay[2] [óvərle] N cubierta *f*; (with metal, wood) revestimiento *m*, chapa *f*

overload[1] [ovərlɔ́d] VT sobrecargar, recargar, saturar

overload[2] [óvərlod] N sobrecarga *f*

overlook[1] [ovərlʊ́k] VT (fail to mention) pasar por alto, omitir; (pardon) perdonar; (look from above) mirar desde arriba; (afford a view of) dar a, tener vista a

overlook[2] [óvərlʊk] N mirador *m*

overly [óvərli] ADV excesivamente

overnight[1] [óvərnaɪt] ADJ **— delivery** entrega al otro día *f*; **— guest** invitado -da a dormir *mf*

overnight[2] [ovərnáɪt] ADV **he succeeded —** tuvo éxito de la noche a la mañana

overpass [óvərpæs] N paso elevado *m*

overpower [ovɚ·páuɚ] VT abrumar
overpowering [ovɚ·páuɚ·ɪŋ] ADJ abrumador
overpriced [ovɚ·práɪst] ADJ demasiado caro
overproduction [ovɚ·prədʌ́kʃən] N superproducción *f*
overqualified [ovɚ·kwɑ́ləfaɪd] ADJ sobrecalificado
overreach [ovɚ·ríʧ] VI **to — oneself** abarcar demasiado
overreact [ovɚ·riǽkt] VI reaccionar exageradamente
override [ovɚ·ráɪd] VT anular
overrule [ovɚ·rúɫ] VT anular
overrun[1] [ovɚ·rʌ́n] VT (overflow) desbordar; (exceed) exceder; (invade) infestar
overrun[2] [óvɚ·rʌn] N exceso de costos *m*
overseas [ovɚ·síz] ADV (beyond the sea) en ultramar; (abroad) en el extranjero
oversee [ovɚ·sí] VI (workers) dirigir, supervisar; (accounts) fiscalizar
overseer [óvɚ·sir] N capataz -za *mf*, supervisor -ora *mf*
overshadow [ovɚ·ʃǽdo] VT eclipsar, opacar
overshoe [óvɚ·ʃu] N chanclo *m*
oversight [óvɚ·saɪt] N (mistake) descuido *m*; (act of overseeing workers) supervisión *f*; (act of overseeing accounts) fiscalización *f*
overstep [ovɚ·stép] VT excederse en
overstrike [óvɚ·straɪk] VT imprimir un carácter directamente encima de otro
overt [ovɚ́·t] ADJ evidente
overtake [ovɚ·ték] VT (pass someone) pasar, rebasar; (befall) abatirse sobre
overtax [ovɚ·tǽks] VT (tax too much) gravar excesivamente; (demand too much) exigir demasiado
overthrow[1] [ovɚ·θró] VT derrocar, derribar
overthrow[2] [óvɚ·θro] N derrocamiento *m*
overtime [óvɚ·taɪm] N (in a game) prórroga *f*, tiempo suplementario *m*; (at work) horas extras *f pl*; **to work —** hacer horas extras
overture [óvɚ·tʃɚ] N (musical composition) obertura *f*; (initial move) propuesta *f*
overturn [ovɚ·ʧ́ɚn] VI/VT volcar[se]; VT (a decision) anular; (a government) derrocar
overview [óvɚ·vju] N vista global *f*, panorama *m*
overweight[1] [ovɚ·wét] ADJ **he's —** pesa demasiado
overweight[2] [óvɚ·wet] N sobrepeso *m*
overwhelm [ovɚ·hwɛ́ɫm] VT abrumar, agobiar
overwhelming [ovɚ·hwɛ́ɫmɪŋ] ADJ (responsibility, task) abrumador, agobiante; (victory) arrollador
overwork[1] [ovɚ·wɝ́·k] VI trabajar demasiado; VT hacer trabajar demasiado
overwork[2] [óvɚ·wɝ·k] N exceso de trabajo *m*
overwrite mode [óvɚ·raɪtmod] VT modo de reescritura *m*
ovulate [ávjəlet] VI ovular
ovulation [ɑvjəléʃən] N ovulación *f*
owe [o] VI/VT deber; (a sum) adeudar, deber
owing [óɪŋ] ADJ debido; **— to** debido a
owl [aʊɫ] N lechuza *f*, búho *m*
own [on] ADJ & PRON propio; **— goal** autogol *m*, gol en contra *m*; **a house of his —** una casa suya; **to be on one's —** ser independiente; **to come into one's —** conseguir lo que uno se merece; **to hold one's —** mantenerse firme; VT poseer; **to — up [to]** confesar
owner [ónɚ] N dueño -ña *mf*, propietario -ria *mf*; **— financing** financiamiento por el propietario *m*
ownership [ónɚ·ʃɪp] N propiedad *f*
ox [ɑks] N buey *m*
oxidation [ɑksɪdéʃən] N oxidación *f*
oxidize [ɑ́ksɪdaɪz] VI/VT oxidar[se]
oxygen [ɑ́ksɪʤən] N oxígeno *m*; **— tent** cámara de oxígeno *f*
oyster [ɔ́ɪstɚ] N ostra *f*; (large) ostión *m*
ozone [ózon] N ozono *m*; **— layer** capa de ozono *f*

Pp

pace [pes] N paso *m*; **—maker** marcapasos *m sg*; VT (traverse) ir y venir por; (set the tempo) marcar al paso; (measure) medir a pasos
pacific [pəsɪ́fɪk] ADJ pacífico; **— Ocean** Océano Pacífico *m*
pacification [pæsɪfɪkéʃən] N pacificación *f*
pacifier [pǽsəfaɪɚ] N chupete *m*
pacifism [pǽsəfɪzəm] N pacifismo *m*
pacify [pǽsəfaɪ] VT (a country) pacificar; (a person) apaciguar
pack [pæk] N (of wolves) manada *f*; (of dogs) jauría *f*; (of cigarettes) cajilla *f*, cajetilla *f*; (of cloth) compresa *f*; (of cards) baraja *f*; (of cyclists) pelotón *m*; **— animal** acémila *f*, bestia de carga *f*; **—rat** rata urraca *f*; (person who saves everything) urraca *f*; **a — of lies** una sarta de mentiras *f*; VT empacar, empaquetar; (carry a gun) portar; (crowd) atestar; (load) cargar; **to — off** despachar; **to — one's bags** hacer las maletas
package [pǽkɪʤ] N paquete *m* (also organized vacation); **— deal** (agreement) acuerdo global *m*; (tourism, travel) paquete turístico *m*; VT (gift) empaquetar; (food) envasar
packaging [pǽkɪʤɪŋ] N embalaje *m*, empaque *m*
packer [pǽkɚ] N empacador -ora *mf*, embalador -ora *mf*
packet [pǽkɪt] N paquete *m*
packing [pǽkɪŋ] N embalaje *m*
pact [pækt] N pacto *m*

pad [pæd] N (cushion) almohadilla *f* (also for ink); (block of paper) bloc *m*; (for aircraft) pista *f*; (for spacecraft) plataforma de lanzamiento *f*; VT (stuff with padding) acolchar; (add to dishonestly) rellenar
padding [pǽdɪŋ] N relleno *m*; (cotton) guata *f*; (of a speech) ripio *m*
paddle [pǽdl] N (for rowing) pala *f*, remo *m*; (for mixing, beating, ping-pong) paleta *f*; **—wheel** rueda de paleta *f*; VI (row) remar; VT hacer avanzar remando; (hit) dar una paletada
paddock [pǽdək] N (field) prado *m*; (enclosure at racetrack) paddock *m*
padlock [pǽdlɑk] N candado *m*; VT cerrar con candado
pagan [pégən] ADJ & N pagano -na *mf*
paganism [pégənɪzəm] N paganismo *m*
page [peʤ] N (sheet) hoja *f*, página *f*; (boy servant) paje *m*; (hotel employee) botones *m sg*; **— break** salto de página *m*; VT (number pages) paginar; (call) llamar por altavoz; *Mex* vocear; **to — through** hojear
pageant [pǽʤənt] N (parade) desfile *m*; (show) espectáculo *m*
pager [péʤɚ] N buscapersonas *m sg*
paid [ped] ADJ pagado; **—-up** liberado, totalmente pagado, pago
paid [ped] *see* pay
pail [peɫ] N balde *m*, cubeta *f*
pain [pen] N dolor *m*; (suffering) sufrimiento *m*; **—killer** analgésico *m*; **on — of** so pena de; **to take —s** esmerarse; **he's a —** es un chinche; ADJ **—staking** esmerado; VT (physical) doler; (mental) apenar
painful [pénfəɫ] ADJ (hurting) doloroso; (distressing) penoso; (difficult) arduo
painless [pénlɪs] ADJ sin dolor, indoloro
paint [pent] N (substance) pintura *f*; (spotted horse) pinto *m*; **—brush** (for art) pincel *m*; (for a house) brocha *f*; VI/VT pintar; **to — the town red** irse de juerga
painter [péntɚ] N pintor -ora *mf*
painting [péntɪŋ] N pintura *f*
pair [pɛr] N par *m*; (married couple) pareja *f*; **a — of scissors** unas tijeras, una tijera; VI/VT aparear[se], emparejar[se]; **to — off** aparearse
pajamas [pəʤǽməz] N pijama/piyama *mf*
Pakistan [pǽkɪstæn] N Paquistán *m*
Pakistani [pǽkɪstǽni] ADJ & N paquistano -na *mf*
pal [pæɫ] N compañero -ra *mf*, compadre *m*, comadre *f*
palace [pǽlɪs] N palacio *m*
palate [pǽlɪt] N paladar *m*
palatial [pəléʃəɫ] ADJ suntuoso
Palau [pɑláʊ] N Paláu *m*
pale [peɫ] ADJ pálido, macilento; N **beyond the —** inaceptable; VI palidecer
paleness [péɫnɪs] N palidez *f*
paleontology [peliəntɑ́ləʤi] N paleontología *f*
Palestine [pǽlɪstaɪn] N Palestina *f*
Palestinian [pæləstínɪən] ADJ palestino; N palestino -na *mf*
palette [pǽlɪt] N paleta *f*
palisade [pǽlɪséd] N empalizada *f*; **—s** acantilados *m pl*
pall [pɔɫ] VT (cover with a cloth) cubrir con un paño mortuorio; (satiate) hartar; VI (tire) cansar; N paño mortuorio *m*; **—bearer** portador del féretro *m*; **to cast a — on** empañar
palliative [pǽliəɪv] N paliativo *m*
pallid [pǽlɪd] ADJ pálido
pallor [pǽlɚ] N palidez *f*
palm [pɑm] N (part of hand) palma *f*; (tree) palmera *f*, palma *f*; **— Sunday** Domingo de Ramos *m*; **—top computer** *Am* computadora de mano *f*, *Sp* ordenador de mano *m*; VT (hide in palm) escamotear; **to — something off on someone** encajar algo a alguien
palpable [pǽɫpəbəɫ] ADJ (perceptible) palpable; (tangible) tangible
palpitate [pǽɫpɪtet] VI palpitar
palpitation [pæɫpɪtéʃən] N palpitación *f*
palsy [pɑ́ɫzi] N parálisis *f*
paltry [pɔ́ɫtri] ADJ miserable, despreciable
pamper [pǽmpɚ] VT mimar, consentir
pamphlet [pǽmflɪt] N (informative) folleto *m*; (political) panfleto *m*
pan [pæn] N (for boiling) cazuela *f*, cacerola *f*, cazo *m*; (for frying) sartén *f*; (for baking) molde *m*; **—handle** mango de sartén *m*; **—handler** pordiosero -ra *mf*; VT criticar duramente; VI **to — for gold** extraer oro; **to — out** dar buen resultado; **to —handle** mendigar, pordiosear
panacea [pænəsíə] N panacea *f*
Panama [pǽnəmɑ] N Panamá *f*
Panamanian [pænəméniən] ADJ & N panameño -ña *mf*
Pan-American [pænəmérɪkən] ADJ panamericano
pancake [pǽnkek] N panqueque *m*; **flat as a —** chato como una tabla
pancreas [pǽnkrɪəs] N páncreas *m*
panda [pǽndə] N panda *m*
pandemic [pændémɪk] ADJ pandémico *m*; N pandemia *f*
pander [pǽndɚ] VI consentir
pane [pen] N vidrio *m*, cristal *m*
panel [pǽnl] N (wall) revestimiento *m*; (group of experts) panel *m*; (of instruments) tablero *m*; VT revestir con paneles
paneling [pǽnlɪŋ] N (wall) panel *m*
pang [pæŋ] N (sharp pain, hunger) punzada *f*; (anguish) remordimientos *m pl*

panic [pǽnɪk] ADJ & N pánico *m*; ADJ **—-stricken** sobrecogido de pánico
panorama [pænərǽmə] N panorama *m*
panoramic [pænərǽmɪk] ADJ panorámico
pansy [pǽnzi] N pensamiento *m*
pant [pænt] VI jadear
panther [pǽnθə˞] N pantera *f*
panties [pǽntiz] N *Sp* bragas *f pl*; *Mex* pantaletas *f pl*; *RP* bombacha *f*
pantomime [pǽntəmaɪm] N pantomima *f*
pantry [pǽntri] N despensa *f*, alacena *f*
pants [pænts] N pantalones *m pl*, pantalón *m*
pantyhose [pǽntihoz] N panty *m*
papa [pápə] N papá *m*
papacy [pépəsi] N papado *m*
papal [pépəł] ADJ papal
papaya [pəpáɪə] N papaya *f*; *Cuba* fruta bomba *f*
paper [pépə˞] N (material) papel *m*; (newspaper) periódico *m*; (assignment) trabajo *m*; (oral contribution) comunicación *f*; (written contribution) artículo *m*; **—back** libro en rústica *m*; **— clip** clip *m*, sujetapapeles *m sg*; **— cutter** guillotina *f*; **— feeder** alimentador de hojas *m*; **— money** papel moneda *m*; **—s** papeles *m pl*; **— shredder** trituradora *f*; **—weight** pisapapeles *m sg*; **—work** (forms) papeleo *m*; (procedures) trámites *m pl*; **on —** por escrito; VI/VT empapelar
paprika [pæpríka] N pimentón *m*, páprika *f*
pap smear [pǽp smir] N citología *f*
Papua New Guinea [pǽpjuənugíni] N Papúa Nueva Guinea *f*
Papua New Guinean [pǽpjuənugíniən] ADJ & N papú *mf*
par [pɑr] N (financial) paridad *f*; (in golf) par *m*; **— value** valor nominal *m*; **at —** a la par; **below —** bajo par; **to be on a — with** estar en pie de igualdad con; **to feel above —** sentirse mejor que lo normal; VT hacer el par
parachute [pǽrəʃut] N paracaídas *m sg*
parachuting [pǽrəʃuɪŋ] N paracaidismo *m*
parachutist [pǽrəʃuɪst] N paracaidista *mf*
parade [pəréd] N (procession) desfile *m*; (military review) parada *f*; **— ground** campo de maniobras *m*; VI desfilar; VT hacer ostentación de
paradigm [pǽrədaɪm] N paradigma *m*
paradise [pǽrədaɪs] N paraíso *m*
paradox [pǽrədɑks] N paradoja *f*
paradoxical [pǽrədɑ́ksɪkəł] ADJ paradójico
paraffin [pǽrəfɪn] N parafina *f*
paragraph [pǽrəgræf] N párrafo *m*; VT dividir en párrafos
Paraguay [pǽrəgwaɪ] N Paraguay *m*
Paraguayan [pǽrəgwáɪən] ADJ & N paraguayo -ya *mf*
parakeet [pǽrəkit] N perico *m*, periquito *m*
parallel [pǽrəlɛł] ADJ & N paralelo *m*; (geometry) paralela *f*; **— port** puerto paralelo *m*; VT (run equidistant from) correr paralelo a; (compare) comparar
paralysis [pərǽləsɪs] N (of the body) parálisis *f*; (of a transportation system) paralización *f*
paralytic [pǽrəlɪ́tɪk] ADJ paralítico -ca
paralyze [pǽrəlaɪz] VT paralizar
paramedic [pǽrəméɪdɪk] ADJ & N paramédico -ca *mf*
parameter [pərǽmɪtə˞] N parámetro *m*
paramilitary [pǽrəmílɪtɛri] ADJ & N paramilitar *mf*
paramount [pǽrəmaʊnt] ADJ supremo, sumo
paranoia [pǽrənɔ́ɪə] N paranoia *f*
paranoid [pǽrənɔɪd] ADJ & N paranoico -ca *mf*; **— delusion** delirio paranoico *m*
paranormal [pǽrənɔ́rməł] ADJ paranormal
paraphernalia [pǽrəfənélja˙] N parafernalia *f*
paraphrase [pǽrəfrez] N paráfrasis *f*; VI/VT parafrasear
paraplegic [pǽrəplíʤɪk] ADJ N parapléjico -ca *mf*
parapsychology [pǽrəsaɪkɑ́ləʤi] N parapsicología *f*
parasite [pǽrəsaɪt] N parásito *m*
parasitic [pǽrəsíɪtɪk] ADJ parasítico; **— disease** enfermedad parasitaria *f*
parasol [pǽrəsɔł] N parasol *m*, sombrilla *f*
paratroops [pǽrətrups] N tropas paracaidistas *f pl*
parcel [pɑ́rsəł] N (package) paquete *m*; (lot) partida *f*; (land) parcela *f*; **— post** paquete postal *m*; VT (land) parcelar; **to — out** repartir
parch [pɑrtʃ] VT secar; **I'm —ed** estoy muerto de sed
parchment [pɑ́rtʃmənt] N pergamino *m*
pardon [pɑ́rdn̩] N perdón *m*, gracia *f*; (legal) indulto *m*; **I beg your —** perdone; VT perdonar, disculpar; (legally) indultar
pare [pɛr] VT mondar, pelar; **to — down expenditures** reducir gastos
parent [pɛ́rənt] N padre *m*, madre *f*; **— directory** directorio padre *m*; **—s** padres *m pl*
parental [pərɛ́ntł] ADJ parental; **— control** control paternal *m*
parenthesis [pərɛ́nθəsɪs] N paréntesis *m*
parenting [pɛ́rəntɪŋ] N **— guide** guía para padres *f*; **— skill** habilidad para educar a los hijos *f*; **good —** buena crianza de los hijos *f*
pariah [pəráɪə] N paria *mf*
parish [pǽrɪʃ] N parroquia *f*; **— priest** [cura] párroco *m*
parishioner [pəríʃənə˙] N feligrés -esa *mf*, parroquiano -na *mf*
parity [pǽrɪɪ́ɪ] N paridad *f*
park [pɑrk] N parque *m*; (for baseball) estadio de béisbol *m*; VI/VT estacionar, aparcar
parking [pɑ́rkɪŋ] N estacionamiento *m*,

aparcamiento *m*; **— lot** estacionamiento *m*, aparcamiento *m*; **— place** lugar de estacionamiento/aparcamiento *m*

Parkinson's disease [párkɪnsənzdɪziz] N enfermedad de Parkinson *f*

parlance [párləns] N habla *f*

parley [párli] N (peace negotiation) parlamento *m*; (discussion) discusión *f*; VI parlamentar

parliament [párləmənt] N parlamento *m*

parliamentary [parləméntri] ADJ parlamentario

parlor [párlɚ] N sala *f*, salón *m*; **— game** juego de salón *m*; **beauty —** salón de belleza *m*

parochial [pərókiəl] ADJ (of a parish) parroquial; (provincial) pueblerino

parody [pǽrədi] N parodia *f*; VT parodiar

parole [pərół] N libertad condicional *f*; VT poner en libertad condicional

parrot [pǽrət] N loro *m*, papagayo *m*; VT repetir como loro

parry [pǽri] VT (a blow) parar; (a remark) eludir; N parada *f*

parse [pars] VT analizar

parser [pársɚ] N analizador *m*

parsing [pársɪŋ] N análisis *m*

parsley [pársli] N perejil *m*

parsnip [pársnɪp] N chirivía *f*

parson [pársən] N pastor -ora *mf*

part [pɑrt] N (component) parte *f*; (role) papel *m*; (in hair) raya *f*; **— and parcel** parte esencial *f*; **— time** tiempo parcial *m*; **in foreign —s** en el extranjero; **spare —s** piezas de repuesto *f pl*, repuestos *m pl*; ADJ **— -time** a tiempo parcial; VI/VT (cut into parts) partir[se]; (divide into parts) dividir[se]; (separate, leave) separar[se]; **to — company** separarse; **to — one's hair** hacerse la raya; **to — with** desprenderse de

partake [parték] VI **to — in** participar; **to — of** (share) compartir; (eat) comer

partial [párʃəl] ADJ parcial

participant [partísəpənt] ADJ & N participante *mf*, partícipe *mf*

participate [partísəpet] VI participar

participation [partɪsəpéʃən] N participación *f*

participle [párdɪsɪpəl] N participio *m*

particle [párdɪkəl] N partícula *f*; **— board** aglomerado *m*

particular [pɚtíkjəlɚ] ADJ particular; (fussy) quisquilloso; N **in —** en particular; **—s** particulares *m pl*

parting [párdɪŋ] N (farewell) despedida *f*; (separation) separación *f*; **— of the ways** encrucijada *f*

partisan [párdɪzən] N (supporter) partidario -ria *mf*, partidista *mf*; (guerrilla) partisano -na *mf*; ADJ (of supporters) partidario, partidista; (of guerrillas) de partisanos

partition [pɑrtíʃən] N (distribution) reparto *m*; (division) división *f*, partición *f*; (wall) tabique *m*, mampara *f*; VT (distribute) repartir; (divide) dividir; (divide with a wall) tabicar

partly [pártli] ADV en parte

partner [pártnɚ] N (in business) socio -cia *mf*; (in an activity) compañero -ra *mf*; (in dancing, sports, marriage) pareja *f*

partnership [pártnɚʃɪp] N (business) sociedad *f*; (relationship) asociación *f*

partridge [pártrɪʤ] N perdiz *f*

party [párdi] N (get-together) fiesta *f*; (political group) partido *m*; (group of people) partida *f*; (litigant) parte *f*; **— of four** mesa para cuatro *f*; **— animal** fiestero -ra *mf*, parrandero -ra *mf*; VI ir de juerga

pass [pæs] VI (to go by) pasar; **to — a kidney stone** expulsar un cálculo renal; **to — away** fallecer; **to — for** pasar por; **to — in review** pasar revista; **to — on** (die) fallecer; (approve) aceptar; (refuse) no querer; **to — out** desmayarse; **to — over** pasar por alto; **to — up an opportunity** dejar pasar una oportunidad; VT (a ball) pasar; (a law) aprobar; (an exam, test) aprobar; **to — judgment** juzgar; **to — oneself off as** hacerse pasar por; **— me the salt** pásame la sal, alcánzame la sal; N (road through mountains) paso *m*; (motion, permission) pase *m*; (for transportation) abono *m*; (over a surface) pasada *f*; (on an exam) aprobación *f*; (of a ball) pase *m*; **—key** llave maestra *f*; **—port** pasaporte *m*; **—word** contraseña *f*, clave de seguridad *f*; **—word protected** protegido por contraseña; **he made a — at her** trató de ligar con ella

passable [pǽsəbəl] ADJ (penetrable) transitable; (mediocre) pasable

passage [pǽsɪʤ] N (fare, musical or textual phrase, alley) pasaje *m*; (passing of time) paso *m*, transcurso *m*; (hallway in a house) pasillo *m*; (secret pathway) pasadizo *m*; (crossing) travesía *f*; (approval of a bill) aprobación *f*; **—way** (corridor) corredor *m*, pasillo *m*; (alley) pasaje *m*

passenger [pǽsənʤɚ] N pasajero -ra *mf*

passerby [pǽsə·baɪ] N transeúnte *mf*, viandante *mf*

passing [pǽsɪŋ] N fallecimiento *m*; ADJ **each — day** cada día que pasa; **— grade** nota de aprobado *f*; **— fancy** capricho pasajero *m*; **— mention** mención al pasar *f*; **— shot** pasante *m*

passion [pǽʃən] N pasión *f*

passionate [pǽʃənɪt] ADJ apasionado

passive [pǽsɪv] ADJ pasivo; N pasiva *f*

past [pæst] ADJ pasado; **— due** en mora, vencido; **— participle** participio pasado *m*; **— perfect** pluscuamperfecto *m*; **— peformance** rendimiento previo *m*; **—**

precedents precedentes anteriores *m pl*; **— tense** tiempo pretérito *m*; **the — president** el expresidente; PREP **— hope** más allá de toda esperanza; **— noon** después de mediodía; **the house — the store** la casa pasando la tienda; **we went — the tower** pasamos al lado de la torre; **half — two** las dos y media; **a woman — forty** una mujer de más de cuarenta años; ADV **for some time —** desde hace algún tiempo; **they drove —** pasaron en coche; N (time) pasado *m*; (tense) pretérito *m*

pasta [pústə] N pasta *f*

paste [pest] N (soft material, puree) pasta *f*; (glue) engrudo *m*; **—board** cartón *m*; VT pegar

pastel [pæstél] ADJ & N pastel *m*

pasteurize [pǽstʃəraɪz] VT pasterizar/pasteurizar

pastime [pǽstaɪm] N pasatiempo *m*

pastor [pǽstɚ] N pastor -ora *mf*

pastoral [pǽstɚəl] ADJ (literary) pastoril; (ecclesiastical) pastoral; N pastoral *f*; (literary work) égloga *f*

pastry [pésɪtri] N (in general) pastelería *f*; (specific) pastel *m*; **— cook** pastelero -ra *mf*, repostero -ra *mf*; **— shop** pastelería *f*, repostería *f*

pasture [pǽstʃɚ] N (grassland) prado *m*; (grass) pasto *m*; (for horses) potrero *m*; VI/VT pastar, pacer, apacentar

pasty [pésti] ADJ pastoso

pat [pæt] ADJ banal; **down —** al dedillo; **to stand —** mantenerse firme; VI/VT dar palmaditas [a]; N palmadita *f*; N **— of butter** porción de mantequilla *f*

patch [pætʃ] N (piece of cloth to repair clothes) remiendo *m*, parche *m* (also for eye, computer); (spot or area, as of ice) tramo [con hielo] *m*; (plot) parcela *f*; VT (repair) remendar; **to — up a quarrel** hacer las paces

patent [pǽtnt] ADJ (evident) patente; (protected by patent) patentado; **— leather** charol *m*; N patente *f*; **— pending** patente en trámite; VT patentar

paternal [pətɝ́nl] ADJ (fatherly) paternal; (of the father's lineage) paterno

paternity [pətɝ́nɪdi] N paternidad *f*; **— test** prueba de paternidad *f*

path [pæθ] N (walkway) senda *f*, sendero *m*; (on a computer) ruta *f*; (of a projectile, storm) trayectoria *f*; **—way** senda *f*, sendero *m*

pathetic [pəθéɛɪk] ADJ (moving) patético; (contemptible) lamentable

pathogen [pǽθəʤən] N patógeno *m*

pathology [pæθáləʤi] N patología *f*

pathos [péθɑs] N patetismo *m*

patience [péʃəns] N paciencia *f*

patient [péʃənt] ADJ & N paciente *mf*

patiently [péʃəntli] ADJ con paciencia

patriarch [pétriɑrk] N patriarca *m*

patriarchal [petriɑ́rkəl] ADJ patriarcal

patrimonial [pætrɪmóniəl] ADJ patrimonial

patrimony [pǽtrəmoni] N patrimonio *m*

patriot [pétriət] N patriota *mf*

patriotic [petriɑ́ɑɪk] ADJ patriótico

patriotism [pétriətɪzəm] N patriotismo *m*

patrol [pətról] VI/VT patrullar, rondar; N patrulla *f*, ronda *f*; **— car** patrullero *m*; **—man** patrullero *m*

patron [pétrən] N (customer) cliente -ta *mf*; (benefactor) benefactor -ora *mf*, mecenas *mf*; (saint) patrono *m*

patronage [pétrənɪʤ] N (support of an artist) mecenazgo *m*; (clientele) clientela *f*; (political) clientelismo *m*; **we appreciate your —** agradecemos su preferencia

patronize [pǽtrənaɪz] VT (be condescending) tratar con condescendencia; (do business with) frecuentar

patter [pǽɚ] VI (strike lightly) golpetear; (chatter) parlotear; N (small blows) golpeteo *m*; (chatter) parloteo *m*

pattern [pǽɚn] N (for sewing) molde *m*; (for drawing) plantilla *f*; (of behavior) patrón *m*; VI/VT **to — something after** modelar algo a imitación de, basarse en el modelo de; **to — oneself after** seguir el ejemplo de

paucity [pɔ́sɪdi] N escasez *f*

paunch [pɔntʃ] N panza *f*, barriga *f*

pause [pɔz] N pausa *f*; VI (while talking) hacer pausa; (while moving) detenerse

pave [pev] VT (with asphalt) pavimentar; (with bricks) enladrillar; (with flagstones) enlosar; **to — the way for** preparar el camino para

pavement [pévmənt] N (roadway) calzada *f*; (of asphalt) pavimento *m*; (of bricks) enladrillado *m*; (of flagstones) enlosado *m*

pavilion [pəvíljən] N pabellón *m*

paw [pɔ] N pata *f*; (with claws) garra *f*; VT (touch with paw) tocar con la pata; (touch with claws) dar zarpazos; (grope) manosear

pawn [pɔn] N (object left in deposit) prenda *f*; (chess piece) peón *m*; (puppet) títere *m*; **—broker** prestamista *mf*; **—shop** casa de empeños *f*, monte de piedad *m*; **in —** en prenda; VT empeñar, dejar en prenda

pay [pe] VT (remit) pagar; VI (be profitable) ser provechoso, convenir; (be worthwhile) valer la pena; **to — attention** prestar atención, fijarse en; **to — back** (return) restituir; (retaliate) vengarse; **to — a compliment** hacer un cumplido; **to — homage** rendir homenaje; **to — one's respects** saludar; **to — off a debt** cancelar una deuda, amortizar una deuda; **to — out** desembolsar, pagar; **to — a visit** hacer una visita; **to — through the nose** pagar demasiado; **I will — for**

your meal te pago la comida; N (payment) pago *m*; (wages) paga *f*, salario *m*; **—back** (payment) restitución *f*; (revenge) venganza *f*; **—check** cheque del sueldo *m*; **— cut** recorte salarial *m*; **—day** día de pago *m*; **— freeze** congelación salarial *f*; **—load** carga útil *f*; **—off** (pay) pago *m*; (reward) recompensa *f*; (bribe) soborno *m*; **— phone** teléfono público *m*; **— raise** aumento salarial / de sueldo *m*; **—roll** nómina *f*, planilla *f*; **— scale** escala salarial *f*; **to hit —dirt** encontrar una mina de oro

payable [péəbəł] ADJ pagadero

payee [peí] N tenedor -ora *mf*, beneficiario -ria *mf*

payment [pémənt] N pago *m*, abono *m*; **— in full** liquidación *f*; **car —s** cuotas del coche *f pl*

payola [peólə] N soborno *m*

PC [písí] N (personal computer) PC *m*; (political correctness) lo políticamente correcto; ADJ (politically correct) políticamente correcto

pea [pi] N guisante *m*; *Am* arveja *f*; **—nut** *Sp* cacahuete *m*; *Mex* cacahuate *m*; *Am* maní *m*; **—nut butter** *Sp* crema de cacahuete *f*; *Mex* crema de cacahuate *f*; *Am* manteca/mantequilla de maní *f*

peace [pis] N paz *f*; **— officer** oficial de policía *m*; **— of mind** serenidad *f*; **at —** en paz; **to keep the —** mantener el orden público; **to hold one's —** callar

peaceful [písfəł] ADJ pacífico, tranquilo

peach [pitʃ] N durazno *m*; *Sp* melocotón *m*; (nice thing or person) delicia *f*, monada *f*; **— tree** durazno *m*, duraznero *m*, *Sp* melocotonero *m*

peacock [píkak] N pavo real *m*, pavón *m*

peak [pik] N (of a mountain) pico *m*, cumbre *f*; (of production, of one's abilities) punto máximo *m*; (of one's career) punto culminante *m*; **— load** carga máxima *f*; **— season** temporada alta *f*; **— time** hora punta *f*

peal [pił] N (of bells) repique *m*; (of laughter) carcajada *f*; VI/VT repicar

pear [per] N pera *f*; **— tree** peral *m*

pearl [pɜł] N perla *f*; **— necklace** collar de perlas *m*

pearly [pɜ́li] ADJ (color) nacarado, perlado; (with pearls) perlado; **the — gates** las puertas del cielo

peasant [pézənt] ADJ & N campesino -na *mf*

peat [pit] N turba *f*

pebble [pébəł] N guijarro *m*, piedrecilla *f*; (smooth) canto *m*

pecan [pɪkán] N pacana *f*

peccary [pékəri] N pecarí/pécari *m*

peck [pek] VI/VT (strike with beak) picar; (eat bit by bit) picotear; (kiss) dar un besito; **—ing order** jerarquía *f*; **to — a hole** agujerear a picotazos; N (quick stroke) picotazo *m*; (kiss) besito *m*; (measure) medida de áridos [9 litros] *f*; **you're in a — of trouble** estás metido en un lío

pectoral [péktə-əł] ADJ & N pectoral *m*

peculiar [pɪkjúljə-] ADJ peculiar, particular

peculiarity [pɪkjuljǽrɪdi] N peculiaridad *f*

pedagogical [pɛdəgɑ́dʒɪkəł] ADJ pedagógico

pedagogue [pédəgɑg] N pedagogo -ga *mf*

pedagogy [pédəgɑdʒi] N pedagogía *f*

pedal [pédl] N pedal *m*; VI/VT pedalear

pedant [pédnt] N pedante *mf*

pedantic [pədǽntɪk] ADJ pedante

peddle [pédl] VI/VT ir vendiendo de puerta en puerta; **to — gossip** repartir chismes

peddler [pédlə-] N buhonero -ra *mf*, mercachifle *m*

pederast [pédərǽst] N pederasta *m*

pederasty [pédərǽsti] N pederastia *f*

pedestal [pédɪstł] N pedestal *m*

pedestrian [pədéstriən] N peatón -ona *mf*; ADJ pedestre

pediatrician [pɪdiətríʃən] N pediatra *mf*

pediatrics [pɪdɪǽtrɪks] N pediatría *f*

pedigree [pédəgri] N (of persons) linaje *m*; (of animals) pedigrí *m*

pedophile [pédəfaił] N pedófilo -la *mf*

pedophilia [pɛdəfíliə] N pedofilia *f*

pee [pi] VI *fam* hacer pipí; N *fam* pipí *m*

peek [pik] VI atisbar; N atisbo *m*

peel [pił] VI/VT (fruit, tree) pelar[se], descortezar[se]; (paint) descascarar[se]; **to keep one's eyes —ed** mantener los ojos abiertos; N cáscara *f*

peeler [pílə-] N pelador *m*

peep [pip] VI/VT (begin to appear) asomar[se]; VI (make sound of chicks) piar; **to — at** atisbar; N (look) atisbo *m*; (sound of chicks) pío *m*; **—hole** mirilla *f*

peer [pir] N par *m* (also nobleman); **— group** grupo paritario *m*; VI (look attentively) escudriñar; (peep out) asomar

peerless [pírlɪs] ADJ incomparable, sin par

peeve [piv] VT irritar; **to get —d** ponerse de mal humor; N cosa que irrita *f*

peevish [pívɪʃ] ADJ malhumorado

peg [peg] N percha *f*; (on violin) clavija *f*; **to take a person down a —** bajarle los humos a alguien; VT (fix with pegs) clavar, clavetear; (set a price) fijar

pejorative [pɪdʒɔ́rədɪv] ADJ peyorativo, despectivo

pelican [pélɪkən] N pelícano *m*

pellet [pélɪt] N (ball) bola *f*, bolita *f*; (shot) perdigón *m*

pell-mell [pélmél] ADJ confuso, tumultuoso; ADV a troche y moche

pelt [pełt] N piel *f*, pellejo *m*; VI/VT acribillar; **to — with stones** apedrear

pelvis [pélvɪs] N pelvis *f*

pen [pɛn] N (fountain) pluma *f*; (ballpoint) bolígrafo *m*; (for pigs) pocilga *f*; (for sheep) redil *m*; (for cows) corral *m*; — **holder** mango de pluma *m*, portaplumas *m sg*; — **name** seudónimo *m*; VT (write) escribir; (shut in) acorralar, encerrar; — **computer** *Am* bolígrafo-computadora portátil *f*, *Sp* bolígrafo-ordenador portátil *m*

penal [pínl̩] ADJ penal

penalize [pénəlaɪz] VT penar; (in sports) penalizar

penalty [pénl̩ti] N (punishment) pena *f*, castigo *m*; (forfeiture) multa *f*; (in sports) penalidad *f*, infracción *f*; — **area** (in soccer) área de penales *f*; — **kick** (in soccer) tiro de penalidad *f*, penalti *m*; — **shootout** (in soccer) definición por penales *f*; — **stroke** (in golf) golpe de penalidad *m*

penance [pénəns] N penitencia *f*

pencil [pénsəl] N (writing instrument) lápiz *m*; (beam of light) haz *m*; — **sharpener** sacapuntas *m sg*

pendant [péndənt] ADJ pendiente

pendent [péndənt] N colgante *m*; ADJ pendiente

pending [péndɪŋ] ADJ pendiente; PREP — **his arrival** hasta que llegue, mientras no llegue

pendulum [péndʒələm] N péndulo *m*

penetrate [pénɪtret] VT penetrar

penetrating [pénɪtreɪdɪŋ] ADJ penetrante

penetration [pɛnɪtréʃən] N penetración *f*

penguin [pénɡwɪn] N pingüino *m*

penicillin [pɛnɪsílɪn] N penicilina *f*

peninsula [pənínsələ] N península *f*

penis [pínɪs] N pene *m*

penitent [pénɪtənt] ADJ & N penitente *mf*

penitentiary [pɛnɪténʃəri] N penitenciaría *f*, penal *m*

penmanship [pénmənʃɪp] N escritura *f*, caligrafía *f*

pennant [pénənt] N banderín *m*, gallardete *m*

penniless [pénɪlɪs] ADJ pobre, sin dinero

penny [péni] N centavo *m*; —**-pincher** tacaño -ña *mf*; **to cost a pretty** — costar un dineral

pension [pénʃən] N (paid to a worker) jubilación *f*; (paid to a worker's survivors) pensión *f*; — **fund** caja de jubilaciones *f*; VT jubilar, pensionar

pensioner [pénʃənɚ] N pensionista *mf*

pensive [pénsɪv] ADJ pensativo

pent [pɛnt] ADJ encerrado; —**-up** acumulado

pentagon [péntəɡɑn] N pentágono *m*

penthouse [pénthaʊs] N penthouse *m*

penultimate [pɪnʌ́ltəmɪt] ADJ penúltimo

people [pípəl] N gente *f*; (national group) pueblo *m*; VT poblar

pep [pɛp] N energía *f*; VI **to — up** animar

pepper [pépɚ] N (black) pimienta *f*; (green) pimiento *m*; (plant, shaker) pimentero *m*; —**mint** menta *f*; VT pimentar; **to — with bullets** acribillar a balazos

peptic ulcer [péptɪk ʌ́lsɚ] N úlcera péptica *f*

per [pɝ] PREP (for each) por; (according to) según; — **capita** per capita; —**cent** por ciento; — **diem** *Am* viático *m*, *Sp* dieta *f*

percale [pɚkét] N percal *m*

perceive [pɚsív] VT percibir

percentage [pɚsɛ́ntɪdʒ] N porcentaje *m*

percentile [pɚsɛ́ntaɪl] N percentil *m*

perceptible [pɚséptəbəl] ADJ perceptible

perception [pɚsépʃən] N percepción *f*

perceptive [pɚséptɪv] ADJ (pertaining to perception) perceptivo; (having keen perception) perspicaz

perch [pɝtʃ] N (rod for birds) percha *f*; (type of fish) perca *f*; VT (alight) posarse; VI/VT (set) encaramar[se]

percolate [pɝ́kəlet] VI/VT filtrar[se]

percussion [pɚkʌ́ʃən] N percusión *f*

perdition [pɚdíʃən] N perdición *f*

perennial [pərɛ́niəl] ADJ perenne; — **plant** planta perenne *f*

perfect[1] [pɝ́fɪkt] ADJ perfecto; **a — stranger** un completo desconocido

perfect[2] [pɚfékt] VT perfeccionar

perfection [pɚfékʃən] N perfección *f*

perfectionist [pɚfékʃənɪst] N perfeccionista *mf*

perfectly [pɝ́fɪktli] ADV (completely) totalmente; (without error) a la perfección, perfectamente; **stand — still** no te muevas

perforate [pɝ́fəret] VI/VT perforar[se]; VT calar

perforation [pɚfəréʃən] N perforación *f*

perform [pɚfɔ́rm] VT (a task) ejecutar, realizar; (a rite, ceremony) celebrar; (a contract) cumplir; (a play) representar; VI (give a performance) actuar; (play music) interpretar; (function) funcionar; (do well) rendir; **to — simultaneously** simultanear

performance [pɚfɔ́rməns] N (of a task) ejecución *f*; (of a ceremony) celebración *f*; (of a contract) cumplimiento *m*; (of a device) desempeño *m*, rendimiento *m*; (of a play) representación *f*; (of an actor) actuación *f*; (of music) interpretación *f*; — **review** evaluación del rendimiento *f*

performer [pɚfɔ́rmɚ] N (drama) artista *mf*, actor *m*, actriz *f*; (music) artista *mf*, intérprete *mf*

perfume[1] [pɝ́fjum] N perfume *m*

perfume[2] [pɚfjúm] VT perfumar

perfumery [pɚfjúməri] N (store) perfumería *f*; (collection) perfumes *m pl*

perhaps [pɚhǽps] ADV tal vez, quizá[s], acaso

peril [pɛ́rəl] N peligro *m*

perilous [pɛ́rələs] ADJ peligroso

perimeter [pərímɪtɚ] N perímetro *m*

period [pírɪəd] N período *m*; (historical) época *f*; (punctuation) punto *m*; (menstruation) período *m*, regla *f*; **you can't go, —!** no

puedes ir, y sanseacabó; **within a — of ten days** en el término de diez días

periodic [pɪriɑ́dɪk] ADJ periódico; **— table** tabla periódica *f*

periodical [pɪriɑ́dɪkəł] ADJ periódico; N revista *f*

peripheral [pərífə-əł] ADJ & N periférico *m*; **— vision** visión periférica *f*

periphery [pərífəri] N periferia *f*

periscope [pérɪskop] N periscopio *m*

perish [pérɪʃ] VI perecer

perishable [pérɪʃəbəł] ADJ perecedero

peritonitis [pɛrɪtnáɪdɪs] N peritonitis *f*

perjure [pɝ́ʤə-] VI **to — oneself** perjurarse, jurar en falso

perjury [pɝ́ʤəri] N perjurio *m*

perks [pɝ-ks] N beneficios adicionales *m pl*

permanence [pɝ́mənəns] N permanencia *f*

permanent [pɝ́mənənt] ADJ permanente; (of a position) titular

permeable [pɝ́miəbəł] ADJ permeable

permeate [pɝ́miet] VI/VT permear

permissible [pə-mísəbəł] ADJ permisible, lícito

permission [pə-míʃən] N permiso *m*

permissive [pə-mísɪv] ADJ permisivo

permit[1] [pə-mɪt] VI/VT (allow) permitir; (make possible) posibilitar

permit[2] [pɝ́mɪt] N permiso *m*

permutation [pɝ-mjutéʃən] N permutación *f*

pernicious [pə-níʃəs] ADJ pernicioso

peroxide [pərɑ́ksaɪd] N peróxido *m*

perpendicular [pɝ-pɪndíkjələ-] ADJ & N perpendicular *f*

perpetrate [pɝ́pɪtret] VT perpetrar

perpetual [pə-pétʃuəł] ADJ perpetuo

perpetuate [pə-pétʃuet] VT perpetuar

perplex [pə-plɛ́ks] VT confundir, dejar perplejo; **—ed** perplejo

perplexity [pə-plɛ́ksɪdi] N perplejidad *f*

persecute [pɝ́sɪkjut] VT perseguir

persecution [pɝ-sɪkjú́ʃən] N persecución *f*

persecutor [pɝ́sɪkjudə-] N perseguidor -ora *mf*

perseverance [pɝ-səvírəns] N perseverancia *f*

persevere [pɝ-səvír] VI perseverar, persistir

Persia [pɝ́ʒə] N Persia *f*

Persian [pɝ́ʒən] ADJ & N persa *mf*

persist [pə-síst] VI (continue, endure) persistir; (to be insistent) insistir

persistence [pə-sístəns] N (endurance) persistencia *f*; (insistence) insistencia *f*

persistent [pə-sístənt] ADJ (lasting) persistente; (insisting) insistente, machacón

person [pɝ́sən] N persona *f*

personable [pɝ́sənəbəł] ADJ agradable

personage [pɝ́sənɪʤ] N personaje *m*

personal [pɝ́sənł] ADJ personal; **— computer** *Sp* ordenador personal *m*; *Am* computadora personal *f*; **— effects** efectos personales *m pl*; **— foul** falta personal *f*; **— identification number** número de identificación personal *m*; **— pronoun** pronombre personal *m*; **— property** bienes muebles *m pl*; **to make a — appearance** presentarse en persona

personality [pɝ-sənɑ́lɪdi] N personalidad *f*; **— disorder** trastorno de la personalidad *m*

personally [pɝ́sənəli] ADV personalmente; **don't take it —** no lo tomes a pecho / a mal

personify [pə-sɑ́nəfaɪ] VT personificar

personnel [pɝ-sənɛ́ł] N personal *m*

perspective [pə-spɛ́ktɪv] N perspectiva *f*

perspicacious [pɝ-spɪkéʃəs] ADJ perspicaz

perspiration [pɝ-spəréʃən] N transpiración *f*

perspire [pə-spáɪr] VI transpirar

persuade [pə-swéd] VT persuadir, convencer

persuasion [pə-swéʒən] N persuasión *f*; (belief) convicción *f*

persuasive [pə-swésɪv] ADJ persuasivo, convincente

pert [pɝ-t] ADJ (insolent) insolente; (lively) vivaz

pertain [pə-tén] VI atañer, corresponder

pertinent [pɝ́tnənt] ADJ pertinente

perturb [pə-tɝ́-b] VT perturbar

Peru [pərú] N Perú *m*

perusal [pərúzəł] N lectura *f*

peruse [pərúz] VT (read carefully) leer con cuidado; (read carelessly) hojear

Peruvian [pərúviən] ADJ & N peruano -na *mf*

pervade [pə-vɛ́d] VT difundirse por

perverse [pə-vɝ́s] ADJ perverso

perversion [pə-vɝ́ʒən] N perversión *f*

perversity [pə-vɝ́sɪdi] N perversidad *f*

pervert[1] [pə-vɝ́t] VT pervertir; (misconstrue) desvirtuar

pervert[2] [pɝ́-vɝ-t] N pervertido -da *mf*

peso [péso] N peso *m*

pessimism [pɛ́səmɪzəm] N pesimismo *m*

pessimist [pɛ́səmɪst] N pesimista *mf*

pest [pɛst] N (insect, disease) peste *f*, plaga *f*; (person) pesado -da *mf*

pester [pɛ́stə-] VT molestar

pesticide [pɛ́stɪsaɪd] N pesticida *m*

pestilence [pɛ́stələns] N pestilencia *f*

pet [pɛt] N (animal) mascota *f*; (favorite) favorito -ta *mf*, preferido -da *mf*; ADJ predilecto; **— name** apodo cariñoso *m*; VT (caress) acariciar; (pat) dar palmaditas a

petal [pɛ́dł] N pétalo *m*

petition [pətíʃən] N petición *f*, solicitud *f*; VI/VT peticionar, solicitar

petrify [pɛ́trəfaɪ] VI/VT petrificar[se]

petroleum [pətróliəm] N petróleo *m*; **— products** productos petrolíferos *m pl*; **— jelly** vaselina *f*

petticoat [pɛ́dɪkot] N enaguas *f pl*

petty [pɛ́di] ADJ (trivial) trivial; (mean) mezquino; **— cash** caja chica *f*; **— larceny** ratería *f*; **— officer** suboficial de marina *m*

petunia [pɪtúnjə] N petunia *f*

pew [pju] N banco *m* / banca *f* de iglesia

pewter [pjúɒə˞] N peltre *m*
peyote [peóɒi] N peyote *m*
phantom [fǽntəm] N fantasma *m*
pharmaceutical [fɑrməsúɒɪkəɫ] ADJ farmacéutico; N producto farmacéutico *m*, fármaco *m*
pharmacist [fárməsɪst] N farmacéutico -ca *mf*
pharmacology [fɑrməkɑ́ɫəʤi] N farmacología *f*
pharmacy [fárməsi] N farmacia *f*
pharynx [fǽrɪŋks] N faringe *f*
phase [fez] N fase *f*; VI **to — out** retirar por etapas; **to — in** incorporar paulatinamente
pheasant [fézənt] N faisán *m*
phenomenon [fɪnɑ́mənɑn] N fenómeno *m*
philanthropy [fɪɫǽnθrəpi] N filantropía *f*
philharmonic [fɪɫhɑrmɑ́nɪk] ADJ filarmónico; N filarmónica *f*
Philippine [fíɫəpin] ADJ & N filipino -na *mf*
Philippines [fíɫəpinz] N filipinas *f pl*
philosopher [fɪɫɑ́səfə˞] N filósofo -fa *mf*
philosophical [fɪɫəsɑ́fɪkəɫ] ADJ filosófico
philosophy [fɪɫɑ́səfi] N filosofía *f*
phishing [fíʃɪŋ] N phishing *m*
phlegm [fɫem] N flema *f*
phobia [fóbiə] N fobia *f*
phone [fon] N teléfono *m*; **— card** tarjeta telefónica *f*; VI/VT telefonear
phonetic [fənɛ́tɪk] ADJ fonético
phonetics [fənɛ́tɪks] N fonética *f*
phonograph [fóna˞ɡræf] N fonógrafo *m*
phonology [fənɑ́ɫəʤi] N fonología *f*
phony [fóni] ADJ falso
phosphate [fɑ́sfet] N fosfato *m*
phosphorus [fɑ́sfə˞əs] N fósforo *m*
photo [fóɒo] N foto *f*; **— finish** final muy reñido *m*
photocopier [fóɒəkɑpiə˞] N fotocopiadora *f*
photocopy [fóɒəkɑpi] N fotocopia *f*; VI/VT fotocopiar
photoelectric [foɒoɪlɛ́ktrɪk] ADJ fotoeléctrico
photogenic [foɒəʤɛ́nɪk] ADJ fotogénico
photograph [fóɒə˞ɡræf] N fotografía *f*; VT fotografiar
photographer [fətɑ́ɡrəfə˞] N fotógrafo -fa *mf*
photography [fətɑ́ɡrəfi] N fotografía *f*
photon [fótɑn] N fotón *m*
photosynthesis [foɒosínθəsɪs] N fotosíntesis *f*
phrase [frez] N frase *f*; VI/VT expresar; (musical) frasear
phylum [fáɪɫəm] N filo *m*
physical [fízɪkəɫ] ADJ físico; **— education** educación física *f*; **— geography** geografía física *f*; **— science** ciencia física *f*; **— therapy** fisioterapia *f*
physician [fɪzíʃən] N médico -ca *mf*; **—'s assistant** ayudante médico -ca sanitario -ria *mf*
physicist [fízɪsɪst] N físico -ca *mf*
physics [fízɪks] N física *f*
physiological [fɪziəɫɑ́ʤɪkəɫ] ADJ fisiológico
physiology [fɪziɑ́ɫəʤi] N fisiología *f*
physique [fɪzík] N físico *m*
pianist [piǽnɪst] N pianista *mf*
piano [piǽno] N piano *m*; **— bench** banqueta de piano *f*; **— hammer** martinete *m*; **— player** pianista *mf*; **— stool** taburete de piano *m*
picaresque [pɪkə˞ésk] ADJ picaresco
piccolo [píkəɫo] N flautín *m*, pícolo *m*
pick [pɪk] VT (choose) escoger, elegir; (gather flowers) juntar; (play a guitar) puntear; (clean teeth) mondarse; (eat with the bill) picotear; (provoke a fight) armar, entablar; VI picar; **to — at** picotear; **to — apart** criticar; **to — a lock** violar una cerradura con ganzúa; **to — on** meterse con; **to — out** (choose) escoger; (distinguish) distinguir; **to — pockets** ratear; **to — up** (gather) recoger; (lift) levantar; (learn) aprender; (order) ordenar; (improve) mejorar; **to — up speed** acelerar la marcha; N (tool) pico *m*; (of a guitar) púa *f*; (act of selecting) selección *f*; (thing or person selected) elección *f*; (the best) lo selecto, lo mejor; **—ax[e]** zapapico *m*; **—lock** ganzúa *f*; **—pocket** ratero -ra *mf*, carterista *mf*; **—up** (taking on freight) recolección *f*; (improvement in business) recuperación *f*; (acceleration) aceleración *f*; **—up truck** camioneta *f*; ADJ **—-proof** a prueba de ladrones
picket [pí̞kɪt] N piquete *m* (also union worker); **— fence** cerca de piquetes *f*; VT (fence) vallar; (block with workers) bloquear, *Am* piquetear
pickle [pí̞kəɫ] N pepinillo en vinagre *m*, curtido *m*; **to be in a —** hallarse en un aprieto; VT encurtir, escabechar; **—d fish** pescado al/en escabeche *m*, pescado adobado *m*
picnic [pí̞knɪk] N picnic *m*; **— area** merendero *m*; VI hacer un picnic
pictorial [pɪktóriəɫ] ADJ pictórico
picture [pí̞ktʃə˞] N (image) imagen *f*; (drawing) dibujo *m*; (photo) fotografía *f*; (situation) panorama *m*; (movie) película *f*; **— frame** marco *m*; **— gallery** galería de pinturas *f*; **— tube** tubo de imagen *m*; **she is the — of unhappiness** es la imagen de la infelicidad; VT (describe) describir; (imagine) imaginar
picturesque [pɪktʃə˞ésk] ADJ pintoresco
pie [paɪ] N pastel *m*, tarta *f*; **— chart** diagrama de pastel *m*; **— graph** gráfica de pastel *f*; **— in the sky** castillos en el aire *m pl*; **it's as easy as —** es pan comido
piece [pis] N (of music, in a board game, of furniture) pieza *f*; (of wood, rock, pie) pedazo *m*, trozo *m*; **—meal** por partes; **— of advice** consejo *m*; **— of cake** pan comido *m*; **— of land** parcela *f*, terreno *m*; **— of one's mind** regaño *m*; **— of news** noticia *f*; **—work** trabajo a destajo *m*; **to go to —s**

descomponerse; VI **to — together** (assemble) armar; (make sense of) atar cabos

pier [pir] N muelle *m*, embarcadero *m*; (breakwater) rompeolas *m sg*

pierce [pirs] VI/VT (make a hole in) agujerear, perforar; (penetrate) penetrar; (cause a sharp pain) punzar

piercing [pírsɪŋ] ADJ (glance, sound) penetrante; (pain) punzante; N perforación *f*

piety [páɪɪdɪ] N piedad *f*

pig [pɪg] N puerco *m*, cerdo *m*, cochino *m*; *Sp* guarro *m*; **—-headed** testarudo, cabezón; **—-iron** hierro en lingotes *m*; **— Latin** jerigonza *f*; **—pen** pocilga *f*; **—tail** coleta *f*

pigeon [pídʒən] N paloma *f*; (young) pichón *m*; **—hole** casilla *f*; **— loft** palomar *m*; VT **to —hole** encasillar

piggy [pígi] N cerdito *m*; **—bank** alcancía *f*; *Sp* hucha *f*; ADV **—back** a hombros, a cuestas

pigment [pígmənt] N pigmento *m*

pike [paɪk] N (weapon) pica *f*; (fish) lucio *m*

pile [paɪł] N (ordered stack) pila *f*; (chaotic group) montón *m*, amontonamiento *m*; (surface of a carpet) pelo *m*; (post) pilote *m*; **— driver** martinete *m*; **—s** almorranas *f pl*; **—-up** accidente múltiple *m*; VI/VT apilar[se], amontonar[se]

pilfer [pɪ́łfɚ] VI/VT ratear, sisar

pilferage [pɪ́łfɚɪdʒ] N ratería *f*

pilgrim [pɪ́łgrəm] N peregrino -na *mf*, romero -ra *mf*

pilgrimage [pɪ́łgrəmɪdʒ] N peregrinación *f*, romería *f*

pill [pɪł] N píldora *f*, pastilla *f*; (naughty child) pesado -da *mf*

pillage [pɪ́lɪdʒ] N pillaje *m*, saqueo *m*, rapiña *f*; VI/VT pillar, saquear

pillar [pɪ́lɚ] N pilar *m*, columna *f*

pillow [pɪ́lo] N almohada *f*; **—case** funda *f*

pilot [páɪlət] N piloto *mf* (also test, light); (of a boat) timonel *m*, piloto *mf*; VT pilotar, comandar

pimple [pɪ́mpəł] N grano *m*, barro *m*

pin [pɪn] N (sewing implement) alfiler *m*; (ornament) prendedor *m*; (rod) pasador *m*, perno *m*; (bowling) bolo *m*; (electric) pata *f*, clavija *f*; **—cushion** alfiletero *m*; **—wheel** molinete *m*, remolino *m*; **to be on —s and needles** estar en ascuas; VT (affix with pins) prender; (in wrestling) inmovilizar; **to — someone down** (hold down) inmovilizar; (force to act) hacer que concrete detalles; **to — one's hopes on** poner sus esperanzas en; **to —point** localizar con precisión; **to — up** sujetar con alfileres

PIN [personal identification number] [pɪn] N PIN *m*

pincers [pínsɚz] N (of lobsters) pinzas *f pl*; (tool) tenazas *f pl*

pinch [pɪntʃ] VT (squeeze with fingers) pellizcar; (squeeze tightly, hamper) apretar; (steal) birlar; (arrest) prender; VI (be too tight) apretar; (economize) economizar; **—ed nerve** nervio pellizcado *m*, nervio pinzado *m*; N (act of pinching) pellizco *m*; (small amount) pizca *f*; (trying circumstances) aprieto *m*, apuro *m*; **— hitter** bateador -ora emergente *mf*; **— runner** corredor emergente *m*

pine [paɪn] N pino *m*; **—apple** piña *f*, ananá[s] *m*; **— cone** piña *f*; **— grove** pinar *m*; **— nut** piñón *m*; VI **to — away** languidecer; **to — for** anhelar, suspirar por

pingpong [pínpɑŋ] N ping-pong *m*, tenis de mesa *m*

pinion [pínjən] N piñón *m*

pink [pɪŋk] N rosado *m*, rosa *m*; **—eye** conjuntivitis *f*; **— slip** notificación de despido *f*; **in the —** rebosante de salud; ADJ rosado, rosa

pinnacle [pínəkəł] N pináculo *m*

pint [paɪnt] N pinta *f*; ADJ **—-sized** diminuto

pinto bean [píntobin] N judía pinta *f*

pioneer [paɪənír] N pionero -ra *mf*; VI ser el primero en hacer algo; VT promover

pious [páɪəs] ADJ (religious) pío, piadoso; (hypocritical) beato

pipe [paɪp] N (for smoking) pipa *f*; (for water) tubo *m*, caño *m*; (of an organ) tubo *m*; (flute) caramillo *m*, flauta *f*; **— dream** ilusiones *f pl*; **—line** (for oil) oleoducto *m*; (for gas) gasoducto *m*; (for water) tubería *f*; **in the —line** en trámite; **— wrench** llave inglesa *f*; VT (convey water) conducir por cañerías; (make music) tocar la flauta; VI chillar; **to — down** callarse

piping [páɪpɪŋ] N (many pipes) cañería *f*, tubería *f*; (border on clothes) ribete *m*; (sound of pipes) sonido de la gaita/flauta *m*; ADJ **— hot** hirviendo

pipsqueak [pípskwik] N chisgarabís *m*, mequetrefe *m*

piracy [páɪrəsi] N piratería *f*

pirate [páɪrɪt] N pirata *mf*; VT piratear

pistol [pístł] N pistola *f*, revólver *m*; VT **to —-whip** dar culatazos

piston [pístn] N pistón *m*, émbolo *m*; **— ring** segmento de compresión *m*; **— rod** eje del pistón *m*

pit [pɪt] N (hole) hoyo *m*, pozo *m*; (in a garage, theater) foso *m*; (trap) trampa *f*; (seed) hueso *m*; (part of a racetrack) box *m*, paddock *m*; (part of the stomach) boca *f*; **—fall** (trap) trampa *f*; (difficulty) dificultad *f*; **this is the —s** esto es lo peor; VI/VT (make holes) picarse; VT **to — against** oponer, enfrentar

pitch [pɪtʃ] VT (throw) tirar, lanzar; (try to sell) pregonar; **to — a tent** armar una tienda; VI

(plane, ship) cabecear; **to — in** colaborar; N (throw) tiro *m*, lanzamiento *m*; (in music) tono *m*; (in printing) espaciado *m*; (slope) grado de inclinación *m*; (tar) brea *f*, pez *f*; **— dark** oscuro como boca del lobo; **—fork** horca *f*, horquilla *f*

pitcher [pítʃə˞] N (vessel) cántaro *m*, jarro *m*, jarra *f*; (in baseball) lanzador -ora *mf*; **—'s mound** montículo *m*

pith [pɪθ] N (in plants, feathers) médula *f*; (essence) meollo *m*

pithy [píθi] ADJ sustancial

pitiful [pítɪfəł] ADJ (deserving pity) lastimoso; (deserving contempt) despreciable

pitiless [pítɪɪlɪs] ADJ despiadado

pituitary [pɪtúɪtɛri] ADJ pituitario; **— gland** glándula pituitaria *f*

pity [pítɪ] N compasión *f*, lástima *f*; **what a —!** ¡qué lástima! VT compadecerse [de]

pivot [pívət] N pivote *m*; VI pivotar

pixel [píksəł] N píxel *m*

pizza [pítsə] N pizza *f*

placard [plǽkə˞d] N cartel *m*

placate [pléket] VT apaciguar

place [ples] N (site) lugar *m*, sitio *m*; (position) puesto *m*; **— mat** mantel individual *m*; **— of birth** lugar de nacimiento *m*; **— of business** oficina *f*; **— of worship** templo *m*; **— setting** cubierto para una persona *m*; **in — of** en lugar de; **it is not my — to do it** no me corresponde a mí hacerlo; VT (put) colocar; (identify) situar, ubicar; **to — an order** hacer un pedido; **to — an ad** poner un anuncio; VI (in sports) clasificarse

placebo [pləsíbo] N placebo *m*

placement [plésmənt] N (in levels, categories) colocación *f*, posicionamiento *m*; (in space) emplazamiento *m*

placenta [pləsɛ́ntə] N placenta *f*

placid [plǽsɪd] ADJ plácido

plagiarism [pléɟɜɪrɪzəm] N plagio *m*

plague [pleg] N plaga *f*, peste *f*; VT atormentar, apestar

plaid [plæd] N tela escocesa *f*

plain [plen] ADJ (without embellishment) sencillo, llano; (clear) claro; (downright, unadulterated) puro; (ordinary) común; (unattractive) poco atractivo; **in — sight** en plena vista; **—clothesman** policía en traje de civil *m*; **—-Jane** sencillo; ADV completamente; N llano *m*, llanura *f*

plaintiff [plɛ́ntɪf] N demandante *mf*, querellante *mf*

plan [plæn] N plan *m*; (drawing, sketch, map, outline) plano *m*; VI/VT planear, planificar; (diagram) hacer el plano de; **—ned parenthood** planificación familiar *f*

plane [plen] N (airplane) avión *m*; (surface) plano *m*; (tool) cepillo *m*; **— tree** plátano *m*; ADJ plano; **— geometry** geometría plana *f*; VI (glide, hover) planear; VT (smooth) cepillar, planear

planet [plǽnɪt] N planeta *m*

planetarium [plænɪtɛ́riəm] N planetario *m*

plank [plæŋk] N (board) tabla *f*, tablón *m*; (tenet) principio *m*, base *f*; VT entarimar

plankton [plǽŋktən] N plancton *m*

planning [plǽnɪŋ] N planeamiento *m*, planificación *f*

plant [plænt] N (vegetation) planta *f*; (industrial installation) fábrica *f*, planta *f*; (mole, spy) topo *m*; VT (plants) plantar; (ideas) sembrar; (a spy, evidence) colocar

plantain [plǽnten] N plátano *m*

plantation [plæntéʃən] N plantación *f*

plaque [plæk] N placa *f*; (on teeth) sarro *m*, placa *f*

plasma [plǽzmə] N plasma *m*, gas ionizado *m*

plaster [plǽstə˞] N (substance) yeso *m*; (preparation applied to body) emplasto *m*; **— of Paris** yeso *m*; VT (cover with plaster) revocar; (apply a preparation) emplastar; (cover with posters) cubrir, empapelar; (defeat) aplastar; **to — down one's hair** achatarse el pelo; **to get —ed** emborracharse

plastic [plǽstɪk] ADJ plástico; **— surgery** cirugía plástica/estética *f*

plate [plet] N (for food) plato *m*; (for collections) bandeja *f*; (metal) plancha *f*, lámina *f*; (license) placa *f*; **— glass** vidrio cilindrado *m*; **— tectonics** tectónica de placas *f*; VT (apply metal covering) chapar, enchapar; (apply armor) blindar

plateau [plætó] N meseta *f*, macizo *m*

platform [plǽtfɔ˞rm] N plataforma *f* (also in politics, computers); (railway) andén *m*; (mobile) tarima *f*, tinglado *m*

platinum [plǽtn̩əm] N platino *m*

platitude [plǽpɪtɪud] N lugar común *m*, perogrullada *f*

platter [plǽɒə˞] N fuente *f*

plausible [plɔ́zəbəł] ADJ plausible

play [ple] VT (game) jugar; (an opponent) jugar contra; (an instrument) tocar; (a drama) representar; (a role) desempeñar; (bet on) apostar; **to — a joke** gastar una broma; **to — cards** jugar a los naipes; **to — havoc** hacer estragos; **to — tennis** jugar al tenis; **to — the fool** hacerse el tonto; VI (divert oneself, gamble) jugar; (kid) bromear; (make music) tocar; **to — along** seguir la corriente; **to — down** minimizar; **to be all —ed out** estar agotado; N (recreational activity, looseness) juego *m*; (instance of playing) jugada *f*; (theater work) obra de teatro *f*; **— on words** juego de palabras *m*; **—boy** playboy *m*; **—ground** recreo *m*, patio *m*; **—ing card** naipe *m*; **—mate** compañero -ra de juego *mf*; **—off [game]** [partido de] desempate *m*; **the**

—**offs** las eliminatorias *f pl*; —**thing** juguete *m*

player [pléə-] N (one who plays, gambler) jugador -ora *mf*; (musician) músico -ca *mf*; (influential person) persona influyente *f*; (womanizer) mujeriego *m*; (actor) actor *m*, actriz *f*; (participant) participante *mf*; — **piano** pianola *f*

playful [pléfəł] ADJ juguetón

playwright [pléraɪt] N dramaturgo -ga *mf*

plea [pli] N (entreaty) súplica *f*, ruego *m*; (allegation) alegato *m*; **to enter a — of guilty** declararse culpable

plead [plid] VI/VT (entreat) suplicar, rogar; (defend) abogar, defender; **to — guilty** declararse culpable

pleasant [plézənt] ADJ agradable, grato, placentero

pleasantry [plézəntri] N cortesía *f*

please [pliz] ADV por favor; VI/VT agradar, complacer; **as you** — como quieras; **to be —d to** tener el gusto de, tener gusto en; **to be —d with** estar satisfecho con

pleasing [plízɪŋ] ADJ agradable

pleasure [pléʒə-] N placer *m*, gusto *m*, agrado *m*; — **trip** viaje de placer *m*

pleat [plit] N pliegue *m*, tabla *f*; (wide) tabla *f*; VT plisar; (wide) tablear

pled [pled] *see* plead

pledge [pleʤ] N (promise) promesa *f*; (security deposit) prenda *f*; (in a fraternity) miembro provisorio *m*; **as a — of** en prenda de; VI/VT (promise) prometer; VT (give as a deposit) empeñar; **to — one's word** dar la palabra; **to — to secrecy** exigir promesa de discreción

plenary [plénəri] ADJ & N plenario *m*

plentiful [pléntɪfəł] ADJ abundante, copioso

plenty [plénti] N abundancia *f*; — **of time** suficiente tiempo *m*; **that's** — con eso basta

pliable [pláɪəbəł] ADJ (flexible) flexible; (docile) dócil

pliant [plaɪənt] ADJ (flexible) flexible; (docile) dócil

pliers [pláɪə-z] N alicates *m pl*, tenazas *f pl*

plight [plaɪt] N aprieto *m*

plod [plɑd] VI (walk) caminar trabajosamente; (work) trabajar laboriosamente

plop [plɑp] VI hacer plaf; VT dejar caer; N plaf *m*

plot [plɑt] N (storyline) trama *f*, argumento *m*; (conspiracy) complot *m*, conspiración *f*; (land) parcela *f*, era *f*; (floor plan) plano *m*; VI/VT (plan secretly) tramar, conspirar, maquinar; VT (make a graph) hacer un gráfico; **to — a course** trazar un curso

plotter [plɑ́ɑə-] N (one who plots) conspirador -ora *mf*; (device) trazador de gráficos *m*

plover [plóvə-] N chorlito *m*

plow [plaʊ] N arado *m*; —**share** reja de arado *f*; VI/VT arar; (uncultivated area) roturar; **to — through** abrirse paso

plowing [pláʊɪŋ] N labranza *f*

pluck [plʌk] VT (a feather, flower) arrancar; (bird) desplumar; (guitar) puntear, pulsar; **to — out/off** desprender; **to — up courage** animarse, cobrar ánimo; N (act of plucking) tirón *m*; (courage) valor *m*

plug [plʌg] N (stopper) tapón *m*; (horse) *pej* penco *m*; (electric) enchufe *m*; (advertisement) mención favorable *f*; (tobacco) rollo *m*; —**-in** (electrical) enchufe *m*; (computer accessory) plug-in *m*; VT (close) tapar; (advertise) hacer una mención favorable de; VI **to — along** no parar; **to — in** enchufar; **to — up** tapar

plum [plʌm] N (fruit) ciruela *f*; — **tree** ciruelo *m*; **that job is a real** — ese trabajo es estupendo

plumage [plúmɪʤ] N plumaje *m*

plumb [plʌm] N (lead weight) plomada *f*; — **bob** plomada *f*; **to be out of** — no estar a plomo; ADJ (perpendicular) a plomo; ADV (in a vertical direction) a plomo; (completely) completamente; VT (measure depth) sondear; (test for verticality) aplomar; (examine) examinar

plumber [plʌ́mə-] N plomero -ra *mf*; *Sp* fontanero -ra *mf*

plumbing [plʌ́mɪŋ] N (work and trade) plomería *f*; *Sp* fontanería *f*; (system of pipes) cañerías *f pl*

plume [plum] N penacho *m*; VT adornar con plumas

plummet [plʌ́mɪt] VI precipitarse; N plomada *f*

plump [plʌmp] ADJ rechoncho, regordete, rollizo; VI/VT **to — down** dejar[se] caer

plunder [plʌ́ndə-] N (act of plundering) pillaje *m*, saqueo *m*; (loot) botín *m*; VI/VT pillar, saquear

plunge [plʌnʤ] VI/VT (into water) zambullir[se], sumergir[se]; (into something solid) hundir[se]; VI (fall) precipitarse; (slope downward) bajar repentinamente; **to — headlong** echarse de cabeza; N zambullida *f*; (rush) salto *m*

plunger [plʌ́nʤə-] N (for a toilet) desatascador *m*; (of a pump) émbolo *m*

pluperfect [plupɚ́fɪkt] N pluscuamperfecto *m*

plural [plʊ́rəł] ADJ & N plural *m*

plurality [plurǽlɪdi] N pluralidad *f*

plus [plʌs] PREP más; N (advantage) ventaja *f*; **two — three** dos más tres *m*; **on the — side** en el lado positivo; — **sign** signo de más *m*

plush [plʌʃ] N felpa *f*; ADJ (fabric) afelpado; (hotel) lujoso

plutonium [plutóniəm] N plutonio *m*

ply [plaɪ] VT (use) manejar; (assail with questions) acosar; (navigate a body of water) surcar; VI (travel regularly) recorrer con regularidad; (work steadily) aplicarse; **to — a trade** ejercer un oficio; N (layer of cloth, rubber) capa *f*; (layer of plywood) chapa *f*; —**wood**

madera compensada *f*, contrachapado *m*

pneumatic [numǽpɪk] ADJ neumático

pneumonia [numónjə] N pulmonía *f*

poach [potʃ] VT (eggs) escalfar; VI/VT (game) cazar furtivamente

pocket [pákɪt] N (in clothes) bolsillo *m*; (vein of ore) filón *m*; (on a pool table) tronera *f*; (of air) bache *m*; (of poverty) bolsa *f*; **—book** cartera *f*, *Sp* bolso *m*; **— book** libro de bolsillo *m*; **—knife** navaja *f*; **— of resistance** foco de resistencia *m*; VT meterse en el bolsillo; (appropriate) embolsar; (knock in a billiard ball) meter en la tronera

pod [pɑd] N (seed vessel) vaina *f*; (herd of cetaceans) manada *f*

podiatrist [pədáɪətrɪst] N podólogo -ga *mf*

podiatry [pədáɪətrɪ] N podiatría *f*

podium [pódɪəm] N podio *m*

poem [póəm] N poema *m*, poesía *f*

poet [póɪt] N poeta *mf*

poetic [poɛ́ɪk] ADJ poético; **— justice** justicia divina *f*; N **—s** poética *f*

poetry [póɪtrɪ] N poesía *f*

poignant [pɔ́ɪnjənt] ADJ conmovedor

poinsettia [pɔɪnsɛ́ɪə] N flor de Pascua *f*

point [pɔɪnt] N (place) punto *m*; (score, in sports) punto *m*, anotación *f*; (sharp end) punta *f*; **— after touchdown** punto extra *m*; **— guard** (basketball) base *mf*, conductor -ora *mf*, guardia *mf*; **— of origin** punto de origen *m*; **— of view** punto de vista *m*; **it is not to the —** no viene al caso; **I don't see the —** no le veo el sentido; **on the — of** a punto de; ADV **—-blank** a quemarropa; VT (direct finger at) apuntar con, señalar con; (indicate) señalar; **to — at** (with finger) señalar; (with a gun) apuntar hacia; **to — out** señalar, indicar; **to — up** enfatizar

pointed [pɔ́ɪntɪd] ADJ (having a point) puntiagudo; (piercing) agudo; **— arch** arco ojival *m*

pointer [pɔ́ɪntɚ] N (stick) puntero *m*; (on a scale) indicador *m*; (dog) perro de muestra *m*; (advice) consejo *m*

pointless [pɔ́ɪntlɪs] ADJ inútil

poise [pɔɪz] N (balance, steadiness) equilibrio *m*; (dignified bearing) aplomo *m*; **to be —d to** estar listo para; VI/VT equilibrar[se]

poison [pɔ́ɪzən] N veneno *m*, ponzoña *f*; **— ivy** hiedra venenosa *f*; VT envenenar, emponzoñar

poisoning [pɔ́ɪzənɪŋ] N (accidental) intoxicación *f*; (intentional) envenenamiento *m*

poisonous [pɔ́ɪzənəs] ADJ venenoso, ponzoñoso

poke [pok] VT (jab) clavar, pinchar; (stir a fire) atizar; (thrust out, as one's head) asomar; **to — out an eye** sacar un ojo; VI **to — along** andar perezosamente; **to — around** husmear; **to — fun at** burlarse de; **to — into** meterse en; **to — out** (project) sobresalir; N pinchazo *m*

Poland [pólənd] N Polonia *f*

polar [pólɚ] ADJ polar; **— bear** oso polar *m*

polarity [pəlǽrɪtɪ] N polaridad *f*

polarization [polərɪzéʃən] N polarización *f*

polarize [pólərɪaɪz] VI/VT polarizar[se]

pole [poɫ] N (long piece of wood, metal) poste *m*; (for a flag) asta *f*; (for vaulting) pértiga *f*, garrocha *f*; (earth's axis) polo *m*; (for skiing) bastón *m*; **— vault** salto con pértiga *m*

Pole [poɫ] N polaco -ca *mf*

polemic [pəlémɪk] ADJ polémico *m*; N polémica *f*

police [pəlís] N policía *f*; **— car** patrullero *m*; **— dog** perro policía *m*; **— force** cuerpo de policía *m*; **—man** policía *m*; **— officer** oficial de policía *mf*, *Am* carabinero -ra *mf*; **— operation** *Am* operativo policial *m*; **— report** parte policial *m*; **— state** estado policíaco *m*; **— station** comisaría de policía *f*; **—woman** policía *f*; VT patrullar

policy [pálɪsɪ] N (procedure) política *f*; (for insurance) póliza *f*

polio [pólio] N polio *f*

Polish [pólɪʃ] ADJ & N polaco -ca *mf*

polish [pálɪʃ] N (sheen) lustre *m*, refinamiento *m*; (refinement) urbanidad *f*, cultura *f*; (substance for furniture) cera *f*; (substance for shoes) betún *m*; VT (a speech) pulir; (a metal) sacar brillo; (a car) encerar; (shoes) lustrar, embetunar; **to — off** despachar; **to — up** (metal) sacar brillo; (speech) pulir

polite [pəláɪt] ADJ cortés

politeness [pəláɪtnɪs] N cortesía *f*

politic [pálɪtɪk] ADJ diplomático, político

political [pəlíɪdɪkəɫ] ADJ político; **— prisoner** preso -sa político -ca *mf*; **— science** ciencias políticas *f pl*

politically correct [pəlíɪdɪklikɔrékt] ADJ políticamente correcto

politician [pɑlɪtíʃən] N político -ca *mf*

politics [pálɪtɪks] N política *f*

polka [póɫkə] N polca *f*; **— dot** lunar *m*

poll [poɫ] N (survey) encuesta *f*; **—s** (elections) comicios *m pl*; (voting place) urna *f*; VT (survey) encuestar; (receive votes) obtener; (record vote of) registrar

pollen [pálən] N polen *m*

pollinate [pálənet] VT polinizar

pollute [pəlút] VI/VT contaminar

pollution [pəlúʃən] N contaminación *f*

polo [pólo] N polo *m*

polyester [pɑliéstɚ] N poliéster *m*

polygamy [pəlígəmi] N poligamia *f*

polyglot [pálɪglɑt] ADJ & N políglota *mf*

polygraph [pálɪgræf] N polígrafo *m*

polymer [páləmɚ] N polímero *m*

polyp [pálɪp] N pólipo *m*

polyunsaturated [pɑliʌnsǽtʃəreɪɪd] ADJ

poliinsaturado
polyurethane [pɑlijúrəθen] N poliuretano *m*
pomegranate [pámıgrænıt] N granada *f*; — **tree** granado *m*
pomp [pɑmp] N pompa *f*, boato *m*, aparato *m*
pompous [pámpəs] ADJ pomposo, aparatoso
pond [pɑnd] N (natural) charca *f*; (artificial) estanque *m*; (for irrigation) balsa *f*
ponder [pándə-] VI meditar; VT considerar
ponderous [pándərəs] ADJ enorme
pontoon [pɑntún] N (on a bridge) pontón *m*; (on an airplane) flotador *m*
pony [póni] N póney *m*; **—tail** colita *f*, cola de caballo *f*; VI **to — up** soltar
Ponzi scheme [pánzi skím] N timo en pirámide *m pl*
poodle [púdl] N caniche *m*
pool [puł] N (puddle of water, blood, etc.) charco *m*; (swimming place) piscina *f*, *Mex* alberca *f*; (association of competitors) pool *m*; (game) pool *m*, billar *m*; (bets) pozo *m*; **— table** billar *m*; **— hall** billar *m*; VI acumularse; VT combinar fondos
poop [pup] N (part of ship) popa *f*; (excrement) *fam* caca *f*; VI *fam* hacer caca
poor [pʊr] ADJ (lacking money) pobre; (deficient) malo; **I'm a — cook** no sé cocinar; **—house** asilo para los pobres *m*; **— little thing** pobrecito -ta *mf*; N **the —** los pobres
pop [pɑp] VI (balloon) reventar, estallar; (eyes, cork) saltar; **to — in** entrar de paso; VT (make explode) hacer reventar; (take out cork) hacer saltar; (put) meter; (take, as pills) tomar; **to — a question** espetar una pregunta; **to — corn** hacer palomitas; N estallido *m*, detonación *f*; **—corn** palomitas *f pl*; **— music** música popular *f*; **— quiz** prueba sorpresa *f*; **— of a cork** taponazo *m*; **— -up menu** menú emergente *m*
pope [pop] N papa *m*
poplar [páplə-] N álamo *m*, chopo *m*; **— grove** alameda *f*
poppy [pápi] N amapola *f*
popular [pápjələ-] ADJ popular; **he's very — with the ladies** tiene mucho éxito con las mujeres
popularity [pɑpjəlǽrıdi] N popularidad *f*
populate [pápjəlet] VT poblar
population [pɑpjəléʃən] N población *f*
populous [pápjələs] ADJ populoso
porcelain [pórsəlın] N porcelana *f*
porch [pórtʃ] N porche *m*
porcupine [pórkjəpaın] N puercoespín *m*
pore [pɔr] N poro *m*; VI **to — over a book** estudiar detenidamente un libro
pork [pɔrk] N carne de cerdo *f*; **— chop** chuleta de cerdo *f*
porn [pɔrn] N porno *m*
pornography [pɔrnágrəfi] N pornografía *f*
porous [pórəs] ADJ poroso
porpoise [pórpəs] N marsopa *f*
port [pɔrt] N (harbor, computer) puerto *m*; (wine) oporto *m*; (left side of ship) babor *m*; **— city** ciudad portuaria *f*; **—hole** ojo de buey *m*; **— of entry** puerto de entrada *m*
portable [pórdəbəł] ADJ portátil
portal [pórdl] N portal *m* (also of Internet)
portent [pórtent] N (omen) presagio *m*, agüero *m*; (marvel, prodigy) portento *m*
portentous [pɔrténtəs] ADJ (ominous) de mal agüero; (prodigious) portentoso
porter [pórdə-] N mozo -za *mf*
portfolio [pɔrtfóliо] N cartera *f*
portion [pórʃən] N porción *f*; VI **to — out** repartir
portly [pórtli] ADJ grueso
portrait [pórtrıt] N (likeness) retrato *m*; (printing orientation) orientación vertical *f*
portray [pɔrtré] VT (draw, describe) retratar; (in a drama) representar
portrayal [pɔrtréəł] N (portrait) retrato *m*; (act of portraying) representación *f*, caracterización *f*
Portugal [pórtʃəgəł] N Portugal *m*
Portuguese [pórtʃəgiz] ADJ & N portugués -esa *mf*
pose [poz] N (posture) pose *f*, postura *f*; (affected attitude) afectación *f*; VI (sit as a model) posar; (act affectedly) afectar una actitud; VT (to make sit as model) hacer posar; (to present) plantear; **to — as** hacerse pasar por
position [pəzíʃən] N (place) posición *f*; (job) puesto *m*, colocación *f*; (political stance) posicionamiento *m*; VI situar, colocar; **to — oneself** posicionarse
positive [pázıdıv] ADJ positivo; **— proof** prueba certera *f*; **I am —** estoy seguro
possess [pəzés] VT poseer
possessed [pəzést] ADJ (by a spirit) poseído; (by an idea) obsesionado
possession [pəzéʃən] N posesión *f*; **to take —** tomar posesión
possessive [pəzésıv] ADJ & N posesivo *m*
possessor [pəzésə-] N poseedor -ora *f*
possibility [pɑsəbílıtıdi] N posibilidad *f*
possible [pásəbəł] ADJ posible, eventual
post [post] N (pole) poste *m*; (position) puesto *m*; (mail) correo *m*; **—card** tarjeta postal *f*; **—haste** a la brevedad; **—man** cartero *m*; **—mark** matasellos *m*; **—master** director de correos *m*; **— office** oficina de correos *f*, casa de correos *f*; **— -office box** apartado postal *m*; ADJ **— paid** porte pagado; VT (affix) fijar; (announce) anunciar; (list) poner en lista; (place) apostar, situar; (mail) echar al correo; **keep me —ed** mantenme al tanto
postage [póstıʤ] N franqueo *m*; **— meter** franqueadora *f*; **— stamp** *Sp* sello *m*; *Am*

estampilla *f*; *Mex* timbre *m*
postal [póstl] ADJ postal; **to go —** perpetrar un ataque homicida, volverse loco
postdate [posdét] VT posfechar
poster [póstə-] N cartel *m*, póster *m*, afiche *m*; **— child** modelo perfecto *m*
posterior [pɑstíriə-] ADJ posterior; N trasero *m*
posterity [pɑstérɪtɪ] N posteridad *f*
postgraduate [postgrǽʤuɪt] ADJ de posgrado; N posgrado -da *mf*
posthumous [pástʃəməs] ADJ póstumo
postnasal [postnézəł] ADJ postnasal
postnatal [postnédl] ADJ posparto; **— care** cuidado posparto *m inv*
postpartum [postpárdəm] ADJ posparto *m*
postpone [postpón] VT posponer, aplazar
postponement [postpónmənt] N aplazamiento *m*
postscript [póstskrɪpt] N posdata *f*
postulate[1] [pástʃəlet] VT postular
postulate[2] [pástʃəlɪt] N postulado *m*
posture [pástʃə-] N (carriage, attitude) postura *f*; (affectation) afectación *f*; VI darse aires
postwar period [póstwár píriəd] N posguerra *f*
posy [pózi] N ramillete *m*
pot [pɑt] N (vessel) olla *f*, marmita *f*; (marijuana) marihuana *f*; **—hole** bache *m*; ADJ **— -bellied** panzudo, barrigón
potable [pódəbəł] ADJ potable
potassium [pətǽsiəm] N potasio *m*
potato [pətédo] N *Sp* patata *f*; *Am* papa *f*; **— chip** patata/papa frita [a la inglesa] *f*, chip *m*
potency [pótnsi] N potencia *f*
potent [pótnt] ADJ potente
potentate [pótntet] N potentado -da *mf*
potential [pəténʃəł] ADJ & N potencial *m*
potion [póʃən] N poción *f*
potter [pádə-] N alfarero -ra *mf*
pottery [pádəri] N (craft, shop) alfarería *f*; (objects) cerámica *f*, objetos de alfarería *m pl*
pouch [pautʃ] N bolsa *f*; (for mail) valija *f*; (for tobacco) petaca *f*
poultry [póltri] N aves de corral *f pl*
pounce [paʊns] VI saltar; **to — upon/on** abalanzarse sobre; **to — on an opportunity** no dejar pasar una oportunidad; N salto *m*
pound [paʊnd] N (unit of weight, British currency) libra *f*; (place for stray dogs) perrera *f*; VT (on a door) golpear; (seeds) machacar; (a military target) bombardear; VI (beat) latir con fuerza
pour [pɔr] VT verter; VI (leave en masse) salir en tropel; (rain) llover a cántaros; **to — out one's feelings** desahogarse
pout [paʊt] VI hacer pucheros; N puchero *m*
poverty [pávə-DI] N pobreza *f*, penuria *f*; ADJ **— -stricken** indigente
powder [páʊdə-] N polvo *m*; (for the face) polvos *m pl*; (for guns) pólvora *f*; **— compact** polvera *f*; **— puff** borla *f*; **to take a —** poner pies en polvorosa; VI/VT (use powder) empolvar[se]; (pulverize) pulverizar[se]
power [páʊə-] N (control, military might) poder *m*, poderío *m*; (in physics, in math) potencia *f*; (physical strength) fuerza *f*; (energy) energía *f*; **— of attorney** poder *m*; **— plant** central eléctrica *f*; **— -save mode** modo de ahorro de energía *m*; **— steering** dirección asistida *f*; **— supply** suministro de energía *m*; **— surge** sobrecarga de voltaje *f*; **in —** oficialista; **legislative —s** atribuciones legislativas *f pl*; VI **—ed by gas** movido por gas; **to — down** apagar; **to — on/up** encender
powerful [páʊə-fəł] ADJ poderoso, potente
powerless [páʊə-lɪs] ADJ impotente
PR [public relations] [píár] N relaciones públicas *f pl*
practical [prǽktɪkəł] ADJ práctico; **— joke** broma pesada *f*, chasco *m*; **— nurse** enfermero -ra sin título *mf*
practically [prǽktɪkli] ADV prácticamente
practice [prǽktɪs] N (repeated exercise) práctica *f*; (habit) costumbre *f*; (doctor's office) consultorio *m*; (lawyer's office) bufete *m*; VI/VT practicar; VT (a profession) ejercer; **in —** en la práctica, prácticamente
practiced [prǽktɪst] ADJ experto, perito
practitioner [prǽktíʃənə-] N practicante *mf*; **general —** médico -ca general *mf*
pragmatic [prægmǽDɪK] ADJ pragmático
prairie [préri] N pradera *f*, llanura *f*
praise [prez] N alabanza *f*, elogio *m*; VT alabar, elogiar; **—worthy** loable, encomiable
prance [præns] VI cabriolar, hacer cabriolas; N cabriola *f*
prank [præŋk] N travesura *f*, chasco *m*; **to play —s** hacer travesuras
prawn [prɔn] N langostino *m*; *Sp* gamba pequeña *f*
pray [pre] VI/VT (religious) rezar, orar; (beg) rogar, suplicar
prayer [prer] N (devout petition to God) oración *f*, rezo *m*; (entreaty) ruego *m*, súplica *f*
praying mantis [préɪŋmǽntɪs] N mantis religiosa *f*
preach [pritʃ] VI/VT predicar; (moralize) sermonear
preacher [prítʃə-] N predicador -ora *mf*
preamble [príæmbəł] N preámbulo *m*
preapproved [priəprúvd] ADJ preaprobado
precancerous [prikǽnsə-əs] ADJ precanceroso
precarious [prɪkériəs] ADJ precario
precaution [prɪkɔ́ʃən] N precaución *f*
precautionary [prɪkɔ́ʃənerɪ] ADJ preventivo
precede [prɪsíd] VI/VT preceder
precedence [présɪDəns] N precedencia *f*, prioridad *f*
preceding [prɪsíDɪŋ] ADJ precedente, anterior

precept [prísɛpt] N precepto *m*
precinct [prísɪŋkt] N distrito *m*; (police station) comisaría *f*; **—s** límites *m pl*
precious [préʃəs] ADJ precioso; (overly refined) preciosista; **— little** muy poco; **— metal** metal precioso *m*; **— stone** piedra preciosa *f*
precipice [présəpɪs] N precipicio *m*, derrumbadero *m*
precipitate[1] [prɪsípɪtet] VI/VT precipitar[se]
precipitate[2] [prɪsípɪtɪt] ADJ & N precipitado *m*
precipitation [prɪsɪpɪtéʃən] N precipitación *f*
precipitous [prɪsípɪtəs] ADJ (steep) escarpado; (hasty) precipitado
precise [prɪsáɪs] ADJ preciso, exacto
precisely [prɪsáɪsli] ADV & INT precisamente, exactamente
precision [prɪsíʒən] N precisión *f*, exactitud *f*; (of expression) propiedad *f*
preclude [prɪklúd] VT excluir; **that doesn't — our considering your application** esto no obsta para que tengamos en cuenta su solicitud
precocious [prɪkóʃəs] ADJ precoz
precursor [prɪkɜ́ʳsəʳ] N precursor *m*
predator [prédətəʳ] N depredador *m*
predatory [prédətəri] ADJ (animal) depredador; (persona) rapaz
predecessor [prédɪsɛsəʳ] N predecesor -ora *mf*, antecesor -ora *mf*
predestine [pridéstɪn] VT predestinar
predetermined [pridɪtɜ́ʳmɪnd] ADJ predeterminado
predicament [prɪdíkəmənt] N aprieto *m*
predicate[1] [prédɪkɪt] ADJ & N predicado *m*
predicate[2] [prédɪket] VT basar
predict [prɪdíkt] VT predecir
prediction [prɪdíkʃən] N predicción *f*, vaticinio *m*
predilection [predlékʃən] N predilección *f*
predispose [prɪdɪspóz] VI/VT predisponer
predisposition [prɪdɪspəzíʃən] N predisposición *f*
predominance [prɪdámənəns] N predominio *m*
predominant [prɪdámənənt] ADJ predominante
predominate [prɪdámənet] VI/VT predominar, preponderar
preeclampsia [priɪklǽmpsiə] N preeclampsia *f*
preexisting [priɪgzístɪŋ] ADJ preexistente
preface [préfɪs] N prefacio *m*, prólogo *m*; VT hacer una introducción; (a book) prologar
prefer [prɪfɜ́ʳ] VT preferir; **to — a claim** presentar una demanda
preferable [préfəʳəbəł] ADJ preferible
preference [préfəʳəns] N preferencia *f*
preferential [prefərénʃəł] ADJ preferente
preferred [prɪfɜ́ʳd] ADJ preferido; **— stocks** acciones preferentes *f pl*
prefix [prífɪks] N prefijo *m*; VT poner un prefijo
pregnancy [prégnənsi] N embarazo *m*; (of an animal) preñez *f*; **— test** prueba de embarazo *f*
pregnant [prégnənt] ADJ (person) embarazada, encinta; (animal) preñada; (full of meaning, rain) preñado, cargado
prehensile [prihénsəł] ADJ prensil
prehistoric [prihɪstɔ́rɪk] ADJ prehistórico
prejudge [priʤʌ́ʤ] VT prejuzgar
prejudice [préʤəɪs] N (bias) prejuicio *m*; (harm) perjuicio *m*; VT (cause bias against) predisponer en contra; (harm) perjudicar
preliminary [prɪlímənɛri] ADJ & N preliminar *m*
prelude [prélud] N preludio *m*; VI/VT preludiar
premarital [primǽrɪdł] ADJ prematrimonial
premature [primətʃúʳ] ADJ prematuro; **— birth** parto prematuro *m*
premeditated [priméɪtɪtɪd] ADJ premeditado
premenstrual [priménstruəł] ADJ premenstrual
premier [prɪmír] N primer ministro *m*; primera ministra *f*; ADJ principal
premiere [prɪmír] N estreno *m*, première *f*
premise [prémɪs] N premisa *f*; **—s** local *m*
premium [prímiəm] N (bonus) premio *m*; (insurance) prima *f*; (surcharge) recargo *m*; **at a —** muy escaso; ADJ superior
premonition [premənífən] N premonición *f*
prenatal [prinédł] ADJ prenatal; **— care** atención prenatal *f*, cuidado prenatal *m*
prenuptial [prinápʃəł] ADJ prenupcial; **— agreement** capitulaciones matrimoniales *f pl*
preoccupy [priákjəpaɪ] VT absorber
preowned [priónd] ADJ de segunda mano
prepacked [pripǽkt] ADJ preempacado
prepaid [pripéd] ADJ pagado de antemano; **to send —** enviar porte pagado
preparation [prɛpəréfən] N (act of preparing) preparación *f*; (substance) preparado *m*; (for a trip) preparativos *m pl*
preparatory [prépəʳətɔri] ADJ preparatorio, preparativo
prepare [prɪpér] VI/VT preparar[se]
preponderance [prɪpándəʳəns] N preponderancia *f*
preponderant [prɪpándəʳənt] ADJ preponderante
preposition [prɛpəzíʃən] N preposición *f*
preposterous [prɪpástəʳəs] ADJ absurdo
prerecorded [prɪrɪkɔ́rɪd] ADJ pregrabado
prerequisite [prɪrékwəzɪt] N prerequisito *m*
prerogative [prɪrágəɪv] N prerrogativa *f*
prescribe [prɪskráɪb] VT (order) prescribir; (medicine) recetar
prescription [prɪskrípʃən] N (order) prescripción *f*; (of medicine) receta *f*
presence [préźəns] N presencia *f*; **— of mind** aplomo *m*, presencia de ánimo *f*
present[1] [prézənt] N (time) presente *m*; (gift)

regalo *m*, presente *m*; **at —** ahora; **for the —** por ahora; ADJ (at a place) presente; (at this time) actual; **— company excepted** con perdón de los presentes; **— participle** gerundio *m*; **— perfect** pretérito perfecto *m*; **—-day** actual

present[2] [prɪzént] VT presentar, entregar

presentable [prɪzéntəbəl] ADJ presentable

presentation [prɛzəntéʃən] N (act of presenting) presentación *f*, entrega *f*; (speech) ponencia *f*; (exposition) planteamiento *m*

presentiment [prɪzéntəmənt] N presentimiento *m*

presently [prézəntli] ADV (soon) pronto; (now) actualmente

preservation [prɛzə-véʃən] N preservación *f*, conservación *f*

preservative [prɪzə́-vəɪv] N conservante *m*

preserve [prɪzə́-v] VI/VT (protect) preservar; (keep food fresh) conservar; N (for game) coto *m*; (for animals) reserva *f*; **—s** mermelada *f*, dulce *m*

preset [prisét] ADJ preestablecido

preside [prɪzáɪd] VI presidir; **to — over a meeting** presidir una reunión

presidency [prézɪdənsi] N presidencia *f*

president [prézɪdənt] N presidente -ta *mf*

presidential [prɛzɪdénʃəl] ADJ presidencial

press [prɛs] VI/VT (bear down, squeeze) apretar, oprimir; (a computer key) oprimir, presionar; (iron) planchar; (force) presionar; (extract juice) prensar; (put under pressure) apremiar; **to — on** avanzar; **to — one's point** insistir en un argumento; **to — through** abrirse paso; N (newspapers) prensa *f*; (printing machine) imprenta *f*; (crowding) empuje *m*; **— conference** conferencia de prensa *f*; **— corps** cuerpo de prensa *m*; **— release** comunicado de prensa *m*

pressing [présɪŋ] ADJ apremiante, urgente

pressure [préʃə-] N presión *f*; **— cooker** olla a presión *f*; **— gauge** manómetro *m*; **— group** grupo de presión *m*; VT apremiar, presionar

prestige [prɛstíʒ] N prestigio *m*

prestigious [prɛstídʒəs] ADJ prestigioso

presumably [prɪzúməbli] ADV **— he is already prepared** es de suponer que ya esté preparado

presume [prɪzúm] VI (be presumptuous) presumir; VT (suppose) suponer; (dare) atreverse a

presumption [prɪzámpʃən] N presunción *f*

presumptuous [prɪzámptʃuəs] ADJ presuntuoso, presumido

presuppose [prisəpóz] VT presuponer

pretax [pritǽks] ADJ antes de impuestos

preteen [pritín] ADJ & N preadolescente *mf*

pretend [prɪténd] VI/VT (make believe) hacer de cuenta que; (feign) fingir; VT (claim) pretender; **to — to the throne** pretender el trono

pretense [prítɛns] N (faked action or belief) engaño *m*; (false show) apariencia *f*; **under — of** so pretexto de

pretension [prɪténʃən] N pretensión *f*; (pretext) pretexto *m*

pretentious [prɪténʃəs] ADJ (full of pretension) pretencioso; (showy) ostentoso

pretext [prítɛkst] N pretexto *m*

pretrial [pritráɪł] ADJ anterior al juicio

pretty [prídi] ADJ bonito; (human only) *Sp* guapo; ADV bastante; **— well** bastante bien, francamente bien; VI/VT **to — up** embellecer

prevail [prɪvél] VI (win) prevalecer; (be widespread, dominant) preponderar, imperar; **to — on/upon** persuadir

prevailing [prɪvélɪŋ] ADJ (opinion) predominante; (feeling) reinante, imperante; **— winds** vientos predominantes

prevalent [prévələnt] ADJ prevaleciente, preponderante

prevent [prɪvént] VT (keep from occurring) prevenir; VI/VT (impede) impedir

prevention [prɪvénʃən] N prevención *f*; (of a disease) prevención *f*, profilaxis *f*

preventive [prɪvéntɪv] ADJ preventivo, cautelar

preview [prívju] N preestreno *m*

previewing [prívjuwɪŋ] N previsualización *f*

previous [príviəs] ADJ previo, anterior

previously [príviəsli] ADV previamente, anteriormente

prey [pre] N (animal) presa *f*; VI **to — on** (animals) alimentarse de; (people) explotar; **it —s upon my mind** me tiene preocupado

price [praɪs] N precio *m*; **at any —** a toda costa; **— control** control de precios *m*; **— fixing** fijación de precios *f*; **— index** índice de precios *m*; **— tag** etiqueta de precio *f*; VT (set price) poner precio a; (ask price) averiguar el precio de

priceless [práɪslɪs] ADJ (without price) invalorable; (amusing) divertidísimo

pricey [práɪsi] ADJ caro

pricing [práɪsɪŋ] N fijación de precios *f*

prick [prɪk] N (puncture) pinchazo *m*; (sharp point) púa *f*; VI/VT pinchar, punzar; **to — up one's ears** parar las orejas

prickly [príkli] ADJ espinoso; **— heat** sarpullido causado por el calor *m*; **— pear** tuna *f*, nopal *m*

pride [praɪd] N orgullo *m*; (excessive) soberbia *f*; VI **to — oneself on** enorgullecerse de

priest [prist] N sacerdote *m*; (Catholic only) cura *m*

priesthood [prísthʊd] N sacerdocio *m*

prim [prɪm] ADJ remilgado

primarily [praɪmérɪli] ADV principalmente, más que nada

primary [práɪmɛri] N elección primaria *f*; ADJ primario; (main) fundamental, principal; — **care** atención primaria *f*; — **colors** colores primarios *m pl*; — **election** elección primaria *f*; — **school** escuela primaria *f*

primate [práɪmet] N primate *m*

prime [praɪm] ADJ (principal) fundamental; (of a number) primo; (select) de primera; — **minister** primer ministro *m*, primera ministra *f*; N (number) número primo *m*; **to be in one's** — estar en la flor de la edad, estar en la plenitud de la vida; — **rate** tasa prima *f*; VT preparar; (a pump) cebar

primer[1] [prímə-] N (first book) manual elemental *m*

primer[2] [práɪmə-] N (pump part) cebador *m*

primitive [prímɪdɪv] ADJ & N primitivo -va *mf*

prince [prɪns] N príncipe *m*

princely [prínsli] ADJ noble, principesco; **a — sum** una suma muy grande

princess [prínsɛs] N princesa *f*

principal [prínsəpəł] ADJ principal; N (money invested) capital *m*; (giver of power of attorney) poderdante *mf*, mandante *mf*; (head of a school) director -ora *mf*

principle [prínsəpəł] N principio *m*

print [prɪnt] VI/VT imprimir; (write in block letters) escribir en letra de molde; **to — out** imprimir; N (type) letra de imprenta *f*; (of art) lámina *f*; (of photographs) copia *f*; (of finger) huella digital *f*; (on cloth) estampado *m*; —**out** versión impresa *f*; **in —** publicado, en venta; **out of —** agotado

printer [príntə-] N (person) impresor -ora *mf*, gráfico -ca *mf*; (machine) impresora *f*; — **driver** controlador de impresora *m*; — **feeder** alimentador de impresora *m*

printing [prɪntɪŋ] N (art, trade) imprenta *f*; (process) impresión *f*, tipografía *f*; (block letters) letra de molde *f*, letra de imprenta *f*; — **press** imprenta *f*; **this book is in its second —** este libro está en su segunda tirada

prior [práɪə-] ADJ previo; — **to** anterior a

priority [praɪɔ́rɪdi] N prioridad *f*; **having —** prioritario

prism [prízəm] N prisma *m*

prison [prízən] N prisión *f*, cárcel *f*, presidio *m*

prisoner [prízənə-] N (captive) prisionero -ra *mf*; (in jail) preso -sa *mf*, presidiario -ria *mf*; — **of war** prisionero -ra de guerra *mf*

pristine [prɪstín] ADJ (immaculate) puro; (perfect) perfecto

privacy [práɪvəsi] N privacidad *f*; — **statement** declaración sobre la privacidad *f*

private [práɪvɪt] ADJ (not public) privado; (individual) particular; — **enterprise** empresa privada *f*; — **eye** detective privado -da *mf*; — **parts** partes pudendas *f pl*; — **property** propiedad privada *f*; —**s** partes pudendas *f pl*; — **school** escuela privada *f*; — **sector** sector privado *m*; **a — citizen** un particular; **in —** en privado; N soldado raso *m*

privation [praɪvéʃən] N privación *f*

privatization [praɪvəɒɪzéʃən] N privatización *f*

privatize [práɪvətaɪz] VT privatizar

privilege [prívəlɪʤ] N privilegio *m*

privileged [prívlɪʤd] ADJ privilegiado

privy [prívi] ADJ **to be — to** estar enterado de; N retrete *m*

prize [praɪz] N (reward) premio *m*; (booty) botín *m*; — **fight** pelea de boxeo profesional *f*; — **fighter** boxeador -ora *mf*, pugilista *mf*; VT apreciar

pro [pro] N profesional *mf*

probability [prɑbəbílɪdi] N probabilidad *f*

probable [prɑ́bəbəł] ADJ probable

probate [próbet] N legalización de una validación testamentaria *f*

probation [probéʃən] N libertad condicional *f*

probationary [probéʃənɛri] ADJ probatorio; — **period** período de prueba *m*

probe [prob] VI/VT (explore with a probe) sondear; (examine) examinar; N sonda *f* (also in space); (investigation) indagación *f*

problem [prɑ́bləm] N problema *m*; —**s** problemática *f*

procedure [prəsíʤə-] N procedimiento *m*; (legal) trámite *m*

proceed [prəsíd] VI (originate) proceder; (continue) proseguir, continuar; **to — against** demandar a; **to — to** proceder a

proceeds [prósidz] N ganancia *f*, lo recaudado

proceedings [prəsídɪŋz] N (events) acontecimientos *m pl*; (record of a conference) actas *f pl*, memoria *f*; (legal action) procedimiento *m*

process [prɑ́sɛs] N proceso *m*; **in the — of** en vías de

processing [prɑ́sɛsɪŋ] N (of applications) tramitación *f*; (of data, substances) procesamiento *m*; — **power** potencia procesadora *f*

procession [prəséʃən] N procesión *f*

processor [prɑ́sɛsə-] N procesador *m*

pro-choice [protʃɔ́ɪs] ADJ pro-elección

proclaim [prəklém] VT proclamar

proclamation [prɑkləméʃən] N proclamación *f*, proclama *f*

procrastinate [prəkrɑ́əstənet] VI/VT dejar para último momento

procreate [prókriet] VI/VT procrear, engendrar

proctology [prɑktɑ́lɑʤi] N proctología *f*

procure [prəkjúr] VT procurar, obtener

prod [prɑd] VT aguijonear; **they —ded me into going / to go** insistieron en que fuera

prodigal [prɑ́dɪgəł] ADJ & N pródigo -ga *mf*

prodigious [prədíʤəs] ADJ prodigioso

prodigy [prɑ́dəʤi] N prodigio *m*

produce[1] [pródus] N (vegetables) verduras *f pl*, hortalizas *f pl*
produce[2] [prədús] VI/VT producir; VT (present) presentar
producer [prədúsə·] N productor -ora *mf*; (of a movie) realizador -ora *mf*
product [prádəkt] N producto *m*
production [prədʌ́kʃən] N producción *f*; (TV, radio) producción *f*, realización *f*; (exaggerated situation) teatro *m*
productive [prədʌ́ktɪv] ADJ productivo
productivity [prɑdəktɪ́vɪdɪ] N productividad *f*
profane [profén] ADJ profano; (vulgar) grosero; VT profanar
profanity [prəfǽnɪdɪ] N groserías *f pl*, palabrotas *f pl*
profess [prəfɛ́s] VI (publicly accept, take vows) profesar; VT (state) afirmar; (claim) pretender
profession [prəféʃən] N profesión *f*
professional [prəféʃənl] ADJ & N profesional *mf*
professor [prəfɛ́sə·] N profesor -ora universitario -ria *mf*; (full) catedrático -ca *mf*
proffer [prɑ́fə·] VT ofrecer; N oferta *f*
proficiency [prəfíʃənsi] N competencia *f*
proficient [prəfíʃənt] ADJ competente
profile [prófaɪl] N (contour) perfil *m*; **a high-— case** un caso muy sonado
profit [prɑ́fɪt] N (gain) ganancia *f*; **— and loss** ganancias y pérdidas *f pl*; **— margin** margen de ganancia *m*; **— sharing** participación en las ganancias de una empresa *f*; **at a —** con ganancia; **to turn a —** dar ganancia; **not for —** sin fines de lucro; VI salir ganando; **to — from** (benefit) aprovechar, sacar provecho de; (use to get an advantage) aprovecharse de; VT servir
profitability [prɑfɪdəbɪ́lɪdɪ] N rentabilidad *f*
profitable [prɑ́fɪdəbəł] ADJ (beneficial) provechoso; (lucrative) lucrativo, rentable
profound [prəfáʊnd] ADJ profundo
profundity [prəfʌ́ndɪdɪ] N profundidad *f*
profuse [prəfjús] ADJ profuso, pródigo
progesterone [prodʒɛ́stəron] N progesterona *f*
prognosis [prɑgnósɪs] N pronóstico *m*
program [prógræm] N programa *m*; VI/VT programar
programmable [prográməbəł] ADJ programable
programmer [prógræmə·] N programador -ora *mf*
programming [prógræmɪŋ] N programación *f*; **— language** lenguaje de programación *m*
progress[1] [prɑ́grɛs] N progreso *m*
progress[2] [prəgrɛ́s] VI progresar
progression [prəgrɛ́ʃən] N progresión *f*
progressive [prəgrɛ́sɪv] ADJ (advancing) progresivo; ADJ & N (liberal) progresista *mf*, progresivo -va *mf*
prohibit [prohíbɪt] VT prohibir, vedar
prohibition [proəbíʃən] N prohibición *f*
project[1] [prɑ́dʒɛkt] N proyecto *m*
project[2] [prədʒɛ́kt] VI/VT (plan) proyectar[se]; VI (jut out) sobresalir
projectile [prədʒɛ́ktəł] N proyectil *m*; ADJ arrojadizo
projection [prədʒɛ́kʃən] N (plan) proyección *f*; (jut) saliente *f*
projector [prədʒɛ́ktə·] N proyector *m*
proletariat [prolɪtɛ́riət] N proletariado *m*
pro-life [prolάɪf] ADJ antiaborto
proliferation [prəlɪfərɛ́ʃən] N proliferación *f*
prolific [prəlífɪk] ADJ prolífico
prologue [prólɔg] N prólogo *m*
prolong [prəlɔ́ŋ] VT prolongar
prolongation [prolɔŋgéʃən] N prolongación *f*
promenade [prɑmənéd] N paseo *m*; (dance) baile *m*; VI/VT pasear[se]
prominent [prɑ́mənənt] ADJ prominente
promiscuous [prəmískjuəs] ADJ promiscuo, liviano
promise [prɑ́mɪs] N promesa *f*; **he showed —** prometía mucho; VI/VT prometer
promising [prɑ́mɪsɪŋ] ADJ prometedor
promissory [prɑ́mɪsɔri] ADJ promisorio; **— note** pagaré *m*
promontory [prɑ́məntɔri] N promontorio *m*
promote [prəmót] VT (foster) promover, fomentar; (advance in rank) ascender; (in school) pasar de año, promover; (advertise) promocionar
promoter [prəmóə·] N (fomenter) propulsor -ora *mf*; (organizer) promotor -ora *mf*
promotion [prəmóʃən] N (act of promoting) promoción *f*; (advance in rank) ascenso *m*
promotional [prəmóʃənl] ADJ promocional
prompt [prɑmpt] ADJ (quick) rápido; (punctual) puntual; VT (cause) inducir; (in theater) apuntar; **to give someone a —** apuntarle a alguien
promptly [prɑ́mptli] ADV (soon) pronto; (punctually) puntualmente
promulgate [prɑ́məłget] VT promulgar
prone [pron] ADJ (disposed) propenso, proclive; (face down) boca abajo; (prostrate) postrado
prong [prɔŋ] N púa *f*, diente *m*
pronoun [prónaʊn] N pronombre *m*
pronounce [prənáʊns] VT (enunciate) pronunciar; (declare) declarar
pronounced [prənáʊnst] ADJ pronunciado
pronouncement [prənáʊnsmənt] N pronunciamiento *m*
pronunciation [prənʌnsiéʃən] N pronunciación *f*
proof [pruf] N (evidence, test, trial printing) prueba *f*; (of alcohol) graduación *f*, grado *m*; **— of purchase** comprobante de compra *m*; **—reader** corrector -ora de pruebas *mf*, revisor -ora de pruebas *mf*; **fifty —**

veinticinco por ciento de graduación alcohólica; **fire—** a prueba de incendios; **water—** impermeable; **bullet—** a prueba de balas

prop [prɑp] N (pole) puntal *m*; (in theater) accesorio *m*; (propeller) hélice *f*; (support) sostén *m*, apoyo *m*; (of a plant) tutor *m*; VT **to — against** apoyar en, sostener en; **to — up** apuntalar, sostener

propaganda [prɑpəgǽndə] N propaganda *f*

propagate [prɑ́pəget] VI/VT propagar[se]

propagation [prɑpəgéʃən] N propagación *f*

propane [prɑ́pen] N propano *m*

propel [prəpɛ́ł] VT propulsar, impulsar

propeller [prəpɛ́lə-] N hélice *f*

propensity [prəpɛ́nsɪdɪ] N propensión *f*

proper [prɑ́pə-] ADJ (appropriate) apropiado; (decorous) decoroso; (genuine) como Dios manda; (correct) correcto; (in math, grammar) propio; **to be — to** ser propio de

properly [prɑ́pə-li] ADV (appropriately) apropiadamente; (correctly) correctamente; (decorously) decorosamente

property [prɑ́pə-dɪ] N (characteristic) propiedad *f*; (real estate) propiedad *f*, finca *f*; (assets) bienes *m pl*; **— damage** daños materiales *m pl*

prophecy [prɑ́fɪsi] N profecía *f*

prophesy [prɑ́fɪsaɪ] VI/VT profetizar

prophet [prɑ́fɪt] N profeta -tisa *mf*

prophetic [prəfɛ́dɪk] ADJ profético

propitious [prəpíʃəs] ADJ propicio

proponent [prəpónənt] N (person who proposes) proponente *mf*; (adherent) defensor -ora *mf*

proportion [prəpɔ́rʃən] N proporción *f*; **out of —** desproporcionado; VT proporcionar; **well —ed** bien proporcionado

proportional [prəpɔ́rʃənł] ADJ proporcional

proportionate [prəpɔ́rʃənɪt] ADJ proporcional

proposal [prəpózəł] N (suggestion) propuesta *f*; (of marriage, dishonest) proposición *f*

propose [prəpóz] VI/VT (suggest) proponer; VI (ask in marriage) declararse, hacer una propuesta de matrimonio; **to — to do something** proponerse hacer algo

proposition [prɑpəzíʃən] N proposición *f*; VT hacer proposiciones deshonestas

proprietor [prəpráɪɪtə-] N propietario -ria *mf*

propriety [prəpráɪɪtɪ] N decoro *m*

propulsion [prəpʌ́łʃən] N propulsión *f*

prorate [prorét] VT prorratear

prosaic [prozéɪk] ADJ prosaico

prose [proz] N prosa *f*

prosecute [prɑ́sɪkjut] VI/VT (take to court) procesar, enjuiciar; VT (pursue) llevar adelante

prosecution [prɑsɪkjúʃən] N (act of prosecuting) procesamiento *m*; (officials who prosecute) ministerio público *m*, fiscalía *f*

prosecutor [prɑ́sɪkjudə-] N fiscal *mf*

proselytize [prɑ́səlɪtaɪz] VT convertir; VI buscar ganar prosélitos

prospect [prɑ́spɛkt] N (outlook, possibility) perspectiva *f*, expectativa *f*; (candidate) candidato -ta *mf*; (possible client) posible cliente -ta *mf*; VT prospectar; VI **to — for** buscar

prospective [prəspɛ́ktɪv] ADJ posible, potencial

prospector [prɑ́spɛktə-] N prospector -ora *mf*

prosper [prɑ́spə-] VI prosperar

prosperity [prɑspɛ́rɪdɪ] N prosperidad *f*, bonanza *f*

prosperous [prɑ́spərəs] ADJ próspero

prostate [prɑ́stet] N próstata *f*; **— gland** próstata *f*

prosthesis [prɑsθísɪs] N prótesis *f*

prostitute [prɑ́stɪtut] N prostituto -ta *mf*; VT prostituir

prostitution [prɑstɪtúʃən] N prostitución *f*

prostrate [prɑ́stret] VT postrar; ADJ (lying flat, overcome) postrado; (lying face down) boca abajo

protagonist [protǽgənɪst] N protagonista *mf*

protect [prətɛ́kt] VI/VT proteger, amparar

protection [prətɛ́kʃən] N protección *f*

protectionist [prətɛ́kʃənɪst] ADJ & N proteccionista *mf*

protective [prətɛ́ktɪv] ADJ protector

protector [prətɛ́ktə-] N protector -ora *mf*

protectorate [prətɛ́ktərɪt] N protectorado *m*

protégé, protégée [prɔ́dəʒe] N protegido -da *mf*

protein [prɔ́tin] N proteína *f*

protest[1] [prɔ́test] N protesta *f*, reclamación *f*

protest[2] [prətɛ́st] VI/VT protestar, reclamar

Protestant [prɑ́dɪstənt] ADJ & N protestante *mf*

protestation [protəstéʃən] N declaración *f*

protocol [prɔ́dəkɔł] N protocolo *m*

proton [prɔ́tɑn] N protón *m*

protoplasm [prɔ́dəplæzəm] N protoplasma *m*

prototype [prɔ́dətaɪp] N prototipo *m*

protozoan [prodəzɔ́ən] N protozoario *m*

protract [protrǽkt] VT prolongar

protrude [protrúd] VI sobresalir, proyectarse

protuberance [prətúbərəns] N protuberancia *f*

proud [praʊd] ADJ orgulloso; (haughty) soberbio; **to be — of** enorgullecerse de, ufanarse de

prove [pruv] VT (demonstrate, verify) probar, demostrar; VI resultar; **events have —d me right** los hechos me han dado la razón

proverb [prɑ́vɜ-b] N proverbio *m*, refrán *m*

provide [prəváɪd] VT (furnish) proveer, proporcionar; (supply) abastecer, aportar; (stipulate) estipular, prevenir; VI **to — for** (support) mantener; (stipulate) estipular; **to — with** proveer de, proporcionar; CONJ **—d [that]** con tal [de] que, siempre que

providence [právɪdəns] N providencia *f*
provider [prəváɪdɚ] N (supplier) proveedor -ora *mf*; (breadwinner) sostén *m*
province [právɪns] N (area) provincia *f*; (competence) competencia *f*
provincial [prəvínʃəł] ADJ (of a province) provincial; (rustic) provinciano, pueblerino; N provinciano -na *mf*
provision [prəvíʒən] N (act of providing, thing provided) provisión *f*, suministro *m*, prestación *f*; (precaution) medida *f*, precaución *f*; (clause) estipulación *f*, prevención *f*; **—s** provisiones *f pl*, víveres *m pl*, bastimentos *m pl*, suministros *m*
provisional [prəvíʒənł] ADJ provisional
proviso [prəváɪzo] N condición *f*, estipulación *f*
provocation [prɑvəkéʃən] N provocación *f*
provoke [prəvók] VT provocar
provost [próvost] N vicerrector -ora *mf*
prow [praʊ] N proa *f*
prowess [práʊɪs] N valentía *f*
prowl [praʊł] VI/VT rondar en acecho
proximity [prɑksímɪdɪ] N proximidad *f*
proxy [prúksi] N (person) apoderado -da *mf*; (power of attorney) poder *m*; **by —** por poder
prude [prud] N mojigato -ta *mf*, gazmoño -ña *mf*
prudence [prúdns] N prudencia *f*
prudent [prúdnt] ADJ prudente
prudery [prúdɚri] N mojigatería *f*, gazmoñería *f*
prudish [prúdɪʃ] ADJ mojigato, gazmoño
prune [prun] N ciruela pasa *f*; VI/VT podar
pry [praɪ] VT curiosear; **to — into** entrometerse; **to — open** abrir por la fuerza; **to — a secret out** extraer/arrancar un secreto
pseudonym [súdnɪm] N pseudónimo/seudónimo *m*
psoriasis [səráɪəsɪs] N psoriasis/soriasis *f*
psych [saɪk] VT **to — out** intimidar psicológicamente
psychedelic [saɪkɪdélɪk] ADJ psicodélico/sicodélico
psychiatrist [saɪkáɪətrɪst] N psiquiatra/siquiatra *mf*
psychiatry [saɪkáɪətri] N psiquiatría/siquiatría *f*
psychic [sáɪkɪk] ADJ psíquico/síquico; N médium *mf*, psíquico -ca / síquico -ca *mf*
psychoanalysis [saɪkoə́nəlaɪz] N psicoanálisis/sicoanálisis *m*
psychological [saɪkəládʒɪkəł] ADJ psicológico/sicológico
psychologist [saɪkáləd̪ʒɪst] N psicólogo -ga / sicólogo -ga *mf*
psychology [saɪkáləd̪ʒi] N psicología/sicología *f*
psychopath [sáɪkəpæθ] N psicópata/sicópata *mf*
psychosis [saɪkósɪs] N psicosis/sicosis *f*
psychosomatic [saɪkosəmǽdɪk] ADJ psicosomático/sicosomático
psychotherapy [saɪkoθérəpi] N psicoterapia/sicoterapia *f*
psychotic [saɪkáɑdɪk] ADJ psicótico/sicótico
puberty [pjúbə·ɚdi] N pubertad *f*
pubic [pjúbɪk] ADJ púbico; **— hair** pelo púbico *m*
public [pʌ́blɪk] ADJ público; **— domain** dominio público *m*; **— health** salud pública *f*; **— relations** relaciones públicas *f pl*; **— school** escuela pública *f*; **— service** servicio público *m*; **to go —** proceder a la venta pública de acciones, salir a bolsa; N público *m*
publication [pʌblɪkéʃən] N publicación *f*
publicity [pʌblísɪdi] N publicidad *f*, propaganda *f*; **— campaign** campaña publicitaria *f*
publicize [pʌ́blɪsaɪz] VT promocionar
publish [pʌ́blɪʃ] VI/VT publicar, editar; **—ing house** [casa] editorial *f*
publisher [pʌ́blɪʃɚ] N editor -ora *mf*
puck [pʌk] N puck *m*
pucker [pʌ́kɚ] VI/VT fruncir[se]; N frunce *m*
pudding [pʊ́dɪŋ] N budín *m*, pudín *m*
puddle [pʌ́dł] N charco *m*
pudendum [pjudéndəm] N partes pudendas *f pl*
Puerto Rican [pɔrd̪əríkən] ADJ & N puertorriqueño -ña *mf*
Puerto Rico [pɔrd̪əríko] N Puerto Rico *m*
puff [pʌf] N (air) resoplido *m*, soplo *m*; (smoke) bocanada *f*; (on a cigarette) pitada *f*, chupada *f*; (of a sleeve) bullón *m*; **— pastry** masa de hojaldre *f*; VI (blow) resoplar; (breathe hard) jadear; (smoke a cigarette) echar bocanadas; **to — up** hincharse; **to — up with pride** henchirse de orgullo
pug [pʌg] N dogo *m*; **— nose** nariz chata *f*
puke [pjuk] VI/VT vomitar, lanzar; N vómito *m*
pull [pʊł] VI/VT (tug) tirar, jalar; (extract) arrancar, extraer; (stretch) estirar; (injure) desgarrar; **to — apart** destrozar; **to — down** (demolish) demoler; (earn) sacar; **to — for** hinchar por; **to — off** conseguir; **to — oneself together** calmarse; **to — over** parar; **to — up** parar; **to — through** salvarse; **to — strings** mover palancas; **to — out** (leave a place) salir; (back out) retirarse; **the train —ed into the station** el tren entró a la estación; N (act of pulling) tirón *m*; (force) fuerza *f*; (influence) influencia *f*; (injury) desgarro *m*; **— -down menu** menú abatible *m*
pullet [pʊ́lɪt] N polla *f*
pulley [pʊ́li] N polea *f*, carrucha *f*
pulmonary [pʌ́łmənɛri] ADJ pulmonar
pulp [pʌlp] N (of paper, wood, fruit) pulpa *f*; (of grape, sugarcane, olive, etc.) bagazo *m*
pulpit [pʊ́łpɪt] N púlpito *m*
pulsar [pʌ́łsɑr] N púlsar *m*
pulsate [pʌ́łset] VI latir
pulse [pʌłs] N pulso *m*; (single pulsation, act of pulsing) pulsación *f*
pulverize [pʌ́łvəraɪz] VT pulverizar[se]
puma [pjúmə] N puma *f*

pumice [pʌ́mɪs] N piedra pómez *f*
pump [pʌmp] N bomba *f*; (shoe) zapatilla *f*, zapato escotado *m*; (for gasoline) surtidor *m*; VI/VT bombear; (inflate) inflar; **to — someone for information** sonsacar [información] a alguien
pumpkin [pʌ́mpkɪn] N calabaza *f*
pun [pʌn] N juego de palabras *m*, retruécano *m*; VI hacer juegos de palabras
punch [pʌntʃ] N (blow) puñetazo *m*; (drink) ponche *m*; (drill) sacabocados *m sg*; (force) fuerza *f*, empuje *m*; **— bowl** ponchera *f*; **— line** remate de un chiste *m*; VI/VT (hit) dar un puñetazo; VT (drive cattle) arriar; (make a hole) agujerear; **to — in/out** marcar tarjeta
punctual [pʌ́ŋktʃuəł] ADJ puntual
punctuality [pʌŋktʃuǽlɪDi] N puntualidad *f*
punctuate [pʌ́ŋktʃuet] VI/VT puntuar; (interrupt) interrumpir; (accentuate) salpicar
punctuation [pʌŋktʃuéʃən] N puntuación *f*
puncture [pʌ́ŋktʃə˞] VI/VT pinchar[se]; *Mex* ponchar[se]; **—d tire** neumático pinchado *m*; N (action of perforating) perforación *f*; (hole) pinchazo *m*; **— wound** herida perforada *f*
pundit [pʌ́ndɪt] N experto -ta *mf*
pungent [pʌ́nʤənt] ADJ (acrid) acre; (sarcastic) mordaz
punish [pʌ́nɪʃ] VT castigar, penar
punishment [pʌ́nɪʃmənt] N castigo *m*
punitive [pjúnɪDɪv] ADJ punitivo; **— damages** daños punitivos *m pl*
punk [pʌŋk] N (inexperienced boy) mocoso *m*; (hoodlum) gamberro *m*; (rock) punk *m*; (punker) punkero -ra *mf*
punt [pʌnt] N (kick) patada de despeje *f*; (boat) balsa *f*; VI/VT despejar; VI andar en balsa
punter [pʌ́ntə˞] N despejador *m*
puny [pjúni] ADJ endeble
pupil [pjúpəł] N (student) escolar *mf*; (part of eye) pupila *f*, niña *f*
puppet [pʌ́pɪt] N títere *m*, monigote *m*; **— show** teatro de títeres *m*
puppy [pʌ́pi] N cachorro *m*
purchase [pɝ́tʃəs] VI/VT comprar, adquirir; N compra *f*; (hold) asidero *m*; **— order** orden de compra *f*; **— price** precio de compra *m*
purchaser [pɝ́tʃəsə˞] N comprador *mf*
purchasing [pɝ́tʃəsɪŋ] N compra *f*; **— agent** agente de compras *mf*; **— power** poder adquisitivo *m*
pure [pjʊr] ADJ puro; ADJ & N **—bred** purasangre *m*
puree [pjʊré] N puré *m*
purgative [pɝ́gəDɪv] ADJ & N purgante *m*
purgatory [pɝ́gətɔri] N purgatorio *m*
purge [pɝ́ʤ] VI/VT purgar[se]; N purga *f*
purify [pjʊ́rəfaɪ] VI/VT purificar[se], depurar[se]
purist [pjʊ́rɪst] N purista *mf*
puritanical [pjʊrɪtǽnɪkəł] ADJ puritano
purity [pjʊ́rɪDi] N pureza *f*
purple [pɝ́pəł] N morado *m*, púrpura *f*; ADJ morado, púrpura
purport[1] [pɝ́pɔrt] N (meaning) significado *m*; (purpose) propósito *m*
purport[2] [pə˞pɔ́rt] VT pretender
purpose [pɝ́pəs] N propósito *m*, objetivo *m*; **on —** adrede, a propósito
purr [pɝ˞] N ronroneo *m* (also motors); VI ronronear
purse [pɝ˞s] N bolso *m*, cartera *f*; VT **to — one's lips** fruncir los labios
pursuant [pə˞súənt] ADV LOC **— to** conforme a, de acuerdo con
pursue [pə˞sú] VT (follow) perseguir; (strive) dedicarse a; (continue) continuar con; (practice a profession) ejercer
pursuer [pə˞súə˞] N perseguidor -ora *mf*
pursuit [pə˞sút] N (chase) persecución *f*, seguimiento *m*, acoso *m*; (striving for) búsqueda *f*; (pastime) pasatiempo *m*; (practice) ejercicio *m*; **in — of** (chasing) detrás de; (striving for) en busca de
pus [pʌs] N pus *m*
push [pʊʃ] VI/VT (shove) empujar; VT (pressure) presionar, promover; (sell drugs) camellear; **to — a button** apretar un botón; VI (in childbirth) pujar; **to — aside/away** apartar; **to — forward** abrirse paso, avanzar; **to — open** abrir de un empujón; **to — through** hacer pasar; N empujón *m*; (military) ofensiva *f*; **—-up** lagartija *f*; ADJ **—-button** de botones
pusher [pʊ́ʃə˞] N camello *mf*
pushy [pʊ́ʃi] ADJ insistente
pussy [pʊ́si] N minino *m*, gatito *m*; **— willow** sauce *m*
put [pʊt] VT poner, colocar; **to — a question** plantear una pregunta; **to — across** expresar; **to — away** guardar; **to — down** (write down) apuntar; (suppress) sofocar; (attribute) atribuir; (humiliate) humillar; (make a down payment) hacer un depósito; (a pet) sacrificar; **to — into** meter; **to — into words** expresar, decir; **to — in writing** poner por escrito; **to — off** (postpone) aplazar, posponer; (perturb) desagradar; (dissuade) disuadir; **to — on** ponerse; **to — on airs** darse tono; **to — on weight** engordar; **to — out** (extinguish) apagar, extinguir; (annoy) molestar; **to — the blame** echar la culpa; **to — to sea** echar al mar; **to — to sleep** sacrificar; **to — up** (construct) levantar; (lodge) alojar; **to — up for sale** poner a la venta; **to — up with** aguantar; **I felt —-upon** sentí que se habían aprovechado de mí; N **— option** opción de venta *f*; **—-down** insulto *m*
putrid [pjʊ́trɪd] ADJ putrefacto

putt [pʌt] VI/VT potear; N pat
putter [pʌ́tə-] VI entretenerse; N (golf) putter *m*
putty [pʌ́ɾi] N masilla *f*; VT rellenar con masilla
puzzle [pʌ́zəł] N (jigsaw) rompecabezas *m sg*; (riddle) acertijo *m*; (problem) enigma *m*; (crossword) crucigrama *m*; VT dejar perplejo, desconcertar; VI **to — out** desentrañar; **to — over** meditar sobre; **to be —d** estar perplejo
pygmy [pígmi] N pigmeo -a *mf*
pylon [páɪlɑn] N pilón *m*
pyramid [pírəmɪd] N pirámide *f*
pyromania [pɪɾoméniə] N piromanía *f*
pyromaniac [pɪɾoméniæk] N pirómano -na *mf*
pyrotechnics [pɪɾətéknɪks] N pirotecnia *f*
python [páɪθɑn] N pitón *mf*

Qq

Qatar [kətár] N Qatar *m*
Qatari [kətári] ADJ & N catarí *mf*
quack [kwæk] N (sound of duck) graznido *m*; (charlatan) matasanos *mf*, charlatán -ana *mf*; ADJ charlatán; VI graznar
quadrilateral [kwɑdrəlǽdə-əł] ADJ & N cuadrilátero *m*
quadriplegic [kwɑdrəplídʒɪk] ADJ & N tetraplégico -ca *mf*
quadruped [kwɑ́drəpɛd] ADJ & N cuadrúpedo *m*
quadruplet [kwɑdrʌ́plɪt] N cuatrillizo -za *mf*
quagmire [kwǽgmaɪr] N (bog) cenagal *m*, atascadero *m*; (crisis) atolladero *m*, atascadero *m*
quail [kweł] N codorniz *f*
quaint [kwent] ADJ pintoresco
quake [kwek] N (instance of quaking) temblor *m*; (earthquake) terremoto *m*; VI temblar
qualification [kwɑləfɪkéʃən] N (for a race) clasificación *f*; (requirement) requisito *m*; **without** — sin reservas
qualify [kwɑ́ləfaɪ] VT (characterize) calificar; (moderate) moderar; (provide with credentials) capacitar; VI (for a race) clasificarse; (for a position) estar capacitado
qualifying [kwɑ́lɪfaɪɪŋ] ADJ calificativo
qualitative [kwɑ́lɪtɛDɪv] ADJ cualitativo
quality [kwɑ́lɪɾi] N (characteristic) cualidad *f*; (excellence) calidad *f*; **— control** control de calidad *m*
qualm [kwɔm] N escrúpulo *m*
quantify [kwɑ́ntəfaɪ] VT cuantificar
quantitative [kwɑ́ntɪtɛDɪv] ADJ cuantitativo
quantity [kwɑ́ntɪDi] N cantidad *f*
quantum mechanics [kwɑ́ntəmmə́kǽnɪks] N mecánica cuántica *f*
quarantine [kwɔ́rəntin] N cuarentena *f*; VT poner en cuarentena
quarrel [kwɔ́rəł] N riña *f*, rencilla *f*; VI reñir, pelear
quarrelsome [kwɔ́rəłsəm] ADJ pendenciero
quarry [kwɔ́ri] N (stone) cantera *f*; (game) presa *f*; VT explotar
quart [kwɔrt] N cuarto de galón [0.9463 litros] *m*
quarter [kwɔ́rDə-] N (one-fourth) cuarto *m*, cuarta parte *f*; (coin) moneda de 25 centavos *f*; (of a sporting match) tiempo *m*; (of a calendar or school year) trimestre *m*; (district) barrio *m*; **—back** mariscal de campo *m*; **—master general** intendente *mf*; **— note** negra *f*; **—s** alojamiento *m*; **from all —s** de todas partes; **to give no — to the enemy** no dar cuartel al enemigo; ADJ cuarto; VT (divide) cuartear, dividir en cuartos; (execute) descuartizar; (lodge troops) acuartelar, acantonar
quarterly [kwɔ́rDə-li] ADV trimestralmente; ADJ trimestral; N publicación trimestral *f*
quartet [kwɔrtét] N cuarteto *m*
quartz [kwɔrts] N cuarzo *m*
quasar [kwézɑr] N cuásar *m*, quásar *m*
quash [kwɑʃ] VT (a rebellion) sofocar; (a decision) anular
quaver [kwévə-] VI temblar; N temblor *m*; (in music) trémolo *m*
queasy [kwízi] ADJ nauseoso
queen [kwin] N reina *f*
queer [kwir] ADJ (strange) raro; (eccentric) excéntrico; **to feel —** sentirse raro; VT comprometer
quell [kwɛł] VT (suppress) reprimir, sofocar; (calm) calmar
quench [kwɛntʃ] VT (flames, thirst) apagar; (passions) aplacar, apagar
query [kwíri] N (question) pregunta *f*; (question mark) signo de interrogación *m*; (doubt) duda *f*; VT (ask) preguntar; (question) expresar dudas; (mark with a question mark) marcar con signo de interrogación
quest [kwɛst] N búsqueda *f*
question [kwéstʃən] N (thing asked) pregunta *f*; (issue) cuestión *f*; **— mark** signo de interrogación *m*; **beyond —** fuera de duda; **that is out of the —** ¡ni pensarlo! VT (ask) preguntar; (interrogate) interrogar; (call into doubt) dudar, cuestionar
questionable [kwéstʃənəbəł] ADJ (doubtful) cuestionable, discutible; (morally dubious) equívoco
questioner [kwéstʃənə-] N interrogador -ora *mf*
questioning [kwéstʃənɪŋ] N interrogatorio *m*; ADJ (asking) interrogador; (doubting) cuestionador
questionnaire [kwɛstʃənér] N cuestionario *m*
queue [kju] N cola *f*, fila *f*; VT poner en la cola
quibble [kwíbəł] VI (split hairs) sutilizar; (evade) evadir; (argue) andar en dimes y diretes; N

(hairsplitting) sutileza *f*; (evasion) evasiva *f*
quiche [kiʃ] N quiche *f*
quick [kwɪk] ADJ rápido, pronto; **—-tempered** irascible, geniudo; **—-witted** agudo; ADV rápido; N (flesh under nails) carne viva *f*; (the living) los vivos; **to cut to the —** herir en lo vivo; **—sand** arena movediza *f*; **—silver** mercurio *m*, azogue *m*
quicken [kwíkən] VI/VT (speed up) acelerar[se], aligerar[se]; (liven) avivar[se]
quickly [kwíkli] ADV rápido, deprisa, de prisa
quickness [kwíknɪs] N (speed) rapidez *f*; (of wit) agudeza *f*
quiet [kwáɪɪt] ADJ (not noisy) silencioso; (not talking) callado; (restrained) tranquilo; (peaceful, still) reposado; **be —!** ¡silencio! ¡cállate! N (freedom from noise) silencio *m*; (tranquillity) tranquilidad *f*, sosiego *m*; VT (make quiet) acallar; (make tranquil) sosegar, tranquilizar, serenar; VI **to — down** calmarse
quietly [kwáɪɪtli] ADV (talk) en voz baja; (walk) silenciosamente; **they — went about buying up shares** fueron comprando acciones sin llamar la atención
quill [kwɪł] N (feather) pluma *f*; (hollow base of feather) cañón *m*; (spine on a porcupine) púa *f*
quilt [kwɪłt] N colcha de retazos *f*; VI/VT hacer una colcha de retazos
quinine [kwáɪnaɪn] N quinina *f*
quip [kwɪp] N ocurrencia *f*; VI decir ocurrencias
quirk [kwɜ-k] N excentricidad *f*
quit [kwɪt] VT (a competition) abandonar; (a place) irse de, salir de; (a job) dejar; (a computer program) salir; **to call it —s** abandonar; **to — smoking** dejar de fumar; VI (withdraw) abandonar; (stop) parar; (resign) renunciar
quite [kwaɪt] ADV (very) bastante; (entirely) del todo, enteramente; **— a person** una persona admirable *f*; **— a lot** bastante; **it's — the fashion** está muy de moda
quiver [kwívə-] VI temblar; N (shake) temblor *m*; (sheath for arrows) carcaj *m*, aljaba *f*
quiz [kwɪz] N (test) prueba *f*; (show) concurso *m*; VI (give a quiz) examinar, poner una prueba; (interrogate) interrogar
quota [kwóʊdə] N cuota *f*
quotation [kwotéʃən] N cita *f*; (of a price) cotización *f*; **— marks** comillas *f pl*
quote [kwot] VI/VT (words) citar; (prices) cotizar; **to — from** citar a; N (of words) cita *f*; (of a price) cotización *f*; **in —s** entre comillas
quotient [kwóʃənt] N cociente *m*

Rr

R & D [research and development] [úrnḍí] N ID *mf*
rabbi [ræbaɪ] N rabino *m*
rabbit [ræbɪt] N conejo *m*
rabble [ræbəł] N chusma *f*, plebe *f*, gentuza *f*
rabid [ræbɪd] ADJ rabioso
rabies [rébiz] N rabia *f*
raccoon [rækún] N mapache *m*
race [res] N (lineage) raza *f*; (competition) carrera *f*; **—horse** caballo de carreras *m*; **—track** (for runners) pista *f*; (for horses) hipódromo *m*; VI (participate in competition) correr, competir en una carrera; (hurry) ir corriendo; (of heart) latir rápido; (of a motor) acelerar; VT (a horse) hacer correr; (an engine) acelerar; **I'll — you** te echo una carrera
racer [résə-] N corredor -ora *mf*; (horse) caballo de carreras *m*
racial [réʃəł] ADJ racial
racism [résɪzəm] N racismo *m*
rack [ræk] N (for clothes) perchero *m*; (for luggage) baca *f*; (for spices) especiero *m*; (for towels) toallero *m*; (for torture) potro de tormento *m*; **— and pinion** cremallera *f* y piñón *m*; VT **to be —ed with pain** estar transido de dolor; **to — one's brain** devanarse los sesos; **to — up** acumular
racket [rækɪt] N (sports) raqueta *f*; (noise of an impact) estrépito *m*, estruendo *m*; (noise of voices and movement) barahúnda *f*, batahola *f*; (swindle) estafa *f*; (extortion) extorsión *f*
racketeer [rækɪtír] N (swindler) trapacero -ra *mf*, estafador -ora *mf*; (extortionist) extorsionista *mf*; VI (swindle) estafar; (extort) extorsionar
radar [réḍɑr] N radar *m*
radial [réḍiəł] ADJ radial
radiance [réḍiəns] N resplandor *m*, fulgor *m*
radiant [réḍiənt] ADJ radiante, resplandeciente
radiate [réḍiet] VI/VT irradiar, radiar
radiation [reḍiéʃən] N radiación *f*; **— sickness** enfermedad por radiación *f*; **— therapy** radioterapia *f*
radiator [réḍieḍə-] N radiador *m*
radical [ræḍikəł] ADJ & N radical *mf*
radicalism [ræḍikəlɪzəm] N radicalismo *m*
radio [réḍio] N (device, system of communication) radio *f*; **— announcer** locutor -ora *mf*; **— listener** radioescucha *mf*; **— station** radiodifusora *f*; **— telescope** radiotelescopio *m*; **— transmitter** radiotransmisor *m*; **by —** por radio; ADJ **—active** radiactivo, radioactivo; VT

(broadcast) transmitir por radio; VI/VT (call) llamar por radio

radiologist [reɒiáləʤɪst] N radiólogo -ga *mf*

radiology [reɒiáləʤi] N radiología *f*

radish [ræɒɪʃ] N rábano *m*

radium [réɒiəm] N radio *m*

radius [réɒiəs] N radio *m*

radon [réɒɑn] N radón *m*

raffle [ræfəł] N rifa *f*, sorteo *m*; VI rifar, sortear

raft [ræft] N balsa *f*

rafter [ræftə˞] N viga *f*

rag [ræg] N (piece of cloth) trapo *m*, guiñapo *m*; (on clothes) harapo *m*, andrajo *m*; **— doll** muñeca de trapo *f*

rage [reʤ] N ira *f*, rabia *f*, cólera *f*; **to be all the —** estar de moda; VI enfurecerse; **to — with anger** bramar de ira

ragged [rǽgɪd] ADJ (ill-clothed) andrajoso, harapiento, desharrapado; (voice) ronco, roto; (on an edge) irregular, desigual; **to be on the — edge** estar al borde

raid [red] N (military) incursión *f*; (by police) allanamiento *m*, redada *f*; (by air) bombardeo aéreo *m*; VI/VT hacer una incursión; VT (attack) atacar; (rob) asaltar; (carry out a police operation on) allanar

raider [réɒə˞] N empresa tiburón *f*

rail [reł] N (of a railroad track) riel *m*, carril *m*; (on a balcony) baranda *f*, barandilla *f*; **— fence** barrera *f*; **—road** ferrocarril *m*; **—road company** empresa ferroviaria *f*; **—road crossing** cruce de ferrocarril *m*; **—road employee** ferroviario -ria *mf*; **—way** ferrocarril *m*; **by —** por ferrocarril; VT **to —road** (goods) transportar por ferrocarril; (laws) hacer aprobar apresuradamente; (a person) condenar injustamente

railing [réɫɪŋ] N (barrier) baranda *f*; (on a bridge) pretil *m*; (on a stairway) pasamano *m*

rain [ren] N lluvia *f*; **—bow** arco iris *m*; **—coat** impermeable *m*; **—drop** gota de lluvia *f*; **—fall** precipitación *f*; **— forest** selva tropical *f*; **— gauge** pluviómetro *f*; **—storm** temporal de lluvia *f*; **— water** agua llovediza *f*; VI/VT llover; **— or shine** llueva o truene; **to — cats and dogs** llover a cántaros

rainy [réni] ADJ lluvioso

raise [rez] VI/VT (voice, hand, a house, spirits) levantar[se]; VT (an alarm) dar; (funds) recaudar, captar; (a salary) aumentar; (a flag) izar; (crops) cultivar; (animals, children) criar; (money) recabar, recaudar; **to — a question** plantear una pregunta; **to — a racket** armar un alboroto; N aumento *m*

raisin [rézɪn] N pasa [de uva] *f*

rake [rek] N rastrillo *m*; VI/VT rastrillar; **to — in money** amasar dinero

rally [rǽli] VI/VT (reorganize troops) reunir[se], juntar[se]; (inspire) reanimar; VI (demonstrate) concentrarse; (recuperate) recuperarse; (reinvigorate) recobrar ánimo; (rise in value) repuntar; (in tennis) pelotear; **to — around someone** apoyar a alguien; N (demonstration) concentración *f*; (recovery) recuperación *f*; (rise in prices) subida *f*; (in tennis) peloteo *m*

RAM [random-access memory] [ræm] N RAM *m*

ram [ræm] N (male sheep) carnero *m*; (tool for battering) ariete *m*; (part of a ship) espolón *m*; VT chocar contra; **to — a boat** embestir un buque con el espolón

ramble [rǽmbəł] VI vagar; **to — on** divagar; N paseo *m*

ramp [ræmp] N rampa *f*

rampage [rǽmpeʤ] N **to go on a —** andar destrozando todo; VI andar destrozando todo

rampant [rǽmpənt] ADJ desenfrenado

ran [ræn] *see* run

ranch [ræntʃ] N hacienda *f*; *Mex* rancho *m*

rancid [rǽnsɪd] ADJ rancio

rancor [rǽŋkə˞] N rencor *m*

random [rǽndəm] ADJ aleatorio, azaroso; **at —** al azar; **— access memory** memoria de acceso directo *f*

randomize [rǽndəmaɪz] VT aleatorizar

rang [ræŋ] *see* ring

range [reɒʤ] N (of types) gama *f*; (of a gun) alcance *m*; (of variation) fluctuación *f*; (of mountains) cadena *f*; (for shooting) campo de tiro *m*; (of an aircraft) autonomía *f*; (grazing place) campo abierto *m*; (stove) cocina *f*; estufa *f*; **— finder** telémetro *m*; **— of vision** alcance visual *m*; VT (align) alinear; (of a gun) tener alcance; VI (vary) oscilar; (be found in an area) extenderse; **his children — in age between 2 and 10** sus hijos van en edad entre 2 y 10

ranger [réɒʤə˞] N (in a park) guardabosque[s] *mf*; (soldier) guardia de asalto *m*

rank [ræŋk] N (in a hierarchy) rango *m*, grado *m*; (line) fila *f*; **— and file** (of an army) tropa *f* sg; **the —s** (soldiers) la tropa; (union members) bases *f pl*; **a sculptor of the first —** un escultor de primer orden; VT (arrange) poner en orden de importancia; VI (rate) figurar; **to — high** tener alto rango; **to — second** estar clasificado en el segundo lugar; ADJ (smelly) hediondo; (growing vigorously) exuberante

ranking [rǽŋkɪŋ] N ránking *m*

ransack [rǽnsæk] VT saquear, desvalijar

ransom [rǽnsəm] N rescate *m*; VT rescatar

rant [rænt] VI/VT despotricar

rap [ræp] VI/VT (strike) golpear; (chat) charlar; VI (in music) rapear, cantar rap; N (blow) golpe *m*; (accusation) cargo *m*; **to take the —** ser el cabeza de turco; **— music** música rap *f*

rapacious [rəpéʃəs] ADJ rapaz
rape [rep] N (violation) violación *f*; (statutory) estupro *m*; (plant) colza *f*; (grape pulp) orujo *m*; VT violar
rapid [ræpɪd] ADJ rápido; N **—s** rápidos *m pl*
rapidity [rəpíDɪti] N rapidez *f*
rapport [rəpɔ́r] N relación *f*
rapt [ræpt] ADJ extasiado
rapture [ræptʃə-] N éxtasis *m*, embeleso *m*; **to go into a —** arrobarse
rare [rɛr] ADJ (infrequent) raro, poco frecuente, extraño; (of gas, earth) raro; (thin, of air) enrarecido; (excellent) excepcional; (not well cooked) crudo; **— earths** tierras raras *f pl*
rarely [rérli] ADV raramente, raras veces
rarity [rérɪDi] N rareza *f*; (of air) enrarecimiento *m*
rascal [ræskəł] N bribón *m*, bellaco *m*, pícaro *m*; *Sp* golfo *m*; **you little —!** ¡bandido! ¡sinvergüenza!
rash [ræʃ] ADJ (thoughtless) precipitado, temerario; N (on skin) sarpullido *m*
raspberry [rǽzbɛri] N frambuesa *f*; **— bush** frambueso *m*
raspy [ræspi] ADJ ronco, áspero
rat [ræt] N rata *f*; **I smell a —** aquí hay gato encerrado; VT (one's hair) cardar; VI **to — on** delatar
ratchet [rǽtʃɪt] N trinquete *m*
rate [ret] N (charge) tarifa *f*; (unit charge for insurance) prima *f*; (pace) paso *m*, ritmo *m*; **— of exchange** tipo de cambio *m*; **— of interest** tasa de interés *f*; **at any —** en todo caso; **at this —** a este ritmo; **at the — of** a razón de; VT (estimate) valorar, estimar; (esteem) considerar; **he —s as the best** se le considera como el mejor; **he —s high** se le tiene en alta estima
rather [rǽðə-] ADV (somewhat) bastante; (more precisely) más bien; **— than** en vez de; **I would — die than** antes la muerte que; **I would — not go** prefiero no ir
ratification [rædɪfɪkéʃən] N ratificación *f*
ratify [rǽdəfaɪ] VT ratificar
rating [rédɪŋ] N (act of adjudging) calificación *f*; (for credit) clasificación *f*; (TV quotient) rating televisivo *m*, índice de audiencia *m*
ratio [réʃio] N razón *f*, proporción *f*
ration [ræʃən] N ración *f*; VT racionar
rational [ræʃənl] ADJ racional
rationale [ræʃənǽł] N motivo *m*
rationalize [ræʃənlaɪz] VI/VT racionalizar
rationing [ræʃənɪŋ] N racionamiento *m*
rattle [rǽdł] VI (bang) golpetear; (move noisily) traquetear; **to — on** parlotear; VT hacer sonar, sacudir; **to — off** recitar; N (banging) golpeteo *m*; (movement) traqueteo *m*; (toy) sonaja *f*, sonajero *m*; (of a rattlesnake) cascabel *m*; (of death) estertor *m*; **—snake** víbora de cascabel *f*
raucous [rɔ́kəs] ADJ (loud) estridente; (rowdy) escandaloso
ravage [rǽvɪʤ] VI/VT asolar, arruinar; N estrago *m*
rave [rev] VI (rant) desvariar, delirar; VI/VT (roar) bramar; **to — about** deshacerse en elogios; N (theater review) crítica muy favorable *f*
raven [révən] N cuervo *m*; ADJ azabache
ravenous [rǽvənəs] ADJ voraz, famélico; **to be —** tener un hambre canina
ravine [rəvín] N quebrada *f*, barranco *m*, cañada *f*
raving [révɪŋ] ADJ delirante; (extraordinary) extraordinario; **— mad** loco de remate; N desvarío *m*
ravish [rǽvɪʃ] VT (kidnap) raptar, secuestrar; (rape) violar
raw [rɔ] ADJ (uncooked, unprocessed, damp and cold) crudo; (of vegetables) fresco, crudo; (unadorned) descarnado; **— flesh** carne viva *f*; **— material** materia prima *f*; **— sugar** azúcar bruto *m*; N **—hide** cuero crudo *m*
ray [re] N (beam) rayo *m*; (stingray) raya *f*
rayon [réɑn] N rayón *m*
raze [rez] VT arrasar, asolar
razor [rézə-] N (device with blade) maquinilla de afeitar *f*, rasuradora *f*; (barber's tool) navaja *f*; (electric) rasuradora electrica *f*; **— blade** hoja de afeitar *f*; **safety —** navaja de seguridad *f*
reach [ritʃ] VI/VT (extend) alcanzar; **to — for** tratar de agarrar; *Sp* tratar de coger; **to — into** meter la mano en; VT (arrive at) llegar a; (contact) ponerse en contacto con; **to — out one's hand** alargar la mano; N alcance *m*; **beyond his —** fuera de su alcance; **within his —** a su alcance; **far —es** zona remota *f*
react [riǽkt] VI reaccionar
reaction [riǽkʃən] N reacción *f*
reactionary [riǽkʃənɛri] ADJ & N reaccionario -ria *mf*
reactor [riǽktə-] N reactor *m*
read [rid] VI/VT leer; VT (interpret) interpretar; (give as a reading, indicate) decir, indicar, marcar; **it —s easily** es fácil de leer; N lectura *f*; **— protect** protección contra lectura *f*; **—/write file** archivo de lectura/escritura *m*
readable [ríDəbəł] ADJ (legible) legible; (nice to read) ameno
reader [ríDə-] N (person who reads) lector -ora *mf*; (schoolbook) libro de lectura *m*, cartilla *f*; (anthology) antología *f*
readership [ríDə-ʃɪp] N lectores *m pl*
readily [rédli] ADV fácilmente
readiness [rédɪnɪs] N estado de preparación *m*; (willingness) buena disposición *f*; **to be in —** estar preparado, estar listo
reading [ríDɪŋ] N lectura *f*; (interpretation) interpretación *f*; **— room** sala de lectura *f*

readjust [riəʤást] VI/VT (improve fit) reajustar; (acclimate) readaptar
readjustment [riəʤástmənt] N (fitting) reajuste *m*; (acclimation) readaptación *f*
ready [rɛ́di] ADJ (prepared) listo, preparado, pronto; (willing) dispuesto; (available) disponible; (quick) rápido; **—-made** de confección
reaffirm [riəfɜ́m] VT reafirmar
reagent [riéʤənt] ADJ & N reactivo *m*
real [rił] ADJ real, verdadero; **— estate** bienes raíces *m pl*, bienes inmuebles *m pl*; **— time** tiempo real *m*
realism [ríəlɪzəm] N realismo *m*
realist [ríəlɪst] N realista *mf*
realistic [riəlístɪk] ADJ realista
reality [riǽlɪɪDi] N realidad *f*; **— check** ajuste de perspectiva *m*
realization [riəlɪzéʃən] N (making real) realización *f*; (understanding) comprensión *f*
realize [ríəlaɪz] VT (achieve) realizar; (comprehend) darse cuenta [de], comprobar, percatarse [de]
really [rili] ADV (extremely) realmente; (truly) verdaderamente; (as question) ¿de veras? ¿verdad? **he's not — a lawyer** en realidad, no es abogado / no es abogado de verdad; **it's — hot in Seville** hace mucho calor en Sevilla; **she's a — good colleague** es una colega superbuena / es una buenísima colega
realm [rɛłm] N (kingdom) reino *m*; (domain) terreno *m*, esfera *f*
realtor™ [ríəłtə-] N agente inmobiliario -ria *mf*
reap [rip] VI/VT (cut with sickle) segar; (harvest) cosechar; **to — a benefit** obtener beneficio, sacar provecho
reaper [rípə-] N (person) segador -ora *mf*; (machine) segadora *f*; (death) la Parca, la Muerte
reappear [riəpír] VI reaparecer
rear [rir] ADJ trasero, posterior; **—guard** retaguardia *f*; N (space at the back) parte de atrás *f*, fondo *m*; (backside) trasero *m*, posaderas *f pl*; **— end** trasero *m*; **—view mirror** espejo retrovisor *m*; VT (raise) criar; VI (rise on back legs) encabritarse, empinarse
reason [rizən] N (faculty) razón *f*; (cause) motivo *m*, razón *f*; **by — of** por causa de; **it stands to —** es lógico; VT razonar; **to — out** resolver por medio de la razón; **to — with** hacer entrar en razón
reasonable [rízənəbəł] ADJ razonable; (in price) módico, moderado
reasoning [rízənɪŋ] N razonamiento *m*, raciocinio *m*; ADJ racional
reassert [riəsɜ́t] VT reafirmar
reassure [riəʃúr] VT tranquilizar
rebate [ríbet] N reembolso *m*, reintegro *m*; VT reembolsar, reintegrar
rebel[1] [rébəł] ADJ & N rebelde *mf*, insurrecto -ta *mf*
rebel[2] [rɪbɛ́ł] VI rebelarse
rebellion [rɪbéljən] N rebelión *f*
rebellious [rɪbéljəs] ADJ rebelde, insurrecto
rebelliousness [rɪbéljəsnɪs] N rebeldía *f*
reboot [ribút] VT reiniciar
rebound[1] [rɪbáʊnd] VI (bounce) rebotar; (catch a rebound) rebotear; (recover) recuperarse
rebound[2] [ríbaʊnd] N (bounce) rebote *m*; (recovery) recuperación *f*; **on the —** de rebote
rebuff [rɪbʌ́f] N desaire *m*, repulsa *f*; VT desairar, rechazar
rebuild [ribłíd] VI/VT reconstruir, reedificar; (car engine) reacondicionar
rebuke [rɪbjúk] VT reprender, reprochar; N reproche *m*, reprimenda *f*
recall[1] [rɪkɔ́ł] VT (remember) recordar; (call back) retirar; (remove from office) destituir
recall[2] [ríkɔł] N (memory) memoria *f*; (of a diplomat, product) retirada *f*; (from office) destitución *f*
recapitulate [rikəpítʃəlet] VI/VT recapitular
recast [rikǽst] VT refundir
recede [rɪsíd] VI retroceder; (of hairline) tener entradas
receipt [rɪsít] N recibo *m*; **upon — of** al recibo de; **—s** entradas *f pl*, ingresos *m pl*
receivable [rɪsívəbəł] ADJ a cobrar
receive [rɪsív] VI/VT recibir; (suggestions) acoger, recibir; (a broadcast) captar, recibir
receiver [rɪsívə-] N recibidor -ora *mf*; (of a telephone) auricular *m*; (of a television or radio, in football) receptor *m*; (in tennis) restador -ora *mf*; (of a bankrupt business) síndico *m*
recent [rísənt] ADJ reciente
receptacle [rɪsɛ́ptəkəł] N receptáculo *m*
reception [rɪsɛ́pʃən] N (hotel, social event, TV) recepción *f*; (act of receiving) recibimiento *m*, acogida *f*; **— room** recibidor *m*
recess [rísɛs] N (niche) nicho *m*; (pause) descanso *m*; (playtime) recreo *m*; **in the —es of** en lo más recóndito de; VI/VT (a meeting) interrumpir; VT (a wall) hacer un nicho en
recession [rɪsɛ́ʃən] N (act of receding) retroceso *m*; (economic) recesión *f*
recessive gene [rɪsɛ́sɪvʤín] N gen recesivo *m*
recidivism [rɪsíDəvɪzəm] N reincidencia *f*
recipe [résəpi] N receta *f*
recipient [rɪsípiənt] N destinatario -ria *mf*
reciprocal [rɪsíprəkəł] ADJ recíproco
reciprocate [rɪsíprəket] VI/VT corresponder [a], *Am* reciprocar
recital [rɪsáɪdł] N recital *m*
recitation [rɛsɪtéʃən] N recitación *f*
recite [rɪsáɪt] VI/VT recitar
reckless [rɛ́klɪs] ADJ (driver) temerario,

imprudente; (speed) desenfrenado
recklessness [réklɪsnɪs] N temeridad *f*, imprudencia *f*
reckon [rékən] VI/VT (calculate) calcular; (consider) considerar; (think) suponer
reckoning [rékənɪŋ] N (computation) cálculo *m*; (settlement of accounts) ajuste de cuentas *m*; **the day of —** el día del juicio *m*
reclaim [rɪklém] VT (win back, recover) recuperar; (make land usable) ganar, sanear
recline [rɪklám] VI/VT reclinar[se], recostar[se]
recluse [réklus] ADJ & N solitario -ria *mf*, ermitaño -ña *mf*
recognition [rekəgníʃən] N reconocimiento *m*
recognizable [rɛkəgnáɪzəbəł] ADJ reconocible
recognize [rékəgnaɪz] VT reconocer
recoil[1] [rɪkɔ́ɪł] VI (firearm) dar un culatazo; (move back) retroceder
recoil[2] [ríkɔɪł] N (of a gun) culatazo *m*; (move back) retroceso *m*
recollect [rekəlékt] VI/VT recordar
recollection [rekəlékʃən] N recuerdo *m*
recommend [rekəménd] VI/VT recomendar
recommendation [rekəmɛndéʃən] N recomendación *f*
recompense [rékəmpɛns] VI/VT recompensar; N recompensa *f*
reconcile [rékənsaɪł] VT (persons) reconciliar; (statements) conciliar; **to — oneself to** resignarse a, conformarse con
reconciliation [rekənsɪliéʃən] N reconciliación *f*
reconnoiter [rikənɔ́ɪdɚ] VT reconocer; VI hacer un reconocimiento
reconsider [rikənsídɚ] VI/VT reconsiderar
reconstruct [rikənstrákt] VT reconstruir
reconstruction [rikənstrákʃən] N reconstrucción *f*
record[1] [rékɚd] N (account) registro *m*, asiento *m*; (account of a meeting) acta *f*; (of criminal acts) antecedentes *m pl*; (of past activities) historial *m*, hoja de servicios *f*; (phonographic) disco *m*; (best performance) récord *m*, plusmarca *f*; **— player** tocadiscos *m sg*; **off the —** extraoficialmente
record[2] [rɪkɔ́rd] VI/VT (write down) registrar, apuntar; (cut a recording) grabar
recorder [rɪkɔ́rɚdɚ] N (archivist) archivero -ra *mf*; (sound device) grabadora *f*; (musical instrument) flauta dulce *f*
recording [rɪkɔ́rɚdɪŋ] N grabación *f*; **— company** grabadora *f*
recount[1] [rɪkáʊnt] VT (tell) narrar, relatar
recount[2] [ríkaʊnt] VT (count again) recontar
recoup [rɪkúp] VI/VT recuperar
recourse [ríkɔrs] N recurso *m*; **to have — to** recurrir a
recover [rɪkʌ́vɚ] VI/VT recobrar[se], recuperar[se]; VI (lost health) restablecerse; VT (lost time, property) recuperar; (damages) obtener indemnización
recovery [rɪkʌ́vərɪ] N (from an illness) recuperación *f*; (of investments) amortización *f*; (through a lawsuit) indemnización *f*; **— room** sala de recuperación *f*
recreation [rekrɪéʃən] N recreación *f*, recreo *m*, esparcimiento *m*
recreational [rekrɪéʃənəł] ADJ recreativo, de recreo; **— vehicle** caravana *f*
recriminate [rɪkrímənet] VI/VT recriminar
recruit [rɪkrút] N recluta *mf*; VI/VT reclutar
recruitment [rɪkrútmənt] N reclutamiento *m*, reclutaje *f*
rectangle [rɛ́ktæŋgəł] N rectángulo *m*
rectangular [rɛktǽŋgjələ·] ADJ rectangular
rectify [rɛ́ktəfaɪ] VT rectificar
rector [rɛ́ktɚ] N rector -ora *mf*
rectum [rɛ́ktəm] N recto *m*
recuperate [rɪkúpəret] VI/VT recuperar[se], recobrar[se]
recur [rɪkɝ́] VI volver a ocurrir, repetirse
recurring [rɪkɝ́ɪŋ] ADJ recurrente
recycle [risáɪkəł] VI/VT reciclar
recycling [risáɪklɪŋ] N reciclaje *m*
red [rɛd] ADJ & N rojo *m*, colorado *m*; **— blood cell** glóbulo rojo *m*; **— card** tarjeta roja *f*; **—-handed** *fam* in fraganti; **—headed** pelirrojo; **—-hot** candente, al rojo vivo; **— light** luz roja *f*; **—neck** granjero -ra blanco -ca pobre *mf*; **— pepper** pimienta de cayena *f*; **— prawn** carabinero *m*; **— snapper** pargo *m*; **— tape** trámites *m pl*; **— wine** vino tinto *m*; **—wood** secoya/secuoya *f*; **in the —** en números rojos; **to see —** enfurecerse
redden [rɛ́dn̩] VI/VT enrojecer, ruborizar[se]
reddish [rɛ́dɪʃ] ADJ rojizo, bermejo
redeem [rɪdím] VT (deliver from sin) redimir; (pay off a mortgage) cancelar; (buy back from pawnshop) desempeñar; (exchange) canjear; (fulfill) cumplir
redemption [rɪdɛ́mpʃən] N redención *f*; (of something pawned) desempeño *m*
redevelopment [rɪdɪvɛ́ləpmənt] N remodelación *f*
redness [rɛ́dnɪs] N rojez *f*; (inflammation) inflamación *f*
redress[1] [rídrɛs] N reparación *f*, desagravio *m*
redress[2] [rɪdrɛ́s] VT reparar, desagraviar
reduce [rɪdús] VI/VT reducir[se]; **she was —d to tears** se echó a llorar
reduction [rɪdʌ́kʃən] N reducción *f*
redundant [rɪdʌ́ndənt] ADJ (repetitive) redundante; (superfluous) superfluo
reed [rid] N caña *f*, junco *m*, carrizo *m*; (of a musical instrument) lengüeta *f*
reef [rif] N (underwater ridge) escollo *m*; (of coral) arrecife *m*
reek [rik] VI heder, apestar; N hedor *m*
reel [rił] N carrete *m*, bobina *f*; VT (on a spool)

bobinar; VI tambalearse; **to — off** recitar; **to — in a fish** sacar un pez del agua

reelect [riːilékt] VT reelegir

reelection [riːilékʃən] N reelección *f*

reemployment [riːimplɔ́ɪmənt] N reinserción laboral *f*

reestablish [riːistǽblɪʃ] VT restablecer

refer [rɪfɝ́] VI/VT referir; (direct to a source of information) remitir; (direct to a doctor) mandar; (mention) referirse a, aludir a

referee [rɛfərí] N árbitro *m*; VT (a game) arbitrar; (a submission) hacer el referato

reference [réfərəns] N (mention) referencia *f*; **— book** libro de consulta *m*; **with — to** con respecto a, respecto de

referendum [rɛfərréndəm] N referéndum *m*

referral [rɪfɝ́əł] N **he gave me a — to a specialist** me mandó con/a un especialista

refill[1] [rifíł] VI/VT rellenar

refill[2] [rifíł] N (for a pen) repuesto *m*; (for a lighter) carga *f*; **may I have a —?** ¿me sirve más?

refinance [rifáɪnæns] VI/VT refinanciar

refine [rɪfáɪn] VT (purify) refinar; (polish) refinar, pulir

refined [rɪfáɪnd] ADJ refinado

refinement [rɪfáɪnmənt] N (of manners) refinamiento *m*, pulimento *m*; (of oil) refinación *f*

refinery [rɪfáɪnəri] N (of oil) refinería *f*; (of sugar) ingenio *m*

reflect [rɪflékt] VI/VT (mirror) reflejar; VI (ponder) reflexionar; **to — poorly on** desacreditar

reflection [rɪflékʃən] N (image) reflejo *m*; (consideration) reflexión *f*; (unfavorable observation) tacha *f*; **on —** pensándolo bien

reflector [rɪfléktɚ] N reflector *m*

reflex [ríflɛks] ADJ & N reflejo *m*

reflexive [rɪfléksɪv] ADJ reflexivo

reflux [ríflʌks] N reflujo *m*

reform [rɪfɔ́rm] VI/VT reformar[se]; N reforma *f*

reformation [rɛfɚ·méʃən] N reforma *f*

reformatory [rɪfɔ́rmətɔri] N reformatorio *m*

reformer [rɪfɔ́rmɚ] N reformador -ora *mf*, reformista *mf*

refraction [rɪfrǽkʃən] N refracción *f*

refractory [rɪfrǽktəri] ADJ (not malleable) refractario; (rebellious) rebelde

refrain [rɪfrén] VI abstenerse; N (of a song) estribillo *m*

refresh [rɪfréʃ] VI/VT refrescar[se]; (computer screen) actualizar, refrescar

refreshing [rɪfréʃɪŋ] ADJ (drink) refrescante; (sleep) reparador; (honesty) agradable

refreshment [rɪfréʃmənt] N (drink) refresco *m*; (food) refrigerio *m*

refrigerate [rɪfrídʒəret] VT refrigerar

refrigeration [rɪfrídʒəréʃən] N refrigeración *f*

refrigerator [rɪfrídʒərendɚ] N frigorífico *m*, nevera *f*, refrigerador *m*; *RP* heladera *f*

refuge [réfjuʤ] N refugio *m*; **to give —** dar albergue

refugee [rɛfjʊʤí] N refugiado -da *mf*

refund[1] [rífʌnd] N reembolso *m*

refund[2] [rɪfʌ́nd] VT reembolsar

refurbish [rɪfɝ́bɪʃ] VT restaurar

refusal [rɪfjúzəł] N negativa *f*, rechazo *m*; **first —** opción *f*

refuse[1] [rɪfjúz] VI/VT (deny a request) negar[se] [a]; **to — to** rehusarse a, negarse a; VT (decline to accept) rechazar, no aceptar

refuse[2] [réfjus] N desechos *m pl*, desperdicios *m pl*

refute [rɪfjút] VT refutar, rebatir

regain [rɪgén] VT (recover) recobrar; (get back to) volver a

regal [rígəł] ADJ regio, real

regard [rɪgárd] VT (consider) considerar; (esteem) estimar; N (consideration) consideración *f*; (esteem) respeto *m*, estima *f*; **—s** recuerdos *m pl*, saludos *m pl*; **as —s** en cuanto a; **with — to** con respecto a

regarding [rɪgárdɪŋ] PREP con respecto a

regardless [rɪgárdlɪs] ADV LOC **— of** independientemente de

regenerate [rɪʤénəret] VI/VT regenerar[se]

regent [ríʤənt] N regente -ta *mf*

reggae [rége] N reggae *m*

regime [rɪʒím] N régimen *m*

regiment [réʤəmənt] N regimiento *m*

region [ríʤən] N región *f*

regional [ríʤənl] ADJ regional

register [réʤɪstɚ] N (recording, range of voice) registro *m*; (entry) asiento *m*; VI/VT (enter into a list) registrar[se]; (enroll) matricular[se], inscribir[se]; VT (indicate) indicar, registrar; (a letter) certificar; VI (appear) aparecer; **that didn't —** no cayó en la cuenta

registered [réʤɪstɚd] ADJ registrado; **— mail** correo certificado *m*; **— nurse** enfermero -ra titulado -da *mf*; **— trademark** marca registrada *f*

registrar [réʤɪstrɑr] N secretario -ria de admisiones *mf*

registration [rɛʤɪstréʃən] N (of a car) matrícula *f*; (of a student) inscripción *f*

regret [rɪgrét] VT (feel sorry) lamentar; (feel rueful) arrepentirse de; N arrepentimiento *m*; **to send —s** enviar sus excusas

regretful [rɪgrétfəł] ADJ lleno de remordimientos

regrettable [rɪgrɛ́dəbəł] ADJ lamentable

regroup [rigrúp] VT reagrupar; VI reorganizarse

regular [régjləɚ] ADJ (symmetrical, uniform) regular; (normal) normal; (habitual) habitual; **a — fool** un verdadero necio; **a —**

guy un buen tipo; (habitual customer) parroquiano -na *mf*; (soldier) soldado de línea *m*

regularity [rɛgjəlǽrɪdi] N regularidad *f*

regulate [régjəlet] VT (control) regular; (make regular) regularizar

regulation [rɛgjəléʃən] N (act of regulating) regulación *f*; **—s** reglamento *m*, reglamentación *f*

regulator [régjəleɪDə·] N regulador *m*

regurgitate [rigə́·ʤɪtet] VI/VT regurgitar

rehabilitate [riəbílɪtet] VI/VT rehabilitar[se]

rehabilitation [riəbɪlɪtéʃən] N rehabilitación *f*

rehearsal [rɪhə́·səł] N ensayo *m*

rehearse [rɪhə́·s] VI/VT ensayar

reign [ren] N reino *m*, reinado *m*; VI reinar

reimburse [riɪmbə́·s] VI/VT reembolsar

reimbursement [riɪmbə́·smənt] N reembolso *m*

rein [ren] N rienda *f* (also control); VI **to — in** dominar, refrenar

reincarnation [riɪnkarnéʃən] N reencarnación *f*

reindeer [réndir] N reno *m*

reinforce [riɪnfɔ́rs] VT reforzar

reinforcement [riɪnfɔ́rsmənt] N refuerzo *m*, reforzado *m*

reinsertion [riɪnsə́·ʃən] N reinserción *f*

reinstate [riɪnstét] VT reinstaurar

reiterate [riíDəret] VT reiterar

reject[1] [rɪʤɛ́kt] VT rechazar

reject[2] [ríʤɛkt] N (thing) cosa rechazada *f*, desecho *m*; (person) rechazado -da *mf*

rejoice [rɪʤɔ́ɪs] VI regocijarse

rejoicing [rɪʤɔ́ɪsɪŋ] N regocijo *m*

rejoin [riʤɔ́ɪn] VT (come again into a group) reincorporarse a; VI/VT (reunite) volver a unir[se]

rejuvenate [rɪʤúvənet] VI/VT rejuvenecer

relapse[1] [rɪlǽps] VI (into bad health) recaer; (into crime) reincidir

relapse[2] [rílæps] N (into bad health) recaída *f*, recidiva *f*; (into crime) reincidencia *f*

relate [rɪlét] VT (tell) relatar, narrar; (connect) relacionar; VI **to — to** relacionarse con

related [rɪlɛ́DɪD] ADJ (connected) relacionado; (kin) emparentado

relation [rɪléʃən] N (association) relación *f*; (act of narrating) narración *f*; (kinship) parentesco *m*; (relative) pariente -ta *mf*; **with — to** con respecto a

relationship [rɪléʃənʃɪp] N relación *f*

relative [rɛ́łəDɪv] ADJ relativo; N pariente -ta *mf*, allegado -da *mf*; **— to** relativo a, referente a

relativity [rɛłətívɪDi] N relatividad *f*

relax [rɪlǽks] VI/VT relajar[se], distender[se]; VT (grip) aflojar

relaxation [rilækséʃən] N (recreation) esparcimiento *m*, recreo *m*; (loosening) relajamiento *m*, relajación *f*

relay[1] [ríle] N relevo *m*, posta *f*; (electrical) relé *m*; **— race** carrera de relevos/postas *f*

relay[2] [ríle, rɪlé] VT transmitir; **to — a broadcast** transmitir un programa

release [rɪlís] VT (let go) soltar; (free prisoners) librar, poner en libertad; (energy) liberar; (news) divulgar; (discharge from hospital) dar de alta; N (liberation) liberación *f*; (permission) permiso *m*; (of film) estreno *m*; (of gas) escape *m*; (of energy) desprendimiento *m*

relegate [rɛ́lɪget] VT relegar

relent [rɪlɛ́nt] VI aplacarse

relentless [rɪlɛ́ntłɪs] ADJ implacable

relevant [rɛ́łəvənt] ADJ pertinente

reliability [rɪlaɪəbɪ́łɪDɪ] N fiabilidad *f*, confiabilidad *f*

reliable [rɪlǽəbəł] ADJ fiable, confiable; (a person) formal

reliance [rɪlǽəns] N (dependency) dependencia *f*; (trust) confianza *f*

relic [rɛ́łɪk] N reliquia *f*

relief [rɪlíf] N (ease) alivio *m*; (aid) ayuda *f*; (projection) relieve *m*; (soldier) relevo *m*; (in golf) alivio *m*; **in —** en relieve; **— map** mapa en relieve *m*

relieve [rɪlív] VT (alleviate) aliviar; (free) liberar; (replace) relevar; VI **to — oneself** orinar

reliever [rɪlívə·] N (baseball) relevista *mf*

religion [rɪlíʤən] N religión *f*

religious [rɪlíʤəs] ADJ religioso

relinquish [rɪlíŋkwɪʃ] VT (give up) renunciar; (let go) soltar

relish [rɛ́łɪʃ] VT (to like the taste) saborear, paladear; (enjoy) disfrutar; N (enjoyment) gusto *m*; (condiment) condimento de pepinillos en vinagre *m*

relocate [rilóket] VI/VT trasladar[se]

reluctance [rɪlʌ́ktəns] N renuencia *f*

reluctant [rɪlʌ́ktənt] ADJ renuente, reacio

rely [rɪláɪ] VI **to — on** (trust) confiar en; (depend on) depender de

REM [rapid eye movement] [áriém] N REM *m*, MOR *m pl*

remain [rɪmén] VI (continue to be) seguir siendo; (stay) quedar[se], permanecer; (to be left) quedar, restar; (to be left over) sobrar; N **—s** restos *m pl*

remainder [rɪménDə·] N (extra) sobrante; (other) restante

remake[1] [rimék] VT rehacer; (film) hacer de nuevo

remake[2] [rímek] N nueva versión *f*

remark [rɪmárk] VT (comment) comentar, observar; (notice) notar, observar; **to — on** comentar; N observación *f*, comentario *m*

remarkable [rɪmárkəbəł] ADJ notable

remedial [rɪmíDɪəł] ADJ (rehabilitative) rehabilitador; (to improve skills) de recuperación

remedy [rémɪdi] N (solution) remedio *m*; (cure) cura *f*; VT (solve) remediar, subsanar; (heal) curar
remember [rɪmémbə˞] VI/VT recordar, acordarse [de]; **— me to him** mándale saludos míos
remind [rɪmáɪnd] VT recordar
reminder [rɪmáɪndə˞] N (of a date, deadline) recordatorio *m*; (warning) advertencia *f*
reminiscence [rɛmənísəns] N reminiscencia *f*, recuerdo *m*
remiss [rɪmís] ADJ negligente
remission [rɪmíʃən] N remisión *f*
remit [rɪmít] VI/VT remitir
remittance [rɪmítn̩s] N remesa *f*, giro *m*
remnant [rémnənt] N (remainder) resto *m*; (of fabric) retazo *m*, retal *m*; (vestige) vestigio *m*
remodel [rimádl̩] VI/VT remodelar
remodeling [rimádl̩ɪŋ] N remodelación *f*
remorse [rɪmɔ́rs] N remordimiento *m*
remote [rɪmót] ADJ (far away) remoto, recóndito; (aloof) distante; (in kinship) lejano; **— access** acceso remoto *m*; **— control** control remoto *m*, mando a distancia *m*; **— login** acceso remoto *m*; **— server** servidor remoto *m*
removal [rɪmúvəł] N (dismissal) deposición *f*, alejamiento *m*; (elimination) eliminación *f*; (extirpation) extirpación *f*
remove [rɪmúv] VT (an obstacle) remover; (take away, take off) quitar; (dismiss) deponer; (eliminate) eliminar; (extirpate) extirpar; **to — from office** separar/apartar del cargo
remunerate [rimjúnəret] VT remunerar *f*, retribuir *f*
remuneration [rɪmjunəréʃən] N remuneración *f*, retribución *f*
renaissance [rénɪsɑns] N renacimiento *m*; **— architecture** arquitectura renacentista *f*
renal [ríni] ADJ renal; **— failure** insuficiencia renal *f*
rend [rɛnd] VI/VT desgarrar[se], rajar[se]
render [réndə˞] VT (give) dar; (cause to become) dejar; (depict) representar; (translate) traducir; (give homage, account) rendir; (provide services, assistance) prestar; (melt down fat) derretir; (deliver a verdict) pronunciar; **to — useless** inutilizar
rendition [rɛndíʃən] N (translation) traducción *f*; (interpretation) interpretación *f*, versión *f*
renegade [rénɪged] N renegado -da *mf*
renegotiate [rinɪgóʃiet] VI/VT renegociar
renegue [rɪníg] VI incumplir
renew [rɪnú] VT (vows, contract) renovar; (furniture) restaurar; (friendship, effort) reanudar; (a loan) prorrogar
renewable [rɪnúəbəł] ADJ renovable
renewal [rɪnúəł] N (of vows, contract) renovación *f*; (of furniture) restauración *f*; (of a city) remodelación *f*; (of friendship, effort) reanudación *f*; (of loan) prórroga *f*
renounce [rɪnáʊns] VT (give up) renunciar a; (repudiate) repudiar, renegar de
renovate [rénəvet] VT renovar
renown [rɪnáʊn] N renombre *m*
renowned [rɪnáʊnd] ADJ renombrado
rent [rɛnt] N (monthly payment) alquiler *m*, arrendamiento *m*; **for —** se alquila, se arrienda; (fissure) rajadura *f*, hendidura *f*; (tear) rasgadura *f*; VI/VT (lease) alquilar, arrendar
rent [rɛnt] *see* rend
rental [rénti] ADJ de alquiler; **— agreement** contrato de alquiler *m*; N alquiler *m*, arrendamiento *m*
renter [rénto˞] N inquilino -na *mf*
renunciation [rɪnʌnsiéʃən] N renuncia *f*
reopen [riópən] VI/VT (doors) reabrir[se]; (negotiations) reanudar[se]
reorganization [riɔrgənɪzéʃən] N reorganización *f*
reorganize [riɔ́rgənaɪz] VI/VT reorganizar[se]
repaginate [ripǽʤɪnet] VT repaginar
repair [rɪpér] VT (fix) reparar, arreglar, componer; (shoes) remendar; **to — to** acudir a; N (fixing) reparación *f*; (of shoes) remiendo *m*, compostura *f*; **in good —** en buen estado; **—man** técnico en reparaciones *m*
reparation [rɛpəréʃən] N reparación *f*, indemnización *f*
repay [rɪpé] VT (return money, favor) devolver; (pay off) pagar
repayment [rɪpémənt] N (of a sum) reembolso *m*; (of a loan) pago *m*
repeal [rɪpíł] VT derogar, revocar, abrogar; N derogación *f*, revocación *f*, abrogación *f*
repeat[1] [rɪpít] VI/VT repetir; N repetición *f*
repeat[2] [rɪpít] N repetición *f*
repeated [rɪpíɪdɪd] ADJ repetido
repel [rɪpɛ́ł] VI/VT repeler; (an attack) rechazar
repellent [rɪpɛ́lənt] ADJ & N repelente *m*
repent [rɪpɛ́nt] VI/VT arrepentirse [de]
repentance [rɪpɛ́ntəns] N arrepentimiento *m*
repentant [rɪpɛ́ntənt] ADJ arrepentido, pesaroso
repercussion [rɛpə˞kʌ́ʃən] N repercusión *f*; **to have —s** repercutir
repertoire [rɛ́pə˞twɑr] N repertorio *m*
repetition [rɛpɪtíʃən] N repetición *f*
replace [rɪplés] VT (place again) volver a colocar; (substitute for) sustituir, reemplazar; (provide a substitute for) reponer
replaceable [rɪplésəbəł] ADJ reemplazable, sustituible
replacement [rɪplésmənt] N (substitute, substitution) sustituto *m*, reemplazo *m*; (making up for) reposición *f*; **— parts** piezas de repuesto *f pl*
replenish [rɪplɛ́nɪʃ] VI/VT (supply) reabastecer;

(fill again) rellenar
replete [rɪplít] ADJ repleto
replica [réplɪkə] N réplica *f*
replicate [réplɪket] VT reproducir, replicar
replication [rɛplɪkéʃən] N reproducción *f*, replicación *f*
reply [rɪplát] VI replicar, contestar; N réplica *f*, contestación *f*
report [rɪpɔ́rt] VT (recount) relatar; (make a crime known, denounce) denunciar; (make an accident known) dar parte de; VI hacer un informe, informar; **to — for duty** presentarse; **to — on** hacer un informe sobre; **to — sick** dar parte de enfermo, reportarse enfermo; **it is —ed that** se dice que; N informe *m*, comunicado *m*; (rumor) rumor *m*; (loud noise) estallido *m*; **— card** boletín de calificaciones *m*
reportedly [rɪpɔ́rdɪdlɪ] ADV según se informa
reporter [rɪpɔ́rdə-] N (news) reportero -ra *mf*; (sports) cronista *mf*
repose [rɪpóz] VI/VT reposar, descansar; N reposo *m*, descanso *m*
repository [rɪpɑ́zɪtɔri] N (object) depósito *m*; (person) depositario -ria *mf*
repossess [ripəzés] VT retomar posesión de
represent [rɛprɪzɛ́nt] VT representar
representation [rɛprɪzɛntéʃən] N representación *f*
representative [rɛprɪzɛ́ntədɪv] ADJ representativo; N representante *mf*
repress [rɪprɛ́s] VI/VT reprimir
repression [rɪprɛ́ʃən] N represión *f*
repressive [rɪprɛ́sɪv] ADJ represivo
reprieve [rɪprív] VT (pardon) indultar; (commute) conmutar; (delay) aplazar; N (pardon) indulto *m*; (commutation) conmutación *f*; (delay) aplazamiento *m*
reprimand [rɛ́prəmænd] N reprimenda *f*, regaño *m*; VT reprender, regañar
reprint[1] [riprínt] VI/VT reimprimir
reprint[2] [rɪ́prɪnt] N (action, result) reimpresión *f*; (offprint) separata *f*
reprisal [rɪprɑ́ɪzəł] N represalia *f*
reproach [rɪprótʃ] VT reprochar; N reproche *m*
reproduce [riprədús] VI/VT reproducir[se]
reproduction [riprədə́kʃən] N reproducción *f*
reproof [rɪprúf] N reprobación *f*
reprove [rɪprúv] VT reprobar
reptile [rɛ́ptaɪł] N reptil *m*
republic [rɪpɑ́blɪk] N república *f*
republican [rɪpɑ́blɪkən] ADJ & N republicano -na *mf*
repudiate [rɪpjúdɪet] VT repudiar
repugnance [rɪpɑ́gnəns] N repugnancia *f*
repugnant [rɪpɑ́gnənt] ADJ repugnante
repulse [rɪpɑ́łs] VT repeler, rechazar; N repulsa *f*, rechazo *m*
repulsive [rɪpɑ́łsɪv] ADJ repulsivo
reputable [rɛ́pjədəbəł] ADJ reputado
reputation [rɛpjətéʃən] N reputación *f*, fama *f*
request [rɪkwɛ́st] N solicitud *f*, petición *f*, requerimiento *m*; **at the — of** a solicitud de, a instancias de; VT solicitar, pedir
require [rɪkwáɪr] VI/VT (need) requerir; (demand) exigir
requirement [rɪkwáɪrmənt] N (demand) requisito *m*; (need) necesidad *f*
requisite [rɛ́kwɪzɪt] ADJ requerido, necesario; N requisito *m*
requisition [rɛkwɪzɪ́ʃən] N (taking over) requisa *f*; (order) pedido *m*; VT (take over) requisar; (order) pedir
rerun [rɪ́rʌn] N refrito *m*
rescind [rɪsɪ́nd] VT rescindir
rescue [rɛ́skju] VT rescatar, salvar; N rescate *m*, salvamento *m*; **to go to the — of** acudir al socorro de, salir al quite de
research[1] [rɪsɜ́-tʃ] N investigación *f*
research[2] [rɪsɜ́-tʃ] VI/VT investigar
researcher [rɪsɜ́-tʃə-] N investigador -ora *mf*
resell [risɛ́ł] VT revender
resemblance [rɪzɛ́mbləns] N semejanza *f*, parecido *m*
resemble [rɪzɛ́mbəł] VT semejar, asemejarse a, parecerse a
resent [rɪzɛ́nt] VT resentirse de
resentful [rɪzɛ́ntfəł] ADJ resentido, rencoroso
resentment [rɪzɛ́ntmənt] N resentimiento *m*
reservation [rɛzə-véʃən] N reserva *f*; *Am* reservación *f*; **to have one's —s** tener reservas
reserve [rɪzɜ́-v] VT reservar; N reserva *f*; (shyness) pudor *m*
reserved [rɪzɜ́-vd] ADJ reservado
reservoir [rɛ́zə-vwar] N (tank) depósito *m*, alberca *f*; (artificial lake) embalse *m*, represa *f*
reset [risɛ́t] VT (computer, machine) reiniciar; **— key** tecla de reinicio *f*
reside [rɪzáɪd] VI residir
residence [rɛ́zɪdəns] N residencia *f*
resident [rɛ́zɪdənt] ADJ & N residente *mf*; (of a neighborhood) vecino -na *mf*
residential [rɛzɪdɛ́ntʃəł] ADJ residencial
residue [rɛ́zɪdu] N residuo *m*
resign [rɪzáɪn] VI/VT renunciar [a], dimitir [de]; **to — oneself to** resignarse a
resignation [rɛzɪgnéʃən] N (act of resigning an office) renuncia *f*, dimisión *f*; (accepting attitude) resignación *f*; **— letter** carta de renuncia *f*
resilience [rɪzɪ́ljəns] N (elasticity) elasticidad *f*; (adaptability) adaptabilidad *f*
resilient [rɪzɪ́ljənt] ADJ (elastic) elástico; (adaptable) adaptable
resin [rɛ́zɪn] N resina *f*
resist [rɪzɪ́st] VT (a temptation) resistir; VI/VT (tyranny) resistirse [a]

resistance [rɪzístəns] N resistencia *f*
resistant [rɪzístənt] ADJ resistente
resolute [rézəlut] ADJ resuelto, decidido
resolution [rezəlúʃən] N resolución *f*
resolve [rɪzɑ́lv] VI/VT resolver[se]; **to — into** convertirse en; **to — to** decidir, resolver; N resolución *f*
resonance [rézənəns] N resonancia *f*
resonate [rézənet] VI/VT resonar
resort [rɪzɔ́rt] N (seaside) centro de veraneo *m*; (for skiing) estación de esquí *f*; **as a last —** como último recurso; VI **to — to** recurrir a
resound [rɪzáʊnd] VI/VT resonar; **—ing victory** victoria contundente *f*
resource [rísɔrs] N recurso *m*
resourceful [rɪzɔ́rsfəł] ADJ ingenioso
respect [rɪspékt] VT respetar; N (esteem) respeto *m*; (detail) aspecto *m*; **with — to** [con] respecto a, respecto de
respectable [rɪspéktəbəł] ADJ respetable
respectful [rɪspéktfəł] ADJ respetuoso
respective [rɪspéktɪv] ADJ respectivo
respiration [respəréʃən] N respiración *f*
respiratory [réspə-ətɔri] ADJ respiratorio; **— failure** insuficiencia respiratoria *f*
respite [réspɪt] N (pause) respiro *f*, tregua *m*; (postponement) prórroga *f*
resplendent [rɪspléndənt] ADJ resplandeciente, refulgente
respond [rɪspɑ́nd] VI/VT responder
respondent [rɪspɑ́ndənt] N (to a lawsuit) demandado -da *mf*; (to a poll) encuestado -da *mf*
response [rɪspɑ́ns] N respuesta *f*
responsibility [rɪspɑnsəbíłɪɪdi] N responsabilidad *f*, reivindicación *f*
responsible [rɪspɑ́nsəbəł] ADJ responsable
rest [rest] N (repose) descanso *m*, reposo *m*; (musical) pausa *f*; (support) apoyo *m*; (remainder) resto *m*; **— home** (for convalescents) casa de reposo *f*; (for the aged) casa de ancianos *f*; **— room** servicio *m*; *Sp* aseo *m*; **an object at —** un objeto en reposo; VI/VT descansar, reposar; VT (one's gaze) posar; (against a wall) reclinar; VI (stop) parar; **to — on** depender de; **let it —** déjalo en paz
restaurant [réstərɑnt] N restaurante *m*; *Am* restorán *m*
restitution [restɪtúʃən] N restitución *f*
restless [réstlɪs] ADJ (worried) inquieto; (fidgety) movedizo
restlessness [réstlɪsnɪs] N inquietud *f*, desasosiego *m*
restoration [rɛstəréʃən] N restauración *f*
restore [rɪstɔ́r] VT restaurar
restrain [rɪstrén] VT (hold back) refrenar, contener, moderar; (bring under control) reducir; **—ing order** medida cautelar *f*
restraint [rɪstrént] N (self-control) compostura *f*, moderación *f*; (device) seguro *m*; **under —** bajo control
restrict [rɪstrík̚t] VT restringir; (someone's liberty) coartar
restriction [rɪstrík̚ʃən] N restricción *f*
restructuring [ristrɑ́ktʃə-ɪŋ] N reestructuración *f*
result [rɪzɑ́łt] VI resultar; **to — from** resultar de; **to — in** dar por resultado; N resultado *m*; **as a —** de resultas, como resultado
resume [rɪzúm] VI/VT (take up again) reasumir, volver a asumir; (continue) reanudar
résumé [rézʊme] N currículum *m*, historial personal *m*
resurrection [rɛzərék̚ʃən] N resurrección *f*
resuscitate [rɪsɑ́sɪtet] VI/VT resucitar
resuscitation [rɪsʌsɪtéʃən] N resucitación *f*
retail [ríteł] N venta al por menor *f*; **— store** tienda minorista *f*; **— trade** comercio minorista *m*; VI/VT vender al por menor; **at —** al por menor, al menudeo
retailer [rítełə-] N minorista *mf*, detallista *mf*
retain [rɪtén] VT (recall, confine, detain) retener; (keep) conservar, quedarse con; (hire) contratar
retainer [rɪténə-] N (device that holds back) retén *m*; (payment) honorarios pagados por adelantado *m pl*
retaliate [rɪtǽliet] VI vengarse
retaliation [rɪtæliéʃən] N venganza *f*
retard [rɪtɑ́rd] VI/VT retardar
retarded [rɪtɑ́rdɪd] ADJ retrasado
retention [rɪtɛ́nʃən] N retención *f*
reticence [rɛ́dɪsəns] N reserva *f*
retina [rɛ́tnə] N retina *f*
retinue [rɛ́tnu] N séquito *m*, comitiva *f*
retire [rɪtáɪr] VI/VT (stop working) retirar[se], jubilar[se]; (withdraw) retirar[se]; (go to bed) acostarse; (withdraw money, troops, machines) retirar
retiree [ritaɪrí] N jubilado -da *mf*
retirement [rɪtáɪrmənt] N retiro *m*, jubilación *f*; **— of debt** retiro de deuda *m*
retort [rɪtɔ́rt] N (reply) réplica *f*; (vessel) retorta *f*
retouch [rɪtɑ́tʃ] VT retocar; N retoque *m*
retrace [ritrɛ́s] VT (mental steps) repasar; (one's route) volver sobre
retract [rɪtrǽkt] VT (a statement) retractar; (claws) retraer[se]; VI desdecirse, retractarse
retreat [rɪtrít] N (place of refuge, period of meditation) retiro *m*, refugio *m*; (military) retirada *f*, repliegue *m*; (bugle call) retreta *f*; VI batirse en retirada, retroceder, replegarse
retrench [rɪtrɛ́ntʃ] VI economizar
retrieval [rɪtrívəł] N recuperación *f*
retrieve [rɪtrív] VT (game animals) cobrar; (something lost) recuperar
retriever [rɪtrívə-] N perro cobrador *m*
retro [rɛ́tro] ADJ retro

retroactive [retroǽktɪv] ADJ retroactivo
retrospect [rétrəspɛkt] ADV LOC **in —** mirando para atrás
retrovirus [rétrovaɪrəs] N retrovirus *m*
return [rɪtə́rn] VI (come back) volver, regresar; VT (put back) devolver, retornar; (deliver a verdict) fallar; **— to sender** devolver al remitente; N (to a place) vuelta *f*, regreso *m*; (of a thing) devolución *f*; (of profit) ganancia *f*; (on a typewriter) retorno de carro *m*; (on a computer) retroceso *m*, salto de línea *m*; **— address** señas del remitente *f pl*; **— game** revancha *f*; **— key** tecla de retorno *f*, tecla de retroceso *f*; **— of service** (tennis) resto *m*; **— ticket** billete de vuelta *m*; **by — mail** a vuelta de correo; **election —s** resultados electorales *m pl*; **in —** a cambio; **in — for** a cambio de; **income tax —** *Sp* declaración de la renta *f*; *Am* declaración de impuestos *f*
reunification [rijunɪfɪkéʃən] N reunificación *f*
reunion [rijúnjən] N reunión *f*
reunite [rijunáɪt] VI/VT reunir[se]
rev [rev] VI/VT acelerar en vacío
reveal [rɪvíł] VT revelar
revealing [rɪvílɪŋ] ADJ revelador; (neckline) atrevido
revel [révəł] VI (enjoy) deleitarse, gozar; (party) parrandear; N parranda *f*
revelation [revəléʃən] N revelación *f*; (book in Bible) Apocalipsis *m sg*
revelry [révəłri] N parranda *f*, jarana *f*
revenge [rɪvénʤ] N venganza *f*, revancha *f*
revengeful [rɪvénʤfəł] ADJ vengativo
revenue [révənu] N (of a government) rentas públicas *f pl*; (of a person) ingresos *m pl*; **— stamp** sello fiscal *m*
reverberate [rɪvə́·bəret] VI reverberar; VT hacer reverberar
revere [rɪvír] VT reverenciar
reverence [révə·əns] N reverencia *f*, veneración *f*; VT venerar
reverend [révə·ənd] ADJ & N reverendo -da *mf*
reverent [révə·ənt] ADJ reverente
reverie, revery [révəri] N ensueño *m*, ensoñación *f*
reverse [rɪvə́·s] ADJ inverso, opuesto; **the — side** el revés; N (opposite) lo opuesto; (back of clothing, mishap) revés *m*; (back of a coin, medal) reverso *m*; (gear) marcha atrás *f*; (back of a piece of paper) dorso *m*; VI/VT invertir[se]; VT (a policy, a vehicle) dar marcha atrás; (a verdict) revocar
revert [rɪvə́·t] VI revertir
review [rɪvjú] N (inspection of a military unit, periodical publication) revista *f*; (repetition of studied material) repaso *m*; (critique of a book, drama) reseña *f*, crítica *f*; (examination of a judicial case) revisión *f*; VI/VT (examine) repasar, revisar; VT (reexamine) revisar, examinar; (inspect troops) pasar revista a; (write a critique of) reseñar
revile [rɪváɪł] VT vilipendiar, denostar
revise [rɪváɪz] VT corregir, enmendar
revision [rɪvíʒən] N (action of revising) corrección *f*; (revised version) versión corregida *f*
revitalize [riváɪdłaɪz] VT revitalizar
revival [rɪváɪvəł] N (of customs) retorno *m*; (of religious feeling) resurgimiento *m*, despertar *m*; (from unconsciousness) resucitación *f*; (of a play) reposición *f*, revisión *f*; (evangelical meeting) asamblea evangelística *f*
revive [rɪváɪv] VT (an unconscious person) reavivar, reanimar; (an apparently dead person) resucitar; (an old play) reponer; (a custom) restablecer; VI revivir, reanimarse; (be reestablished) restablecerse
revocation [rɛvəkéʃən] N revocación *f*
revoke [rɪvóḱ] VT revocar
revolt [rɪvółt] N revuelta *f*, sublevación *f*; VI rebelarse, sublevarse; **it —s me** me da asco
revolting [rɪvółtɪŋ] ADJ repugnante, asqueroso
revolution [rɛvəlúʃən] N revolución *f*
revolutionary [rɛvəlúʃənɛri] ADJ & N revolucionario -ria *mf*
revolve [rɪváłv] VI/VT girar
revolver [rɪváłvə·] N revólver *m*
revolving credit [rɪváłvɪŋ] N crédito rotativo *m*
revue [rɪvjú] N revista *f*
revulsion [rɪváłʃən] N repugnancia *f*, asco *m*
reward [rɪwɔ́rd] N recompensa *f*; VT recompensar
rewind [riwáɪnd] VI/VT rebobinar
rewrite[1] [riráɪt] VI/VT reescribir
rewrite[2] [ríraɪt] N corrección *f*
rhea [ríə] N ñandú *m*
rhetoric [rɛ́də·ɪk] N retórica *f*
rheumatic [rumǽdɪk] ADJ reumático; **— fever** fiebre reumática *f*
rheumatism [rúmətɪzəm] N reumatismo *m*, reuma *m*
rheumatoid [rúmətɔɪd] ADJ reumatoide
Rh factor [árétʃfǽktə·] N factor Rh *m*
rhinoceros [raɪnɑ́sərəs] N rinoceronte *m*
rhinoplasty [ráɪnoplæsti] N rinoplastia *f*
rhinovirus [ráɪnovaɪrəs] N rinovirus *m*
rhododendron [roʊdədéndrən] N rododendro *m*
rhubarb [rúbarb] N (vegetable) ruibarbo *m*; (brawl) reyerta *f*
rhyme [raɪm] N rima *f*; **without — or reason** sin ton ni son; VI/VT rimar
rhythm [ríðəm] N ritmo *m*
rhythmical [ríðmɪkəł] ADJ rítmico; (breathing) acompasado
rib [rɪb] N (of person, animal) costilla *f*; (of umbrella) varilla *f*; (in garment) canalé *m*, cordoncillo *m*; **— cage** caja torácica *f*; VT burlarse de

ribbon [ríbən] N (of cloth) cinta *f*; (of land) franja *f*, faja *f*
rice [raɪs] N arroz *m*; **— field** arrozal *m*
rich [rɪtʃ] ADJ rico; (tasty) sabroso; (buttery) mantecoso; (colorful) vivo; **— text format** formato de texto enriquecido *m*; N **—es** riquezas *f pl*
rickety [ríkɪdɪ] ADJ (shaky) desvencijado; (affected with rickets) raquítico
ricochet [ríkəʃe] N rebote *m*; VI rebotar
rid [rɪd] VT librar, desembarazar; **to get — of** librarse de, deshacerse de
ridden [rídn̩] *see* ride
riddle [rídl̩] N (puzzle) acertijo *m*, adivinanza *f*; (something puzzling) enigma *m*; VI hablar en enigmas; VT acribillar, perforar; **to be —d with graft** estar plagado de corrupción
ride [raɪd] VI (on a horse) cabalgar, jinetear; (on a bicycle) montar; (in a vehicle) andar/viajar/ir en; **this car —s well** este coche anda bien; **his hopes are riding on that** tiene las esperanzas puestas en eso; **just let it —** déjalo tranquilo; VT (travel on horse, bicycle) montar; (travel on bus) andar en; (harass) hostigar; **to — away** irse; **to — by** pasar; **to — out** capear; **to — up** subirse; N (in a vehicle) paseo *m*, viaje *m*; (at an amusement park) aparato *m*; **to give someone a —** llevar/acercar en coche; **to go on a —** dar un paseo
rider [ráɪdɚ] N (on a horse) jinete *m*; (on a bicycle) ciclista *mf*; (on an insurance policy) cláusula añadida *f*; (law) anexo *m*
ridge [rɪʤ] N (back of an animal) espinazo *m*, lomo *m*; (chain of hills) cadena *f*; (of a roof) caballete *m*; (of cloth) cordoncillo *m*
ridicule [rídɪkjuɫ] N burla *f*, mofa *f*; VT ridiculizar, poner en ridículo
ridiculous [rɪdíkjələs] ADJ ridículo
riffraff [rífræf] N *pej* gentuza *f*, chusma *f*
rifle [ráɪfəɫ] N rifle *m*, fusil *m*; VT robar; **to — through** revolver
rift [rɪft] N (opening) grieta *f*, hendidura *f*; (disagreement) desavenencia *f*
rig [rɪg] VT (sails) aparejar, equipar; (an election) amañar; **to — up** armar; N (on a ship) aparejo *m*, equipo *m*; (apparatus) aparato *m*; (truck) camión *m*
rigging [rígɪŋ] N jarcia *f*
right [raɪt] ADJ (not left) derecho; (not wrong) correcto, acertado; (suitable) adecuado; **— angle** ángulo recto *m*; **—-hand** derecho; **—-hand man** brazo derecho *m*; **—-handed** diestro; **— justification** alineación a la derecha *f*; **—-to-life** antiaborto, pro vida; **— triangle** triángulo recto *m*; **—-wing** derechista, de derecha; **at the — moment** en el momento justo; **the — people** la gente indicada; **to be —** tener razón; **to be all —** estar bien; **he's not in his — mind** no está en sus cabales; **to turn out —** salir bien; ADV (straight) derecho, directamente; (correctly) correctamente; (to the right) a la derecha; **— after** justo después de; **—-face** media vuelta a la derecha; **— now** ahora mismo, ahorita; **— there** allí mismo; **it is — where you left it** está exactamente donde lo dejaste; **to hit — in the eye** darle de lleno en el ojo; **— click** pulsación en el botón derecho del ratón *f*; N (just claim) derecho *m*; (moral good) bien *m*; (direction, political persuasion) derecha *f*; **— of way** prioridad *f*, preferencia *f*; **— to work** derecho al trabajo *m*; **make a — at the corner** gira/dobla a la derecha; **to the —** a la derecha; **to be in the —** tener razón; VI/VT (make upright) enderezar[se]; **to — click** pulsar el botón derecho del ratón; VT (correct) corregir
righteous [ráɪtʃəs] ADJ recto, justo; **— anger** rabia justificada *f*
righteousness [ráɪtʃəsnɪs] N rectitud *f*, superioridad moral *f*
rightful [ráɪtfəɫ] ADJ legítimo
rightist [ráɪdɪst] N derechista *mf*
rightly [ráɪtli] ADV con razón
rigid [ríʤɪd] ADJ rígido
rigidity [rɪʤídɪtɪ] N rigidez *f*
rigor [rígɚ] N rigor *m*
rigorous [rígɚəs] ADJ riguroso
rim [rɪm] N (edge) borde *m*; (on a car) llanta *f*; *Am* rin *m*; (on a bicycle) aro *m*; (on a plate) filete *m*; (of glasses) montura *f*
rind [raɪnd] N (cheese) corteza *f*; (fruit) cáscara *f*
ring [rɪŋ] N (on finger, of smoke) anillo *m*; (for women only) sortija *f*; (under the eyes) ojeras *f pl*; (in the nose) argolla *f*; (circle) círculo *m*, redondel *m*, ruedo *m*; (in a circus) pista *f*; (for bullfights) plaza de toros *f*; (for boxing) cuadrilátero *m*; (for gymnastics) anillas *f pl*; (of criminals) banda *f*; (undertone) tono *m*; (sound of telephone) timbrazo *m*, telefonazo *m*; (sound of bells) retintín *m*, repique *m*; **— finger** anular *m*; **—leader** cabecilla *mf*; **—worm** tiña *f*; VT (surround) cercar; (make doorbell sound) tocar; (make bell sound) tañer; VI (of ears) zumbar; (make sound of a doorbell) sonar; (make sound of a bell) repicar, repiquetear; **to — the nose of an animal** ponerle una argolla en la nariz a un animal; **to — the hour** dar la hora; **to — true** parecer verdad; **to — up the sale** marcar la venta
ringlet [ríŋlɪt] N (curl) rizo *m*, bucle *m*, sortija *f*; (small ring) sortija pequeña *f*
rink [rɪŋk] N pista de patinaje *f*
rinkydink [ríŋkidɪŋk] ADJ de pacotilla
rinse [rɪns] VI/VT enjuagar, aclarar; N enjuague *m*, aclarado *m*

riot [ráɪət] N (uprising) motín *m*, tumulto *m*; (excess) exceso *m*; **he's a —** es un cómico; VI amotinarse

riotous [ráɪəDəs] ADJ (wanton) desenfrenado; (funny) graciosísimo

rip [rɪp] VI/VT rasgar[se], rajar[se]; VT (something sewn) descoser; **to — away** desprender; **to — into** asaltar; **to — off** robar; **to — out a seam** descoser una costura; N rasgadura *f*, rajadura *f*; **— cord** cordón de apertura *m*; **—off** robo *m*

ripe [raɪp] ADJ maduro; **to be — for** estar preparado/listo para; **— old age** edad avanzada *f*

ripen [ráɪpən] VI/VT madurar[se], sazonar[se]

ripeness [ráɪpnɪs] N madurez *f*

ripening [ráɪpənɪŋ] N maduración *f*

ripple [rípəł] VI/VT (water) rizar[se]; (grass) agitar[se]; N ondulación *f*, rizo *m*

rise [raɪz] VI (go up) subir; (increase) aumentar; (get up, stand up) levantarse; (slope up) elevarse; (arise) surgir; (of mist) levantarse; (of the sun, moon) salir; (of dough) crecer, leudar; **to — up in rebellion** sublevarse, alzarse; **to — above** superar; **to — to the challenge** aceptar el desafío y triunfar; N (of prices, volume) subida *f*, aumento *m*; (of an empire, talent) surgimiento *m*; (slope upward) elevación *f*; **to get a — out of someone** provocar a alguien; **to give — to** ocasionar

risen [rízən] *see* rise

risk [rɪsk] N riesgo *m*; **— factors** factores de riesgo *m pl*; **at —** a riesgo; ADJ **—-free** sin riesgo; VT arriesgar, aventurar; **to — defeat** correr el riesgo de perder, exponerse a perder

risky [rískɪ] ADJ arriesgado, aventurado

risqué [rɪskė] ADJ subido de tono, atrevido, picante

Ritalin hydrochloride [rídəlɪnhaɪdrəklóraɪd] N clorhidrato de Ritalina *m*

rite [raɪt] N rito *m*

ritual [rítʃuəł] ADJ & N ritual *m*

ritzy [rítsi] ADJ elegante

rival [ráɪvəł] ADJ & N rival *mf*; VT rivalizar con, competir con

rivalry [ráɪvəłrɪ] N rivalidad *f*

river [rívə-] N río *m*; **—bank** orilla *f*, ribera *f*; **— transport** transporte fluvial *m*

rivet [rívɪt] N remache *m*; VT (put rivets) remachar; (fix) fijar, clavar

riveting [rívɪDɪŋ] N (action) remache *m*; ADJ (fascinating) fascinante

RNA [ribonucleic acid] [árénė] N ARN *m*

roach [rotʃ] N cucaracha *f*

road [rod] N (in the country) camino *m*; (highway) carretera *f*; **on the — to recovery** en vías de recuperación; **— map** mapa carretero *m*; **— rage** ira caminera *f*; **—side** borde del camino *m*; **—way** camino *m*

roam [rom] VI/VT vagar [por], errar [por], rodar [por]; VI vagabundear

roar [rɔr] VI/VT rugir, bramar; **to — with laughter** reír a carcajadas; N rugido *m*, bramido *m*; **— of laughter** risotada *f*, carcajada *f*

roast [rost] VI/VT (meat, potatoes) asar[se]; (coffee, nuts) tostar, torrar; (criticize) criticar; N (meat) asado *m*; (party) barbacoa *f*; **— beef** rosbif *m*

rob [rab] VI/VT robar; **to — someone of something** robarle algo a alguien

robber [rábə-] N ladrón -ona *mf*

robbery [rábəri] N robo *m*

robe [rob] N manto *m*, traje talar *m*, túnica *f*; (ceremonial dress) toga *f*; (bath wrap) bata *f*

robin [rábɪn] N petirrojo *m*

robot [róbɑt] N robot *m*

robotics [robádɪks] N robótica *f*

robust [robást] ADJ (strong) robusto; (hearty) saludable; (solid) sólido

rock [rɑk] N roca *f*; (crag) peñasco *m*, peñón *m*; (diamond) diamante *m*; (music style) rock *m*; **— crystal** cristal de roca *m*; **— salt** sal de piedra *f*, sal gema/mineral *f*; **on the —** en las rocas; **to go on the —s** tropezar en un escollo; *Am* escollar; **to hit —-bottom** tocar fondo; VI/VT (move to and fro) mecer[se]; (stagger) sacudir, estremecer; **to — to sleep** arrullar

rocker [rákə-] N (chair) mecedora *f*; (fan or performer of rock music) roquero -ra *mf*

rocket [rákɪt] N cohete *m*

rocketry [rákɪtri] N cohetería *f*

rocking [rákɪŋ] N **— chair** mecedora *f*; **— horse** caballito de madera *m*, caballito mecedor *m*

rocky [rákɪ] ADJ (with rocks) rocoso; (difficult) difícil

rod [rɑd] N (stick) vara *f*, varilla *f*; (in engine) vástago *m*; (measure of length) aproximadamente 5 metros *f*

rode [rod] *see* ride

rodent [róDənt] N roedor *m*

rodeo [róDio] N rodeo *m*

rogue [rog] N pícaro -ra *mf*, bribón -ona *mf*; ADJ solitario y bravo

roguish [rógɪʃ] ADJ (rascally) pícaro, bribón; (mischievous) travieso

role [roł] N (in a drama) papel *m*, rol *m*; **— model** modelo ejemplar *m*; **—-playing** improvisación *f*

roll [roł] VI (move on wheels, rotate) rodar; (rotate one's eyes) revolear; (sway) balancearse, bambolearse; (reverberate) retumbar; (flow as waves) ondular; VT (steel) aplanar; (cigarettes) liar; (a drum) redoblar; (one's *r*'s) pronunciar la erre; **to — over in**

the snow revolcarse en la nieve; **to — up** arrollar, enrollar; **to — around** llegar; **to — back** reducir, rebajar; **to — by** pasar; **to — out** (products) lanzar; **to — over** (physically) volcar, darse vuelta; (investments) reinvertir; **to get —ing** ponerse en marcha; N (of paper, fabric, etc.) rollo *m*; (of coins) cartucho *m*; (of a ship) balanceo *m*; (of thunder) retumbo *m*; (of a drum) redoble *m*; (of members) lista *f*; (of waves) ondulación *f*; (of a typewriter) carro *m*; (of bread) bollo *m*, panecillo *m*; (of dice) tiro *m*; ADJ **—-on** de bolita

roller [róləʳ] N (for painting, moving things) rodillo *m*; (hair) rulo *m*, rulero *m*; **— coaster** montaña rusa *f*; **— skate** patín de ruedas *m*

rolling [róliŋ] ADJ (countryside) ondulado; (wheel) rodante; **— pin** rodillo *m*, palote *m*

roly-poly [rólipóli] ADJ rechoncho

ROM [read-only memory] [rɑm] N ROM *f*, memoria de ROM *f*, memoria de sólo lectura *f*

Roman [rómən] ADJ & N romano -na *mf*; **— numeral** número romano *m*

romance [rómæns] N (love affair, story) romance *m*; (romantic atmosphere) romanticismo *m*; VT cortejar; ADJ (linguistic) romance, románico

romanesque [romənésk] ADJ románico

Romania [roméniə] N Rumania *f*

Romanian [roméniən] ADJ & N rumano -na *mf*

romantic [romǽntɪk] ADJ romántico

romanticism [romǽntəsɪzəm] N romanticismo *m*

romp [ramp] VI (frolic) retozar, brincar; (win easily) arrasar; N (frolic) retozo *m*; (victory) victoria fácil *f*

roof [ruf] N (ceiling) techo *m*, tejado *m*; (flat roof) azotea *f*; **— of the mouth** paladar *m*; **to hit the —** poner el grito en el cielo; VT techar

rookie [rúki] N novato -ta *mf*

room [rum] N (in building) cuarto *m*; (large) sala *f*; (in a hotel) habitación *f*; (space) lugar *m*, sitio *m*; **— and board** pensión completa *f*; **—mate** compañero -ra de cuarto *mf*; **— service** servicio a la habitación *f*; **to take up —** ocupar espacio; **the whole — laughed** todos los presentes se rieron; VI hospedarse, alojarse

roomy [rúmi] ADJ espacioso, amplio

roost [rust] N vara *f*; VI posarse [para dormir]

rooster [rústəʳ] N gallo *m*

root [rut] N raíz *f*; **— canal** (part of tooth) canal radicular *m*, tratamiento de conducto *m*; **— directory** directorio de raíz *m*, directorio raíz *m*; **to take —** (a plant) echar raíces, prender; (an idea) arraigar[se]; VI (grow roots) arraigar[se], echar raíces; (dig) hozar; **to — for** animar; **to — out/up** (uproot) arrancar de raíz; (eradicate) erradicar

rope [rop] N (cord) soga *f*, cuerda *f*; (lasso) reata *f*, lazo *m*; (on a ship) cabo *m*; (thick) maroma *f*; **to be at the end of one's —** no dar más; **to know the —s** conocer el paño, sabérselas todas; VT enlazar; **to — off** acordonar; **to — someone in** agarrar a alguien

Rorschach test [rɔ́rʃɑk test] N prueba de Rorschach *f*

rosary [rózəri] N rosario *m*

rose [roz] N rosa *f*; (color) rosa *m*; **—bud** capullo de rosa *m*, pimpollo de rosa *m*; **—bush** rosal *m*; ADJ **—-colored** de color rosa

rose [roz] *see* rise

rosemary [rózmɛri] N romero *m*

roseola [rozíələ] N roséola *f*

roster [rústəʳ] N lista *f*

rostrum [rústrəm] N tribuna *f*

rosy [rózi] ADJ (pink) rosado, color de rosa; (of cheeks) sonrosado; **— future** porvenir halagüeño *m*

rot [rɑt] VI/VT pudrir[se]; N podredumbre *f*

rotary [róbəri] ADJ rotatorio, rotativo

rotate [rótet] VI/VT rotar

rotation [rotéʃən] N rotación *f*, giro *m*

rotor [róbəʳ] N rotor *m*

rotten [rátn] ADJ (decomposing) podrido; (stinking) hediondo; (morally corrupt) corrupto; (despicable) odioso

rotund [rotǽnd] ADJ rollizo

rouge [ruʒ] N colorete *m*

rough [raf] ADJ (coarse) áspero, rugoso; (violent) violento; (rude) tosco; (approximate) aproximado; (bumpy) desigual, irregular; (rugged) agreste, bronco; (stormy) picado, revuelto; **— diamond** diamante en bruto *m*; **— draft** borrador *m*; **— estimate** aproximación *f*; **— weather** mal tiempo *m*; **he had a — time** le fue mal; VI **to — it** vivir sin lujos ni comodidades

roughly [rǽfli] ADV (not smoothly) ásperamente; (rudely) groseramente, rudamente; (approximately) aproximadamente; **to estimate —** tantear

roughness [rǽfnɪs] N (lack of smoothness) aspereza *f*; (rudeness) rudeza *f*; (unevenness) desigualdad *f*; **the — of the sea** lo picado del mar

roulette [rulét] N ruleta *f*

round [raʊnd] ADJ redondo; **— number** número redondo *m*; **— trip** viaje de ida y vuelta *m*; N (of talks, drinks, dance) ronda *f*; (of cheese) rodaja *f*; (in cards, sports) vuelta *f*; (in boxing) round *m*, asalto *m*; (of golf) partido *m*, ronda *f*; (canon) canon *m*; **— of ammunition** carga de municiones *f*; **— of applause** aplauso *m*; **—up** (of cattle) rodeo *m*; (of criminals) redada *f*; **to make the —s** hacer la ronda; PREP & ADV **—about** indirecto; **— -the-clock** veinticuatro horas al día; **all year —** todo el año; **to come —**

pasar; **to go — a corner** doblar una esquina; VT (a corner) doblar; (an edge, a number) redondear; **to — off/out** redondear; **to — up** juntar, reunir; **to — up cattle** juntar el ganado

roundness [ráʊndnɪs] N redondez *f*

rouse [raʊz] VI/VT (wake) despertar[se]; VT (instigate) incitar

rout [raʊt] N (defeat) derrota aplastante *f*; (flight) huida en desbandada *f*; VT (defeat) derrotar, destrozar; (cause to flee) poner en fuga

route [raʊt, rut] N ruta *f*, trayecto *m*, recorrido *m*; (of newspaper delivery) reparto *m*; VT dirigir

routine [rutín] N rutina *f*

rove [rov] VI/VT vagar [por], errar [por]

rover [róvə-] N vagabundo -da *mf*

row[1] [raʊ] N (fight) riña *f*, pelea *f*, bronca *f*

row[2] [ro] N (line) fila *f*, hilera *f*, ringlera *f*; **four times in a —** cuatro veces seguidas; VI/VT (propel with oars) remar, bogar; **—boat** bote de remos *m*, barca *f*

rowdy [ráʊdɪ] ADJ (person) alborotador; (party) bullicioso; N camorrista *mf*

rower [róə-] N remero -ra *mf*

royal [rɔ́ɪəł] ADJ real; **— blue** azul marino *m*; **— flush** escalera real *f*

royalty [rɔ́ɪəłti] N (group) realeza *f*; (person) miembro de la realeza *m*; **royalties** derechos *m pl*, regalías *f pl*

RSVP [répondez s'il vous plaît] [árésvípí] LOC S.R.C.

rub [rʌb] VI/VT (apply friction) frotar[se]; (massage) friccionar; (spread on) aplicar frotando; (make sore) rozar; **to — off** quitar[se] frotando; **to — out** borrar; **to — shoulders with** codearse con; **to — the wrong way** peinar a contrapelo; **don't — it in!** ¡no me lo refriegues por la cara! N (act of rubbing) fricción *f*; (difficulty) dificultad *f*; (abraded area) roce *m*, frote *m*

rubber [rʌ́bə-] N caucho *m*, goma *f*; **— band** goma elástica *f*; **—s** chanclos *m pl*; **— stamp** sello de goma *m*; **— tree** gomero *m*; VT **to —-stamp** autorizar automáticamente

rubbing alcohol [rʌ́bɪŋ ǽłkəhɔł] N alcohol para fricciones *m*

rubbish [rʌ́bɪʃ] N (trash) basura *f*; (nonsense) pamplinas *f pl*

rubble [rʌ́bəł] N (debris) escombros *m pl*; (stone fragments) ripios *m pl*, cascote *m*

rubella [rubélə] N rubéola/rubeola *f*, sarampión alemán *m*

rubric [rúbrɪk] N rúbrica *f*

ruby [rúbi] N rubí *m*

ruckus [rʌ́kəs] N barahúnda *f*, jaleo *m*

rudder [rʌ́də-] N timón *m*

ruddy [rʌ́dɪ] ADJ rubicundo

rude [rud] ADJ (impolite) grosero; (uncouth, crude, simple) tosco; (harsh) rudo

rudeness [rúdnɪs] N (impoliteness) grosería *f*; (crudeness) tosquedad *f*; (harshness) rudeza *f*

rueful [rúfəł] ADJ (inspiring pity) triste; (repentant) arrepentido

ruffian [rʌ́fiən] N rufián *m*

ruffle [rʌ́fəł] VI/VT (gather cloth) fruncir[se]; (raise feathers) erizar[se]; (ripple water) agitar[se], rizar[se]; (muss hair) desgreñar[se]; (bother a person) molestar[se], fastidiar[se]; N (frill on clothes) volante *m*; (gathering in cloth) frunce *m*, pliegue *m*; (ripples in water) ondulación *f*, rizo *m*

rug [rʌg] N alfombra *f*; (hairpiece) peluquín *m*

rugby [rʌ́gbi] N rugby *m*

rugged [rʌ́gɪd] ADJ (terrain) escarpado, áspero, fragoso; (face) recio; (manners) tosco; (way of life) duro; (man) robusto

ruin [rúɪn] N ruina *f*; **to go to —** arruinarse, venirse abajo; VI/VT arruinar[se], estropear[se]; (spoil) echar[se] a perder

ruinous [rúɪnəs] ADJ ruinoso

rule [ruł] N (principle) regla *f*; (line separating newspaper columns) filete *m*; (government) mando *m*, gobierno *m*; **—s and regulations** reglamentos y disposiciones administrativas *m pl*; **the — of law** el imperio de la ley; **as a — of thumb** por regla general, a ojo de buen cubero; VI/VT (govern) reinar, gobernar; (decree) fallar, dictaminar, sentenciar; (put lines on paper) rayar, poner renglones; **to — out** excluir; **to — over** reinar, gobernar

ruler [rúlə-] N (governor) gobernante *mf*; (measuring instrument) regla *f*

ruling [rúlɪŋ] N (decision) fallo *m*, sentencia *f*, dictamen *m*; (line on paper) renglón *m*; ADJ (governing) gobernante, reinante

rum [rʌm] N ron *m*

rumba [rʌ́mbə] N rumba *m*; VI rumbear

rumble [rʌ́mbəł] VI (as thunder) retumbar; (as a stomach) hacer ruido; (fight) pelear; N (roar) retumbo *m*; (growl) ruido *m*; (fight) pelea *f*

ruminate [rúmənet] VI rumiar

rummage [rʌ́mɪdʒ] VI/VT rebuscar, hurgar; N cachivaches *m pl*; **— sale** venta de beneficencia *f*

rumor [rúmə-] N rumor *m*; VT murmurar; **it is —ed that** se rumorea que, corre la voz que

rump [rʌmp] N (of quadruped) anca *f*, grupa *f*; (of bird) rabadilla *f*; (of person) trasero *m*

run [rʌn] VI (person, tears, water) correr; (stockings, dyes) correrse; (machines) funcionar; (faucet) chorrear; (candidate) presentarse como candidato; (sore) supurar; VT (a mile, a risk) correr; (one object through another) pasar; (a business) manejar, dirigir; (a red light) comerse; (a news story) publicar; (a sum of money) costar; (a computer program) ejecutar; (a fever) tener; **— along**

now! ¡vete! **to — across someone** encontrarse con alguien; **to — after** perseguir; **to — around with** andar con; **to — away** fugarse, escaparse; **to — down** (stop working) dejar de funcionar; (capture) aprehender; (criticize) hablar mal de; (run over) atropellar; (tire) cansar; **to — dry** secarse; **to — into** (encounter) tropezarse con, encontrarse con; (collide) chocar con; **to — out** salir corriendo; **to — out of money** quedarse sin dinero; **to — over** (spill) derramarse; (run down) atropellar, arrollar; (move along a surface) deslizar por; **to — through** (stab) atravesar; (squander) despilfarrar; **to — up** acumular; **the play ran for three months** la obra estuvo en cartel durante tres meses; **it —s in the family** es un rasgo de familia; N (act of running) carrera *f*, corrida *f*; (point in baseball) carrera *f*, anotación *f*; (defect in stockings) carrera *f*, corrida *f*; (routine trip) recorrido *m*; (of newspapers) tirada *f*; (of a play) temporada en cartel *f*; (on a bank) pánico *m*, corrida *f*; **—away** fugitivo -va *mf*; **—away horse** caballo desbocado *m*; **— batted in** carrera impulsada *f*; **— of good luck** racha de buena suerte *f*; **— of the mill** del montón; **—way** (for planes) pista *f*; (for models) pasarela *f*; **to be on the —** estar huyendo; **in the long —** a la larga; **he gave me the —around** contestó con evasivas; **she gave us a —down** nos hizo un resumen; ADJ **— -down** desvencijado

rung [rʌŋ] N (of a chair) barrote *m*; (of a ladder) peldaño *m*

rung [rʌŋ] *see* ring

runner [rʌ́nə-] N (one who runs) corredor -ora *mf*; (on a table) tapete *m*; (on a sled) patín *m*; (on a skate) cuchilla *f*; (on a plant) estolón *m*; (of drugs, contraband) contrabandista *mf*; **— -up** segundo -da *mf*

running [rʌ́nɪŋ] N (of a race) corrida *f*, carrera *f*; (of a business) manejo *m*, dirección *f*; (of water) flujo *m*; (of machines) funcionamiento *m*; (of a car) rodaje *m*; **to be out of the —** estar fuera de combate; **— board** estribo *m*; ADJ (sore) supurante; **— water** agua corriente *f*; **in — condition** en buen estado; **for ten days —** durante diez días seguidos

runt [rʌnt] N (animal) animal más pequeño de la camada *m*; (person) *pej* mequetrefe *m*

rupture [rʌ́ptʃə-] N (of relations, internal organ) ruptura *f*; (of a tire) rotura *f*; (hernia) hernia *f*; VI/VT romper[se], reventar[se]

rural [rʊ́rəł] ADJ rural

rush [rʌʃ] VI/VT (hurry) apresurar[se]; *Am* apurar[se]; VT (a parcel) llevar con prisa, llevar rápido; (an enemy) precipitarse, abalanzarse sobre; **to — by/past** pasar corriendo; **to — out** salir corriendo; N (haste) prisa *f*; *Am* apuro *m*; (attack) acometida *f*; (hurried activity) bullicio *m*; (plant) junco *m*; **— hour** hora punta *f*; **— of air** ráfaga *f*; **— of people** tumulto *m*; **— of water** torrente *m*; **— order** pedido urgente *m*

Russia [rʌ́ʃə] N Rusia *f*

Russian [rʌ́ʃən] ADJ & N ruso -sa *mf*

rust [rʌst] N (oxidation) herrumbre *f*, orín *m*; (disease) tizón *m*; ADJ **— -colored** color herrumbre; **— -proof** inoxidable; VI/VT herrumbrar[se]

rustic [rʌ́stɪk] ADJ rústico; N campesino -na *mf*, paleto -ta *mf*

rusting [rʌ́stɪŋ] N oxidación *f*

rustle [rʌ́sət̬ł] VI susurrar, crujir; VT hacer susurrar, hacer crujir; **to — cattle** robar ganado; N susurro *m*, crujido *m*

rusty [rʌ́sti] ADJ (oxidized) herrumbrado, oxidado; (rust-colored) color herrumbre; (out of practice) falto de práctica; **my German is —** se me ha olvidado el alemán

rut [rʌt] N (furrow) surco *m*; (of a wheel) rodada *f*; (routine) rutina *f*; (heat) celo *m*; **to be in a —** ser esclavo de la rutina; VI estar en celo

ruthless [rʊ́θlɪs] ADJ despiadado

ruthlessness [rʊ́θlɪsnɪs] N crueldad *f*

Rwanda [ruʊ́ndə] N Ruanda *f*

Rwandan [ruʊ́ndən] ADJ & N ruandés -esa *mf*

rye [rɑɪ] N centeno *m*; **— bread** pan de centeno *m*

Ss

saber [sébə-] N sable *m*

sabotage [sǽbət̬ɑʒ] N sabotaje *m*; VT sabotear

sac [sæk] N bolsa *f*, saco *m*

saccharine [sǽkə-ɪn] ADJ empalagoso; N sacarina *f*

sack [sæk] N (bag) saco *m*, bolso *m*; (looting) saqueo *m*; (in football) captura *f*; **in the —** en la cama; VT (bag) embolsar, ensacar; (loot) saquear; (fire) despedir

sacrament [sǽkrəmənt] N sacramento *m*

sacred [sé́krɪd] ADJ sagrado

sacrifice [sǽkrəfɑɪs] N (also in baseball) sacrificio *m*; **at a —** con pérdida; VT sacrificar

sacrilege [sǽkrəlɪʤ] N sacrilegio *m*

sacrilegious [sæ̀krəlí́ʤəs] ADJ sacrílego

sacrum [sé́krəm] N sacro *m*

sad [sæd] ADJ triste

sadden [sǽdn̩] VI/VT entristecer[se]; VT pesar

saddle [sǽdł] N (for horse) silla de montar *f*, montura *f*; (for bicycle) sillín *m*; **—bag** alforja *f*; **— horse** caballo de silla *m*; **— pad** carona *f*; **— tree** arzón *m*; VT ensillar; **to — up** ensillar; **to — someone with**

responsibilities cargar a alguien de responsabilidades
sadism [séɑɪzəm] N sadismo *m*
sadistic [səɑ́ɪstɪk] ADJ sádico
sadness [sǽɑnɪs] N tristeza *f*
safari [səfáɪi] N safari *m*
safe [sef] ADJ (secure) seguro, salvo; (trustworthy) digno de confianza; (careful) precavido, prudente; **— and sound** sano y salvo; **— deposit box** caja de seguridad *f*; **—guard** salvaguarda *f*; **—keeping** custodia *f*; **— mode** modo a prueba de fallos/errores *m*; N caja fuerte *f*; **—-conduct** salvoconducto *m*; ADV (in baseball) safe; VT **to —guard** salvaguardar
safely [séfli] ADV (without danger) sin peligro; (without incident) sin percances; **I can — say** puedo decir con toda seguridad
safety [séfti] N seguridad *f*; **— belt** cinturón de seguridad *m*; **— device** mecanismo de seguridad *m*, seguro *m*; **— glass** vidrio inastillable *m*; **— net** red *f*; **— pin** imperdible *m*
saffron [sǽfrən] N (spice) azafrán *m*; (color) color azafrán *m*
sag [sæg] VI/VT (wall) combar[se], pandear[se]; VI (stock market, breast) caer; (spirits) decaer; (rope) aflojarse; (pants) abolsarse; **his shoulders —** tiene las espaldas caídas; N (of a wall) pandeo *m*, comba *f*; (in prices) caída *f*
sage [seɑ̃ʒ] ADJ sabio; N (wise person) sabio -bia *mf*; (plant) salvia *f*
said [sɛd] *see* say
sail [seɪ] N (part of a boat) vela *f*; (trip) viaje en barco *m*; **—boat** velero *m*; **—fish** pez vela *m*; **under full —** a toda vela; **to set —** zarpar; VI/VT (travel by boat) navegar; (set sail) zarpar; **to — along** deslizarse, navegar; **to — along the coast** costear; **to — through an exam** aprobar un examen con facilidad
sailor [séɪlə-] N marinero -ra *mf*
saint [sent] N santo -ta *mf*; **— John** San Juan
saintly [séntli] ADJ santo, piadoso
sake [seɪk] N **for the — of** por; **for my —** por mí; **for pity's —** por el amor de Dios; **for brevity's —** para ser breve; **for the — of argument** por vía de argumento; **art for art's —** el arte por el arte
salad [sǽləd] N ensalada *f*; **— dressing** aderezo *m*
salamander [sǽləmændə-] N salamandra *f*
salary [sǽləri] N sueldo *m*, retribución *f*; **— bracket** categoría salarial *f*; **— range** escala de sueldos *f*, escala salarial *f*
sale [seɪl] N (act of selling) venta *f*; (special sales event) liquidación *f*, saldo *m*; **—s clerk** dependiente -ta *mf*; **—s force** personal de ventas *m*; **—sperson** dependiente -ta *mf*; **—s tax** impuesto sobre las ventas *m*; **for —** en venta; **on —** con rebaja, rebajado
salient [séliənt] ADJ & N saliente *m*
saline [sélin] ADJ salino; **— solution** solución salina *f*
saliva [səláɪvə] N saliva *f*
sally [sǽli] N (sortie) salida *f*; (excursion) excursión *f*; VI salir, hacer una salida; **to — forth** salir
salmon [sǽmən] N salmón *m*
salmonella [sǽlmənɛ́lə] N salmonela *f*
salon [səlán] N salón *m*; (beauty parlor) salón de belleza *m*, peluquería *f*
saloon [səlún] N salón *m*, taberna *f*, bar *m*
salt [sɔ́ɪt] N sal *f*; (for smelling) sales *f pl*; **—cellar** salero *m*; **— lick** salegar *m*; **— mine** salina *f*; **—peter** salitre *m*; **—shaker** salero *m*; **—water** agua salada *f*; **old —** lobo de mar *m*; **the — of the earth** la sal de la tierra; VT salar; **to — away** ahorrar
salty [sɔ́lti] ADJ (food, water) salado; (soil, water) salobre
salutation [sæljətéʃən] N saludo *m*
salute [səlút] N saludo *m*; (of guns) salva *f*; VI/VT (greet) saludar; (acknowledge) reconocer
Salvadoran, Salvadorian [sǽlvədɔ́r[i]ən] ADJ & N salvadoreño -ña *mf*
salvage [sǽlvɪɑ̃ʒ] N (recovery) salvamento *m*; (objects recovered) objetos salvados *m pl*; VT salvar
salvation [sǽlvéʃən] N salvación *f*
salve [sæv] N ungüento *m*, pomada *f*
salvo [sǽlvo] N salva *f*
same [sem] ADJ (identical) mismo; (similar) igual; **—-day delivery** entrega el mismo día *f*; **it is all the — to me** me da igual, me da lo mismo; **the — to you** igualmente; **all the —** de todos modos
Samoa [səmóə] N Samoa *f*
Samoan [səmóən] ADJ & N samoano -na *mf*
sample [sǽmpəɫ] N muestra *f*; VT (try) probar; (take samples) muestrear
sampling [sǽmplɪŋ] N muestreo *m*
sanatorium [sǽnətɔ́rɪəm] N sanatorio *m*
sanctify [sǽŋktəfaɪ] VT santificar
sanction [sǽŋkʃən] N sanción *f*; VT sancionar
sanctity [sǽŋktɪɑ̃ɪ] N santidad *f*
sanctuary [sǽŋktʃuɛri] N (church auditorium, place of refuge) santuario *m*; (game preserve) reserva *f*
sand [sænd] N arena *f*; **—box** arenero *m*; **— dollar** erizo de mar plano *m*; **—paper** papel de lija *m*; **to —paper** lijar; **—stone** arenisca *f*; **—storm** tormenta de arena *f*; **—trap** trampa de arena *f*; VT lijar, pulir
sandal [sǽndl] N sandalia *f*
sandwich [sǽndwɪtʃ] N bocadillo *m*, emparedado *m*; VT intercalar; **to be —ed between** quedar apretado entre
sandy [sǽndi] ADJ (full of sand) arenoso,

arenisco; (yellowish red) rubio
sane [sen] ADJ cuerdo
sang [sæŋ] *see* sing
sanitary [sǽnɪtɛri] ADJ sanitario; **— napkin** paño higiénico *m*
sanitation [sænɪtéʃən] N (sewers) saneamiento *m*; (hygiene) salubridad *f*
sanity [sǽnɪDi] N cordura *f*
sank [sæŋk] *see* sink
San Marinese [sænmærəníz] ADJ & N sanmarinense *mf*, sanmarinés -esa *mf*
San Marino [sænməríno] N San Marino *m*
Sanskrit [sǽnskrɪt] N sánscrito *f*
Santa Claus [sǽntəklɔz] N Papá Noel *m*, Santa Claus *m*
São Tomean [saʊtoméən] ADJ & N santotomense *mf*
São Tome and Principe [saʊtoméændprínsipe] N Santo Tomé y Príncipe *m*
sap [sæp] N (juice) savia *f*; (fool) tonto -ta *mf*; VT (exhaust) agotar
sapling [sǽplɪŋ] N (tree) árbol joven *m*; (person) jovenzuelo -la *mf*
sapphire [sǽfaɪr] N zafiro *m*
sarcasm [súrkæzəm] N sarcasmo *m*, socarronería *f*
sarcastic [sɑrkǽstɪk] ADJ sarcástico, socarrón
sarcoma [sɑrkómə] N sarcoma *m*
sarcophagus [sɑrkúfəgəs] N sarcófago *m*
sardine [sɑrdín] N sardina *f*
sardonic [sɑrdánɪk] ADJ sardónico
sash [sæʃ] N (around waist) faja *f*; (around shoulder) banda *f*; (on window) marco *m*, bastidor *m*
sassy [sǽsi] ADJ insolente
sat [sæt] *see* sit
satanic [sətǽnɪk] ADJ satánico
satchel [sǽtʃəl] N cartera *f*
satellite [sǽdlaɪt] N satélite *m*; **— dish** [antena] parabólica *f*
satiate [séʃiet] VT saciar, hartar
satin [sǽtn] N raso *m*, satén *m*
satire [sǽtaɪr] N sátira *f*
satirical [sətírɪkəl] ADJ satírico
satirize [sǽDəraɪz] VT satirizar
satisfaction [sæDɪsfǽkʃən] N satisfacción *f*
satisfactory [sæDɪsfǽktəri] ADJ satisfactorio
satisfied [sǽDɪsfaɪd] ADJ satisfecho
satisfy [sǽDɪsfaɪ] VI/VT satisfacer
saturate [sǽtʃəret] VI/VT (impregnate) saturar[se]; (soak) empapar[se]; **—d fat** grasa saturada *f*
Saturday [sǽDə-De] N sábado *m*
sauce [sɔs] N salsa *f*; **—pan** cacerola *f*; VT aderezar con salsa
saucer [sɔ́sə-] N platillo *m*
saucy [sɔ́si] ADJ (insolent) fresco, descarado, insolente; (who talks back) respondón
Saudi Arabia [sɔ́Diərébiə] N Arabia Saudí *f*, Arabia Saudita *f*
Saudi Arabian [sɔ́Diərébiən] ADJ & N saudí *mf*, saudita *mf*
saunter [sɔ́ntə-] VI pasearse, deambular
sausage [sɔ́sɪʤ] N (thick) chorizo *m*; (thin) salchicha *f*; (cured) longaniza *f*; **— -making** charcutería *f*
savage [sǽvɪʤ] ADJ (uncivilized) salvaje; (furious) rabioso; (rugged) agreste; N salvaje *m*; VT hacer trizas de
savagery [sǽvɪʤri] N salvajismo *m*, barbarie *f*
savannah [səvǽnə] N sabana *f*
save [sev] VT (a sinner, a person in danger) salvar; (furniture) salvaguardar, proteger; (money, time, energy) ahorrar, economizar; (data) guardar; VI (lay up money, be economical) ahorrar; (protect) salvaguardar; **to — from** librar de; **— as** (on a computer) almacenar como, guardar como; **to — one's eyes** cuidarse la vista; N (in baseball) salvado *m*; PREP salvo, menos
savings [sévɪŋz] N ahorros *m pl*; **— account** cuenta de ahorros *f*; **— bank** caja de ahorros *f*
savior [sévjə-] N salvador -ora *mf*
savor [sévə-] N (taste) sabor *m*; (trace) dejo *m*; VT saborear
savory [sévəri] ADJ (delicious) sabroso; (not sweet) salado
savvy [sǽvi] N astucia *f*; ADJ astuto
saw [sɔ] N sierra *f*; **—horse** caballete *m*; VI/VT aserrar[se]; **—dust** aserrín *m*, serrín *m*; **—mill** aserradero *m*
saw [sɔ] *see* see
sawn [sɔn] *see* saw
saxophone [sǽksəfon] N saxofón *m*
say [se] VT (something interesting) decir; (a prayer) rezar; VI (a clock) marcar; (a sign) rezar, decir; **—!** ¡oye! **that is to —** es decir; **— I bought it** supongamos que yo lo compraría; **it goes without —ing** huelga decir[lo]; **there's a lot to be said for** es muy recomendable; **when all is said and done** al fin y al cabo; **you can — that again** tú lo has dicho; N **the final —** la última palabra; **to have one's —** dar su opinión; ADV **you could earn, —, a million dollars** podrías ganar, pongamos, un millón de dólares
saying [séɪŋ] N dicho *m*, refrán *m*
scab [skæb] N (of a wound) costra *f*; (on plants) roña *f*; (strikebreaker) esquirol *m*, amarillo -lla *mf*; VI (wound) formar una costra; (break a strike) ser esquirol
scabby [skǽbi] ADJ (wound) costroso; (plant) roñoso
scaffold [skǽfəld] N (in construction) andamio *m*; (of a gallows) patíbulo *m*
scald [skɔld] VI/VT escaldar[se]; N escaldadura *f*
scale [skel] N (progression) escala *f*; (for weighing) balanza *f*; (heavy-duty) báscula *f*;

(on fish, reptiles, human skin) escama *f*; **pair of —s** balanza *f*; VT (climb) escalar; (remove scales) escamar; VI/VT (adjust proportionately) graduar, escalar; **to — down** rebajar proporcionalmente

scallion [skǽljən] N cebollino *m*

scallop [skǽləp] N (mollusk) vieira *f*; (of beef) escalope *m*; (of fabric) festón *m*; VT festonear

scalp [skælp] N cuero cabelludo *m*; VT (to skin) arrancar la cabellera; (to resell) revender

scalpel [skǽlpəł] N bisturí *m*

scalper [skǽlpə˞] N revendedor -ora *mf*

scam [skæm] N timo *m*, estafa *f*

scamp [skæmp] N pícaro -ra *mf*, tunante -ta *mf*, pillo -lla *mf*

scamper [skǽmpə˞] VI (run) escabullirse, escaparse; (caper) cabriolar

scan [skæn] VT (horizon) escudriñar, escrutar; (brain) hacer una tomografía; (page) echar un vistazo a; (verse) escandir; (digitalize for computer) escanear; N tomografía *f*

scandal [skǽndl] N escándalo *m*

scandalize [skǽndlˌaɪz] VT escandalizar

scandalous [skǽndlˌəs] ADJ escandaloso

scanner [skǽnə˞] N escáner *m*

scanning [skǽnɪŋ] N escaneado *m*

scant [skænt] ADJ escaso

scanty [skǽnti] ADJ (provisions) escaso; (skirt) muy corto; (bikini) breve

scapegoat [sképgot] N chivo expiatorio *m*, cabeza de turco *m*

scapula [skǽpjə̌lə] N escápula *f*, omóplato *m*

scar [skɑr] N cicatriz *f*, lacra *f*; VT dejar una cicatriz

scarce [skɛrs] ADJ escaso; **to be —** escasear

scarcely [skérsli] ADV (barely) apenas; **he's — a genius** no es un genio ni mucho menos

scarcity [skérsɪdi] N escasez *f*, pobreza *f*, carestía *f*

scare [skɛr] VI/VT espantar[se], asustar[se]; **to — away** ahuyentar; **to — up** reunir; N susto *m*, sobresalto *m*; (of war, of a heart attack) amago *m*; **—crow** espantapájaros *m sg*

scared [skɛrd] ADJ asustado; **I'm — of spiders** tengo miedo de las arañas / las arañas me dan miedo

scarf [skɑrf] N (woolen) bufanda *f*; (silk, cotton) pañuelo *m*; VI **to — up** engullir

scarlet [skɑ́rlɪt] N escarlata *m*, grana *f*; **— fever** escarlatina *f*

scary [skéri] ADJ (causing fright) de miedo; (easily frightened) asustadizo

scat [skæt] INTERJ ¡fuera!

scatter [skǽtə˞] VI/VT (seeds) esparcir[se], desparramar[se], desperdigar[se]; (crowd) dispersar[se]; **—brained** atolondrado; N **—brain** cabeza de chorlito *mf*

scattered [skǽtə˞d] ADJ disperso

scavenge [skǽvɪnʤ] VT recoger, rescatar; VI hurgar

scenario [sɪnério] N guión *m*; **worst-case —** el peor de los casos

scene [sin] N escena *f*; (sphere of activity) ambiente *m*, ámbito *m*; **to make a —** montar una escena; **behind the —s** entre bastidores

scenery [sínəri] N paisaje *m*; (on a stage) decorado *m*

scenic [sínɪk] ADJ panorámico

scent [sɛnt] N (smell) olor *m*; (fragrance) perfume *m*; (trace) pista *f*, rastro *m*; (sense of smell) olfato *m*; VI/VT (perceive through smell) olfatear; (intuit) presentir; (give fragrance to) perfumar

schedule [skéʤUł] N (plan) calendario *m*; (timetable) horario *m*; (appendix) apéndice *m*; (list) lista *f*; **on —** al día, a la hora prevista; **ahead of —** adelantado; VT programar, fijar

scheme [skim] N (plan) plan *m*, proyecto *m*; (plot) ardid *m*, trama *f*; (of colors) combinación *f*; VI/VT maquinar, intrigar, tramar

schemer [skímə˞] N maquinador -ora *mf*, intrigante *mf*

scheming [skímɪŋ] ADJ intrigante; N maquinación *f*

schizophrenia [skɪtsəfréniə] N esquizofrenia *f*

scholar [skɑ́lə˞] N (student) alumno -na *mf*; (fellow) becario -ria *mf*; (erudite person) erudito -ta *mf*, estudioso -sa *mf*

scholarly [skɑ́lə˞li] ADJ erudito

scholarship [skɑ́lə˞ʃɪp] N (erudition) erudición *f*; (award) beca *f*

school [skuł] N (primary) escuela *f*, colegio *m*; (secondary) secundaria *f*; Sp instituto *m*; (university) universidad *f*; (of law, etc.) facultad *f*; (of language, driving) academia *f*; (of thought) escuela *f*; (of fish) banco *m*, cardumen *m*; **—boy** escolar *m*; **—girl** escolar *f*; **—house** escuela *f*; **—master** maestro -tra *mf*; **—mate** compañero -ra de escuela *mf*; **—room** aula *f*, sala de clase *f*; **—teacher** maestro -tra *mf*; **— year** año lectivo *m*; VT instruir, entrenar

schooling [skúlɪŋ] N instrucción *f*

schooner [skúnə˞] N goleta *f*

sciatic nerve [saɪǽʤɪknɑ́˞v] N nervio ciático *m*

science [sáɪəns] N ciencia *f*; **— fiction** ciencia ficción *f*

scientific [saɪəntífɪk] ADJ científico; **— method** método científico *m*

scientist [sáɪəntɪst] N científico -ca *mf*

scintillate [síntˌlet] VI (diamonds) centellear, destellar; (stars) titilar

scissor [sízə˞z] VT cortar con tijera; N **—s** tijera *f*, tijeras *f pl*; **— kick** tijera *f*, tijereta *f*

sclerosis [sklərósɪs] N esclerosis *f*

scoff [skɑf] N mofa *f*, burla *f*; VI mofarse; **to — at** mofarse de, burlarse de

scold [skoʊld] VI/VT reprender, regañar, reñir; N regañón -ona *mf*
scolding [skóʊldɪŋ] N regaño *m*, reprimenda *f*
scoliosis [skoliósɪs] N escoliosis *f*
scoop [skup] N (ladle) cucharón *m*; (spoon for ice cream) cuchara *f*; (shovel) pala *f*; (news item) primicia *f*; VT sacar con cuchara; (report first) adelantarse a; **to — in a good profit** sacar buena ganancia; **to — out** (water) achicar; (a hole) cavar; **to — up** recoger
scoot [skut] VI (go fast) correr; (go away) largarse
scooter [skúʊtə̵-] N (with motor) scooter *m*; (toy) monopatín *m*, patinete *m*
scope [skop] N (range) alcance *m*, ámbito *m*; (sphere) esfera *f*; VT observar
scorch [skɔrtʃ] VI/VT chamuscar[se], quemar[se]; N chamuscadura *f*; *Am* quemadura *f*
score [skor] N (partial result) tanteo *m*; (total result) resultado *m*; (on a test) calificación *f*; (scratch) arañazo *m*; (twenty) veintena *f*; (of music) partitura *f*; **—board** marcador *m*; **on that —** a ese respecto; **to keep —** llevar la cuenta; **to settle old —s** ajustar cuentas; **what is the —?** ¿cómo va el marcador? VT (grade) calificar; (orchestrate) orquestar; (scratch) arañar; VI/VT (make points) marcar, tantear; (hook up with someone) ligar; **to — a goal** marcar/meter un gol
scorn [skɔrn] N desdén *m*, menosprecio *m*; VI/VT desdeñar, menospreciar
scornful [skɔ́rnfəł] ADJ desdeñoso
scorpion [skɔ́rpiən] N escorpión *m*, alacrán *m*
Scotch [skɑtʃ] ADJ escocés; **— whisky** whisky escocés *m*
Scotland [skátlənd] N Escocia *f*
Scotsman [skátsmən] N escocés *m*
Scotswoman [skátswʊmən] N escocesa *f*
Scottish [skáʊɪʃ] ADJ escocés
scoundrel [skáʊndrəł] N bellaco *m*, infame *m*, truhán *m*
scour [skaʊr] VT (clean) fregar, restregar; (search an area) inspeccionar
scourge [skɜ̵ʤ] N (affliction, means of affliction) azote *m*; VT azotar
scout [skaʊt] N (military) explorador -ora *mf*; (child explorer) explorador -ora *mf*, scout *mf*; (for talent) cazatalentos *mf sg*; **a good —** una buena persona; VI/VT explorar; VI **to — for** buscar
scowl [skaʊł] N ceño fruncido *m*; VI fruncir el ceño
scram [skræm] VI largarse
scramble [skrǽmbəł] VI (climb) subir a gatas; **to — for** pelearse por; **to — up** subir a gatas; VT (eggs) revolver; (numbers) mezclar; **—d eggs** huevos revueltos *m pl*; N (difficult climb) subida difícil *f*; (struggle for possession) arrebatiña *f*
scrap [skræp] N (fragment) fragmento *m*, pedacito *m*; (of truth) ápice *m*; (fight) riña *f*, reyerta *f*; **—book** álbum de recortes *m*; **— iron** chatarra *f*; **— paper** papel borrador *m*; **—s** sobras *f pl*, desperdicios *m pl*; VT (break apart) desguazar; (discard) desechar; VI (fight) pelearse, reñir
scrape [skrep] VI/VT (rub) raspar; (damage) arañar; **to — along** ir tirando, ir pasándola; **to — by** arreglárselas; **to — together** reunir; **to bow and —** ser muy servil; N (act of scraping) raspado *m*; (injury) raspón *m*, raspadura *f*; (sound) chirrido *m*; (fight) pelea *f*; (difficult situation) aprieto *m*
scraper [skrépə̵-] N raspador *m*
scratch [skrætʃ] VI/VT (mark) arañar, rasguñar; (relieve itching) rascar[se]; (cancel from a race) retirar[se]; (cause itching) picar; VI (to dig, as a hen) escarbar; **to — out** (words) tachar; (eyes) sacar; N (injury) arañazo *m*, rasguño *m*; (sound) chirrido *m*; **to start from —** empezar de cero; **— test** examen dérmico de alergias *m*
scrawny [skrɔ́ni] ADJ esmirriado
scream [skrim] N grito *m*, alarido *m*; **he's a —** es un payaso; VI/VT gritar
screech [skritʃ] N (of brakes) chirrido *m*; (of voice) chillido *m*; **— owl** lechuza *f*; VI (of brakes) chirriar; (of voice) chillar
screen [skrin] N (movie, computer) pantalla *f*; (divider) biombo *m*; (on window) mosquitero *m*; (sifter) tamiz *m*; **— door** puerta con mosquitero *f*; **—ing test** prueba de detección *f*; **—pass** pase pantalla *m*; **—play** guión *m*; **— saver** protector de pantalla *m*, salvapantallas *m sg*; **—writer** guionista *mf*; VT (conceal) tapar; (sift) tamizar; (project) proyectar; (select) seleccionar
screw [skru] N (device) tornillo *m*; (one turn) vuelta *f*; (propeller) hélice *f*; **—driver** destornillador *m* (also cocktail); VT atornillar; **to — on** enroscar; **to — up one's courage** cobrar ánimo; **to — around** perder tiempo
scribble [skríbəł] VI/VT garabatear, garrapatear; N garabato *m*
scrimp [skrɪmp] VI hacer economías
script [skrɪpt] N (writing) escritura *f*; (screenplay) guión *m*
scripture [skrɪ́ptʃə̵-] N escritura sagrada *f*
scroll [skroł] N (roll) rollo *m*; (adornment) voluta *f*; VI **to — down** bajar el cursor
scrub [skrʌb] VI/VT (rub) fregar, restregar; **to — up** lavarse las manos; VT (cancel) cancelar; N (cleaning) friega *f*, fregada *f*; (bushes) maleza *f*; (rough terrain) breña *f*; **— pine** pino achaparrado *m*; **— team** equipo suplente *m*; **—woman** fregona *f*
scruple [skrúpəł] N escrúpulo *m*
scrupulous [skrúpjələs] ADJ escrupuloso
scrutinize [skrúṭnaɪz] VI/VT escrutar,

escudriñar

scrutiny [skrútṇi] N escrutinio *m*, examen minucioso *m*

scuba [skúbə] N escafandra *f*; VI **to — -dive** bucear

scuff [skʌf] VT (shoes) rayar; (floor) marcar; N (on shoes) raya *f*; (on floor) marca *f*

scuffle [skʌ́fəł] N refriega *f*, riña *f*; VI (fight) pelear, reñir; (shuffle) arrastrar los pies

sculptor [skʌ́łptə-] N escultor -ora *mf*

sculpture [skʌ́łptʃə-] N escultura *f*; VI/VT esculpir

scum [skʌm] N (in a glass) capa de suciedad *f*; (on a pond) verdín *m*; (people) *pej* escoria *f*; (vile person) *pej* canalla *mf*; **—bag** *pej* canalla *mf*; VI cubrirse de espuma; VT espumar

scurrilous [skɜ́-ələs] ADJ (coarse) grosero

scurry [skɜ́-i] VI correr; **to — away/off** escabullirse

scurvy [skɜ́-vi] N escorbuto *m*

scuttle [skʌ́dł] VI (run) correr; **to — away/off** escabullirse; VT (sink a ship) hundir; (abandon a plane) abandonar

scythe [saɪð] N guadaña *f*

sea [si] N mar *mf*; **— battle** batalla naval *f*; **—board** costa *f*, litoral *m*; **—coast** costa *f*, litoral *m*; **— cow** vaca marina *f*; **— current** corriente marina *f*; **—food** frutos del mar *m pl*; **— green** verdemar *m*; **—gull** gaviota *f*; **— horse** caballito de mar *m*; **— level** nivel del mar *m*; **— lion** léon marino *m*; **—man** marino *m*, marinero *m*; **—plane** hidroavión *m*; **—port** puerto de mar *m*; **— power** potencia naval *f*; **—shore** costa *f*; **—sickness** mareo *m*; **—side** costa *f*, litoral *m*; **— turtle** tortuga marina *f*; **— urchin** erizo de mar *m*; **—weed** alga [marina] *f*; **at —** (on the ocean) en el mar; (confused) perdido; **by —** por barco; **to put to —** hacerse a la mar; **on the high —s** en alta mar; ADJ marino; **—faring** marinero; **—sick** mareado; **to get —sick** marearse; **—worthy** marinero

seal [siɫ] N (stamp) sello *m*; (on a jar) precinto *m*; (animal) foca *f*; **to set one's — to** sellar; VT (put a seal on) sellar; (close with a seal) precintar; **—ing wax** lacre *m*; **to — one's fate** determinar el destino de uno; **to — off** acordonar; **to — in** cerrar herméticamente; **to — with wax** lacrar

seam [sim] N (sewing) costura *f*; (in rock) grieta *f*; (in ore deposits) veta *f*; VT coser

seamstress [símstrɪs] N costurera *f*

seamy [sími] ADJ sórdido

sear [sir] VT chamuscar

search [sɜ-tʃ] VI/VT (an area) rastrear, requisar; (a suitcase) registrar; (a person) cachear; **— me!** ¡a mí que me registren! ¡yo que sé! **to — for** buscar; N (for something) búsqueda *f*; (of baggage, ships) registro *m*; (of an area) rastreo *m*; **— and replace** buscar y reemplazar; **— engine** motor de búsqueda *m*, máquina de búsqueda *f*; **— function** función de búsqueda *f*; **—light** reflector *m*; **— warrant** orden de registro *m*; **in — of** en busca de

season [sízən] N (of the year) estación *f*; (period of time) temporada *f*, época *f*; (sports schedule) temporada *f*; **in —** en temporada/época; **— ticket** billete de abono *m*; **open —** temporada de caza/pesca *f*; **out of —** fuera de temporada/época; VT (to spice) sazonar, aderezar; VI (wood) secarse; **a —ed pilot** un piloto experimentado

seasonal [sízənəł] ADJ estacional

seasoning [sízənɪŋ] N condimento *m*, aliño *m*

seat [sit] N (furniture) asiento *m*; (of bicycle) sillín *m*; (in parliament) escaño *m*; (of government) sede *f*; (in the theater) localidad *f*; (buttocks) asentaderas *f pl*; (of clothes) fondillos *m pl*; **to take a —** sentarse, tomar asiento; **— belt** cinturón de seguridad *m*; VT (cause to sit) sentar; (accommodate with seats) tener capacidad para; (place) colocar; **to — oneself** sentarse

seborrhea [sɛbərí́ə] N seborrea *f*

seclude [sɪklúd] VT aislar; **to — oneself from** recluirse de, aislarse de

secluded [sɪklúdɪd] ADJ apartado, aislado, recogido

seclusion [sɪklúʒən] N recogimiento *m*, aislamiento *m*

second [sɛ́kənd] ADJ segundo; **— base** segunda base *f*, intermedia *f*; **— baseman** segunda base *mf*, camarero -ra *mf*, intermediarista *mf*; **— child** segundón -ona *mf*; **— cousin** primo -ma segundo -da *mf*; **— fiddle** segundón -ona *mf*; **— floor** primer piso *m*; **— half** (sports) segundo tiempo *m*; **—hand** de segunda mano; **— lieutenant** subteniente *mf*; **— mortgage** segunda hipoteca *f*; **— nature** automático; **—-rate** mediocre, de segunda; **to get —s** repetir, servirse por segunda vez; **— serve** segundo servicio *m*; **on — thought** pensándolo bien; N (part of a minute) segundo *m*; (helper in a duel) padrino *m*; **—s** (inferior wares) artículos de segunda *m pl*; (additional helping) segunda ración *f*; **in a —** ahorita; **may I have —s?** ¿puedo repetir? VT (support) secundar, apoyar; (assist in duels) apadrinar; (support a motion) apoyar; **to —-guess** cuestionar

secondary [sɛ́kəndɛri] ADJ secundario; **— school** escuela secundaria *f*

secondly [sɛ́kəndli] ADV en segundo lugar

secrecy [sí́krɪsi] N secreto *m*

secret [sí́krɪt] ADJ & N secreto *m*

secretariat [sɛkrɪtɛ́riət] N secretaría *f*

secretary [sékrɪtɛri] N (assistant) secretario -ria *mf*; (government) ministro -tra *mf*; (furniture) escritorio *m*
secrete [sɪkrít] VT (discharge) secretar, segregar; (hide) ocultar
secretion [sɪkríʃən] N secreción *f*
secretive [síkrɪdɪv] ADJ hermético
sect [sɛkt] N secta *f*
section [sékʃən] N (component) sección *f*; (of a chapter) apartado *m*; (of a text) trozo *m*; (of a city) sector *m*; (incision) corte *m*; (of orange) gajo *m*; VT seccionar
sector [séktə-] N sector *m*
sectorial [sɛktɔ́riəł] ADJ sectorial
secular [sékjələ-] ADJ secular; N (person) seglar *mf*, lego -ga *mf*
secure [sɪkjúr] ADJ (certain, safe) seguro; (firm) firme; VT (make certain, guarantee) asegurar, afianzar; (make firm) afirmar, cimentar; (obtain) obtener; (protect) proteger; (lock) cerrar con llave; (capture) capturar; (tie) amarrar
security [sɪkjúrɪdi] N (safety, freedom from worry) seguridad *f*; (guarantee) fianza *f*, garantía *f*; (guarantor) fiador -ora *mf*; **—deposit** depósito de garantía *m*; **securities** valores *m pl*
sedan [sɪdǽn] N sedán *m*
sedate [sɪdét] ADJ sosegado, tranquilo; VT sedar
sedation [sɪdéʃən] N sedación *f*
sedative [sédətɪv] ADJ & N calmante *m*, sedante *m*
sedentary [sédn̩tɛri] ADJ sedentario
sediment [sédəmənt] N sedimento *m*; (dregs) heces *f pl*
sedition [sɪdíʃən] N sedición *f*
seduce [sɪdús] VI/VT seducir [a]
seduction [sɪdʌ́kʃən] N seducción *f*
see [si] VI/VT (perceive, find out, meet, visit) ver; (understand) entender; (make sure) fijarse, asegurarse; (date) salir con; **—ing-eye dog** perro guía *m*; **let me —** a ver; **to — to** encargarse de, atender; **to — off** despedir; **to — through someone** calar a alguien; **to — about** ocuparse de; **to — out** acompañar a la puerta; N sede *f*
seed [sid] N (grains) semilla *f*; (in tennis) cabeza de serie *f*; **to go to —** echarse a perder; **— bed** semillero *m*; VI/VT (sow) sembrar; VT (remove seeds) despepitar, quitar las semillas; (player) clasificar; VI producir semillas
seedy [sídi] ADJ sórdido
seek [sik] VT (search for) buscar; (ask for) pedir; **to — after** buscar; **to — to** tratar de, esforzarse por
seem [sim] VI parecer; **they — to be here** parece que están aquí; **it —s to me** me parece
seemingly [símɪŋli] ADV aparentemente
seen [sin] *see* see
seep [sip] VI/VT rezumar[se]
seer [sir] N vidente *mf*
seesaw [sísɔ] N balancín *m*, subibaja *m*; VI oscilar
seethe [sið] VI bullir, hervir; **he was seething** hervía de rabia
segment [ségmənt] N segmento *m*
segregate [ségrɪgɛt] VI/VT segregar
seismic [sáɪzmɪk] ADJ sísmico
seize [siz] VT (grab) asir, agarrar; (take possession) apoderarse de; (take advantage of) aprovecharse de; (confiscate) embargar, incautarse de, secuestrar; **to — upon** asir; VI **to — [up]** (mechanism, motor) agarrotarse; **to — upon** valerse de
seizure [sízə-] N (of power) toma *f*; (of property) confiscación *f*; (of drugs, guns) incautación *f*, secuestro *m*; (epileptic) ataque *m*
seldom [sɛ́łdəm] ADV rara vez, raramente
select [sɪlɛ́kt] ADJ selecto; VI/VT elegir, seleccionar
selection [sɪlɛ́kʃən] N selección *f*, elección *f*
selective [sɪlɛ́ktɪv] ADJ selectivo
self [sɛłf] N (ego) yo *m*; **—-assurance** desenvoltura *f*; **—-control** autocontrol *m*; **—-defense** defensa propia *f*; (juridical term) legítima defensa *f*; **—-denial** abnegación *f*; **—-determination** autodeterminación *f*; **—-discipline** autodisciplina *f*; **—-esteem** autoestima *f*; **—-government** autogobierno *m*; **—-help** autoayuda *f*; **—-image** autoimagen *f*; **—-improvement** mejora personal *f*; **—-interest** interés personal *m*; **—-made man** hombre que debe su éxito a sus propios esfuerzos *m*; **—-pity** autocompasión *f*; **—-reliance** independencia *f*, autosuficiencia *f*; **—-respect** amor propio *m*; **—-sacrifice** sacrificio *m*; **—-satisfaction** autosatisfacción *f*; **his better —** su lado bueno *m*; **his former —** lo que era antes; ADJ **—-assured** desenvuelto; **—-centered** egocéntrico; **—-composed** tranquilo; **—-confident** con confianza de sí mismo; **—-conscious** (shy) cohibido; (with complexes) acomplejado; **—-destructive** autodestructivo; **—-employed** que trabaja por cuenta propia; **—-evident** evidente; **—-explanatory** claro, fácil de entender; **—-propelled** autopropulsado; **—-righteous** que afecta superioridad moral; **—-satisfied** pagado de sí, satisfecho de sí; **—-service** autoservicio; **—-serving** interesado; **—-sufficient** autosuficiente
selfish [sɛ́łfɪʃ] ADJ egoísta
selfishness [sɛ́łfɪʃnɪs] N egoísmo *m*
selfless [sɛ́łflɪs] ADJ desinteresado, generoso
sell [sɛł] VI/VT vender[se]; **his books — well** se venden bien sus libros; **to be sold on** estar entusiasmado con; **to — off** liquidar; **to — out** (dispose of) liquidar; (betray) traicionar,

vender; (run out) agotarse; N —**-off** (liquidation) liquidación *f*; (decline) baja *f*; —**out** traición *f*

seller [sɛlɚ] N vendedor -ora *mf*

selling [sɛ́lɪŋ] N venta *f*

semantics [sɪmǽntɪks] N semántica *f*

semblance [sɛ́mbləns] N apariencia *f*

semester [səméstɚ] N semestre *m*

semicircle [sɛ́mɪsɝkəl] N semicírculo *m*

semicolon [sɛ́mɪkolən] N punto y coma *m*

semiconductor [sɛmɪkəndʌ́ktɚ] N semiconductor *m*

semifinal [sɛ́mɪfaɪnl̩] ADJ & N semifinal *f*

seminar [sɛ́mənɑr] N seminario *m*

seminary [sɛ́mənɛri] N seminario *m*

Semitic [səmɪ́tɪk] ADJ semítico

senate [sɛ́nɪt] N senado *m*

senator [sɛ́nətɚ] N senador -ora *mf*

send [sɛnd] VT enviar, mandar; **that sent chills down my spine** me dio escalofríos; **to — away** hacer salir; **to — back** devolver; **to — for** mandar buscar a; **to — in** remitir; **to — out for** encargar; **to — word** mandar decir

sender [sɛ́ndɚ] N remitente *m*

Senegal [sɛ́nɪgəl] N Senegal *m*

Senegalese [sɛnɪgəlíz] ADJ & N senegalés -esa *mf*

senile [sí́naɪl] ADJ senil, chocho

senility [sɪnɪ́lɪtɪ] N senilidad *f*, chochera *f*, chochez *f*

senior [sí́njɚ] ADJ (with more seniority) más antiguo; (in school) de cuarto año; (for the elderly) para ancianos; **John Smith** — John Smith padre; N (person of higher rank) superior *mf*; (fourth-year student) estudiante de cuarto año *mf*; (elderly person) persona de la tercera edad *f*; **to be somebody's —** ser mayor que alguien; **— citizen** persona de la tercera edad *f*; **— partner** socio -cia principal *mf*

seniority [sinjɔ́rɪtɪ] N antigüedad *f*

sensation [sɛnséʃən] N sensación *f*

sensational [sɛnséʃənl̩] ADJ sensacional

sense [sɛns] N (of humor, honor, direction) sentido *m*; (of pain, insecurity) sensación *f*; (meaning) significado *m*, sentido *m*; **— of hearing** sentido del oído *m*; **— of humor** sentido del humor *m*; **— of sight** sentido de la vista *m*; **— of smell** sentido del olfato *m*; **— of taste** sentido del gusto *m*; **— of touch** sentido del tacto *m*; **to make —** tener sentido; **to make — of something** entender algo; **in a —** en cierto sentido; **to take leave of one's —s** volverse loco; **to come to one's —s** (wake up) volver en sí; (be reasonable) recobrar el juicio; VT (perceive) percibir, sentir; (intuit) intuir

senseless [sɛ́nslɪs] ADJ (meaningless) sin sentido; (unconscious) inconsciente

sensibility [sɛnsəbɪ́lɪtɪ] N sensibilidad *f*

sensible [sɛ́nsəbəł] ADJ sensato, razonable, juicioso

sensitive [sɛ́nsɪtɪv] ADJ (to emotions) sensible; (to stimuli) sensitivo

sensitivity [sɛnsɪtɪ́vɪtɪ] N sensibilidad *f*

sensitize [sɛ́nsɪtaɪz] VT sensibilizar

sensor [sɛ́nsɔr] N sensor *m*

sensory [sɛ́nsəri] ADJ sensorial; **— overload** sobrecarga sensorial *f*

sensual [sɛ́nʃuəł] ADJ sensual

sensuality [sɛnʃuǽlɪtɪ] N sensualidad *f*

sensuous [sɛ́nʃuəs] ADJ sensual

sent [sɛnt] *see* send

sentence [sɛ́ntəns] N (to prison) sentencia *f*, condena *f*; (phrase) oración *f*; VT condenar, sentenciar

sentiment [sɛ́ntəmənt] N sentimiento *m*

sentimental [sɛntəmɛ́ntl̩] ADJ sentimental; (excessively) sensiblero

sentimentality [sɛntəmɛntǽlɪtɪ] N sentimentalismo *m*; (excessive) sensiblería *f*

sentinel [sɛ́ntnəł] N centinela *m*

sentry [sɛ́ntri] N centinela *m*; **— box** garita *f*

separate[1] [sɛ́prɪt] ADJ (apart) separado

separate[2] [sɛ́pəret] VI/VT separar[se]

separation [sɛpəréʃən] N separación *f*

Sephardi [səfɑ́rdi] N sefardí *mf*, sefardita *mf*

September [sɛptɛ́mbɚ] N septiembre *m*, setiembre *m*

sequel [sí́kwəł] N continuación *f*

sequence [sí́kwəns] N secuencia *f*; (of events) serie *f*; **in —** en orden; VT secuenciar

Serb [sɝb] N (person) serbio -bia *mf*

Serbian [sɝ́biən] ADJ serbio; N (language) serbio *m*; (person) serbio -bia *mf*

serenade [sɛrənɛ́d] N serenata *f*, ronda *f*; VI/VT dar [una] serenata [a], rondar [a]

serene [sərí́n] ADJ sereno

serenity [sərɛ́nɪtɪ] N serenidad *f*

sergeant [sɑ́rdʒənt] N sargento *m*

serial [sí́riəł] N (novel) novela por entregas *f*; ADJ (published in installments) por entregas; (murder) en serie; **— bus** bus en serie *m*; **— connector** conector en serie *m*; **— killer** asesino -na en serie *mf*; **— mouse** ratón en serie *m*; **— number** número de serie *m*; **— port** puerto serie/serial *m*; **— printer** impresora en serie *f*

series [sí́riz] N serie *f*

serious [sí́riəs] ADJ serio; (illness) grave

seriously [sí́riəsli] ADV (consider) en serio; (injure) gravemente; **—, what do you want?** hablando en serio, ¿qué es lo que quieres?

seriousness [sí́riəsnɪs] N seriedad *f*; (of an illness) gravedad *f*

sermon [sɝ́mən] N sermón *m*

serpent [sɝ́pənt] N sierpe *f*, serpiente *f*

serrated [sɛ́rɛdɪd] ADJ serrado

serum [sírəm] N suero *m*
servant [sɝ́vənt] N sirviente -ta *mf*, criado -da *mf*
serve [sɝv] VI/VT (in a restaurant, in a store) servir, atender; (in tennis) sacar; **to — a term in prison** cumplir una condena; **to — a warrant** entregar una orden judicial; **to — as** servir de; **to — notice** advertir; **to — one's purpose** resultarle útil a alguien; **it —s me right** me lo merezco; N (in tennis) saque *m*; **— and volley** saque y volea *m*
server [sɝ́vɚ] N (one who serves) servidor -ora *mf*; (in a restaurant) camarero -ra *mf*; (for pie) utensilio para servir *m*; (computer) servidor *m*; (tennis player) sacador -ora *mf*
service [sɝ́vɪs] N servicio *m*; (in tennis) saque *m*, servicio *m*; (of a warrant) entrega *f*; **— break** rotura de servicio *f*; **— entrance** entrada de servicio *f*; **—man** (soldier) militar *m*; (for repairs) reparador *m*; **— station** gasolinera *f*, estación de servicio *f*; **at your —** a su servicio; VT (a car) revisar; (an industry) atender, servir; (a debt) pagar; **in- — training** capacitación para empleados; **out of —** (broken) averiado, fuera de servicio
serviceable [sɝ́vɪsəbəɫ] ADJ (practical) práctico; (durable) duradero
servile [sɝ́vaɪɫ] ADJ servil
servitude [sɝ́vɪtud] N servidumbre *f*
sesame [sɛ́səmi] N sésamo *m*, ajonjolí *m*
session [sɛ́ʃən] N (meeting) sesión *f*; (semester) semestre *m*; (of Congress) período de sesiones *m*
set [sɛt] VT (place) colocar; (fix) fijar, establecer; (sic) azuzar; (print) componer; VI (cement) fraguar; (jelly) cuajar; (sun) ponerse; (glue) endurecerse; **to — a bone** reducir un hueso dislocado; **to — a diamond** engastar un diamante; **to — an example** dar ejemplo; **to — a poem to music** ponerle música a un poema; **to — a precedent** establecer un precedente; **to — a trap** tender una trampa; **to — a watch** poner el reloj en hora; **to — about** disponerse a; **to — aside** (move an object) apartar; (money) ahorrar; (a claim) rechazar; (a verdict) anular; **to — back** (hinder, make earlier) atrasar; (cost) costar; (a clock) retrasar; **to — forth** exponer; **to — forth on a journey** ponerse en camino; **to — free** librar; **to — off** (make explode) hacer estallar; (start on a journey) ponerse en camino; (intensify) resaltar; **to — one's heart on** tener la esperanza puesta en; **to — one's mind on** resolverse a; **to — out for** partir para; **to — out to** proponerse; **to — right** rectificar; **to — the table** poner la mesa; **to — up** (assemble) armar; (set a trap for) tender; (establish) establecer; (a computer program) instalar; **to — upon someone** acometer a alguien; ADJ (fixed) fijo; (ready) listo; (hard) duro; N (ensemble) juego *m*; (group) conjunto *m*; (TV) aparato *m*; (scenery) escenario *m*; (of tennis) set *m*, manga *f*; **—back** revés *m*; **— of teeth** dentadura *f*; **— point** punto de set/manga *m*; **—up** (arrangement) arreglo *m*; (assembly) montaje *m*; (installation) instalación *f*; (trap) tongo *m*, timo *m*; **—up program** programa de instalación *m*
setter [sɛ́dɚ] N sétter *m*
setting [sɛ́dɪŋ] N (act of putting down) colocación *f*; (jewel) engaste *m*; (in theater) escenario *m*; (of sun, moon) puesta *f*; (of dial) posición *f*; **— sun** sol poniente *m*
settle [sɛ́dl] VT (a territory) colonizar, poblar; (affairs) arreglar; (argument) zanjar; (lawsuit) arreglar; (an estate) liquidar; (a bill) saldar, solventar; (one's nerves) calmar; VI (end a dispute) llegar a un arreglo; (take up residence) establecerse; (alight) posarse; (sink to bottom) depositarse; **to — down** (get married) casarse; (mend one's ways) sentar cabeza; (take up residence) instalarse; (become calm) calmarse; **to — on a date** fijar/señalar una fecha; **to — for** conformarse con; **to — up** pagar
settlement [sɛ́dlmənt] N (community) colonia *f*, población *f*; (act of establishing) asentamiento *m*; (agreement) acuerdo *m*; (of a lawsuit) arreglo *m*; (of a bill) pago *m*, finiquito *m*; (final disposition) liquidación *f*
settler [sɛ́tlɚ] N colono -na *mf*, poblador -ora *mf*
settling [sɛ́dlɪŋ] N asentamiento *m*
seven [sɛ́vən] NUM siete; **— hundred** setecientos
seventeen [sɛvəntín] NUM diecisiete
seventh [sɛ́vənθ] ADJ séptimo
seventy [sɛ́vənti] NUM setenta
sever [sɛ́vɚ] VT (an arm) cortar; (relations) romper
several [sɛ́vəɚəɫ] ADJ varios
severance pay [sɛ́vərənspe] N indemnización por despido *f*
severe [səvír] ADJ (criticism, standards) severo; (winter, test) duro; (storm, heat) intenso; (illness) grave
severity [səvɛ́rɪti] N (of criticism, standards) severidad *f*; (of water, test) dureza *f*; (of storm, heat) intensidad *f*; (of illness) gravedad *f*
Sevillian [səvíɪ̈jən] ADJ & N sevillano -na; **— dances** sevillanas *f pl*
sew [so] VI/VT coser
sewage [súɪʤ] N aguas negras *f pl*; **— system** alcantarillado *m*
sewer [súɚ] N alcantarilla *f*, cloaca *f*, colector *m*
sewing [sóɪŋ] N costura *f*; **— machine** máquina de coser *f*
sewn [son] *see* sew

sex [sɛks] N sexo *m*; **— appeal** atractivo sexual *m*; **— symbol** símbolo sexual *m*; VT sexar
sexism [sɛ́ksɪzəm] N sexismo *m*
sexist [sɛ́ksɪst] ADJ & N sexista *mf*
sexton [sɛ́kstən] N sacristán *m*
sexual [sɛ́kʃuəł] ADJ sexual; **— assault** violación *f*; **— discrimination** discriminación sexual *f*; **— harassment** acoso sexual *m*
sexuality [sɛkʃuǽlɪɪDɪ] N sexualidad *f*
sexy [sɛ́ksi] ADJ sexy, morboso
Seychelles [seʃɛ́ł] N Seychelles *f pl*
shabby [ʃǽbi] ADJ (worn) gastado; (slovenly) andrajoso; (tawdry) sórdido; (mean) mezquino; **not too —** no está mal
shack [ʃæk] N casucha *f*, choza *f*
shackle [ʃǽkəł] N grillete *m*; **—s** cadenas *f pl*, grillos *m pl*; VT (put in chains) engrillar; (impede) estorbar
shad [ʃæd] N sábalo *m*
shade [ʃɛd] N (shadow) sombra *f*; (nuance) matiz *m*; (for windows) persiana *f*; (phantom) espectro *m*; (of a lamp) pantalla *f*; **a — longer** un poco más largo; **in the —** a la sombra; **—s** (sunglasses) *Am* lentes negros/oscuros *m pl*; *Sp* gafas de sol *f pl*; VT (protect from sun) sombrear, dar sombra
shadow [ʃǽdo] N (dark image, shade) sombra *f*; (phantom) espectro *m*; **in the — of** a la sombra de; **without a — of doubt** sin sombra de duda; VT (darken) sombrear; (make gloomy) ensombrecer; **to — someone** seguirle la pista a alguien
shady [ʃéDɪ] ADJ sombreado, umbrío; **— character** sospechoso -sa *mf*; **— dealings** negocios turbios *m pl*
shaft [ʃæft] N (of a mine) pozo *m*; (of a feather) cañón *m*; (of an elevator) hueco *m*; (of an arrow) asta *f*
shaggy [ʃǽgi] ADJ peludo, lanudo
shake [ʃek] VI (tremble) temblar; VI/VT (move back and forth) sacudir[se]; (in order to mix) agitar[se]; (elude) deshacerse de; **to — hands** darse la mano; **to — one's head** menear la cabeza; **to — with cold** tiritar; **to — with fear** temblar de miedo; **to — off** (a cold, disappointment, etc.) deshacerse de; (depression) librarse de; **to — up** (a liquid) agitar; (a person) trastornar; N (violent) sacudida *f*; (of milk) batido *m*; **hand—** apretón de manos *m*; **the —s** escalofríos *m pl*; **—-up** reorganización *f*
shaken [ʃékən] *see* shake
shaky [ʃéki] ADJ (hand) temblroroso; (start) vacilante
shall [ʃæł] V AUX **I — come** vendré; **— I help you?** ¿te ayudo? **thou shalt not steal** no robarás
shallow [ʃǽlo] ADJ (plate) llano; (water) poco profundo; (breathing) superficial; (explanation) superficial, somero
shallowness [ʃǽlonɪs] N (of plate) lo llano; (of water) poca profundidad *f*; (of person) superficialidad *f*
sham [ʃæm] N (hoax) farsa *f*; (impostor) impostor -ora *mf*; **— battle** simulacro de batalla *m*
shambles [ʃǽmbəłz] N desorden *m*, caos *m*
shame [ʃem] N (embarrassment) vergüenza *f*; (dishonor) deshonra *f*; (pity) lástima *f*; **— on you!** ¡qué vergüenza! **to bring — upon** deshonrar; VT avergonzar
shameful [ʃémfəł] ADJ vergonzoso
shameless [ʃémlɪs] ADJ desvergonzado, descarado
shamelessness [ʃémlɪsnɪs] N desvergüenza *f*
shampoo [ʃæmpú] N (product) champú *m*; (act of washing) lavado del cabello *m*; VI/VT lavar con champú
shamrock [ʃǽmrɑk] N trébol *m*
shank [ʃæŋk] N (part of leg) canilla *f*, espinilla *f*; (cut of meat) pierna *f*, pata *f*
shanty [ʃǽnti] N casucha *f*; *Sp* chabola *f*; **—town** suburbio *m*
shape [ʃep] N (form) forma *f*; (condition) condición *f*; (silhouette) bulto *m*; **to be in bad —** andar mal; **to get in —** ponerse en forma; **to take —** configurarse; VT plasmar, dar forma a; **to — up** reformarse
shapeless [ʃéplɪs] ADJ informe
share [ʃɛr] N (portion) parte *f*, porción *f*; (stock) acción *f*; **—cropper** aparcero *m*; **—holder** accionista *mf*; VI/VT compartir; **to — in** participar en
shark [ʃɑrk] N (fish) tiburón *m*; (swindler) estafador -ora *mf*
sharp [ʃɑrp] ADJ (blade) afilado, filoso; (needle) puntiagudo; (curve) cerrado; (contrast) marcado, nítido; (smell) acre; (wind) cortante; (pain) punzante; (remark) mordaz, agudo; (mind) perspicaz; (musical note) sostenido; (dresser) elegante; (cheese) picante; (ear) fino; **— eye** vista aguzada *f*; **—shooter** tirador -ora de primera *mf*; **—-tongued** mordaz; **—-witted** agudo; N (in music) sostenido *m*
sharpen [ʃárpən] VI/VT (knife) afilar[se]; VT (pencil) sacar punta a; (skill) afinar
sharply [ʃárpli] ADV (contrast) marcadamente; (respond) bruscamente, con aspereza; (turn) bruscamente
sharpness [ʃárpnɪs] N (of a blade) lo afilado; (of a needle) lo puntiagudo; (of a curve) lo cerrado; (of a contrast) nitidez *f*; (of a smell) acritud *f*; (of pain) intensidad *f*; (of a remark) mordacidad *f*; (of a mind) perspicacia *f*, agudeza *f*; (of cheese) lo picante
shatter [ʃǽDə-] VI/VT (glass) astillar[se], hacer[se] añicos; (nerves) destrozar[se]; (health)

quebrantar[se]; (hopes) frustrar

shave [ʃev] VI/VT (remove hair) afeitar[se], rasurar[se]; VT (cut thin slices) cepillar; (graze) rozar; **to — off** rapar; N afeitado *m*, rasurado *m*; **he had a close —** se salvó por poco

shaven [ʃévən] *see* shave

shaver [shévɚ] N afeitadora *f*

shavings [ʃévɪŋz] N virutas *f pl*

shawl [ʃɔł] N mantón *m*, chal *m*

she [ʃi] PRON ella; **— who** la que, quien; N **—-bear** osa *f*

sheaf [ʃif] N (of corn) gavilla *f*; (of arrows) haz *m*; (of paper) fajo *m*

shear [ʃir] VT esquilar, trasquilar; N **—s** (for sheep) tijeras para esquilar *f pl*; (for plants) tijeras para podar *f pl*; (for metal) cizallas *f pl*; (for hair) tijeras de peluquero *f pl*

shearing [ʃírɪŋ] N esquila *f*, esquileo *m*

sheath [ʃiθ] N (of sword, peas) vaina *f*; (of knife, umbrella) funda *f*

sheathe [ʃið] VT (a sword) envainar; (a knife) enfundar

shed [ʃɛd] N cobertizo *m*, tinglado *m*, *Am* galpón *m*; VT (tears) derramar; (light) arrojar; (leaves) perder; (skin, hair) mudar, perder; VI (be waterproof) ser impermeable; (lose hair) pelechar; (lose leaves) deshojarse; (lose skin) mudar la piel

sheen [ʃin] N brillo *m*

sheep [ʃip] N oveja *f*; **—dog** perro pastor *m*, ovejero *m*; **—skin** (hide) piel de oveja *f*; (leather) badana *f*; (parchment) pergamino *m*; (diploma) diploma *m*

sheepish [ʃípɪʃ] ADJ vergonzoso, tímido

sheer [ʃir] ADJ (absolute) puro, total; (fine) fino; (vertical) vertical, acantilado

sheet [ʃit] N (bedding) sábana *f*; (of ice) capa *f*; (of paper) hoja *f*; (of glass) lámina *f*; (of rain) cortina *f*; **— metal** chapa de metal *f*; **— music** música en hojas de partitura *f*

shelf [ʃɛłf] N estante *m*, repisa *f*, anaquel *m*; (of rock) saliente *f*

shell [ʃɛł] N (turtles, snail) caparazón *f*; (of mollusk) concha *f*; (of egg, nut) cáscara *f*; (of peas) vaina *f*; (of a ship) casco *m*; (of a building) armazón *m*; (of artillery) proyectil *m*; (of a rifle) cartucho *m*; **—fish** mariscos *m pl*; VT (nuts, eggs) pelar; (peas) desgranar; (military target) bombardear

shelter [ʃéłtɚ] N (refuge) refugio *m*, resguardo *m*, abrigo *m*; **to take —** refugiarse, guarecerse; VI/VT (take or give refuge) refugiar[se], resguardar[se], abrigar[se]

shelve [ʃɛłv] VT (place on a shelf) colocar en un estante; (defer) archivar

shepherd [ʃépɚd] N pastor *m*; (dog) perro pastor *m*

sherbet [ʃɝbɪt] N sorbete *m*

sheriff [ʃérɪf] N alguacil *m*

sherry [ʃéri] N jerez *m*

shield [ʃiłd] N escudo *m*; VI/VT (protect) escudar[se]; VT (conceal) ocultar

shift [ʃɪft] VI/VT (gears) cambiar; **to — for oneself** arreglárselas solo; **to — the blame** echar la culpa a otro; N (of gears, of wind) cambio *m*; (dress) vestido suelto *m*; (of workers) turno *m*; **— key** tecla de [cambio a] mayúsculas *f*

shiftless [ʃíftlɪs] ADJ holgazán

shimmer [ʃímɚ] VI titilar; N titileo *m*

shin [ʃɪn] N espinilla *f*, canilla *f*; VI **to — up** trepar

shine [ʃaɪn] VI brillar, relucir; VT (shoes) limpiar, lustrar; (furniture) lustrar; N brillo *m*, resplandor *m*; (of shoes) lustre *m*

shingle [ʃíŋgəł] N (on roof) teja *f*; (sign) chapa *f*; **—s** (skin disorder) culebrilla *f*, zona *f*; **to hang out one's —** abrir un consultorio; VT cubrir con tejas

shiny [ʃáɪni] ADJ (bright) brillante; (worn) brilloso

ship [ʃɪp] N (on water) buque *m*, navío *m*; (in air) avión *m*; **—builder** constructor -ora naval *mf*; **—mate** camarada de a bordo *mf*; **—wreck** naufragio *m*; **—yard** astillero *m*; ADJ **—shape** ordenado; VT transportar; **to — off** sacarse de encima; VI **to —wreck** naufragar

shipment [ʃípmənt] N cargamento *m*, remesa *f*

shipper [ʃípɚ] N (sender) expedidor -ora *mf*; (carrier) transportista *mf*

shipping [ʃípɪŋ] N envío *m*; **— charges** gastos de envío *m pl*; **— and handling** gastos de envío *m pl*

shirk [ʃɝk] VT evadir, esquivar, rehuir

shirt [ʃɝt] N camisa *f*; **in —sleeves** en mangas de camisa; **—tail** faldón *m*

shiver [ʃívɚ] VI (from cold) tiritar; (from cold, fear, etc.) temblar; N temblor *m*; **—s** escalofríos *m pl*

shoal [ʃoł] N (sandbank) bajío *m*, banco de arena *m*; (school of fish) banco *m*, bandada *f*

shock [ʃɑk] N (impact, disturbance) choque *m*; (of electricity) sacudida *f*; (of wheat) hacina *f*; (physical convulsion) shock *m*, choque *m*; **— absorber** amortiguador *m*; **— of hair** guedeja *f*; **— therapy** terapia de electroshock *f*, terapia electroconvulsiva *f*; **— troops** tropas de choque *f pl*; **— wave** onda expansiva *f*; VT (bewilder) chocar, horrorizar; (discharge electricity) dar una descarga eléctrica; (make bundles of grain) hacinar, hacer gavillas de

shocking [ʃáɑkɪŋ] ADJ chocante, escandaloso

shod [ʃɑd] *see* shoe

shoddy [ʃáɑdi] ADJ chapucero

shoe [ʃu] N zapato *m*; (for brakes) zapata *f*; (for

horses) herradura *f*; **—horn** calzador *m*; **—lace** cordón *m*; **—maker** zapatero -ra *mf*; **— polish** betún *m*; **— repairman** zapatero -ra remendón -ona *mf*; **— store** zapatería *f*; **—string** cordón *m*; **to live on a —string** vivir con poco dinero; **to tie one's —s** atarse los zapatos; VT (a person) calzar; (a horse) herrar

shone [ʃon] *see* shine

shoo-in [ʃúɪn] N favorito -ta *mf*

shook [ʃʊk] *see* shake

shoot [ʃut] VT (wound with a bullet) pegar un tiro; (discharge a firearm) disparar; (film a movie) rodar; (hit a soccer ball) chutar; VI (discharge bullet, arrow) disparar, tirar; (be discharged) dispararse; (hunt with a gun) cazar; (germinate) brotar; (throw) lanzar; (take a photo) fotografiar; (film) filmar; (try to score, in soccer) chutar; (try to score, in basketball) tirar; **to — at** disparar a, tirar a; **to — at goal** patear al arco; **to — by** pasar rápidamente; **to — down** (plane) derribar; (argument) refutar; **to — forth** brotar; **to — up** (grow) crecer rápidamente; (damage by shooting) tirotear; (inject drugs) chutar; N (new growth) yema *f*, retoño *m*, vástago *m*; (filming) rodaje *m*

shooter [ʃúɚə-] N (of guns) tirador -ora *mf*; (of balls, soccer) goleador -ora *mf*

shooting [ʃúɚɪŋ] N (discharge of a gun) tiro *m*, disparo *m*; (exchange of shots) tiroteo *m*; (filming) filmación *f*; **— guard** escolta *mf*; **— match** concurso de tiro *m*; **— pain** punzada *f*; **— star** estrella fugaz *f*

shop [ʃɑp] N (store) tienda *f*; (artisan's place of business, carpentry course) taller *m*; (business) planta *f*; **—keeper** tendero -ra *mf*; **—lifter** ladrón -ona de tiendas *mf*; **—lifting** hurto en las tiendas *m*; **— window** escaparate *m*, vitrina *f*; **to talk —** hablar de negocios; VI ir de compras; **to — for** ir a comprar; **to —lift** hurtar [en las tiendas]

shopper [ʃápə-] N cliente -ta *mf*, comprador -ora *mf*

shopping [ʃápɪŋ] N **to go —** ir de compras; **— center** centro comercial *m*

shore [ʃɔr] N costa *f*, ribera *f*; (of a lake) orilla *f*; VT **to — up** apuntalar

shorn [ʃɔrn] *see* shear

short [ʃɔrt] ADJ (not long in duration) corto, breve; (not long in length) corto; (not tall) bajo; (scanty) escaso; (curt) brusco; **— circuit** cortocircuito *m*; **—comings** limitaciones *f pl*; **—cut** atajo *m*, cortada *f*; **—fall** déficit *m*, insuficiencia *f*; **—hand** taquigrafía *f*; **—-handed** escaso de personal; **—-legged** pernicorto; **—sighted** miope, corto de vista; **— stop** torpedero -ra *mf*, campocorto *mf*; **— story** cuento *m*; **—wave** onda corta *f*; **in the — run/haul/term** a corto plazo; **for —** para abreviar; **in —** en resumen, en suma; **in — order** rápidamente; **to be — on** estar escaso de, estar alcanzado de; **to be — on something** faltarle a uno algo; **to cut —** interrumpir; **I'm running — on sugar** se me está acabando el azúcar; ADV **to stop —** parar de repente, parar en seco; **to come up —** quedarse corto; N (circuit) cortocircuito *m*; **—s** short *m*, pantalón corto *m*; VI/VT (a circuit) cortocircuitar[se]; (change) dar de menos; **to —change** dar de menos; **to — out** fundir

shortage [ʃɔ́rdɪʤ] N escasez *f*, penuria *f*

shorten [ʃɔ́rtn̩] VI/VT acortar[se]; VT recortar

shortening [ʃɔ́rtn̩ɪŋ] N (lard) manteca *f*; (abbreviation) acortamiento *m*

shortly [ʃɔ́rtli] ADJ (soon) en breve, pronto; (curtly) bruscamente, secamente

shortness [ʃɔ́rtnɪs] N (of length, height) cortedad *f*; (of time) brevedad *f*; (of breath) falta *f*; (of a reply) brusquedad *f*

shot [ʃɑt] N (discharge) tiro *m*, disparo *m*; (photograph) foto *f*; (pellet) perdigón *m*, plomo *m*; (ball in shot-putting) bala *f*; (injection) inyección *f*; (swallow) trago *m*; (throw) tirada *f*; (in soccer) tiro *m*, disparo *m*; **—gun** escopeta *f*; **— put** lanzamiento de bala *m*; **not by a long —** ni con mucho; **he is a good —** tiene buena puntería; **to take a —** disparar; **to take a — at** intentar

shot [ʃɑt] *see* shoot

should [ʃʊd] V AUX **I — think so** ya lo creo; **you — arrive before nine** deberías llegar antes de las nueve; **you — eat less** tendrías que comer menos; **you — have seen her** tendrías que haberla visto; **were he to come, I — be pleased** si viniera, me alegraría

shoulder [ʃóɫdə-] N (of a person, coat) hombro *m*; (cut of meat) paletilla *f*; (of a road) arcén *m*; **— blade** (person) homóplato *m*; (animal) paletilla *f*; **— pad** hombrera *f*; **to turn a cold — to** hacerle el vacío a; **the responsibility is on your —s** tú tienes la responsabilidad; VT (a load) cargar al hombro; (a task, an expense) cargar con, asumir; (a door) empujar con el hombro

shout [ʃaʊt] VI/VT gritar; N grito *m*

shove [ʃʌv] VI/VT empujar; **to — aside** echar a un lado; **to — off** (go away) largarse; (push off) desatracar; N empujón *m*, empellón *m*

shovel [ʃʌ́vəɫ] N pala *f*; VT echar con la pala

show [ʃo] VT (exhibit) mostrar, manifestar; (prove) demostrar; (indicate) indicar, marcar; (a film, a TV program) dar; VI (be visible) verse, asomar; (make an appearance) aparecerse; **— him in** hazle entrar; **to —case** presentar; **to — mercy** tener piedad; **to —**

off hacer alarde, aparentar; **to — up** aparecer; **to — someone up** poner a alguien en evidencia; **to — the way** señalar el camino; N (exhibition) exposición *f*; (display) demostración *f*; (ostentation) ostentación *f*, alarde *m*; (performance) espectáculo *m*; (showing) función *f*; (on TV) programa *m*; (movie theater) cine *m*; **— business** farándula *f*; **—case** vitrina *f*; **—down** confrontación *f*; **— -off** fanfarrón -ona *mf*; **to go to the —** ir al cine; **for —** para impresionar

shower [ʃáʊə-] N (rain) aguacero *m*, chubasco *m*; (bath) ducha *f*; (for brides) fiesta para novias *f*; (of sparks, blows) lluvia *f*; VI (bathe) ducharse; (rain) llover; VT (with gifts) inundar; (with praise) colmar

shown [ʃon] *see* show

showy [ʃói] ADJ ostentoso; (attractive) vistoso

shrank [ʃræŋk] *see* shrink

shred [ʃred] N (of paper) tira *f*; (of evidence) pizca *f*; **to be in —s** estar hecho jirones; **to tear to —s** hacer trizas; VI/VT (documents) triturar; (vegetables) rallar

shrew [ʃru] N (animal) musaraña *f*; (woman) arpía *f*

shrewd [ʃrud] ADJ astuto, sagaz

shriek [ʃrik] VI/VT chillar; N chillido *m*

shrill [ʃrɪł] ADJ chillón

shrimp [ʃrɪmp] N (animal) camarón *m*; (small person) renacuajo *m*; VI pescar camarones

shrine [ʃraɪn] N (chapel) capilla *f*; (altar) altar *m*

shrink [ʃrɪŋk] VI/VT (in size) encoger; VI (in value) reducirse; **to — from** retroceder; N (psychiatrist) *fam* loquero -ra *mf*; **—wrap** envoltura de plástico transparente *f*

shrinkage [ʃríŋkɪʤ] N (of clothes) encogimiento *m*; (of value) reducción *f*

shrivel [ʃrívəł] VI/VT secar[se], marchitar[se]

shroud [ʃraʊd] N mortaja *f*; VT (to wrap for burial) amortajar; (to hide) cubrir

shrub [ʃrʌb] N arbusto *m*

shrug [ʃrʌg] VI encogerse de hombros; VT encogerse de; **to — off** minimizar, ignorar; N encogimiento de hombros *m*

shrunk [ʃrʌŋk] *see* shrink

shrunken [ʃrʌ́ŋkən] *see* shrink

shudder [ʃʌ́də-] VI (from cold) tiritar; (from fear) temblar, estremecerse; N temblor *m*, estremecimiento *m*

shuffle [ʃʌ́fəł] VI/VT (cards) barajar; VT (mix) mezclar; VI (walk) arrastrar los pies; (dance) bailar arrastrando los pies; **to — along** ir arrastrando los pies; N (of cards) barajadura *f*; (of feet) arrastrapiés *m sg*

shun [ʃʌn] VT rehuir, evitar

shut [ʃʌt] VI/VT cerrar[se]; **to — down** cerrar; **to — off** cortar; **to — out** impedir la entrada de; **to — up** (close) cerrar bien; (lock up) encerrar; (be quiet) callarse; N **— -down** cese de actividades *m*; **— -eye** sueño *m*; **— -in** enfermo -ma confinado -da a la casa *mf*

shutter [ʃʌ́də-] N (of a window) postigo *m*, contraventana *f*; (of a camera) obturador *m*

shuttle [ʃʌ́dł] N (in loom) lanzadera *f*; (spaceship) transbordador espacial *m*; (airplane) puente aéreo *m*; (bus, train) servicio regular *m*; VI ir y venir; VT llevar y traer

shy [ʃaɪ] ADJ tímido, retraído; (wary) esquivo; (lacking) escaso; VI asustarse, respingar; **to — away** (start) asustarse, respingar; (avoid) esquivar

shyness [ʃáɪnɪs] N timidez *f*, retraimiento *m*

shyster [ʃáɪstə-] N *fam* picapleitos *m sg*

sibling [síblɪŋ] N hermano *m*; hermana *f*; **— rivalry** rivalidad entre hermanos *f*

sic [sɪk] VT azuzar

sick [sɪk] ADJ (ill) enfermo; (deranged) enfermizo, morboso; (at heart) angustiado; **— and tired** harto; **to be — of** estar harto de; **to be — to one's stomach** tener náuseas; **to make —** (disgust) dar asco; (anger) dar rabia, enfermar; **— leave** licencia por enfermedad *f*

sicken [sɪ́kən] VI/VT (with illness) enfermar[se], poner[se] enfermo; (with disgust) dar asco; (with anger) dar rabia, enfermar

sickening [sɪ́kənɪŋ] ADJ repugnante

sickle [sɪ́kəł] N hoz *f*; **— cell anemia** anemia falciforme *f*

sickly [sɪ́kli] ADJ enfermizo, enclenque

sickness [sɪ́knɪs] N enfermedad *f*

side [saɪd] N lado *m*; (of a coin, piece of paper) cara *f*; (of a person) costado *m*; (of a hill) ladera *f*; (of beef) media res *f*; (of a boat) banda *f*; (team) equipo *m*; (garnish) acompañamiento *m*; **—arm** arma de mano *f*; **—bar** ladillo *m*; **—board** aparador *m*; **—burns** patillas *f pl*; **— -glance** mirada de soslayo/reojo *f*; **—light** (illumination) luz lateral *f*; (detail) detalle incidental *m*; **—line** (in sports) banda *f*, línea de banda *f*; (in business) negocio suplementario *m*; **to sit on the —lines** no intervenir; **—walk** acera *f*; *Caribe* andén *m*; *Am* vereda *f*; *Mex* banqueta *f*; **—wall** flanco *m*; **—ways** (walk) de costado; (glance) de soslayo; **— by —** uno al lado del otro; **by his —** a su lado; **by the — of** al lado de; **on all —s** por todos lados; ADJ (on the side) lateral; (secondary) secundario; VI **to —step** evitar, esquivar; **to —track** (a train) desviar; (attention) distraer; **to — with** ponerse del lado de

siding [sáɪdɪŋ] N revestimiento *m*

SIDS [sudden infant death syndrome] [sídz] N síndrome de muerte súbita infantil *m*

siege [siʤ] N sitio *m*, asedio *m*, cerco *m*; **to lay — to** sitiar

Sierra Leone [siérəlıón] N Sierra Leona *f*
sieve [sɪv] N tamiz *m*, cedazo *m*
sift [sɪft] VT cerner, tamizar; **to — through** revisar
sigh [saɪ] VI suspirar; N suspiro *m*
sight [saɪt] N (sense) vista *f*; (attraction) punto de interés *m*; (ridiculous thing or person) adefesio *m*, mamarracho *m*; (on a gun) mira *f*; **—seeing** turismo *m*; **in —** a la vista; **on —** en el acto; **he is out of —** ya no se ve; **at first —** a primera vista; **to catch — of** divisar; **to lose — of** perder de vista; **you're a — for sore eyes** dichosos los ojos que te ven; VT (a ship) avistar, divisar; (a gun) apuntar
sign [saɪn] N (gesture) seña *f*, señal *f*; (indication) muestra *f*, señal *f*, indicio *m*; (placard) letrero *m*; (omen) agüero *m*, presagio *m*; (astrological, mathematical) signo *m*; (on road) cartel *m*, letrero *m*; **— language** lenguaje de signos *m*; VI/VT (write name) firmar; (signal) hacer señas [de]; VT (hire) contratar; (use sign language) hablar por señas; **to — off on** aprobar; **to — over property** ceder una propiedad; **to — up** (in a club) anotarse; (in the army) alistarse
signal [sígnl] N señal *f*; VI/VT señalar, hacer señas [a]; ADJ notable
signature [sígnətʃə-] N firma *f*
signer [sáɪnə-] N firmante *mf*, signatario -ria *mf*
significance [sɪgnífɪkəns] N significación *f*
significant [sɪgnífɪkənt] ADJ significativo; **my — other** mi media naranja *f*
significantly [sɪgnífɪkəntlɪ] ADV (considerably) apreciablemente, considerablemente; **he looked at me —** me dio una mirada significativa/expresiva
signify [sígnəfaɪ] VT significar
silence [sáɪləns] N silencio *m*; VT (child, fears) acallar; (criticism) silenciar, enmudecer
silencer [sáɪlənsə-] N silenciador *m*
silent [sáɪlənt] ADJ (machine) silencioso; (person) callado, silencioso; **— agreement** acuerdo tácito *m*; **— film** película muda *f*
silhouette [sɪluét] N silueta *f*; VT **to be —d against** perfilarse contra
silicon [sílɪkən] N silicio *m*; **— chip** chip de silicio *m*
silk [sɪłk] N seda *f*; **— industry** industria sedera *f*; **—worm** gusano de seda *m*
silken [sɪłkən] ADJ (of silk) de seda; (like silk) sedoso
silky [sɪłkɪ] ADJ sedoso
sill [sɪł] N alféizar *m*, antepecho *m*
silly [sílɪ] ADJ necio, bobo, lelo
silo [sáɪlo] N silo *m*
silt [sɪłt] N cieno *m*, limo *m*
silver [sɪłvə-] N (metal, color) plata *f*; (tableware) cubiertos de plata *m pl*; ADJ (of silver) de plata; (silver-colored) plateado; **— anniversary** las bodas de plata *f pl*; **—-plated** bañado en plata; **—-plating** plateado *m*; **—smith** platero -ra *mf*; **—ware** cubiertos de plata *m pl*; VT platear; (a mirror) azogar
similar [símələ-] ADJ semejante, similar
similarity [sɪməlǽrɪdɪ] N semejanza *f*, similitud *f*
similarly [símɪlə-lɪ] ADV de manera similar; **—, a mile is longer than a kilometer** del mismo modo, una milla es más larga que un kilómetro; **they were — surprised** quedaron igualmente sorprendidos
simile [símə-lɪ] N símil *m*
simmer [símə-] VI/VT hervir a fuego lento; **to — down** calmarse
simple [símpəł] ADJ (uncomplicated) simple, sencillo; (naive) simple; **—minded** simple, simplón
simpleton [símpəłtən] N simplón -ona *mf*, mentecato -ta *mf*
simplicity [sɪmplísɪdɪ] N (lack of complication) sencillez *f*, simplicidad *f*; (naiveté) simpleza *f*
simplify [símpləfaɪ] VI/VT simplificar
simplistic [sɪmplístɪk] ADJ simplista
simply [símplɪ] ADV (in a simple manner) con sencillez; (merely) simplemente; **it is — ridiculous** francamente, es ridículo
simulate [símjəlet] VI/VT simular
simulation [sɪmjəléʃən] N simulación *f*
simultaneous [saɪmałténɪəs] ADJ simultáneo
sin [sɪn] N pecado *m*; VI pecar
since [sɪns] CONJ (continuously) desde que; (inasmuch as) puesto que, ya que; PREP (continuously) desde; (from a past time) a partir de; **we have been here — five** estamos aquí desde las cinco; ADV desde entonces; **ever —** desde entonces; **he died long —** murió hace mucho tiempo; **she has — agreed** después de eso consintió
sincere [sɪnsír] ADJ sincero
sincerity [sɪnsérɪdɪ] N sinceridad *f*
sine [saɪn] N seno
sinew [sínju] N tendón *m*
sinewy [sínjuɪ] ADJ (full of tendons) nervudo; (robust) membrudo; (chewy) estropajoso
sinful [sínfəł] ADJ (act) pecaminoso; (person) pecador
sing [sɪŋ] VI/VT cantar; N **—song** sonsonete *m*
Singapore [sínəpɔr] N Singapur *m*
Singaporean [sɪŋəpóriən] ADJ & N singapurense *mf*
singe [sɪnʤ] VT chamuscar, socarrar; N chamusquina *f*, socarrina *f*
singer [sínə-] N cantante *mf*; intérprete *mf*
single [síŋgəł] ADJ (only one) solo, único; (for one person) individual; (unmarried) soltero; **— bed** cama de una plaza *f*; **—-entry bookkeeping** teneduría por partida simple *f*; **—-family home** vivienda unifamiliar *f*; **—**

file fila india *f*; **—-handed** solo, sin ayuda; **—-minded** resuelto; **—-spacing** sencillo *m*; **every — one** cada uno; **not a — word** ni una sola palabra; N (bill) billete de uno *m*; (unmarried person) soltero -ra *mf*; (record) disco sencillo *m*; (in baseball) sencillo *m*; **—s** (in tennis) individuales *m pl*; VT **to — out** elegir

singular [sínŋgjələ˞] ADJ & N singular *m*

sinister [sínɪstə˞] ADJ siniestro

sink [sɪŋk] VI/VT (ship) hundir[se]; VT (money) invertir; (a well) cavar; (a pipeline) enterrar; **it finally sank in** finalmente nos dimos cuenta de eso; **to — one's teeth into** clavar los dientes en; **to — to one's knees** caer de rodillas; **sunk in thought** absorto; **my heart sank** se me fue el alma al piso; **the sun was —ing** se iba poniendo el sol; N (in the kitchen) fregadero *m*; (in bathroom) lavabo *m*; (pond for sewage) pozo negro *m*; **—hole** socavón *m*, sumidero *m*

sinner [sínə˞] N pecador -ora *mf*

sinuous [sínjuəs] ADJ sinuoso

sinus [sáɪnəs] N seno *m*

sinusitis [saɪnəsáɪDɪs] N sinusitis *f*

sip [sɪp] VI/VT sorber; N sorbo *m*

siphon [sáɪfən] N sifón *m*; VI/VT (liquid) sacar con sifón; (money) desviar

sir [sɜ˞] N señor *m*

siren [sáɪrən] N sirena *f*

sirloin [sɜ˞lɔɪn] N solomillo *m*

sister [sístə˞] N hermana *f*; **—-in-law** cuñada *f*; **— Mary** Sor María *f*

sit [sɪt] VI sentar[se]; (pose) posar; (be seated) estar sentado; (be located) estar situado; **to — down** sentarse; **to — in on a class** ir de oyente a una clase; **to — on** posponer; **to — out a dance** saltearse una pieza; **to — still** estarse quieto; **to — tight** mantenerse firme en su puesto; **to — up** incorporarse; **to — up all night** quedarse en vela; **to — well** caer bien; N **—-in** sentada *f*; **—-up** abdominal *m*

sitcom [sítkɑm] N comedia de situación *f*

site [saɪt] N (for construction) terreno *m*, solar *m*; (on the Internet) sitio *m*; **— license** licencia de sitio *f*; **on- — training** capacitación en el lugar de trabajo

sitter [sítə˞] N niñera *f*, *Sp* canguro *mf*

sitting [sítɪŋ] N sesión *f*; **in one —** de una sentada, de un tirón; ADJ **— duck** blanco fácil *m*; **— room** cuarto de estar *m*

situated [sítʃuɛDɪd] ADJ situado, ubicado

situation [sɪtʃuéʃən] N situación *f*

Sitz bath [síts bæθ] N baño de asiento *m*

six [sɪks] NUM seis; **— hundred** seiscientos; N **—-pack** paquete de seis *m*; **—-shooter** revólver de seis tiros *m*

sixteen [sɪkstín] NUM dieciséis

sixth [sɪksθ] ADV & N sexto *m*

sixty [síksti] NUM sesenta

size [saɪz] N tamaño *m*; (of clothing) talla *f*; VT clasificar según el tamaño; **to — up** juzgar

sizable, sizeable [sáɪzəbəł] ADJ de tamaño considerable

sizzle [sízəł] VI chisporrotear; N chisporroteo *m*

skate [sket] N patín *m*; **—board** monopatín *m*; VI/VT patinar

skein [sken] N madeja *f*

skeletal [skélɪdł] ADJ esquelético

skeleton [skélɪtən] N esqueleto *m*, osamenta *f*; (of a building) armazón *m*; **— key** llave maestra *f*

skeptic, sceptic [sképtɪk] N escéptico -ca *mf*

skeptical [sképtɪkəł] ADJ escéptico

skepticism [sképtɪsɪzəm] N escepticismo *m*

sketch [sketʃ] N (drawing) boceto *m*, croquis *m*; (outline) esbozo *m*, bosquejo *m*; (skit) sketch *m*; VI/VT (draw) dibujar; (outline) bosquejar

skew [skju] VT (cloth) sesgar; (data) tergiversar

skewer [skjúə˞] N brocheta *f*

ski [ski] N esquí *m*; **— jump** (sport) salto con esquís *m*; (course) pista de saltos *f*; **— lift** telesquí *m*; VI/VT esquiar [en]

skid [skɪd] N patinazo *m*; VI patinar

skiing [skíɪŋ] N esquí *m*

skill [skɪł] N destreza *f*, habilidad *f*, maña *f*

skilled [skɪłd] ADJ diestro, habilidoso; **— worker** obrero -ra calificado -da *mf*

skillet [skílɪt] N sartén *f*

skillful, skilful [skíłfəł] ADJ diestro, habilidoso

skim [skɪm] VT (milk) desnatar; (a broth) espumar; (pass near surface) rozar; VI/VT (read) leer por encima, repasar; **to — over** rozar; N **— milk** *Sp* leche desnatada *f*; *Am* leche descremada *f*

skimp [skɪmp] VI escatimar; **to — on** escatimar

skimpy [skímpi] ADJ (funds) escaso; (dress) corto; (bikini) pequeño

skin [skɪn] N piel *f* (also of animal, sausage, potato); (of the face) cutis *m*, tez *f*; (for carrying wine) pellejo *m*; (of boiled milk) nata *f*; (of grapes) hollejo *m*; **—-deep** superficial; **—-diving** natación submarina *f*; **—flint** roña *mf*; **—head** cabeza rapada *mf*; **to save one's —** salvar el pellejo; **to be saved by the — of one's teeth** salvarse por un pelo; VT (animal) despellejar, desollar; (fruit) pelar; (a person) quitarle a uno el dinero

skinny [skíni] ADJ flaco; **to —-dip** nadar desnudo

skip [skɪp] VI (jump) brincar, ir dando saltos; (omit) saltarse; (bounce) rebotar; VT (a page) saltar[se]; (class) faltar a; (a stone) hacer rebotar; **to — out** escaparse; N salto *m*, brinco *m*

skipper [skípə˞] N (captain) patrón -ona *mf*, capitán -ana *mf*; (jumper) saltador -ora *mf*

skirmish [skɜ˞mɪʃ] N escaramuza *f*; VI

escaramuzar

skirt [skɜ̞t] N falda *f*; VT bordear; **to — an issue** evitar un tema

skit [skɪt] N sketch *m*

skull [skʌɫ] N cráneo *m*, calavera *f*; **— and crossbones** calavera *f*

skunk [skʌŋk] N mofeta *f*; *Am* zorrillo *m*

sky [skaɪ] N cielo *m*; **— blue** azul celeste *m*; **—diving** paracaidismo extremo *m*; **—-high** muy alto; **—lark** alondra *f*; **—light** claraboya *f*; **—line** horizonte *m*; **—scraper** rascacielos *m sg*; VI **to —rocket** subir vertiginosamente

slab [slæb] N (of wood) trozo *m*; (of stone) losa *f*, laja *f*; (of meat) tajada *f*

slack [slæk] ADJ (not taut) flojo; (careless) descuidado; (sluggish) lento; **— season** temporada baja *f*; **to take up the —** llenar el vacío; **—s** pantalones *m pl*; VI holgazanear; **to — off** holgazanear

slag [slæg] N escoria *f*

slain [slen] *see* slay

slalom [slɑ́ləm] N slalom *m*

slam [slæm] VI/VT cerrar[se] de un golpe; VI (hit) chocar; VT (throw down) hacer golpear; (criticize) criticar; **to — on the brakes** dar un frenazo; **to — the door** dar un portazo; N (blow) golpazo *m*; (criticism) crítica *f*; (of a door) portazo *m*; **—-dunk** (easy decision) éxito seguro *m*

slander [slǽndə̞-] N calumnia *f*, difamación *f*; VT calumniar, difamar

slanderous [slǽndə̞əs] ADJ calumnioso, difamatorio

slang [slæŋ] N (jargon) jerga *f*; (argot) argot *m*

slant [slænt] N (orientation, bias) sesgo *m*; (of a roof) inclinación *f*; VI/VT (bias) sesgar; (slope) inclinar[se], ladear[se]

slap [slæp] N (to the body) palmada *f*; (to the face) bofetada *f*, torta *f*, cachetada *f*; (with a glove) guantada *f*; **—-happy** aturdido; **—stick** de golpe y porrazo; **a — in the face** un desaire; **a — on the wrist** un tirón de orejas; **a — on the back** una palmadita en la espalda; VT abofetear; **to — down** reprimir

slash [slæʃ] VI/VT (cut) acuchillar; *Am* tajear; VT (whip) azotar; (reduce) reducir, rebajar; N (sweeping stroke, wound) cuchillada *f*, tajo *m*; (typographical sign) barra *f*

slat [slæt] N tablilla *f*

slate [slet] N (rock, roofing) pizarra *f*; (color) color pizarra *m*; (list of candidates) lista de candidatos *f*; VT empizarrar; **this building is —d for destruction** se ha programado la demolición de este edificio

slaughter [slɔ́ɫə̞-] N matanza *f*; **—house** matadero *m*; VT (animals) matar; (people, opponents) masacrar

slave [slev] N esclavo -va *mf*; **—driver** capataz de esclavos *m*; **— labor** (workers) mano de obra esclava *f*; (work) trabajo de esclavos *m*; VI trabajar como esclavo -va

slavery [slévə̞ri] N esclavitud *f*

Slavic [slɑ́vɪk] ADJ eslavo

sleazy [slízi] ADJ (squalid) sórdido; (contemptible) despreciable

sled [sled] N trineo *m*

sledgehammer [slédʒhæmə̞-] N almádena *f*

sleek [slik] ADJ (hair) lustroso; (sports car) elegante

sleep [slip] VI/VT dormir; **it —s three** tiene espacio para que duerman tres personas; **to — around** ser promiscuo; **to — in** dormir hasta tarde; **to — it off** dormir la mona; **to — something off** dormir para que desaparezca algo; **to — over** dormir en casa ajena; **to — together** acostarse juntos; **to — with** acostarse con; **to — on it** consultarlo con la almohada; N sueño *m*; **— apnea** apnea obstructiva del sueño *f*; **— disorder** trastorno del sueño *m*; **— mode** modo de dormir *m*; **—walker** sonámbulo -la *mf*; **to go to —** dormirse; **to put to —** (put to bed) dormir a; (euthanize) sacrificar

sleeper [slípə̞-] N (one who sleeps) persona que duerme *f*; (beam) durmiente *m*; (on a train) coche cama *m*; (unexpected success) éxito inesperado *m*; (sofa bed) sofá-cama *m*

sleepily [slípɪli] ADV con somnolencia

sleepiness [slípɪnɪs] N sueño *m*, somnolencia *f*

sleeping [slípɪŋ] N sueño *m*; ADJ dormido; **— bag** saco de dormir *m*; **— pill** píldora para dormir *f*, somnífero *m*; **— sickness** enfermedad del sueño *f*

sleepless [slípɪɫɪs] ADJ (person) desvelado; (night) en blanco

sleepy [slípi] ADJ somnoliento, adormilado; **to be —** tener sueño

sleet [slit] N cellisca *f*; VI caer cellisca

sleeve [sliv] N manga *f*; **to have something up one's —** tener algo en la manga

sleigh [sle] N trineo *m*; **—bell** cascabel *m*; VI pasear en trineo

sleight of hand [sláɪd əvhǽnd] N prestidigitación *f*

slender [slɛ́ndə̞-] ADJ delgado, esbelto

slept [slɛpt] *see* sleep

sleuth [sluθ] N sabueso -sa *mf*

slew [slu] *see* slay

slice [slaɪs] N (of bread, cheese) rebanada *f*; (of fruit) tajada *f*, raja *f*; (of meat) lonja *f*; (in tennis) cortado *m*, golpe cortado *m*; VT cortar, rebanar, tajar

slick [slɪk] ADJ (unctuous) untuoso; (sly) astuto; (slippery) resbaladizo

slicker [slɪ́kə̞-] N impermeable *m*

slid [slɪd] *see* slide

slide [slaɪd] VI/VT deslizar[se]; **to — in** cerrar[se]

deslizando; **to — out** abrirse deslizando; **to let something —** dejar pasar algo; N deslizamiento *m*; (playground equipment) tobogán *m*; (of a trombone) vara corredora *f*; (photographic) diapositiva *f*; (for microscopes) portaobjeto *m*

slight [slaɪt] N desaire *m*; VT (snub) desairar; (neglect) descuidar; ADJ (slim) delgado; (delicate) delicado, tenue; (small in degree) leve, ligero

slightly [sláɪtlì] ADV algo, un poco

slim [slɪm] ADJ delgado, esbelto; **a — chance** una posibilidad remota

slime [slaɪm] N (in rivers) limo *m*, fango *m*; (of snails) baba *f*; (despicable person) asqueroso -sa *mf*

slimy [sláɪmì] ADJ (muddy) fangoso; (slobbery) baboso, gomoso; (despicable) asqueroso

sling [slɪŋ] N (weapon) honda *f*; (for arm) cabestrillo *m*; **—shot** (toy) tirachinas *m sg*, tirador *m*; (weapon) honda *f*; VT lanzar; **to — a rifle over one's shoulder** ponerse el rifle en bandolera

slink [slɪŋk] VI (move furtively) andar furtivamente; (move provocatively) caminar provocativamente; **to — away** escurrirse

slip [slɪp] VI (slide) deslizarse; (slide accidentally) resbalar[se]; (fail to engage) patinar; (deteriorate) empeorar; VT (make slip) hacer resbalar; (put) meter; **to — away** escaparse, escabullirse; **to — by** correr; **to — in** meter[se]; **to — one's dress on** ponerse el vestido; **to — out** (leave) salir inadvertido; (say inadvertently) escapársele a uno algo; **to — up** meter la pata; **to let an opportunity — by** dejar pasar una oportunidad; **it —ped my mind** se me olvidó; **it —ped off** se zafó; N (act of slipping) resbalón *m*, traspié *m*; (mistake) equivocación *f*; (pillow cover) funda *f*; (underskirt) viso *m*; (piece of paper) papeleta *f*, tira de papel *f*; (space for boats) embarcadero *m*; **— of the tongue** lapsus [linguae] *m*; **—knot** nudo corredizo *m*; **Freudian —** acto fallido *m*

slipper [slípə-] N zapatilla *f*, pantufla *f*

slippery [slípərì] ADJ resbaloso, resbaladizo; (evasive) evasivo, escurridizo

slipshod [slípʃɑd] ADJ chapucero

slit [slɪt] VT cortar a lo largo; **to — someone's throat** degollar a alguien; **to — into strips** cortar en tiras; N raja *f*, hendidura *f*

slither [slíðə-] VI serpentear, culebrear; N serpenteo *m*, culebreo *m*

sliver [slívə-] N astilla *f*; VI/VT astillar[se]

slob [slɑb] N (unkempt) dejado -da *mf*; (uncouth) bruto -ta *mf*

slobber [slábə-] N baba *f*; VI/VT babosear, babear[se]

slogan [slógən] N eslogan *m*, lema *m*

slop [slɑp] VT (splash) salpicar; (feed) dar de comer; N (pigswill) bazofia *f*; (mud) fango *m*

slope [slop] VI/VT inclinar[se]; N vertiente *f*, declive *m*, cuesta *f*, cortado *m*; (in math) pendiente *f*

sloppiness [slápɪnɪs] N chapucería *f*

sloppy [slápì] ADJ (muddy) fangoso; (splashed) salpicado; (slovenly) cochino; (poorly done) chapucero

slot [slɑt] N (for coins, letters) ranura *f*; (in a computer) bahía *f*, ranura *f*; (place in a series) casilla *f*; (job) puesto *m*; **— machine** tragamonedas *mf sg*, tragaperras *mf sg*; VT hacer una ranura

sloth [slɔθ] N (vice) pereza *f*; (animal) perezoso *m*

slouch [slaʊtʃ] N (posture) encorvamiento *m*; (inept person) torpe *mf*; (lazy person) holgazán -ana *mf*; VI/VT (crouch) andar agachado, encorvar[se]; (shuffle) andar caído de hombros

Slovakia [slovákiə] N Eslovaquia *f*

Slovakian [slovákiən] ADJ & N eslovaco -ca *mf*

Slovene [slóvin] ADJ & N esloveno -na *mf*

Slovenia [slovíniə] N Eslovenia *f*

slovenliness [slávənlɪnɪs] N (of a person) desaseo *m*, desaliño *m*; (of work) descuido *m*

slovenly [slávənlì] ADJ (unclean) desaseado; (unkempt) desaliñado; (poorly done) descuidado

slow [slo] ADJ (not fast) lento, tardo; (running behind) atrasado; (sluggish) lerdo, torpe, pesado; **in — motion** en cámara lenta; ADV lentamente, despacio; VI/VT **to — down/up** andar más despacio, frenar; N **—down** (in business) disminución de actividades *f*; (in labor disputes) huelga de celo *f*

slowly [slólì] ADV despacio, lento, lentamente; **— but surely** lenta pero seguramente

slowness [slónɪs] N (of speed) lentitud *f*; (of intelligence) torpeza *f*

slug [slʌg] N (bullet) bala *f*; (coin) moneda falsa *f*; (animal) babosa *f*; (swallow) trago *m*; (blow with fist) puñetazo *m*; VT aporrear; **to — it out** agarrarse a puñetazos

sluggard [slʌ́gə-d] N holgazán -ana *mf*

sluggish [slʌ́gɪʃ] ADJ (slow) lento; (torpid) aletargado, torpe

sluggishness [slʌ́gɪʃnɪs] N torpeza *f*

sluice [slus] N (channel with a gate) esclusa *f*; (channel) canal *m*; **— gate** compuerta *f*

slum [slʌm] N barrio bajo *m*; **—s** tugurios *m pl*; **—lord** propietario de tugurio *m*; VI visitar los barrios bajos; **to — it** divertirse en lugares de poca categoría

slumber [slʌ́mbə-] VI dormir; N sueño *m*; **— party** fiesta de niñas que se quedan a dormir *f*

slump [slʌmp] VI (a person) desplomarse; (prices, markets) bajar repentinamente; N (in

prices) baja repentina *f*; (in the economy) ralentización *f*; (in sports) mala racha *f*

slung [slʌŋ] *see* sling

slunk [slʌŋk] *see* slink

slur [slɜ˞] VT (pronounce indistinctly) pronunciar mal; (connect notes) ligar; N (connection of notes) ligado *m*; (insult) insulto *m*

slush [slʌʃ] N (melted snow) nieve a medio derretir *f*; (sludge) nieve fangosa *f*; (mud) fango *m*; (refuse) desperdicios *m pl*; **— fund** (illicit fund) cuenta para fines ilícitos *f*; (petty cash) caja chica *f*

sly [slaɪ] ADJ astuto, taimado; **on the —** a escondidas

smack [smæk] N (taste) dejo *m*; *Sp* deje *m*; (kiss) beso ruidoso *m*; (loud eating) chasquido *m*; (slap) palmada *f*, sopapo *m*; (heroin) *fam* caballo *m*; VT (kiss) dar un beso ruidoso; (eat loudly) chascar, chasquear; (slap) dar una palmada; **to — of** tener un dejo de

small [smɔł] ADJ (not large) pequeño, chico; (of build) menudo; (narrow) estrecho; (lowercase) minúsculo; (petty) mezquino; **— caps** versalillas *f pl*, versalitas *f pl*; **— change** cambio suelto *m*; **— fry** gente menuda *f*; **— intestine** intestino delgado *m*; **—pox** viruela *f*; **— talk** cháchara *f*; **to feel —** avergonzarse; N (size) pequeño *m*; **— of the back** baja espalda *f*

smallness [smɔ́łnɪs] N pequeñez *f*

smart [smart] ADJ (intelligent) listo, inteligente; (astute) astuto; (stylish) elegante; **— aleck/alec** sabihondo -da *mf*; **— bomb** bomba inteligente *f*; **— card** tarjeta de circuito integrado *f*, tarjeta inteligente *f*; **— money** inversión inteligente *f*; **— remark** insolencia *f*; N (pain) escozor *m*; VI picar; **I'm —ing from his rude remarks** todavía me duelen sus groserías

smash [smæʃ] VT (destroy) estrellar, destrozar; (a rebellion) aplastar; **to — into** estrellarse contra; N (sound) estrépito *m*; (blow) choque violento *m*; (tennis shot) remate *m*; **a — hit** un exitazo

smear [smɪr] VT (daub) untar; (spot, vilify) manchar; (blur) correrse; (defeat) reventar; **to — with paint** pintorrear, pintarrajear; N (stain) mancha *f*; (culture) frotis *m*; **— campaign** campaña de difamación *f*

smell [smɛł] VI/VT oler; **to — of** oler a; **that —s** huele mal, apesta; **to — up** apestar; N (odor) olor *m*; (sense) olfato *m*; **— of** olor a

smelly [smɛ́lɪ] ADJ hediondo, apestoso

smile [smaɪł] VI sonreír[se]; N sonrisa *f*

smiling [smáɪlɪŋ] ADJ risueño, sonriente

smirk [smɜ˞k] N sonrisa suficiente *f*; VI sonreír con suficiencia

smith [smɪθ] N herrero -ra *mf*

smitten [smítn̩] *see* smite

smog [smɑg] N smog *m*

smoke [smok] N humo *m*; (cigarette) cigarro *m*, cigarrillo *m*; **— detector** detector de humo *m*, detector de incendios *m*; **— inhalation** inhalación de humo *f*; **— screen** cortina de humo *f*; **—stack** chimenea *f*; **to have a —** fumar; VI (put off smoke) echar humo; (go fast) volar; VT (tobacco) fumar; (ham, fish, glass) ahumar; **to — out** (drive out) ahuyentar con humo; (expose) poner al descubierto

smoker [smókə˞] N fumador -ora *mf*; (train car) vagón de fumar *m*

smoking [smókɪŋ] ADJ humeante; **— car** vagón de fumar *m*; **— gun** prueba irrefutable *f*; **— room** cuarto de fumar *m*; N (use of tobacco) tabaquismo *m*, fumar *m*

smoky [smóki] ADJ humoso

smolder, smoulder [smółdə˞] VI arder

smooth [smuð] ADJ (surface) liso; (skin) suave, terso; (tire) gastado; (sea) sereno, tranquilo; (manners) agradable, fino; (flatterer) zalamero; VT (make surface even) alisar; (make easy) allanar; **to — away** hacer desaparecer; **to — one's hair** atusarse el cabello; **to — over** limar asperezas

smoothness [smúðnɪs] N (of a surface) lisura *f*; (of skin) tersura *f*, suavidad *f*; (of sea) tranquilidad *f*; (of manners) fineza *f*; (of a flatterer) zalamería *f*

smote [smot] *see* smite

smother [smʌ́ðə˞] VT (stifle) ahogar[se], sofocar[se], asfixiar[se]; (envelop) cubrir; (overprotect) sobreproteger

smudge [smʌʤ] N borrón *m*, mancha *f*; VI/VT borronear[se], manchar[se]

smug [smʌg] ADJ suficiente, petulante

smuggle [smʌ́gəł] VI/VT contrabandear, hacer contrabando; **to — in** entrar de contrabando; **to — out** sacar de contrabando

smuggler [smʌ́glə˞] N contrabandista *mf*

smut [smʌt] N (soot) hollín *m*; (pornography) pornografía *f*; (parasite) tizon *m*

snack [snæk] N tentempié *m*, bocadillo *m*; **— bar** cafetería *f*, tizón *m*

snafu [snæfú] N relajo *m*

snag [snæg] N (branch) gancho *m*; (in fabric) enganchón *m*; (any obstacle) pega *f*, obstáculo *m*, contrariedad *f*; **to hit a —** tropezar con un obstáculo; VI/VT enganchar[se]; VT (a ball) agarrar

snail [sneł] N caracol *m*; **— mail** correo regular *m*; **—'s pace** paso de tortuga *m*

snake [snek] N serpiente *f*; **—bite** mordedura de serpiente *f*; **— in the grass** víbora *f*; **—skin** piel de serpiente *f*; VI serpentear

snap [snæp] VI (make sound) chasquear, dar un chasquido; (lose control) estallar, perder los estribos; VT (take a photograph) sacar; VI/VT

(break) quebrar[se]; **to — at** (try to bite) tirar un mordiscón; (speak harshly) ladrar; **to — one's fingers** chasquear los dedos, castañetear con los dedos; **to — out of** recuperarse de; **to — shut** cerrar[se] de golpe; **to — together** abrochar; **to — up** llevarse; N (sound) chasquido *m*; (fastener) broche *m*; (bite) tarascada *f*; **it's a —** es pan comido; **— judgment** decisión atolondrada *f*; **—dragon** dragón *m*; **—shot** instantánea, foto *f*

snappy [snǽpi] ADJ (biting) mordedor; (elegant) elegante; **make it —!** ¡date prisa!

snare [snɛr] N (trap) trampa *f*; **— drum** tambor con bordón *m*; VT atrapar

snarl [snɑrl] VI/VT (growl) regañar; (tangle) enmarañar[se], enredar[se]; N (growl) gruñido *m*; (tangle) maraña *f*, enredo *m*

snatch [snætʃ] VT (seize) arrebatar; (kidnap) secuestrar; VI **to — at** dar manotazos; N (act of snatching) arrebato *m*; (fragment) fragmento *m*

snazzy [snǽzi] ADJ llamativo

sneak [snik] VI andar furtivamente; **to — in** entrar a escondidas; **to — out** salir a hurtadillas; VT **to — something in** meter algo a escondidas; **to — something out** sacar a escondidas; **to — a cigarette** fumar a escondidas; N persona solapada *f*

sneakers [sníkɚz] N zapatillas [deportivas] *f pl*, tenis *m pl*

sneer [snɪr] VI (smile) sonreír con sorna; **to — at** mofarse de; N expresión de sorna *f*

sneeze [sniz] VI estornudar; **that's nothing to — at** no es nada desdeñable; N estornudo *m*

snicker [sníkɚ] VI reírse burlonamente; N risita burlona *f*

snide [snaɪd] ADJ malévolo

sniff [snɪf] VI/VT husmear, olfatear; **to — at** husmear; (ridicule) menospreciar; N (act of sniffing) husmeo *m*, olfateo *m*; (smell) bocanada *f*

sniffle [snífəl] VI (with a cold) sorberse los mocos; (when crying) gimotear; N (when crying) gimoteo *m*; **the —s** un resfrío

snip [snɪp] VT tijeretear; **to — off** cortar de un tijeretazo; N (act of snipping) tijeretada *f*, tijeretazo *m*; (piece cut off) pedacito *m*, recorte *m*; **— of conversation** retazo de conversación *m*

sniper [snáɪpɚ] N francotirador -ora *mf*

snitch [snɪtʃ] VI (tell on) chivar, chivatar; VT (rob) ratear; N soplón -ona *mf*, chivato -ta *mf*

snob [snɑb] N esnob *mf*

snoop [snup] VI fisgar, fisgonear; N fisgón -ona *mf*

snooze [snuz] VI dormitar; N siesta *f*; **to take a —** echar un sueñecito / un sueñito / una siesta

snore [snɔr] VI roncar; N ronquido *m*

snorkel [snɔ́rkəl] N esnórquel *m*

snort [snɔrt] VI resoplar, bufar; VI/VT (drugs) esnifar; N resoplido *m*, bufido *m*; (drink) trago *m*

snout [snaʊt] N hocico *m*, jeta *f*, morro *m*; (nose) *fam* napias *f pl*

snow [sno] N nieve *f* (also cocaine, heroin); **—ball** bola de nieve *f*; **—board** monopatín de nieve *m*; **—drift** ventisquero *m*; **—fall** nevada *f*; **—flake** copo de nieve *m*; **—man** muñeco de nieve *m*; **—mobile** motonieve *f*; **—plow** quitanieves *m sg*; **—shoe** raqueta *f*; **—storm** ventisca *f*; VI nevar; **the airport was —ed in** cerraron el aeropuerto por nieve; **to — under** (cover in snow) cubrir de nieve; (overwhelm) abrumar; **to —ball** aumentar rápidamente

snowy [snóɪ] ADJ nevado; (white) níveo

snub [snʌb] VT volverle la cara a, desairar, despreciar; N desaire *m*, desprecio *m*; **—-nosed** chato; *Am* ñato

snuck [snʌk] *see* sneak

snuff [snʌf] VI **to — out** apagar, extinguir; N (tobacco product) rapé *m*; **to be up to —** dar la talla

snug [snʌg] ADJ (tight-fitting) ajustado; (comfortable) cómodo

so [so] ADV (in this way) así; (to this degree) tan; (so much) tanto; **— am I** yo también; **—-and-—** fulano [de tal]; **—-called** llamado; **— as to** para; **— far as I know** que yo sepa; **— many** tantos; **— much** tanto; **—-—** regular; **— much the better** tanto mejor; **— that** de modo que; **I was — a beauty queen!** ¡sí que fui reina de belleza! **— long!** ¡hasta luego! **and — forth** etcetera, y así sucesivamente; **I believe —** creo que sí; **is that —?** ¿en serio? ¡no me digas! **ten minutes or —** unos diez minutos; INTERJ (upon discovering a secret) ajajá; CONJ (in order that) de modo que; (consequently) así que, entonces

soak [sok] VI/VT (immerse) remojar[se]; (drench) empapar[se]; **to — through** colarse por; **to — up** absorber, embeber; **to be —ed through** estar empapado, estar calado hasta los huesos; N remojón *m*

soap [sop] N jabón *m*; (television show) telenovela *f*; **— bubble** pompa de jabón *f*; **— dish** jabonera *f*; VT enjabonar

soapy [sóɪpi] ADJ jabonoso

soar [sɔr] VI/VT (airplane) elevar[se]; (kite) remontar[se]; (hopes) aumentar[se]; (prices) disparar[se]; (glider) planear[se]; VI (bird) volar

sob [sɑb] VI sollozar, hipar; N sollozo *m*, hipo *m*

sober [sóbɚ] ADJ (not drunk) sobrio; (temperate) moderado; (serious, subdued) serio, sobrio; VI **to — up** (get over drunkenness) despejarse; (become more serious) sentar

cabeza

sobriety [səbráɪɪDi] N (not being drunk) sobriedad *f*; (moderation) moderación *f*; (seriousness) seriedad *f*

soccer [sákə-] N fútbol *m*, balompié *m*; **— ball** esférico *m*; **— field** campo de juego *m*, cancha *f*; **— player** futbolista *mf*; **— World Cup** Campeonato Mundial de Fútbol *m*

sociable [sóʃəbəł] ADJ sociable

social [sóʃəł] ADJ (of society) social; (friendly) sociable; **— climber** arribista *mf*; **— science** ciencias sociales *f pl*; **— security** seguridad social *f*; **— welfare** asistencia social *f*; **— work** asistencia social *f*; N reunión social *f*

socialism [sóʃəlɪzəm] N socialismo *m*

socialist [sóʃəlɪst] ADJ & N socialista *mf*

socialize [sóʃəlaɪz] VT socializar; VI salir, tener trato social

society [səsáɪIDi] N sociedad *f*; (companionship) compañía *f*

socioeconomic [sosioɛkənámɪk] ADJ socioeconómico

sociology [sosiáladʒi] N sociología *f*

sociopath [sósiəpæθ] N sociópata *mf*

sock [sak] N (garment) calcetín *m*; (blow) puñetazo *m*, zumbido *m*; VT pegar, zumbar; **to — away** ahorrar

socket [sákɪt] N (of eye) cuenca *f*; (electrical outlet) enchufe *m*; (for bulb) portalámparas *m sg*, casquillo *m*

sod [sad] N (lawn) césped *m*; (piece) tepe *m*; VT cubrir de césped

soda [sóDə] N (drink) gaseosa *f*; (sodium hydroxide) soda *f*, sosa *f*; **— fountain** bar de bebidas sin alcohol *m*; **— pop** gaseosa *f*; **— water** agua con gas *f*

sodium [sóDiəm] N sodio *m*

sodomy [sádəmi] N sodomía *f*

sofa [sófə] N sofá *m*; **— bed** sofá-cama *m*

soft [sɔft] ADJ (butter, bed, water, penalty) blando; (life) fácil, cómodo; (hair, skin) suave; (light) tenue; **—ball** softball *m*; **—-boiled eggs** huevos pasados por agua *m pl*; **— coal** carbón bituminoso *m*; **— drink** gaseosa *f*; **— page break** salto de página suave/automático *m*; **— palate** velo del paladar *m*; **— return** salto de línea suave *m*; **—ware** software *m*

soften [sɔ́fən] VI/VT (butter) ablandar[se]; (skin) suavizar[se]; VT (a blow) amortiguar; (voice) bajar

softly [sɔ́ftli] ADV (talk) en voz baja; (walk) sin hacer ruido

softness [sɔ́ftnɪs] N (of butter) blandura *f*; (of hair, skin) suavidad *f*; (of light) tenuidad *f*

soggy [sági] ADJ (clothes) empapado; (day) húmedo

soil [sɔɪł] N suelo *m*, tierra *f*; VI/VT ensuciar[se], manchar[se]

solace [sálɪs] N consuelo *m*; VT consolar

solar [sólə-] ADJ solar; **— eclipse** eclipse de sol *m*; **— energy** energía solar *f*; **— plexus** plexo solar *m*; **— system** sistema solar *m*

sold [soɪd] *see* sell

solder [sádə-] VI/VT soldar[se]; N soldadura *f*; **—ing iron** soldador *m*

soldier [sóɪłʤə-] N (of low rank) soldado *m*; (of any rank) militar *m*

sole [soɪ̯] ADJ solo, único; N (of a foot) planta *f*; (of a shoe) suela *f*; (fish) lenguado *m*

solely [sóɪ̯li] ADV solamente; **you are — responsible** eres el único responsable

solemn [sáləm] ADJ solemne

solemnity [səlémnɪDi] N solemnidad *f*

solenoid [sólənɔɪd] N solenoide *m*

solicit [səlísɪt] VT (aid) pedir; (a prostitute) ofrecerse; VI (sell) vender, ofrecer productos

solicitor [səlísɪDə-] N abogado *m*; **— general** subsecretario -ria de justicia *mf*

solicitous [səlísɪDəs] ADJ solícito

solid [sálɪd] ADJ (firm) sólido; (dense) denso; **— blue** azul liso *m*; **— geometry** geometría del espacio *f*; **— gold** oro puro *m*; **— line** línea continua *f*; **—-state** de estado sólido; **for one — hour** por una hora entera; N sólido *m*

solidarity [sɑlɪdǽrɪDi] N solidaridad *f*

solidify [səlídəfaɪ] VI/VT solidificar[se]

solidity [səlíDɪti] N solidez *f*

solitary [sálɪteri] ADJ solitario; **to be in — confinement** estar incomunicado

solitude [sálɪtud] N soledad *f*

solo [sólo] N (in music) solo *m*

soloist [sóloɪst] N solista *mf*

Solomon Islander [sáləmənáɪləndə-] N salomonense *mf*

Solomon Islands [sáləmənáɪləndz] N Islas Salomón *f pl*

solstice [sɔ́łstɪs] N solsticio *m*

soluble [sáljəbəł] ADJ soluble

solution [səlúʃən] N solución *f*

solve [sɑłv] VT resolver, solucionar

solvent [sɑ́łvənt] N solvente *m*, disolvente *m*

Somalia [somáljə] N Somalia *f*

Somalian [somáljən] ADJ & N somalí *mf*

somber [sámbə-] ADJ sombrío

some [sʌm] ADJ algún, alguno; **I worked for — time** trabajé por un rato; **that is — dog!** ¡menudo perro! PRON algunos; **and then —** y más todavía; ADV **— twenty people** unas veinte personas; **I like it —** me gusta un poco

somebody [sʌ́mbɑDi] PRON alguien

someday [sʌ́mde] ADV algún día

somehow [sʌ́mhau] ADV de alguna manera; **— or other** de alguna manera u otra

someone [sʌ́mwʌn] PRON alguien, alguno

somersault [sʌ́məɪsɔłt] N (on ground) voltereta *f*; (in air) salto mortal *m*; VI (on ground) dar una voltereta; (in air) dar un salto mortal

something [sámθɪŋ] PRON algo *m*; **— else** otra cosa; **thirty—** (age) treinta y tantos; (person) treintañero -ra *mf*
sometime [sámtaɪm] ADV algún día, en algún momento; **—s** a veces, de vez en cuando
somewhat [sámhwɑt] ADV algo
somewhere [sámhwɛr] ADV en alguna parte; **— else** en alguna otra parte
son [sʌn] N hijo *m*; **— -in-law** yerno *m*; **— of a gun** *fam* hijo de su madre *m*
sonar [sónɑr] N sonar *m*
song [sɔŋ] N canción *f*; (of a bird) canto *m*; **— and dance** cuento chino *m*; **—writer** compositor -ora *mf*; **—bird** ave canora *f*, pájaro cantor *m*; **to buy something for a —** comprar algo muy barato
sonic barrier [sánɪkbǽri·ɚ] N barrera del sonido *f*
sonnet [sánɪt] N soneto *m*
sonority [sə·nɔ́rɪDi] N sonoridad *f*
sonorous [sə́nə·əs] ADJ sonoro
soon [sun] ADV pronto; **— after nine** poco después de las nueve; **as — as** tan pronto como, en cuanto; **see you —** hasta pronto; **how — do you want it?** ¿para cuándo lo necesitas? **he arrived —er** llegó antes; **—er or later** tarde o temprano; **I'd —er stay here** prefiero quedarme aquí
soot [sʊt] N hollín *m*, tizne *m*
soothe [suð] VT calmar, aliviar
soothsayer [súθseə·] N agorero -ra *mf*
sooty [sʊ́Di] ADJ tiznado
sop [sɑp] VT empapar; **to — up** absorber; **to be —ping wet** estar empapado; N **—s** sopas *f pl*
sophisticated [sə·fístɪkeDɪd] ADJ sofisticado
sophomore [sáfə·mɔr] N estudiante de segundo año *mf*
soprano [sə·prǽno] N soprano *m*
sorcerer [sɔ́rsə·rə·] N brujo *m*, hechicero *m*
sorceress [sɔ́rsə·ɪs] N hechicera *f*
sordid [sɔ́rDɪd] ADJ sórdido, escabroso
sore [sɔr] ADJ (painful) dolorido, doloroso; (grieved) dolorido; (angry) enojado; **—head** cascarrabias *mf*; **my arm is —** me duele el brazo; **to have a — throat** tener dolor de garganta; N llaga *f*, úlcera *f*
soreness [sɔ́rnɪs] N dolor *m*
sorority [sə·rɔ́rɪDi] N asociación femenina de estudiantes *f*
sorrow [sáro] N (sadness) pena *f*, pesar *m*, pesadumbre *f*; (cause of sadness) disgusto *m*
sorrowful [sáro·fəł] ADJ triste, pesaroso
sorry [sári] ADJ **I am —** lo siento; **I am — about that** lo lamento; **I am — for her** la compadezco; **—?** ¿Cómo? **you'll be —** te arrepentirás; **he was in — shape** estaba en un estado lamentable
sort [sɔrt] N clase *f*, tipo *m*; **— of tired** algo cansado; **all —s of** toda clase de; **out of —s** (depressed) de mal humor; (ill) indispuesto; **— key** tecla de ordenación *f*; **— order** orden de clasificación *m*; VT (classify) clasificar; (put in order) ordenar; **to — out** separar, apartar; **to — out a problem** resolver un problema
SOS [ésoés] N SOS *m*
sought [sɔt] *see* seek
soul [soł] N alma *f*; **— music** música soul *f*; **not a —** nadie, ni un alma; **the — of tact** la imagen del tacto
sound [saʊnd] N sonido *m*; (inlet) brazo de mar *m*; **— barrier** barrera del sonido *f*; **— card** tarjeta de sonido *f*; **—proof** a prueba de sonido; **—track** banda sonora *f*; **— wave** onda sonora *f*; ADJ (healthy) sano; (sane) cuerdo; (well founded) bien fundado, lógico; **— advice** buen consejo *m*; **— sleep** sueño profundo *m*; **a — beating** una buena paliza; **of — mind** en su sano juicio; **safe and —** sano y salvo; VI sonar; VT (an alarm) tocar; (a channel) sondar; (opinion) sondear; **to — out** tantear, sondear
soup [sup] N sopa *f*; **— dish** plato sopero *m*; **—spoon** cuchara sopera *f*; **— tureen** sopera *f*
sour [saʊr] ADJ (acidic) agrio, ácido; (peevish) agrio, avinagrado; **to go —** (milk) cortarse, agriarse; (a relationship) estropearse; **— cream** *Sp* nata agria *f*; *Am* crema agria *f*; **— milk** leche cortada *f*; **—puss** cascarrabias *mf*; avinagrado -da *mf*; VI/VT agriar[se], avinagrar[se]; (milk) cortar[se]
source [sɔrs] N fuente *f*, origen *m*; **— code** código fuente *m*
sourness [sáʊrnɪs] N acidez *f*
souse [saʊs] VI/VT (plunge) zambullir[se]; (soak) empapar[se]; N borracho -cha *mf*, esponja *f*
south [saʊθ] N sur *m*, mediodía *f*; ADJ meridional, sureño; **— Africa** Sudáfrica *f*; **— African** sudafricano -na *mf*; **— America** América del Sur *f*, Sudamérica *f*; **— American** sudamericano -na *mf*; **—bound** con rumbo al sur; **—east** sureste, sudeste; **—eastern** sureste, sudeste; **— Korea** Corea del Sur *f*; **— Korean** surcoreano -na *mf*; **—paw** zurdo -da *mf*; **— pole** polo sur *m*; **—west** sudoeste, suroeste; **—western** sudoeste, suroeste; ADV hacia el sur
southern [sə́ðə·n] ADJ meridional, sureño
southerner [sə́ðə·nə·] N sureño -ña *mf*, meridional *mf*, habitante del sur *mf*
southward [sáʊθwə·d] ADV hacia el sur, rumbo al sur
souvenir [suvə·nír] N recuerdo *m*
sovereign [sə́və·ɪn] ADJ & N soberano -na *mf*
sovereignty [sə́və·ɪnti] N soberanía *f*
sow[1] [saʊ] N puerca *f*
sow[2] [so] VI/VT sembrar
sown [son] *see* sow[2]
soy [sɔi] N *Sp* soja *f*; *Am* soya *f*; **—bean** *Sp* semilla

de soja *f*; *Am* semilla de soya *f*; **— sauce** *Sp* salsa de soja *f*; *Am* salsa de soya *f*

spa [spɑ] N balneario *m*

space [spes] N espacio *m*; **—-age** de la era espacial; **—bar** barra espaciadora *f*; **—craft** nave espacial *f*; **—ship** nave espacial *f*; **— shuttle** transbordador espacial *m*; **— station** estación espacial *f*; **— suit** traje espacial *m*; VT espaciar; **to — out** distraerse

spacious [spéʃəs] ADJ espacioso, amplio

spade [sped] N (shovel) pala *f*; (in cards) pica *f*; **to call a — a —** al pan, pan y al vino, vino

Spain [spen] N España *f*

spam [spæm] N correo electrónico basura *m*, spam *m*

span [spæn] N (of hand) palmo *m*; (of time) espacio *m*; (of attention) lapso *m*, período *m*; (of bridge) tramo *m*; (of wing) envergadura *f*; (of life) duración *f*; VT (time) abarcar; (a river) atravesar, salvar

Spaniard [spǽnjɚd] N español -ola *mf*

Spanish [spǽnɪʃ] ADJ (of Spain) español; (Spanish-speaking) hispano; N (language) español *m*; **— America** Hispanoamérica *f*

spank [spæŋk] VT dar nalgadas; N palmada *f*, nalgada *f*

spanking [spǽŋkɪŋ] N zurra en las nalgas *f*; ADJ **— new** flamante

spare [spɛr] VT (embarrassment) ahorrar, evitar; (money) prestar; (an enemy) perdonar la vida a; (a worker) prescindir de; **— me!** ¡ten piedad de mí! **to — no expense** no escatimar gastos; **to have time to —** tener tiempo de sobra; ADJ (austere) austero; (extra) de sobra, de más; **— cash** dinero disponible *m*; **— parts** repuestos *m pl*; **— time** tiempo libre *m*; N (part) repuesto *m*; (tire) neumático de repuesto *m*

spark [spɑrk] N chispa *f*; **— plug** bujía *f*; VI chispear, echar chispas; VT (a riot) desencadenar; (interest, criticism) provocar

sparkle [spárkəł] VI (diamond) centellear; (sparkler) chispear; (eyes) brillar; N (flashing) brillo *m*, centelleo *m*; (spirit) viveza *f*, animación *f*

sparkling [spárklɪŋ] ADJ (diamond) centelleante; (eyes) brillante; **— water** agua con gas *f*; **— wine** vino espumoso *m*

sparrow [spǽro] N gorrión *m*

sparse [spɑrs] ADJ escaso; (hair) ralo

spasm [spǽzəm] N espasmo *m*

spasmodic [spæzmɑ́dɪk] ADJ espasmódico

spastic [spǽstɪk] ADJ espástico

spat [spæt] N riña *f*

spat [spæt] *see* spit

spatial [spéʃəł] ADJ espacial

spatter [spǽdɚ] VI/VT salpicar; N salpicadura *f*

spatula [spǽtʃələ] N espátula *f*

spawn [spɔn] VI desovar; VT engendrar; N (of fish) huevas *f pl*; (of frogs) huevos *m pl*

spay [spe] VT esterilizar, castrar

speak [spik] VI hablar; VT (a language) hablar; (the truth) decir; (one's lines) recitar, decir; **so to —** por decirlo así, valga la expresión; **to — for** hablar en nombre de / a favor de; **to — one's mind** hablar sin rodeos; **to — out against** denunciar; **to — out for** defender; **to — up** hablar fuerte

speaker [spíkɚ] N orador -ora *mf*; (at a conference) conferenciante *mf*; (of a language) hablante *mf*; **— of the House** presidente -ta de la cámara de representantes *mf*; **—phone** teléfono con parlante *m*

spear [spir] N (weapon) lanza *f*; (for fishing) arpón *m*; (sprout) brote *m*; VT (a person, animal) alancear, herir con lanza; (a fish) arponear

spearmint [spírmɪnt] N mentaverde *f*

special [spéʃəł] ADJ especial; **— delivery** entrega inmediata *f*; **— education** educación especial *f*; **— effects** efectos especiales *m pl*; **— interest [group]** grupo de presión *m*; N (sale item) especialidad *f*; (TV program) especial *m*

specialist [spéʃəlɪst] N especialista *mf*

specialization [spɛʃəlɪzéʃən] N especialización *f*, especialidad *f*

specialize [spéʃəlaɪz] VI/VT especializar[se]

specially [spéʃəli] ADV especialmente, específicamente

specialty [spéʃəłti] N especialidad *f*

species [spíʃiz] N especie *f*

specific [spɪsífɪk] ADJ específico, determinado; **— gravity** peso específico *m*; N **—s** detalles *m pl*

specifically [spɪsífɪkli] ADV concretamente, específicamente

specify [spésəfaɪ] VI/VT especificar

specimen [spésəmən] N (representative) espécimen *m*, ejemplar *m*; (sample) muestra *f*

speck [spɛk] N (small dot) mota *f*, manchita *f*; (small amount) pizca *f*

speckle [spékəł] N manchita *f*, mota *f*; VT salpicar, motear; **—d** moteado

spectacle [spɛ́ktəkəł] N espectáculo *m*; **—s** gafas *f pl*, anteojos *m pl*; **to make a — of oneself** dar un espectáculo, ponerse en ridículo

spectacular [spɛktǽkjəlɚ] ADJ espectacular

spectator [spɛ́ktɛɚ] N espectador -ora *mf*

spectrum [spɛ́ktrəm] N espectro *m*

speculate [spɛ́kjəlet] VI/VT especular

speculation [spɛkjəléʃən] N especulación *f*

speculative [spɛ́kjələtɪv] ADJ especulativo

speculator [spɛ́kjəlɛɚ] N especulador -ora *mf*

sped [spɛd] *see* speed

speech [spitʃ] N (faculty of speaking) habla *f*; (formal) discurso *m*; (in a play) parlamento *m*; **— defect** defecto de pronunciación *m*; **—**

recognition reconocimiento de habla *m*; — **synthesis** síntesis de habla *m*; **to make a** — pronunciar un discurso

speechless [spítʃlɪs] ADJ (dumb) mudo; (astonished) estupefacto

speed [spid] N (rapidity) velocidad *f*, rapidez *f*; (gear) velocidad *f*; (amphetamine) anfeta *f*; — **limit** límite de velocidad *m*; **at full** — a toda velocidad; VI (break speed limit) ir con exceso de velocidad; **to** — **by** pasar a toda velocidad; **to** — **off/away** irse a toda velocidad; **to** — **up** (a car, work) acelerar; (a delivery) hacer llegar a toda velocidad

speedometer [spɪdámɪdə˞] N velocímetro *m*

speedy [spídɪ] ADJ veloz, rápido

spell [spɛł] N (charm) hechizo *m*, sortilegio *m*, conjuro *m*; (period) temporada *f*; (sickness) ataque *m*; **to put under a** — hechizar; ADJ —**bound** hechizado; VT (spoken) deletrear; (written) escribir; (represent) significar, representar; **to** — **-check** comprobar la ortografía; **I** —**ed it out for him** se lo dije con todas las letras

spelling [spélɪŋ] N ortografía *f*; — **bee** concurso de ortografía *m*

spend [spɛnd] VT (money) gastar; (time) pasar; —**thrift** derrochador -ora *mf*, gastador -ora *mf*, pródigo -ga *mf*

spending [spéndɪŋ] N gastos *m pl*; — **cut** recorte de gastos *m*; **to go on a** — **spree** salir a gastar dinero a lo loco

spent [spɛnt] *see* spend

sperm [spɜ˞m] N esperma *mf*; — **whale** cachalote *m*

spermicide [spɜ́˞məsaɪd] N espermicida *m*

sphere [sfɪr] N esfera *f*; — **of influence** esfera de influencia *f*

spherical [sférɪkəł] ADJ esférico

sphincter [sfíŋktə˞] N esfínter *m*

spice [spaɪs] N especia *f*; VT condimentar; **to** — **up** dar sal

spiciness [spáɪsɪnɪs] N lo picante

spick and span [spíkənspǽn] ADJ impecable

spicy [spáɪsi] ADJ picante

spider [spáɪdə˞] N araña *f*; — **monkey** mono araña *m*; —**'s web** telaraña *f*

spigot [spígət] N grifo *m*, espita *f*

spike [spaɪk] N (sprout) espiga *f*; (sharp object) púa *f*, pincho *m*; (on shoes) clavo *m*; —**s** zapatillas con clavos *f pl*; VT (impale) clavar; (add alcohol to) echar alcohol a; (hit a volleyball) picar

spill [spɪł] VI/VT volcar[se], derramar[se], verter[se]; VT (a rider) hacer caer; **to** — **the beans** descubrir el pastel; VI **to** — **over** (a liquid) desbordarse; (a conflict) extenderse; N (of water) derrame *m*; (of blood) derramamiento *m*; (fall) caída *f*

spilt [spɪłt] *see* spill

spin [spɪn] VT (wool) hilar; (a top, one's partner) hacer girar; VI dar vueltas, girar; **to** — **yarns** contar cuentos; N (turning) giro *m*, vuelta *f*; (of an airplane) barrena *f*; (political) sesgo *m*; **to take a** — dar una vuelta

spinach [spínɪtʃ] N espinaca *f*

spinal [spáɪnl] ADJ espinal, vertebral; — **column** columna vertebral *f*, espina dorsal *f*; — **cord** médula espinal *f*

spindle [spíndl] N (for weaving) huso *m*; (on machines) eje *m*

spine [spaɪn] N espina *f*, espinazo *m*

spinning [spínɪŋ] N (action) hilado *m*; (art) hilandería *f*; — **machine** máquina de hilar *f*; — **mill** hilandería *f*; — **top** trompo *m*, peonza *f*; — **wheel** rueca *f*

spinster [spínstə˞] N solterona *f*

spiral [spáɪrəł] ADJ & N espiral *m*; — **notebook** cuaderno de espiral *m*; — **staircase** escalera de caracol *f*

spire [spaɪr] N aguja *f*, chapitel *m*

spirit [spírɪt] N (ghost) espíritu *m*; (animation) ánimo *m*, brío *m*; (alcohol) alcohol *m*; **low** —**s** abatimiento *m*; **to be in good** —**s** estar de buen humor; VT **to** — **away** llevar como por arte de magia

spirited [spírɪtɪd] ADJ fogoso, brioso

spiritual [spírɪtʃuəł] ADJ & N espiritual *m*

spirituality [spɪrɪtʃuǽlɪtɪ] N espiritualidad *f*

spit [spɪt] VI/VT escupir; N (saliva) escupitajo *m*; (for roasting) asador *m*, espeto *m*, espetón *m*; (of sand) banco *m*

spite [spaɪt] N despecho *m*, inquina *f*; **in** — **of** a pesar de; **out of** — por despecho; VT contrariar

spiteful [spáɪtfəł] ADJ malicioso

splash [splæʃ] VI/VT salpicar; VI chapotear, chapalear; N salpicadura *f*, chapoteo *m*; **to make a** — hacer olas

splatter [splǽdə˞] VI/VT salpicar; N salpicadura *f*

spleen [splin] N bazo *m*; (ill humor) mal humor *m*

splendid [spléndɪd] ADJ espléndido

splendor [spléndə˞] N esplendor *m*

splice [splaɪs] VT (tape, genes) empalmar, unir; N empalme *m*, unión *f*

splint [splɪnt] N tablilla *f*; VT entablillar

splinter [splíntə˞] N astilla *f*; VI/VT astillar[se]

split [splɪt] VI/VT (stone, wood) hender[se], rajar[se]; (candy bar) partir[se], dividir[se]; **to** — **hairs** hilar fino; **to** — **one's sides with laughter** desternillarse de risa; **to** — **the difference** partir la diferencia; ADJ (wood) partido, hendido; (a group) dividido; —**-level** en desnivel; — **personality** doble personalidad *f*; — **screen** pantalla dividida *f*; — **second** fracción de segundo *f*; N hendidura *f*, grieta *f*; (in a group) escisión *f*, división *f*

spoil [spɔɪł] VI (milk) cortar[se]; (food) echarse a perder; VT (vacation, performance) estropear, arruinar; (plans) desbaratar; (enjoyment) aguar; (child) malcriar, mimar demasiado; N **—s** botín *m*

spoiler [spɔ́ɪlə-] N alerón *m*

spoke [spok] N rayo *m*

spoke [spok] *see* speak

spoken [spókən] *see* speak

spokesperson [spókspɜ-sən] N portavoz *mf*, vocero -ra *mf*

sponge [spʌnʤ] N (animal, utensil) esponja *f*; (parasite) gorrón -ona *mf*; **— bath** baño de esponja *m*; **— cake** *Am* bizcochuelo *m*; *Sp* bizcocho *m*; VI **to — off** (clean) quitar con esponja; (take advantage of) gorronear; **to — up** absorber con una esponja

sponger [spʌ́nʤɜ-] N gorrón -ona *mf*, parásito *m*

spongy [spʌ́nʤi] ADJ esponjoso, esponjado

sponsor [spɑ́nsɜ-] N (of the arts) mecenas *mf*; (of sports, TV program) patrocinador -ora *mf*; (of a bill) proponente *mf*; VT (a child) apadrinar; (arts, sports, TV show) patrocinar; (bill) proponer

sponsorship [spɑ́nsɜ-ʃɪp] N patrocinio *m*

spontaneity [spɑntənéɪDi] N espontaneidad *f*

spontaneous [spɑnténiəs] ADJ espontáneo; **— abortion** aborto espontáneo *m*

spook [spuk] N (ghost) espectro *m*; (spy) espía *mf*

spool [spuł] N carrete *m*, carretel *m*; VT (wool) devanar; (tape) enrollar

spoon [spun] N cuchara *f*; VT cucharear, poner con una cuchara; **to — -feed** dar de comer en la boca

spoonful [spúnfuł] N cucharada *f*

spore [spɔr] N espora *f*

sport [spɔrt] N deporte *m*; **to be a good —** tener espíritu deportivo; **— utility vehicle** vehículo utilitario deportivo *m*; **—s car** coche deportivo *m*; **—s jacket** saco de sport *m*, americana *f*; **—sman** (hunter) cazador *m*; (in sports) hombre de espíritu deportivo *m*; **—smanship** espíritu deportivo *m*, deportividad *f*; **—swriter** cronista deportivo -va *mf*; ADJ deportivo; VT lucir

sporty [spɔ́rti] ADJ deportivo

spot [spɑt] N (stain) mancha *f*, mota *f*; (blemish) espinilla *f*; (insect bite) roncha *f*; (place) lugar *m*, paraje *m*; (difficult situation) aprieto *m*; **on the —** en el acto; **—-check** inspección al azar *f*; **—light** (in theater) foco *m*; (outdoors) reflector *m*; **to be in the —light** ser el centro de atención; **— remover** quitamanchas *m sg*; VI/VT (stain) manchar, ensuciar; VT (see in the distance) divisar; (notice) notar; (give advantage) dar como ventaja

spotless [spátlɪs] ADJ inmaculado

spotted [spáDɪd] ADJ manchado, moteado

spouse [spaʊs] N cónyuge *mf*; **— abuse** abuso conyugal *m*

spout [spaʊt] VT (throw) arrojar chorros de; (talk) soltar tonterías; VI (flow out) salir a chorros; (talk) perorar; N (of a fountain) caño *m*; (of a gutter) canalón *m*; (of a teapot) pico *m*

sprain [spren] VT torcerse; N torcedura *f*

sprang [spræŋ] *see* spring

sprawl [sprɔł] VI (spread limbs) despatarrarse; (extend) extenderse; (fall) tumbarse; N postura despatarrada *f*

spray [spre] VI/VT rociar[se]; N (of liquid) rociada *f*; (foam) espuma *f*; (of flowers) ramillete *m*; **— can** aerosol *m*; **— paint** pintura en aerosol *f*

spread [spred] VI/VT (arms, newspaper) extender[se]; (butter) untar[se]; (map) desdoblar[se]; (legs) abrir[se]; (seeds) esparcir[se]; (news) difundir[se], diseminar[se]; (odor) difundir[se], expandirse; (rumor) propalar; (panic) sembrar; VT (panic, news) sembrar; N (of ideas) difusión *f*; (of opinion) diseminación *f*; (of disease) propagación *f*; (of nuclear weapons) proliferación *f*; (for a bed) cubrecama *m*; (for bread) pasta *f*; (of food) festín *m*; (ranch) hacienda *f*; **—sheet** (paper) planilla de cálculo *f*; (program) planilla electrónica *f*

spree [spri] N parranda *f*, farra *f*; **to go on a —** ir de parranda/farra; **to go on a shopping —** gastar dinero desenfrenadamente

spring [sprɪŋ] VI saltar; **to — at** abalanzarse sobre; **to — from** nacer de; **to — open** abrir[se] de golpe; **to — to mind** venir a la mente; **to — up** surgir; VT **to — a leak** (boat) hacer agua; (pipe) comenzar a gotear; **to — news** dar una noticia de sopetón; N (season) primavera *f*; (coil) muelle *m*, resorte *m*; (elasticity) elasticidad *f*; (jump) salto *m*; (water) manantial *m*, fuente *f*; **—board** trampolín *m*; **— fever** fiebre de primavera *f*; **— mattress** colchón de muelles *m*; **—time** primavera *f*; **— water** agua de manantial *f*; **he's no — chicken** no se cuece en el primer hervor

sprinkle [spríŋkəł] VT (with sugar) espolvorear; (with droplets) salpicar, rociar; (rain) gotear, chispear

sprint [sprɪnt] VI (run) echarse una carrera; (run a competitive race) [e]sprintar; N (run) corrida corta *f*; (race) [e]sprint *m*

sprocket [sprákɪt] N piñón *m*, rueda dentada *f*

sprout [spraʊt] VI (leaf) brotar, salir; (plants) retoñar; (seeds) germinar; (houses) surgir; VT echar; **he —ed horns** le salieron cuernos; N retoño *m*, brote *m*, renuevo *m*

spruce [sprus] N picea *f*; VI **to — up** arreglarse

sprung [sprʌŋ] *see* spring

spun [spʌn] *see* spin
spunk [spʌŋk] N agallas *f pl*
spur [spɝ] N (on stirrups) espuela *f*; (stimulus) aguijón *m*; (of a rooster) espolón *m*; (of a mountain) estribación *f*; (of a railroad track) ramal *m*; **on the — of the moment** espontáneamente; VT espolear; **to — on** animar
spurious [spjúriəs] ADJ espurio
spurn [spɝn] VT rechazar, desdeñar
spurt [spɝt] VI salir a chorros; N (of water) chorro *m*; (of a runner) esfuerzo repentino *m*; **in —s** por rachas
sputter [spʌ́dɚ] VI (fire) chisporrotear; (person) refunfuñar; N (fire) chisporroteo *m*
sputum [spjúdəm] N esputo *m*
spy [spaɪ] N espía *mf*; **—glass** catalejo *m*; VI espiar; **to — on** espiar
squabble [skwábəł] VI reñir; N reyerta *f*
squad [skwɑd] N (of police) patrulla *f*; (for execution) pelotón *m*; (of athletes) equipo *m*; (for guarding) retén *m*; **— car** [coche] patrullero *m*
squadron [skwádrən] N (in navy) escuadra *f*; (in army) escuadrón *m*
squalid [skwɑ́lɪd] ADJ escuálido
squall [skwɔł] N (rain) chubasco *m*, borrasca *f*; (sound) berrido *m*; VI berrear
squalor [skwɑ́lɚ] N miseria *f*, escualidez *f*
squander [skwándɚ] VT despilfarrar, derrochar, disipar
squanderer [skwándərɚ] N derrochador -ora *mf*
square [skwɛr] N (shape) cuadrado *m*; (on a pattern) cuadro *m*; (plaza) plaza *f*, *Mex* zócalo *m*; (tool in carpentry) escuadra *f*; (on chessboard) casilla *f*; **— brackets** corchetes *m pl*; **— dance** cuadrilla *f*; **— knot** nudo de rizo *m*; **— meal** comida completa *f*; **— root** raíz cuadrada *f*; **he is a —** es muy conservador; VT (make square) cuadrar; (draw squares on) cuadricular; (multiply by itself) elevar al cuadrado; **to — one's shoulders** erguirse; ADJ (in shape) cuadrado; (at ninety degrees) en ángulo recto; (tied) empatado; (frank) franco; **to be — with someone** estar a mano con alguien; ADV **right — between the eyes** justo entre los ojos
squash [skwɑʃ] N (gourd) calabaza *f*; (sport) squash *m*; VT (smash) aplastar, despachurrar
squat [skwɑt] VI (sit low) acuclillarse; (occupy) ocupar sin autorización; ADJ (sitting low) acuclillado; (thickset) rechoncho, achaparrado; N (nothing) nada; **he doesn't know—** no sabe un comino; **in a —** en cuclillas
squawk [skwɔk] VI (of chickens) cacarear; (complain) quejarse; N (of chickens) cacareo *m*; (complaint) quejido *m*
squeak [skwik] VI (door) rechinar, chirriar; (shoe) rechinar; (mouse) chillar; N (of door) rechinamiento *m*, chirrido *m*; (of shoe) rechinamiento *m*; (of mouse) chillido *m*
squeaky [skwíki] ADJ (door) chirriante; (shoes) rechinante
squeal [skwił] VI chillar; (complain) protestar; (snitch) chivatar, delatar; N chillido *m*
squeamish [skwímɪʃ] ADJ delicado
squeegee [skwíʤi] N escurridor de goma *m*, limpiavidrios *m sg*
squeeze [skwiz] VT apretar; (press very hard) estrujar; (an orange) estrujar, exprimir; (hug) abrazar; **to — into** meter[se] con dificultad en, encajar[se] en; **to — out** (an orange) exprimir; (a towel) escurrir; **to — through a crowd** abrirse paso entre la multitud; N (of hands) apretón *m*; (excessive squeeze) estrujón *m*; (hug) abrazo *m*; (lack) restricción *f*
squelch [skwɛłtʃ] VT (revolt) aplastar, sofocar; (criticism) acallar
squid [skwɪd] N calamar *m*
squint [skwɪnt] VI (partially close eyes) entrecerrar los ojos; (look askance) mirar de soslayo; N (look with partially closed eyes) mirada con los ojos entrecerrados *f*; (side glance) mirada de soslayo *f*
squirm [skwɝm] VI retorcerse; **to — out of a difficulty** zafarse de un aprieto
squirrel [skwɝ́əł] N ardilla *f*
squirt [skwɝt] VT echar un chisguete en; VI salir a chorritos; N chisguete *m*, chorrito *m*; **— gun** pistola lanzaagua *f*, pistola de agua *f*
Sri Lanka [srilɑ́ŋkə] N Sri Lanka *f*
Sri Lankan [srilɑ́ŋkən] ADJ & N cingalés -esa *mf*
stab [stæb] VI/VT apuñalar, acuchillar; **to — at** tirar puñaladas a; N (with a dagger) puñalada *f*; (with a knife) cuchillada *f*; (with a pocketknife) navajazo *m*; (of pain) punzada *f*, pinchazo *m*; **to take a — at** intentar; **— wound** cuchillada *f*
stability [stəbílɪDi] N estabilidad *f*
stabilization [stebəlɪzéʃən] N estabilización *f*
stable [stébəł] ADJ estable; N establo *m*, cuadra *f*; (for horses only) caballeriza *f*; VT poner en el establo
stack [stæk] N (ordered) pila *f*; (chaotic) montón *m*; (of a chimney) chimenea *f*; (in a library) estantería *f*; VT amontonar, apilar
stadium [stéDɪəm] N estadio *m*
staff [stæf] N (stick) cayado *m*; (of a flag) asta *f*; (personnel) personal *m*, plantel *m*; (of music) pentagrama *m*; **— of life** pan de cada día *m*; **— officer** oficial de estado mayor *m*; **editorial —** redacción *f*; **teaching —** cuerpo docente *m*; VT contratar personal para
stag [stæg] N (deer) venado *m*, ciervo *m*; (other animals) macho *m*; **— beetle** ciervo volante *m*; **— party** fiesta para hombres *f*

stage [stedʒ] N (showplace) escenario *m*; (for popular entertainment) tablado *m*; (theater) teatro *m*, las tablas *f pl*; (period) etapa *f*, estadio *m*; (distance) etapa *f*; **—coach** diligencia *f*; **— fright** miedo al escenario *m*, fiebre de candilejas *f*; **—hand** tramoyista *mf*; **by —s** por etapas; VT (a play) poner en escena; (an attack) organizar

stagger [stǽgɚ] VI (totter) tambalearse, dar tumbos; VT (hit hard) hacer tambalear; (overwhelm) dejar azorado; (alternate) escalonar; N tambaleo *m*

stagnant [stǽgnənt] ADJ estancado

stagnate [stǽgnet] VI estancarse

stagnation [stægnéʃən] N estancamiento *m*

staid [sted] ADJ envarado

stain [sten] N (spot) mancha *f*; (color) tinte *m*, tintura *f*; VI/VT (spot) manchar[se]; (color) teñir[se]; **—ed-glass window** vitral *m*

stainless [sténlɪs] ADJ sin mancha; **— steel** acero inoxidable *m*

stair [stɛr] N peldaño *m*, escalón *m*; **—case** escalera *f*; **—s** escalera *f*; **—way** escalera *f*

stake [stek] N (pole) estaca *f*; (investment) interés *m*; (bet) apuesta *f*; **at —** en juego; **to die at the —** morir en la hoguera; VT estacar; **to — out** vigilar

stalactite [stəlǽktaɪt] N estalactita *f*

stalagmite [stəlǽgmaɪt] N estalagmita *f*

stale [steł] ADJ (bread) duro; (air) viciado; (joke) viejo; **—mate** punto muerto *m*

stalk [stɔk] N tallo *m*; VT acechar

stall [stɔł] N (at a market) puesto *m*; (at a fair) caseta *f*, barraca *f*; (in a stable) compartimiento *m*; VI (airplane) entrar en pérdida; (talks) llegar a un punto muerto; (motor) pararse; **he is —ing** está arrastrando los pies; VT (airplane) hacer entrar en pérdida; (talks) paralizar; (motor) parar

stallion [stǽljən] N semental *m*

stamina [stǽmənə] N resistencia *f*, aguante *m*

stammer [stǽmɚ] VI balbucear; N balbuceo *m*

stamp [stæmp] VT (a letter) sellar; *Mex* timbrar; *Am* estampillar; (an official document) sellar, timbrar; (a coin) acuñar; VI (with foot) pisotear, patalear; (with hoof) piafar; **to — out** eliminar; N (on a letter) *Sp* sello *m*; *Mex* timbre *m*; *Am* estampilla *f*; (on an official document) sello *m*, timbre *m*; (instrument, character) sello *m*; (on the ground) pisotón *m*; (sound) paso *m*; **— tax** timbre *m*

stampede [stæmpíd] N estampida *f*; VI huir en estampida; VT hacer huir en estampida

stance [stæns] N posición *f*, postura *f*; (political) posicionamiento *m*

stanch, staunch [stɔntʃ] VT restañar; ADJ (strong) firme; (loyal) fiel

stand [stænd] VI (take a standing position) ponerse de pie, levantarse; *Am* parar[se]; (to be in a standing position) estar de pie; *Am* estar parado; (stop) detenerse; (withstand, tolerate) aguantar, tolerar, soportar; (remain valid) mantenerse; **to — aside** apartarse; **to — back** retroceder; **to — behind someone** respaldar a alguien; **to — by** (be uninvolved) mantenerse al margen; (be alert) estar alerta; (support) respaldar; **to — for** (denote) significar; (tolerate) tolerar; **to — one's ground** mantenerse firme; **to — out** destacarse, sobresalir; **to — up for** defender; **it —s to reason** es razonable; **it —s one meter tall** mide un metro de alto; **to — a chance of** tener posibilidad de; **where do you — on this issue?** ¿qué opinas al respecto? N (at a market) puesto *m*; (at a fair) caseta *f*; (of trees) bosque *m*; (opinion) posición *f*; (for music) atril *m*; (for taxis) parada *f*; **—by** recurso viejo *m*; **—by passenger** pasajero -ra en la lista de espera *mf*; **—off** empate *m*; **—point** punto de vista *m*; **to come to a —still** pararse; **to be at a —still** estar parado; ADJ **—alone** autónomo

standard [stǽndɚd] N (of behavior) norma *f*; (of living, performance) nivel *m*; (of weights) patrón *m*; (banner) estandarte *m*; **gold —** patrón oro *m*; **—-bearer** portaestandarte *mf*; **— deviation** desviación estándar *f*; **— of living** nivel de vida *m*; **— time** hora oficial *f*; **to be up to —** satisfacer los requisitos; ADJ (normal) normal; (standardized) estándar

standardization [stændɚ·ɪzéʃən] N estandarización *f*

standardize [stǽndɚ·daɪz] VT estandarizar, uniformar

standby [stǽndbaɪ] ADV **we're flying —** estamos volando standby

standing [stǽndɪŋ] N (position) posición *f*; (rank) rango *m*; (reputation) reputación *f*; ADJ (not seated) derecho, en pie; (permanent) permanente; (stagnant) estancado; **— order** pedido fijo *m*; **— ovation** ovación de pie *f*

stank [stæŋk] *see* stink

stanza [stǽnzə] N estrofa *f*

staple [stépəł] N (for paper) grapa *f*; (main product) producto principal *m*; (food) alimento básico *m*; ADJ (principal) principal; (basic) básico; VT engrapar

stapler [stépləɚ] N grapadora *f*

star [stɑr] N estrella *f* (also actor); (asterisk) asterisco *m*; **— attraction** atracción principal *f*; **—fish** estrella de mar *f*; **—light** luz de las estrellas *f*; **—-spangled** salpicado de estrellas; **a — student** un[a] estudiante sobresaliente; VT (act in) protagonizar; (put asterisk on) marcar con asterisco; (cover with stars) estrellar

starboard [stárbərd] N estribor *m*; ADV a estribor

starch [stɑrtʃ] N almidón *m* (also food); VT almidonar
stardom [stárdəm] N estrellato *m*
stare [stɛr] VI/VT mirar fijamente; N mirada fija *f*
stark [stɑrk] ADJ (landscape) yermo; (truth) descarnado, desnudo; (contrast) marcado; ADV — **naked** en cueros; — **raving mad** loco de remate
starling [stárlɪŋ] N estornino *m*
starry [stárɪ] ADJ estrellado
start [stɑrt] VI/VT (begin) comenzar, empezar; (a car) poner[se] en marcha, arrancar; VT (a fire) provocar; VI (jump) sobresaltarse; **to — off/out/up** empezar; **don't get him —ed** no le des cuerda; N (beginning) comienzo *m*, principio *m*; (of a race) salida *f*; (nervous jump) sobresalto *m*; (nervous jump of a horse) respingo *m*; — **-up** compañía recién establecida *f*; — **-up funds** capital inicial *m*; — **button** botón de inicio *m*; — **menu** menú de inicio *m*
starter [stárdə-] N (on an automobile) arranque *m*; (for a race) juez de salida *mf*; **for —s** para empezar
startle [stárdl] VI/VT asustar[se], sobresaltar[se]
startling [stárdlɪŋ] ADJ asombroso, sorprendente
starvation [stɑrvéʃən] N inanición *f*
starve [stɑrv] VI/VT hambrear; VI morirse de hambre; VT matar de hambre; (for affection) privar de cariño
starving [stárvɪŋ] ADJ hambriento, muerto de hambre
stash [stæʃ] VI **to — away** ir ahorrando; N alijo *m*
state [stet] N estado *m*; — **of the art** con los últimos avances; —**room** (on a ship) camarote *m*; (on a train) compartimiento *m*; — **-run company** compañía estatal *f*; —**sman** estadista *m*; —**swoman** estadista *f*; VT (declare) declarar, aseverar, manifestar; (describe) exponer
stately [stétli] ADJ majestuoso, imponente
statement [stétmənt] N (declaration) declaración *f*, aseveración *f*; (bill) estado de cuentas *m*
static [stǽɪk] ADJ estático; N interferencia *f*; — **electricity** electricidad estática *f*; **don't give me any** — no me compliques la vida
station [stéʃən] N estación *f*; (on the radio) emisora *f*; (on television) canal *m*; (social rank) condición *f*; — **wagon** camioneta *f*; VT (a sentry) apostar; (troops) estacionar
stationary [stéʃənɛrɪ] ADJ (not moving) estacionario; (stopped) detenido; (fixed) fijo
stationery [stéʃənɛrɪ] N (material) artículos de papelería *m pl*; (paper) papel de carta *m*
statistical [statístɪkəl] ADJ estadístico
statistics [stətístɪks] N (science) estadística *f*; (data) estadísticas *f pl*
statue [stǽtʃu] N estatua *f*
stature [stǽtʃə-] N (physical) estatura *f*; (moral) talla *f*
status [stǽɪdəs] N (prestige, rank) status *m*; (legal, financial) situación *f*; (marital) estado *m*; — **bar** (computer) barra de estado *f*; — **symbol** símbolo de status *m*
statute [stǽtʃut] N (bylaw) estatuto *m*; (law) ley *f*; — **of limitations** ley de prescripción *f*
statutory [stǽtʃətɔri] ADJ estatutario; — **rape** estupro *m*
stave [stev] N (of a barrel) duela *f*; VI **to — off** evitar
stay [ste] VI (remain) quedarse, permanecer; **to — away** mantenerse alejado; **to — in** quedarse en casa; **to — out of trouble** no meterse en líos; **to — up** quedarse levantado; VT **to — an execution** aplazar una ejecución; N (time spent) estancia *f*, estadía *f*, permanencia *f*; (support) sostén *m*, soporte *m*
stead [sted] N **in her —** en su lugar; **to stand one in good —** ser de provecho para uno
steadfast [stédfæst] ADJ fijo, firme
steadiness [stédɪnɪs] N (firmness) firmeza *f*; (of the hand) pulso *m*; (constancy) constancia *f*; (continuity) continuidad *f*
steady [stédɪ] ADJ (not shaky) firme; (constant) constante; (continuous) continuo; — **boyfriend** novio formal *m*; — **customer** cliente -ta asiduo -dua *mf*; — **income** ingreso fijo *m*; VI/VT (an object) asegurar; (nerves) calmar
steak [stek] N bistec *m*, churrasco *m*
steal [stiɫ] VT (a thing, a base) robar, hurtar; (a girlfriend) soplar; VI **to — away/out** escabullirse, escaparse; N (bargain) ganga *f*
stealth [steɫθ] N sigilo *m*; **by —** furtivamente
stealthy [stéɫθi] ADJ furtivo
steam [stim] N (evaporated water) vapor *m*; (arising from an object) vaho *m*; — **engine** máquina de vapor *f*; — **roller** apisonadora *f*, aplanadora *f*; — **ship** [buque de] vapor *m*; — **shovel** excavadora *f*; VT (cook) cocer al vapor; VI (give off steam) echar vapor; **to get —ed up** (angry) indignarse; (covered with vapor) empañarse
steamer [stímə-] N buque de vapor *m*
steed [stid] N corcel *m*
steel [stiɫ] N acero *m*; — **blue** azul acero *m*; — **industry** siderurgia *f*; — **mill** acería *f*; — **wool** lana de acero *f*; VT acerar; **to — oneself** prepararse
steep [stip] ADJ (hill) empinado, escarpado, acantilado; (decline) marcado; (price) excesivo; VT (tea) infusionar; VI (tea) estar en infusión, infusionarse
steeple [stípəɫ] N (spire) aguja *f*, chapitel *m*; (bell tower) campanario *m*
steer [stir] N (young bovine) novillo *m*; (grown

bovine) buey *m*; VI/VT (a car) conducir, manejar; (a ship) gobernar, timonear; VI (turn) girar, doblar; **to — clear of** evitar; **to — a conversation** desviar una conversación; **the car —s easily** el coche es fácil de conducir; **—ing** dirección *f*; **—ing wheel** volante *m*

stellar [stélə-] ADJ estelar

stem [stɛm] N (of a plant) tallo *m*; (of a leaf) pedúnculo *m*, rabo *m*; (of a glass) pie *m*; (of a pipe) cañón *m*; **— cell** célula estaminal/embrional *f*; VT detener, contener, estancar; **to — from** provenir de

stench [stɛntʃ] N hedor *m*, hediondez *f*, tufo *m*

stencil [sténsəl] N plantilla *f*, matriz *f*

stenographer [stənɑ́grəfə-] N taquígrafo -fa *mf*

step [stɛp] N (in walking, dancing) paso *m*; (on stairs) peldaño *m*, escalón *m*; (in music) tono *m*; **— by —** paso a paso; **—ladder** escalera *f*; **to take —s** (walk) dar pasos; VI dar un paso; **— this way** pase por aquí; **to — aside** hacerse a un lado; **to — back** retroceder; **to — down** (descend) bajar; (resign) renunciar; **to — off** bajar; **to — off a distance** medir a pasos una distancia; **to — on** pisar, pisotear; **to — on the gas** pisar el acelerador; **to — out** salir; (act) tomar medidas; **to — up** subir; **in — with the music** al compás de la música

stepbrother [stépbrʌðə-] N hermanastro *m*

stepdaughter [stépdɔ́tə-] N hijastra *f*

stepfather [stépfɑðə-] N padrastro *m*

stepmother [stépmʌðə-] N madrastra *f*

steppe [stɛp] N estepa *f*

stepsister [stépsɪstə-] N hermanastra *f*

stepson [stépsʌn] N hijastro *m*

stereo [stério] ADJ & N estéreo *m*

stereotype [stériətaɪp] N estereotipo *m*

sterile [stérəl] ADJ estéril

sterility [stərílɪtɪ] N esterilidad *f*

sterilize [stérəlaɪz] VT esterilizar

stern [stɜ-n] ADJ austero, severo, adusto; N (of a ship) popa *f*

sternum [stɜ́-nəm] N esternón *m*

steroid [stérɔɪd] N esteroide *m*

stethoscope [stéθəskop] N estetoscopio *m*

stew [stu] VI/VT (cook) estofar[se], guisar[se]; VI (worry) preocuparse; N estofado *m*, guiso *m*; **to be in a —** estar preocupado

steward [stúə-d] N (manager) administrador *m*; (on a ship) camarero *m*; (on an airplane) auxiliar de vuelo *m*

stewardess [stúə-dɪs] N (on a ship) camarera *f*; (on an airplane) auxiliar de vuelo *f*, azafata *f*

stick [stɪk] N (of wood) palo *m*, vara *f*; (of firewood) raja *f*; (of dynamite) cartucho *m*; **— shift** palanca de cambios *f*; **—-up** atraco *m*, asalto *m*; VI/VT (adhere) pegar[se], adherir[se]; VT (place) poner, meter; (stab) clavar, pinchar; VI (become jammed) atascarse; **— 'em up!** ¡arriba las manos! **to — out** salir, sobresalir; **to — out one's head** asomar la cabeza; **to — out one's tongue** sacar la lengua; **to — to a job** persistir en una tarea; **to — up** (point up) estar parado de punta; **to — up for** defender; **to — someone up** asaltar/atracar a alguien

sticker [stíkə-] N (thistle) abrojo *m*; (adhesive) etiqueta adhesiva *f*

sticky [stíki] ADJ pegajoso

stiff [stɪf] ADJ (leather, cardboard) tieso, duro; (drink) fuerte, cargado; (shirt) almidonado; (back) entumecido; (test) difícil; (breeze) fuerte; (personality) envarado; (climb) arduo; (price) alto; **to get —** entumecerse; N (cadaver) *fam* fiambre *m*

stiffen [stɪfən] VI/VT (leather) endurecer[se]; (back) entumecer[se]; (shirt) almidonar[se]; **to — up** agarrotar[se]

stiffness [stífnɪs] N (of leather) dureza *f*, tiesura *f*; (of one's back) entumecimiento *m*; (of one's personality) envaramiento *m*; (of resistance) firmeza *f*

stifle [stáɪfəł] VI/VT ahogar[se], sofocar[se]; **to — a yawn** contener un bostezo

stigma [stígmə] N estigma *m*

stigmatize [stígmətaɪz] VI/VT estigmatizar

still [stɪł] ADJ (not moving) quieto; (quiet) silencioso; **—born** nacido muerto; **— life** naturaleza muerta *f*; VT acallar; ADV todavía, aún; **he's — here** todavía está [aquí]; CONJ de todos modos, en todo caso; **—, it's a good buy** en todo caso, es una ganga; N (for distilling) alambique *m*; (quiet) silencio *m*

stillness [stíłnɪs] N (not moving) quietud *f*; (silence) silencio *m*

stilt [stɪłt] N (for walking) zanco *m*; (support) pilote *m*

stilted [stíłtɪd] ADJ (personality) envarado; (style) afectado

stimulant [stímjələnt] ADJ & N estimulante *m*

stimulate [stímjəlet] VT estimular

stimulation [stɪmjəléʃən] N estimulación *f*

stimulus [stímjələs] N estímulo *m*

sting [stɪŋ] VI/VT (insects, thorns) picar; (insects) aguijonear; VT (shampoo) hacer picar; (rain) azotar; (cheat) timar; N (pain) picadura *f*; (stinger) aguijón *m*; (confidence game) golpe *m*; **— of remorse** punzada de remordimiento *f*; **—ray** manta raya *f*

stinger [stíŋə-] N aguijón *m*

stinginess [stínʤɪnɪs] N tacañería *f*, mezquindad *f*

stingy [stínʤi] ADJ mezquino, tacaño

stink [stɪŋk] VI (smell bad) heder, apestar; **to — of** heder a; **to — up** dar mal olor a; **your performance —s** tu actuación es un desastre; N hedor *m*

stipend [stáɪpɪnd] N (fellowship) beca *f*; (salary) estipendio *m*
stipulate [stípjəlet] VT estipular
stipulation [stɪpjəléʃən] N estipulación *f*
stir [stɜ˞] VI (move) bullir, rebullir; (awaken) despertar; VT (mix) revolver; (move emotionally) conmover; (stoke) atizar; **to — up** (trouble) provocar, suscitar; (an old grudge) remover; **to —-fry** saltear; N —-**crazy** claustrofóbico; **to give something a** — revolver algo; **to cause a** — causar revuelo
stirring [stɜ́˞ɪŋ] ADJ (moving) conmovedor
stirrup [stɜ́˞rəp] N estribo *m*
stitch [stɪtʃ] N (in sewing) puntada *f*; (on a wound) punto *m*; **to be in —es** desternillarse de risa; VI/VT coser
St. Kitts and Nevis [sentkítsənnívɪs] N San Cristóbal y Nieves *m*
St. Lucia [sentlúʃə] N Santa Lucía *f*
St. Lucian [sentlúʃən] ADJ & N santalucense *mf*
stock [stɑk] N (selection) surtido *m*; (reserves) existencias *f pl*; (livestock) ganado *m*; (lineage) estirpe *f*; (shares) acciones *f pl*, valores *m pl*; (in grafting) patrón *m*; (broth) caldo *m*; **—broker** corredor -ora de bolsa *mf*, bolsista *mf*; **— company** sociedad anónima *f*; **— exchange** bolsa de valores *f*; **—holder** accionista *mf*; **— market** mercado de valores *m*, bolsa de valores *f*; **— market trends** tendencias bursátiles *f pl*; **— options** opciones *f pl*; **—pile** acopio *m*; **—room** depósito *m*; **— size** tamaño ordinario *m*; **—yard** corral *m*; **in** — en existencia; **out of** — agotado; VT (sell) vender; (fill shelves) abastecer; **to — up on** surtirse de, acumular; **to —pile** acopiar; ADJ (trite) trillado
stockade [stɑkéd] N (fence) estacada *f*, empalizada *f*; (prison) prisión militar *f*
stocking [stɑ́kɪŋ] N (hose) media *f*; (sock) calcetín *m*
stocky [stɑ́ki] ADJ robusto
stoic [stóɪk] ADJ & N estoico -ca *mf*
stoke [stok] VT (fire) atizar; (engine) alimentar
stole [stol] (fur) estola *f*
stole [stol] *see* steal
stolen [stólən] *see* steal
stomach [stʌ́mək] N (organ) estómago *m*; (belly) panza *f*, barriga *f*; **he has a big** — es barrigón; **to lie on one's** — estar panza abajo; VT (tolerate) aguantar
stomp [stɑmp] VI pisar fuerte; VT (crush) pisotear; (defeat) aplastar
stone [ston] N (rock, gem) piedra *f*; (in fruit) hueso *m*; (in kidneys) cálculo *m*; **within a —'s throw** a tiro de piedra; **— Age** Edad de Piedra *f*; ADJ —-**deaf** sordo como una tapia; VT (a person) lapidar; (a fruit) deshuesar; **to —wall** bloquear, ignorar
stony [stóni] ADJ (made of stone) pétreo; (driveway) pedregoso; (silence) sepulcral
stood [stʊd] *see* stand
stool [stuł] N (furniture) taburete *m*, banqueta *f*; (excrement) materia fecal *f*; **— pigeon** soplón -ona *mf*, chivato -ta *mf*
stoop [stup] VI (bend over) agacharse; (have bad posture) encorvarse; **to — to** rebajarse a; N (posture) encorvamiento *m*; (porch) entrada *f*, porche *m*; **to walk with a** — andar encorvado; ADJ —-**shouldered** encorvado, cargado de espaldas
stop [stɑp] VI (halt) parar, detenerse; (malfunction) parar[se]; VT (halt) parar, detener; (cancel) cancelar; (suspend) suspender; (plug) tapar; **to — at nothing** no tener escrúpulos; **to — by/in** visitar; **to — from** impedir; **to — over at** hacer escala en; **to — short** parar en seco; **to — up** tapar, atascar; **it —ped raining** paró/dejó de llover; N parada *f*, detención *f*; (on organ) registro *m*; **—gap** arreglo provisorio *m*; **—light** semáforo *m*; **—over** escala *f*; **— sign** *Sp* stop *m*; *Am* señal de pare *f*; *Mex* alto *m*; **—volley** (tennis) dejada de volea *f*; **—watch** cronómetro *m*; **to bring to a** — parar; **to make a** — parar
stoppage [stɑ́pɪdʒ] N interrupción *f*; (strike) huelga *f*
stopper [stɑ́pə˞] N tapón *m*
storage [stɔ́ɹɪdʒ] N almacenaje *m*, almacenamiento *m*; (of electronic data) almacenamiento *m*; **— battery** acumulador *m*; **— device** dispositivo de almacenamiento *m*; **to keep in** — almacenar
store [stɔr] N (shop) tienda *f*, almacén *m*; (supply) reserva *f*, provisión *f*; **—house** (warehouse) almacén *m*, depósito *m*; (source) mina *f*, fuente *f*; **—keeper** tendero -ra *mf*, almacenista *mf*; **—room** almacén *m*, depósito *m*; **what is in — for us?** ¿qué nos espera? VT (commercial goods) almacenar; (personal effects) guardar; **to — up** acumular
stork [stɔ˞k] N cigüeña *f*
storm [stɔ˞m] N (on land) tormenta *f*; (at sea) tempestad *f*, temporal *m*; (of protest) ola *f*; **— troops** tropas de asalto *f pl*; VT (attack) tomar por asalto; VI **to — in/out** entrar/salir en tromba
stormy [stɔ́˞mɪ] ADJ tormentoso, tempestuoso
story [stɔ́ɹi] N (tale) cuento *m*, historia *f*; (newspaper article) artículo *m*; (lie) mentira *f*; (information) información *f*; (plot) argumento *m*, trama *f*; (floor) piso *m*
stout [stʌʊt] ADJ (fat) corpulento; (robust) robusto, fornido; (strong) fuerte; (courageous) valiente
stove [stov] N (for heating) estufa *f*; (for cooking) cocina *f*; estufa *f*
stow [sto] VT (keep) guardar; (hide) esconder;

(put in cargo hold) estibar; **to — away on a ship** viajar de polizón

stowaway [stóəwe] N polizón -ona *mf*

straddle [strǽdl] VI/VT estar a horcajadas; VT (a fence) ponerse a horcajadas; (one's legs) abrir; (not take sides) no comprometerse

strafe [stref] VT ametrallar

straggle [strǽgəl] VI **to — along/behind** rezagarse; **to — in** entrar de a pocos

straight [stret] ADJ (not curved) recto; (not tilted) derecho; (in succession) seguido; (hair) lacio, liso; (teeth) parejo; (frank) franco; (heterosexual) heterosexual; **— A's** sobresaliente en todo; **—edge** regla *f*; **— face** cara seria *f*; **— flush** escalera de color *f*; ADJ **—forward** (honest) honesto; (simple) sencillo, campechano; (clear) claro; ADV **— ahead** todo derecho, todo recto; **for two hours —** dos horas seguidas; **to come — home** volver derecho a casa; **to leave — after lunch** irse justo después de comer; **to set a person —** aclararle algo a alguien; **tell me —** dímelo francamente; **he can't think —** no puede pensar con claridad; N (of a racetrack) recta *f*

straighten [stréṭn̩] VI/VT enderezar[se]; (situation) arreglar[se]; VT (hair) alisar, *RP* laciar; **to — out a child** enderezar a un niño

straightness [strétnɪs] N derechura *f*

strain [stren] VI (pull) tironear; (try hard) esforzarse; VT (exhaust) agotar; (hurt voice) forzar; (injure a joint) torcer; (injure a muscle) sufrir un tirón en; (hurt a relationship) crear una tirantez en; VI/VT (filter) colar[se]; N (effort) esfuerzo *m*; (injury) torcedura *f*; (pressure) presión *f*; (trouble in a relationship) tirantez *f*; (lineage) cepa *f*

strainer [strénə-] N colador *m*

strait [stret] N estrecho *m*; **in dire —s** en aprietos; **—jacket** camisa de fuerza *f*, chaleco de fuerza *m*; ADJ **—laced** puritano

strand [strænd] VI/VT (a ship) encallar, varar; VT (a person) dejar plantado; **to be —ed** (boat) estar encallado; (person) quedar plantado; N (beach) costa *f*, playa *f*; (of rope) ramal *m*; (of thread) hebra *f*; (of hair) mechón *m*

strange [strenʤ] ADJ (bizarre) extraño, raro; (unknown) desconocido

strangeness [strénʤnɪs] N (unusualness) lo extraño, rareza *f*; (unexpectedness) lo inesperado

stranger [strénʤə-] N (unknown person) extraño -ña *mf*, desconocido -da *mf*; (outsider) forastero -ra *mf*; **to be no — to something** tener experiencia con algo

strangle [strǽŋgəl] VI/VT estrangular[se]; VT (creativity) coartar; N **—hold** (in wrestling) llave al cuello *f*; (in markets) monopolio *m*

strap [stræp] N (leather band) correa *f*, tira *f*; (on a dress) tirante *m*; VT atar con correa; **to — in** amarrar[se], abrochar[se]

stratagem [strǽDəʤəm] N estratagema *f*

strategic [strətíʤɪk] ADJ estratégico

strategy [strǽDəʤi] N estrategia *f*

stratosphere [strǽDəsfɪr] N estratosfera *f*

stratum [strǽDəm] N estrato *m*

straw [strɔ] N paja *f* (also for drinking); **—berry** fresa *f*; **— man** testaferro *m*; **— vote** votación de prueba *f*; ADJ **—-colored** pajizo

stray [stre] VI (deviate, digress) desviarse; (get lost) perderse; (wander) vagar; (sin) descarriarse, perderse; ADJ extraviado, perdido; N perro/gato mostrenco *m*

streak [strik] N (line) raya *f*; (vein) vena *f*; (of luck) racha *f*; (of light) rayo *m*; VI (run naked) correr desnudo; (get discolored) aclararse

stream [strim] N (jet) chorro *m*; (river) río *m*; (brook) arroyo *m*; ADJ **—lined** (vehículo) aerodinámico; (business) racionalizado; VI (water) correr, fluir; (blood) derramar; **to — out** brotar, manar; **to — in** entrar a raudales

streaming [strímɪŋ] N corriente *f*, flujo *m*; **— audio** flujo continuo de datos de audio *m*; **— video** flujo continuo de datos de vídeo *m*

street [strit] N calle *f*; **—car** tranvía *f*; **—lamp** farol *m*, poste de alumbrado *m*; **— sweeper** barrendero -ra *mf*

strength [strɛnθ] N fuerza *f*; (spiritual) firmeza *f*; **on the — of** en base a

strengthen [strɛ́ŋθən] VI/VT fortalecer[se], reforzar[se]

strengthening [strɛ́ŋθənɪŋ] N fortalecimiento *m*

strenuous [strénjuəs] ADJ arduo

strep throat [strépθrót] N infección por estreptococo *f*

stress [stres] N (tension) tensión *f*; (strain) estrés *m*; (pressure) esfuerzo *m*; (emphasis) énfasis *m*; (accent) acento *m*; **— test** prueba de esfuerzo *f*; VT (emphasize) enfatizar; (accentuate) acentuar; (exert force) someter a un esfuerzo; (put under pressure) estresar; **to — out** estresarse

stressful [strésfəl] ADJ estresante

stretch [strɛtʃ] VI/VT (make or become longer) estirar[se], alargar[se]; (extend) extender[se]; (exaggerate) exagerar; **to — oneself** estirarse, desperezarse; **to — out** (lengthen) extender[se]; (lie) tumbarse, tenderse; N (act of stretching) desperezo *m*; (segment of road) trecho *m*, tramo *m*; (period of time) período *m*; (exaggeration) exageración *f*; **— mark** estría *f*

stretcher [strétʃə-] N camilla *f*

strew [stru] VT esparcir

strewn [strun] *see* strew

stricken [stríkən] ADJ (with disease) aquejado; (by a flood) afectado; (with fear) aterrado

stricken [stríkən] *see* strike

strict [strɪkt] ADJ estricto; **in — confidence** en absoluta confianza
stridden [strídn̩] *see* stride
stride [straɪd] VI caminar a paso largo, dar zancadas; N (gait) paso *m*; (long step) zancada *f*, tranco *m*
strident [stráɪdənt] ADJ estridente
strife [straɪf] N conflictos *m pl*
strike [straɪk] VI/VT (hit) golpear, pegar; (stop work) hacer huelga [contra]; VT (find oil, etc.) dar con, encontrar; (occur to) ocurrírsele a uno; (cross out) tachar; (mark by chimes) dar; (light a match, etc.) encender; (make a coin) acuñar; **to — a compromise/deal** llegar a un acuerdo; **to — one's fancy** antojársele a uno; **to — out** (cross out) tachar; (set forth) encaminarse; (fail) fracasar; (in baseball) poncharse; **to — someone out** ponchar a alguien; **to — up a conversation** entablar conversación; **to — up a friendship** trabar amistad; **how does she — you?** ¿qué tal te parece? N (work stoppage) huelga *f*; (attack) ataque *m*; (finding of oil) descubrimiento *m*; (in baseball) strike *m*; **—breaker** esquirol *m*, rompehuelgas *m sg*; **—out** ponchado *m*, ponche *m*; **—through** tachado *m*; **— zone** zona de strike *f*; **called —** strike cantado *m*
striker [stráɪkɚ] N (person on strike) huelguista *mf*; (of a bell) badajo *m*; (in soccer) artillero -ra *mf*
striking [stráɪkɪŋ] ADJ (unusual, conspicuous) notable; (attractive) llamativo; (on strike) en huelga
string [strɪŋ] N (cord) cuerda *f*, cordel *m*; (of pearls, lies) sarta *f*; (of questions) serie *f*; (of data) secuencia *f*; (of beans) fibra *f*; (of garlic, peppers) ristra *f*; **— bean** habichuela *f*, judía verde *f*; **—s** (in an orchestra) cuerdas *f pl*; (on a tennis racket) cordaje *m*, encordado *m*; **no —s attached** sin condiciones; VT (beads) ensartar; (a musical instrument) encordar; **to — along** tener en ascuas; **to — out** extender[se], prolongar[se]; **to — up** colgar, ahorcar; **to be strung out** estar muy tenso
stringent [strínd͡ʒənt] ADJ (law, need) riguroso; (time limit) estrecho, ajustado
strip [strɪp] VI/VT (make/get naked) desnudar[se]; VT (remove bark) descortezar; (remove leaves) deshojar; (remove sheets) deshacer; (remove varnish) quitar el barniz; (damage gears) estropear el engranaje; **to — search** registrar al desnudo; **to —-mine** explotar a cielo abierto; N (of a thing) tira *f*; (of land) faja *f*; **— mall** centro comercial *m*; **— search** registro al desnudo *m*
stripe [straɪp] N (band) raya *f*, lista *f*, banda *f*; (military insignia) galón *m*; (type) tipo *m*
striped [straɪpt, stráɪpɪd] ADJ listado, rayado
strive [straɪv] VI esforzarse por, luchar por
striven [strívən] *see* strive
strode [strod] *see* stride
stroke [strok] N (in golf, tennis, of luck, of genius) golpe *m*; (cerebral hemorrhage) derrame cerebral *m*; (movement in swimming) brazada *f*; (style in swimming) estilo *m*; (of a piston) carrera *f*; (of a painter's brush) pincelada *f*, trazo *m*; (of lightning) rayo *m*; **at the — of ten** al dar las diez; VT (pet) acariciar; (praise) halagar
stroll [stroł] VI dar un paseo, pasearse; N paseo *m*, caminata *f*
stroller [stróləɚ] N cochecito de bebé *m*
strong [strɔŋ] ADJ fuerte; (husky) recio; (eyesight, probability) bueno; (protest) enérgico; (views, faith, support) firme; (features, resemblance) marcado; (argument) sólido; **—hold** (fortress) fortaleza *f*; (center of activity) baluarte *m*; **—-willed** (resolute) resuelto, decidido; (stubborn) terco; ADV **to be going —** seguir activo; VT **to —-arm** intimidar
strongly [strɔ́ŋli] ADV (argue, object) enérgicamente; (pull) con fuerza
strove [strov] *see* strive
struck [strʌk] *see* strike
structural [stráktʃərəł] ADJ estructural
structure [stráktʃəɚ] N (the way parts are arranged) estructura *f*; (thing constructed) construcción *f*; VT estructurar
structuring [stráktʃəɚɪŋ] N estructuración *f*
struggle [strʌ́gəł] VI (with difficulties) luchar, bregar; (with an assailant) forcejear; **she —s in math** la pasa mal en matemáticas; N lucha *f*; (of ideas) pugna *f*, lucha *f*; (fight) contienda *f*, forcejeo *m*; **it's a —** da mucho trabajo
strung [strʌŋ] *see* string
strut [strʌt] VI pavonearse; N pavoneo *m*; (support) tirante *m*, puntal *m*; (shock absorber) amortiguador *m*
strychnine [stríknaɪn] N estricnina *f*
stub [stʌb] N talón *m*; VT **to — one's toe** dar[se] un tropezón, reventarse el dedo
stubble [stʌ́bəł] N (of a crop) rastrojo *m*; (of a beard) barba de unos días *f*
stubborn [stʌ́bə-n] ADJ terco, testarudo
stubbornness [stʌ́bə-nnɪs] N terquedad *f*, testarudez *f*
stucco [stʌ́ko] N estuco *m*; VT estucar
stuck [stʌk] ADJ (unable to move) atascado; (adhering) pegado; **to be — on someone** estar loco por alguien; **—-up** estirado, presumido
stuck [stʌk] *see* stick
stud [stʌd] N (knob) tachuela *f*, tachón *m*; (earring) arete *m*; (cufflink) gemelo *m*; (on shirtfront) botón *m*; (horse, man) semental *m*; (horse) garañón *m*; VT tachonar
student [stúdn̩t] N alumno -na *mf*; (secondary,

university) estudiante *mf*; **— body** alumnado *m*; ADJ estudiantil

studio [stúDio] N estudio *m*, taller *m*; **— apartment** estudio *m*

studious [stúdiəs] ADJ estudioso

study [stʌ́di] N estudio *m*; VT estudiar

stuff [stʌf] N (material) materia *f*, material *m*; (things) trastos *m pl*, bártulos *m pl*; (cloth) paño *m*, tela *f*; (affair) cosa *f*; (junk) cachivaches *m pl*; VT (mattress) rellenar; (dead animal) embalsamar, disecar; **to — into** meter en; **I'm —ed** estoy lleno

stuffing [stʌ́fɪŋ] N relleno *m*

stuffy [stʌ́fi] ADJ (person) envarado; (air) viciado; (nose) tapado

stumble [stʌ́mbəł] VI (trip) tropezar, trastabillar, dar un traspié; (stutter) balbucear; **to — out** salir a tropezones; **to — upon** tropezar con; **stumbling block** obstáculo *m*; N tropezón *m*, tropiezo *m*, traspié *m*

stump [stʌmp] N (of a tree) tocón *m*, cepa *f*; (of a tooth) raigón *m*; (of a limb) muñón *m*; **to be on the —** hacer una campaña electoral; VT (baffle) dejar perplejo; (remove stumps) arrancar los tocones de; **to — the country** recorrer el país haciendo campaña

stun [stʌn] VT (shock, surprise) dejar atónito, pasmar; (render unconscious) dejar sin sentido; **— gun** pistola tranquilizante *f*

stung [stʌŋ] *see* sting

stunk [stʌŋk] *see* stink

stunning [stʌ́nɪŋ] ADJ (shocking) pasmoso; (beautiful) elegante, bellísimo

stunt [stʌnt] VT (stop growth) atrofiar; (do acrobatic tricks) hacer acrobacia; N (feat) acrobacia *f*; (for publicity) maniobra *f*; **—man** doble *m*; **—woman** doble *f*; **to pull a —** hacerse el listo

stupefy [stúpəfaɪ] VT (make lethargic) atontar, embrutecer; (astonish) dejar estupefacto, alelar

stupendous [stupéndəs] ADJ estupendo

stupid [stúpɪd] ADJ tonto, estúpido, majadero

stupidity [stupídɪDi] N tontería *f*, estupidez *f*, majadería *f*

stupor [stúpə-] N estupor *m*

sturdy [stɜ́-Di] ADJ (person) fornido, fuerte; (construction) sólido, robusto

stutter [stʌ́Də-] VI tartamudear, tartajear; VT decir tartamudeando; N (act of stuttering) tartamudeo *m*; (speech defect) tartamudez *f*

stutterer [stʌ́Dərə-] N tartamudo -da *mf*

stuttering [stʌ́DərIŋ] ADJ tartamudo; N (act of stuttering) tartamudeo *m*; (speech defect) tartamudez *f*

St. Vincent and the Grenadines [sentvínsəntənðəgrénədinz] N San Vicente y las Granadinas *m*

sty [staɪ] N (for pigs) pocilga *f*; (in eye) orzuelo *m*

style [staɪł] N estilo *m*; (type) modelo *m*; **— sheet** página de estilo *f*; **out of —** fuera de moda; **like it's going out of —** como loco; VT (a book) intitular; (hair) peinar; **he —s himself Professor Smith** se hace llamar Profesor Smith

stylish [stáɪlɪʃ] ADJ elegante, de moda

stylistic [staɪlístɪk] ADJ estilístico

stylistics [staɪlístɪks] N estilística *f*

stymie, stymy [stáɪmi] VT obstaculizar

Styrofoam™ [stáɪrəfom] N poliestireno *m*

suave [swɑv] ADJ urbano, educado

subcommittee [sʌ́bkəmɪDi] N subcomité *m*

subconscious [sʌbkʌ́nʃəs] ADJ subconsciente

subcontract [sʌbkʌ́ntrækt] VT subcontratar

subdivide [sʌbdɪváɪd] VT subdividir

subdivision [sʌ́bdɪvɪʒən] N subdivisión *f*; (of land) parcelación *f*

subdue [səbdú] VT (overcome, vanquish) sojuzgar, someter, rendir; (repress) reprimir; (attenuate) atenuar

subdued [səbdúd] ADJ (atmosphere) tranquilo; (mood) deprimido; (lighting, color) tenue

subject[1] [sʌ́bʤɪkt] N (of a king) súbdito -ta *mf*; (of a sentence, in an experiment) sujeto *m*; (in school) asignatura *f*, materia *f*; **— matter** tema *m*; ADV LOC **— to** (changes, laws, conditions) sujeto a; (depression, earthquakes) propenso a

subject[2] [səbʤ́ékt] VT someter

subjection [səbʤ́ékʃən] N sometimiento *m*

subjective [səbʤ́éktɪv] ADJ subjetivo

subjectivity [sʌbʤ́ektívɪDi] N subjetividad *f*

subjugate [sʌ́bʤəget] VT sojuzgar, avasallar

subjunctive [səbʤʌ́ŋktɪv] ADJ & N subjuntivo *m*

sublet [sʌ́blét] VI/VT subarrendar

sublime [səbláɪm] ADJ sublime

submarine [sʌbmərín, sʌ́bmərin] ADJ submarino; N submarino *m*

submerge [səbmɜ́ʤ] VI/VT sumergir[se]

submerged [səbmɜ́ʤd] ADJ inmerso, sumergido

submission [səbmíʃən] N (humility) sumisión *f*; (subjugation) sometimiento *m*, sumisión *f*; (sending) entrega *f*, envío *m*

submissive [səbmísɪv] ADJ sumiso

submit [səbmít] VI/VT someter[se]; (to a judge) elevar[se]; **to — a report** presentar un informe

subordinate[1] [səbórdnɪt] ADJ & N subordinado -da *mf*, subalterno -na *mf*

subordinate[2] [səbórdnet] VT subordinar

subpar [sʌ́bpár] ADJ inferior

subpoena [səpínə] N citación *f*, orden de comparecencia *f*

subroutine [sʌ́brutin] N subrutina *f*

subscribe [səbskráɪb] VI (underwrite, sign) suscribir; (receive a magazine) abonarse,

suscribirse; (agree with) adherirse a

subscriber [səbskráɪbɚ] N (to shares) suscriptor -ora *mf*; (to services) abonado -da *mf*; (to a magazine) suscriptor -ora *mf*, abonado -da *mf*; (to an idea) partidario -ria *mf*

subscript [sʌ́bskrɪpt] N subíndice *m*

subscription [səbskrípʃən] N suscripción *f*, abono *m*

subsequent [sʌ́bsɪkwənt] ADJ subsiguiente

subsequently [sʌ́bsɪkwəntli] N posteriormente, con posterioridad *f*

subservient [səbsɝ́viənt] ADJ servil

subside [səbsáɪd] VI (sediment) hundirse; (water level) bajar; (volcano, storm, anger) calmarse, aquietarse

subsidiary [səbsídɪɛri] ADJ subsidiario; N sucursal *f*, filial *f*

subsidize [sʌ́bsɪdaɪz] VT subvencionar, subsidiar

subsidy [sʌ́bsɪdɪ] N subvención *f*, subsidio *m*

substance [sʌ́bstəns] N sustancia *f*; **— abuse** abuso de sustancias *m*

substandard [sʌbstǽndɚd] ADJ de calidad inferior

substantial [səbstǽnʃəl] ADJ (changes) sustancial; (food, lecture) sustancioso; (furniture) sólido; (amount) considerable, importante; **to be in — agreement** estar básicamente de acuerdo

substantiate [səbstǽnʃiet] VT (verify) verificar; (prove) probar

substantive [sʌ́bstəntɪv] ADJ & N sustantivo *m*

substitute [sʌ́bstɪtut] VT sustituir, reemplazar; **I —d water for milk** usé agua en vez de leche, sustituí/reemplacé la leche por agua; VI **John —d for Mary** Juan sustituyó/reemplazó a María; N (one who substitutes) sustituto *m*, reemplazo *m*; (teacher, athlete) suplente *mf*; (thing) sucedáneo *m*

substitution [sʌbstɪtúʃən] N sustitución *f*; **the — of water for milk** la sustitución de leche por agua

subterfuge [sʌ́btə-fjuʤ] N subterfugio *m*

subterranean [sʌbtərénɪən] ADJ subterráneo

subtitle [sʌ́btaɪdl] N subtítulo *m*

subtle [sʌ́dl] ADJ sutil

subtlety [sʌ́dlti] N sutileza *f*

subtotal [sʌ́btoʊdl] N subtotal *m*

subtract [səbtrǽkt] VT (deduct) restar; (take away) sustraer

subtraction [səbtrǽkʃən] N sustracción *f*, resta *f*

suburb [sʌ́bɝb] N barrio residencial periférico *m*

suburban [səbɝ́bən] ADJ (residential) residencial; (on the outskirts) periférico

subversive [səbvɝ́sɪv] ADJ subversivo

subway [sʌ́bwe] N metropolitano *m*, metro *m*, subterráneo *m*

succeed [səksíd] VI (be successful) tener éxito; (manage) lograr; **to — to** heredar; VT (follow) suceder a

success [səksés] N éxito *m*

successful [səksésfəl] ADJ (person) exitoso; (effort) productivo, satisfactorio; **to be —** tener éxito

succession [səksséʃən] N sucesión *f*

successive [səksésɪv] ADJ sucesivo

successor [səksésə-] N sucesor -ora *mf*

succinct [səksíŋkt] ADJ sucinto, escueto

succor [sʌ́kɚ] N socorro *m*; VT socorrer

succumb [səkʌ́m] VI sucumbir

such [sʌtʃ] ADJ tal; **— as** tal como; **at — and — a place** en tal o cual lugar; **he's — an idiot!** ¡es tan idiota! **in — a case** en tal caso / en semejante caso; **there's no — thing** eso no existe; PRON **hobbies, pastimes, and —** hobbies, pasatiempos y cosas por el estilo; **a car — as yours** un coche como el tuyo; ADV **— nice neighbors** vecinos tan simpáticos

suck [sʌk] VI/VT chupar; (suckle) mamar; (vacuum, pump) aspirar; **to be —ed into** ser arrastrado a; VI; **to — in air** aspirar

sucker [sʌ́kɚ] N (gullible person) primo -ma *mf*; (lollipop) *Sp* piruli *m*; *Mex* paleta *f*; *RP* chupetín *m*

sucrose [súkros] N sacarosa *f*

suction [sʌ́kʃən] N succión *f*, aspiración *f*

Sudan [sudǽn] N Sudán *m*

Sudanese [sudn̩íz] ADJ & N sudanés -esa *mf*

sudden [sʌdn̩] ADJ súbito, repentino, brusco; **— death** (also in sports) muerte súbita *f*; **— infant death syndrome** síndrome de muerte infantil súbita *m*; **all of a —** de repente, de improviso

suddenly [sʌdn̩li] ADV de repente, repentinamente

suddenness [sʌdn̩nɪs] N brusquedad *f*, lo repentino

suds [sʌdz] N espuma *f*

sue [su] VI/VT demandar, poner pleito; **to — for** pedir, suplicar; **to — for damages** demandar por daños y perjuicios

suede [swed] N gamuza *f*, ante *m*

suffer [sʌ́fə-] VI/VT (feel pain) sufrir, padecer; VT (tolerate) tolerar

sufferer [sʌ́fərɚ] N paciente *mf*

suffering [sʌ́fə-ɪŋ] N sufrimiento *m*, padecimiento *m*

suffice [səfáɪs] VI/VT bastar, ser suficiente

sufficient [səfíʃənt] ADJ suficiente, bastante

suffix [sʌ́fɪks] N sufijo *m*

suffocate [sʌ́fəket] VI/VT ahogar[se], sofocar[se]; (to die, kill) asfixiar[se]

suffocation [sʌfəkéʃən] N ahogo *m*, sofoco *m*

suffrage [sʌ́frɪʤ] N sufragio *m*

sugar [ʃúgɚ] N azúcar *mf*; (endearment) cariño *m*; **— cane** caña de azúcar *f*; VT azucarar; **to — the pill** dorar la píldora

suggest [səgʤ́ést] VT (propose) sugerir; (hint) insinuar; **—ed retail price** precio

sugerido *m*

suggestion [səgʤéstʃən] N (proposal) sugerencia *f*; (in hypnosis) sugestión *f*

suggestive [səgʤéstɪv] ADJ insinuante; **to be — of** evocar

suicide [súɪsaɪd] N (act) suicidio *m*; (person) suicida *mf*; **to commit —** suicidarse

suit [sut] N (clothes) traje *m*; (in cards) palo *m*, color *m*; (lawsuit) demanda *f*, pleito *m*, querella *f*; **—case** maleta *f*, valija *f*; VT (adapt) adaptar, ajustar; (satisfy) satisfacer; (look good) quedarle bien a, sentarle bien a; (be convenient, appropriate) convenir, venir bien; **— yourself** haz lo que te parezca

suitable [súʊəbəł] ADJ (appropriate) apropiado; (apt) apto

suitably [súʊəbli] ADV como corresponde

suite [swit] N (series) serie *f*; (series of rooms, musical composition) suite *f*; (furniture) juego *m*; (software) paquete de programas de productividad *m*

suitor [súʊə-] N pretendiente *m*, galán *m*

sulfate, sulphate [sʌ́łfet] N sulfato *m*

sulfide, sulphide [sʌ́łfaɪd] N sulfuro *m*

sulfur, sulphur [sʌ́łfə-] N azufre *m*

sulfuric, sulphuric [sʌłfjúrɪk] ADJ sulfúrico

sulk [sʌłk] VI enfurruñarse; N **to be in a —** estar enfurruñado

sulky [sʌ́łki] ADJ malhumorado, enfurruñado

sullen [sʌ́lən] ADJ hosco, huraño

sully [sʌ́li] VT mancillar, ensuciar

sultry [sʌ́ltri] ADJ (hot) bochornoso, sofocante; (sensual) sensual

sum [sʌm] N suma *f*; **in —** en resumen; VI **to — up** resumir, recapitular

summarize [sʌ́mərəɪz] VI/VT resumir

summary [sʌ́mərɪ] N resumen *m*; ADJ sumario

summer [sʌ́mə-] N verano *m*, *lit* estío *m*; **— resort** balneario *m*, lugar de veraneo *m*; **— school** cursos de verano *m pl*; **—time** verano *m*; VI veranear

summit [sʌ́mɪt] N cumbre *f*, cima *f*

summon [sʌ́mən] VT (a witness) citar; (an employee, the police) llamar; N **—s** citación judicial *f*

sumptuous [sʌ́mptʃuəs] ADJ suntuoso

sun [sʌn] N sol *m*; **to —bathe** tomar el sol; **—beam** rayo de sol *m*; **—block** protector solar *m*; **—burn** quemadura de sol *f*; **—dial** reloj de sol *m*; **—down** puesta de[l] sol *f*; **—flower** girasol *m*; **—glasses** gafas de sol *f pl*, anteojos de sol *m pl*; **— lamp** lámpara solar *f*; **—light** luz del sol *f*; **—rise** salida de[l] sol *f*, amanecer *m*; **—screen** protector solar *m*; **—set** puesta de[l] sol *f*; **—shine** luz [del sol] *f*; **—spot** mancha solar *f*; **—stroke** insolación *f*; **—tan** bronceado *m*; **—up** salida del sol *f*; VI **to — oneself** tomar el sol; **to —burn** quemar[se] al sol

Sunday [sʌ́nde] N domingo *m*; **— school** escuela dominical *f*

sundry [sʌ́ndri] ADJ diversos

sung [sʌŋ] *see* sing

sunk [sʌŋk] *see* sink

sunny [sʌ́ni] ADJ (day, patio) soleado; (disposition) alegre

super [súpə-] N (of a building) conserje *m*, portero -ra *mf*; ADJ (wonderful) súper, bárbaro

superb [sʊpɝ́b] ADJ excelente

supercharger [súpə-tʃarʤə-] N sobrealimentador *m*

supercomputer [súpə-kəmpjʊtə-] N *Am* supercomputadora *f*; *Sp* superordenador *m*

superego [supə-ígo] N superego *m*, superyó *m*

superficial [supə-fíʃəł] ADJ superficial

superfluous [sʊpɝ́fluəs] ADJ superfluo

superhuman [supə-hjúmən] ADJ sobrehumano

superimpose [supə-ɪmpóz] VT superponer, sobreponer

superintendent [supə-ɪnténdənt] N (of work) superintendente *mf*, supervisor -ora *mf*; (of building) conserje *mf*, portero -ra *mf*

superior [sʊpíriə-] ADJ & N superior *mf*

superiority [sʊpiriɔ́rɪdɪ] N superioridad *f*

superlative [sʊpɝ́ləɪdɪv] ADJ & N superlativo *m*

supermarket [súpə-mɑrkɪt] N supermercado *m*, súper *m*

supernatural [supə-nǽtʃə-əł] ADJ sobrenatural

superpower [súpə-paʊə-] N superpotencia *f*

superscript [súpə-skrɪpt] N superíndice *m*

supersede [supə-síd] VT reemplazar

supersonic [supə-sʌ́nɪk] ADJ supersónico

superstar [súpə-stɑr] N superestrella *f*

superstition [supə-stíʃən] N superstición *f*

superstitious [supə-stíʃəs] ADJ supersticioso

superstore [súpə-stɔr] N hipermercado *m*

supervise [súpə-vaɪz] VI/VT supervisar, fiscalizar

supervision [supə-víʒən] N supervisión *f*, fiscalización *f*

supervisor [súpə-vaɪzə-] N supervisor -ora *mf*

supine [súpaɪn] ADJ supino

supper [sʌ́pə-] N cena *f*

supplant [səplǽnt] VT suplantar

supple [sʌ́pəł] ADJ (flexible) flexible, elástico; (agile) ágil, grácil

supplement[1] [sʌ́pləmənt] N (of a newspaper) suplemento *m*; (of a book) apéndice *m*; (of one's diet) complemento *m*

supplement[2] [sʌ́pləmɛnt] VT complementar, suplementar

supplemental [sʌpləméntəł] ADJ suplementario

supplier [səpláɪə-] N abastecedor -ora *mf*, proveedor -ora *mf*

supply [səpláɪ] VT abastecer, suministrar; N (act of supplying) abastecimiento *m*; **— and demand** oferta y demanda *f*; **in short —**

escaso; **supplies** suministros *m pl*, provisiones *f pl*; **office supplies** artículos de oficina *m pl*; **military supplies** pertrechos *m pl*

support [səpɔ́rt] VT (keep from falling) sostener, soportar; (encourage) apoyar; (facilitate) potenciar; (corroborate) corroborar; (help with computers) soportar; **to be —ed by** fundamentarse en/sobre; N (of a structure) sostén *m*, soporte *m*; (of a family) sustento *m*; (of a candidate, idea) apoyo *m*; (of a theory) respaldo *m*; (for a computer) soporte *m*; **— group** grupo de apoyo *m*

supporter [səpɔ́rdə˞] N partidario -ria *mf*, simpatizante *mf*; (in sports) hincha *mf*

supportive [səpɔ́rdɪv] ADJ solidario; **you've always been very — of us** siempre nos has apoyado

suppose [səpóz] VT suponer; **we are —d to go** tenemos que ir

supposedly [səpózɪdli] ADV supuestamente

supposition [sʌpəzíʃən] N suposición *f*, supuesto *m*

suppository [səpázɪtɔ̈ri] N supositorio *m*

suppress [səprés] VT (repress) reprimir; (eliminate) suprimir; (a revolt) sofocar

suppression [səpréʃən] N (repression) represión *f*; (elimination) supresión *f*; (of a revolt) sofocación *f*

supremacy [suprémə̈si] N supremacía *f*

supreme [suprím] ADJ supremo

surcharge [sɝ́tʃɑ̈rʤ] N recargo *m*, prima *f*

sure [ʃur] ADJ seguro; (judgment) certero; (hand) firme; **to make — of** asegurarse de; ADV **he — drinks a lot** es una esponja; **may I sit here?** —¡ ¿me puedo sentar? ¡cómo no!

surely [ʃúrli] ADV seguramente, ciertamente; **— you jest** no hablarás en serio; **he will — come** seguramente vendrá

surf [sɝf] N (breaking waves) rompientes *mf pl*; (foam) espuma *f*; (undertow) resaca *f*; **—board** tabla de surf *f*; VI/VT (on water) hacer surfing [en], surfear; (on the Internet) navegar, surfear

surface [sɝ́fɪs] N superficie *f*; (of a solid) cara *f*; VI (come to top) emerger; (turn up) salir a la luz; VT (a submarine) sacar a la superficie; (a road) revestir

surfeit [sɝ́fɪt] N (excess) exceso *m*; (feeling of fullness) hartazgo *m*; VI/VT hartar[se]

surfing [sɝ́fɪŋ] N (on water) surfing *m*; (on the Internet) navegación *f*

surge [sɝ˞ʤ] N (of people, disgust) oleada *f*; (of waves) oleaje *m*; (of electricity) sobrecarga de voltaje *f*; **— protector** protector contra sobrecargas de voltaje *m*; VI (people) precipitarse; (current) subir

surgeon [sɝ́ʤən] N cirujano -na *mf*

surgery [sɝ́ʤəri] N cirujía *f*; (room) quirófano *m*

surgical [sɝ́ʤɪkəł] ADJ quirúrgico; **— dressing** vendaje quirúrgico *m*; **— instruments** instrumentos quirúrgicos *m pl*

Suriname, Surinam [sʊ́rɪnɑm] N Surinam *m*

Surinamese [sʊrɪnɑmíz] ADJ & N surinamés -esa *mf*

surly [sɝ́li] ADJ malhumorado, hosco, arisco

surmise [sɝ˞máɪz] VT conjeturar, suponer; N conjetura *f*, suposición *f*

surmount [sɝ˞máʊnt] VT superar

surname [sɝ́nem] N apellido *m*

surpass [sɝ˞pǽs] VT superar, sobrepujar

surpassing [sɝ˞pǽsɪŋ] N superación *f*

surplus [sɝ́plʌs] N excedente *m*, sobrante *m*, sobra *f*; (of funds) superávit *m*

surprise [sɝ˞práɪz] N sorpresa *f*; VT sorprender

surprising [sɝ˞práɪzɪŋ] ADJ sorprendente

surprisingly [sɝ˞práɪzɪŋli] ADV sorprendentemente; **not —** como era de esperar

surreal [sɝríəł] ADJ surrealista

surrealism [sɝríəlɪzəm] N surrealismo *m*

surrealist [sɝríəlɪst] N surrealista *mf*

surrealistic [sɝriəlístɪk] ADJ surrealista

surrender [sɝréndə˞] VI (accept defeat) rendir[se], darse por vencido; (give oneself up) entregarse; VT entregar; N rendición *f*

surreptitious [sɝ˞ɔptíʃəs] ADJ subrepticio

surrogate [sɝ́ɔgɪt] ADJ sustituto; **— mother** madre de alquiler *f*

surround [sɝ˞áʊnd] VT rodear, circundar; (a city) sitiar

surrounding [sɝ˞áʊndɪŋ] ADJ circundante; N **—s** alrededores *m pl*, inmediaciones *f pl*, entorno *m*

surtax [sɝ́tæks] N sobretasa *f*

surveillance [sɝ˞véləns] N vigilancia *f*

survey[1] [sɝ˞vé] VT (evaluate) evaluar; (measure) medir; (contemplate) contemplar; (poll) encuestar

survey[2] [sɝ́ve] N (inspection) reconocimiento *m*, inspección *f*; (measure) medición *f*; (overview) panorama *m*; (poll) encuesta *f*, sondeo *m*; **— course** curso general *m*

surveyor [sɝ˞véə˞] N agrimensor -ora *mf*

survival [sɝ˞váɪvəł] N supervivencia *f*, sobrevivencia *f*; (subsistence) subsistencia *f*; **the — of the fittest** la supervivencia del más apto

survive [sɝ˞váɪv] VI/VT sobrevivir (also live longer than); (subsist) subsistir

surviving [sɝ˞váɪvɪŋ] ADJ superviviente

survivor [sɝ˞váɪvə˞] N sobreviviente *mf*, superviviente *mf*

susceptible [səséptəbəł] ADJ susceptible; **to be — of proof** poderse demostrar; **to be — to pneumonia** ser propenso a la pulmonía

suspect[1] [sʌ́spekt] N sospechoso -sa *mf*

suspect[2] [səspékt] VT sospechar, recelar

suspend [səspénd] VT suspender
suspenders [səspéndə·z] N tirantes *m pl*
suspense [səspéns] N (uncertainty) incertidumbre *f*; (in movie) suspenso *m*; *Sp* suspense *m*; **to keep in —** mantener en suspenso, tener en vilo
suspension [səspénʃən] N suspensión *f*; (of a ban) levantamiento *m*; **— bridge** puente colgante *m*
suspicion [səspíʃən] N sospecha *f*
suspicious [səspíʃəs] ADJ (causing suspicion) sospechoso; (experiencing suspicion) suspicaz, desconfiado
sustain [səstén] VT (weight) sostener, sustentar; (pretense, effort) mantener; (an injury) sufrir; (an objection) admitir; (a musical note) sostener
sustainable [səsténəbəł] ADJ sostenible, sustentable
sustenance [sástənəns] N sustento *m*, alimento *m*
suture [sútʃə·] N sutura *f*
swab [swɑb] N bola de algodón *f*, *RP* hisopo *m*; VT pasar un hisopo sobre
swagger [swǽgə·] VI (walk) pavonearse, contonearse; (boast) fanfarronear; N (walk) pavoneo *m*, contoneo *m*; (bluster) fanfarronería *f*
swallow [swálo] N (drink) trago *m*; (bird) golondrina *f*; VI/VT tragar; **to — up** consumir
swallowing [swáloɪŋ] N deglución *f*
swam [swæm] *see* swim
swamp [swɑmp] N pantano *m*, ciénaga *f*; **—land** cenagal *m*; VI/VT (flood) inundar[se]; (overwhelm) abrumar[se], agobiar[se]
swampy [swámpi] ADJ pantanoso, cenagoso
swan [swɑn] N cisne *m*; **— dive** salto del ángel *m*; **— song** canto de cisne *m*
swap [swɑp] VT cambiar, canjear; N cambio *m*, canje *m*
swarm [swɔrm] N enjambre *m*; VI (of bees) salir en enjambre; (of people, tourists) pulular, hormiguear; **to be —ing with** ser un hervidero de, abundar en
swarthy [swɔ́rði] ADJ trigueño, moreno
swat [swɑt] VT (a person) pegar; (flies) aplastar; **to — at** manotear; N manotazo *m*
sway [swe] VI/VT (move to and fro) balancear[se], bambolear[se]; (move hips) menear[se]; (influence) influir [en]; N (movement) balanceo *m*, vaivén *m*, bamboleo *m*; (influence) influencia *f*; **to hold — over** dominar
Swazi [swázi] N suazi *mf*
Swaziland [swázilænd] N Suazilandia *f*
swear [swɛr] VI/VT (vow) jurar; (use profanity) decir palabrotas; *Sp* soltar tacos; **to — in** (give oath) juramentar; (take oath) prestar juramento; **she —s by canned peaches** para ella no hay nada como los duraznos enlatados; **to — off** renunciar a; **to — to** jurar por
sweat [swɛt] VI (perspire) sudar; (ooze) exudar, sudar; (worry) preocuparse; N sudor *m*; **— glands** glándulas sudoríparas *f pl*; **—shirt** sudadera *f*; **—suit** equipo deportivo *m*; *Sp* chándal *m*; **no —** no hay problema
sweater [swɛ́tə·] N suéter *m*, jersey *m*
sweating [swɛ́tɪŋ] N sudor *m*, sudoración *f*, transpiración *f*
sweaty [swɛ́tɪ] ADJ sudoroso, sudado
Swede [swid] N sueco -ca *mf*
Sweden [swídn] N Suecia *f*
Swedish [swídɪʃ] ADJ sueco
sweep [swip] VI/VT (clean with broom, scan) barrer; (dredge) dragar; VT (touch) rozar; (search) rastrear; VI (spread) extenderse; **to — away** llevar, arrastrar; **to — down upon** caer sobre, asolar; **to — off** limpiar; **to — into** (enter majestically) entrar majestuosamente; (enter quickly) entrar rápidamente; **to — up** recoger; N (cleaning) barrida *f*; (extension) extensión *f*; (movement) barrido *m*; (search) rastreo *m*
sweeper [swípə·] N (for cleaning) barredora *f*; (in soccer) líbero *m*
sweeping [swípɪŋ] ADJ (statement) [demasiado] general; (victory) aplastante
sweet [swit] ADJ (in flavor, personality) dulce; (in smell) bueno, fragante; **—-and-sour** agridulce; **—heart** querido -da *mf*; **— pea** *Sp* guisante de olor *m*; **— potato** batata *f*, boniato *m*; *Mex* camote *m*; **to have a — tooth** ser goloso; N dulce *m*, golosina *f*; **my —** mi vida, mi alma; VT **to —-talk** halagar
sweeten [swítn] VI/VT (a food) endulzar[se]; (an experience) dulcificar[se]
sweetener [swítnə·] N endulzante *m*, edulcorante *m*
sweetness [swítnɪs] N (of personality) dulzura *f*; (of taste) dulzor *m*
swell [swɛł] VI/VT (limbs, with pride) hinchar[se], henchir[se]; VI (river) crecer; (population) crecer, engrosar[se]; VT (make grow) hacer crecer, hacer aumentar, engrosar; N (of ocean) oleaje *m*; ADJ regio, bárbaro
swelling [swɛ́łɪŋ] N hinchazón *f*
swelter [swɛ́łtə·] VI sofocarse de calor
swept [swɛpt] *see* sweep
swerve [swɜ·v] VI/VT (in a car) virar; (from a goal) desviar[se]; N viraje *m*
swift [swift] ADJ ligero, veloz, raudo; N vencejo *m*
swiftness [swíftnɪs] N velocidad *f*, rapidez *f*
swim [swɪm] VI/VT nadar; (float) flotar; **to — across** atravesar nadando; **my head is —ming** me da vueltas la cabeza; **I love**

—ming me encanta nadar; N *Mex* alberca *f*; **—suit** traje de baño *m*; **to take a —** ir a nadar, dar una nadada

swimmer [swímə-] N nadador -ora *mf*; **—'s ear** otitis externa *f*

swimming [swímɪŋ] N natación *f*; **— pool** piscina *f*

swindle [swíndł] VT estafar; N estafa *f*, trapacería *f*

swine [swaɪn] N puerco *m*, cerdo *m*; (person) *offensive* puerco -ca *mf*, sinvergüenza *mf*

swing [swɪŋ] VI/VT (on a swing) columpiar[se]; (move to and fro) balancear[se], bambolear[se]; (baseball, golf) dar un swing [con]; VI (change) virar; **to — and miss** abanicar; **to — around** dar vueltas; **to — open** abrirse; VT (make turn) hacer girar; (influence) influir sobre; **to — a deal** concretar un negocio; **I can't — a new car** no me puedo dar el lujo de comprar un auto nuevo; N (playground toy) columpio *m*; (oscillation) balanceo *m*, vaivén *m*, bamboleo *m*; (in golf, baseball, music) swing *m*; (change) cambio *m*; **— and a miss** abanico *m*; **in full —** en su apogeo; **to get into the — of things** agarrarle la onda a algo, cogerle el tranquillo a algo

swipe [swaɪp] VT (steal) afanar, sisar; (slide) deslizar; **to — a card** pasar una tarjeta por un lector; N (insult) insulto *m*; **to take a — at someone** (physical) tirarle un manotazo a alguien; (verbal) insultar

swirl [swɝł] VI/VT arremolinar[se]; (dancers) girar; N remolino *m*; (smoke) espiral *f*

Swiss [swɪs] ADJ & N suizo -za *mf*; **— cheese** queso suizo *m*

switch [swɪtʃ] N (change) cambio *m*; (electrical) interruptor *m*, llave *f*; (stick for whipping) varilla *f*; (on railways) agujas *f pl*; **—blade** navaja automática *f*; **—board** centralita *f*; **—man** guardagujas *m sg*; **—-hitter** (in baseball) bateador -ora ambidiestro *mf*; VI/VT cambiar [de]; (train cars) desviar; **to — off** (current) cortar; (light, TV) apagar; **to — on** encender, prender

Switzerland [swítsə-lənd] N Suiza *f*

swivel [swívəł] N pivote *m*; **— chair** silla giratoria *f*

swollen [swólən] ADJ hinchado

swollen [swólən] *see* swell

swoon [swun] VI desvanecerse, desmayarse; **to — over someone** morirse por alguien; N vahído *m*

swoop [swup] VI **to — down upon** abalanzarse sobre; N descenso súbito *m*; **at one fell —** de un tirón

sword [sɔrd] N espada *f*; **—fish** pez espada *m*

swore [swɔr] *see* swear

sworn [swɔrn] *see* swear

swum [swʌm] *see* swim

swung [swʌŋ] *see* swing

sycamore [síkəmɔr] N sicomoro *m*

syllable [síləbəł] N sílaba *f*

syllabus [síləbəs] N programa [de estudios] *m*

syllogism [sílədʒɪzəm] N silogismo *m*

symbiosis [sɪmbióʊsɪs] N simbiosis *f*

symbol [símbəł] N símbolo *m*

symbolic [sɪmbúlɪk] ADJ simbólico

symbolism [símbəlɪzəm] N simbolismo *m*

symbolize [símbəlaɪz] VT simbolizar

symmetrical [sɪmétrɪkəł] ADJ simétrico

symmetry [símɪtri] N simetría *f*

sympathetic [sɪmpəθétɪk] ADJ (compassionate) compasivo; (understanding) comprensivo, solidario; (favoring) favorable; (nervous system) simpático

sympathize [símpəθaɪz] VI (be compassionate) compadecer[se]; (be understanding) comprender; (be in favor) favorecer; **to — with** estar a favor de

sympathizer [símpəθaɪzə-] N simpatizante *mf*

sympathizing [símpəθaɪzɪŋ] ADJ simpatizante

sympathy [símpəθi] N (compassion) compasión *f*; (understanding) comprensión *f*; (condolence) condolencia *f*, pésame *m*; **to extend one's —** dar el pésame

symphony [símfəni] N sinfonía *f*; **— orchestra** orquesta sinfónica *f*

symposium [sɪmpóziəm] N simposio *m*

symptom [símptəm] N síntoma *m*

synagogue [sínəgɑg] N sinagoga *f*

synchronize [síŋkrənaɪz] VI/VT sincronizar[se]

synchronous [síŋkrənəs] ADJ sincrónico

syndicate[1] [síndɪkɪt] N sindicato *m*

syndicate[2] [síndɪket] VI/VT (form a syndicate) sindicar[se]; VT (sell rights) vender los derechos de

syndrome [síndrom] N síndrome *m*

synergy [sínə-dʒi] N sinergia *f*

synonym [sínənɪm] N sinónimo *m*

synonymous [sɪnánəməs] ADJ sinónimo

synopsis [sɪnápsɪs] N sinopsis *f*

syntax [síntæks] N sintaxis *f*

synthesis [sínθəsɪs] N síntesis *f*

synthesize [sínθəsaɪz] VI/VT sintetizar

synthesizer [sínθəsaɪzə-] N sintetizador *m*

synthetic [sɪnθétɪk] ADJ sintético

syphilis [sífəlɪs] N sífilis *f*

Syria [síriə] N Siria *f*

Syrian [síriən] ADJ & N sirio -ria *mf*

syringe [sərínʤ] N jeringa *f*

syrup [sírəp] N (food) almíbar *m*, jarabe *m*; (medicine) jarabe *m*

system [sístəm] N sistema *m*; **— crashes** caídas del sistema *f pl*

systematic [sɪstəmǽtɪk] ADJ sistemático

systematize [sístəmətaɪz] VI/VT sistematizar

systemic [sɪstémɪk] ADJ sistémico
systolic [sɪstálɪk] ADJ sistólico

Tt

tab [tæb] N (on a keyboard) tabulador *m*; (on index cards) pestaña *f*, ceja *f*; (bill) cuenta *f*; **— key** tecla de tabulación *f*; VI tabular
table [tébəł] N (furniture) mesa *f*; (list) tabla *f*; **— lamp** lámpara de mesa *f*; **— of contents** tabla de contenido *f*, índice *m*; **at —** a la mesa; VT posponer indefinidamente, dar carpetazo a; **—cloth** mantel *m*; **—spoon** (spoon) cuchara grande *f*; (measurement) cucharada *f*; **—spoonful** cucharada *f*; **— tennis** tenis de mesa *m*; **—ware** vajilla *f*, servicio de mesa *m*
tablet [tǽblɪt] N (pill) pastilla *f*, tableta *f*; (paper) bloc *m*; (stone) tabla *f*, lápida *f*; (portable writing surface) tablilla *f*
tabloid [tǽblɔɪd] N (paper size) tabloide *m*; (type of press) prensa amarilla/sensacionalista *f*
taboo [tæbú] N tabú *m*
tabulate [tǽbjəlet] VT tabular
tachometer [tækámɪDə·] N tacómetro *m*
tacit [tǽsɪt] ADJ tácito
taciturn [tǽsɪtɜ·n] ADJ taciturno
tack [tæk] N (nail) tachuela *f*; (stitch) hilván *m*; (heading of a boat) rumbo *m*; (course of action) táctica *f*; (equipment for a horse) arreos *m pl*; VT (to nail) clavar con tachuelas; (to stitch) hilvanar; **to — on** agregar; VI virar, cambiar de rumbo
tackle [tǽkəł] N (for fishing, hoisting) aparejo *m*; (in rugby, football) placaje *m*, parada *f*; (person) atajador *m*; VT (a problem) enfrentar, abordar; (a task) emprender; (a horse) poner arreos; VI/VT (rugby, American football) placar, atajar
tacky [tǽki] ADJ (in bad taste) de mal gusto, chabacano; *Sp* hortera; (sticky) pegajoso
tact [tǽkt] N tacto *m*
tactful [tǽktfəł] ADJ que tiene tacto
tactics [tǽktɪks] N táctica *f*
tactile [tǽktɪl] ADJ táctil
tactless [tǽktlɪs] ADJ falto de tacto
tag [tæg] N (label) etiqueta *f*; (question) coletilla *f*; (nickname) apodo *m*; **to play —** jugar al pillapilla; VT etiquetar; (in the game of tag) pillar; **to — along** acompañar
tail [teł] N cola *f*, rabo *m*; (of a shirt) faldón *m*; (pursuer) perseguidor -ora *mf*; **—bone** rabadilla *f*; **— end** (of a concert) final *m*; (of a procession) cola *f*; **—light** luz trasera *f*; **—pipe** tubo de escape *m*; **—s** (of a coin) cruz *f*; (of a tuxedo) frac *m*; **—spin** barrena *f*; **to —gate** seguir demasiado de cerca [a otro coche]
tailor [télə·] N sastre *m*; **— shop** sastrería *f*; VT hacer a medida; (adapt) adaptar
taint [tent] N (stain) mancha *f*; (contamination) contaminación *f*; VI/VT (stain) manchar[se]; (contaminate) contaminar[se]
Taiwan [taɪwán] N Taiwán *m*
Taiwanese [taɪwanís] ADJ & N taiwanés -esa *mf*
Tajik [tadʒík] ADJ & N tayiko -ka *mf*
Tajikistan [tadʒíkɪstæn] N Tayikistán *m*
take [tek] VT (a load) llevar; (someone else's property) robar, llevarse; (one number from another) restar; (prisoner, medicine, measures, a course) tomar; (one of a set) elegir, coger; (a bribe) aceptar; (a prize) recibir; (advice) seguir; (a walk) dar; (a vacation) irse; (a trip) hacer; (a piece of news) recibir; (a photo) sacar; **to — a bath** bañarse; **to — after** parecerse a; **to — a look at** echar un vistazo a; **to — a notion to** ocurrírsele a uno; **to — apart** desarmar, desmontar; **to — aside** apartar; **to — away** (carry away) llevarse; (steal) sustraer; **to — back** devolver; **to — back one's words** retractarse; **to — by surprise** tomar desprevenido; **to — care of** (a person) cuidar de; (a matter) atender a; **to — charge of** encargarse de; **to — down in writing** anotar, apuntar; **to — effect** entrar en vigencia; **to — exercise** hacer ejercicio; **to — in** (include) incluir; (observe) observar; (deceive) embaucar; (provide shelter for) albergar; (make smaller) tomar, achicar; **to — leave** despedirse; **to — off** (remove) quitar[se]; (conduct) llevar; (discount) rebajar; (start flight) despegar; **to — offense** ofenderse; **to — office** asumir un cargo; **to — on** (accept) asumir; (hire) tomar, contratar; (acquire) adquirir; **to — out** (withdraw) sacar; (carry out [food], take on a date) llevar; **to — over** hacerse cargo [de]; **to — place** tener lugar; **to — revenge** vengarse; **to — stock** hacer un balance; **to — stock in** tener confianza en; **to — the floor** tomar la palabra; **to — to heart** tomar a pecho; **to — to one's heels** poner pies en polvorosa; **to — to task** reprender, regañar; **to — up a matter** tratar un asunto; **to — up again** retomar; **to — up space** ocupar espacio; **I — it that** supongo que; **it —s ten minutes** lleva diez minutos; **the vaccination didn't —** la vacuna no prendió; N (profits) ingresos *m pl*; (of fish) pesca *f*, captura *f*; (of a film production) toma *f*; (opinion) opinión *f*; (approach) enfoque *m*; **—off** (of an airplane) despegue *m*; (parody) parodia *f*; **—over** (of a government) toma de poder *f*; (of a company) adquisición *f*
taken [tékən] *see* take
talcum [tǽłkəm] N talco *m*; **— powder** polvo de

talco *m*

tale [teɪl] N (story) cuento *m*, relato *m*; (lie) mentira *f*

talent [tǽlənt] N talento *m*

talented [tǽləntɪd] ADJ talentoso

talk [tɔk] VI/VT hablar; (chat) charlar; VT (nonsense) decir; (a language) hablar; (politics) hablar de; **to — back** contestar con impertinencia; **to — down to** hablar con arrogancia a; **to — someone into something** convencer a alguien para que haga algo; **to — out of** disuadir de; **to — over** discutir; **to — up** alabar, hacer propaganda; N (formal speech) charla *f*; (gossip) habladurías *f pl*; (lingo) habla *f*; **— of the town** la comidilla del pueblo *f*; **— show** programa de entrevistas *m*

talkative [tɔ́kəɾɪv] ADJ hablador, parlanchín, charlatán

tall [tɔl] ADJ alto; **— order** misión imposible *f*; **— tale** cuento chino *m*, patraña *f*; **six feet —** de seis pies de altura; **how — are you?** ¿cuánto mides?

tallow [tǽlo] N sebo *m*

tally [tǽli] N (account) cuenta *f*; VT llevar la cuenta; **to — up** sumar; **to — with** concordar con

tambourine [tæmbərín] N pandereta *f*

tame [tem] ADJ (docile) manso, dócil; (domesticated) domesticado; (dull) aburrido; VT (make docile) amansar, domar; (domesticate) domesticar

tamper [tǽmpɚ] VI **to — with** (a jury) sobornar; (a lock) intentar forzar; (a document) alterar, amañar; ADJ **—-proof** a prueba de alteración

tampon [tǽmpɑn] N tampón *m*

tan [tæn] VI/VT (cure) curtir[se]; (darken skin) broncear[se], tostar[se]; VT (cure) adobar; (spank) zurrar; N color tostado *m*; (of skin) bronceado *m*; ADJ (car) color tostado; (skin) bronceado, tostado

tandem [tǽndəm] N tándem *m*; **in — with** en colaboración con

tangent [tǽnʤənt] ADJ & N tangente *f*; **to go off on a —** salirse por la tangente

tangerine [tǽnʤərín] N mandarina *f*; *Am* tangerina *f*

tangible [tǽnʤəbəɫ] ADJ tangible

tangle [tǽŋgəɫ] VI/VT enredar[se], enmarañar[se]; N enredo *m*, maraña *f*; (in hair) nudo *m*, enredijo *m*

tank [tæŋk] N tanque *m* (also military), depósito *m*; VT guardar en un tanque; VI **to — up** (with gasoline) llenar el tanque; (with alcohol) emborracharse

tannery [tǽnəɾi] N curtiduría *f*, tenería *f*; *Am* curtiembre *f*

tantalize [tǽntəɫaɪz] VT atormentar con tentaciones

tantamount [tǽntəmaʊnt] ADJ **to be — to** equivaler a

tantrum [tǽntrəm] N berrinche *m*, perrera *f*, rabieta *f*

Tanzania [tænzəníə] N Tanzania *f*

Tanzanian [tænzéniən] ADJ & N tanzano -na *mf*

tap [tæp] N golpecito *m*; (repeated) golpeteo *m*; (with the hand) palmadita *f*; (faucet) llave *f*; *Sp* grifo *m*; **— dance** claqué *m*; **— water** agua de llave *f*; VI/VT (once) tocar; (repeatedly) golpetear; (with fingers) tamborilear; (utilize) explotar; (draw off liquid) extraer; **to — a tree** sangrar un árbol; **to — a telephone** intervenir un teléfono

tape [tep] N (adhesive, magnetic) cinta *f*; **— measure** cinta métrica *f*; **— recorder** grabadora *f*, grabador *m*; **— recording** grabación *f*; **—worm** lombriz *f*, solitaria *f*; VT (affix) atar con cinta; VI/VT (record) grabar; **to —-record** grabar

taper [tépɚ] N (diminished size) estrechamiento *m*; (candle) vela *f*, candela *f*; VI/VT afinar[se]; **to — off** (become smaller) afinar[se]; (diminish) ir disminuyendo

tapestry [tǽpɪstri] N (wall hanging) tapiz *m*; (art, industry) tapicería *f*

tapioca [tæpiókə] N tapioca *f*

tapir [tépɚ] N tapir *m*

tar [tɑɾ] N alquitrán *m*, brea *f*; VT alquitranar; **to — and feather** emplumar

tarantula [tərǽntʃələ] N tarántula *f*

tardy [tɑ́ɾdi] ADJ **to be —** llegar tarde

target [tɑ́rgɪt] N blanco *m*; **— practice** tiro al blanco *m*

tariff [tǽrɪf] N tarifa *f*, arancel *m*

tarnish [tɑ́rnɪʃ] VI/VT (metal) deslustrar[se], empañar; (reputation) manchar[se]

tart [tɑɾt] ADJ (fruit) agrio, ácido; (remark) mordaz; N (pie) tarta *f*

tartar [tɑ́rdɚ] N (in wine) tártaro *m*; (on teeth) sarro *m*; **— sauce** salsa tártara *f*

task [tæsk] N tarea *f*, labor *f*; **— bar** barra de tareas *f*; **— force** fuerza de tarea *f*; **—master** tirano -na *mf*; **to take to —** reprender, regañar

tassel [tǽsəɫ] N borla *f*

taste [test] VT (perceive) sentir el gusto/sabor de; (try) probar; (try wine) catar; VI **to — of onion** saber a cebolla; **it —s sour** tiene un sabor agrio; N (sense, aesthetic judgment) gusto *m*; (flavor) sabor *m*; (small amount of food) bocadito *m*; (small amount of drink) sorbo *m*; **— bud** papila gustativa *f*

tasteless [tésttlɪs] ADJ (with no taste) soso, desabrido; (in bad taste) de mal gusto

tasty [tésti] ADJ sabroso

tatter [tǽdɚ] N andrajo *m*, harapo *m*, pingajo *m*

tattered [tǽdɚd] ADJ harapiento, andrajoso

tattle [tǽdɫ] VI acusar; **to — on** acusar a; N

—**tale** acusetas *mf sg*
tattoo [tætú] N tatuaje *m*; VI/VT tatuar[se]
taught [tɔt] *see* teach
taunt [tɔnt] VT provocar, burlarse de; N provocación *f*, pulla *f*
taut [tɔt] ADJ tenso, tirante
tavern [tǽvə-n] N taberna *f*, cantina *f*
tawdry [tɔ́dri] ADJ (affair) sórdido; (outfit) charro
tax [tæks] N impuesto *m*, contribución *f*, gravamen *m*; (burden) carga *f*; VT (a product) gravar; (a person) cobrarle impuestos a; (patience, resources) poner a prueba; —**attorney/lawyer** abogado -da tributarista *mf*; —**code** código impositivo *m*; —-**deductible** desgravable; —**deduction** deducción impositiva *f*; —**evasion** evasión de impuestos *f*; —**payer** contribuyente *mf*; —**return** declaración de impuestos *f*; —**shelter** abrigo impositivo *m*, refugio fiscal *m*; —**withholding** retención impositiva *f*; ADJ —-**exempt** no gravable, exento de impuestos; —-**free** libre de impuestos
taxable [tǽksəbəł] ADJ imponible, tributable
taxation [tækséʃən] N (result of taxing) impuestos *m pl*; (act of taxing) imposición de contribuciones *f*
taxi [tǽksi] N taxi *m*; VI ir en taxi; (an airplane) rodar por la pista; —**cab** taxi *m*
taxidermy [tǽksɪdɜ-mi] N taxidermia *f*
taxonomy [tæksɑ́nəmi] N taxonomía *f*
tea [ti] N té *m*; —**bag** bolsita de té *f*; —**cup** taza de té *f*; —**kettle/pot** tetera *f*; —**party** té *m*; —**spoon** (spoon) cucharita *f*, cucharilla *f*; (measurement) cucharadita *f*; —**spoonful** cucharadita *f*; —**time** hora del té *f*
teach [titʃ] VI/VT enseñar; **to — a class** dar clase
teacher [títʃə-] N (primary school) maestro -tra *mf*; (secondary school) profesor -ora *mf*; —**s college** [escuela] normal *f*
teaching [títʃɪŋ] N enseñanza *f*; —**s** enseñanzas *f pl*; —**activities** actividades pedagógicas *f pl*; —**profession** magisterio *m*
team [tim] N equipo *m*; (of yoked animals) yunta de bueyes *f*; (of horses) tiro *m*, enganche *m*; —**mate** compañero -ra de equipo *mf*; VI **to — up** unirse, formar un equipo
teamster [tímstə-] N transportista *mf*, camionero -ra *mf*
tear[1] [tɪr] N lágrima *f*; —**drop** lágrima *f*; —**gas** gas lacrimógeno *m*; **to burst into —s** romper a llorar
tear[2] [tɛr] VI/VT (rip) rasgar[se]; (rip a hole) hacer[se] un siete; VT **to — along** ir a toda velocidad; **to — apart** (rip up) romper, destrozar; (separate) separar; **to — away** apartar[se]; **to — down** (a building) demoler, derribar; (a machine) desarmar, desmontar; (a person) denigrar; **to — one's hair** arrancarse los cabellos; N desgarrón *m*, desgarradura *f*, rasgón *m*
tearful [tírfəł] ADJ (look) lloroso; (farewell) triste
tease [tiz] VT (make fun of a person) molestar, fastidiar; (tantalize sexually) provocar; (comb wool, hair) cardar; **to — out** sacar; N provocadora *f*
teat [tit] N teta *f*
techie [tɛ́ki] N *fam* experto -ta en computación *mf*
technical [tɛ́knɪkəł] ADJ técnico; —**support** soporte técnico *m*
technician [tɛkníʃən] N técnico -ca *mf*, perito -ta *mf*
technique [tɛkník] N técnica *f*
technological [tɛknəlɑ́dʒɪkəł] ADJ tecnológico
technology [tɛknɑ́lədʒi] N tecnología *f*, técnica *f*
tectonics [tɛktɑ́nɪks] N tectónica *f*
tedious [tíɒiəs] ADJ tedioso, aburrido
tedium [tíɒiəm] N hastío *m*
tee [ti] N (T-shirt) camiseta *f*; (golf ball support) tee *m*; (start of hole in golf) punto de salida *m*
teem [tim] VI **to — with** abundar en, estar lleno de
teen [tin] *see* teenager
teenager [tínedʒə-] N adolescente *mf*
teens [tinz] N (teenage years) adolescencia *f*; (numbers 13–19) números de trece a diecinueve *m pl*
teethe [tiðd] VI **the baby is teething** al bebé le están saliendo los dientes
teetotaler [títódlə-] N abstemio -mia *mf*
telecast [tɛ́ləkæst] N teledifusión *f*
telecommunication [tɛlɪkəmjunɪkéʃən] N telecomunicación *f*; —**s** telecomunicaciones *f pl*
telecommuting [tɛlɪkəmjúɒɪŋ] N teletrabajo *m*
teleconference [tɛ́lɪkɑnfə-əns] N teleconferencia *f*
telegram [tɛ́ləgræm] N telegrama *m*
telegraph [tɛ́ləgræf] N telégrafo *m*; VI/VT telegrafiar
telegraphic [tɛləgrǽfɪk] ADJ telegráfico
telemarketing [tɛləmɑ́rkɪɒɪŋ] N telemercadeo *m*, telemarketing *m*
telepathy [təlɛ́pəθi] N telepatía *f*
telephone [tɛ́ləfon] N teléfono *m*; —**book** guía telefónica *f*; —**booth** cabina telefónica *f*; —**number** número telefónico *m*; —**operator** telefonista *mf*; —**receiver** auricular *m*, tubo de teléfono *m*; VI/VT telefonear, llamar por teléfono
telescope [tɛ́lɪskop] N telescopio *m*; VI plegarse
televisable [tɛləvǽɪzəbəł] ADJ televisivo
televise [tɛ́ləvaɪz] VT televisar
television [tɛ́ləvɪʒən] N (medium) televisión *f*; (device) televisor *m*; —**program** programa televisivo *mf*; —**viewer** televidente *mf*
tell [tɛł] VI/VT (the truth) decir; (a story) contar;

to — apart distinguir; **to — on someone** acusar a alguien; **to — someone off** regañar a alguien; **to — time** decir la hora; **I can't — if he's old or young** no sé si es viejo o joven; **his age is beginning to —** se le comienza a notar la edad; ADJ **a —tale sign** una señal reveladora; **he is a —tale** es un acusica

teller [téllə-] N (narrator) narrador -ora *mf*; (in a bank) cajero -ra *mf*

temerity [təmérɪDi] N temeridad *f*

temp [tɛmp] N empleado -da temporal *mf*

temper [témpə-] N (hardness) temple *m*; (bad humor) mal genio *m*; **to keep one's —** mantener la calma; **to lose one's —** perder los estribos, encolerizarse; VT templar

temperament [témpə-əmənt] N temperamento *m*, genio *m*, talante *m*

temperance [témpə-əns] N (moderation) templanza *f*, temperancia *f*; (abstinence from alcohol) abstinencia de bebidas alcohólicas *f*

temperate [témpə-ɪt] ADJ (weather) templado; (opinions, habits) moderado

temperature [témpə-əʧur] N temperatura *f*; **to have a —** tener fiebre

tempest [témpɪst] N tempestad *f*

tempestuous [tɛmpéstʃuəs] ADJ tempestuoso

template [témplɪt] N plantilla *f*

temple [témpəł] N (church) templo *m*; (side of the forehead) sien *f*

temporal [témpə-əł] ADJ temporal

temporary [témpərɛri] ADJ temporal, eventual

tempt [tɛmpt] VT tentar

temptation [temptéʃən] N tentación *f*

tempting [témptɪŋ] ADJ tentador

ten [tɛn] NUM diez; N **—s of candidates** decenas de candidatos *f pl*

tenacious [tənéʃəs] ADJ tenaz

tenacity [tənǽsɪDi] N tenacidad *f*

tenant [ténənt] N inquilino -na *mf*, arrendatario -ria *mf*

tend [tɛnd] VT (care for) cuidar; **to —** to (take care of) ocuparse de; (lean toward) tender, inclinarse

tendency [téndənsi] N tendencia *f*

tender [téndə-] ADJ tierno; (painful) sensible; N (offer) oferta *f*; (legal currency) curso legal *m*; (person who tends) cuidador -ora *mf*, vigilante *mf*; VT presentar, ofrecer

tenderness [téndə-nɪs] N (of feeling) ternura *f*; (of meat) terneza *f*, ternura *f*; (sensitivity to pain) sensibilidad *f*

tendinitis [tɛndənáɪDɪs] N tendinitis *f*

tendon [téndən] N tendón *m*

tendril [téndrəł] N zarcillo *m*

tenement [ténəmənt] N casa de vecindad *f*

tenet [ténɪt] N principio *m*

tennis [ténɪs] N tenis *m*; **— court** cancha de tenis *f*, pista de tenis *f*; **— elbow** codo de tenista *m*; **— player** tenista *mf*; **— shoes** tenis *m pl*

tenor [ténə-] N tenor *m*

tense [tɛns] ADJ tenso; N (grammatical) tiempo *m*

tension [ténʃən] N (stress) tensión *f*; (tautness) tirantez *f*

tent [tɛnt] N (camping) tienda de campaña *f*; (circus) carpa *f*; VI acampar

tentacle [téntəkəł] N tentáculo *m*

tentative [téntətɪv] ADJ tentativo

tenth [tɛnθ] ADJ & N décimo *m*

tenuous [ténjuəs] ADJ (light, color, cloth) tenue; (peace) frágil

tenure [ténjə-] N (of professorship) titularidad *f*; (of an office) ocupación *f*

tepid [tépɪd] ADJ tibio

terabyte [térəbaɪt] N terabyte *m*

term [tɜ-m] N (word, mathematical expression) término *m*; (period) período *m*; (time in office) mandato *m*; (semester) semestre *m*; (trimester) trimestre *m*; (set date for payment) plazo *m*; **— life insurance** seguro de vida a término *m*; **— paper** trabajo final *m*; **—s** condiciones *f pl*; **at —** a término; **to be on good —s** estar en buenas relaciones; **not to be on speaking —s** no hablarse; **to come to —s** aceptar; VT denominar

terminal [tɜ-mənł] ADJ terminal; N (of airport, computer) terminal *mf*; (electric) terminal *m*

terminate [tɜ-mənet] VI/VT terminar[se]

termination [tɜ-mənéʃən] N terminación *f*; (of an employee) despido *m*

terminology [tɜ-rmənáłəʤi] N terminología *f*

termite [tɜ-maɪt] N termita *f*

terrace [térɪs] N terraza *f*, escalón *m*; VT poner terrazas en, escalonar

terrain [tərén] N terreno *m*

terrestrial [tərɛ́strɪał] ADJ terrestre

terrible [térəbəł] ADJ terrible, tremendo

terrier [térɪə-] N terrier *m*

terrific [tərífɪk] ADJ estupendo

terrify [térəfaɪ] VT aterrar, aterrorizar, espeluznar

territory [térɪtɔri] N territorio *m*

terror [térə-] N terror *m*

terrorism [térə-ɪzəm] N terrorismo *m*

terrorist [térə-ɪst] N terrorista *mf*

terrorize [térə-aɪz] VT aterrorizar

terse [tɜ-s] ADJ lacónico

test [tɛst] N (trial, experiment) prueba *f*; (of intelligence, multiple choice) test *m*; (examination) examen *m*, prueba *f*; **— market** mercado de prueba *m*; **— pilot** piloto de pruebas *m*; **— tube** tubo de ensayo *m*, probeta *f*; **—-tube baby** bebé de probeta *m*; **to undergo a —** someterse a una prueba; **to take a —** dar un examen; **to give a —** poner un examen; **to put to the —** poner a prueba; VT (put to the test) probar, poner a prueba; (give an exam) poner una prueba, examinar; **—ing** pruebas *f pl*; **to —-drive**

probar; VI **girls — better than boys** en los exámenes salen mejor las niñas que los niños
testament [tɛ́stəmənt] N testamento *m*; (testimony) testimonio *m*
testicle [tɛ́stɪkəł] N testículo *m*
testify [tɛ́stəfaɪ] VI (serve as witness) testificar; (confirm) dar fe
testimony [tɛ́stəmoni] N testimonio *m*
testosterone [testɑ́stəron] N testosterona *f*
tetanus [tɛ́tnəs] N tétano[s] *m*
tetracycline [tɛtrəsáɪklɪn] N tetraciclina *f*
Teutonic [tutɑ́nɪk] ADJ teutónico
text [tɛkst] N texto *m*; **—book** libro de texto *m*; **— editor** editor de texto[s] *m*; **— message** mensaje de texto *m*; VT enviar mensajes de texto, *RP* textear
textile [tɛ́kstaɪł] ADJ textil; N textil *m*, tejido *m*; **— mill** fábrica de tejidos *f*
texture [tɛ́kstʃə˞] N textura *f*
Thai [taɪ] ADJ & N (person) tailandés -esa *mf*; (language) tailandés *m*
Thailand [tɑ́ɪlænd] N Tailandia *f*
than [ðæn] CONJ que; **I have more — you** tengo más que tú; **more — once** más de una vez
thank [θæŋk] VT dar las gracias, agradecer; **to have oneself to — for** tener la culpa de; INTERJ **— heaven!** ¡gracias a Dios! **— you** gracias; **—-you letter** carta de agradecimiento *f*; N **—s** gracias *f pl*
thankful [θǽŋkfəł] ADJ agradecido
thankfulness [θǽŋkfəłnɪs] N gratitud *f*, agradecimiento *m*
thankless [θǽŋklɪs] ADJ ingrato
thanksgiving [θæŋksgɪ́vɪŋ] N acción de gracias *f*; **— Day** día de acción de gracias *m*
that [ðæt] ADJ (something nearer the speaker) ese, esa; (something more remote from speaker) aquel, aquella; **— dog** ese/aquel perro *m*; **— one** (nearer) ese, esa; DEMON PRON (nearer to speaker) ese, esa; (more remote from speaker) aquel, aquella; (neuter) eso, aquello; **— is my daughter** esa/aquella es mi hija; **— was a nightmare** eso/aquello fue una pesadilla; REL PRON que; **the bike — disappeared** la bici que desapareció; **the pen — I was writing with** la lapicera con la que / la cual escribía; **— is** es decir; CONJ que; **she said — she would come** dijo que vendría; ADV tan; **it's not — far** no queda tan lejos; **— much** tanto; **she was — tall** era así de alta
thatch [θætʃ] N paja *f*; *Am* quincha *f*; VT techar con paja; *Am* quinchar; **—ed roof** techo de paja *m*; *Am* techo de quincha *m*
thaw [θɔ] VI/VT (food) descongelar[se]; (ice and snow) derretir[se]; (relations, refrigerator) deshelar[se]; N deshielo *m*
the [ðə, ði] DEF ART (singular) el *m*, la *f*; **— boy** el chico *m*; (plural) los *m*, las *f*; **— girls** las chicas *f pl*; **— good thing about that** lo bueno de eso; ADV **— more I work, — less I accomplish** cuanto más trabajo, menos consigo
theater, theatre [θíəDə˞] N teatro *m*
theatrical [θiǽtrɪkəł] ADJ teatral
theft [θɛft] N hurto *m*, robo *m*
their [ðɛr] POSS ADJ **this is — dog** este es su perro, este es el perro de ellos
theirs [ðɛrz] PRON **this book is —** este libro es suyo, este libro es de ellos/ellas; **these things are —** estas cosas son suyas / de ellos / de ellas; **— is bigger** el suyo / la suya / el de ellos / la de ellos es más grande; **a friend of —** un amigo suyo, un amigo de ellos
them [ðɛm] PRON los *m pl*, las *f pl*; **I see —** los/las veo; **I talk to —** les hablo a ellos; **I went with —** fui con ellos/ellas
thematic [θɪmǽDɪK] ADJ temático
theme [θim] N (topic) tema *m*; (essay) ensayo *m*, redacción *f*; **— park** parque temático *m*; **— song** tema *m*
themselves [ðɛmsɛ́lvz] PRON **they — built their house** ellos mismos se construyeron la casa; **they are not — today** hoy no son los mismos de siempre; **they were sitting by —** estaban sentados solos; **they looked at — in the mirror** se miraron en el espejo; **they talk to —** hablan solos; **they bought — a yacht** se compraron un yate
then [ðɛn] ADV (at that time) entonces, en aquel tiempo; **it was cheaper —** era más barato en aquel tiempo; (after) luego, después; **from — on** a partir de entonces; **now and —** de vez en cuando; **until —** hasta entonces; **I ate, — I paid** comí, luego pagué; **now —** ahora bien; **are you sorry —?** ¿estás arrepentido pues? ADJ entonces; **the — president** el entonces presidente; CONJ entonces; **if not, — you should stay** si no, entonces deberías quedarte
theologian [θiəlóʤən] N teólogo -ga *mf*
theological [θiəlɑ́ʤɪkəł] ADJ teológico
theology [θiɑ́ləʤi] N teología *f*
theoretical [θiərɛ́DɪKəł] ADJ teórico
theory [θíəri] N teoría *f*; **in —** en teoría
therapeutic [θɛrəpjúDɪK] ADJ terapéutico
therapist [θɛ́rəpɪst] N terapeuta *mf*; (psychologist) psicólogo -ga *mf*
therapy [θɛ́rəpi] N terapia *f*
there [ðɛr] ADV ahí; *Am* allí; (more remote) allá; *Sp* allí; **—abouts** por ahí, más o menos; **—after** (later) después; (always subsequently) de allí en adelante; **—by** así, de ese modo; **— ensued a war** a continuación hubo una guerra; **—fore** por consiguiente, por lo tanto; **—in** en eso, allí; **— is/are** hay; **— goes the bus** ahí va el autobús; **— —**

bueno, bueno; **—of** de eso; **—on** (on that) encima; (later) luego, después; **—upon** (after) luego, después; (for this reason) por consiguiente; (upon that) encima; **—with** (with that) con eso; (after that) luego, en seguida; **who's —?** ¿quién es? **is Mary —?** ¿está María? **we got — at 5** llegamos a las 5

thermal [θɝ́məł] ADJ termal; **— energy** energía térmica *f*

thermal [θɝ́məł] ADJ térmico

thermodynamic [θɝ›modaɪnǽmɪk] ADJ termodinámico

thermometer [θɚ›mámɪdɚ›] N termómetro *m*

thermonuclear [θɝ›monúkliɚ›] ADJ termonuclear

thermos [θɝ́məs] N termo *m*

thermostat [θɝ́məstæt] N termostato *m*

thesaurus [θɪsɔ́rəs] N (synonym dictionary) diccionario de sinónimos *m*; (large dictionary) diccionario *m*

these [ðiz] ADJ & PRON estos, estas

thesis [θísɪs] N tesis *f*

they [ðe] PRON ellos, ellas

thick [θɪk] ADJ (slice) grueso; (fog, soup) espeso; (accent) marcado; (wit) torpe; **one inch —** una pulgada de espesor; **— as thieves** como carne y uña; ADJ **—headed** estúpido; **—set** grueso; **—-skinned** insensible; N **the — of the fight** lo más reñido de la pelea; **through — and thin** pase lo que pase

thicken [θíkən] VI/VT espesar[se], trabar[se]; **the plot —s** la trama se complica

thicket [θíkɪt] N soto *m*, matorral *m*, boscaje *m*

thickness [θíknɪs] N (of paper, wood) espesor *m*, grosor *m*; (of soup) lo espeso; (of lips) lo grueso; (of a beard) lo tupido; (of hair) lo abundante

thief [θif] N ladrón -ona *mf*

thieve [θiv] VI/VT hurtar, robar

thigh [θaɪ] N muslo *m*

thimble [θímbəł] N dedal *m*

thin [θɪn] ADJ (ice, wire) delgado, fino; (person) flaco; (vegetation, beard, hair) ralo; (voice) tenue, fino; (air) enrarecido; (excuse) débil; (soup) aguado; VI/VT (paint, soup, sauce) diluir; (hair) entresacar; **to — out** (hair) ralear; (crowd) dispersarse

thing [θɪŋ] N cosa *f*; **there's no such —** eso no existe; **that is the — to do** eso es lo que hay que hacer; **the — about Mary** lo que pasa con María

thingamajig [θíŋəmədʒɪg] N chisme *m*, coso *m*

think [θɪŋk] VI/VT (reason) pensar, razonar; (believe) creer, opinar; **to — about** pensar en; **to — back** recordar; **to — it over/through** pensarlo bien, reflexionar sobre; **I'm —ing of you** pienso en ti; **what do you — of Mary?** ¿qué piensas de María? **I thought of a plan** se me ocurrió un plan; **to — up an excuse** inventar/elucubrar una excusa; **I don't — so** no creo; **who does he — he is?** ¿quién se cree que es? **to — well of** tener buena opinión de; **she —s nothing of spending $1000** no le importa nada gastar $1000

thinking [θíŋkɪŋ] N **current —** la opinión actual *f*; **to my way of —** a mi parecer; ADJ pensante

thinner [θínɚ›] N disolvente *m*

thinness [θínnɪs] N (of ice, person) delgadez *f*, flacura *f*; (of hair) escasez *f*; (of air) enrarecimiento *m*; (of soup) fluidez *f*

third [θɝd] ADJ tercer[o]; **— base** tercera base *f*, antesala *f*; **— baseman** tercero *m*, antesalista *m*; **— chapter** capítulo tercero *m*, tercer capítulo *m*; **— person** tercera persona *f*; **—-rate** de poca categoría; **— World** Tercer Mundo *m*; ADV tercero; N tercio *m*; (gear, musical interval) tercera *f*; **the — of March** el tres de marzo

thirst [θɝst] N sed *f*; VI tener sed; **to — for** tener sed de, estar sediento de

thirsty [θɝ́sti] ADJ sediento; **to be —** tener sed

thirteen [θɝ›tín] NUM trece

thirty [θɝ́ɪ] NUM treinta; ADJ & N **—something** treintañero -ra *mf*

this [ðɪs] ADJ & PRON este *m*, esta *f*, esto (neuter); **— dog** este perro; **— is a disaster** esto es un desastre

thistle [θísəł] N cardo *m*

thong [θɔŋ] N (strip of leather) correa *f*; (garment) tanga *mf*; (shoe) chancleta *f*

thorax [θɔ́ræks] N tórax *m*

thorn [θɔrn] N (sharp growth) espina *f*; (plant) espino *m*

thorny [θɔ́rni] ADJ espinoso, escabroso

thorough [θɝ́o] ADJ (exhaustive) exhaustivo, minucioso, detenido; (conscientious) concienzudo; **—bred** ADJ de pura sangre; N purasangre *m*

those [ðoz] ADJ & PRON (nearer) esos *m*, esas *f*; PRON (more remote) aquellos *m*, aquellas *f*; **— of you** los de vosotros/ustedes; **— that/who** los/las que

though [ðo] CONJ aunque; **as —** como si; ADV sin embargo

thought [θɔt] N (act, product of thinking) pensamiento *m*; (idea) idea *f*; (opinion) opinión *f*; (concern) consideración *f*; **to be lost in —** estar abstraído; **to give it no —** no darle importancia; **the very —** la mera idea; **at the — of** ante la idea de; **on second —** pensándolo bien; **my —s are with you** te acompaño en el sentimiento

thought [θɔt] *see* think

thoughtful [θɔ́tfəł] ADJ (considerate) considerado, atento; (well thought out) bien pensado; (reflective) pensativo, reflexivo

thoughtfulness [θɔ́tfəłnɪs] N consideración *f*
thoughtless [θɔ́tlɪs] ADJ (inconsiderate) desconsiderado; (careless) descuidado; (not reflective) irreflexivo
thoughtlessness [θɔ́tlɪsnɪs] N (lack of consideration) desconsideración *f*; (carelessness) descuido *m*; (lack of reflection) falta de reflexión *f*
thousand [θáʊzənd] NUM mil
thrash [θræʃ] VI/VT (whip, defeat) zurrar, vapulear, apalear; (thresh) trillar, desgranar; **to — around** revolverse, agitarse; **to — out a matter** ventilar un asunto
thread [θrɛd] N (in fabric) hilo *m*; (on a screw) rosca *f*; ADJ **—bare** raído; VT (a needle) enhebrar; (beads) ensartar; (a screw) enroscar; **to — one's way** abrirse paso
threat [θrɛt] N amenaza *f*
threaten [θrɛ́tn] VI/VT amenazar
threatening [θrɛ́tnɪŋ] ADJ amenazador, amenazante
three [θri] NUM tres; **— hundred** trescientos; ADJ **— -dimensional** tridimensional; **— -point basket** triple *m*; **— -point play** jugada de tres puntos *f*
thresh [θrɛʃ] VT trillar
threshold [θrɛ́ʃhołd] N umbral *m*
threw [θru] *see* throw
thrift [θrɪft] N economía *f*
thrifty [θrɪ́fti] ADJ económico, ahorrativo
thrill [θrɪł] VI/VT emocionar[se], ilusionar[se]; N emoción *f*, ilusión *f*
thrive [θraɪv] VI (person, economy) prosperar, florecer; (plants) crecer mucho
throat [θrot] N garganta *f*
throb [θrɑb] VI latir, palpitar; N latido *m*, palpitación *f*
throes [θroz] ADV LOC **in the — of war** en plena guerra; **in the — of death** agonizando
throne [θron] N trono *m*
throng [θrɔŋ] N muchedumbre *f*, turbamulta *f*; VI apiñarse, llegar en tropel
throttle [θrɑ́dł] N (of a motor) válvula reguladora / de aceleración *f*, regulador *m*; (of a motorcycle) puño giratorio del gas *m*; VT ahogar, estrangular
through [θru] PREP por, a través de; (as intermediary) por medio de; **Monday — Friday** de lunes a viernes; **all — the night** toda la noche; ADV (completely) de un lado a otro; (from beginning to end) de principio a fin, de cabo a rabo; **loyal — and —** leal a toda prueba; **he's an aristocrat — and —** es un aristócrata de pura cepa; **to carry —** llevar a cabo; ADJ (ticket, train) directo; **to be —** (with a task) haber terminado; (in a profession) estar acabado; **we're —!** (with a boyfriend) ¡se acabó entre nosotros!
throughout [θruáʊt] PREP (all through) por todo; (during) a lo largo de, durante; ADV (duration) de principio a fin; (space) por todas partes
throw [θro] VI/VT (a ball) tirar, lanzar; (a light, voice) arrojar; (a switch) conectar; (a pot on a wheel) modelar; (a punch) lanzar; (a wrestler) tumbar; (a game for a bribe) dejarse perder; (a rider) desmontar; (a party) dar, organizar; **that really threw me** eso me confundió; **to — away** (dispose of) tirar, arrojar; (squander) malgastar; **to — down** tirar al suelo; **to — in** añadir; **to — into gear** engranar; **to — in the clutch** embragar; **to — out** (garbage) tirar, arrojar; (unruly guest) echar; **to — up** vomitar, devolver; N (act or instance of throwing) tiro *m*; (of dice) tirada *f*; (shawl) chal *m*; (blanket) manta *f*; **— -in** (soccer) saque de banda *m*; ADJ **—away** desechable
thrown [θron] *see* throw
thrush [θrʌʃ] N tordo *m*, zorzal *m*
thrust [θrʌst] VT (stab) clavar; (shove) empujar; **to — oneself upon** meterse en; **to — a task upon someone** imponerle una tarea a alguien; **to — aside** echar a un lado; VI (push) dar un empujón; (stab at) lanzar una estocada; (push through) empujar para pasar; N (stab) estocada *f*; (force of a jet engine) empuje *m*; (shove) empujón *m*; (military assault) arremetida *f*, acometida *f*
thud [θʌd] N golpe sordo *m*; VI caer con un golpe sordo
thug [θʌg] N matón *m*
thumb [θʌm] N pulgar *m*; **—tack** chinche *f*, tachuela *f*; **under the — of** bajo la bota de; VT hojear; **to give a —s up** aprobar
thump [θʌmp] N golpe sordo *m*; VI hacer un ruido sordo
thunder [θʌ́ndə˞] N trueno *m*; **—bolt** rayo *m*; **—head** nubarrón *m*; **—storm** tormenta eléctrica *f*, tronada *f*; VI tronar
thunderous [θʌ́ndə˞əs] ADJ atronador, estruendoso
Thursday [θɝ́zde] N jueves *m*
thus [ðʌs] ADV así; **— far** (space) hasta aquí; (time) hasta ahora
thwart [θwɔrt] VT frustrar
thyme [taɪm] N tomillo *m*
thyroid [θáɪrɔɪd] N tiroides *m sg*
Tibet [tɪbɛ́t] N Tíbet *m*
Tibetan [tɪbɛ́tn] ADJ & N tibetano -na *mf*
tic [tɪk] N tic *m*, manía *f*
tick [tɪk] N (sound of a clock) tic tac *m*; (cover of a pillow) funda *f*; (checkmark) marca *f*; (insect) garrapata *f*; VI hacer tic tac; **to — off** (check off) marcar; (anger) enojar
ticket [tɪ́kɪt] N billete *m*; *Am* boleto *m*; (slate of candidates) candidatura *f*; (summons) multa *f*; (tag) etiqueta *f*; **— office** taquilla *f*; VT (give passage) vender billetes; (give summons)

multar

tickle [tíkəł] VT (poke) cosquillear, hacer cosquillas; (amuse) dar ilusión; VI picar; N picazón *f*, cosquilleo *m*

ticklish [tíklɪʃ] ADJ (prone to tickling) cosquilloso; (delicate) delicado

tidal [táɪdl] ADJ — **wave** (tsunami) tsunami *m*, maremoto *m*; (large wave) marejada *f*

tidbit [tídbɪt] N (snack) golosina *f*; (gossip) chisme jugoso *m*

tide [taɪd] N marea *f*; (of opinion) corriente *f*; —**water** (water) agua de marea *f*; (land) marisma *f*; VT **to — over** cubrir

tidy [táɪdɪ] ADJ (orderly) ordenado; (large) considerable; VI/VT arreglar; **to — oneself up** arreglarse

tie [taɪ] VI (fasten) atarse; (make same score) empatar; VT (fasten) atar; (make a knot) hacer un nudo en; (make same score as) empatar con; **to — a record** empatar una marca; **to — down** atar; **to — in** cuadrar; **to — one on** emborracharse; **to — tight** atar fuerte; **to — up** (bind) atar; (hinder) bloquear; (occupy) ocupar; (moor a ship) amarrar; N (cord) cuerda *f*; (relations) lazo *m*, vínculo *m*; (cravat) corbata *f*; (railway) durmiente *m*, traviesa *f*; (score) empate *m*; —-**break** (in sports) desempate *m*; (in tennis) muerte súbita *f*

tier [tɪr] N nivel *m*

tiger [táɪgɚ] N tigre *m*

tight [taɪt] ADJ (knot, nut) apretado, ajustado; (clothes) ceñido, ajustado; (control) firme, estricto; (race) reñido; (stingy) tacaño, mezquino; (drunk) borracho; — **end** (football) receptor cerrado *m*; —-**fisted** agarrado; —**rope** cuerda floja *f*; —**wad** tacaño -ña *mf*; **to be in a — spot** estar en un aprieto; ADV bien, herméticamente; **to hold on —** agarrarse bien

tighten [táɪtn̩] VI/VT (knot, nut, belt) apretar[se]; (control) estrechar[se]

tightness [táɪtnɪs] N (narrowness) estrechez *f*; (stinginess) tacañería *f*

tilde [tɪ́łdə] N tilde *f*

tile [taɪł] N (on a roof) teja *f*; (on a floor) baldosa *f*; (on a wall) azulejo *m*; — **roof** tejado *m*; VT (roof) tejar; (floor) embaldosar; (wall) azulejar

till [tɪł] PREP hasta; CONJ hasta que; VI/VT (plow) labrar, arar; N (cash drawer) caja *f*

tilt [tɪłt] VI/VT ladear[se], inclinar[se]; N (act or instance of tilting) ladeo *m*, inclinación *f*; (incline) declive *m*; (joust) justa *f*; **at full —** a toda velocidad

timber [tímbɚ] N (cut wood) madera [de construcción] *f*; (trees) árboles para madera *m pl*; (beam) viga *f*; —**line** límite de la vegetación arbórea *m*; — **wolf** lobo gris *m*

timbre [tímbɚ] N timbre *m*

time [taɪm] N (past, present, future) tiempo *m*; (on the clock) hora *f*; (occasion) vez *f*; (period) período *m*, momento *m*, época *f*; —-**and-a-half pay** paga de tiempo y medio *f*; — **bomb** bomba de tiempo *f*; — **frame** plazo aproximado de tiempo *m*; —**keeper** cronometrador -ora *mf*; — **limit** límite de tiempo *m*; — **out** descanso *m*; —**piece** reloj *m*; —**share** tiempo compartido *m*; — **signature** compás *m*; —**table** horario *m*; — **zone** huso horario *m*; **at —s** a veces; **at the same —** a la vez, al mismo tiempo; **at this —** en este momento; **behind —** atrasado; **lunch—** hora del almuerzo *f*; **from — to —** de vez en cuando; **for the — being** por el momento; **in —** a tiempo; **in no —** en seguida; **it's about —** ya era hora; **on —** puntual; **to buy on —** comprar a plazo; — **after —** una vez tras otra; **to do —** cumplir una condena; **to have a good —** divertirse; **what — is it?** ¿qué hora es? VT (a race) cronometrar; (a test) fijar la duración de; (one's arrival) fijar la hora de; **to — an attack well** atacar en el momento oportuno

timeless [táɪmlɪs] ADJ eterno

timely [táɪmlɪ] ADJ oportuno

timer [táɪmɚ] N (person) cronometrador -ora *mf*; (device) reloj *m*

timid [tímɪd] ADJ tímido, apocado

timidity [tɪmídɪdɪ] N timidez *f*, apocamiento *m*

timing [táɪmɪŋ] N (measurement) cronometraje *m*; (synchronization) sincronización *f*; **that was good —** lo hiciste en el momento oportuno

timorous [tímɚəs] ADJ timorato

tin [tɪn] N (metal) estaño *m*; (tin plate) hojalata *f*; — **can** lata *f*; —**foil** papel de estaño *m*, papel de aluminio *m*; VT estañar

tincture [tíŋktʃɚ] N tintura *f*

tinder [tíndɚ] N yesca *f*

tinge [tɪnʤ] VT (tint) teñir; (affect slightly) matizar; N (of color) tinte *m*, matiz *m*; (of taste) dejo *m*; (of irony) matiz *m*

tingle [tíŋgł] VI sentir hormigueo, hormiguear; **to — with excitement** estremecerse de entusiasmo; N hormigueo *m*

tinker [tíŋkɚ] VI ocuparse, entretenerse; **to — with** hacer ajustes

tinkle [tíŋkł] VT (ring lightly) tintinear; (urinate) *fam* hacer pipí; N tintineo *m*

tinnitus [tɪnáɪdəs] N tinitus *m*

tinsel [tínsł] N (Christmas trim) espumillón *m*, guirnalda *f*; (tawdry decoration) oropel *m*

tint [tɪnt] N (hue) matiz *m*; (for hair) tinte *m*, tintura *f*; (for glass) coloreado *m*; VT (hair) teñir; (glasses) colorear

tiny [táɪnɪ] ADJ diminuto, chiquito

tip [tɪp] N (point) punta *f*; (gratuity) propina *f*;

(piece of advice) consejo *m*; VI/VT (tilt) inclinar[se], ladear[se]; (give a gratuity) dar propina [a]; **to — a person off** advertir a alguien; **to — one's hat** sacarse/quitarse el sombrero; **to — over** volcar[se]

tipsy [típsi] ADJ alegre

tiptoe [típto] N punta del pie *f*; **on —s** de puntillas; VI andar de puntillas

tirade [táɪred] N diatriba *f*

tire [taɪr] N neumático *m*; *Mex* llanta *f*; *Am* goma *f*; VI/VT cansar[se], fatigar[se]; **to — out** cansar, fatigar

tired [taɪrd] ADJ cansado, fatigado; **— out** agotado; **I'm — of your complaining** estoy harto de tus quejas

tireless [táɪrlɪs] ADJ incansable

tiresome [táɪrsəm] ADJ aburrido, pesado, plasta

tissue [tɪʃu] N (cell aggregate) tejido *m*; (handkerchief) pañuelo de papel *m*; **— paper** papel tisú *m*

tit [tɪt] N paro *m*

titanic [taɪtǽnɪk] ADJ titánico

titanium [taɪténiəm] N titanio *m*

tithe [taɪð] N diezmo *m*; VI pagar el diezmo

titillate [tídḷet] VT (sexually) excitar; (interest) despertar interés

title [táɪdl] N título *m*; (of a painting) rótulo *m*; **— deed** título de propiedad *m*; **— page** portada *f*

TNT [tíénti] N TNT *m*

to [tu] PREP **I gave it — you** te lo di a ti; **to count — ten** contar hasta diez; **I called — find out** llamé para averiguar; **— my surprise** para mi sorpresa; **a quarter — five** las cinco menos cuarto; **bills — be paid** cuentas por pagar; **things — do** cosas que hacer; **frightened — death** muerto de susto; **from house — house** de casa en casa; ADV **— and fro** de acá para allá; **to come —** volver en sí

toad [tod] N sapo *m*; **—stool** seta *f*, hongo no comestible *m*

toast [tost] VI/VT (brown) tostar[se]; VT (congratulate) brindar por; N (bread) tostada *f*; (congratulation) brindis *m*

toaster [tóstə-] N tostadora *f*; **— oven** horno tostador *m*

tobacco [təbǽko] N tabaco *m*

today [tədé] ADV hoy; (nowadays) hoy día

toddler [tádlə-] N niño pequeño *m*, niña pequeña *f*

toe [to] N dedo del pie *m*; (of shoe, sock) punta *f*; **—nail** uña del dedo del pie *f*; VT (touch with toe) tocar con el dedo del pie; **to — the line** hacer buena letra, entrar en vereda

together [təgéðə-] ADV (in union) juntos; (at the same time) al mismo tiempo; **— with** junto con; **all —** todos juntos

Togo [tógo] N Togo *m*

Togolese [togəlíz] ADJ & N togolés -esa *mf*

toil [tɔɪł] VI trabajar, esforzarse, bregar; N trabajo *m*, esfuerzo *m*

toilet [tɔ́ɪlɪt] N (bowl) inodoro *m*; (lavatory) aseo *m*, lavabo *m*; **— paper** papel higiénico *m*; ADJ **—-trained** que ya no usa pañales

token [tókən] N (symbol) señal *f*; (keepsake) recuerdo *m*; (coinlike metal piece) ficha *f*; **— payment** pago nominal *m*; **as a — of friendship** en prenda de amistad

told [tołd] *see* tell

tolerance [tálə-əns] N tolerancia *f*

tolerant [tálə-ənt] ADJ tolerante

tolerate [tálə-ret] VT tolerar

toll [tołˌ] N (of bells) tañido *m*; (payment) peaje *m*; (charges) tarifa *f*; (of victims) balance *m*; **— bridge** puente de peaje *m*; **— road** carretera de peaje *f*; ADJ **— -free** libre de cargos; VI/VT tañer [a muerto]

tomato [təméɪDo] N tomate *m*

tomb [tum] N tumba *f*, sepulcro *m*, sepultura *f*; **—stone** lápida *f*

tomcat [tómkæt] N gato macho *m*

tomorrow [təmɔ́ro] ADV & N mañana *f*; **— morning** mañana por la mañana *f*

ton [tʌn] N tonelada *f*

tone [ton] N (pitch) tono *m*; (of a voice, instrument) sonoridad *f*; (of a speech) tono *m*, tónica *f*; VI **to — down** moderar, matizar

toner [tóna-] N tóner *m*; **— cartridge** cartucho de tóner *m*

Tonga [tɑ́ŋgə] N Tonga *m*

Tongan [tɑ́ŋgən] ADJ & N tongano -na *mf*

tongs [tɔŋz] N tenazas *f pl*

tongue [tʌŋ] N (body part, language, of a flame) lengua *f*; (of a shoe) lengüeta *f*; **— depressor** depresor de lengua *m*; **— in cheek** irónicamente; **— twister** trabalenguas *m sg*; **on the tip of my —** en la punta de la lengua; **to hold one's —** callarse la boca; VI tocar con la lengua; **to — -lash** reprender; **to be — -tied** tener trabada la lengua

tonic [tánɪk] ADJ tónico; N (medicine) tónico *m*; (water, key note) tónica *f*; **— water** agua tónica *f*

tonight [tənáɪt] ADV esta noche

tonsil [tánsəł] N amígdala *f*

tonsillitis [tɑnsəláɪDɪs] N amigdalitis *f*, anginas *f pl*

too [tu] ADV (in addition) también; (excessively) demasiado; **— bad!** ¡qué lástima! **— many** demasiados; **— much** demasiado

took [tʊk] *see* take

tool [tuł] N herramienta *f*; **—bar** barra de herramientas *f*; **—box/kit** caja de herramientas *f*; **—shed** cobertizo para herramientas *m*

toot [tut] VI/VT (horn) sonar; (whistle) pitar; (trumpet) tocar; **to — one's own horn** darse

autobombo; N (of horn, trumpet) toque *m*; (of horn) bocinazo *m*; (of whistle) pitido *m*

tooth [tuθ] N (front) diente *m*; (back) muela *f*; **—ache** dolor de muelas *m*; **—brush** cepillo de dientes *m*; **— decay** caries [dental] *f* sg; **— fairy** ratoncito Pérez *m*; **— mark** dentellada *f*; **—paste** pasta dental *f*, pasta dentífrica *f*; **—pick** mondadientes *m* sg, palillo de dientes *m*; **to fight — and nail** luchar a brazo partido; **to have a sweet —** ser goloso

toothed [tuθt] ADJ dentado

toothless [túθlɪs] ADJ desdentado

top [tɑp] N (of a mountain) cumbre *f*, cima *f*; (of a page) parte superior *f*; (of a jar) tapa *f*; (of a convertible) capota *f*; (of a table) superficie *f*; (of a tree) copa *f*; (toy) trompo *m*, peonza *f*; (blouse) blusa *f*; **—coat** abrigo *m*; **— dollar** precio exorbitante *m*; **— hat** sombrero de copa *m*; **—spin** liftado *m*; **at — speed** a velocidad máxima; **to be — dog** ir a la cabeza; **to be at the — of the class** ser el mejor de la clase; **at the — of one's voice** a voz en cuello; **filled up to the —** lleno hasta el tope; **from — to bottom** de arriba abajo; **on — of** encima de; ADJ (officer, floor) superior; (shelf, step) más alto; **—-flight** de primera; **—-heavy** desbalanceado; **—most** superior; **—-rated** de la más alta categoría; **—-secret** altamente confidencial; **—-notch** de primera; VT (a tree) desmochar; (a list) encabezar; (a performance) superar; (a level) exceder; **to — off** (an action) rematar; (a tank) llenar hasta el tope; **that —s everything!** ¡eso es el colmo!

topaz [tópæz] N topacio *m*

topic [tápɪk] N tema *m*, materia *f*, *Am* tópico *m*

topical [tápɪkəł] ADJ (of medicine) tópico; (current) de actualidad

topless [táplɪs] ADJ topless; **— swimsuit** monokini *m*

topple [tápəł] VT (knock over) derribar; (overthrow) derrocar; VI (fall) volcarse; (lose power) caer; **to — over** volcarse

topsy-turvy [tápsitɝvi] ADJ & ADV patas arriba

torch [tɔrtʃ] N antorcha *f*

tore [tɔr] *see* tear

torment[1] [tɔ́rmɛnt] N tormento *m*

torment[2] [tɔrmɛ́nt] VT atormentar, martirizar

torn [tɔrn] *see* tear[2]

tornado [tɔrnéɪdo] N tornado *m*

torpedo [tɔrpíɪdo] N torpedo *m*; **— boat** torpedero *m*; VT torpedear

torpid [tɔ́rpɪd] ADJ torpe

torpor [tɔ́rpɚ] N letargo *m*, torpor *m*

torque [tɔrk] N par de torsión *m*

torrent [tɔ́rənt] N torrente *m*

torrential [tɔrɛ́nʃəł] ADJ torrencial

torrid [tɔ́rɪd] ADJ tórrido

torsion [tɔ́rʃən] N torsión *f*

torso [tɔ́rso] N torso *m*, tronco *m*

tortoise [tɔ́rɪtɪs] N tortuga *f*

tortuous [tɔ́rtʃuəs] ADJ tortuoso

torture [tɔ́rtʃɚ] N tortura *f*; VT torturar

torturous [tɔ́rtʃɚəs] ADJ torturante, torturador

toss [tɔs] VT (a ball, coin) tirar; (one's head) echar; (a salad) revolver; **to — aside** echar a un lado; VI (waves) cabecear; (a person in bed) dar vueltas; N (of coin, ball) tiro *m*; (of head) sacudida *f*

total [tódł] ADJ & N total *m*; **— amount** importe total *m*, montante *m*; **— loss** pérdidas totales *f* pl

totalitarian [totælɪtɛ́riən] ADJ totalitario

totter [tápɚ] VI tambalear[se], titubear

touch [tʌtʃ] VI/VT (have physical contact with) tocar; (move deeply) conmover, enternecer; (compare with) compararse con, igualar; (affect) afectar; **to — down** aterrizar; **to — off** provocar; **to — up** retocar; **to — upon** mencionar; N (contact) contacto *m*, roce *m*, toque *m*; (sense) tacto *m*; (knack) mano *f*; (slight amount) poquito *m*; ; **—down** anotación *f*; **—down pass** envío de anotación *m*, pase de anotación *m*; **— screen** pantalla táctil *f*; **—-sensitive display** pantalla táctil *f*; **—stone** piedra de toque *f*; **a woman's —** un toque femenino; **finishing —** toque final *m*; **to keep in —** mantenerse en contacto; ADJ **—-and-go** precario; **—-tone** de botones

touching [tʌ́tʃɪŋ] ADJ conmovedor

touchy [tʌ́tʃi] ADJ hipersensible

tough [tʌf] ADJ (leather) fuerte, resistente; (fighter) duro, fuerte; (steak) duro, correoso; (situation) difícil; (neighborhood) bravo

toughen [tʌ́fən] VI/VT (leather) curtir[se]; (meat) endurecer[se]; (person) endurecerse

toughness [tʌ́fnɪs] N (of leather) resistencia *f*; (of a fighter, steak) dureza *f*; (of a situation) dificultad *f*; (of a neighborhood) lo bravo

toupee [tupé] N peluquín *m*

tour [tur] N (professional, artistic) gira *f*; (touristic) tour *m*, excursión *f*; (of a building) visita *f*; VI/VT (artistic, political) hacer una gira [por]; (touristic) hacer un tour

tourism [túrɪzəm] N turismo *m*

tourist [túrɪst] N turista *mf*; **— attraction** atracción turística *f*; **— class** clase turista/turística *f*

tournament [tɝ́nəmənt] N torneo *m*

tourniquet [tɝ́nɪkɪt] N torniquete *m*

tow [to] VT remolcar; N (pull) remolque *m*; (fiber) estopa *f*; **—rope** cuerda de remolque *f*; **— truck** remolque *m*, grúa *f*, *Am* guinche *m*; **in —** a cuestas

toward, towards [təwɔ́rd[z]] PREP (in the direction of) hacia; (for) para; **— four o'clock** a eso de las cuatro; **to feel angry —**

estar enojado con

towel [táʊəɫ] N toalla *f*

tower [táʊə-] N torre *f*, — **model** *Am* computadora torre *f*, *Sp* ordenador torre *m*; VI **to — over** elevarse sobre, dominar

towering [táʊə-ɪŋ] ADJ (tall) elevado, muy alto; (excessive) desmedido

town [taʊn] N (large) ciudad *f*; (small) pueblo *m*, localidad *f*; (downtown) centro *m*; — **hall** ayuntamiento *m*; **out of —** de viaje

toxic [táksɪk] ADJ tóxico; — **shock syndrome** síndrome de choque tóxico *m*

toxin [táksɪn] N toxina *f*

toy [tɔɪ] N juguete *m*; — **poodle** caniche enano *m*; VI **to — with** (fiddle with) juguetear con; (consider) considerar

trace [tres] N (path, mark, footprint) huella *f*; (mark) rastro *m*, traza *f*; (vestige) vestigio *m*; VT (a plan) trazar; (history) examinar; (an image) calcar; (a criminal) rastrear

trachea [tréki͡ə] N tráquea *f*

tracheotomy [trekiáɒəmi] N traqueotomía *f*

track [træk] N (of a heel, animal) huella *f*; (of a wheel) rodada *f*; (for racing) pista *f*; (path) senda *f*, sendero *m*; (of a railroad) vía *f*; (on a record) surco *m*; (on a CD) tema *m*, pista *f*; (of study) orientación *f*; — **and field** atletismo *m*; — **meet** encuentro de atletismo *m*; — **record** trayectoria *f*; **to be off the —** estar descarrilado; **to keep — of** seguir el hilo de; VI/VT (a criminal) rastrear, seguir la pista de; (an aircraft, a student, progress) seguir; VI (wheels) estar alineado; (stylus) seguir los surcos; **to — down** perseguir; **to — in mud** traer lodo en los pies

tract [trækt] N (of land) terreno *m*; (political) octavilla *f*; (digestive) tubo *m*

traction [trǽkʃən] N tracción *f*

tractor [trǽktə-] N tractor *m*; —**-trailer** tractocamión *m*

trade [tred] N (buying and selling) comercio *m*, trato *m*; (industry) industria *f*; (swap) canje *m*, cambio *m*; (manual labor) oficio *m*; (profession) profesión *f*; (people in a business) gremio *m*; —**-in** entrega como parte de pago *f*; —**-off** compensación *f*; —**mark** marca registrada *f*, marca de fábrica *f*; — **agreement** acuerdo comercial *m*; — **balance** balanza comercial *f*; — **barrier** barrera comercial *f*; — **name** (of product) nombre comercial *m*; (of company) razón social *f*; — **school** escuela industrial *f*; — **union** sindicato *m*; VI/VT (buy and sell) comerciar, negociar; (exchange) canjear; (traffic) traficar; **to — in** entregar

trader [trédə-] N (dealer) comerciante *mf*; (at fairs) feriante *mf*; (of slaves) tratante *mf*

trading [tréɪdɪŋ] N transacciones *f pl*, comercio *m*; — **partners** socios comerciales *m pl*

tradition [trədíʃən] N tradición *f*

traditional [trədíʃənəɫ] ADJ tradicional

traffic [trǽfɪk] N (of drugs) tráfico *m*; (of vehicles) tránsito *m*, tráfico *m*; — **accident** accidente de tránsito *m*; — **jam** atasco circulatorio *m*; — **light** semáforo *m*; VI traficar

tragedy [trǽdʒɪdi] N tragedia *f*

tragic [trǽdʒɪk] ADJ trágico

trail [treɫ] VI/VT (drag) arrastrar[se]; (follow in a race) ir detrás [de]; (track) seguir la pista [de], rastrear; VT (leave a trace) dejar una estela / un reguero de; VI **to — off** desvanecerse, apagarse; N (trace) rastro *m*, huella *f*; (path) trocha *f*, sendero *m*, senda *f*; (of smoke) estela *f*; (of blood) reguero *m*; — **bike** motocicleta de trail *f*

trailer [trélə-] N (of a truck) remolque *m*; (of a film) sinopsis *f*, trailer *m*, avance *m*; (house) caravana *f*

train [tren] N (railroad) tren *m*; (part of a dress) cola *f*; — **of thought** hilo de pensamiento *m*; VI/VT (worker) capacitar[se]; (troops, athlete) adiestrar[se]; *Am* entrenar[se]; VT (an animal) amaestrar; (a child) educar, formar; (a cannon) apuntar; **to — on** (a camera, eye) enfocar

trainee [trení] N aprendiz -iza *mf*, practicante *mf*

trainer [trénə-] N (of animals) amaestrador -ora *mf*; (of workers, troops, athletes) entrenador -ora *mf*

training [trénɪŋ] N (of animals) amaestramiento *m*; (of workers) capacitación *f*; (of troops, athletes) entrenamiento *m*, adiestramiento *m*; (of children) educación *f*

trait [tret] N rasgo *m*, seña *f*

traitor [trédə-] N traidor -ora *mf*

trajectory [trədʒéktəri] N trayectoria *f*

tramp [træmp] VT (trample) pisar; VI andar con pasos pesados; (roam, as a hobo) vagabundear; N (hobo) vagabundo -da *mf*

trample [trǽmpəɫ] VT pisotear; **to — on/over** pisotear, atropellar; **to — out** apagar de un pisotón

trampoline [trǽmpəlín] N trampolín *m*, cama elástica *f*

trance [træns] N trance *m*

tranquil [trǽŋkwɪɫ] ADJ tranquilo

tranquilizer [trǽŋkwɪlaɪzə-] N tranquilizante *m*

tranquillity [trænkwílɪɫɪdi] N tranquilidad *f*

transact [trænzǽkt] VT llevar a cabo

transaction [trænzǽkʃən] N transacción *f*, negocio *m*; —**s** actas *f pl*

transatlantic [trænzɪtlǽntɪk] ADJ transatlántico

transcend [trænsénd] VI/VT trascender

transcendence [trænséndəns] N trascendencia *f*

transcendental [trænsendéntɫ] ADJ trascendental, trascendente

transcribe [trænskráɪb] VT transcribir
transcript [trǽnskrɪpt] N transcripción *f*
transfer [trænsfɚ̵] VI/VT (on a bus, train) trasbordar; (a prisoner, worker) trasladar[se]; VT (loyalty, rights, money, data) transferir; (property) traspasar; N (on a bus, train) trasbordo *m*; (of loyalty, rights, money, data) transferencia *f*; (of a prisoner, worker) traslado *m*; (of property) traspaso *m*; **— of ownership** traspaso de propiedad *m*; **— rate** velocidad de transferencia *f*
transferable [trænsfɚ̵əbəɫ] ADJ transferible
transfix [trænsfíks] VT (impale) traspasar, atravesar; (paralyze) paralizar
transform [trænsfɔ́rm] VI/VT transformar[se]
transformation [trænsfɚ̵méʃən] N transformación *f*
transformer [trænsfɔ́rmɚ̵] N transformador *m*
transfusion [trænsfjúʒən] N transfusión *f*; **to give a —** dar una transfusión de sangre, poner sangre
transgress [trænzgrɛ́s] VT transgredir; **to — against** pecar contra; **to — the bounds of** traspasar los límites de
transgression [trænzgrɛ́ʃən] N transgresión *f*, pecado *m*
transient [trǽnziənt] ADJ transeúnte, pasajero; N transeúnte *mf*, vagabundo -da *mf*
transistor [trænzístɚ̵] N transistor *m*
transit [trǽnzɪt] N tránsito *m*; **in —** en tránsito, de paso
transition [trænzíʃən] N transición *f*
transitive [trǽnzɪdɪv] ADJ transitivo
transitory [trǽnzɪtɔ̀ri] ADJ transitorio, pasajero
translate [trǽnzlet] VI/VT traducir
translation [trænzléʃən] N (rendering in different language) traducción *f*; (movement) translación *f*
translator [trǽnzleɪɚ̵] N traductor -ora *mf*
transmission [trænzmíʃən] N transmisión *f*
transmit [trænzmít] VI/VT transmitir
transmitter [trænzmídɚ̵] N transmisor *m*
transnational [trænznǽʃənəɫ] ADJ transnacional
transom [trǽnsəm] N travesaño *m*, montante *m*
transparency [trænzpɛ́rənsi] N transparencia *f*
transparent [trænspɛ́rənt] ADJ transparente; **to be —** traslucirse
transpire [trænspáɪr] VI (happen) ocurrir; (become known) descubrirse; VI/VT (perspire) transpirar
transplant[1] [trænsplǽnt] VI/VT trasplantar
transplant[2] [trǽnsplænt] N trasplante *m*
transport[1] [trænspɔ́rt] VT transportar, acarrear
transport[2] [trǽnspɔrt] N (moving) transporte *m*, acarreo *m*; (airplane) avión de transporte *m*; (rapture) éxtasis *m*; (of freight) flete *m*
transportation [trænspɚ̵téʃən] N transporte *m*
transpose [trænspóz] VI/VT (letters) transponer; (a song) transportar
transverse [trænsvɚ̵́s] ADJ transversal; (flute) transverso
trap [træp] N trampa *f*; (for hunting) trampa *f*, cepo *m*; (under a sink) sifón *m*; **—door** trampilla *f*; VI/VT (to capture animals) cazar con trampa, atrapar; VT (to pin) aprisionar
trapeze [trǽpíz] N trapecio *m*
trapezoid [trǽpəzɔɪd] N & ADJ trapezoide *m*
trash [trǽʃ] N basura *f*, desechos *m pl*; (people) *pej* gentuza *f*; **— can** cubo de basura *m*
trashy [trǽʃi] ADJ ordinario
trauma [trɔ́mə] N (physical) traumatismo *m*; (psychological) trauma *m*
traumatic [trəmǽɪɪk] ADJ traumático
travel [trǽvəɫ] VI/VT viajar [por]; VI (sound waves) propagarse; (in basketball) caminar, hacer pasos; N viaje *m*; **— agency** agencia de viajes *f*; **— expenses** gastos de viaje *m pl*, gastos de desplazamiento *m pl*; **—s** viajes *m pl*
traveler [trǽvəlɚ̵] N viajero -ra *mf*; **—'s check** cheque de viajero *m*
traverse [trəvɚ̵́s] VI/VT atravesar, cruzar; (skiing) bajar en diagonal; N (crossbar) travesaño *m*; (crossing) travesía *f*
travesty [trǽvɪsti] N farsa *f*
tray [tre] N bandeja *f*
treacherous [trɛ́tʃɚ̵əs] ADJ traicionero, alevoso
treachery [trɛ́tʃəri] N traición *f*, alevosía *f*
tread [trɛd] VI/VT (trample) pisar, pisotear; VI (walk) andar, caminar; N (step) paso *m*; (on tire) banda de rodadura/rodaje *f*; (on shoe) dibujo *m*; **—mill** cinta rodante *f*
treason [trízən] N traición *f*
treasure [trɛ́ʒɚ̵] N tesoro *m*; **— hunt** búsqueda del tesoro *f*; VT atesorar
treasurer [trɛ́ʒərɚ̵] N tesorero -ra *mf*
treasury [trɛ́ʒəri] N tesorería *f*, tesoro *m*; **secretary of the —** ministro -tra de hacienda *mf*
treat [trit] VI/VT (act toward, discuss in writing, give medical aid) tratar; **I —ed myself to ice cream** me di un festín de helado; N (pleasure) placer *m*; (gift) regalo *m*; **my —** yo invito
treatable [tríɪdəbəɫ] ADJ tratable
treatise [tríɪdɪs] N tratado *m*
treatment [trítmənt] N trato *m*, tratamiento *m*; (artistic handling) interpretación *f*
treaty [tríɪdi] N tratado *m*
treble [trɛ́bəɫ] ADJ (triple) triple; (of higher clef) de tiple; **— clef** clave de sol *f*; N tiple *m*; VI/VT triplicar
tree [tri] N árbol *m*; **— hugger** ecologista *mf*; **—top** copa de árbol *f*; **up a —** en aprietos
treeless [tríɪɪs] ADJ pelado, sin árboles
trek [trɛk] N expedición *f*; VI viajar con dificultad
tremble [trɛ́mbəɫ] VI temblar; N temblor *m*
tremendous [trɪméndəs] ADJ tremendo

tremor [trémə-] N temblor *m*, sacudida *f*
tremulous [trémjələs] ADJ trémulo
trench [trɛntʃ] N (military) trinchera *f*; (for pipes) zanja *f*; (on sea floor) fosa *f*; **— coat** trinchera *f*, gabardina *f*
trend [trɛnd] N tendencia *f*
trendy [tréndi] ADJ de moda
trespass [trɛ́spæs] N (illegal entry) entrada ilegal *f*; (religious) deuda *f*; VI (enter illegally) entrar ilegalmente; **to — against** (violate) violar; (sin) pecar; **no —ing** prohibido el paso
triage [triáʒ] N triaje *m*, clasificación *f*
trial [tráiəl] N (testing) ensayo *m*, prueba *f*; (attempt) tentativa *f*; (affliction) aflicción *f*; (in a court of law) juicio *m*, proceso *m*; **— balloon** globo sonda *m*; **— by fire** prueba de fuego *f*; **— flight** vuelo de prueba *m*; **— offer** oferta de prueba *f*; **— period** período de prueba *m*; **— run** ensayo *m*, prueba *f*; **by — and error** por ensayo y error
triangle [tráiæŋgəł] N triángulo *m*
triangular [traiǽŋgjələ-] ADJ triangular
tribe [traib] N tribu *f*
tribulation [trɪbjəléʃən] N tribulación *f*
tribunal [traɪbjúnəł] N tribunal *m*
tributary [tríbjəteri] ADJ & N tributario *m*, afluente *m*
tribute [trɪ́bjut] N (tax) tributo *m*; (testimonial) homenaje *m*
triceps [tráɪsɛps] N tríceps *m sg*
trick [trɪk] N (ruse) treta *f*, trampa *f*, trapisonda *f*; (magician's) truco *m*; (prank) broma *f*; (in cards) baza *f*; **to be up to one's old —s** hacer de las suyas; **to play a — on someone** gastarle una broma a alguien; VT hacer trampa, engañar; **to — someone into something** hacer que alguien haga algo por medio de artilugios
trickery [trɪ́kəri] N engaños *m pl*, argucias *f pl*
trickle [trɪ́kəł] VI gotear; **to — in [out]** llegar [irse] de a poco; N goteo *m*
trickster [trɪ́kstə-] N embustero -ra *mf*
tricky [trɪ́ki] ADJ (artful) mañoso; (difficult) complicado
tricycle [tráɪsɪkəł] N triciclo *m*
trifle [tráɪfəł] N (worthless thing) fruslería *f*, nadería *f*, bobada *f*; (cheap purchase) bagatela *f*; (small sum) miseria *f*; VI **to — with** jugar con; **to — away** perder
trigger [trɪ́gə-] N gatillo *m*; VT desencadenar
trill [trɪł] VI/VT (birds) trinar; (musical instrument) tremolar; (the rsound) pronunciar con vibración; N (of birds, etc.) trino *m*; (of the rsound) vibración *f*
trillion [trɪ́ljən] N billón *m*
trilogy [trɪ́ləʤi] N trilogía *f*
trim [trɪm] VT (adorn) adornar, guarnecer; (an edge) bordear; (fingernails, hair, threads) recortar; (hedge) podar; (airplane) equilibrar; (a wick) despabilar; ADJ (neat) cuidado; (slim) delgado; (fit) en buen estado físico; N (embellishment) adorno *m*; (of sails) orientación *f*; (cutting of hair) recorte *m*; (cutting of hedge) poda *f*; (of an airplane) equilibrio *m*
trimming [trɪ́mɪŋ] N (act of cutting) recorte *m*; (on a uniform) orla *f*, ribete *m*; **—s** (embellishments) adornos *m pl*; (food) guarniciones *f pl*; (parts cut off) recortes *m pl*
Trinidad and Tobago [trɪ́nɪdǽdəntəbégo] N Trinidad y Tobago *f*
Trinidadian [trɪnɪdǽdiən] ADJ & N trinitense *mf*
trinket [trɪ́ŋkɪt] N chucheria *f*, baratija *f*
trio [trío] N trío *m*
trip [trɪp] N (journey, drug-induced condition) viaje *m*; (experience) experiencia *f*; (accidental stumble) tropezón *m*; (making fall) zancadilla *f*; **— planner** planificador de rutas *m*; VT (cause to stumble) hacer una zancadilla a; (trip up) confundir; (release a catch) soltar; (blow a fuse) hacer saltar; VI (stumble) tropezar; (skip) andar con paso ligero; (make a mistake) equivocarse; (hallucinate) viajar; (blow a fuse) saltar
triphthong [trɪ́fθɔŋ] N triptongo *m*
triple [trɪ́pəł] ADJ & N (also in baseball) triple *m*; VI (in baseball) pegar un triple; VT (multiply by three) triplicar
triplet [trɪ́plɪt] N trillizo *m*
tripod [tráɪpad] N trípode *m*
trite [traɪt] ADJ trivial, trillado
triumph [tráiəmf] N triunfo *m*; VI triunfar
triumphant [traɪʌ́mfənt] ADJ triunfante, triunfador
trivial [tríviəł] ADJ trivial, baladí, fútil
trod [trɑd] *see* tread
trodden [trɑdn̩] *see* tread
trolley [tráli] N (electric bus) trole *m*, trolebús *m*; (on tracks) tranvía *m*
trombone [trɑmbón] N trombón *m*
troop [trup] N (of scouts) tropa *f*; (of soldiers) escuadrón *m*; (of tourists) horda *f*; **—s** tropas *f pl*
trophy [trófi] N trofeo *m*
tropic [trápɪk] N trópico *m*
tropical [trápɪkəł] ADJ tropical
trot [trɑt] VI trotar; VT hacer trotar; **to — out** sacar a relucir; N trote *m*
trouble [trábəł] VT (afflict) aquejar; (make turbid) enturbiar; VI/VT (bother) molestar[se]; (disturb) preocupar[se]; **to —shoot** solucionar problemas; N (problem) problema *m*; (difficulty) dificultad *f*, sinsabor *m*; (disturbance) disturbio *m*; (effort) molestia *f*; (ailment) enfermedad *f*, trastorno *m*; (mechanical breakdown) avería *f*, desperfecto *m*; **—maker** agitador -ora *mf*, revoltoso -sa

mf; **—shooter** solucionador -ora *mf*, localizador -ora de averías *mf*; **to be in —** estar en un aprieto; **it is not worth the —** no vale la pena; **to make —** causar problemas; **to take the —** tomarse la molestia; ADJ **—-free** sin problemas

trough [trɔf] N (for food) pesebre *m*, comedero *m*; (for water) abrevadero *m*, bebedero *m*; (of weather, on ocean floor) depresión *f*

trousers [tráʊzɚz] N pantalones *m pl*

trousseau [trúso] N ajuar *m*

trout [traʊt] N trucha *f*

trowel [tráʊəł] N (for mortar) llana *f*, paleta *f*; (for digging) desplantador *m*

truant [trúənt] N alumno -na que falta a clase sin permiso *mf*

truce [trus] N tregua *f*

truck [trʌk] N (vehicle) camión *m*; *Mex* troca *f*; (dealings) trato *m*; (vegetables) hortalizas *f pl*; **— driver** camionero -ra *mf*; *Mex* troquero -ra *mf*; VI/VT transportar en camión; *Mex* transportar en troca

trudge [trʌdʒ] VI andar con dificultad

true [tru] ADJ verdadero; (story) verídico; (copy, translation) fiel; (well) a plomo; (wheel) alineado, centrado; **—-blue** leal; **—-false test** prueba de verdadero o falso *f*; **his dream came —** su sueño se hizo realidad

truly [trúli] ADV (surprisingly) verdaderamente; (sincerely) sinceramente; (actually) en realidad, realmente; (accurately) fielmente; **very — yours** su seguro servidor, atentamente

trumpet [trʌ́mpɪt] N trompeta *f*; VI/VT (musician) trompetear; (elephant) barritar

trunk [trʌŋk] N (of tree, body) tronco *m*; (receptacle) baúl *m*; (of elephant) trompa *f*; (of a car) maletero *m*, *Mex* cajuela *f*; **—s** traje de baño *m*

trust [trʌst] N (confidence) confianza *f*; (charge) cargo *m*; (firm) trust *m*; (fund) fondo fideicomiso *m*; VI/VT (rely on) confiar en, fiarse de; VT (believe) creer; (hope) esperar

trustee [trʌstí] N (person holding property of another) fideicomisario -ria *mf*; (administrator) administrador -ora *mf*

trusteeship [trʌstíʃɪp] N (position of holding property) fideicomiso *m*; (administrative position) cargo de administrador *m*

trustful [trʌ́stfəł] ADJ confiado

trusting [trʌ́stɪŋ] ADJ confiado

trustworthy [trʌ́stwɝ-ði] ADJ fidedigno, digno de confianza

trusty [trʌ́sti] ADJ leal

truth [truθ] N verdad *f*

truthful [trúθfəł] ADJ (account) verídico; (person) veraz

truthfulness [trúθfəlnɪs] N veracidad *f*

try [traɪ] VT (attempt) tratar de, intentar; (test, taste) probar; (strain) poner a prueba; (put on trial) procesar, enjuiciar; **to — on** probarse; **to — one's luck** probar fortuna; **to — and** tratar de; **to — out** (test) probar; (for a team) presentarse para; N intento *m*, tentativa *f*; **—out** prueba *f*

trying [tráɪɪŋ] ADJ penoso

tryst [trɪst] N cita romántica *f*

T-shirt [tíʃɝt] N camiseta *f*

tub [tʌb] N (for bathing) bañera *f*; (for butter) envase *m*; (for washing) tina *f*

tuba [túbə] N tuba *f*

tube [tub] N tubo *m* (also electronic); (television) televisor *m*

tuberculosis [tʊbɝkjəlósɪs] N tuberculosis *f*

tubular [tʊ́bjələr] ADJ tubular

tuck [tʌk] VT (stick in) meter; (make fold) alforzar; **to — in one's shirt** meter la camisa dentro del pantalón; **to — into bed** arropar; **to — something under one's arm** meterse algo bajo el brazo; N alforza *f*

Tuesday [túzde] N martes *m*

tuft [tʌft] N (of feathers) penacho *m*; (of hair) mechón *m*, copete *m*; (of plants) mata *f*

tug [tʌg] VI/VT (pull) tirar, jalar; (drag) arrastrar; **to — at** tironear; N (pull) tirón *m*; (boat) remolcador *m*

tuition [tuíʃən] N matrícula *f*

tulip [túlɪp] N tulipán *m*

tumble [tʌ́mbəł] VI (fall) caer; (collapse) venirse abajo; (do handsprings, etc.) dar volteretas; **to — down** rodar; **to — dry** secar en la secadora; **to — over** tropezarse; N (fall) caída *f*; (gymnastic trick) voltereta *f*

tumbler [tʌ́mblɚ] N (glass) vaso *m*; (person) acróbata *mf*

tummy [tʌ́mi] N barriguita *f*

tumor [túmɚ] N tumor *m*

tumult [túmʌłt] N tumulto *m*

tumultuous [tumʌ́łtʃuəs] ADJ tumultuoso

tuna [túnə] N (fish) atún *m*, bonito *m*; (prickly pear) tuna *f*

tune [tun] N (melody) tonada *f*, aire *m*; (electronic adjustment) sintonía *f*; **—-up** afinación *f*; **to be in —** (in pitch) estar afinado; (adjusted) sintonizado; **to be out of —** estar desafinado; VT (engine) afinar; (musical instrument) afinar, templar; (radio) sintonizar; **to — in** sintonizar; **to — out** ignorar

tuner [túnɚ] N afinador -ora *mf*; (electronic) sintonizador *m*

tungsten [tʌ́ŋstən] N tungsteno *m*

tunic [túnɪk] N túnica *f*

Tunisia [tunízə] N Túnez *m*

Tunisian [tunízən] ADJ & N tunesino -na *mf*

tunnel [tʌ́nəł] N túnel *m*; (for traffic) viaducto *m*; **— vision** visión en túnel *f*; VI cavar; VT hacer un túnel

turban [tɝ́bən] N turbante *m*
turbine [tɝ́baɪn] N turbina *f*
turbocharger [tɝ́botʃɑrʤɚ] N turbocompresor *m*
turbojet [tɝ́boʤɛt] N turborreactor *m*
turbulence [tɝ́bjələns] N turbulencia *f*
turbulent [tɝ́bjələnt] ADJ turbulento
turf [tɝf] N (lawn) césped *m*; (peat) turba *f*; (track for horse races) pista *f*; (territory) territorio *m*; VT cubrir con césped
Turk [tɝk] N turco -ca *mf*
turkey [tɝ́ki] N pavo *m*; **— vulture** buitre pavo *m*
Turkey [tɝ́ki] N Turquía *f*
Turkish [tɝ́kɪʃ] ADJ turco; **— bath** baño turco *m*
Turkmen [tɝ́kmən] ADJ & N turcomano -na *mf*
Turkmenistan [tɝ́kmɛnɪstǽn] N Turkmenistán *m*
turmoil [tɝ́mɔɪł] N confusión *f*, agitación *f*
turn [tɝn] VT (corner) doblar, dar vuelta; (wheel, key) girar, dar vuelta; (page) dar vuelta; (soil) labrar; (stomach) revolver; (ankle) torcer[se]; (a river) desviar; VI (change color) cambiar de color; (become) ponerse; (rotate) girar; (change direction) girar, dar la vuelta; **to — against** volverse en contra de; **to — around** dar la vuelta, girar; **to — away** (face) volver; (eyes) apartar; (person) rechazar; **to — back** (return) volver; (a clock) atrasar; **to — down** (offer, request) rechazar; (radio) bajar; **to — in** (hand in/over) entregar; (go to bed) acostarse; **to — inside out** dar vuelta al revés; **to — into** convertir[se] en; **to — off** (light) apagar; (faucet) cerrar; (a road) salir de; (person in general sense) disgustar; (person in sexual sense) quitarle las ganas a alguien; **to — on** (light) encender, prender; (faucet) abrir; (person) excitar; **to — out** (light) apagar; (people) expulsar; (product) producir; **to — out well** salir bien; **to — over** (car) volcar[se]; (engine) arrancar; (thought, idea, etc.) dar vueltas a; (criminal, weapon, etc.) entregar; **—table** plato giratorio *m*; **to — to** (have recourse to) acudir a, recurrir a; (become) volver[se]; **to — up** aparecer; **to — up one's nose** desdeñar; **to — up one's sleeves** arremangarse; **to — upside down** dar vuelta; N (rotation) vuelta *f*, revolución *f*; (change of direction) giro *m*, vuelta *f*; (change in condition) cambio *m*; (curve) recodo *m*, curva *f*; (opportunity) turno *m*; **— of mind** actitud *f*; **—off** (disgusting thing) asco *m*; (road exit) salida *f*; **— of phrase** giro *m*; **—out** concurrencia *f*; **—over** (of employees) renovación *f*; (of merchandise) volumen *m*; (in football) pérdida de balón *f*; (pastry) empanada *f*, pastelito *m*; (of a ball) pérdida *f*; **—pike** autopista *f*; **—stile** torniquete *m*, molinete *m*; **— signal** intermitente *m*; **at every —** a cada paso; **bad —** mala pasada *f*; **good —** favor *m*; **his bad teeth are a —off** sus feos dientes me dan asco / me repugnan; **his foreign accent is a —-on** su acento extranjero me excita; **it's my —** me toca a mí; **to take —s** turnarse
turnip [tɝ́nɪp] N nabo *m*
turpentine [tɝ́pəntaɪn] N trementina *f*, aguarrás *m*
turquoise [tɝ́kɔɪz] N turquesa *f*
turret [tɝ́ɪt] N (small tower, gun tower) torreta *f*; (on a ship) torre *f*
turtle [tɝ́dł] N tortuga *f*; **—dove** tórtola *f*; **—neck** cuello vuelto *m*
tusk [tʌsk] N colmillo *m*
tutor [túdɚ] N profesor -ora particular *mf*; VI/VT dar clases particulares
tutorial [tutɔ́riəł] ADJ de tutoría; N (computer) tutorial *m*; (math, Spanish) cursillo *m*
Tuvalu [túvəlu] N Tuvalu *m*
Tuvaluan [tuvəlúən] ADJ & N tuvaluano -na *mf*
tuxedo [tʌksído] N esmoquin *m*
TV [television] [tíví] N *fam* tele *f*
twang [twæŋ] N (in music) tañido *m*; (of speech) nasalidad *f*; VI (vibrate) vibrar; VT hacer vibrar; VI/VT (speak nasally) ganguear
twangy [twǽŋi] ADJ gangoso
tweak [twik] VT (pinch) pellizcar; (adjust) ajustar; N (pinch) pellizco *m*; (adjustment) ajuste *m*
tweed [twid] N tweed *m*
tweezers [twízɚz] N pinzas *f pl*
twelve [twɛłv] NUM doce
twentieth [twɛntiɪθ] NUM vigésimo; **it's his — birthday** hoy cumple veinte años; **it's the — time I've told you** ya te lo dije veinte veces
twenty [twɛ́nti] NUM veinte; **—-five** veinticinco
twerp [twɝp] N idiota *mf*, papanatas *mf sg*
twice [twaɪs] ADV dos veces
twig [twɪg] N ramita *f*
twilight [twáɪlaɪt] N crepúsculo *m*, ocaso *m*; **— zone** zona gris *f*
twin [twɪn] ADJ & N (fraternal) mellizo -za *mf*; (identical) gemelo -la *mf*; **— bed** cama individual *f*
twine [twaɪn] N cuerda *f*; VI/VT (twist) enroscar[se]; (interlace) entrelazar[se]
twinge [twɪnʤ] N (of pain, remorse) punzada *f*
twinkle [twíŋkəł] VI (star) titilar, parpadear; (eyes) brillar; N (of stars) titileo *m*, parpadeo *m*; (of eyes) brillo *m*
twirl [twɝł] VI/VT girar, dar vueltas [a]; N giro *m*, vuelta *f*; (of ice cream) espiral *m*
twist [twɪst] VI/VT (wind, coil) torcer[se]; (distort) tergiversar[se]; (writhe) retorcer[se]; (coil) enroscar[se]; N (of an ankle) torcedura *f*; (distortion) tergiversación *f*; (in a road, coil)

vuelta *f*; (unforeseen event) vuelta de tuerca *f*
twister [twístə˞] N tornado *m*
twitch [twɪtʃ] VI/VT crispar[se], mover[se]; N (tic) tic *m*; (pang) punzada *f*; (tug) tirón *m*
twitter [twítə˞] VI gorjear; N gorjeo *m*
two [tu] NUM dos; **— hundred** doscientos; **—-point conversion** conversión de dos puntos *f*; **my — cents' worth** mi opinión *f*; **to put — and — together** atar cabos; ADJ **—-bit** de chicha y nabo; **—-edged** de doble filo; **—-faced** (with two faces) de dos caras; (hypocritical) hipócrita, falso; **—-fisted** pendenciero; **—-way** de dos sentidos
tycoon [taɪkún] N magnate *mf*
type [taɪp] N tipo *m*, índole *f*; **—face** tipo de letra *m*; **—script** texto escrito a máquina *m*; **—writer** máquina de escribir *f*; **—writing** mecanografía *f*; VI/VT (a letter) escribir a máquina, mecanografiar, digitar, teclear, tipiar, tipear; VT (blood) determinar el grupo sanguíneo; **to —set** componer; **to —write** escribir a máquina; ADJ **—written** escrito a máquina
typhoid [táɪfɔɪd] N tifoidea *f*; **— fever** fiebre tifoidea *f*, tifus *m*
typhoon [taɪfún] N tifón *m*
typhus [táɪfəs] N tifus *m*
typical [típɪkəl] ADJ típico
typist [táɪpɪst] N mecanógrafo -fa *mf*
typo [táɪpo] N error tipográfico *m*
typographical [taɪpəgrǽfɪkəl] ADJ tipográfico; **— error** error de imprenta *m*, errata *f*
typology [taɪpɑ́lə̌ʤi] N tipología *f*
tyrannical [tɪrǽnɪkəl] ADJ tiránico
tyranny [tírəni] N tiranía *f*
tyrant [táɪrənt] N tirano -na *mf*

Uu

ubiquitous [jubíkwɪdəs] ADJ ubicuo
U-boat [júbot] N submarino alemán *m*
udder [ʌ́də˞] N ubre *f*
UFO [unidentified flying object] [júéfó] N OVNI *m*
Uganda [jugǽndə] N Uganda *f*
Ugandan [jugǽndən] ADJ & N ugandés -esa *mf*
ugliness [ʌ́glɪnɪs] N fealdad *f*
ugly [ʌ́gli] ADJ feo; (incident) deplorable; (mood) de perros
uh-huh [ʌhʌ́] INTERJ *fam* sí
Ukraine [jukrén] N Ucrania *f*
Ukrainian [jukréniən] ADJ & N ucraniano -na *mf*
ulcer [ʌ́lsə˞] N úlcera *f*
ulcerate [ʌ́lsəret] VI ulcerar
ulcerous [ʌ́lsə˞əs] ADJ ulceroso
ulna [ʌ́lnə] N cúbito *m*
ulterior [ʌltíri˞ə˞] ADJ ulterior; **— motive** segunda intención *f*
ultimate [ʌ́ltəmɪt] ADJ (destination) último, final; (authority) final, máximo; (principle) fundamental; (vacation) perfecto; N súmmum *m*
ultimately [ʌ́ltəmɪtli] ADV en última instancia
ultimatum [ʌltəméɪ̌ʔəm] N ultimátum *m*
ultralight [ʌ́ltrəlaɪt] ADJ & N ultraligero *m*
ultramodern [ʌltrəmɑ́də˞n] ADJ ultramoderno
ultrasound [ʌ́ltrəsʌʊnd] N ultrasonido *m*; **— imaging** imágenes por ultrasonido *f pl*
ultraviolet [ʌ́ltrəvɪ́ə̌ləɪt] ADJ & N ultravioleta *m*
umbilical cord [ʌmbílɪkəlkɔ˞d] N cordón umbilical *m*
umbrella [ʌmbrélə] N paraguas *m sg*
umpire [ʌ́mpaɪr] N árbitro *m*; (in tennis) juez -eza de silla *mf*; VI/VT arbitrar
unable [ʌnébəl] ADJ **to be — to** no poder
unabridged [ʌnə˞bríʤd] ADJ íntegro
unaccented [ʌnǽksɛntɪd] ADJ sin acento
unacceptable [ʌnɪksépt̬əbəl] ADJ inaceptable, inadmisible
unaccustomed [ʌnə˞kʌ́stə˞md] ADJ (not used to) no acostumbrado; (uncommon) insólito
unadjusted [ʌnə˞ʤʌ́stɪd] ADJ no ajustado
unadulterated [ʌnə˞dʌ́ltə˞eɪ̌dɪd] ADJ puro
unaffected [ʌnə˞fɛ́ktɪd] ADJ (not affected) no afectado; (sincere) natural, sincero; (unpretentious) sin afectación
unaffiliated [ʌnə˞fílɪeɪ̌dɪd] ADJ no afiliado
unanimity [junə˞nímɪdi] N unanimidad *f*
unanimous [junə˞nə˞məs] ADJ unánime
unarmed [ʌnə˞rmd] ADJ desarmado
unassuming [ʌnə˞súmɪŋ] ADJ modesto, sin pretensiones
unattached [ʌnə˞tǽtʃt] ADJ (piece of paper) suelto; (person) soltero
unauthorized [ʌnɔ́θə˞raɪzd] ADJ no autorizado
unavailable [ʌnə˞vélə̌bəl] ADJ no disponible
unavoidable [ʌnə˞vɔ́ɪ̌dəbəl] ADJ inevitable, ineludible
unaware [ʌnə˞wér] ADJ inconsciente; ADV **to be — of** ignorar; **—s** sin darse cuenta
unbalanced [ʌnbǽlə˞nst] ADJ desequilibrado
unbearable [ʌnbér̬əbəl] ADJ inaguantable, insoportable
unbeatable [ʌnbíd̬əbəl] ADJ imbatible
unbeaten [ʌnbítn̩] ADJ invicto
unbecoming [ʌnbɪkʌ́mɪŋ] ADJ (behavior) impropio; (clothes) que no [le] luce
unbelief [ʌnbɪlíf] N incredulidad *f*, descreimiento *m*.
unbelievable [ʌnbɪlívəbəl] ADJ increíble
unbeliever [ʌnbɪlívə˞] N descreído -da *mf*
unbending [ʌnbéndɪŋ] ADJ inflexible
unbiased [ʌnbáɪəst] ADJ imparcial
unbounded [ʌnbáʊndɪd] ADJ illimitado

unbridled [ʌnbráɪdld] ADJ desenfrenado
unbroken [ʌnbrókən] ADJ (intact) intacto; (not tamed) indomado; (uninterrupted) ininterrumpido
unbuckle [ʌnbákəl] VT desabrochar
unbutton [ʌnbátn] VI/VT desabotonar, desabrochar
uncalled-for [ʌnkółdfɔr] ADJ injustificado
uncanny [ʌnkǽni] ADJ inexplicable, misterioso
uncertain [ʌnsə́·tn] ADJ incierto
uncertainty [ʌnsə́·tnti] N incertidumbre *f*
unchanged [ʌntʃéndʒd] ADJ inalterado
uncharitable [ʌntʃǽrɪɪdəbəl] ADJ duro, poco caritativo
uncivilized [ʌnsívəlaɪzd] ADJ incivilizado
uncle [ǽŋkəl] N tío *m*; **to say —** darse por vencido
unclean [ʌnklín] ADJ (dirty) sucio; (impure) impuro
uncollectable [ʌnkəléktəbəl] ADJ incobrable
uncomfortable [ʌnkámfə·bəbəl] ADJ incómodo
uncommon [ʌnkámən] ADJ (unusual) poco común; (extraordinary) extraordinario
uncompromising [ʌnkámprəmaɪzɪŋ] ADJ (intransigent) intransigente; (unfailing) incondicional
unconcerned [ʌnkənsə́·nd] ADJ indiferente
unconditional [ʌnkəndíʃənəl] ADJ incondicional
unconfirmed [ʌnkənfə́·md] ADJ no confirmado
unconscious [ʌnkánʃəs] ADJ inconsciente
unconstitutional [ʌnkɑnstɪtúʃən] ADJ inconstitucional
uncontrollable [ʌnkəntróləbəl] ADJ (movement) incontrolable; (urge, laughter) incontenible
unconventional [ʌnkənvénʃənəl] ADJ poco convencional
uncouth [ʌnkúθ] ADJ tosco
uncover [ʌnkávə·] VI/VT descubrir[se]; VI (remove bedcovers) destaparse
uncovered [ʌnkávə·d] ADJ descubierto
unctuous [ǽŋktʃuəs] ADJ untuoso, zalamero
uncultivated [ʌnkáltəvedɪd] ADJ (person) inculto, no cultivado; (land) no cultivado
uncultured [ʌnkáltʃə·d] ADJ inculto
undaunted [ʌndɔ́ntɪd] ADJ impávido, intrépido
undecided [ʌndɪsáɪdɪd] ADJ indeciso
undeclared [ʌndɪkléɪrd] ADJ no declarado
undefined [ʌndɪfáɪnd] ADJ indefinido
undelete utility [ʌndɪlít jutɪlɪtɪ] N programa para recuperar datos borrados *m*
undeniable [ʌndɪnáɪəbəl] ADJ innegable, indudable
under [ʌndə·] PREP (below) bajo, debajo de, abajo de; (in a ranking) por debajo de; (less) menos de; **— the Democrats** durante el mandato de los Demócratas; **— a pseudonym** bajo un pseudónimo; **— cost** a menos del costo/coste, por debajo del costo/coste; **— contract** bajo contrato; **— wraps** oculto; ADV (below) debajo, abajo; (less than) menos; **to be —** estar inconsciente
underage [ʌndə·éʤ] ADJ menor de edad; **— drinking** consumo de alcohol por menores de edad *m*
underarm [ʌ́ndə·ɑrm] N axila *f*
underbrush [ʌ́ndə·brʌʃ] N maleza *f*
undercharge [ʌndə·tʃárʤ] VI cobrar de menos
underclass [ʌ́ndə·klæs] N subproletariado *m*
undercover [ʌndə·kávə·] ADJ clandestino, secreto
undercut [ʌndə·kát] VT (undermine) socavar; (sell for less) vender por menos que
underdeveloped [ʌndə·dɪvéləpt] ADJ subdesarrollado
underdog [ʌ́ndə·dɔg] N el de abajo *m*, la de abajo *f*
underemployed [ʌndə·ɛmplɔ́ɪd] ADJ subempleado
underestimate [ʌndə·éstəmet] VT (person) subestimar; (price) subvaluar
underfed [ʌndə·fɛ́d] ADJ desnutrido
underfoot [ʌndə·fʊ́t] ADJ (beneath the feet) bajo los pies; (in the way) estorbando
undergird [ʌndə·gə́·d] VT reforzar
undergo [ʌndə·gó] VT (an operation) someterse a; (a change) experimentar, sufrir
undergraduate [ʌndə·grǽʤuɪt] N estudiante de pregrado *mf*; **— course** clase de pregrado *f*
underground[1] [ʌndə·gráʊnd] ADV (under the earth) bajo tierra; (secretly) en secreto
underground[2] [ʌ́ndə·graʊnd] ADJ (under the earth) subterráneo; (secret) clandestino; N resistencia *f*, grupo clandestino *m*
underhanded [ʌndə·hǽndɪd] ADJ (secret) secreto, solapado; (illicit) ilícito
underlie [ʌndə·láɪ] VI/VT subyacer [a]
underline [ʌ́ndə·laɪn] VT subrayar
underlying [ʌndə·láɪɪŋ] ADJ (inflation, racism) subyacente; (problems) de fondo
undermine [ʌndə·máɪn] VT minar, menoscabar
underneath [ʌndə·níθ] PREP bajo, debajo de, abajo de; ADV debajo, abajo; N la parte inferior
undernourished [ʌndə·nə́·ɪʃt] ADJ desnutrido
underpants [ʌ́ndə·pænts] N (for men) calzoncillos *m pl*; (for women) *Sp* bragas *f pl*; *Mex* pantaletas *f pl*; *RP* bombacha *f*
underrated [ʌndə·rɛ́dɪd] ADJ infravalorado
underscore [ʌndə·skɔ́r] N subrayado *m*; VT subrayar
undersecretary [ʌndə·sɛ́krətɛrɪ] N subsecretario -ria *mf*
undersell [ʌndə·sɛ́l] VT (to sell at a low price) malbaratar; (to sell cheaper) vender a menos precio
undershirt [ʌ́ndə·shə·t] N camiseta *f*

underside [ándəsaɪd] N parte inferior *f*
undersigned [ʌndəsáɪnd] N abajo firmante *mf*, infrascrito -ta *mf*
underskirt [ándəskɚt] N enaguas *f pl*
understaffed [ʌndəstǽft] ADJ falto de personal
understand [ʌndəstǽnd] VI/VT comprender, entender; **I — you're leaving** tengo entendido que te vas; **to — about** saber de/entender de
understandable [ʌndəstǽndəbəɫ] ADJ comprensible
understanding [ʌndəstǽndɪŋ] N (comprehension) comprensión *f*, entendimiento *m*; (tolerance) comprensión mutua *f*; (agreement) acuerdo *m*; ADJ comprensivo
understate [ʌndəstét] VT minimizar
understood [ʌndəstúd] ADJ entendido; (implicit) sobreentendido
understood [ʌndəstúd] *see* understand
understudy [ándəstʌdi] N suplente *mf*, sobresaliente *mf*; VI/VT suplir [a], servir de sobresaliente [para]
undertake [ʌndəték] VT emprender, acometer; **to — to** comprometerse a
undertaken [ʌndətékən] *see* undertake
undertaker [ándətekɚ] N director -ora de funeraria / pompas fúnebres *mf*, funerario -ria *mf*
undertaking [ʌndətékɪŋ] N empresa *f*
under-the-table [ándəðətébəɫ] ADJ ilícito, bajo cuerda
undertone [ándətoɫn] N (low voice) voz baja *f*; (undercurrent) tónica *f*
undertook [ʌndətúk] *see* undertake
undertow [ándətoɫ] N resaca *f*
undervalued [ʌndəvǽljud] ADJ infravalorado
underwater [ándəwɔtɚ, ándəwɔ́tɚ] ADJ submarino; ADV por debajo del agua
underwear [ándəwɛr] N ropa interior *f*
underweight [ándəwet] ADJ de peso insuficiente
underworld [ándəwɝɫd] N (of criminals) hampa *f*; (netherworld) el más allá
underwrite [ʌndəraɪt] VI/VT (finance) financiar; (sign) suscribir; (insure) asegurar
underwriter [ʌndəraɪdɚ] N (insurance) asegurador -ora *mf*; (stock exchange) suscriptor -ora *mf*
undesirable [ʌndɪzáɪrəbəɫ] ADJ indeseable
undetermined [ʌndɪtɝ́mɪnd] ADJ indeterminado
undid [ʌndíd] *see* undo
undisclosed [ʌndɪsklózd] ADJ no divulgado
undisturbed [ʌndɪstɝ́bd] ADJ (unworried, uninterrupted) tranquilo; (unspoiled) virgen
undivided [ʌndɪváɪdɪd] ADJ indiviso
undo [ʌndú] VT (reverse an action) deshacer, anular; (unfasten) desabrochar, desabotonar; (destroy) destruir; (loosen hair) soltar
undocumented [ʌndákjəmɛntɪd] ADJ indocumentado
undoing [ʌndúɪŋ] N (reversal) deshacer *m*; (destruction) destrucción *f*, perdición *f*; (of buttons) desabrochar *m*
undone [ʌndʌ́n] ADJ (unfinished) sin terminar; (ruined) perdido; (unfastened) desabrochado; **to come —** (clothing) desabrocharse; (person) desquiciarse
undone [ʌndʌ́n] *see* undo
undoubtedly [ʌndáʊdɪdli] ADV indudablemente, sin duda
undress [ʌndrés] VI/VT desnudar[se], desvestir[se]
undue [ʌndú] ADJ (inappropriate) indebido; (excessive) excesivo
undulate [ándʒəlet] VI/VT ondular
undying [ʌndáɪɪŋ] ADJ imperecedero, eterno
unearned [ʌnɝ́nd] N inmerecido; **— run** (baseball) carrera sucia *f*
unearth [ʌnɝ́θ] VT desenterrar
uneasiness [ʌnízɪnɪs] N (feeling) inquietud *f*, desasosiego *m*, desazón *f*; *Sp* grima *f*; (of peace) precariedad *f*; (of silence, situation) incomodidad *f*; (of sleep) agitación *f*
uneasy [ʌnízi] ADJ (feeling) inquieto; (peace) precario; (silence) incómodo; (situation) molesto; (sleep) agitado
uneducated [ʌnédʒəkeɪdɪd] ADJ inculto, ignorante
unemployable [ʌnɪmplɔ́ɪəbəɫ] ADJ inempleable
unemployed [ʌnɪmplɔ́ɪd] ADJ (jobless) desocupado, desempleado, *Sp* parado; (unused) ocioso
unemployment [ʌnɪmplɔ́ɪmənt] N desocupación *f*, desempleo *m*, *Sp* paro *m*; **— compensation** seguro de paro *m*; *Sp* paro *m*; **— rate** *Am* tasa de desempleo *f*, *Sp* tasa de paro *f*
unending [ʌnéndɪŋ] ADJ interminable
unequal [ʌníkwəɫ] ADJ desigual; **to be — to a task** no ser capaz de cumplir una tarea
unequivocal [ʌnɪkwívəkəɫ] ADJ inequívoco, tajante
unerase [ʌnɪrés] VT recuperar archivos borrados
unethical [ʌnéθɪkəɫ] ADJ no ético
uneven [ʌnívən] ADJ (rough) irregular, accidentado; (inequitable) desigual; (not uniform) desparejo; (odd, of numbers) impar
uneventful [ʌnɪvéntfəɫ] ADJ sin incidente
unexpected [ʌnɪkspéktɪd] ADJ inesperado
unexpressive [ʌnɪksprɛ́sɪv] ADJ inexpresivo
unfailing [ʌnféɪɪŋ] ADJ (inexhaustible) inagotable; (dependable) infalible
unfair [ʌnfɛ́r] ADJ (measure, price) injusto; (competition) injusto, desleal
unfaithful [ʌnféθfəɫ] ADJ infiel
unfamiliar [ʌnfəmíljɚ] ADJ (unknown) poco

familiar, desconocido; (unacquainted) poco familiarizado

unfasten [ʌnfǽsən] VI/VT desabrochar[se], desprender[se]

unfavorable [ʌnfévərəbəl] ADJ desfavorable

unfeeling [ʌnfíliŋ] ADJ insensible

unfettered [ʌnfétərd] ADJ (untied) desatado; (free) libre

unfinished [ʌnfíniʃt] ADJ (matter) inacabado, inconcluso; (business) pendiente; (wood) sin terminar, sin barnizar; (task) inconcluso, sin terminar

unfit [ʌnfít] ADJ (unsuitable) no apto; (incapable) incapaz

unfold [ʌnfóld] VT (open out) desdoblar, desplegar; VI (happen) desarrollarse; (reveal) revelarse

unforced error [ʌnfɔ́rst érər] N (tennis) error no forzado *m*

unforeseen [ʌnfɔrsín] ADJ imprevisto

unforgettable [ʌnfər-gétəbəl] ADJ inolvidable

unfortunate [ʌnfɔ́rtʃənɪt] ADJ desgraciado, desafortunado, desventurado

unfortunately [ʌnfɔ́rtʃənətli] ADV desafortunadamente, lamentablemente

unfounded [ʌnfáʊndɪd] ADJ infundado

unfriendly [ʌnfréndli] ADJ (forces) hostil; (person) antipático

unfurl [ʌnfɜ́-l] VI/VT desplegar[se]

unfurnished [ʌnfɜ́-nɪʃt] ADJ sin amueblar, desamueblado

ungainly [ʌngénli] ADJ (ungraceful) desgarbado, desmadejado; (clumsy) torpe

ungrateful [ʌngrétfəl] ADJ ingrato, desagradecido

unguarded [ʌngárdɪd] ADJ (incautious) descuidado, desprevenido; (unattended) sin vigilancia; (defenseless) indefenso; **an — moment** un momento de descuido

unhappiness [ʌnhǽpinɪs] N infelicidad *f*

unhappy [ʌnhǽpi] ADJ (sad) infeliz, desdichado, desgraciado; (dissatisfied) insatisfecho; (infelicitous) poco afortunado

unharmed [ʌnhármd] ADJ ileso

unhealthy [ʌnhélθi] ADJ (climate, food, lifestyle) malsano, insalubre; (complexion, obsession) enfermizo

unheard-of [ʌnhɜ́-dʌv] ADJ inaudito, desconocido

unhinge [ʌnhínʤ] VT desquiciar

unholy [ʌnhóli] ADJ (noise) infernal; (alliance) nefasto

unhook [ʌnhʊ́k] VT (disentangle) desenganchar; (undo) desabrochar

unhurt [ʌnhɜ́-t] ADJ ileso

uniform [júnəfɔrm] ADJ & N uniforme *m*

uniformity [junəfɔ́rmɪdi] N uniformidad *f*

unify [júnəfaɪ] VI/VT unificar[se]

unilateral [junəlǽdə-əl] ADJ unilateral

unimportant [ʌnɪmpɔ́rtn̩t] ADJ insignificante, sin importancia

uninhabited [ʌnɪnhǽbɪdɪd] ADJ deshabitado

uninhibited [ʌnɪnhíbɪdɪd] ADJ desinhibido, desenfadado

uninspired [ʌnɪnspáɪrd] ADJ poco inspirado

uninstall [ʌnɪnstɔ́l] VT desinstalar

uninsured [ʌnɪnʃʊ́rd] ADJ sin seguro médico

unintelligible [ʌnɪntélɪʤəbəl] ADJ ininteligible

uninterrupted [ʌnɪntər-ʌ́ptɪd] ADJ ininterrumpido

union [júnjən] N unión *f*; (labor) sindicato *m*, gremio *m*; **— dues** cuotas sindicales *f pl*; **— labor** mano de obra sindicalizada/agremiada *f*; **— leader** dirigente sindical *mf*

unionize [júnjənaɪz] VI/VT sindicar[se], agremiar[se]

unique [juník] ADJ único, singular; **that feature is — to the South** ese rasgo es peculiar del sur

unisex [júnəseks] ADJ unisex

unison [júnəsən] ADV LOC **in —** al unísono

unit [júnɪt] N (part of a whole) unidad *f*; (part of a machine) módulo *m*

unitarian [junɪtériən] ADJ unitario

unitary [júnɪtɛri] ADJ unitario

unite [junáɪt] VI/VT unir[se]

United Arab Emirates [junáɪdɪdǽrəbémə-ɪts] N Emiratos Árabes Unidos *m pl*

United Kingdom [junáɪdɪdkíŋdəm] N Reino Unido *m*

United States [junáɪdɪdstéts] N Estados Unidos *m pl*

unity [júnɪdi] N unidad *f*; (concord) unión *f*

universal [junəvɜ́-səl] ADJ universal; **— donor** donante universal *mf*; **— joint** acoplamiento universal de cardán *m*

universe [júnəvɜ-s] N universo *m*

university [junəvɜ́-sɪdi] N universidad *f*; **— degree** título universitario *m*

unjust [ʌnʤʌ́st] ADJ injusto

unjustifiable [ʌnʤʌstəfáɪəbəl] ADJ injustificable

unkempt [ʌnkémpt] ADJ (uncombed) desgreñado, despeinado; (messy) desaliñado

unkind [ʌnkáɪnd] ADJ antipático, poco amable

unknown [ʌnnón] ADJ desconocido; **— quantity** incógnita *f*; **it is —** se ignora

unlawful [ʌnlɔ́fəl] ADJ ilegal

unleaded [ʌnlédɪd] ADJ sin plomo

unleash [ʌnlíʃ] VT desatar

unless [ənlés] CONJ a menos que, a no ser que

unlicensed [ʌnláɪsənst] ADJ (without permission) sin permiso, ilícito; (without credentials) no acreditado

unlike [ʌnláɪk] ADJ distinto, diferente; **he is — me** es diferente de mí; PREP a diferencia de; **how — you to forget!** ¡me extraña que te hayas olvidado!

unlikely [ʌnláɪkli] ADJ (improbable) improbable; (not realistic) inverosímil; (exotic) exótico; **I am — to come** es improbable que venga
unlimited [ʌnlímɪdɪd] ADJ ilimitado
unload [ʌnlód] VI/VT (take cargo from) descargar; VI (pour out one's feelings) desahogarse; (sell) liquidar
unlock [ʌnlák] VI/VT abrir con llave
unlucky [ʌnláki] ADJ (unfortunate) desafortunado; (ominous) aciago, funesto; **an — number** un número de mala suerte
unmanageable [ʌnmǽnɪʤəbəł] ADJ (crisis, situation) inmanejable; (person) rebelde
unmanned [ʌnmǽnd] ADJ (deprived of courage) achicado; (with no crew) no tripulado
unmarked [ʌnmárkt] ADJ sin marcar
unmarried [ʌnmǽrid] ADJ soltero
unmask [ʌnmǽsk] VI/VT desenmascarar[se]
unmistakable [ʌnmɪstékəbəł] ADJ inconfundible
unmitigated [ʌnmídɪgeɪdɪd] ADJ absoluto
unmoved [ʌnmúvd] ADJ (unflinching) impasible; (indifferent) indiferente
unnatural [ʌnnǽtʃə-əł] ADJ (contrary to nature) no natural; (unloving) desnaturalizado; (monstrous) monstruoso; (affected) afectado
unnecessary [ʌnnésəsɛri] ADJ innecesario
unnoticed [ʌnnóʊɪst] ADJ inadvertido, desapercibido
unobserved [ʌnəbzɝ́vd] ADJ inadvertido
unobtrusive [ʌnəbtrúsɪv] ADJ discreto
unoccupied [ʌnákjəpaɪd] ADJ (house) desocupado; (territory) no ocupado
unofficial [ʌnəfíʃəł] ADJ extraoficial, no oficial
unoriginal [ʌnərídʒənəł] ADJ poco original
unorthodox [ʌnɔ́rθədɑks] ADJ heterodoxo
unpack [ʌnpǽk] VT (a suitcase) deshacer, desempacar; (a carton) desembalar
unpaid [ʌnpéd] ADJ (debt) impagado, por pagar; (work) no remunerado
unplayable [ʌnpléəbəł] ADJ (golf) injugable
unpleasant [ʌnplézənt] ADJ desagradable
unpleasantness [ʌnplézəntnɪs] N (quality or state of being unpleasant) lo desagradable; (unpleasant episode) desavenencia *f*, disgusto *m*
unplug [ʌnplʌ́g] VI/VT desenchufar
unpopular [ʌnpápjələ-] ADJ (decision) impopular; **she was — in school** tenía pocos amigos en la escuela
unprecedented [ʌnprésɪdɛntɪd] ADJ sin precedente, inaudito
unpredictable [ʌnprɪdíktəbəł] ADJ impredecible, imprevisible
unpremeditated [ʌnprimédɪteɪdɪd] ADJ impremeditado; (murder) sin premeditación
unprepared [ʌnprɪpɛ́rd] ADJ (surprised) desprevenido; (not ready) no preparado
unpretentious [ʌnprɪténʃəs] ADJ modesto, sin pretenciones
unprincipled [ʌnprínsəpəłd] ADJ sin escrúpulos, falto de principios
unprintable [ʌnpríntəbəł] ADJ impublicable
unproductive [ʌnprədʌ́ktɪv] ADJ improductivo
unprofessional [ʌnprəfɛ́ʃənəł] ADJ poco profesional
unprofitable [ʌnpráfɪdəbəł] ADJ no rentable
unpublished [ʌnpʌ́blɪʃt] ADJ inédito, sin publicar
unpunished [ʌnpʌ́nɪʃt] ADJ impune
unqualified [ʌnkwáləfaɪd] ADJ (worker) *Sp* no cualificado; *Am* no calificado; (support) incondicional; (disaster) absoluto
unquestionable [ʌnkwéstʃənəbəł] ADJ incuestionable, indiscutible
unravel [ʌnrǽvəł] VI/VT (a rope) desenredar[se]; (a sweater) destejer[se]; (cloth) deshilachar[se]; (a plan) deshacer[se]; VT (a mystery) desentrañar
unreal [ʌnríəł] ADJ (not real) irreal; (unbelievable) increíble
unreasonable [ʌnrízənəbəł] ADJ (excessive) exagerado; (irrational) irracional, poco razonable
unrecognizable [ʌnrɛkəgnáɪzəbəł] ADJ irreconocible
unrefined [ʌnrɪfáɪnd] ADJ (oil, sugar) no refinado; (behavior) inculto, grosero
unrelated [ʌnrɪlédɪd] ADJ no relacionado
unreliable [ʌnrɪláɪəbəł] ADJ (person) informal; (machine, information) *Sp* poco fiable; *Am* poco confiable
unreported [ʌnrɪpɔ́rdɪd] ADJ sin declarar
unrest [ʌnrést] N malestar *m*, agitación *f*
unrestricted [ʌnrɪstríktɪd] ADJ no restringido
unroll [ʌnrół] VI/VT desenrollar[se]
unruly [ʌnrúli] ADJ (student) indisciplinado, revoltoso, díscolo; (country) ingobernable; (hair) rebelde
unsafe [ʌnséf] ADJ (risky) arriesgado; (dangerous) peligroso
unsanitary [ʌnsǽnɪtɛri] ADJ (behavior) antihigiénico, insalubre; (place, climate) insalubre
unsatisfactory [ʌnsǽdɪsfǽktəri] ADJ no satisfactorio, insatisfactorio
unscrew [ʌnskrú] VT desatornillar, destornillar
unscrupulous [ʌnskrúpjələs] ADJ sin escrúpulos
unseasonable [ʌnsízənəbəł] ADJ impropio de la estación
unseat [ʌnsít] VT derribar
unsecured [ʌnsɪkjʊ́rd] ADJ sin garantía
unseen [ʌnsín] ADJ invisible, oculto
unselfish [ʌnsɛ́lfɪʃ] ADJ desinteresado
unselfishness [ʌnsɛ́lfɪʃnɪs] N desinterés *m*
unsettled [ʌnsɛ́dl̩d] ADJ (situation)

desordenado; (wilderness) sin colonizar; (case) pendiente; (weather) variable

unsightly [ʌnsáɪtli] ADJ feo, antiestético

unskilled [ʌnskíld] ADJ (not trained) inexperto; (not qualified) *Sp* no cualificado; *Am* no calificado

unsolicited [ʌnsəlísɪdɪd] ADJ no solicitado

unsophisticated [ʌnsəfístɪkeɪd] ADJ sencillo, no sofisticado

unsound [ʌnsáʊnd] ADJ (argument) erróneo, falso; (body) enfermizo; (mind) demente; (foundation) poco sólido; (investment) poco seguro

unspeakable [ʌnspíkəbəl] ADJ indecible

unspecified [ʌnspésɪfaɪd] ADJ no especificado

unsportsmanlike [ʌnspórtsmənlaɪk] ADJ antideportivo

unstable [ʌnstébəl] ADJ inestable

unsteady [ʌnstédɪ] ADJ (walk) inseguro, inestable; (flame) temboloroso; (pulse) irregular

unsuccessful [ʌnsəksésfəl] ADJ sin éxito, infructuoso

unsuitable [ʌnsúːdəbəl] ADJ (person) no apto; (place) inadecuado, inapropiado

unsuspected [ʌnsəspéktɪd] ADJ insospechado

untenable [ʌnténəbəl] ADJ insostenible

unthinkable [ʌnθíŋkəbəl] ADJ impensable

untidy [ʌntáɪdɪ] ADJ (dress) desaliñado, desastrado; (room) desordenado

untie [ʌntáɪ] VI/VT desatar[se], destrabar[se]

until [ʌntíl] PREP hasta; CONJ hasta que

untimely [ʌntáɪmli] ADJ (ill-timed) inoportuno; (premature) prematuro

untiring [ʌntáɪrɪŋ] ADJ incansable, denodado

untold [ʌntóld] ADJ (riches) incalculable; (suffering) inaudito

untouched [ʌntátʃt] ADJ (not injured) ileso; (not affected) no afectado; **he left his dessert** — no tocó el postre

untrained [ʌntrénd] ADJ (worker) *Sp* no cualificado; *Am* no calificado; (animal) no amaestrado; (eye) inexperto

untried [ʌntráɪd] ADJ (untested) no probado, no ensayado; (not taken to trial) no juzgado

untrue [ʌntrú] ADJ (incorrect) falso; (unfaithful) infiel; (disloyal) desleal

untutored [ʌntúːdə-d] ADJ (unschooled) sin instrucción; (unsophisticated) inculto

untwist [ʌntwíst] VT desenroscar

unused [ʌnjúzd] ADJ (no used) sin usar; (unaccustomed) no habituado

unusual [ʌnjúːʒuəl] ADJ (infrequent) desacostumbrado, raro; (highly abnormal) inusitado, insólito

unvarnished [ʌnvárnɪʃt] ADJ (without varnish) sin barnizar; (straightforward) puro

unveil [ʌnvél] VT (remove a veil) quitar el velo a; (reveal) descubrir

unwarranted [ʌnwórəntɪd] ADJ injustificado

unwelcome [ʌnwélkəm] ADJ (untimely) inoportuno; (unpleasant) desagradable; (poorly received) mal recibido

unwholesome [ʌnhóləsəm] ADJ malsano

unwieldy [ʌnwíldi] ADJ poco manejable, difícil de manejar

unwilling [ʌnwílɪŋ] ADJ **to be — to** no estar dispuesto a

unwise [ʌnwáɪz] ADJ imprudente

unwonted [ʌnwóntɪd] ADJ inusitado, inacostumbrado

unworthy [ʌnwə́ːði] ADJ indigno

unwrap [ʌnrǽp] VT desenvolver

unwritten [ʌnrítn] ADJ no escrito; (agreement) de palabra

unzip [ʌnzíp] VT abrir la cremallera

up [ʌp] ADV (position) arriba; (direction) hacia arriba; **—-front** (paid in advance) inicial; (frank) franco; **— and down** de arriba para abajo; **— against** enfrentado con; **he's — for reelection** se presenta para la reelección; **I'm feeling —** me siento optimista; **I'm — for golf** tengo ganas de jugar al golf; **prices are —** los precios han subido; **that is — to you** queda en tus manos, es cosa tuya; **the children are already —** ya se levantaron los niños; **the moon is —** salió la luna; **the wheat is —** germinó el trigo; **time is —** se terminó el tiempo; **to be — on the news** estar al corriente de las noticias; **to be — to one's old tricks** hacer de las suyas; **what's —?** ¿qué pasa? **he — and went** agarró ý se fue; PREP **— the current** contra la corriente; **— the river** río arriba; **— the street** calle arriba; **— to now** hasta ahora; N **—s and downs** altibajos *m pl*; VI; ADJ (assembled) armado; (finished) terminado, concluido; **—-and-coming** prometedor; **—-to-date** actualizado

upbeat [ʌ́pbit] ADJ optimista

upbringing [ʌ́pbrɪŋɪŋ] N crianza *f*

update [ʌpdét] VT actualizar; N actualización *f*

upend [ʌpénd] VI/VT (stand on end) poner[se] de punta; (defeat) derrotar

upgrade [ʌ́pgred] VT (facilities) mejorar; (computer) actualizar; N (facilities) mejora *f*; (computer) actualización *f*

upheaval [ʌphívəl] N trastorno *m*

upheld [ʌphéld] *see* uphold

uphill[1] [ʌ́phɪl] ADV cuesta arriba

uphill[2] [ʌ́phɪl] ADJ penoso, arduo

uphold [ʌphóld] VT sostener, apoyar; (legal decision) refrendar

upholster [ʌphóləstə-] VT tapizar

upholstery [ʌphóləstəri] N tapicería *f*

upkeep [ʌ́pkip] N mantenimiento *m*

uplift [ʌplíft] VT (physically) elevar; (spiritually)

edificar
upload [ápload] VT cargar, subir; N carga *f*
upon [əpán] PREP sobre, encima de; **— arriving** al llegar; **once — a time** érase una vez
upper [ápɚ] ADJ (higher) superior; (high) alto; **to have the — hand** dominar, llevar la ventaja; N (of shoe) pala *f*; (of berth) litera superior *f*; **— class** clase alta *f*; **— crust** flor y nata *f*; **—case** mayúsculo; **—cut** (in boxing) gancho al mentón *m*; **—most** (highest) de más arriba; (most important) mayor; **— respiratory infection** infección respiratoria alta *f*; **—s** dentadura postiza superior *f*
uppity [ápɪdɪ] ADJ presumido
upright [ápraɪt] ADJ (posture) erecto, erguido; (position) vertical; (character) íntegro, recto, cabal; **— piano** piano vertical *m*; N (column) montante *m*; (piano) piano vertical *m*; (post) poste *m*
uprightness [ápraɪtnɪs] N (physical) verticalidad *f*; (moral) rectitud *f*
uprising [ápraɪzɪŋ] N alzamiento *m*, levantamiento *m*
uproar [áprɔr] N tumulto *m*, alboroto *m*, bulla *f*
uproarious [aprórɪəs] ADJ (tumultuous) tumultuoso; (funny) graciosísimo
uproot [ʌprút] VT arrancar de raíz, desarraigar
upscale [ápskeɪl] ADJ de lujo
upset[1] [ʌpsét] VI/VT (overturn) volcar[se], tumbar; (distress) trastornar[se], perturbar[se], alterar[se]; VT (in sports) derrotar al favorito; ADJ (overturned) volcado; (ill) indispuesto; (distressed) disgustado, enojado
upset[2] [ápsɛt] N (overturning) vuelco *m*; (unexpected defeat) derrota inesperada *f*; (emotional state) trastorno *m*, disgusto *m*; (illness) malestar *m*
upshot [ápʃɑt] N consecuencia *f*
upside [ʌpsaɪd] N (upper part) parte superior *f*; (positive prospect) lo bueno; ADJ & ADV **— down** al revés, patas arriba
upstage [ʌpstédʒ] VT eclipsar
upstairs[1] [ʌpstérz] ADV (location) arriba, en el piso de arriba; (movement) [para] arriba
upstairs[2] [ʌpstɛrz] ADJ de arriba; N piso de arriba *m*
upstart [ʌpstɑrt] N advenedizo -za *mf*
uptake [ʌptek] N **quick on the —** listo; **slow on the —** duro de entendederas
uptight [ʌptáɪt] ADJ (nervous) nervioso; (conventional) estreñido
up-to-the-minute [ʌptəðəmínɪt] ADJ actualizado
upturn [ʌptɚn] N (prices) aumento *m*, subida *f*; (markets) tendencia alcista *f*
upward [ʌpwɚd] ADV (toward a higher place) hacia arriba; **— of** más de; ADJ ascendente; **— mobility** ascenso social *m*; **— trend** tendencia al alza *f*
uranium [jʊréniəm] N uranio *m*
urban [ɝbən] ADJ urbano; **— blight** tugurización *f*; **— legend** leyenda urbana *f*; **— renewal** renovación urbana *f*; **— sprawl** expansión urbana *f*
urbanism [ɝbənɪzəm] N urbanismo *m*
urchin [ɝtʃɪn] N pilluelo -la *mf*, guaje -ja *mf*
urethra [jʊríθrə] N uretra *f*
urge [ɝdʒ] VT (exhort) exhortar, urgir; (beg) rogar; (propose) propugnar; **to — on** animar; N impulso *m*, gana *f*
urgency [ɝdʒənsi] N urgencia *f*
urgent [ɝdʒənt] ADJ urgente
urinal [júrənl] N urinario *m*, mingitorio *m*
urinalysis [jʊrənǽlɪsɪs] N análisis de orina *m*
urinary [júrəneri] ADJ urinario; **— tract** vías urinarias *f pl*
urinate [júrɪnet] VI/VT orinar
urine [júrɪn] N orina *f*
URL [Uniform Resource Locator] [júɑ́rél] N URL *m*
urn [ɝn] N urna *f*
urologist [jʊrɑ́lədʒɪst] N urólogo -ga *mf*
Uruguay [júrəgwaɪ] N Uruguay *m*
Uruguayan [jʊrəgwáɪən] ADJ & N uruguayo -ya *mf*
us [ʌs] PRON nos; **she saw —** nos vio; **he came with —** vino con nosotros; **he gave it to —** nos lo dio [a nosotros]
USA [United States of America] [júésé] N EEUU *m sg/pl*
usable [júzəbəł] ADJ utilizable, aprovechable
usage [júsɪdʒ] N uso *m*, costumbre *f*
USB [Universal Serial Bus] [júésbí] N USB *m*; **— port** puerto USB *m*
use[1] [juz] VT usar, utilizar (also exploit); (consume) gastar; (take advantage of) aprovecharse de; VI **to — up** gastar, agotar
use[2] [jus] N (application) uso *m*; (utilization) empleo *m*, utilización *f*, aprovechamiento *m*; (usefulness) utilidad *f*; **it is of no —** es inútil; **out of —** en desuso; **to have no — for** no soportar; **to make — of** usar, utilizar; **to put to —** utilizar; **what is the — of it?** ¿para qué sirve?
used[1] [juzd] ADJ usado
used[2] [just] VI **to be — to** estar acostumbrado a; **it — to be green** antes era verde
useful [júsfəł] ADJ útil
usefulness [júsfəłnɪs] N utilidad *f*
useless [júslɪs] ADJ inútil, inservible
uselessness [júslɪsnɪs] N inutilidad *f*
user [júzɚ] N usuario -ria *mf*; **—-friendly** fácil de utilizar; **— group** grupo de usuarios *m*; **—name** nombre del usuario *m*
usher [ʌ́ʃɚ] N acomodador -ora *mf*; VT conducir, acompañar; **to — in** (a person) acompañar;

(an era) anunciar, marcar el comienzo de
usual [júʒuəł] ADJ (habitual) usual, habitual; (everyday) de todos los días; **as —** como siempre; **she wasn't her — self** no era la de siempre; **the — thing** lo normal; **more than —** más que de costumbre
usually [júʒuəli] ADV generalmente, normalmente; **he — doesn't mind** no suele importarle
usurp [juśᵊp] VI/VT usurpar
usury [júʒəri] N usura *f*
utensil [juténsəł] N utensilio *m*, útil *m*
uterine [júdə-ɪn] ADJ uterino
uterus [júdə-əs] N útero *m*
UTI [urinary tract infection] [jútíáɪ] N infección del tracto urinario *f*
utilitarian [jutɪlɪtériən] ADJ utilitario
utility [jutílɪdi] N (usefulness) utilidad *f*; (public service) empresa de servicio público *f*, empresa de agua o electricidad *f*; **— furniture** muebles prácticos *m pl*; **— program** programa utilitario *m*; **— room** lavadero *m*
utilization [judḷɪzéʃən] N utilización *f*
utilize [júdḷaɪz] VT utilizar
utmost [ʌ́tmost] ADJ (extreme) sumo, extremo; (farthest) más distante; N máximo *m*; **he did his —** hizo cuanto pudo; **to the —** al máximo
utopia [jutópiə] N utopía *f*
utter [ʌ́də-] VT (emit) dar, proferir; (say) decir, pronunciar; (make circulate) poner en circulación; ADJ absoluto, completo
utterance [ʌ́də-əns] N (of words) enunciado *m*; (of money) emisión *f*
uvula [júvjələ] N campanilla *f*, úvula *f*
Uzbek [úzbɛk] ADJ & N uzbeko -ka *mf*
Uzbekistan [uzbɛ́kɪstæn] N Uzbekistán *m*

Vv

vacancy [vékənsi] N (job) vacante *f*; (room in hotel) habitación libre *f*; **no —** completo
vacant [vékənt] ADJ (position) vacante; (expression) vacío; (seat, room) libre
vacate [véket] VI/VT (a room) desalojar, desocupar; (a contract) anular; (a position) dejar vacante
vacation [vekéʃən] N vacaciones *f pl*; **on —** de vacaciones
vaccinate [vǽksənet] VI/VT vacunar
vaccination [vǽksənéʃən] N vacunación *f*
vaccine [vǽksín] N vacuna *f*
vacillate [vǽsəlet] VI vacilar
vacuum [vǽkjum] N vacío *m*; **— cleaner** aspiradora *f*; **— tube** tubo de vacío *m*; ADJ **— -packed** envasado al vacío; VI/VT pasar la aspiradora
vagabond [vǽgəbɑnd] ADJ & N vagabundo -da *mf*
vagina [vəʤáɪnə] N vagina *f*
vaginal [vǽʤən!] ADJ vaginal; **— bleeding** hemorragia vaginal *f*; **— discharge** flujo vaginal *m*; **— itching** escozor vaginal *m*
vaginitis [vǽʤɪnáɪdɪs] N vaginitis *f*
vagrancy [végrənsi] N vagancia *f*
vagrant [végrənt] ADJ & N vagabundo -da *mf*
vague [veg] ADJ vago, indistinto
vain [ven] ADJ (futile) vano, hueco; (proud of appearance) vanidoso; **in —** en vano
Valencian [vəlénsiən] ADJ & N valenciano -na
valentine [vǽləntaɪn] N (card) tarjeta del día de San Valentín *f*; (person) querido -da *mf*; **—'s Day** día de San Valentín *m*, día de los enamorados *m*
valet [vælé] N (manservant) criado *m*; (in a hotel) mozo de habitación *m*; (car parker) aparcacoches *m sg*
valiant [vǽljənt] ADJ valiente
valid [vǽlɪd] ADJ válido, valedero; **to be/become —** tener efectividad
validity [vəlídɪti] N validez *f*
valise [vəlíz] N maleta *f*, valija *f*
valley [vǽli] N valle *m*
valor [vǽlə-] N valor *m*, valentía *f*
valorize [vǽləraɪz] VT valorar
valorous [vǽlə-əs] ADJ valeroso, valiente
valuable [vǽljəbəł] ADJ valioso, preciado; N **—s** objetos de valor *m pl*
valuation [vǽljuéʃən] N (value) valoración *f*; (appraisal) tasación *f*, valuación *f*
value [vǽlju] N valor *m*; VT valorar
valve [vǽv] N válvula *f*; (on mollusks) valva *f*
vamp [vǽmp] N vampiresa *f*; VT seducir
vampire [vǽmpaɪr] N vampiro *m*
van [vǽn] N camioneta *f*
vandal [vǽnd!] N vándalo *m*
vane [ven] N (for weather) veleta *f*; (of a fan, windmill) aspa *f*; (of propeller) paleta *f*
vanilla [vənílə] N vainilla *f*
vanish [vǽnɪʃ] VI desaparecer, esfumarse
vanity [vǽnɪdi] N vanidad *f*; **— table** tocador *m*
vanquish [vǽnkwɪʃ] VT vencer
vantage point [vǽntɪʤpɔɪnt] N mirador *m*
Vanuatu [vanuútu] N Vanuatu *m*
Vanuatuan [vanuútuən] ADJ & N vanuatuense *mf*
vapor [vépə-] N vapor *m*, humo *m*
vaporize [vépə-aɪz] VI/VT vaporizar[se]
variable [vériəbəł] ADJ & N variable *f*; **— annuity** anualidad variable *f*
variance [vériəns] N discrepancia *f*, desacuerdo *m*; **to be at —** no concordar
variant [vériənt] N variante *f*, modalidad *f*
variation [vɛriéʃən] N variación *f*
varicose [vǽrɪkos] ADJ varicoso; **— veins** *Sp*

varices *f pl*; *Am* vários *f pl*

varied [vérid] ADJ variado, vario

variegated [vériɪgeɒɪd] ADJ variopinto

variety [vəráɪɪɒɪ] N variedad *f*

various [vériəs] ADJ vario

varnish [várnɪʃ] N barniz *m*, charol *m*; VT barnizar, charolar

varsity [vársɪɒɪ] N equipo universitario *m*

vary [véri] VI/VT variar

vascular [vǽskjələ˞] ADJ vascular

vase [ves] N jarrón *m*; (for flowers) florero *m*

vasectomy [vəséktəmi] N vasectomía *f*

Vaseline™ [vǽsəlín] N vaselina *f*

vast [væst] ADJ vasto, inmenso

vastly [vǽstli] ADV enormemente

vastness [vǽstnɪs] N inmensidad *f*

vat [væt] N tina *f*, barrica *f*

VAT [value-added tax] [víéti] N IVA *m*

Vatican City [vǽɒɪkənsíɒi] N Ciudad del Vaticano *f*

vaudeville [vɔ́dɒɪł] N vodevil *m*

vault [vɔłt] N (arched structure) bóveda *f*; (burial chamber) panteón *m*; (place for valuables) cámara acorazada *f*; (jump) salto *m*; VT (cover with a vault) abovedar; VI/VT (jump) saltar

VCR [videocassette recorder] [vísiár] N *Am* video *m*; *Sp* vídeo *m*

veal [vił] N ternera *f*; **— cutlet** chuleta de ternera *f*

vector [vɛktə˞] N vector *m*

veer [vir] VI/VT virar; N virada *f*

vegan [vígən] ADJ & N vegan *mf*

vegetable [véʤtəbəł] N (food) verdura *f*, hortaliza *f*; (plant, comatose person) vegetal *m*; **— garden** huerto *m*; (large) huerta *f*; **— kingdom** reino vegetal *m*; **— oil** aceite vegetal *m*

vegetarian [vɛʤɪtériən] ADJ & N vegetariano -na *mf*

vegetate [véʤɪtet] VI vegetar

vegetation [vɛʤɪtéʃən] N vegetación *f*

vegetative [véʤɪtɛɒɪv] ADJ vegetativo

vehemence [víəməns] N vehemencia *f*

vehement [víəmənt] ADJ vehemente

vehicle [víɪkəł] N vehículo *m*

veil [vẽł] N velo *m*; VT velar

vein [ven] N (blood vessel, style) vena *f*; (small deposit of ore) veta *f*; (large deposit of ore) filón *m*

veined [vend] ADJ (marble) veteado; (leaf) nervado

velocity [vəlásɪɒi] N velocidad *f*

velvet [vɛ́łvɪt] N terciopelo *m*; ADJ (of velvet) de terciopelo; (like velvet) aterciopelado

velvety [vɛ́łvɪɒi] ADJ aterciopelado

vendetta [vɛndɛ́ɒə] N vendetta *f*

vending machine [vɛ́ndɪŋməʃin] N expendedor automático *m*, máquina expendedora *f*

vendor [vɛ́ndə˞] N vendedor -ora *mf*, proveedor -ora *mf*; (in a stall) puestero -ra *mf*

veneer [vənír] N (layer of wood) chapa *f*; (outward appearance) barniz *m*; VT chapar, enchapar

venerable [vɛ́nə˞əbəł] ADJ venerable

venerate [vɛ́nə˞et] VT venerar

veneration [vɛnə˞éʃən] N veneración *f*

venetian blind [vəníʃənblɑ́ɪnd] N veneciana *f*

Venezuela [vɛnɪzwélə] N Venezuela *f*

Venezuelan [vɛnɪzwélən] ADJ & N venezolano -na *mf*

vengeance [vɛ́nʤəns] N venganza *f*; **with a —** (violently) con furia; (energetically) con ganas

vengeful [vɛ́nʤfəł] ADJ vengativo

venison [vɛ́nə˞sən] N carne de venado *f*

venom [vɛ́nəm] N veneno *m*

venomous [vɛ́nə˞məs] ADJ venenoso

vent [vɛnt] N (outlet for air) ventilación *f*; (opening of a volcano) chimenea *f*; **to give — to anger** desahogar la ira; VI/VT desahogar[se], descargar[se]

ventilate [vɛ́ntɪlet] VI/VT ventilar[se]

ventilation [vɛntɪléʃən] N ventilación *f*

ventilator [vɛ́ntɪleɒə˞] N ventilador *m*

ventricle [vɛ́ntrɪkəł] N ventrículo *m*

venture [vɛ́ntʃə˞] N (adventure) aventura *f*; (business enterprise) empresa *f*; **— capital** capital de riesgo *m*; VI/VT aventurar[se], arriesgar[se]

venue [vɛ́nju] N lugar *m*

veranda [vərǽndə] N porche *m*, terraza *f*

verb [vɜ˞b] N verbo *m*

verbal [vɜ́˞bəł] ADJ (linguistic, related to verbs) verbal; (not written) oral

verbatim [və˞béɒəm] ADJ textual; ADV textualmente

verbiage [vɜ́˞bɪɪɒʤ] N palabrerío *m*

verbose [və˞bós] ADJ verboso

verdict [vɜ́˞ɒɪkt] N veredicto *m*

verdure [vɜ́˞ʤə˞] N *lit* verdura *f*

verge [vɜ˞ʤ] ADV LOC **on the — of** al borde de, a punto de; VI **to — on** rayar en, lindar con

verification [vɛrɪfɪkéʃən] N verificación *f*, comprobación *f*

verify [vɛ́rɪfaɪ] VT verificar, constatar, comprobar

veritable [vɛ́rɪɒəbəł] ADJ verdadero

vermillion [və˞míljən] ADJ & N bermellón *m*

vermin [vɜ́˞mɪn] N bichos *m pl*

vermouth [və˞múθ] N vermú *m*

vernacular [və˞nǽkjələ˞] ADJ vernáculo; N (plain language) lengua vernácula *f*

versatile [vɜ́˞səɖł] ADJ versátil

verse [vɜ˞s] N verso *m*; (stanza) estrofa *f*; (line of poem) verso *m*; (in Bible) versículo *m*

versed [vɜ˞st] ADJ versado

version [vɜ́˞ʒən] N versión *f*

versus [vɜ́˞səs] PREP contra; (in sports) versus

vertebra [vɝ́·Dəbrə] N vértebra *f*
vertebrate [vɝ́·Dəbrɪt] ADJ vertebrado
vertical [vɝ́·DɪkəɫI] ADJ vertical
vertigo [vɝ́·DɪGo] N vértigo *m*
very [véri] ADV muy; **— many** muchísimos; **— much** muchísimo; **it is — cold today** hace mucho frío hoy; ADJ (same) mismo; (mere) mero
vessel [vésəɫ] N (container) vasija *f*; (duct) vaso *m*; (ship) nave *f*
vest [vest] N chaleco *m*; VT conferir; **—ed interests** intereses creados *m pl*
vestibule [véstɪbjuɫ] N vestíbulo *m*, zaguán *m*
vestige [véstɪʤ] N vestigio *m*
vet [vet] N (veterinarian) veterinario -ria *mf*; (veteran) veterano -na militar *mf*; VT evaluar
veteran [vɛ́Dərən] ADJ & N veterano -na *mf*
veterinarian [vɛDə·ə́nɛriən] N veterinario -ria *mf*
veterinary [vɛ́Də·ənɛri] ADJ veterinario; **— medicine** veterinaria *f*
veto [víto] N veto *m*; VT vetar
vex [vɛks] VT molestar, irritar
via [váɪə, víə] PREP (by way of) vía; (by means of) por
viability [vaɪəbíɫɪDI] N viabilidad *f*
viable [váɪəbəɫ] ADJ viable
vial [váɪəɫ] N ampolla *f*, frasco *m*
vibrate [váɪbret] VI/VT vibrar
vibration [vaɪbréʃən] N vibración *f*
vibrator [váɪbreDə·] N vibrador *m*
vicarious [vaɪkérɪəs] ADJ indirecto
vice [vaɪs] N vicio *m*
vice president [váɪsprézɪDənt] N vicepresidente -ta *mf*
viceroy [váɪsrɔI] N virrey *m*
viceroyalty [vaɪsrɔ́ɪəɫti] ADJ virreinato
vice versa [váɪsə·vɝ́·sə] ADV viceversa
vicinity [vɪsínɪDI] N vecindad *f*, cercanías *f pl*, aledaños *m pl*
vicious [víʃəs] ADJ (violent) violento, sanguinario; (evil) maligno, perverso; (malicious) malicioso; **— circle** círculo vicioso *m*; **— dog** perro fiero *m*, perro bravo *m*
vicissitude [vɪsísɪtud] N vicisitud *f*, peripecia *f*
victim [víktɪm] N víctima *f*
victimize [víktəmaɪz] VT (make victim) victimizar; (dupe) estafar
victor [víktə·] N vencedor -ora *mf*
victorious [vɪktɔ́riəs] ADJ victorioso
victory [víktəri] N victoria *f*
video [vídio] N *Am* video *m*; *Sp* vídeo *m*; **—cassette** *Am* video *m*; *Sp* vídeo *m*; **—cassette recorder** videocasete *m*; **—conference** videoconferencia *f*; **— console** videoconsola *f*; **— game** videojuego *m*; **— portal** *Am* portal de videos *m*; *Sp* portal de vídeos *m*; **—tape** *Am* cinta de video *f*; *Sp* cinta de vídeo *f*; **— clip** videoclip *m*
vie [vaɪ] VI competir; **to — for power** disputarse el poder
Vietnam [vieɪtnám] N Vietnam *m*
Vietnamese [viɪtnəmíz] ADJ & N vietnamita *mf*
view [vju] N (field of vision) vista *f*; (opinion) opinión *f*; (panorama) visión panorámica *f*; **—point** punto de vista *m*; **in — of** en vista de; **to be within —** estar a la vista; **with a — to** con el propósito de; VT (see) ver; (consider) enfocar
viewer [vjúə·] N telespectador -ora *mf*, televidente *mf*
vigil [víʤəɫ] N vigilia *f*, vela *f*; **to keep —** velar
vigilance [víʤələns] N vigilancia *f*
vigilant [víʤələnt] ADJ vigilante
vigor [víGə·] N vigor *m*, pujanza *f*, dinamismo *m*
vigorous [víGə·əs] ADJ vigoroso
vile [vaɪɫ] ADJ (evil) vil, ruin; (foul, bad) pésimo
villa [vílə] N quinta *f*, casa de campo *f*
village [vílɪʤ] N aldea *f*, villa *f*
villager [vílɪʤə·] N aldeano -na *mf*
villain [vílən] N villano -na *mf*
villainous [vílənəs] ADJ vil, villano
villainy [víləni] N villanía *f*, vileza *f*
vindicate [víndɪket] VT reivindicar, vindicar
vindication [vɪndɪkéʃən] N reivindicación *f*, vindicación *f*
vindictive [vɪndíktɪv] ADJ vengativo
vine [vaɪn] N (grapevine) vid *f*; (decorative) parra *f*; (stem) sarmiento *m*; (climbing plant) enredadera *f*
vinegar [vínɪGə·] N vinagre *m*
vineyard [vínjə·d] N viña *f*, viñedo *m*
vintage [víntɪʤ] N (act or season of gathering grapes) vendimia *f*; (harvest of grapes) cosecha *f*; (year) año *m*; ADJ (wine) añejo; (classic) excelente; (old) antiguo, de colección; (typical) típico
vinyl [váɪnɪ]] N vinilo *m*
viola [vióɫə] N viola *f*
violate [váɪəɫet] VT violar; (a law) violar, quebrantar
violation [vaɪəɫéʃən] N violación *f*; (traffic) infracción *f*
violence [váɪəɫəns] N violencia *f*
violent [váɪəɫənt] ADJ violento
violet [váɪəɫɪt] N (flower) violeta *f*; (color) violeta *m*; ADJ violeta
violin [vaɪəɫín] N violín *m*
violinist [vaɪəɫínɪst] N violinista *mf*
VIP [very important person] [víáɪpí] N & ADJ VIP *m*
viper [vápə·] N víbora *f*
viral [váɪrəɫ] ADJ viral
virgin [vɝ́·ʤɪn] ADJ & N virgen *f*; (uninitiated) no iniciado -da *mf*; **— Islands** Islas Vírgenes *f pl*
virginal [vɝ́·ʤənɪ]] ADJ virginal
virile [vírəɫ] ADJ viril

virility [vərílɪɪ̈dɪ] N virilidad *f*
virology [vaɪrɑ́ləʤi] N virología *f*
virtual [vɝ́tʃuəł] ADJ virtual; **— community** comunidad virtual *f*; **— reality** realidad virtual *f*; **— stores** tiendas virtuales *f pl*
virtually [vɝ́tʃuəli] ADV (remotely) virtualmente; (almost) prácticamente
virtue [vɝ́tʃu] N virtud *f*
virtuosity [vɝtʃuɑ́sɪɪ̈dɪ] N virtuosismo *m*
virtuoso [vɝtʃuóso] ADJ & N virtuoso -sa *mf*
virtuous [vɝ́tʃuəs] ADJ virtuoso
virulent [vírə́lənt] ADJ virulento
virus [vɑ́rəs] N virus *m*; **—-free** libre de virus; **— protection software** programas de protección contra virus *m pl*
visa [vízə] N *Am* visa *f*; *Sp* visado *m*
vis-à-vis [vízəví] PREP con respecto a
visceral [vísə́-əł] ADJ visceral
viscous [vískəs] ADJ viscoso
vise [vaɪs] N tornillo de banco *m*
visibility [vɪzɪbílɪɪ̈dɪ] N visibilidad *f*
visible [vízəbəł] ADJ visible
Visigoth [vízɪgɔθ] N visigodo -da *mf*
vision [víʒən] N (sense, apparition) visión *f*; (eyesight) vista *f*
visionary [víʒənɛ́ri] ADJ & N visionario -ria *mf*
visit [vízɪt] VT visitar; (afflict) infligir; VI estar de visita; **to — with** charlar con; N (stay) visita *f*; (chat) charla *f*
visitation [vɪzɪtéʃən] N (apparition) visitación *f*; (punishment) castigo *m*; (parental right) régimen de visita *m*
visiting [vízɪɪ̈dɪŋ] ADJ (team) visitante
visitor [vízɪɪ̈dɚ] N visita *f*, visitante *mf*
visor [vɑ́ɪzɚ] N visera *f*
vista [vístə] N (visual) vista *f*; (mental) perspectiva *f*
visual [víʒuəł] ADJ visual; **— recognition** reconocimiento visual *m*
visualize [víʒuəlaɪz] VT visualizar, imaginar
vital [vɑ́ɪdł] ADJ vital; **— signs** signos vitales *m pl*
vitality [vaɪtǽlɪɪ̈dɪ] N vitalidad *f*
vitamin [vɑ́ɪɪ̈dəmɪn] N vitamina *f*
vituperation [vaɪtupərə́fən] N vituperación *f*, vituperio *m*
vivacious [vaɪvé́fəs] ADJ vivaz, vivaracho
vivacity [vaɪvǽsɪɪ̈dɪ] N vivacidad *f*
vivid [vívɪɪ̈d] ADJ vívido, vivo
vivisection [vívɪsɛ́kʃən] N vivisección *f*
vocabulary [vokǽbjəlɛ́rɪ] N vocabulario *m*
vocal [vókół] ADJ (musical) vocal; (outspoken) vociferante; **— cords** cuerdas vocales *f pl*
vocalic [vokǽlɪk] ADJ vocálico
vocation [vokéʃən] N vocación *f*
vociferous [vosífə́-əs] ADJ vociferante
vodka [vɑ́dkə] N vodka *m*
vogue [vog] N boga *f*, moda *f*; **in —** en boga, de moda
voice [vɔɪs] N voz *f*; **—mail** correo de voz *m*, contestador automático *m*; **— recognition** reconocimiento de voz *m*; **— synthesis** síntesis de voz *f*; VT expresar
voicing [vɔ́ɪsɪŋ] N sonoridad *f*
void [vɔɪd] ADJ (devoid, empty) vacío; (not binding) nulo, inválido; **— of** desprovisto de; N vacío *m*; VT (bowels) evacuar; (a check) anular; **—ed check** cheque anulado *m*
volatile [vɑ́łədł] ADJ (liquid) volátil; (political situation) explosivo, conflictivo; (stock market) voluble; (temperament) cambiante
volcanic [vołkǽnɪk] ADJ volcánico
volcano [vołkéno] N volcán *m*
volition [vəlíʃən] N volición *f*; **of one's own —** por su propia voluntad
volley [vɑ́li] N (of firearms) descarga *f*; (of protests, arrows, stones) lluvia *f*; (of a tennis ball) volea *f*; **—ball** voleibol *m*, balonvolea *m*; VI/VT (shoot bullets) descargar; (hit tennis balls) volear
volt [vołt] N voltio *m*
voltage [vółtɪɪ̈ʤ] N voltaje *m*
volume [vɑ́ljəm] N volumen *m*, tomo *m*
voluminous [vəlúmɪnəs] ADJ voluminoso
voluntary [vɑ́lənt̬ɛ́rɪ] ADJ voluntario
volunteer [vɑ́lənt̬ír] ADJ & N voluntario -ria *mf*; VI/VT (offer) ofrecer[se], brindar[se]; RP comedir[se]; VI (do volunteer work) trabajar de voluntario -ria
voluptuous [vəlɑ́ɪ̈ptʃuəs] ADJ voluptuoso
vomit [vɑ́mɪt] N vómito *m*; VI/VT vomitar
voodoo [vúɪ̈du] N vudú *m*
voracious [vɔ́ɹéʃəs] ADJ voraz
vortex [vɔ́ɹt̬ɛ́ks] N vórtice *m*
vote [vot] N (right, ballot) voto *m*; (act of voting) votación *f*; VI votar; VT (a bill) aprobar; (a political party) votar a/por; **to — against** votar en contra; **to — in favor** votar a favor; **to — to do something** votar por hacer algo
voter [vóɪ̈dɚ] N votante *mf*
voting [vóɪ̈dɪŋ] N votación *f*
vouch [vɑʊt̬ʃ] VI **to — for** dar fe de, salir de fiador a, fiar a; VT **to — that** dar fe de que
voucher [vɑ́ʊt̬ʃɚ] N (receipt) comprobante *m*; (coupon) vale *m*; (person) fiador -ora *mf*, garante *mf*
vow [vɑʊ] N voto *m*; **to take a —** prometer; VT jurar
vowel [vɑ́ʊł] N vocal *f*
voyage [vɔɪ́ɪ̈ʤ] N (long trip) viaje *m*; (trip by sea) travesía *f*; VI viajar
voyeur [vɔɪɚ́] N mirón -ona *mf*
VP [vice president] [vípí] N vice presidente -ta *mf*
vulgar [vɑ́łgə-] ADJ (rude) ordinario, grosero, soez; (popular, vernacular) vulgar
vulgarity [vałgǽrɪɪ̈dɪ] N ordinariez *f*, vulgaridad *f*
vulnerable [vɑ́łnə-əbəł] ADJ vulnerable
vulture [vɑ́łtʃə-] N buitre *m*

Ww

wacky [wǽki] ADJ (person) chiflado; (idea) descabellado

wad [wɑd] N (for artillery, for filling) taco *m*; (ball) pelota *f*, pelotón *m*; (of money) rollo *m*, fajo *m*; (of cotton) bola *f*; VI/VT (a firearm) atacar; (a piece of paper) hacer una pelota [con]

waddle [wɑ́dl̩] VT anadear, andar como un pato; N anadeo *m*

wade [wed] VI andar por el agua; **to — through a book** leer con dificultad un libro

wafer [wéfɚ] N (cookie) oblea *f*; (in Catholic ritual) hostia *f*; (computer) lámina/oblea de silicio *f*

waffle [wɑ́fɚl] ADJ *Sp* gofre *m*; *Am* wafle *m*; **— iron** *Sp* plancha para hacer gofres *f*; *Am* waflera *f*

waft [wæft] VI flotar; VT llevar por el aire; N (of air) ráfaga *f*; (of odor) ola *f*

wag [wæg] VI/VT menear[se], mover[se]; **to — the tail** colear; N (movement) meneo *m*, movimiento *m*; (joker) bromista *mf*

wage [wedʒ] N salario *m*; **— earner** asalariado -da *mf*; (paid daily) jornalero -ra *mf*; **—s** salario *m*; (daily) jornal *m*; **— scale** escala salarial *f*; VT (war) hacer; (battle) librar

wager [wédʒɚ] N apuesta *f*; VI/VT apostar

wagon [wǽgən] N (horsedrawn) carro *m*; (covered) carreta *f*; (toy) carrito *m*; **to fix someone's —** vengarse de alguien; **to be on the —** abstenerse de bebidas alcohólicas

wail [wel] VI lamentar; N lamento *m*

waist [west] N cintura *f*; (of garment) talle *m*; **—band** pretina *f*; **—coat** chaleco *m*; **—line** talle *m*, cintura *f*

wait [wet] VI/VT esperar; **to — for** esperar; **to — on** servir; **to — tables** trabajar de camarero -ra; N espera *f*; **to lie in — for** estar en/al acecho de

waiter [wéɪɚ] N camarero *m*, mozo *m*, mesero *m*

waiting [wéɪɪŋ] N espera *f*; **— list** lista de espera *f*; **— room** sala de espera *f*

waitress [wétrɪs] N camarera *f*, moza *f*, mesera *f*

waive [wev] VT (rights) renunciar a; (a rule) hacer una excepción

waiver [wévɚ] N (of rights) renuncia *f*; (of rules) excepción *f*

wake [wek] VI/VT despertar[se]; **to — up** despertar[se]; N (at death) velatorio *m*; (of a ship) estela *f*, surco *m*; **—-up call** (in a hotel) llamada del servicio despertador *f*; (to action) llamada de atención *f*; **in the — of** después de, detrás de

wakeful [wékfəl] ADJ (awake) despierto; (insomniac) insomne

waken [wékən] VI/VT despertar[se]

Wales [welz] N Gales *m sg*

walk [wɔk] VI andar, caminar; (to a place) ir a pie; (go away) marcharse; (in baseball) sacar una base por bolas *f*; **to — back** volver a pie; **to — down** bajar a pie; **to — in** entrar caminando; **to — out** (to go out) salir caminando; (to abandon) dejar; (to strike) declararse en huelga; **to — up** subir a pie; VT (to cause to walk) hacer caminar; (to trace on foot) recorrer; **to — the streets** callejear; **to — someone** (baseball) darle una base por bolas; N (period of walking) paseo *m*, caminata *f*; (pace) paso *m*; (gait) andar *m*; **— of life** condición *f*; **—out** huelga *f*; **to take a —** pasear, dar un paseo

walker [wɔ́kɚ] N (device to aid walking) andador *m*; (one who walks) caminante *mf*; (in sports) marchista *mf*

walking [wɔ́kɪŋ] ADJ andante; **— papers** despido *m*; **— stick** bastón *m*

wall [wɔl] N (interior) pared *f*; (garden) muro *m*, tapia *f*; (fort) muralla *f*; (of silence) barrera *f*; **—paper** papel de empapelar *m*; **—flower** alhelí *m*; **—-to-—** de pared a pared; **to have one's back to the —** estar entre la espada y la pared; **to drive someone up the —** sacar a alguien de quicio; **I was climbing the —s** me moría de aburrimiento; **she was a —flower** no la sacaban a bailar; VT **to —paper** empapelar

wallet [wɑ́lɪt] N cartera *f*, billetera *f*

wallow [wɑ́lo] VI (roll) revolcarse; (indulge oneself) regodearse

walnut [wɔ́lnʌt] N nuez *f*; **— tree** nogal *m*

walrus [wɔ́lrəs] N morsa *f*

waltz [wɔlts] N vals *m*; VI valsar

wand [wɑnd] N (rod) vara *f*; (magic) varita *f*

wander [wɑ́ndɚ] VI/VT vagar [por], errar [por]; **to — away** perderse; **my mind —s easily** me distraigo fácilmente

wanderer [wɑ́ndərɚ] N vagabundo -da *mf*

wane [wen] VI menguar, flaquear; N **to be on the —** ir menguando

wannabe [wɑ́nəbi] N aspirante *mf*

want [wɑnt] VI/VT (desire) querer; **he —s judgment** le falta juicio; **he's —ed in Texas** se lo busca en Texas; N (desire) deseo *m*; (lack) falta *f*; (scarcity) escasez *f*; **to be in —** estar necesitado; **— ad** [anuncio] clasificado *m*

wanting [wɑ́ntɪŋ] ADJ (lacking) falto; (deficient) deficiente

wanton [wɑ́ntən] ADJ (immoderate) desenfrenado; (immoral) lascivo; (senseless, unprovoked) gratuito

war [wɔr] N guerra *f*; **— crime** crimen de guerra *m*; **—fare** guerra *f*; **— games** juegos de

guerra *m pl*, simulacro de batalla *m*; **—head** ojiva *f*; **—ship** acorazado *m*; VI guerrear, hacer la guerra; **—like** bélico *f*

warble [wɔ́rbəł] VI gorjear; N gorjeo *m*

warbler [wɔ́rblə·ɚ] N (European) curruca *f*; (American) arañero *m*

ward [wɔrd] N (district) distrito *m*; (of a hospital) pabellón *m*; (of a tutor) pupilo -la *mf*; VI **to — off** resguardarse de, conjurar

warden [wɔ́rdɪn] N (of prison) alcaide *m*

wardrobe [wɔ́rdrob] N (room) guardarropa *m*; (furniture) armario *m*, ropero *m*; (garments) vestuario *m*, guardarropa *m*

warehouse [wɛ́rhaʊs] N almacén *m*, depósito *m*

wares [wɛrz] N mercancías *f pl*

warm [wɔrm] ADJ (bath) caliente; (clothes) abrigado; (weather) caluroso; (colors, reception) cálido; **—-blooded** de sangre caliente; **—hearted** de buen corazón; **it is — today** hace calor hoy; N **—up** precalentamiento *m*; VI/VT calentar[se]; **to — over** recalentar; **to — up** calentar[se], templar[se]; **it —s my heart** me alegra el corazón; **she —ed to the idea** se entusiasmó con la idea

warmth [wɔrmθ] N calor *m*, tibieza *f*

warn [wɔrn] VI/VT (advise of danger) advertir; (urge to behave) amonestar

warning [wɔ́rnɪŋ] N (of danger) advertencia *f*; (of punishment) amonestación *f*

warp [wɔrp] N (yarn) urdimbre *f*; (curve) comba *f*, alabeo *m*; VI/VT (wood) combar[se], alabear[se]; (character) deformar[se]; **he has a —ed personality** tiene una personalidad retorcida

warrant [wɔ́rənt] N orden *f*; **a — for his arrest** una orden de arresto contra él; VT garantizar

warranty [wɔ́rənti] N garantía *f*; VT garantizar

warrior [wɔ́riə·ɚ] N guerrero -ra *mf*

wart [wɔrt] N verruga *f*

wary [wɛ́ri] ADJ cauteloso, cauto; **to be — of** desconfiar de

was [wʌz] *see* be

wash [wɑʃ] VI/VT lavar[se]; **to — out** (a bottle) lavar; (a substance) quitar lavando; (a creekbed) erosionar; **to — up** lavarse; **the bottle was —ed up on the shore** la botella fue traída por el mar; **he was —ed away by the waves** fue arrastrado por las olas; **his excuse won't —** su excusa no va a colar; N (act of washing) lavado *m*; (clothes to be washed) ropa para lavar *f*; (washed clothes) ropa lavada *f*; **—cloth** toallita para lavarse *f*; **—out** (erosion) derrubio *m*; (failure) fracaso *m*; **—room** lavabo *m*, lavatorio *m*; ADJ **—-and-wear** de lava y pon, de no planchar; **—ed-up** fracasado; **—ed-out** desteñido

washable [wɑ́ʃəbəł] ADJ lavable

washer [wɑ́ʃə·ɚ] N (washing machine) lavadora *f*, máquina de lavar *f*; (metal ring) arandela *f*; **—woman** lavandera *f*

washing [wɑ́ʃɪŋ] N lavado *m*; **— machine** lavadora *f*, máquina de lavar *f*

wasp [wɑsp] N avispa *f*

WASP [White Anglo-Saxon Protestant] [wɑsp] N persona blanca, anglosajona y protestante *f*

waste [west] VI/VT (squander resources) malgastar, desperdiciar; **to — away** consumirse; VT (squander time) perder; (murder) liquidar; N (of resources) desperdicio *m*, malgasto *m*, derroche *m*; (of time) pérdida *f*; (refuse) desperdicios *m pl*, desechos *m pl*; (liquid refuse) vertido *m*; **—land** tierra yerma *f*, páramo *m*; **— of time** pérdida de tiempo *f*; **—paper basket** papelera *f*; **— products** productos de desecho *m pl*; **— treatment** tratamiento de residuos *m*; **to go to —** desperdiciarse; **to lay — to** asolar

wasted [wéstɪd] ADJ (squandered) desperdiciado; (debilitated) consumido; (drunk) borracho

wasteful [wéstfəł] ADJ (person) despilfarrador, gastador; (method) antieconómico

watch [wɑtʃ] VI (look) mirar; (be careful) cuidarse; (be vigilant) vigilar; VT (view) mirar, ver; (observe) observar; (tend) cuidar; **— out for the cars!** ¡cuidado con los coches! **to — for** estar a la espera de; **to — over** proteger; N (timepiece) reloj *m*; (period of wakefulness) vela *f*, vigilia *f*; (vigilant guard) guardia *mf*; (duty shift) guardia *f*; (lookout) centinela *m*; **—band** pulsera *f*; **—dog** (type of dog) perro guardián *m*; (organization) organismo de control *m*; **—maker** relojero -ra *mf*; **—making** relojería *f*; **—man** vigilante *m*, sereno *m*; **—tower** atalaya *f*, torre de vigilancia *f*; **—word** (password) contraseña *f*; (motto) consigna *f*, lema *m*; **to be on the —** estar alerta; **to keep — on/over** vigilar a

watchful [wɑ́tʃfəł] ADJ alerta, atento

water [wɔ́ɔɚ·ɚ] N agua *f*; **—bed** cama de agua *f*; **—bird** ave acuática *f*; **— buffalo** búfalo de agua *m*; **—color** acuarela *f*; **—cress** berro *m*; **—fall** (small) cascada *f*; (large) catarata *f*; **—front** muelles *m pl*; **—fountain** fuente *f*, *Mex, RP* bebedero *m*; **— heater** calentador de agua *m*; **— lily** nenúfar *m*; **—melon** sandía *f*; **— pistol** pistola de agua *f*; **— power** energía hidráulica *f*; **—shed** vertiente *f*; **— ski** esquí acuático *m*; **— softener** ablandador de agua *m*; **— sports** deportes acuáticos *m pl*; **—spout** (pipe) tubo de desagüe *m*; (tornado) tromba *f*; **— supply** abastecimiento de agua *m*; **— table** capa freática *f*; **— vapor** vapor de agua *m*; **—way** vía navegable *f*; **my — broke** se me rompieron las aguas, se me rompió la

fuente; ADJ **—logged** empapado; **—proof** (fabric) impermeable; (watch) sumergible; **—tight** hermético; VT (irrigate) regar; (dilute) aguar; VI/VT (animals) abrevar; **—ed-down** (with water) aguado; (simplified) simplificado; (softened) suavizado; **to —proof** impermeabilizar; **to — -ski** hacer esquí acuático; **my eyes are —ing** me lloran los ojos; **it makes my mouth —** se me hace agua la boca

watery [wɔ́də-i] ADJ (watered-down) aguado; (like water) acuoso; (boggy) húmedo

watt [wɑt] N vatio *m*

wattage [wɑ́dɪʤ] N vataje *m*

wave [wev] N (radio) onda *f*; (water, heat, fashion) ola *f*; (of disgust, of people) oleada *f*; (with the hand) saludo *m*; **—length** longitud de onda *f*; **on the same —length** en la misma onda, en sintonía; VI (flag) ondear; (hair) ondular[se]; VI (greet) saludar con la mano; **to — good-bye** decir adiós con la mano

waver [wévə-] VI (hesitate) vacilar, titubear; (falter) flaquear

wavy [wévi] ADJ ondeado, ondulado

wax [wæks] N cera *f*; (for seals) lacre *m*; **— paper** papel encerado *m*; VT (cover with wax) encerar; (defeat) derrotar; VI (moon) crecer; **to — poetic** ponerse poético

way [we] N (road) camino *m*; (manner) modo *m*, manera *f*; **—farer** caminante *mf*; **— in** entrada *f*; **— out** salida *f*; **—s** costumbres *f pl*; **—side** borde del camino *m*; **— through** paso *m*, pasaje *m*; **a long — off** muy lejos; **by — of London** por Londres; **by — of comparison** a modo de comparación; **by the —** a propósito; **in no —** de ningún modo; **on the — to** rumbo a; **to get out of the —** apartarse; **to go out of one's — to** desvivirse por; **to look the other —** hacer la vista gorda; **to lead the —** ir a la cabeza; **to be in a bad —** hallarse mal de salud; **to give —** (yield) ceder; (break) quebrarse; **to get one's —** salirse con la suya; **to make — for** abrir paso para; ADJ **— -out** estrafalario; VT **to —lay** (wait in ambush) estar al acecho de; (attack) asaltar; (stop) detener

wayward [wéwə-d] ADJ (disobedient) desobediente; (willful) porfiado

we [wi] PRON nosotros -as *mf*

weak [wik] ADJ débil; (deficient) flojo; **— force** fuerza débil *f*; **— -kneed** achicado; **— sister** (coward) cobarde *mf*; **— link** parte más delgada del hilo *f*

weaken [wíkən] VI/VT debilitar[se], quebrantar[se]

weakling [wíklɪŋ] N alfeñique *m*

weakness [wíknɪs] N debilidad *f*, flaqueza *f*; (deficiency) flojedad *f*

wealth [wɛłθ] N riqueza *f*

wealthy [wɛ́łθi] ADJ rico, adinerado, pudiente

wean [win] VT destetar; **to — oneself of** quitarse el vicio de

weapon [wɛ́pən] N arma *f*

wear [wɛr] VT (have on) llevar, tener puesto; (dress in habitually) usar; VI/VT (waste away) desgastar[se]; **to — away** gastar[se], desgastar[se]; **to — down** (a person) agotar; (a pencil) desgastar; **to — off** perder efecto; **to — on** prolongarse; **to — out** (make unfit) gastar[se], degastar[se], sobar[se]; (expend) agotar; **it —s well** es duradero; N (use) gasto *m*; (clothes) ropa *f*; (durability) durabilidad *f*; (deterioration) desgaste *m*; **— and tear** desgaste *m*

weariness [wírɪnɪs] N cansancio *m*, fatiga *f*

wearing [wérɪŋ] ADJ (causing wear) desgastante; (causing fatigue) cansado

wearisome [wírisəm] ADJ fastidioso

weary [wíri] ADJ cansado, fatigado; VI/VT cansar[se], fatigar[se]

weasel [wízəł] N comadreja *f*

weather [wɛ́ðə-] N tiempo *m*; (storm) tempestad *f*; **— -beaten** desgastado/curtido por la intemperie; **— bureau** oficina meteorológica *f*; **— conditions** condiciones atmosféricas *f pl*; **—man** meteorólogo *m*; **— report** parte meteorológico *m*; **—vane** veleta *f*; **it is fine —** hace buen tiempo; **to be under the —** estar enfermo; ADJ **—proof** resistente a la intemperie; VI/VT (a surface) gastar[se]; (skin) curtir; (crisis, storm) capear

weave [wiv] VT (cloth, basket) tejer, entretejer; (to put together) urdir, tramar; **to — together/into** entretejer, entrelazar; **to — one's way** zigzaguear; N tejido *m*

weaver [wívə-] N tejedor -ora *mf*

web [wɛb] N (of a spider) telaraña *f*; (of lies) sarta *f*; (membrane) membrana *f*; (Internet) web *f*; (animal) palmípedo *m*; **— browser** navegador [web] *m*; **—cast** transmisión por la web *f*; **—foot** pata palmada *f*; **— hosting** alojamiento web *m*; **—master** administrador -ora de un sitio web *mf*; **— page** página web *f*; **—site** sitio web *m*; VT; ADJ **—footed** palmípedo; VI/VT **to —cast** transmitir por la web

wed [wɛd] VI/VT casarse [con]; VT casar a

wedding [wɛ́dɪŋ] N boda *f*, casamiento *m*; **— day** día de boda *m*; **— dress** traje de novia *m*; **— ring** anillo de boda *m*

wedge [wɛʤ] N cuña *f*; **to drive a — between** separar; VT acuñar, meter cuñas entre; **to be —d between** estar apretado entre

Wednesday [wénzde] N miércoles *m*

wee [wi] ADJ chiquito, pequeñito

weed [wid] N mala hierba *f*; (marijuana) hierba *f*; **—killer** herbicida *m*; VT deshierbar,

escardar; **to — out** eliminar

week [wik] N semana *f*; **—day** día de semana *m*; **—end** fin de semana *m*; **a — from today** de aquí en una semana

weekly [wíkli] ADJ semanal; ADV semanalmente; N semanario *m*

weep [wip] VI llorar, lagrimear

weeping [wípɪŋ] ADJ lloroso; **— willow** sauce llorón *m*; N llanto *m*

weevil [wívəł] N gorgojo *m*

weigh [we] VI/VT pesar; (consider) ponderar, sopesar, barajar; **to — anchor** levar anclas; **to — down** agobiar, abrumar; **to — on one's conscience** pesar en la conciencia de uno

weight [wet] N (heaviness, importance) peso *m*; (for clocks, scales, barbells) pesa *f*; **—lifting / —training** levantamiento de pesas *m*, halterofilia *f*; **—-watcher** persona a dieta *f*; **to put on —** engordar; **to lose —** adelgazar; VT (add weight) añadir peso; (in statistics) ponderar; **to — someone down** agobiarle a uno

weightless [wétlɪs] ADJ ingrávido

weighty [wédi] ADJ importante

weird [wírd] ADJ (strange) extraño; (supernatural) misterioso

weirdo [wírdo] N bicho raro *m*, ente *m*

welcome [wéłkəm] N bienvenida *f*; ADJ bienvenido; **— mat** alfombrilla *f*, felpudo *m*; **— rest** descanso agradable *m*; **you are —** no hay de qué, de nada; **you are — here** estás en tu casa; **you are — to use it** a tus órdenes; VT dar la bienvenida a, acoger

weld [wełd] VI/VT soldar[se]; N soldadura *f*

welfare [wéłfer] N (good fortune) bienestar *m*; (public assistance) asistencia social *f*; **— state** estado de bienestar *m*

well [weł] ADV bien; **— then** pues bien; **—-being** bienestar *m*; **—-nigh** casi, muy cerca de; **he is — over fifty** tiene mucho más de cincuenta años; **all is —** todo está bien; INTERJ ¡bueno! ADJ (healthy) bien de salud, sano; N (of water, oil) pozo *m*; (of staircase) caja *f*; **—spring** fuente *f*, manantial *m*; ADJ **—-bred** bien educado; **—-defined** bien definido; **—-done** (steak) bien cocido; (a task) bien hecho; **—-fed** bien alimentado; **—-founded** bien fundamentado; **—-groomed** bien arreglado, aseado; **—-heeled** adinerado; **—-informed** bien informado; **—-known** (of a fact) bien sabido; (of a person) bien conocido, notorio; **—-made** bien hecho; **—-meaning** bien intencionado; **—-off** adinerado, acomodado; **—-read** leído, educado; **—-rounded** completo; **—-spoken** bien hablado; **—-to-do** adinerado; VI **tears —ed up in his eyes** se le llenaron los ojos de lágrimas

wellness [wéłnɪs] N (health) salud *f*; (health care) medicina preventiva *f*

welsh [wełʃ] VI **to — on** (a debt) no pagar; (a promise) no cumplir

Welsh [wełʃ] ADJ & N galés -esa *mf*

welt [wełt] N verdugón *m*

went [went] *see* go

wept [wept] *see* weep

were [wɜ-] *see* be

west [west] N (cardinal point) oeste *m*; (hemisphere) occidente *m*; **— Berlín** Berlín occidental *m*; **— Indies** Antillas *f pl*; ADJ **— wind** viento del oeste *m*; ADV (direction) hacia el oeste; (location) al oeste

western [wéstə-n] ADJ occidental, del oeste; N (movie genre) película del oeste *f*

westerner [wéstə-nə-] N occidental *mf*

westward [wéstwə-d] ADV hacia el oeste; ADJ occidental

wet [wet] ADJ (drenched) mojado; (damp, rainy) húmedo; **— blanket** aguafiestas *mf* sg; **—land** humedal *m*; **— nurse** nodriza *f*; **— paint** pintura fresca *f*; **— suit** traje de buzo *m*; VI/VT (soak) mojar[se]; (dampen) humedecer[se]

wetness [wétnɪs] N humedad *f*

whack [hwæk] VI/VT (hit) golpear, pegar; (assassinate) *fam* liquidar; **to — off** (cut) cortar; N (blow) golpazo *m*; *Sp vulg* hostia *f*; **to take a — at** hacer un intento de; **out of —** descompuesto, averiado

whale [hweł] N ballena *f*; VI pescar ballenas

wharf [hwɔrf] N muelle *m*, embarcadero *m*

what [hwɑt] INTERR PRON & N qué; **— did you say?** ¿qué dijiste? **— for?** ¿para qué? **—'s the matter?** ¿qué pasa? **—'s the score?** ¿cómo va el marcador? **and —not** y demás; REL PRON lo que; **come — may** venga lo que venga; **anyplace —soever** en cualquier lugar; **so —?** y qué? **take — you need** toma lo que necesites; ADJ qué; **— books did you want?** ¿qué libros querías? **take — books you need** toma los libros que necesites; INTERJ cómo, qué; **— happy children!** ¡qué niños más felices! **— luck!** ¡qué buena suerte!

whatever [hwɑtévə-] PRON lo que; **do it, — happens** hazlo, pase lo que pase; **— you may think** pienses lo que pienses; **— do you mean?** ¿qué demonios quieres decir? **take — you need** toma lo que necesites; ADJ **any person —** una persona cualquiera / cualquier persona; **no money —** nada de dinero; INTERJ (anything) ¡lo que sea! (I give up) ¡lo que tú digas!

wheat [hwit] N trigo *m*; **— germ** germen de trigo *m*

wheel [hwił] N (disc) rueda *f*; (of cheese) horma *f*; (for pottery) torno *m*; (for steering a car) volante *m*; (for steering a ship) timón *m*;

—barrow carretilla *f*; **—base** batalla *f*, paso *m*; **—chair** silla de ruedas *f*; **—s** (car) *fam* coche *m*; VT (a round object) hacer rodar; (a person, bicycle, wheelchair) empujar; VI **to — out** sacar rodando; **to — in** entrar rodando; **to — around** girar sobre los talones

wheeze [hwiz] N resuello ruidoso *m*; VI resollar

when [hwɛn] ADV & CONJ cuando; INTERJ, ADV, & N cuándo

whenever [hwɛnévə˞] CONJ **— I see him** (each time) cada vez que lo veo; ADV (at a future time) **— I see him** cuando lo vea

where [hwɛr] ADV, N, & INTERR PRON dónde *m*; (direction) adónde; CONJ donde; (direction) adonde

whereabouts [hwérəbaʊts] N paradero *m*; INTERR ADV dónde

whereas [hwɛrǽz] CONJ mientras que; (in preambles) visto que, considerando que

whereby [hwɛrbáɪ] ADV por lo cual

wherefore [hwérfɔr] ADV por lo cual

wherein [hwɛrín] ADV en donde

whereof [hwɛráv] REL PRON de que; INTERR PRON de qué

whereupon [hwɛrəpán] ADV después de lo cual

wherever [hwɛrévə˞] ADV dondequiera que

werewithal [hwɛ́rwɪðɔł] N medios *m pl*, fondos *m pl*

whet [hwɛt] VT (stimulate) estimular; (sharpen) afilar; **—stone** piedra de afilar *f*

whether [hwɛ́ðə˞] CONJ **— we like it or not** nos guste o no nos guste; **I doubt — we can do it** dudo [de] que lo podamos hacer; **he asked — I was coming** me preguntó si venía

which [hwɪtʃ] INTERR PRON cuál[es]; **— do you want?** ¿cuál[es] quieres? REL PRON que; **the apple, — I just bought** la manzana, que acabo de comprar; **the book of — I spoke** el libro del que / del cual hablé; **that — you don't know can hurt you** lo que no sabes puede hacerte daño; INTERR ADJ qué, cuál[es] de; **— house is it?** ¿qué casa es? ¿cuál de las casas es?

whichever [hwɪtʃévə˞] PRON & ADJ (no matter which) cualquiera [que]; **— you choose, you'll regret it later** elijas el que elijas, te arrepentirás después; (anyone that) el que / la que; **choose — you like** elije el que quieras

whiff [hwɪf] N (waft) soplo *m*; (odors, scandal) bocanada *f*, tufillo *m*; **to take a —** oler

while [hwaɪł] N rato *m*; **a short —** un ratito; **a short — ago** hace poco; CONJ (during) mientras; (whereas) mientras que; (even though) aunque; VT **to — away** pasar

whim [hwɪm] N capricho *m*, antojo *m*

whimper [hwímpə˞] VI/VT lloriquear, gimotear; N lloriqueo *m*, gimoteo *m*

whimsical [hwímzɪkəł] ADJ caprichoso, antojadizo

whine [hwaɪn] VI (whimper) gemir; (complain) quejarse; N (whimper) gemido *m*; (complaint) quejido *m*; **stop whining!** ¡deja de quejarte!

whiner [hwáɪnə˞] N llorón -ona *mf*, quejica *mf*

whiny [hwáɪni] ADJ quejoso, quejica

whip [hwɪp] N azote *m*, látigo *m*, rebenque *m*; VT (hit with a whip) azotar, fustigar; (spank) zurrar, dar una paliza; (beat to a froth) batir; (defeat) vencer; **to — out** sacar; **to — up** (prepare) preparar rápidamente; (incite) incitar

whipping [hwípɪŋ] N zurra *f*, paliza *f*; **— cream** crema para batir *f*

whir [hwɜ˞] VI zumbar; N zumbido *m*

whirl [hwɜ˞ł] VI girar; **to — around** arremolinarse; **my head —s** me da vueltas la cabeza; N (rotation) giro *m*; (of water) remolino *m*; **—pool** remolino *m*; **—pool bath** baño de remolino *m*; **—wind** torbellino *m*, remolino de viento *m*; **—wind tour** gira relámpago *f*; **my head is in a —** me da vueltas la cabeza; **to give it a —** probarlo

whisk [hwɪsk] VT (sweep) barrer; (beat) batir; **to — away** llevarse de prisa; VI **to — by** pasar rápidamente; N (broom) escobilla *f*; (beater) batidor *m*

whisker [hwískə˞] N (hair of beard) pelo de la barba *m*; (sideburn) patilla *f*; (of animals) bigote *m*

whiskey, whisky [hwíski] N whisky *m*

whisper [hwíspə˞] VI/VT (person) cuchichear, secretear; (leaves, water) susurrar; N (people) cuchicheo *m*; (leaves, water) susurro *m*; **to talk in a —** cuchichear

whistle [hwísəł] VI/VT silbar; (loud) chiflar; (in protest) rechiflar; VI (referee, train) pitar; **to — for someone** llamar a uno con un silbido; N (sound) silbido *m*; (loud sound) chiflido *m*; (of a referee) pitido *m*; (instrument) silbato *m*, pito *m*; **—-blower** acusador -ora *mf*

white [hwaɪt] ADJ (color, ethnicity) blanco; **— blood cell** glóbulo blanco *m*; **— bread** pan blanco *m*; **—caps** cabrillas *f pl*; **—-collar** administrativo, de cuello blanco; **— gold** oro blanco *m*; **— hair** cana *f*; **— lie** mentirilla *f*; **— noise** ruido blanco *m*; **—wash** (paint) lechada *f*; (cover-up) encubrimiento *m*; N blanco *m* (also ethnicity); (of egg) clara *f*; VT **to —wash** (paint) blanquear, enjalbegar; (cover up) encubrir

whiten [hwaɪtn̩] VI/VT blanquear[se], emblanquecer

whiteness [hwáɪtnɪs] N blancura *f*

whitish [hwáɪdɪʃ] ADJ blancuzco, blanquecino

whittle [hwídł] VI/VT tallar; **to — away** ir gastando; **to — down expenses** reducir los gastos

whiz [hwɪz] VI zumbar; **to — by** pasar zumbando; VT hacer zumbar; N (sound)

zumbido *m*; (ace) as *m*; **— kid** niño -ña prodigio *mf*

who [hu] REL PRON quien[es]; INTERR PRON quién[es]; **he —** el que

WHO [World Health Organization] [dábəɫjuétʃó] N OMS *f*

whoa [hwo] INTERJ (to express amazement) ¡jo! (to stop a horse) ¡so!

whoever [huévɚ] REL PRON (whatever person) quienquiera que, el/la que; INTERR PRON (who) quién

whole [hoł] ADJ (complete) completo, íntegro; (unbroken) entero; (uninjured) ileso; **—-grain** integral; **—hearted** sincero; **—heartedly** de todo corazón; **— life insurance** seguro de vida permanente *m*; **— milk** leche entera *f*; **— note** redonda *f*; **—sale** (in bulk) al por mayor; (massive) masivo; **—sale slaughter** matanza *f*; **—-wheat** integral; **the — day** todo el día; **to go — hog** tirar la casa por la ventana; N todo *m*; (for amounts) totalidad *f*; **—sale** venta al por mayor *f*, mayoreo *m*; **—saler** comerciante al por mayor *mf*, mayorista *mf*, almacenista *mf*; **as a —** en su totalidad; **on the —** en general; ADV **—sale** al por mayor; VI/VT **to —sale** vender al por mayor

wholesome [hółsəm] ADJ sano

whom [hum] REL PRON a quien[es]; **for/to/with —** para/a/con quien; INTERR PRON a quién[es]

whoop [hwup] N (shout) grito *m*; (gasp) respiración convulsiva *f*; VI (person) gritar; (owl) ulular; **to — it up** armar jaleo

whopper [hwápɚ] N (large thing) cosa enorme *f*; (lie) mentira *f*, trola *f*

whopping [hwápɪŋ] ADJ enorme

whose [huz] REL PRON cuyo; **the man — son is here** el hombre cuyo hijo está aquí; INTERR PRON de quién; **— book is this?** ¿de quién es este libro?

why [hwaɪ] ADV & CONJ por qué; **that's the reason — he left** es por eso que se fue; N porqué *m*; INTERJ **—, of course!** ¡pero claro!

wick [wɪk] N mecha *f*, pabilo *m*

wicked [wíkɪd] ADJ malvado, perverso

wickedness [wíkɪdnɪs] N maldad *f*, perversidad *f*

wicker [wíkɚ] N mimbre *m*; **— chair** silla de mimbre *f*

wide [waɪd] ADJ (broad) ancho; (of great range) amplio; (spacious) vasto, extenso; **— apart** muy apartados; **—-awake** muy despierto, despabilado; **— body** avión de fuselaje ancho *m*; **—-eyed** ojiabierto, con los ojos bien abiertos; **— of the mark** lejos del blanco; **—-open** abierto de par en par; **— receiver** receptor abierto *m*; **—spread** (over a wide area) extendido; (among many people) generalizado; **to open —** (a door) abrir de par en par; (one's mouth) abrir bien; **two feet —** dos pies de ancho

widely [wáɪdli] ADV **it is — known that** es bien sabido que; **he is a — known artist** es un artista muy conocido; **he is — read** es muy leído; **— different versions** versiones muy diferentes

widen [wáɪdn̩] VI/VT ensanchar[se], ampliar[se]

widow [wído] N viuda *f*

widower [wídoɚ] N viudo *m*

width [wɪdθ] N ancho *m*, anchura *f*

wield [wiłd] VT (power) ejercer; (tool) manejar; (weapon) blandir, esgrimir

wife [waɪf] N esposa *f*, señora *f*, *Sp* mujer *f*

wifi [wireless fidelity] [wáɪfɪɪ] N wifi *f*

wig [wɪg] N peluca *f*

wiggle [wígəł] VI/VT (hips) menear[se]; (toes) mover[se]; N (of hips) meneo *m*; (of toes) movimiento *m*; **— room** flexibilidad *f*

wigwam [wígwɑm] N tienda indígena *f*

wild [waɪłd] ADJ (animal, savage) salvaje, bravío, bronco; (plant) silvestre; (party) desenfrenado; (conduct) alocado; (storm, temperament) violento; (hair) desordenado; (look) extraviado, desencajado; (enthusiasm) delirante; **— boar** jabalí *m*; **— card** comodín *m*; **—cat** gato montés *m*; **—-eyed** de mirada extraviada, con los ojos desencajados; **—fire** fuego arrasador *m*; **—flower** flor silvestre *f*; **— goose chase** búsqueda inútil *f*; **—life** fauna *f*; **I'm just — about Mary** estoy loco por María; **not in your —est dreams** ni lo pienses; **to drive someone —** volver loco a alguien; **to talk —** decir disparates; N **—s** regiones salvajes *f pl*

wilderness [wíłdəɚnɪs] N (near mountains) monte *m*; (desert) desierto *m*; (jungle) jungla *f*

wile [waɪł] N artimaña *f*, treta *f*

will [wɪł] VT (use willpower) conseguir a fuerza de voluntad; (bequeath) legar, dejar; V AUX **if you —** si quieres; **she — come** va a venir, vendrá; **this motorcycle — go 100 mph** esta motocicleta puede hacer 100 millas por hora; **in spite of everything, he — not stop complaining** a pesar de todo, no deja de quejarse; **she — just sit for hours doing nothing** se pasa horas sentada sin hacer nada; **that — do** basta; N (wish) voluntad *f*; (testament) testamento *m*; **—power** fuerza de voluntad *f*; **at —** a discreción, a voluntad

willful [wíłfəł] ADJ testarudo, porfiado

willies [wíliz] N escalofríos *m pl*

willing [wílɪŋ] ADJ dispuesto, voluntarioso

willingly [wílɪŋli] ADV de buena gana, gustosamente

willingness [wílɪŋnɪs] N buena voluntad *f*, buena gana *f*

willow [wílo] N sauce *m*

wilt [wɪlt] VI/VT (plant) marchitar[se]; VI (person) languidecer
wily [wáɪli] ADJ astuto, artero
wimp [wɪmp] N pelele *m*
win [wɪn] VI/VT ganar; VT (support, fame, affection) ganarse; (victory) alcanzar, conseguir; **to — out** ganar, triunfar; **to — over** conquistar; **a — - — situation** una situación beneficiosa para ambas partes; N victoria *f*
wince [wɪns] VI hacer una mueca; N mueca *f*
winch [wɪntʃ] N cabrestante *m*, torno *m*, *Am* guinche *m*
wind[1] [wɪnd] N (air) viento *m*; (gas) gases *m pl*; **—bag** charlatán -ana *mf*; **—breaker**™ cazadora *f*; **—fall** ganancia inesperada *f*; **— instrument** instrumento de viento *m*; **—mill** molino de viento *m*; **—pipe** tráquea *f*; **— power** energía eólica *f*; **—shield** parabrisas *m sg*; **—shield wiper** limpiaparabrisas *m sg*; **—sock** manga de viento *f*; **—surfing** windsurf *m*; **— tunnel** túnel aerodinámico *m*; **to get — of** enterarse de; **to break —** ventosear; **to catch one's —** recobrar el aliento; ADJ **—ward** de barlovento; ADV **—ward** hacia/a barlovento
wind[2] [waɪnd] VT enrollar; (watch) dar cuerda a; VI (take a bending course) serpentear; **to — around** enrollarse; **to — down** (relax) tranquilizarse; (come to a conclusion) irse terminando; **to — up** (string) enrollar; (a clock) dar cuerda; (a project) completar; (in jail) acabar; N (turn) vuelta *f*; (bend) recodo *m*; **—up** conclusión *f*
winding [wáɪndɪŋ] ADJ sinuoso; **— staircase** escalera de caracol *f*
window [wíndo] N (in building, on screen) ventana *f*; (in building, large) ventanal *m*; (in car, plane) ventanilla *f*; (in a shop) escaparate *m*; *Am* vidriera *f*; **—pane** cristal *m*, vidrio *m*; **— shade** visillo *m*; **—sill** alféizar *m*
windy [wíndi] ADJ ventoso; **it is —** hace/hay viento
wine [waɪn] N vino *m*; **— cellar** bodega *f*; **—glass** copa *f*; **—grower** viticultor -ora *mf*, viñatero -ra *mf*; **— industry** industria vinícola *f*; **—skin** odre *m*; **— tasting** cata de vinos *f*
winery [wáɪnəri] N bodega *f*
wing [wɪŋ] N (of bird, plane, building, table) ala *f*; **— nut** tuerca [de] mariposa/palomilla *f*; **—span/—spread** envergadura *f*; **—tip** extremo del ala *m*; **in the —s** en los bastidores; **under one's —** al amparo de alguien; **to take —** levantar vuelo; VI volar; VT (wound slightly) herir en el ala/brazo; **to — it** improvisar
winger [wíŋə-] N (in soccer) ala *mf*, extremo *mf*
wink [wɪŋk] VI/VT guiñar; **to — approval** guiñar en aprobación; **to — at** hacer la vista gorda; N guiño *m*, guiñada *f*; **I didn't sleep a —** no pegué un ojo
winner [wínə-] N ganador -ora *mf*, triunfador -ora *mf*
winning [wínɪŋ] ADJ (successful) ganador, vencedor; (charming) atractivo; **—s** ganancias *f pl*
wino [wáɪno] N *pej* borracho -cha *mf*
winter [wíntə-] N invierno *m*; **— weather** clima invernal *m*; VI invernar
wintry [wíntri] ADJ invernal
wipe [waɪp] VT (sweat, tears) enjugar; (wet surfaces) secar; (dry surface) limpiar; **to — away** enjugar; **to — off** limpiar; **to — out** aniquilar; **to — up** limpiar
wiper [wáɪpə-] N limpiaparabrisas *m sg*
wire [waɪr] N (filament) alambre *m*; (telegram) telegrama *m*; **— fence** alambrado *m*; **—tap** intervención del teléfono *f*, pinchazo *m*; **— transfer** transferencia electrónica *f*; **by —** por telégrafo; VT (an appliance) alambrar; (a house) electrificar; VI/VT (a message) telegrafiar; (money) girar; **to — together** atar con alambre; **to —tap** intervenir un teléfono, pinchar un teléfono
wired [waɪrd] ADJ (installed) alambrado; (tied) atado con alambre; (electrified) electrificado; (enthusiastic) sobreexcitado
wireless [wáɪrlɪs] ADJ inalámbrico; **— Internet** internet inalámbrico *m*
wiring [wáɪrɪŋ] N cableado *m*
wiry [wáɪri] ADJ (skinny) nervudo; (like wire) crespo
wisdom [wízdəm] N (moral) sabiduría *f*; (scholarly) saber *m*; **— tooth** muela del juicio *f*
wise [waɪz] ADJ (discerning) sabio; (prudent) sensato, prudente; (erudite) erudito; **—crack** broma *f*, chiste *m*; **— guy** sabihondo *m*; **the Three — Men** los Tres Reyes Magos; N **in no —** de ningún modo; VI **to — up** avisparse
wish [wɪʃ] VT desear; **I — you were here** ojalá estuvieras aquí; **I — you the best** te deseo lo mejor; **to — for** pedir; **to — upon a star** pedir un deseo; N deseo *m*; **to make a —** pedir un deseo; **best —es** saludos
wishy-washy [wíʃiwɑʃi] ADJ indeciso
wistful [wístfəł] ADJ (pensive) pensativo; (nostalgic) nostálgico
wit [wɪt] N (intelligence) agudeza *f*, ingenio *m*; (verbal humor) gracejo *m*, sal *f*, chispa *f*; (person) persona aguda *f*, persona ingeniosa *f*; **to be at one's —s' end** no saber qué más hacer; **to live by one's —s** vivir de su ingenio; **to lose one's —s** perder el juicio; **to use one's —s** valerse de su ingenio
witch [wɪtʃ] N bruja *f*; **—craft** brujería *f*; **— hunt** cacería de brujas *f*

with [wɪθ, wɪð] PREP con; **rice — chicken** arroz con pollo *m*; **the man — glasses** el hombre de gafas; **I left my son — Mary** dejé a mi hijo al cuidado de María; **to be — it** está al día; **— me** conmigo; **— you** contigo, con usted

withdraw [wɪðdrɔ] VI/VT retirar[se]

withdrawal [wɪðdrɔəɫ] N (of troops) retirada *f*; (from public office) alejamiento *m*; (from a bank) *Am* retiro *m*; *Sp* retirada *f*; **— [symptoms]** síndrome de abstinencia *m*

withdrawn [wɪθdrɔn] *see* withdraw

withdrew [wɪθdrú] *see* withdraw

wither [wíðə-] VI/VT (of a plant) marchitar[se]; (of a person) consumir[se]; **she —ed him with a look** lo fulminó con la mirada

withheld [wɪθhéɫd] *see* withhold

withhold [wɪθhóɫd] VT (approval) negar; (funds) retener; (truth) ocultar

withholding tax [wɪθhóɫdɪŋtæks] N impuesto deducido del salario *m*

within [wɪðín] PREP dentro de; **— five miles** a menos de cinco millas; ADV dentro, adentro

without [wɪðáʊt] PREP sin; **— my seeing him** sin que yo lo vea; ADV fuera, afuera

withstand [wɪθstǽnd] VI/VT resistir

withstood [wɪθstʊ́d] *see* withstand

witness [wítnɪs] N (person) testigo *mf*; (testimony) testimonio *m*; **to bear —** atestiguar; VT (see) presenciar; (sign) firmar como testigo

witticism [wídɪsɪzɛm] N ocurrencia *f*

witty [wídi] ADJ ocurrente, dicharachero

wizard [wízə-d] N (sorcerer) mago *m*, brujo *m*, hechicero *m*; (computer expert) experto -ta *mf*; (genius) genio *m*

wobble [wábəɫ] N tambaleo *m*, bamboleo *m*; VI/VT tambalear[se], bombolear[se]

woe [wo] N aflicción *f*; **— is me!** ¡pobre de mí!

woeful [wófəɫ] ADJ lamentable

wok [wɑk] N wok *m*

woke [wok] *see* wake

woken [wókən] *see* wake

wolf [wʊɫf] N lobo *m*; **— spider** araña lobo *f*

woman [wúmən] N mujer *f*; *fam* tía *f*; **a —'s touch** un toque femenino; **women's lib[eration]** movimiento de liberación femenina *m*; **women's rights** derechos de la mujer *m pl*

womanhood [wúmənhʊd] N (condition) condición de mujer *f*; (all women) las mujeres *f pl*

womanizer [wúmənaɪzə-] N mujeriego *m*

womankind [wúmənkaɪnd] N las mujeres *f pl*

womanly [wúmənli] ADJ femenino

womb [wum] N (uterus) útero *m*, matriz *f*; (insides of something) vientre *m*; (center) seno *m*

won [wʌn] *see* win

wonder [wʌ́ndə-] VI/VT preguntarse; **to — at** admirarse de, maravillarse de; **I — what time it is** ¿qué hora será? N (marvel) maravilla *f*; (surprise) asombro *m*; (miracle) milagro *m*; **it's a — that** es asombroso que; **it's no — that** no es de extrañar que

wonderful [wʌ́ndə-fəɫ] ADJ maravilloso, estupendo

woo [wu] VI/VT cortejar

wood [wʊd] N (material, also golf club) madera *f*; (firewood) leña *f*; **—cutter** leñador -ora *mf*; **—louse** cochinilla *f*; **—pecker** pájaro carpintero *m*; **—s** bosque *m*; **— shaving** viruta *f*; **—shed** leñera *f*; **—sman** leñador *m*; **—winds** maderas *f pl*; **—work** carpintería *f*, maderaje *m*; **to come out of the —work** salir de la nada

wooded [wʊ́dɪd] ADJ arbolado

wooden [wʊ́dn̩] ADJ (of wood) de madera; (lifeless) inexpresivo

woody [wʊ́di] ADJ (with trees) arbolado; (like wood) leñoso

woof [wʊf] N (of fabric) trama *f*; INTERJ (sound made by a dog) ¡guau!

wool [wʊɫ] N lana *f*; **— sweater** suéter de lana *m*

woolen [wʊ́ɫən] ADJ de lana; N **—s** (fabric) tejido de lana *m*; (clothes) ropa de lana *f*

woolly [wʊ́li] ADJ lanudo

word [wɜ-d] N (lexical unit) vocablo *m*, palabra *f*; (promise) palabra *f*; (news) noticia *f*, aviso *m*; (order) mandato *m*, orden *m*; **— for —** palabra por palabra; **— processing** procesamiento de textos *m*; *Sp* tratamiento de texto[s] *m*; **—s [of a song]** letra [de una canción] *f*; **— spacing** espaciado de palabras *m*; **— wrap** retorno de línea automático *m*; **I found out by — of mouth** me lo dijeron; **may I have a — with you?** ¿podemos hablar? **to eat one's —s** tragarse/comerse las palabras; VT (oral) expresar; (written) formular

wording [wɜ́-dɪŋ] N formulación *f*

wordy [wɜ́-di] ADJ verboso, prolijo

wore [wɔr] *see* wear

work [wɜ-k] N (effort) trabajo *m*; (employment) empleo *m*, trabajo *m*; (artistic product, fortification) obra *f*; **—book** cuaderno/libro de trabajo *m*; **—day** día laborable *m*; **— environment** entorno de trabajo *m*; **— flow** flujo de trabajo *m*; **—force** mano de obra *f*; **—load** cantidad/carga de trabajo *f*; **—man** obrero *m*; **— of art** obra de arte *f*; **—out** sesión de ejercicio *f*; **— permit** permiso de trabajo *m*; **—place** lugar de trabajo *m*; **— schedule** horario de trabajo *m*; **—sheet** planilla *f*, hoja de ejercicios *f*; **—shop** taller *m*; **—station** estación de trabajo *f*; **— stoppage** huelga *f*, paro laboral *m*; **—s** fábrica *f*; **the —s** todo; **—week**

semana de trabajo *f*; **he's hard at —** está trabajando duro; ADJ **—-related** laboral; VI (labor) trabajar; (function) funcionar; VT (change) efectuar; (metal, land) trabajar; (a crowd) manipular; (a mine) explotar; (employees) hacer trabajar; **to — in[to]** introducir; **to — loose** soltar[se], aflojar[se]; **to — on** (repair) arreglar; (improve) tratar de mejorar; **to — one's way through college** pagarse los estudios trabajando; **to — one's way up** ascender a fuerza de trabajo; **to — out** (a plan) urdir; (a problem) resolver; **he —s out every day** hace ejercicio todos los días; **to — overtime** trabajar horas extras; **it all —ed out** al final todo salió bien; **to be all —ed up** estar sobreexcitado; **to get —ed up** agitarse

workaholic [wɜ́kəhɑ́lɪk] N adicto -ta al trabajo *mf*

worker [wɜ́kɚ] N trabajador -ora *mf*; (in a factory) obrero -ra *mf*; (in an office) oficinista *mf*

working [wɜ́kɪŋ] N (act of someone who works, shaping of metals) trabajo *m*; (operation) funcionamiento *m*, operación *f*; (of a problem) cálculo *m*; (of a mine) explotación *f*; ADJ (class) obrero, trabajador; (majority) suficiente; **— class** clase obrera/trabajadora *f*; **— lunch** comida de trabajo *f*; **—man** obrero *m*

workmanship [wɜ́kmənʃɪp] N (skill) habilidad *f*, destreza *f*; (quality of work) confección *f*

world [wɜ́ld] N mundo *m*; **— Bank** Banco Mundial *m*; **— Cup** Copa del Mundo *f*; **—view** cosmovisión *f*; **— war** guerra mundial *f*; **— Wide Web** web *f*, red [mundial electrónica] *f*; ADJ **—-class** de categoría mundial; **—-famous** de fama mundial; **—-shaking** trascendental; **—wide** mundial

worldly [wɜ́ldli] ADJ (mundane) mundano, temporal; (sophisticated) de mundo, corrido; (material) material

worm [wɜ́m] N gusano *m*; ADJ **—-eaten** comido por los gusanos, carcomido; VT desparasitar, quitar las lombrices; **to — a secret out of someone** extraerle/sonsacarle un secreto a alguien; **to — oneself into** insinuarse en

worn [wɔrn] ADJ desgastado, usado

worn [wɔrn] *see* wear

worrisome [wɜ́isəm] ADJ preocupante, inquietante

worry [wɜ́i] VI/VT preocupar[se], inquietar[se]; VT (harass) hostigar; VI **to — with** juguetear con; N preocupación *f*, inquietud *f*, zozobra *f*; **—wart** preocupón -ona *mf*

worse [wɜ́s] ADJ & ADV peor; **— and —** cada vez peor; **— than ever** peor que nunca; **from bad to —** de mal en peor; **so much the —** tanto peor; **to be — off** estar peor que antes; **to change for the —** empeorar[se]; **to get —** empeorar[se]

worship [wɜ́ʃɪp] N (act of worshiping) adoración *f*; (ceremony) culto *m*; VT (revere) adorar, venerar; VI (attend services) asistir al culto

worshiper [wɜ́ʃɪpɚ] N (one who worships) adorador -ora *mf*; **—s** fieles *mf pl*

worst [wɜ́st] ADJ & ADV **the — one** el/la peor; **the — thing** lo peor; **—-case scenario** el peor de los casos; VT derrotar

worth [wɜ́θ] ADJ **to be — a dollar** valer un dólar; **to be — hearing** ser digno de oírse; **to be —while** valer la pena; **it's — doing** vale la pena hacerlo; N valor *m*, valía *f*; **ten cents' — of** diez centavos de; **to get one's money's — out of** aprovechar al máximo

worthless [wɜ́θlɪs] ADJ (useless) inútil; (despicable) despreciable; **— check** cheque sin fondos *m*

worthy [wɜ́ði] ADJ (meritorious) digno, meritorio; (esteemed) benemérito; **— cause** causa noble *f*; **— of praise** digno de elogio; N persona ilustre *mf*

would [wʊd] V AUX **I — do it if I could** lo haría si pudiera; **— you please open the door?** ¿podrías abrir la puerta por favor? **he said he — do it** dijo que lo haría; **as a child, I — play all the time** de niño, jugaba todo el tiempo; **— that she were alive!** ¡ojalá estuviera viva!

wound[1] [wund] N herida *f*; VI/VT herir; (with an arrow) flechar

wound[2] [waund] *see* wind

wove [wov] *see* weave

woven [wóvən] *see* weave

wow [wɑʊ] VT impresionar; INTERJ ¡huy!

wrangle [rǽŋgəl] VI/VT (quarrel) discutir; (obtain) agenciarse de; VT (herd) juntar; *Am* rodear; N riña *f*, pendencia *f*

wrangler [rǽŋglɚ] N vaquero -ra *mf*

wrap [ræp] VT envolver; **to — up** (a present) envolver; (a baby) arropar; (a task) terminar; (against the cold) abrigar[se]; **to be —ped in** estar envuelto en; **to be —ped up in** estar absorto en; N (coat) abrigo *m*; (shawl) chal *m*; **—-up** (summary) resumen *m*; (end) final *m*; **keep under —s** mantener secreto

wrapper [rǽpɚ] N envoltura *f*, envoltorio *m*

wrapping [rǽpɪŋ] N envoltura *f*; **— paper** papel para envolver *m*

wrath [ræθ] N ira *f*, cólera *f*

wreak [rik] VT **to — havoc** hacer estragos

wreath [riθ] N corona *f*; **— of smoke** espiral de humo *f*

wreck [rɛk] N (building) ruina *f*; (car, plane) restos *m pl*; (a ship) pecio *m*; (shipwreck) naufragio *m*; (person) desastre *m*, ruina *f*; (accident) accidente *m*; VI tener un accidente; VT (a ship) naufragar; (a car, totally)

destrozar; (a car, with minor damage) chocar; (a building) demoler

wreckage [rékɪʤ] N (of a building) escombros *m pl*; (of a car, plane) restos de un accidente *m pl*; (of a ship) pecio *m*

wrecker [rékə˞] N (tow truck) grúa *f*, camión de remolque *m*; (worker) obrero -ra de demolición *mf*

wrench [rɛntʃ] N (twist) torcedura *f*; (pull) tirón *m*; (tool) llave de tuercas *f*; VT torcer, retorcer; **to — off/out** arrancar de un tirón, arrebatar

wrest [rɛst] VT (pull) arrancar; (take away) arrebatar

wrestle [résəɫ] VI/VT luchar [con/contra]; N lucha *f*

wrestler [réslə˞] N luchador -ora *mf*

wrestling [réslɪŋ] N lucha libre *f*

wretch [rɛtʃ] N miserable *mf*, infeliz *mf*

wretched [rɛ́tʃɪd] ADJ (unfortunate) desdichado, infeliz; (despicable) vil, miserable, arrastrado; (inferior) pésimo

wriggle [rígəɫ] VI culebrear, serpentear; **to — out of** escabullirse de; VT menear, retorcer

wring [rɪŋ] VT (twist) torcer, retorcer; (extract) arrancar; **to — one's hands** retorcerse las manos; **to — out** escurrir

wrinkle [rɪ́ŋkəɫ] N arruga *f*, surco *m*; (problem) problema *m*; VI/VT arrugar[se]

wrist [rɪst] N muñeca *f*; **—watch** reloj [de] pulsera *m*

writ [rɪt] N auto *m*, mandato *m*

write [raɪt] VI/VT escribir; (transfer data) grabar; **to — back** contestar; **to — down** apuntar; **to — off** cancelar; **to — out** escribir en forma completa; **to — -protect** proteger contra grabación; **to — up** hacer un reportaje sobre; **it's written all over his face** se le ve en la cara; **she —s for a living** es escritora; N **—-up** reportaje *m*; **— protection** protección contra grabación *f*

writer [ráɪdə˞] N escritor -ora *mf*, literato -ta *mf*

writhe [raɪð] VI retorcerse

writing [ráɪdɪŋ] N (act of writing) escritura *f*; (handwriting) letra *f*, escritura *f*; (style) estilo *m*; **— desk** escritorio *m*; **— paper** papel de escribir *m*; **—s** obra *f*; **to put in —** poner por escrito

written [rɪ́tn̩] *see* write

wrong [rɔŋ] ADJ (incorrect) incorrecto, equivocado; (improper) inapropiado; **what's — with you?** ¿qué te pasa? **you are —** estás equivocado; **the — side of a fabric** el revés de una tela; **— side out** con lo de adentro para afuera; **to be on the — side of the road** ir a contramano / en sentido contrario; **that is the — book** ese no es el libro; **it is in the — place** está fuera de lugar; ADV mal; **to go —** salir mal; N (evil) mal *m*; (injustice) injusticia *f*; **to be in the —** (not be right) estar equivocado; (be to blame) tener la culpa; **to do —** hacer mal; VT perjudicar

wrongful [rɔ́ŋfəɫ] ADJ injusto, injustificado

wrongly [rɔ́ŋli] ADV (reported) incorrectamente; (accused) injustamente

wrote [rot] *see* write

wrought [rɔt] ADJ forjado; **— iron** hierro forjado *m*

wrung [rʌŋ] *see* wring

wry [raɪ] ADJ (smile) torcido; (remark, humor) irónico; **to make a — face** torcer la cara

WTO [World Trade Organization] [dʌ́bəɫjutío] N OMT *f*

WWW [World Wide Web] [dʌ́bəɫjudʌ́bəɫjudʌ́bəɫju] N web *f*

Xx

xenophobia [zɛnəfóbiə] N xenofobia *f*

Xerox™ [zírɑks] N fotocopia *f*; VI/VT fotocopiar

x-rated [éksrɛDɪd] ADJ pornográfico

x-ray [éksre] N rayos X *m pl*, radiografía *f*; VI/VT radiografiar

xylophone [záɪləfon] N xilofón *m*, xilófono *m*

Yy

yacht [jɑt] N yate *m*; VI navegar en yate

y'all [jəɫ] PRON *Am* ustedes *mf*; *Sp* vosotros -as *mf*

Yankee [jǽŋki] ADJ & N estadounidense del norte del país *mf*

yard [jɑrd] N (measure) yarda [0.9144m] *f*; (spar) verga *f*; (courtyard) patio *m*; (grassy area) jardín *m*; **—stick** (stick) vara de medida [de una yarda] *f*; (criterion) patrón *m*, norma *f*

yarn [jɑrn] N (material) hilo *m*; (story) cuento *m*

yawn [jɔn] VI bostezar; N bostezo *m*

yeah [jɛ́ə] ADV *fam* sí; *fam* **— right!** ¡de eso, nada! ¡qué va!

year [jir] N año *m*; **—book** anuario *m*; ADJ **—-end** de fin de año; **—-round** de todo el año; **—-to-date** del año hasta la fecha

yearling [jírlɪŋ] N animal de un año *m*; (of cows) añojo -ja *mf*

yearly [jírli] ADJ anual; ADV anualmente

yearn [jɝn] VI anhelar, suspirar por

yearning [jɝ́nɪŋ] N anhelo *m*

yeast [jist] N levadura *f*

yell [jɛɫ] VI/VT gritar; N grito *m*

yellow [jɛ́lo] ADJ (color) amarillo; (coward)

cobarde; **— card** (in soccer) tarjeta amarilla *f*; **— fever** fiebre amarilla *f*; **— jacket** avispa *f*; **— pages** páginas amarillas *f pl*; N amarillo *m*; VI/VT poner[se] amarillo, amarillear

yellowish [jéloɪʃ] ADJ amarillento

yelp [jɛłp] VI gañir, aullar; N gañido *m*, aullido *m*

Yemen [jémən] N Yemen *m*

Yemeni [jéməni] ADJ & N yemení *mf*

yen [jen] N (currency of Japan) yen *m*; (desire) anhelo *m*; VI anhelar

yes [jes] ADV sí; **—-no question** pregunta de sí o no *f*

yesterday [jéstə-de] ADV & N ayer *m*; **the day before** — anteayer

yet [jet] ADV & CONJ **are they here —?** ¿ya llegaron? **they aren't here** — todavía no llegan, aún no han llegado; **— another** otro más; **ugly — charming** feo pero encantador; **as —** todavía, aún

yield [jiłd] VI/VT (surrender, give in) ceder; (produce) rendir, redituar; **to — 5 percent** dar un cinco por ciento de interés; N (production) rendimiento *m*, producción *f*; (of stocks) rédito *m*

yodel [jódl] VI cantar a la tirolesa; N canto tirolés *m*

yoga [jógə] N yoga *m*

yogurt [jógə-t] N yogur *m*

yoke [jok] N (crossbar) yugo *m*; (pair of animals) yunta *f*; (on a shirt) canesú *m*; VT uncir

yolk [jok] N yema *f*

yonder [jándə-] ADJ aquel; ADV (location) allá; (direction) hacia allá

yore [jɔr] N **in days of** — antaño

you [ju] SUBJ PRON (sg informal) tú; *RP, Central Am* vos; (sg formal) usted; (pl informal) *Sp* vosotros; *Am* ustedes; (pl formal) ustedes; **I see** — (sg informal) te veo; (sg formal) lo veo; (pl informal) *Sp* os veo; *Am* los veo; (pl formal) los veo; **I talk to** — (sg informal) te hablo; (sg formal) le hablo; (pl informal) *Sp* os hablo; *Am* les hablo; (pl formal) les hablo; **I went with** — (sg informal) fui contigo; (sg formal) fui con usted; (pl informal) *Sp* fui con vosotros; *Am* fui con ustedes; (pl formal) fui con ustedes; **it's for** — (sg informal) es para ti; (sg informal) *RP, Central Am* es para vos; (sg formal) es para usted; (pl informal) *Sp* es para vosotros; *Am* es para ustedes; (pl formal) es para ustedes; **this is how — make bread** así se hace el pan

young [jʌŋ] ADJ joven; **— man** joven *m*; **— people** gente joven *f*; **— woman** joven *f*; N (offspring) cría *f*

youngster [jʌ́ŋstə-] N muchacho -cha *mf*, jovencito -ta *mf*

your [jɔr] POSS ADJ **this is — dog** (sg informal) este es tu perro; (sg formal) este es su perro; (pl informal) *Sp* este es vuestro perro, *Am* este es su perro; (pl formal) este es su perro

yours [jɔrz] PRON **this book is** — (sg informal) este libro es tuyo; (sg formal) este libro es suyo / de usted; (pl informal) *Sp* este libro es vuestro; *Am* este libro es suyo / de ustedes; (pl formal) este libro es suyo / de ustedes; **— is bigger** (sg informal) el tuyo / la tuya es más grande; (sg formal) el suyo / el de usted / la suya / la de usted es más grande; (pl informal) *Sp* el vuestro / la vuestra es más grande; *Am* el suyo / el de ustedes es más grande; (pl formal) el suyo / el de ustedes es más grande; **a friend of** — (sg informal) un amigo tuyo; (sg formal) un amigo suyo / de usted; (pl informal) *Sp* un amigo vuestro; *Am* un amigo suyo / de ustedes; **— truly** atentamente

yourself [jɔrsɛ́łf] PRON **you — wrote the letter** (sg informal) tú mismo escribiste la carta; (sg formal) usted mismo escribió la carta; **you yourselves wrote the letter** (pl informal) *Sp* vosotros mismos escribisteis la carta; *Am* ustedes mismos escribieron la carta; (pl formal) ustedes mismos escribieron la carta; **you are not — today** (sg informal) hoy no eres el mismo de siempre; (sg formal) hoy no es el mismo de siempre; **you are not yourselves today** *Sp* hoy no sois los mismos de siempre; *Am* hoy no son los mismos de siempre; (pl formal) hoy no son los mismos de siempre; **you were sitting by** — (sg informal) tú estabas sentado solo; (sg formal) usted estaba sentado solo; **you were sitting by yourselves** (informal) *Sp* vosotros estabais sentados solos; *Am* ustedes estaban sentados solos; (pl formal) ustedes estaban sentados solos; **you look at — at the mirror** (sg informal) tú te miras en el espejo; (sg formal) usted se mira en el espejo; **you look at yourselves at the mirror** (pl informal) *Sp* vosotros os mirais en el espejo; *Am* ustedes se miran en el espejo; (pl formal) ustedes se miran en el espejo; **you bought — a house** (sg informal) te compraste una casa; (sg formal) usted se compró una casa; **you bought yourselves a house** (pl informal) *Sp* os comprasteis una casa; *Am* se compraron una casa; (pl formal) se compraron una casa

youth [juθ] N (person) joven *m*; (young age) juventud *m*

youthful [júθfəł] ADJ juvenil

yo-yo [jójo] N yo-yo *m*

yuan [juán] N yuan *m*

yucca [jákə] N yuca *f*

yuck [jʌk] INTERJ puaj, puaf

Yugoslavia [jugoslávia] N Yugoslavia *f*

Yugoslavian [jugoslávian] ADJ & N yugoslavo -va *mf*

Yuletide [júłtaɪd] N Navidad *f*

yummy [jámi] ADJ delicioso; INTERJ ¡qué rico!
yuppie [jápi] N yuppie *mf*

Zz

Zambia [zǽmbiə] N Zambia *f*
Zambian [zǽmbiən] ADJ & N zambiano -na *mf*
zany [zéni] ADJ loco, chiflado
zap [zæp] VT liquidar
zeal [ziɫ] N celo *m*, fervor *m*
zealot [zélət] N fanático -ca *mf*
zealous [zéləs] ADJ celoso, fervoroso
zebra [zíbrə] N cebra *f*
zenith [zínɪθ] N cenit *m*
zephyr [zéfɚ] N céfiro *m*
zeppelin [zépəlɪn] N zepelín *m*, dirigible *m*
zero [ziro] NUM cero *m*; **there's — possibility that he'll come** las posibilidades de que venga son nulas
zest [zɛst] N entusiasmo *m*
zigzag [zígzæg] N zigzag *m*; ADJ & ADV en zigzag; VI zigzaguear, andar en zigzag; VT hacer zigzaguear
Zimbabwe [zɪmbábwe] N Zimbabue *m*
Zimbabwean [zɪmbábweən] ADJ & N zimbabuo -bua *mf*
zinc [zɪŋk] N cinc *m*, zinc *m*
zip [zɪp] VI/VT cerrar/abrir con cremallera; **to — by** pasar volando; **to — over** ir corriendo; N cero *m*; **— code** código postal *m*
zipper [zípɚ] N cremallera *f*, cierre [relámpago] *m*
zirconium [zɚkóniəm] N circonio *m*
zodiac [zódɪæk] N zodíaco *m*
zombie [zámbi] N zombi *mf*
zone [zon] N zona *f*; **— defense** defensa en zonas *f*; VT dividir en zonas
zoning [zónɪŋ] N zonificación *f*
zoo [zu] N zoológico *m*; *Sp* zoo *m*; **—keeper** guardián -ana del zoológico *mf*
zoological [zoəlɑ́ʤɪkəɫ] ADJ zoológico
zoology [zoɑ́ləʤi] N zoología *f*
zoom [zum] VI (make sound) zumbar; **to — in** ampliar una imagen; **to — off** salir zumbando; **to — out** achicar la imagen; N zumbido *m*; **— lens** teleobjetivo *m*, zoom *m*
zucchini [zukíni] N calabacín *m*
zygote [záigot] N cigoto *m*, zigoto *m*